OXFORD COMME
INTERNATIONAL LAW

General Editors: *Professor Philip Alston*, Professor of International Law
at New York University, and *Vaughan Lowe QC*, Essex Court Chambers,
London and Emeritus Fellow of All Souls College, Oxford

THE UN CONVENTION ON THE ELIMINATION OF ALL FORMS OF DISCRIMINATION AGAINST WOMEN

A Commentary

The UN Convention on the Elimination of All Forms of Discrimination against Women

A Commentary

Edited by

MARSHA A. FREEMAN
CHRISTINE CHINKIN
BEATE RUDOLF

Assistant Editors

SUSANN KROWORSCH
ALLISON SHERRIER
SARAH WITTKOPP

OXFORD
UNIVERSITY PRESS

OXFORD
UNIVERSITY PRESS

Great Clarendon Street, Oxford, OX2 6DP,
United Kingdom

Oxford University Press is a department of the University of Oxford.
It furthers the University's objective of excellence in research, scholarship,
and education by publishing worldwide. Oxford is a registered trade mark of
Oxford University Press in the UK and in certain other countries

Published in the United States of America by Oxford University Press
198 Madison Avenue, New York, NY 10016, United States of America

British Library Cataloguing in Publication Data
Data available

Library of Congress Data available

ISBN 978–0–19–956506–1
ISBN 978–0–19–968224–9 (pbk.)

Printed and bound by CPI Group (UK) Ltd, Croydon, CR0 4YY

Foreword

Few causes championed by the United Nations have generated as wide and strong support as that to promote and protect the equal rights of women. The Charter of the United Nations reaffirms the equal rights of men and women. The United Nations has created a strong framework of internationally agreed norms, strategies, and programmes to eliminate discrimination against women in all its manifestations wherever it occurs, and guarantee their equal enjoyment with men of all human rights. The Convention on the Elimination of All Forms of Discrimination against Women and its Optional Protocol form the basis of this framework. The Convention was adopted by the General Assembly in 1979 and by the end of 2010, had been accepted by 186 States parties from all regions of the world. Of these, 100 had ratified or acceded to its Optional Protocol which provides for petitions and inquiries.

The Convention is the result of the determination of international women's rights activists—inside and outside government—to ensure that a comprehensive treaty setting out women's human rights and the obstacles to their full implementation is at the core of international human rights law. Its Optional Protocol resulted from that same determination, carried through to the next generation.

Setting out the steps that States are obliged to take to eliminate discrimination against women and ensure their equality with men in the civil, cultural, economic, political, and social spheres, the Convention is one of the first human rights treaties to incorporate the ideas of universality, indivisibility, and interdependence of all human rights. It is a milestone in bridging human rights and development, in particular through requiring States parties to take all appropriate measures to eliminate discrimination against rural women and ensure that they participate in, and benefit from, rural development on an equal basis with men. The Convention pioneered recognition of the concept of substantive equality for women by requiring that they enjoy equality with men in real terms, as well as formal equality in law and policy. By requiring States parties to take all appropriate measures to modify the social and cultural patterns of conduct of women and men to eliminate prejudices and practices based on ideas of inferiority or superiority of either of the sexes or stereotyped roles for them, the Convention requires the transformation of States, communities, and families to achieve full gender equality.

Progress made by States in implementing the Convention is overseen by the Committee on the Elimination of Discrimination against Women, which from its first session in 1982, has provided a distinct and dynamic interpretation of the treaty's terms. The Committee has contributed to our understanding of human rights, placed women's human rights high on the international agenda, and empowered individual women to claim them. Its jurisprudence, developed through general recommendations which provide the Committee's collective view of the measures States should take to fulfil their Convention obligations, and 'views' adopted after consideration of petitions have been profoundly influential. Indeed, its jurisprudence has guided regional and national courts and tribunals. Most importantly, the Committee has sought to identify solutions and examples of best practices so that the Convention will benefit all women.

Since its adoption, the Convention has captured the imagination of women world-wide, and has been used by many to transform their lives. Recognizing this, one of the Committee's longest-serving members, Hanna Beate Schöpp-Schilling, became determined to make the Convention, the Optional Protocol, and the work of the Committee as widely known as possible through a substantive commentary. She brought together the scholars and activists who have contributed to this volume, and gained their commitment to the project. Under Dr Schöpp-Schilling's guidance and inspired by her vision of the Convention as a living instrument, the authors began work on this volume in 2008. Sadly, Dr Schöpp-Schilling passed away in July 2009 after a short illness. Her vision and commitment motivated the authors to complete the commentary.

I am convinced that this commentary will be an important tool for States, human rights mechanisms, intergovernmental agencies, and civil society, especially women's groups, to advance their understanding of how the Convention and its Optional Protocol can be used to achieve true equality for women. It also highlights the promise these instruments hold, that the standards and procedures they set out will be brought home to all women in every community and every country in the world. I acknowledge the expertise of those who contributed to the commentary and the quality of their work. I believe the world will be indebted to the care and passion they brought to their task.

Navi Pillay
United Nations High Commissioner for Human Rights
May 2011

Dedication

This Commentary is the inspiration of Hanna Beate Schöpp-Schilling, who served as a member of the Committee on the Elimination of Discrimination against Women from 1989 through 2008. Beate envisioned the Commentary as a summation of and a tribute to the Committee's work in establishing the Convention on the Elimination of All Forms of Discrimination against Women as the international standard for women's human rights and a continuing inspiration for women and men working towards equality throughout the world. She and her co-editor Beate Rudolf organized the project and recruited the authors to reflect the breadth and depth of the Committee's work and of the Convention's content and potential.

A few months after the first authors' meeting, held in Berlin in September 2008, Beate Schöpp-Schilling was diagnosed with pancreatic cancer. Among all the obligations she had taken on as she ended her twenty years of work on the Committee, her first concern was continuity of the Commentary project. At her request, Marsha Freeman took on the sharing of editorial tasks with Beate Rudolf. A few months later Christine Chinkin joined the editorial team.

Beate Schöpp-Schilling passed away in July 2009, when the Commentary was barely under way. The editors and authors have missed her knowledge, her passion, her vision, and her good sense, at every stage of the project.

We have lost not only one of the great experts, but a great friend. In dedicating this Commentary to her, we recall her dedication to equality for women everywhere.

Thank you, Beate.

Preface

This Commentary reflects thirty years of work by the United Nations Committee on the Elimination of Discrimination against Women to establish the framework for applying the norms of the Convention on the Elimination of All Forms of Discrimination against Women. In that time, 104 independent experts have served on the Committee, from all the regions of the world and, as the Convention states, representing the 'different forms of civilization as well as the principal legal systems'. Those thirty years have also seen dramatic change in the global political and economic context—the 'civilizations' mentioned in the Convention—greatly affecting both the make-up of the Committee and the issues that come before it.

The Commentary also reflects thirty years of authors' and editors' experience, first and foremost, that of Hanna Beate Schöpp-Schilling. She and her co-editor Beate Rudolf organized the project as a collaboration, commencing with a meeting in Berlin in 2008 in which all but one of the original fourteen authors participated. Representing five regions and a broad range of knowledge, the authors worked out a common framework for all the chapters and a list of cross-cutting historical and conceptual issues to be discussed in the introduction. They also established a process for sharing comments on each chapter as it was produced and decided that the original plan of holding introductory and wrap-up meetings should be expanded to allow for discussion of all the chapters and exploration of additional issues as they came up. Consequently, authors met again in The Hague in May 2009, Berlin in August 2009, and Bellagio in July 2010. The editors finalized the substantive production in London in December 2010.

As the project progressed through the latter three authors' meetings, the most difficult issue was the one we can only refer to as Missing Beate. When Beate Schöpp-Schilling passed away in July 2009, it was clear that it would take more than one person to succeed her as an editor—and certainly nobody could replace her. Accordingly the editorial team was expanded to three, adding Marsha A. Freeman and Christine Chinkin. Beate Rudolf remained the literal anchor, as the editorial support staffing was established through her post at the Free University of Berlin. In 2010, she became the Director of the German Institute for Human Rights, and during the final months of the project we benefited from the German Institute hosting a graduate research fellow who became a valuable member of the editorial support team. Throughout the process, we have missed Beate Schöpp-Schilling's comprehensive knowledge, clear judgement, and above all, her vision.

The Commentary is designed as an in-depth account of the Convention norms, and their meaning and application, as developed by the CEDAW Committee. For reasons of both space and focus, we leave to others the detailed exploration of substantive issues as experienced by women in various systems and spaces. The Committee's work is informed by accounts of these experiences, from NGOs, UN agencies, and sometimes from the States parties themselves. Its primary purpose is to develop the legal standards against which States parties' actions are measured, and to engage them in a dialogue under both the review process and the Optional Protocol, that explains to them where they have met the standards, where they fall short, and how to move forward. The Commentary documents the achievement of that purpose. The individual chapters include references to works of scholarship, United Nations and other organizations' reports, and regional and domestic jurisprudence that have advanced the substantive discussion of particular issues, but its focus is on the work of the Committee. The Introduction reflects contextual and cross-cutting issues and concerns that inform the application of the Convention as a whole. Bibliographies and tables are included as Appendices for further reference.

In producing this book, the editors and authors have consulted many colleagues around the globe. Acknowledgments are listed in each author chapter. In addition, CEDAW expert Cees Flinterman contributed significantly to the early stages of the project. The editors have received encouragement and thoughtful responses from former CEDAW Chairpersons Elizabeth Evatt and Ivanka Corti, for which we are truly grateful.

We are also grateful to the institutions that have provided support for the Commentary project: The Free University of Berlin, for our staff and for supporting meetings in Berlin in September 2008 and August 2009; the German Institute for Human Rights for hosting the September 2008 meeting; the German Federal Foreign Office for financing the August 2009 meeting; the Netherlands Ministry of Foreign Affairs and the Hague campus of Leiden University for the Hague meeting of May 2009; the Rockefeller Foundation Bellagio Conference Center for hosting our meeting in July 2010, and the Women in Law Program of American University Washington College of Law for its extensive work on the Bellagio application. The University of Minnesota Law School and the London School of Economics Faculty of Law have provided significant infrastructure and collegial support for Dr Freeman and Prof Chinkin respectively. Our editors at Oxford University Press, John Louth and Merel Alstein, have been supportive of the entire project and extremely helpful as we sorted out technical and schedule issues.

Special mention must be made and thanks given to our editorial staff, who have dealt promptly and professionally with special, frequently unforeseen requests requiring additional research as well as the mundane toil of correcting citations and formatting text. Two assistant editors, Sarah Wittkopp and Susann Kroworsch, also are authors—the rising generation, whom we have been very happy to have working with us. Susann especially rose to the occasion of taking on chapters when their original author left the project. Assistant editor Allison Sherrier joined the staff in September 2010 as part of her research fellowship with the German Institute for Human Rights, and she has proven to be not only a quick study but an extremely good-natured one, exhibiting great equanimity in dealing with multiple chapter versions and the minutiae of punctuation styles. Throughout the project we had excellent help from student research assistants at the Free University of Berlin: Sahrah Al-Nasrawe-Sözeri, Benjamin Feyen, Ines Franke, Michael Gläsner, Anna-Maria Paulus, and Eric Veillerobe.

We also thank Jane Connors for taking on the Reservations chapter when the original author became unavailable. The most profound thanks, however, go to Frances Raday and Ineke Boerefijn, who agreed to write the chapters that Beate Schöpp-Schilling had been planning to produce—and met a challenge well beyond the intellectual.

Marsha A. Freeman
Christine Chinkin
Beate Rudolf
Minneapolis, London and Berlin,
April 2011

Preface to the Paperback Edition

The Commentary editors are delighted with the opportunity to provide this preface to the softcover edition, which Oxford University Press decided to offer unusually soon after publication of the hardcover. The hardcover edition has been extraordinarily well received, and all involved have had many requests for a more economically accessible version. We know that this edition will find its way into many more hands and help many more women and organizations in their advocacy and research to promote women's human rights.

The softcover edition is an exact replica of the hardcover, with minor text corrections made by the authors. The publication process, requiring that pagination remain the same as that of the hardcover, regrettably does not allow for major revision or addition of material relating to State party reviews and events that occurred after the original publication cutoff date of December 31, 2010. We note for the record, however, that since then the Committee has adopted views on several individual complaints and has adopted General Recommendation 29, on Economic Consequences of Marriage and Family Relationships and Their Dissolution. These documents are of course available on the Web site of the Office of the High Commissioner for Human Rights.

We thank our OUP editors for making this edition possible so quickly. And once again we express our gratitude for the inspiration of our late friend and mentor Beate Schoepp-Schilling, who envisioned the *Commentary* as a resource for those who care about, or should care about, equality–NGOs, scholars, UN human rights experts, government officials. We hope that this edition will truly become a source of inspiration for all.

Marsha A Freeman
Christine Chinkin
Beate Rudolf

Authors' Contributions

Table of Contents

A Note on the Authors

Fareda Banda, BL(Hons), LLB, D. Phil, is Professor of the Laws of Africa at the School of Oriental and African Studies in the University of London. She is the author of *Women, Law and Human Rights: An African Perspective* and a report on *Laws that Discriminate against Women*. She is on the editorial boards of the *Journal of African Law, the International Journal of Law, Family and Policy* and is an associate editor (Africa) of the *International Survey of Family Law*. She sits on the international advisory boards of the *Africa Journal of Human Rights, Africa Law Reports*, and the *East Africa Journal of Peace and Human Rights*.

Ineke Boerefijn, PhD, is an associate professor at the Netherlands Institute of Human Rights, held the Opzij Chair at the Centre for Gender and Diversity at Maastricht University, and was Julius Stone Visiting Researcher at the University of New South Wales and the Australian Human Rights Centre. She is an editor of the *Nederlands Tijdschrift voor de Mensenrechten* and of the *International Studies Journal (Iran)*, and a member of the Advisory Board of the Institute for Human Rights of Åbo Akademi University. She is Rapporteur of the Committee on International Human Rights Law and Practice of the International Law Association (ILA).

Andrew Byrnes, BA (Hons), LLB (Hons), LLM, is Professor of Law at the University of New South Wales and Chair of the Australian Human Rights Centre, and was previously at the Universities of Sydney and Hong Kong, and the Australian National University. He is a member of the editorial boards of the *Australia Yearbook of International Law* and the *Australia Journal of Human Rights*. His publications include *International Women's Rights Cases* (co-editor) and *Bills of Rights in Australia – History, Politics and Law* (co-author).

Christine Chinkin, LLB, LLM, PhD, is Professor of International Law at the London School of Economics and Political Science and William W. Cook Global Law Professor, University of Michigan. She is a member of Matrix Chambers, a Fellow of the British Academy and Director of Studies of the International Law Association. She is author of *Third Parties in International Law*, co-author of *The Boundaries of International Law: a Feminist Analysis* and of *The Making of International Law*, and an editor of the *American Journal of International Law*.

Janie Chuang, JD, is an Associate Professor of Law at American University, Washington College of Law. She serves on the Executive Council of the American Society of International Law, and as the U.S. Representative to the International Law Association's Feminism and International Law Committee.

Jane Connors, LLM, is the Chief of the Special Procedures Branch at the Office of the High Commissioner for Human Rights (OHCHR). From 1980 to 1996, she taught law at universities in Australia and the United Kingdom, spending fourteen years at the School of Oriental and African Studies, London. In 1996, she joined the UN Division for the Advancement of Women as the Chief of the Women's Rights Section. In 2002, she took a position in the Human Rights Treaty Bodies Division at the OHCHR. She has written extensively on women's rights, including in respect of violence against women, and CEDAW.

Rebecca J. Cook, JD, JSD, holds the Faculty Chair in International Human Rights at the University of Toronto Law Faculty and is Co-Director of the International Programme on Reproductive and Sexual Health Law. She is editor of *Human Rights of Women: National and International Perspectives*, co-editor of *Health and Human Rights*, and co-author of *Reproductive Health and Human Rights*, and *Gender Stereotyping: Transnational Legal Perspectives*. She serves as an editor for the *International Journal of Gynecology and Obstetrics*.

Marsha A. Freeman, PhD, JD, is Senior Fellow at the University of Minnesota Human Rights Center, where she is Director of the International Women's Rights Action Watch. She also is Adjunct Professor of Law at the University of Minnesota Law School. Dr. Freeman is editor of *Assessing the Status of Women*, a guide for reporting under the Convention. She has published numerous articles, reports, and technical papers on the Convention's content and procedures and on advocacy using its provisions, and supervised production of shadow reports on more than fifty States parties from 1992 through 2002.

Savitri W.E. Goonesekere, LLB, LLM, D.Lit (h.c.) mult., Attorney at Law, is Emeritus Professor of Law and former Vice Chancellor University of Colombo Sri Lanka. She served as an expert on the UN Committee on All Forms of Discrimination against Women and edited and contributed to *Violence Law and Women's Rights in South Asia*.

Rikki Holtmaat, LLM, PhD, is professor of International Non-Discrimination Law at Leiden University and a freelance researcher and consultant in the area of gender equality. She is a member of the European Commission's Network of Legal Experts in the field of Gender Discrimination and of the Dutch Working Group of Feminism and International Law. She is author of, *inter alia*, *Towards Different Law and Public Policy; The Significance of Article 5a CEDAW for the Elimination of Structural Gender Discrimination* and of *Women's Human Rights and Culture: From Deadlock to Dialogue*.

Susann Kroworsch, works as a graduate research fellow and is a PhD candidate at Freie Universität Berlin. She studied law at Humboldt Universität zu Berlin and Université Montesquieu Bordeaux (first and second state exam in law). During her legal clerkship (*Referendariat*) she worked, *inter alia*, at the Federal Foreign Office and the Human Rights Committee of the German Federal Parliament (*Bundestag*).

Frances Raday, LLB, LLD, who was a member of the CEDAW Committee 2000–2003, is Director of the Concord Research Center for Integration of International Law in Israel, Haim Stricks Law School, COLMAN; Chair, Advisory Board of Israel's Equal Employment Opportunity Commission; member of the UN Human Rights Council Working Group on Discrimination against Women; Lieberman Chair of Labour Law (emerita) Hebrew University, Jerusalem; Honorary Professor University College London; and Doctor Honoris Copenhagen University. She is the author of numerous academic books and articles on human rights, labour law, and feminist legal theory.

Beate Rudolf, Dr. iur., Professor of Law, is Director of the German Institute for Human Rights, the National Human Rights Institution of Germany according to the UN Paris

Principles. Until 2010, she was Junior Professor of Public Law and Equality Law at the Faculty of Law of Freie Universität Berlin. She is a vice-president of the European Women Lawyers Association (EWLA) and a member of the ILA Committee 'Feminism in International Law'.

Verónica Undurraga, JD, LLM, JSD candidate, is Director of the Women's Program at the Human Rights Center, University of Chile Law School. She is a member of the Latin American Law Professors' Network and the Seminar in Latin America on Constitutional and Political Theory. She is a board member of Fundación Pro Bono and a founding member of the Chilean Society for Public Policy.

Sarah Wittkopp, is a PhD candidate at Freie Universität Berlin and law clerk (*Referendarin*) at the Higher Regional Court of Berlin, including a traineeship at the Federal Ministry for Economic Cooperation and Development. She studied law at Freie Universität Berlin and Stockholms Universitet, Sweden. She was a research fellow at the Collaborative Research Center 'Governance in Areas of Limited Statehood' and at Freie Unversität Berlin.

A Note on Citation Formats

The primary material on which the Commentary relies is the CEDAW Committee's concluding observations on State party reviews. As the Optional Protocol has been in force only for ten years, relatively few cases have been decided under it. Because of the very large number of citations to the Committee's conclusions on State party reviews, the editors adopted a short form of citation to the concluding observations, approved by the Oxford University Press.

The designation system for CEDAW documents has changed over the years. After the Committee began to formulate specific conclusions and recommendations, they were designated as Concluding Comments through the Fortieth Session in January 2008. Since the Forty-first Session in July 2008, the conclusions have been designated as Concluding Observations, in conformity with the usage of the other human rights treaty bodies. However, some search protocols produce documents labelled 'Concluding Observations' in a general heading and 'Concluding Comments' per State party. For purposes of simplicity, the Commentary uses the term Concluding Observations (or CO) for most of these citations.

From its inception through 2008, the Committee's conclusions have been included in an annual report to the General Assembly (UN Doc. A/ numbers), and since 1997 divided into parts corresponding to the first, second, and, where relevant, third session held in each calendar year. In 2005, the Committee's secretariat began to provide individual document numbers for the conclusions for each State party in each session (using CEDAW/C/ numbers). Search tools, including the United Nations' Universal Index to Human Rights Documents, may designate the documents with either number. Accordingly, the citations in this Commentary to documents published in those years may use either number format. Since 2009, the CEDAW documents carry only CEDAW/C numbers.

The Commentary reflects the Committee's record through 31 December 2010.

A Note on Citations to the Commentary

The authors suggest that citations to the Commentary be as follows:

Author, Article [No], p [No], in Freeman, Chinkin, Rudolf (eds), CEDAW Commentary (Oxford: OUP, 2012)

eg A Byrnes, Article 1, p xx in Freeman, Chinkin, Rudolf (eds), CEDAW Commentary (Oxford: OUP, 2012)

Table of Acronyms

ACHR	American Convention on Human Rights
ACRWC	African Charter on the Rights and Welfare of the Child
CAT	Convention against Torture and Other Cruel, Inhuman or Degrading Treatment or Punishment
CCPR	Human Rights Committee
CEDAW	Convention on the Elimination of All Forms of Discrimination against Women
CERD	Committee on the Elimination of Racial Discrimination
CESCR	Committee on Economic, Social and Cultural Rights
CESR	Center for Economic and Social Rights
CPED	International Convention for the Protection of All Persons from Enforced Disappearance
CRC	Convention on the Rights of the Child
CRPD	Convention on the Rights of Persons with Disabilities
CSW	Commission on the Status of Women
DAW	Division for the Advancement of Women
DEDAW	Declaration on the Elimination of Discrimination against Women
DEVAW	Declaration on the Elimination of Violence against Women
ECHR	European Convention on Human Rights
ECtHR	European Court of Human Rights
ECJ	European Court of Justice
ECOSOC	Economic and Social Council
FAO	Food and Agricultural Organization
HRC	Human Rights Council
ICCPR	International Covenant on Civil and Political Rights
ICERD	International Convention on the Elimination of all Forms of Racial Discrimination
ICESCR	International Covenant on Economic, Social and Cultural Rights
ICJ	International Court of Justice
ICRMW	International Convention on the Protection of the Rights of All Migrant Workers and Members of their Families
ILO	International Labour Organization
IWRAW	International Women's Rights Action Watch
NGO	Non-governmental organization
OHCHR	Office of the High Commissioner for Human Rights
OP	Optional Protocol
OPCAT	Optional Protocol to the Convention against Torture and Other Cruel, Inhuman or Degrading Treatment or Punishment
UDHR	Universal Declaration of Human Rights

UNDP	United Nations Development Programme
UNHCHR	UN High Commissioner for Human Rights
UNFPA	United Nations Population Fund
UNGA	UN General Assembly
UNIFEM	United Nations Development Fund for Women
UNMIK	United Nations Interim Administration Mission in Kosovo
UNSC	United Nations Security Council
UN SG	United Nations Secretary-General
UNTAET	United Nations Transitional Administration in East Timor
UNTS	United Nations Treaty Series
VCLT	Vienna Convention on the Law of Treaties
WHO	World Health Organization

Table of Cases

Australia

Belize

Table of Legislation

NATIONAL LEGISLATION

INTERNATIONAL INSTRUMENTS

Introduction

A. Introduction

The Convention on the Elimination of All Forms of Discrimination against Women (CEDAW or the Convention) is a key international human rights instrument and the only one exclusively addressed to women. Indeed, it has been described as the United Nations' (UN) 'landmark treaty in the struggle for women's rights', and as constituting 'an international bill of rights for women'.[1] The Convention applies to all forms of discrimination against women and is not limited to the specific fields spelled out within it. Discrimination against women is defined in terms of its impact on women's equal enjoyment of their human rights and fundamental freedoms. Its scope is wide, requiring States parties to address how the enjoyment of recognized human rights is adversely affected by gender-based distinctions, exclusions, and stereotypes. While it binds States parties with respect to public actions, laws, and policies, like the earlier ICERD it extends the understanding of human rights by requiring the State party to prevent or impose sanctions on acts of discrimination by non-State (private) actors, including within the family, the community, and the commercial sector.

This volume is the first comprehensive commentary on the Convention and its Optional Protocol (OP) as interpreted through the work of its monitoring body, the Committee on the Elimination of Discrimination against Women (the Committee). The Commentary comprises detailed analyses of the Preamble and each article of the Convention and of the Optional Protocol. It also includes a separate chapter on the cross-cutting substantive issue of violence against women. The sources relied on in every chapter are primarily the language of the article in question and the general recommendations, concluding observations and case law under the Optional Protocol, through which the Committee has interpreted and applied the Convention. The drafting process for each article is described only briefly, as two commentaries on the *travaux préparatoires* already exist.[2] However, a fuller drafting history of the Optional Protocol, which the existing commentaries do not cover, is included in that chapter. Jurisprudence from national courts and international bodies, including the regional human rights institutions, is included if it refers directly to the Convention or, exceptionally, if it has made a particularly significant contribution to understanding the legal guarantee of women's equality.

Although the chapters are self-contained, the Commentary is conceived of as an integral whole. In that vein, the concepts and ideas that are repeated across Convention articles are cross-referenced. And while each chapter of the Commentary is attributed to an author(s), all the contributors have had the opportunity to comment on drafts and make suggestions. Bringing the contributors together in working meetings (Berlin in 2008, The Hague and Berlin in 2009, and Bellagio in 2010) greatly facilitated the development of shared thinking and approach.

As a commentary on the Convention, this work does not purport to offer a detailed analysis of the status or position of women under international law, or developments in the international protection of women's human rights outside the framework of the

---

[1] *The United Nations and The Advancement of Women, 1945–1995*, UN Blue Books Series, Vol. VI (rev. edn, 1996) 5.

[2] L Rehof, *Guide to the Travaux Préparatoires of the United Nations Convention on the Elimination of All Forms of Discrimination against Women* (1993); Japanese Association of International Women's Rights, *Convention on the Elimination of All Forms of Discrimination against Women: A Commentary* (1995).

Convention. These issues have been the subject of a great deal of research and analysis, and we acknowledge our debt to those whose work we have drawn upon.

This Introduction to the Commentary provides an overview of the Convention and its embedding in the international law of human rights. It briefly outlines the Convention's adoption, structure, and key concepts. It summarizes the most significant issues of Convention application and interpretation and the ways in which the Committee has sought to ensure the Convention's continuing relevance for women around the world. It introduces some issues that are pervasive throughout the Convention, and where they are addressed in more detail elsewhere in the Commentary it directs readers to the appropriate chapters. A few matters are touched upon only in the Introduction, such as the principles of general international law which affect interpretation and implementation of the Convention.

B. Towards a Convention on Elimination of Discrimination against Women

I. The League of Nations

The long history of the idea of women's human rights is still largely unrecorded, especially in the global South.[3] The struggle for their guarantee has taken place across multiple sites worldwide, has involved women from many sectors of society, and has manifested itself in diverse forms. It has involved considerable courage and commitment from those seeking to secure the advancement of women, which has too often been violently resisted.

In international institutional terms the story commences with the League of Nations, established in the aftermath of World War I.[4] The International Council of Women argued unsuccessfully for the inclusion of women's rights in the League Covenant. In 1935, the question of the status of women was placed on the League's agenda, and in 1937, a Committee of Experts was appointed to carry out an inquiry into the legal status of the world's women. The outbreak of World War II and subsequent dissolution of the League brought its work to an end.

In the absence of any general international provisions on women's rights, some measures were adopted to address limited and specified circumstances. For example, in 1919, the International Labour Organization adopted the Convention Concerning the Employment of Women before and after Childbirth[5] and the Convention Concerning the Employment of Women during the Night.[6] These treaties were narrow in scope and protective in nature[7] rather than directed towards women's enjoyment of rights. Indeed, their protective stance restricted women's choices with respect to forms of employment (night work) and the consequences of maternity and thus undermined women's autonomy, as discussed in the chapter on Article 11. The League of Nations also addressed trafficking of women through the 1921 Convention for the Suppression of Traffic in Women and

---

[3] A Fraser, 'Becoming Human: The Origins and Development of Women's Human Rights' (1999) 21 *Human Rights Quarterly* 853–906.

[4] H Pietilä, *The Unfinished Story of Women and the United Nations* (2007).

[5] ILO Convention No 3.   [6] ILO Convention No 4.

[7] Natalie Hevener Kaufman describes three categories of treaties dealing specifically with women: protective, corrective and non-discriminatory. 'International Law and the Status of Women: An Analysis of International Legal Instruments Related to the Treatment of Women' (1978) 1 *Harv Women's LJ* 131.

Children and the 1933 Convention for the Suppression of the Traffic in Women of Full Age, as discussed in the chapter on Article 6.

At the regional level, in 1928, the Sixth International Conference of American States, meeting in Havana, Cuba founded the Inter-American Commission of Women, the first intergovernmental body mandated expressly to work on issues related to the status of women. The Inter-American Commission was responsible for the 1933 Montevideo Convention on the Nationality of Married Women, a forerunner to CEDAW Article 9.

II. The UN Charter

The UN Charter was the first international agreement to deal expressly with the question of discrimination on the basis of sex. It refers in its preamble to 'the equal rights of men and women' and Article 1(3) includes among the purposes of the UN the promotion and encouragement of respect for human rights and fundamental freedoms for all without distinction based, *inter alia*, on sex.[8] These references to non-discrimination on the basis of sex were inserted in the Charter as the result of concerted lobbying by women delegates (notably women from Latin American States)[9] and support from non-governmental organizations (NGOs) accredited to the Founding Conference of the UN at San Francisco in 1945. This dual focus—the right to equal treatment and non-discrimination in the enjoyment of human rights—is continued in the general human rights instruments: the UDHR, Article 2,[10] the ICCPR Articles 2(1) and 3, and the ICESCR Articles 2(2) and 3. The ICCPR Article 26 goes further, asserting equality before the law and a free-standing (independent) prohibition of discrimination, including on the basis of sex.

At the time the UN Charter was adopted, responsibility for women's development and the promotion of women's status was placed in the hands of a specialist and separate women's commission. This was first designated as a sub-commission of the Commission on Human Rights, but by 1946 the Commission on the Status of Women (CSW) was a separate functional commission of the ECOSOC under UN Charter Article 68, having the same status within the UN system as the Commission on Human Rights. The CSW's functions included making recommendations to ECOSOC 'on promoting women's rights' and 'on urgent problems requiring immediate attention in the field of women's rights'.[11] ECOSOC agreed that the CSW should be represented at meetings of the UN Commission on Human Rights 'when sections of the draft of the international bill of human rights concerning the particular rights of women are under discussion'.[12] The CSW was instrumental in ensuring that the phrase 'equal rights of men and women' in the Preamble of the UN Charter was retained in the UDHR[13] and subsequently was responsible for the drafting of three 'corrective' conventions which sought to address particular areas in which women suffered disadvantage. The Convention on the Political Rights of Women, 1952 (discussed in the chapter on Article 7),[14] the Convention on the Nationality of Married Women, 1957, and the Convention on Consent to Marriage, Minimum Age for Marriage and

---

[8] See also UN Charter arts 55(c), 56 and, in the context of the trusteeship system, 76(c).

[9] For women delegates at the San Francisco Conference see Pietilä (n 4 above) 9–10.

[10] UDHR art 7 asserts that '[a]ll are equal before the law and are entitled without discrimination to equal protection of the law'. It does not spell out the prohibited categories of discrimination.

[11] ECOSOC Res 48 E/RES/48 (IV) (29 March 1947).   [12] Ibid para 3.

[13] Pietilä (n 4 above) 17–19.

[14] UNGA Res 640 (VII) (20 December 1952) (recommending member States to 'grant the same political rights to women as to men').

Registration of Marriages, 1962 (both discussed in the chapter on Article 16), establish significant and binding principles of equality but are specific and narrow in subject matter and lack accountability mechanisms.[15]

By the 1960s, it was becoming evident that despite the principle of non-discrimination in women's enjoyment of rights included in the UN Charter and the UDHR 'extensive discrimination against women continue[d] to exist'.[16] Women had been active in national self-determination movements, but decolonization and development projects had failed to deliver the anticipated benefits to women.[17] A change in the traditional roles of women and men was needed to ensure equality between women and men.[18] Even before the adoption of the two UN Covenants, the ICCPR and ICESCR,[19] women realized the shortcomings of general equality and non-discrimination provisions and were seeking an instrument identifying and condemning the particular and multiple manifestations of discrimination faced by women worldwide. Accordingly, demands began to be made for a more comprehensive and well-targeted international focus on women, including development of a norm of non-discrimination against women within the emerging human rights legal framework.

III. The Declaration on the Elimination of Discrimination against Women, 1967

The first step was adoption of the Declaration on the Elimination of Discrimination against Women[20] (DEDAW), sponsored by developing and socialist States.[21] It was drafted by the CSW and debated in the UNGA Third Committee before being adopted in 1967.[22] It follows the structure of the UDHR, comprising a Preamble and eleven articles. Article 1 declares discrimination against women to be an offence against human dignity, and Article 2 states that 'appropriate measures shall be taken . . . to establish adequate legal protection for equal rights of men and women'. Article 3 recognizes the part custom and prejudice play in denying women's equality and requires appropriate measures for their eradication as well as abolition of practices 'based on the idea of the inferiority of women'. Subsequent articles identify particular areas of discrimination against women—public life, nationality of married women, the family, penal codes, trafficking and exploitation of prostitution, education, and economic and social life—and state that 'appropriate measures shall be taken' to address them. Finally, the Declaration asserts that the general principle of 'equality of rights of men and women demands implementation in all States in accordance with the principles of the Charter of the United Nations and of the Universal Declaration of Human Rights'.

---

[15] M Galey, 'Promoting Non-Discrimination against Women: The UN Commission on the Status of Women' (1979) 23 *Intl Studies Quarterly* 273, 277–81.

[16] CEDAW Preamble para 6. [17] E Boserup, *Women's Role in Economic Development* (1970).

[18] CEDAW Preamble para 6.

[19] The ICCPR and ICESCR were adopted by UNGA Res 2200 PartA (XXI) para 14 (16 December 1966) the ICESCR came into force on 3 January 1976; the ICCPR on 23 March 1976.

[20] UNGA Res 2263 (XXII) (7 November 1967).

[21] UNGA Res 1921 (XVIII) (5 December 1963), requested ECOSOC to invite CSW to prepare a draft declaration on elimination of discrimination against women.

[22] A Fraser, ' The Convention on the Elimination of All Forms of Discrimination against Women (The Women's Convention)' in A Winslow (ed), *Women, Politics and the United Nations* (1995) 78–85.

IV. The UN Decade for Women 1975–1985 and the Decade World Conferences

The process of gaining legal commitment to women's equality was an element of the evolving global women's movement[23] epitomized by (but by no means limited to) three world conferences on women. In 1972, the twenty-fifth anniversary of the first CSW session, the UNGA accepted a CSW recommendation to hold a world summit on women in Mexico City in 1975, focusing on the themes of equality, development, and peace and designating 1975 International Women's Year.[24] Following the Mexico City Conference the UNGA proclaimed 1975–85 as the UN Decade for Women.[25] The UNGA agreed to convene further world conferences on women at the mid-point of the Decade[26] (Copenhagen, 1980)[27] and at its end (Nairobi, 1985).[28] The final documents adopted at these Conferences provided important—albeit legally non-binding—blueprints for future strategy and action. The Nairobi Forward Looking Strategies (FLS) adopted at the final Conference of the Decade presented 'concrete measures to overcome the obstacles to the Decade's goals and objectives for the advancement of women'.[29]

As meeting spaces for ever-increasing numbers of women from around the globe, the three world conferences held during the Decade provided the impetus for networking and organizing at local and international levels. In the more open political environment after the end of the Cold War, the 1990s saw a further 'continuum of conferences' on diverse aspects of development, with 'goals dependent on the advancement of women'.[30] Women participated effectively in these global conferences and important affirmations of women's human rights were achieved at Rio de Janeiro (1992),[31] Vienna (1993),[32] Cairo (1994),[33] and Copenhagen (1995).[34] This activity culminated in the Fourth World Conference on Women (Beijing, 1995), a high point for international activism on women's human rights and status. The Rome Statute of the International Criminal Court, a binding treaty adopted in 1998, brought violent crimes committed against women into the ambit of international criminal law.[35] The CEDAW story is closely entwined with these global commitments.

V. Adoption of the Convention, 1979

As a UNGA resolution DEDAW is not legally binding, and its language is primarily aspirational. Nevertheless, agreement on these principles facilitated the process of moving from a non-binding instrument to a binding treaty, which was initiated

---

[23] P Antrobus, *The Global Women's Movement: Origins, Issues and Strategies* (2004).

[24] UNGA Res 3010 (XXVII) (18 December 1972) UN Doc A/RES/3010 (XXVII).

[25] UNGA Res 3520 (XXX) (15 December 1975) para 2.   [26] Ibid para 20.

[27] The second World Conference was to have been held in Tehran, but the 1979 Iranian revolution resulted in a change of venue.

[28] UNGA Res 35/136 (11 December 1980) UN Doc A/RES/35/136 para 17.

[29] 'Report of the World Conference to Review and Appraise the Achievements of the United Nations Decade for Women: Equality, Development and Peace', Nairobi, Kenya, 15–26 July 1985, UN Doc A/CONF.116/28/Rev.1 (85.IV.10) (1986) para 8.

[30] *The United Nations and the Advancement of Women 1945–1995* (n 1 above) 54.

[31] UN Conference on Environment and Development, Rio de Janeiro, Brazil 2–14 June 1992.

[32] World Conference on Human Rights, Vienna, Austria, 14–25 June 1993.

[33] UN International Conference on Population and Development, Cairo, Egypt, 5–13 September 1994.

[34] World Summit for Social Development, Copenhagen, Denmark, 6–12 March 1995.

[35] The Rome Statute, especially arts 7(1)(g); 7(1)(h); 7(3); 8(2)(b)(xxii); 8(2)(e)(vi); 36(8)(a) and (b).

when the Polish delegate to the CSW proposed an international convention, less than a year after DEDAW was adopted.[36] In 1972, the CSW received a report of the UN Secretary–General (UNSG) discussing the various international instruments appertaining to women's rights and the views of governments on the concept of a convention. A CSW working group was formed to consider a possible convention, and the Philippines prepared a draft text,[37] without implying any commitment by that government. The working group continued to follow the strategy of governmental non-commitment by not attributing positions to any particular delegate, thereby creating 'free spaces' for discussion between members.[38] The Philippines and the USSR ultimately presented a joint draft convention.[39]

Many of the provisions in DEDAW are reflected in the final text of the Convention. While ICERD, 1965, also was a source of some language (including the definition of discrimination) and structure, the Convention, like DEDAW drafted primarily by women, reflected an understanding of women's lives. Significant differences between racial discrimination and sex-based discrimination had to be taken into account, most notably the need to prohibit the discrimination against women that occurs from within their own families and communities.

The 1975 Mexico City World Plan of Action had recommended that '[h]igh priority should be given to the preparation and adoption of the convention on the elimination of discrimination against women, with effective procedures for its implementation'.[40] The CSW completed its work on a draft in 1977 and forwarded it to the UNGA, where it was scrutinized by a working group of the GA Third Committee. The full Third Committee, sitting as a Working Group of the Whole, considered it in November and early December, 1979. The Convention was adopted by the UNGA Resolution 34/180 on 18 December 1979, with 130 votes in favour, none against and 10 abstentions.[41] It was opened for signature at the mid-Decade Conference at Copenhagen in 1980, where sixty-four States signed the treaty at a special ceremony, and two States submitted their instruments of ratification. It entered into force on 3 September 1981, thirty days after the twentieth State, St Vincent and the Grenadines, submitted its instrument of accession to the UN SG in accordance with Article 27(1). As of 31 December 2010, there are 186 States parties, making it the second most widely ratified UN human rights treaty.[42] The seven UN member States that have not ratified or acceded to the Convention are Iran, Nauru, Palau, Somalia, Sudan, Tonga, and the United States of America (which signed the Convention on 17 July 1980). By signing the Convention, the USA is obliged to refrain from acts which would defeat the object and purpose of the treaty.[43]

---

[36] Fraser (n 22 above) 84.   [37] UN Doc E/CN.6/573 (6 November 1973).
[38] Fraser (n 3 above) 894.   [39] UN Doc E/CN.6/AC.1/L.4 (8 January 1974).
[40] World Plan of Action for the Implementation of the Objectives of the International Women's Year, the Declaration of Mexico on the Equality of Women and their Contribution to Development and Peace, UN Doc E/CONF.66/34 (76.IV.1) (1976) Part 1 para 198.
[41] UN Doc A/Res/34/180 Bangladesh, Brazil, Comoros, Haiti, Mali, Mauritania, Mexico, Morocco, Saudi Arabia, and Senegal abstained; Albania, Djibouti, Dominica, Equatorial Guinea, Iran, Malawi, Papua New Guinea, Saint Lucia, Seychelles, Solomon Islands, South Africa, and United Republic of Cameroon did not vote.
[42] As of 31 December 2010, there were 193 States parties to the CRC. The four Geneva Red Cross Conventions have achieved 194 ratifications making them universally applicable; website of the International Committee of the Red Cross, <http://www.icrc.org/Web/eng/siteeng0.nsf/htmlall/genevaconventions#a1> accessed 31 December 2010.
[43] VCLT art 18.

C. Structure of the Convention

The Convention formally comprises a Preamble and six parts. The parts are not labelled although they were during the drafting process. Part I (Articles 1–6) deals with States parties' general obligations; Part II (Articles 7–9) with public life and civil and political rights; Part III (Articles 10–14) with economic and social rights; Part IV (Articles 15–16) with legal status, including within the family; Part V (Articles 17–22) with the Committee; and Part VI (Articles 23–30) with the final provisions. The structure might be more easily understood for purposes of application as comprising Articles 1–5, which describe the general obligations of States parties under the Convention and form an overarching interpretive framework for the application of the subject specific obligations in Articles 6–16. Articles 17–22 establish the monitoring mechanism, and the final articles set out administrative and other details. Consistency between many of the substantive articles is achieved through some repetition of language (for example 'all appropriate measures', 'eliminate discrimination against women'). Some issues are alluded to in more than one article, such as references to maternity in Articles 4, 5(b), and 11(2); family planning in 10(h), 12, 14(2)(b), and 16(1)(e); pregnancy in 11(2) and 12(2); and Article 14 on rural women touches on many issues, with reference to the special obstacles to equality women experience in rural areas. Such repetition reflects the realities of women's lives, which resist rigid compartmentalization between, *inter alia,* their working lives, their family lives, and their health needs.

I. Preamble

The Preamble follows and develops the wording of the preamble to DEDAW. Its basic premise is that despite the existence of other human rights instruments, extensive discrimination continues, that this discrimination violates the principles of equality of rights, and that the Convention aims to implement the principles of the DEDAW by requiring States parties to undertake specific measures. It links the 'promotion of equality between men and women' to the significant political and economic concerns of the day, including the New International Economic Order, eradication of apartheid and colonialism, nuclear disarmament, and development. These issues are discussed further in the chapter on the Preamble.

II. Articles 1 to 5

'The Convention is an innovative human rights treaty'[44] and much of the innovation is found in the first five articles, which set out the purpose of the Convention and States parties' general obligations under it. The purpose is elimination of discrimination against women, in order, in the words of Article 3, 'to ensure the full development and advancement of women', and thus their enjoyment of human rights 'on a basis of equality with men'. Since human rights law operates within a State-centric framework, the Convention addresses equality between women and men within States, not between women across States. Elimination of discrimination and achievement of equality are at the heart of the

---

[44] HB Schöpp-Schilling, 'The Nature and Scope of the Convention' in HB Schöpp-Schilling and C Flinterman (eds), *The Circle of Empowerment: Twenty-five Years of the UN Committee on the Elimination of Discrimination against Women* (2007) 10, 16.

Convention. Writings in philosophy, theology, political, legal, and feminist theory have explored the different meanings and understandings of these concepts.[45] The Convention defines discrimination widely (drawing upon the definition in ICERD Article 1) and encompasses both formal (*de jure*) and substantive (*de facto*) equality, as discussed in the chapter on Article 1. The acceptance of this definition by the CCPR[46] and the CESCR[47] has strengthened the link between the Convention and the Covenants and entrenched it in international human rights law.

The Convention not only prohibits sex-based discrimination but expressly prohibits discrimination against women, irrespective of their marital status, that adversely impacts upon their enjoyment of their human rights and fundamental freedoms.[48] The importance of the distinction is that CEDAW is not gender–neutral but addresses explicitly the need to eliminate discrimination against women. As a corollary to this premise, discrimination which seeks to redress the historical subordination of women and to accelerate the achievement of equality—that is, preferential treatment for women through the adoption of temporary special measures—is provided for by the Convention, as is explained in its General Recommendation 25 and discussed in the chapter on Article 4. Further, achieving equality requires addressing the structural nature of discrimination that is rooted in patriarchy, social and cultural patterns of conduct of men and women, prejudices, customary and other practices, and stereotyped roles for men and women, as described in Article 5. At the time of its adoption the Convention was unique in requiring States parties to modify such types of behaviour,[49] as is discussed in the chapter on Article 5.

Articles 1 to 5 are complementary and should be read in conjunction with each other and Article 24.[50] Taken together they indicate the comprehensive nature of the Convention's vision and States parties' obligations. Articles 2 and 24 require States parties to undertake the requisite measures at the national level to ensure the prohibition of all discrimination against women and the existence of competent national institutions to make the prohibition effective. The Convention is not limited to achievement of formal and substantive equality. Rather, States parties 'shall take measures' in all spheres of life for the 'full development and advancement of women' (Article 3). This looks to transformation of society and gender relations—what might be termed transformative equality. Such progressive transformation does not depend upon rigid adherence to the applicability of the 'same' rights to women and men but gives effect and legitimacy to areas of difference. Positive obligations under the Convention involve changing social and institutional structures, for example, public life (Articles 7 and 8), the workplace (Article 11(2)), education (Article 10(2)), and common parental responsibilities as described in the Preamble and Articles 5(2), 11(2)(c), and 16(1)(d)–(f). They also require according differential treatment to women to take account of their specific situation, in particular that of maternity (pregnancy and childbirth), covered in Articles 4(2), 11(2), and 12(2). Human rights law offers

---

[45] See the discussion in chs on arts 1–5.

[46] CCPR, 'General Comment 18' (1994) UN Doc HRI/GEN/1/Rev.1 para 6.

[47] CESCR, 'General Comment 16' (2005) UN Doc E/C.12/2005/4 para 11; CESCR, 'General Comment 20' (2009) UN Doc E/C.12/GC/20 para 7.

[48] The ICCPR and ICESCR make an express commitment to the 'equal right of men and women' to enjoyment of the rights in the respective Covenants; ICCPR art 3; ICESCR art 3.

[49] CRPD art 8 (1) requires States parties 'to adopt immediate, effective and appropriate measures...to combat stereotypes, prejudices and harmful practices relating to persons with disabilities, including those based on sex'.

[50] GR 28 para 7.

a vision of the good life—self-determination and freedom from fear and want—to women and men. What is required through societal transformation is that women and men have the same opportunities for achievement of this vision: true equality achieved through recognition of difference. These issues run through all the chapters on Articles 1–16.

Human rights law is centred on the relationship between the individual and the State, but in many instances the threat to women's enjoyment of their human rights comes not from State agents but from private individuals, such as members of their family and community. Inequality within the private sphere of the family undermines women's access to and enjoyment of rights in the public sphere of the workplace and politics. It is, therefore, crucial to the success of the Convention as an instrument condemning discrimination against women that it is not limited to the vertical relationship between the State and individuals but that it also applies, through the instrumentality of the State, to the horizontal relationships between individuals. Article 2(e) accordingly requires the State party to 'take all appropriate measures to eliminate discrimination against women by any person, organization or enterprise'. This imposes a positive obligation on States parties to protect individuals from violations of their human rights by other individuals. It has been developed through the concept of due diligence, most specifically in the context of combating violence against women. These issues are therefore discussed primarily in the chapters on Article 2 and violence against women.

III. Articles 6 to 16

Articles 6 to 16 cover the specific substantive areas of the Convention. Article 6 is formally located in Part I. While it deals with particular abuses– trafficking and exploitation of prostitution—it is phrased in terms of a general obligation. It is a transitional article between the general obligations of Part I and the specificities of Part II. It also differs from other articles in that it makes no reference to equality between women and men. Article 6 does not state that women have an equal right to be free from being trafficked, or from being exploited in prostitution, but that the State party shall suppress these activities as harmful to women. The practices addressed in Article 6 are linked to Article 5 in that they are fostered by attitudes and prejudices relating to the subordination of women and must therefore be eradicated. In this sense, too, Article 6 belongs in Part I of the Convention. Article 6 is important in recognizing the gendered nature of human trafficking and in bringing it into the framework of human rights law in addition to that of criminal justice. However, the provision lacks specificity, for example, as to the means of suppression. This is one area in which the Convention has been significantly supplemented by other global and regional treaties. These issues are discussed in the chapter on Article 6.

Many Convention articles require States parties to take 'all appropriate measures to eliminate discrimination': in political and public life (Article 7); international organizations (Article 8); the acquisition and retention of nationality and the transmission of nationality to children (Article 9); education (Article 10); employment (Article 11); health care (Article 12); family benefits, financial credit, and participation in recreational activities, sport, and cultural life (Article 13); the rural sector (Article 14); equality before the law, legal capacity, freedom of movement (Article 15); and within the family (Article 16). Some of these Articles are detailed, setting out multiple situations and requirements (for example, Articles 10, 11, 14, and 16) while others are perhaps surprisingly brief (for example, Article 12). There is no explicit reference to gender-based violence in

Articles 7–16 (and only by implication in Article 6). However, the Committee rectified this omission through its General Recommendation 19, which explains such violence as a form of discrimination within Article 1 and links it to all the substantive articles.[51]

The substantive articles of the Convention '[b]ring together in a comprehensive legally binding form, internationally accepted principles on the rights of women—and make clear that they are applicable to women in all societies.'[52] In contrast to the International Covenants on Human Rights, the Convention defines discrimination and requires in a single instrument the adoption of appropriate measures for the elimination of discrimination in civil, political, economic, social, and cultural fields. It thereby recognizes that guarantees of civil and political rights are incomplete without taking account of the economic, social, and cultural environment in which they operate for women, and that exercise of civil and political rights is critical to full enjoyment of economic, social, and cultural rights. In this way the Convention identifies areas in which discrimination against women is most marked and where special attention by States parties is required. It also challenges the public/private dichotomy historically observed in international law.[53] For example, it asserts women's equal rights to participate in public decision-making bodies at all levels, including the international (Articles 7 and 8) and also explicitly affirms women's right to equality within the 'private' arena of the family (Articles 15(4) and 16) and private contractual arrangements (Article 15(2) and (3)).

IV. Articles 17 to 22

Part V of its Convention deals with its implementation through the establishment of an independent monitoring mechanism, the CEDAW Committee. However, this was controversial, and the precedents for establishing monitoring bodies in the UN human rights treaties existing at the time were not uniform.

DEDAW does not specify an implementing mechanism. Although it is formally non-binding, ECOSOC nevertheless requested States to inform the UN SG 'of action taken by them in compliance with the principles of the Declaration' and the SG to submit a report on the information received for consideration by the CSW.[54] This system of reporting to the CSW was largely ineffective. It was, therefore, extremely important that provision for effective implementation—as recommended by the Mexico City World Plan of Action—was included in the Convention.

Monitoring bodies had been established by the ICCPR Article 28 (the Human Rights Committee) and the ICERD Article 8 (CERD). In contrast, the ICESCR did not provide for any such body. States parties' reports on their progress in implementing the ICESCR were [to be] submitted to the ECOSOC,[55] a body comprising elected States members of the UN, not all of which would necessarily be party to the ICESCR. The CSW was the UN body mandated to promote women's rights and eliminate discrimination on the grounds of sex.[56] It already had a role in receiving reports, and the ICESCR model suggested it as the appropriate body under the Convention. Some delegations were reluctant

---

[51] See the discussion in the ch on Violence against Women.
[52] *The United Nations and the Advancement of Women 1945–1995* (n 1 above) 41.
[53] H Charlesworth and C Chinkin, *The Boundaries of International Law A Feminist Analysis* (2000) 30–1; 56–9.
[54] ECOSOC Res 1325 (XLIV) (31 May 1968) paras 6–7.   [55] ICESCR art 17.
[56] ECOSOC Res 48 (IV) (29 March 1947).

to establish a new body, which would have different membership, be formally independent, and thus might diminish the CSW's authority in the field. However, Article 17 was adopted, providing for the establishment of the Committee as (at that time) the UN human rights treaty body with the largest membership of independent experts. Elections to the Committee and other issues relating to its membership are discussed in the chapter on Article 17.

Article 18 provides for State party reporting to the Committee and Article 19 gives the Committee competence to determine its own Rules of Procedure. The Committee's work in drafting guidelines for State party reporting and the ongoing process of developing its working methods are detailed in the chapter on Article 19. Article 20 provides that the Committee 'shall normally meet for a period of not more than two weeks annually' in order to consider States parties' reports. No other UN human rights treaty limits the meeting time for its monitoring body in this way, and the problems it has presented for the Committee and the struggle for amendment of Article 20 are described in that chapter. Article 21 describes the Committee's reporting obligations to the ECOSOC and UNGA and provides the basis for its adoption of general recommendations.

The situation of women is relevant to the programmes of all specialized agencies, and several have participated in the Committee's sessions. The interaction between the specialized agencies and the Committee is discussed in the chapter on Article 22. The Convention does not provide for 'other competent bodies' (for example, NGOs) to provide advice to the Committee, as does the CRC Article 45(b). Nevertheless, the Committee has over the years developed a highly productive relationship with NGOs, notably women's NGOs, and with other stakeholders such as national human rights institutions and UN Human Rights Council special procedure mandate holders.[57]

V. Articles 23 to 30

Part VI of the Convention covers various concluding provisions common to other human rights treaties, as discussed in the chapters on these articles. In order to provide the highest level of protection for women's equality, Article 23 provides that where there are national or international provisions more conducive to its achievement, they shall prevail. Article 24 on necessary measures which States parties undertake to adopt at the national level reinforces the obligations of States parties under the Convention, in particular Articles 2 and 3. Articles 25–27 cover a range of technical issues required by international law: the modalities of becoming bound by the Convention, revision, and entry into force. Article 28 reiterates the general international law position[58] that 'a reservation incompatible with the object and purpose of the Convention' is not permitted. Article 29 provides for the resolution of disputes including the possibility of referral of a dispute on the interpretation or application of the Convention to the International Court of Justice (ICJ)[59] Finally, Article 30 provides for the authenticity of the text in all six languages of the UN.

---

[57] Report of the Secretary-General, 'Status of the Convention on the Elimination of All Forms of Discrimination against Women' (2009) UN Doc A/64/342. See also M Freeman, 'The Committee on the Elimination of Discrimination against Women and the Role of Civil Society in Implementing International Women's Human Rights Norms' (spring 2010) 16 *New England J of Intl & Comparative L* 25.

[58] VCLT art 19(c).

[59] *Armed Activities on the Territory of the Congo* (New Application: 2002) (*Democratic Republic of the Congo v Rwanda*) (3 February 2006) 1996 ICJ Rep paras 80–93.

VI. The Optional Protocol

Unlike the two UN human rights treaty bodies that existed in 1979 (CCPR and CERD), the CEDAW Committee was not mandated to hear individual or inter-State complaints about non-compliance with Convention obligations. Its original competence was restricted to the consideration of States parties' reports under Article 18 of the Convention. The 1993 Vienna World Conference on Human Rights called for the adoption of new procedures 'to strengthen implementation of the commitment to women's equality and the human rights of women'.[60] The CSW and the Committee were to 'quickly examine' the possibility of introducing the right of individual petition through the preparation of an optional protocol. Following the Vienna Conference a non-governmental expert group developed a draft, which was taken up by the Committee and the CSW.[61] The Optional Protocol, adopted in 1999, provides for individual communications from individuals and groups and for an inquiry procedure into grave or systematic violations. It thus significantly extends the Committee's jurisdiction under the Convention for those States that have become parties to it. The drafting, text and application of the Optional Protocol are described in that chapter.

D. Issues of Definition and Interpretation

I. The Committee as Interpretive Body

The Convention is the only universal legally binding instrument to concentrate comprehensively on the achievement of women's equality. However, partly because it is a product of its time, some key terms are not defined and some issues that are critical to women's full enjoyment of their human rights are not mentioned, or are addressed only in general and indeterminate language. But, like other human rights treaties, it is a 'dynamic instrument that accommodates the development of international law'.[62] Since the Convention does not include provisions on interpretation, it should be interpreted in accordance with the normal rules of public international law as encapsulated in the Vienna Convention on the Law of Treaties (VCLT).[63] In particular, every Article should be interpreted in 'good faith in accordance with the ordinary meaning to be given to the terms of the treaty in their context and in the light of its object and purpose',[64] that is, of the Convention as a whole. *Travaux préparatoires* are a supplementary means of interpretation which should be consulted only when the above process leads to ambiguity or to a result that is 'manifestly absurd or unreasonable'.[65]

The Committee has the task of interpreting the Convention. It commenced work in Vienna in 1982. Its primary responsibility under the Convention was to receive States parties' initial and periodic reports. Progress in its early sessions was impeded by Cold War-inspired ideological differences between its members, which prevented it 'from

---

[60] Vienna Declaration and Programme of Action II para 40.

[61] A Byrnes and J Connors, 'Enforcing the Human Rights of Women: A Complaints Procedure for the Women's Convention? Draft Optional Protocol to the Convention on the Elimination of All Forms of Discrimination against Women' (1996) 21 *Brooklyn J Intl L* 679.

[62] GR 28 para 2. See also GR 25 para 3: 'The Convention is a dynamic instrument'.

[63] The VCLT provisions on interpretation are widely accepted as customary international law.

[64] VCLT art 31(1).   [65] Ibid art 32.

making effective use of its functions for some years'.[66] Nevertheless, from the outset Committee members shared a commitment, experience, and expertise in women's rights, which has continued.[67] Through a range of activities, including self-appraisal, interaction with NGOs and participation in the Meetings of Chairpersons of the UN Human Rights Treaty Bodies, the Committee has adapted its working methods and practices, expanded its activities, and enhanced its impact and visibility.[68] It has also provided authoritative interpretations and definitions to clarify States parties' legal obligations under the Convention. In the words of General Recommendation 28, paragraph 2, the Committee along with 'other actors at the national and international levels, [has] contributed to the clarification and understanding of the substantive content of the Convention's articles, the specific nature of discrimination against women and the various instruments required for combating such discrimination'. This section looks at how the Committee's work and practical experience in implementing and monitoring the Convention have expanded global understanding of Convention norms and the obstacles to their achievement. The following section examines the instrumentalities engaged by the Committee in applying the Convention to States parties with widely differing legal, social, and cultural environments.

II. Definitions

1. Woman

While the Convention defines discrimination in Article 1, it does not define either 'woman'[69] (or man) or 'sex'. Although it does not spell out that 'women' includes girls under the age of Eighteen[70] (as does for example, the Protocol on the Rights of Women in Africa[71]), this is evidently the case. Equality in education is essential for girls. They are mentioned explicitly in Article 10(f) in the context of prematurely dropping out of school and implicitly in provisions relating to school premises (Article 10(b)) and programmes (Article 10(c)). Many of the concerns addressed in the Convention, such as trafficking, marriage, health, exploitation, and violence have immediate and important consequences for girls. Indeed, social recognition of the transition from girlhood to womanhood may depend upon a girl's perceived readiness for sexual intercourse, marriage, or childbearing. These are often forced upon girls before they are physically or mentally prepared, constituting harmful discrimination. The Committee refers readily

---

[66] E Evatt, 'Finding a Voice for Women's Rights: The Early Years of CEDAW' (2002) 34 *George Washington Intl L Rev* 515, 520.

[67] Ibid 525.

[68] M Bustelo, 'The Committee on the Elimination of Discrimination against Women at the Crossroads' in P Alston and J Crawford (eds), *The Future of UN Human Rights Treaty Monitoring* (2000) 79; HB Schöpp-Schilling, 'The Nature and Mandate of the Committee' in Schöpp-Schilling and Flinterman (n 44 above) 248–61.

[69] ILO Convention No 3 art 2 stated that 'the term woman signifies any female person, irrespective of age or nationality, whether married or unmarried, and the term child signifies any child whether legitimate or illegitimate'.

[70] CRC art 1 defines a child as 'every human being below the age of eighteen years unless under the law applicable to the child, majority is attained earlier'.

[71] The Protocol on the Rights of Women in Africa art 1(a) states that "Women" means persons of female gender, including girls'.

to girls (or children)[72] and requires that States parties pay particular 'attention to the specific needs of (adolescent) girls'.[73]

2. *Gender*

Like the UN Charter, the UDHR, ICCPR, and ICESCR, the language of the Convention is that of sex and sex-based discrimination, understood as a biological category. Since the word 'gender' was not an understood concept in international human rights law in 1979 it does not appear in the Convention and was therefore not defined. Over time the term has appeared in international instruments, although its translation into certain languages has remained problematic. The Committee introduced the concept in its general recommendations[74] but without definition. In General Recommendation 25, the Committee stated that 'biological as well as socially and culturally constructed differences between women and men must be taken into account' and noted the definition of gender that had been used in the 1999 World Survey on the Role of Women.[75] In General Recommendation 28, it has provided its own definition. Paragraph 5 states that:

(a) The term gender refers to socially constructed identities, attributes and roles for women and men and society's social and cultural meaning for these biological differences resulting in hierarchical relationships between women and men and in the distribution of power and rights favouring men and disadvantaging women. This social positioning of women and men is affected by political, economic, cultural, social, religious ideological and environmental factors and can likewise be changed by culture, society and community.

This understanding of gender clarifies that the term is not to be equated with women (as is often the case) but is concerned with the relations, notably those of the distribution of power, between women and men. The Committee seeks to address the adverse practical consequences for women of discrimination rooted in gender as a social construct, for example, the role of women as carers, or the violence that is committed against women who deviate from their assigned gender roles.

The definition of gender in General Recommendation 28 should be compared with the more limited definition in the Rome Statute of the International Criminal Court, Article 7(3):

For the purpose of this Statute, it is understood that the term 'gender' refers to the two sexes, male and female, within the context of society. The term 'gender' does not indicate any meaning different from the above.

This indicates that 'gender ha[d] become a "loaded" term'[76] in international negotiations, with certain religious and other groups and States inaccurately characterizing it as referring to sexual orientation and rejecting it on that basis.

---

[72] Including in concluding observations, eg CO Papua New Guinea, CEDAW/C/PNG/CO/3 (2010) para 25 (concern that customs and practices perpetuate discrimination against women and girls) and statements, eg 'Statement on the international financial crisis and its consequences for the human rights of women and girls' UN Doc A/64/38 (Supp), 43rd Session (2009) Decision 43/II, 144.

[73] GR 28 para 21; see also GR 19; GR 21; GR 24.

[74] eg GR 17 ('statistics disaggregated by gender'), GR 19 ('gender-based violence'), GR 24 ('gender discrimination' and 'gender equality'), GR 26 (sex and gender-based concerns related to migrant women).

[75] *UN 1999 World Survey on the Role of Women in Development* (1999) ix, cited in GR 26 n 2.

[76] Schöpp-Schilling (n 44 above) 19–20.

The Committee's approach to the specific issues of discrimination faced by lesbian women has a long evolution. Between 1994 and 2001, it referred to sexual orientation in several concluding observations but then stopped doing so. In 2008, activists briefed the Committee on the impact of State and non-State violence against lesbians, bisexual women, and transgender individuals.[77] Intersexual persons argued before the Committee that the Convention protects 'all persons who are physically and clearly not belonging to the male gender' and that medical treatment of intersexual children constitutes discrimination against women because the aim is to 'visually and mentally adjust them to what is perceived as "female" in the respective cultural context.'[78] The Committee has again begun to express its concern about discrimination and harassment of women because of their sexual orientation or gender identity.[79] General Recommendation 28 paragraph 31 affirms that lesbian women are particularly vulnerable to discrimination, although it does not explicitly refer to bisexual, transgender, and intersexual persons.

3. Domestic Implementation

Under Articles 2, 5, 6, 7, 8, 10, 11, 12, 13, 14, and 16 States parties are required to take 'all appropriate measures' to eliminate discrimination in the respective fields. This wording, also found in DEDAW and the ICESCR, allows States parties flexibility in determining how best to give effect to the Convention within their own legal systems. As stated by a former chairperson of the Committee, there 'would be no benefit in adopting a rigid interpretation of an instrument intended to apply for the benefit of women in all regions of the world, in States at different stages of development and with many different cultures and legal systems'.[80] The obligation is one of conduct (or means) but also of result, and a State party 'must be able to justify the appropriateness of the particular means it has chosen and to demonstrate whether it will achieve the intended effect and result'.[81] 'Appropriate' may entail consideration of available resources, but the language of the Convention is more forceful than that of the ICESCR Article 2, in which 'all appropriate means' is expressly qualified by reference to 'the maximum of available resources' and 'progressive realisation'. CEDAW Article 2 also requires that appropriate measures be adopted 'without delay' (again in contrast to the ICESCR). Article 2 sets out in more detail States parties' obligations with respect to appropriate measures, and Article 3 indicates that these include, but are not limited to, legislation. The Committee's interpretation of the phrase is considered more fully in the chapters on those articles.

The status of the Convention in domestic legal systems, and the ability of courts to apply it directly without incorporating or enabling legislation, depends upon the constitutional

---

[77] International Gay and Lesbian Human Rights Commission '30 Years of CEDAW: Achievements & Continuing Challenges Towards the Realization of Women's Human Rights' (2009) available at <http://www.iglhrc.org/cgi-bin/iowa/article/takeaction/partners/872.html> accessed 31 December 2010.

[78] Association of Intersexed People/XY Women, Shadow Report to the 6th National Report of Germany on the UN Convention on Elimination of All Forms of Discrimination against Women, 5 online at <http://intersex.shadowreport.org/public/Association_of_Intersexed_People-Shadow_Report_CEDAW_2008.pdf> accessed 31 December 2010.

[79] eg CO Kyrgyzstan, CEDAW/C/KGZ/CO/3 (2008) para 43; CO Germany, CEDAW/C/DEU/CO/6 (2009) paras 61–2 (requesting 'the State party to enter into dialogue with non-governmental organizations of intersexual and transsexual people in order to better understand their claims and to take effective action to protect their human rights').

[80] Evatt (n 66 above) 536.   [81] GR 28 para 23.

framework of each State party, notably whether it has a monist or dualist legal system,[82] as discussed in the chapter on Article 2. The Committee has urged States parties in which the Convention is not automatically part of the domestic legal order to consider taking the requisite steps to 'domesticate' it—that is expressly to incorporate it through legislation.[83] Whether or not the Convention is incorporated, States parties must ensure the rights within their domestic legal system[84] and provide for their effective enforcement through sanctions and remedies as provided for under Article 2 and reinforced by Article 24. In this regard it should be noted that the judiciary does not always rigidly adhere to the theoretical monist-dualist distinction. In some cases domestic judges have ruled that international obligations accepted by the State should be given effect in national legal systems, regardless of whether there has been formal incorporation. The *Victoria Falls Declaration of Principles for the Promotion of the Human Rights of Women*, adopted by the Commonwealth Secretariat in 1994, emphasizes the importance of judges being guided by the Convention when applying national constitutions and laws, including the common law and customary law. Cases where domestic judges have applied the Convention are discussed in the relevant chapters. Judges and legal advocates must be aware of the Convention to promote incorporation and other forms of inclusion. The Committee has proposed training sessions for lawyers and judges, and some such training has been undertaken by international organizations and NGOs.

III. Core Concepts

1. *The Equality Model*

The Convention's focus is on non-discrimination against women. It requires elimination of discrimination against women in the context of identified fields as set out in Articles 7–16, which are primarily those included in the ICCPR and ICESCR. The Covenants are expressed in gender-neutral language, but the nature of assumed harm is based on men's life experiences. The non-discrimination/equality model fits less readily where women's life experiences differ from those of men, and this has constrained the understanding of 'the full spectrum of abuses committed against women'.[85] Moreover, when the Convention was drafted, violence against women was not yet recognized as widespread, structural, and serious, requiring effective response from States parties as a matter of law and policy; unplanned and unwanted pregnancy was largely a taboo subject; abortion was unmentionable in any international arena; and the value of household and caregiving work was not recognized by policy-makers. Accordingly, some of the realities of women's lives are not explicitly accounted for in the Convention, such as women's unpaid work and gender-based violence committed against them.

---

[82] I Brownlie, *Principles of International Law* (7th edition 2008) 31–3; J Combacau and S Sur, *Droit international public*, 6th edn (2004) 181–6; S Kadelbach, 'The Transformation of Treaties into Domestic Law' (1999) 42 *German Ybk Intl L* 66; J Nijman and A Nollkaemper, *New Perspectives on the Divide between National and International Law* (2007).

[83] GR 28 para 31.

[84] This is in accordance with the VCLT art 27 which provides that '[a] party may not invoke the provisions of its internal law as justification for its failure to perform a treaty'.

[85] S Cartwright, 'Interpreting the Convention' in Schöpp-Schilling and Flinterman (n 44 above) 30.

Women's childbearing role is the basis for much stereotyping and discrimination against them, but the Convention's provisions related to fertility and reproduction are limited by adherence to the equality model and locate reproductive rights primarily in the context of the family. For example, States parties are required to take 'all appropriate measures to eliminate discrimination against women' to ensure 'access to specific educational information to help to ensure the health and well-being of families, including information and advice on family planning' (Article 10(h)). Similarly, Article 16(1)(e) requires women and men to have 'the same rights to decide freely and responsibly on the number and spacing of their children'. The language of Article 12 is not specifically limited to the family context, but it does not clearly take account of needs such as contraception for unmarried women, forced pregnancy, or access to safe abortion. The Committee has had to develop through its concluding observations and General Recommendation 24 the premise that 'birth control is at the very heart of male/female relationships'.[86]

The human rights guarantee of the right to life and to bodily integrity applies equally to women and men. However, this gender-neutral approach does not take account of how violence and loss of life usually occur in women's lives differently from those of men, notably at the hands of non-State actors such as family members. The chapters on Article 1, on particular substantive articles, and on violence against women describe the Committee's endeavours to address these omissions and to promote understanding that women-specific measures are required to achieve substantive equality and thus to give effect to the Convention's transformative potential.

2. *Equality and Equity*

Some States parties and other actors have challenged the meaning of 'equality' and its consistent use in the Convention and all other human rights treaties, arguing that elimination of discrimination against women can be achieved by assigning women and men different roles according to sex, but which are complementary and equally valued. Alternative concepts such as equity, complementarity, or 'rights equivalent to those of men' are thus proffered to substitute for 'equality'. Islamic States, along with the Holy See and certain other States, proposed using 'equity' instead of equality in the Beijing Platform for Action. Although the proposal was defeated, it generated strong controversy. Equity is based on subjective notions of fairness: 'equity is an illusive social goal which allows governments to offer all types of justifications when they fall short, whereas equality is a human right and therefore a legal obligation which cannot legally be avoided'.[87]

The Committee has adopted a forceful response to these attempts to displace the language of equality. It has stressed that the normative concepts of equality and equity are not the same and noted with concern States parties' tendency to use the terms synonymously and interchangeably. It has stated that this is not correct, and that such usage can lead to conceptual confusion[88] and has urged the expansion of 'dialogue among public entities, civil society and academia in order to clarify the understanding of equality in accordance with the Convention'.[89] In General Recommendation 28 paragraph 22, the Committee

---

[86] Fraser (n 3 above) 882.
[87] A Facio and M Morgan, 'Equity or Equality for Women? Understanding CEDAW's Equality Principles' (2009) *IWRAW Asia Pacific Occasional Papers Series* (2009) No 14, 21.
[88] CO Guyana, A/60/38, 33rd Session (2005) paras 287–8; CO Paraguay, A/60/38, 32nd Session (2005) paras 277–8; CO Dominican Republic, A/59/38, 31st Session (2004) paras 288–9.
[89] eg CO Vanuatu, CEDAW/C/VUT/CO/3 (2007) paras 14–15.

again calls upon States parties 'to use exclusively the concepts of equality of women and men or gender equality and not to use the concept of gender equity in implementing their obligations under the Convention'. This denotes the need for continuing resistance to attempts to dilute the obligations of the Convention. Finally, it should be noted that even within those societies where commitment to women's equality is supposedly accepted in the twenty-first century, this position has not been achieved without struggle and confrontation.[90]

IV. Women's Multiple Identities

The 1999 World Survey on the Role of Women, cited by the Committee in General Recommendation 25, stated that 'gender is a social stratifier . . . similar to other stratifiers such as race, class, ethnicity, sexuality, and age.'[91] The Convention itself does not stress the importance of social signifiers in addition to those of sex and gender and apart from Article 14 on rural women relies on the single signifier—women. This fails to capture the diversity of women and thus the range of their experiences. Nor does it recognize the complexity of discriminatory practices which may be directed at a multiplicity of intersecting identities.

The Committee has identified intersectionality as a 'basic concept for understanding the scope' of States parties' obligations.[92] Accordingly, to ensure that all women enjoy freedom from discrimination, specific measures must be taken to address the ways in which women are affected in their enjoyment of a right as a result of the intersection of discrimination based on sex with discrimination based on any other identity factor(s). Intersecting discrimination can determine the form or nature that discrimination takes, the circumstances in which it occurs, its consequences and the availability of appropriate remedies.[93] In its concluding observations to States parties' reports and general recommendations the Committee has identified 'certain groups of women' who are susceptible to and experience particular forms of discrimination, including 'women deprived of their liberty, refugees, asylum-seeking and migrant women, stateless women, lesbian women, disabled women, women victims of trafficking, widows, and elderly women'[94] and has generally recommended to States parties that they take the necessary steps to address such discrimination. In addition, through general recommendations concerning particular groups such as disabled women,[95] women migrant workers,[96] and older women[97] the Committee has made more detailed and targeted recommendations for the protection of their human rights.

V. Respect, Protect, Fulfil

The imprecise language of many human rights provisions creates uncertainty as to what is expected of States parties to ensure compliance with their obligations. Human rights

---

[90] Report of the Special Rapporteur on Violence against Women, 'Intersections between Culture and Violence against Women' UN Doc A/HRC/4/34 (17 January 2007) paras 23–6.
[91] GR 25 n 2 quoting *1999 World Survey on the Role of Women in Development*, United Nations, New York, ix.
[92] GR 28 para 18.
[93] CERD, 'General Recommendation XXV' UN Doc HRI/GEN/1/Rev.9 (Vol. II) 287 (considering the intersectionality between race and gender).
[94] GR 28 para 31.   [95] GR 18.   [96] GR 26.   [97] GR 27.

bodies have sought to rectify this uncertainty. One such attempt is that of the CESCR in developing and applying a model of multilayered State obligations: the obligations to respect, protect, and fulfil rights.[98] The Committee has adopted this typology, as a useful tool for analysis, at first with respect to particular situations such as violence against women[99] and women's right to health care,[100] and then more generally in the context of Article 4.[101] General Recommendation 25 paragraph 4 states that:

(b) **States parties to the Convention are under a legal obligation to respect, protect, promote and fulfil this right to non-discrimination for women and to ensure the development and advancement of women in order to improve their position to one of de jure as well as de facto equality with men.**

This legal obligation towards women continues throughout their lifespan.[102] In General Recommendation 28 paragraph 9 the Committee has explained the different levels of obligation. The obligation to respect, what is often called the negative State obligation, requires that States parties refrain from adopting laws and policies that interfere directly or indirectly with a woman's equal enjoyment of her rights. States parties must therefore ensure that their policies do not have unseen or unintended adverse consequences for women. Nor must States parties make matters worse, for example, by restricting individuals' agency and prohibiting (or interfering with) self-help measures without providing human rights compliant alternatives.[103] The obligation to protect—or to ensure respect—is the positive obligation of States parties to protect women from discrimination by non-State actors, and to 'take steps directly aimed at eliminating customary and all other practices that prejudice and perpetuate the notion of inferiority or superiority of either of the sexes'.[104] The obligation to fulfil (or promote) is forward-looking, requiring States parties and other relevant actors to adopt short-, medium- and long-term public policies, programmes, and institutional frameworks to combat discrimination against women in all its forms and manifestations, aiming at the eventual complete fulfilment of the right to non-discrimination and the full development of women's potential on an equal basis with men. It requires States parties to take positive steps to ensure that in practice, men and women enjoy rights on a basis of equality. Where appropriate the chapters in the Commentary have analyzed States parties' obligations in accordance with this typology.

E. Interpretive Processes and Mechanisms

I. General Recommendations

In common with the other UN human rights treaty bodies, the Committee has adopted general recommendations (or general comments), obliquely provided for under Article 21. The Committee was at first divided on whether Article 21 did in fact

---

[98] eg CESCR, 'General Comment 12' (1999) UN Doc E/C.12/1999/5 para 15. In CESCR, 'General Comment 16' (2005) UN Doc E/C.12/2005/4 the CESCR explained the different levels of obligation in the context of non-discrimination against women.
[99] *Ms AT v Hungary* CEDAW Communication No 2/2003 (2005) CEDAW/C/32/D/2003 para 9.6.
[100] GR 24 para 13.   [101] GR 25 para 4.   [102] GR 28 para 31.
[103] eg the Committee noted that a woman victim of domestic violence had made 'positive and determined efforts' to save her own life. *Fatma Yildirim (deceased) v Austria* CEDAW Communication No 6/2005 (2007) CEDAW/C/39/D/6/2005 para 12.1.3.
[104] GR 28 para 9.

authorize it to adopt general recommendations and in 1986 sought the advice of the Legal Counsel of the UN on the issue, as discussed in the chapter on Article 21.

The Committee as of 31 December 2010 had adopted twenty-eight general recommendations, some of which relate to working methods and others to the substantive articles of the Convention.[105] Early general recommendations tended to be brief and some only procedural, relating primarily to the State party reporting system. Since 1992, the Committee has adopted a number of significant and substantive general recommendations which clarify the content of States parties' obligations as to specific rights. Some articulate the content of rights stated expressly in the Convention, such as equality in the family (General Recommendation 21, Articles 9, 15, and 16), participation in political and public life (General Recommendation 23, Articles 7 and 8) and health care (General Recommendation 24, Article 12). Each of these is discussed in the chapters on the respective article. General Recommendation 12 and General Recommendation 19 on violence against women are significant substantive and dynamic interpretive recommendations, as violence is not explicitly addressed within the Convention. General Recommendation 16 and General Recommendation 17 respectively address another omission from the Convention, women's unpaid work within family enterprises and generally. Several general recommendations spell out the applicability of the Convention to women who are in situations of particular disadvantage, for example, those infected with HIV or AIDS (General Recommendation 15), disabled women (General Recommendation 18), women migrant workers (General Recommendation 26), and older women (General Recommendation 27), thereby expanding the vision of women's lives and circumstances addressed by the Convention. Other general recommendations address miscellaneous issues of general concern, such as the need for adequate resources for the Committee (General Recommendation 7), statistical data (General Recommendation 9), and reservations (General Recommendation 4 and General Recommendation 20). A comprehensive general recommendation (General Recommendation 25) on temporary special measures elucidates States parties' obligations under Article 4(1), with additional relevance to the other articles in Part I of the Convention. Article 2 is more fully covered in General Recommendation 28, which also explains the Committee's understanding of such concepts as gender, equality, and intersectionality. General Recommendation 25 is discussed in the chapter on Article 4 and General Recommendation 28 in that on Article 2. As of the end of 2010, a further general recommendation relating to States parties' obligations under Article 16 is under consideration.[106]

General recommendations provide guidance to States parties and others in understanding the obligations of the Convention and facilitate consistency in its application. In preparing general recommendations the Committee draws on its extensive experience in the consideration of States parties' reports, as well as seeking input *inter alia* from the secretariat and from academic and NGO experts.

---

[105] See Annexe with General Recommendations.

[106] The general approach is outlined in the Concept Note on the General Recommendation on Economic Consequences of Marriage and its Dissolution, CEDAW/C/2009/II/WP.2 (2009). A general recommendation on 'women in armed conflict and post conflict situations' is also planned as well as a joint general recommendation with the Committee on the Rights of the Child on harmful practices; closing remarks by Ms Zou Xiaoqiao, 47th Session of the Committee on the Elimination of Discrimination against Women, Geneva, 4 to 22 October 2010.

II. Concluding Observations

In 1993, at its 12th Session, the Committee agreed on a process for drafting concluding observations (or comments[107]) in response to States parties' reports.[108] Since 1994, it has adopted concluding observations to indicate its concerns about States parties' implementation of the Convention. Concluding observations allow the Committee 'to speak with one voice'[109] in identifying its priorities, obstacles to progress in Convention implementation, and practices that it considers contrary to Convention norms. Unlike the broader brush of the general recommendations, they are tailored to the situation in each State party and make recommendations for practical measures addressed to the specific issues raised by each State party's report. As the number of States parties has increased to near-universal ratification and some have been subjected to multiple reviews, the Committee has had ample opportunity to develop its views. Concluding observations are thus a primary source of information about the Committee's approach and are referred to throughout the Commentary.

III. Individual Communications and Inquiry

The coming into force of the Optional Protocol has provided the Committee with two further avenues for interpretation of the Convention—individual complaints and the inquiry procedure. As of the end of 2010, only one inquiry had been completed under the Optional Protocol, Article 8, into the many deaths and disappearances of women in *Ciudad Juarez*;[110] this is discussed in the chapter on violence against women. Gender-based violence against women has been the subject of four individual communications that have been found admissible to date; the substantive issues raised are also discussed in that chapter. A further communication found admissible concerned access to information with respect to health and well-being in the context of sterilization of a Roma woman.[111] Discussion of the grounds for admissibility and the follow-up procedures to a decision of the Committee is found in the chapter on the Optional Protocol. An important issue yet to be addressed is whether the general obligations contained in Articles 1–5 (including the definition of discrimination in Article 1) can be invoked on their own or whether they must be invoked in conjunction with substantive provisions of the Convention. Although the Committee has not directly answered this, it has found violations of Articles 2 and 5 in conjunction with Article 16,[112] of Articles 2 and 3 in conjunction with Article 1,[113] and of 2 and 5 in conjunction with Article 1.[114] This issue is discussed in the chapter on the Optional Protocol.

[107] In 2008, the Committee changed its language from 'concluding comments' to 'concluding observations' to harmonize with the other UN treaty bodies; decision 40/III, UN Doc A/63/38, Part I, ch I.

[108] Prior to that time, the Committee's concerns and recommendations were included in the general record of each State party review but were not organized as a separate comprehensive statement.

[109] Evatt (n 66 above) 534.

[110] 'Report on Mexico produced by the Committee on the Elimination of Discrimination against Women under Article 8 of the Optional Protocol to the Convention, and reply from the Government of Mexico', CEDAW/C/2005/OP8/Mexico (27 January 2005) (*Mexico Inquiry*).

[111] *AS v Hungary* CEDAW Communication No 4/2004 (2006) CEDAW/C/36/D/4/2004.

[112] *Ms AT v Hungary* (n 99 above).

[113] *Şahide Goekce v Austria* CEDAW Communication No 5/2005 (2007) CEDAW/C/39/D/5/2005; *Fatma Yildirim (deceased) v Austria* (n 103 above).

[114] *Vertido v the Philippines* CEDAW Communication No 18/2008 (2010) CEDAW/C/46/18/2008.

Decisions on communications are those of the Committee. Following the practice of other UN human rights treaty bodies, individual members of the Committee have upon occasion attached separate (and dissenting) opinions. The desirability of this practice is contested. Individual opinions (as for example, those entered by Judges of the International Court of Justice) allow for the expression of diverse views about the application of the Convention in particular situations and suggest approaches that might be preferred in the future and thus contribute to progressive and dynamic interpretation of the Convention. However, separate and dissenting opinions also indicate that consensus was not possible.

The Committee, like all the treaty monitoring bodies, lacks the power to enforce its views. Nevertheless, its competence to make recommendations in response to States parties' violations is important because it provides the opportunity for the Committee to expand upon the individual circumstances of the case to address root causes and structural discrimination. Accordingly, in the *Mexico Inquiry* and in views on individual communications the Committee has made detailed recommendations that go to both the particularities of the case in hand and their wider context. In the *Mexico Inquiry* a broad array of recommendations was directed to the Mexican government, to the officials responsible for investigation and punishment of perpetrators, and to those responsible for prevention of harm and the promotion and protection of women's human rights. Since Article 2 does not expound on what constitutes appropriate reparations for victims of violation, the Committee has considerable discretion in making its recommendations.[115]

IV. Suggestions, Decisions, and Statements

The Committee does not limit itself to the issues placed immediately before it through States parties' reports and proceedings under the Optional Protocol. It performs a wider role by issuing statements and decisions that confirm the relevance of the Convention in various exceptional situations (natural disasters,[116] conflict,[117] peace processes[118]) and the necessity of incorporating women's interests and concerns in policy- and decision-making.[119] It has adopted suggestions as to adopting or expanding procedures, addressed to UN bodies that are empowered to deal with them, for example, to the CSW with respect to the Optional Protocol and to the UNGA for extension of its sessions, as discussed in the chapters on the Optional Protocol and Article 20, respectively.

V. Status of Interpretive Mechanisms as Sources of International Law

The status of these mechanisms as a source of international human rights law is uncertain. None—general recommendations, concluding observations, opinions and views,

---

[115] See the discussion in ch on art 2.

[116] 'Statement of the Committee on the Elimination of Discrimination against Women on the Situation in Haiti, 45th Session' (January 2010) UN Doc E/CN.6/2010/CRP.2, Annex IV.

[117] Decision 43/III, Statement of the Committee on the Elimination of Discrimination against Women on the Situation in Gaza, UN Doc A/64/38 (Supp) (2009) Annex II.

[118] eg 'Statement on the Inclusion of the Afghan Women in the Process of Peace building, Security and Reconstruction in Afghanistan', 45th Session (January 2010) UN Doc E/CN.6/2010/CRP.2, Annex V.

[119] eg 'Gender and Sustainable Development', UN Doc A/57/38 (Supp) (2002) para 429(j); Decision 26/III, 'Ending Discrimination against Older Women through the Convention', A/57/38, Part I, para 430 (2002) (on the occasion of the Second World Assembly on Ageing in Madrid).

statements—are legally binding instruments under general international law.[120] However, their formal legal status must be weighed against their source: the Committee which 'was established specifically to supervise the application of [the] treaty'.[121] Its views may be accepted as offering 'more or less authoritative statements of interpretation'.[122] This position is supported by the International Court of Justice which has asserted that it 'should ascribe great weight' to the views of the Human Rights Committee with respect to the interpretation of the ICCPR. The same must be true of the views of the CEDAW Committee vis-à-vis the Convention. In the words of the ICJ: 'The point here is to achieve the necessary clarity and the essential consistency of international law, as well as legal security, to which both the individuals with guaranteed rights and the States obliged to comply with treaty obligations are entitled.'[123] Through these diverse methods the Committee clarifies the scope of the Convention and States parties' obligations pursuant to it. States parties' responses may generate subsequent State practice for interpretation of the Convention in accordance with VCLT Article 31(3)(b).[124] These processes contribute to the required certainty and consistency while also allowing for flexibility and progress.

VI. Contributions by NGOs

NGOs have made a considerable contribution to the articulation of rights under the Convention and more generally to the gendered analysis of human rights principles. In addition to providing academic analysis, background documentation, and input into the preparation of general recommendations and Committee statements, they have on occasion developed guidelines and recommendations on particular subjects.

Two examples are the Montréal Principles on Women's Economic, Social and Cultural Rights, 2004[125] and the Nairobi Declaration on Women's and Girls' Right to a Remedy and Reparation, 2007.[126] The Montréal Principles built on earlier NGO guidelines[127] that sought to assist in 'understanding and determining violations of economic, social and cultural rights and in providing remedies thereto' by adding a gender dimension. The Nairobi Declaration addressed the lack of reference to gender-based violations of human rights and humanitarian law in the UNGA Resolution on the Basic Principles and Guidelines

---

[120] The sources of international law are set out in the Statute of the International Court of Justice (1945) art 38(1): treaties, customary international law, and general principles of law.

[121] *Case Concerning Ahmadou Sadio Diallo* (Republic of Guinea v Democratic Republic of the Congo) (2010) ICJ Rep (Judgment of 30 November 2010) para 66.

[122] H Steiner, P Alston, and R Goodman, *International Human Rights in Context: Law Politics Morals*, 3rd edn (2007).

[123] *Case Concerning Ahmadou Sadio Diallo* (n 121 above) para 66.

[124] VCLT art 31 states that a treaty shall be interpreted 'in good faith in accordance with the ordinary meaning to be given to the terms of the treaty in their context.' Art 31(3)(b) provides for 'subsequent practice in the application of the treaty which establishes the agreement of the parties regarding its interpretation' to be taken into account, together with the context.

[125] 26 *Human Rights Quarterly* 760–80 (2004).

[126] Available at <http://www.womensrightscoalition.org/site/reparation/signature_en.php> accessed 31 December 2010.

[127] Limburg Principles on the Implementation of the International Covenant on Economic, Social and Cultural Rights (adopted 8 January 1987) UN Doc E/CN.4/1987/17/Annex; The Maastricht Guidelines on Violations of Economic, Social and Cultural Rights 1997 at <http://www1.umn.edu/humanrts/instree/Maastrichtguidelines_.html> accessed 31 December 2010.

on the Right to a Remedy and Reparation for Victims of Gross Violations of International Human Rights Law and Serious Violations of International Humanitarian Law.[128]

As instruments produced by non-State bodies, these efforts fall outside the formal sources of international (and hence human rights) law as set out in the Statute of the ICJ, Article 38(1). They are prepared in the hope that they will be adopted by other international actors, cited and applied by decision and policy-makers and thus come to be accepted as contributing to the corpus of international law. Their influence will depend in each instance on such factors as the quality of the text, the standing of the authors and the degree of acceptance.

F. Interpreting and Applying Convention Norms: Substantive and Contextual Issues

I. The Convention as a Human Rights Instrument

In December 1999, twenty years after the adoption of the Convention, and on the opening of the Optional Protocol for signature, UN Secretary-General Kofi Annan asserted that 'this "Women's Bill of Rights" stands as a milestone'.[129] Yet upon its adoption the Convention was not immediately and universally accorded the weight appropriate to an international human rights instrument by States or by scholars and activists.

The Convention's place of origin within the UN system served to distance it and the Committee from other human rights activities and developments. Unlike the other international human rights treaties, the Convention was drafted by the CSW, a UN Charter body that is not specifically mandated to address human rights. Nor does the CSW focus on State accountability in the same manner as the former Commission on Human Rights and current Human Rights Council. As a functional commission of ECOSOC, the CSW is fundamentally a policy body and is serviced by the UN Division for the Advancement of Women (DAW), part of the Department of Economic and Social Affairs, which was based for many years in Vienna and currently is based in New York. Because of the CSW's position in the UN structure, the draft Convention was vetted by the Third Committee of the UNGA (responsible for social affairs) rather than the Sixth Committee (responsible for legal affairs, including human rights). Upon adoption of the Convention, DAW (then designated only as a Branch) became the secretariat for the Committee, and the Committee's staffing and sessions were located in Vienna and New York rather than at the Office of the High Commissioner for Human Rights (formerly the Human Rights Centre) in Geneva. This history cut off the Convention and the Committee from the Geneva-based human rights bodies in physical as well as conceptual terms.

The Convention was isolated conceptually despite the fundamental principle that the human rights of women cannot be separated from the human rights of all people. The UDHR states that 'everyone' is entitled to the enjoyment of all the rights and freedoms contained therein without discrimination, *inter alia*, on the basis of sex and on a basis of equality between women and men. It does not indicate that women have a separate set of human rights. The two UN Covenants reinforce the principle of non-discrimination and include specific statements on women's right to equal enjoyment of all human rights.

---

[128] UNGA Res 60/147 (16 December 2005) UN Doc A/RES/60/147.
[129] UN Press Release (10 December 1999) SG/SM/7258 WOM/1152.

All the other international and regional human rights treaties either state the principle of non-discrimination explicitly or, in language derived from the UDHR, specify their application without discrimination on the basis of sex.

None the less, for many years the existence of the Convention seemed to provide a rationale for States and other human rights actors to consider women's human rights as a marginal concern, assigned solely to the attention of the Committee. The uniquely short working time provided for the Committee in the Convention and the struggle to increase it, as discussed in the chapter on Article 20, underscored this marginalization.[130] The physical separation from the secretariat for the other UN human rights treaty bodies (and from the many Geneva-based human rights NGOs) resulted in the Committee's jurisprudence and practices developing with less reference to those of the other treaty bodies than might otherwise have been the case.[131] The separation also rendered the Committee's work less visible to the other treaty monitoring bodies.

The Committee's growing connection with the work of the other treaty monitoring bodies is discussed below, section F. IV. Most significantly, as part of the UN reform process, the Committee's base for meeting and staff servicing was moved to the OHCHR in Geneva as of January 2008.

II. Relationship to Other International Instruments

It is beyond the scope of this Introduction to detail the numerous international instruments relevant to the issues addressed in the Convention that have been adopted since 1979, and especially since the end of the Cold War. These have emanated primarily from the world conferences discussed above and other UN bodies, including the specialized agencies. One of the most significant was the assertion at the Vienna World Conference on Human Rights in 1993 that the 'human rights of women and of the girl-child are an inalienable, integral and indivisible part of universal human rights'.[132] Women's reproductive rights were guaranteed at the 1994 Conference on Population and Development in Cairo.[133] The affirmation of women's human rights was reiterated at the Fourth World Conference on Women, Beijing, 1995,[134] which included the human rights of women as a Critical Area of Concern. Other issues included in the Convention were amplified in the Beijing Platform for Action, including education, health, and decision-making, as well as issues taken up in general recommendations and concluding observations, notably violence against women and specifically in armed conflict.

The Beijing Platform for Action and the Convention are 'mutually reinforcing in achieving gender equality and the empowerment of women'.[135] The Conference called upon governments to ratify, accede to, and implement the Convention,[136] a call reiterated

---

[130] A Byrnes, 'The "Other" Human Rights Treaty Body: The Work of the Committee on the Elimination of Discrimination Against Women' (1989) 14 *Yale J Intl L* 1.

[131] Bustelo (n 68 above) 83.

[132] UN World Conference on Human Rights, Vienna Declaration and Programme of Action (25 June 1993) UN Doc A/Conf.157/23, 1993 (hereinafter Vienna Declaration or Vienna Programme of Action) paras 1 and 18.

[133] 'Report of the International Conference on Population and Development, Cairo' (1994) UN Doc A/Conf. 171/13.

[134] Declaration and Platform for Action, Beijing (1995) UN Doc A/Conf. 177/20 para 213.

[135] Declaration on the Occasion of the Fifteenth Anniversary of the Fourth World Conference on Women, ECOSOC OR 2010 (Supp No 7) E/2010/27, UN Doc E/CN.6/2010/11, Annex, para 4.

[136] Beijing Platform for Action (n 134 above) para 230.

in the Five-Year Review and Appraisal Outcome Document.[137] In turn, the UNGA imme-diately post-Beijing requested the Committee to 'to take into account the Platform for Action when considering reports submitted by States parties, and invite[d] States parties to include information on measures taken to implement the Platform for Action in their reports'.[138] This the Committee has done, particularly in relation to seeking information about national plans of action, allocated resources, and national machinery for implemen-tation. Upon occasion (but not systematically), the Committee links the commitments of Beijing with those under Convention Articles 3 and 24.

Within the UN, the CSW and other women-specific bodies have continued to work on matters addressed within the Convention or associated with it. In 2010, the UNGA adopted by consensus a resolution on 'enhanced system-wide coherence' that included 'strengthening the institutional arrangements for support of gender equality and the empowerment of women'.[139] The functions and mandates of four existing UN enti-ties that dealt with gender issues—the Office of the Special Adviser on Gender Issues and Advancement of Women (OSAGI), the DAW, United Nations Development Fund for Women (UNIFEM), and the International Research and Training Institute for the Advancement of Women (INSTRAW)—were replaced by a single body, 'the United Nations Entity for Gender Equality and the Empowerment of Women, to be known as UN Women', operational from 1 January 2011.[140] This title demonstrates the famil-iar confusion between 'women' and 'gender'. The approach of UN Women to women's human rights and its level of interaction with the Committee remain to be seen.

Many other UN bodies have adopted resolutions and programmes of work on general and specific issues relating to women. The UNGA Millennium Declaration asserts that 'the equal rights and opportunities of women and men must be assured'[141] and resolves to implement the Convention.[142] In its concluding observations the Committee rou-tinely emphasizes that compliance with the Convention is critical to achievement of the Millennium Development Goals (MDGs). In turn, success of the MDGs would enhance women's advancement and development in accordance with Convention Article 3, as dis-cussed in the chapter on that article. The Committee has drawn upon UNSC resolutions on women, peace, and security,[143] in emphasizing the importance of women's participa-tion in peace processes as a significant factor in ending violence against women in armed conflict.[144] The UN Human Rights Council has urged all stakeholders 'to take into full account both the rights of women and a gender perspective in its universal periodic review process, including in the preparation of information submitted for the review, during the review dialogue, in the review outcome and in the review follow-up'.[145] In turn, the Committee has drawn upon commitments made in that process to reinforce its own recommendations to States parties.[146] In its resolutions on elimination of discrimination

---

[137] UNGA Res S-23/3, rev. 1. Further actions and initiatives to implement the Beijing Declaration and Platform for Action (16 November 2000) UN Doc A/RES/S-23/3 para 68(c).

[138] UNGA Res 50/203 (23 February 1996) UN Doc A/RES/50/203 para 36.

[139] UNGA Res 64/289, (2 July 2010) UN Doc A/RES/64/289.   [140] Ibid para 49.

[141] UNGA Res 55/2 (8 September 2000) UN Doc A/RES/55/2 paras 6 and 20.   [142] Ibid para 25.

[143] UNSC Res 1325 (31 October 2000) UN Doc S/RES/1325; UNSC Res 1820 (19 June 2008) UN Doc S/RES/1820; UNSC Res 1888 (30 September 2009) UN Doc S/RES/1888; UNSC Res 1889 (5 October 2009) UN Doc S/RES/1889.

[144] eg CO Myanmar, CEDAW/C/MMR/CO/3 (2008) para 25.

[145] Human Rights Council Res 6/30 (14 December 2007) UN Doc A/HRC/RES/6/30.

[146] eg CO Finland, CEDAW/C/FIN/CO/6 (2008) para 174.

against women the Council welcomes the Committee's work 'on women's equality before the law'.[147]

Unlike the Convention, resolutions of international institutions (including those of the UNSC unless adopted under UN Charter, chapter VII) and instruments adopted by world conferences are not formally binding but are statements of political aspiration and commitment. Many of them recognize the special status of the Convention and make pre-ambular reference to it, or bring it within their operative paragraphs. Its continued importance is therefore maintained and even strengthened by these later, often more politically significant, instruments. As with the Beijing Platform for Action, the Convention and these later instruments are mutually reinforcing.

III. The Convention, Non-derogability, and Customary International Law

As an international human rights treaty, the Convention confirms that women have a right not to be subject to sex- or gender-based discrimination and an entitlement to equality. Articles 1 and 3 integrate all 'human rights and fundamental freedoms' into the Convention, providing a rights-based approach to women's development and advancement, as discussed in more detail in the chapters on those articles. The Convention does not allow for derogation in times of public emergency, nor is the commitment to women's equality made subject to such 'claw-backs' as protection of national security, public order, public health, morals or the rights of freedoms of others. Indeed, in those Conventions that provide for derogation, adopted measures must not involve discrimination 'solely on the ground of [*inter alia*] sex'.[148] Non-derogability (even without implementation) conveys 'a special place in the hierarchy of rights.'[149]

Another question is whether the principle of non-discrimination on the basis of sex has attained the status of customary international law, binding upon all States including non-parties to the Convention. In some respects this question is theoretical, since its inclusion in the UN Charter as a purpose of the Organization means that all member States have made the basic commitment. Its repetition in the UDHR and UN Covenants reinforces this point. This view appears to be widely accepted, with leading academic commentators in agreement.[150] Indeed, the Inter-American Court of Human Rights has taken the position that it has *jus cogens* status[151]—a 'peremptory norm of general international law...accepted and recognized by the international community of States as a whole as a norm from which no derogation is permitted'.[152] Beyond this fundamental principle, claims of customary international law status for particular articles of the Convention and for the prohibition of violence against women must be scrutinized for their compatibility with uniform and consistent State practice and *opinio juris*.[153]

---

[147] Human Rights Council Res 12/17 (12 October 2009) UN Doc A/HRC/RES/12/17.

[148] ICCPR art 4(1); see also ECHR art 14; IACHR art 27.

[149] M Shaw, *International Law*, 6th edn (2008) 275.

[150] eg Brownlie (n 82 above) 572–3; K Doehring, *Völkerrecht*, 2nd edn (2005) § 20, marginal note 987; Shaw (n 149 above) 286–7.

[151] Juridical Condition and Rights of the Undocumented Migrants (Advisory Opinion) OC-18/03 (17 September 2003) 23.

[152] VCLT art 53.

[153] These are the requirements for a rule of customary international law; Brownlie (n 82 above) 6–10. See *Military and Paramilitary Activities in and against Nicaragua* 1986 ICJ Rep 14 paras 188–9 on the status of resolutions as *opinio juris*.

IV. Integrating Gender Perspectives into the Human Rights Work of the United Nations

The 1993 Vienna World Conference on Human Rights asserted that '[t]he equal status of women and the human rights of women should be integrated into the mainstream of United Nations system-wide activity'.[154] In 1995, subsequent to an OHCHR Expert Group Meeting on the Development of Guidelines for the Integration of Gender Perspectives into Human Rights Activities and Programmes,[155] the annual Meetings of the Chairpersons of the Human Rights Treaty Bodies took up the matter of integration,[156] and the Commission on Human Rights adopted a series of resolutions confirming the principle.[157] A 1998 UN SG's report on 'The Question of Integrating the Human Rights of Women throughout the United Nations System', confirming the recommendations of the 1995 Expert Group, states the goal:

(c) to ensure that the inevitable social construction of men's and women's respective roles does not permit a discriminatory bias which subordinates women to men or places women in any kind of inferior position. ... In the field of human rights, this primarily involves understanding that every occurrence of a human rights violation has a gender dimension.158

The OHCHR and the treaty monitoring bodies have made some progress in integrating gender perspectives. CCPR General Comment 28 on Equality of Rights between Men and Women and CESCR General Comment 16 on The Equal Right of Men and Women to the Enjoyment of all Economic, Social and Cultural Rights analyze the ICCPR and ICESCR respectively from the perspective of women's experiences and the violations of their human rights. CAT and CERD also have adopted general comments on the application of those treaties to the situation of women.[159] All of the treaty monitoring bodies have taken up violations of women's human rights, although some more consistently than others. Some of the Human Rights Council Special Procedures also have given attention to women-specific issues in their reports,[160] and as of 2010 a new special procedure (a working group) has been established to address discrimination against women.[161] Some of the Human Rights Council's Universal Periodic Reviews have noted violations of women's human rights.

---

[154] Vienna Programme of Action II (n 132 above) para 37.

[155] 'Report of the Expert Group' (20 November 1995) UN Doc E/CN.4/1996/105 para 71.

[156] See eg Improving the Operation of the Human Rights Treaty Bodies: Follow-up Action on the Conclusions and Recommendations of the Sixth Meeting of Persons Chairing the Human Rights Treaty Bodies, UN Doc HRI/MC/1996/2 (1996) paras 100–8; 'Report of the Persons Chairing the Human Rights Treaty Bodies on their Tenth Meeting', UN Doc A/53/432 Annex (1998) paras 53–4.

[157] eg 'Question of Integrating the Human Rights of Women into the Human Rights Mechanisms of the United Nations', CHR Res 1995/86, ESCOR Supp (No 4) 253, UN Doc E/CN.4/1995/86 (1995); 'Question of Integrating the Human Rights of Women throughout the United Nations System', CHR Res 1996/48, ESCOR Supp (No 3) 159, UN Doc E/CN.4/1996/48.

[158] 'Report of the Secretary General on the Question of Integrating the Human Rights of Women Throughout the United Nations System' (25 March 1998) UN Doc E/CN.4/1998/49 paras 8–9.

[159] CAT, 'General Comment 2' (2007) UN Doc CAT/C/GC/2 para 22; CERD, 'General Comment XXV' (2000) UN Doc HRI/GEN/1/Rev.9 (Vol. II).

[160] eg 'Special Rapporteur on Torture: Mission to Cambodia' (2008) UN Doc A/HRC/7/3/Add.5 paras 88 and 97; 'Special Rapporteur on the Right to Adequate Housing, Mission to South Africa' (2008) UN Doc A/HRC/7/16/Add.3 paras 84–7; 'Special Rapporteur on the Right of Everyone to the Enjoyment of the Highest attainable Standard of Physical and Mental Health, Mission to India' (2010) UN Doc A/HRC/14/20/Add.2.

[161] Human Rights Council Report (24 September 2010) UN Doc A/HRC/15/L.15.

The High Commissioner for Human Rights, in a 2009 report, summarized these developments and made recommendations to remedy continuing shortcomings.[162] Notably, the report refers to 'integration of the gender perspective', the terminology that has been used consistently by the OHCHR and its predecessor Centre for Human Rights. This language is telling. While the project has been far from perfect, and the accomplishments incremental, the language of 'integrating the gender perspective' is somewhat more concrete than the language of 'mainstreaming' used elsewhere throughout the UN system, and the human rights mechanisms offer a defined area in which results can be seen and evaluated. The terminology and application of 'mainstreaming', in contrast, are highly problematic. The word itself connotes a narrow and exclusionary vision of women's place in the world, suggesting that they are a group that has to be deliberately included by those in power rather than rightfully enjoying their engagement as half of humankind. Measurement of and accountability for its impact also have proven problematic.

As a concept unknown in international institutions in 1979, gender mainstreaming is not mentioned in the Convention. Nevertheless, in line with UN policy on gender mainstreaming the Committee commends its introduction as a practical and appropriate tool for the advancement of women and the enhancement of their human rights. The Committee has also recognized that successful gender mainstreaming requires use of tools such as gender impact analysis, the compilation of sex-disaggregated statistics, and gender-based budget allocations. Article 3, seeking the 'the full development and advancement of women', may be seen as the basis for the adoption of gender mainstreaming, as discussed in that chapter. However, the Committee is also aware of the limitations of gender mainstreaming and questions States parties closely about its implementation and impact.

V. Challenges Based on Religion and Culture

The Convention is intended to be universal, to apply to all women across the globe regardless of the prevailing ideology or economic development of the State in which they live, or its dominant cultural and religious belief systems. The Convention does not subscribe to any particular theory of law or politics but builds on the overlapping consensus of different moral, cultural, and legal approaches. However, its commitment to women's equality and empowerment are at odds with the beliefs associated with certain religious communities and cultural traditions.

During the drafting process a number of Islamic States expressed concerns related in particular to Articles 9, 15, and 16. Most Islamic States have become parties to the Convention but in many instances with significant reservations, some general and some specific, primarily of Articles 2, 9, 15, and 16. Reservations to specific articles are discussed in the relevant chapters and more generally in the chapter on Article 28. While other States parties have entered reservations, those of the Islamic States parties refer directly or indirectly to Sharia—religious law—as the basis for the reservations, and as noted in the chapter on Article 28, the Committee has found reservations to Articles 2 and 16 to be contrary to the object and purpose of the Convention. A number of the reservations to Article 9 have been withdrawn, but those relating to Articles 2, 15, and 16, in particular, remain problematic.

---

[162] 'Integrating the Human Rights of Women throughout the United Nations System: Report of the Office of the United Nations High Commissioner for Human Rights' (2009) UN Doc A/HRC/12/46 para 18.

The Committee's concluding observations on many States parties' reports also reflect the continuing challenge of dealing with the patriarchal culture and resistance to change that are not associated with any particular religion or tradition but are widely present in almost all societies. The Committee has underscored States parties' obligation to address cultural obstacles to equality rather than relying on culture as an excuse for lack of progress. In more recent years it has encouraged States parties to address cultural issues by viewing culture as dynamic rather than as monolithic or immutable. It has accordingly encouraged the expression of different understandings of culture, as well as seeking to persuade Islamic States parties to re-examine their reservations in view of the evolving interpretations of religious law seen in some of the Islamic States parties.

VI. The Challenges of Globalization

When the Convention was adopted, a global redistribution of wealth, formulated as the New International Economic Order, was promoted by developing States and was reflected in its Preamble.[163] The NIEO was opposed by many economically developed States and although endorsed by the UNGA[164] remained controversial. Instead, global economic development has been characterized since the 1980s by adherence to the liberal (market-oriented) economic agenda. Although in some instances the globalized economy has opened opportunities for women, for example, through employment and migration, economic globalization has also had significant adverse effects on women's advancement, as well as contributing in diverse ways to the feminization of poverty.[165]

State commitment to women's human rights has been weakened by undemocratic forces of 'globalization from above'—corporate enterprises, markets, and movements of capital—undermining the decision- and policy-making power of the State, notably with respect to economic and labour policies. Some governments have been unwilling to uphold their workers' human rights if doing so might discourage investment, and corporate actors remain largely unregulated by international law. Consequences such as social exclusion, unemployment, or low-paid employment, and weakening of trade union organization all have gendered dimensions, for '[e]conomic systems which value profits often do so at the expense of female labour'.[166] Women are seen as a passive, compliant, temporary work-force that will accept low wages (or lower wages than their male comparators) without demanding rights. The traditional sexual division of labour (the location of women in employment regarded as inherently suitable for them, for example, the caring professions) has been amplified through the addition of new locations and forms of work (eg services industry, tourism). What remains constant is the low economic value accorded to work performed primarily by women, often migrants, frequently in poor and unsafe working

---

[163] CEDAW Preamble (9th para): 'convinced that the establishment of the new international economic order based on equity and justice will contribute significantly towards the promotion of equality between men and women'.

[164] Declaration on the Establishment of a New International Economic Order, UNGA Res 3201 (S-VI) (1 May 1974) UN Doc A/RES/S-6/3201; Charter of Economic Rights and Duties of States, UNGA Res 3281 (XXIX) (12 December 1974) UN Doc A/RES/29/3281.

[165] Beijing Platform for Action (n 134 above) paras 47–68; S Fukuda-Parr, 'What does Feminization of Poverty Mean? It isn't Just Lack of Income' (1999) 5(2) *Feminist Economics* 99.

[166] 'Preliminary Report submitted by the Special Rapporteur on Violence against Women, its causes, and consequences, Ms Radhika Coomaraswamy', UN Doc E/CN.4/1995/42 para 55.

conditions, accompanied by lack of job security and by violence.[167] Globalization has also tended to deepen women's property disadvantage as the cash economy has displaced communal or household-based land use.[168]

The impact of economic privatization and structural adjustment programmes upon the enjoyment of human rights, particularly economic and social rights, has attracted the attention of the Committee,[169] of other UN human rights bodies,[170] and of NGOs.[171] The Committee has also noted the effect on women of economic crisis. These issues are addressed in the chapter on Article 3. Together with the opposition to women's advancement presented by religious and cultural traditionalism, this may present the greatest challenge to the achievement of the Convention's objectives.

G. The Convention in the Twenty-first Century

The first task undertaken by the CSW after its inception was to carry out a global survey of the state of the world's women. It found four areas of particular concern: women's political rights and legal rights, women's access to education, and their working life.[172] All these and other issues have been addressed by specific treaties and through the lens of non-discrimination in the Convention.

Nevertheless, discrimination against women remains a fact of life worldwide. Nowhere in the world do women participate equally with men in government, and women represent 25 per cent or more of elected legislators in only twenty-two countries.[173] Although illiteracy rates have steadily declined over the past three decades, largely because of efforts to increase basic educational opportunities for girls,[174] nearly two-thirds of the world's billion people who are still illiterate are women.[175] Of all the health measures monitored by the World Health Organization, the largest discrepancy between rich and poor countries occurs in maternal mortality. Violence against women is endemic. Discriminatory inheritance and property ownership laws are still widely in effect around the world. Property discrimination in agrarian economies is particularly striking—women typically work the fields, grow and harvest the food but cannot own the land under civil, customary or religious laws. If women do not own or control land they cannot get credit. In industrialized countries, fewer women than men own their homes. Even where there is no legal

---

[167] Such conditions are seen in the *Mexico Inquiry* (n 110 above).

[168] Progress of the World's Women 2000: UNIFEM Biennial Report. See also: 'Report of the Special Rapporteur on Violence against women, its Causes and Consequences', Ms Yakin Ertürk, on 'Political Economy of Women's Human Rights', UN Doc A/HRC/11/6 (18 May 2009).

[169] See especially the discussion in ch on art 3.

[170] Effects of Structural Adjustment Policies on the Full Enjoyment of Human Rights, Report by the independent expert, Mr Fantu Cheru, submitted in accordance with Commission decisions 1998/102 and 1997/103, UN Doc E/CN.4/1999/50 (24 February 1999); 'Report of the Special Rapporteur on violence against women, its causes, and consequences, Ms Radhika Coomaraswamy, on trafficking in women, migration, and violence against women submitted in accordance with Commission on Human Rights resolution 1997/44', UN Doc E/CN.4/2000/68, 29.

[171] eg the Montreal Principles (n 125 above).   [172] Pietilä (n 4 above) 21.

[173] The Inter-Parliamentary Union: <http://www.ipu.ovrg/wmn-e/world.htm> accessed 30 June 2010.

[174] Ibid 76.

[175] Beijing Platform for Action (n 134 above) para 70. In 2010, UNDP asserted the continuation of this reality; 'Empowering women through literacy empowers us all', UNDP Newsroom (8 September 2010) <http://content.undp.org/go/newsroom/2010/september/empowering-women-through-literacy-empowers-us-all.en> accessed 31 December 2010.

discrimination, women are subject to social pressures or economic realities that create unequal access to land, property, and wealth.

The Convention is a forceful statement that such discrimination against women is unacceptable. States in all regions of the world have agreed to its significance, if not to all of its terms. And that global agreement in itself is a catalyst for change. The Convention has become a human rights process, and, as former Chairperson Ivanka Corti notes, its success lies in that process.

Thirty years after its adoption, many States parties have changed laws and established programmes to address discrimination, and where this has occurred the Committee has shifted emphasis from formal equality—adoption of laws and policies—to substantive equality—questioning States parties on their implementation and impact. It also has become very clear in its insistence that culture, tradition, religion, and community identity are no excuse for failure to address discrimination. International civil society is deeply engaged in helping the Committee understand the obstacles to and opportunities for domestic implementation as well as in using the Convention and the work of the Committee to promote that implementation.

Legal and policy reform that improves the position of women generally cannot be attributed to a single change factor. Greater global attention to women's and girls' education, explosive global growth of communications and therefore of access to information, and the impact of communications on the capacity to organize are all major factors in promoting change.

Further social change is not induced through legislative and governmental policies alone. Most importantly, the Convention has been used and relied upon in multiple ways by women across the world who have devised ways best suited to their local contexts, both in conjunction with governments and through their own initiatives. International agencies may assist them.[176] Unlike legislation and judicial decisions, localized applications of the Convention and the Committee's General Recommendations do not enter the annals of the UN or of international law, but are important in providing openings for change in women's lives.[177]

In 1975, the Decade for Women invigorated global discussion of women's human rights that has widened and deepened beyond the imagining of the 14,000 women who participated in the NGO Forum at Nairobi in 1985. The adoption of the Convention was the crowning accomplishment of the Decade for Women. Its development to encompass a vision of structural equality and transformed attitudes and institutions is the Committee's accomplishment of today. The continuation of this process remains the challenge for today and the future.

---

[176] eg UNIFEM, *Time for Action Implementing CEDAW in Southeast* Asia (2009).
[177] SE Merry, *Human Rights and Gender Violence: Translating International Law into Local Justice* (2006).

Preamble

The States Parties to the present Convention,

(1) Noting that the Charter of the United Nations reaffirms faith in fundamental human rights, in the dignity and worth of the human person and in the equal rights of men and women,

(2) Noting that the Universal Declaration of Human Rights affirms the principle of the inadmissibility of discrimination and proclaims that all human beings are born free and equal in dignity and rights and that everyone is entitled to all the rights and freedoms set forth therein, without distinction of any kind, including distinction based on sex,

(3) Noting that the States Parties to the International Covenants on Human Rights have the obligation to ensure the equal rights of men and women to enjoy all economic, social, cultural, civil and political rights,

(4) Considering the international conventions concluded under the auspices of the United Nations and the specialized agencies promoting equality of rights of men and women,

(5) Noting also the resolutions, declarations and recommendations adopted by the United Nations and the specialized agencies promoting equality of rights of men and women,

(6) Concerned, however, that despite these various instruments extensive discrimination against women continues to exist,

(7) Recalling that discrimination against women violates the principles of equality of rights and respect for human dignity, is an obstacle to the participation of women, on equal terms with men, in the political, social, economic and cultural life of their countries, hampers the growth of the prosperity of society and the family and makes more difficult the full development of the potentialities of women in the service of their countries and of humanity,

(8) Concerned that in situations of poverty women have the least access to food, health, education, training and opportunities for employment and other needs,

(9) Convinced that the establishment of the new international economic order based on equity and justice will contribute significantly towards the promotion of equality between men and women,

(10) Emphasizing that the eradication of apartheid, all forms of racism, racial discrimination, colonialism, neo-colonialism, aggression, foreign occupation and domination and interference in the internal affairs of States is essential to the full enjoyment of the rights of men and women,

(11) Affirming that the strengthening of international peace and security, the relaxation of international tension, mutual co-operation among all States irrespective of their social and economic systems, general and complete disarmament, in particular nuclear disarmament under strict and effective international control, the affirmation of the principles of justice, equality and mutual benefit in relations among countries and the realization of the right of peoples under alien and colonial domination and foreign occupation to self-determination and independence, as well as respect for national sovereignty and territorial integrity, will promote social progress and development and as a consequence will contribute to the attainment of full equality between men and women,

(12) Convinced that the full and complete development of a country, the welfare of the world and the cause of peace require the maximum participation of women on equal terms with men in all fields,

(13) Bearing in mind the great contribution of women to the welfare of the family and to the development of society, so far not fully recognized, the social significance of maternity and the role of both parents in the family and in the upbringing of children, and aware that the role of women in procreation should not be a basis for discrimination but that the

upbringing of children requires a sharing of responsibility between men and women and society as a whole,

(14) Aware that a change in the traditional role of men as well as the role of women in society and in the family is needed to achieve full equality between men and women,

(15) Determined to implement the principles set forth in the Declaration on the Elimination of Discrimination against Women and, for that purpose, to adopt the measures required for the elimination of such discrimination in all its forms and manifestations,[1]

Have agreed on the following:

	TABLE OF CONTENTS
A. Introduction	36
B. Travaux Préparatoires	38
C. Issues of Interpretation	38
I. Structure of the Preamble	38
II. Contents of the Preamble Paragraphs	39

A. Introduction

There is no required form or content to a treaty preamble; 'everything depends on the circumstances'.[2] The Preamble to the Convention on the Elimination of All Forms of Discrimination against Women (the Convention), like most preambles, introduces the subject matter of the treaty, explains its background and foreshadows its articles, and indicates the context and object and purpose of the treaty. The Convention Preamble also locates the Convention within international human rights law, in particular the prohibition of discrimination on the basis of sex, and within the wider international political and legal scene of 1979. It draws the link between rights and economic development, of women and also of society. In addition, it makes 'what are essentially political statements',[3] some of its paragraphs couched as political rhetoric, raising contemporaneous issues not immediately directed to the core goal of the Convention—to eliminate discrimination against women.

The Convention Preamble is unusually long, fifteen paragraphs in contrast to the five paragraphs of the ICCPR and ICESCR and the twelve of ICERD. It was drafted against the backdrop of both the evolving human rights standard-setting in the UN Commission on Human Rights and the different strands of political debate about the best approaches to achieving women's equality at the global level. The former—the legal element—is reflected in the allusions to prior human rights instruments. The political elements reflect the themes of the International Decade for Women adopted by the UNGA that encompass the primary geopolitical concerns of the time: to promote equality between men and women—the focus of the West; to ensure the full integration of women in the total development effort—the concern of the developing world; and to recognize the importance of women's increasing contribution to the development of friendly relations and cooperation among States and to the strengthening of world peace—the stated concern of the Soviet Union and the Eastern bloc.[4] These themes were widely discussed at the World

---

[1] The numbering is added for ease of reference, following L Rehof, *Guide to the Travaux Préparatoires of the UN Convention on the Elimination of All Forms of Discrimination against Women* (1993) 30–1.
[2] A Aust, *Modern Treaty Law and Practice*, 2nd edn (2007) 425.   [3] Ibid.
[4] UNGA Res 3010 (XXVII) (18 December 1972).

Conference of the International Women's Year (Mexico City 1975), the first of the three World Conferences on Women that marked the International Decade for Women, and continued to dominate debates at the subsequent Conferences at Copenhagen in 1980 and Nairobi in 1985. From the outset 'these three objectives were considered interrelated and mutually reinforcing, such that the advancement of one contributes to the advancement of the others'.[5] Many of the issues alluded to in the Preamble are foreshadowed in the Declaration and Resolutions adopted at the Mexico City Conference.[6] Equality and development are basic themes in the Convention, although peace is not.[7]

In addition to these themes the Preamble reflects the issues of concern in international affairs and the norms of international law at the time the Convention was adopted. Similarly, its language is that of its time; for instance, the concept of gender had not yet appeared on the international agenda in 1979. In this respect, the Preamble seems somewhat outdated. Nevertheless, it also contains progressive and forward-looking language: 'maximum participation of women', 'change in the traditional role of men as well as the role of women in society'. It is to the credit of the CEDAW Committee (the Committee) that it has built upon the progressive language in making the Convention a 'dynamic instrument'.[8]

The Preamble is not an operative part of the treaty and thus does not directly create binding legal obligations. However, it is an integral part of the treaty and contextually significant for the purpose of interpretation under VCLT Article 31.[9] Article 31(2) provides that for the purpose of interpretation the treaty shall include its preamble. Traditionally, the preamble is resorted to for determination of the object and purpose of the treaty.[10] It is, therefore, important that there should not be inconsistency between the treaty text and the preamble,[11] and the latter can also be useful in addressing gaps in the text. The preamble is particularly significant for the interpretation of human rights treaties, which are lawmaking treaties intending to set up an 'objective' system as opposed to a conventional one based on reciprocity,[12] where the parties' interest in balancing their

---

[5] H Pietilä, *The Unfinished Story of Women and the United Nations* (2007) 42.

[6] 'Report of the World Conference of the International Women's Year, Mexico City, Mexico', 19 June–2 July 1975 (Mexico Conference) UN Doc E/CONF.66/34.

[7] The linkage between women, peace, and security did not regain prominence until 2000, when the UNSC adopted its ground-breaking resolution 1325, which stressed the 'importance of [women's] equal participation and full involvement in all efforts for the maintenance and promotion of peace and security'. UNSC Res 1325 (31 October 2000) UN Doc S/RES/1325. See also UNSC Res 1889 (5 October 2009) UN Doc S/RES/1889 ('need for the full, equal and effective participation of women at all stages of peace processes').

[8] GR 28 para 2.

[9] 'A treaty shall be interpreted in good faith in accordance with the ordinary meaning to be given to the terms of the treaty in their context and in the light of its object and purpose', VCLT art 31(1). VCLT art 4 states that the Convention applies only to conventions adopted after its coming into force. This occurred on 27 January 1980, subsequent to the adoption of CEDAW. However, the VCLT is accepted as the authoritative statement of modern treaty law; Aust (n 2 above) 12–13.

[10] International Law Commission, Commentary on the Draft Convention on the Law of Treaties, reprinted 61 *Am J Intl L* (1967) 285, 355. See M Villiger, *Commentary on the 1969 Vienna Convention on the Law of Treaties* (2009) 428.

[11] Villiger (n 10 above) 426.

[12] The ICJ, speaking of the Convention for the Prevention and Punishment of Genocide, stated that:'In such a convention the contracting States do not have any interests of their own; they merely have, one and all, a common interest, namely, the accomplishment of those high purposes which are the *raison d'être* of the convention. Consequently, in a convention of this type one cannot speak of individual advantages or disadvantages to States, or of the maintenance of a perfect contractual balance between rights and duties.'*Reservations to the Convention on Genocide* (Adv Op) 1951 ICJ Reports 15, 23.

respective rights and duties calls for an inquiry into their respective intentions. However, the Convention Preamble does not make a forceful statement condemning discrimination against women,[13] instead largely referring to equality as instrumental to furthering the welfare of the family, the development of society and state, and world peace in general.[14] Such a clause would have been appropriate particularly as the Convention does not include an operative provision comparable to DEDAW Article 1, which states that discrimination against women 'is fundamentally unjust and constitutes an offence against human dignity'. The Committee has only rarely cited the Preamble in its interpretation and application of the Convention.[15]

B. Travaux Préparatoires

The Preamble was the subject of considerable discussion during the drafting process.[16] The Philippines draft did not include a preamble,[17] but that put forward by the USSR did,[18] following the example of other UN human rights instruments, including the UDHR, ICCPR, ICESCR, and ICERD and especially the Declaration on the Elimination of Discrimination against Women (DEDAW).[19] Within the Commission on the Status of Women (the CSW) it quickly became accepted that the future convention would include a preamble. Most preamble paragraphs of DEDAW are included in the Convention preamble, albeit with some considerable adaptations. The exception is DEDAW Preamble paragraph 8, which considered it 'necessary to ensure the universal recognition in law and in fact of the principle of equality of men and women'. In its place the Convention Preamble notes States' obligations under the ICCPR and ICESCR to 'ensure the equal rights of men and women to enjoy all economic, social, cultural, civil and political rights', as well as other international conventions that promote equal rights of men and women.[20] Additional paragraphs primarily reflect changes in the international political and economic environment between 1967 and 1979. The United Kingdom opposed the inclusion of these paragraphs,[21] and upon ratification, France and the Netherlands made declarations protesting them.[22] These declarations do not purport to be reservations and have no legal effect.

C. Issues of Interpretation

I. Structure of the Preamble

Preamble paragraphs 1 to 5 refer to other international legal instruments that contain a prohibition of discrimination on the basis of sex. These texts served as an inspiration for the Convention and evidence the international legal commitment to this prohibition and

---

[13] As contrasted to the ICERD preamble, which strongly condemns racial discrimination. See n 56 on ICERD preamble below and related text.
[14] Paras 12 and 13.   [15] GR 23 paras 1 and 2, citing Preamble paras 7 and 12.
[16] Rehof (n 1 above) 30–41.   [17] UN Doc E/CN.6/573 (1973).
[18] UN Doc E/CN.6/AC.1/L.2 (1974).   [19] UNGA Res 2263 (XXII) (7 November 1967).
[20] Paras 3 and 4.   [21] W McKean, *Equality and Discrimination under International Law* (1983) 192.
[22] 1343 UNTS 370 (France); For The Netherlands, see <http://www.un.org/womenwatch/daw/cedaw/reservations-country.htm> accessed 31 December 2010. Moreover, the Federal Republic of Germany made its standard declaration according to which the right to self-determination is not limited to peoples under foreign or colonial domination, see ibid.

its corollary, ensuring the equal rights of men and women to enjoyment of all human rights. Preamble paragraphs 6 to 8 then turn to the reality of women's situation and the major problems that are to be addressed through the Convention: the continued existence of extensive discrimination against women, which is an obstacle to women's participation in all aspects of life within their own State, and which, in turn, has negative consequences for economic development at the macro-level of the State and the micro-level of the family, and, more broadly still, for humanity. Paragraph 8 recognizes the impact of poverty on women, although it falls short of characterizing the effect of poverty as a violation of women's human rights.

The assertion of women's human dignity captures the essential nature of human identity and thus the universal commitment to women's human rights and their inalienability. However, these paragraphs are simultaneously instrumentalist in their endorsement of equality as necessary to the development of women's potentialities 'in the service of their countries and of humanity'.

Preamble paragraphs 9 to 11 emphasize the factors that States considered conducive to realizing the purposes of the Convention and locate them within contemporary international affairs: the establishment of a new international economic order, the eradication of colonialism and apartheid, and strengthening international peace and security.[23] These paragraphs reflect the ethos of the first global conference on women in Mexico City in 1975 where 'many male delegates...used it to test the political waters on such questions as development, the new international economic order (NIEO), and the influence of colonialism on developing countries, many of them newly independent. Soviet and American delegates sparred over Cold War issues in the plenary sessions'.[24] These paragraphs are not pursued through the Convention's operative articles.

Preamble paragraphs 12 to 14 underline the roles of women in all spheres of human life, whether recognized or not, and make a commitment to changed relations between women and men, including shared responsibility for the upbringing of children, for the achievement of substantive equality. Finally, paragraph 15 emphasizes the overall purpose of the Convention, to implement the principles of the non-binding predecessor instrument, DEDAW, through adoption of measures to eliminate discrimination against women 'in all its forms and manifestations'.

In negotiating an international instrument, delegates draw upon existing accepted language. Despite the innovative nature of the Convention as an asymmetrical treaty targeted not at prohibition of sex-based discrimination but at discrimination against women, in many provisions the language is taken from or echoes that of earlier instruments, regardless of their direct relevance to women. Some wording foreshadows evolution of further concepts and ideas.

II. Contents of the Preamble Paragraphs

The States Parties to the present Convention,

(1) Noting that the Charter of the United Nations reaffirms faith in fundamental human rights, in the dignity and worth of the human person and in the equal rights of men and women,

---

[23] Debates during the drafting of these paragraphs reflect States' differing Cold War ideologies; see Rehof (n 1 above) 37–9.

[24] A Fraser, 'Becoming Human: The Origins and Development of Women's Human Rights' (1999) 21 *Human Rights Quarterly* 853, 895.

The wording of this first paragraph was uncontested[25] as it reiterates the second paragraph of the preamble to the United Nations Charter, thus making it secondary only to the Charter's primary objective 'to save succeeding generations from the scourge of war'. The Convention's opening Preamble paragraph omits only the final words of the second paragraph of the Charter preamble, 'and of nations large and small'. The Charter provided the authority for the subsequent development of human rights instruments through its promotion and encouragement of respect for human rights without distinction, *inter alia,* on the basis of sex,[26] but as it did not set out member States' obligations in this respect there was a clear need for further instruments. The first such instrument, the UDHR, repeats the same wording in its fifth preamble paragraph.[27] The inclusion of this same text in the Convention affirms its status as a UN human rights treaty that sets out States' obligations in fulfilling the objectives of the UN Charter and the UDHR.

The paragraph emphasizes human rights, dignity, and equality as the three pillars of the Convention. It also closely resembles the introductory preamble paragraph of DEDAW, although the latter is drafted in the names of the peoples of the United Nations (as is the preamble of the UN Charter itself). The Convention, in conformity with regular treaty practice, is drafted in the name of States parties,[28] which affirms their position as the duty holders under the Convention.

(2) **Noting that the Universal Declaration of Human Rights affirms the principle of the inadmissibility of discrimination and proclaims that all human beings are born free and equal in dignity and rights and that everyone is entitled to all the rights and freedoms set forth therein, without distinction of any kind, including distinction based on sex,**

The second Preamble paragraph evokes the UDHR Articles 1 and 2. Article 1 proclaims that 'all human beings are born free and equal in dignity and rights'. Equality in dignity denotes the essential quality of being human and the equal worth of all human beings.[29] During the drafting of the UDHR Eleanor Roosevelt argued that the concept of dignity was necessary 'to emphasize that every human being is worthy of respect . . . it was meant to explain why human beings have rights to begin with'.[30] It entails the normative postulate of equal respect for all individuals as autonomous subjects responsible for their own choices and actions. Equality thus rules out alternative concepts such as 'equity' or 'equitable treatment' whereby the measure of worth and respect due are based on features socially ascribed to women and men respectively and their constructed social roles.[31] Article 1 of the UDHR also affirms that rights follow from dignity, and as dignity is equal dignity, so too must rights be equal rights. The wording also underscores the interrelationship between equality and freedom: equality is indispensable to ensuring that all human beings have the same opportunity to live their lives according to their own aspirations and choices, and that they enjoy the freedoms to realize those choices. By noting these concepts embedded in the UDHR, the second Preamble paragraph links the Convention to this same conceptual framework.

---

[25] Rehof (n 1 above) 34.   [26] UN Charter arts 1(3), 13, 55, 56, 62, 68, and 76.
[27] UNGA Res 217 (III) (10 December 1948).   [28] Aust (n 2 above) 424.
[29] For an overview of the use of 'dignity' in historical and contemporary national and international texts, see C McCrudden, 'Human Dignity and Judicial Interpretation of Human Rights' (2008) 19 *Eur J Intl L* 655.
[30] MA Glendon, *A World Made New: Eleanor Roosevelt and the Universal Declaration of Human Rights* (2001) 146.
[31] See the discussion in the Introduction chapter.

Allusion to dignity as the basis of human worth and choice has been misused to suggest that women do not need rights as long as their dignity is protected. Such arguments may disguise discriminatory stereotyping of women.[32] Indeed, just prior to the Fourth World Conference on Women the Holy See, using the opportunity of having a global audience far more diverse than the usual, attempted to redefine women's dignity as a matter of 'complementarity' to that of men and not as a basis of the right to make choices.[33]

Reference to dignity is not repeated in the operative provisions of the Convention, which consistently frame States parties' obligations in terms of equality and rights. However, the fundamental connection of equality and dignity in its positive sense is retained throughout the Convention. The exercise of rights is based in freedom and in human choice as to determining one's purpose in life and pursuing it, the elements of dignity in the philosophical sense.[34] Human beings are the subjects of responsibility, and equally so; no individual should be able to reduce another's responsibility by forcing choices on her and thus diminishing her human dignity.

The use of the inclusive 'all human beings' in place of 'all men' in the UDHR Article 1 was at the insistence of a number of women delegates to the UN Commission on Human Rights. The Indian delegate, Hansa Mehta, feared 'all men' might be interpreted to exclude women[35] and resisted the argument that 'all men' would be read generically to include all persons. She was strongly supported by Bodil Begtrup (as chair of CSW) and Minerva Bernardino of the Dominican Republic (chair of CSW, 1953–55) who also understood that recognizing rights for 'everyone' did not necessarily translate into inclusion of women's rights.[36]

The second phrase in Preamble paragraph 1 ('everyone...based on sex') reflects the UDHR Article 2 which lays down a general prohibition of distinction, *inter alia*, on the basis of sex, in entitlement to the rights contained in the UDHR. The reiteration of this phrase in the Convention Preamble brings the UDHR prohibition of sex-based discrimination into the Convention. However, the Convention is not directed at sex-based discrimination, but at discrimination against women. Further, the UDHR Article 2 is not a free-standing non-discrimination or equality clause, but is limited to the rights contained in the Declaration.

The Convention Preamble paragraph 1 largely follows the first preamble paragraph of DEDAW, but differs in that it affirms 'the principle of inadmissibility of discrimination' whereas DEDAW asserts only the 'principle of non-discrimination'. The Convention wording was controversial during the drafting process and shifted back and forth several

[32] S Baer, 'Dignity, Liberty, Equality: A Fundamental Rights Triangle of Constitutionalism' (2009) 59(4) *University of Toronto LJ* 417–68; Orit Kamir, 'Honor and Dignity Cultures: The Case of *Kavod* and *Kvod Ha-Adam* in Israeli Society and Law' in D Kretzmer and E Klein (eds), *The Concept of Human Dignity in Human Rights Law* (2002) 231–62.

[33] Letter of His Holiness John Paul II to Mrs Gertrude Mongella, Secretary-General of the Fourth World Conference on Women of the United Nations, 26 May 1995, para 3, <http://www.vatican.va/holy_father/john_paul_ii/letters/1995/documents/hf_jp-ii_let_19950526_mongella-pechino_en.html> accessed 31 December 2010.

[34] N Petersen, 'Human Dignity' in R Wolfrum (ed), *The Max Planck Encyclopedia of Public International Law* (2008) paras 5 and 9, online edition <www.mpepil.com> accessed 31 December 2010.

[35] Fraser (n 24 above) 88. The USSR maintained 'steady pressure' to ensure the 'lack of sexisim' in the UDHR; J Morsink, *Universal Declaration of Human Rights* (1999) 117.

[36] J Morsink (n 35 above) 116–29; J Morsink, 'Women's Rights in the Universal Declaration' 13 *Human Rights Quarterly* (1991) 229, 233–6.

times.[37] The reasons are not clear: arguably 'inadmissibility' conveys a stronger repudiation of discrimination than merely the 'principle of non-discrimination'. The concept of inadmissibility does not appear elsewhere in the Convention (and neither does that of non-discrimination). The terminology difference thus has no legal consequence.

(3) Noting that the States Parties to the International Covenants on Human Rights have the obligation to ensure the equal rights of men and women to enjoy all economic, social, cultural, civil and political rights,

The wording of Preamble paragraph 3 reflects that of Article 3 of the ICCPR and the ICESCR, which are phrased in identical terms with respect to the rights contained in each Covenant.[38] This paragraph shifts from the negative concept of non-discrimination to the positive obligation of equality. An attempt to downplay the legally binding force of the Covenant provisions was defeated during the drafting process.[39] Some States considered that the international covenants should be named.[40] Article 3 of each Covenant is limited to the rights guaranteed by the respective Covenant, while the Convention goes further, guaranteeing women equality in 'all fields' of life, irrespective of any specific mention in the Covenants.[41]

Read with the preceding Preamble paragraph, the Convention is explicitly linked to the International Bill of Rights, inviting the use of those instruments in its interpretation.[42] This helps deflect the issue that because some States parties to the CEDAW Convention are not parties to the Covenants, Article 3 of the Covenants might not qualify as 'relevant rule[s] of international law applicable in the relations between the parties', which are additional sources of interpretation under the VCLT.[43] Consequently, ICCPR and ICESCR Article 3 help to determine the meaning of 'equal rights of men and women'. Nevertheless, any Convention interpretation must take account of its asymmetrical approach, whereby women are guaranteed 'the exercise and enjoyment of human rights and fundamental freedoms on a basis of equality with men'.[44]

The DEDAW preamble does not include a comparable provision. This may be because the two Covenants had been adopted just under a year prior to DEDAW and were not yet in force.[45]

(4) Considering the international conventions concluded under the auspices of the United Nations and the specialized agencies promoting equality of rights of men and women,

By not listing the relevant instruments in this Preamble paragraph, comprehensive coverage is ensured. By 1979, several UN treaties relating to rights had been adopted through the work of the CSW: the Convention on the Political Rights of Women, 1952 (discussed

---

[37] Rehof (n 1 above) 35.

[38] ICCPR art 3: 'The States Parties to the present Covenant undertake to ensure the equal right of men and women to the enjoyment of all civil and political rights set forth in the present Covenant.' ICESCR art 3: 'The States Parties to the present Covenant undertake to ensure the equal right of men and women to the enjoyment of all economic, social and cultural rights set forth in the present Covenant.'

[39] Ecuador proposed the wording 'the international covenants on human rights indicate to States the obligation' in place of 'under the international covenants . . . States have the obligation', Rehof (n 1 above) 35.

[40] Byelorussia and the USSR, ibid.   [41] See the discussion in chs on arts 1 and 3.

[42] eg GR 19 para 7 lists rights that are not included directly in the CEDAW Convention but are included in the Covenants.

[43] VCLT art 31(3)(c).   [44] CEDAW art 3.

[45] The ICCPR and ICESCR were adopted by the UNGA on 16 December 1966; the ICCPR entered into force on 23 March 1976 and the ICESCR on 3 January 1976.

in the chapter on Article 7), the Convention on the Nationality of Married Women, 1957 (discussed in the chapter on Article 9), and the Convention on Consent to Marriage, Minimum Age for Marriage and Registration of Marriages, 1962 (discussed in the chapter on Article 16). Conventions concluded under the auspices of the specialized agencies include those of the ILO, for example, the Equal Remuneration Convention,[46] Maternity Protection Convention (Revised),[47] and the Discrimination (Employment and Occupation) Convention.[48] The ILO had also adopted a number of conventions relevant to women during the period of the League of Nations, which technically do not come within the terms of 'under the auspices of the United Nations'.[49] UNESCO Convention against Discrimination in Education, 1960, has considerable bearing on the CEDAW Convention Article 10.[50] Other relevant treaties are those for the suppression and combating of trafficking, which foreshadow Convention Article 6.[51]

Unlike the preceding Preamble paragraph, this paragraph makes no explicit reference to States' obligations arising out of these treaties. Arguably, its purpose is to enable the Convention to be interpreted in light of these treaties, or to see it as complementary to them.

In contrast to the second preamble paragraph of DEDAW, the Convention Preamble paragraph 4 does not characterize the international treaties referred to as 'designed to eliminate all forms of discrimination' but more narrowly as 'promoting equality of rights'. This seems to indicate a somewhat restricted understanding of their reach because 'all forms of discrimination' encompass (at least) direct and indirect discrimination, whereas equality of rights seems to disregard *de facto* inequality, often resulting from indirect discrimination.

(5) Noting also the resolutions, declarations and recommendations adopted by the United Nations and the specialized agencies promoting equality of rights of men and women,

The preamble to DEDAW had combined reference to conventions and other legal instruments such as resolutions and declarations within a single paragraph, while the Convention separates them into Preamble paragraphs 4 and 5. Paragraph 5 was introduced during the drafting process from wording that had earlier been deleted from the preceding paragraph.[52] It ensures the Convention's linkage with the totality of pre-existing instruments adopted under the auspices of the UN by including legally non-binding resolutions and declarations, so-called 'soft law'. However, the hierarchy between binding legal obligation and soft law is maintained in that the former is to be 'considered' and the latter only 'noted'. By 1979, the UNGA had adopted many such resolutions, commencing with a resolution in its first session on the political rights of women.[53] They include resolutions that specifically address equality and non-discrimination,[54] as well as other relevant issues such as the advancement of women, women's integration into development, women's economic status, and rural women. In the 1970s, the UNGA adopted a spate of resolutions relating

---

[46] ILO Convention No 100.   [47] ILO Convention No 103.   [48] ILO Convention No 111.

[49] One of these, the Night Work (Women) Convention, 1919, and its Protocol were both revised in 1948; ILO Convention No 89 and Protocol 89.

[50] Adopted by the UNESCO General Conference, 11th Session, Paris, 14 December 1960.

[51] eg Convention for the Suppression of the Traffic in Persons and of the Exploitation of the Prostitution of Others.

[52] Rehof (n 1 above) 36. The new paragraph was proposed by Denmark.

[53] UNGA Res 56 (I) (11 December 1946).

[54] UNGA Res 3521 (XXX) (15 December 1975).

to International Women's Year, the Decade for Women, and follow-up resolutions to the Mexico City World Plan of Action. The most significant forerunner UNGA resolution is DEDAW, which is also the explicit subject of the final Preamble paragraph.

(6) **Concerned, however, that despite these various instruments extensive discrimination against women continues to exist,**

Preamble paragraph 6 turns from the normative background to the reality, the factual situation of discrimination against women worldwide, which continues today.[55] It is striking that the Preamble to the Convention does not use strong language to condemn persistent discrimination against women as morally unjust, as does the preamble to ICERD with respect to racial discrimination.[56] Unlike DEDAW preamble paragraph 4 which included some positive wording ('despite the progress made in the matter of equality rights'), the Convention focuses on the prevailing challenges. In DEDAW preamble paragraph 4, discrimination against women is described as 'considerable', but in Convention paragraph 6 the adjective is 'extensive', which implies that it is more widespread and far-reaching. Emphasizing the continuation of extensive discrimination against women despite the various instruments alluded to in earlier paragraphs, justifies the adoption of this Convention directed at discrimination against women and covering all fields.

During the drafting process a number of States opposed the inclusion of this paragraph. Some argued in favour of restricting the broad geographic sweep through alternative wording such as 'in a number of regions', or 'in parts of the world', while others contended that they had succeeded in eliminating discrimination against women.[57] The unrestricted wording that was finally adopted is a strong reminder that no State or society is free from sex-based discrimination.[58]

(7) **Recalling that discrimination against women violates the principles of equality of rights and respect for human dignity, is an obstacle to the participation of women, on equal terms with men, in the political, social, economic and cultural life of their countries, hampers the growth of the prosperity of society and the family and makes more difficult the full development of the potentialities of women in the service of their countries and of humanity,**

Preamble paragraph 7 was adopted by consensus. It returns to the themes of equality of rights and respect for human dignity addressed in paragraphs 1 and 2. Since both are violated by discrimination against women, there can be no doubt that such discrimination is of itself a clear violation of rights. In addition, discrimination is an obstacle to women's participation in political, social, economic, and cultural fields, the areas specified in Convention Article 3. The paragraph also links discrimination and development, presaging the concept of rights-based development, through the term 'growth of the prosperity

---

[55] eg in 2010, the CSW welcomed 'the progress made...towards achieving gender equality' and stressed that challenges and obstacles remain. Declaration on the occasion of the fifteenth anniversary of the Fourth World Conference on Women, ECOSOC, 'Report on the fifty-fourth session' (2010) UN Doc E/CN.6/2010/11.

[56] ICERD preamble para 5 states: 'Convinced that any doctrine of superiority based on racial differentiation is scientifically false, morally condemnable, socially unjust and dangerous, and that there is no justification for racial discrimination, in theory or in practice, anywhere.'

[57] Rehof (n 1 above) 36. Socialist countries claimed that discrimination had been eliminated from their countries.

[58] eg UN HRC Res 15/23 (8 October 2010) UN Doc A/HRC/RES/15/23 (deeply concerned that women everywhere are still subject to significant disadvantage as the result of discriminatory laws and practices and that *de jure* and *de facto* equality has not been achieved in any country in the world).

of society'. The contemporaneous International Development Strategy for the Second UN Development Decade (commencing 1 January 1971) maintains the importance of growth through its goal of 6 per cent annual average growth for developing countries,[59] but also declares its ultimate goal to 'bring about sustained improvement in the well-being of the individual and bestow benefits on all',[60] now termed 'human development'.

According to this Preamble paragraph, discrimination against women also affects the prosperity of the family, described in the International Covenants as the 'natural and fundamental group unit of society'.[61] However, this instrumental approach is not continued into Convention Article 16, where elimination of discrimination in the family is required as a goal in itself. Finally, the paragraph turns to the development of women, still tied to their potentialities in service to their countries and humanity. This view of women's service was presaged by the reference in the Mexico Declaration on the Equality of Women and Their Contribution to Development and Peace (the Mexico Declaration), paragraph 10, which asserts that equality of rights carries with it the assumption of duties, making it therefore 'a duty of women to make full use of opportunities available to them and to perform their duties to the family, the country and humanity'.[62] This again contrasts with Convention Article 3, in which women's full development and advancement is 'for the purpose of guaranteeing them the exercise and enjoyment of human rights', not for any economic or other service they might offer.

(8) Concerned that in situations of poverty women have the least access to food, health, education, training and opportunities for employment and other needs,

Eradication of the gap in wealth between developed and developing countries was a major concern of the 1970s, as evidenced by the commitment to a New International Economic Order (NIEO) as referred to in Preamble paragraph 9. Poverty within States also was a concern, expressed for instance in the 1975 Mexico City World Plan of Action. This included various references to poverty, including as an obstacle to the enjoyment of basic human rights.[63] It also asserted that denial of women's rights lies at the root of mass poverty.[64] It did not, however, focus on economic disparities between women and men, nor did it identify women's experience of poverty.[65] The preamble to DEDAW makes no reference to the factual realities of poverty for women. Preamble paragraph 8 redresses this omission:[66] poor women have the least access to the basic conditions of life, food and health, and to services and conditions that could lift them out of poverty, and to education, training, and employment. The operative articles of the Convention do not articulate a right to be free from poverty or hunger,[67] although Articles 10, 11, and 12 address States parties' obligations in the fields of education, employment, and

---

[59] UNGA Res 2626 (XXV) (24 October 1970) Part B, para 13.   [60] Ibid, Part A, preamble para 7.
[61] ICESCR art 10(1); ICCPR art 23(1).
[62] Declaration of Mexico on the Equality of Women and their Contribution to Development and Peace (adopted at the Mexico Conference (n 6 above)).
[63] Ibid 98.   [64] Ibid 125.
[65] Women's poverty is again addressed in 'Report of the World Conference to Review and Appraise the Achievements of the United Nations Decade for Women: Equality, Development and Peace', Nairobi, Kenya, 15–26 July 1985 and the Beijing Platform for Action makes the 'feminisation of poverty' its first critical area of concern.
[66] This new paragraph was proposed by Bangladesh, Indonesia, Pakistan, Singapore, and Somalia; Rehof (n 1 above) 37.
[67] UDHR art 25 includes food as an element of an adequate standard of living; ICESCR art 11(2) recognizes the 'fundamental right of everyone to be free from hunger'.

health respectively, and Article 13 more broadly requires elimination of discrimination 'in other areas of economic and social life.'[68]

(9) **Convinced that the establishment of the new international economic order based on equity and justice will contribute significantly towards the promotion of equality between men and women,**

The 'continuing severe economic imbalance in the relations between developed and developing countries'[69] made the establishment of a NIEO a primary objective of the newly independent States, in particular those of Africa and Asia, that by the 1970s formed a majority within the UNGA. The demands of the NIEO included those of the UN Decade for Women, equality, development, and peace, but the equality envisaged is as between States, rather than as between individuals within States. Like other documents of the time, the Charter of Economic Rights and Duties of States[70] asserts the right and obligation 'to eliminate colonialism, apartheid, racial discrimination...' but makes no mention of sex-based discrimination. Indeed, there is no mention of women in any of the constitutive documents of the NIEO, the Charter, the Declaration,[71] or the Programme of Action. DEDAW does not include any provision equivalent to the Convention's Preamble paragraph 9, which also asserts (without any empirical justification) that implementation of the NIEO based on equity and justice would contribute to the promotion of equality between women and men.

(10) **Emphasizing that the eradication of apartheid, all forms of racism, racial discrimination, colonialism, neo-colonialism, aggression, foreign occupation and domination and interference in the internal affairs of States is essential to the full enjoyment of the rights of men and women,**

As Preamble paragraph 9 addressed the major economic concerns of the newly independent States in the UNGA, Preamble paragraph 10 addresses their major political concerns. They are also linked in that the Declaration on the Establishment of a NIEO includes the right to restitution and compensation for 'all States, territories and peoples under foreign occupation, alien and colonial domination or apartheid'. Similar language was reiterated in other instruments of the decade, for instance, the Mexico Declaration[72] and the International Development Strategy for the Second United Nations Development Decade.[73] Non-intervention in the affairs of States was a core norm in the 1970 UNGA Declaration on Friendly Relations among States, which was widely regarded as a reaffirmation of the principles of the UN Charter on its twenty-fifth anniversary.[74] Preamble paragraph 10 is not directed solely at women; eradication of these evils is necessary for the full enjoyment of rights by men and women.[75]

---

[68] Article 13 addresses an adequate standard of living and other economic, social, and cultural rights. See the discussion in ch on art 13.

[69] UNGA Res 3202 (S-VI) (1 May 1974).

[70] Charter of Economic Rights and Duties of States, UNGA Res 3281 (XXIX) (12 December 1974); Declaration on the Establishment of a New International Economic Order, UNGA Res A/RES/3201 (S-VI) (1 May 1974).

[71] Ibid.

[72] See (n 62 above) paras 24 and 25.   [73] UNGA Res 2626 (XXV) (24 October 1970) para 5.

[74] Declaration on Principles of International Law concerning Friendly Relations and Cooperation among States in accordance with the Charter of the United Nations, UNGA Res 2625 (XXV) (24 October 1970).

[75] The Netherlands considered that the paragraph should include women and men. Rehof (n 1 above) 38.

(11) **Affirming that the strengthening of international peace and security, the relaxation of international tension, mutual co-operation among all States irrespective of their social and economic systems, general and complete disarmament, in particular nuclear disarmament under strict and effective international control, the affirmation of the principles of justice, equality and mutual benefit in relations among countries and the realization of the right of peoples under alien and colonial domination and foreign occupation to self-determination and independence, as well as respect for national sovereignty and territorial integrity, will promote social progress and development and as a consequence will contribute to the attainment of full equality between men and women,**

This Preamble paragraph continues the pattern of addressing themes of contemporary political importance and addresses explicitly that of peace. It posits a link between the strengthening of international peace and security through attention to a range of identified issues that were causing tension in the international order and the attainment of equality between women and men. The political context of the Cold War is evidenced by the wording 'mutual co-operation among all States irrespective of their social and economic systems'. Nuclear disarmament was another concern of the newly independent (non-nuclear) States. The Nuclear Non-Proliferation Treaty, 1968 came into force in 1970, and disarmament was the subject of a number of UNGA resolutions in the 1970s.[76] It also features in the Mexico Declaration through the exhortation that '[w]omen as well as men should promote real, general and complete disarmament under effective international control'. The Brandt Commission Report made the important connection between disarmament and development, including because of the 'burden the arms race imposes on national economies, and of the resources it diverts from peaceful development'.[77]

The right to self-determination is contained in UN Charter Article 1(2), and Article 1 of the ICCPR and ICESCR.[78] Here it is made applicable not just to colonialism but also to alien domination and foreign occupation.[79] The language replicates closely that of another instrument of the time, Protocol I to the Geneva Conventions, 1977,[80] which includes as international armed conflict, in accordance with Common Article 2, conflicts where 'peoples are fighting against colonial domination and alien occupation and against racist regimes in the exercise of their right of self-determination'.[81] National sovereignty and territorial integrity are key concepts in the UN Charter and reiterated in the 1970 Declaration on Principles of Friendly Relations. The linkage between these concerns and promotion of women's equality is quite indirect: mutual cooperation on these issues will promote social progress and development which, in turn, will contribute to full equality between women and men. This appears to envisage a form of 'trickle down' effect.

---

[76] eg UNGA Res 3484 (XXX) 'General and Complete Disarmament' (12 December 1975); UNGA Res 31/189 'General and Complete Disarmament' (21 December 1976); UNGA 32/88 'Special Session of the GA devoted to Disarmament' (12 December 1977); UNGA Res 33/91 'General and Complete Disarmament' (16 December 1978).

[77] Brandt Commission, *North-South: A Programme for Survival* (1980).

[78] Self-determination is core to the important UNGA Res 1514 (XV) (14 December 1960). This resolution also includes in its preamble the wording contained in Convention Preamble para 1.

[79] While there were many other examples of foreign occupation in 1979 (including but by no means limited to Western Sahara, East Timor) the World Conference at Mexico linked these words directly to Palestine, Mexico Conference (n 6 above) 111.

[80] Protocol Additional to the Geneva Conventions of 12 August 1949, and relating to the Protection of Victims of International Armed Conflicts (Protocol I), 8 June 1977, art 1(4).

[81] See the four Geneva Conventions of 12 August 1949 and Protocols I and II, referenced in the Treaty Table in the Appendix.

(12) Convinced that the full and complete development of a country, the welfare of the world
      and the cause of peace require the maximum participation of women on equal terms with
      men in all fields,

Preamble paragraph 12 is highly instrumental and far-reaching, linking women's participation 'in all fields' to development and peace. It largely repeats the language of both DEDAW preamble paragraph 7 and paragraph 15 of the Mexico Declaration ('[t]he full and complete development of any country requires the maximum participation of women as well as of men in all fields'). However, the Convention paragraph additionally emphasizes women's participation 'on equal terms with men'. This paragraph gives greater weight to the importance of women in development than does the International Development Strategy for the Second United Nations Development Decade, which failed to incorporate women other than asserting that 'the full integration of women in the total development effort should be encouraged'.[82] Hilkka Pietilä describes what she calls an impressive 'countermove' by CSW which was to propose to the UNGA 'a comprehensive resolution outlining "a programme of concerted international action for the advancement of women"'.[83] The UNGA too stressed that 'women must play an important role in the promotion, achievement and maintenance of international peace'.[84] The ideas in this paragraph project forward to the Millennium Development Goals, in which gender equality and the empowerment of women are perceived—again evidencing the instrumental approach to equality in development—as 'effective ways to combat poverty, hunger and disease and to stimulate development that is truly sustainable'.[85]

(13) Bearing in mind the great contribution of women to the welfare of the family and to the devel-
      opment of society, so far not fully recognized, the social significance of maternity and the role
      of both parents in the family and in the upbringing of children, and aware that the role of
      women in procreation should not be a basis for discrimination but that the upbringing of chil-
      dren requires a sharing of responsibility between men and women and society as a whole,

DEDAW preamble paragraph 6 itemizes women's contribution to society ('social, political, economic and cultural life'). While not using the language of gender, Convention Preamble paragraph 13 identifies maternity as a matter of social significance (rather than as a 'women's issue'), implying that it is also socially constructed. By alluding to the use of women's biological role in procreation as a basis for sex discrimination and stating that this should not be so, paragraph 13 goes to the heart of the Convention.[86] Convention Preamble paragraph 13 differs quite sharply from DEDAW preamble paragraph 6 in that the former refers to the role of both parents in the family, while the latter is limited to the role of women in the family 'and particularly in the rearing of children'. In this, the Convention is closer to the Mexico Declaration, which asserted that '[w]omen and men have equal rights and responsibilities in the family and in society'. Both these latter instruments are also significant in the weight they give to the responsibilities involved in bringing up children, which according to the Convention should be shared between women, men and society as a whole. This Preamble paragraph is made operative through Convention

---

[82] UNGA Res 2626 (XXV) (24 October 1970) Part B, para 18 (h).
[83] Pietilä (n 5 above) 38. The resolution is: UNGA Res 2716 (XXV) (15 December 1970).
[84] UNGA Res 3520 (XXX) (15 December 1975).
[85] UNGA Res 55/2 (18 September 2000) UN Doc A/Res/55/2 para 20. See also the discussion in ch on art 3.
[86] See also the discussion in ch on art 16.

Article 5(2); both are forward looking in the commitment to social transformation and changed gender relations.

(14) **Aware that a change in the traditional role of men as well as the role of women in society and in the family is needed to achieve full equality between men and women,**

Preamble paragraph 14 builds on the previous paragraph.[87] In contrast to the instrumentality of other paragraphs, the language is solely about achieving full equality between women and men. There is no equivalent provision in DEDAW, but the paragraph picks up on the Mexico Declaration, which had implicitly made the same point by asserting that '[m]en should participate more actively, creatively and responsibly in family life for its sound development in order to enable women to be more intensively involved in the activities of their communities and with a view to combining effectively home and work possibilities of both partners'. Preamble paragraph 14 is given operative effect in Convention Article 5, a provision that had no forerunner in the UN Covenants or ICERD.

(15) **Determined to implement the principles set forth in the Declaration on the Elimination of Discrimination against Women and, for that purpose, to adopt the measures required for the elimination of such discrimination in all its forms and manifestations,**

This final paragraph affirms the purpose of the Convention, to give legal effect to and implement the principles in the non-binding DEDAW. It does not indicate that in fact the Convention goes further than DEDAW in a number of ways, described in the other chapters in this Commentary. The wording 'adopt the measures required' indicates the obligations imposed upon States parties throughout the operative articles of the Convention.

---

[87] This additional paragraph was proposed by Sweden; Rehof (n 1 above) 40.

Article 1

For the purposes of the present Convention, the term 'discrimination against women' shall mean any distinction, exclusion or restriction made on the basis of sex which has the effect or purpose of impairing or nullifying the recognition, enjoyment or exercise by women, irrespective of their marital status, on a basis of equality of men and women, of human rights and fundamental freedoms in the political, economic, social, cultural, civil or any other field.

* I would like to thank Professor Dianne Otto for her comments on this and the chapter on art 2; Luke Beck, Renée Chartres, Maria Herminía Graterol, and Eleanor Bath for their research assistance, and the University of New South Wales for Goldstar and Faculty of Law funding to support research for this chapter and the chapters on arts 2, 23, and 24.

A. Introduction

I. Background

The concept of 'discrimination against women', defined in Article 1, is fundamental to the Convention: nearly every substantive article of the treaty identifies elimination of such discrimination as the core of the State party's obligations. The drafters of the treaty brought to the task a deep understanding of the social and political contexts in which sex discrimination and injustice occurred. They saw that the inequality of women and discrimination against them were complex phenomena, reflected in and perpetuated by laws, customs and traditions, beliefs about what it meant to be a woman or a man, social and economic institutions, and power relations within and between societies and between women and men. Discrimination took many forms—exclusion from or limited rights to participate in the political and public spheres of community life, economic marginalization and dependence, the prevalence of stereotypes that limited life opportunities or valued predominantly 'male' activities and characteristics over 'female' ones, inequality in the family, and violence against women in the community and in the family. The organization of societies to institutionalize many of these forms of discrimination often made the discrimination seem 'natural' or 'normal', and frequently concealed the systematic nature of the preference given to 'male' interests. The drafters also understood that while a person's sex was an important determinant of discrimination against her, sex and gender interact with other characteristics to compound the effect of discrimination.

The goal of the drafters—to eliminate *all* forms of discrimination against women—was extremely ambitious. While the drafters drew on a number of existing international instruments which obliged or called on States to eliminate discrimination against women in specific areas, the Convention goes well beyond those in the extent of the obligations States parties assume under it. A number of States would have preferred that the Convention address discrimination on the ground of sex generally, thereby also covering discrimination against men on the basis of sex, rather than focusing only on discrimination against women. However, the overwhelming view was that such a symmetrical approach would fail to recognize the pervasive discrimination against women on the basis of their sex, and that an asymmetric guarantee was needed in the form of a sex-specific instrument.[1] The definition of discrimination against women in Article 1 and the related concept of equality must be viewed in this context. As the Committee has noted:

The Convention goes beyond the concept of discrimination used in many national and international legal standards and norms. While such standards and norms prohibit discrimination on the grounds of sex and protect both men and women from treatment based on arbitrary, unfair and/or unjustifiable distinctions, the Convention focuses on discrimination against women, emphasizing that women have suffered, and continue to suffer from various forms of discrimination because they are women.[2]

Much of the Committee's discussion of this fundamental article occurs in the context of the other articles of the Convention, both under the general obligations of Article 2 and

---

[1] N Burrows, 'The 1979 Convention on the Elimination of All Forms of Discrimination Against Women' (1985) 32 *Netherlands International Law Review* 419, 425; LA Rehof, *Guide to the Travaux Préparatoires of the United Nations Convention on the Elimination of All Forms of Discrimination against Women* (1993) 44.

[2] GR 25 para 5.

also under specific articles. Its most complete discussions of the Article 1 definition are found in General Recommendation 25 and General Recommendation 28.

II. Concepts of Equality and Discrimination

The concept of equality has given rise to philosophical, theoretical, and political debate for thousands of years.[3] This chapter first identifies a number of different understandings of equality and discrimination and strategies for achieving equality and eliminating discrimination, and examines how these have been embodied in the text of the Convention. It then explores how the approaches to equality and the elimination of discrimination have been developed by the Committee in its practice under the Convention.

The central purpose of the Convention, as reflected in its title, is the elimination of all forms of discrimination against women; the complementary[4] purpose of ensuring the enjoyment of rights 'on the basis of equality of women and men' also appears in many of the treaty's provisions. Each of these concepts implies the obligation of non-discrimination: the elimination of classifications, acts, or practices which are based explicitly on sex or which have an indirectly discriminatory effect, so that women enjoy access to the benefits and opportunities available within existing social structures. But beyond this, the Convention requires States parties to take positive steps to address the exclusion of women, ensuring not just formal entitlements but the substantive enjoyment of those opportunities, and it requires systemic change to modify exclusionary social structures that enshrine the perspectives and interests of privileged groups.

Discussions of equality in the human rights context employ a range of terms representing different understandings of the concept: formal equality, substantive equality, equality of opportunity, equality of results, and transformative equality, among others. Scholars and commentators do not always use particular terms in the same way, and the meanings of some terms overlap.

1. Formal Equality

This term is commonly used to refer to an approach to equality which has its roots in the principles of Aristotelian philosophy according to which equality and justice require like things to be treated in a like manner, while unlike things are to be treated in an unlike manner. 'Formal equality' often refers to the first aspect of this approach, sometimes known as the 'sameness', 'similarly situated', or 'identical treatment' approach to equality. It embodies the presumption that equality means that all persons are to be treated identically, and a failure to do so amounts to discrimination or a denial of equality. In its legal formulations it gives effect to the belief that certain individual or group characteristics are irrelevant to particular decisions, and makes unlawful the use of those characteristics as the basis for decision-making. At the same time it does permit the rebuttal of the assumption that all persons are similarly situated by allowing those who seek to justify differential treatment to show that there is an 'objective and reasonable justification' for that treatment.

---

[3] See generally S Gosepath, 'Equality' (March 2001, revised June 2007) in Edward N Zalta (ed), *Stanford Encyclopedia of Philosophy* <http://plato.stanford.edu/archives/spr2009/entries/equality/> accessed 29 November 2010.

[4] See A Bayefsky, 'The Principle of Equality or Non-Discrimination in International Law' (1990) 12 *Human Rights Law Journal* 1; OM Arnardóttir, *Equality and Non-Discrimination under the European Convention on Human Rights* (2003) 8–10.

The starting point of this approach to equality is that women and men should be considered to be the same in relevant respects and that identical treatment should be the norm. This approach sees as suspect differential treatment based on sex or on assumptions about the capabilities of and appropriate roles for women or men because of their sex; any differentiation of this sort must be justified as reasonable. In international human rights law this approach is reflected in instruments such as the ICCPR and the European Convention on Human Rights and is expressed in the jurisprudence of bodies such as the CCPR[5] and the European Court of Human Rights.[6]

Formal equality focuses on the content of laws and practices and their even-handed application. To the extent that it enables those who have been denied opportunities or rights that others enjoy to do so, it can advance the equal enjoyment of rights. However, its primary focus is not on the impact of apparently neutral criteria or practices, and approaches based on formal equality are criticized on the ground that they fail to give proper weight to differences and diversity among humans or that they insufficiently take into account underlying discriminatory social structures. The formal equality approach has also been criticized as dependent on finding appropriate comparators and thereby reinforcing existing androcentric structures and values: women can only claim to be entitled to those things that men already enjoy, but the recognition of such claims does little to change existing social structures or to recognize the respects in which women are different from men.

2. Substantive Equality[7]

This concept is contrasted with formal equality and the term is also employed in a variety of senses. First, it has been used in relation to the second aspect of the Aristotelian prescription that equality means that unlike things should be treated in an unlike manner, in proportion to their unlikeness. Sometimes known as the 'difference approach', it holds not only that differential (or non-identical) treatment may not be discriminatory, but also that in certain circumstances equality will require differential treatment of persons who are not similarly situated. Like the 'sameness approach', this model does not itself provide guidance as to the particular differences that result in persons not being similarly situated, nor does it indicate how those differences should be taken into account. This approach is also reflected in the jurisprudence of international bodies such as the CCPR[8] and the European Court of Human Rights,[9] as the second limb of an Aristotelian approach.

---

[5] The dominant approach of the CCPR has been a presumption that equality requires identical treatment, any departure from which must be justified by 'objective and reasonable criteria' (see CCPR 'General Comment 18' (1989) UN Doc HRI/GEN/1/Rev.9 (Vol. I) paras 8 and 13), though it has also endorsed a substantive/disadvantage approach under the ICERD and the CEDAW Convention (GC 18 paras 6 and 7). See generally M Nowak, *UN Covenant on Civil and Political Rights: CCPR Commentary* (2nd rev edn, 2005), especially at 76–82 (art 3) and 597–634 (art 26).

[6] Arnardóttir (n 4 above), DJ Harris, M O'Boyle, EP Bates, and CM Buckley, *Law of the European Convention on Human Rights* (2nd edn, 2009) ch 15, especially at 581–90.

[7] See the discussion in Arnardóttir (n 4 above) 24–6 (drawing on Kimber's analysis).

[8] CCPR notes that 'not every differentiation of treatment will constitute discrimination, if the criteria for such differentiation are reasonable and objective and if the aim is to achieve a purpose which is legitimate under the Covenant.' CCPR 'General Comment 18' (1989) UN Doc HRI/GEN/1/Rev.9 (Vol. I) para 13. But this does not articulate a positive duty to consider and respond to difference, but rather seems a more reactive approach to it.

[9] See C Overy and RCA White, *Jacobs & White: The European Convention on Human Rights* (4th edn, 2006) 412–31.

The term 'substantive equality' is also used to refer to the practical (or *de facto*) disadvantageous impact of particular laws, policies, or practices, whether sex-neutral or sex-specific. Laws or policies that are neutral on their face may in fact disproportionately and unjustifiably exclude women, or a subgroup of women, from opportunities, resulting in disparate impact or indirect discrimination. Substantive equality may also be seen as reflecting a 'law in action' analysis, which critiques law and policy for a failure to realize in practice the goals they purport to pursue. While broader than a formal equality approach, a substantive equality approach based on an indirect discrimination model is still a comparative approach. Obligations to avoid indirect discrimination are generally qualified by the existence of exceptions based on justifiability or reasonableness that reflect prevailing social arrangements. This approach, therefore, tends to leave intact social and institutional structures that are exclusionary and based on androcentric assumptions and models.

The notion of 'substantive equality' is also used in theories of sex or gender inequality which focus on 'asymmetrical structures of power, dominance and disadvantage at work in society'.[10] This 'disadvantage' model examines the structural and ideological conditions that lead to the oppression of women and denial of their rights and is not constrained to the same extent to find comparators in order to demonstrate unequal treatment as are the other models. A 'disadvantage' model, for example, would readily find discrimination in the adverse treatment of women on the ground of pregnancy, where no male comparator is appropriate or available, while other more limited formal analysis might have difficulty in reaching such a conclusion.

3. Transformative Equality

Some scholars have advanced a formulation of the concept of equality, termed 'transformative equality', which sees full and genuine equality as likely to be achieved only when the social structures of hierarchy and dominance based on sex and gender are transformed.[11] In some cases sex would become irrelevant; in other cases the differences that exist between women and men would be appropriately recognized and valued in social arrangements. A leading scholar describes the concept:

Equality as transformation does not aim at a gender-neutral future, but one which appropriately takes gender into account. The future is not simply one of allowing women into a male-defined world. Instead, equality for women entails a re-structuring [of] society so that it is no longer male-defined. Transformation requires a redistribution of power and resources and a change in the institutional structures which perpetuate women's oppression. It requires a dismantling of the public-private divide and a reconstruction of the public world so that child-care and parenting are seen as valued common responsibilities of both parents and the community. It aims to facilitate the full expression of women's capabilities and choices, and the full participation of women in society. ... This shows that equality as transformation requires not just the removal of barriers, but also positive measures to bring about change.[12]

[10] See eg Arnardóttir (n 4 above) 27; CA MacKinnon, *Feminism Unmodified* (1987) 32–45; R Hunter, *Indirect Discrimination in the Workplace* (1992) 1–9; J Bridgeman and S Millns, *Feminist Perspectives on Law: Law's Engagement with the Female Body* (1998) 69–107.

[11] S Fredman, 'Beyond the Dichotomy of Formal and Substantive Equality: Towards a New Definition of Equal Rights' in I Boerefijn *et al* (eds), *Temporary Special Measures: Accelerating de facto Equality of Women under Article 4(1) UN Convention on the Elimination of All Forms of Discrimination Against Women* (2003) 111.

[12] Ibid 115.

This might also be seen as a form of substantive equality with systemic and structural dimensions, and the terms do overlap. This Commentary uses the term 'transformative equality' to denote change of a fundamental and far-reaching nature, an objective which is embodied in the text and spirit of the Convention.

4. *Equality of Opportunity*

This concept, on its face intuitively straightforward, is complex and has given rise to much philosophical discussion[13] as well as debate over the proper and most effective ways of measuring and achieving it. In one sense it reflects the idea of a 'level playing field'—that everyone should be in the same position to take advantage of the opportunities offered by society—while recognizing that people will make different choices, with different outcomes for members of different groups.

Equality of opportunity encompasses both the formal and the substantive. 'Formal' equality of opportunity refers to the absence of any formal legal or other explicit barriers to participation by an affected group, without reference to the practical circumstances that may make it difficult or impossible for members of the disadvantaged group to take advantage of these opportunities.

'Substantive' equality of opportunity refers to the reality that identical treatment and lack of formal barriers to participation often will not provide persons who have been subject to discrimination a real chance to take advantage of opportunities, and that specific measures may be needed in order to ensure that they are in fact able to do so.[14] Removing a restriction on women attending universities, for example, will have little practical impact if women have not been able to undertake the secondary education necessary to lay the foundation for university studies. Ensuring equality of opportunity involves taking steps to ensure that girls receive an education equal in all respects to that provided to boys, so they can apply for university admission against the same standards and have a reasonable prospect of meeting them.

5. *Equality of Result or Equality of Outcome*

This concept posits as confirmation of equality, a proportionate level of participation by or distribution of particular benefits or opportunities to different groups in society. The claim that equality of opportunity only really exists if it leads to equality of outcome is controversial, as substantively equal opportunity may not lead to equal outcomes, due to the role of 'personal' choices, which are often limited by external factors, in influencing results. However, inequality of outcome may be an indication that there is in fact no substantive equality of opportunity, and equality of outcome may be advanced as a legitimate goal in itself.[15]

---

[13] See R Arneson, 'Equality of Opportunity' (2002) in EN Zalta (ed), *Stanford Encyclopedia of Philosophy* at <http://plato.stanford.edu/entries/equal-opportunity/> accessed 31 December 2010.

[14] Fredman (n 11 above) 113–14, using the phrase 'equality of opportunity' to refer to substantive equality of opportunity.

[15] A Phillips, 'Defending equality of outcome' (2004) 12(1) *Journal of Political Philosophy* 1 at <http://eprints.lse.ac.uk/533/1/equality_of_outcome.pdf> accessed 31 December 2010.

III. Comparison with Corresponding Articles in Other Human Rights Instruments

The definition of 'discrimination against women' in Article 1 draws on similar definitions in earlier human rights treaties.[16] These include ILO Convention No 111,[17] the UNESCO Convention against Discrimination in Education,[18] and the ICERD. The ILO and UNESCO Conventions address discrimination on the basis of sex generally rather than discrimination against women on the basis of sex exclusively. Article 1 of the Convention mirrors the definition of 'racial discrimination' in ICERD Article 1.

The ICERD approach is directed against discrimination on the basis of race, so is a form of symmetrical protection—any form of racial discrimination is prohibited— while the Convention addresses only one category of discrimination on the basis of sex, discrimination against women. Apart from this difference (and the inclusion of the word 'preference' in the ICERD definition), the critical difference in wording between the Convention definition and the ICERD definition lies in the final phrase of each: the ICERD definition of racial discrimination applies to the specific fields enumerated as well as to 'any other field of public life', while the Convention applies to those same fields, but also applies to the 'civil or any other field'. This wording represents a deliberate decision by the drafters to ensure that the scope of the Convention was not confined to the realm of public life,[19] but also addressed the fundamental inequalities that women suffered in the private sphere, in particular within the family.[20]

B. Travaux Préparatoires

The major issues of concern to the drafters were:

- whether the Convention should be limited to discrimination against women or provide a more general guarantee against discrimination on the basis of sex;[21]
- whether a reference to 'preference [on the ground of sex]' should be included in the definition of 'discrimination against women';
- whether the Convention should be expressed to apply only to fields of 'public life';
- how to ensure that discrimination against unmarried mothers and their children was included.

The negotiations eventually concluded that the treaty should address discrimination against women and should not become a convention protecting against discrimination on the ground of sex generally.

---

[16] DEDAW did not contain a definition of discrimination, though one was originally proposed along the lines of that which appears in the Convention. AS Fraser, 'The Convention on the Elimination of All Forms of Discrimination against Women (the Women's Convention)' in A Winslow (ed), *Women, Politics, and the United Nations* (1995) 81, 83.

[17] Art 1.   [18] Art 1.

[19] K Hirose, 'Article 1: Definition of Discrimination against Women', in Japanese Association of International Women's Rights, *Convention on the Elimination of All Forms of Discrimination against Women: A Commentary* (1995) 46–7.

[20] Protocol on the Rights of Women in Africa art 1 also contains a definition of discrimination against women in very similar terms to that in the CEDAW Convention.

[21] Rehof (n 1 above) 44 and 46.

A number of drafts of a definition of discrimination were put before the CSW. Those which attracted the most detailed consideration drew on ICERD but sought to adapt it to the position of women. The two most influential were alternative drafts proposed by the CSW Working Group which were in turn based on a Philippines draft[22] and an amended version of that draft proposed by the United Kingdom.[23]

The Working Group's alternative drafts were very similar. The first, based closely on the Philippines draft, read:[24]

'Article 1

In this Convention, the term 'discrimination against women' shall mean any distinction, exclusion, restriction made on the basis of sex which has the effect of or the purpose of nullifying or impairing the recognition, enjoyment or exercise, on an equal footing, of human rights and fundamental freedoms in the political, economic, social, cultural or any field of public life.'[25]

The second followed the United Kingdom's amendments to the Philippines draft, which included the term 'preference'.

The text adopted by consensus by the CSW was the first alternative, with minor modifications:[26]

'Article 1

For the purpose of the present Convention the term 'discrimination against women' shall mean any distinction, exclusion, restriction made on the basis of sex which has the purpose or effect of nullifying or impairing the recognition, enjoyment or exercise by women, on an equal footing with men, of human rights and fundamental freedoms in the political, economic, social, cultural or any other field of public life.'

The word 'preference' was omitted by the CSW because some States were concerned that prohibiting 'preferences' based on sex might limit their discretion to adopt positive action to redress historical or systemic discrimination against women,[27] or might place at risk the particular benefits or protection that women had been given under labour legislation and other protective schemes.[28]

Two further changes to the CSW draft were subsequently made by the Working Group of the Third Committee of the General Assembly.[29] The first was the removal of the words 'of public life', ensuring that the Convention applied to areas of private life as well; a reference to the 'civil' field was also included.[30] The second was the addition of the phrase 'irrespective of their marital status' to the CSW definition;[31] This was partly in response to proposals related to Article 16 that would have made explicit that unmarried mothers

---

[22] Draft art 1 (1973), UN Doc E/CN.6/573. Annex I.

[23] The UK amendment to the Philippines draft Article 1 reads: 'The term "discrimination" for the purposes of this Convention shall mean any distinction, exclusion, restriction or preference which has the purpose or effect of nullifying or impairing the recognition, enjoyment or exercise by women, on an equal footing with men, of human rights and fundamental freedoms in the political, economic, social, cultural or any other field of public life.' Draft art 1 (1974), UN Doc E/CN.6/AC.1/L.3. The USSR had proposed a different definition (UN Doc E/CN.6/AC.1/L.2 (1974)).

[24] UN Doc E/CN.6/574 7 (1974) 7.   [25] Ibid.

[26] Burrows (n 1 above) 425; Rehof (n 1 above) 47.

[27] Hirose (n 19 above) 46. In the event, the removal of the words does not appear to have had any significant impact on the coverage of the Convention.

[28] Ibid 46.   [29] Ibid 46–7.   [30] Ibid.

[31] UN Doc A/C.3/33/L.47/Add.2 paras 263–4; Hirose (n 19 above) 47–8; Burrows (n 1 above) 426.

and children of unmarried parents should not be discriminated against on that ground.[32] These proposals were withdrawn on the understanding that the phrase 'irrespective of marital status' would be included in Article 1.[33]

C. Issues of Interpretation

I. Analysis of the Text

1. 'Any Distinction, Exclusion or Restriction Made on the Basis of [Sex]'

This phrase, in conjunction with the following ones, is intended to be read broadly to encompass the many ways in which women might be denied equality because of gendered assumptions, practices and social structures. 'Distinction' would include explicit sex-based differential treatment of women and men; 'exclusion' refers to patterns of belief and social practices (including gender stereotypes) which deny to women the opportunities and rights that are available to men; and 'restriction' refers to limitations on the enjoyment of rights to a greater extent than may apply to men's enjoyment of those rights.[34]

The Article 1 reference to any distinction, exclusion, or restriction made 'on the basis of sex', does not mean that an explicit reference to sex or sex-related characteristics is required for an action to be discriminatory.[35] Read in the context of Article 1 and the entire Convention, as well as taking into account ICERD practice relating to similar language, it is clear that such an explicit reference is not required. The phrase 'on the basis of sex' covers situations where sex is explicitly mentioned as a basis of differential treatment (direct discrimination) or where application of a 'neutral' criterion or a particular practice results in a disparate impact on women (indirect discrimination). To insist that an explicit reference to sex is required in order to invoke the Convention's norms, would significantly frustrate the achievement of its purposes.

2. 'Sex, Gender and Sexuality'

The Convention uses the term 'sex' as the central marker for deciding what types of differential treatment or disparate impact are (im)permissible. Underpinning the Convention are the assumptions both of sexual difference—that there exist two different sexes and that there are biological differences of significance between men and women, as well as culturally constructed differences—and of shared humanity: that women and men share many characteristics and are equally entitled to respect for their individual human dignity.

When the Convention was being drafted, the distinction between 'sex' and 'gender' was not invoked at the international level to any great extent. The central role played by Article 5 in the scheme of the Convention and its emphasis on the social construction of women's and men's roles shows that the drafters of the Convention were determined

---

[32] UN Doc A/C.3/33/L.47/Add.2 paras 258–62.

[33] UN Doc A/C.3/33/L.47/Add.2 paras 194, 258–64; Hirose (n 19 above) 47–8.

[34] Cook and Cusack provide examples: RJ Cook and S Cusack, *Gender Stereotyping; Transnational Legal Perspectives* (2009) 107–11.

[35] See eg Cook and Cusack, who argue that 'a law, policy or practice that fails to treat similar interests of men and women in the same way, or that fails to treat a significantly different interest between them in a way that adequately respects that difference, creates a *distinction between men and women*' within the meaning of art 1. Ibid 108 (emphasis in original).

to address the many ways in which biological sex differences were relied on to construct gender identities that disadvantaged women.

Another issue is whether 'sex' includes sexual orientation or sexuality, providing for application of the Convention to discrimination against women on the grounds of their sexuality, either as a form of sex discrimination or because such discrimination reflects harmful stereotypes about the roles of women and men. The extent to which the Convention provides protection to transgendered and intersexual persons, transsexuals is also unclear. The Committee has been cautious in addressing the issue of sexuality but has expressed concern about discrimination against women based on their sexuality or gender identity.[36]

3. 'Which has the Effect or Purpose of'

Acts which treat women differentially based on a rationale other than sex may none the less constitute discrimination against women if they involve disadvantageous treatment or impact. An intention to discriminate is not required; the critical criterion is whether a difference in treatment impairs their enjoyment of their rights. This reading concurs with the Convention purpose of eliminating 'all forms' of discrimination. As the Committee has noted, the effect of the definition is that 'even where discrimination was not intended':

> an identical or neutral treatment of women and men might constitute discrimination against women if such treatment resulted in or had the effect of women being denied the exercise of a right because there was no recognition of the pre-existing gender-based disadvantage and inequality that women face.[37]

4. 'Impairing or Nullifying the Recognition, Enjoyment or Exercise by Women'

The test of what constitutes discrimination is a substantive one: it must be shown that the act or practice in question is based on sex, and has an adverse impact on women's enjoyment of their human rights and fundamental freedoms. A sex-based action or practice which enhances women's enjoyment of their rights and freedoms is not discrimination against them within the meaning of the Convention.[38] Nor is it discrimination against men on the basis of sex under other international treaties, provided it is a measure to achieve substantive equality—and thus has an 'objective and reasonable justification'—or is a temporary special measure designed to overcome past disadvantage, which is permissible and may be required both under the Convention and other treaties.[39]

The words 'by women' were added to the end of this phrase during the drafting. The intention was to emphasize that the purpose of the Convention is to address sex discrimination against women rather than sex discrimination generally.[40]

---

[36] eg CO Albania, CEDAW/C/ALB/CO/3 (2010) paras 42–3; CO Uganda, CEDAW/C/UGA/CO/7 (2010) paras 43–4. See also GR 28 para 18; GR 29 para 13. See also the discussion in ch on art 5.

[37] GR 28 para 5.   [38] Art 4(1) and GR 28 para 18.

[39] See CCPR, 'General Comment 18' (1989) UN Doc HRI/GEN/1/Rev.9 (Vol. I) 18 paras 6 and 10 and 'General Comment 28' (2000) UN Doc CCPR/C/21/Rev.1/Add.10 para 3; CESCR, 'General Comment 16' (2005) UN Doc E/C.12/2005/4 para 15.

[40] The United Kingdom expressed concern that otherwise 'a distinction made on the basis of sex and resulting in the impairment of the rights of a man would . . . be classified as "discrimination against women".' UN Doc E/CN.6/591 para 33.

5. 'Irrespective of Their Marital Status'

This phrase was added relatively late in the drafting. It acknowledges that women's marital status has frequently been a reason for their experiencing discrimination, sometimes because they are married and at other times because they are not. Prohibition of discrimination against women 'irrespective of their marital status' could protect married women against discrimination on the ground of their marital status as compared to women who are not married, as well as by comparison with married men. Conversely, it could protect women who are not married from being discriminated against on that basis, both as regards men who are not married and women who are married. If the phrase extended this far, the Convention would in effect cover marital status discrimination between different categories of women, as well as discriminatory treatment clearly based on sex between the categories of married/unmarried women and married/unmarried men.

Thus, the issue is whether all of these forms of differential treatment are captured by Article 1, or whether Article 1 covers only discrimination between married women and married men, or between unmarried women and unmarried men. Logically, it would be possible to read the treaty as protecting women who are not married from being discriminated against on that basis, both as compared to men who are not married and women who are married. Understood this way, the Convention would cover marital status discrimination between women. The Convention recognizes that not every form of disadvantage suffered by women can be neatly reduced to a simple comparator-based test (reproductive issues and maternity are examples). Many cases will involve discrimination between women of a particular marital status and men of the same marital status. In addition, in some areas a difference in treatment between married women and unmarried women may reflect gender-based stereotypes as referred to in Article 5, clearly falling within the contextual approach to equality articulated in the Convention. Nevertheless, the drafting history is fairly clear that the drafters were contemplating protecting married women against discriminatory treatment compared with married men, and unmarried women as compared with unmarried men.[41]

6. 'On a Basis of Equality of Men and Women'

This phrase underlines the nature of the Convention as a treaty addressing discrimination against women. Some have seen this phrase (and similar phrases occurring in other provisions of the Convention) as reinforcing an 'equality as sameness' framework for the Convention—in other words, women are only entitled to what men already have.[42] Yet this conclusion depends on how one understands equality, as discussed above: a broad approach to equality does not limit the Convention to merely guaranteeing women an equal right to what men already have.

---

[41] See the discussion of the drafting history in *AB v Registrar of Births, Deaths and Marriages* [2007] FCAFC 140 (2007) 162 FCR 528. The United Kingdom's instrument of ratification stated that 'the phrase "irrespective of their marital status" shall not be taken to render discriminatory any difference of treatment accorded to single persons as against married persons, so long as there is equality of treatment as between married men and married women and as between single men and single women.' In 1995, the UK withdrew this reservation, noting that this was the correct interpretation of the provision but that there was 'no need for this to be explicitly stated.' CEDAW/C/UK/3 Annex A 126 (1995).

[42] eg H Charlesworth, 'Concepts of Equality in International Law' in G Huscroft & P Rishworth (eds), *Litigating Rights: Perspectives from Domestic and International Law* (2002) 137, 145 and 146.

7. 'Of Human Rights and Fundamental Freedoms in the Political, Economic, Social, Cultural, Civil or any Other Field'

States parties are obliged to eliminate discrimination against women not only in the fields explicitly covered by the Convention, but also in relation to a much broader range of human rights and fundamental freedoms. In this respect, the Convention adopts a different approach from that in Article 2(1)(a) of the ICCPR and ICESCR respectively or in Article 14 of the European Convention on Human Rights,[43] each of which limits the obligation of non-discrimination to the rights set out in the respective treaties.[44] The Convention imposes an obligation to work towards equality on the basis of sex and gender in relation to the many human rights and fundamental freedoms which are not specifically mentioned in the text of the Convention but which are recognized under other treaties and customary international law, and arguably even under some instruments which might not have treaty or customary international law status. These rights include, for example, the right to life, the right to be free from torture, the right to freedom of expression, the right to privacy, the right to freedom of opinion, belief, and religious expression, the rights of members of minorities, the right to adequate housing, and the many rights or protections guaranteed under international humanitarian law or other specialized areas of international law—none of which are explicitly mentioned in the Convention. These matters are covered by the general obligations, especially Articles 2, 3, and 24.[45]

II. Interpretation by the Committee

1. General Approach

The Committee has adopted a flexible approach to the meaning of equality and its application in the specific practical circumstances that arise under the different articles. Since the Convention came into force a number of different conceptions or models of equality have been employed, ranging from identical treatment of women and men, to models of substantive equality which require a contextual and structural analysis of the effect of particular laws, policies, and practices.

The Committee has used a number of different terms relating to equality, regularly referring to *de jure* and *de facto* equality, formal equality, substantive equality, direct discrimination, indirect discrimination, and other related terms. The variety of terminology and the different aspects of equality and non-discrimination to which they refer (and the attendant obligations) can be seen in the extended discussions in General Recommendations 25[46] and 28.[47] In General Recommendation 25, the Committee set

---

[43] By contrast, the ICERD, in addition to the general obligation in art 2(1)(a) to eliminate 'racial discrimination in all its forms', also contains in art 5 a detailed list of specific rights in the enjoyment of which equality is to be guaranteed. In its 'General Recommendation XX' (1996) UN Doc HRI/GEN/1/Rev.9 (Vol. II) on article 5, para 1, CERD noted that 'the rights and freedoms mentioned in article 5 do not constitute an exhaustive list'.

[44] Though ICCPR art 26 extends beyond the civil and political rights contained in that treaty, and Protocol 12 to the European Convention on Human Rights provides for a freestanding right to equality and non-discrimination.

[45] In this regard, the Committee's statement in GR 28 para 7 that 'the spirit of the Convention covers other rights' than those specifically listed in the Convention understates the position—the letter of the Convention, not just its spirit, effects this coverage.

[46] GR 25 para 12.   [47] GR 28 paras 4–5, 18–19, and 22.

out the underlying obligations of States parties contained in the general provisions of the treaty (Articles 1, 2, 3, 5, and 24):[48]

Firstly, States parties' obligation is to ensure that there is no direct or indirect discrimination against women in their laws and that women are protected against discrimination—committed by public authorities, the judiciary, organizations, enterprises or private individuals—in the public as well as the private spheres by competent tribunals as well as sanctions and other remedies. Secondly, States parties' obligation is to improve the de facto position of women through concrete and effective policies and programmes. Thirdly, States parties' obligation is to address prevailing gender relations and the persistence of gender-based stereotypes that affect women not only through individual acts by individuals but also in law, and legal and societal structures and institutions.

The essence of the flexible approach is ensuring substantive equality.[49] The Committee has underlined the necessity of formal equality to achieving the purpose of the Convention— women are entitled to the same rights as men, such as the right to vote, to contract, to freely practise their religion.[50] However, it has also stressed that this approach is not sufficient to eliminate discrimination against women:

[A] purely formal legal or programmatic approach is not sufficient to achieve women's de facto equality with men, which the Committee interprets as substantive equality. In addition, the Convention requires that women be given an equal start and that they be empowered by an enabling environment to achieve equality of results. It is not enough to guarantee women treatment that is identical to that of men. Rather, biological as well as socially and culturally constructed differences between women and men must be taken into account. Under certain circumstances, non-identical treatment of women and men will be required in order to address such differences. Pursuit of the goal of substantive equality also calls for an effective strategy aimed at overcoming underrepresentation of women and a redistribution of resources and power between men and women.[51]

Finally, the Committee stresses that it is necessary to strive for transformative equality to fully realize the goals of the Convention, noting that fundamental social changes are required, as '[t]he position of women will not be improved as long as the underlying causes of discrimination against women, and of their inequality, are not effectively addressed'.[52]

---

[48] Ibid para 7. This passage is much influenced by the similar approach taken by the report of the Groenman Commission, established by the Netherlands Government to provide an overview of Convention implementation in the Netherlands: *Het Vrouwenverdrag in Nederland anno 1997, Verslag van de Rapportagecommissie Internationaal Verdrag tegen Discriminatie van Vrouwen* (1997) para 2.1.2 [translated in R Holtmaat, Towards Different Law and Public Policy: The Significance of Article 5a CEDAW for the Elimination of Structural Gender Discrimination (2004) Appendix, 139]. That report argued that the Convention had three sub-aims: (1) achieving full equality before the law and in public administration, (2) improving the *de facto* position of women, and (3) combatting the dominant gender ideology.

[49] GR 25 para 6 notes that a State party's obligations under the Convention 'extend beyond a purely formal legal obligation of equal treatment of women with men'.

[50] See eg CO Malawi, CEDAW/C/MWI/CO/6 (2010) paras 12–15; CO Jamaica, A/61/38 36th Session (2006) paras 391–2; CO Burundi, A/56/38 24th Session (2001) paras 55–6.

[51] GR 25 para 8. See also CO Timor-Leste, CEDAW/C/TLS/CO/1, (2009) para 17 ('equality of opportunities' in Constitution not the same as 'equality' under CEDAW); CO Singapore, CEDAW/C/SGP/CO/3 (2007) para 14.

[52] Ibid para 10.

2. *Sex and Gender*

The Committee distinguishes between 'sex' and 'gender' but has affirmed that the Convention covers discrimination against women (and girls[53]), whether based on sex or gender:

> The term sex refers to biological differences between men and women. The term gender refers to socially constructed identities, attributes and roles for women and men and society's social and cultural meaning for these biological differences resulting in hierarchical relationships between women and men and in the distribution of power and rights favouring men and disadvantaging women. This social positioning of women and men is affected by political, economic, cultural, social, religious, ideological and environmental factors and can likewise be changed by culture, society and community. The application of the Convention to gender-based discrimination is made clear by the definition of discrimination contained in article 1.[54]

3. *Sexuality/Sexual Orientation*

The Committee has been cautious in its approach to issues relating to discrimination against women on the ground of their sexuality. It has referred with approval to legislation which prohibits discrimination on the ground of sexual orientation[55] and has noted with concern the criminalization of same-sex relationships,[56] in one case recommending that penalties for same-sex relationships be removed from a State party's criminal code.[57] There is, in principle, no reason why the Convention should not be applied to provide protection for women who are discriminated against because of their sexuality where it 'has been used to subordinate women and reinforce male superiority', for example, where 'a lesbian's right to life is violated when she is subjected to death threats for not conforming to dictated heterosexual norms'.[58] General Recommendation 21 underlines women's autonomy in relation to marriage and family matters and recognizes the existence of 'various forms of family',[59] though it is not clear how far this would extend with respect to treatment of same-sex couples. In its discussion of multiple discrimination in General Recommendation 27 and General Recommendation 28, the Committee noted that women experience discrimination not only as women but also on the basis of 'other factors', of which sexuality is one.[60] The Committee has also raised the issue in its dialogues with States parties.[61]

4. *Concepts of Equality*

a) **Formal and Substantive Equality**

While insisting in many contexts that the Convention requires guarantees of formal equality to bring about the elimination of discrimination, the Committee has stressed

---

[53] GR 28 para 21.

[54] GR 28 para 5. The Committee made a statement to similar effect in GR 25 para 7 n 2.

[55] See tan beng hui, Exploring the Potential of the UN Treaty Body System in Addressing Sexuality Rights, International Women's Rights Action Watch Asia Pacific Occasional Paper Series, No 11 (2007) 7–11; JE Bond, 'International Intersectionality: A Theoretical and Pragmatic Exploration of Women's International Human Rights' (2003) 52 *Emory LJ* 71.

[56] CO Mexico, A/53/38 (Supp) part I, 18th Session (1998) para 420.

[57] CO Kyrgyzstan, A/54/38 (Supp) part I, 20th Session (1999) paras 127–8.

[58] t b hui (n 55 above) 8. See CO Guatemala, CEDAW/C/GUA/CO/7 (2009) paras 19–20; CO Lithuania, CEDAW/C/LTU/CO/4 (2008) para 23; CO Kyrgyzstan, CEDAW/C/KGZ/CO/3 (2008) para 43.

[59] GR 21 para 16.   [60] GR 27 para 13; GR 28 para 18.   [61] t b hui (n 55 above) 10–11.

the need for States parties to adopt laws and practices that embody a substantive equality approach.[62] For example, the Committee commended a State party on the legislative measures it had taken but expressed its concern at 'the limited scope of the existing legislation to eliminate discrimination on various grounds, including sex, which merely aims at equal treatment of individuals and does not fully reflect the principle of substantive equality embodied in the Convention'.[63] The Committee expressed the same view in General Recommendation 25.[64]

b) *De Jure* and *De Facto* Equality

Similarly, the Committee has regularly expressed its concern that States parties ensure not only *de jure* but also *de facto* equality. This appears to be another way of expressing the difference between formal and substantive equality.[65] This is made clear in General Recommendation 25 and in its reviews of State party implementation.[66] An example of its frequently expressed concern about the need to go beyond *de jure* equality is the Committee's criticism of one State party for its 'narrow focus primarily on *de jure* equality rather than the realization also of *de facto*, or substantive, equality of women as required under the Convention' and 'about [its] lack of efforts to assess the impact of laws and policies on women's equality in such sectors as decision-making, education, employment and health'.[67]

c) Direct and Indirect Discrimination

As discussed above, the language of Article 1 and its history show that both direct discrimination and indirect or disparate impact discrimination are intended to fall within the scope of the Convention. In its practice the Committee has stressed the importance of addressing both forms of discrimination to achieve substantive equality. Direct discrimination is 'different treatment explicitly based on grounds of sex and gender differences',[68] while:

[i]ndirect discrimination against women occurs when a law, policy, programme or practice appears to be neutral as it relates to men and women, but has a discriminatory effect in practice on women, because pre-existing inequalities are not addressed by the apparently neutral measure. Moreover, indirect discrimination can exacerbate existing inequalities owing to a failure to recognize structural and historical patterns of discrimination and unequal power relationships between women and men.[69]

---

[62] eg CO Benin, A/60/38, 33rd Session (2005) paras 145–6; CO Malaysia, A/61/38, 35th Session (2006) paras 64–5; CO St Lucia, A/61/38, 35th Session (2006) para 254; CO China, A/61/38, 36th Session (2006) paras 425–6; CO Armenia, CEDAW/C/ARM/CO/4/Rev.1, 43rd Session (2009) paras 12–13; CO Germany, CEDAW/C/DEU/CO/6, 43rd Session (2009) paras 25–6.

[63] CO Slovakia, A/63/38, 41st Session (2008) para 22.

[64] GR 25 para 8 (citing *1999 World Survey on the Role of Women in Development* (United Nations, 1999)) ix.

[65] GR 25 para 7.

[66] See eg CO Equatorial Guinea, A/59/38, 31st Session (2004) paras 185–6; CO Democratic People's Republic of Korea, A/60/38, 33rd Session (2005) para 38.

[67] CO Benin, A/60/38, 33rd Session (2005) para 145. See also CO Ecuador, A/58/38 (Supp) part II, 29th Session (2003) para 301; CO Brazil, A/58/38, 29th Session (2003) para 98; CO Andorra, A/56/38, 25th Session (2001) paras 49–50.

[68] GR 28 para 16.   [69] GR 28 para 16. See also GR 25 n 1.

The Committee has regularly called on States parties to ensure that indirect discrimination be addressed in law and policy, ideally by incorporating the Article 1 definition into domestic law.[70]

d) Equality of Opportunity/Equality of Outcome or Result

The Committee has on a number of occasions referred to the concepts of equality of opportunity and equality of outcome. It has criticized States parties for focusing only on achieving (formal) equality of opportunity at the expense of substantive equality.[71] The Committee has also stated that:

[e]quality of results is the logical corollary of de facto or substantive equality. These results may be quantitative or qualitative in nature, or both; that is, women enjoying their rights in various fields in fairly equal numbers with men, enjoying the same income levels, equality in decision-making and political influence, and women enjoying freedom from violence.'[72]

e) Equality and Equity

The Committee has stressed on a number of occasions that the normative concept of equality stated in the Convention and the concept of equity are not the same.[73] Some States parties have argued that their pursuit of the goal of 'equity' is consistent with the Convention because 'equity' is in essence substantive equality, as required by the Convention.[74] However, this view assumes that 'equality' is limited to formal equality only, rather than including substantive equality.[75] Other States parties have argued that their goal is to achieve the elimination of discrimination against women by ensuring that women and men have different roles, assigned according to sex, that are complementary and equally valued. The Committee has been forthright in its response to this approach, noting that despite the States parties' statements that 'equity' meant 'substantive' or '*de facto* equality', 'the terms "equity" and "equality" are not synonymous or interchangeable and can lead to conceptual confusion.'[76] The Committee also has noted with concern one State party's 'distinctive understanding of the principle of equality, which implies similar rights of women and men as well as complementarities and harmony between women and men, rather than equal rights of women and men'.[77]

---

[70] eg CO Botswana, CEDAW/C/BOT/CO/3 (2010) paras 9–10; CO Madagascar, CEDAW/C/MDG/CO/5 (2008) paras 10–11; CO Kyrgyzstan, CEDAW/C/KGZ/CO/3 (2008) paras 9–10; CO Bhutan, A/59/38, 30th Session (2004) para 99; CO Kuwait, A/59/38, 30th Session (2004) paras 64–5; CO Japan, A/58/38, 29th Session (2003) paras 357–8; CO Morocco, A/58/38, 29th Session (2003) para 161.

[71] eg CO The United Kingdom, A/63/38, 41st Session (2008) paras 264–5.

[72] GR 25 at para 9.

[73] eg CO Guyana, A/60/38, 33rd Session (2005) paras 287–8; CO Paraguay, A/60/38, 32nd Session (2005) paras 277–8; CO Dominican Republic, A/59/38, 31st Session (2004) paras 288–9; CO Venezuela, CEDAW/C/VEN/CO/6 (2006) para 22; CO Vanuatu, A/62/38, 38th Session (2007) paras 316–17; CO Nicaragua, CEDAW/C/NIC/CO/6 (2007) para 16. See generally A Facio and MI Morgan, 'Equity or Equality for Women? Understanding CEDAW's Equality Principles' (2009) 60 *Alabama L Rev* 1133.

[74] Facio (n 73 above) 1135–7.   [75] Ibid.

[76] eg CO Guyana, A/60/38, 33rd Session (2005) para 288, and similar formulations in the other concluding observations at n 73 above. See also GR 28 para 22.

[77] CO Saudi Arabia, A/63/38, 40th Session (2008) para 28.

5. *Relationship between Article 1 and Article 4*

The relationship between prohibitions of discrimination and the permissibility of tempo-rary special measures (or positive action or affirmative action) often gives rise to confu-sion. The question is whether positive or preferential measures, which 'discriminate' in favour of women in order to redress the effects of past or continuing discrimination, are a justifiable exception to the principle of non-discrimination, or whether such measures are not discriminatory at all, as they promote substantive equality by taking social context and power relations into account.[78] These issues are discussed in detail in the chapter on Article 4.

6. *Rights and Freedoms to Which the Convention Applies*

The definition of 'discrimination against women' extends to discrimination in the enjoy-ment of human rights and fundamental freedoms in any field and is not limited to those rights or fields explicitly mentioned in the Convention. This understanding of the broad coverage of the Convention has been at the heart of the Committee's approach for many years. It appears prominently in General Recommendation 19, in which the Committee referred to a number of rights not specifically mentioned in the Convention which may be violated by the subjection of women to violence in the family, in the community, or at the hands of the State. The Committee states clearly that States parties' obligations extend to eliminating inequality in the enjoyment of those rights that results from gender-based violence. It also appears in the Committee's consideration of intersectionality (the position of particular groups of women, such as ethnic minorities or indigenous peoples, migrant workers, and women with disabilities, all of whom may be subject to multiple discrimination)[79] and other cross-cutting themes.

In the case of *Cristina Muñoz-Vargas y Sainz de Vicuña v Spain*, a number of Committee experts offered the view that the Convention may not apply to all forms of differential treatment based on sex that reflect stereotyped roles of women and men. That case involved a claim by a complainant whose younger brother had succeeded to the title of Count pursuant to the Spanish laws providing for male primacy in succession to titles of nobil-ity. The complainant argued that these rules constituted a violation of the Convention in general, and of Article 2(f) in particular.[80] A majority of the Committee rejected the complaint on the ground that the relevant events had occurred before the entry into force of the Convention and the Optional Protocol for Spain. In a concurring opinion, eight members rejected the claim on a different ground, that because 'the title of nobility in question is of a purely symbolic and honorific nature, devoid of any legal or material effect', the claim was incompatible with the Convention, which was directed to protect-ing women from discrimination which actually impaired or nullified the enjoyment of their rights.[81] One member of the Committee dissented explicitly from this view, arguing that the Convention was directed to the elimination of 'the negative effects of conduct based on culture, custom, tradition and the ascription of stereotypical roles that entrench

---

[78] See GR 25 para 18, echoing art 4(1): 'The Committee considers that States parties that adopt and imple-ment such measures under the Convention do not discriminate against men.'

[79] eg GR 18 (disabled women); GR 25 para 12.

[80] Communication No 7/2005, decision on admissibility, A/62/38, 39th Session (2007), Annex VII.C, 474.

[81] Ibid 482 (individual opinion by Committee members Magalys Arocha Dominguez, Cees Flinterman, Pramila Patten, Silvia Pimentel, Fumiko Saiga, Glenda P. Simms, Anamah Tan, Zou Xiaoqiao (concurring)).

the inferiority of women', that 'the immediate material consequence of such patterns of behaviour does not have to be demonstrated', that the rules of primogeniture embodied such traditional stereotypes, and that the conclusion that the claim was incompatible with the Convention did not reflect 'the intent and spirit' of the treaty.[82]

a) Broader Application: Violence against Women

Parsing the individual elements of the Convention definition does not necessarily capture all of the ways in which the Convention may be interpreted to address the manifold forms of discrimination against women. As a human rights instrument, the Convention must be interpreted dynamically in response to later developments or issues that were not considered—or understood as human rights issues—at the time the Convention was formulated.[83]

The Committee has adopted a broad remedial approach to interpretation in a number of areas. The first is in relation to violence against women, which the Committee has interpreted as a form of discrimination against women involving denial of a range of fundamental rights and freedoms, including many not explicitly mentioned in the Convention. This approach was first comprehensively stated in General Recommendation 19,[84] and it has since that time been consistently reflected in the Committee's concluding comments and observations and in its jurisprudence under the OP. In General Recommendation 19, the Committee stated:[85]

The Convention in article 1 defines discrimination against women. The definition of discrimination includes gender-based violence, that is, violence that is directed against a woman because she is a woman or that affects women disproportionately. It includes acts that inflict physical, mental or sexual harm or suffering, threats of such acts, coercion and other deprivations of liberty. Gender-based violence may breach specific provisions of the Convention, regardless of whether those provisions expressly mention violence.

Gender-based violence, which impairs or nullifies the enjoyment by women of human rights and fundamental freedoms under general international law or under human rights conventions, is discrimination within the meaning of article 1 of the Convention.

7. Intersectionality

Although the Convention does not explicitly refer to multiple discrimination that women suffer by virtue of their sex and other status,[86] it recognizes that particular groups of women may be subject to specific forms of discrimination based on both their sex and on other characteristics.[87] This is reflected in references in the Preamble to women living in

---

[82] Individual dissenting opinion of Shanthi Dairiam, ibid 483.

[83] GR 25 para 3: 'The Convention is a dynamic instrument. Since the adoption of the Convention in 1979, the Committee, as well as other actors at the national and international levels, have contributed through progressive thinking to the clarification and understanding of the substantive content of the Convention's articles and the specific nature of discrimination against women and the instruments for combating such discrimination.' See also GR 28 para 15.

[84] GR 19 refers to the following rights that are not specifically referred to in the Convention: (a) the right to life; (b) the right not to be subject to torture or to cruel, inhuman, or degrading treatment or punishment; (c) the right to equal protection according to humanitarian norms in time of international or internal armed conflict; and (d) the right to liberty and security of person. See chapter on violence against women.

[85] GR 19 paras 6–7. See also GR 28 para 19.   [86] Compare CRPD preamble para (p).

[87] See generally Bond (n 55 above), and International Women's Rights Action Watch Asia Pacific, *Addressing Intersectional Discrimination with Temporary Special Measures*, International Women's Rights Action Watch Asia Pacific Occasional Paper Series, No 8 (2006) 25–6.

poverty and elsewhere in the Convention to women of a particular marital status, pregnant women, and women living in rural areas. The Committee in its practice has identified many groups of women to whom the Convention extends protection on the basis of their sex in combination with another status. The Committee explained the concept of intersectionality and its significance in General Recommendation 28:

Intersectionality is a basic concept for understanding the scope of the general obligations of States parties contained in article 2. The discrimination [against] women based on sex and gender is inextricably linked with other factors that affect women, such as race, ethnicity, religion or belief, health, status, age, class, caste, and sexual orientation and gender identity. Discrimination on the basis of sex or gender may affect women belonging to such groups to a different degree or in different ways than men. States parties must legally recognize and prohibit such intersecting forms of discrimination and their compounded negative impact on the women concerned.[88]

This approach can also be seen in General Recommendation 26 on women migrant workers. The Committee states that women migrant workers are entitled to the protection of their rights under the Convention as well as under other treaties and the UDHR,[89] noting that '[d]iscrimination based on race, ethnicity, cultural particularities, nationality, language, religion or other status may be expressed in sex- and gender-specific ways'.[90]

In General Recommendation 24 on the right to health care, the Committee noted that in addition to biological differences between women and men, 'there are societal factors that are determinative of the health status of women and men and can vary among women themselves' and that as a result 'special attention should be given to the health needs and rights of women belonging to vulnerable and disadvantaged groups, such as migrant women, refugee and internally displaced women, the girl child and older women, women in prostitution, indigenous women and women with physical or mental disabilities'.[91]

In other instances the Committee has referred to many different groups of women, including rural women, women with disabilities,[92] women belonging to ethnic minorities (including Roma),[93] immigrant and refugee women, indigenous women, migrant women, elderly women,[94] women in prison, and women belonging to sexual minorities.[95] In its Treaty-specific Reporting Guidelines for periodic reports, the Committee requests information 'on the implementation of the Convention with respect to different groups of women, in particular those subject to multiple forms of discrimination',[96] and has called

---

[88] GR 28 para 18. See also GR 25 para 12.   [89] GR 26 paras 6–7.   [90] Ibid para 14.
[91] GR 24 para 6.
[92] eg CO Tajikistan, CEDAW/C/TJK/CO/3 (2007) paras 39–40; CO Mali, CEDAW/C/MLI/CO/5 (2005) para 32.
[93] See, in particular, GR 27 and the Committee's earlier decision, *Ending Discrimination against Older Women through the Convention*, Decision 26/III, A/57/38 (Supp) part I, 26th Session (2002) paras 430–6. See also CEDAW CO Finland, A/56/38 (2001) para 305; CO Sweden, A/56/38 (Supp) part II, 25th Session (2001) para 356; CO Greece, A/57/38, Exceptional Session (2002) para 293 (2002); CO Brazil, CEDAW/C/BRA/CO/6 (2007) para 27; CO Former Yugoslav Republic of Macedonia, CEDAW/C/MKD/CO/3, 34th Session (2006) para 28(r)(i); CO Slovakia, CEDAW/C/SVK/CO/4 (2008) para 23; CO Italy, A/60/38, 32nd Session (2005) para 35; CO Denmark, A/57/38, 27th Session (2002) para 343.
[94] eg CO Tajikistan, CEDAW/C/TJK/CO/3 (2007) para 39.
[95] eg CO Ecuador, CEDAW/C/ECU/CO/7 (2008) para 28. See also GR 28 paras 18 and 31.
[96] CEDAW Decision 40/I, *Convention-Specific Reporting Guidelines of the Committee on the Elimination of Discrimination against Women*, A/63/38 (Supp) part I, 40th Session (2008), Annex I, para 21. See also *Harmonised Guidelines on Reporting under the International Human Rights Treaties, including Guidelines on a Core Document and Treaty-Specific Documents*, HRI/GEN/2/Rev.6 (2009) paras 51, 54, and 55.

on States parties to ensure that they address 'intersecting forms of discrimination' through legislation and other means.[97]

D. Reservations

Few reservations have been entered specifically to Article 1, though some of the general reservations to the Convention in effect reject the scope of its definition of discrimination against women. A number of reservations have related to succession to the throne or other titles of nobility and hereditary privileges in countries which retain preferential male succession.[98] For example, the United Kingdom, referring specifically to Article 1, stated that its ratification 'is subject to the understanding that none of its obligations under the Convention shall be treated as extending to the succession to, or possession and enjoyment of, the Throne, the peerage, titles of honour, social precedence or armorial bearings', or as extending to the affairs of religious denominations or orders, or to the admission into or service in the Armed Forces of the Crown (this last limited since 2005 to any act done for the purpose of ensuring the combat effectiveness of the Armed Forces of the Crown).[99] While there is no specific human right to succeed to a monarchy or title of nobility, rules which discriminate between males and females in the transmission of these titles would appear to fall within the scope of Article 7 of the Convention, to the extent that they can be seen as relating to public and political life, or if seen as relating to private or family life would fall within the general obligations of Article 2 read with the reference to human rights and fundamental freedoms in Article 1, or Articles 15 and 16.

The United Kingdom also declared that it understood 'the main purpose of the Convention, in the light of the definition contained in Article 1, to be the reduction, in accordance with its terms, of discrimination against women, and does not therefore regard the Convention as imposing any requirement to repeal or modify any existing laws, regulations, customs or practices which provide for women to be treated more favourably than men, whether temporarily or in the longer term; the United Kingdom's undertakings under Article 4, paragraph 1, and other provisions of the Convention are to be construed accordingly'. This appears to essentially affirm that the Convention is directed to discrimination against women, and restating the UK position on the effect of Article 23 of the Convention.[100]

---

[97] CO Belarus, CEDAW/C/BLR/CO/7 (2011) para 12; CO Hungary, CEDAW/C/HUN/CO/6 (2007) para 30. See also CO Albania, CEDAW/C/ALB/CO/3 (2010) paras 18–19.

[98] See eg the reservations of Liechtenstein, Monaco, and Luxembourg (withdrawn 2008); see the discussion in ch on reservations.

[99] See L Lijnzaad, *Reservations to UN-Human Rights Treaties: Ratify and Ruin?* (1995) 306–7, noting that it is not clear which of the provisions of the Convention are engaged by such issues, but suggesting that arts 5, 7, and 15 may be relevant.

[100] See the discussion in ch 31 on art 23.

Article 2

States Parties condemn discrimination against women in all its forms, agree to pursue by all appropriate means and without delay a policy of eliminating discrimination against women and, to this end, undertake:

(a) To embody the principle of the equality of men and women in their national constitutions or other appropriate legislation if not yet incorporated therein and to ensure, through law and other appropriate means, the practical realisation of this principle;

(b) To adopt appropriate legislative and other measures, including sanctions where appropriate, prohibiting all discrimination against women;

(c) To establish legal protection of the rights of women on an equal basis with men and to ensure through competent national tribunals and other public institutions the effective protection of women against any act of discrimination;

(d) To refrain from engaging in any act or practice of discrimination against women and to ensure that public authorities and institutions shall act in conformity with this obligation;

(e) To take all appropriate measures to eliminate discrimination against women by any person, organisation or enterprise;

(f) To take all appropriate measures, including legislation, to modify or abolish existing laws, regulations, customs and practices which constitute discrimination against women;

(g) To repeal all national penal provisions which constitute discrimination against women.

* I would like to thank Professor Dianne Otto for her comments on this and the chapter on art 1; Luke Beck, Renée Chartres, Maria Herminía Graterol, and Eleanor Bath for their research assistance, and the University of New South Wales for Goldstar and Faculty of Law funding to support research for this chapter and the chapters on arts 1, 23, and 24.

A. Introduction

Article 2 has been described by the Committee as 'the very essence of the Convention' and 'crucial to [its] full implementation'.[1] This provision, together with Articles 1, 3, 4, 5(a), and 24 sets out the general obligations assumed by States parties.[2] These articles state the broad aspirations of the Convention and the accompanying legal obligations in all fields, at the international and national levels.[3] While the Convention addresses many of the most significant areas and forms of discrimination in specific articles (Articles 6–16), it does not explicitly address all issues; these general articles ensure that the coverage of the Convention is comprehensive, giving effect to its purpose of eliminating discrimination against women in all its forms in every field.

Although Articles 2, 3, and 24 overlap significantly, each has a distinct focus that reflects its origin and the role that the Convention drafters saw for it. According to general principles of treaty interpretation, inclusion of all three articles is assumed to be deliberate and not duplicative. The differences in wording may be significant in determining the scope of each provision.

Article 2 focuses on law and the role of legislation and legal institutions in ensuring that women are not subject to discrimination, whether formal (*de jure*) or in practice (*de facto*). It emphasizes the importance of providing positive legal guarantees of equality and protection against discrimination and eliminating existing discriminatory laws and customs. However, it is not confined to legal measures, as it obliges States parties to adopt policy and other 'appropriate measures' to eliminate discrimination.

The relationship between Articles 3 and 24 and Article 2 is not clear. Article 3 requires States parties to take 'all appropriate measures' to ensure the full enjoyment of rights on a basis of equality; it is broad-ranging as to the type of measures required and the fields it covers, and emphasizes the positive aspects of the enjoyment and exercise of rights, and the broader goals of the development and advancement of women.[4] Article 3 affirms, together with Article 2 and the broad definition of 'discrimination against women' in Article 1, that the Convention requires States parties to work towards the elimination of discrimination against women in the enjoyment of all fundamental human rights and freedoms, not just those explicitly addressed in the treaty.[5] This understanding of the scope of the Convention has been at the heart of the Committee's approach for many

---

[1] GR 28 paras 41 and 6.
[2] Art 6 may also be seen as a general provision: see the discussion in ch on art 6.   [3] GR 19 para 10.
[4] See the discussion in ch on art 3.
[5] See the discussion in ch on art 1. In contrast, ICERD art 5 includes a detailed list of specific rights the equal enjoyment of which is to be guaranteed.

years.[6] It appears in General Recommendation 19, in which the Committee refers to a number of rights not specifically mentioned in the Convention which may be violated by the subjection of women to violence in the family, in the community or at the hands of the State, and emphasizes that the State party's obligations extend to eliminating the inequality in enjoyment of these rights that gender-based violence causes.[7] It also appears in the Committee's consideration of the issue of intersectionality (its approach to discrimination against particular groups of women—such as ethnic minorities or indigenous peoples, migrant workers, and women with disabilities)[8] and other cross-cutting themes.

Article 24 requires States parties to take 'all necessary measures at the national level' to fully realize the rights in the Convention. Its emphasis on national level action restates a fundamental principle of international law. It underlines that the Convention is not just a collection of aspirational statements, but imposes legal obligations to take steps at the national level to give effect to the 'rights recognized in the present Convention'.[9] In the reporting procedure the Committee has tended to address under Article 2 many issues relating to the institutional procedures and arrangements for the implementation of the Convention that might also have been addressed under Articles 3 or 24.

In General Recommendation 28, the Committee sets out a comprehensive statement of its understanding of States parties' obligations under the Convention, in particular Article 2. Other UN human rights treaty bodies have adopted corresponding statements on the general obligations of States parties under those treaties; the general comments of these other bodies, in particular of the CCPR[10] and the CESCR[11] are of particular importance.[12] Taken together, these interpretive statements set out a body of jurisprudence and commentary that informs the interpretation and application of Article 2 and other provisions of the Convention.

B. Travaux Préparatoires

Article 2 draws most significantly on DEDAW and ICERD, as well as on other treaties. A version of Article 2 was included in the original Philippines and USSR drafts presented to the CSW and the combined draft on which much of the discussion was

---

[6] Notwithstanding the Committee's comment that the 'spirit' of the Convention extends protection against discrimination in the enjoyment of rights 'not explicitly mentioned in the Convention' (GR 28 para 7), this protection is firmly anchored in the letter of the Convention, in particular in arts 1, 2, and 3.

[7] Rights referred to in GR 19 which are not explicitly stated in the Convention: the right to life; the right not to be subject to torture or to cruel, inhuman, or degrading treatment or punishment; the right to equal protection according to humanitarian norms in time of international or internal armed conflict; and the right to liberty and security of person.

[8] See eg GR 18; GR 25 para 12, and GR 26.   [9] See the discussion in ch on art 24.

[10] CCPR, 'General Comment 31: Nature of the General Legal Obligation on States Parties to the Covenant' (2004) UN Doc HRI/GEN/1/Rev.9 (Vol. I).

[11] CESCR, 'General Comment 3' UN Doc E/1991/23, 5th Session. See also CESCR, 'General Comment 9' (1998) UN Doc E/C.12/1998/24, 'General Comment 10' (1998) UN Doc E/C.12/1998/25, and 'General Comment 20' (2009) UN Doc E/C.12/GC/20. See also CCPR, 'General Comment 28' (2000) UN Doc CCPR/C/21/Rev.1/Add.10 and CESCR, 'General Comment 16' (2005) UN Doc E/C.12/2005/4, which address the issue of the equal rights of women and men to the enjoyment of the rights governed by the two Covenants.

[12] See also CRC, 'General Comment 5' (2003) UN Doc HRI/GEN/1/Rev.9 (Vol. II) and CAT, 'General Comment 2' (2007) UN Doc CAT/C/GC/2.

based. One element which disappeared was the original Philippines proposal that States 'shall, if circumstances warrant, ratify, accede to and fully implement as soon as practicable the international instruments of the United Nations and the specialized agencies relating to the elimination of discrimination against women.'[13] The final structure of the article was put in place by the Belgian redraft,[14] which contained most of the elements of the version finally adopted. One element contained in that draft that did not survive was a provision that each State party 'undertakes to promote organizations and movements whose purpose is to advance the status of women and eliminate all discrimination against them'.[15] The current Article 2(g), which had been a separate provision in the Philippines and combined Philippines/USSR draft, was added in the final version.

C. Issues of Interpretation

The Committee has stated that Article 2 'is central to the objects and purpose of the Convention'.[16] States parties 'which ratify the Convention do so because they agree that discrimination against women in all its forms should be condemned and that the strategies set out in Article 2(a) to (g), should be implemented by States parties to eliminate it'.[17] Article 2 embodies the three major obligations assumed by States parties to the Convention: elimination of direct and indirect discrimination in laws and the actions of public authorities and at the hands of private individuals; improvement of the *de facto* situation of women through policies and programs; and addressing prevailing gender relations and harmful gender stereotypes in law, social structures, and attitudes.[18]

The Committee has also drawn on analyses of the nature of human rights obligations developed under other treaties to explicate the meaning and scope of Convention obligations. Of particular importance has been the tripartite framework developed initially in relation to economic, social, and cultural rights,[19] but now applied to civil and political rights as well: the obligations to respect, protect, and fulfil/promote the rights guaranteed. The obligation to respect requires the State itself to refrain from taking actions that involve discrimination against women; the obligation to protect requires that States protect women against discrimination by non-State actors; and the obligation to promote or fulfil involves taking a range of measures to create the conditions under which women can enjoy *de jure* and *de facto* equality.[20] This tripartite framework can illuminate State party obligations under Article 2 and, indeed, other general and specific provisions of the

---

[13] UN Doc E/CN.6/573, draft art 2(d)(ii) (1973).   [14] UN Doc E/CN.6/591/Add 1 (1976).

[15] UN Doc E/CN.6/591/Add 1, draft art 2(g).

[16] Statement on reservations to the Convention on the Elimination of All Forms of Discrimination against Women adopted by the Committee on the Elimination of Discrimination against Women, UN Doc A/53/38, 19th Session (1998) 47, 49 para 16.

[17] Ibid.   [18] GR 25 para 7.

[19] For early articulations of the approach, see A Eide, *Right to Adequate Food as a Human Right* (1989) paras 169–81, UN Sales No E.89.XIV.2; and A Eide, 'Economic, Social and Cultural Rights as Human Rights' in A Eide et al (eds), *Economic, Social and Cultural Rights: A Textbook* (1995) 21, 37–8. See generally M Craven, *The International Covenant on Economic, Social and Cultural Rights: A Perspective on its Development* (1995) 109–114; MM Sepúlveda, *The Nature of the Obligations under the International Covenant on Economic, Social, and Cultural Rights* (2003) 157–248; M Dowell-Jones, *Contextualising the International Covenant on Economic, Social and Cultural Rights: Assessing the Economic Deficit* (2004) 28–34.

[20] GR 28 para 9.

Convention, especially those requiring States parties to take 'necessary' or 'appropriate' measures.[21]

After only briefly referring to this framework in earlier general recommendations,[22] in General Recommendation 28, the Committee endorsed this approach to characterizing and interpreting Convention obligations[23] and drew attention to its utility in ascertaining the scope of obligations to adopt 'appropriate measures'.[24] Thus, for example, Article 2(d) reflects the obligation to respect the right of persons not to be discriminated against by government, and Article 2(e) the obligation to protect against discrimination by non-State actors. The obligation to fulfil relates to some of the measures required to be taken under Article 2, as well as under Articles 3, 4, 5, 23, and 24.

I. Chapeau

The chapeau of Article 2, like much of the article, closely follows the wording of the corresponding provision of ICERD.[25] States parties:

- **formally condemn discrimination against women in all its forms**
- **agree to pursue . . . without delay a policy of eliminating discrimination against women**
- **by all appropriate means.**

The first part of the chapeau is an important symbolic statement that is a powerful expression of the international community's attitude towards discrimination against women— the language of condemnation is also used in the context of racial discrimination. The second part of the chapeau states an unambiguous legal obligation ('agree') to adopt a policy of eliminating discrimination and to work towards the implementation of that policy 'without delay'.

1. 'States Parties Condemn Discrimination against Women in all its Forms'

The language of 'condemnation' is among the strongest forms of disapproval used in international treaties and thus expresses States parties' deep abhorrence[26] of discrimination against women and a strong commitment to eliminating it, placing it on the same level as racial discrimination.[27] In General Recommendation 28, the Committee noted that States parties 'have an immediate and continuous obligation to condemn discrimination' and:

are obliged to proclaim their total opposition to all forms of discrimination against women to all levels and branches of Government, to their population and to the international community, and their determination to bring about the elimination of discrimination against women.[28]

---

[21] Cook and Cusack, apply the typology in elaborating application of the Convention to the elimination of harmful gender stereotypes. RJ Cook and S Cusack, *Gender Stereotyping: Transnational Legal Perspectives* (2009) 76–84.

[22] See eg GR 25 para 4.   [23] GR 28 para 9.   [24] GR 28 para 37.

[25] ICERD art 2(1): 'States Parties condemn racial discrimination and undertake to pursue by all appropriate means and without delay a policy of eliminating racial discrimination in all its forms and promoting understanding among all races'. See E Schwelb, 'The International Convention on the Elimination of All Forms of Racial Discrimination' (1966) 15 *Intl and Comparative L Quarterly* 996, 1015.

[26] International Women's Rights Action Watch Asia Pacific, *Possible Elements for Inclusion in a General Recommendation on to Article 2 of CEDAW, Outcome Document of the Expert Group Meeting on CEDAW Article 2: National and International Dimensions of State Obligation (IWRAW AP Article 2 Report)* (2007) para 21.

[27] Ibid. One commentator suggests that the pursuit of a policy of eliminating discrimination 'would provide the normative content of the obligation to condemn'. N Burrows, 'The 1979 Convention on the Elimination of All Forms of Discrimination Against Women' (1985) 32 *Netherlands Intl L Rev* 419, 426.

[28] GR 28 para 15.

The reference to 'all forms' of discrimination underlines the drafters' intent that States 'be vigilant in condemning all forms of discrimination, including forms that are not explicitly mentioned in the Convention or that may be emerging'.[29] The treaty thus applies to discrimination by public and private entities, whether it is embodied in law, custom, tradition, culture, or other practices, or is direct, intentional, indirect, individual, or systemic.

2. 'Agree to Pursue by all Appropriate Means and Without Delay a Policy of Eliminating Discrimination against Women'

This general obligation contains a number of important elements which the Committee explicated in General Recommendation 28.[30] The agreement of States parties 'to pursue...a policy' requires them to adopt a framework for identifying all forms of discrimination against women, and develop a policy for eliminating them and a strategy for implementing the policy. While States enjoy a considerable degree of flexibility in fashioning a policy, it must be concrete and targeted towards the achievement of specific goals, with an ultimate goal of completely eliminating discrimination.[31] Accordingly, the State must:

immediately assess the de jure and de facto situation of women and take concrete steps to formulate and implement a policy that is targeted as clearly as possible towards the goal of fully eliminating all forms of discrimination against women and achieving women's substantive equality with men. The emphasis is on forward movement, from the evaluation of the situation to the formulation and initial adoption of a comprehensive range of measures to building on those measures continuously, in the light of their effectiveness and new or emerging issues, towards the Convention's goals.[32]

The obligation to adopt a policy is an immediate one[33]—a point underlined by the phrase 'without delay';[34] a State cannot justify delay 'on any grounds, including political, social, cultural, religious, economic, resource or other considerations or constraints within the State'.[35] The obligation to 'pursue' the policy also is continuing and includes responsibility to monitor progress and adjust the policy as time passes.

The Committee has set out a number of elements of State policy that will be conducive to the fulfilment of Article 2 obligations.[36] The policy should include both legal and non-legal measures,[37] and should cover all fields of life within the scope of the Convention;[38] ensure that all branches and levels of government are appropriately engaged in implementation;[39] identify women as rights-bearers under the policy, 'with particular emphasis on the groups of women who are most marginalized and who may suffer from various forms of intersectional discrimination';[40] ensure that women are able to 'participate actively in the development, implementation and monitoring of the policy'[41] and

---

[29] GR 28 para 15.   [30] GR 28 paras 23–9.   [31] GR 28 para 23.

[32] GR 28 para 24. The Committee has required States parties to carry out a comprehensive assessment of the position of women in formulating a policy of gender equality, and to monitor the policy's implementation against specific indicators of progress. See eg CO Kazahkstan, A/62/38, 37th Session (2007) para 75; CO Namibia, A/62/38, 37th Session (2007) paras 258–9; CO Austria, A/62/38, 37th Session (2007) paras 493–4; CO Poland, A/62/38, 37th Session (2007) paras 379–80.

[33] GR 28 para 29.   [34] GR 28 para 29.   [35] GR 28 para 29.

[36] See, in particular, *IWRAW AP Article 2 Report* (n 26 above) paras 28–34.   [37] GR 28 para 24.

[38] Ibid para 25.   [39] Ibid para 25.

[40] Ibid para 26.   [41] Ibid para 27.

that they have access to information about their Convention rights and are able to claim them.[42] The policy should also be action-oriented and result-driven,[43] with appropriate indicators and timelines, be adequately resourced (as part of 'mainstream governmental budget processes');[44] ensure that there is an effective national women's machinery within the executive branch and with direct access to the highest levels of government;[45] ensure that independent monitoring institutions, such as national human rights institutions or independent women's commissions, are established, or that the mandates of existing national institutions extend to the rights guaranteed under the Convention;[46] and 'engage the private sector, including business enterprises, the media, organizations, community groups and individuals, and enlist their involvement in adopting measures that will fulfil the goals of the Convention in the private economic sphere'.[47]

Consistent with its general practice,[48] the Committee reiterated in General Recommendation 28 the importance of establishing 'mechanisms that collect relevant sex-disaggregated data, enable effective monitoring, facilitate continuing evaluation and allow for the revision or supplementation of existing measures and the identification of any new measures that may be appropriate'.[49]

3. 'All Appropriate Means'/'(All) Appropriate Measures'[50]

The concept of '(all) appropriate measures/means' appears in a number of Convention articles. This phrase acknowledges that situations vary and allows the State party the flexibility to select and design the most effective measures for its national context. The word 'all' underlines the obligation to adopt a comprehensive range of measures, given the widespread and diverse nature of discrimination against women. These must include legislative measures,[51] but also include other types of measures, a point underlined by the Article 18 obligation of States parties to submit regular reports 'on the legislative, judicial, administrative and other measures' they have adopted to give effect to the Convention.

'Appropriate measures' also includes temporary special measures as one means of achieving the practical realization of equality. In General Recommendation 25, the Committee noted that these measures fall within Article 2 as well as under other provisions of the Convention, and that States parties should 'report on the legal or other basis for such measures, and their justification for choosing a particular approach. States parties are further invited to give details about any legislation concerning temporary special measures, and in particular whether such legislation provides for the mandatory or voluntary nature of temporary special measures'.[52] The Committee reaffirmed this position in General Recommendation 28, noting that the adoption of temporary special measures is

---

[42] Ibid para 27.   [43] Ibid para 28.   [44] Ibid para 28.

[45] Ibid para 28. On national machineries, see UN Doc E/CN.6/1999/4 paras 43–78, and the Beijing Platform for Action, para 201. The obligation to establish effective national machinery could be seen as arising under any of arts 2, 3, or 24, though arts 2 and 24 seem the most appropriate. See GR 25 para 34.

[46] GR 28 para 28.   [47] Ibid.

[48] See GR 9 (1989) and also CO Azerbaijan, A/62/38, 37th Session (2007) paras 108–9; CO India, A/62/38, 37th Session (2007) paras 151–2; CO Namibia, A/62/38, 37th Session (2007) paras 296–7; CO Poland, A/62/38, 37th Session (2007) paras 397–8; CO Nicaragua, A/62/38 (Supp), 37th Session (2007) paras 567–8.

[49] GR 28 para 28.   [50] GR 28 para 23.

[51] eg CO Equatorial Guinea, A/59/38, 31st Session (2004) paras 187–8.

[52] GR 25 para 30.

one aspect of the States parties' obligation to 'fulfil' women's rights to non-discrimination and equality,[53] and that States parties should have in place a legislative framework for temporary special measures.[54]

4. *'And, to this End, Undertake'*

The final part of the chapeau also involves an unequivocal obligation ('States parties...undertake'), linked to a number of specified outcomes. In some cases, the obligation is specific, required to be implemented immediately, and capable of being achieved immediately (for example, Article 2(a), (c), (d), and (g)). In other cases, the language of the treaty allows greater discretion to the State party to determine the measures appropriate to achieve the goal (which may or may not be seen as immediately achievable). The reference in a number of articles to '(all) appropriate measures' introduces a level of flexibility and thus uncertainty into understanding what the obligation in question means and the pace at which the measures are to be taken. For example, Article 2(a) plainly requires legislative measures, as well as other measures which will serve the purpose of eliminating discrimination. Article 2(b) and (f) are to similar effect. In these cases the challenge is to identify the measures that are appropriate to particular circumstances. In Article 2(e), no mention is made of legislative measures—the reference is only to 'all appropriate measures'—but legislative measures of some sort (in addition to any other measures) would plainly be required, particularly in light of the requirement in Article 2(c) to establish effective legal protection of women's human rights. These obligations must also be read in light of the first part of the chapeau, in particular that the stated objectives must be pursued without delay.

II. Article 2(a)

Article 2(a), in common with other parts of Article 2, places great importance on the role of law in contributing to the elimination of discrimination against women as well as implicitly recognizing the role that law plays in embodying and perpetuating that discrimination.

Article 2(a) draws on DEDAW Article 2(a).[55] The Philippines[56] and joint Philippines/USSR[57] proposals that formed its basis, and the draft adopted by the CSW in January 1974,[58] provided that each State party 'shall embody the principle of equality of rights in its Constitution, if not yet incorporated, or shall guarantee by law, the practical realization of this principle'. The version of the draft paragraph adopted by the CSW in 1976 reiterated the requirement of a constitutional guarantee and added the further requirement that a State 'ensure through law or other appropriate means, the practical realization of this principle',[59] suggesting that constitutional level guarantees of equality—not just legislative ones—were mandatory.

---

[53] GR 28 paras 9, 20, and 37(d).

[54] eg CO Ukraine, A/57/38, Exceptional Session (2002) paras 282–3; CO Democratic Republic of Congo, CEDAW/C/COD/CO/5 (2006) para 20; CO Mongolia, CEDAW/C/MNG/CO/7 (2008) para 12.

[55] DEDAW art 2(a): 'The principle of equality of rights shall be embodied in the constitution or otherwise guaranteed by law'.

[56] UN Doc E/CN/6/573 (1973) draft art 2(d)(i).

[57] UN Doc E/CN.6/AC.1/L.4 (1974) draft art 2(d)(i).   [58] UN Doc E/CN.6/589 (1974) 35.

[59] UN Doc E/CN.6/608 (1976) 3, draft art 2(a).

The provision was amended in the later drafting stages by the substitution of the phrase 'or [in] other appropriate legislation', clarifying that something less than a constitutional guarantee of equality is sufficient to satisfy the obligation. Use of the adjective 'appropriate' does not suggest that it would be acceptable to have no legislative embodiment of the principle—that would run counter to the purpose of the article. Rather, the phrase acknowledges that because the legal traditions and legislative structures of the States parties differ, the principle of equality can be legislatively guaranteed by a variety of means. For example, a Gender Equality Law, a general sex discrimination law, or the inclusion of equality guarantees in sector-specific laws (such as a labour code), could effectively provide legislative recognition of the equality principle. Despite this language, the Committee regularly recommends that States parties guarantee women's human rights in the national constitution—and thus ensure that they prevail over inconsistent laws of less than constitutional status[60]—and that such rights be enforceable in national courts.[61] The Committee has also urged States parties to take advantage of 'constitutional moments' or transitional situations to ensure that constitutions and other laws include guarantees of women's equality and give effect to the State party's Convention obligations.[62]

1. Direct Incorporation of the Convention into Domestic Law

The fundamental international law obligation of States parties is to ensure that domestic legislation and practice implement the obligations they have accepted under the Convention, so women may effectively enjoy the right to be free from discrimination. Where the Convention requires legislative implementation, or where legislation is an 'appropriate measure', the State party must enact laws consistent with the Convention obligations.

To secure the enforceability of its provisions at the national level, 'States parties undertake to incorporate the Convention in their domestic legal system or to give it otherwise appropriate legal effect within their domestic legal orders in order to secure the enforceability of its provisions at the national level'.[63] The Convention, thus, does not explicitly require direct incorporation of its provisions as a whole into domestic law, but leaves it to States parties to decide in light of their constitutional systems. In States parties with monist systems, ratification will normally have the effect of

---

[60] eg CO Yemen, A/63/38 (Supp), 41st Session (2008) paras 361–2; CO the Philippines, A/61/38, 36th Session (2006) paras 517–18; CO Fiji, A/57/38, 26th Session (2002) paras 46–7; CO Niger, CEDAW/C/NER/CO/2 (2007) paras 11–12; CO Singapore, A/62/38, 39th Session (2007) paras 107–8, and the concluding observations cited in nn 82 and 83 below.

[61] eg CO Suriname, A/57/38, 27th Session (2002) paras 39–40.

[62] eg CO Kenya, CEDAW/C/KEN/CO/7 paras 11–12 (2011); CO Timor–Leste, CEDAW/C/TLS/CO/1 (2009) para 14; CO Spain, CEDAW/C/ESP/CO/6 (2009) paras 11–12; CO Angola, A/59/38, 31st Session (2004) paras 142–3; CO Jordan, A/55/38, 22nd Session (2000) paras 168–9. See also the Committee's statements relating to the post-2003 war reconstruction efforts in Iraq: *Letter Addressed to the Special Representative of the Secretary-General for Iraq and High Commissioner for Human Rights*, UN Doc A/58/38 (Supp) part II, 29th Session (2003), Annex VII, 201; *Statement by the Committee on the Elimination of Discrimination against Women on the Situation of women in Iraq*, UN Doc A/59/38 (Supp) part I, 30th Session (2004), Annex II, 87; *Statement on the Situation of Women in Iraq, Addressed to the Iraqi Interim Government*, UN Doc A/59/38 (Supp) part II, 31st Session (2004), Annex XI, 268; and *Statement by the Committee on the Elimination of Discrimination against Women on the Situation of Women in Iraq*, UN Doc A/60/38 part II, 33rd Session (2005), Annex X, 244.

[63] GR 28 para 31.

directly incorporating the Convention into domestic law, and its provisions may thus be enforceable as domestic law.[64] Where this occurs, the treaty's provisions may enjoy the status of ordinary legislation or in some cases a more elevated status, depending on the State party's constitutional arrangements.[65] Whether a particular provision of the Convention is justiciable (that is, can be the basis of a claim before a national court or tribunal and applied by that body), depends both on the text of the provision itself and the domestic rules relating to the direct applicability or effect (self-executing nature) of treaty provisions.[66] Some national courts have held provisions of the Convention generally to be directly applicable in domestic law,[67] while others have held that the majority of its provisions not to be directly applicable because of their non-self-executing nature (but even so have recognized that particular provisions of the Convention might none the less be justiciable).[68]

The Committee has consistently urged States parties to 'domesticate' the Convention, that is, to incorporate its provisions into domestic law so individuals may invoke them as a source of rights before national courts and other institutions, whether or not the treaty as such is part of national law.[69] The Committee has welcomed such incorporation, whether by operation of constitutional rules relating to the incorporation of treaties in the legal system, or by virtue of a special law enacting the Convention as domestic law (generally required where a State party has a dualist system).[70] The Committee has also regularly sought clarification as to whether the Convention forms part of domestic law and its status in the hierarchy of domestic norms,[71] and of the practical impact where the treaty does form part of domestic law, by requesting information about whether courts and

---

[64] See discussion in the Introduction.

[65] See generally A Byrnes and C Renshaw, 'Within the State' in D Moeckli, S Shah, S Sivakumaran, and D Harris (eds), *International Human Rights Law* (2010) 498, 500–6.

[66] See GR 28 para 31; see generally K Kaiser, 'Treaties, Direct Applicability' in R Wolfrum (ed) *The Max Planck Encyclopedia of Public International Law* (2008) online edition <www.mpepil.com> accessed 31 December 2010.

[67] eg in Costa Rica; A Facio and MI Morgan, 'Equity or Equality for Women? Understanding CEDAW's Equality Principles' (2009) 60 *Alabama L Rev* 1133, 1160–5; NC Subedi, 'Elimination of Gender Discriminatory Legal Provision by the Supreme Court of Nepal with Reference to Women's Rights to Property' (2009) 26(1) *Tribhuvan University J* 37, 45–51 (the Nepal Treaty Act, 2047 (1990) provides that treaties form part of domestic law).

[68] Examples are Germany, Switzerland, and Japan: see B Simma, D-E Khan, M Zöeckler, and R Geiger, 'The Role of German Courts in the Enforcement of International Human Rights' in B Conforti and F Francioni (eds), *Enforcing International Human Rights in Domestic Courts* (1997) 71, 86; R Kägi-Diener, 'Die Bedeutung internationaler Diskriminierungsverbote, insbesondere von CEDAW, für die schweizerische Rechtsprechung', *Frauenfragen* 1.2009, 42, 48; *Grüne Bewegung Uri et al v Landrat des Kantons Uri*, Swiss Federal Court (Bundesgericht), judgment of 7 October 1998, BGE 125 I 21, §4; and Y Iwasawa, *International Law, Human Rights, and Japanese Law: The Impact of International Law on Japanese Law* (1998) 61–3.

[69] See eg CO Guinea-Bissau, CEDAW/C/GNB/CO/6 (2009) para 10; CO Denmark, CEDAW/C/DEN/CO/7 (2009) paras 14–15; CO Bhutan, CEDAW/C/BTN/CO/7 (2009) paras 11–12; CO Timor-Leste, CEDAW/C/TLS/CO/1 (2009) paras 15–16; CO Tuvalu, CEDAW/C/TUV/CO/2 (2009) paras 11–12; CO Mauritius, CEDAW/C/MAR/CO/5 (2006) paras 10–11; CO Malaysia, CEDAW/C/MYS/CO/2 (2006) paras 7–8; CO Angola, A/59/38, 31st Session (2004) para 140.

[70] See eg CO Argentina, CEDAW/C/ARG/CO/6 (2010) para 13; CO Guyana, A/60/38, 33rd Session (2005) para 280; CO Gabon, A/60/38, 32nd Session (2005) para 223; CO Turkey, A/60/38, 32nd Session (2005) para 355.

[71] See eg CO Kuwait, CEDAW, A/59/38 part I, 30th Session (2004) paras 62–3; CO Albania, CEDAW/C/ALB/CO/3 (2010) paras 12–13; CO The Philippines, CEDAW/C/PHI/CO/6 (2006) paras 9–10; CO Kazakhstan, A/56/38, 24th Session (2001) para 88; CO Lao PDR, CEDAW/C/LAO/CO/7 (2009) paras 9–10.

tribunals have invoked the Convention in their decisions.[72] On occasions, the Committee has urged States parties to ensure that the Convention has at least the same status as other human rights treaties under domestic law, in order to ensure that its norms prevail over inconsistent laws.[73] The Committee has expressed its concern that the question of the self-executing nature or justiciability of Convention provisions has been left to the courts, lest this lead to gaps in implementation at the national level.[74]

The Committee has commented that the rights guaranteed by the Convention 'may receive enhanced protection in those States where the Convention is automatically or through specific incorporation part of the domestic legal order'.[75] However, simply incorporating the Convention as a whole into domestic law will not be sufficient to fully implement the obligation to give the treaty legal effect, as implementation also requires legislation to provide for situation-specific norms and remedies. In some States parties the precise status of incorporated treaties or whether they prevail over inconsistent national laws is not clear[76] and, in most of the States parties that directly incorporate treaties, the Convention has not been explicitly invoked before or applied by domestic courts with any great frequency.[77] Accordingly, the Committee has often urged States parties to take steps to ensure greater awareness of the Convention among the judiciary and members of the legal profession.[78] The Committee has also noted that States parties 'must ensure that courts are bound . . . to interpret the law, to the maximum extent possible, in line with the obligations of States parties to the Convention', and that where this is not possible, the courts should draw inconsistencies to the attention of the appropriate authorities.[79]

The Committee has underlined the need for detailed implementing legislation even where the Convention forms part of domestic law,[80] and *a fortiori* where it is not.[81] It has also regularly urged States parties to ensure that constitutional or legislative guarantees of equality and non-discrimination on the basis of sex are consistent with the Convention

---

[72] See eg CO Mali, A/61/38, 34th Session (2006) para 185.

[73] See eg CO Norway, CEDAW/C/NOR/CO/7 (2007) paras 12–13.

[74] See eg CO The Netherlands, CEDAW/C/NLD/CO/5 (2010) paras 12–13. See also CO Switzerland, CEDAW/C/CHE/CO/3 (2009) paras 15–16.

[75] GR 28 para 31.

[76] See eg CO Timor-Leste, CEDAW/C/TLS/CO/1 (2009) paras 15–16; CO Yemen, CEDAW/C/YEM/CO/6 (2008) paras 12–13; CO Morocco, A/63/38, 40th Session (2008) paras 223–4; CO The Philippines, CEDAW/C/PHI/CO/6 (2006) paras 9–10.

[77] See eg CO Belgium, CEDAW/C/BEL/CO/6 (2008) paras 17–18; CO El Salvador, CEDAW/C/SLV/CO/7 (2008) para 11; CO Syrian Arab Republic, A/62/38, 38th Session (2007) para 123; CO Paraguay, A/60/38, 32nd Session (2005) para 275; CO Mali, CEDAW/C/MLI/CO/5 (2006) para 9.

[78] See eg CO Switzerland, CEDAW/C/CHE/CO/3 (2009) paras 15–16; CO Indonesia, CEDAW/C/IDN/CO/5 (2007) para 9; CO Suriname, A/62/38, 37th Session (2007) para 293; CO Japan, A/58/38, 29th Session (2003) para 358; CO Italy, A/60/38, 32nd Session (2005) para 317; CO Madagascar, CEDAW/C/MDG/CO/5 (2008) para 11; CO El Salvador, CEDAW/C/SLV/CO/7 (2008) paras 11–12; CO Syrian Arab Republic, CEDAW/C/SYR/CO/1 (2007) para 14.

[79] GR 28 para 33.

[80] See eg CO Argentina, CEDAW/C/ARG/CO/6 (2010) para 13; CO Haiti, CEDAW/C/HTI/CO/7 (2009) paras 10–11; CO Guatemala, CEDAW/C/GUA/CO/7 (2009) paras 11–12; CO Estonia, A/57/38, 26th Session (2001) para 81.

[81] See eg CO Thailand, A/61/38, 34th Session (2006) para 231; CO Gambia, A/60/38, 33rd Session (2005) paras 187–8; CO Bangladesh, A/59/38, 31st Session (2004) paras 239–40.

and to adopt the definition of 'discrimination against women' in Article 1;[82] a general constitutional or legislative guarantee of equality is not enough.[83]

2. *'And to Ensure, Through Law and Other Appropriate Means, the Practical Realization of this Principle'*

The requirement that legal guarantees of equality provide not just formal protection for women but effective practical protection appears in a number of Article 2 provisions. Article 2(a) underlines the importance of the enjoyment of rights in fact (*de facto*), as well as in formal legal terms (*de jure*), a distinction that the Committee clearly and regularly notes.[84] A wide range of measures is thus required.[85] In its Treaty-specific Reporting Guidelines the Committee requests information in State party reports 'of a more analytical nature on the impact of laws, the interaction of plural legal systems, policies, programmes on women' and 'on the progress made in ensuring enjoyment of the provisions of the Convention by all groups of women throughout their lifecycle within the territory or jurisdiction of the State party'.[86] In the guidelines for preparing initial reports, the Committee requests that each State party provide 'a detailed analysis of the impact of legal norms on women's factual situation and the practical availability, implementation and effect of remedies for violations of provisions of the Convention'.[87]

Similarly, in its Convention-specific guidelines for subsequent (periodic) reports, the Committee requests information 'on any remaining or emerging obstacles to the exercise and enjoyment by women of their human rights and fundamental freedoms...as well as information on measures envisaged to overcome those obstacles',[88] and the reports should 'in particular, address the impact of measures taken'.[89] The Committee has also requested States parties to include in their Common Core Document (an overview document that every State party must produce for use by all the treaty monitoring bodies[90]) an account of both legal measures taken and their impact, in accordance with the requirement that States parties provide information about the measures taken to promote both formal and substantive equality, and the enjoyment of the right to equality in practice.[91]

---

[82] See eg CO Germany, A/55/38, 22nd Session (2000) para 312; CO Kazakhstan, A/56/38, 24th Session (2001) paras 87–8; CO Guinea, A/56/38, 25th Session (2001) paras 118–99; CO Estonia, A/57/38, 26th Session (2002) paras 87–8; CO Congo, A/58/38, 28th Session (2003) paras 158–9; CO Thailand, A/61/38, 34th Session (2006) paras 270–1; CO Japan, CEDAW/C/JPN/CO/6 (2009) paras 21–2; CO Tuvalu, CEDAW/C/TUV/CO/2 (2009) paras 13–14; CO Uruguay, CEDAW/C/URY/CO/7 (2008) paras 10–11.

[83] See eg CO Singapore, CEDAW/C/SGP/CO/3 (2007) paras 13–14; CO Democratic Republic of Congo, CEDAW/C/COD/CO/5 (2006) paras 19–20; CO Algeria, A/60/38, 32nd Session (2005) paras 139–40; CO Cuba, CEDAW/C/CUB/CO/6 (2006) paras 11–12; CO Eritrea, CEDAW/C/ERI/CO/3 (2006) paras 10–11; CO China, CEDAW/C/CHN/CO/6 (2006) paras 9–10; CO Jamaica, CEDAW/C/JAM/CO/5 (2006) paras 19–20.

[84] See eg CO Singapore, A/62/38, 39th Session (2007) para 108; CO Benin, A/60/38, 33rd Session (2005) paras 145–6.

[85] See eg CO India, A/62/38, 37th Session (2007) paras 149–50 and CO Vietnam, A/62/38, 37th Session (2007) paras 451–2.

[86] *Convention-Specific Reporting Guidelines of the Committee on the Elimination of Discrimination against Women (Treaty-Specific Guidelines)*, CEDAW Decision 40/I, A/63/38, 40th Session (2008), Annex I para 6.

[87] *Treaty-Specific Guidelines* (n 86 above) para 14.   [88] Ibid para 19(c).   [89] Ibid para 20.

[90] *Harmonised Guidelines on Reporting under the International Human Rights Treaties, including Guidelines on a Core Document and Treaty-Specific Documents*, HRI/GEN/2/Rev.6 (2009) paras 50–9.

[91] Ibid paras 51 and 53.

III. Article 2(b)

Article 2(b) and (c) are closely related and, indeed, overlap in a number of respects with each other as well as with Article 2(a). Article 2(b) requires that a State party adopt a range of measures prohibiting discrimination against women. The word 'prohibit' implies that an effective legal proscription of discrimination is required, and the language of 'appropriate legislative' measures goes to the particular form that this legislation might take rather than whether legislative measures are appropriate at all.

The Committee has regularly called on States parties to introduce comprehensive gender equality or sex discrimination laws where such laws do not already exist and to include in those laws a definition of discrimination against women based on Article 1 of the Convention.[92] For example, the Committee has noted that even if a State party had enacted legislation covering direct and indirect sex discrimination in the area of employment, it was, nevertheless, a matter of concern that it did not have a 'general anti-discrimination law that contains a definition of discrimination against women in accordance with Article 1, encompassing both direct and indirect discrimination, and covering all areas of the Convention'.[93]

The Committee sees Article 2(b) (as well as (Article 2(c)) as the source of a State party's obligation to ensure the availability of remedies for women subject to discrimination.[94] This paragraph provides the States parties with some measure of discretion, but effective legal and practical protection against discrimination requires some form of sanctions. The provision originated in the USSR draft which proposed the requirement that States parties should enact legislation 'providing for punishment',[95] and appeared in a slightly different version in a Belgian proposed amendment which emphasized that the provision 'should be understood in the broadest sense to include all types of remedy and all types of penalty, whether penal or civil'.[96] The CSW changed the wording to include a reference to legislative or 'other appropriate measures' and replaced the word 'penalties' with 'sanctions'.[97] Thus, laws 'prohibiting' discrimination cannot be hortatory, but must embody some form of legal or other material consequence for those who violate them. However, the nature and extent of sanctions may vary according to the particular subject and the nature of the infringement. 'Sanctions' would include penal, civil, or administrative sanctions, depending on the forum that has jurisdiction over particular claims.

---

[92] See eg CO Sri Lanka, CEDAW/C/LKA/CO/7 (2011) para 15; CO Timor-Leste, CEDAW/C/TLS/CO/1 (2009) para 18; CO Yemen, A/63/38, 41st Session (2008) para 360; CO Morocco, A/63/38, 40th Session (2008) para 222; CO Syrian Arab Republic, A/62/38, 38th Session (2007) para 126. Where the right to gender equality is enshrined in national constitutions or other human rights instruments, States parties are reminded that a specific provision is required prohibiting *de jure* and *de facto* discrimination on the basis of sex. See eg CO Jordan, A/55/38, 22nd Session (2000) para 168.

[93] CO Poland, A/62/38, 37th Session (2007) paras 374–5. See also CO Haiti CEDAW/C/HTI/CO/7 (2009) paras 10–11; CO Maldives, A/62/38, 37th Session (2007) para 219; CO Kazahkstan, A/62/38, 37th Session (2007) para 75; CO Cameroon, CEDAW/C/CMR/CO/3 (2009) paras 10–11.

[94] GR 28 para 32.   [95] UN Doc E/CN.6/AC.1/L.2 (1974).

[96] Draft art 3 read: 'to adopt legislative measures *accompanied by penalties*', UN Doc E/CN.6/591/Add.1/Corr.1 (1976) 2.

[97] UN Doc E/CN.6/608 (E/5909) (1976) Annex IV, 102.

In General Recommendation 28, the Committee states that the obligation to ensure remedies means that States parties must 'provide reparation to women whose rights under the Convention have been violated':[98]

Such remedies should include different forms of reparation, such as monetary compensation, restitution, rehabilitation, and reisnstatement; measures of satisfaction, such as public apologies, public memorials and guarantees of non-repetition; changes in relevant laws and practices; and bringing to justice the perpetrators of violations of human rights of women.[99]

IV. Article 2(c)

Article 2(c) draws on ICERD Article 6. It requires effective judicial and other protection of women's entitlement to enjoy rights on an equal basis with men. The 'national' tribunals referred to are municipal tribunals at all levels; depending on the constitutional structure of the State party, these may include national or central (federal) tribunals, state or provincial tribunals, or other, lower-level tribunals.[100] Remedies may also be available through administrative bodies, national human rights institutions, anti-discrimination agencies, or ombudsman procedures.[101]

The undertaking to 'ensure ... the effective protection' of the women's human rights under their national systems is a stringent obligation of result. 'Effective' protection means both providing for a legally binding or effective remedy for a violation of rights, and a practically available one.[102] The Committee has stated that 'while ... the text of the Convention does not expressly provide for a right to a remedy, [it] considers that such a right is implied in the Convention, in particular, in Article 2(c)',[103] though in General Recommendation 28, the Committee also states that Article 2(b) requires States parties to ensure the availability of appropriate remedies.[104]

The obligation entails effective protection, requiring that remedies be in fact accessible to women who wish to assert their rights before the relevant courts and tribunals and other institutions. To ensure that the protection provided by law is 'effective', States parties must ensure that all women are made aware of their rights;[105] that free legal services are made available so women have the practical means to seek vindication of their rights;[106] and

---

[98] GR 28 para 32. See generally *Basic Principles and Guidelines on the Right to a Remedy and Reparation for Victims of Gross Violations of International Human Rights Law and Serious Violations of International Humanitarian Law*, UNGA resolution 60/147, Annex (2005).

[99] GR 28 para 32. See also CO Tajikistan, CEDAW/TJK/CO/3 (2007) paras 11–12.

[100] See Schwelb (n 25 above) 1027–8, in relation to the similar phrase in the ICERD.

[101] See eg CO Papua New Guinea, CEDAW/C/PNG/CO/3 (2010) paras 19–20. For further discussion of the role of national human rights institutions in Convention implementation, see the discussion in ch on art 24.

[102] See eg CO Burundi, A/63/38, 40th Session (2008) paras 128–9; CO Gabon, A/60/38, 32nd Session (2005) paras 229–30; CO Algeria, A/60/38, 32nd Session (2005) paras 145–6.

[103] *Vertido v Philippines*, CEDAW Communication No 18/2008 (2010), CEDAW/C/46/D/18/2008 para 8.3.

[104] GR 28 para 32.

[105] See eg CO Madagascar, CEDAW/C/MDG/CO/5 (2008) para 11; CO Syrian Arab Republic, CEDAW/C/SYR/CO/1 (2007) para 16; CO Thailand, CEDAW/C/THA/CO/5 (2006) para 16; CO Switzerland, CEDAW/C/CHE/CO/3 (2009) para 15.

[106] See eg CO India, A/62/38, 37th Session (2007) paras 155–6, and in relation to women migrant workers, GR 26 para 26(c).

that data on the number and nature of complaints and their disposition are collected.[107] States parties also have a duty to take concrete action to ensure that judges, magistrates, law enforcement personnel, employers, and the legal profession, are familiar with the legislative reforms.[108] The provision also requires an appropriately resourced and focused criminal law enforcement process that ensures that criminal violations of women's human rights are properly investigated and prosecuted.

In General Recommendation 19 relating to violence against women, the Committee urged States parties to provide 'effective complaints procedures and remedies, including compensation',[109] and 'effective legal measures, including penal sanctions, civil remedies and compensatory provisions to protect women against all kinds of violence, including inter alia violence and abuse in the family, sexual assault and sexual harassment in the workplace'.[110]

In its General Recommendation 26 on women migrant workers, the Committee addressed the requirements of legal protection, stressing the need for access to remedies when their rights were violated (citing Articles 2(c) and (f) and Article 3) and stating that 'adequate legal remedies and complaint mechanisms' and 'easily accessible dispute resolution mechanisms' should be put in place;[111] that States parties should repeal laws that effectively prevent women from bringing claims before courts or other authorities;[112] the need for 'access to legal assistance and to the courts and regulatory systems charged with enforcing labour and employment laws, including free legal aid',[113] and that temporary shelter and safe accommodation during trial should be provided.[114]

In addition to any remedy granted to a particular claimant, States parties are obligated to address systemic issues that may have led to the violation. In the analogous situation under the Optional Protocol, for example, the Committee has recommended to States parties that they address the specific needs of the complainant (guarantee of physical safety, provision of a safe home and of support and legal assistance, as well as reparation proportionate to the injuries suffered)[115] and adopt a number of systemic measures as well.[116]

V. Article 2(d)

Article 2(d) obliges a State party to ensure that the State and its organs do not engage in discrimination against women. This is an articulation of the State's 'obligation to respect' the right of women not to be subject to discrimination at the hands of the State. The obligation is a fundamental one, since States parties 'undertake to refrain' from the conduct in question, and 'undertake to ensure' that all public authorities and institutions

---

[107] See eg CO Myanmar, CEDAW/C/MMR/CO/3 (2008) para 15; CO Azerbaijan, CEDAW/C/AZE/CO/4, 44th Session (2009) para 111.

[108] See eg CO Croatia, A/60/38, 32nd Session (2005) para 189.   [109] GR 19 para 24(i).

[110] GR 19 para 24(t)(i). See also CO Peru, CEDAW/C/PER/CO/6 (2007) para 20 and *Report on Mexico Produced by the Committee on the Elimination of Discrimination against Women under Article 8 of the Optional Protocol to the Convention, and Reply from the Government of Mexico* (*Mexico Inquiry*), CEDAW/C/2005/OP.8/MEXICO paras 271–86.

[111] GR 26 para 26 (c)(i).   [112] Ibid para 26 (c)(ii).   [113] Ibid para 26 (c)(iii).

[114] Ibid para 26 (c)(iv).

[115] See *Goekce v Austria*, CEDAW Communication No 5/2005 (2007) CEDAW/C/39/D/5/2005 paras 12.1.6, 12.3; *Yildirim v Austria*, CEDAW Communication No 6/2005 (2007) CEDAW/C/39/D/6/2005 paras 12.1.6, 12.3.

[116] *AT v Hungary*, CEDAW Communication No 2/2003 (2005) CEDAW/C/32/D/2003 para 9.6.

also do so. This represents an obligation of result, which is violated by a failure to achieve the specified outcome. It may be contrasted with the obligation in relation to actions of non-State actors in Article 2(e), which requires States parties 'to take all appropriate measures' to eliminate discrimination by non-State actors and which leaves to the State party considerable discretion as to how it goes about achieving that goal. This latter obligation has been described as an obligation of 'due diligence' in relation to the acts of private or non-State actors.[117]

Under the international law of State responsibility, the obligation under Article 2(d) is binding on all organs of the State at all levels of government.[118] This includes not only the executive government and other public bodies that are established by statute as independent bodies, but also the judicial and legislative organs of the State.[119] The reference to 'public bodies' and 'public institutions' in this paragraph is intended to be broad in scope;[120] all levels of the legislative and judicial organs of the State, including those of component units of federal states or autonomous regions,[121] would in any case be covered by the Convention as a matter of general international law. Thus, a ruling or procedure adopted by a court that constitutes or upholds discrimination against women would be a failure by the State party to refrain from discrimination (subject to the possibility that rectification or remedy on appeal, or a successful appeal, would mean that the State had carried out its obligation).[122]

This provision applies directly to all acts of State organs and the acts of other persons or entities which are attributable to the State under the law of State responsibility.[123] The legislative framework referred to in Article 2(a)–(c) is one of the measures required of the State party to ensure that public officials and authorities do not engage in discrimination against women. In addition, States parties are required to put in place appropriate administrative measures such as training and education, in order to prevent discrimination, and procedures for the investigation of cases in which discrimination appears to have occurred. More generally, the Committee has recommended that States parties adopt procedures for assessing the gender implications of any proposed new laws, policies, or projects before giving approval to proceed.[124]

VI. Article 2(e)

This provision is a highly significant component of the Convention, emphasizing that States parties are required to address discrimination against women by private or non-State actors. This obligation extends both to the specific areas covered in Articles 6–16 of the Convention and to the enjoyment of other guaranteed human rights and fundamental

---

[117] See the discussion below under art 2(e).

[118] cf CCPR, 'General Comment 31' (2004) UN Doc HRI/GEN/1/Rev.9 (Vol. I) para 4.

[119] United Nations International Law Commission, *Articles on State Responsibility* (*ILC Articles on State Responsibility*), art 4 and Commentary paras 9–10, *Report of the International Law Commission on the Work of its Fifty-Third Session,* UN Doc A/56/10 (Supp) 43 (2001) 84. See also *Vertido v Philippines* (n 103 above) para 8.4.

[120] LA Rehof, *Guide to the Travaux Préparatoires of the United Nations Convention on the Elimination of All Forms of Discrimination against Women* (1993) 57–8.

[121] *ILC Articles on State Responsibility* (n 119 above), art 4 and Commentary paras 6–8.

[122] See *Vertido v Philippines* (n 103 above) para 8.2.   [123] See the discussion under art 2(e).

[124] See eg CO Mexico, CEDAW/C/MEX/CO/6 (2006) paras 20–1; CO Samoa, A/60/38, 32nd Session (2005) para 63; CO Gabon, A/60/38, 32nd Session (2005) paras 229–30.

freedoms.[125] The early drafts of this paragraph were based closely on ICERD Article 2(1)(d) and provided that each State party 'undertakes not to sponsor, defend or support discrimination against women by any person or organization'. This was superseded by a provision in the CSW draft providing that each State party 'shall endeavour to take all preventive measures to eliminate discrimination against women by any person or organization'.[126]

Article 2(e) explicitly obliges the State to take measures to eliminate discrimination by non-State actors (also addressed by Articles 2(f) and (5).[127] Owing to the different formulation of the obligations under Article 2(1)(d) and (e), it may be necessary to determine whether non-State actors can ever be 'public authorities and institutions'. Under Article 2(1)(d), a State party must itself 'refrain' from discrimination and 'ensure' that public authorities do so, while under Article 2(e) the State's obligation is to 'take all appropriate measures' to eliminate discrimination by non-State actors. The latter obligation is arguably a less stringent one, because States parties cannot necessarily be held to account for all discrimination committed by non-State actors, such as private individuals, corporations, or other organizations. The State party's obligation as to these actors is that of 'due diligence'. In General Recommendation 28, the Committee explains the obligation in terms that appear to conflate the obligations under Article 2(1)(d) and (e), stating that:[128]

Article 2 is not limited to the prohibition of discrimination against women caused directly or indirectly by States parties. Article 2 also imposes a due diligence obligation on States parties to prevent discrimination by private actors. In some cases a private actor's acts or omission of acts may be attributed to the State under international law. States parties are thus obliged to ensure that private actors do not engage in discrimination against women, as defined in the Convention.

Under the international law of State responsibility[129] the acts of non-State actors can be treated as those of the State in a variety of circumstances. In some cases, 'non-State actors' may in fact be acting as the State, or their acts or omissions may be directly attributable to the State because the State has delegated its role to the non-State actor or has authorized the non-State actor to take action on its behalf. In such cases the acts of the non-State actor are imputed to the State and the obligation under Article 2(1)(d) is applicable, so the State party must ensure that the non-State actor does not engage in prohibited discrimination. For example, the acts of a private contractor operating a prison are those of the State, rather than those of a non-State actor, for the purposes of the law of State responsibility. Therefore, the Convention requires the State party to ensure that the contractor does not engage in discrimination against women, such as committing violence against them.

Under Article 2(e), the State party's obligation is to take 'all appropriate measures' to 'eliminate' discrimination against women. At first sight this may seem much less

---

[125] See generally in relation to corporations, *State Responsibilities to Regulate and Adjudicate Corporate Activities under the United Nations' Core Human Rights Treaties, Individual Report on the United Nations Convention on the Elimination of All Forms of Discrimination against Women, Report No 4, prepared for the Special Representative of the Secretary-General on Human Rights and Transnational Corporations and Other Business Enterprises (Ruggie CEDAW Report)* (2007).

[126] Y Yamashita, 'Article 2: Obligations of States Parties to Eliminate Discrimination against Women' in Japanese Association of International Women's Rights, *Convention on the Elimination of All Forms of Discrimination against Women: A Commentary* (1995) 59, 67.

[127] The obligations of the State party to regulate the acts of private individuals is underlined in GR 19 para 9, GR 25 para 7, and GR 28. GR 28 para 36 states that art 2(e) establishes an obligation 'to eliminate discrimination by any public or private actor'. To the extent that 'public actors' are part of the State, this obligation appears to be subsumed in art 2(d).

[128] GR 28 para 13.   [129] See *ILC Articles on State Responsibility* (n 119 above).

demanding than the State party's own obligation to refrain from discrimination and to ensure that public institutions generally do so. However, given the condemnation of discrimination and the obligation to pursue without delay a policy of eliminating it, and the requirements in Article 2(a), (b) and (c) relating to legislative measures, laws addressing discrimination by private enterprises and organizations are an essential component of the obligation, and the Committee has urged States parties to ensure that not only State actors are covered by legislation prohibiting discrimination, but private actors as well.[130] The standard of due diligence (taking 'all appropriate measures') is a demanding one, as States parties may be obliged to take measures in addition to legislation, as the Committee underlines in General Recommendation 25 in relation to the adoption of temporary special measures:

States parties should provide adequate explanations with regard to any failure to adopt temporary special measures. Such failures may not be justified simply by averring powerlessness, or by explaining inaction through predominant market or political forces, such as those inherent in the private sector, private organizations, or political parties. States parties are reminded that article 2 of the Convention, which needs to be read in conjunction with all other articles, imposes accountability on the State party for action by these actors.[131]

The critical question here is what constitutes 'appropriate measures' in a particular context. Some guidance can be obtained from the jurisprudence that has emerged around the concept of 'due diligence' in human rights law (though in certain circumstances the standard of appropriateness may be higher than the standard of conduct required by 'due diligence'). The jurisprudence which has developed in relation to the obligation to 'protect' rights may also provide additional resources for interpreting this phrase.

The due diligence standard, which has its origins in the general international law of State responsibility for injury to aliens,[132] has been extensively examined under a number of human rights treaties, with some of the leading cases arising within the Inter-American human rights system.[133] The American Convention on Human Rights, along with other human rights treaties of general application, has been held to impose obligations on the State in relation to the acts of private individuals who violate the rights of others.[134] The responsibility lies in the failure of the State to take reasonable measures to prevent or to investigate and punish any violation by non-State actors of the rights recognized by the treaty in question.[135] The State should also, if possible, attempt to restore the status quo and provide compensation for damage resulting from the violation.[136] However, in

---

[130] See eg CO Sri Lanka, CEDAW/C/LKA/CO/7 (2011) para 15(b); CO India, A/55/38, 22nd Session (2000) paras 66–7.

[131] Para 29.

[132] R Pisillo-Mazzeschi, 'The Due Diligence Rule and the Nature of the International Responsibility of States' (1992) 35 *German Ybk of Intl L* 9, 22–36; RP Barnidge Jr, 'The Due Diligence Principle Under International Law' (2006) 8 *Intl Community L Rev* 81, 91–121.

[133] See generally C Benninger-Budel (ed), *Due Diligence and its Application to Protect Women from Violence* (2008). See also *Opuz v Turkey* (2009) ECHR 33401/02.

[134] See, in particular, *Velásquez Rodríguez v Honduras*, Inter-American Court of Human Rights Series C No 4 (29 July 1988); *Maria da Penha Maia Fernandes v Brazil*, Inter-American Commission on Human Rights, Case 12.051, Report No 54/01 (16 April 2001) para 56.

[135] See J Bourke-Martignoni, 'The History and Development of the Due Diligence Standard in International Law and Its Role in the Protection of Women against Violence' in Benninger-Budel (n 133 above) 47.

[136] *Godínez Cruz case*, Inter-American Court of Human Rights Series C No 8 (20 January 1988) para 175.

the context of the discussions about violence against women in particular and contrary to the traditional use of the concept in relation to the acts of non-State actors,[137] some commentators have applied the term 'due diligence' to the obligation of the State itself in relation to the actions of State organs, in particular, as it concerns preventive, punitive, and compensatory measures that must be taken where an act attributable to the State involves a violation of the Convention.[138] This approach is of concern because it may have the effect of diluting the strict liability nature of the State's obligations in respect of the conduct of its own organs to an obligation based on fault (that is, a failure to take reasonable measures or exercise due diligence).

The Committee endorsed the notion of due diligence as applicable under the Convention in General Recommendation 19. It stressed that gender-specific violence against women is a form of discrimination under the Convention and that States parties are not only directly responsible for the acts of State organs but 'may also be responsible for private acts if they fail to act with due diligence to prevent violations of rights or to investigate and punish acts of violence, and for providing compensation'.[139]

In a number of its decisions under the Optional Protocol and in its report on the *Mexico Inquiry*,[140] the Committee has used the concept of due diligence in explaining the nature of the State party's obligation to take appropriate measures to eliminate discrimination by non-State actors. For example, in *Yildirim v Austria*,[141] the Committee found that Austria had a comprehensive system of legislation and other measures to address domestic violence but that 'in order for the individual woman victim of domestic violence to enjoy the practical realization of the principle of equality of men and women and of her human rights and fundamental freedoms, the political will that is expressed in the aforementioned comprehensive system of Austria must be supported by State actors, who adhere to the State party's due diligence obligations'.[142]

State officials, therefore, must put appropriate law and policy measures in place and must properly administer and give effect to them. The Committee has adopted a demanding standard in its cases involving domestic violence, all of which involved sustained and serious injury and threats of injury of which the authorities were aware. In *Yildirim*, for example, it held that the failure to coordinate the activities of law enforcement authorities properly, the failure to detain the deceased complainant's husband following a pattern of actual and threatened violence, and the failure to provide other effective protection to the victim involved a violation of the State's due diligence obligation.[143]

While the content of the obligation of due diligence has been explored quite extensively at the international level in relation to violence against women, as noted in General

---

[137] See I Boerefijn, 'De blinddoek opzij: een mensenrechtenbenadering van geweld tegen vrouwen' (2006) 19–23, available at <http://arno.unimaas.nl/show.cgi?did=16239> accessed 31 December 2010, cited in C Benninger-Budel (n 133 above), 'Introduction', 1, 14.

[138] See eg 'The due diligence standard as a tool for the elimination of violence against women', *Report of the Special Rapporteur on Violence against Women, its Causes and Consequences, Yakin Ertürk*, E/CN.4/2006/61 paras 14–105, especially para 30; and Inter-American Commission on Human Rights, 'Access to Justice for Women Victims of Violence in the Americas', OEA/Ser.L/V/II. Doc. 68 (20 January 2007) 11–19 paras 23–45.

[139] GR 19 para 9.

[140] *Mexico Inquiry* (n 110 above). See also the Committee's comments in relation to the Gujarat massacre in 2002: CO India, CEDAW/C/IND/CO/SP.1 (2010).

[141] Communication No 5/2005.

[142] Ibid para 12.1.2. See also *AT v Hungary* (n 116 above) and *Goekce v Austria* (n 115 above).

[143] *Yildirim v Austria* (n 115 above) paras 12.13–12.6.

Recommendation 28 [144] the concept of due diligence is applicable not just to those rights which are violated by the infliction of violence, but also to violations by non-State actors of other rights guaranteed by or falling within the ambit of the Convention—though what is required by way of due diligence would vary from case to case. For example, in General Recommendation 26 on migrant women workers, the Committee, citing Article 2(e), noted that States parties must ensure that employers and recruiters do not discriminate against women migrant workers by confiscating travel documents or preventing them from leaving the premises where they work.[145]

'Appropriate measures' to eliminate discrimination against women by non-State actors are not limited to legislation. For instance, the Committee has urged States parties to develop both formal and informal strategies to promote the reconciliation of family and work responsibilities so women will not be disadvantaged when applying for full-time positions.[146] Other policies directed at non-State actors include the promotion of positive images of women in the mainstream media and awareness-raising campaigns.[147]

VII. Article 2(f)

In requiring States parties to 'modify or abolish' discriminatory 'laws, regulations, customs and practices', this provision is closely related to the obligations in Article 5(a).

Under Article 2(f), States parties have a duty to repeal legislative provisions that discriminate against women. Failure to do so is regarded by the Committee as a breach of the State party's obligations under the Convention. The Committee has identified many examples of laws and regulations that discriminate against women that must be amended or repealed.[148] Key areas of concern in this regard include the legal grounds and procedures for divorce[149] and post-divorce arrangements, including child custody and property distribution; laws regulating inheritance rights, in particular, those allowing priority to male relatives over women;[150] laws permitting polygamy;[151] criminal laws relating to marital rape and violence against women;[152] and citizenship laws that discriminate against female nationals and their children when they marry a non-national.[153]

Other laws have also drawn the Committee's attention, from almost every area of social life. For example, General Recommendation 26 on migrant workers (reiterated in General Recommendation 28[154]), refers specifically to the obligation under Article 2(f) in relation to discriminatory restrictions on women's immigration and to laws that 'prohibit migrant women workers from getting married to nationals or permanent residents, becoming pregnant or securing independent housing'.[155] Other groups which the Committee has identified as 'particularly vulnerable to discrimination through civil and penal laws,

---

[144] GR 28 paras 9, 10, 13, 36, and 37(b).

[145] GR 26 para 26(d).   [146] See CO Algeria, A/60/38, 32nd Session (2005) para 158.

[147] See eg eg CO Myanmar, CEDAW/C/MMR/CO/3 (2008) para 21; CO Morocco, A/63/38, 40th Session (2008) paras 229–30; CO Tajikistan, A/62/38, 37th Session (2007) paras 36–7.

[148] In addition to the examples in the following footnotes, see also the examples in chs on arts 9, 16, and violence against women.

[149] See eg CO Thailand, A/61/38, 34th Session (2006) paras 274–5.

[150] See eg CO Uganda, A/57/38 (Supp) part II, Exceptional session (2002) paras 153–4; CO Mozambique, A/62/38, 38th Session (2007) paras 167–8.

[151] See eg CO Gabon, A/60/38, 32nd Session (2005) para 231.

[152] See eg CO Singapore, A/62/38, 39th Session (2007) paras 121–2.

[153] See eg CO Suriname, A/62/38, 37th Session (2007) paras 294–5.

[154] GR 28 para 31.   [155] GR 26 para 26(a).

regulations and customary laws and practices' are 'women deprived of their liberty, refugees, asylum-seeking women, migrant women, stateless women, lesbian women, disabled women, women victims of trafficking, widows and elderly women'.[156]

While the Convention requires amendment of individual inconsistent laws, the Article 2(f) obligation can most effectively be met by an initial comprehensive review of legislation following ratification, a gender impact analysis of new legislation, and a regular updating review (the reporting procedure may be part of this process).[157] The Committee has encouraged States parties to undertake gender impact analysis of new and existing legislation on a regular basis[158] and to carry out regular reviews.[159]

In relation to States parties which have plural legal systems, the Committee has regularly noted that provisions of personal status law that discriminate against women must be amended or repealed.[160] It has called on States parties to consult with the relevant communities, in particular the women, as part of the process of reforming discriminatory laws and practices.[161]

The prevalence of discriminatory traditional practices and customs which accentuate stereotypes is frequently described by the Committee as delaying the advancement of women and their attaining full equality. The Committee has addressed these issues under both Article 2(e) and Article 2(f), and has interpreted these provisions (and Article 5(a)) to impose an obligation on States parties to intervene positively in the activities and practices of religious, cultural, or ethnic groups that either directly or indirectly discriminate against women. States parties are reminded that a policy of non-intervention 'perpetuates sexual stereotypes... and discrimination against women' and is contrary to the Convention.[162] The Committee has noted the importance of taking steps to address discriminatory attitudes embodied in personal status laws, religious law, or custom,[163] and gender stereotypes more generally.[164]

The Committee has identified different types of measures that might be appropriate to implement this obligation. These include the criminalization of discriminatory practices and the provision of civil remedies for the victims. Non-legal approaches should include the adoption of programmes to raise awareness of the Convention and to challenge stereotypical attitudes and perceptions about the roles and responsibilities

---

[156] GR 28 para 31.

[157] cf CRC, 'General Comment 5' (2003) UN Doc CRC/GC/2003/5 para 18 (Convention imposes obligation to undertake comprehensive, holistic, and continuing review of legislation and administrative practice for consistency with CRC standards).

[158] CO Kyrgyzstan, CEDAW/C/KGZ/CO/3 (2008) paras 11–12; CO Kenya, CEDAW/C/KEN/CO/6 (2007) paras 17–18.

[159] See eg CO Tuvalu, CEDAW/C//TUV/CO/2 (2009) paras 15–16; CO Mongolia, CEDAW/C/MNG/CO/7 (2008) para 17; CO Guinea, A/56/38, 25th Session (2001) para 119; CO Cameroon, CEDAW/C/CMR/CO/3 (2009) paras 14–15; CO Mozambique, A/62/38, 38th Session (2007) paras 165 and 168; CO Nicaragua, A/62/38, 37th Session (2007) paras 561–2; CO The Philippines, CEDAW/C/PHI/CO/6 (2006) paras 11–12; CO Thailand, A/61/38, 34th Session (2006) paras 268–9; CO Lebanon, A/60/38, 33rd Session (2005) paras 97–8: CO Gabon, A/60/38, 32nd Session (2005) paras 231–2.

[160] See eg CO Cameroon, CEDAW/C/CMR/CO/3 (2009) para 14; CO Namibia, CEDAW/C/NAM/CO/3 (2007) paras 28–9; CO The Philippines, CEDAW/C/PHI/CO/6 (2006) paras 11–12; CO Lebanon, A/60/38, 33rd session (2005) paras 99–100.

[161] See eg CO The Philippines, CEDAW/C/PHI/CO/6 (2006) paras 11–12.

[162] See eg CO India, A/55/38, 22nd Session (2000) para 60.   [163] GR 21 para 50.

[164] See eg GR 28 para 22; GR 27 paras 16 and 36; CO Namibia, CEDAW/C/NAM/CO/3 (2007) paras 16–17; CO Yemen, CEDAW/C/YEM/CO/6 (2008) paras 15–16; CO Spain, CEDAW/C/ESP/CO/6 (2009) paras 17–18. See also *Vertido v Philippines* (n 103 above) para 8.9.

of women and men. According to the Committee, such policies should involve non-governmental organizations, national ministries, or other agencies for women, the media, and intellectuals, with the primary goal of encouraging a change in people's way of thinking. Law reform, information, education, and communications, particularly in rural areas, are critical to the attainment of this objective.[165] Efforts to integrate the equality principle into the curricula for instructing teachers and trainers, also serve the purpose of Article 2(f).[166]

VIII. Article 2(g)

Included as a separate article in early drafts of the Convention, this provision was eventually added as a final paragraph to Article 2. A number of States made the point that it was redundant since the other general obligations to modify or abolish discriminatory legislation applied to discriminatory penal laws as much as to other forms of legislation.[167] A proposal that the provision be removed from the draft on this basis was rejected: Egypt, supported by India and Senegal, as well as other delegations, successfully argued for its retention on the ground that '[r]ules of a discriminatory nature abounded in penal codes in particular'.[168] The obligation is one which is subject to immediate implementation.

The Committee has identified a range of legislation that falls under this provision. It includes laws that criminalize abortion,[169] do not prohibit marital rape,[170] allow a defence of 'honour' to charges of homicide or assault,[171] discriminate against women in relation to the rules of evidence (for example, corroboration requirements in sexual offence cases), or establish offences of 'public decency' that are used to target women,[172] or criminal offences which blame and criminalize the female victim.[173] The Committee has also expressed concern about legislation that permits a man to avoid a prosecution for rape if he marries the victim,[174] or that provides for maximum but not minimum sentences for sexual offences, concerned that this 'could lead to light sentences for sexual offences that are not commensurate with the gravity of those offences'.[175]

---

[165] See eg CO Burkina Faso, A/55/38, 22nd Session (2000) para 266.

[166] See eg CO Argentina, CEDAW/C/ARG/CO/6 (2010) para 34; CO Liberia, CEDAW/C/LBR/CO/6 (2009) paras 32–3; CO Finland, A/63/38, 41st Session (2008) paras 181–2; CO Pakistan, A/62/38, 38th Session (2007) paras 285–6; CO Croatia, A/60/38, 32nd Session (2005) paras 200–1; CO Bahrain, CEDAW/C/BHR/CO/2 (2008) paras 32–3.

[167] See UN Doc E/CN.6/SR.638 paras 29–39.   [168] UN Doc E/CN.6/SR.638 para 32.

[169] See eg CO The Philippines, CEDAW/C/PHI/CO/6 (2006) para 28.

[170] See eg CO Tuvalu, CEDAW/C//TUV/CO/2 (2009) paras 31–2; CO Lebanon, CEDAW/C/LBN/CO/3 (2008) para 26; CO Singapore, A/62/38, 39th Session (2007) paras 121–2; CO Syrian Arab Republic, A/62/38, 38th Session (2007) paras 129–30.

[171] See eg CO Lebanon, A/60/38, 33rd Session (2005) paras 103–4; CO Iraq, A/55/38, 22nd Session (2000) paras 193–4; CO Jordan, A/55/38, 22nd Session (2000) paras 178–9; CO Syrian Arab Republic, A/62/38, 38th Session (2007) paras 129–30.

[172] CO Yemen, CEDAW/C/YEM/CO/6 (2008) paras 18–19.

[173] See eg CO Tuvalu, CEDAW/C//TUV/CO/2 (2009) paras 31–2 (any female person fifteen years of age or above who allows her grandfather, father, brother, or son to have sexual intercourse with her is guilty of a felony).

[174] CO Bolivia, CEDAW/C/BOL/CO/4 (2008) para 7; CO Cameroon, CEDAW/C/CMR/CO/3 (2009) para 14; CO Syrian Arab Republic, A/62/38, 38th Session (2007) paras 129–30.

[175] CO Tuvalu, CEDAW/C/TUV/CO/2 (2009) para 31.

D. Other Issues of Application

I. Federal States/States with Decentralized or Devolved Governance Arrangements

Some States parties have a constitutional division of power under which the federal or central government represents the State on the international level, while the power to take legislative or other measures required to implement a treaty lies solely in the political subdivisions or is shared with the federal authority.[176] Under international law the State party through the central government is accountable for any failure to carry out obligations under the treaty, even if the failure is caused by the refusal by the subdivisions to implement the treaty's terms.[177] As to States parties with such distributed arrangements, the Committee has expressed concern that they ensure consistent implementation at all government levels and establish coordination mechanisms to ensure that this takes place.[178]

II. Territorial Application of the Convention

Unlike some other human rights treaties, the Convention makes no specific provision in relation to its territorial or personal application. Accordingly, the general rule set out in Article 29 of the VCLT, that treaties apply to the entire territory of a State party, would apply, and the obligations of the State party apply in relation to all persons within that territory. The Committee has frequently called on States parties to ensure that protections against discrimination apply *de jure* and *de facto* to all parts of their territory, for example, urging them to ensure that export processing or free trade zones not be exempted from or be governed by lower standards than those contained in national laws.[179]

The Committee has also emphasized that States parties have a responsibility to uphold the rights of all women and girls, including non-citizens, in their territory or under their jurisdiction or control. Thus, States parties must ensure that non-citizen women are aware of their rights and have access to effective remedies when their rights are violated.[180] The Committee also frequently identifies as a concern the legislative and social protection offered to women asylum seekers, and it urges States parties to address the continuing discrimination experienced by women asylum seekers and other minority groups by, *inter alia*, ratifying additional international treaties that deal specifically with the situation of such individuals, such as the CMW.[181]

---

[176] This is the default rule. Some treaties, such as the ICCPR in art 50, make explicit provision for the application of the treaty to all parts of a federal State.

[177] *ILC Articles on State Responsibility* (n 119 above), art 4 and Commentary paras 8–10. This may also be seen as a specific instance of the rule embodied in VCLT art 27 that a State may not rely on its internal law to justify a failure to carry out its treaty obligations.

[178] See eg CO India, CEDAW/C/IND/CO/SP.1 (2010) para 6; CO Australia, CEDAW/C/AUL/CO/7 (2010) paras 16–17; CO Argentina, CEDAW/C/ARG/CO/6 (2010) paras 11–12; CO Canada, CEDAW/C/CAN/CO/7 (2008) paras 11–12; CO Nigeria, A/63/38, 41st Session (2008) para 312; CO Mexico, CEDAW/C/MEX/CO/6 (2006) paras 8–9; CO Italy, A/60/38, 32nd Session (2005) paras 320–1; CO Switzerland, A/58/38, 28th Session (2003) paras 110–11; CO Belgium, A/57/38, 27th Session (2002) paras 143–4.

[179] See eg CO Jamaica, A/56/38, 24th Session (2001) paras 229–30. CO Dominican Republic, A/59/38, 31st Session (2004) para 307; CO Nicaragua, A/62/38 (Supp) part I, 37th Session (2007) paras 577–8; CO Fiji, A/57/38, 26th Session (2002) paras 56–7.

[180] See eg CO Germany, A/55/38, 22nd Session (2000) para 318.

[181] See eg CO Ethiopia, A/59/38, 30th Session (2004) para 266.

III. Extraterritorial Application of the Convention

States parties' conduct outside their territory which affects the rights of individuals, raises the issue of whether treaty obligations apply outside the State party's formal geographic boundaries.[182] In General Recommendation 28, the Committee indicates that States parties 'are responsible for all their actions affecting human rights, regardless of whether the affected persons are in their territories'.[183]

Actions undertaken outside the territory of a State party by State agents which involve the exercise of State functions such as the issuing of passports, would normally fall within the scope of the human rights treaties (for example, if a consulate refused to renew a passport because of the political activities of the citizen or on sex-discriminatory grounds).[184] A more controversial issue is whether treaty obligations apply to activities of the State in territory which is not geographically within the State but over which it may have effective control—for example, where a territory is leased to a State party (such as Guantánamo Bay, leased to the United States by Cuba), or where the agents of one State exercise powers in another State's territory for a relatively short period (for example, a kidnapping or abduction on foreign soil). In such cases, a number of international bodies have held that, where the State exercises powers of this sort on the territory of another State, its own human rights obligations will be engaged if it is in effective control of the person or situation in question.[185]

Moreover, if a State is present in the territory of another State or in a territory which does not form part of any sovereign State, the CCPR and other UN and regional treaty bodies have taken the position that the occupying State is obliged to observe its human rights obligations under treaties and customary international law in so far as it is in 'effective control' of persons or of territory.[186] Most of these cases have involved the conduct of military operations or belligerent occupation. For example, the CCPR and the ICJ have both found that Israel's obligations under the ICCPR extend to the actions of Israeli authorities in the West Bank and Gaza,[187] and in its *Advisory Opinion on the Wall*, the ICJ held that even though the ICESCR did not contain a territorial clause similar to that which appears in the ICCPR, the ICESCR nevertheless applied to Israeli actions in the Occupied Territories.[188] This view is shared by the CESCR (though contested by Israel on the ground that aspects of the occupation were governed solely by the humanitarian laws of armed conflict).

---

[182] See generally F Coomans and MT Kamminga (eds), *Extraterritorial Application of Human Rights Treaties* (2004), and M Gondak, *The Reach of Human Rights in a Globalising World: Extraterritorial Application of Human Rights Treaties* (2009).

[183] GR 28 para 12.

[184] See eg *Lichtensztejn v Uruguay*, HRC Communication No 77/1980 (1983), A/38/40 (Supp), 38th Session, 146.

[185] See eg *López Burgos v Uruguay*, HRC Communication No 52/1979 (1981), A/36/40 (Supp), 36th Session, 176.

[186] CCPR, 'General Comment 31' (2004) UN Doc HRI/GEN/1/Rev.9 (Vol. I) para 10; CAT, 'General Comment 2' (2007) UN Doc CAT/C/GC/2 para 16 (obligations extending to 'all areas where the State party exercises, directly or indirectly, in whole or in part, *de jure* or *de facto* effective control').

[187] See CCPR, CO Israel, CCPR/CO/78/ISR (2003) para 11; International Court of Justice, *Legal Consequences of the Construction of a Wall in the Occupied Palestinian Territory (Advisory Opinion)* [*Wall Opinion*] [2004] ICJ Rep 136 para 112.

[188] *Wall Opinion* (n 187 above) para 112.

The ICJ has also expressed the view in an application for interim measures in a case brought by Georgia against the Russian Federation that even though ICERD Articles 2 and 5 contain no specific territorial application provision, they 'generally appear to apply, like other provisions of instruments of that nature, to the actions of a State party when it acts beyond its territory'.[189] Similarly, the former European Commission on Human Rights and the European Court of Human Rights have on various occasions held that Turkey's occupation of and presence in northern Cyprus engage its obligations under the European Convention on Human Rights because of its effective control, notwithstanding the existence of a purportedly independent separate government of the 'Turkish Republic of Northern Cyprus'.[190]

The same principle applies to obligations under the Convention, despite its lack of specific language on territorial scope.[191] For example, the Committee addressed these issues in relation to Israel,[192] regretting the State party's stated position that 'the Convention does not apply beyond its own territory' and its refusal on that basis to report on the Occupied Territories or respond to questions about women in those areas.[193] The Committee's statement in General Recommendation 28 that the Convention also applies in situations of armed conflict[194] indicates that a State party may be bound in respect of its actions outside its territory when engaged in an armed conflict or occupation.[195]

The extent of the responsibility of a State party for the actions of an interim local administration in occupied territory with limited international personality, where various responsibilities have been delegated to that administration (as is the case with Israel and the Palestinian Authority in the West Bank) is complex, but the Committee's position has been that the State party to the Convention has overall responsibility for reporting and ensuring the observance of the Convention in that territory.[196]

Conversely, where a State party is not in a position to exercise control over part of its territory, it will not generally be responsible for securing the enjoyment of human rights in that territory.[197] The Committee has recognized this in the case of Cyprus, which had reported to the Committee in 2004 that 'due to the continuing illegal occupation and effective control of 37 per cent of its territory by Turkish military forces, the Government is unable to ensure the enjoyment of the rights provided for in the CEDAW'.[198]

---

[189] *Case Concerning Application of the International Convention on the Elimination of All Forms of Racial Discrimination (Georgia v Russian Federation), Request for the Indication of Provisional Measures,* Order of 15 October 2008 [2008] ICJ Rep 353, 386 para 109.

[190] See eg *Loizidou v Turkey (Preliminary Objections),* Series A No 310 (1995) 20 EHRR 99; and *Cyprus v Turkey* Reports 2001-IV and the cases are discussed by Gondak (n 182 above) 126–31, and by R Lawson, 'Life After *Banković*: On the Extraterritorial Application of the European Convention on Human Rights' in Coomans and Kamminga (n 182 above) 83, 96–9.

[191] GR 28 para 12.

[192] See UN Doc CEDAW/C/SR.685 (2005) (Israeli Ministry of Foreign Affairs and Ministry of Justice discussions with the Committee on the issue of applicability of the Convention to the West Bank and the Gaza Strip).

[193] CO Israel, A/60/38, 33rd Session (2005) paras 243–4. The Committee reiterated its view in 2001 CO Israel, CEDAW/C/ISR/CO/5, paras 12–13 (2011) (referring to GR 28 para 12).

[194] GR 28 para 11.

[195] See also *Statement by the Committee on the Elimination of Discrimination against Women on the situation in Gaza,* Decision 43/III, UN Doc A/64/38, 43rd Session (2009), Annex II, 141, para 3.

[196] CO Israel, CEDAW/C/ISR/CO/5 paras 12–13 (2011).

[197] ILC, *Articles on State Responsibility* (n 119 above) art 23 (force majeure) and Commentary para 3.

[198] *Combined 3rd to 5th Reports of Cyprus,* UN Doc CEDAW/C/CYP/3–5 (2004) para 10.

The Committee 'note[d] with concern the political environment which impedes the implementation of the Convention in the entire territory of the Republic of Cyprus'.[199]

The Convention does not explicitly address the issue of whether a State party has an obligation to regulate the acts of its nationals or its corporations outside its territory. In General Recommendation 28, the Committee stated that the obligations of States parties to establish effective legal protection of the rights of women 'also extend to acts of national [private] corporations operating extraterritorially'.[200] Although the Committee has on occasions commended States for regulating certain activities of their nationals abroad (eg assisting or performing female genital mutilation,[201] sex tourism, and trafficking), it has not developed this aspect of Convention application to a significant degree.[202]

IV. Conduct of States Parties as Participants in International Organizations

While the extent to which international organizations are bound by international human rights obligations is disputed, there is authority to suggest that States parties do not absolve themselves of their human rights obligations by establishing an international organization to deal with particular areas.[203] Indeed, it may be argued that States parties should conduct themselves consistently with those obligations as they participate in international organizations and endeavour to ensure that the actions taken by those organizations do not involve or cause human rights violations. Given the collective nature of international organizations and their status as independent legal entities, the content of a State party's obligation is a complex issue, particularly if an individual State party is not in a position to control or even influence significantly decisions which may have the effect of violating the human rights of persons in other States.

The Committee and the other UN human rights treaty bodies urge States parties to ensure that any international agreement or decision they undertake does not violate the respective treaties. This would include:

- ensuring that gender impact is taken into account when designing, delivering, and accepting development assistance;[204]
- taking Convention obligations into account in States parties' negotiations with international financial institutions for loans and other forms of financing for domestic projects;[205]

---

[199] CO Cyprus, CEDAW/C/CYP/CO/5 (2006) para 33. Turkey has not included material on northern Cyprus in its reports under the Convention, and the Committee does not appear to have raised with Turkey at any stage the extent of its responsibility under the Convention in relation to northern Cyprus.

[200] GR 28 para 36.   [201] CO Denmark, CEDAW/C/DEN/CO/6 (2006) para 20.

[202] See *Ruggie CEDAW Report* (n 125 above) 53–8.

[203] A Clapham, *Human Rights Obligations of Non-State Actors* (2006) 109. See also 'Maastricht Guidelines on Violations of Economic, Social and Cultural Rights', para 19 in (1998) 20(3) *Human Rights Quarterly* 691, 698.

[204] See eg CO Canada, A/58/38, 28th Session (2003) para 340; CO Spain, CEDAW/C/ESP/CO/6 (2009) para 8; CO Switzerland, CEDAW/C/CHE/CO/3 (2009) para 8; CO Luxembourg, A/58/38, 28th Session (2003) para 299; CO New Zealand, A/58/38, 29th Session (2003) para 404; CO Japan, A/58/38, 29th Session (2003) para 355, CO Ireland, A/60/38, 33rd Session (2005) para 377; CO Guinea-Bissau, CEDAW/C/GNB/CO/6 (2009) para 16 and CO Tuvalu, CEDAW/C/TUV/CO/2 (2009) para 56.

[205] See eg CESCR, 'General Comment 18' (2005) UN Doc HRI/GEN/1/Rev.9 (Vol. I) para 30; CESCR, 'General Comment 12' (1999) UN Doc HRI/GEN/1/Rev.9 (Vol. I) para 36; CERD, 'General Comment XXIX' (2002) UN Doc HRI/GEN/1/Rev.9 (Vol. II) para 7(ii). See also Principle 19 of the

- ensuring that international agreements relating to trade liberalization do not have an adverse impact on protected rights;[206]
- taking steps in their capacity as members of international organizations, including the international financial institutions, to ensure that those institutions duly take protected rights into account in their activities.[207]

The Committee has also in other contexts called on States parties to enter into bilateral or regional agreements with other States in order to address trans-border problems. For example, in General Recommendation 26 dealing with women migrant workers, the Committee notes, referring to Convention Article 3, that to prevent discrimination against women migrant workers, States parties that are sending, receiving, or transit countries should 'enter into bilateral or regional agreements or memorandums of understanding protecting the rights of women migrant workers' and associated sharing of information, including best practices and details of alleged violations of relevant laws.[208] Conversely, the Committee has called on States parties to analyze carefully the impact of free trade agreements and trade liberalization policies on women in their jurisdiction.[209]

V. Ratification of Other Instruments

In addition to legislative measures, the Committee encourages States parties to consider ratifying other international treaties to which they are not yet a party, with the object of enhancing women's enjoyment of their human rights and fundamental freedoms in all aspects of life.[210] Regional conventions relating to women, such as the Convention of Belém do Pará, are also promoted as an effective way to strengthen the States parties' programmes in particular areas.[211]

E. Reservations

Article 2 has drawn a significant number of reservations[212] in which States parties purport to limit their obligations under the article generally[213] or under its specific provisions. Many of the reservations are coupled with reservations to Articles 5, 15, and 16, and

---

'Montréal Principles on Women's Economic, Social and Cultural Rights', in (2004) 26(3) *Human Rights Quarterly* 772.

[206] See CESCR, 'General Comment 15' (2002) UN Doc HRI/GEN/1/Rev.9 (Vol. I) para 35; CESCR, 'General Comment 14' (2000) UN Doc HRI/GEN/1/Rev.9 (Vol. I) para 39; CESCR, 'General Comment 13' (1999) UN Doc HRI/GEN/1/Rev.9 para 56; CESCR, 'General Comment 12' UN Doc HRI/GEN/1/Rev.9 (Vol. I) (1999) paras 19 and 36. See also *Montréal Principles* (n 205 above) Principle 19.

[207] See eg CESCR, 'General Comment 14' (2000) UN Doc HRI/GEN/1/Rev.9 (Vol. I) para 39. See also *Montréal Principles* (n 205 above) Principle 19.

[208] GR 26 para 27(a).

[209] See eg CO Guatemala, CEDAW/C/GUA/CO/6 (2006) para 32; CO Mexico, CEDAW/C/MEX/CO/6 (2006) para 20; CO Colombia, CEDAW/C/COL/CO/6 (2007) para 28; CO The Philippines, CEDAW/C/PHI/CO/6 (2006) para 26; CO Niger, CEDAW/C/NER/CO/2 (2007) para 35; CO Jamaica, CEDAW/C/JAM/CO/5 (2006) para 38.

[210] 'Ratification of other treaties' appears as a standard heading in the 'Subject headings (titles) to be used in concluding observations', UN Doc A/63/38, 41st Session (2008), Annex X, 261.

[211] See eg CO Jamaica, A/56/38, 24th Session (2001) para 226.

[212] For the text of reservations and objections, see United Nations, *Multilateral Treaties Deposited with the Secretary-General*, Chapter IV <http://treaties.un.org/pages/ParticipationStatus.aspx> accessed 31 December 2010.

[213] See eg the reservations entered by Egypt, Morocco, Bangladesh, and Singapore.

refer to actual or perceived inconsistencies between Convention obligations and the requirements of religious or customary law or traditional practices and attitudes, or seek to preserve the operation of existing constitutional provisions or national law—often without specifying what those inconsistencies might be. There is also a significant number of general reservations to the Convention,[214] which have a particular impact on Article 2 obligations; many of these also refer to possible inconsistencies with religious or customary law or traditional practices, or to existing constitutional arrangements, and frequently do not detail the inconsistencies.

Many of these reservations may be incompatible with the object and purpose of the treaty and are therefore not permitted under Article 28, which embodies general international law on this issue. But frequently, because of the lack of detail in the reservations, it is difficult to assess the extent of the inconsistency between the Convention obligations and the various laws and practices that are invoked as their basis.[215]

Some States have entered reservations to specific provisions of Article 2 which appear to be significant in impact and may be incompatible with the object and purpose of the Convention.[216] A number of States parties have entered narrower reservations to Article 2, such as those claiming inconsistency between the Convention and the laws or practices relating to the succession to the throne, to other hereditary titles or honours, or to positions of traditional leadership.[217]

The Committee has made a number of statements on the issue of reservations to Article 2 and consistently encourages States parties which have made such reservations to clarify their impact and to review them with the goal of eventually removing them. The Committee has stated that it considers Article 2 to be 'the very essence of the obligations of States parties under the Convention'[218] and Article 2 (and 16) to be 'core provisions of the Convention' and continues to be concerned 'at the number and extent of reservations entered to those articles'.[219] In its treaty-specific reporting guidelines, the Committee has asked States parties to provide details of the impact of their general reservations and their plans to work towards their withdrawal.[220] The Committee has also stated its view that such general reservations are inconsistent with the object and purpose of the Convention.[221]

The Committee maintains a strong position on the incompatibility of general reservations to the Convention and specific reservations to Article 2,[222] at least where the reservation lacks detail about the claimed inconsistency between the domestic situation and the Convention.

---

[214] See eg the reservations entered by Saudi Arabia, Tunisia, Mauritania, the Maldives, and Malawi (original reservation, withdrawn in 1991) (n 212 above).

[215] A number of other States parties have objected to these broad reservations, while still maintaining that the Convention is in force between the reserving State and themselves. See the discussion in ch on art 28.

[216] See eg the United Arab Emirates (art 2(f)), the Democratic People's Republic of Korea (art 2(f)).

[217] See eg the reservations entered by Lesotho, the Federated States of Micronesia, Spain, Qatar, Morocco, the United Kingdom, and the Cook Islands (the last withdrawn in 2007, which the Committee welcomed: CEDAW/C/COK/CO/1).

[218] GR 28 para 41.   [219] CEDAW 1998 Statement (n 16 above) para 6.

[220] *Treaty-Specific Guidelines* (n 86 above) para 10.

[221] A/49/38 (Supp) (1994) xix, and GR 28 para 41.

[222] See eg CO Singapore, A/62/38, 39th Session (2007) paras 105–6.

The intent is to encourage States parties to keep their reservations under review and to modify or withdraw them, especially where they have not entered comparable reservations to similar obligations under other treaties,[223] and the Committee commends States parties when they do so.[224] As of the end of December 2010, no case had been decided under the Optional Protocol involving the validity of a reservation to Article 2.

---

[223] See eg CO Niger, CEDAW/C/NER/CO/2 (2007) para 9.
[224] See eg CO Syrian Arab Republic, A/62/38, 38th Session (2007) paras 121–2.

Article 3

States Parties shall take in all fields, in particular in the political, social, economic and cultural fields, all appropriate measures, including legislation, to ensure the full development and advancement of women, for the purpose of guaranteeing them the exercise and enjoyment of human rights and fundamental freedoms on a basis of equality with men.

A. Introduction

Article 3 is located in Part I of the Convention on the Elimination of All Forms of Discrimination against Women (CEDAW) as one of the provisions that describe States parties' general obligations under the Convention. Read in conjunction with Articles 1, 2, 4, 5, and 24, it forms part of the overarching interpretative framework for the application of the specific obligations set out in Articles 6–16.[1] Article 24 in Part VI is somewhat repetitive of Article 3. The obligations and concepts introduced in these initial articles apply to all other articles in the Convention. The Committee has on occasion viewed

  * I would like to thank Lena Skoglund for her valuable contribution as a research assistant; I would also like to thank Professor Hilary Charlesworth for her helpful comments on the chapter on Article 3 and the chapter on Violence against Women and, as always, for her encouragement and support.
  [1] eg GR 25 para 6; GR 28 para 7.

Article 3 as 'catching' matters that fall outside the express terms of other articles. However, as it often refers to Article 3 alongside other articles, notably Article 2, it is not always clear how the articles might be separated, or the extent to which it is desirable to do so.

Article 3 is a rare provision in the Convention schemata in that it does not explicitly identify elimination of discrimination against women as its goal. Rather, it emphasizes States parties' obligations to take positive steps to ensure the full development and advancement of women on a basis of equality with men. It thus affirms and complements the clauses calling for positive equality between women and men in the ICCPR, Article 3 and ICESCR, Article 3, as well as the non-discrimination clauses, ICCPR Articles 2(1) and 26 and ICESCR Article 2(2).

Article 3 is also the only substantive article in the Convention that explicitly guarantees women their human rights and fundamental freedoms. By echoing the language of the UN Charter Articles 1(3) and 55 and the preamble to the UDHR it connects the Convention with those instruments. But Article 3 goes further than simply providing a guarantee of women's human rights. By linking the full development and advancement of women with the exercise and enjoyment of their human rights, it is purposeful and instrumental, providing the legal basis for structural—transformative—change in the lives of women. Paragraph 7 of the Convention Preamble also refers to the 'full development of the potentialities of women', noting that discrimination against women makes this more difficult to achieve. However, unlike the Preamble, where the full development of women is sought 'in the service of their countries and of humanity', Article 3 is directed towards the full development and advancement of women, as a goal in its own right. It thus provides a notable statement of the importance of equality of women and men as a freestanding legal objective.

Article 3 is to some extent analogous to ICERD Article 2(2), which states:

States Parties shall, when the circumstances so warrant, take, in the social, economic, cultural and other fields, special and concrete measures to ensure the adequate development and protection of certain racial groups or individuals belonging to them, for the purpose of guaranteeing them the full and equal enjoyment of human rights and fundamental freedoms.

There are some textual differences between Article 3 and ICERD Article 2(2), most of which were a subject of discussion during the drafting process. Article 3 assumes a more immediate obligation by omitting the qualifying clause '[w]hen the circumstances so warrant'; the Convention expressly includes the 'political' field while ICERD does not, although it may be implied under 'other fields'; ICERD requires that States parties take 'special and concrete measures' while in the Convention the obligation is to take 'all appropriate measures'; there is no explicit mention of legislation in ICERD, Article 2(2) although there is in Article 2(1)(d); ICERD requires 'adequate' development and the Convention 'full' development, coupled with the 'advancement of women'. The final sentence in ICERD, Article 2(2) has no counterpart in the Convention:

These measures shall in no case entail as a consequence the maintenance of unequal or separate rights for different racial groups after the objectives for which they were taken have been achieved.

Article 3 has no directly equivalent provision in the ICCPR or ICESCR, although it imports the Covenants into the Convention through the inclusion of human rights and fundamental freedoms and specification of 'political, social, economic and cultural fields'.

Like Article 3 (and more fully Article 2), the ICCPR and ICESCR also specify legislation as a means of implementation of States parties' obligations.[2]

Article 3 has attracted little focused attention from either States parties or the Committee. There was no equivalent provision to Article 3 in DEDAW. No State party has reserved Article 3 explicitly, and the Committee has not adopted a general recommendation on it.

B. Travaux Préparatoires

Article 3 as finally adopted is little different from the first draft put forward by the Philippines and was subject to remarkably little discussion throughout the drafting process. The Philippines proposed:[3]

States Parties shall when the circumstances so warrant undertake, in the social, economic, cultural and other fields, concrete measures to ensure the adequate development and advancement of women, for the purpose of guaranteeing them the exercise and enjoyment of human rights and fundamental freedoms.

The joint Philippines/USSR draft omitted 'when the circumstances so warrant' but was otherwise unchanged. The wording of the Philippines' draft closely followed that of ICERD Article 2(2) and received wide support, except from Finland which considered it to be unnecessary in light of the substantive Articles 10–14.

C. Issues of Interpretation

Article 3 replicates and reinforces other provisions of the Convention. The open-endedness of some of the language allows for teleological interpretation of the Convention as a dynamic,[4] living instrument. Its focus on 'advancement' makes it especially forward-looking.

I. 'States Parties Shall Take in All Fields'

Under international law, treaty obligations rest with the State party, regardless of the constitutional order within the State, such as its federal structure.[5] The State party therefore ensures compliance by sub-State units. The mandatory language ('shall take') denotes positive State action 'in all fields'. This holistic approach 'anticipates the emergence of new forms of discrimination that had not been identified at the time of its drafting'[6] and emphasizes that the Convention is not limited to specified fields of application, as is the case with the two UN Covenants, but is to apply to all areas of relevance to women and their lives, both the public and the private.

An insight into how States parties may view the Convention's scope is provided by the UK. In its *One Year On Report* (2009) to the Committee, the UK explained the difference

---

[2] ICCPR art 2(2); ICESCR art 2(1).

[3] (6 November 1973); UN Doc E/CN.6/573, L Rehof, *Guide to the Travaux Préparatoires of the United Nations Convention on the Elimination of All Forms of Discrimination against Women* (1993) 62–5.

[4] eg GR 25 para 3, repeated GR 28 para 2: 'The Convention is a dynamic instrument'.

[5] eg CO Nigeria, CEDAW/C/NGA/CO/6 (2008) para 9.   [6] GR 28 para 8.

between its proposed equality legislation and the Convention. The former protects against discrimination in 'specific fields only, namely work, the provision of goods, facilities and services and the exercise of public functions, premises, education in schools and in further and higher education institutions, and in associations including private clubs'. In contrast, the UK stated (but without referring to Article 3), 'the CEDAW covers all fields including in particular social and cultural fields'.[7]

The phraseology 'all fields' is sufficiently indeterminate to provide Convention authority for an expansive interpretation that encompasses areas of activity not spelled out in subsequent provisions of the Convention. The Committee's concluding observations to States parties' reports, general statements, and recommendations suggest that it implicitly endorses this approach. 'All fields' encompasses, *inter alia*, the provision of goods, facilities, and services, economic and sustainable development,[8] property,[9] technology,[10] armed conflict,[11] detention,[12] climate change[13] and pollution, aftermath of natural disaster,[14] such as the tsunami[15] and cyclones,[16] and post-conflict reconstruction[17] and management.[18]

'All fields' also ensures the Convention's applicability to all women. For example, General Recommendation 18 refers specifically and only to Article 3 as the basis for its recommendations to States parties with respect to women with disabilities. Although this is the only general recommendation in which the Committee finds its competence explicitly in Article 3, the Committee has drawn upon Article 3 in other general recommendations to reinforce its position. Thus, Article 3 (along with Article 2) is expressly declared in General Recommendation 19 on violence against women as the basis for establishing 'a comprehensive obligation to eliminate discrimination in all its forms in addition to the specific obligations under Articles 5–16'.[19] In General Recommendation 21 paragraph 43, Article 3 is mentioned along with Articles 2 and 24 as requiring gradual progress towards equality in the family and thus that States parties should withdraw reservations; in General Recommendation 25 paragraph 6, Article 3 is read jointly with Articles 1, 2,

---

[7] Government Equalities Office, *Response By the United Kingdom (UK) and Northern Ireland (NI) to Select Recommendations of the United Nations Committee on the Elimination of All Forms of Discrimination against Women following the examination of the UK and NI's 5th and 6th Periodic Reports on 10 July 2008* (2009) (hereinafter UK, *One Year On Report*).

[8] CEDAW, 'Working Paper on the World Summit on Sustainable Development' UN Doc CEDAW/C/2002/I/WP.2, 26th Session (2002).

[9] K Rittich, 'The Properties of Gender Equality' in P Alston and M Robinson (eds), *Human Rights and Development Towards Mutual Reinforcement* (2005) 87.

[10] Art 14(2)(g). The Committee has also raised this with States parties, eg CO Bhutan, A/59/38, 30th Session (2004) paras 113–14.

[11] eg CO Croatia, A/50/38, 14th Session (1995) paras 585–6; CO Bosnia-Herzegovina, A/49/38 (Supp) 13th Session (1994) para 736; Decision 43/III, Statement by the Committee on the Elimination of Discrimination against Women on the Situation in Gaza, A/64/38 (Supp) Annex II (2009).

[12] eg CO Russian Federation, A/57/38, 26th session (2002) para 392.

[13] Decision 44/II, Statement by the Committee on the Elimination of Discrimination against Women on Gender and Climate Change, UN Doc A/65/38, 44th Session (2009).

[14] GR 28 para 11.   [15] eg CO Indonesia, CEDAW/C/IDN/CO/5 (2007) para 38.

[16] eg CO Myanmar, CEDAW/C/MMR/CO/3 (2008) para 22; Statement of the Committee on the Elimination of Discrimination against Women on the Situation in Haiti, UN Doc A/65/38 (Supp) 45th session, (2010).

[17] Statement by the Committee on the Elimination of Discrimination against Women on the Situation of Women in Iraq, Decision 30/III, UN Doc A/59/38 (Supp) (2004) Annex II.

[18] CEDAW, 'Gender and Sustainable Development' (2002) para 423.

[19] GR 19 para 10; see discussion in ch on violence against women below.

4, 5, and 24 to set out the 'general interpretative framework' of States parties' obligations under the Convention; and in General Recommendation 28 paragraph 8, the Committee notes that Articles 2 and 3 'anticipate the emergence of new forms of discrimination that had not been identified at the time of [the Convention's] drafting'.

II. 'In Particular in Political, Economic, Social, and Cultural Fields'

While providing for the application of the Convention in non-specified fields, Article 3 also spells out those to which it applies 'in particular': 'political,[20] social, economic and cultural fields'. This language largely echoes that of Article 1, although after discussion, the field of civil activity (included in Articles 1 and 15(2)) was omitted from Article 3.[21] While it is unclear why Articles 1 and 3 differ in this respect, taken together they incorporate all the rights contained in the UDHR, ICCPR, and ICESCR that are not expressly mentioned in the Convention.[22] This approach has been adopted by the Committee,[23] which has asserted that '[t]he spirit of the Convention covers other rights, which are not explicitly mentioned in the Convention but which have an impact on the achievement of equality of women with men and which represent a form of discrimination against women'.[24] For example, General Recommendation 19 paragraph 16 specifies its applicability to refugee women and paragraph 14 to single mothers, neither of whom are expressly addressed in the Convention.

Further, by describing the relevant fields of activity, rather than specifying political, social, economic, and cultural rights—the approach taken in the ICCPR and ICESCR and the Beijing Platform for Action[25]—Article 3 allows an interpretation that goes beyond the identified Covenant rights. This is important because denial of women's rights in the political, economic, social, and cultural fields 'contributes to their economic dependence, denial of personal autonomy'[26] and more generally to their lack of power.

Enumeration of these multiple fields of activity highlights the importance of women's human rights in political organization, representation, participation, and action,[27] in the allocation of and access to economic and social resources, and in cultural life. General Recommendation 23 on political and public life, paragraph 1 recalls the Preamble of the Convention in considering the role of women in the development of the State that is undermined by unequal political participation and representation. The Committee has

---

[20] The Philippines' draft of art 3 did not include the 'political' field (n 3 above).

[21] Rehof (n 3 above).

[22] Andrew Byrnes notes the rights to freedom of expression, privacy, and to be free from arbitrary detention; A Byrnes, 'The Convention on the Elimination of All Forms of Discrimination against Women' in W Benedek, E Kisaakye, and G Oberleitner (eds), *Human Rights of Women International Instruments and African Experiences* (2002) 119, 124.

[23] GR 28 para 3 states that 'the Convention is part of a comprehensive international human rights legal framework' and lists a wide range of international treaties that are explicitly or implicitly 'grounded in the concept of non-discrimination on the basis of sex and gender'.

[24] GR 28 para 7.

[25] Beijing Declaration and Platform for Action, adopted by the Fourth World Conference on Women (15 September 1995) para 213.

[26] Montréal Principles on Women's Economic, Social and Cultural Rights, 26 *Human Rights Quarterly* (2004) 760, 762.

[27] Art 3 (with arts 2 and 7) 'require that women be guaranteed equal access to organisations'. N Hevener Kaufman and SA Lindquist, 'Critiquing Gender-Neutral Treaty Language: The Convention on the Elimination of All Forms of Discrimination against Women' in J Peters and A Wolper (eds), *Women's Rights, Human Rights* (1995) 114, 120.

also expressed concern about the 'absence of an enabling environment... [that] prevents women from fully participating in all aspects of public life in accordance with articles 3, 7 and 8 of the Convention'.[28] Public life is widely understood to include governmental bodies,[29] law enforcement, the judiciary, and the diplomatic corps.[30] Economic and social rights[31] overlap and are mutually reinforcing in that both are directed at ensuring women's economic independence and free choices within society. Denial of employment, inheritance, and property rights (including marital property) undermines women's economic activity.[32] The economic field[33] encompasses both the wage sector and the informal economy, where women are especially active but may remain invisible and lack social and legal protections.[34] Social rights have been described as aiming at 'securing the ability to live a life of dignity for everyone, without dependence on others (other than the State), while reasonably fulfilling all basic needs, including welfare rights, rights in the sphere of employment, and rights to education and health'.[35]

The inclusion of the cultural field is a reminder that culture can be empowering (as well as the basis of harmful practices) for women. It echoes ICESCR Article 15(1), which has no direct comparator in the Convention, although Article 13(c) requires States parties to take all appropriate measures to eliminate discrimination against women 'in all aspects of cultural life'. Culture as a 'broad, inclusive concept encompassing all manifestations of human existence... shapes and mirrors the values of well-being, as well as the economic, social and political life of individuals, groups of individuals and communities'.[36] As such, it is empowering for women when they receive sustenance and support from their community. However, women are also disproportionately affected by social and cultural marginalization which adversely impacts upon their access to and enjoyment of other rights.[37] Article 3 must be read in conjunction with Article 5(1) requiring modification of those aspects of culture that sustain prejudice and stereotypical roles for women and men and thus undermine women's enjoyment of their rights.

General Recommendation 19 emphasizes the importance of addressing discrimination in all fields—political, economic, social, and cultural—in the context of violence against women. It explains that the 'comprehensive obligation to eliminate discrimination in all its forms' established by Article 3 (with Article 2) includes the need for positive action by States parties in the economic field to combat violence against women. It notes that cultural—sexist—attitudes that regard women as subordinate to men 'contribute to the propagation of pornography and the depiction and other commercial exploitation of women as sexual objects, rather than as individuals'. General Recommendation 25, referring to Article 3 (along with Articles 1, 2, 4, and 5) reinforces this point by requiring

---

[28] CO Belarus, A/55/38, 22nd Session (2000) para 355.

[29] eg CO Bhutan, A/59/38, 30th Session (2004) para 108.

[30] eg CO Kuwait, A/59/38, 30th Session (2004) para 75.

[31] L Farha, 'Women Claiming Economic, Social and Cultural Rights—The CEDAW Potential' in M Langford (ed), *Social Rights Jurisprudence Emerging Trends in International and Comparative Law* (2008) 553.

[32] Rittich (n 9 above) 87; CEDAW GR 21 paras 30–5.

[33] Art 13 refers to 'areas of economic and social life'; see discussion in ch on art 13.

[34] eg CO The Philippines, CEDAW/C/PHI/CO/6 (2006) para 25; CO Vietnam, CEDAW/C/VNM/CO/6 (2007) paras 22–3. See also R King and C Sweetman, *Gender Perspectives on the Economic Crisis* (2010) 6.

[35] D Barak-Erez, 'Social Rights as Women's Rights' in D Barak-Erez and AM Gross (eds), *Exploring Social Rights Between Theory and Practice* (2007) 397, 398.

[36] CESCR, 'General Comment 21' (2009) UN Doc E/C.12/GC/21.

[37] Montréal Principles on Women's Economic, Social and Cultural Rights (n 26 above) 760.

States parties to take measures across all fields 'to address prevailing gender relations and the persistence of gender-based stereotypes'.[38]

III. 'All Appropriate Measures'

States parties have the positive obligation to take 'all appropriate measures' to achieve the objectives laid down in Article 3. These are in addition to the specific measures, including constitutional and legal reform, spelled out in Article 2. The original draft had specified 'concrete' measures',[39] which was changed to 'all appropriate measures' reflecting the language of ICESCR Article 2(1) ('all appropriate means'). It is less forceful than that of ICERD, Article 2(2), which stipulates 'special and concrete measures'.[40] The parallel requirement under ICESCR, according to CESCR General Comment 3, is that Article 2(2) be given 'its full and natural meaning'.[41]

'Appropriate measures' affords States parties flexibility in determining how best to achieve the objectives of the Convention within their own particular social, economic, and political contexts, recognizing that this may not always be through legislation.[42] The Committee has not explicitly stated its understanding of 'appropriate measures', but in its general recommendations it has suggested a range of social (for example, removal of obstacles[43]), economic (for example, gender budgeting[44] and resource allocation[45]), educational,[46] and administrative[47] mechanisms for monitoring and implementation of the Convention, which demonstrate a similarly broad approach to that taken by the CESCR. States parties should thus adopt 'appropriate measures' in all fields in order for women to enjoy all human rights, not just those specified in the substantive Articles 6–16 of the Convention.

The language of Article 3 ('shall take') and the Committee's application of 'all appropriate measures' make it clear that Convention obligations are subject to immediate implementation rather than progressive realization. Nor does Article 3 reiterate the wording of ICESCR, Article 2(1) relating to progressive realization. It might be argued that General Recommendation 21 undermines this conclusion by stating in paragraph 43 that '[c]onsistent with articles 2, 3 and 24 . . . the Committee requires that all States parties gradually progress to a stage where, . . . each country will withdraw its reservation'. However, this paragraph is not directed at the totality of States parties' obligations under the Convention but only at the removal of reservations, which is not applicable to Article 3 itself.

Temporary special measures, where needed, are included among appropriate measures, as set out in Article 4 and General Recommendation 25. The latter replicates the

---

[38] GR 25 para 7.

[39] Belgium proposed the change to 'all appropriate measures'; Rehof (n 3 above) 64.

[40] The Committee has requested examples of 'concrete measures'; eg question to Niger, UN Doc CEDAW/C/NER/Q/2 (2003) art 3 para 9.

[41] CESCR, 'General Comment 3' (1990) UN Doc E/1991/23 para 4.

[42] GR 28 para 23. The UK, for example, has asserted that 'it is not appropriate, nor indeed possible, for legislation to address such obligations'. UK, *One Year on Report* (n 7 above) para 6.

[43] eg GR 23 para 45(c); GR 24 para 31(b).

[44] H Hofbauer, 'Gender-Sensitive Budget Analysis: A Tool to Promote Women's Rights' (2002) 14 *Canadian J of Women and the L* 98–117.

[45] eg GR 24 para 30.

[46] eg GR 19 para 24(f): 'States should introduce education and public information programmes to help eliminate prejudices that hinder women's equality (recommendation No 3, 1987)'.

[47] eg GR 19 para 24(c); GR 23 para 45(c); GR 24 para 31(d).

language of Article 3 in asserting that 'States Parties to the Convention are under a legal obligation . . . to ensure the development and advancement of women in order to improve their position to one of de jure as well as de facto equality with men'.[48] Article 3 lays the ground for the introduction of temporary special measures and is referenced in General Recommendation 25 (along with Articles 1, 2, 5, and 24) which establishes that States parties may have an obligation to take such measures with respect to any of the substantive Articles 6–16.[49]

IV. 'Including Legislation'

Article 3 reinforces Article 2 by affirming that legislation is included among 'appropriate measures'. The importance of enacting and implementing effective legislative reform to achieve the objectives of the Convention is more fully spelled out in the Committee's general recommendations.[50] Without referring explicitly to Article 3, the Committee may remind States parties of their obligation 'to raise the awareness of legislators about the need to give priority attention to legislative reforms in order to achieve de jure equality for women and compliance with the State party's international treaty obligations'.[51]

Legislation may be required in multiple fields of law, such as those addressing family, civil, penal, labour, commercial, and administrative matters. The Outcome Document adopted at the Beijing + 5 General Assembly Special Session recognized that in many States a gender perspective has not been integrated into the laws or codes, administrative rules or regulations within these diverse fields.[52] Article 3 provides a legal basis for requiring States parties to do so. This encompasses full and systematic incorporation of the Convention throughout domestic law,[53] and such legislation should prevail over other domestic law.[54]

The Committee has referred to many other practical and legal instrumentalities, which are discussed more fully in the section on the nature of States parties' obligations (section E below).

V. 'To Ensure the Full Development and Advancement of Women'

This language spells out the fundamental objective of eliminating discrimination against women and thus of the Convention:[55] ensuring the full development and advancement of women. The stronger word 'full' was preferred to the originally proposed weaker word 'adequate'.[56] Neither 'development' nor 'advancement' is defined in the Convention and both are multifaceted. They denote forward movement and progress, especially when read together. Thus, practices and policies that put back women's advancement are not

---

[48] GR 25 para 4.   [49] Ibid para 24.
[50] eg GR 19 para 24(r)(ii); GR 21 para 49; CEDAW GR 23 para 47(a).
[51] eg CO Myanmar, CEDAW/C/MMR/CO/3 (2008) para 11.
[52] Outcome Document adopted by the 23rd UNGA Special Session, 'Women 2000: Gender Equality, Development and Peace for the 21st Century' (2000) para 27.
[53] eg CO Indonesia, CEDAW/C/IDN/CO/5 (2007) para 8.
[54] eg CO Myanmar, CEDAW/C/MMR/CO/3 (2008) para 9.
[55] D Gierycz, 'Human Rights of Women at the Fiftieth Anniversary of the United Nations' in Benedek, Kisaakye and Oberleitner (n 22 above) 30, 34.
[56] The Philippines' draft (n 3 above).

in conformity with Article 3, and the Committee has expressed concern about such situations, sometimes,[57] but not always, mentioning Article 3.[58]

Women have had a somewhat uneasy relationship with policies and programmes for economic development and growth. State development has not always been for, or resulted in, the advancement of women, and without exploration of the gender dimension the adverse consequences for women of development projects too often remain invisible.[59] The Committee has implicitly invoked Article 3 in asserting 'the urgent need to ensure that globalisation and transition to market economic policies improve the quality of life of women';[60] in recommending that development projects be assessed from a gender perspective;[61] and in emphasizing that 'megaprojects' and global economic trends must not be allowed to disadvantage women.

The Committee, in common with other bodies, has turned its attention to the impact of gender inequality on development. It has noted that 'if sustainable development is to realise economic, social and environmental goals, women's needs and concerns must be given equal priority with those of men'.[62] The Beijing Declaration emphasizes that women's empowerment and equal participation are essential elements for development.[63] Similarly, the World Bank has reported that 'ignoring gender disparities comes at great cost to people's well-being and to countries' abilities to grow sustainably, to govern effectively, and thus to reduce poverty'.[64] Poverty too is feminized as was spelled out in the first Critical Area of Concern in the Beijing Platform for Action.[65] It is, thus, crucial to promote gender equality, including in national development plans, as 'an important part of a development strategy that seeks to enable all people—women and men alike—to escape poverty and improve their standard of living'.[66] This also requires taking into account women's access to health care, social security, education, clean water and sanitation services, fertile land, income-generation opportunities, and participation in decision-making processes.[67]

---

[57] eg under the heading 'art 3', the Committee expressed disappointment at the abolition of the Cabinet Committee for Emancipation Policy. General Observations, the Netherlands, UN Doc A/49/38 (Supp) 13th Session (1994) para 267.

[58] eg CO Russian Federation, UN Doc A/57/38, 26th Session (2002) para 381 (steadily decreasing representation of women in the political arena), para 383 ('deteriorating situation of women in employment'); Statement by the Committee on the Elimination of Discrimination against Women on the Situation of Women in Iraq, Decision 30/III, UN Doc A/59/38, 30th Session (2004), Annex II (repeal of civil statutes governing issues related to marriage, divorce, child custody and inheritance); CO Italy, A/60/38, 32nd Session (2005) para 318.

[59] On the gendered differential of development policies see E Boserup, *Women's Role in Economic Development* (1970); F Banda, *Women, Law and Human Rights: an African Perspective* (2005) 269–95.

[60] CEDAW, 'Working Paper on the World Summit on Sustainable Development' (n 8 above) para 2; see also the discussion in ch on art 14.

[61] eg CO Samoa, A/60/38, 32nd Session (2005) para 63.

[62] CEDAW, 'Working paper on the World Summit on Sustainable Development' (n 8 above) para 4; it has repeated this in concluding observations, eg CO Botswana, CEDAW/C/BOT/CO/3 (2010) para 40.

[63] Beijing Platform for Action (n 25 above) para 56.

[64] World Bank Policy Research Report, '*Engendering Development: Through Gender Equality in Rights, Resources and Voice*' (2001).

[65] The 'feminization of poverty' refers to both the gendered ways in which women become poor (eg through divorce or discriminatory property laws) and their experience of poverty; Beijing Platform for Action (n 25 above) para 48; CEDAW, 'Working paper on the World Summit on Sustainable Development' (n 8 above) para 6(a); CO Russian Federation, A/57/38, 26th Session (2002) para 338.

[66] World Bank Policy Research Report (n 64 above).

[67] CO The Philippines, CEDAW/C/PHI/CO/6 (2006) para 30.

Article 3 places women's own development and advancement at the forefront, rather than that of States or of peoples as a collectivity. Further, by explicitly guaranteeing the exercise and enjoyment of human rights and fundamental freedoms as the purpose of the full development and advancement of women, Article 3 locates women as rights-holders, not just as objects (or subjects) or prospective beneficiaries of development policy.[68]

The rights-based approach requires recognizing women's legal entitlement to development and advancement as an end in itself and not primarily as instrumentalities for State economic development. It moves away from the utilitarian language of development economists[69] to that of entitlement to equal choices and opportunities to be enshrined within the formal legal system. The Convention 'recognizes the inextricability of subordination and the economic and social structures that generate and perpetuate it'.[70] Understood in this way, Article 3 foreshadows, with gender specificity, the UN Declaration on the Right to Development which asserts that '[t]he right to development is an inalienable human right'.[71]

The Committee has taken up these issues, but generally without referring to Article 3. It has considered the relationship between gender and economic development, for example, seeking information and expressing concern about the impact on women of economic crisis, structural adjustment programmes,[72] and macroeconomic policies,[73] including that economic growth and development may not benefit women as much as men.[74] It has requested States parties to ensure that all poverty alleviation programmes fully benefit women[75] and to enhance 'monitoring of the impact of economic development and changes on women and to take proactive and corrective measures, including increasing social spending, so that women can fully and equally benefit from growth and poverty reduction'.[76] The Committee has welcomed the introduction of micro-credit or micro-enterprise schemes that facilitate women's independence through enhancement of their economic self-sufficiency.[77]

Economic globalization may have created new employment opportunities for women in the formal economy, enhancing their opportunities for economic independence. However, it also has its downsides, such as 'economic restructuring as well as, in a certain number of countries, persistent, unmanageable levels of external debt and structural adjustment

---

[68] UNGA Res 41/128 (1986) states that the 'human person should be the active participant and beneficiary of the right to development'.

[69] H Steiner, 'Social Rights and Economic Development: Converging Discourses' (1998) 4 *Buffalo Human Rights L Rev* 25.

[70] C Romany, 'State Responsibility goes Private: the Feminist Critique of the Public/Private Distinction in International Human Rights Law' in RJ Cook (ed), *Human Rights of Women: National and International Perspectives* (1994) 85, 108 (citing art 3).

[71] UNGA Res 41/128 (1986). This resolution was preceded by the Commission on Human Rights resolution 4 (XXXIII), 21 February 1977. See also World Conference on Human Rights, Vienna Declaration and Programme of Action, (12 July 1993) UN Doc A/Conf. 157/23 para 10.

[72] CO Trinidad and Tobago, A/57/38, 26th Session (2002) para 156.

[73] eg question to Turkey, UN Doc CEDAW/PSWG/2005/I/CRP.1/Add.8, para 1. It noted 'the lack of information on the integration of a gender perspective in the State party's economic planning'. CO Turkey, A/60/38, 32nd Session (2005) para 379.

[74] eg CO China, CEDAW/C/CHN/CO/6 (2006) paras 15–16.

[75] eg CO Belarus, A/59/38, 30th session (2000) para 354.

[76] CO China, CEDAW/C/CHN/CO/6 (2006) paras 15–16.

[77] eg CEDAW, 'Working paper on the World Summit on Sustainable Development' (n 8 above) para 6(i); CO Mauritius, CEDAW/C/MAR/CO/5 (2006) para 8.

programmes'.[78] The gendered division of labour, trapping women in low-paid, unregulated work, for example, in export processing zones, poses a particular risk to women who are especially vulnerable.[79] The Committee has explained that while it is appreciative of the need for 'economic growth, it is concerned that the human rights of vulnerable groups such as tribal populations may be adversely affected by large-scale economic projects'.[80] More broadly, it has expressed concern about women's poverty and social exclusion,[81] which are exacerbated by global economic downturns.[82] It has recommended that 'the promotion of gender equality and sensitisation to gender equality issues is an explicit component of, and is fully implemented in, its national development plans and policies, in particular, those aimed at poverty alleviation, sustainable development and natural disaster management'.[83]

The Committee has linked sustainable development with 'gender-sensitive people-centred human development, based on equality and equity, participation of government and civil society, transparency and accountability in governance'.[84] The combined civil and political rights and socio-economic rights in the Convention, the Beijing Declaration and Platform for Action, and the Beijing + 5 Outcome Document constitute 'important legal, policy and programmatic instruments that also provide a clear agenda that must be integrated into sustainable human development'.[85]

In addition to issues relating to economic development the Committee has explicitly addressed women's development in the context of health and family relations, for example, recognizing family responsibilities as inhibiting personal development,[86] and the fallacy that women and men have different rates of intellectual development.[87] It has seen the 'health, development and well-being' of family members as linked objectives and noted that these are all enhanced where there are 'freely available appropriate measures for the voluntary regulation of fertility'.[88] The Convention does not explicitly adopt the life cycle approach to the guarantee of women's human rights but the language of Article 3 implicitly does so, confirmed by the Committee (without reference to Article 3) in General Recommendation 24:[89] securing women's advancement and full development as a lifespan[90] project from infancy and childhood through to old age. Perhaps surprisingly, General Recommendation 19 does not describe how gender-based violence inhibits women's development.[91]

---

[78] Beijing Platform for Action (n 25 above) para 47.

[79] SE Sweeney, 'Government Respect for Women's Economic Rights' in S Hertel and L Minkler (eds), *Economic Rights Conceptual, Measurement and Policy Issues* (2007) 233, 236–9.

[80] CO India, CEDAW/C/IND/CO/3 (2007) para 46.

[81] See E Evatt, 'Private Global Enterprises, International Trade and Finance' in HB Schöpp-Schilling and C Flinterman (eds), *The Circle of Empowerment: Twenty-Five Years of The UN Committee on The Elimination of Discrimination against Women* (2007) 106, 117.

[82] Decision 43/II, Statement by the Committee on the Elimination of Discrimination against Women on the international financial crisis and its consequences for the human rights of women and girls, UN Doc A/64/38 (Supp), 43rd Session (2009), Annex I.

[83] eg CO Indonesia, CEDAW/C/IDN/CO/5 (2007) para 39; CO Ireland, A/60/38, 33rd session (2005) para 393; Statement of the Committee on the Elimination of Discrimination against Women on the situation in Haiti, UN Doc A/65/38, 45th Session (2010).

[84] CEDAW, 'Working paper on the World Summit on Sustainable Development' (n 8 above) para 2.

[85] Ibid para 425. [86] GR 21 para 21. [87] Ibid para 38. [88] Ibid para 23.

[89] GR 24 para 7. See also the Beijing Declaration and Platform for Action (n 25 above) para 216.

[90] GR 28 para 31 (using the language of 'lifespan').

[91] UNGA Res 48/104 (1993) recognizes that violence against women has led to the 'prevention of the full advancement of women'.

States parties must identify where sex- and gender-based inequality exist and ensure that their measures, policies, and practices, including those for economic development, advance the position of women and do not merely accommodate women's difference. The Committee's almost routine request for gender-disaggregated statistics reflects a concern that without the data thus provided women's advancement in any of the relevant fields cannot be measured or monitored. Measures need not be applied equally to women and men, rather their impact must be subject to effective gender analysis 'through inter-institutional involvement at all levels'[92] and their application adapted to redress any *de facto* inequality. Some women are subject to further, particular disadvantage and additional, special, or corrective measures are needed to secure their entitlement to advancement and enjoyment of human rights.[93]

Article 3 provides the authority for the radical rethinking of development strategies that a rights-based—and gender-sensitive—approach to development requires. Accordingly, government actions, whether of a legislative, administrative, policy, or programmatic nature, must be considered in light of the obligations inherent in human rights[94]: individual entitlement and State accountability for failure to perform.

VI. 'For the Purpose of Guaranteeing them the Exercise and Enjoyment of Human Rights and Fundamental Freedoms'

States parties' obligations under Article 3 are expressly to guarantee women's exercise and enjoyment of human rights and fundamental freedoms, as stipulated in international treaties and customary international law. Article 3 (along with Article 1) implicitly lays the groundwork for the assertion in the Vienna Declaration and Programme for Action that '[t]he human rights of women and of the girl-child are an inalienable, integral and indivisible part of universal human rights'.[95] In similar language General Recommendation 19 also refers to women's enjoyment of 'human rights and fundamental freedoms under general international law or under human rights conventions' and notes that gender-based violence that impairs the enjoyment of such rights constitutes discrimination under Convention Article 1.

By not listing the relevant human rights and fundamental freedoms (or other international instruments), Article 3 allows for progressive development as the understanding of rights is extended, for example, through 'declarations, programmes and platforms for action adopted by relevant United Nations conferences, summits and special sessions'.[96] Ensuring women's social, political, and economic advancement facilitates their enjoyment of human rights, while the full and equal enjoyment of human rights underpins women's advancement and development and is essential for its achievement.[97]

---

[92] eg CO Bolivarian Republic of Venezuela, CEDAW/C/VEN/CO/6 (2006) para 18.

[93] eg GR 18; CO Myanmar, CEDAW/C/MMR/CO/3 (2008) para 33; CO India, CEDAW/C/IND/CO/3 (2007) para 15. The Convention on the Rights of Persons with Disabilities, art 6 identifies the multiple discriminations faced by women with disabilities.

[94] S Goonesekere, 'The Conceptual and Legal Dimensions of a Rights-Based Approach, and its Gender Dimensions' in UN Division for the Advancement of Women, *A Rights-Based Approach to Women's Empowerment and Advancement and Gender Equality* (1998).

[95] Vienna Declaration and Programme of Action, (1993) UN Doc A/CONF.157/23 part I para 18; part II para 36.

[96] Relevant conferences are listed in a number of concluding observations, eg CO Samoa, A/60/38, 32nd Session (2005) para 68.

[97] Beijing Declaration and Platform for Action para 213.

The UN Millennium Declaration,[98] from which the Millennium Development Goals (MDGs) were articulated, uses the language of the 'empowerment of women' rather than that of advancement and development.[99] The MDGs are goals, not rights.[100] They are 'elaborated in very limiting terms that refer to eliminating the gender gap in education and increasing women's employment in the formal sector and political participation in national parliaments' and thus fail to capture the 'wide sweep of CEDAW'.[101] Nor are they subject to the treaty monitoring system.

The UN OHCHR has engaged with the MDGs as the central global development programme, stating that a 'human rights-based approach means ensuring that the MDG lens is sufficiently focused on the rights of women; for example, those entrenched in the Convention on the Elimination of All Forms of Discrimination against Women'.[102] The Committee has routinely raised their implementation with States, giving some effect to the mutuality between the MDGs and rights.[103] The Committee also uses the language of women's empowerment, a language that 'aims to enhance women's self-awareness, self-esteem, self-confidence and self-reliance'.[104]

While the shift of language from victimization to empowerment[105] is evidently beneficial for women, some caution must also be exercised. It may be used to turn the focus away from the State's obligation to ensure measures for women's advancement and development by identifying and removing obstacles and ensuring an appropriate legal environment, to women having to determine their own actions to achieve these goals. Self-reliance must not be substituted for States parties' obligations. If women within a particular society are deemed to be 'empowered', failure to achieve advancement and development may be attributed to their failings, either individually or as a group, while the location of these objectives within the language of rights in the Convention emphasizes States parties' obligations. The Committee's repeated emphasis on the 'full and effective implementation of the Convention as indispensable for achieving the MDGs'[106] underlines the importance of a holistic approach, including women's autonomy and empowerment within a rights-based framework. It regularly calls upon States parties to integrate 'a gender perspective and the explicit reflection of the provisions of the Convention in all efforts' for achieving the MDGs and has requested States parties to report on their efforts in this regard. The rights-based approach to women's advancement summarized in Article 3 entails participation, agency, transparency, and accountability.

---

[98] UNGA Res 55/2, United Nations Millennium Declaration, UN Doc A/RES/55/2 (2000) para 20.

[99] eg the MDGs, Goal Three: 'Promote Gender Equality and Empower Women'.

[100] P Alston, 'Ships Passing in the Night: The Current State of the Human Rights and Development Debate seen through the Lens of the Millennium Development Goals' (2005) 27 *Human Rights Quarterly* 755.

[101] S Goonesekere, 'Universalizing Women's Human Rights through CEDAW' in Schöpp-Schilling and Flinterman (eds) (n 81 above) 52, 65.

[102] OHCHR, *Claiming the Millennium Development Goals: A Human Rights Approach* (2008) 7.

[103] P Alston and M Robinson (eds), *Human Rights and Development: Towards Mutual Reinforcement* (2005).

[104] *The Mandate of the Special Rapporteur on Violence Against Women (1994–2009)—A Critical Review*, 35.

[105] 'From victimization towards empowerment', ibid 34.

[106] eg CO Indonesia, CEDAW/C/IDN/CO/5 (2007) para 43; CO Myanmar, CEDAW/C/MMR/CO/3 (2008) para 53; CO India, CEDAW/C/IND/CO/3 (2007) para 63; CO Israel, CEDAW/C/ISR/CO/3 (2005) para 45.

VII. 'On a Basis of Equality with Men'

These last words of Article 3 had been deleted by the CSW and were reintroduced by the style committee.[107] They locate Article 3 in the overall context of the Convention: to eliminate discrimination against women and to achieve equality between women and men. This phrase is repeated from Article 1, and when read with the earlier wording of Article 3 and all other substantive articles, most especially Article 2 (which does not mention equality between women and men), it is apparent that women's equality does not always require a male comparator. Rather, the phrase makes clear that practices that are detrimental to women 'as such' must be eliminated to accord women the same opportunities as men to achieve their 'full development and advancement' *as women*.[108] Article 3 encapsulates transformative equality, as discussed below.

D. Equality in Context

I. Formal, Substantive, and Transformative Equality

Article 3 must be understood in conjunction with Articles 1, 2, 4, 5, and 24,[109] which together set out States parties' core obligations under the Convention. They require formal equality (for example, through the adoption of legislation to ensure a non-discriminatory legal framework) and substantive equality (for example, through temporary special measures). Article 3 catches 'those discriminatory practices that do not come within the scope of the Article 1 definition'.[110] The powerful language in General Recommendation 19 that 'Articles 2 and 3 establish a comprehensive obligation to eliminate discrimination in all its forms'[111] encompasses direct and indirect discrimination, harassment, cultural prejudice, and stereotyping. Article 3 thus complements and reinforces Articles 1, 2, and 5.

The goal of ensuring women's full development and advancement requires positive and corrective action not only to achieve *de facto* equality, but also to ensure the elimination of structural inequalities that impede women's access to enjoyment of rights. This requires removal of pre-existing inequalities. Article 3 provides the framework for the specific measures for structural transformation that are set out in Articles 4 and 5 and reinforces the means by which this must be done ('all appropriate measures including legislation' as also spelled out in Article 2). The UK in its *One Year On Report* (2009) refers to Article 3 in noting that the Convention standards are higher than those typically included in non-discrimination legislation, such as its own, the aim of which is to 'prohibit discrimination and promote equality of opportunity'. The Convention's provisions 'are not to do with the conferral of rights on people'[112] but with transforming institutional structures (such as those of the workplace), as well as social and economic assumptions and behaviours. The Committee has explained that the Convention requires States to progress towards 'a real transformation of opportunities, institutions, and systems so that they are no longer grounded in historically determined male paradigms of power and life patterns'.[113]

---

[107] Rehof (n 3 above) 64.

[108] R Cook, 'State Accountability under the Convention on the Elimination of All Forms of Discrimination against Women' in Cook (ed), (n 70 above) 228, 236.

[109] GR 25 para 6.   [110] Ibid.

[111] The earlier general recommendation on Violence against Women, GR 12, did not mention art 3.

[112] UK, *One Year on Report* (n 7 above) para 6. The UK mentions art 5(b).   [113] GR 25 para 10.

Article 3 is at the core of this obligation and clarifies that positive actions are required across all fields—political, social, economic, and cultural interpreted broadly as discussed above—to ensure progress in all aspects of women's lives. It thus requires reassessment of legislation, policies, and programmes, including those for economic development and poverty reduction, to evaluate their impact upon women's equality and advancement.

E. States Parties' Obligations

I. Implementation: Respect, Protect, Promote and Fulfil

General Recommendation 25, paragraph 4 draws upon the language of Article 3 in asserting that 'States parties to the Convention are under a legal obligation to respect, protect, promote and fulfil this right to non-discrimination for women and to ensure the development and advancement of women in order to improve their position to one of de jure as well as de facto equality with men'.[114] The Committee invites States parties to report on the 'institution(s) responsible for designing, implementing, monitoring, evaluating and enforcing such temporary special measures'.[115] Since it understands Article 3 as constituting one of the bases for requiring States parties to report on their adoption of temporary special measures, they also should report on all measures intended for the advancement and development of women within national jurisdictions.

The Committee has frequently questioned States parties on their chosen methods for ensuring the advancement of women and it invariably returns to the matter in its concluding observations. As already observed, the overarching and imprecise character of Article 3 overlaps with Articles 1, 2, 4, and 5, and especially Article 24. The Committee has questioned States parties under Article 3 about their national women's machinery and it is not always apparent whether its appraisal of such machinery is under Article 3 or Article 24. The Committee has also asked States parties' representatives about other issues under Article 3 that might just as easily have been brought under another article,[116] or have induced responses that could do so.[117]

The Committee has also raised general questions without reference to any specific article but which can be understood as coming within the terms of Article 3. Concerns about poverty reduction, economic empowerment of women, and promotion of women's autonomy through sponsorship of income-generating activities, access to micro-credit, and loan schemes are often addressed without reference to Article 3, although of relevance to that article as well as others, such as Article 14.[118] Nor has the Committee explicitly identified what is required by each of the layers of obligation, or clarified what States parties must do to comply with Article 3. It is, therefore, useful to examine the issues about which members of the Committee have questioned States parties, the steps for which the Committee has commended States, and gaps and omissions in implementation about

---

[114] See also GR 28 para 16.　　[115] Ibid para 34.

[116] eg the questions asked of Japan about educational programmes for women; CO Japan, UN Doc A/49/38 (Supp) 13th Session (1994) art 3 para 561 could have been located under art 10.

[117] eg asked about programmes for the advancement of women, the Russian representative described programmes of support for women to enter public life which could have been supplied under art 7; CO Russia, UN Doc A/57/38, 14th Session (1995) art 3 para 504.

[118] eg CO Madagascar, CEDAW/C/MDG/CO/5 (2008) para 32.

which it has expressed concern, to determine how they illuminate the normative content of Article 3.

1. *Obligation to Respect*

The obligation to respect requires States parties not to take measures that undermine the full advancement and development of women and their enjoyment of human rights and fundamental freedoms. Article 3 also requires positive State action through the imposition of a direct government obligation to advance women in and through State agencies, for example, through effective integration of gender into budgetary policy. It also requires the State party to remove obstacles and to introduce measures directed at encouraging full compliance with the principles of the Convention, particularly where religious or private law or custom conflict with those principles.[119] States parties' actions to this end will vary, and 'with the help of the Committee, [States parties must] decide what action is required to fulfil the treaty obligation'.[120]

The Committee has more generally given attention to national legal and political institutions[121] for the advancement of women,[122] especially welcoming the allocation of human and material resources for this purpose. Article 3 requires States parties to make available to women institutions appropriate to their needs where those needs differ from those of men.[123] This interpretation is supported by Article 24 and General Recommendation 25, which in paragraph 24 commends a range of institutions, including 'women's ministries, women's departments within ministries or presidential offices, ombudspersons, tribunals or other entities of a public or private nature with the requisite mandate to design specific programmes, monitor their implementation, and evaluate their impact and outcomes.' States parties have reported on such measures—and others—aimed at institutional capacity building and awareness-raising for the achievement of the Convention's objectives. Practices vary according to individual States parties' constitutional, political, social, and economic order and the Committee is receptive to diverse approaches. In general, it welcomes 'various measures in the areas of law, policy and institutions aimed at the advancement of women to a position of equality with men'[124] and expresses concern where there are no such measures.[125]

Some steps on which the Committee has commended States include the adoption of equal opportunity laws; the establishment of institutions within local, regional, and federal governments for advising on matters of concern to women, or 'coordinating, supporting, monitoring and advocating for women's equality';[126] the setting up of appropriate offices such as an equality ombudsperson,[127] gender focal points,[128] Women Liaison

---

[119] GR 21 para 50. This obligation is said to be required by arts 2, 3, and 24.

[120] Z Ilic and I Corti, *UNITAR Manual on Human Rights Reporting*, UN Doc HR/PUB/91/1 (1991).

[121] GR 6 does not refer to art 3 or 24.

[122] eg CO Bolivarian Republic of Venezuela, CEDAW/C/VEN/CO/6 (2006) para 6 (welcoming efforts at strengthening the national machinery for the advancement of women).

[123] S Cusak and RJ Cook, 'Combating Discrimination Based on Sex and Gender' in C Krause and M Scheinin (eds), *International Protection of Human Rights: A Textbook* (2009) 205, 208.

[124] eg CO Bolivarian Republic of Venezuela, CEDAW/C/VEN/CO/6 (2006) para 7.

[125] eg CO Italy, A/60/38, 32nd session (2005) para 318.

[126] eg CO Indonesia, CEDAW/C/IDN/CO/5 (2007) para 14.

[127] CO Japan, UN Doc A/49/38, 13th Session (1994) art 3, para 563.

[128] eg CO Malaysia, CEDAW/C/MYS/CO/2 (2006) para 5.

Officers (especially within rural areas),[129] regional desk offices;[130] the development and adoption of a national gender policy,[131] strategy,[132] or plan of action,[133] in particular, in accordance with the Beijing Declaration and Platform for Action.[134] Instead of forming a government department (or unit within a department) or statutory body a State party may designate an NGO as the predominant institution for the advancement of women. While appreciating that the body in question may have significant expertise and advocacy skills the Committee has expressed some caution about this approach, apprehending that non-governmental status may constrain its 'authority and influence' within the national hierarchy and undermine the government's accountability for Convention implementation.[135]

The Committee has not been satisfied with reports that simply itemize or describe the machinery for the advancement of women without providing details of their mandate,[136] operation, allocation of responsibility for performance, or means of evaluation.[137] Members have sought quantitative and qualitative assessment of national policies for the coordination of policies dealing with women and questioned States parties on weaknesses.[138] They have also asked about responsibility for financing at the national, regional, and provincial levels, including with respect to women's centres.[139] Where equality laws have been introduced the Committee has queried how often women have availed themselves of their protections and with what results.[140]

A particular area of concern relates to inadequate human, legal, and material resources[141] to support institutions relied upon by States parties for securing women's advancement and gender equality. The Committee has expressed its concern where national machinery may have insufficient decision-making power or financial and human resources[142] and has sought clarification about the appropriateness of the level of funding.[143] It has recommended that sufficient funds be allocated in the State party budget to ensure that the relevant mechanism has the 'power and authority to carry out its work'.[144] It has also asked about gender responsive budgeting[145] and auditing and has commended their institution.[146]

---

[129] CO Samoa, A/60/38, 32nd Session (2005) para 41.

[130] eg CO Sierra Leone, CEDAW/C/SLE/Q/5 (2007) art 3, para 8 (questioning about government plans to deploy regional desk officers outside of Freetown).

[131] eg CO Bolivarian Republic of Venezuela, CEDAW/C/VEN/CO/6 (2006) para 17; CO Nigeria, CEDAW/C/NGA/CO/6 (2008) para 9.

[132] eg CO Ireland, A/60/38, 33rd Session (2005) para 385.

[133] eg question to DPR Korea, CEDAW/PSWG/2005/II/CRP.1/Add.3 (2005) art 3, para 5.

[134] The Committee regularly refers to the Beijing Platform, eg CO New Zealand, CEDAW/C/NZL/CO/6 (2006) para 6.

[135] CO Eritrea, CEDAW/C/ERI/CO/3 (2006) para 12.

[136] eg CO Benin, CEDAW/PSWG/2005/II/CRP.1/Add.1 (2005) art 3, para 7.

[137] eg CO Guatemala, A/57/38, Exceptional Session (2002) para 180.

[138] eg General Observations Russian Federation, UN Doc A/50/38 (Supp) 14th Session (1995) para 503.

[139] eg General Observations, The Netherlands, UN Doc A/49/38 (Supp) 13th Session (1994) para 265.

[140] eg CO St Lucia, CEDAW/C/LCA/Q/6, (2006) art 3, para 5; CO Pakistan, CEDAW/C/PAK/Q/3 (2007) art 3, para 6.

[141] eg CO Lithuania, CEDAW/C/LTU/CO/4 (2008) para 72.

[142] eg CO Peru, CEDAW/C/PER/CO/6 (2007) para 14.

[143] eg question to the FYROM, 34th Session CEDAW/C/MKD/Q/1–3 (2005) art 3, para 3.

[144] eg CO Lithuania, CEDAW/C/LTU/CO/4 (2008) para 73.

[145] eg question to Mauritius, CEDAW/C/MAR/Q/5 (2006) para 5.

[146] eg CO Denmark, CEDAW/C/DEN/CO/6 (2006) para 5.

The Committee has also made recommendations relating to the status, visibility, and workload of those responsible for the advancement of women within national governments. It seeks to ensure that such tasks are assigned the appropriate priority and weight.[147]

The Committee has particularly commended the use of gender mainstreaming[148] of policies at all levels as a tool for securing women's equality, encouraged its introduction, and recommended training in gender mainstreaming and sensitivity. It has commended gender mainstreaming in development strategies,[149] including development aid[150] and cooperation.[151] It does not, however, unreservedly accept gender mainstreaming as satisfactory and has expressed concern about its effective implementation and impact.[152] One concern is that the relevant body responsible for implementing gender mainstreaming may lack the requisite visibility, decision-making power, or human and financial resources to be able to 'effectively promote the advancement of women and gender equality across all branches and sectors of Government and at the national and local levels'.[153]

A related concern is that mainstreaming women's issues into a non-specialist government department or unit may dilute their significance and diminish attention to 'the issue of discrimination against women, including its quantitative predominance and its qualitative cross-cutting nature'.[154] An overall integrated approach to gender mainstreaming, including into business, politics, and administration, is essential and the Committee has appreciated processes that seek to achieve this.[155] Gender impact studies at the highest political levels[156] are required to determine any differential impact of existing policies, practices, and laws on women and men, as well as before the adoption of all potential new measures.[157] Lack of coordination among government bodies tasked with the oversight of gender issues and a failure to allocate responsibility for performance may compromise gender mainstreaming activities.[158] The Committee has sought specific information on the impact of gender mainstreaming[159] and recommended that States parties implement measures for assessment.[160]

The Committee has also focused on the importance of women's participation in developing policies and practices for achieving gender equality. General Recommendation 25 paragraph 34 states in the context of temporary special measures that women in general,

---

[147] eg ibid (concern that the Gender Equality Division had only four employees and that the work of the gender focal points was in addition to their regular tasks).

[148] eg CO Indonesia, CEDAW/C/IDN/CO/5 (2007) para 5; CO Estonia, A/57/38, 26th Session (2002) para 91.

[149] eg question to Lao People's Democratic Republic, CEDAW/PSWG/2005/I/CRP.1/Add.5 (2005) art 3, para 4.

[150] CO Ireland, A/60/38, 33rd Session (2005) para 377.

[151] eg CO Germany, A/59/38, 30th Session (2004) para 382.

[152] See generally H Charlesworth, 'Not Waving But Drowning: Gender Mainstreaming and Human Rights in the United Nations' (2005) 18 *Harvard Human Rights J* 1–18; S Kouvo, 'The United Nations and Gender Mainstreaming: Limits and Possibilities' in D Buss and A Manji (eds), *International Law: Modern Feminist Approaches* (2005) 237–52.

[153] CO Indonesia, CEDAW/C/IDN/CO/5 (2007) para 14.

[154] CO Lithuania, CEDAW/C/LTU/CO/4 (2008) para 72.

[155] eg CO Germany, A/59/38, 30th Session (2004) para 378.

[156] eg CO New Zealand, CEDAW/C/NZL/CO/6 (2006) para 15; CO Czech Republic, CEDAW/C/CZE/CO/3 (2006) para 12.

[157] eg CO China, CEDAW/C/CHN/CO/6 (2006) para 16.

[158] eg CO Trinidad and Tobago, A/57/38, 26th Session (2002) para 143.

[159] eg CO Iceland, A/57/38, 26th Session (2002) para 254.

[160] eg CO Mauritania, CEDAW/C/MRT/CO/1 (2007) para 24.

and affected groups of women in particular, should be able to participate in the design, implementation, and evaluation of national machinery and policies. This principle must have general application.

2. *Obligation to Protect*

The obligation to protect includes the State party's duty to exercise due diligence in ensuring that women's advancement and development is not impeded by non-State actors, including the economic policies of private enterprises.[161] It has recommended the formulation and implementation of codes of ethics and action programmes for multinational corporations, especially those operating in export processing zones.[162] The Committee drew upon Article 3 (and Articles 1, 2, 5, 6, and 15) in explaining Mexico's accountability for failure to exercise due diligence in its inquiry into multiple deaths of women in Ciudad Juárez[163] and in two individual communications brought under the Optional Protocol to the Convention.[164] In *Şahide Goekce v Austria*[165], the authors complained of violations of Articles 1, 2, 3, and 5 with respect to the killing of Şahide Goekce by her husband because the State party had not actively taken all appropriate measures to protect her right to personal security and life. The Committee concluded that Austria had violated its obligations under Articles 2 and 3 of the Convention, read in conjunction with Article 1 and General Recommendation 19.[166] The reasoning and conclusions in the companion case of *Fatma Yildirim v Austria*[167] are similar.[168]

In neither case did the Committee explicate on what particular obligation under Article 3 had been violated, or on what language of the article it was basing its conclusion. However, the facts in each instance (as well those determined by the inquiry into deaths and disappearances of women in Ciudad Juárez, Mexico) demonstrate the failure by State authorities to secure the victims' protection from third parties and their advancement, development, or full enjoyment of their human rights, as required by Article 3. The rights to life and physical integrity are not spelled out in the Convention but are incorporated into it through Article 3 and General Recommendation 19. More explicitly, the obligation to exercise due diligence with respect to the advancement of women requires States parties to ensure equal access to justice,[169] including accessible legal aid and advice, and procedures for dealing with complaints of gender-based discrimination.[170]

---

[161] E Evatt, 'Private Global Enterprises, International Trade and Finance' in Schöpp-Schilling and Flinterman (eds) (n 81 above) 106.

[162] CEDAW, 'Working Paper on the World Summit on Sustainable Development' (n 8 above) para 6(g).

[163] 'Report on Mexico produced by the Committee on the Elimination of Discrimination against Women under art 8 of the Optional Protocol to the Convention, and reply from the Government of Mexico', CEDAW/C/2005/OP.8/MEXICO para 50.

[164] Art 3 was not mentioned in earlier individual communications: *Ms AT v Hungary* CEDAW Communication No 2/2003 (2005), CEDAW/C/32/D/2003 or *Ms AS v Hungary* CEDAW Communication No 4/2004 (2006), CEDAW/C/36/D/4/2004. *Ms NSF v the UK* CEDAW Communication No 10/2005, did not invoke any Convention article but the Committee remarked that the asylum claim appeared 'to raise issues under arts 2 and 3 of the Convention'. The Communication was found inadmissible for failure to exhaust domestic remedies.

[165] Communication No 5/2005 (6 August 2007) CEDAW/C/39/D/5/2005.   [166] Ibid para 12.1.6.

[167] Communication No 6/2005 (1 October 2007) CEDAW/C/39/D/6/2005.

[168] Ibid paras 3.1 and 12.1.6. See also discussion in ch on violence against women below.

[169] eg questions to Gambia, CEDAW/PSWG/2005/II/CRP.1/Add.4, 33rd Session (2005) art 3, para 3.

[170] Question to DPR Korea, CEDAW/PSWG/2005/II/CRP.1/Add.3, 33rd Session (2005) art 3, para 6.

3. *Obligation to Promote and Fulfil*

The obligation to promote and fulfil imposes an ongoing and dynamic obligation to adopt and apply the measures needed to secure women's advancement. Many of the measures commended by the Committee and described under the obligation to respect are also long-term measures directed towards fulfilling States' parties' obligations under Article 3. However, 'long-term' does not denote delay or deferral of positive action, nor is compliance with Article 3 to be withheld until 'circumstances so warrant'.[171] States are obliged to determine a timetable for the achievement of equality between women and men[172] and, if necessary, to speed up the proposed strategy for women's advancement.[173]

Education and training for all women in economic empowerment, including those in remote areas,[174] are important measures for their advancement as is recognized by Article 10. The experts have questioned States parties about women's access to education under Article 3.[175]

Promotion of the Convention and of the Committee's concluding observations to States parties must be ensured through their wide dissemination in an accessible form to women throughout the country (especially to rural areas or to women who face added disadvantage). This is essential to facilitate women's advocacy and lobbying at the national level and thus is another key element in fulfilment of the State party's obligations.

The Committee has repeatedly emphasized the importance of setting benchmarks and measurable indicators, and collecting appropriate and accurate gender-disaggregated statistics[176] developed over time. Without such a database it is impossible to analyze trends, and thus to determine level of progress in the practical realization of women's *de facto* equality and advancement.[177] Lack of consistent statistical data 'may also constitute an impediment to the State party itself in designing and implementing targeted policies and programmes'.[178] Statistics should be disaggregated not only by sex, but by other categories of disadvantage and exclusion, such as caste, minority status, ethnicity,[179] urban and rural locations.[180]

The role of women's NGOs in achieving the objectives of Article 3 is not expressly referred to in the Convention. Nevertheless, the Committee has noted their beneficial work[181] and recommended that States parties collaborate and consult with civil society 'representing various groups of women',[182] including inviting their contribution to legislative processes[183] and to preparation of States parties' reports.[184] It has asked about

---

[171] This phrase from the Philippines' draft was removed during drafting; Rehof (n 3 above) 63.

[172] eg CO Romania, CEDAW/C/2000/II/CRP.3/Add.7 (2000) para 300; CO Cook Islands, CEDAW/C/COK/CO/1 (2007) para 13.

[173] eg CO Ireland, A/60/38, 33rd Session (2005) para 385.

[174] CO Cook Islands, CEDAW/C/COK/CO/1 (2007) para 27.

[175] General Observations Japan, A/49/38 (Supp) 13th Session (1994) art 3, para 561. See also discussion in ch on art 10.

[176] GR 9 does not refer to art 3, although the Committee has done so elsewhere in relation to statistics.

[177] eg CO China CEDAW/C/CHN/CO/6 (2006) para 16.

[178] CO Peru, CEDAW/C/PER/CO/6 (2007) para 10.

[179] CO India, CEDAW/C/IND/CO/3 (2007) para 15.

[180] CO Peru, CEDAW/C/PER/CO/6, (2007) para 11.

[181] eg CO Uzbekistan, CEDAW/C/UZB/CO/3 (2006) para 17.

[182] GR 25 para 34; question to Cambodia, CEDAW/C/KHM/Q/1–3 (2005) art 3, para 8.

[183] CO Nigeria, CEDAW/C/NGA/CO/6 (2008) para 7.

[184] eg CO Malaysia, CEDAW/C/MYS/CO/2 (2006) para 32.

registration processes for NGOs[185] and expressed concern about the lack of an enabling environment,[186] or any threats to the effective operation of women's NGOs.[187]

The Committee recognizes that fulfilling the objectives of Article 3 (and thus implementation of the Convention) is not easy and requires technical expertise and financial resources. It recommends to States that they avail themselves of the assistance available within the international community, including international donors and UN agencies such as the UNDP,[188] in accordance with the Beijing Platform for Action and the Outcome Document of the 23rd special session of the General Assembly.[189]

F. Conclusions

The language of Article 3 is imprecise but has considerable potential for progressive interpretation that supports women's advancement and full development. While it has not been explicitly used by the Committee on many occasions as the basis for imposing freestanding obligations (with the exception of General Recommendation 18) it has been relied upon (in conjunction with other articles of the Convention) as the basis for asserting States parties' obligations with respect to violence against women, removing reservations, and establishing effective national processes for the achievement of the Convention's objectives. Its open-ended wording confers a residual capacity allowing for the inclusion of matters which do not come within the express wording of other articles. The Committee has not been consistent in placing certain issues as obligations under particular articles. Sometimes it has used the heading 'Article 3' but it also uses thematic headings such as 'institutional framework' or 'national machinery', thereby raising issues of Article 3 as well as of other articles (notably Articles 2 and 24). The choice of headings does not seem to correlate with whether the State has used the Convention's structure in its report.

The main issues the Committee mentions under the heading of Article 3 are the following:

- Collection of gender disaggregated data.
- 'National machinery' for advancement of women: many questions relate to the resources, mandate, 'authority', and impact of the institutions set up (or missing) for achieving gender equality.
- National plans and policies for implementing the Convention and monitoring the impact of the policies, including in accordance with the requirements of the Beijing Platform for Action, the Beijing + 5 Outcome Document, and the MDGs.
- Investigating impediments to women's advancement.
- Gender mainstreaming of policies, including development policies.
- Monitoring gender impact of development strategies.
- The role of civil society, including women's NGOs and identity-based minority groups, in the formation of legislative and development strategy.

---

[185] eg question to Turkmenistan, CEDAW/C/TKM/Q/2 (2006) art 3, para 9.

[186] eg CO Belarus, A/59/38, 30th Session (2004) paras 343–4.

[187] eg CO Uzbekistan, CEDAW/C/UZB/CO/3 (2006) para 17.

[188] eg CO Cook Islands, CEDAW/C/COK/CO/1, (2007) para 17; question to Syria, 38th Session CEDAW/C/SYR/Q/1, (2006) art 3, para 9.

[189] eg CO Eritrea, CEDAW/C/ERI/CO/3 (2006) para 32.

- The place and role of women's NGOs more generally, including whether they were involved in the reporting process.
- Equal access to justice and redress.
- Measures taken to publicize the Convention.
- Gender impact of structural adjustment and macroeconomic policies; women and poverty.
- Financial resources devoted to advancement of women both within designated institutions and outside of the particular designated ministry.

Since the adoption of the Convention other hard and soft international law instruments have pushed boundaries and expanded women's human rights across many fields. These have emanated from multiple bodies, for example, the UNSC (resolutions 1325 (2000) 1820 (2008); 1888 (2009) and 1889 (2009; 1960 (2010)); the UNGA (the outcome document of the twenty-third special session of the UNGA, the MDGs); UN agencies; the outcome documents of global conferences (for example, the World Conference on Human Rights, the Conference on Population and Development, the Fourth World Conference on Women and their follow-up processes). Many of these documents reinforce the Convention and refer to States parties' obligations under it. The open-ended language of Article 3 coupled with its essential purpose—'to ensure the full development and advancement of women'—allows a progressive and dynamic interpretation and a holistic approach to women's human rights.

Article 4

1. Adoption by States Parties of temporary special measures aimed at accelerating de facto equality between men and women shall not be considered discrimination as defined in the present Convention, but shall in no way entail as a consequence the maintenance of unequal or separate standards; these measures shall be discontinued when the objectives of equality of opportunity and treatment have been achieved.

2. Adoption by States Parties of special measures, including those measures contained in the present Convention, aimed at protecting maternity shall not be considered discriminatory.

* I would like to thank my chief research assistant Revital Tordjman and also research assistants Belle Spivak and Julie Asila for their excellent and indispensable research assistance on this chapter and the chapter on art 11.

A. Introduction[1]

I. Background

Article 4, in both its paragraphs, introduces the concept of special measures into the Convention, in the first paragraph temporary special measures (TSMs) to accelerate *de facto* equality for women and, in the second, special measures to protect maternity, which are not of a temporary nature.[2] The 'special measures' referred to in the two sections serve divergent purposes and differ in their conceptual basis. Article 4(1) TSMs are promotional measures of assistance, compensation, and correction to ensure women equal opportunities in all fields of life. Article 4(2) focuses on the specific issue of maternity, legitimizing protective measures for women's needs associated with maternity.

In its entirety, encompassing special measures to promote *de facto* equality and to protect maternity, Article 4 addresses the need to protect women's right to equality and an obligation to guarantee their capabilities. The capabilities approach recognizes the need to guarantee those functions particularly crucial to women as dignified free beings who shape their own lives in cooperation and reciprocity with others. Central capabilities include the right to hold property or seek employment on an equal basis with others; to participate effectively in political choices; to move freely from place to place; to have one's bodily boundaries treated as sovereign; to be secure against sexual abuse; to have the social bases of self-respect and non-humiliation; and to be treated as a dignified being whose worth is equal to that of others.[3]

Not all measures directed to improving the situation of women are either TSMs or measures for protection of maternity. In addition to the special measures required by Article 4 and distinct from them, States parties are obliged to take permanent measures which ensure the full development and advancement of women and will guarantee women's equality and human dignity, such as those called for in Article 3. The Committee has drawn attention to this distinction:

> States parties should clearly distinguish between temporary special measures taken under article 4, paragraph 1, to accelerate the achievement of a concrete goal for women of de facto or substantive equality, and other general social policies adopted to improve the situation of women and the girl child. Not all measures that potentially are, or will be, favourable to women are temporary special measures. The provision of general conditions in order to guarantee the civil, political, economic, social and cultural rights of women and the girl child, designed to ensure for them a life of dignity and non-discrimination, cannot be called temporary special measures.[4]

Article 4 addresses both of the major barriers to women's *de facto* equality. First, achievement of *de facto* equality for women is constrained by gender stereotyping and ongoing discriminatory practices. Second, women's participation in social, political,

---

[1] I am writing this chapter in homage to Hanna Beate Schöpp-Schilling, who chaired the drafting committee for General Comment 25, in which I participated. She was a remarkable exponent of a clear view of women's right to substantive equality and a wonderful friend. Her unexpected death sadly prevented her from giving us the commentary on Article 4, which she had initially undertaken to write. I can only hope that I have done justice to her vision.

[2] HB Schöpp-Schilling, 'Reflections on a General Recommendation on Article 4(1) of the Convention on the Elimination of All Forms of Discrimination Against Women' in I Boerefijn, F Coomans, J Goldschmidt, R Holtmaat, and R Wolleswinkel (eds), *Temporary Special Measures: Accelerating de facto Equality of Women under Article 4(1) UN Convention on the Elimination of All Forms of Discrimination against Women* (2003) 18.

[3] MC Nussbaum, *Sex and Social Justice* (1999) 39,105.   [4] GR 25 para 19.

and economic fields is hampered by failure to integrate women's reproductive role into social and economic structures. These result in a wide gap between the right to equality and its translation into living law and social practice. Article 4 provides the tools to close this gap.

Article 4(1) provides for TSMs as promotional measures to ensure women equal opportunities in all fields of life. Article 4(1) adds an additional conceptual tool to the definition and guarantees of *de facto* equality, already provided in Articles 1, 2, 3, and 5, by recognizing the need to accelerate the process of achieving *de facto* equality between men and women. The word 'accelerate' was at the time of its adoption[5] unique to the Convention; it was not used in either the ILO Conventions or in ICERD. No prejudice has left a deeper imprint on social expectations and behaviour than that which has resulted from socialization to gender roles. Article 4(1) in mandating an obligation to accelerate the implementation of women's right to *de facto* equality grants recognition to the intransigence and persistence of cultural and institutional barriers to women's equality and to the urgency of eliminating them.

Article 4(1) promotional measures, similar to affirmative action or positive action measures in national jurisdictions, are among the most controversial provisions in the Convention. They are debated in political and academic circles, as noted by the UNCHR Sub-Commission's Special Rapporteur on the concept and practice of affirmative action:

Affirmative preference is the most controversial form of affirmative action.... Discrimination takes place through the rationing of social goods and this will mean that some members of other groups will no longer be considered for these social goods which are now only in limited supply.[6]

In the context of the Convention, promotional measures constitute an integral aspect of *de facto* equality for women. Article 4(1) makes it clear that TSMs are a legitimate and necessary strategy for the achievement of *de facto* equality. Furthermore, the Committee's interpretation and application of Article 4(1), in both its concluding observations and its general recommendations, provide a convincing response to the theoretical problems raised by the Special Rapporteur.

Article 4(2) special measures are directed to guaranteeing proper conditions for maternity and to facilitating integration of that role with women's full participation in all aspects of civil, social, and economic life. Maternity, insofar as it concerns the childbearing functions of pregnancy, childbirth, and breast-feeding, represents a biological difference, which requires permanent special measures for women.

It is not clear whether the recognition accorded to special measures for protection of 'maternity' extends only to childbearing or also to childrearing. While childbearing is biologically determined, attribution of childrearing as a woman's role is a gender construct. There is variation between different articles of the Convention regarding the conceptual category of maternity. In Article 5(b), maternity is regarded as a 'social function', while the upbringing and development of children is the common responsibility of men and women.[7] Article 11(2) prohibits discrimination on grounds of 'marriage or maternity',

---

[5] It was later adopted in the Convention on the Rights of Persons with Disabilities.

[6] UNCHR (Sub-Commission), 'Comprehensive Examination of Thematic Issues Relating to Racial Discrimination, Preliminary report submitted by Mr Marc Bossuyt, Special Rapporteur, in accordance with Sub-Commission resolution 1998/5' (2000) UN Doc E/CN.4/Sub.2/2000/11 paras 38 and 78.

[7] See the discussion in ch on art 5.

apparently relating to the role of childrearing as well as the biological role of reproduction; however, Article 11(2)(b), which requires support for social services to enable parents to combine family obligations with work responsibilities and participation in public life, refers to parents and not mothers. Article 16(1)(d) and (f) underscore the premise that parenting is a shared responsibility.

The Convention clearly visualizes the elimination of stereotyped roles for men and women. However, the transition from the traditional patriarchal family, in which women are solely responsible for child care, to the egalitarian family in which all roles are shared, in a gender-neutral fashion, is far from fully implemented in the social realities of States parties. In the interim, in traditionalist family contexts, special protective measures for mothers regarding not only childbearing but also childrearing may be necessary.

II. Conceptual Framework of Article 4

1. *Special Measures are Integral to De Facto Equality*

Both paragraphs of Article 4 introduce special measures as a means to realize *de facto* as well as substantive equality for women.[8] As such, these special measures are inherent in the concept of equality under the Convention and not an exception to it: Article 4(1) 'TSMs *aimed at accelerating de facto equality*' is by self-definition, one of the means to realize *de facto* equality. Article 4(2) 'special measures... *aimed at protecting maternity*' is also inherent in *de facto* equality and not an exception to it. The need to give differential treatment to those who are differently situated, in proportion to their unlikeness, is an integral part of the concept of equality.

The Committee affirmed, in General Recommendation 25, regarding Article 4(1), that special measures constitute an inherent part of the concept of equality:

The Committee views the application of these measures not as an exception to the norm of non-discrimination, but rather as an emphasis that temporary special measures are part of a necessary strategy by States parties directed towards the achievement of de facto or substantive equality of women with men in the enjoyment of their human rights and fundamental freedoms.[9]

The Committee's approach contrasts with that of the Special Rapporteur, who adopted the view that affirmative action is an exception to the principle of non-discrimination.[10] Various regional instruments and the States parties' legal systems offer varying approaches to the issue of whether affirmative or positive action is an integral part of equality or an exception to the principle of non-discrimination.[11] One scholar effectively sums up the problem of characterizing TSMs as an exception:

Positioning affirmative action as an exception to anti-discrimination law means that affirmative action measures are in principle 'suspect' of being discriminatory and need special justification.

---

[8] See the discussion in ch on art 1.

[9] GR 25 para 18; See analogously CERD, 'General Recommendation 32' (2009) UN Doc CERD/C/GC/32 para 20.

[10] UNCHR (Sub-Commission), 'Prevention of Discrimination, The Concept and Practice of Affirmative Action, Final report submitted by Mr Marc Bossuyt, Special Rapporteur, in accordance with Sub-Commission resolution 1998/5' (2002) UN Doc E/CN.4/Sub.2/2002/21 para 113; See also B Hepple, M Coussey, and T Choudhury, *Equality: A New Framework: Report of the Independent Review of the Enforcement of UK Anti-discrimination Legislation* (2000).

[11] J Swiebel, 'What Could the European Union Learn From the CEDAW Convention?' in Boerefijn et al (eds) (n 2 above) 51, 52–61.

This, in turn, means accepting that the current social rules, which tend to exclude the targeted groups, are not suspect of being discriminatory and are accepted as generally fair. The gendered character of those rules is ignored.[12]

The wording of Article 4(1), and the Committee's interpretation of it, indicate clearly that States parties are obligated under Article 4(1) to adopt the inclusive view of TSMs as an integral element of *de facto* equality and not as an exception to non-discrimination principles.[13]

Analogously, Article 4(2) protective special measures for maternity should be considered an integral aspect of equality, in interpretation of the same language: 'shall not be considered discriminatory.' Article 4(2) special measures are, like TSMs, essential to achieve *de facto* equality.

2. *Protecting Maternity is Integral to Development and Sustainability*

Special protective measures for maternity are not only necessary to secure *de facto* equality for women, they are also essential for economic development and sustainability. Maternity protection is vital to achieve goals of development and sustainability: optimal use of human capital resources, including the human capital of women; avoidance of female and child poverty, which are aggravated by the absence of proper social and economic support for maternity; and planning to ensure conditions for the growth of the next generation, which is essential to long-term social and economic development.

3. *'Special'*

Both paragraphs of Article 4 employ the term 'special' measures. The term 'special', used in both paragraphs, as in ICERD, expresses States parties' commitment to provide means to enable women to participate and compete in society on an equal basis with men.

General Recommendation 25 explains the use of the word 'special' in Article 4(1):

> The term 'special', though being in conformity with human rights discourse, also needs to be carefully explained. Its use sometimes casts women and other groups who are subject to discrimination as weak, vulnerable and in need of extra or 'special' measures in order to participate or compete in society. However, the real meaning of 'special' in the formulation of article 4, paragraph 1, is that the measures are designed to serve a specific goal.[14]

The use of special measures does not suggest charity but rather entitlement. The goal for which Article 4(1) TSMs are employed is the achievement of *de facto* equal opportunity for women. In Article 4(2), the concept of 'protecting' maternity is a recognition of women's entitlement to conditions which facilitate 'maternity as a social function'.[15] Special measures are essential to secure equal opportunity in participation and competition in various fields of social life, where social, health, and economic burdens may be placed on women as a result of gender stereotypes or of their role in maternity.

---

[12] C Bacchi, 'The Practice of Affirmative Action Policies: Explaining Resistances and How These Affect Results' in Boerefijn et al (eds) (n 2 above) 75, 79.

[13] S Fredman, 'Beyond the Dichotomy of Formal and Substantive Equality: Towards a New Definition of Equal Rights' in Boerefijn et al (eds) (n 2 above) 111, 117.

[14] GR 25 para 21. [15] Art 5.

4. *Mandatory Nature*

The obligation to adopt TSMs can be understood from the object and purpose of the Convention and, more particularly, from the obligation to adopt all appropriate measures to ensure the practical realization of the principle of equality and the effective protection of women from discrimination.[16] TSMs are mandatory in various circumstances because they constitute the most appropriate means to accelerate *de facto* equality for women under Articles 6 to 16.

Article 4(1) provides that special measures shall not be considered discriminatory, thus not expressly indicating that TSMs are mandatory, and the view has been expressed that they are merely permissive.[17] However, in General Recommendation 25, para 24, the Committee clarifies the obligatory nature of TSMs:

[T]he Committee considers that States parties are obliged to adopt and implement temporary special measures in relation to any of these articles if such measures can be shown to be necessary and appropriate in order to accelerate the achievement of the overall, or a specific goal of, women's de facto or substantive equality.

Analogously, Article 4(2) is mandatory, as it too is expressly linked to other articles of the Convention that impose an obligation on States parties to adopt appropriate maternity protection measures.

5. *Financing of Special Measures*

Special measures may require financial support. Special measures for maternity in particular require financial support. Maternal health care, additional nutrition, and absences from the workplace for requirements of maternity, such as fertility treatments, pregnancy, birth, post-natal recovery, and breast-feeding, all create costs. The potential cost-bearers may be public (the state or national insurance) or private—either the woman and her family or the private employer or private insurer.

The Committee has noted that allocating the cost to private concerns acts as a disincentive to take on women of childbearing age as employees and that government failure to deal with maternity as a social function places women at a 'structural disadvantage...with regard to their employment rights'.[18] Analogously, the principle seems to be that costs for all special measures, including TSMs, should preferably be borne by the State rather than private concerns.

---

[16] R Cook, 'Obligations to Adopt Temporary Special Measures Under the Convention on the Elimination of All Forms of Discrimination Against Women' in Boerefijn et al (eds) (n 2 above) 119, 129–31; Schöpp-Schilling (n 2 above); UNCHR, M Bossuyt (n 6 above) para 38; E Vogel-Polsky, *Positive Action and the Constitutional and Legislative Hindrances to its Implementation in the Member States of the Council of Europe* (1989) 13. The CERD Committee, addressing the issue of promotional and protective special measures under CERD, also affirmed their mandatory nature. However, the Committee relied on direct language in CERD art 2(2) to the effect that States parties shall, when circumstances so warrant, take 'special and concrete measures', CERD 'General Recommendation 32' (2009) UN Doc CERD/C/GC/32 paras 30 and 32.

[17] UNCHR (Sub-Commission), 'Comprehensive Examination of Thematic Issues Relating to Racial Discrimination, Preliminary report submitted by Mr Marc Bossuyt, Special Rapporteur, in accordance with Sub-Commission resolution 1998/5 (2000) UN Doc E/CN.4/Sub.2/2000/11; *EFTA Surveillance Authority v The Kingdom of Norway* (Case E-1/02) (24 January 2003) para 58; the EFTA Court said that art 4(1), like all provisions of international conventions dealing with affirmative action, is 'clearly permissive rather than mandatory'.

[18] CO Jordan, A/55/38, 22nd Session (2000) para 185; CO New Zealand, A/53/38/Rev.1, 19th Session (1998) para 269.

6. *Time Scale*

The Committee has carefully elaborated the rationale for differing time scales for application of special measures:

The purpose of article 4, paragraph 1, is to accelerate the improvement of the position of women to achieve their de facto or substantive equality with men, and to effect the structural, social and cultural changes necessary to correct past and current forms and effects of discrimination against women, as well as to provide them with compensation. These measures are of a temporary nature.[19]

Article 4, paragraph 2, provides for non-identical treatment of women and men due to their biological differences. These measures are of a permanent nature, at least until such time as the scientific and technological knowledge referred to in article 11, paragraph 3, would warrant a review.[20]

III. Comparison to Corresponding Articles in Other Human Rights Instruments

The concept of special measures was first introduced in ILO Convention No 111, which provided that special measures designed to meet the particular requirements of 'persons who, for reasons such as sex, age, disablement, family responsibilities or social or cultural status, are generally recognised to require special protection or assistance', shall not be deemed to be discrimination.[21] ICERD provides that special measures 'shall not be deemed racial discrimination' and States parties 'shall, when the circumstances so warrant... take special measures'.[22] The 1975 ILO Declaration on Equality of Opportunity and Treatment for Women Workers stated that positive special treatment during a transitional period to promote effective equality between the sexes shall not be regarded as discriminatory.[23] UNESCO decided in 1979, that until 'full equality' of education and training opportunities was assured, special programmes for girls and women were needed to eliminate the gap.[24]

Article 4 expands the special measures provided for women beyond those under other international instruments. It requires promotional measures to accelerate *de facto* equality for the full range of social contexts in which women live their lives. It also provides widely defined protective measures for maternity.[25] A comparative study of affirmative action for women under European Community and international law concludes that 'the most significant binding international norm on affirmative action for women is Article 4(1) of CEDAW'.[26]

---

[19] GR 25 para 15.   [20] Ibid para 16.

[21] Discrimination (Employment and Occupation) Convention art 5.   [22] ICERD art 1.

[23] International Labour Conference (60th Session): Declaration on Equality of Opportunity and Treatment for Women Workers (25 June 1975).

[24] UNESCO (1979) UN Doc E/CN.6/632.

[25] Protection for maternity in other Conventions will be discussed below under art 4(2).

[26] A Peters, *Women, Quotas, and Constitutions: A Comparative Study of Affirmative Action for Women under American, German, EC, and International Law* (1999) 275.

B. Travaux Préparatoires

In the early stages of the drafting, there were differing opinions regarding 'measures to achieve *de facto* equality of rights of women with men', as proposed by Russia. France and the UK opposed 'discrimination in favour of women', while Canada, Sweden, and Denmark wished to see provision for equality of the sexes. The UK observed that temporary measures should be permitted but not required to equalize opportunities for women where it is necessary to overcome historical discrimination. State representatives emphasized that unequal standards must be discontinued when objectives are reached (the US, the Netherlands, and Colombia). The Working Group adopted the final text of Article 4(1), suggested by Canada, Denmark, Kenya, the USSR, and the US.

There were also differing opinions regarding measures protecting maternity. The UK draft introduced a provision that protection of women at work due to 'their physical nature' and for 'promotion of the welfare of mothers' does not violate the principle of equality. Canada, with the support of Panama, Portugal, and Hungary, suggested changing this to 'protection of maternity'. Other States' representatives suggested deleting the paragraph (Norway) or regarded it as redundant in view of the detailed provisions of Article 11 (Portugal and France). The United States, Sweden, and the Federal Republic of Germany had reservations regarding the paragraph for various reasons, Sweden being of the opinion that measures to protect the social functions of reproduction should cover both men and women. The USSR failed to understand this, since 'maternal functions were the lot of women'. Egypt, opposed by the Philippines and the USSR, suggested restricting the protective measures to pregnancy. In the result, Article 4(2) provided that special measures protecting maternity shall not be considered discriminatory.[27]

C. Issues of Interpretation–Article 4(1)

I. Promotional Equality

Article 4(1) TSMs are promotional measures of assistance, compensation, and correction to accelerate *de facto* equality and thus ensure women equal opportunities and capabilities in all fields of life.

1. Accelerating De Facto Equality

Measures to accelerate *de facto* equality are necessary because the right to formal equality is inadequate to give women a genuinely equal start. Formal removal of barriers to women's opportunities and prohibition of discrimination are not enough to secure implementation of equality *de facto*. Enforcing the right to equality only by responding to proven cases of discrimination cannot effect systemic change and bring about equality *de facto*. Systemic discrimination requires a systemic solution:

In the Committee's view:

A purely formal legal or programmatic approach is not sufficient to achieve women's de facto equality with men, which the Committee interprets as substantive equality. In addition, the

---

[27] LA Rehof, *Guide to the Travaux Préparatoires of the United Nation Convention on the Elimination of All Forms of Discrimination against Women* (1993) 66–76.

Convention requires that women be given an equal start and that they be empowered by an enabling environment to achieve equality of results.[28]

It is the role of special measures, required under Article 4(1), to create an enabling environment which will give women an equal start and empower them to participate and compete in all fields of social, political, and economic life. Special measures are necessary to dismantle the social mechanisms and gender constructs which have disempowered women.

2. 'Special Measures'

The method for accelerating *de facto* equality is adoption of TSMs. Special measures of this kind clearly entail treating men and women differently, giving preference to women. Indeed, in General Recommendation 25, the Committee affirmed:

It is not enough to guarantee women treatment that is identical to that of men. Rather, biological as well as socially and culturally constructed differences between women and men must be taken into account. Under certain circumstances, non-identical treatment of women and men will be required in order to address such differences. Pursuit of the goal of substantive equality also calls for an effective strategy aimed at overcoming underrepresentation of women and a redistribution of resources and power between men and women.[29]

The term 'special measures' may be functionally analogous to measures taken by States parties which have been variously described as affirmative action, positive action, positive measures, or preferential treatment. Nevertheless, special measures under Article 4(1) should be regarded as having an autonomous meaning, developed in accordance with the context and principles of the Convention. Indeed, the Committee avoids the use of terms other than 'TSMs'.[30]

3. Special Measures Are Not Discriminatory

Special measures are sometimes characterized as reverse discrimination or positive discrimination and regarded as discriminatory against men. This terminology misinterprets the aim of TSMs, which is to promote *de facto* equality in the context of the Convention's asymmetrical goal of eliminating discrimination against women. The terminology of reverse discrimination also runs counter to the express provision of Article 4(1) that TSMs shall not be considered discrimination.[31]

4. Systemization of TSMs in Different Contexts

Promotional measures must be properly engineered to meet the goal of accelerating *de facto* equality.[32] The Committee indicates the kind of measures required and cautions that the type of measure must be adapted to context and to the specific goals of the measure:

The choice of a particular 'measure' will depend on the context in which article 4, paragraph 1, is applied and on the specific goal it aims to achieve.[33]

---

[28] GR 25 para 8.   [29] Ibid.   [30] Ibid para 17.
[31] CERD, 'General Recommendation 32' (2009) UN Doc CERD/C/GC/32 para 12; UNCHR (Sub-Commission), 'Prevention of Discrimination, The Concept and Practice of Affirmative Action, Final report submitted by Mr Marc Bossuyt, Special Rapporteur, in accordance with Sub-Commission resolution 1998/5' (2002) UN Doc E/CN.4/Sub.2/2002/21 para 5.
[32] See section C. II: *Issues of Policy* below.   [33] GR 25 para 22.

The European Court of Justice has ruled certain kinds of temporary special measures to be contrary to equality provisions of the European Community law,[34] and in some States certain kinds of affirmative action have been held unconstitutional.[35] However, systematizing the application of different kinds of TSMs so that they are proportionate to the circumstances can justify the impact of the measures on equality between the sexes.[36]

The Committee's directives for implementation of TSMs show awareness of the need to devise proportionate measures:

(1) The Committee has recommended TSMs for allocating resources in areas where this can correct prior discrimination and disadvantage in education and training;[37] gender studies; eradication of adult illiteracy amongst women; and public awareness programmes.[38] Corrective of systemic discrimination, such measures are proportional in their aim and impact.

(2) The Committee has systematically called for plans of action, with setting of goals and timetables, either by the State or private institutions, and for monitoring mechanisms.[39] These TSMs promote self-regulation and are thus in essence proportional.

(3) The Committee has recommended adoption of quota systems almost exclusively in the context of political representation and public appointments, only on rare occasion recommending quotas for the private sector.[40] Quota systems set a numerical target for advancement of women to positions in which they are under-represented. The quota system may require exclusive appointment of women until parity between men and women is reached or it may require a lesser percentage of women appointees. Quotas are proportional in the context of public sector discrimination, since, as the Committee states, '[f]or appointment, selection or election to public and political office, factors other than qualification and merit, including the application of the principles of democratic fairness and electoral choice, may also have to play a role'.[41] The Special Rapporteur has concurred: 'Particularly in the public sector... the determining factor is "representativity".'[42] This approach finds support in the jurisprudence of the CCPR, which found no violation of the ICCPR in the imposition of a gender requirement for appointment to a High Council of Justice.[43]

---

[34] *Katarina Abrahamsson and Leif Anderson v Elisabet Fogelqvist* (Case C-407/98) [2000] ECR I-5539; HB Schöpp-Schilling, 'Background Paper for a General Recommendation on CEDAW Article 4.1' (2001) UN Doc CEDAW/C/2002/I/WP.1 para 34.

[35] Report by the Secretariat, 'Committee's Approach to Article 4, Paragraph 1of the Convention' (2001) UN Doc CEDAW/C/2001/II/5, 13.

[36] F Raday, 'Systematizing the Application of Different Types of Temporary Special Measures Under Article 4 of CEDAW' in Boerefijn et al (eds) (n 2 above) 35, 36. There are four theories of social justice which can be used to legitimize the use of temporary special measures: distributive justice (ensuring equity in the distribution of social goods), compensatory justice (corrective measures to compensate for group discrimination), social utilitarianism (increasing the overall happiness of members of society), and liberalism (economic efficiency theory).

[37] 'Committee's Approach to Article 4, Paragraph 1 of the Convention' (n 35 above) 10–11.

[38] Ibid 12.

[39] CO Israel, A/60/38, 33rd Session (2005) para 252; CO Nepal, A/59/38, 30th Session (2004) para 215; CO Angola, A/59/38, 31st Session (2004) para 155; CO Canada, A/58/38 (Supp), 28th Session (2003) para 372.

[40] See the discussion in section C. III. *Areas of Application* below.   [41] GR 25 para 23.

[42] UNCHR (Sub-Commission), Prevention of Discrimination, The Concept and Practice of Affirmative Action, Final report submitted by Mr Marc Bossuyt, Special Rapporteur, in accordance with Sub-Commission resolution 1998/5 (2002) UN Doc E/CN.4/Sub.2/2002/21 para 104.

[43] *Guido Jacobs v Belgium* CCPR Communication No 943/2000 (2004) CCPR/C/81/D/943/2000.

(4) Unlike quotas, preferential treatment may be restricted to situations where a woman's qualifications are equal to those of the male candidate.[44] Preferential treatment where the woman has equal qualifications to those of the male merely shifts the evidentiary burden, requiring the party making the appointment to show reason justifying the choice of the male candidate to a position in which women are under-represented. Shifting the evidentiary burden helps to overcome stereotypes which would otherwise weigh in favour of the male and exclude the female.[45] This form of preferential treatment is at the core of the Article 4(1) requirement of accelerating *de facto* equality and can appropriately be applied to employment,[46] training and educational opportunity, economic activity, and credit, in the private as well as the public sphere.

5. *Temporary*

Promotional measures under Article 4(1) are expressly termed 'temporary': 'TSMs shall in no way entail as a consequence the maintenance of unequal or separate standards; these measures shall be discontinued when the objectives of equality of opportunity and treatment have been achieved'. The temporal test is thus functional.

The Committee indicates monitoring as the method for ensuring the proper time scale for special measures.[47] This would not of course invalidate other methods such as 'sunset clauses', which include predetermined dates for expiry or provide a statistical or other indicator as a benchmark for discontinuation of the special measure. However, if the special measure has not yet achieved its goal, the State party might be required to renew it in order to fulfil its Article 4(1) obligation.[48] Interpreting the ICERD requirement that special measures be discontinued after achievement of the objects for which they were taken, the High Court of Australia[49] said, '[t]he fact that it may prove necessary to continue the regime indefinitely does not involve an infringement of the proviso. What it requires is a discontinuance of the special measures after achievement of the objects for which they were taken'.

There are two contesting visions of the aims of TSMs: equality of opportunity and equality of results.[50] Equality of opportunity as a goal rests on the view that the role of anti-discrimination law is to eliminate discrimination in access to opportunity and

---

[44] AH Goldman, 'Affirmative Action' in M Cohen, T Nagel and T Scanlon (eds), *Equality and Preferential Treatment* (1977) 192; Schöpp-Schilling (n 2 above) 30.

[45] Bacchi (n 12 above) 94, argues that the term preferential treatment is a misnomer: ' "Affirmative action" is not "preferential treatment", but an acknowledgement that power and bias are at work in appointments'. In contrast, Special Rapporteur Bossuyt groups weak preferential treatment together with the strong form of preferential treatment, without distinction, as the 'most controversial form of affirmative action'; UNCHR (Sub-Commission), 'Comprehensive Examination of Thematic Issues Relating to Racial Discrimination, Preliminary report submitted by Mr Marc Bossuyt, Special Rapporteur, in accordance with Sub-Commission resolution 1998/5' (2000) UN Doc E/CN.4/Sub.2/2000/11 para 78.

[46] See ECJ, eg *Katarina Abrahamsson and Leif Anderson v Elisabet Fogelqvist* (n 34 above) para 60; *Marschall v Land Nordrhein-Westfalen* (Case C-409/95) (1997) ECR I-6363.

[47] GR 25 para 11, 'continuous monitoring of laws, programmes and practices directed at the achievement of women's *de facto* or substantive equality is needed so as to avoid a perpetuation of non-identical treatment that may no longer be warranted'.

[48] Cook (n 16 above) 127–8.

[49] *David Alan Gerhardy v Robert John Brown* [1985] HCA 11; (1985) 159 CLR 70 (Gibbs CJ) para 21, (Mason J) para 47, (Deane J) para19.

[50] UNCHR (Sub-Commission), 'Comprehensive Examination of Thematic Issues Relating to Racial Discrimination, Preliminary report submitted by Mr Marc Bossuyt, Special Rapporteur, in accordance with Sub-Commission resolution 1998/5' (2000) UN Doc E/CN.4/Sub.2/2000/11 para 31.

choices, and that equality cannot be achieved if individuals begin the race from different starting points; it reflects a vision of society that is based on respect for efficiency and individual merit and achievement.[51] Equality of results as a goal rests on the view that skills and talents are distributed uniformly and that the test of whether opportunity is equal in every sense is whether the outcomes are equal. Beate Schöpp-Schilling, noting that the goal of equality of results is controversial, nevertheless, maintained that 'substantive equality requires that results be achieved. . . . [E]quality of results is the logical corollary of substantive equality'.[52]

The Committee takes the view that:

[e]quality of results is the logical corollary of de facto or substantive equality. These results may be quantitative and/or qualitative in nature; that is, women enjoying their rights in various fields in fairly equal numbers with men, enjoying the same income levels, equality in decision-making and political influence, and women enjoying freedom from violence.[53]

II. Issues of Policy

1. Merit

Where TSMs are used to facilitate women's entry to functions which are based on a merit requirement, they are usually conditioned upon the woman's equal qualifications. Establishing quotas without a condition of equal qualifications in functions which require merit might lead to claims that individuals promoted within the quota are incompetent, or that the method perpetuates stereotypes or undermines economic efficiency.

The Committee points out that merit requirements may themselves exclude women from eligibility so careful scrutiny for gender bias in the requirements themselves is required: 'questions of qualification and merit, in particular in the area of employment in the public and private sectors, need to be reviewed carefully for gender bias as they are normatively and culturally determined'.[54] The Committee did not, however, take the view that merit is in itself an inherently gendered concept.[55]

2. Target Beneficiaries

Discrimination against women has been pervasive and affects women in every social category and context. Hence, TSMs are intended to accelerate *de facto* equality as a systemic goal and the social background of an individual female beneficiary is not relevant.

The Committee's monitoring of Article 4(1) targets women at all socio-economic levels and in all areas of social, political, and economic activity.[56] This policy counters any concern[57] that preferential treatment may be regressive in its social impact, benefiting women in the social elite rather than women who have been disadvantaged by societal discrimination.

---

[51] Ibid para 32.   [52] Schöpp-Schilling (n 2 above) 26–7.
[53] GR 25 para 9.   [54] Ibid para 23.
[55] T Rees, *Mainstreaming Equality in the European Union: Education, Training and Labour Market Policies* (1998) 39. See also Bacchi (n 12 above) 89. Both take the view that merit is itself a gendered concept.
[56] See section C. III. 2. 'Intersectionality' below.
[57] UNCHR (Sub-Commission), Comprehensive Examination of Thematic Issues Relating to Racial Discrimination, Preliminary report submitted by Mr Marc Bossuyt, Special Rapporteur, in accordance with Sub-Commission resolution 1998/5 (2000) UN Doc E/CN.4/Sub.2/2000/11 paras 11, 12, and 37.

3. Burden on Third Parties

Preferential measures are criticized as requiring innocent individuals, who have neither been responsible for past discriminatory practices nor beneficiaries of them, to make sacrifices to compensate members of target groups.[58] This is not always the case. Although in some instances an identifiable male third party may be disadvantaged, in others the cost of the measure will be distributed diffusely.[59] Where a third party is directly affected, so long as the TSM is proportionate as discussed above,[60] the express goal of accelerating *de facto* equality for women takes precedence, and the temporary setback experienced by some men is the inevitable cost of promoting equality between men and women. The CCPR has found preferential treatment in the public service to be permissible as a 'remedy' for persons who had been previously disadvantaged, despite claims that it adversely affected other employees.[61]

III. Areas of Application

1. Scope of Promotional Special Measures

The Committee states:

The term 'measures' encompasses a wide variety of legislative, executive, administrative and other regulatory instruments, policies and practices, such as outreach or support programmes; allocation and/or reallocation of resources; preferential treatment; targeted recruitment, hiring and promotion; numerical goals connected with time frames; and quota systems.[62]

This description of the measures required includes both the regulatory sources which should be employed for the purposes of introducing TSMs and also the types of TSMs which might be introduced.

The Committee has indicated the wide range of fields in which TSMs might be applied:[63] 'education and training at all levels, the economy, politics, employment, political and public life, representing Government at the international level, participating in the work of international organizations, health services, credit and loans, sports, culture and recreation, and legal awareness.'[64] These are each separately considered in the chapters on Articles 7–16. A central focus of the Committee's application of Article 4(1) has been to increase women's representation in all areas of public life, including at the decision-making level, and in law enforcement, the judiciary, and the diplomatic corps. It has called on States parties to promote the adoption of quota systems for women candidates in elections,[65] or numerical goals and timetables to increase the representation of women in decision-making positions at all levels.[66]

---

[58] Ibid para 37.
[59] Ibid para 74.   [60] See section C. I. 4 'Systemization of TSMs in Different Contexts' above.
[61] *RD Stalla Costa v Uruguay* Communication No 198/1985 (1987) A/42/40 paras 10–11.
[62] GR 25 para 22.   [63] Ibid paras 37–8.   [64] See also Schöpp-Schilling (n 2 above) 32.
[65] CO Haiti, CEDAW/C/HTI/CO/7 (2009) para 29; CO Denmark, CEDAW/C/DEN/CO/7 (2009) para 23; CO Guatemala, A/57/38, Exceptional Session (2002) paras 190–1.
[66] CO Haiti, CEDAW/C/HTI/CO/7 (2009) para 19; CO Tuvalu, CEDAW/C/TUV/CO/2 (2009) paras 26 and 36; CO Peru, CEDAW/C/PER/CO/6 (2007) para 17; CO Malta, A/59/38 (Supp), 31st Session (2004) paras 107–10; CO Canada, A/58/38 (Supp), 28th Session (2003) paras 371–2.

2. Intersectionality

Where necessary, TSMs should be directed to benefit women subjected to multiple discrimination, including rural women[67] and women belonging to ethnic minorities.[68] The Committee has called on States parties to apply TSMs to eradicate poverty and illiteracy, especially amongst rural women and Roma women.[69]

D. Issues of Interpretation–Article 4(2)

I. Maternity

Article 4(2) exempts special measures aimed at protecting maternity from the prohibition of discrimination. This provision is central to the integration of women's special needs associated with maternity in the political, economic, social, cultural, civil, or any other field.[70] The Committee has said little about Article 4(2) and did not include analysis of it in General Recommendation 25.

Maternity is to be understood as a social function, under Article 5(b). States parties shall take all appropriate measures to ensure that family education includes a proper understanding of maternity as a social function and the recognition of the common responsibility of men and women in the upbringing and development of their children. They must also, under Article 16(1)(e), take all appropriate measures to ensure, on a basis of equality of men and women, 'the same rights to decide freely and responsibly on the number and spacing of their children'. However, these goals have still to be reached in many societies. Furthermore, motherhood is not always voluntary. It may be the result of lack of access to contraception, rape, or patriarchal domination in which the woman had no choice. The Committee has pointed out the kind of pressure that may be imposed on women to be mothers:

The Committee also expresses concern about the limited autonomy that women have over decisions on the number and spacing of their children, and the limited sex education and knowledge of family planning. The Committee is also concerned about prevalent social attitudes that measure a man's masculinity by the number of children he fathers.[71]

Protection for maternity requires measures which safeguard the voluntary nature of motherhood in all cultural settings.[72]

1. Procreation—Biological Difference

Article 4(2) special measures are directed to 'protecting maternity'. Maternity in this context refers primarily to 'women's biologically determined permanent needs and experiences'[73] relating to their reproductive role: fertility treatments, pregnancy, childbirth, post-natal physiological manifestations, and breast-feeding. In order to achieve *de facto* equality, women's biological maternity needs must be met to place them on an equal

---

[67] CO Vanuatu, CEDAW/C/VUT/CO/3 (2007) para 21; CO Argentina, A/57/38, Exceptional Session (2002) paras 356–7.

[68] CO Israel, A/60/38, 33rd Session (2005) paras 251–2, 255–6, and 259–60.

[69] CO Bolivia, CEDAW/C/BOL/CO/4 (2008) para 33; CO Vanuatu, CEDAW/C/VUT/CO/3 (2007) para 31; CO Peru, CEDAW/C/PER/CO/6 (2007) para 27.

[70] See the discussion in ch on art 1.

[71] CO Guatemala, A/57/38, Exceptional Session (2002) para 194.

[72] See the discussion in chs on arts 12 and 16(1)(e).   [73] GR 25 para 11.

footing with men in combining parenthood with equal opportunity in social, economic, and political life.

The equality measures required to address biological aspects of maternity are both elimination of discrimination and special measures.[74] Even where formal equality and equal allocation of resources are achieved, they may not be enough to protect biological aspects of maternity. For instance, basing the right of absence from work for maternity leave on a comparison to sick leave is not an appropriate basis for comparison, nor does it provide proper coverage to protect women's physiological needs in pregnancy or during the post-natal or breast-feeding periods.

Identification of maternity needs as being an exception rather than the norm has been challenged by some feminist writers, who regard it as creating a 'difference dilemma' which leads to marginalization of the needs of those who are labelled different,[75] or an 'out-group'. As one scholar puts it:

the way in which some ... theorists deal with maternity confirms this tendency to see members of out-groups as the problem. In some places policies dealing with maternity are called forms of positive action and an 'exception' from anti-discrimination law. This framework of understanding leaves unchallenged the gendered character of those laws. If these were genuinely gender-neutral, women's bodies would not be constituted as exceptional.[76]

Insofar as the aims of protecting maternity can be achieved by eliminating discrimination, this critique is valid and valuable. However, where additional measures are needed to protect the biological aspects of maternity, it is difficult to see how provision can be made for women's needs as the 'in-group'. Biological maternity gives rise to needs for specific health care, specific rights in the workplace, and additional nutrition, which are not required by non-pregnant people, male or female. Women themselves do not have pregnancy or post-natal needs for most of their lives and hence measures to ensure protection of biological maternity are measures of accommodation for an exceptional state for women. In order to achieve *de facto* equality, it is legitimate and necessary to make provision for the role of women in procreation and to supply special measures as needed to address women's specific needs in this role. Though these measures are special, in that they target women—and only women in their reproductive roles—they should be dealt with as normal and indeed obligatory under Article 4(2).

2. Childrearing

Unlike procreation, parenting or childrearing is a non-biological aspect of maternity. Either parent or, indeed, a biologically unrelated carer may fill the role of childrearer. Nevertheless, childrearing has been gender-constructed as a 'natural female role'. The woman is constructed as a mother and wife, whose primary obligations are to bear children and take care of her home and family. Her paid work is accepted, if at all, as a secondary contribution to the family livelihood.[77]

---

[74] See the discussion in ch on art 12.

[75] M Minow, *Making All the Difference: Inclusion, Exclusion and American Law* (1999).

[76] Bacchi (n 12 above) 90.

[77] S Fogiel-Bijaoui, 'Familism, Post-Modernity and the State: The Case of Israel' (2002) 21 *The Journal of Israeli History* 38. See the discussion in ch on art 5.

The stereotypically imposed gendered division of labour restricts women's range of choice and limits their ability to participate in public, political, and economic life. The Committee has expressed concern where:

the responsibility of family and childcare is placed exclusively on women, particularly as the population policy encourages women to have large families. This situation encourages their marginalization in the economy and exacerbates poverty.[78]

The allocation of childrearing to women is directly related to women's exclusion from public power and their subjection to patriarchal power within the family. Attributing to them the exclusive nurturing and caring role with respect to children is not merely a matter of 'separate but equal' role division; rather, it has been central in the construction of a stereotype of woman's inferiority, subordination, and/or 'difference'.[79]

There is a danger that special protective measures for women in childrearing will perpetuate disadvantageous stereotypes regarding women's ability to participate in the marketplace and in public life. The Committee, aware of this danger, has expressed concern 'over the continuing prevalence of sex-role stereotypes and the reintroduction of such symbols as a Mothers' Day and a Mothers' Award, which are seen as encouraging women's traditional roles'[80] and at the stereotyping of women, which perceives them exclusively as care-givers and homemakers, assigning them, in education and employment, to spheres suitable to their 'characteristics'.[81]

In view of this complexity, special measures to protect childrearing functions should be available to both parents, on a gender-neutral basis. The gender-neutral designation of the parental services contributes to the transformative equality required by Article 5(b) and to recognition of the common responsibility of men and women in the upbringing and development of their children. The CEDAW Committee and the CESCR have encouraged the introduction of parental leave, have called for incentives for men to take up parental leave,[82] and have commended a number of countries for their successful introduction of parental leave.[83]

Nevertheless, Article 4(2) also allows for special measures to protect maternity, which includes maternal parenting. Hence, special measures to encourage women to integrate work and family, such as giving first priority to women workers for places for their children in child care programmes or special family allowances for women to participate in extracurricular training programmes, could be justified as special measures to increase the workforce participation or promotion potential of women with small children. Transfer of social security child benefits by National Insurance to mothers or giving women the first choice as to whether to retain custody of children in the case of divorce or death may, in some contexts, be justified on grounds that women remain, as a rule, in many families,

---

[78] CO Mongolia, A/56/38, 24th Session (2001) para 269.

[79] See eg NJ Chodorow, *Feminism and Psychoanalytic Theory* (1989).

[80] CO Belarus, A/55/38, 22nd Session (2000) para 361.

[81] CO Democratic People's Republic of Korea, A/60/38, 33rd Session (2005) para 53.

[82] CESCR CO New Zealand, UN Doc E/2004/22 (2003) para 181; CO Canada, A/58/38, 28th Session (2003) para 381; CEDAW CO Luxembourg, A/58/38, 28th Session (2003) para 381; CEDAW CO Finland, A/56/38, 24th Session (2001) para 298; CESCR CO China, Macao Special Administrative Region, UN Doc E/2006/22 (2005) 38 para 248.

[83] CO Luxembourg, A/58/38, 28th Session (2003) para 298; CO New Zealand, A/58/38 (Supp), 29th Session (2003) para 400; CO Slovenia, A/58/38, 29th Session (2003) para 199. See more detailed discussion in chs on arts 11 and 16.

the primary caretakers. Such measures for the continuing protection of maternal parenting will be necessary where women's family roles as primary care-givers remain largely unchanged.

Transformative measures are required to allow women, like men, to rear children as well as participating fully in all fields of social, political, and economic activity.

Transformation requires a redistribution of power and resources and a change in the institutional structures which perpetuate women's oppression. It requires a dismantling of the public-private divide and a reconstruction of the public world so that child care and parenting are seen as valued common responsibilities of both parents and the community. . . . [E]quality as transformation requires not just the removal of barriers, but also positive measures to bring it about.[84]

Article 4 provides the tools for the positive measures needed to realize the 'change in the traditional role of men as well as the role of women in society and in the family', which is recognized in the Preamble of the Convention as necessary in order to achieve full equality between men and women.

---

[84] Fredman (n 13 above) 115.

Article 5

States Parties shall take all appropriate measures

(a) To modify the social and cultural patterns of conduct of men and women, with a view to achieving the elimination of prejudices and customary and all other practices which are based on the idea of the inferiority or the superiority of either of the sexes or on stereotyped roles for men and women;

(b) To ensure that family education includes a proper understanding of maternity as a social function and the recognition of the common responsibility of men and women in the upbringing and development of their children, it being understood that the interest of the children is the primordial consideration in all cases.

* I want to express my thanks to Anna van Duin (LLM/Mjur) who acted as my research assistant.

A. Introduction

I. The Place and Function of Article 5 in the Convention

1. Gender Stereotypes and Fixed Parental Gender Roles

The drafters of the Convention stressed the need to see maternity as a positive value instead of a ground to discriminate against women, and they were fully aware that a change in the traditional role of men and women in society and in the family is a prerequisite for achieving full equality between men and women.[1] While Article 5(a) obliges States parties to eliminate all harmful practices 'based on the idea of the inferiority or the superiority of either of the sexes or on stereotyped roles for men and women', Article 5 (b) concerns 'the most universal traditionalist cultural norm that disadvantages women, which is the stereotypical assignment of sole or major responsibility for childcare to women'.[2] Negative and detrimental traditional, cultural, customary, or religious beliefs, ideas, rules, and practices concerning women's role in private and public life, should be replaced by a positive appreciation of women's contribution to society and by a practice of sharing parental roles. The sub-sections of Article 5, therefore, are two sides of the same coin.

The social and cultural patterns of conduct, prejudices, customary, and all other practices, and ideas about the inferiority or superiority of either of the sexes, mentioned in Article 5(a) may be comprised in the single term gender stereotypes. Similarly, the core

---

[1] CEDAW, Preamble paras 13–14.

[2] F Raday, 'Culture, Religion, and CEDAW's Article 5(a)' in HB Schöpp-Schilling and C Flinterman (eds), *The Circle of Empowerment: Twenty-Five Years of The UN Committee on The Elimination of Discrimination against Women* (2007) 74.

concern of Article 5(b), that is, the recognition of the common responsibilities of men and women in the upbringing and development of their children, is parental gender roles. The content and scope of Article 5 can therefore be summarized as the obligation to modify gender stereotypes and fixed parental gender roles.

2. The Place of Article 5 in the Convention

As a general provision, the norms of Article 5 should be regarded along with the other articles in Part I on their own merits. They also lay a framework for the interpretation and implementation of the Convention as a whole. The Committee explicitly recognized the article's cross-cutting relevance, describing, for example, the discriminatory situation in a State party 'in which extremely stereotyped social, economic, political and cultural roles were assigned to men and women; that situation resulted in subordination of . . . women in virtually all the areas and at all the levels covered by the articles of the Convention'.[3] Article 5 is especially connected to Articles 2(f) and 10(c), which respectively refer to 'existing laws, regulations, customs and practices' and to 'stereotyped concept of the roles of men and women'.[4] These two provisions specify particular methods States parties should employ to reach the overall goal of the modification of gender stereotypes and fixed parental gender roles.

3. Transformative Equality and Structural Discrimination

Article 5 exemplifies that the Convention is a living instrument and that its provisions are subject to a continuous dynamic and progressive interpretation.[5] It appears that originally its meaning and scope were widely underestimated. Although many States parties entered reservations (in particular to Articles 2 and 16) with the argument that their religion or tradition(s) was at odds with the principle of full (legal) equality of women, few States parties reserved Article 5.[6] The language of Article 5 provides no clarity as to how it might be implemented. The wording suggests that the Article is solely directed at modifying the social and cultural patterns of conduct of men and women and to ensure family education, which would obligate States parties only to launch information and education campaigns.[7] This restrictive reading of Article 5 was prevalent in the legal literature until the end of the 1990s.[8] The Convention as a whole was criticized for not being progressive enough, precisely because it supposedly only addressed gender ideology, not systemic or structural discrimination against women.[9]

The Committee's interpretation of the content and scope of Article 5, and the way this article co-determines the scope of the whole Convention, refutes these criticisms. As early as its 5th session in 1986, the Committee appealed to the States parties to consider the

---

[3] CO Guatemala, A/49/38, 13th Session (1994) para 78.
[4] See the discussion in ch on arts 2 and 10.   [5] GR 25 para 3.
[6] Raday (n 2 above); E Sepper, 'Confronting the "Sacred and Unchangeable": The Obligation to Modify Cultural Patterns under the Women's Discrimination Treaty' (2008) 30 *University of Pennsylvania J Intl L* 585, 596. See also the discussion in ch on art 28.
[7] eg L Lijnzaad, 'Over rollenpatronen en de rol van het Verdrag' in A W Heringa, J Hes, and L Lijnzaad (eds), *Het Vrouwenverdrag. Een beeld van een verdrag* (1994) 43–57; M Wadstein, 'Implementation of the UN Convention on the Elimination of all Forms of Discrimination Against Women' (1988) 10 *Human Rights Quarterly* 5–21.
[8] R Holtmaat, Towards Different Law and Public Policy: The significance of Article 5a CEDAW for the elimination of structural gender discrimination (2004) 61–8; Sepper (n 6 above) 589 n 13.
[9] H Charlesworth, C Chinkin and S Wright, 'Feminist Approaches to International Law' (1991) 85 *American J of Intl L* 613, 634.

introduction of appropriate measures to implement Article 5(a).[10] One of its first general recommendations was on Article 5.[11] Over the years, the Committee continuously stressed that gender stereotypes and fixed parental gender roles have a 'pronounced impact' on women's human rights.[12] This process found its culmination in General Recommendation 25, where Article 5 was characterized as the pillar under the third objective of the Convention, ie to 'address prevailing gender relations and the persistence of gender-based stereotypes'.[13] These phenomena, according to the Committee, 'affect women not only through individual acts by individuals, but also in the law, and legal and societal structures and institutions'.[14] Through the inclusion of Article 5, the Convention, therefore, not only addresses gender ideology, but also the systemic and structural inequality of women, and—in order to overcome the discrimination resulting from it—calls for understanding equality as a transformative principle.[15]

4. *The Relationship between Article 5 and Discrimination against Women*

Although Article 5 does not speak of discrimination, and although the definition of discrimination in Article 1 does not mention gender stereotypes or fixed parental gender roles, these phenomena are closely related to discrimination against women. In the first place, Article 5 acknowledges that gender stereotypes and fixed parental gender roles lie at the basis of discrimination against women. The elimination of all forms of discrimination against women is impossible without eradicating these causes.[16] In the second place, prejudices and all customs and practices which are based on the inferiority of women and on stereotyped roles for men and women are discriminatory in themselves.[17] The Committee has adopted both approaches, stating that it:

continues to be concerned about the persistence of patriarchal attitudes and deep-rooted stereotypes regarding the role and responsibilities of men and women in society, which discriminate against women. The Committee is also concerned that the preservation of negative cultural practices and traditional attitudes serves to perpetuate women's subordination in the family and society and constitutes a serious obstacle to women's enjoyment of their fundamental rights.[18]

The Committee uses various terms to express the nature of the relationship between gender stereotyping and discriminating against women. For example, it states that stereotypes

---

[10] UN Doc A/41/45 para 365, as cited by M Wadstein (n 7 above) 13.
[11] GR 3 was adopted in 1987.   [12] eg CO Korea, CEDAW/C/PRK/CO/1 (2005) para 35.
[13] GR 25 para 7. This interpretation was first developed in an independent expert report for the Dutch Government; L Groenman, T van Vleuten, R Holtmaat, I van Dijk, and J de Wildt Groenman, *Het Vrouwenverdrag in Nederland anno 1997,* The Hague: Ministerie van SZW (1997).
[14] GR 25 para 7; eg CO Luxembourg, A/55/38, 22nd Session (2000) para 404.
[15] S Fredman, 'Beyond the Dichotomy of Formal and Substantive Equality: Towards a New Definition of Equal Rights' in I Boerefijn, F Coomans, J Goldschmidt, R Holtmaat, and R Wolleswinkel (eds), *Temporary Special Measures: Accelerating De Facto Equality of Women under Article 4(1) UN Convention on the Elimination of all Forms of Discrimination Against Women* (2003) 116; D Otto, 'Rethinking the "Universality" of Human Rights Law'(1997–1998) 29 *Columbia Human Rights L Rev* 1–46.
[16] The Committee sometimes speaks of 'adverse cultural norms' eg CO Madagascar, CEDAW/C/MDG/CO/5 (2008) para 16.
[17] Confirmed in art 2(f) and CESCR, 'General Comment 20' (2009) UN Doc E/C.12/GC/20 para 20. The discriminatory nature of gender stereotypes has been acknowledged in some important court cases, eg in US Supreme Court in *Price Waterhouse v Hopkins,* 490 US 228 (1989). RJ Cook and S Cusack, *Gender Stereotyping; Transnational Legal Perspectives* (2010).
[18] CO Burundi, CEDAW/C/BDI/CO/4 (2008) para 17.

'constitute barriers',[19] that they 'constitute the most serious obstacles',[20] or that they 'present impediments to . . . and are a root cause of' the disadvantaged position of women.[21] Sometimes, stereotypes are described as discriminatory in themselves.[22]

5. *Equality, Dignity, and Diversity*

The Convention Preamble mentions the principles of equality of rights and respect for human dignity.[23] This refers to UDHR Article 1, where the same principles are mentioned. The underlying presumption is that all human beings, irrespective of national or ethnic origin, class or caste, race, sex, sexual orientation, or any other classification that human beings can possibly construct between themselves, are potentially rational and morally responsible beings with an authentic desire to control their own lives. The social and cultural patterns of conduct and stereotyped roles that are addressed by Article 5, which are based on prejudice and on traditional or customary ideas about the inferiority of women, deny individual women the possibility to be a person in their own right and to employ all of their human capacities and capabilities to lead a meaningful life as a human being.[24] Gender stereotypes and fixed parental gender roles, therefore, not only deny women the right to be treated respectfully as an equal and dignified human being; they also deny women the autonomy to live their lives according to their own choices and convictions about their personal and unique contribution to sustaining and developing humanity.

Women and men have a fundamental right not to be confined to culturally defined constructions of femininity or masculinity, or to pre-fixed (and fixated) female and male parental roles that are entrenched in their 'culture'[25] as well as in primary social and legal institutions.[26] The Committee has made it clear that implementation of the Convention requires 'the recognition that women can have various roles in society, not only the important role of mother and wife, exclusively responsible for children and the family, but also as an individual person and actor in her community and in the society in general'.[27] All human beings are equal and have equal rights and deserve equal respect for their human dignity, but at the same time they may have very diverse ideas and wishes about what they actually want to do with their lives.[28] Therefore, the principles of individual autonomy and diversity are essential to a proper understanding of the content and scope of Article 5 and of the Convention as a whole.[29]

---

[19] CO Cook Islands, CEDAW/C/COK/CO/1 (2007) para 28.

[20] CO Cyprus, A/51/38, 15th Session (1996) para 45.

[21] CO New Zealand, CEDAW/C/NZL/CO/6 (2007) para 22.

[22] CO Guinea, CEDAW/C/EST/GIN/CO/6 (2007) para 23.

[23] Preamble para 7. See the discussion in ch on Preamble.

[24] M Nussbaum, *Women and Human Development. The Capabilities Approach* (2000).

[25] In this chapter, unless otherwise indicated, 'culture' is used in the broad sense, including cultural expressions, language, custom, religion, tradition, institutional settings, etc.

[26] Cook and Cusack (n 17 above) 68.

[27] CO Suriname, A/57/38, 27th Session (2002) para 48. Similarly CO Uzbekistan, A/56/38, 24th Session (2001) para 169.

[28] Lijnzaad (n 7 above) 57.

[29] A similar position is taken in South African Supreme Court 1999 1 SA 6 (CC), *National Coalition for Gay and Lesbian Equality v Ministry of Justice*, para 143.

II. Gender Stereotypes and Fixed Parental Gender Roles

1. *Ideas about the Inferiority or Superiority of either of the Sexes*

Article 5 addresses ideas about the inferiority or superiority of either of the sexes. The drafters exhibited a fundamental insight about the persistent unequal nature of relations between men and women. A woman, according to patriarchal traditions, is destined to be a species whose very existence is derived from and depends upon that of a man. During the long history of humanity—with the rare exception of a few matriarchal cultures—'woman' has always been and is persistently constructed as 'the other', that is: not-a-man.[30] At the basis of this binary construction lies a hierarchy of the two sexes: 'woman' being the negative or inferior side of the two poles, thereby justifying male domination. Patriarchy and misogyny are of all times and places, including the twenty-first century and the world's most 'emancipated' societies. The crucial question is not whether societies or cultures are patriarchal, but how they are differently so.[31] There exists a close link between patriarchy and ideas about what it means to be a 'real man' and the persistence of violence against women.[32]

In many patriarchal narratives about gender, women are described not as inferior, but as inherently different from men. The leading principle is that men and women are equal in worth and in dignity. This is often expressed by using the word 'equity' instead of equality. Statements to this effect can be found in some States parties' contributions in the constructive dialogue with the Committee, where they stress 'that the notions of the role of women in the family should not be changed. A misunderstanding of equality would not benefit any society. It is said to be more important to encourage the idea of the complementarity of men and women'.[33] Occasionally, 'woman' is characterized as superior to 'man', especially with respect to her caring or nurturing capacities. 'Woman', thus, is put on a pedestal, deserving a special degree of respect and concern from men, from civil society and/or from the government. However, women occupy this sacred position only when and in as far as they fulfil the traditionally, customary, or religiously determined duties that come along with primarily or exclusively being a mother/care-giver. The other side of celebrating women's 'relational orientation' or her 'special nurturing capacities' is that any transgression of her traditional gender identity or gender role is legally impossible or inconceivable and/or may be severely punished in the society or in the family, even to the point of murder. In many States a form of secular and state controlled reproduction of the patriarchal system exists, in which women are conceived of as needing protection under special legal and policy measures, mainly relating to reproduction and motherhood. This protection is often constructed to restrict women's human rights, most significantly the right to be economically active and financially independent and the right to choose an education or a spouse. Men, in such systems, are seen as head of the household or bread-winner and on that ground are regarded as deserving special rights in the area of economic subsistence and have control of family members' actions.

---

[30] S de Beauvoir, *The Second Sex* (1949), various editions and translations.

[31] L Volpp, 'Feminism versus Multiculturalism' (2001) 101 *Columbia L Rev* 1181, 1217.

[32] Human Rights Council, 'Intersections Between Culture and Violence Against Women, Report of the UN Special Rapporteur on Violence Against Women, its Causes and Consequences' Y Ertürk (17 January 2007) UN Doc A/HRC/4/34.

[33] eg CO Guatemala, A/49/38, 13th Session (1994) para 68.

2. Gender and Gender Stereotypes

The term 'gender' refers to 'the social construction of differences between women and men and ideas of "femininity" and "masculinity"—the excess cultural baggage associated with biological sex'.[34] Gender is constantly produced and reproduced and is more a process than a fixed condition with static content. Gender is active; every person and every existing social structure contributes to it,[35] including the law.[36] Male and female gender identities are experienced as real but are imposed by society in the same way as (*inter alia*) a national, racial, ethnic, or a sexual orientation identity may take on an appearance of reality or truth.[37] The Committee stresses that gender is a product of culture and society, but it immediately adds that it 'can likewise be changed by culture, society and community'.[38]

A stereotype is 'a generalized view or preconception of attributes or characteristics possessed by, or the roles that are or should be performed by, members of a particular group'.[39] Gender stereotypes tend to freeze gender identities and gender roles and make them appear as real, universal, eternal, natural, essential, and/or unchangeable. Gender stereotypes can be about differences between the biological sexes, assumed or real psychological characteristics, male and female sexuality, sex roles, or they can be a compound of these factors.[40] They come in two main forms: descriptive and prescriptive (or normative).[41] The line between descriptive and prescriptive stereotypes is very thin since many descriptions of what women are, also function as prescriptions of how they should behave.[42]

Stereotypes, including gender stereotypes, play a positive role in shaping people's personal identity. However, not all gender stereotypes are useful instruments in the shaping of a dignified personal identity.[43] According to the language of Article 5, only stereotyped representations of 'woman', or 'femaleness' that play a role in the construction of social, economic, cultural, and legal deprivation or inequality between men and women or leads to subordination of women should be modified.[44] Stereotypes which are favourable for women—sometimes called benevolent stereotypes[45]—should also be questioned, such as those in which women are put on a pedestal of celebrated motherhood.

3. Fixed Parental Gender Roles

In most cultures a woman's sexuality, her reproductive capacity, and her nurturing and caring role as regards her children, her husband, and the wider family are crucial in the

---

[34] H Charlesworth, 'Feminist Methods in International Law' (1999) 93 *Am J Intl L* 379, 379; see also UN Department of Economic and Social Affairs, Division for the Advancement of Women, '1999 World Survey on the Role of Women in Development' (1999) UN Doc ST/ESA/326, ix. The Committee has defined gender in GR 28 para 5, as discussed in the Introduction.

[35] S Gherardi, 'The Gender We Think, the Gender We Do in our Everyday Organizational Lives' (1994) 6 *Human Relations* 591–610.

[36] C Smart, 'The Women in Legal Discourse' (1992) 1 *Social and Legal Studies* 29–44; R Holtmaat, 'The Power of Legal Concepts: the Development of a Feminist Theory of Law' (1989) 5 *Intl J of the Sociology of L* 481–502.

[37] AM Gross, 'Sex, Love, and Marriage: Questioning Gender and Sexuality Rights in International Law' (2008) 21 *Leiden J of Intl L* 235, 251.

[38] GR 28 para 5.   [39] Cook and Cusack (n 17 above) 9.   [40] Ibid 25.

[41] ST Fiske et al, 'Social Science Research on Trial: Use of Sex Stereotyping Research in Price Waterhouse v Hopkins' (1991) 46 *American Psychologist* 1049–60; Descriptive stereotypes are often subdivided into 'statistical' and 'false' stereotypes.

[42] KA Appiah, 'Stereotypes and the Shaping of Identity' (2000) 88 *Californian L Rev* 41, 49.

[43] Appiah (n 42 above) 52.   [44] Ibid 43.

[45] M Baretto and N Ellemers, 'The Burden of Benevolent Sexism: How it Contributes to the Maintenance of Gender Inequalities' (2005) 35 *European J of Social Psychology* 633–42.

construction of her inferiority, subordination, and/or her difference from men.[46] Women are not only the birth mothers of the next generations, but they are also in charge of reproducing the group's culture; they feed their children with the meals they prepare, but also with the norms, practices, values, beliefs, and traditions that are crucial for the group's or nation's identity. Gender relations are thus seen as constituting the essence of a particular culture, to be passed by women from generation to generation.[47] This 'natural female role' serves as the ultimate excuse to keep women in the 'safe haven' of the male-controlled family.[48] The gender identity or role of 'man' in the patriarchal system of unequal gender relations is that of the person in charge of maintaining and preserving the 'natural family order' and preventing 'his' women (wife, sister, daughter, or any other female relative) from casting a shade of shame on the family. Gender stereotypes and fixed parental gender roles are also oppressive for men; those who do not live up to them bring shame upon the family and may be punished socially and/or legally.

4. The Persistence of Gender Stereotypes

It is sometimes argued that when discrimination against women has been eliminated, or when women participate in social and economic or political life in equal numbers with men, gender stereotypes and fixed parental gender roles will automatically disappear.[49] The history of women's legal emancipation and their increased participation in public and economic life, for example, in northern American and European countries, shows that gender stereotyping and the unequal sharing of family responsibilities between men and women remain as persistent obstacles to women's *de facto* equality.

Abolishing, eradicating, or eliminating[50] gender stereotypes, or even modifying them, is a long and slow process.[51] Gender stereotypes fulfil an important cognitive function because they 'provide structure and meaning, and they shape perceptions most when the data themselves are open to multiple interpretations'.[52] In turn, this function is based on the basic cognitive structure of the human mind, in which it is easiest to learn things when they fit into pairs of concepts that are opposed to each other. A system of fixed gender stereotypes of 'female' and 'male' characteristics and behaviour helps to construct such pairs. This construction of differences between 'man' and 'woman' is also closely related to sexuality or sexual attractiveness (to the other or to the same sex).[53] Because gender stereotypes play an important role in the construction of identity, of individuals, communities, and

---

[46] eg N Chodorow, *Feminism and Psychoanalytic Theory* (1989).

[47] M van den Brink, 'Gendered Sovereignty? In Search of Gender Bias in the International Law Concept of State Sovereignty' in I Boerefijn and J Goldschmidt (eds), *Changing Perceptions of Sovereignty and Human Rights. Essays in Honour of Cees Flinterman* (2008) 77.

[48] Raday (n 2 above) 69.

[49] eg N Burrows, 'The 1979 Convention on the Elimination of all forms of Discrimination Against Women' (1985) 32 *Netherlands Intl L Rev* 419, 248; C Jolls, 'Antidiscrimination's Law's Effects on Implicit Bias' Working Paper No 148, 16, <http://ssrn.com/abstract=959228> accessed 31 December 2010; Cook and Cusack (n 17 above) 174.

[50] This language was used in first drafts of art 5.

[51] J Wyttenbach, 'Violence against Women, Culture/Religious Traditions and the International Standard of Due Diligence' in C Benninger-Budel (ed), *Due Diligence and its Application to Protect Women from Violence* (2008) 225, 237; R Holtmaat and J Naber, *Women's Human Rights and Culture: From Deadlock to Dialogue* (2010) 68 ff.

[52] Fiske et al (n 41 above) 1050.   [53] Appiah (n 42 above) 43.

States,[54] eradicating or abolishing them would remove the basis of this gender identity, which would most probably lead to uncertainty and anxiety.

Gender stereotypes are so deeply inscribed in our language, images, practices, norms, and values, that we are not aware that we continuously use them. They only become visible when certain 'natural' practices or beliefs are confronted with other practices and beliefs in other communities or in other parts of the world. A final obstacle to change is that gender stereotypes—and the practices that are based upon them—are embedded in strong social norms. A characteristic of such norms is that it is very difficult for an individual or even for one family, to adopt practices or behaviour that contravenes them. Change can only be brought about when a whole community is involved in the process.[55]

Because stereotyping is so fundamental to human thought and action, the purpose of the Convention cannot be to eradicate or abolish all gender stereotypes, but only to transform or modify those stereotypes that are detrimental to the realization of women's human rights. The text of Article 5(a) speaks of the elimination of prejudices and customary and all other practices which lead to discrimination. This is not the same as requiring the elimination of all gender stereotypes.

5. Gender Stereotypes and Intersectional Discrimination

The construction of gender stereotypes and fixed parental gender roles ultimately rests upon the assumption that there are two opposite and mutually exclusive biological sexes. This means that intersexual people by definition do not fit into the picture.[56] Heterosexual sexuality takes a central place in this construction.[57] The most blatant transgression of the patriarchal female gender identity and her fixed gender (motherly) role is the lesbian woman who chooses to renounce a male sexual partner and thereby also rejects the protection of the male head of household and all other forms of male supervision and control of her life. Lesbian women experience severe forms of violence, including (gang) rape in order to 'cure' their 'abnormal' sexual preference.[58] Through the mechanism of gender stereotyping, discrimination on the ground of sexual orientation and discrimination against transsexual and intersexual people intersects[59] with discrimination on the basis of sex and—from the perspective of Article 5—should be eliminated and combated by all States parties.

Gender stereotyping may also intersect with a wide range of other identities that are constructed in the social, legal, and cultural order, such as the identity of a divorcee, a single woman, a childless woman, a housewife, a working mother, a welfare mother, a widow, a battered woman, an immigrant woman, an indigenous woman, a rural woman,

---

[54] Ibid 52.

[55] G Mackie and J LeJeune, '*Social Dynamics of Abandonment of Harmful Practices*' UNICEF Innocenti Working Papers Series, IWP-2009-06 (2009) V and 10.

[56] J Butler, '*Gender Trouble: Feminism and the Subversion of Identity*' (1990) 1–34 and 110–28.

[57] Gross (n 37 above) 251, summarizing the work of Judith Butler.

[58] eg UN Commission on Human Rights 'Torture and Other Cruel, Inhuman or Degrading Treatment or Punishment, Report of the Special Rapporteur M Nowak' (March 2006) UN Doc E/CN.4/2006/6/Add.1 paras 180 and 183.

[59] K Crenshaw 'Demarginalizing the Intersection of Race and Sex, a Black Feminist Critique of Antidiscrimination Doctrine, Feminist Theory, and Antiracist Politics' (1989) *University of Chicago Legal Forum* 139–67: Related terms are 'compounded discrimination' or 'multiple discrimination'.

a woman of colour, a prostitute, or a criminal woman. Economic position, class or caste, religion, sexual orientation, legal status, health, age, social status, nationality, ethnic origin or race, all lie at the basis of discrimination sustained by descriptive and prescriptive stereotypes that combine and intersect with gender stereotypes.[60] The Committee acknowledges that certain groups of women 'in addition to being affected by gender stereotypes, face multiple forms of discrimination, on grounds such as their ethnicity or their sexual orientation'.[61]

III. The Concept of Culture in the Context of Article 5

Article 5 addresses culture in terms of 'patterns of conduct' and 'customary practices', but it does not mention the words tradition or religion. In practice, the Committee uses the terms religion, culture, tradition, and customs in the context of Article 5. Religious beliefs and practices are seen as a specimen of social, cultural, or traditional practices and customs that (when damaging for women's rights) must all be modified. Included in this wide concept of culture are also social and economic arrangements, political structures, and legal regulations.

Culture may be an important positive (re)source for the construction of gender identities.[62] However, most often it contributes to damaging or negative gender stereotypes or fixed parental gender roles that stand in the way of women's equality and dignity and lead to discrimination against them. Article 5 does not address only 'exotic', 'backward', 'traditionalist', or 'oppressive' cultures, but all human relations and institutions or structures in which gender stereotypes and fixed parental gender roles are used in a way that is detrimental to the full realization of women's human rights. Culture is intrinsic to human existence; exoticizing it should be avoided.[63] In the same vein, culture should not be seen as having a particular essence which is monolithic, static, and unchangeable.[64] Since the content of each culture is constructed by human beings, its structure and content is subject to continuous change.[65] 'The expression "cultural life" is an explicit reference to culture as a living process, historical, dynamic and evolving, with a past, a present and a future.'[66] Not only is cultural change possible, according to Article 5, it is also obligatory.

---

[60] eg *Yilmaz-Dogan v the Netherlands*, CERD Committee (29 September 1988) CERD/C/36/D/1/1984, for a clear case of intersection between gender and racial/ethnic stereotyping.

[61] The Committee mentions sexuality: CO Guatemala, CEDAW/C/GUA/CO7 (2009) para 19; sexual orientation and gender identity: CO Panama, CEDAW/C/PAN/CO/7 (2010) para 22; minority or immigrant status: eg CO New Zealand, CEDAW/C/NZL/CO/6 (2007) para 22; CO France, CEDAW/C/FRA/CO/6 (2008) para 18, CO The Netherlands, CEDAW/C/NLD/CO/5 (2010) para 24; CO Cyprus, CEDAW/C/CYP/CO/5 (2006) para 31; Roma women: eg CO Hungary, CEDAW/C/EST/HUN/CO/6 (2007) para 31; CO Romania, CEDAW/C/ROM/06 (2006) para 26, 27; widows: eg CO Nepal, A/59/38, 31st Session (2004) para 206; and rural women: eg CO Cameroon, CEDAW/C/CMR/CO/3 (2009) para 42.

[62] Recognized by the Committee in eg CO Antigua and Barbuda, A/52/38, 17th Session (1997) para 270.

[63] Generally, UN Human Rights Council, 'Intersections Between Culture and Violence Against Women' (n 32 above); L Volpp, 'Blaming Culture for Bad Behaviour' (2000) 12 *Yale J of the Humanities* 89–115; SE Merry, *Human Rights and Gender Violence: Translating International Law into Local Justice* (2006).

[64] Essentialist approaches to culture may not only be found with defenders of the values of a certain culture, but also with advocates for human rights. R Holtmaat and J Naber (n 51 above).

[65] M Sunder, 'Piercing the Veil' (2002–2003) 112 *Yale L J* 1399, 1423, discussing this stance in relation to religion.

[66] eg CESCR, 'General Comment 21' (2009) UN Doc E/C.12/GC/21 para 11.

IV. Related Provisions in Other Human Rights Documents

The necessity of modifying gender stereotypes and of fixed parental gender roles can be found in many international human rights documents.[67] A most clear example is included in CESCR General Comment 16, acknowledging that gender stereotypes and fixed parental gender roles stand in the way of the fulfilment of all of women's human rights.[68] The CESCR calls gender stereotyping a form of discrimination against women,[69] thereby reflecting a wide acceptance of the CEDAW Committee's analysis of the causes and consequences of discrimination against women. Some international documents use wording similar to that of Article 5.[70] A wide range of documents express the recognition of maternity as a positive social function and the sharing of responsibilities of parents as important values and approaches.[71] Traditional gender roles, prejudices, and stereotypes are seen as important obstacles to the full enjoyment of women's social and economic rights.[72] Other international human rights documents recognize that stereotypes lie at the root of many different forms of discrimination, most notably racial and ethnic discrimination,[73] and discrimination on the ground of disability.[74]

B. Travaux Préparatoires

I. The Basis for the Article

Article 5 has its origins in DEDAW Article 3:[75]

All appropriate measures shall be taken to educate public opinion and to direct national aspirations towards the eradication of prejudice and the abolition of customary and all other practices which are based on the idea of inferiority of women.[76]

A combination of the proposals of the Philippines and the USSR resulted in the following draft:

1. States parties shall adopt all necessary measures with a view to educating public opinion for the complete eradication of prejudices, customs and all other practices based on the concept of women and for the recognition that the protection of motherhood is a common interest of the entire society which should bear responsibility for it.
2. Any advocacy of the superiority of one sex over the other and of discrimination on the basis of sex shall be prohibited by law.[77]

---

[67] Cook and Cusack (n 17 above) 145, 146, and 174 n 2.
[68] CESCR, 'General Comment 16' (2005) UN Doc E/C.12/2005/4 para 14.
[69] CESCR, 'General Comment 20' (2009) UN Doc E/C.12/GC/20 para 20.
[70] eg the Convention of Belém do Para: arts 7(e) and 8(b); the Protocol to the Banjul Charter on the Rights of Women in Africa, arts 2(2) and 4(d) and arts 6 and 13.
[71] eg CRC Preamble and art 18(1); ACHR art 17; CCPR, 'General Comment 19' (1990) UN Doc HRI/GEN/1/Rev.1 para 8.
[72] eg CESCR, 'General Comment 16' (2005) UN Doc E/C.12/2005/4 para 14; CCPR 'General Comment 28' (2000) UN Doc CCPR/C/21/Rev.1/Add.10 paras 5 and 25.
[73] CERD Preamble and arts 4 and 7; CERD, 'General Recommendation XXVII' (2000) UN Doc A/55/18, 57th Session and CERD, 'General Recommendation 30' (2004) UN Doc A/59/18, 64th Session.
[74] CRPD art 8(1)(b).
[75] LA Rehof, *Guide to the Travaux Préparatoires of the United Nations Convention on the Elimination of All Forms of Discrimination against Women* (1993) 79–88 for references to the relevant UN documents.
[76] DEDAW; Rehof (n 75 above) 78.   [77] Art 6, later renumbered to art 5; Rehof (n 75 above) 79.

II. Developments during the Drafting Process

The scope of what finally became Article 5(a) is both broader and narrower than DEDAW Article 3. The element 'to direct national aspirations' disappeared from the text. The element of the education of public opinion was moved to Article 5(b); consequently, this part of Article 5 became directed (positively) towards informing the public about the 'proper' understanding of maternity as a social function and the shared responsibility of men and women for the upbringing of the children. The duty to eliminate prejudices remained in Article 5(a), but the original verb 'to educate' was replaced by 'to modify'. An obligation to modify human behaviour, based in social and cultural patterns of conduct, is a very compelling and difficult one. In this respect, one could disagree with Rehof, who concludes that the final text is weaker at this point.[78] Rehof also points out that the final text 'replaced "eradication of prejudice" with the weaker "elimination of prejudices". It mentioned stereotyped roles for both men and women and not only women's stereotyped roles'.[79] Instead of explicitly naming the problem of customary ideas about the inferiority of women, the final text mentions the inferiority or superiority of either of the sexes. It thereby recognizes that sometimes women (mainly as mothers) are put on a pedestal; this, however, does not mean that they are seen as full members of society and can equally participate in all aspects of public life.

In the first (joint) drafts a prohibition of 'any advocacy of hatred for the feminine sex that constitutes incitement to discrimination against women' was included.[80] This proposal was removed from the draft, because it was argued that such a prohibition would be problematic in the view of freedom of speech. The discussions on this issue do not seem to have been very thorough or deep. For example, it is not clear why a similar prohibition was deemed possible in ICERD (Article 4) and not in the context of this Convention.

The USSR proposal included three aspects concerning the protection of motherhood: a duty 'to enable women to combine the fulfilment of their maternal obligations and participation in all spheres of national life', an obligation to ensure the 'protection of mothers and children', and 'the special protection of women workers'. In fact, the last two elements—in a different form—have been included in Article 11(2).[81] In the framework of Article 5(b), the element of protection by the State through social laws, was changed into a duty to educate the general public about the positive social value of maternity and about the responsibilities of both parents towards their children. The effect is that States parties are given a duty to educate instead of a duty to make appropriate laws. The observation made by many State delegations that protection of motherhood all too often leads to undermining women's rights or to stigmatization and stereotyping was honoured in two ways: the word 'protection' was taken out altogether and the word 'motherhood' was consequently replaced by 'maternity'. The choice of the word 'maternity' indicates that the drafters exclusively wanted to protect the biological aspects of giving birth to children,[82] and were aware of the fact that protection of the social and cultural construction of the motherly role all too often leads to fixed parental gender roles, which according to Article 5(b) should be subjected to change.

---

[78] Rehof (n 75 above) 84.   [79] Ibid.
[80] Para 2 of both the Philippines and the joint USSR/Philippine proposal.
[81] See the discussion in ch on art 11.
[82] This is reflected in art 4(2). See the discussion in ch on art 4.

The phrase about the best interest of the child, added at the very last stage of the drafting process, seems like an afterthought, one that from a perspective of improving women's rights could in fact weaken the provision when it leads to the interpretation that the primary purpose of Article 5(b) is to serve the best interests of children. However, this concept should be interpreted and implemented in a manner that does not reinforce gender stereotypes or fixed parental gender roles.[83]

C. The Committee's Interpretation of Article 5

I. References in Committee Documents

In its 6th session (1987), the Committee adopted General Recommendation 3, in which it emphasizes the importance of implementing Article 5(a). In many other general recommendations the Committee directly or indirectly refers to Article 5[84] and voices 'its concerns regarding gender stereotyping and States parties' failure to adequately address this phenomenon'.[85] Authors of several communications under the Optional Protocol based their claims on (*inter alia*) Article 5.[86] The Committee concluded that Article 5(a) was violated in the Hungarian case concerning protection against domestic violence.[87] In the two other cases, both involving Austria's lack of protection against domestic violence, the Committee recognized the linkages between traditional attitudes by which women are regarded as subordinate to men and domestic violence.[88] Violation of Articles 2(f) and 5(a) were the main issue in the Philippines case, in which the Committee found that criminal court judgments concerning rape reflected gender stereotypes and myths about male and female sexuality and sexual behaviour.[89] In one case in which the claim was not based on Article 5, one of the dissenters none the less extensively discussed the provision.[90] Article 5 was also discussed in the report of the Committee's inquiry into the rapes and murders of women in and around Ciudad Juárez, Mexico under the Optional Protocol.[91]

---

[83] See the discussion in ch on art 16. M van den Brink, *Moeders in de Mainstream; Een genderanalyse van het werk van het VN-kindercomité*, dissertation Utrecht University with a summary in English: *Mothers in the Mainstream—A Gender Analysis of the Work of the UN Committee on the Rights of the Child* (2006).

[84] GR 12, Preamble, consideration 1; GR 14, Preamble, considerations 2, 5, and 6 and Recommendations (a)(iii), (a)(iv), and (b); GR 19, Comments and Recommendations 11, 12, 21–3, and 24(d), (e), (f), (t)(ii); GR 21, Consideration 3 and Comments 11, 12, 14, 16–21, 32, 41–4, 46, 48(b), and 50; GR 23, Comments 8, 10–12, 20(c), and 44; GR 24, Comments 12(b) and 28; GR 25, Considerations 6, 7, 10, and 38.

[85] Cook and Cusack (n 17 above) 134.

[86] eg CEDAW OP decisions/views in cases *Ms B-J v Germany*, CEDAW Communication No 1/2003 (2004) Excerpt from UN Doc A/59/38, 31st Session; *Ms AT v Hungary* CEDAW Communication No 2/2003(2005), CEDAW/C/32/D/2003; CEDAW Communication No 2/2003(2005) CEDAW/C/32/D/2003; *Şahide Goekce v Austria*, CEDAW Communication No 5/2005 (2007) CEDAW/C/39/D/5/2005; *Fatma Yildirim (deceased) v Austria*, CEDAW Communication No 6/2005 (2007) CEDAW/C/39/D/6/2005; *Vertido v the Philippines*, CEDAW Communication No 18/2008 (2010) CEDAW/C/46/D/18/2008; Cook and Cusack (n 17 above) 135–7.

[87] *Ms AT v Hungary* (n 86 above).

[88] *Şahide Goekce v Austria* and *Fatma Yildirim (deceased) v Austria* (n 86 above) para 12.2; these cases were decided on the basis of other provisions in the Convention.

[89] *Vertido v the Philippines* (n 86 above).

[90] S Dairam dissenting in *Cristina Muñoz-Vargas y Sainz de Vicuña v Spain*, CEDAW Communication No 7/2005, CEDAW/C/39/D/7/2005 paras 13.5 and 13.7.

[91] Report on Mexico produced by the Committee on the Elimination of Discrimination against Women under art 8 of the Optional Protocol to the Convention, and reply from the Government of Mexico, CEDAW/C/2005/OP.8/Mexico (2005). See also VAW discussion in ch on art 9.

The Committee's concluding observations exemplify the role of Article 5 as co-determining the content and scope of all other substantive articles in the Convention. Occasionally, the Committee expresses its general concerns about 'the pervasiveness of patriarchal attitudes and deep-rooted stereotypes regarding the roles and responsibilities of women and men in the family, in the workplace, in political life and society'.[92] Most often, it discusses the issues of gender stereotyping and fixed parental gender roles in comments and observations concerning the various substantive rights that are guaranteed under the Convention.[93]

II. Article 5 in Relation to the Prohibition of Discrimination against Women

1. *Direct Discrimination*

Often, official laws and policies attribute different (unequal) rights and responsibilities to men and women on the basis of gender stereotypes and fixed parental gender roles.[94] Instances of such direct discrimination are sometimes justified with a call upon the preservation of culture, or with the argument that women need special protection because of their roles as mothers or care-givers.[95] Men in such systems have special rights as breadwinners or heads of households. The Committee recommends that States parties undertake 'changes in laws and administrative regulations to recognize women as heads of households, and the concept of shared economic contribution and household responsibilities'.[96] In other instances it has expressed concerns about 'stereotypes, including the State party's explicit recognition of women's alleged primary responsibility in rearing children, providing care to family members and providing moral advice in the community'[97] or about discriminatory provisions in national law 'which perpetuate stereotypes by providing that men are the heads of households and women are relegated to domestic roles, allow polygamy and set a legal minimum age of marriage of 16 for girls'.[98]

Many States parties, although not allowing sex discrimination in their own laws and policies, officially recognize the validity of customary or religious laws in the constitution and/or state (federal) laws, even when such laws are contrary to the principle of sex equality.[99] This issue touches upon the general question of how far a State party can justify violations of human rights on its territory on the basis of legally guaranteed autonomy of certain cultural or religious groups (often ethnic and religious minorities).[100] On the basis of Articles 5 and/or 2(f), the Committee rejects direct discrimination against women

---

[92]   CO Guatemala, CEDAW/C/GUA/CO7 (2009) para 19.

[93]   As a consequence, the issues of gender stereotyping and fixed parental gender roles are also discussed in most other chapters in this Commentary.

[94]   This issue is closely related to the obligations under art 2(f), see the discussion in ch on art 2.

[95]   This argument is also rejected by the European Court of Human Rights: 'To the extent that the difference [in treatment] was founded on the traditional gender roles, that is on the perception of women as primary child-carers and men as primary breadwinners, these gender prejudices cannot, by themselves, be considered by the Court to amount to sufficient justification for the difference in treatment, any more than similar prejudices based on race, origin, colour or sexual orientation.' *Konstantin Markin v Russia*, 7 October 2010, ECHR, Appl n 30078/06 para 58.

[96]   CO Fiji Islands, A/57/38, 26th Session (2002) para 32.

[97]   CO Uzbekistan, CEDAW/C/UZB/CO/3 (2006) para 19.

[98]   CO Indonesia, CEDAW/C/EST/IDN/CO/5 (2007) para 18.

[99]   eg CO Botswana, CEDAW/C/BOT/CO/3 (2010) para 23.

[100] See also the discussion in ch on art 2.

that flows from the official recognition of religious or customary laws.[101] The Committee makes the same point as to reservations on the ground of respect for religious or customary law[102]

Direct discrimination against women sometimes results from the State party's *de facto* recognition of customary, traditional, or religious laws and practices. State authorities, including the judiciary, often do not stand up against religious authorities or community leaders who argue that their customs or religious prescriptions do not allow for women's equality. The Committee 'notes with great concern that, although the national laws guaranteed the equal status of women, the continued existence of and adherence to customary laws perpetuated discrimination against women, particularly in the context of the family'.[103]

2. *Indirect Discrimination*

The Committee clearly states that providing formal equal rights by law or making laws formally sex neutral, is not enough; the gender stereotypes that underlie these laws must be questioned.[104] Sex neutral categorizations in law which in fact reflect and/or sustain existing unequal gender relations and gender stereotypes, may lead to indirect discrimination. For example, the Committee connects the persistence of stereotypical and traditional attitudes to the prevalence of women among part-time workers and to their differential treatment in social laws and policies.[105]

3. *Structural Discrimination*

In General Recommendation 25[106] and in many concluding observation, the Committee points out that traditional and stereotypical attitudes 'are reflected in people's behaviour and in legislation and policy, and limit women's full enjoyment of all their rights guaranteed under the Convention.'[107] This expands the effect of Article 5 far beyond a mere transformation of certain 'ideas' or 'ideologies' about men's and women's different (and inherently inferior or unequal) characteristics or roles and includes the obligation to put an end to structural discrimination and to aim for transformative equality.

III. The Committee's Approach to Culture

1. *The Committee's Response to Cultural Essentialism*

The conception of culture as having a fixed and eternal essence regarding the relationships between the sexes obstructs implementation of Article 5.[108] Time and again, the Committee 'urges the State party to view culture as a dynamic aspect of the country's

---

[101] eg CO Burundi, CEDAW/C/BDI/CO/4 (2008) para 13; CO Vanuatu, CEDAW/C/VUT/CO/3 (2007) para 10; CO Namibia, CEDAW/C/NAM/CO/3 (2007) para 16; CO Niger, CEDAW/C/NER/CO/2 (2007) para 15; CO Indonesia, CEDAW/C/EST/IDN/CO/5 (2007) para 12.

[102] eg CO Israel, CEDAW/C/ISR/CO/3 (2005) para 25; CO India, CEDAW/C/IND/CO/3 (2007) para 10.

[103] CO Zimbabwe, A/53/38, 18th Session (1998) para 139; CO Albania, A/58/38, 28th Session (2003) para 68.

[104] CO Slovenia, A/52/38, 16th Session (1997) para 89.

[105] CO Germany, A/55/38, 22nd Session (2000) para 313 and 314; similarly in CO UK and Northern Ireland, A/54/38, 21st Session (1999) para 308; CO Slovakia, A/53/38, 19th Session (1998) para 74.

[106] GR 25 para 7.   [107] CO Luxembourg, A/55/38, 17th Session (1997) para 404.

[108] The term 'essentialism' refers to an epistemological approach in which it is presumed that we are able to capture the essence of 'beings' by means of giving a fixed description of them. This is opposed to the

social fabric and life and therefore subject to change'.[109] The Committee in its early days at some point went rather far in suggesting that a culture or religion could or should be changed or even abolished.[110] It now phrases these concerns more cautiously, but it is still quite firm about the necessity of intervention by the State party when women's rights are violated based on culture, including religious practices or beliefs.[111] The Committee sees that a change of culture requires the strong political will of a State party.[112] It often stresses the desirability of engaging in a dialogue with civil society about the necessary cultural changes, urging the State party 'to intensify co-operation in this regard with civil society organizations, women's groups and community leaders, traditional and religious leaders, as well as teachers and the media'[113] in order 'to facilitate social and cultural change and the creation of an enabling environment that is supportive of gender equality'.[114]

2. *Cultural Practices and Beliefs under the Scope of Article 5*

The Committee acknowledges that all human societies suffer from gender stereotypes and fixed parental gender roles.[115] In its constructive dialogue with States parties and in drafting its concluding observations, the Committee to a large extent depends upon the issues that are raised by the States parties' reports or by NGOs in their shadow reports.[116] Based on this input, the Committee most often refers to harmful practices that result from gender stereotyping in relation to culture in the context of Article 5(a) as to the situation of women in economically developing States, and mainly discusses the damaging effects of fixed parental gender roles and the implementation of Article 5(b) with respect to Eastern European, former Soviet Union, and Western States.[117] By not often expressly naming certain practices in the latter States (such as pornography, sexist advertising, or cosmetic surgery) as 'cultural', the process runs the risk of exoticizing or orientalizing culture.[118]

a) Traditional Harmful Practices and Beliefs

Apart from frequently expressing a general concern about the discriminatory effects of gender stereotypes and damaging cultural practices (including violence against women) which are based upon them,[119] the Committee has commented on a great variety of particular harmful customary, traditional, or religious laws and practices. It discusses, *inter alia,* polygamy, inhumane rites undergone by widows, female circumcision and similar customs,[120] son-preference and illegal sex-selective abortion,[121] traditional practices

---

understanding of culture and gender as something that not 'is', but that is constantly being produced and reproduced, as being fluid and a process. Holtmaat and Naber (n 51 above) 68.

[109] eg CO Angola, A/59/38, 31st Session (2004) para 147; CO Jordan, CEDAW/C/EST/JOR/CO/4 (2007) para 20; CO Mozambique, CEDAW/C/MOZ/CO/2 (2007) paras 20–1; CO Madagascar, CEDAW/C/MDG/CO/5 (2008) para 17.

[110] eg CO Libyan Arab Jamahiriya, A/49/38, 13th Session (1994) para 130; CO Morocco, A/52/38, 16th Session (1997) para 71.

[111] eg CO Pakistan, CEDAW/C/PAK/CO/3 (2007) para 29.

[112] CO Ecuador, A/49/38, 13th Session (1994) para 524.

[113] CO Nigeria, CEDAW/C/NGA/6 (2008) para 323.

[114] CO Nicaragua, CEDAW/C/NIC/CO/6 (2007) para 12.   [115] eg GR 23 para 10.

[116] Merry (n 63 above) 90 ff.   [117] Holtmaat and Naber (n 51 above).

[118] UN Human Rights Council, 'Intersections between Culture and Violence against Women' (n 32 above) ch 3.

[119] eg CO Mozambique, CEDAW/C/MOZ/CO/2 (2007) paras 20 and 21. S Koukoulis-Spiliotopoulos, 'The Limits of Cultural Traditions' (2008) *Annuaire International des Droits de l'Homme III* 412, 420 n 33.

[120] CO Nigeria, A/53/38, 19th Session (1998) para 153.

[121] CO China, CEDAW/C/CHN/CO/6 (2006) para 17.

related to dowries, adultery and the practice of pre-marriage,[122] bride price and dowry,[123] forced and early marriage and female genital mutilation, ritual bondage, levirate, and repudiation,[124] widowhood rites and food taboos,[125] *trokosi* (ritual slavery),[126] and the customary right of married men to treat their wives in the same way as minor children.[127] Also, the Committee frequently notices that cultural barriers may exist which prevent women from owning land and participating in the decision-making process.[128] It expresses concerns about customary law that has a detrimental impact on the rights of women with regard to inheritance, matrimonial regimes, and gifts,[129] and on the concept of male guardianship over women (*mehrem*).[130]

b) Machismo

The Committee has expressed concern about the effects of a Latin American and Caribbean machismo culture which encourages adolescent and young males to engage in high-risk sexual behaviour as a proof of manhood. The Committee makes clear that 'as long as stereotyped roles persisted in education and mothers encouraged their sons to adopt macho attitudes whereas girls were brought up to be docile and obedient, no change was imminent'.[131] And it notes 'that the prevailing gender stereotypes and patriarchal culture attitude of machismo, affected women in all walks of life and expressed itself also in violence against women, which was largely accepted'.[132]

c) Protective Maternity Laws

The Committee forcefully criticizes the persistence of protective maternity laws which stretch beyond the mere protection of the biological or physical consequences of pregnancy and childbirth, and thereby perpetuate the stereotype of women's primary role as mothers and childminders.[133] It notes 'that protective labour laws had the sole effect of restricting women's economic opportunities, and were neither legitimate nor effective as a measure for promoting women's reproductive health. Women should have a right to free choice as to their employment'.[134] The overemphasis on legislative protection and cultural promotion of motherhood and family roles for women, rather than on women as

---

[122] CO Congo, A/58/38, 28th Session (2003) para 180; CO Bhutan, A/59/38, 31st Session (2004) paras 31 and 32.

[123] CO Timor-Leste, CEDAW/C/TLS/CO/1 (2009) para 29; CO Botswana, CEDAW/C/BOT/CO/3 (2010) para 23; CO Albania, A/58/38, 28th Session (2003) para 69.

[124] CO Togo, CEDAW/C/TGO/CO/5 (2006) para 14.

[125] CO Guinea-Bissau, CEDAW/C/GNB/CO/6 (2009) para 23.

[126] CO Ghana, CEDAW/C/GHA/CO/5 (2006) para 21.

[127] CO Botswana, CEDAW/C/BOT/CO/3 (2010) para 23.

[128] eg CO Paraguay, A/51/38, 15th Session (1996) para 126; CO Kyrgyzstan, A/59/38, 31st Session (2004) para 171.

[129] CO Burundi, CEDAW/C/BDI/CO/4 (2008) para 13.

[130] CO Saudi Arabia, CEDAW/C/SAU/CO/4 (2008) para 15.

[131] CO Ecuador, A/49/38, 13th Session (1994) para 523; similarly eg CO Dominican Republic, A/53/38, 18th Session (1998) para 334; and CO Nicaragua, A/56/38, 25th Session (2001) para 294.

[132] CO Ecuador, A/49/38, 13th Session (1994) para 524; similarly CO Cuba, A/55/38, 23rd Session (2000) para 261; CO Jamaica, CEDAW/C/JAM/CO/5 (2006) para 15.

[133] This issue is also discussed in chs on arts 4 and 11.

[134] CO Ukraine, A/51/38, 15th Session (1996) para 286; similarly CO Armenia, A/52/38, 17th Session (1997) para 58; CO Czech Republic, A/53/38, 18th Session (1998) para 196; CO China, A/54/38, 20th Session (1999) paras 280 and 296; CO Kazakhstan, A/56/38, 24th Session (2001) paras 101–2; CO Kuwait, A/59/38, 31st Session (2004) para 72.

individuals in their own right, limits women's possibilities and reinforces fathers' lack of participation in child care.[135]

d) Breadwinner Models and Sharing Responsibilities within the Family

The Committee is also concerned about the persistence of male breadwinner models and the lack of facilities that would stimulate the sharing of responsibilities within the family.[136] This situation is based on 'entrenched stereotypical attitudes to women in society, and the idea of an exclusively male head of household' and it 'encourages segregation in employment, and a denial of the economic contribution of women.'[137] The Committee connects this issue to 'women's predominance in part-time work, their main responsibility for family and caring work, occupational segregation, men's extremely low participation in parental leave . . . and the taxation of married couples'.[138] The Committee expressly rejects the encouragement of part-time work as a solution to the problem of the combination of paid work and care activities.[139] It sees the fact that mainly women work part-time as an indication of hidden or indirect discrimination.[140] Governments are urged to take measures allowing women to choose to work full time.[141] In the same vein, the Committee links gender stereotyping to the persistence of the gender pay gap[142] and warns that job evaluation and pay schemes may be based on gender stereotypes.[143] Gender stereotyping and fixed parental gender roles may lead to a lack of social arrangements, in both the private and the public sectors, that could facilitate the reconciliation of paid work and care obligations of both men and women. In this context, the Committee often mentions child care facilities and parental leave for both fathers and mothers.[144] Sometimes, the Committee finds that a country is setting a good example in this respect, for example, where it praised a State party 'for directing attention to the necessary changes in men's roles and tasks as an important element in achieving true gender equality, including men's encouragement to use their right to paternity leave and to increase their involvement as caretakers in the labour market'.[145]

---

[135] CO Slovakia, A/53/38, 19th Session (1998) para 74; similarly CO Armenia, A/52/38, 17th Session (1997) para 58.

[136] CO Austria, CEDAW/C/AUT/CO/6 (2007) para 17; similarly CO Greece, CEDAW/C/GRC/CO/6 (2007) para 13; CO Germany, A/59/38, 31st Session (2004) para 384; CO Cape Verde, CEDAW/C/CPV/CO/6 (2006) para 17; CO China, CEDAW/C/CHN/CO/6 (2006) para 17; CO Poland, CEDAW/C/POL/CO/6 (2007) para 16; CO Italy, CEDAW/C/ITA/CC/4–5 (2005) para 25; CO Estonia, A/57/38, 26th Session (2002) paras 25–6; CO Lithuania, A/55/38, 23rd Session (2000) paras 138–9; CO Egypt, A/56/38, 24th Session (2001) para 332.

[137] CO Fiji Islands, A/57/38, 26th Session (2002) para 31. Women's economic and social rights are further discussed in chs on arts 11 and 13.

[138] CO Germany, A/55/38, 22nd Session (2000) paras 313–14; similarly CO Germany, A/59/38, 31st Session (2004) para 384.

[139] CO Australia, A/50/38, 14th Session (1995) para 600.

[140] CO Belgium, A/51/38, 15th Session (1996) para 187; CO Iceland, A/51/38, 15th Session (1996) para 96; CO Germany, A/55/38, 22nd Session (2000) paras 313–14.

[141] eg CO The Netherlands, A/56/38, 25th Session (2001) para 214.

[142] eg CO The United Kingdom, A/54/38, 21st Session (1999) para 308; CO Germany, A/55/38, 22nd Session (2000) paras 313–14; CO Norway, A/50/38, 14th Session (1995) para 491.

[143] CO Finland, A/56/38, 24th Session (2001) para 298.

[144] eg CO France, CEDAW/C/FRA/CO/6 (2008) para 27; CO Saudi Arabia, CEDAW/C/SAU/CO/4, (2008) para 32.

[145] CO Norway, A/50/38, 14th Session (1995) para 486; similarly CO Finland, A/50/38, 14th Session (1995) para 388.

e) Gender Stereotyping in Education and the Media

Time and again, the Committee has stated that it is 'concerned about the consequences of gender stereotyping in curricula and the impact of the fact that girls take traditional "female" courses and boys traditional "male" courses on women's employment options and income',[146] and has drawn attention to stereotypical cultural attitudes which are reflected in the segregation of the labour market and in educational choices of girls and boys.[147] As a result, 'women continue to be concentrated in a narrow range of employment'.[148] In this context, the Committee has often urged the elimination of gender stereotypes in educational materials in order to facilitate 'the diversification of the educational choices of boys and girls'.[149]

The Committee also frequently makes comments on the way in which women are depicted in advertising and in the media as sex objects and in traditional roles.[150] On a few occasions, it notes with concern 'that a process of mainstreaming pornography, also known as "sexualization of the public sphere", is occurring in the State party',[151] and that media and advertising 'are becoming increasingly pornographic, and that the over-sexualized depiction of women strengthens the existing stereotypes of women as sex object and girls' low self-esteem'.[152]

3. *Culture and Religion Cannot Justify Discrimination against Women*

The Committee acknowledges 'that culture is a positive vehicle for influencing the advancement of women, and suggested that cultural art forms be used as a vehicle to promote respect for women'.[153] However, such considerations are often followed by the Committee's serious concerns about the negative impact that the same culture may have on women's human rights.[154] When confronted with damaging cultural beliefs and practices, it always reminds States parties of Article 5, often in combination with Article 2(f), and argues that 'cultural characteristics could not be allowed to undermine the principle of the universality of human rights, which remained inalienable and non-negotiable, nor to prevent the adoption of appropriate measures in favour of women'.[155] With respect to religion, it has noticed that States parties do not make sufficient effort to counteract the damaging effects of some (fundamentalist) religious beliefs or practices.[156] It sees

---

[146] eg CO Trinidad and Tobago, A/57/38, 26th Session (2002) para 33. See also the discussion in ch on art 10.

[147] CO Norway, CEDAW/C/NOR/CO/7 (2007) para 17.

[148] eg CO France, CEDAW/C/FRA/CO/6 (2008) para 18; CO Lebanon, CEDAW/C/LBN/CO/3 (2008) para 24; CO Belize, CEDAW/C/BLZ/CO/4 (2007) para 23.

[149] eg CO Estonia, CEDAW/C/EST/CO/4 (2007) para 13.

[150] CO Germany, A/59/38, 31st Session (2004) para 384; similarly CO Germany, CEDAW/C/DEU/CO/6 (2009) para 27; CO Italy, CEDAW/C/ITA/CC/4-5 (2005) para 25. In this context the Committee regularly uses the words 'sexist' or 'sexism', eg CO Ukraine, CEDAW/C/UKR/CO/7 (2010) para 24.

[151] CO Sweden, CEDAW/C/SWE/CO/7 (2008) para 22.

[152] CO Finland, CEDAW/C/FIN/5 and 6 (2008) para 177.

[153] CO Antigua and Barbuda, A/52/38, 17th Session (1997) para 270; similarly CO Guyana, A/49/38, 13th Session (1994) para 101.

[154] CO Bhutan, A/59/38, 31st Session (2004) para 115; CO Cambodia, CEDAW/C/KHM/CO/3 (2006) para 17; CO Cook Islands, CEDAW/C/COK/CO/1 (2007) para 22.

[155] CO Morocco, A/52/38, 16th Session (1997) para 64; similarly CO Indonesia, A/53/38, 18th Session (1998) para 282; CO Vanuatu, CEDAW/C/VUT/CO/3 (2007) para 10; CO Algeria, A/54/38, 20th Session (1999) para 71.

[156] CO Azerbaijan, A/53/38, 18th Session (1998) para 58; CO Turkey, A/52/38, 16th Session (1997) para 164; CO Indonesia, CEDAW/C/EST/IDN/CO/5 (2007) para 12.

traditionalism under the mask of preserving national identity as a cause of discrimination[157] and in a similar vein expresses concern 'that the concept of Asian values[158] regarding the family, including that of the husband having the legal status of head of household, might be interpreted so as to perpetuate stereotyped gender roles in the family and reinforce discrimination against women'.[159]

According to the Committee, the principles of equality and non-discrimination and respect for women's dignity clearly prevail over claims about the values of religion, culture, or tradition and the wish of States parties to preserve these values. This issue touches on the debate about the concept of the universality of human rights in the light of claims made by some cultures or religions that their (internal) norms should be respected, protected, and sustained, even when they contravene women's human rights.[160] The Committee frequently talks of a dialogue that it deems necessary in order to find solutions for the conflicts that may arise between norms and practices that are based in culture and the human rights standards that are set by the Convention.[161] In that context, the Committee urges States parties 'to create the conditions for a wide intercultural dialogue that would respect diversity while guaranteeing full compliance with the principles, values and international norms for the protection of human rights, including women's rights'.[162]

The Committee's position conforms to many other international legal instruments, which acknowledge the right of all human beings to live according to cultural traditions and a right to practise one's beliefs. These rights exist under the condition that the human rights of others, including women, are not in any way restricted or violated.[163] This position is reflected in (*inter alia*) the UNESCO Convention on the Protection and Promotion of the Diversity of Cultural Expressions (2005), stating in Article 2 that 'no one may invoke the provisions of this Convention in order to infringe human rights and fundamental freedoms as enshrined in the Universal Declaration of Human Rights or guaranteed by international law, or to limit the scope thereof'. Similarly, the (1981) UN Declaration on the Elimination of All Forms of Intolerance and of Discrimination Based on Religion or Belief stipulates in Article 5(5) that a child may not be injured under the pretext of religion or belief.[164]

Some international documents that guarantee the freedom of religion also contain clauses in which this freedom is restricted by the rights and freedoms of others.[165] Automatic preference of women's human rights over the freedom of religion cannot be

---

[157] CO Mozambique, CEDAW/C/MOZ/CO/2 (2007) para 22.

[158] Reference is made to the Bangkok Declaration (7 April 1993) UN Doc A/Conf.157/ASRM/8-A/CONF.157/PC/59.

[159] CO Singapore, A/56/38, 25th Session (2001) para 79.

[160] eg S Moller Okin, 'Is Multiculturalism Bad for Women?' (1997) *Boston Review* 22, 25–32; CI Nyamu, 'How Should Human Rights and Development Respond to Cultural Legitimization of Gender Hierarchy in Developing Countries?' (2000) 41 *Harvard Intl L J* 381–418; Volpp (n 31 above) 1181–218; F Raday 'Culture, Religion, and Gender' (2003) 1 *Intl J of Constitutional L* 663–715; Sunder (n 65 above) 1393–472; A Phillips, *Multiculturalism Without Culture* (2007); D Otto, 'Rethinking the "Universality" of Human Rights Law' (1997–1998) 29 *Columbia Human Rights L Rev* 1–46; Holtmaat and Naber (n 51 above).

[161] eg CO Nigeria, CEDAW/C/NGA/6 (2008) para 323; CO Nicaragua, CEDAW/C/NIC/CO/6 (2007) para 12.

[162] eg CO Bolivia (2008) CEDAW/C/BOL/CO-4 para 23.

[163] Koukoulis-Spiliotopoulos (n 119 above) 418.

[164] UNGA Res 36/55 (25 November 1981) UN Doc A/RES/36/55. C Packer, *Using Human Rights to Change Tradition* (2002) 74.

[165] eg ICCPR art 18(3).

induced from such exception clauses. When invoking such a provision, it needs to be demonstrated that a certain religious practice is indeed damaging for women's rights and interests and therefore justifies a restriction of religious freedom.[166] In its General Comment on ICCPR Article 18, the Human Rights Committee has stated 'that the fact that a religion is recognized as a state religion or that it is established as official or traditional or that its followers comprise the majority of the population, shall not result in any impairment of the enjoyment of any of the rights under the Covenant.'[167] In a similar vein, it expressly stated that the rights that are guaranteed under Article 27 do not authorize any State, group, or person to violate women's human rights under the Covenant.[168]

D. Issues of Implementation

I. The Nature of the Obligations under Article 5

1. All Appropriate Measures to Modify Patterns of Conduct and to Ensure Education

The drafters of the Convention left open what States parties should do to implement their obligations under Article 5.[169] The Chapeau of Article 5 speaks of taking 'all appropriate measures' to 'modify' (section a) and to 'ensure' (section b). States parties' obligations under international human rights law may be divided into obligations to respect, to protect and to fulfil.[170] The Committee does not use this typology when discussing obligations under Article 5.[171] It mentions first, measures to modify stereotyped ideas or ideologies that are expressed in educational materials, in advertising and in the media, and second, the obligation of States parties to scrutinize their own laws, policies, and practices and the structural features of society in order to reveal and redress the presence of gender stereotypes and fixed parental gender roles and to amend such laws and policies, including the removal of obstacles to the sharing of family responsibilities between men and women.

2. Measures to Modify Stereotyped Representations of Women in Educational Materials, in Advertising, and in the Media

a) The State Party's Obligation to Change Stereotypes

States parties have a responsibility to eliminate damaging gender stereotypes.[172] This may be done through extensive information campaigns that promote an image of women that is different from the traditional stereotypes.[173] The Committee mentions

---

[166] F Raday, 'Traditionalist Religious and Cultural Challengers: International and Constitutional Human Rights Responses' (2008) 41 *Israel L Rev* 596, 600.

[167] HRC GC 22, UN Doc CCPR/C21/Rev.1/Add.4 (1993) para 9.

[168] CCPR, 'General Comment 28' (2000) UN Doc CCPR/C/21/Rev.1/Add.10 para 32; UN Commission on Human Rights, 'Study on Freedom of Religion or Belief and the Status of Women in the Light of Religion, Report submitted by Mr A Amor, Special Rapporteur, in accordance with Commission on Human Rights resolution 2001/42' (2002) UN Doc E/CN.4/2002/73/Add.2 paras 58 and 64.

[169] Rehof (n 75 above) 77 ff; Holtmaat (n 8 above) 64 ff.

[170] See the discussion in ch on art 1 and Introduction.

[171] Cook and Cusack (n 17 above) 76 ff analyze the obligations following from art 5(a) along these lines.

[172] GR 3.

[173] CO Czech Republic, A/53/38, 18th Session (1998) para 206; CO Estonia, A/57/38, 26th Session (2002) paras 25–6. See for a positive appraisal of such campaigns CO Cyprus, A/51/38, 15th Session (1996) para 51.

(mass) media and education as the two most important sectors in this respect.[174] States parties have a special responsibility with respect to educational materials, as is also stressed in Article 10(c). They have the obligation to put an end to gender segregation in professional education and employment by changing the content of educational curricula and materials and providing gender-sensitive teacher training programmes.[175]

b) The State Party's Obligation to Intervene in Public Expressions of Gender Stereotypes

Although a proposal to make it obligatory for States to prohibit incitement to discrimination against women was rejected during the drafting process, States parties have duties concerning the protection of women against damaging gender stereotypes produced by non-State (private) actors. Under Article 5, States parties are obliged to ensure that there are no damaging stereotypes in the media, in educational materials, and similar forms of expression, even when these are presented by private actors.[176] The Committee commends legislative measures (such as a legal obligation to install a Code of Ethics),[177] but a State party may also take measures that stimulate voluntary cooperation by private actors.[178] With regard to pornography, the Committee has welcomed new censorship laws, which 'would place greater restrictions on the availability of violent and pornographic material, introduce new controls on the displaying of the material and set penalties for the possession of banned materials'.[179] Where the Government does not have the authority to intervene directly because it would risk violating freedom of expression, the freedom of religion, and/or the freedom of education,[180] the Committee 'urges the State party to encourage the mass media to promote cultural changes with regard to the roles and tasks attributed to women and men, as required by article 5 of the Convention'.[181] Incidentally, it 'calls upon the State party to strengthen its strategies to combat sexualization of the public sphere and to take proactive measures to ensure that media production and coverage are non-discriminatory and increase awareness of these issues among media proprietors and other relevant actors in the industry'.[182]

---

[174] CO Lithuania, A/55/38, 23rd Session (2000) para 139; similarly CO Romania, A/55/38, 23rd Session (2000) para 303; CO Egypt, A/56/38, 24th Session (2001) paras 334–5; CO Vietnam, A/56/38, 25th Session (2001) para 251; CO Estonia, A/57/38, 26th Session (2002) paras 25–6.

[175] eg CO France, CEDAW/C/FRA/CO/6 (2008) para 18; CO Lebanon, CEDAW/C/LBN/CO/3 (2008) para 24; CO Belize, CEDAW/C/BLZ/CO/4 (2007) para 23; CO Estonia, CEDAW/C/EST/CO/4 (2007) para 13; CO Belgium (2008) CEDAW/C/BEL/CO/6, para 24; CO Guinea-Bissau, CEDAW/C/GNB/CO/6 (2009) para 23.

[176] This can be seen as the obligation to protect.

[177] CO Lithuania, A/55/38, 23rd Session (2000) para 139; CO Romania, A/55/38, 23rd Session (2000) para 303; CO Egypt, A/56/38, 24th Session (2001) paras 334–5; CO Vietnam, A/56/38, 25th Session (2001) para 251; CO Estonia, A/57/38, 26th Session (2002) paras 25–6.

[178] CO France, CEDAW/C/FRA/CO/6 (2008) para 18.

[179] CO New Zealand, A/49/38, 13th Session (1994) para 641.

[180] The Committee recognizes this constitutional limitation in CO Germany, CEDAW/C/DEU/CO/6 (2009) para 28.

[181] CO Ukraine, A/57/38, 27th Session (2002) para 296; similarly CO El Salvador, CEDAW/C/SLV/CO/7 (2008) para 23; CO Bahrain, CEDAW/C/BHR/CO/2 (2008) para 23.

[182] CO Sweden, CEDAW/C/SWE/CO/7 (2008) para 23; similarly CO Japan, CEDAW/C/JPN/CO/6 (2009) para 29.

3. Measures to Eliminate Structural Discrimination and to Promote the Sharing of Family Responsibilities

a) Revealing Structural Discrimination

Article 5 requires that the systemic or structural nature of discrimination against women be brought to the surface.[183] Stereotypical gender identities and fixed parental gender roles are very deeply entrenched in all cultures.[184] They are reflected in and sustained by State laws.[185] Revealing the way gender stereotypes and fixed parental gender roles are entrenched in laws and in government practices and policies requires education and training of lawyers and civil servants on the issue of gender stereotypes.[186] States parties must undertake gender impact assessments and integrate gender perspectives in all areas of government action, such as 'legal provisions on the taxation of married couples ("splitting") and its impact on the perpetuation of stereotypical expectations for married women'.[187] This requires gender expertise at a high government level and commitment of the leading political and administrative stakeholders. NGOs should be involved as a resource and not as holders of the obligation. The Committee 'recommends that the Government take advantage of existing bodies of knowledge relating to indirect and structural patterns of discrimination. It emphasizes that the Government, rather than women themselves, have primary responsibility for implementing strategies to eliminate these forms of discrimination'.[188] In order to fulfil the obligations under Articles 5(a) and 2(f), the Committee has recommended 'that the State party further clarify the causes of persistent inequality between women and men, including through studies on the institutional rules that reinforce gender-role stereotyping, [and] the specific manifestations of stereotypical ideology in the State party'.[189]

b) Abolishing and Amending Laws and Policies that Sustain Structural Discrimination

Article 5 calls for transformative equality, including the abolition of all forms of direct, indirect, or structural discrimination that exists as a consequence of gender stereotypes and fixed gender parental roles.[190] The Committee regularly has urged States parties to 'review and reform personal laws of different ethnic and religious groups to ensure *de jure* gender equality and compliance with the Convention'.[191] The Committee has offered a far-reaching warning that a State party's constitution reflected a stereotyped image of the roles of women 'in the home and as mothers', and urged the Parliamentary Committee

---

[183] This could be seen as a duty to fulfil. In Holtmaat (n 8 above) ch 15, a methodology of revealing and abolishing instances of structural discrimination is included. Cook and Cusack (n 17 above) 45 ff.

[184] Cook and Cusack (n 17 above) in ch 2, emphasize that for the elimination of gender stereotypes it is crucial to reveal them.

[185] CO Ecuador, A/49/38, 13th Session (1994) para 523.

[186] CO Italy, A/52/38, 17th Session (1997) para 357; CO Cook Islands, CEDAW/C/COK/CO/1 (2007) para 15.

[187] CO Germany, A/55/38, 22nd Session (2000) para 314; similarly CO Germany, CEDAW/C/DEU/CO/6 (2009) para 30.

[188] CO Croatia, UN Doc A/53/38, 18th Session (1998) para 113; similarly CO Equatorial Guinea, A/59/38, 31st Session (2004) para 195; CO Togo, CEDAW/C/TGO/CO/5 (2006) para 14.

[189] CO Greece, CEDAW/C/GRC/CO/6 (2007) para 14; similarly CO Morocco, A/52/38, 16th Session (1997) para 72.

[190] This can be seen as an obligation to respect.

[191] eg CO India, CEDAW/C/IND/CO/3 (2007) para 11; CO Fiji Islands, A/57/38, 26th Session (2002) para 32; CO Indonesia, CEDAW/C/EST/IDN/CO/5 (2007) para 18.

working on a revision of the constitution to be fully aware of the 'obligations under the Convention, including article 5'.[192] In that regard the Committee suggested 'that the State party consider replacing male-oriented language with gender-sensitive language in the Constitution to convey the concept of gender equality more clearly'.[193]

c) Adopting New Laws and Public Policies

The Committee also calls for the enactment of new laws and policies in the areas of economic and social rights, including the right to child care and the right to parental leave, for example, where it asks a State party to ensure that 'legislation and policies create the structural and systemic framework that will lead to women's long-term participation in the labour force on a basis of equality with men'.[194] The Committee, in the context of discussing Article 5 and/or Article 11, repeatedly insists that concrete measures are needed to promote the role of men in unpaid care activities.[195] The enactment of pregnancy leave and/or parental leave is not deemed sufficient for that purpose, as it cannot be guaranteed that they will lead to a substantial change in (fixed) gender roles.[196] In fact, such policies may 'continue to place primary responsibility for family work and childcare on women, rather than emphasizing the shared responsibility of men and women'.[197]

4. *Temporary Special Measures to Implement Article 5*

The obligation to modify gender stereotypes and fixed parental gender roles cannot be fulfilled without the States parties undertaking measures to bring about the necessary changes in attitudes, beliefs, and practices, both at the level of individuals and private parties and at State level.[198] In General Recommendation 25, the Committee reminds States parties 'that temporary special measures should be adopted to accelerate the modification and elimination of cultural practices and stereotypical attitudes and behaviour that discriminate against or are disadvantageous for women'.[199] Occasionally, the Committee has stated that it is concerned about the lack of 'temporary special measures in order to eliminate these stereotypes'.[200] Temporary special measures are also mentioned in relation to changing men's roles in the family.[201] Measures that are presented by States parties as a positive measure for women may be stereotypical themselves, for example, when a programme concerns 'non-academic training such as embroidery, industrial sewing, etc., conducted as a positive discrimination programme', which 'would only contribute to keeping women to the feminized sector of the economy'.[202]

---

[192]   CO Ireland, A/54/38, 21st Session (1999) paras 193–4. The Committee here refers to art 41(2) of the Irish Constitution.

[193]   CO Ireland, CEDAW/C/IRL/CO/4-5 (2005) para 25.

[194]   CO Ireland, A/54/38, 21st Session (1999) para 182.

[195]   eg CO Ukraine, A/51/38, 15th Session (1996) para 300; CO Iceland, A/57/38, 26th Session (2002) para 28.

[196]   CO Iceland, A/51/38, 15th Session (1996) paras 94–5; CO Sweden, CEDAW/C/SWE/CO/7 (2008) para 26.

[197]   CO Ireland, A/54/38, 21st Session (1999) para 183; similarly CO Finland, A/56/38, 24th Session (2001) para 298.

[198]   Cook and Cusack (n 17 above) 82.   [199]   GR 25 para 38.

[200]   CO Estonia, A/57/38, 26th Session (2002) paras 25–6; CO Lithuania, A/55/38, 23rd Session (2000) paras 138–9; CO Ireland, A/54/38, 21st Session (1999) para 190.

[201]   CO Czech Republic, A/53/38, 18th Session (1998) para 206.

[202]   CO Mauritius, A/50/38, 14th Session (1995) para 213.

II. The Extent of the Obligations

1. Immediate or Gradual Implementation

States parties are under all circumstances required to implement Convention obligations (including Article 5) in a timely fashion and in good faith.[203] The subject matter of Article 5 suggests that this Article obliges States parties to start implementing its provisions immediately after ratification. On several occasions the Committee has 'emphasized the fact that, despite the country's current economic problems, initiatives could be developed in favour of equality at minimal expense, and indeed must be developed'.[204] The Committee regularly stresses that a State party should implement its obligations under this Article 'without delay'.[205] Sometimes, the Committee adds to this that the State party is urged 'to put in place, without delay, a comprehensive strategy, including clear goals and timetables, to modify and eliminate negative cultural attitudes and practices and deep-rooted stereotypes that discriminate against women, in conformity with articles 2(f) and 5(a) of the Convention'.[206] The obligation to eliminate structural discrimination requires that States parties (re-)examine and amend their laws and policies. This requires gender expertise and the existence of an adequate machinery to fulfil the obligations in this respect, which may take some time to develop.

In 2002, the Committee decided that its concluding observations would include a section on 'factors and difficulties' affecting the implementation of the Convention only in the most exceptional circumstances. 'The persistence of stereotypical attitudes relating to the roles of women and men would not be categorized as such a factor or difficulty'.[207] The Committee has confirmed that position by declining to accept a State party's claim of societal support for discriminatory practices as a rationale for failing to deal with them.[208]

Gender stereotypes and ideas about the inferiority of women, as well as traditional (fixed) gender roles concerning fatherhood and motherhood, are deeply entrenched in all cultures and societies. Gradual implementation of Article 5 and support from the population[209] may be required to avoid a backlash.[210] The Committee has indicated that it 'recognizes that changing mentality is a long-term endeavour and calls upon the State party to continue, in a comprehensive manner, its efforts until these gender-role stereotypes are eliminated'.[211]

---

[203] RJ Cook, 'State Accountability under the Convention on the Elimination of All Forms of Discrimination Against Women' in RJ Cook (ed), *Human Rights of Women. National and International Perspectives* (1994) 229 ff.

[204] CO Ecuador, A/49/38, 13th Session (1994) para 540; similarly CO Morocco, A/52/38, 16th Session (1997) para 71.

[205] eg CO Gabon, CEDAW/C/GAB/CC 2-5 (2005) para 31; CO Niger, CEDAW/C/NER/CO/2 (2007) para 18; CO Malawi, CEDAW/C/MWI/CO/5 (2006) para 20.

[206] eg CO Nicaragua, CEDAW/C/NIC/CO/6 (2007) para 12.

[207] UN Doc A/57/38 (Part II) ch VI: 'Ways and Means of Expediting the Work of the Committee' para 374.

[208] CO Gabon, CEDAW/C/GAB/CC 2-5 (2005) para 30.

[209] CO Morocco, A/52/38, 16th Session (1997) para 71.

[210] Raday (n 166 above) 596–634, concerning a backlash caused by some judgments of constitutional courts condemning traditional or religious practices as violations of women's human rights.

[211] CO Luxembourg, CEDAW/C/LUX/CO/5 (2008) para 16.

2. *Public and Private Life*

From the wording of Article 5(a) it appears that it is directed in the first instance at the sphere of (open or covert) expressions of negative and damaging stereotypes about the roles of men and women in public, both in vertical and horizontal relationships.[212] In addition, Article 5(b) addresses the issue of education, which also is generally an aspect of public life. However, measures to combat damaging stereotyped expressions and to educate the public about the proper understanding of the shared responsibilities of both parents can have an impact on the private or intimate relationships between men and women and the way they organize their family life. The Committee has recognized that a State party that bans gender stereotypes from its laws and policies and tries to transform fixed parental gender roles will thereby influence the private relations within the family, observing that it is 'difficult for the Government to promote new concepts of men's and women's roles without appearing to interfere, once again, with individual choices and desires'.[213]

Even if a State party limits its actions to implement Article 5 to the public sphere, the question may arise as to how far other constitutionally guaranteed human rights (such as freedom of speech or freedom of religion or education) may be curtailed. In relation to Articles 5(b) and 10(c) the issue may arise whether and how far a State party has the liberty to prescribe certain educational materials or programmes, especially when the school belongs to a particular religious denomination or is funded privately. Nevertheless, such freedoms cannot prevent the application or implementation of Article 5. In theory and practice they can be limited by other rights, such as the right not to be discriminated against on grounds of sex.[214] The Convention protects women against gender stereotyping and advocating women's inferiority. A State party that really wants to put an end to this type of discrimination and takes measures to that effect, must argue that such measures are justifiable on the ground that Article 5 requires them to be taken.[215]

3. *Justiciability*

Article 5(a) has been invoked by the authors of several communications under the Optional Protocol. The Committee has held States parties accountable for violating their obligations under this provision. This means that, within the framework of the individual complaints procedure, Article 5 is conceived of as a right that an individual can invoke against her own government. The justiciability of Article 5 on the domestic level (in individual court cases) is a subject of debate. According to some commentators, the provision lacks determinacy as there is no definition of key concepts such as stereotyped roles and the inferiority or superiority of either of the sexes[216] and the article encompasses 'the objective of eradicating role models, and thereby enlarging the freedom of choice of women, [which] is an extra-legal objective and that its realization is outside the scope of the law'.[217] However, the function of Article 5 may be of a different nature, providing both a basis on which to evaluate the norms and customs of one's society and to modify its social and cultural behaviours and beliefs which cause or sustain human rights violations. The emphasis, therefore, is on States parties' obligations to be proactive in implementing

---

[212] The fact that the Convention may have horizontal effect also follows from art 2(e), see the discussion in ch on art 2.
[213] CO Bulgaria, A/53/38, 18th Session (1998) para 233.   [214] Cook and Cusack (n 17 above) 241.
[215] Lijnzaad (n 7 above) 55.   [216] Ibid 45 and 57.   [217] Ibid 46.

Article 5 concretely. Therefore, it seems incorrect to describe Article 5 as soft law.[218] In addition, Article 5 may very well play a role in determining in individual domestic cases what should qualify as direct or indirect discrimination against women.[219] In that sense, the article helps to strengthen women's legal and *de facto* positions in terms of their right not to be subjected to any form of discrimination, including gender stereotyping.

4. Reservations

A remarkably small number of States parties have entered reservations to Article 5, considering its far-reaching content and scope.[220] Article 5, in combination with Article 2(f), belongs to the very core of the Convention.[221] These reservations are therefore incompatible with the object and purpose of the Convention under Article 28(2), as has been argued by several objecting States parties, including Mexico, Norway, France, and the Netherlands. The Committee has noted that reservations to the Convention cannot be justified with reference to traditions and religion.[222] This point of view has also been laid down in a general statement about the acceptability of reservations: 'Neither traditional, religious or cultural practice nor incompatible domestic laws and policies can justify violations of the Convention.'[223]

---

[218] Packer (n 164 above) 54, stating that 'the undertaking is of a softer character than a legal claim'.

[219] Cook and Cusack (n 17 above) discuss a range of judgments of national and international or regional courts which directly or indirectly refer to the standards of art 5.

[220] See also the discussion in ch on art 28.

[221] Cusack and Cook, 'Combating Discrimination on Sex and Gender' in C Krause and M Scheinin (eds), *International Protection of Human Rights: A Textbook* (2009) 223.

[222] eg CEDAW CO Israel, A/52/38, 17th Session (1997) para 157.

[223] CEDAW, 'General Statement on the Impact of Reservations' UN Doc A/53/38, 19th session (1998) part II para 17.

Article 6

States Parties shall take all appropriate measures, including legislation, to suppress all forms of traffic in women and exploitation of prostitution of women.

* I would like to thank Anne Gallagher, Nathan Briggs, Matthieu Riviere, Kyle Ingram, Meredith Owen, and Sara Waldron.

A. Introduction

I. Historical Context and Main Concepts

Article 6 of the Convention addresses the obligation of States parties to suppress the trafficking and exploitation of prostitution[1] of women. When the Convention was drafted, these issues were already addressed in international treaties, specifically the 1949 Convention for the Suppression of the Traffic in Persons and of the Exploitation of the Prostitution of Others[2] (1949 Trafficking Convention). Declaring trafficking (for sexual purposes only) and prostitution to be 'incompatible with the dignity and worth of the human person' and a 'danger to the welfare of the individual, the family and the community', the 1949 Trafficking Convention punishes the (undefined) practices of trafficking, procurement, and exploitation of prostitution, irrespective of the victim's age or consent, and whether internal or cross-border. Due to the existing coverage under international law, the Convention drafters believed that trafficking needed only brief mention. Bringing trafficking into a human rights treaty regime denoted an important conceptual shift, however, by subjecting, for the first time, States' anti-trafficking efforts to the scrutiny of an expert treaty monitoring body.

Like the 1949 Trafficking Convention, Article 6 of the Convention does not define the terms 'trafficking' and 'exploitation of prostitution'. While exploitation of prostitution is generally understood to refer to pimping, the meaning of trafficking has evolved (and been deeply contested) over time.[3] The CEDAW Committee has embraced a more expansive conception of trafficking than that of the 1949 Trafficking Convention. In its General Recommendation 19, for example, the Committee identified 'new forms of trafficking' including 'the recruitment of domestic labour from developing countries to work in developed countries and organized marriages between women from developing countries and foreign nationals'. Even this characterization is outdated, as migratory flows are now understood to run from poorer countries to *relatively* wealthier countries, rather than necessarily from developing to developed countries.

---

[1] Following the usage of art 6, this text uses the terms 'prostitution' or 'prostitutes' and not 'sex-work' or 'sex-worker'.

[2] Convention for the Suppression of the Traffic in Persons and of the Exploitation of the Prostitution of Others (Trafficking Convention) (opened for signature 21 March 1950, entered into force 15 July 1951) 96 UNTS 271.

[3] A Gallagher, *The International Law of Human Trafficking* (2010) 12–42.

The 2000 UN Protocol to Prevent, Suppress and Punish Trafficking in Persons, Especially Women and Children[4] (Trafficking Protocol), supplementing the 2000 UN Convention against Transnational Organized Crime[5] (Organized Crime Convention), finally defined 'trafficking' as a matter of international law and States' obligations to address this problem were specifically articulated. The Committee has called upon States parties to ratify the Trafficking Protocol and to adopt the new international legal definition of trafficking contained therein.[6]

(a) 'Trafficking in persons' shall mean the recruitment, transportation, transfer, harbouring or receipt of persons, by means of the threat or use of force or other forms of coercion, of abduction, of fraud, of deception, of the abuse of power or of a position of vulnerability or of the giving or receiving of payments or benefits to achieve the consent of a person having control over another person, for the purpose of exploitation. Exploitation shall include, at a minimum, the exploitation of the prostitution of others or other forms of sexual exploitation, forced labour or services, slavery or practices similar to slavery, servitude or the removal of organs;

(b) The consent of a victim of trafficking in persons to the intended exploitation set forth in subparagraph (a) of this article shall be irrelevant where any of the means set forth in subparagraph (a) have been used.[7]

The international legal definition of trafficking has thus evolved significantly to encompass trafficking of women, men, and children, for the purpose of placing them into a wide range of exploitative labour practices beyond forced prostitution. Consistent with this broader view, the Committee, in its consideration of States parties' reports, has called upon States parties, for example, to protect women and girls from forced marriage,[8] and those working as domestic servants and in maquiladoras from exploitation and abuse.[9]

II. Role of the Convention

As recognized in the Committee's practice, trafficking is a phenomenon inexorably linked to the socio-economic impact of globalization, with wealth disparities feeding increased intra- and transnational labour migration as livelihood options decrease in less wealthy countries and communities. Women are over-represented among those migrating for survival, the gender disparity often attributed to the 'feminization of poverty'[10] arising from the failure of existing social structures to provide equal and just educational and employment opportunities for women. This results in a feminization of migration, as women accept dangerous migration arrangements to escape the

---

[4] Protocol to Prevent, Suppress and Punish Trafficking in Persons, Especially Women and Children, supplementing the United Nations Convention against Transnational Organized Crime (Trafficking Protocol) (adopted 15 November 2000, entered into force 25 December 2003) 2237 UNTS 319.

[5] Convention Against Transnational Organized Crime (Organized Crime Convention) (adopted 15 November 2000, entered into force 29 September 2003) 2225 UNTS 209.

[6] CO Poland, CEDAW/C/POL/CO/6 (2007) para 21; CO Guinea-Bissau, CEDAW/C/GNB/CO/6 (2009) para 30.

[7] Trafficking Protocol art 3(a)-(b).

[8] CO India, A/55/38, 22nd Session (2000) para 62; CO Democratic Republic of the Congo, A/55/38, 22nd Session (2000) para 215; CO Cameroon, A/55/38, 23rd Session (2000) para 54.

[9] CO Nicaragua, A/56/38, 25th Session (2001) para 315; CO Mauritania, CEDAW/C/MRT/CO/1 (2007) para 32.

[10] CO Belarus, A/59/38, 30th Session (2004) paras 350–4; CO Portugal, CEDAW/C/PRT/CO7 (2007) paras 44–5.

entrenched discrimination, including unequal employment, gender-based violence, and the lack of access to basic resources for women.[11] Current data indicating that women and girls form the majority of trafficked persons suggest that trafficking is a gender-based harm.[12] Women experience discrimination at every stage of the trafficking cycle. Gender-based discrimination and violence in their home communities increase women's vulnerability to traffickers; women are forced into gender-specific exploitative labour (for example, forced prostitution, domestic work); and they suffer gender-specific harms from trafficking (for example, unwanted pregnancy, forced marriage, rape, forced abortion, STDs). The Convention's broad framework for eliminating discrimination against women in all spheres of life thus offers unique potential to address the underlying root causes of women's and girls' particular vulnerabilities to trafficking.

The Convention is one of several different sources of international laws relevant to the prevention and punishment of trafficking, and the protection of trafficking survivors. These include, in addition to trafficking-specific treaties,[13] treaties relating to slavery and the slave trade,[14] forced labour,[15] human rights, and criminal justice.[16] Within the area of human rights alone, trafficking can be approached from a number of different angles—for example, women's rights, labour rights, children's rights, migrant workers' rights. The Convention is one of only two international human rights treaties that mention trafficking specifically, the Convention on the Rights of the Child (CRC) being the other.[17] While subsequent law and policy developments have culminated in a much broader understanding of trafficking than that held by the CEDAW Convention drafters (eg as also affecting men and boys and involving non-sexual exploitation), the Convention's identification of trafficking as a problem rooted in discrimination is an important paradigm for exploring the root causes of the phenomenon and for identifying specific rights and State obligations. Moreover, the fact that no State party has entered a reservation to Article 6 heightens the Convention's potential for establishing a baseline anti-discrimination approach to trafficking of women and girls.

---

[11] UNCHR, 'Integration of the Human Rights of Women and the Gender Perspective: Violence against Women' (2000) UN Doc E/CN.4/2000/68 paras 54–60.

[12] eg US Department of State, 'Trafficking in Persons Report' (2008) 7 (claiming 80 per cent of transnational trafficking victims are female). This statistic reflects, however, that trafficking has been seen, until very recently, exclusively as an issue of sexual exploitation affecting women and children.

[13] Council of Europe Convention on Action against Trafficking in Human Beings (Council of Europe Trafficking Convention) (opened for signature 16 May 2005, entered into force 1 February 2008) CETS 197; Convention on Preventing and Combating Trafficking in Women and Children for Prostitution by the South Asian Association for Regional Cooperation (SAARC Convention) (adopted 5 January 2002).

[14] Convention to Suppress the Slave Trade and Slavery (Slavery Convention) (adopted 25 September 1926; entered into force 9 March 1927) 60 LNTS 253; Supplementary Convention on the Abolition of Slavery, the Slave Trade and Institutions and Practices Similar to Slavery (Supplementary Slavery Convention) (adopted 7 September 1956, entered into force 30 April 1957) 226 UNTS 3.

[15] ILO Convention concerning Forced or Compulsory Labour (ILO Convention No 29) (adopted 28 June 1930, entered into force 1 May 1932) 39 UNTS 55; ILO Convention concerning the Abolition of Forced Labour (ILO Convention No 105) (adopted 25 June 1957, entered into force 17 January 1959) 320 UNTS 291; ILO Convention concerning the Prohibition and Immediate Action for the Elimination of the Worst Forms of Child Labor (ILO Convention No 182) (adopted 17 June 1999, entered into force 19 November 2000) 2133 UNTS 161.

[16] The Rome Statute art 7(2)(c); Organized Crime Convention.

[17] Convention on the Rights of the Child (CRC) (adopted 20 November 1989, entered into force 2 September 1990) 1577 UNTS 3 arts 32, 34, and 35.

III. CEDAW Committee Practice

1. *Concluding Observations*

The Committee's assessments of States parties' reports under Article 6 have consisted of recommending broad, programmatic measures and providing, at times inconsistent, interpretations of the scope of Article 6 vis-à-vis the issue of prostitution. It has called upon States parties, for example, to incorporate and implement legislative measures to prevent trafficking and prosecute traffickers; to take measures aimed at poverty alleviation and women's economic empowerment; to provide victim assistance through counselling, reintegration, and rehabilitation; to collect data on trafficking and the impact of anti-trafficking interventions; and to increase international, regional, and bilateral cooperation with other countries.[18] The Committee has also discussed the discrimination that feeds trafficking, such as rural women's unequal access to food, lack of access to alternative livelihoods, discriminatory measures taken against prostitutes and not the pimps, customers, or traffickers. But the Committee has not linked States parties' obligations to address these root causes to specific provisions of the Convention, and instead has situated them generally within the context of Article 6.[19] States parties' obligations under Article 6 thus remain broadly programmatic, and could greatly benefit from specific elaboration in the form of a general recommendation on trafficking and exploitation of prostitution. Inconsistencies in the Committee's reviews of States parties' reports with regard to prostitution are a potential obstacle, however, to the development of a general recommendation on Article 6. Not surprisingly, given the deep divides within the international feminist community over prostitution reform, the Committee members themselves have divergent views as to how States parties should address prostitution.[20] The Committee members' contrasting positions over whether States parties should seek abolition of all prostitution or target only the exploitation of prostitution are evident in the Committee's review of States parties' reports.[21] While, in recent years, the Committee has more consistently followed the text of the Convention by calling upon States parties to target the exploitation of prostitution, its specific guidance has also included recommendations that target prostitution more generally, such as efforts to prevent women from entering into prostitution, and to discourage the demand for prostitution.

2. *General Recommendations*

The Committee addresses trafficking and exploitation of prostitution in General Recommendation 19 on violence against women and briefly references trafficking in General Recommendation 26 on women migrant workers. The Committee initially considered addressing trafficking in General Recommendation 26 on migrant workers, but ultimately decided that trafficking should be addressed separately.[22]

---

[18] See the discussion in section E: *State Obligation* below.

[19] Economic and Social Commission for Asia and the Pacific, *Violence against and Trafficking in Women as Symptoms of Discrimination: The Potential of CEDAW as an Antidote* (Gender and Development Discussion Paper Series No 17, 2005).

[20] E Novikova, 'Poverty, Prostitution, and Trafficking' and K Morvai, 'Personal Reflection: Rethinking Prostitution and Trafficking' in HB Schöpp-Schilling and C Flinterman (eds), *The Circle of Empowerment: Twenty-Five Years of the UN Committee on the Elimination of Discrimination Against Women* (2007) 124–40, 141–4.

[21] See discussion in section C (nn 50–1 below).   [22] GR 26 n 4.

General Recommendation 19 identifies trafficking as a form of violence against women, and *ipso facto*, a form of discrimination on the basis of sex. As a form of gender-based violence, trafficking violates a wide range of rights, including the right to life, right not to be subjected to torture or to cruel, inhuman, or degrading treatment of punishment, right to equal protection according to humanitarian norms in time of international or internal armed conflict, right to liberty and security of the person, right to equal protection under the law, right to equality in the family, right to the highest attainable standard of physical and mental health, and right to just and favourable conditions of work.[23] General Recommendation 19, paragraph 15 notes that poverty and unemployment increase opportunities for trafficking in women and force many women, including young girls, into prostitution. Because prostitutes are 'especially vulnerable to violence' since their status, which may be unlawful, 'tends to marginalize them', prostitutes 'need the equal protection of laws against rape and other forms of violence'. General Recommendation 19, paragraph 16 further notes that 'wars, armed conflicts and occupation of territories often lead to prostitution, trafficking in women and sexual assault of women, which require specific protective and punitive measures'.[24]

General Recommendation 26 addresses women migrant workers in low-paid jobs who may be at high risk of abuse and discrimination and who may never acquire eligibility for permanent stay or citizenship in the country of destination.[25] The Committee recognized that 'while women migrant workers may become victims of trafficking due to various degrees of vulnerability they face', the trafficking phenomenon 'is complex and needs more focused attention'. It noted that many elements of General Recommendation 26 would also be relevant where women migrants have been victims of trafficking.[26]

3. *Optional Protocol*

In *Zhen Zhen Zheng v Netherlands*, Article 6 was the basis of an individual communication filed under the Optional Protocol.[27] The Committee did not reach the merits of the claim, finding the communication inadmissible due to failure to exhaust domestic remedies. The author of the communication, a minor, was trafficked from China into the Netherlands for purposes of forced prostitution. She had not identified herself as a trafficking victim to the Dutch authorities and had unsuccessfully applied for asylum and a resident permit to remain in the Netherlands after she became pregnant and was released from her trafficking situation. The applicant claimed that the Netherlands had violated its obligation under Article 6 for failing to notify her of the possibility of pursuing relief under the 'B9' scheme, which permitted trafficked persons to apply for temporary residency status. The Committee found that the applicant had not exhausted domestic remedies because she had yet to pursue B9 relief after learning of the option and, moreover, judicial review of the decision on the applicant's residency permit application was still pending.

In a dissenting opinion, three Committee members considered the complaint to be admissible and emphasized the State party's obligation to exercise due diligence in identifying potential victims of trafficking and informing them of their rights. The dissent explicitly relied on the UN Trafficking Protocol to interpret States parties' obligations under the Convention Article 6. Finding a violation of Article 6, the dissent

---

[23] GR 19 para 7.   [24] See also the discussion in ch on violence against women.

[25] GR 26 n 4.   [26] Ibid.

[27] *Zhen Zhen Zheng v Netherlands*, Communication 15/2007 (2008) CEDAW/C/42/D/15/2007 para 7.4.

recommended that the Netherlands take steps to determine whether the applicant was trafficked and, if so, to provide the protections required under the Protocol. Moreover, the dissent recommended that the Netherlands take measures to ensure that law enforcement officials are appropriately trained to interview and recognize trafficked persons at an early stage, including interview techniques that account for the vulnerable status of trafficked persons suffering post-traumatic stress disorder. The State party should also require that those identified as trafficked are referred for services and counselling and informed of procedures for seeking protection.[28]

B. Travaux Préparatoires

I. Article 6 Placement and Brevity

The placement and brevity of Article 6 are notable when compared to the other provisions of the Convention. Its placement in Part I, alongside the framework articles, seems odd at first glance, as its subject matter—trafficking and exploitation of prostitution—is more akin to the substantive articles located in the Convention Parts II to IV. The *travaux préparatoires* suggest that placement of the trafficking article in Part I was intentional, but offer no insight as to the rationale behind this choice.

With the exception of an early draft proposed by the USSR, which placed the trafficking article later in the Convention, with provisions labelled 'Civil and Family Rights',[29] all drafts placed it with the framework articles in the first section of the treaty. Until shortly before the final draft, this first section was labelled 'General Provisions', in contrast to the headings 'Political Rights', 'Social and Economic Rights', and 'Civil and Family Rights' that organized the remaining articles.[30] The final draft of the Convention deleted these headings, preferring the labels Parts I through IV, respectively.

One can only speculate as to why the trafficking article was placed in Part I (formerly 'General Provisions') of the Convention. One possibility is that the severity of the harms of trafficking and exploitation of prostitution, as compared to the other substantive articles, warranted elevating its status to the beginning of the Convention. Another possible rationale for article placement could stem from a recognition that effective suppression of trafficking and exploitation of prostitution would require compliance with all of the substantive obligations of the Convention. Yet another possibility is that the drafters conceived of trafficking and exploitation of prostitution as manifestations of discrimination distinct from, but of similar stature to, those described in the framework articles. Unlike the other framework articles, which set out States parties' obligations in terms of measures to achieve equality, Article 6 requires States parties 'to suppress' trafficking and exploitation of prostitution. This unique framing suggests that trafficking is a particular form of discrimination, though it was not formulated as such until General Recommendation 19. Placement of the trafficking article in Part I ultimately does not appear, however, to have been factored into its interpretation by the Committee.

As to the brevity of the text of Article 6, the *travaux préparatoires* make clear that the drafters considered trafficking and exploitation of prostitution to be already sufficiently

---

[28] Ibid para 9.1.   [29] UN Doc E/CN.6/AC.1/L.2 (1974) 9.
[30] eg UN Doc E/CN.6/AC.1/L.6 (1974) 3; UN Doc E/CN.6/591 (1976) 113; UN Doc A/C.3/34/WG.1/CRP.6 (1979) 3–5.

addressed under the 1949 Trafficking Convention, and, thus, 'a detailed article [was] not considered necessary'.[31] The final text of Article 6 was almost entirely derived from Article 8 of DEDAW.[32] The earliest versions of the draft Convention article added to the DEDAW text a phrase obliging States parties to combat trafficking and exploitation of prostitution 'in accordance with international conventions and agreements in this regard',[33] but this explicit reference to international law was soon deleted.[34]

II. Scope of Subject Matter

1. 'All Forms of Traffic'

The Convention does not define 'all forms of traffic'. The *travaux préparatoires* suggest, however, that the drafters intended the term to encompass only trafficking into the sex sector, despite a growing recognition that trafficking can occur for non-sexual purposes. When the Convention was drafted, the phenomenon of 'exploitation of labour through illicit and clandestine trafficking' outside the sex sector was actively being studied within the UN, including by the CSW, Commission on Human Rights, its Sub-Commission on the Prevention of Discrimination and Protection of Minorities, and the International Labour Organization. Whenever 'exploitation of labour and illicit and clandestine trafficking in foreign labour' was discussed specifically in relation to women and girls, however, it was always in the context of trafficking for forced prostitution.[35] Indeed, in the course of the UN's ongoing study, the CSW was explicitly directed to draw attention to the 'plight of young girls and women who were lured into lives of prostitution by false promises of overseas jobs'.[36]

2. 'Exploitation of Prostitution'

As the text of the Convention and its *travaux préparatoires* make clear, the Convention was not intended to suppress prostitution as such, but rather to suppress only the 'exploitation of prostitution'. During the drafting process, a few delegations attempted to expand the scope of the provision to encompass all prostitution. Early on, Norway proposed rewording the draft article to read: 'States Parties agree to take all appropriate measures, including legislation, to combat prostitution and the illicit traffic in women', to bring it into line with the Mexico City World Plan of Action.[37] Shortly thereafter, Denmark proposed, and subsequently withdrew, an amendment to the same effect.[38] Near the end of the drafting process, Morocco offered the following oral amendment: 'States Parties shall take all appropriate measures, including legislation, to suppress prostitution, traffic in women and exploitation of prostitution

---

[31] UN Doc E/CN.6/573 (1973) para 77. Report of the Secretary General, 'Draft Convention on the Elimination of Discrimination against Women' (1977) UN Doc A/32/218 para 50.

[32] DEDAW art 8: 'All appropriate measures, including legislation, shall be taken to combat all forms of traffic in women and exploitation of prostitution of women.' UNGA Res 2263 (XXII) (7 November 1967) UN Doc A/RES/48/104. Aside from changing 'combat' to 'suppress', art 6 is identical.

[33] UN Doc E/CN.6/AC.1/L.6 (1974) 3.   [34] UN Doc CN.6/AC.1/L.17 (1974) 10.

[35] UNCHR, 'Report of the Special Rapporteur: Exploitation of Labour through Illicit and Clandestine Trafficking' (1975) UN Doc E/CN.4/Sub.2/L.640 paras 82–9.

[36] Ibid paras 6, 31, and 32; see also UN Doc E/CN.6/SR.613–28 (1974) 71–3.

[37] UN Doc E/CN.6/591 (1976) 19, 61; World Plan of Action for the Implementation of the Objectives of the International Women's Year, Mexico City 19 June–2 July 1975, UN Doc E/CONF.66/34 (1976) para 159.

[38] UN Doc E/CN.6/SR.638 (1976) paras 40–9.

of women in all its forms.'[39] The Netherlands and Italy objected that the Moroccan amendment was inconsistent with the 1949 Trafficking Convention, which referred only to the exploitation of prostitution, and, thus, that it introduced a new element that their delegations could not accept. Ireland, Ethiopia, and Zambia objected that the phrase 'exploitation of prostitution of women in all its forms' was imprecise and ambiguous. Morocco's amendment was rejected by forty-eight votes to nineteen, with forty-six abstentions.[40] In the final text, Article 6 targets only the 'exploitation of prostitution'.

3. *Other Harms*

There was some discussion during the drafting process of expanding Article 6 to include harms other than prostitution and trafficking. A proposed amendment, that was later withdrawn owing to lack of support, was to broaden Article 6 to include 'attacks on the physical integrity of women'.[41] The need for such a provision dealing with attacks on the physical integrity of women was later noted,[42] and it was proposed that Article 6 should refer to 'combating also those forms of commercial advertisement and exploitation which use the female body in a way contrary to human dignity'.[43] Another was for media exploitation to be taken into account.[44] Ultimately, however, the drafters decided to keep the original text of the Article, limiting its coverage to trafficking and exploitation of prostitution.

C. Issues of Interpretation

I. 'All Forms of Traffic'

Given the Trafficking Protocol definition of trafficking,[45] international law now supports a much broader conception of the term 'trafficking' than that likely contemplated by the Convention drafters. Though the Committee has remained heavily focused on sex trafficking, consistent with evolving international anti-trafficking law, it has interpreted 'all forms of traffic' also to include trafficking for non-sexual purposes. General Recommendation 19, paragraph 14 notes that '[i]n addition to established forms of trafficking there are new forms of sexual exploitation, such as sex tourism, the recruitment of domestic labour from developing countries to work in developed countries and organized marriages between women from developing countries and foreign nationals'. These practices are 'incompatible with the equal enjoyment of rights by women and with respect for their rights and dignity', placing women at special risk of violence and abuse. Accordingly, the Committee has called upon States parties to monitor and address the continuing phenomenon of sex

---

[39] UN Doc A/C.3/34/SR.72 (1979) para 17.

[40] Ibid paras 17–32. During discussions of the final text of the Convention, Guinea and Jordan stated that they would have preferred that art 6 include suppression of prostitution itself, 13 UNYB (31 December 1979) 849.

[41] UN Doc E/CN.6/SR/638 (1976) para 40 (Belgium); UN Doc A/32/218 (1977) para 51 (Portugal).

[42] L Rehof, *Guide to the Travaux Préparatoires of the United Nations Convention on the Elimination of All Forms of Discrimination against Women* (1993) 91.

[43] UN Doc E./CN.6/591 (1976) para 68 and Annex I, 61.   [44] Rehof (n 42 above) 92.

[45] Trafficking Protocol art 3.

tourism[46] and to address trafficking for non-sexual purposes,[47] particularly the trafficking of women and girls for exploitative domestic work[48] and forced marriage.[49]

II. 'Exploitation of Prostitution'

Also not defined in the text of the Convention, 'exploitation of prostitution' has been interpreted to cover any acts to obtain profit from prostitution such as pimping.[50] CEDAW aims to suppress the *exploitation of* prostitution, as opposed to suppression of prostitution generally. International instruments adopted since the Convention, including, in particular, the Trafficking Protocol, have also not required suppression of prostitution generally, focusing instead on the suppression of its exploitation. As explained in the Trafficking Protocol interpretive notes and reiterated in subsequent UN guidance, States parties decided to leave the legal treatment of prostitution to the discretion of individual States.[51]

With international law decidedly agnostic on the issue, whether 'trafficking' encompasses non-coerced prostitution remains actively debated. On one side of the divide are the self-described 'abolitionists', who believe that all prostitution is inherently exploitative and degrading to women and amounts to sexual slavery. Consequently, 'abolitionists' believe that the failure of States to prohibit *all* prostitution violates a woman's right to sexual autonomy. On the other side of the divide are those who oppose the 'abolitionist' view for diverse reasons. Some believe that women can choose prostitution as a viable livelihood option because the absence of adequate protections for prostitutes—not the sex industry itself—opens the door to trafficking and other abuses. Under this view, State action to penalize adults choosing to engage in prostitution amounts to a denial of individual liberty. Others acknowledge discomfort with the concept of sex as labour, yet none the less oppose the 'abolitionist' agenda on pragmatic grounds, believing that such policies—even those that seek to decriminalize the prostitute while penalizing all other actors involved in the sex industry—can work to harm prostitutes, for example, by driving the sex industry further underground.

Reflecting this deep divide, States vary enormously in how they characterize and address prostitution in their domestic laws, adopting one of three general approaches: (1) criminalization; (2) decriminalization; or (3) legalization/regulation of prostitution. The criminalization paradigm views prostitution as a social evil that should be subject to penal measures, though approaches vary as to whether prostitutes themselves are targeted. 'Prohibitionist' approaches criminalize all actors, whereas 'toleration' excludes the prostitute from penal measures. Decriminalization views prostitution as a personal choice between consenting adults, leaving relationships between prostitutes and pimps, brothel owners and clients outside the criminal framework and punishing only

---

[46] CO Thailand, CEDAW/C/THA/CO/5 (2006) para 28.

[47] CO Gabon, CEDAW/C/GAB/CC/2–5 (2005) paras 28–9; CO Saudi Arabia, CEDAW/C/SAU/CO/2 (2008) para 24.

[48] CO Mauritania, CEDAW/C/MRT/CO/1 (2007) paras 31–2; CO Singapore, CEDAW/C/SGP/CO/3 (2007) para 22.

[49] CO China, CEDAW/C/CHN/CO/6 (2006) paras 33–4.

[50] Working Group on Trafficking in Persons, 'Analysis of Key Concepts of the Trafficking in Persons Protocol' (9 December 2009) CTOC/COP/WG.4/2010/2 paras 9–12.

[51] Trafficking Protocol art 3; Interpretive notes on the Trafficking Protocol (2000) UN Doc A/55/383/Add.1 para 64.

non-consensual acts. Legalization also seeks to address prostitution outside criminal law, and instead to regulate prostitution through zoning, licensing, and at times, mandatory health checks.

The Committee's approach to prostitution in its consideration of States parties' reports has been inconsistent, reflecting the ambiguity of the text and the prostitution reform debates.[52] On the one hand, the Committee has expressed concern that criminalization of the purchase of sex could lead to clandestine prostitution and, consequently, increased vulnerability of women and girls to trafficking.[53] On the other hand, it has equated prostitution with exploitation under Article 6,[54] noting in particular that decriminalization could have unintended negative effects on migrant prostitutes.[55] Rather than take a position on the legal treatment of prostitution, the Committee has focused on the need for States parties to assess the impact on prostitutes of whatever framework each State party has adopted, for example, the possibility that rehabilitation measures may stigmatize the prostitute, or that administrative detention of prostitutes may lead to denial of due process rights.[56] The Committee has been clear, however, that any legal penalties attached to prostitution should not disproportionately penalize the prostitutes relative to traffickers, those who arrange for the exchange of sex for money (pimps), and those who purchase sex (johns).[57]

The Committee has increasingly targeted prostitution generally, however, expressing its concern that prostitution continues to thrive in some countries, and that it even involves 'educated' women.[58] It has called upon States parties to discourage demand for prostitution,[59] to develop programmes to prevent women from entering into prostitution,[60] to provide information regarding the causes and extent of prostitution,[61] and to monitor and address the link between sex tourism and prostitution.[62] The Committee has

---

[52] A Gallagher, 'Human Rights and the New UN Protocols on Trafficking and Migrant Smuggling: A Preliminary Analysis' (2001) 23 *Human Rights Quarterly* 975, 1001–2.

[53] CO Sweden, A/56/38, 25th Session (2001) paras 354–5; CO Norway, CEDAW/C/NOR/CO/7 (2007) para 22; CO Fiji, CEDAW/C/FIJI/CO/4 (2010) para 25.

[54] CO Ecuador, A/58/38, 29th Session (2003) para 313; CO Republic of Korea, CEDAW/C/KOR/CO/6 (2007) para 20.

[55] CO The Netherlands, A/56/38, 25th Session (2001) para 210; CO New Zealand, A/58/38, 29th Session (2003) para 414); CO New Zealand, CEDAW/C/NZL/CO/6 (2007) paras 28–9; CO The Netherlands, CEDAW/C/NLD/CO/4 (2007) paras 21–2.

[56] CO China, CEDAW/C/CHN/CO/6 (2006) para 19; CO Vietnam, CEDAW/C/VNM/CO/6 (2007) para 18.

[57] CO Guyana, A/56/38, 25th Session (2001) para 180; CO Mauritius, CEDAW/C/MAR/CO/5 (2006) paras 20–1; CO China, CEDAW/C/CHN/CO/6 (2006) para 19.

[58] CO Malawi, CEDAW/C/MWI/CO/5 (2006) para 23; CO Thailand, CEDAW/C/THA/CO/5 (2006) para 28; CO Cuba, CEDAW/C/CUB/CO/6 (2006) para 21; CO Egypt, CEDAW/C/EGY/CO/7 (2010) para 25.

[59] CO Latvia, A/59/38, 31st Session (2004) para 60; CO Spain, A/59/38, 31st Session (2004) para 337; CO Syrian Arab Republic, CEDAW/C/SYR/CO/1 (2007) para 24; CO Cook Islands, CEDAW/C/COK/CO/1 (2007) para 27; CO Honduras, CEDAW/C/HON/CO/6 (2007) para 21; CO Japan, CEDAW/C/JPN/CO/6 (2009) para 40; CO Libya, CEDAW/C/LBY/CO/5 (2009) para 28; CO Botswana, CEDAW/C/BOT/CO/3 (2010) para 28.

[60] CO Australia, CEDAW/C/AUS/CO/5 (2006) para 21; CO Denmark, CEDAW/C/DEN/CO/6 (2006) para 25; CO Luxembourg, CEDAW/C/LUX/CO/5 (2008) para 30.

[61] CO Venezuela, CEDAW/C/VEN/CO/6 (2006) para 28; CO Saint Lucia, CEDAW/C/LCA/CO/6 (2006) para 20; CO Mauritius, CEDAW/C/MAR/CO/5 (2006) para 21; CO Luxembourg, CEDAW/C/LUX/CO/5 (2008) para 29.

[62] CO Cook Islands, CEDAW/C/COK/CO/1 (2007) para 27; CO Belize, CEDAW/C/BLZ/CO/3 (2007) para 22; CO Kenya, CEDAW/C/KEN/CO/6 (2007) para 30.

noted its concern, for example, over the existence of illegal strip clubs[63] and the lack of data concerning clandestine prostitution in massage parlours.[64] It has also urged States parties to support women who want to stop practising prostitution, to provide training and/or education for alternative livelihoods, and to take measures to rehabilitate and reintegrate prostitutes.[65] For example, noting how the impact of famine and natural disasters, particularly on rural women, can result in vulnerability to prostitution, the Committee called upon North Korea to ensure that rural women have equal access to food supplies.[66] Similarly, it has called upon States parties to provide rural women with economic alternatives to prostitution,[67] including specifically women who have lost their livelihoods due to changes in the agricultural sector.[68]

The Committee has also targeted the root causes of prostitution by focusing on the need to change society's perception of women as sex objects. For example, it has urged States parties to 'encourage a positive change of atmosphere regarding sex phone lines as they run counter to the efforts being made to portray women positively, and not as "sex objects", in the media';[69] to 'take appropriate measures to protect [cabaret dancers] from all forms of exploitation and to take action aimed at changing men's and society's perception of women as sex objects';[70] and has commended the use of regular mass media programmes, conferences, and seminars on violence, trafficking in human beings, prostitution, and elimination of stereotypes.[71]

D. Equality in Context

While the Committee's analysis of Article 6 has been limited, a comprehensive understanding of the processes of trafficking and exploitation of prostitution and their impact on women reveals how the phenomena are rooted in diverse forms of discrimination.

I. Formal and Substantive Equality

General Recommendation 19 explicitly identifies trafficking as a form of gender-based violence against women, and *ipso facto* a violation of the norm prohibiting discrimination on the basis of sex.[72] *De jure* and *de facto* discrimination feeds the trafficking cycle in countries of origin, transit, and destination.

In countries of origin, the lack of formal equal rights with respect to citizenship, inheritance and other property rights, employment, educational opportunities, and access to financial resources, all contribute to the feminization of migration, causing women to look beyond their home communities for income-earning options. Compounding the

---

[63] CO Iceland, CEDAW/C/ICE/CO/6 (2008) paras 23–4.

[64] CO Finland, CEDAW/C/FIN/CO/6 (2008) para 17.

[65] CO The Netherlands, A/56/38, 25th Session (2001) para 210; CO New Zealand, A/58/38, 29th Session (2003) para 414; CO Angola, A/59/38, 31st Session (2004) para 157; CO Maldives, CEDAW/C/MDV/CO/3 (2007) para 22; CO Suriname, CEDAW/C/SUR/CO/3 (2007) para 22; CO Botswana, CEDAW/C/BOT/CO/3 (2010) para 28; CO Egypt, CEDAW/C/EGY/CO/7 (2010) para 26; CO Fiji, CEDAW/C/FJI/CO/4 (2010) para 25.

[66] CO Democratic People's Republic of Korea, CEDAW/C/PRK/CO/1 (2005) paras 41–2.

[67] CO Colombia, CEDAW/C/COL/CO/6 (2007) para 21.

[68] CO Saint Lucia, CEDAW/C/LCA/CO/6 (2006) para 20.

[69] CO Finland, A/56/38, 24th Session (2001) para 304.

[70] CO Switzerland, A/58/38, 28th Session (2003) para 123.

[71] CO Hungary, A/57/38, Exceptional Session (2002) para 308.   [72] GR 19 paras 13–16.

vulnerabilities are formal restrictions on women's rights to out-migration based on sex or sex combined with age, marital status, pregnancy, or maternity status, occupation-specific restrictions, or requirements that women have written permission of male relatives to obtain a passport or migrate.

Women's unequal access to training and education may restrict their access to reliable information on migration, thus increasing their vulnerability to being trafficked. These factors, in turn, can make women even more susceptible to the exploitative offers of third parties to facilitate their migration and search for employment. Since women generally have fewer assets than men, they tend to be more financially dependent on third parties who can charge usurious rates of interest or use their positions of power to exploit the women.[73]

Multiple forms of *de jure* and *de facto* discrimination may confront women upon their arrival in the destination countries.[74] Governments may ban the formal employment of women, conforming to gendered notions of appropriate work for women that track women's traditional roles as providers of domestic care and sex.[75] Thus relegated to the informal labour market, women are often denied labour rights,[76] such as minimum wage and overtime pay guarantees. Since prostitution is illegal in most countries, prostitutes tend not to benefit from labour protections. Moreover, because they are often stigmatized as inviting misfortune on themselves, prostitutes may be denied equal protection of laws against rape and other forms of violence.

Upon return to their home countries, compounding the push factors that led them to migrate in the first instance, trafficked women may face the social stigma attached to their having been trafficked, especially those trafficked for forced prostitution.[77] Some countries of origin may not recognize their victim status as trafficked persons and deprive them of rights to nationality and social services otherwise provided to victims of crime. Other countries of origin may even prosecute trafficked persons for their unauthorized departure.[78]

Suppression of trafficking and the exploitation of prostitution thus requires the achievement of formal and substantive equality in many if not all of the political, social, economic, and cultural fields covered by the Convention.[79] Only by achieving substantive equality in these fields can the root causes of trafficking be addressed and women's and girls' vulnerability to trafficking eliminated.

II. Transformative Equality

Article 5 of the Convention requires the elimination of stereotypes or prejudices based on sex. The legal, political, and economic constraints on women that create vulnerability to trafficking and exploitation of prostitution are often deeply rooted in stereotypes, customs, and norms that promote a narrow view of women's roles in their families and communities.[80]

---

[73] GR 26 para 13.   [74] Ibid para 14.   [75] See the discussion in ch on art 11.

[76] CO Saudi Arabia, CEDAW/C/SAU/CO/2 (2008) paras 38–9 (excluding migrant domestic workers from labour law protections).

[77] CO Armenia, CEDAW/C/ARM/CO/4/Rev.1 (2009) para 24; CO Azerbaijan, CEDAW/C/AZE/CO/4 (2009) para 23.

[78] Gallagher (n 3 above) 161 (discussing Lao PDR as example).

[79] See the discussion in ch on art 3.   [80] See the discussion in ch on art 5.

Transformative equality necessitates the elimination of negative cultural stereotypes and expectations of women, and demands greater recognition and valuing of the social and economic contributions of women workers, particularly in the informal sector. Family structures based on traditional sex roles and division of labour impede women's access to the formal labour sector and, hence, legally mandated workplace protections.[81] Moreover, socio-cultural expectations of a woman's subservience to her family can lead her to remit her earnings to a degree not expected of men; indeed, the income stream may bypass the woman wage-earner entirely and run directly to her spouse or extended family members. A sense of familial obligation to maintain the income stream may even override any concerns regarding the woman's exploitive working conditions.

Stereotypes regarding women in the sex industry render them particularly vulnerable to exploitation and violence. Prostitutes are a marginalized group to whom significant social stigma is attached. As Justices Sachs and O'Regan of the South African Constitutional Court opined in their dissenting opinion in the *Jordan* case, anti-prostitution laws that characterize the prostitute as the primary offender reinforce a pattern of sexual stereotyping that conflicts with gender equality. The prostitute, typically female, is stereotyped as a social outcast, a fallen woman 'who bring[s] misfortune on [herself] and invite[s] disregard for [her] bod[y]'; the male client, on the other hand, is regarded as having 'given in to temptation, or as having done the sort of thing that men do' and, thus, he 'has not acted in a morally reprehensible fashion'. The difference in social stigma 'tracks a pattern of applying different standards to the sexuality of men and women'.[82]

III. Direct and Indirect Discrimination

Direct and indirect discrimination against women can feed the causes and exacerbate the consequences of trafficking and exploitation of prostitution. Laws that directly restrict, on the basis of sex, a woman's right to employment in the formal sector, to education, to migrate, to access bank accounts, to claim, retain, or change her nationality, and to inherit property, are all examples of direct discrimination that increase women's vulnerability to trafficking and exploitation of prostitution. Causal factors also can be found in laws that indirectly discriminate[83] against women including, for example, labour laws that do not apply to the informal sector, including domestic work and prostitution. Similarly, laws criminalizing prostitution activities that target prostitutes with greater sanctions than their pimps or clients may constitute indirect discrimination on the basis of sex. Such discrimination can perpetuate the stigma against prostitutes, in turn denying them, in practice, equal protection of laws against rape and physical mistreatment. While the Committee has not directly made these linkages, they flow from an understanding of Article 1 as it operates in the trafficking context.

IV. Intersectional Discrimination

As noted by the Human Rights Committee, 'racism, racial discrimination and xenophobia contribute to discrimination against women and other violations of their rights, including

---

[81] See the discussion in chs on arts 11 and 16.

[82] *Jordan and Others v the State* [2 October 2002] Constitutional Court of South Africa CCT 31/01 (dissenting opinion, Sachs, J and O'Regan, J) paras 64 and 87.

[83] See the discussion in ch on art 1.

cross-border trafficking of women and children, and enforced trafficking and other forms of forced labour disguised, *inter alia,* as domestic or other kinds of personal service'.[84]

Trafficking is often the product of multiple discriminations operating simultaneously, including discrimination on the basis of sex, class, race, ethnicity, nationality, immigration status, and age.[85] Sociologists studying the demand for persons trafficked into domestic work and prostitution have found that racism, xenophobia, and prejudice against ethnic minority groups make it easier for consumers of such exploitation to justify the practice.[86] The migrant comes from an impoverished and 'uncivilized' country, 'and so is neither familiar with nor entitled to the rights, freedoms and respect owed to local workers, and even paying them for their labour can be construed as a favor'.[87] Women and girls who are socially, economically, and politically marginalized are also devalued by employers and clients and are considered 'the 'natural' or 'ideal' occupants of the lowliest positions in domestic work and prostitution.[88]

Regulating domestic work and prostitution does not, by itself, counteract racism, prejudice, and xenophobia against migrants and ethnic minority groups. Governments must address directly the social devaluation of migrants and their social, political, and economic marginalization.[89] The Committee's analysis of the rights of women migrant workers in General Recommendation 26 illustrates how sex-based discrimination renders this population at risk of trafficking 'due to the various degrees of vulnerability they face'. Migrant women workers may not enjoy the protection of the laws of the origin, transit, or destination countries, at either *de jure* or *de facto* levels.[90] Female migrants are in a different position from male migrants with respect to the availability of legal migration channels, the sectors into which they migrate, the forms of abuse they suffer, and the consequences thereof. The push and pull factors impelling women to migrate—poverty, the desire for new opportunities, natural disasters and wars, gendered cultural practices, and gender-based violence in countries of origin—are 'exacerbated by sex-specific divisions of labour in the formal and informal manufacturing and service sectors in countries of destination, as well as a male-centred culture of entertainment' that creates demand for women.[91]

E. States Parties' Obligation

I. Nature of the Obligation

1. *'All Appropriate Measures'*

The prohibition of trafficking and exploitation of prostitution should be analyzed with reference to the Convention's overarching commitment to eliminating discrimination against women and promoting equality between women and men, including the requirements set out in Articles 2 and 5 of the Convention.

---

[84] CCPR, 'Contributions to the World Conference against Racism, Racial Discrimination, Xenophobia, and Related Intolerance' (13 March 2001) UN Doc A/CONF.189/PC.2/14 para 18.

[85] eg CO Germany, A/59/38, 30th Session (2004) para 394; CO The Philippines, CEDAW/C/PHI/CO/6 (2006) para 21; CO Ecuador, CEDAW/C/ECU/CO 7 (2008) para 23; CO Albania, CEDAW/C/ALB/CO/3 (2010) para 29.

[86] J O'Connell Davidson and B Andersen, 'Is Trafficking in Human Beings Demand Driven? A Multi-Country Pilot Study' ('Demand Study') [2003] International Organization for Migration (IOM) Migration Research Series, No 15, 42.

[87] Ibid.   [88] Ibid; CO Ecuador, CEDAW/C/ECU/CO/7 (2008) para 22.

[89] Demand Study (n 86 above) 44.   [90] GR 26 para 4.   [91] Ibid para 8.

Given that trafficking and exploitation of prostitution are perpetrated primarily by non-State actors, by extending the reach of State party responsibility to encompass private persons, organizations, and enterprises, Article 2(e) is of critical importance in the trafficking context. As General Recommendation 19, paragraph 9 states, under general international law and specific human rights covenants, 'States may also be responsible for private acts if they fail to act with due diligence to prevent violations of rights or to investigate and punish acts of violence', and may be obliged to provide compensation.[92] Recent developments in international anti-trafficking law can be brought within this Convention obligation to exercise due diligence. They have clearly established States parties' obligations to criminalize trafficking,[93] to quickly and accurately identify victims of trafficking,[94] to investigate and prosecute trafficking cases with due diligence,[95] to provide victims with support and protection,[96] to prevent trafficking,[97] and to engage in international cooperation with other States.[98] As discussed in detail below,[99] measures to respect, protect, and fulfil these obligations include not just legislative measures, but also administrative measures and programmes, ideally developed with the input of civil society organizations.[100]

2. *Immediate Implementation*

Article 6 places an immediate obligation on States parties to take measures to suppress trafficking and exploitation of prostitution. By using the language 'States Parties *shall* take all appropriate measures' (emphasis added)—as opposed to the aspirational language of States parties being required to 'endeavour' or 'consider' such measures—Article 6 does not contemplate the possibility of gradual implementation.

3. *Specific and Non-specific Obligations*

The language of Article 6 is specific with respect to the end result it seeks to obtain—the suppression of trafficking and exploitation of prostitution—but is non-specific with respect to how States parties are to achieve this result. As discussed below, established and evolving international anti-trafficking norms developed within the last decade help provide specific substantive content to Article 6. The Committee appears to have been informed by these developments in its responses to States parties' reports.

---

[92] For an analysis of States' duty of due diligence, see the discussion in chs on Violence Against Women and art 2. See also, GR 28 paras 13 and 19.

[93] Trafficking Protocol art 5.   [94] Council of Europe Trafficking Convention art 10.

[95] UNCHR, 'Recommended Principles And Guidelines On Human Rights And Human Trafficking, Report Of The United Nations High Commissioner For Human Rights To The Economic And Social Council, Addendum' ('UNRPGs') (20 May 2002) UN Doc E/2002/68/Add.1 principle 2; *Velasquez-Rodriguez Case* Inter-American Court of Human Rights Series C No 4 (29 July 1988) 28 ILM 291 (1989).

[96] Trafficking Protocol arts 6–8; Council of Europe Trafficking Convention arts 11–16; UNRPGs (n 95 above) principles 7–11, guideline 6.

[97] Trafficking Protocol art 9; Council of Europe Trafficking Convention arts 5–6; UNRPGs (n 95 above) principles 4–6, guideline 7.

[98] Trafficking Protocol art 2(c); Council of Europe Trafficking Convention art 32; UNRPGs (n 95 above) guideline 11.

[99] See section E. II. below.

[100] Trafficking Protocol art 6(3); Council of Europe Trafficking Convention art 35; UNRPGs (n 95 above) guidelines 1(3), 1(7), and 5(2).

II. Implementation

Recent developments in international anti-trafficking law have given rise to a set of specific norms that complement and augment the Committee's practice in guiding States parties towards compliance with its Article 6 obligations.

The adoption of the Trafficking Protocol in 2000 marked the beginning of a decade of rapid and progressive development of anti-trafficking norms at the international, regional, and national levels. The Trafficking Protocol created a much-needed international cooperation framework for preventing trafficking, prosecuting traffickers, and protecting trafficked persons. Developed in response to States' concerns over the impact of trafficking on crime and border control, the Trafficking Protocol emphasizes criminal justice aspects of trafficking. By contrast, the Convention situates trafficking in a human rights framework. Recognizing that anti-trafficking measures tended to neglect the rights of trafficked persons in 2002, the Office of the UN High Commissioner for Human Rights developed the Recommended Principles and Guidelines on Human Rights and Human Trafficking (UNRPGs).[101] The UNRPGs draw upon existing international human rights law, including Convention Article 6, and their accompanying Commentary provides practical, rights-based policy guidance on the trafficking issue, and reflects trends in normative development. The Council of Europe Trafficking Convention, adopted in 2005, codifies a number of these standards, confirming the significance of human rights protection to the effectiveness of anti-trafficking efforts, thus remedying (for European States parties to this Convention) a key weakness in the Trafficking Protocol.[102]

The Committee has called upon States parties to ratify the Trafficking Protocol,[103] to comply with the UNRPGs,[104] to adopt specific legislation on trafficking[105] (including laws to deal with forced labour[106]) and national plans of action that include gender, race, and age dimensions,[107] and to ensure that the laws and policies are fully implemented.[108] Although the Committee has rarely provided detailed examples of what Article 6 requires, its recommendations are consistent with specific norms contained in international and regional anti-trafficking instruments, international human rights law, and relevant soft law.

---

[101] UNRPGs (n 95 above).

[102] A Gallagher, 'Recent Legal Developments in the Field of Human Trafficking: A Critical Review of the 2005 European Convention and Related Instruments' (2006) 8 *Eur J of Migration and L* 163.

[103] eg CO Mauritius, CEDAW/C/MAR/CO/5 (2006) para 21; CO Vietnam, CEDAW/C/VNM/CO/6 (2007) para 19; CO Mongolia, CEDAW/C/MNG/CO/7 (2008) para 28; CO Yemen, A/63/38, 41st Session (2008) para 370; CO Papua New Guinea, CEDAW/C/PNG/CO3 (2010) para 32.

[104] eg CO Switzerland, CEDAW/C/CHE/CO/3 (2009) para 30.

[105] eg CO Romania, A/55/38, 23rd Session (2000) para 309; CO Estonia, A/57/38, 26th Session (2002) para 102; CO Ireland, A/60/38, 33rd Session (2005) para 389 bis; CO Malaysia, CEDAW/MYS/CO/2 (2006) para 24; CO Syria, CEDAW/C/SYR/CO/1 (2007) para 22; CO Guatemala, CEDAW/C/GUA/CO/7 (2009) para 24; CO Egypt, CEDAW/C/EGY/CO/y (2010) para 26.

[106] eg CO Mauritania, CEDAW/C/MRT/CO/1 (2007) para 32.

[107] eg CO Brazil, CEDAW/C/BRA/CO/6 (2007) paras 23–4.

[108] eg CO Macedonia, CEDAW/C/MKD/CO/3 (2006) para 22; CO Kazakhstan, CEDAW/C/KAZ/CO/2 (2007) para 35; CO Bahrain, CEDAW/C/BHR/CO/2 (2008) para 27; CO Lao People's Democratic Republic, CEDAW/C/LAO/CO/7 (2009) para 28; CO Russian Federation, CEDAW/C/USR/CO/7 (2010) para 27.

1. *Obligation to Respect*

a) No Prosecution of Trafficked Women for Status Offences

Trafficked persons are victims of crime and human rights violations. In countries of transit or destination, however, trafficked persons are often arrested, detained, and even prosecuted for unlawful activities related to their trafficking experiences, including illegal entry into the country, working without a permit, or engaging in prostitution or begging. In countries of origin, trafficked persons are sometimes penalized upon their return for unlawful departure. The Committee has explicitly stated that trafficked women should not be criminalized or penalized for violations of immigration, anti-prostitution, or other laws for involvement in illegal activities that result from their trafficking.[109]

b) No Routine Detention of Trafficked Women

Trafficked persons are often routinely detained in immigration detention centres or other facilities, sometimes for long periods of time. This frequently occurs when the victim is not correctly identified and is detained as an illegal migrant pending deportation, or when the victim is identified correctly but is unwilling or unable to cooperate with law enforcement in the criminal investigation of the alleged trafficker.[110]

The practice of victim detention is highly gendered,[111] with females comprising the overwhelming majority of trafficked persons in detention.[112] Women and girls are more likely to be identified through official channels as trafficked than men and boys, who are often misidentified as illegal migrants. Once identified as trafficked, female trafficked persons are assumed to be more in need of protection from harm than their male counterparts and therefore more likely to be detained.[113]

While the Committee has made clear that victims should not be sent to prisons or juvenile detention facilities,[114] it has not provided a substantive assessment of detention practices. Strongly advising against such detention practices, the UNRPGs provides relevant guidance.[115] When the detention is overwhelmingly directed at women and girls, it amounts to unlawful discrimination on the basis of sex, and may also be sufficient to support a claim of unlawful deprivation of liberty and/or arbitrary detention.[116]

c) Respect for Established Rights

In an effort to prevent trafficking, countries of origin may take measures to prevent individuals from migrating, preventing, for example, women within a certain age group from emigrating to specified destinations and for specified occupations.[117] Moreover, coun-

---

[109] eg CO Cambodia, CEDAW/C/KHM/CO/3 (2006) paras 19–20; CO Malaysia, CEDAW/C/MYS/CO/2 (2006) para 23; CO Uzbekistan, CEDAW/C/UZB/CO/3 (2006) para 25; CO Vietnam, CEDAW/C/VNM/CO/6 (2007) paras 18–19; CO Syria, CEDAW/C/SYR/CO/1 (2007) para 24; CO Pakistan, CEDAW/C/PAK/CO/3 (2007) para 30; CO Singapore, CEDAW/C/SGP/CO/3 (2007) paras 21–2; CO Cook Islands, CEDAW/C/COK/CO/1 (2007) para 26; CO Lebanon, CEDAW/C/LBN/CO/3 (2008) paras 28–9.

[110] A Gallagher and E Pearson, 'The High Cost of Freedom: A Legal and Policy Analysis of Shelter Detention for Victims of Trafficking' (2010) 74 *Human Rights Quarterly* 73; OHCHR, *UNRPG: Commentary* (2009) s 7.1.

[111] UNRPG: Commentary (n 110 above) s 7.4.   [112] Ibid.   [113] Ibid.

[114] eg CO Syria, CEDAW/C/SYR/CO/1 (2007) para 24; CO The Netherlands, CEDAW/C/NLD/CO/5 (2010) para 29.

[115] UNRPGs (n 95 above) guidelines 2(6) and 6(1).

[116] UNRPG: Commentary (n 110 above) s 7.4.

[117] Gallagher (n 3 above) 161–4; UNCHR, 'Report of the Special Rapporteur on Violence against Women' UN Doc E/CN.4/2000/68 (2000) para 48.

tries of destination may take (or not prevent private actors from taking) foreign victims of trafficking into 'protective' custody, and may prevent their return home until certain conditions are met, such as that the trafficked person provides testimony in criminal prosecution of the trafficker.[118] States' misidentification of a trafficked person as an illegal immigrant deserving of deportation rather than as a victim of crime and human rights violations can result in the failure to recognize the trafficked person as a seeker of asylum or other international refugee protection.[119] Even where an individual is identified as a trafficking victim, States may believe, inaccurately, that the fact of the trafficking or the illegal migration involved in the trafficking is a basis for denying refugee status. Moreover, the State may fail to respect the individual's right of 'non-refoulement' (non-return),[120] applicable in situations where there are substantial grounds for believing the person would be subjected to persecution or torture if returned to her country of origin.

Anti-trafficking measures shall not affect the rights, obligations and responsibilities of States and individuals under international law.[121] The Committee has not dealt specifically with the emigration restrictions—passed in the name of addressing trafficking—that violate the right to freedom of movement.[122] However, the Committee has called upon destination countries either to ensure that the country of origin provides full protection to trafficked women, or to grant trafficked women asylum or refugee status in accordance with gender-based persecution grounds under international refugee law.[123]

d) Trafficked Women's and Girls' Citizenship and Nationality Rights

The Committee has expressed its concern over reports that trafficked women and their children born abroad encounter social and legal difficulties resettling in their home State and lose their rights as nationals.[124] The Committee has clearly noted that citizenship and nationality laws must not cause trafficked women to lose their nationality or their ability to convey their citizenship on their children born abroad, especially women who are trafficked as brides or for commercial sexual exploitation.[125]

e) Discrimination against Prostitutes

General Recommendation 19, paragraph 15 notes that prostitutes are especially vulnerable to violence because their status, which may be unlawful, tends to marginalize them. Prostitutes who are also migrants may be particularly vulnerable to exploitation and violence, given the added layer of discrimination due to their migrant status generally, and migrant prostitutes' relatively low status within the sex sector specifically. The Committee has noted that laws criminalizing prostitution have, in practice, penalized the prostitute

---

[118] UNRPG: Commentary (n 110 above) s 3.3.   [119] Ibid s 3.4.

[120] See CAT art 3(1); ICCPR art 7; CRC art 22; CAT (2000) UN Doc CAT/C/SR.422 para 31.

[121] Trafficking Protocol art 14; Council of Europe Trafficking Convention art 40(4); UNRPGs (n 95 above) principle 3.

[122] See Gallagher (n 3 above) 162–4 discussing the right to leave.

[123] eg CO The Netherlands, A/56/38, 25th Session (2001) para 21; CO Spain, A/59/38, 31st Session (2004) para 337; CO Spain, CEDAW/C/ESP/CO/6 (2009) para 22; CO Argentina, CEDAW/C/ARG/CO/6 (2010) para 46. For discussion of when trafficked persons may qualify for refugee status, see UNHCR, 'Guidelines on International Protection: the application of Article 1A(2) of the 1951 Convention and/or 1967 Protocol relating to the status of refugees to victims of trafficking and persons at risk of being trafficked' (2006) HCR/GIP/06/07.

[124] CEDAW, 'Summary Record of the 759th meeting (Chamber B)' (2007) CEDAW/C/SR.759 paras 30 and 33; CO Vietnam, CEDAW/C/VNM/CO/6 (2007) para 18.

[125] eg CO Indonesia, CEDAW/C/IDN/CO/3 (2007) para 28. See also the discussion in ch on art 9.

rather than the exploiters of prostitution such as pimps and johns.[126] Anti-prostitution laws should only penalize the actions of those who profit from the sexual exploitation of women, not the women themselves.[127] The Committee has further directed that where laws permit women to work as prostitutes, they should not discriminate against migrant prostitutes.[128] It did not, however, address this issue in its General Recommendation 26 on women migrant workers.

f) Prompt and Accurate Identification of Trafficked Women

Prompt and accurate identification is critical to ensuring that a trafficked person does not suffer a further denial of her rights.[129] Without adequate training of immigration and law enforcement officials, the additional elements that distinguish trafficking from illegal migration and migrant smuggling—the presence of force, coercion, or deception used for the purpose of placing the person in exploitation[130]—can be difficult to detect or to prove without active investigation.

Consistent with the UNRPGs and the European Trafficking Convention,[131] the Committee has called upon States parties to ensure that training of border police and law enforcement officials provide them with requisite skills to recognize victims of trafficking and to provide support for them.[132]

2. Obligation to Protect

Because the Convention obligates States parties to 'overcome all forms of gender-based violence, whether by public or private act',[133] they must exercise due diligence with respect to the acts committed by non-State actors. As the European Court of Human Rights found in *Rantsev v Cyprus and Russia*, a State may be held accountable for failing to prevent, prosecute, and punish non-State actors subjecting persons to servitude and forced labour and for failing to provide appropriate protection for victims.[134] In a similar vein, States parties' duty of due diligence under Article 6 requires a wide range of measures. In some instances, the Committee has refrained from addressing in detail issues that have been dealt with elsewhere under international law, or to which the Committee has previously alluded—for example, the reference in General Recommendation 19 to trafficking of girls and trafficking in the context of armed conflict. The open-ended language of Article 6

---

[126] eg CO Japan, CEDAW/C/JPN/CO/6 (2009) para 29.

[127] eg CO Fiji, A/57/38, 26th Session (2002) para 65; CO Korea CEDAW/C/KOR/CO/6 (2007) para 20; CO Kenya CEDAW/C/KEN/CO/6 (2007) paras 28–9.

[128] eg CO The Netherlands, A/56/38, 25th Session (2001) paras 209–10; CO The Netherlands, CEDAW/C/NLD/CO/4 (2007) paras 21–2.

[129] See *Zhen Zhen Zheng v Netherlands* (n 27 above) dissenting opinion.

[130] Compare Protocol against the Smuggling of Migrants by Land, Sea and Air, supplementing the UN Convention against Transnational Organized Crime (adopted 8 January 2001, entered into force 28 January 2004) 2241 UNTS 507.

[131] See Council of Europe Trafficking Convention art 10; UNRPGs (n 95 above) guideline 2. Also, UNRPGs (n 95 above) guidelines 2(1)-(3).

[132] eg CO Portugal, A/57/38, 26th Session (2002) para 336; CO Slovenia, A/58/38, 28th Session (2003) para 424; CO Nigeria, A/59/38, 31st Session (2004) para 244; CO Maldives, CEDAW/C/MDV/CO/3 (2007) para 20; CO Guatemala, CEDAW/C/GUA/CO/7 (2009) para 24; CO Tanzania, CEDAW/C/TZA/CO/6 (2008) para 28.

[133] GR 19 para 24(a). See Convention arts 2(e)-(f) and (5); GR 28 paras 13 and 19. For in-depth analysis of due diligence, see the discussion in ch on Violence against Women.

[134] *Rantsev v Cyprus and Russia* [2010] ECHR 25965/04. Note that because the decision pre-dates the Council of Europe Trafficking Convention, the decision does not reference 'trafficking' per se.

would provide the Committee the scope to address these issues in greater detail, especially when read with other provisions of the Convention.

a) Criminal Justice Responses to End Impunity

Any prohibition on trafficking would be meaningless in the absence of an obligation to criminalize trafficking, which is a central and mandatory provision of the UN Trafficking Protocol,[135] and a requirement of all other regional and international anti-trafficking instruments.[136] The Committee has called upon States parties to strengthen their law enforcement responses to trafficking, including increased prosecution and punishment of traffickers.[137] It has also encouraged States parties to target demand for prostitution, though it has not explicitly called for its criminalization.

b) Protection and Support for Victims

Consistent with the standards of the UN Trafficking Protocol, the European Trafficking Convention, the SAARC Convention, and the UNRPGs,[138] the Committee has called upon States parties to provide victim assistance through counselling, reintegration, and rehabilitation programmes,[139] and to provide victims with special shelter.[140] The Committee has advised that protection measures be human-rights based, and that reintegration be long-term.[141]

In most national legal frameworks, victim support and protection is explicitly conditioned on the victim's cooperation with law enforcement, and even where there is no conditionality as a matter of law, victims are pressured into providing information and testimony.[142] As the UNRPG Commentary explains, separating protection and support from victim cooperation is a 'fundamental tenet of a human rights approach to trafficking'.[143] Conditional assistance can have negative consequences in that compelled testimony from a trafficked person, particularly one suffering from psychological and physical trauma, is unlikely to be helpful to the prosecution, and can foster distrust between the trafficked person and law enforcement bodies.

Like other human rights treaty bodies,[144] and consistent with the UNRPGs and the European Trafficking Convention,[145] the Committee has recognized the need to de-link

---

[135] Trafficking Protocol art 5.

[136] Council of Europe Trafficking Convention art 18; SAARC Convention art 1.

[137] eg CO India, A/55/38, 22nd Session (2000) para 77; CO Kazakhstan, A/56/38, 24th Session (2001) para 98; CO Switzerland, A/58/38, 28th Session (2003) para 125; CO Korea, CEDAW/C/KOR/CO/6 (2007) para 20; CO Nicaragua, CEDAW/C/NIC/CO/6 (2007) para 22.

[138] Trafficking Protocol art 6(3); Council of Europe Trafficking Convention art 12; SAARC Convention art IX(3); UNRPGs (n 95 above) principles 7–11, guideline 6.

[139] eg CO Lithuania, A/55/38, 23rd Session (2000) para 153; CO Vietnam, A/56/38, 25th Session (2001) para 261; CO Estonia, A/57/38, 26th Session (2002) para 102; CO France, A/58/38, 29th Session (2003) para 274; CO Nigeria, A/59/38, 30th Session (2004) para 302; CO The Netherlands, CEDAW/C/NLD/CO/4 (2007) para 24; CO Honduras, CEDAW/C/HON/CO/6 (2007) para 21; CO Pakistan, CEDAW/C/PAK/CO/3 (2007) paras 31–2; CO Armenia, CEDAW/C/ARM/CO/4/Rev.1 (2009) para 25; CO Turkey, CEDAW/C/TUR/CO/6 (2010) para 27.

[140] eg CO Latvia, A/59/38, 31st Session (2004) para 58; CO Azerbaijan, CEDAW/C/AZE/CO/4 (2009) para 24; CO Cameroon, CEDAW/C/CMR/CO/3 (2009) para 31; CO Ukraine, CEDAW/C/UKR/CO/7 (2010) para 31.

[141] eg CO Serbia, CEDAW/C/SCG/CO/1 (2007) para 26; CO Brazil, CEDAW/C/BRA/CO/6 (2007) para 24.

[142] UNRPG: Commentary (n 110 above) s 8.2.   [143] Ibid.

[144] CAT CO Australia, CAT/C/AUS/CO/1 (2008) para 32.

[145] UNRPGs (n 95 above) principle 8; Council of Europe Trafficking Convention art 5(6).

victim support and protection from cooperation. It has called upon States parties to provide for the extension of temporary protection visas, reintegration, and support services to all victims of trafficking, including those who are unable or unwilling to cooperate in the investigation and prosecution of traffickers due to, for example, fear of retaliation by their traffickers.[146] The Committee has also emphasized the importance of allowing victims a 'reflection and recovery period'. This measure allows trafficked persons who lack immigration status a temporary stay of deportation to allow them to recover and escape the influence of their traffickers so that they can make an informed decision as to whether to cooperate in the investigation and prosecution of their traffickers.[147] While the Committee has not specified an acceptable length of time for a reflection period, it has concluded that thirty days 'is insufficient for the victims to recover from their ordeal and prepare for re-entry to their countries of origin'.[148]

c) Legal Assistance, Protection, and Temporary Residence Permits

International law requires that trafficked persons be afforded the legal and other assistance necessary to ensure that they are able to participate in any proceedings against their traffickers in a fully informed and safe manner.[149] Given these security concerns, the UNRPGs and the European Trafficking Convention recommend specific measures to protect victims' privacy.[150] While the Committee has not addressed privacy issues specifically, it has called upon States parties to provide trafficked persons the support necessary for them to participate in the prosecution of their traffickers,[151] including witness protection,[152] and residence permits[153] regardless of whether the victims testify[154] or the perpetrators are punished.[155]

d) Safe and Preferably Voluntary Return and Options for Residency in Appropriate Cases

Trafficked persons are routinely deported from countries of transit and destination, often due to a failure to identify the individual as having been trafficked, and sometimes notwithstanding the authorities' knowledge of the trafficking. Deportation can result in

---

[146]   Eg CO The Netherlands, CEDAW/C/NLD/CO/4 (2007) para 24; CO The United Kingdom, CEDAW/C/UK/CO/6 (2009) para 283; CO The Netherlands, CEDAW/C/NLD/CO/5 (2010) para 28.

[147]   See eg Council of Europe Trafficking Convention art 13.

[148]   CO Denmark, CEDAW/C/DEN/CO/6 (2006) paras 22–3.

[149]   Trafficking Protocol art 6(2); SAARC Convention art V; Council of Europe Trafficking Convention art 12(1)(c)-(e); UNRPGs (n 95 above) principle 9, guideline 6(5).

[150]   eg the UNRPGs and the Council of Europe Trafficking Convention recommend specific measures to protect victims' privacy. UNRPGs (n 95 above) principle 9; UNRPG Commentary (n 110) s 9.4; Council of Europe Trafficking Convention art 11(3). Victim protection should not, however, be at the expense of the accused's right to a fair trial. UNRPG: Commentary (n 110 above) s 8.4.

[151]   eg CO Portugal, A/57/38, 26th Session (2002) para 336; CO Albania, A/58/38, 28th Session (2003) para 71; CO Bangladesh, A/59/38, 31st Session (2004) para 244; CO Singapore, CEDAW/C/SGP/CO/3 (2007) para 22; CO Guatemala, CEDAW/C/GUA/CO/7 (2009) para 24; CO Panama, CEDAW/C/PAN/CO/7 (2010) para 31.

[152]   eg CO Russia, A/57/38, 26th Session (2002) para 396; CO Nigeria, CEDAW/C/NGA/CO/6 (2008) para 26; CO Albania, CEDAW/C/ALB/CO/3 (2010) para 29.

[153]   eg CO Switzerland, A/58/38, 28th Session (2003) para 125; CO Belgium, CEDAW/C/BEL/CO/6 (2008) para 42; CO Switzerland, CEDAW/C/CHE/CO/3 (2009) para 30. See also Trafficking Protocol art 8(2); Council of Europe Trafficking Convention arts 16(2) and 14(1)(b).

[154]   eg CO France, A/58/38, 29th Session (2003) para 274; CO The Netherlands, CEDAW/C/NLD/CO/4 (2007) paras 27–8; CO The United Kingdom, CEDAW/C/UK/CO/6 (2008) para 283.

[155]   eg CO France, A/58/38, 29th Session (2003) para 274. See also Council of Europe Trafficking Convention art 28; Organized Crime Convention art 24.

trafficked persons being subjected to intimidation and violence by their traffickers, stigmatization and rejection by their families and communities, and detention and prosecution by their countries of origin for unauthorized departure and other alleged offences.[156] Such conditions can place the trafficked person at risk of re-victimization and possibly re-trafficking. On the other hand, some trafficked persons prefer to return to their countries of origin and are entitled to do so without unreasonable or undue delay as a matter of international human rights law.[157] In either case, safe[158] and preferably voluntary repatriation, combined with reintegration assistance[159], is critical to protecting the trafficked person from re-victimization and re-trafficking.[160]

The UNRPGs and the European Trafficking Convention make clear that where return would place the trafficked person at ongoing risk, or where there are humanitarian concerns, alternatives to repatriation such as temporary or permanent residency permits should be considered.[161] Consistent with these standards, the Committee has called upon States parties to ensure that trafficked women are either provided with full protection in their countries of origin, or granted asylum or refugee status in the countries of transit or destination,[162] for example, in accordance with gender-based persecution grounds under the 1951 Refugee Convention.[163]

e) Safe, Fair, and Equal Labour Migration Opportunities

General Recommendation 26 notes that women migrant workers are vulnerable to trafficking.[164] One critical source of vulnerability for women is the lack of safe labour migration options and the lack of information regarding the dangers associated with trafficking.

The European Trafficking Convention requires States parties to take measures to enable migration to take place legally, particularly through dissemination of accurate information on the conditions enabling legal entry and stay in the territory.[165] In a similar vein, the Committee recommended that a State party ensure adequate wages, decent working conditions, including days off, benefits, medical insurance, and access to complaint and redress mechanisms.[166] It also urged that a law requiring employers to post a security bond for domestic workers must not limit the domestic worker's freedom of movement under any circumstances.[167]

f) Special Protective and Punitive Measures in Conflict Contexts

General Recommendation 19 paragraph 16 notes that wars, armed conflicts, and the occupation of territories often lead to increased prostitution, trafficking in women, and sexual assault of women, which require specific protective and punitive measures. During conflict, individuals may be trafficked by military groups to provide labour, soldiers, and sexual services, while post-conflict civilian populations may be under extreme economic or other pressure to move and thus are vulnerable to traffickers' threats, coercion, and

---

[156] UNRPG: Commentary (n 110 above) s 11.1.   [157] UDHR art 13(2); ICCPR art 12(4).
[158] UNRPG: Commentary (n 110 above) s 11.2.   [159] Ibid s 11.3.
[160] Trafficking Protocol arts 8 and 9; Council of Europe Trafficking Convention art 16(1)-(4).
[161] Council of Europe Trafficking Convention art 14(1); UNRPGs (n 95 above) principle 11.
[162] eg CO The Netherlands, A/56/38, 25th Session (2001) para 212; CO Denmark, CEDAW/C/DEN/CO/7 (2009) para 33.
[163] eg CO Spain, CEDAW/C/ESP/CO/6 (2009) para 22; CO Argentina, CEDAW/C/ARG/CO/6 (2010) para 46.
[164] GR 26 n 4.   [165] Council of Europe Trafficking Convention art 5(4).
[166] eg CO Singapore, CEDAW/C/SGP/CO/3 (2007) paras 23–4.   [167] Ibid.

deception.[168] Weak criminal justice systems can create a culture of impunity for trafficking, and even the presence of international military and peacekeeping forces can present a threat of trafficking of women and girls, in particular.[169]

In noting the need for special protections in the conflict context in General Recommendation 19, the Committee has expanded upon international anti-trafficking treaty law, but the Committee has not developed the point further through concluding observations. The UNRPGs thus provide useful guidance in this area, recommending that States focus on transforming socio-cultural norms that prescribe roles and encourage privilege based on sex, rebuilding family and community support systems, and improving accountability mechanisms, among other examples.[170]

g) Special Protection for Girl Victims of Trafficking

While child victims of trafficking are entitled to the same rights and protections as adults, they should be treated separately from adults and provided special protections due to their increased vulnerability to exploitation and the particular physical and psychosocial harm suffered.[171] Although the Committee has yet to address this issue, relevant international norms establish that the best interests of the child are to be paramount at all times.[172] Accordingly, measures include, for example, the appointment of a guardian and special procedures with respect to a child's participation in criminal proceedings, among others.[173]

3. Obligation to Fulfil

a) Access to Remedies

As victims of crime and human rights violations, trafficked persons have a right to access effective and appropriate remedies under international human rights law. In General Recommendation 19, the Committee identified as among the measures necessary to provide effective protection of women against gender-based violence 'civil remedies and compensatory provisions to protect women against all kinds of violence'.[174] The Committee has specifically emphasized the need for States parties to provide trafficked women access to remedies.[175] While the Committee has not elaborated on this recommendation, evolving international anti-trafficking norms recommend that States provide options for civil or criminal actions against traffickers, compensation measures for trafficked persons, and residency permits to enable trafficked persons to pursue these remedies.[176]

b) Data Collection

Comprehensive understanding of the extent and nature of the trafficking phenomenon remains elusive. The clandestine nature of the activity complicates data collection and statistical analysis. Notwithstanding the adoption of an international legal definition of trafficking under the Trafficking Protocol, States parties vary in their interpretation of the

---

[168] UNRPG: Commentary (n 110 above) s 5.6.   [169] Ibid.   [170] Ibid.

[171] UNRPGs (n 95 above) guideline 8; UNRPG: Commentary (n 110 above) s 10.

[172] CRC arts 32–9; SAARC Convention art III; UNICEF 'Guidelines for the Protection of the Rights of Child Victims of Trafficking' (2006) guideline 2; UNRPGs (n 95 above) principle 10.

[173] Ibid.   [174] GR 19 paras 24(t)(1) and 24(i).

[175] eg CO Singapore, CEDAW/C/SGP/CO/3 (2007) para 22; CO Australia, CEDAW/C/AUS/CO/7 (2010) para 31.

[176] Trafficking Protocol art 6(6); Legislative Guide to the Organized Crime Convention and its Protocols (2004) para 368; Council of Europe Trafficking Convention art 15(2)-(4); UNRPGs (n 95 above) principle 17, guideline 9(3).

range of activities that qualify as 'trafficking'. Moreover, the impact of trafficking interventions adopted around the world remains gravely under-explored with the few studies conducted thus far revealing serious deficiencies.[177]

Consistent with the Trafficking Protocol, the European Trafficking Convention, and the UNRPGs, the Committee has called upon States parties to collect data, including comprehensive statistics, on trafficking and the impact of measures taken to address the phenomenon.[178] Specifically, they should evaluate the causes of trafficking,[179] monitor and compile data regarding victims' ages and national origins,[180] trends in trafficking, and on court cases, prosecutions, and victims assisted, as well as results achieved in prevention.[181] With an eye to vulnerability factors, the Committee has called upon a State party to collect statistics on the situation of migrant women in employment, education, and health, and on the various forms of violence they experience so the Committee can get a clear picture of their *de facto* situation.[182] States parties are to monitor the effects of anti-trafficking laws and policies[183] and conduct gender impact assessments, including with respect to laws and policies concerning immigration[184] and prostitution. The unintended effects of laws concerning prostitution—whether they criminalize or decriminalize the practice—are to be assessed, particularly with respect to migrant prostitutes.[185]

c) Addressing Demand as a Root Cause of Trafficking

Trafficking is perpetuated by a global market that seeks cheap, exploitable labour and the goods it produces. Demand reduction is an important component of any effective prevention strategy.[186] Exploring the demand side of trafficking requires inquiry into what shapes demand, who are the individuals that exploit or consume trafficked labour, and how States—whether through action or inaction—construct or facilitate the conditions under which such exploitation can occur.[187]

[177] eg Global Alliance Against Trafficking in Women, *Collateral Damage: the Impact of Anti-Trafficking Measures on Human Rights Around the World* (2007); Gallagher and Pearson (n 110 above).

[178] CO Kazakhstan, A/56/38, 24th Session (2001) para 98; CO Portugal, A/57/38, 26th Session (2002) para 336; CO El Salvador, A/58/38, 28th Session (2003) para 313; CO Bhutan, A/59/38, 30th Session (2004) para 124; CO Korea, CEDAW/C/KOR/CO/6 (2007) para 20; CO Niger, CEDAW/C/NER/CO/2 (2007) paras 26 and 32; CO Peru, CEDAW/C/PER/CO/6 (2007) para 31; CO Myanmar, CEDAW/C/MMR/CO/3 (2008) para 27; CO Guinea-Bissau, CEDAW/C/GNB/CO/6 (2009) para 30; CO Egypt, CEDAW/C/EGY/CO/7 (2010) para 26. See also Trafficking Protocol art 9(2); UNRPGs (n 95 above) guideline 3; Council of Europe Trafficking Convention arts 5(2) and 6(a).

[179] CO Belarus, A/59/38, 30th Session (2004) para 350; CO Austria, CEDAW/C/AUT/CO/6 (2007) paras 25–6; CO Nicaragua, CEDAW/C/NIC/CO/6 (2007) para 22.

[180] CO Japan, A/58/38, 29th Session (2003) para 364.

[181] CO Indonesia, CEDAW/C/IDN/CO/3 (2007) para 25.

[182] CO Switzerland, A/58/38, 28th Session (2003) para 123.

[183] CO Belize, CEDAW/C/BLZ/CO/3 (2007) para 22; CO Serbia, CEDAW/C/SCG/CO/1 (2007) para 26; CO Brazil, CEDAW/C/BRA/CO/6 (2007) paras 20 and 24; CO Kazakhstan, CEDAW/C/KAZ/CO/2 (2007) para 28; CO Austria, CEDAW/C/AUT/CO/6 (2007) paras 26 and 30; CO Indonesia, CEDAW/C/IDN/CO/3 (2007) para 25; CO Hungary, CEDAW/C/HUN/CO/6 (2007) para 23; CO Sierra Leone, CEDAW/C/SLE/CO/5 (2007) para 29.

[184] CO Canada, A/58/38, 28th Session (2003) paras 357–8.

[185] CO Sweden, A/56/38, 25th Session (2001) para 355; CO The Netherlands, A/56/38, 25th Session (2001) para 210; CO New Zealand, A/58/38, 29th Session (2003) para 414; CO The Netherlands, CEDAW/C/NLD/CO/4 (2007) para 22; CO Iceland, CEDAW/C/ICE/CO/6 (2009) para 24.

[186] UNRPGs (n 95 above) principle 4; Trafficking Protocol art 9(5); Council of Europe Trafficking Convention art 6.

[187] Demand Study (n 86 above) 44.

International law obliges States to adopt measures (legislative, educational, social, or cultural) to discourage the demand that fosters all forms of exploitation.[188] The Committee thus far has addressed demand only with respect to trafficking into the sex sector. It has called upon States parties to discourage the demand for prostitution,[189] including by combating sex tourism[190] and taking action to change men's and society's perception of women as sex objects.[191]

d) Promoting Trafficking Awareness in All Sectors of Society

Key to combating trafficking is the need to encourage awareness of the problem of trafficking among both public officials and the general population. Though most countries have adopted some form of anti-trafficking legislation and/or plans of action, more training of judicial and law enforcement officials to recognize and address trafficking is necessary.

International law obliges States to develop public awareness campaigns to prevent demand for trafficked persons' labour or exploitation and to lessen vulnerability to trafficking among at-risk populations.[192] In a similar vein and consistent with Covention Article 5, General Recommendation 19 calls upon States parties to ensure that the media respect and promote respect for women, and to use public information and education programmes to eliminate prejudices and change attitudes concerning the roles and status of men and women.[193] The Committee specifically has called upon States parties to encourage awareness in all sectors, particularly judicial and public security authorities, educators, and parents, with a view to implementing measures to prevent sexual exploitation.[194] Information and training on anti-trafficking laws should be provided to the judiciary, law enforcement agents, including border police, public officials, and social workers.[195]

e) Structural Remedies to Address the Causes of Trafficking and Exploitation of Prostitution

As General Recommendation 19, paragraph 14 notes, poverty and unemployment increase opportunities for trafficking in women, and force many women into prostitution. Because poverty severely restricts a person's opportunities to pursue one's well-being with respect to basic capabilities (eg, adequate food, clothing, and shelter), it can lead one to make decisions that increase vulnerability to trafficking.[196] Inequality within and between countries and inequality of opportunity between the sexes—eg, manifested

---

[188] CO Sweden, A/56/38, 25th Session (2001) para 355; CO The Netherlands, A/56/38, 25th Session (2001) para 210; CO New Zealand, A/58/38, 29th Session (2003) para 414; CO Belarus, A/59/38, 30th Session (2004) para 352.

[189] CO Latvia, A/59/38, 31st Session (2004) para 60; CO Syria, CEDAW/C/SYR/CO/1 (2007) para 24; CO Cook Islands, CEDAW/C/COK/CO/1(2007) para 27; CO Honduras, CEDAW/C/HON/CO/6 (2007) para 21.

[190] CO Cook Islands, CEDAW/C/COK/CO/1 (2007) para 27; CO Kenya, CEDAW/C/KEN/CO/6 (2007) paras 29–30; CO Belize, CEDAW/C/BLZ/CO/3 (2007) paras 21–2.

[191] CO Switzerland, A/58/38, 28th Session (2003) para 123; CO Finland, A/56/38, 24th Session (2001) para 285.

[192] Trafficking Protocol art 9(2); Council of Europe Trafficking Convention art 6.

[193] GR 19 para 24(d), (f), and (t)(2).

[194] CO Nigeria, A/59/38, 30th Session (2004) para 312; CO Niger, CEDAW/C/NER/CO/2, 38th Session (2007) para 26; CO Colombia CEDAW/C/COL/CO/6 (2007) para 21.

[195] CO Mozambique, CEDAW/C/MOZ/CO/2 (2007) para 29.

[196] UNRPG Commentary (n 110 above) s 5.3.

in discriminatory nationality, property, migration, and migrant labour laws—further compound this vulnerability.

International law obligates States to take measures to alleviate the poverty and inequality that render individuals vulnerable to trafficking.[197] Recommended measures include improved education opportunities; improved access to credit, finance, and productive resources; elimination of any *de jure* or *de facto* barriers to employment; legal and social measures to ensure rights in employment including a minimum wage that ensures an adequate standard of living; and the provision of technical and other assistance to countries of origin to enable them to address inequalities that contribute to trafficking-related vulnerabilities.[198] The Committee has called upon States parties to focus on the causes of trafficking and exploitation of prostitution through measures aimed at poverty alleviation and women's economic empowerment.[199] Recognizing that vulnerability to exploitation begins at an early age, the Committee has specifically called upon States parties to protect girl domestic workers from exploitation and abuse and to ensure that they can exercise their right to education.[200] It has also encouraged States parties to develop advocacy programs to prevent forced prostitution and trafficking,[201] with the cooperation of NGOs.[202] States parties are also encouraged to establish programmes to rehabilitate and reintegrate prostitutes and to support women who want to stop practising prostitution[203] through providing shelter, subsistence, health services, and education and training for alternative livelihoods.[204] The Committee has cautioned, however, against rehabilitation measures (for example, administrative camps) that may stigmatize victims of prostitution and deny them due process rights.[205]

By taking the same approach as the specialist treaties on trafficking, the Committee contributes to consistency and coherence in the development of international anti-trafficking law while ensuring that the human rights of women and girls remain a priority. These measures, combined with those recommended with respect to other articles of the Convention—particularly Articles 10 (education), 11 (employment), 13 (economic and

---

[197] Trafficking Protocol art 9(4).   [198] UNRPG Commentary (n 110 above) s 5.3.

[199] eg CO Romania, A/55/38, 23rd Session (2000) para 309; CO Vietnam, A/56/38, 25th Session (2001) para 269; CO Ecuador, A/58/38, 29th Session (2003) para 310; CO Kyrgyzstan. A/59/38, 30th Session (2004) para 164; CO Mauritania, CEDAW/C/MRT/CO/1 (2007) para 32; CO Cook Islands, CEDAW/C/COK/CO/1 (2007) paras 27 and 32; CO Niger, CEDAW/C/NER/CO/2 (2007) paras 26 and 32; CO Austria, CEDAW/C/AUT/CO/6 (2007) para 26; CO Indonesia, CEDAW/C/IDN/CO/3 (2007) para 25; CO Nicaragua, CEDAW/C/NIC/CO/6 (2007) para 22; CO Estonia, CEDAW/C/EST/CO/4 (2007) para 13; CO Colombia, CEDAW/C/COL/CO/6 (2007) para 21; CO Hungary, CEDAW/C/HUN/CO/6 (2007) para 23; CO Sierra Leone, CEDAW/C/SLE/CO/5 (2007) para 29.

[200] eg CO Mauritania, CEDAW/C/MRT/CO/1 (2007) paras 31–2.

[201] eg CO Democratic Republic of Congo, A/55/38, 22nd Session (2000) para 220.

[202] eg CO Lithuania, A/55/38, 23rd Session (2000) paras 153 and 168.

[203] eg CO Equatorial Guinea, A/59/38, 31st Session (2004) para 204; CO Norway, CEDAW/C/NOR/CO/7 (2007) para 22; CO Korea, CEDAW/C/KOR/CO/6 (2007) para 20; CO Maldives, CEDAW/C/MDV/CO/3 (2007) para 22. CO Norway, CEDAW/C/NOR/CO/7 (2007) para 22; CO Kenya, CEDAW/C/KEN/CO/6 (2007) para 30; CO Tajikistan, CEDAW/C/TJK/CO/3 (2007) para 24.

[204] CO Guyana, A/56/38, 25th Session (2001) para 181; CO Russian Federation, A/57/38, 26th Session (2002) para 394; CO Switzerland, A/58/38, 28th Session (2003) para 123; CO Latvia, A/59/38, 31st Session (2004) para 58; CO Korea, CEDAW/C/KOR/CO/6 (2007) para 20; CO The Netherlands, CEDAW/C/NLD/CO/4 (2007) para 32; CO Suriname CEDAW/C/SUR/CO/3 (2007) para 30; CO Maldives CEDAW/C/MDV/CO/3 (2007) para 22.

[205] CO Vietnam, CEDAW/C/VNM/CO/6 (2007) para 18.

social life), 14 (rural women), and 15 (legal capacity)—provide a comprehensive approach to eliminating the conditions that render women and girls vulnerable to trafficking.

f) Bilateral and Multilateral Cooperation

Effective efforts to combat trafficking require a comprehensive, collaborative approach among countries of origin, transit, and destination. Trafficking cases often involve alleged offenders, trafficked persons, and evidence that are located in more than one country, giving rise to criminal investigations and prosecutions in multiple jurisdictions.[206] Cooperation mechanisms between national law enforcement agencies, as well as legal mechanisms such as extradition and mutual legal assistance are thus critical to ensuring that traffickers do not enjoy impunity. Cooperation regarding adoption and enforcement of labour migration agreements could also help eliminate trafficking and related exploitation.[207] Consistent with a core purpose of international anti-trafficking laws,[208] the Committee has called upon States parties to engage in bilateral and multilateral collaboration and cooperation in their efforts to combat trafficking.[209]

g) Cooperation with Civil Society in the Design and Implementation of Anti-Trafficking Interventions

Civil society organizations play a crucial role in efforts to combat trafficking. Often the first point of contact with trafficked persons, NGOs have rare and valuable access to victim perspectives and a practical understanding of victim needs. The Committee has clearly stated that governments should work in partnership with civil society organizations and to increase their funding.[210] But governments should also fully fund national anti-trafficking plans, rather than outsource their implementation to NGOs.[211]

The multiple and overlapping areas of State obligation identified above highlight the need for a holistic social and legal approach to the trafficking of women and girls. The Convention's broad framework for eliminating discrimination against women in all spheres of life thus holds tremendous potential for addressing this human rights problem.

---

[206] International anti-trafficking laws establish jurisdictional rules to coordinate States' exercises of jurisdiction in trafficking cases. See, eg, Council of Europe Trafficking Convention arts 15, 21, and 31.

[207] UNRPGs (n 95 above) guideline 11.

[208] Trafficking Protocol art 2; Council of Europe Trafficking Convention art 1.

[209] CO Lithuania, A/55/38, 23rd Session (2000) para 153; CO Finland, A/56/38, 24th Session (2001) para 304; CO Iceland, A/57/38, 26th Session (2002) para 248; CO Brazil, A/58/38, 29th Session (2003) para 116; CO Bhutan, A/59/38, 30th Session (2004) para 124; CO Israel, CEDAW/C/ISR/CO/3 (2005) para 30; CO Gambia, CEDAW/C/GMB/CO/1–3 (2005) para 28; CO Malaysia, CEDAW/C/MYS/CO/2 (2006) para 24; CO Cape Verde, CEDAW/C/CPV/CO/6 (2006) para 22; CO Colombia, CEDAW/C/COL/CO/6 (2007) para 21; CO Morocco, CEDAW/C/MAR/CO/4 (2008) para 23; CO Nigeria, CEDAW/C/NGA/CO/6 (2008) para 26; CO Saudi Arabia, CEDAW/C/SAU/CO/2 (2008) para 24.

[210] CO Australia, CEDAW/C/AUS/CO/5 (2006) para 32; CO The Philippines, CEDAW/C/PHI/CO/6 (2006) para 20.

[211] CO Moldova, CEDAW/C/MDA/CO/3 (2006) para 25.

Article 7

States Parties shall take all appropriate measures to eliminate discrimination against women in the political and public life of the country and, in particular, shall ensure to women, on equal terms with men, the right:

(a) To vote in all elections and public referenda and to be eligible for election to all publicly elected bodies;

(b) To participate in the formulation of government policy and the implementation thereof and to hold public office and perform all public functions at all levels of government;

(c) To participate in non-governmental organizations and associations concerned with the public and political life of the country.

* I would like to thank Sahrah Al-Nasrawe-Sözeri, Andrea Eriksson, Benjamin Feyen, Ines Franke, Heidi Matthews, Anna-Maria Paulus, Eric Veillerobe, and Professor Susan Williams for their assistance and helpful comments on the chapters on arts 7 and 8 of this Commentary.

A. Introduction

Article 7 comprehensively addresses States parties' obligations in realizing women's political rights. These include the right to participate directly in the formulation of public policy as elected representatives (Article 7(a)) or as appointed public officials (Article 7(b)), as well as indirectly through voting (Article 7(a)). Article 7 is unique in human rights law because it also encompasses non-discrimination with regard to the participation in non-governmental organizations and associations (Article 7(c)). In these respects, States parties must strive to realize formal, substantive, and transformative equality which includes the adoption of temporary special measures (TSMs) under Article 4(1) to accelerate its realization. The article plays a major role in the work of the Committee, and the Committee has elaborated upon the meaning and scope of Article 7 in its analysis of Articles 7 and 8 in 1994[1] and in its General Recommendation 23 in 1997.[2]

Historically, men have dominated the public and political sphere, while women have been assigned to the private sphere of the household and the family exclusively.[3] Perceptions on the rights of women to participate in all spheres of life have changed through the work of women's movements during the twentieth century.[4] Although the invidious stereotypes that lie at the basis of this dichotomy persist, the participation of women in political and public life is viewed as a requirement for the realization of democracy[5] and as inherent in the right to development[6]. The overall purpose of the Convention, substantive equality of men and women and women's advancement, requires that women must be given the same possibility to influence the decision-making process and thereby the outcomes in State laws and policies that govern all sectors of economic, social, and cultural life.[7] To reach this end, Article 7 aims at enhancing the presence as well as the representation of women in public and political life. However, the mere presence of women in decision-making bodies is not a goal in itself, but rather, in the sense of *meaningful* presence, requires that

---

[1] CEDAW Committee, 'Implementation of Article 21 of the Convention on the Elimination of All Forms of Discrimination Against Women. Analysis of Articles 7 and 8 of the Convention. Report by the Secretariat (30 November 1993)' UN Doc CEDAW/C/1994/4.

[2] GR 23.

[3] F Gaspard, 'Unfinished Battles: Political and Public Life' in HB Schöpp-Schilling and C Flinterman, *The Circle of Empowerment* (2007) 145–58, 146.

[4] Ibid 146.

[5] GR 23 para 14; UNGA Res 'Women and Political Participation' (10 February 2004) UN Doc A/RES/58/142, Preamble section 8; IPU, Paper for the United Nations Office of the Special Adviser on Gender Issues and Advancement of Women, Expert Group Meeting on 'Enhancing Women's Participation in Electoral Processes in Post-Conflict Countries', EGM/ELEC/2004/E3 (2004) 3, 27.

[6] UNGA Res, 'Declaration in the Right to Development' (4 December 1986) UN Doc A/RES/41/128 2nd recital.

[7] S Fredman, *Discrimination Law* (2002) 22.

women be given the opportunity to have a real and viable input in all decision-making processes. Given that women are continuously under-represented, State measures are needed to compensate for past and prevent future discrimination.

There are several approaches to explain the objective of increased participation of women. While it is often stated that quantitative increase in the number of women holding elected political office will necessarily effect a substantive change in outcomes,[8] the link between the two is not easy to make. Some writers contend that essential differences between men and women render representation across the sexes impossible: 'only women can represent women'.[9] Including a 'critical mass' of women ensures that the concerns and needs of all women will be taken into account. This might imply that the number of women matters only if they are 'distinct' from men in their priorities and legislative activities,[10] and runs the risk of replicating a stereotypical view of women.[11] But the impact of the presence of women in decision-making bodies on the content and style of decisions is uncertain;[12] the political context, for example, allegiance to party platforms, might constrain their representation of women's interests.[13] Moreover, in view of the heterogeneity of women and the impact of intersecting grounds of discrimination, the term 'women's interests' seems misleading.[14] Therefore, as women will not share a common view on all matters, in order to reflect the complex and diverse perspectives, opinions, and interests within the group, women's full proportional representation is necessary.[15]

Other writers explain the objective of increased participation by the historically grounded and continually existing patterns of domination and subordination between men and women.[16] What women share is the lack of access to political power. Indeed, decision-making bodies which are male-dominated tend to exclude the perspectives of the under-represented sex and to perpetuate their existing composition.[17] Thus, the historically grounded exclusion of women creates a need for greater 'descriptive representation'[18] of women. Due to shared experiences of marginalization, women will be equipped to bring the interests of other women into the deliberative process, especially with respect to newly emerging issues that have a bearing on gender relations.

---

[8] B Meyer, 'Much Ado About Nothing? Political Representation Policies and the Influence of Women Parliamentarians in Germany' (2003) 20:3 *Review of Policy Research* 401–21, 416; S Thomas 'The Impact of Women on State Legislative Policies' (1991) 53: 4 *J of Politics* 958–76, 974.

[9] C Boyle, 'Home Rule for Women: Power Sharing between Men and Women' (1983) 7:3 *Dalhousie L J* 790–809, 797.

[10] K Cowell-Meyers, 'Gender, Power, and Peace: A Preliminary Look at Women in the Northern Ireland Assembly' (2001) 23:3 *Women & Politics* 55–88, 57, 60.

[11] Fredman (n 7 above) 154.

[12] K Beckwith and K Cowell-Meyers, 'Sheer Numbers: Critical Representation Thresholds and Women's Political Representation' (2007) 5:3 *Perspectives on Politics* 553–65, 553f.

[13] H Charlesworth and C Chinkin, *The Boundaries of International Law* (2000) 192; Sandra Fredman gives the example of Margaret Thatcher as demonstrating women in power do not necessarily represent women's interests, Fredman (n 7 above) 154; S Childs and ML Krook, 'Theorizing Women's Political Representation: Debates and Innovations in Empirical Research' (2008) 17:2 *Femina Politica* 20–30, 23.

[14] A Phillips, *Engendering Democracy* (1991) 72; Childs/Krook (n 13 above) 25.

[15] J Mansbridge, 'The Descriptive Political Representation of Gender: An Anti-Essentialist Argument' in J Klausen and CS Maier (eds), *Has Liberalism Failed Women?* (2001) 19–38, 24f; the diversity approach is also discernible in the Committee's COs on intersectional discrimination, see below D.5.

[16] eg Mansbridge (n 15 above) 19–38.   [17] Fredman (n 7 above) 155.

[18] Mansbridge (n 15 above) 19–38.

Increased participation of women is a prerequisite for social change in many other fields and therefore a precondition for the realization of women's economic, social, and cultural rights.[19] The Committee noted in its General Recommendation 23, that where there is full and equal participation of women in decision-making, the implementation of the Convention improves.[20] Hence, the aim of Article 7 is the realization of equal participation in the political and public field as an intrinsic value indispensable for the realization of full equality of men and women in general.

Within the UN system, political rights of women were asserted in 1952 in the Convention on the Political Rights of Women and were reiterated without much change in the Declaration on the Elimination of Discrimination against Women (DEDAW).[21] While both earlier instruments referred to the right to vote, to be elected, and the right to hold public office and exercise public functions without discrimination, Articles 7 and 8 of the Convention added substantial elements.

B. Travaux Préparatoires

Throughout the drafting process only a few substantial changes were made to the drafts by the Philippines[22] and the USSR[23] as well as their combined draft[24] and the version in the draft report of the Working Group to the CSW[25]. Non-discrimination in political participation was seemingly rather uncontroversial and the discussions were primarily driven by the wish to make the Article more comprehensive. The text of the chapeau was changed to be more specific and firm: States parties 'shall take all appropriate measures' and 'ensure...the right'.[26] Article 7(a) in the USSR draft,[27] the entitlement to vote or be eligible for election to 'any central or local representative State organ or public organization' was broadened substantially to include 'all elections and public referenda', as well as 'all elected bodies'.[28] Regarding Article 7(b), the wording 'at the national and local level' relating to the right to participate in government policy and hold public office in the combined draft[29] was changed to encompass 'all levels of government' in order to include

---

[19] K Kawamata, 'Article 7: Equality in Political and Public life' in Japanese Association of Women's Rights (ed), *Convention on the Elimination of All Forms of Discrimination against Women. A Commentary* (1995) 139–50, 139.

[20] GR 23 para 14; CO Kuwait CEDAW/C/KWT/CO/2 (2004) para 60.

[21] UNGA Res 2263 (7 November 1967) (XXII) UN Doc A/6880, art 4.

[22] ECOSOC Text of the Draft Convention on the Elimination of Discrimination against Women proposed by the Philippines (6 November 1973) UN Doc E/CN.6/573, art 5.

[23] ECOSOC Working Group on a new Instrument or Instruments of International Law to Eliminate Discrimination against Women, Working Paper submitted by the Union of Soviet Socialist Republics (7 January 1974) UN Doc E/CN.6/AC.1/L.2, art 7.

[24] ECOSOC Working Group on a new Instrument or Instruments of International Law to Eliminate Discrimination against Women, Working Paper submitted by the Philippines and the Union of Soviet Socialist Republics (9 January 1974) UN Doc E/CN.6/AC.1/L.4/Add.1, 1.

[25] ECOSOC Commission on the Status of Women Working Group on a new Instrument or Instruments of International Law to Eliminate Discrimination against Women, Draft Report of the Working Group to the Commission on the Status of Women (14 January 1974) UN Doc E/CN.6/AC.1/L.12, 10.

[26] LA Rehof, *Guide to the Travaux Préparatoires of the United Nations Convention on the Elimination of All Forms of Discrimination against Women* (1993) 94.

[27] ECOSOC, UN Doc E/CN.6/AC.1/L.2, art 7.   [28] Rehof (n 26 above) 94.

[29] ECOSOC, UN Doc E/CN.6/AC.1/L.4/Add.1, 1.

regional and provincial levels.[30] In Article 7(c), reference was added to 'the public and political life of the country' the NGO with which has to be concerned. This was included in response to a concern that the entitlement might interfere with the freedom of association of private single-sex social clubs and that interference with the autonomy of such organizations falls beyond the power of the State.[31] Governmental representation at the international level was thought to be implicit in the idea 'to hold public office and perform all public functions' in Article 7(b);[32] it was later agreed to include a separate Article on the matter (the final Article 8).[33]

C. Issues of Interpretation

I. Chapeau

'The chapeau lays down the overarching obligation for States Parties to take all appropriate measures to eliminate discrimination against women in the political and public life of the country. In particular, they shall ensure to women, on equal terms with men, the rights contained in Article 7(a)–(c).' This enumeration is not exhaustive as indicated by the wording 'in particular' in the chapeau, which bestows on women the right not to be discriminated against in all other aspects of political and public life.[34] All three sub-headings of Article 7 raise issues that go beyond their precise wording relating to the structure and organization of political life within a State. In the context of ICCPR Article 25, protecting political and public life, the Human Rights Committee has stated that freedom of expression (implying a free press and other media) and freedom of assembly and association are also covered as *essential adjuncts* to the political and public rights protected by this provision.[35] Although these rights are not specified in other articles of the Convention, the rights protected by ICCPR Article 25 are sufficiently analogous to those protected by Article 7 to warrant the proposition that they are none the less integrated into the realization of Article 7 rights, a view strengthened by Article 3.[36]

1. Political and Public Life of the Country

The 'political and public life of the country' is a concept closely related to—but even broader than—the concept of 'public affairs' in ICCPR Article 25. Under the Convention, this concept extends to civil society, as specified in Article 7(c), and includes 'public boards and local councils and the activities of organizations such as political parties, trade unions, professional or industry associations, women's organizations, community-based organizations or other organizations concerned with public and political life'.[37] The concept of public affairs in ICCPR Article 25 thus more closely resembles the narrower concept of 'government policy' in Article 7(b).

---

[30] ECOSOC Commission on the Status of Women, Draft Convention on the Elimination of all Forms of Discrimination against Women Working-paper prepared by the Secretary-General (21 June 1976) UN Doc E/CN.6/591, Annex 1 Amendments and new Versions Proposed, 62.

[31] Ibid para 84; the first concern was expressed by Canada and the United Kingdom; the second by Finland.

[32] Rehof (n 26 above) 100.

[33] UNGA, 'Addendum to the Working Paper Prepared by the Secretary-General, Decisions Taken by the Working Group of the Whole of the Convention on the Elimination of Discrimination against Women during the 32nd session of the General-Assembly' (2 October 1978) UN Doc A/C.3/33/WG.1/CR1/Add.1, 9.

[34] GR 23 para 5.

[35] HRC, 'General Comment No 25' UN Doc CCPR/C/21/Rev.1/Add.7 (1996) paras 26–7.

[36] See the discussion in ch on art 3.   [37] GR 23 para 5.

II. Article 7(a)

Article 7(a) is a distant result of the women's struggle to achieve the right to vote, which started in the late eighteenth century. The movement, which originated in France and Great Britain, set out to fight women's exclusion from the political realm and acquire women's suffrage.[38] Article 7(a) contains the twofold obligation of ensuring the right to vote and to stand for election; in these respects, women are to have the same rights as men. The right to vote refers to the right of the individual to take part in the governing of their country through freely chosen representatives. The requirements for elections to suffice as a realization of the right to vote are universal and equal suffrage, secret ballot,[39] and periodicity. This ensures the accountability of representatives for the exercise of the legislative or executive powers vested in them and guarantees that governmental authority continues to be based on the free expression of the will of the electorate.[40] In scope, (a) refers to all elections, including those to Parliament, Government, Senate, and local government. The concept of 'public referenda' complements the concept of elections to encompass all direct ballots and plebiscites where the people of a constituency are asked to accept or reject a certain policy or legislative proposal. The right to be elected refers to the right of women to be nominated as candidates for election and to have the democratic chance of winning a seat in the elected body. It also extends to the right not to be discriminated against during tenure of political office. The term 'publicly elected bodies' is the counterpart to the concept of elections, encompassing even those bodies that have only an advisory role.

1. Political System

The Convention does not expressly require any particular form of political system. The political system of a State is one factor amongst many which determine the degree of integration of women into political and public life and, as yet, no political system has realized full integration of women.[41] None the less, General Recommendation 23 requires, as a minimum, that 'each citizen enjoys the right to vote and be elected at genuine periodic elections held on the basis of universal suffrage and by secret ballot, in such a way as to guarantee the free expression of the will of the electorate'.[42] Thus, the implementation of Article 7 demands a form of governance where the will of the people plays a substantial role in determining State policy.

2. Choice of Electoral System

The Committee is silent on the issue and does not prescribe the form of electoral system in its dialogue with States parties. General Recommendation 23, paragraph 22 notes the impact of the system of balloting, the distribution of seats in the legislature, and the choice of district on the right to be elected. Research has also shown some systems to be more effective in increasing the number of women in elected office.[43] Proportional

---

[38] cf AS Fraser, 'Becoming Human: The Origins and Development of Women's Human Rights' (1999) *Human Rights Quarterly* 4, 853–906.

[39] ICCPR, art 25(b).

[40] cf CCPR, 'General Comment No 25' UN Doc CCPR/C/21/Rev.1/Add.7 (1996) para 9.

[41] CSW, 'Report of the Secretary General' E/CN.6/1995/3/Add.6, 1 (39th Session, 1995) para 21 ff; comparing obstacles to women's participation in different political systems: IWRAW Asia Pacific, 'Regional Consultation on Women's Right to Participate in Political and Public Life: Report' (2004) 23.

[42] GR 23 para 6.

[43] S Larserud and R Taphorn, '*Designing for Equality. Best-fit, Medium-fit and Non-favourable Combinations of Electoral Systems and Gender Quotas*' (2007) 12ff.

representation systems with multi-member-districts have been shown to achieve greater representation of women than plurality/majority systems[44] as parties nominate several candidates which creates incentives to nominate women (as well as candidates from other groups in society) in order to create greater diversity, thereby attracting a variety of voters. Majoritarian systems, on the other hand, usually allow for single-member districts, and parties tend to nominate the most powerful or most likely to be elected (typically male) candidate.[45] Other electoral factors that can influence women's level of participation are electoral thresholds, district magnitude, and the use of closed or open voting lists.[46] Changing electoral systems promises enhanced inclusion of women on a short-term basis because they are more malleable and easier to change than the overall cultural and social position of women.[47]

III. Article 7(b)

Article 7(b) moves beyond formal participation and voting to substantial issues: the right to participate in formulating and implementing government policy and the right to hold public office and perform public functions without discrimination. It covers the vast variety of non-elective public sector employment and the right to influence politics not only through voting but also through other, less formal channels.

1. Government Policy

The term 'government policy' is a broad concept congruent with the concept 'conduct of public affairs' in ICCPR Article 25. In its General Recommendation 23, paragraph 5, the Committee adopted the interpretation of the CCPR in its General Comment 25, paragraph 5: 'The conduct of public affairs...is a broad concept which relates to the exercise of political power, in particular the exercise of legislative, executive and administrative powers. It covers all aspects of public administration, and the formulation and implementation of policy at international, national, regional and local levels'.

2. Public Office and Public Functions

Complementing Article 7(a), 'public office' encompasses all non-elective public posts. The lack of a definition of the term 'public office' in 7(b) allows for greater flexibility according to the different understandings States parties have given the term in their internal law. The public sector has been defined as all market and non-market activities which at each institutional level are controlled and mainly financed by public authority.[48] Public sector occupation ranges from administrative posts to government ministry posts, judges, police

[44] RE Matland, 'Enhancing Women's Political Participation: Legislative Recruitment and Electoral Systems' in J Ballington and A Karam, *Women in Parliament: Beyond Numbers* (2005) 93–111, 99; UNDAW, 'Report of the Expert Group Meeting on Equal Participation of Women and Men in Decision-Making Processes with Particular Emphasis on Political Participation and Leadership' EGM/EPDM/2005/Report 15.

[45] J Ballington and RE Matland, 'Political Parties and Special Measures: Enhancing Women's Participation in Electoral Processes' EGM/ELEC/2004/E8 3.

[46] UNDAW (n 44 above) 15; Ballington and Matland (n 45 above) 5f.

[47] Ballington and Matland (n 45 above) 4.

[48] M Hammouya, 'Statistics on Public Sector Employment. Methodology, Structures and Trends' (1999) 3f; 'System of National Accounts', Commission of the European Communities, International Monetary Fund, Organization for Economic Cooperation and Development, United Nations, World Bank (1993) chapter IV: Institutional units and sectors, 102–4.

and security forces, the military, religious life (in case of a State religion), educational and academic institutions,[49] boards of trustees of foundations under public law, district health boards, municipal councils, advisory councils and mayors to government advisory boards and publicly owned companies.

Similarly, States parties give the term 'public functions' varied meanings. Under the Convention, the term serves as a blanket clause, completing the term 'public office' to cover every State-related occupation in public and political life. The Committee has interpreted it more broadly than under the international law on State responsibility, encompassing not only all areas in which acts of individuals can be attributed to the State according to Chapter II of the ILC's Articles on State Responsibility,[50] but also privatized companies that are heavily regulated by the State. In a word, 'public functions' are all activities that are carried out in the interest and for the benefit of the public. They need not be controlled by public authority, for example, in the case of the judiciary, and need not necessarily be carried out by public officers, as where public functions are outsourced to private entities.

The phrase 'at all levels' refers to both public offices and public functions and was inserted during the drafting process to clarify that women have the right to be represented at all branches and levels of government and all levels of seniority. In *Calderon v President of the Republic*, the Constitutional Chamber of the Supreme Court of Justice of Costa Rica held that a failure to include female candidates on a list of candidates submitted to the Parliament for the Board of Directors of the Monitoring Body for Public Services (*Junta Directiva de la Autoridad Reguladora de los Servicos Públicos*) was inconsistent with the State's obligation under Convention Article 7 to ensure equality in public life. It ordered the government to take active steps to reach this goal by including a representative number of women in the future.[51]

3. *Women in the Military*

The participation of women in all levels of the armed forces is controversial. Several States parties have entered reservations in relation to the issue (although many have subsequently withdrawn them).[52] In many States parties, women are either prohibited from entering military service altogether or at least from serving in positions involving armed combat.[53] In two judgments, *Sirdar* in 1999[54] and *Kreil* in 2000[55], the ECJ opened positions within the military to men and women alike.[56] The Court held, *inter alia*, that women cannot be excluded from specific employment on the ground that they should be given greater protection generally than men from risks which are not connected to women's specific needs.[57] The exclusion of women from the military service relies on and perpetuates stereotypical views of typically male and female spheres of life; it also depicts women as

---

[49] CO Hungary CEDAW/C/HUN/CO/6 (2007) paras 22, 25; CO Liechtenstein CEDAW/C/LIE/CO/3 (2007) para 17; CO Austria CEDAW/C/AUT/CO/6 (2007) para 28. Art 7(b) covers only State universities; private universities are a matter of art 7(c).

[50] ILC, 'Draft Articles on State Responsibility for Internationally Wrongful Acts' (Fifty-third session, 2001) Part of UN Doc A/56/10.

[51] *Calderon v President of the Republic and another* (Vote no. 716–98), (1998) 6 BHRC 306.

[52] See the discussion in ch on art 28.

[53] eg Australia, New Zealand, Italy, Portugal, Spain, United Kingdom, United States.

[54] ECJ Case C-273/97, *Angela Maria Sirdar v The Army Board and Secretary of State for Defence* [1999] ECR I-7403.

[55] ECJ Case C-285/98, *Tanja Kreil v Bundesrepublik Deutschland* [2000] ECR I-69.

[56] B Rudolf, '*European Union: Compulsory Military Service*' (2005) I-CON 637–79, 674, 678.

[57] ECJ (n 55 above) para 30.

'second-class-citizens' who share neither the same rights nor the same duties with men. States parties must open up the military to provide women with career opportunities and the possibility of shaping public policy concerning military issues.[58] This even requires States parties to accommodate women's differences, for example, by changing entry level physical requirements that amount to indirect discrimination.

4. *Privatization*

Privatization, the transfer of public functions of government to the private sector, is a common economic policy in market economies. However, outsourcing of the delivery of public services must not result in the erosion or circumvention of States parties' human rights obligations,[59] including women's equal access to these privatized entities. The Committee's view seems to be that these functions continue to be 'public functions' under Article 7(b) subjecting States to the strict liability standard for acts of privatized entities. This high standard may be difficult to realize under the internal law of many States parties. This, however, is no defence under public international law. Privatized functions could also be covered by Article 7(c), but only with respect to participation. States parties' obligation would then be that of due diligence with respect to non-State actors under Convention Articles 2(e) and 7(c). Before any liberalization measure is taken, its impact on women must be assessed and measures must be taken to avoid detrimental outcomes.[60] Further, in the process of privatization itself States parties must regulate, set normative standards to ensure women's equal participation, and monitor behaviour when drawing up, negotiating, and enforcing contracts.[61]

5. *Women's Access to Traditional Forms of Power*

For many women in rural areas[62] the arena of formal politics is far away from their everyday lives. They are more affected by traditional fora of dispute resolution and decision-making which often overlap with the local administrative and judicial structures created by appointment, such as clan committees, leadership councils, councils of elders, traditional chiefs, land administration committees, and local council courts.[63] Such leadership positions are traditionally male-dominated.[64] For instance, women are often not allowed to attend clan meetings or have a voice in decision-making processes, despite the impact

---

[58] CEDAW Committee, 'Implementation of Article 21 of the Convention on the Elimination of All Forms of Discrimination against Women. Analysis of articles 7 and 8 of the Convention. Report by the Secretariat' (30 November 1993) CEDAW/C/1994/1 para 29ff.

[59] UN High Commission of Human Rights, Economic, Social and Cultural Rights, 'Liberalisation of Trade in Services and Human Rights', Report of the High Commissioner, E/CN.4/Sub.2/2002/9, 25 June 2002, paras 4–14; K de Feyter/F Gómez Isa, 'Privatisation and Human Rights. An Overview' in Id. (eds), *Privatisation and Human Rights in the Age of Globalisation* (2005) 1, 3.

[60] eg CO New Zealand, A/53/38/Rev.1 (Part II), 19th Session (1998) para 276.

[61] For human rights in general: UN High Commission of Human Rights, Economic, Social and Cultural Rights: 'Liberalisation of Trade in Services and Human Rights', Report of the High Commissioner (25 June 2002) UN Doc E/CN.4/Sub.2/2002/9 paras 39, 50.

[62] See the discussion in ch on art 14; art 14 does not explicitly refer to participation in political decision-making, but does refer to 'all' community activities and the implementation etc of development planning.

[63] For informal justice systems cf C Nyamu-Musembi, 'For or Against Gender Equality? Evaluating the Post-Cold War "Rule of Law" Reforms in Sub-Saharan Africa' (2005) UNRISD Occasional Paper No 7, 14; for the Kenyan context cf C Nyamu-Musembi, 'Are Local Norms and Practices Fences or Pathways? The Example of Property Rights' in Abdullahi A An-Na'im (ed), *Cultural Transformation and Human Rights in Africa* (2002) 126–50, 129ff.

[64] S Düsing, *Traditional Leadership and Democratisation in Southern Africa. A Comparative Study of Botswana, Namibia and South Africa* (2002) 252.

of clan membership on women's lives.[65] Under Article 7(b) and (c), States parties must ensure that women are included even in these customary mechanisms, including through the application of temporary special measures (TSMs). The Committee has asked States parties, *inter alia*, to conduct awareness-raising programmes with traditional chiefs.[66] Some laws governing traditional mechanisms provide for gender-sensitive provisions,[67] with contended success.[68]

6. *Women in Post-conflict Reconstruction*

The Beijing Platform for Action Critical Area of Concern E on women and armed conflict sought the inclusion of women into all aspects of peace processes.[69] In 2000, women's important role in the reconstruction of war-torn societies, that is, in the maintenance of international peace and security, was recognized in Security Council Resolution 1325 on women, peace, and security,[70] which provides a comprehensive political framework on all gender-related aspects of peace processes. Article 7 reinforces these provisions on women's participatory rights with normative strength,[71] and has been used as such by the Committee.[72] States parties are obligated to secure women's access to and effective participation in formal and informal peace processes as well as to adopt a gender perspective in all peacemaking efforts.[73] The obligations outlined above apply similarly to recovery efforts and disaster management after natural catastrophes.[74]

IV. Article 7(c)

Article 7(c) is unique in human rights law; it specifies the right of women not to be discriminated against in participating in 'non-governmental organizations' (NGOs) and associations, that are concerned with public and political life. The paragraph brings private actors into the realm of political rights and, thus, challenges the public-private divide.

This paragraph raises the possible conflict with the human right of freedom of association, which allows associations to define their own rules of admission. It is clear from the *travaux préparatoires* that the drafters of the Convention considered the problem, and concluded that as to organizations and associations concerned with public life, the prohibition

---

[65] C Nyamu-Musembi (n 63 above) 139f.

[66] CO Niger CEDAW/C/NER/CO/2 (2007) para 28; CO Togo CEDAW/C/TGO/CO/5 (2006) para 21.

[67] Namibian Council of Traditional Leaders Act 1997, Act No 13, 1997, Official Government Gazette No 1706, (16 October 1997) art. 3 (1) g); Communal Land Rights Bill of the Republic of South Africa, Government Gazette No 25492, (3 October 2003) art 30(4), art 34(1)d)(i); Tanzanian Village Land Act of 1999, art 53(2).

[68] L Khadiagala, 'The failure of popular justice in Uganda: Local councils and women's property rights' (2001) 32 *Development and Change* 55–76, 64.

[69] Beijing Declaration and Platform for Action UN Docs A/CONF.177/20 (1995), A/CONF.177/20/Add.1 (1995) Strategic Objective E.1 para 142 a).

[70] Security Council Resolution 1325, UN Doc S/RES/1325 (2000). See also the follow-up resolutions: Resolution 1820, UN Doc S/RES/1820 (2008); Resolution 1888, UN Doc S/RES/1888 (2009), and Resolution 1889, UN Doc S/RES/1889 (2009).

[71] UNIFEM, 'Women, Peace & Security. CEDAW and Security Council Resolution 1325. A Quick Guide' (2001) 5.

[72] CO Serbia CEDAW/C/SCG/CO/1 (2007) para 28.

[73] cf CO Serbia CEDAW/C/SCG/CO/1 (2007) para 27; CO Rwanda CEDAW/C/RWA/CO/6 (2009) para 5; Committee, 'Statement on the Situation of Women in Iraq' Decision 30/III, A/59/38 (Supp.), Annex II (2004); see the discussion in chapter on violence against women.

[74] CO Indonesia CEDAW/C/IDN/CO/5 (2007) para 38; CO Myanmar CEDAW/C/MMR/CO/3 (2008) para 22.

of discrimination prevails over freedom of association. The Committee has stated that Article 7(c) in conjunction with Article 7(b) requires State parties to secure the effective functioning of women's NGOs and associations through consultative processes, cooperation, membership in task forces or committees, contribution to legislative processes, as well as through financing.[75]

1. Non-governmental Organizations

There is no generally accepted definition of NGO in international law.[76] In the context of rules providing for consultation by international organizations with NGOs,[77] the term is often understood as referring to national or international private organizations.[78] In actual usage, the term is often used to describe non-profit organizations only.[79] As the antonym of governmental organizations, the term covers the vast variety of organizations that are neither created nor directed by the State, including women's NGOs and human rights NGOs.

2. Associations Concerned with Political and Public Life

In its reviews of States parties' reports, the Committee has broadly interpreted the notion of 'associations' to cover all associations that are private in nature, but operate within public and political life. It applies, therefore, to political parties, trade unions,[80] religious organizations,[81] employer's associations,[82] and employee's associations. While General Recommendation 23 does not expressly include corporations, the Committee regularly incorporates in its concluding observations references to State obligations regarding the conduct of corporations under Article 7. It has, *inter alia*, urged States parties to take measures in the private business sector[83] and economy,[84] for example, with respect to positions as senior managers, and membership on boards of directors.[85] 'NGO' in UN parlance generally refers to non-profit organizations; the inclusion of 'associations' emphasizes that the activities of profit-oriented organizations are covered by Article 7 as well.[86]

---

[75] One of the drafts of the Working Group of the CSW stipulated that '[e]ach Party shall endeavour to promote organizations and movements whose purpose is to advance the status of women and eliminate discrimination against them', art 2 of the Draft Convention of the Working Group of the CSW, Report of the 26th Session 1976 Official Record, UN Doc E/CN.6/608, 4; CO Mozambique CEDAW/C/MOZ/CO/2 (2007) para 8; CO Nigeria CEDAW/C/NGA/CO/6 (2008) para 310; CO Democratic People's Republic of Korea CEDAW/C/PRK/CO/1 (2005) para 52.

[76] AK Lindblom, *The Legal Status of Non-Governmental Organisations in International Law* (2001) 46.

[77] eg art 71 UN Charter; Council of Europe Resolution (51) 30 F, Relations with International Organisations, both Intergovernmental and Non-governmental, 3 May 1951; OAS, AG/RES. 57 (I-0/71, Standards on Cooperative Relations Between the Organization of American States and the United Nations, its Specialised Agencies, and Other National and International Organizations, 23 April 1971.

[78] Lindblom (n 76 above) 48ff.

[79] Kawamata (n 19 above) 142; Lindblom (n 76 above) 48; cf *World Bank Handbook on Good Practices Relating to Non-Governmental Organisations*, 19; Council of Europe, Convention in the Recognition of the Legal Personality of International Non-Governmental Organisations, 1986, ETS no 124, art 1 a).

[80] eg CO Greece CEDAW/C/GRC/CO/6 (2007) para 23

[81] eg CO Cook Islands CEDAW/C/COK/CO/1 (2007) para 28.

[82] eg CO Greece CEDAW/C/GRC/CO/6 (2007) para 23.

[83] eg CO Finland CEDAW/C/FIN/CO/6 (2008) para 22; CO Liechtenstein CEDAW/C/LIE/CO/3 (2007) para 17; CO Republic of Korea CEDAW/C/KOR/CO/6 (2007) para 24; CO The Netherlands CEDAW/C/NLD/CO/4 (2007) para 17; CO Bosnia-Herzegovina CEDAW/C/BIH/CO/3 (2006) para 30.

[84] eg CO Austria CEDAW/C/AUT/CO/6 (2007) paras 27, 28.

[85] eg CO Finland CEDAW/C/FIN/CO/6 (2008) para 21; CO Sweden CEDAW/C/SWE/CO/7 (2008) para 24; CO Iceland CEDAW/C/ICE/CO/6 (2008) para 25.

[86] Kawamata (n 19 above) 144.

3. *Women in Political Parties*

Because political parties play a mediating role between the electorate and formal political process, they can exert great influence on the gender balance and sensitivity of formal politics in selection and nomination of prospective political candidates.[87] However, their internal structure and organization can be an obstacle to women's participation.[88] As the 'gatekeepers' of formal politics they are a useful target of gender-oriented strategies. The State party's obligation is to ensure that political parties realize equality by increasing the number of female candidates.[89] Potential measures range from information and awareness-raising campaigns and training sessions for prospective candidates[90] to financial aid for female candidates' campaigns and encouraging parties to adopt party quotas.[91] The Committee, however, prefers legal quotas in the Constitution or in law,[92] as the enforcement of political party measures relies on the goodwill of party leaders.[93]

A prominent example of the States parties' obligations under Article 7(c) is the prohibition of internal party policies that deny women membership. In the case of the SGP, a Christian religious party in the Netherlands, the Committee twice disapproved of the State's inaction in failing to prohibit such party policies.[94] The Dutch courts were divided on the question of whether State failure to take measures to ensure compliance with non-discrimination constituted an infringement of Article 7 and whether it outweighed freedom of association and freedom of religion.[95] The Convention, however, expressly states that religious beliefs and cultural traditions cannot serve as justifications for infringements of the right to equality.[96] If there are no appropriate remedies at hand to compel the party to allow women to be elected, the State is under an obligation under Articles 7(c) and 2(f) to amend its laws.[97]

4. *Women in Trade Unions*

Ensuring equality of men and women in their access to trade unions is another obligation arising under Article 7(c). Trade unions play a critical role for women's equality:[98] they can address women's remaining marginalization and their being trapped in low-paying jobs and high vulnerability to discrimination in the workplace (see Article 11). States parties must take adequate measures, in accordance with Articles 2(e) and 7(c) to increase the number

---

[87] GR 23 para 34; CEDAW (n 58 above) para 13.

[88] UNDAW (n 44 above) 15.   [89] CO Guinea CEDAW/C/GIN/CO/6 (2007) para 31;

[90] UNDAW (n 44 above) 18; CO Guinea CEDAW/C/GIN/CO/6 (2007) para 31; CO Syrian Arab Republic CEDAW/C/SYR/CO/1 (2007) para 26.

[91] eg CO Bahrain CEDAW/C/BHR/CO/2 (2008) para 29; CO Jordan CEDAW/C/JOR/CO/4 (2007) para 28; CO Syrian Arab Republic CEDAW/C/SYR/CO/1 (2007) para 26.

[92] CO Morocco CEDAW/C/MAR/CO/4 (2008) para 25.

[93] T Sacchet, 'Political Parties: When do they Work for Women?' (2005) EGM/EPWD/2005/E10 3.

[94] CO The Netherlands A/56/38 25th Session (2001) paras 219–20; CO The Netherlands CEDAW/C/NLD/CO/4 (2007) paras 25–6.

[95] The Hague Court of First Instance, *Stichting Proefprocessenfonds Clara Wichmann et al v the Netherlands* (7 September 2005) LJN: AU2088; the Hague Court of Appeal, *the State of The Netherlands and the SGP v Stichting Proefprocessfonds Clara Wichmann et al* (20 December 2007) LJN: BC0169. Administrative Jurisdiction Division of the Council of State, *SGP v the Minister of the Interior* (5 December 2007) LJN: BB9493.

[96] cf art 5(a); art 2(f) and the discussion in the ch on arts 2 and 5.

[97] I Boerefijn, 'The Right to Political Participation: the Case of the SGP' in R Holtmaat and I Boerefijn (eds), *Women's Human Rights and Culture/Religion/Tradition: International Standards as Guidelines for Discussion?* (2010) SIM Special No 32, 121–139.

[98] ILO, 'The Role of Trade Unions in Promoting Gender Equality' (2002) 5.

of women in trade unions.[99] The case of *Jacomb v Australian Municipal Administrative Clerical and Services Union* is illustrative. The Federal Court of Australia had to decide whether affirmative action measures for the union's branch executive and State conference constituted discrimination against men. Drawing on Convention Articles 4(1) and 7(c), the Court held that the relevant provisions of the Sex Discrimination Act allowing for such measures were to be interpreted in conformity with the Convention, and, thus, did not constitute discrimination.[100] From the viewpoint of the Convention, this decision entails that Article 7(c) not only obliges States parties to ensure formal equality of access to NGOs, but also, in conjunction with Article 4(1), substantive equality which can be reached through affirmative action measures.

5. Fair Representation on Corporate Boards

One of the consequences of the inclusion of private enterprises under the term 'non-governmental association' in Article 7(c) is that States parties' obligations extend to securing women's fair and equal representation on corporate governing boards.[101] The Committee commends States to adapt temporary special measures applicable in the private sector,[102] for example, National Action Plans aimed at increasing the number of women in such positions.[103]

D. Equality in Context

I. Formal Equality

Women's formal right to equality in the public sphere is recognized almost universally, although some States parties reserve certain areas of public service for men, such as military posts, succession to the throne, titles of nobility, and religious positions.[104] Formal equality continues to be an important step, but is insufficient to fulfil the demands of Article 7.

II. Substantive Equality

Representation and participation of women in political and public life remain far from equal in practice.[105] *De facto* equality is reached when women have substantive equality of opportunity, that is, where men and women benefit from substantially the same starting positions to participate in public and political life in the way they deem fit. Under Article 7, the Committee even employs the concept of equality of results even

---

[99] eg CO Greece CEDAW/C/GRC/CO/6 (2007) para 24; CO Argentina CEDAW/C/ARG/CO/5 (2004) para 368 (Argentina adopted a Trade Union Quota Law in 2002 requiring a 30 per cent quota of women on lists for all internal elections, as well as a 30 per cent quota for all collective bargaining units).

[100] *Jacomb v Australian Municipal Administrative Clerical and Services Union*, Decision of the Federal Court of Australia of 24 September 2004, [2004] FCA 1250, paras 44, 60.

[101] The issue is connected with Articles 11 and 13, but the committee's focus is on Article 7.

[102] eg CO Sweden CEDAW/C/SWE/CO/7 (2008) para 25; CO Mauritius CEDAW/C/MAR/CO/5 (2006) para 23.

[103] CO Finland CEDAW/C/FIN/CO/6 (2008) para 21.

[104] See the discussion in chapter on art 28. cf also Communication 7/2005, *Christina Muñoz-Vargas y Sainz de Vicuñ v Spain* CEDAW/C/39/D/7/2005.

[105] According to the IPU Database on Women in National Parliaments the average percentage of women in national parliaments is 19.2 per cent, <http://www.ipu.org/wmn-e/world.htm> accessed 31 December 2010.

when it asks States parties to adopt quotas.[106] Under Article 7(a), this would require not only the *de jure* ability to vote and stand for election, but the creation of a situation where men and women have substantially the same democratic chances of winning a seat in a publicly elected body. Ensuring this state of affairs might necessitate unequal treatment of men and women in order to counter historically determined under-representation. According to this interpretation, 'equality' under Article 7(a) includes being able to make meaningful use of the right to political participation and the States parties' corresponding obligation to create encouraging, supportive, and enabling conditions for such participation.

Under Article 7(b), substantive equality entails that all requirements and conditions for entering and remaining in public service are equally accessible to and capable of being satisfied by women, in the sense that they are no longer modelled along male life-styles but appropriately take women's differential needs into account. This goal has been realized in exceptionally few States parties.[107] Equality as regards the right to participate in the formulation and implementation of government policy is more difficult to measure, but here again substantive equality of chances encompasses favourable conditions that are gender-sensitive.

Equality under Article 7(c) is substantive. The right to join all NGOs and associations must be guaranteed effectively, and all overt and hidden obstacles to women's participation must be eliminated. Equality under Article 7(c) has a more substantial aspect: in conjunction with and complementing Article 7(b), NGOs must be accorded the possibility of participating in the formulation and implementation of government policy.[108]

The threshold for achievement of substantive equality is unclear. Parity in representation would be a strong indication of substantive equality of opportunity in the area of public and political life, but due to personal choice actual representation can fall short of parity. Much of the advocacy for increased female participation in public life has centred on the so-called 'critical mass' which allows for gender-sensitive and women-friendly outcomes. Activists have widely applied this concept to political and public life. 'Critical mass' is referred to in the Beijing Platform[109] and in General Recommendation 23, in which the Committee observes that when women's rate of participation reaches 30–35 per cent, there is an appreciable impact on the political style and content of decisions. The Committee cited the example of Nordic States parties, where the critical mass of women in decision-making positions led to improvements in areas such as equal rights, women's control over their bodies, child care, and protection against violence.[110] The application

[106] GR 24 paras 8, 9; D Dahlerup, 'Women in Parliament: Beyond Numbers' (1998); updated version of ch 4 on 'Using Quotas to Increase Women's Political Representation' (2002), <http://www.onlinewomen inpolitics.org/beijing12/Chapter4_Dahlerup.pdf> accessed 31 December 2010.

[107] Women currently (status as of July 2008) account for 60 per cent of ministerial positions in Finland, CO Finland CEDAW/C/FIN/CO/6 (2008) para 6, and for 52 per cent of managers in municipal, county, council, and central government in Sweden, <http://www.sweden.se/eng/Home/Society/Equality/Facts/Gender-equality-in-Sweden> accessed 31 December 2010.

[108] Kawamata (n 19 above) 144.

[109] GR 23 para 16; Beijing Declaration and Platform for Action (n 69 above) Strategic objective G.1 para 194(a).

[110] CEDAW Committee, 'Implementation of Article 21 of the Convention on the Elimination of All Forms of Discrimination against Women. Analysis of Articles 7 and 8 of the Convention. Report by the Secretariat' (1993) CEDAW/C/1994/1 para 11.

of the 'critical mass' concept to political life has lately been subjected to some criticism.[111] None the less, a gender-sensitive perspective seems more likely to develop when a critical mass of women are in decision-making positions.[112]

III. Transformative Equality Including Elimination of Structural Obstacles and Gender Stereotyping

Transformative equality in the public and political fields implies a real transformation of all public and political institutions as well as society at large so that gender relations in public and political life are no longer grounded in historically determined male paradigms of power. This entails the elimination of structural obstacles to the realization of women's political rights and a change in social relations and society's attitude towards women in public life.

Two spheres of human life and legal systems, the private and the public, have long been viewed as distinct,[113] with men invariably dominant in the public sphere associated with politics, government, economics, and the workplace.[114] Although the Committee challenges this dichotomy,[115] the stereotypical view that women belong to the private sphere remains prevalent in many societies.[116] Women, it is thought, should have no say in politics because they lack the knowledge, ability, or interest. Convention Articles 7 and 5 compel States parties to eliminate stereotypical perceptions of male and female behaviour and role in the political and public field. Cultural and social, sometimes religious, stereotypes discourage women from exercising their political rights and are often at the root of women's disadvantaged position.[117] Accordingly, the Committee often highlights the relationship between invidious stereotypes about women and their under-representation and recommends that States parties undertake measures to change these perceptions of women's role in political life,[118] for example, through revision of school textbooks and teaching materials.[119]

---

[111] S Grey, 'Does Size Matter? Critical Mass Theory and New Zealand's Women MPs' (2002) 55 *Parliamentary Affairs* 19–29, 29; S Childs and ML Krook, 'Critical Mass Theory and Women's Political Representation' (2008) 56 *Political Studies* 725–36, 725f; S Childs and ML Krook (n 13 above) 22.

[112] E Rehn and E Johnson Sirleaf, *Women, War, Peace. The Independent Expert Assessment on the Impact of Armed Conflict on Women and Women's Role in Peacebuilding* (2002) 80.

[113] SB Boyd (ed), *Challenging the Public/Private Divide: Feminism, Law and Public Policy* (1997); J Motijunaite (ed), *Women's Rights: the Public/Private Dichotomy* (2005).

[114] CO Turkmenistan CEDAW/C/TKM/CO/2 (2006) para 14; D Sullivan, 'The Public/Private Distinction in International Human Rights Law' in J Peters/A Wolper (eds), *Women's Rights, Human Rights. International Feminist Perspectives* (1995) 126–33, 128; H Charlesworth, 'Human Rights as Men's Rights' in JS Peters and A Wolper (eds), *Women's Rights, Human Rights. International Feminist Perspectives* (1995) 103–13, 106.

[115] CO Cape Verde CEDAW/C/CPV/CO/6 (2006) para 24, (asking the State to encourage men to undertake their fair share of domestic responsibilities so that women can devote time to public and political life).

[116] eg Slovakia explained the low representation of women as due to insufficient social demand for such participation; the Committee saw this as indicating the State's lack of understanding of the importance of equal participation of women and of the responsibilities of States in promoting and supporting that participation; CO Slovakia CEDAW/C/SVK/CO/4 (2008) para 38.

[117] eg CO Indonesia CEDAW/C/IDN/CO/3 (2007) para 16; CO Azerbaijan CEDAW/C/AZE/CO/3 (2007) para 21; CO Kyrgyzstan CEDAW/C/KGZ/CO/3 (2008) para 23.

[118] eg CO Uruguay A/57/38, 26th Session (2002) para 27; CO Kazakhstan A/56/38, 24th Session (2001) paras 89, 90; CO Estonia CEDAW/C/EST/CO/4 (2007) para 12; CO Cuba A/55/38, 23rd Session (2000) para 262; CO Hungary CEDAW/C/HUN/CO/6 (2007) para 17.

[119] eg CO Estonia CEDAW/C/EST/CO/4 (2007) para 13; CO Turkmenistan CEDAW/C/TKM/CO/2 (2006) para 15.

Many structural obstacles have emerged as a result of this dichotomous allocation of spheres of action which continue to contribute to the absence of women from the political sphere. Women's inequality in education (contributing to disproportionately high rates of illiteracy in comparison with men)[120] and in access to information on their rights, violence against women, restrictions on their movement, hindered access to resources, and financial constraints all impede women's access to political posts.[121] Media coverage of male and female political candidates differs.[122] The double burden of economic dependence and household duties prevents or restricts women from taking an active part in public life.[123] Working conditions in elected and non-elected bodies, especially the long and inflexible working hours, hamper women's pursuit of such careers if they have additional family duties. Moreover, the political sphere, still dominated by men, is shaped by male networking patterns, posing further obstacles to women. When engaged in public activities, women are often restricted to 'soft' areas such as education, health, 'women's issues', children, and the environment. Finance, security, foreign policy, and the economy remain male-dominated sectors, and stereotypes based on these assignments are often perpetuated by the media.[124] In some countries, political violence and harassment of women has become a notorious issue. In this respect, the Committee has commended Bolivia for its adopting a law against political harassment of women in government posts, while expressing concern that such violence existed at all.[125]

Without addressing these structural impediments, 'there will be no long-term political empowerment of women'.[126] The institutions will, however, not change by themselves; States parties must adopt proactive measures to change their own institutions as well as societal norms; all political bodies as well as social institutions must fundamentally change their attitudes.

IV. Direct vs Indirect Discrimination

Direct discrimination by States parties is rather rare, as most guarantee formal equality in their constitution or other laws. It persists, however, for example, where the State prohibits women from voting or from standing for election.[127] However, direct discrimination also occurs more often when private individuals (for example, family members) hinder women from exercising their right to vote or be elected. Discrimination in the legal requirements for recruitment to public office is rare, but it does happen, as when the law excludes women from certain posts: royal titles and power, service as judges in religious or traditional tribunals, or posts within the military.[128] These institutions are the traditional bearers of symbolic, and sometimes real, power in a society. In the view of the Committee, such

---

[120] See the discussion in ch on art 10.   [121] IWRAW Asia Pacific (n 41 above) 3; IPU (n 5 above) 5f.

[122] Third Periodic Report of States Parties: Lebanon CEDAW/C/LBN/3 (2006) para 154.

[123] CEDAW (n 58 above) para 35f.   [124] GR 23 para 12.

[125] CO Bolivia CEDAW/C/BOL/CO/4 (2008) para 30.

[126] D Dahlerup, 'Conclusion' in Drude Dahlerup (ed), *Women, Quotas and Politics* (2006) 293, 294; consenting: Philipps (n 14 above) 82.

[127] CO Saudi Arabia CEDAW/C/SAU/CO/2 (2008) para 25.

[128] F Banda, *Project on a Mechanism to Address Laws that Discriminate Against Women* (2008), <http://www.ohchr.org/Documents/Publications/laws_that_discriminate_against_women.pdf> accessed 31 December 2010.

exclusion clearly is discrimination against women and contravenes the principles of the Convention, especially Article 2.[129]

Indirect discrimination, however, is omnipresent. A number of outwardly gender-neutral factors present obstacles to women's participation; for example, voting procedures can pose obstacles more difficult to overcome for women such as requiring a photograph for voter registration,[130] or long distances to polling stations.[131] Indirect discrimination regarding the right to stand for election occurs when certain requirements for candidacy privilege men over women, for example, educational requirements in countries where access to higher education is gender-biased, minimum property qualifications, literacy,[132] or the requirement to pay a nomination or registration fee.[133] The widespread practice of family voting constitutes indirect discrimination (and electoral fraud) through private individuals that disproportionately deprives women and younger family members of their individual voting rights.[134] States parties have an obligation to sanction and prevent such practices.

These obstacles apply similarly to the right to enter public service posts. Under Article 7(b), recruitment and promotion requirements can amount to indirect discrimination, especially when they include requirements that men can meet more readily than women because of current or historical differences in life patterns, such as education or work experience. Expectations as to candidates' biographies and life history must be evaluated and changed to appropriately take gender differences into account.

V. Intersectional Discrimination

Indigenous and minority women are regularly even more severely under-represented than women belonging to the dominant ethnic group in a given State. In the view of the Committee, political and public bodies must represent the full diversity of the population;[135] it therefore calls on States parties to increase the participation of women from ethnic minorities, indigenous groups, and religious minorities, for example, through implementing temporary special measures.[136] The Committee also requests States parties to provide disaggregated data on the participation of migrant, refugee, and minority

---

[129] GR 23 para 31; CO Maldives CEDAW/C/MDV/CO/3 (2007) para 12.

[130] In Afghanistan, women were allowed to use voter registration cards without photographs to counter the women's fear of retaliation when exercising their right to vote, Human Rights Watch 'Campaigning against Fear. Women's Participation in Elections in Afghanistan's 2005 Elections' (2005) 9.

[131] A Lippincott, 'Is Uganda's "No Party" System Discriminatory of Women and a Violation of International Law?' (2002) 3 *Brooklyn J of Intl* L 1137–66, 1146.

[132] GR 23 para 23.

[133] In Mongolia candidates are required by party bylaw to pay 20 million MNT to their party to be nominated for election which poses a particular obstacle for women, CO Mongolia CEDAW/C/MNG/CO/7 (2008) para 29; similarly, in Tajikistan, candidates have to pay a registration fee; the Committee asked the State party to waive it for women candidates, CO Tajikistan CEDAW/C/TJK/CO/3 (2007) para 26.

[134] Congress of Local and Regional Authorities of Europe Rec III (2002) para 10.

[135] CO France CEDAW/C/FRA/CO/6 (2008) para 25; CO The Netherlands CEDAW/C/NLD/CO/4 (2007) para 18.

[136] CO New Zealand CEDAW/C/NZL/CO/6 (2007) para 31; see also: CO Colombia CEDAW/C/COL/CO/6 (2007) paras 26, 27, asking the State for enhanced effort to increase the number of afro-descendent and indigenous women; CO Suriname CEDAW/C/SUR/CO/3 (2007) para 26, asking the State to extend TSMs to indigenous women and women from other racial minorities; CO Philippines CEDAW/C/PHI/CO/6 (2006) para 24, asking the State to adopt TSMs to indigenous and Muslim women.

women in political and public life.[137] It should be noted, however, that the right to vote and to stand for election as well as the right to perform certain public functions essential to the security of the State can be restricted to citizens of the State, as is underscored in ICCPR Article 25. Thus, female non-citizens such as migrant women and asylees cannot claim these participatory rights under Article 7 if they are not granted to men in the same situation.

E. States Parties' Obligations

I. Nature of the Obligations

1. *'All Appropriate Measures' including the Need for the Application of TSMs*

Article 7 requires States parties to take 'all appropriate measures' to ensure certain political rights to women. In order to ensure these rights, States parties have to adopt, *inter alia*, the measures set out in the general Articles 2, 4, and 5. Thus, the measures to be taken range from legislative to administrative and other policy measures, including TSMs.[138] The Committee invariably recommends that States parties adopt TSMs in the area of Article 7.[139] In light of the obligation under Article 3 that States parties take 'all appropriate measures... to ensure the full development and advancement of women', and the ineffectiveness of measures many States parties have taken in the political and public fields during the thirty years since the Convention came into force, TSMs to accelerate implementation of Article 7 are warranted in most States parties.

a) Types of TSMs in Political and Public Life

The Committee recommends that States parties employ a variety of TSMs, ranging from less to more interventionist. General Recommendation 23, paragraph 15 and concluding observations mention recruiting, financially assisting, and training women candidates on leadership and negotiation skills,[140] amending electoral procedures,[141] developing campaigns directed at equal participation, establishing benchmarks, setting numerical goals and timetables,[142] and establishing quotas targeting women for election and appointment to public positions such as the judiciary or other professional groups that play an essential part in the everyday life of all societies.

The Committee often recommends that States parties employ quota systems,[143] and the absence or unwillingness to do so provokes criticism by the Committee.[144] The

---

[137] CO Norway CEDAW/C/NOR/CO/7 (2007) para 24; CO The Netherlands CEDAW/C/NLD/CO/4 (2007) para 18.

[138] See the discussion in ch on art 4.

[139] The Committee has in its COs to the reports of States from the 39th Session, '23 June–10 July 2007' to the 48th Session (17 January–14 February 2011) commended all States to adopt or strengthen TSMs in political and public life.

[140] eg CO Estonia CEDAW/C/EST/CO/4 (2007) para 21; CO Hungary CEDAW/C/HUN/CO/6 (2007) para 25.

[141] eg CO Chile CEDAW/C/CHI/CO/4 (2006) para 14.

[142] eg CO Estonia CEDAW/C/EST/CO/4 (2007) para 21.

[143] eg CO Honduras CEDAW/C/HON/CO/6 (2007) para 19; CO Sierra Leone CEDAW/C/SLE/CO/5 (2007) para 19; CO Maldives CEDAW/C/MDV/CO/3 (2007) para 24.

[144] GR 23 para 29; eg CO Belize CEDAW/C/BLZ/CO/3 (2007) para 17; CO The Netherlands CEDAW/C/NLD/CO/4 (2007) para 17.

Committee is unclear as to whether quotas constitute TSMs: sometimes quotas are mentioned in the enumeration of TSMs that should be adopted, and sometimes they are mentioned as separate (presumably because they are deemed permanent). Quotas must be differentiated from measures taken to implement them: while the former are permanent in that they formulate a ratio that should at least be reached and maintained,[145] the measures taken to implement them whilst the goal has not yet been reached are temporary in nature, restricted to the period in which the quota, meaning the ratio of representation, cannot perpetuate itself without further special measures by the State party. According to the Committee, a legal basis for quotas is necessary, either in a State party's constitution or in other law.[146] The quotas must be mandatory[147] and efficient,[148] meaning that they have to include measures that ensure compliance with the quota, for example, sanctions or other enforcement measures[149] including incentives.[150] Effective monitoring and accountability mechanisms must be established and must be applied systematically, and implementation procedures must be simple to perform. It is important to the Committee that quotas should not be applied as a ceiling, but as a minimum requirement.[151] An alternative design would be a 'reverse quota' stipulating that no sex should constitute more than two thirds of an elected body.[152] The quota should provide for an appropriate goal of at least 30 per cent (critical mass); otherwise the quota is considered too low.[153] The Committee employs a wide interpretation with respect to the proportionality of a quota,[154] stating that even giving preference to allegedly lesser qualified women, might be allowed as the qualification or merit in question has to be reviewed for a possible gender bias.[155]

2. *Immediate vs Gradual Implementation*

The question of immediate or gradual realization has seldom arisen in the work of the Committee. In the field of women's political representation in legislatures and public service, the Committee seems to be of the opinion that low overall representation of women indicates a violation of Article 7.[156] In these cases, the Committee asks the State party to comply with or enhance compliance with Articles 7 and 8.[157] This indicates that a

---

[145] An example of a permanent measure is the French Law on Parity, Loi no 2000–493 du 6 juin 2000 tendant à favoriser l'égal access des femmes et des hommes aux mandats électoraux et fonctions électives, in: Journal Officiel 2000 No 131 8560.

[146] eg CO Belize CEDAW/C/BLZ/CO/3 (2007) para 18.

[147] Non-mandatory provisions evoke criticism by the Committee (ad hoc moral commitments by political parties are not enough), eg CO Morocco CEDAW/C/MAR/CO/4 (2008) para 25; CO Indonesia CEDAW/C/IDN/CO/3 (2007) para 27; CO Vanuatu CEDAW/C/VUT/CO/3 (2007) para 27.

[148] eg CO Brazil CEDAW/C/BRA/CO/6 (2007) para 25.

[149] eg CO Indonesia CEDAW/C/IDN/CO/3 (2007) paras 26-7; CO Honduras CEDAW/C/HON/CO/6 (2007) para 22.

[150] eg CO Mauritania CEDAW/C/MRT/CO/1 (2007) para 6. Another aspect of efficiency is the requirement of the chosen quota to fit with the electoral system; cf. Larserud/Taphorn (n 43 above).

[151] eg CO Burundi CEDAW/C/BDI/CO/4 (2008) paras 19, 20.

[152] eg CO Liechtenstein CEDAW/C/LIE/CO/3 (2007) para 17.

[153] eg CO Jordan CEDAW/C/JOR/CO/4 (2007) para 28 (10 per cent quota); CO Niger (2007) CEDAW/C/NER/CO/2 para 28 (10 per cent quota).

[154] See the discussion in ch on art 4 for the ECJ approach. [155] GR 25 para 23.

[156] eg CO Morocco CEDAW/C/MAR/CO/4 (2008) para 24; CO Nigeria CEDAW/C/NGA/CO/6 (2008) para 27; CO Yemen CEDAW/C/YEM/CO/6 (2008) para 22; CO The United Kingdom CEDAW/C/UK/CO/6 (2008) para 37; CO Kenya CEDAW/C/KEN/CO/6 (2007) para 27.

[157] eg in CO Kenya CEDAW/C/KEN/CO/6 (2007) paras 27, 28; CO Vanuatu CEDAW/C/VUT/CO/3 (2007) para 27.

minimum threshold of representation is an immediate obligation of the State; in reverse, the obligation to reach parity in political life is seen as a goal to be implemented gradually. Therefore, it is sufficient for the State to prove that all appropriate measures are being taken to increase the ratio of women. The evaluation of the appropriateness of the measures lies with the Committee, as it reviews States parties' measures in the reporting procedure and suggests other or more appropriate solutions.

II. Implementation

1. *Obligation to Respect*

This obligation refers to the State's own conduct; *de jure* realization is brought about by enacting pertinent constitutional or legislative provisions. The *de facto* realization of these rights, however, requires additional legislative measures to abolish indirect discrimination in public and political life. The requirements for entering public service and public functions have to be carefully designed to work with the realities of female and male lifestyles,[158] and educational choices for pursuing a career must be made available to men and women alike by dealing similarly with eligibility criteria.

2. *Obligation to Protect*

Under Article 7(c) in particular, which entails mainly indirect obligations, the State party is required to exercise due diligence over the activities of NGOs and associations by taking preventive, remedial, punitive, or compensatory measures against interference by third parties, especially political parties, trade unions, corporations, and the media. In this respect, Article 2(e) deserves close attention. In contrast, third-party interference with rights under Article 7(b) is rare.

States parties have the obligation to adapt procedures in order to prevent interference with women's rights to participate in public life, for example, by improving voter registration procedures to ensure women's free exercise of the vote.[159] Penal law provisions and other legal remedies can protect women against reprisals by third parties (for example, husbands and relatives) when women exercise their political rights. Deprecating and threatening behaviour towards female representatives by male colleagues should be effectively sanctioned.

The Committee views awareness-raising and public education campaigns as particularly well-suited measures to address deep-rooted stereotypes and patriarchal attitudes regarding the role and responsibilities of men and women in public life.[160] Such measures, aimed at the public or at corporations and political parties, can guide public opinion to change attitudes, held by both women and men, regarding their respective roles in the household, in the family, at work, and in society as a whole,[161] and that discourage women's involvement in political and public life. Legal measures must be taken to ensure equal allocation

---

[158] HB Schöpp-Schilling, 'Reflections on a General Recommendation on Article 4 (1) of the Convention on the Elimination of All Forms of Discrimination against Women' in I Boerefijn et al (eds), *Temporary Special Measures. Accelerating the de-facto Equality of Women under Art. 4 (1) UN Convention on the Elimination of All Forms of Discrimination against Women* (2003) 15, 26.

[159] eg CO Guatemala CEDAW/C/GUA/CO/7 (2009) paras 25-6.

[160] eg CO Republic of Korea CEDAW/C/KOR/CO/6 (2007) paras 25-6.

[161] eg CO Uruguay CEDAW/C/URY/CO/7 (2008) para 31.

of media coverage of male and female political candidates, and various policy measures must address the media's role in perpetuating discriminatory gender stereotypes.[162]

States parties must enact legislation prohibiting NGOs and associations from discriminating against women and excluding them from membership.[163] One mechanism is to make the granting of financial support to NGOs conditional upon their adoption of a gender equality perspective.[164]

3. Obligation to Fulfil

According to the Committee, additional measures are needed besides the *de jure* realization to secure the effective enjoyment of the entitlements under Article 7—for example, the establishment of numerical goals, benchmarks, timetables, and quotas for nomination, selection, and promotion.[165]

To enable the Committee to assess States parties' implementation of Article 7 rights effectively, they must include sufficient information and sex-disaggregated data in their reports on women's participation and representation in the various sectors and levels of political and public life.[166] They must monitor the effectiveness of measures taken and report on progress and failures.[167]

States parties should develop targeted training and mentoring programmes on leadership and negotiation skills for women candidates and women wanting to join the public service.[168] Training programmes on effective participation in policy-making can also be directed at NGOs.[169] In addition, States parties could invest in formal education for participation, such as scholarships for women to attend law schools and public policy schools[170] and leadership programmes for young women in high school ('pipeline projects').

States parties are obliged to support measures aimed at identifying and reducing specific barriers that reduce the percentage of women in office. They should support the equal sharing of family responsibilities by adopting measures to enhance the work/life-balance for both women and men in the public sector.[171] Examples include measures to extend

---

[162] Lebanon had noticed in its report the unequal media coverage allocated to male and female candidates for election, Third Periodic Report of States Parties, Lebanon, CEDAW/C/LBN/3, para 154. As Lebanon had not taken any corrective measures ('Responses to the list of questions of the Committee on the Elimination of Discrimination against Women with regard to the consideration of the third periodic report of Lebanon on implementation of the Convention', CEDAW/C/LBN/Q/3/Add.1, Question 13), the Committee commended the State to encourage the media to project the equal status of men and women in private as well as public life, CO Lebanon CEDAW/C/LBN/CO/3 (2007) para 25; see also: CO Switzerland CEDAW/C/CHE/CO/3 (2009) para 33.

[163] CO The Netherlands A/56/38, 25th Session (2001) paras 219f.

[164] Sweden Combined sixth and seventh report CEDAW/C/SWE/7 (2008) para 198.

[165] GR 23 para 15.

[166] eg CO Slovakia CEDAW/C/SVK/CO/4 (2008) para 24; CO Finland CEDAW/C/FIN/CO/6 (2008) para 22; CO France CEDAW/C/FRA/CO/6 (2008) para 25.

[167] eg CO Korea CEDAW/C/KOR/CO/6 (2007) para 24; CO Belgium CEDAW/C/BEL/CO/6 (2008) paras 20, 21.

[168] eg CO Estonia CEDAW/C/EST/CO/4 (2007) para 21; CO Guinea CEDAW/C/GIN/CO/6 (2007) para 31; CO Mali CEDAW/C/MLI/CO/5 (2006) para 26.

[169] CO Lithuania CEDAW/C/LTU/CO/4 (2008) para 83, recommending training programmes on how to participate effectively in European Gender Equality Programmes.

[170] Mansbridge (n 15 above) 31.

[171] eg CO Singapore CEDAW/C/SGP/CO/3 (2007) para 32; CO Republic of Moldova CEDAW/C/MDA/CO/3 (2006) para 27.

opportunities of taking leave of absence from employment and receiving compensation for child care,[172] as well as providing high-quality public day care for officials.[173]

Sufficient and sustained government financial support for women's NGOs would increase their capacity to support women's human rights.[174] At the same time, financial aid must be provided in an impartial manner that ensures the continued independence of the NGOs as regards their work and conduct.

Improving conditions for women in public and political life relates directly to facilitating the work of civil society organizations. This includes working with political parties to increase the number of women candidates by encouraging them to use quotas or numerical goals, or legislation that provides financial incentives to parties to achieve greater gender balance in their own leadership positions.[175] General Recommendation 23 also proposes that States parties must consult with and incorporate the advice of civil society groups that represent women's views and interests.[176] States parties should encourage the nomination of qualified women as members of advisory bodies to Government.[177]

III. Justiciability

The chapeau entails an obligation to 'take all appropriate measures,' accompanied by the explicit obligations to 'ensure' rights as specified in Article 7(a)–(c). The justiciability of the obligation to take all appropriate measures is problematic as the formulation is quite broad and vague. Nevertheless, it creates certain minimum justiciable performance obligations, including assessing discrimination in the field and the adoption by States parties of a plan to address discrimination.[178] The Committee can evaluate whether a State party has taken the minimum steps necessary to demonstrate a *bona fide* effort to fulfil its obligation,[179] and can suggest additional measures.

Article 7 (a)–(c) creates obligations to ensure a right. The obligations under (a) to ensure the right to vote and be elected, are justiciable, as the content of the right and the concrete steps to be taken in order to fulfil the obligation are clearly identifiable.[180] The wording 'government policy' in the first part of (b) is rather vague. Its content can, however, be specified by referring to the related concept of 'conduct of public affairs' found in ICCPR Article 25(a).[181] The second part of Article 7(b), obliging States parties to ensure that women have equal rights with men to perform all public functions at all levels of government, is more clear. Because it is possible to identify the scope of activities and offices encompassed, the obligation is justiciable.[182] Finally, the scope of the obligations created by Article 7(c) is quite clear, and they are therefore justiciable.

IV. Reservations

A number of States parties have entered reservations that materially affect implementation of Article 7, although not all of them expressly note the article.[183] Most concern the

---

[172] Sweden Combined sixth and seventh periodic report para 170 (n 164 above).
[173] Mansbridge (n 15 above) 19, 31.   [174] eg CO Lithuania CEDAW/C/LTU/CO/4 (2008) para 83.
[175] eg CO Czech Republic CEDAW/C/CZE/CO/3 (2006) para 20.   [176] GR 23 para 26.
[177] GR 23 para 29.
[178] A Byrnes and J Connors, 'Enforcing the Human Rights of Women: A Complaints Procedure for the Women's Convention? Draft Optional Protocol to the Convention on the Elimination of All Forms of Discrimination against Women' (1996) 21 *Brooklyn J Intl L* 679–797, 729.
[179] Ibid 717.   [180] Ibid 721.   [181] Ibid 721.   [182] Ibid 721.
[183] Discussed at length in ch on art 28.

obligations under Article 7(b).[184] The Committee has urged the respective governments to withdraw them.[185] A number of reservations to Article 7 on service in the military have recently been withdrawn.[186]

[184] Australia on 30 August 2000 concerning combat duties, United Nations, Treaty Series, Vol. 1325, 378; the United Kingdom of Great Britain and Northern Ireland, concerning any act done for the purpose of ensuring the combat effectiveness of the Armed Forces of the Crown, United Nations, Treaty Series, Vol. 1423, 412, art A c) as modified on 6 June 2005; Monaco concerning police enforcement duties; New Zealand and the Cook Islands, as to police duties involving serving in situations of violence or threat of violence. The Cook Islands withdrew its reservations on 30 July 2007, CEDAW, CO Cook Islands CEDAW/C/COK/CO/1 (2007) para 5; Israel, concerning the appointment of women to serve as judges in religious courts where it is prohibited by the laws of any of the religious communities.

[185] CEDAW CO Maldives A/56/38 (2001) 24th Session para 131; CO Malaysia CEDAW/C/MYS/CO/2 (2006) para 10; CO Israel CEDAW/C/ISR/CO/3 (2005) para 26.

[186] New Zealand withdrew its reservation on 5 July 2007; the Cook Islands withdrew its reservation on 30 July 2007; Austria had a similar reservation, United Nations, Treaty Series, Vol. 1272, 456, but withdrew it on 11 September 2000; Belgium withdrew its reservation, United Nations, Treaty Series, Vol. 1402, 376, on 14 September 1998 and 8 July 2002; similarly, Germany withdrew its reservation, United Nations, Treaty Series, Vol. 1402, 378, on 10 December 2001; Switzerland on 29 April 2004; Thailand, United Nations, Treaty Series, Vol. 1404, 419, on 1 August 1996.

Article 8

States Parties shall take all appropriate measures to ensure to women, on equal terms with men and without any discrimination, the opportunity to represent their Governments at the international level and to participate in the work of international organisations.

A. Introduction

Article 8 codifies women's participatory entitlement in international affairs, thus complementing their participatory rights as stated in Article 7. Many of the States parties' obligations under Article 7(b) correspond to obligations under Article 8; hence, States parties must ensure the full participation of women at all levels and all areas of international

* I would like to thank Sahrah Al-Nasrawe-Sözeri, Andrea Eriksson, Benjamin Feyen, Ines Franke, Anna-Maria Paulus, Eric Veillerobe, and Professor Susan Williams for their assistance and helpful comments on the chapters on arts 7 and 8 of this Commentary.

affairs.[1] In the drafting of Article 7, the negotiating States decided to formulate a separate article on women's international representation rather than including it as a paragraph in Article 7. This decision pays tribute to the immense importance of decision-making in international fora, on matters such as peacemaking, conflict resolution, military expenditure and nuclear disarmament, development and the environment, foreign affairs and economic restructuring. Despite the influence of such decisions on peoples' lives,[2] and its considerable reference in General Recommendation 23, Article 8 has played a comparatively minor role in the Committee's reviews and in scholarship on the Convention.

The Convention is the only human rights treaty that refers expressly to participation in international matters.[3] In contrast, UDHR Article 21 and ICCPR Article 25(c) refer to 'the government of his country' and 'public service in his country' respectively. However, the CCPR interpreted the phrase 'conduct of public affairs' in Article 25(a) to cover 'all aspects of public administration, and the formulation and implementation of public policy at the international, national, regional and local levels'.[4]

Similarly to Article 7, the object of Article 8 is the realization of equality of men and women in all spheres of public life. As the decisions taken in international fora greatly influence national politics and, thus, everyday life, women must be given the opportunity to participate equally in the process. Parity in participation can ensure that the greatest possible plurality and diversity of views are brought into the deliberative process in international bodies to prevent gender-biased outcomes.[5]

B. Travaux Préparatoires

The original drafts of the Philippines and the USSR did not mention the right of women to represent their government at the international level.[6] It was arguably thought to be implicit in the idea of 'holding public office and performing public functions'.[7] During the drafting process, it was first proposed to include a reference to the international level in Article 7,[8] but it was later agreed to formulate a separate article on the right to international representation.[9] The wording of the newly-born Article 8 was uncontroversial; the draft of the Ukrainian SSR, bringing together three earlier proposals for (then) Article 9,

---

[1] GR 23 para 35.   [2] GR 23 para 39.

[3] K Nose, 'Article 8: Participation in International Activities' in Japanese Association of International Women's Rights (ed) *Convention on the Elimination of All Forms of Discrimination against Women. A Commentary* (1995) 151, 157.

[4] CCPR, 'General Comment No 25' UN Doc CCPR/C/21/Rev.1/Add.7 (1996) para 5.

[5] S Fredman, *Discrimination Law* (2002) 155.

[6] LA Rehof, *Guide to the Travaux Préparatoires of the United Nations Convention on the Elimination of All Forms of Discrimination against Women* (1993) 99f.

[7] Ibid 100.

[8] ECOSOC Commission on the Status of Women, Draft Convention on the Elimination of all Forms of Discrimination against Women Working-paper prepared by the Secretary-General (21 June 1976) UN Doc E/CN.6/591 para 83; ECOSOC Commission on the Status of Women, Draft Convention on the Elimination of all Forms of Discrimination against Women Working-paper prepared by the Secretary-General, Addendum (25 June 1976) UN Doc E/CN.6/591/Add.1 p. 4 (Draft version by Belgium).

[9] UNGA, 'Addendum to the Working Paper Prepared by the Secretary-General, Decisions Taken by the Working Group of the Whole of the Convention on the Elimination of Discrimination against Women during the thirty-second session of the General-Assembly' UN Doc A/C.3/33/WG.1/CRP.1/Add.1 (1987) 9; Rehof (n 6 above) 100.

was discussed and adopted with only minor changes.[10] The Convention became the first international treaty to address explicitly the issue of women's participation at the international level.[11]

C. Issues of Interpretation

Article 8 states a twofold obligation: States parties must take all appropriate measures to ensure to women the opportunity to represent their governments at the international level and the opportunity to participate in the work of international organizations. Unlike Article 7, Article 8 does not refer to a 'right' that has to be ensured by the State, but an 'opportunity'. This does not mean that Article 8 is not a legal obligation; as the Convention is a non-discrimination treaty directed at States, all the provisions are binding regardless of how the obligation is framed.[12] As part of a human rights treaty, Article 8 creates a corresponding subjective right of individual women to non-discrimination.

I. Opportunity to Represent their Governments at the International Level

The wording of Article 8—representation of one's government—is somewhat startling since representation at the international level is attributable to the State, not to a particular government. The wording might refer to the usual practice of the executive representing the State party internationally.[13] The Committee's work under Article 8 has focused mainly on diplomacy.[14] States parties must realize their obligation towards women in relation to all positions on the diplomatic staff of embassies and missions, including permanent missions to international organizations (Article 1(d) VCDR). Women must be given equal opportunity to be recruited, selected, and promoted to these positions, and they must be assigned to deal with substantive matters, including traditionally male-dominated areas such as international security and economic policy.[15] The obligation applies to all other posts within the foreign service and other international departments within the executive. In a broad understanding of the term 'representation', Article 8 also refers to international cooperation by the State party's administrative, legislative, or judicial branches.

II. Opportunity to Participate in the Work of International Organizations

Two categories of 'participation' in the work of international organizations exist: as staff (international civil service) and as special representatives who represent the organization on a short-term basis. International civil servants exercise a public function in the service of an international organization in a continuous and exclusive manner, under a specific international legal regime,[16] and their acts are directly attributable to the international

---

[10] UNGA, 'Report of the Working Group of the Third Committee, Additions to the Proposal by the Ukrainian SSR' (6 December 1977) UN Doc A/C.3/32/WG.1/CRP.6/Add.7, 1–2.

[11] CEDAW, 'Implementation of Article 21 of the Convention on the Elimination of All Forms of Discrimination against Women. Analysis of Articles 7 and 8 of the Convention, Report by the Secretariat' (30 November 1993) CEDAW/C/1994/1 para 22.

[12] See the discussion in the Introduction.

[13] CCPR, 'General Comment No 31: The Nature of the General Legal Obligation Imposed on States Parties to the Covenant' UN Doc CCPR/C/21/Rev.1/Add.13 (2004) para 4.

[14] Art 3(1)(a) VCDR.   [15] GR 23 para 35.

[16] Y Beigbeder, 'International Civil Service' in R Wolfrum (ed), *Max Planck Encyclopedia of International Law* online edition para 1 <http://www.mpepil.com> accessed 31 December 2010.

organization. Special representatives have appointments such as special rapporteurs and other experts on missions, representing the international organization for specific tasks.[17] They act in their personal capacity when exercising their task, but their acts are attributable to the organization that has mandated the task.

The obligations of States parties relate to these two categories only to the extent that the State can exert influence on their regulation.[18] States parties must, when creating international organizations, negotiate and agree on gender-sensitive internal organizational rules, staff regulations, and rules for appointment, in conformity with Article 8. Accordingly, States parties sometimes report on the participation of women in the international civil service.[19] Additionally, States parties must ensure a gender balance in making nominations for election or appointment to international organizations and their subordinate bodies.[20]

According to the International Law Commission, the term 'international organizations' denotes organizations established by a treaty or other instrument governed by international law and possessing their own international legal personality; in addition to States, they may include other entities as members.[21] Article 8 encompasses regional organizations as well. All departments within these organizations are covered, including courts, subsidiary bodies, funds and programmes, specialized agencies, and treaty bodies.[22] In light of the object and purpose of Article 8 to effectively provide women with the chance of influencing policy-making at the international level the provision encompasses informal and non-permanent cooperation structures without a public international law foundation, such as international conferences and expert meetings.[23]

III. Specifications of Article 8 in International Organizations

Many international organizations have regulations that relate to States parties' obligations under Article 8, compelling member States to include women in delegations or in nomination of candidates. UN Charter Article 8 in current understanding binds only UN organs, not the member States, but serves as a 'source of inspiration' for them.[24]

---

[17] H Keller, 'Special Representative' in R Wolfrum (ed), *Max Planck Encyclopedia of International Law online edition* para 1 <http://www.mpepil.com> accessed 31 December 2010.

[18] States could possibly be held responsible for violations of the Convention committed by organs of an international organization, cf art 28 of the Draft Articles on Responsibility of International Organizations in: UNGA, 'Report of the International Law Commission on the Work of its Fifty-Eight Session,' UN Doc A/61/10 Chapter VII p 252 ff. The draft articles are the ongoing work of the International Law Commission (ILC) on the responsibility of international organizations which can serve as a valuable guide to the current position of customary international law in this area.

[19] cf Sixth Periodic Report of States Parties: Germany CEDAW/C/DEU/6 (2007) p 34f; Combined Fifth and Sixth Periodic Report of States Parties: Belgium CEDAW/C/BEL/6 (2007) p 73f; Combined Sixth and Seventh Periodic Reports of States Parties: Ecuador CEDAW/C/ECU/7 (2007) para 253; Sixth Periodic Report of States Parties: Nigeria CEDAW/C/NGA/6 (2006) p 65f; Combined Fourth and Fifth Periodic Report: Indonesia CEDAW/C/IDN/4–5 (2005) para 88; Sixth Periodic Reports of States Parties: New Zealand CEDAW/C/NZL/6 (2006) para 125ff.

[20] The Beijing Declaration and Platform for Action reiterated the obligation to ensure a gender balance; UN Docs A/CONF.177/20 (1995) and A/CONF.177/20/Add.1 (1995) para 190(j).

[21] UNGA, 'Report by the International Law Commission at its Fifty-Eight Session' UN Doc A/61/10, 61st Session (2006) 277–8; Draft Articles on the International Responsibility of States art 2.

[22] Nose (n 3 above) 156.   [23] GR 23 para 35.

[24] S von Schorlemer, 'Article 8' in B Simma (ed), *The Charter of United Nations. A Commentary*, 2nd edn (2002) Vol. I 230, 232. It was originally thought to apply to member States as well as UN organs; RB Russell, *A History of the United Nations Charter: The Role of the United States 1940–1945* (1958) 793f.

However, the wording of Article 8 allows for a broader interpretation and is not limited to addressing UN organs. Similarly, the Council of Europe[25] and the African Union[26] have adopted rules that promote gender balance within their organization; the statutes or rules for the International Criminal Court,[27] the European Court of Human Rights,[28] and the International Criminal Tribunals for Rwanda and Yugoslavia[29] provide similar regulations as to the judges.

IV. International Civil Service

Article 8 does not directly bind international organizations. However, several international and regional organizations have regulations providing for equal opportunities in international civil service.[30] UN Charter Article 8 prescribes conditions of equality of men and women in the organs.[31] The UN Administrative Tribunal adjudicated in *Mullan v Secretary-General* that Article 8 creates legal obligations,[32] and extended the meaning of the provision to equality in conditions of employment.[33] The General Assembly has stated the need for gender parity in the UN system,[34] and the Secretariat has instituted TSMs to achieve this goal throughout the organization.[35] The application

---

[25] Council of Europe 4th European Ministerial Conference on equality between women and men, 'Declaration on Equality between the Women and Men as a Fundamental Criterion of Democracy' (Istanbul, 13–14 November 1997); Council of Ministers, 'Recommendation 3 on Balanced Participation of Women and Men in Political and Public Decision-making' (12 March 2003) H/Inf (2003) 6; Parliamentary Assembly, Resolution 1348 (2003) Gender-balanced Representation in the Parliamentary Assembly (30 September 2003); Council of Europe, Parliamentary Assembly, Rules of Procedure 2009, Rule 6.2 a and 7.1 b.

[26] AU, 'Protocol to the Treaty Establishing the African Economic Community Relating to the Pan-African Parliament' (Sirte, Libya, 2 March 2001), art 4(2); AU, 'African Union Gender Policy' REV 2 (10 February 2009) 1ff; Maputo Declaration on Gender Mainstreaming and the Effective Participation of Women in the African Union (24 June 2003).

[27] Rome Statute of the International Criminal Court art 36 Nr. 8 (a)(iii).

[28] European Court of Human Rights, Rules of the Court, Strasbourg, December 2008 Rule 14; Council of Europe Parliamentary Assembly, Res. 1366(2004) 'Candidates for the European Court of Human Rights' (30 January 2004) para 3 ii.

[29] Art 12 ter 1. (b) Statute of the International Criminal Tribunal for Rwanda; art 13 ter 1. (b) Statute of the International Criminal Tribunal for Yugoslavia.

[30] Council of Europe, 4th European Ministerial Conference on equality between women and men (Istanbul, 13–14 November 1997) 'Declaration on Equality between Women and Men as a Fundamental Criterion of Democracy' para 11; AU Solemn Declaration on Gender Equality in Africa (Addis Ababa, 6–8 July 2004) Assembly/AU/Decl.12 (III) preamble; Assembly of the African Union, Statutes of the Commission of the African Union (9–10 July 2002) ASS/AU/2(I)–d art 6 (3); Report of the Secretary-General on the Implementation of the 'Inter-American Program of Women's Human Rights and Gender Equity and Equality', pursuant to Resolution AG/RES.2124 (XXXV-O/05), Annex 1; OAS General Assembly, UN Docs AG/RES. 1303 (XXIV-O/94); AG/RES. 1422 (XXVI-O/96); AG/RES. 1588 (XXVIII-O/98); AG/RES. 1627 (XXIX/O-99).

[31] von Schorlemer (n 24 above) 230.

[32] UNAT Decision No 162 (*Mullan v Secretary General*), 10 October 1972, AT/DEC/114–166 (1974) 392.

[33] Ibid 394.

[34] UNGA UN Docs A/RES/47/226, (30 April 1993) section C; A/RES/51/67 (31 January 1997) para 3; A/RES/53/119 (25 April 1997) section C; A/Res/52/96 (10 December 1997) para 4; A/RES/53/119 (05 February 1999) para 2; A/Res/54/139 (10 February 2000) paras 2–4, 8, 12, 18; A/RES/57/180 (30 January 2003) para 3.

[35] UN Secretariat Administrative Instruction. Special Measures for the Achievement of Gender Equality UN Doc ST/AI/1999/9 (21 September 1999) para 1.1, 1.8(a). It seems symptomatic for the issue that the Secretariat felt the need to stress the self-evident obligation to consider favourably women who have superior qualifications.

of Article 8 is, however, complicated by Charter Article 101(3) which also governs the appointment of staff within the UN.[36] Within the treaty body system, representation of women has been very low in all treaty bodies except for the two dealing with women and children.[37]

V. Women in Conflict Resolution, Peace-keeping, and Peace-building Missions

Other areas covered by Article 8 are conflict resolution, peace-keeping, and peace-building missions.[38] States are obliged under Article 8 to include women in all international conflict resolution efforts, such as in peace conferences, mediation, and negotiation. They must also include women when supplying military personnel to UN missions.[39] The persistent lack of women in peace-keeping forces reflects the lack of women in the military of the participating States, which itself is a shortcoming of UN member States with respect to Convention Article 7.[40]

The Security Council has begun to recognize the importance of including women in its efforts to restore peace and security in conflict zones.[41] SC Resolution 1325 on women, peace, and security calls for increasing women's participation in peace-keeping as military observers, civilian police, human rights and humanitarian personnel,[42] in conflict resolution,[43] and as special representatives of the Secretary-General and envoys[44]. It also urges the Security Council to include a gender component in field missions.[45] Human rights components of UN missions serving as interim administrators refer to the Convention as a legal basis for the activities of the mission.[46] Article 8 could thus become the standard for the selection and promotion of international staff for the mission. NATO and OSCE have both adopted Action Plans on increasing the number of women within those organizations.[47]

---

[36] UNGA Resolution 3416 (XXX) on the Employment of Women in the Secretariat (08 December 1975) para 3. For further reading: H Charlesworth and C Chinkin, *The Boundaries of International Law A feminist Analysis* (2000) 185.

[37] AF Bayefsky *The UN Human Rights Treaty System: Universality at the Crossroads* (2001) 104f.

[38] GR 23 para 40.

[39] cf UNSC, 'Resolution 1325 on women, peace and security' (31 October 2000) UN Doc S/RES/1325 (2000) para 1.

[40] CEDAW, 'Implementation of Article 21 of the Convention on the Elimination of All Forms of Discrimination against Women. Analysis of articles 7 and 8 of the Convention. Report by the Secretariat' (30 November 1993) CEDAW/C/1994/1 para 33.

[41] C Pampell Conaway and J Shoemaker, 'Women in United Nations Peace Operations: Increasing the Leadership Opportunities' (2008) *Women in International Security* 10f.

[42] UNSC (n 39 above) paras 4, 6.   [43] Ibid paras 1, 2.

[44] Ibid para 3.   [45] Ibid para 5.

[46] UNTAET, 'Regulation on the Authority of the Transitional Administration in East-Timor', UNTAET/REG/1999/1 (27 November 1999) Section 2; UNMIK, Regulation on the Law applicable in Kosovo UNMIK/REG/1999/24 (12 December 1999) para 1.3(f). Arguably, such international civil administration is obliged to adhere to internationally recognized human rights standards as it is effectively acting as a sovereign power; F Mégret and F Hoffmann, 'The UN as a Human Rights Violator? Some Reflections on the United Nations Changing Human Rights Responsibilities' (2003) 25 *Human Rights Quarterly* 314–42, 328.

[47] NATO, 'Gender Balance and Diversity 2007–2010' (June 2007); OSCE Ministerial Council '2004 OSCE Action Plan for the Promotion of Gender Equality' (7 December 2004) MC.DEC/14/04 Annex.

D. Equality in Context

I. Formal Equality

A constitutional or legal guarantee of equality has been affirmed in most States parties;[48] this guarantees formal equality in representing the State at the international level.[49]

II. Substantive Equality

As in all other spheres of public and political life the formal guarantee of equality is not reflected in reality. Women remain grossly under-represented in States parties' diplomatic corps and in international and regional organizations, especially in high-ranking posts.[50] The Committee regularly expresses its concern at the low number of women in foreign service and diplomacy.[51] The under-representation of women in these formal structures is in stark contrast to the widespread engagement of women in NGOs on matters of international concern.[52]

The ultimate goal of Article 8 is the realization of substantive equality,[53] which calls for an enabling environment that makes *de facto* equality a viable possibility. Recruitment requirements for the foreign service and other international posts must be revised to appropriately take gender differences into account, educational chances for women have to be improved, targeted recruitment needs to address particularly young women in universities.

III. Transformative Equality including Elimination of Structural Obstacles and Gender Stereotyping

Transformative equality aims at the elimination of the invidious gender stereotypes that form the basis of the continuing under-representation of women and the structural obstacles that originate from them.[54] Stereotypical views on women's natural place in society originate from the public/private divide that has long confined women to the private life of home and family as their main sphere of action:[55] It follows from this that women should have no say in political, hence in international affairs. The belief that such work cannot be fulfilled by married women, especially when they are posted overseas as this will collide with their family duties, hinders women from service in the diplomatic corps,[56] and the remuneration policy for diplomatic service in some States parties reflects this stereotype. Women are not universally entitled to the same spousal and family benefits as men in the foreign service due to the belief that the husband will be employed as well. Women who do enter international service continue to be subjected to stereotyping, often

---

[48] GR 23 para 13; cf in State reports: Combined Sixth and Seventh Periodic Reports of States Parties: Ecuador CEDAW/C/ECU/7 (2007) para 245; Sixth Periodic Report of States Parties: Nigeria CEDAW/C/NGA/6 (2006) 65.

[49] eg Combined Sixth and Seventh Periodic Reports of States Parties: Ecuador CEDAW/C/ECU/7 (2007) para 245; Sixth Periodic Report of States Parties: Nigeria CEDAW/C/NGA/6 (2006) 65.

[50] GR 23 para 36.

[51] CO Suriname CEDAW/C/SUR/CO/3 (2007) para 25; CO Cuba CEDAW/C/CUB/CO/6 (2006) para 23; CO Mexico CEDAW/C/MEX/CO/6 (2006) para 28; CO Kuwait CEDAW/C/KWT/CO/2 (2004) para 74.

[52] GR 23 para 39. [53] GR 25 para 8. [54] See the discussion in the ch on art 5.

[55] GR 23 para 8; F Raday, 'Culture, Religion and CEDAW's Article 5(a)' in HB Schöpp-Schilling and C Flinterman *The Circle of Empowerment: Twenty-Five Years of The UN Committee on The Elimination of Discrimination against Women* (2007) 68, 71.

[56] IWRAW Asia-Pacific, 'Report of the Regional Consultation on Women's Right to Participate in Political and Public Life' (2004) 11.

assigned to departments and projects that are deemed 'suitable' for women, such as human rights, children, women, and health. International security, armed conflict, disarmament, finance, trade, and global economic policy remain male-dominated areas. Additionally, such stereotypes can preclude women from seeking positions of leadership.[57] Especially in UN field missions, women's under-representation has been justified by referring to the dangerous nature of such positions and their emergency basis. The invidious stereotypical view that women are physically and emotionally incapable of dealing with hardship situations has posed the greatest obstacle to their participation in the military.[58]

A multitude of structural obstacles poses difficulties for women wanting to work in international affairs, many of them comparable to the obstacles to the realization of the rights under Article 7(b). Inequality in access to education in many States parties limits women's career choices. The long hours and inflexible working conditions in diplomatic service and international organizations make this a difficult choice for individuals who have family responsibilities—and under current structural conditions, that primarily affects women. Male dominance in foreign service and international organizations, generating closed male networks, also works in favour of male candidates.

IV. Direct vs Indirect Discrimination

Direct discrimination as to international representation clearly occurs when women are excluded from public office that may have international duties, such as certain posts within the military.[59] A State party's refusal to accept female diplomats from other States is also discriminatory, particularly contravening Article 2.[60] Indirect discrimination is widespread, such as recruitment and promotion requirements in the foreign service, under conditions described above.

V. Intersectional Discrimination

Article 8 requires States parties to increase the participation of women of ethnic minorities and indigenous groups as all political and public bodies should represent the full diversity of the country.[61] The Committee also requested disaggregated data on the participation of minority women in political and public life.[62]

E. States Parties' Obligations

I. Nature of the Obligations

1. 'All Appropriate Measures'

The 'appropriate measures' required by Article 8 include the requirements set out under the general Articles 2, 4, and 5 of the Convention. Obligations to respect, protect, and

---

[57] CO Nigeria CEDAW/C/NGA/CO/5 (2004) para 309.
[58] GJ DeGroot, 'A Few Good Women: Gender Stereotypes, the Military and Peacekeeping' in L Olsson and TL Tryggestad, *Women and International Peacekeeping* (2001) 23.
[59] eg in Australia, New Zealand, Italy, Portugal, Spain, United Kingdom, United States.
[60] GR 23 para 31; CO Maldives (2 February 2007) CEDAW/C/MDV/CO/3 para 12.
[61] CO France CEDAW/C/FRA/CO/6 (2008) para 25; CO The Netherlands CEDAW/C/NLD/CO/4 (2007) para 18.
[62] CO New Zealand CEDAW/C/NZL/CO/6 (2007) para 31; CEDAW CO Colombia CEDAW/C/COL/CO/6 (2007) paras 26, 27; CO Suriname CEDAW/C/SUR/CO/3 (2007) para 26; CO Norway CEDAW/C/NOR/CO/7 (2007) para 24; CO The Netherlands CEDAW/C/NLD/CO/4 (2007) para 18.

fulfil under Article 8 entail a range of legislative as well as administrative measures and programmes, as well as TSMs.

2. Need for the Application of TSMs

As the formal guarantee of equality has proven insufficient and women remain significantly under-represented in almost all international fora, TSMs are clearly needed. The Committee's reasoning in General Comments 23 and 25 applies equally to Article 8.[63] States parties are obligated to adopt TSMs as they are necessary and the most appropriate to reach substantive equality in public and political life, including at the international level.[64] A wide range of TSMs are applicable in implementing Article 8, including recruiting, targeting, financially assisting, and training potential candidates for the foreign service or similar representative functions; developing campaigns aimed at equal participation, and setting benchmarks, timetables, numerical goals, and quotas.[65] Quotas are viewed as especially suitable in case of nomination lists for posts in international organizations. The ECHR, however, referring to Convention Articles 4, 7, and 8, stated in its Advisory Opinion on the election of judges to the ECHR that exceptions to the quota requirements for the nomination of candidates are necessary.[66]

3. Immediate vs Gradual Implementation

To implement Article 8, States parties must ensure the specific goal of providing substantively the same opportunities for men and women to participate in international affairs. Similar to Article 7(b), the obligations arising from Article 8 are to be implemented immediately as to the obligation to respect and protect. The obligation to fulfil the goal of parity of men and women at the international level, requires the State party to take concrete steps for its realization, although the goal itself can and will be implemented only gradually. States must report on steps taken which the Committee will evaluate in the review dialogue.

II. Implementation

1. Obligation to Respect

The obligation to respect pledges States parties to codify the constitutional or legal guarantee of equal opportunities to represent one's government at the international level as well as to eliminate indirectly and directly discriminatory legislation that affects opportunities. It obliges States parties to review existing legislation and practice on recruitment, selection, and promotion procedures in diplomatic service and other areas of international representation for possible gender bias. Qualifications such as age requirements for

---

[63] See the discussion in ch on art 7.

[64] GR 23 para 15; GR 25 para 24; cf CO Guinea CEDAW/C/GIN/CO/6 (2007) para 31; CO Hungary CEDAW/C/HUN/CO/6 (2007) para 25; CO Indonesia CEDAW/C/IDN/CO/3 (2007) para 27; CO Serbia CEDAW/C/SCG/CO/1 (2007) para 27; CO Tajikistan CEDAW/C/TJK/CO/3 (2007) para 25; CO Cuba CEDAW/C/CUB/CO/6 (2006) para 24.

[65] GR 23 para 15.

[66] ECHR, 'Advisory Opinion on certain legal questions concerning the lists of candidates submitted with a view to the election of judges to the European Court of Human Rights' (12 February 2008); cf A Mowbray, 'The Consideration of Gender in the Process of Appointing Judges to the European Court of Human Rights' (2008) 8:3 *Human Rights L Rev* 549, 559.

entering the foreign service must be reviewed and modelled along female and male life realities.

2. *Obligation to Protect*

The obligations of Article 8 can be fulfilled solely by the State party; third party interference is, therefore, rare. None the less, States parties must effectively prevent interference by private persons. There is no Committee practice on obligations to protect under Article 8.

3. *Obligation to Fulfil*

The Committee's work under Article 8 focuses on the States parties' obligations to fulfil. Such measures must include TSMs if substantive equality cannot be reached by other means. States should include sufficient information on implementation and gender-disaggregated data on women in diplomacy and delegations to international organizations in their reports.[67] They must also monitor the effectiveness of measures taken and the results achieved and report on progress and failures.[68]

Information campaigns on career choices available in the foreign service targeting female students,[69] are a useful tool. Such campaigns, painting a positive picture of women in the foreign service and in international organizations and addressing stereotypical views of career choices suitable for women, should also be directed to the general public. They should stress the importance of women's equal participation in public life.[70]

States parties are obligated to increase the number of women studying for a career in the foreign service.[71] Scholarships for female students are especially important. Similarly, educational programmes in high schools addressing young women ('pipeline projects') can have a transformative impact on how women are socialized into leadership roles.

Proactive measures in recruitment to international posts must address women candidates specifically and can give women preference over male candidates. Goals and benchmarks for selection, recruitment, and promotion of women should accompany such measures. States parties should identify and abolish the barriers women encounter during employment in the foreign service. They must support measures that encourage the equal sharing of family responsibilities between men and women, providing compensation for child care and procuring part-time and other flexible working time models.

States parties are obliged to place their influence behind equality-focused regulations and appointments to international organizations.

III. Justiciability

Article 8 contains the obligation to 'take all appropriate measures' to achieve a specified goal, without further qualification. Assessment of the measures can be made by evaluating

---

[67] CO Slovakia CEDAW/C/SVK/CO/4 (2008) para 24; CO Finland CEDAW/C/FIN/CO/6 (2008) para 22; CO France CEDAW/C/FRA/CO/6 (2008) para 25.
[68] CO Korea CEDAW/C/KOR/CO/6 (2007) para 24; CO Belgium CEDAW/C/BEL/CO/6 (2008) paras 20, 21.
[69] CO Belgium CEDAW/C/BEL/CO/6 (2008) para 22.
[70] CO Malawi CEDAW/C/MWI/CO/5 (2006) para 26; CO Gabon CEDAW/C/GAB/CC/2–5 (2005) para 34; CO Vanuatu CEDAW/C/VUT/CO/3 (2007) para 27; CO Guatemala CEDAW/C/GUA/CO/7 (2009) para 26; CO Brazil CEDAW/C/BRA/CO/6 (2007) para 26; CO Kyrgyzstan CEDAW/C/KGZ/CO/2 (2004) para 165.
[71] CO Chile CEDAW/C/CHI/CO/4 (2006) para 14.

the numbers of women within the foreign service and the State parties' record in nominating women to positions in international organizations. As the scope of State obligation is sufficiently precise, these matters are justiciable on the international level.[72] States parties' performance is justiciable on the national level as well; obligations under Article 8 have been litigated domestically.[73]

IV. Reservations

There are no reservations to Article 8. However, reservations as succession to royal titles and on engagement in the military service have a bearing on Article 8, as these functions include representative duties in international fora.

---

[72] A Byrnes and J Connors, 'Enforcing the Human Rights of Women: A Complaints Procedure for the Women's Convention? Draft Optional Protocol to the Convention On the Elimination of All Forms of Discrimination against Women' (1996) 21 *Brooklyn J Int l L* 679, 728.

[73] See *Secretary of the Dep't of Foreign Affairs & Trade v Styles* [1989] EOC para 92 (challenge to over-seas posting decision by foreign service).

Article 9

1. States Parties shall grant women equal rights with men to acquire, change or retain their nationality. They shall ensure in particular that neither marriage to an alien nor change of nationality by the husband during marriage shall automatically change the nationality of the wife, render her stateless or force upon her the nationality of the husband.

2. States Parties shall grant women equal rights with men with respect to the nationality of their children.

A. Introduction

Article 9 of the Convention deals with States parties' obligation to grant women equal rights with men in relation to their own nationality and their children's nationality. The term 'nationality' historically has been differentiated from 'citizenship', which is considered to have a broader meaning.[1] 'Nationality' is an international law concept, under which an individual, with a recognized link to a sovereign State, is given the international protection afforded by that State in relation to other sovereign States. Citizenship is the entitlement

* I would like to thank Allison Sherrier for her research assistance on the chapters on arts 9 and 15.

[1] 'Final Report on Women's Equality and Nationality in International Law' in *Report of the Sixty-Ninth Conference*, International Law Association, London, 2000, 248–304, esp 258–9; *Women 2000 and Beyond: Women Nationality and Citizenship*, June 2003, UN Division for the Advancement of Women, Department of Economic and Social Affairs, 2–22.

to full membership within a State or its domestic jurisdiction. Nationality was thus perceived as a term of international law, differentiated from the status of citizenship within a domestic jurisdiction and legal system of individual States. However, nationality and citizenship have come to be treated synonymously 'as an instrument for securing the rights of the individual in the national and international spheres'.[2] The Committee's General Recommendation 21 clarifies that the term 'nationality' in the Convention includes the concept of citizenship and is used synonymously. This general recommendation recognizes that a 'nationality is critical for full participation in society' and provides examples of the denial of rights in domestic jurisdictions that result from a lack of 'status as nationals or citizens'.[3]

The term 'nation' is used by diverse non-western communities across the world to describe their connectivity as a group with a common ethnic, religious, or cultural identity. Tribal or minority groups within a State may describe themselves as 'a nation', sometimes claiming a right to self-determination and territory within the State. Article 9, derived from a Western legal tradition of international law, does not accommodate that concept of nation. When States parties apply a universal norm of equality between men and women relating to nationality as specified by the Article, they are challenged to apply the universal norm in a context of competing claims regarding respect for minority group rights based on ethnic, religious, and cultural diversity within the State.

The text of Article 9 responds to developments in legal systems influenced by the English common law and civil law on family relations.[4] The English common law concept of a married woman's 'coverture' or coming within what the jurist Blackstone described as the 'wing of protection' of her husband, meant that she had no separate personal identity.[5] This lack of personal identity and the male breadwinner/head of family concept created the norm of a married woman's dependent nationality or her nationality being determined exclusively by reference to her husband's nationality. It followed that a child's nationality through a link to the natal family had to be derived from the married man. On the basis that maternity was identified at birth, the natal relationship to the mother determined a non-marital child's legal status. The civil law tradition was influenced by the Roman law on *patria potestas* (power of the father), but did not recognize the concept of coverture. However, the civil law concept of the husband's marital power and preferred guardian-ship rights, and the illegality of non-marital relationships created similar norms.[6] Not surprisingly, many domestic legal systems influenced by these legal concepts recognize the principle of a married woman's dependent nationality and her incapacity to pass her nationality to her children.

Gender-biased nationality laws became an issue that early feminists raised as part of their campaign for equality and non-discrimination on the ground of sex. The link between elimination of discrimination in this area and women's broader access to public

---

[2] H Lauterpacht, 'Foreword to the First Edition' in P Weis (ed), *Nationality and Statelessness in International Law*, 2nd edn (1979) xi.

[3] GR 21 paras 5–6.

[4] 'Final Reports on Women's Equality and Nationality in International Law' (n 1 above).

[5] W Blackstone, *Commentaries on the Laws of England*, 16th edn (1825) 366, 454–9.

[6] Ibid. See also *Lord Advocate v Jaffrey* [1921] AC 146, *Attorney General for Alberta v Cook* [1926] AC 144; HR Hahlo and E Kahn, *The South African Law of Husband and Wife*, 5th edn (1985) 13; E Spiro, *Law of Parent and Child*, 4th edn (1985).

life was, therefore, made very early.[7] Nationality came to be recognized as a 'right to have rights', essential to the agenda on gender equality, political participation, and women's enjoyment of human rights in the private and public spheres, as full members of a State.[8]

International law on women's nationality rights began to develop from the 1930s. The issue was raised at the Hague Codification Conference in 1930 and was followed by a campaign at the League of Nations for a separate treaty eliminating discrimination in nationality law. The Montevideo Convention on Nationality of Women 1933[9] adopted by the Inter-American Commission expressed the Commission's mandate to take on issues relating to the civil and political equality of women.[10] The UDHR Articles 2, 7, and 15 also recognized the importance of nationality as a human right of all men and women and a dimension of achieving equality and non-discrimination on the ground of sex.

The evolution of international standards on women's nationality reflects changes in the family relations norms that had prevented women from enjoying equal right to citizenship. The first nationality convention affecting women was the Convention on the Nationality of Married Women,[11] which provides in Article 1 that marriage, change of nationality by the husband, or dissolution of the marriage should not automatically affect the wife's nationality.

DEDAW Article 5 deals specifically with nationality, following Article 4 on political rights, emphasizing that the equal right to nationality is a critical civil and political right of equal citizenship, full membership in a State, and equal entitlements of women in all areas of private and public life. However, like the 1957 Convention, DEDAW focused on the specific issue of women's nationality as related to marriage—the private sphere—to address problems of dual nationality and statelessness that could arise through discriminatory nationality laws.[12] This connection between nationality rights as a dimension of equal civil and political rights in the public sphere, and stereotypical attitudes to women's role in the family and in private law remains a key dimension of Article 9 and of evolving standards on women's right to nationality in international law.

B. Travaux Préparatoires

The discussions on Article 9(1) among States participating in the drafting of the Convention refer to provisions in DEDAW Article 5 as well as the Convention on the

---

[7] K Knop and C Chinkin, 'Remembering Chrystal Macmillan: Women's Equality and Nationality in International Law' (2001) 22 *Michigan J of Intl L* 523, 524; 'Final Report on Women's Equality and Nationality in International Law' (n 1 above).

[8] *Perez v Brownell* 356 US 44, 64 (1958); Knop and Chinkin (n 7 above); A Shachar, 'The Worth of Citizenship in an Unequal World' (2007) 8 *Theoretical Inquiries in Law* 367.

[9] See Convention on the Rights and Duties of States adopted by the Seventh International Conference of American States (Montevideo Convention) (adopted 26 December 1933, entered into force 26 December 1934) 165 LNTS 19.

[10] 'Final Reports on Women's Equality and Nationality in International Law' (n 1 above); Knop and Chinkin (n 7 above).

[11] Convention on the Nationality of Married Women (adopted 29 January 1957, entered into force 11 August 1958) 309 UNTS 65, arts 1 and 3.

[12] DEDAW arts 1 and 3.

Nationality of Married Women.[13] There was some discussion of whether nationality should be included at all, due to the diversity in approaches in domestic jurisdictions and the difficulty of harmonizing standards with religious teachings in Islamic jurisdictions. Ultimately, a consensus emerged on the importance of incorporating an article on nationality that covered acquisition, change, and retention of nationality, naturalization procedures after marriage, and transmission of nationality to children.

There was some difference of opinion in regard to whether gender-neutral language referring to 'persons' or 'spouses' rather than 'women' should be used in regard to acquisition, change, and retention of nationality and naturalization procedures after marriage. Canada wanted gender-neutral language to be used, which would also include the rights of men.[14] Belgium and Kenya supported this approach.[15] Other delegates said that the Convention on Nationality of Married Women had focused on a standard that referred specifically to women's rights, and using gender-neutral language would dilute that focus. The language that was eventually adopted, proposed by the USSR, set a general standard of women's equal right to nationality and specifically required the elimination of any concept of dependent nationality. Concern with rights of both men and women was accommodated by accepting an amendment from Mexico which added a reference to a male comparator in stating the equal rights regarding acquisition, change, and retention of nationality.[16]

Initial proposals also suggested that States parties should be permitted to limit naturalization procedures on grounds such as national security and public policy.[17] However, these proposals were not accepted.

One of the original proposals referred to recognizing women's equal rights with men in the transmission of nationality to their children. Criticisms focused on the prospect of the child having dual nationality or none at all if there was a disagreement between the parents in regard to transmitting nationality to a child.[18] A compromise draft suggested by the Netherlands was eventually adopted, stating the norm as women's equal right with men 'with respect to the nationality of their children'. This clarified that the father's nationality could not be the sole determining factor in the child's nationality, without specifically mentioning the right of both to transmit nationality at their discretion.[19] This also meant that States which do not recognize transmission through descent could facilitate nationality through both parents.

Different views on the child's nationality were expressed by Islamic States, with Pakistan referring to women's right to legal capacity and custody in Islam as supportive of the article on nationality,[20] and the Syrian Arab Republic focusing on the child automatically acquiring the nationality of the father.[21]

[13] LA Rehof, *Guide to the Travaux Préparatoires of the UN Convention on the Elimination of All Forms of Discrimination against Women* (1993) 103; T Junko, 'Article 9: Equality with Respect to Nationality' in Japanese Association of International Women's Rights (ed), *Convention on the Elimination of All Forms of Discrimination against Women: A Commentary*, Japanese Association of International Women's Rights (1992) 163, 164–9.

[14] UN Doc E/CN.6/591 (1976) para 92; UN Doc E/CN.6/SR.638 (1976) 75.

[15] UN Doc E/CN.6/591/Add.1 (1976) 4.   [16] Rehof (n 13 above) 105.   [17] Ibid 106.

[18] UN Doc A/C.3/32/L.59 (1977) paras 158–9.   [19] Rehof (n 13 above) 107.

[20] UN Doc E/CN.6/606 (1976) 2.   [21] UN Doc A/C.3/34/SR.70 (1979) para 35.

C. Issues of Interpretation

The CEDAW Convention was the first international treaty to refer specifically to women's rights in regard to their own nationality and their children's nationality. The Convention both reflects the history on nationality rights and breaks new ground. It includes Article 9 on women's equal right to nationality in Part II of the Convention, with other articles on civil and political rights. Article 9(1) recognizes that nationality is a critically important status for women's full political participation and voice as equal partners with men in the community. Equal citizenship rights are an essential dimension of women's empowerment and recognition of their identity as persons with all the entitlements of full membership in the State. This link between women's empowerment and nationality has been underlined in General Recommendation 21, which states that '[n]ationality is critical to [women's] full participation in society' and '[w]ithout status as nationals or citizens, women are deprived of the right to vote or to stand for public office and may be denied access to public benefits and a choice of residence'.[22] This reinforces the concept of indivisibility of women's human rights in the Convention, focusing on the link between the right to nationality and exercise of both civil and political rights and socio-economic rights such as access to education, health care, and housing.

Article 9(1) is the culmination of the movement to eliminate women's dependent nationality. Article 9(2) specifically addresses an aspect that should have been incorporated into the earlier international standards, recognizing women's equal rights with men with respect to the nationality of children. The Convention, therefore, seeks to eliminate the concept of one nationality for family members based on a male head of household/breadwinner in a family unit created through legal marriage, which can negatively affect women's nationality rights. Not only is nationality an issue of a woman's identity and full participation in the political process and public sphere, but it is also critical to recognizing the responsibility of men and women as equals or partners within the family. Ten years after the Convention was adopted, the CRC incorporated the same values on joint and shared parental responsibility in the family recognizing, as the Convention does in other articles, the interface between gender equality in family relations and children's rights.

In formulating these standards the Convention establishes norms which require a complete reversal of the approach to family relations in legal systems that focus on a single male head of household/breadwinner. To this extent, the private law dimensions of Article 9 reinforce the norms of Convention Articles 5 and 16, requiring elimination of stereotypical attitudes based on ideas of male superiority, and providing for equal roles and responsibilities in the family.[23] This connection to family relations has been recognized and emphasized by the Committee in General Recommendation 21. The reference to the nationality issue and the inclusion of an analysis of Article 9 as one of three articles that have 'special significance for the status of women in the family'[24] is an acknowledgement that in many countries, it is the patriarchal values on women's role and responsibility in the family that has prevented States parties from eliminating discrimination in nationality laws, in relation to women themselves and to their children.

---

[22] GR 21 para 6.   [23] See the discussion on elimination of stereotypes in ch on art 5.
[24] GR 21 paras 5–6.

The male comparator is used as the standard of equality and non-discrimination in both paragraphs of Article 9, emphasizing the importance of citizenship identity and status for both men and women. However, the language of Article 9 is not gender-neutral, focusing on the need to take into account the specificities of women's situations in achieving the standard of an equal right to acquire nationality. The discussion of the scope of Article 9(1) and (2) indicates that eliminating this discrimination may indeed involve measures to confer nationality on women and on their children. In international law every sovereign State has discretion to decide according to its domestic law on citizenship and immigration who will be a national, and the preconditions for granting nationality. The Convention clarifies that this discretion is now limited by the obligations to achieve a standard of equality according to international human rights law[25] and regional human rights instruments.[26]

Article 9(1) does not guarantee women a right to acquire a State party's nationality. It differs in this respect from the regional instruments which grant every person the right to the nationality of the state in whose territory that person is born if that person does not have the right to any other nationality.[27] The Convention provision also contrasts with some other international conventions and UDHR Article 15(1). ICCPR Article 24(3) and CERD Article 5(d)(iii) recognize a right to acquire nationality. CRC Article 7(1) refers to a child's right to acquire a nationality. The CEDAW Convention only requires non-arbitrary methods of transmission of nationality that can amount to gender-based discrimination against women.

I. Article 9(1) Equality and Non-discrimination in Respect of Women's Nationality

Most States adopt general principles for determining how nationality is acquired in their domestic jurisdiction. These principles are described as *jus sanguinis*—a blood relationship of descent through a national, or *jus soli*—birth within the territory of the State. Some States may adopt a combination of these principles in conferring nationality.[28]

When nationality is acquired exclusively on the basis of birth within a state, men, women, and children can acquire this status, irrespective of sex, although even the gender-neutral principle of nationality by birth can have a discriminatory impact for women and lead to indirect discrimination. However, nationality by descent, unless interpreted in harmony with the Convention's gender-equality norms, tends to entrench discriminatory approaches to nationality.

The interpretation of nationality by descent in domestic jurisdictions as a connection exclusively with the husband and father in the marital family, and the mother only in the non-marital family, can be traced to patriarchal legal values derived from an English common law or Roman civil law tradition. Inevitably, nationality laws reflected a patriarchal view of family relations in interpreting family unity and determining acquisition of

---

[25] *Nationality Decrees Issued in Tunis and Morocco on November 8th*, Advisory Opinion (1923) PCIJ Series B No 4, 24; *Nottebohm Case* (1955) ICJ Rep 4; I Brownlie, *Principles of Public International Law*, 7th edn (2008) 573.

[26] ACHR arts 1 and 20; Protocol on the Rights of Women in Africa art 6(g) and (h).

[27] European Convention on Nationality (opened for signature 6 November 1997, entered into force 1 March 2000) ETS 166 art 4(a); ACHR art 20.

[28] Brownlie (n 25 above) 388–91; Shachar (n 8 above).

nationality by marital children through their biological link and descent from the father. The Committee's concluding observations on many Asian, African, and Middle Eastern States parties[29] and scholarship[30] demonstrate how colonialism impacted on legal systems to entrench English common law and civil law approaches, which also influenced nationality law.

In many newly independent nations women had joined with men in freedom struggles. The failure to recognize women's rights to equality, including political participation and voice as full members of the State at the dawn of a new era of independence from colonial rule and the adoption of new constitutions, was sometimes a restatement of what the new elites perceived as 'traditional' family values or an automatic reception of colonial legal values without review.

General Recommendation 21 and the Committee's concluding observations[31] confirm that this gender-biased interpretation of nationality by descent violates the norms of Article 9(1). It also conflicts with Articles 15 and 16 on women's rights to equality in legal capacity and in family relations. The concept of nationality by descent, in order to conform to Convention Article 9(1), must therefore be interpreted on the basis of proof of the biological link to the mother, or on proof or acknowledgement of biological paternity. Patriarchal fictions in family law and policy that deny the reality of the child's biological link to the mother or father in the marital and non-marital family can no longer be used in interpreting the concept of *jus sanguinis* in nationality law. Since an adopted child acquires the legal status of a child born to adoptive parents, such a child will also benefit from *jus sanguinis*.[32]

Nationality can also be acquired by a naturalization procedure. States have a right to determine these procedures as well as requirement for the grant of resident visas. General Recommendation 21 clarifies that according to Article 9(1) 'nationality should be capable of change by an adult woman.'[33] Some States, however, apply different criteria to married men and married women. In such States, for example, an alien woman married to a male national can become a naturalized citizen by choice or with minimal requirements, whereas an alien man married to a female national must satisfy stringent requirements.

---

[29] CO Nigeria, A/63/38, 41st Session (2008) para 316; CO Burundi, A/63/38, 40th Session (2008) paras 127–8; CO Lebanon, A/63/38, 40th Session (2008) para 202; CO Morocco, A/63/38, 40th Session (2008) paras 215 and 252; CO Jordan, A/62/38, 39th Session (2007) para 182; CO Pakistan, A/62/38, 38th Session (2007) paras 254, 265, and 266; CO Kenya, CEDAW/C/KEN/CO/6 (2007) para 32; CO Ghana, CEDAW/C/GHA/CO/5 (2006) paras 25–6; CO Malaysia, CEDAW/C/MYS/CO/2 (2006) paras 9–14; CO Japan, CEDAW/C/JPN/CO/6 (2009) para 6.

[30] AE Mayer, 'Reform of Personal Status Laws in North Africa: A Problem of Islamic or Mediterranean Laws?' (1995) 49 *Middle East J* 432; S Sardar Ali, 'A Comparative Perspective of the Convention on the Rights of the Child and the Principles of Islamic Law: Law Reform and Children's Rights in Muslim Jurisdictions' in *Protecting the World's Children* (2007) 141–8; S Sardar Ali (ed), *Conceptualising Islamic Law, CEDAW and Women's Human Rights in Plural Legal Settings*, UNIFEM South Asia Regional Office New Delhi (2006). P Kasemsup, 'Reception of law in Thailand–a Buddhist society' in M Chiba (ed), *Asian Indigenous Law in Interaction with Received Law* (1986) 267; ES Yassin, 'Development of plural structures of law in Egypt' in M Chiba (ed), *Asian Indigenous Law in Interaction with Received Law* (1986) 13.

[31] CO Nigeria, A/63/38, 41st Session (2008) para 316; CO Burundi, A/63/38, 40th Session (2008) para 128; CO Lebanon, A/63/38, 40th Session (2008) para 202; CO Morocco, A/63/38, 40th Session (2008) paras 252–3; CO Saudi Arabia, CEDAW/C/SAU/CO/2 (2008) paras 27–8; CO Jordan, A/62/38, 39th Session (2007) para 182; CO Pakistan, A/62/38, 38th Session (2007) paras 265–6; CO Kenya, CEDAW/C/KEN/CO/6 (2007) para 32; CO Ghana, CEDAW/C/GHA/CO/5 (2006) paras 25–6; CO Japan, CEDAW/C/JPN/CO/6 (2009) para 6. GR 21 paras 2, 6, 9, and 10.

[32] Brownlie (n 25 above) 392.   [33] GR 21 para 6.

These differences are based on the legal concept of a man as breadwinner and head of the marital family and on States' concern that an alien man is more likely by virtue of being male to take advantage of economic opportunities. They discriminate against women and men of different nationalities who marry, and in particular discriminate against the citizen spouse who is a woman.

The nationality jurisprudence of regional courts and the CCPR, interpreting general guarantees of equality, also clarifies that different treatment of alien wives who marry male nationals and alien husbands who marry female nationals, amounts to gender-based discrimination as to visas and in naturalization procedures.[34] Some domestic courts apply constitutional guarantees of equality and non-discrimination to reject such differences in visa requirements, concluding that they amount to gender-based discrimination and a denial of women's right to equality.[35] The Pakistan Supreme Court has, however, adopted a different interpretation. The court focused on the advantage conferred on alien women marrying Pakistani men as positive discrimination on behalf of these women, and refused to accept the argument that denying this right to the alien husband of Pakistani women was a violation of the constitutional norm on gender equality. Pakistan's nationality law was amended later to permit a child to obtain the mother's nationality, but the provision discriminating against female spouses remains.[36]

In addition to the reinforcement of Article 9(1) guarantees by regional and domestic courts, judicial interpretation of related rights has also reinforced the right of non-discrimination as to nationality. A woman's right to freedom of movement and choice of residence, and the right to family unity and spousal contribution to family support guaranteed in national constitutions and other laws, have been applied by domestic courts in Botswana and Zimbabwe to challenge administrative denials of resident visas to spouses of female nationals.[37] These rights have also been cited in other major decisions.[38] The South African Constitutional Court has also used the woman's right to dignity to challenge the arbitrary exercise of discretion in visa procedures which the court found interfered with family life.[39] This jurisprudence and General Recommendation

---

[34] CO Thailand, CEDAW/C/THA/CO/5 (2006) paras 31–2; CO Egypt, CEDAW/C/EGY/CO/7 (2010) para 37; CO Bangladesh, A/59/39, 31st Session (2004) paras 249–50; *Abdulaziz, Cabales and Balkandali v United Kingdom* Applications 9214/80; 9473/81; 9474/81 (1985) 7 EHRR 471; *Proposed Amendments to the Naturalization Provisions of the Constitution of Costa Rica*, Advisory Opinion OC-4/84, Inter-American Court of Human Rights Series A No 4 (1984); *In re Aumeeruddy–Cziffra v Mauritius*, ICCPR Communication No 35/1978 (1981) UN Doc A/36/40.

[35] *Meera Gurung v Department of Immigration* (decision 4858) NLR 2051 (1994) [Supreme Ct of Nepal]; *D'Souza v Attorney General & Fisher v Controller of Immigration*, unreported cases from Sri Lanka, cited in S Goonesekere (ed), *Violence, Law and Women's Rights in South Asia* (2004) 46; *Unity Dow v Attorney General of Botswana* (1992) LRC Const 623 (CA, Botswana); *Rattigan and Others v Chief Immigration Officer* (1994) 2 ZLR 54; *Salem v Chief Immigration Officer* (1994) 2 ZLR 28, followed in *Kohilhas v Chief Immigration Officer* (1997) 2 RLR 441; *Hambly v Chief Immigration Officer* (1999) 9 BCLR 966 (ZS, Zimbabwe).

[36] Writ Petition 275 of 1994 *Sharifan v Federation of Pakistan* (1998) Lahore 59 [Pakistani High Court]; Pakistan's Nationality Act (1951) (s 5 amended but s 10(2) discrimination remains regarding foreign spouses); Sardar Ali, *Conceptualising Islamic Law* (n 30 above) 348.

[37] *Unity Dow v Attorney General of Botswana* (n 35 above); *Rattigan and Others v Chief Immigration Officer* (n 35 above); *Salem v Chief Immigration Officer* (n 35 above); *Hambly v Chief Immigration Officer* (n 35 above).

[38] *Abdulaziz, Cabales and Balkandali v United Kingdom* (n 34 above); *Proposed Amendments to the Naturalization Provisions of the Constitution of Costa Rica* (n 34 above); *In re Aumeeruddy–Cziffra v Mauritius* (n 34 above).

[39] *Dawood v Minister of Home Affairs* (2000) 3 SA 936.

21 indicate how the general norm of equality, and other human rights guaranteed in the Convention especially in Articles 15(4) and 16, reinforce the Article 9(1) right to nationality.

1. Eliminating the Concept of Dependent Nationality

The principle of the married woman's dependent nationality which undermined the right to equality and individual autonomy is described in standard texts on Public International Law as one of several 'principles' of involuntary naturalization.[40] Yet it was rooted in patriarchal perceptions of the family. If a married woman came under 'coverture' or marital power she would become the 'other' when she married an alien, and an alien married woman would be absorbed into her husband's nation. These principles were not incorporated in the same manner in Islamic law or customary laws in Asia and Africa, but the impact of received colonial common or civil law meant that transmission of nationality was perceived exclusively as a male prerogative.[41] General Recommendation 21, as well as the Committee's concluding observations,[42] highlight the necessity of amending laws on family relations in countries with a received colonial legal tradition to create a context for reforms that reject the norm of dependent nationality.

States parties' obligation to protect married women's nationality is underlined by the specificity of the Article 9(1) language: States parties are 'in particular' called upon to ensure 'that neither marriage to an alien nor change of nationality by the husband during marriage shall automatically change the nationality of the wife, render her stateless or force upon her the nationality of the husband.'

The reference to the wife's statelessness covers the possibility of a woman losing her original nationality upon marriage and becoming stateless if she is unable to acquire the husband's nationality or if she acquires the husband's nationality upon marriage and subsequently loses it upon the dissolution of that marriage. General Recommendation 21 recognizes this risk of statelessness, emphasizing that nationality 'should not be arbitrarily removed because of marriage or dissolution of marriage or because her husband or father changes his nationality'.[43] Article 9(1), therefore, complements the international instruments that relate to the reduction of statelessness,[44] a problem that is particularly relevant to women affected by displacement and to victims of trafficking.

The Committee has rarely discussed the issue of statelessness. A joint session of the Committee and the United Nations High Commissioner for Refugees held in 2009

---

[40] eg Brownlie (n 25 above) 391.

[41] Mayer (n 30 above); Sardar Ali, 'A Comparative Perspective of the Convention on the Rights of the Child and the Principles of Islamic Law' (n 30 above); Sardar Ali, *Conceptualising Islamic Law* (n 30 above).

[42] CO Nigeria, A/63/38, 41st Session (2008) para 316; CO Burundi, A/63/38, 40th Session (2008) para 127; CO Lebanon, A/63/38, 40th Session (2008) para 202; CO Morocco, A/63/38, 40th Session (2008) paras 215 and 252; CO Saudi Arabia, CEDAW/C/SAU/CO/2 (2008) paras 27–8; CO Jordan, A/62/38, 39th Session (2007) para 182; CO Pakistan, A/62/38, 38th Session (2007) paras 265–6; CO Kenya, CEDAW/C/KEN/CO/6 (2007) para 32; CO Ghana, CEDAW/C/GHA/CO/5 (2006) paras 25–6; CO Malaysia, CEDAW/C/MYS/CO/2 (2006) paras 13–14; CO Japan, CEDAW/C/JPN/CO/6 (2009) para 6; CO Guinea, A/56/38, 25th Session (2001) paras 124–5; CO Egypt, A/56/38, 24th Session (2001) para 330; CO Jamaica, A/56/38, 24th Session (2001) paras 209 and 214; CO Vietnam, A/56/38, 25th Session (2001) para 235; CO Singapore, CEDAW/C/SGP/CO/3 (2007) para 26.

[43] GR 21 para 6.

[44] Convention on the Reduction of Statelessness (1961); UDHR art 15(1); ICCPR art 24(3); CERD art 5(d)(iii).

attempted to address this gap.[45] The background paper for this joint session suggested ways in which the Committee can help to ensure reduction of statelessness by stronger implementation of the Convention norms on gender equality in regard to nationality rights.[46]

Article 9(1) reaffirms Article 1 of the Convention on the Nationality of Married Women, replacing the concept of married women's dependent nationality with their right to autonomy and independence from the husband in this regard. Neither the solemnization of a marriage or its dissolution, nor the husband's subsequent acquisition of nationality by naturalization, therefore, should affect the wife's nationality. Article 9(1) does not, however, retain the provision of the Convention on the Nationality of Married Women which enables only the alien wife of a national to acquire her husband's nationality by naturalization procedures.[47] The jurisprudence on visas and naturalization procedures, referred to earlier, clarifies that such laws and procedures amount to gender-based discrimination against a citizen spouse, though they create the impression of protecting women's rights. The Committee has also reiterated this position,[48] and indicated that such provisions violate Article 9(1).

States parties that provide for naturalization of foreign spouses can place a married woman, especially one who has entered into a token marriage in situations of trafficking or migration for employment, at risk of violence and abuse during the waiting period for acquisition of the husband's nationality. The Committee has noted this possibility and the need for a response from the State party.[49]

Article 9(1) cannot be interpreted in a manner that disadvantages a married woman who exercises personal choice in regard to nationality. Article 9(1) promotes the concept of dual nationality and resident visa regulations that permit a married woman to live and work in the country in which her husband and children reside, while retaining her nationality. She should not be pressured to lose her nationality because she wishes to live with her family. The jurisprudence on equality and non-discrimination in visa regulations[50] is relevant in interpreting the standard set in Article 9(1) and General Recommendation 21 on the right of an adult woman to independent choice in changing or retaining nationality. Such a right is as important to women as giving them the right voluntarily to acquire the husband's

---

[45] UN High Commissioner for Refugees, Displacement, Statelessness and Questions of Gender Equality under the Convention on the Elimination of All Forms of Discrimination against Women (August 2009) UN Doc PPLAS/2009/02, 1, 38 available at <http://www.unhcr.org/refworld/docid/4a8aa8bd2.html> accessed 31 December 2010; CO Bhutan, CEDAW/C/BTN/CO/3 (2004) paras 127–8.

[46] UN High Commissioner for Refugees (n 45 above) 57–8.

[47] Convention on the Nationality of Married Women art 3(1).

[48] See the discussion in Section C. I. of this Ch. See also cases in national courts: *Meera Gurung v Department of Immigration* (n 35 above); *D'Souza v Attorney General* (n 35 above); *Fisher v Controller of Immigration* (n 35 above); *Unity Dow v Attorney General of Botswana* (n 35 above); *Rattigan and Others v Chief Immigration Officer* (n 35 above); *Salem v Chief Immigration Officer* (n 35 above); *Hambly v Chief Immigration Officer* (n 35 above). CO Thailand, CEDAW/C/THA/CO/5 (2006) paras 31–2; CO Morocco, A/63/38, 40th Session (2008) para 252.

[49] Knop and Chinkin (n 7 above); 'Final Reports on Women's Equality and Nationality in International Law' (n 1 above); CO The Netherlands, A/62/38, 37th Session (2007) para 348; CO Singapore, CEDAW/C/SGP/CO/3 (2007) para 26.

[50] *Abdulaziz, Cabales and Balkandali v United Kingdom* (n 34 above); *Proposed Amendments to the Naturalization Provisions of the Constitution of Costa Rica* (n 34 above); *In re Aumeeruddy–Cziffra v Mauritius* (n 34 above) (See also n 35 above).

nationality.[51] If nationality laws compel a woman to give up her nationality in order to live with her spouse or children in the country of her husband's nationality, the norm of equality is clearly violated. General Recommendation 21 also includes a new dimension of discrimination in interpreting Article 9 in stating that nationality 'should not be arbitrarily removed because... [an adult woman's] father changes his nationality.'[52]

II. Article 9(2) Equality with Respect to the Nationality of Children

Many States interpret nationality by descent by reference to the father's nationality in the case of a marital child and the mother's nationality only in the case of a non-marital child.[53] While the principle of the wife's dependent nationality was rejected by the Nationality Convention, equality of men and women as to transmission of nationality to children was not mentioned.[54] The CEDAW Convention was the first international treaty to recognize that the norm of non-discrimination and gender equality requires that men and women have equal rights 'with respect to the nationality of their children'. Though the need to prevent the child's statelessness is not specifically referred to in Article 9(2), interpreting nationality by descent exclusively through the father could result in the child of an unknown or stateless father becoming stateless. The child of a mother who cannot transmit nationality is also placed at risk of statelessness if the father's country bases nationality on birth in the country and the child is born overseas.[55]

Article 9(2) complements Article 9(1) and CRC Article 7(1) on a child's right to acquire a nationality. There is a clear interface between the nationality rights of women and those of children. Women who participated in sessions at the NGO Forum parallel to the Fourth World Conference on Women in Beijing highlighted the problems they faced when a child had a different nationality from theirs because of the male-biased interpretation of nationality by descent. *Unity Dow v Attorney General of Botswana* created a jurisprudence of global relevance, highlighting the discrimination faced by women when the link between women's right to nationality and children's nationality is not recognized.[56] A range of women's human rights in regard to child custody, personal travel and freedom of movement, as well as a child's rights pertaining to health, education, and child support in the country of the mother's nationality, can be undermined when a woman has a right to nationality but cannot transmit her nationality to her children. Women's rights as nationals to freedom of movement, to dignity, and to maintain family life with care and support for family members including children, and the responsibilities these rights create, can be used to challenge nationality laws and administrative procedures that prevent the child acquiring the mother's nationality.

Specific provisions on other rights in both the Convention and CRC are relevant in interpreting the CEDAW Convention Article 9(2). Articles 16(1)(d) and 15(4), and articles on joint and shared parental responsibilities of women and men in CRC can be

---

[51] See the European Convention on Nationality (n 27 above) for an example of a regional instrument that recognizes that dual nationality is possible, focusing on avoiding statelessness and ensuring equality and non-discrimination in nationality law.

[52] GR 21 para 6.   [53] Brownlie (n 25 above) 389, 392.

[54] Knop and Chinkin (n 7 above) 572.

[55] UN High Commissioner for Refugees (n 45 above) 40–2.

[56] *Unity Dow v Attorney General of Botswana* (n 35 above); *Meera Gurung v Department of Immigration* (n 35 above).

used to accommodate the rights of women in passing nationality to children in harmony with Convention Article 9(2). Similarly, a child's right under CRC Article 7(1) to have a relationship with his or her parents, as a dimension of nationality rights, makes an important connection to women's rights in regard to transmitting nationality to children without discrimination. The child's right not to be discriminated against on the ground of national origin or status, to have equal access to health services and education, and have decisions made in his or her best interests as determined within the scope of these CRC standards, can help States to formulate laws and policies that confer the same rights on men and women in regard to transmission of nationality.[57]

The *travaux préparatoires* clarify that the drafters used the language in Article 9(2) to avoid recognizing an equal right to transmit nationality on the argument that this could result in a child's dual nationality or a risk of statelessness where there was parental disagreement. General Recommendation 21 on an adult woman's right to personal choice in nationality[58] and the jurisprudence that has emerged in national and regional courts on naturalization and visas suggests that the Convention must now be interpreted in a manner that gives equal rights in transmission of nationality even when this creates a situation of dual nationality for children. The Committee has pointed out that dual nationality of children is supported by the Convention's equality norm, rather than being a problem that should be avoided, and that the prospect of dual nationality cannot justify a State party's determination of children's nationality only according to the father's nationality when a child of an alien father and a citizen mother is born overseas.[59] The Committee has also stated that failure to amend discriminatory laws in this area cannot be justified by arguments based on diversity in culture or religion.[60]

In referring to equal rights of women and men with respect to the nationality of 'their children', Article 9(2) contemplates both biological and adoptive relationships, since the latter seeks to simulate the relationship of parent and child. In regard to biological parentage, Article 9(2) and CRC Article 2 also depart from the traditionally accepted norms of both international law and many States' domestic laws, on the distinction between marital and non-marital children in the area of nationality.[61] Nationality by descent must now be interpreted as descent from either parent. The only requirement would be proof of parentage. The Committee has indicated that laws and regulations which recognize a concept of conferring nationality to children on the basis of birth in the State, but deny it when the father is a non-national, or permit women to transmit nationality but deny it when the child is born outside the territory and the father is a non-national, clearly violate Article 9(2).[62]

---

[57] CEDAW arts 15(4), 16(1)(c), 16(1)(d), 16(1)(f), 5(4), and 11(2)(c); CRC arts 2, 3, 5, 18, 24, and 28. See also, GR 21 para 6; CESCR, 'General Comment 20' (25 May 2009) UN Doc E/C.12/GC/20 para 40.

[58] GR 21 para 6.

[59] CO Singapore, A/56/38, 25th Session (2001) para 75; CO Guinea, A/56/38, 25th Session (2001) paras 124–5; CO Iraq, A/55/38, 23rd Session (2000) paras 187–8.

[60] CO Singapore, A/56/38, 25th Session (2001) para 74; CO Egypt, A/56/38 (2001) paras 318, 319, and 326; CO Malaysia, CEDAW/C/MYS/CO/2 (2006) para 9.

[61] Knop and Chinkin (n 7 above) 548; *Protecting the World's Children*, UNICEF (2007) 34 and 209; Brownlie (n 25 above) 389 and 392.

[62] eg Constitution of Malaysia arts 14 and 15; Constitution of Singapore arts 122(1) and 123(2) as amended 1967; CO Singapore, A/56/38, 25th Session (2001) para 75; CO Guinea, A/56/38, 25th Session (2001) paras 124–5. cf *Nguyen v Immigration and Naturalisation Service* 121 S Ct 2053 (2001).

III. The Right to a Passport and Article 9

One of the attributes of nationality is the right to leave and re-enter the country of nationality. Article 15(4) of the Convention states the norm of gender equality with regard to freedom of movement. This right, together with a nationality, entitles a woman to a passport (although other requirements, which must be non-discriminatory, may have to be satisfied according to a State party's laws). The State party's discretion must be exercised in a manner which is in harmony with the equal rights to freedom of movement stated in Articles 9 and 15(4).

Restrictions on women's right to travel on a passport as autonomous individuals, and their right to have a minor child included in their passport, violate the norms of Article 9. These restrictions usually take the form of requiring a husband or father's consent. Domestic jurisprudence interpreting constitutional guarantees of equality as well as the right to freedom of movement has clarified that these restrictions violate Article 9.[63] The Committee has considered domestic laws that restrict a woman's right to a separate passport or to have a child's name on her passport, as contravening the norms of both Article 9(1) and 9(2).[64] Because the Convention also provides for joint and shared parental responsibilities, a court order would be required in the event of a parental dispute on taking the child out of a jurisdiction. The consent of each parent may also be required for entry of a child on either parent's passport, where the State party permits a child to acquire the nationality of either parent and the child has dual nationality. These legal procedures would have to be accommodated within the interpretation of Article 9.

D. Equality in Context

I. Formal Equality

States parties must put in place constitutional or legislative provisions that aim to achieve equality between men and women in relation to the specific areas of nationality. Eliminating discrimination and the legal concept of dependent nationality, and recognizing an adult woman's independent right to nationality and the capacity to transfer nationality to children through descent are important formal equality measures within the aims and objectives of the core Articles 1, 2, and 16. Providing remedies for infringement of these provisions through courts or mechanisms such as ombudspersons and national human rights institutions is critical to the achievement of formal equality. The requirement of legal reform to achieve formal equality is stated in Convention Article 2(a), (b), and (c), a number of the Committee's concluding observations, and national and regional jurisprudence.[65]

---

[63] *Unity Dow v Attorney General of Botswana* (n 35 above); *Nawakw v Attorney General of Zambia* (1993) 3 Law Rep Commonwealth 231.

[64] CO Egypt, A/56/38, 24th Session (2001) para 315; CO Jamaica, A/56/38, 24th Session (2001) para 214; CO Maldives, A/56/38, 24th Session (2001) para 118; CO Uganda, A/57/38, Exceptional Session (2002) para 141; CO Jordan, A/62/38, 39th Session (2007) paras 182–3.

[65] See *Abdulaziz, Cabales and Balkandali v United Kingdom* (n 34 above); *Proposed Amendments to the Naturalization Provisions of the Constitution of Costa Rica* (n 34 above); *In re Aumeeruddy–Cziffra v Mauritius* (n 34 above); *Meera Gurung v Department of Immigration* (n 35 above); *Fisher v Controller of Immigration* (n 35 above); *Unity Dow v Attorney General of Botswana* (n 35 above); *Rattigan and Others v Chief Immigration Officer* (n 35 above); *Salem v Chief Immigration Officer* (n 35 above); *Hambly v Chief Immigration Officer* (n 35 above); CO Andorra, A/56/38, 25th Session (2001) para 34; CO Singapore, A/56/38, 25th Session (2001)

II. Substantive Equality

The discriminatory impact of formal nationality laws, particularly with respect to visas, naturalization procedures, the avoidance of statelessness, and recognition of dual nationality, is a matter of substantive equality. To achieve substantive equality, proactive measures are necessary. Such measures could include providing migrant women, domestic workers, women victims of domestic violence, or trafficked women, with access to legal literacy and assistance in order to obtain residence permits which could precede naturalization procedures. Facilitating dual nationality for women and children can help women actually to enjoy the benefit of formal laws that give men and women equal right to acquire, retain, or change their nationality. CESCR General Comment 20 notes the importance of ensuring that nationality laws facilitate and do not prevent access to adequate food and health care and children's access to education.[66] In short, States parties must pay attention to the context in which nationality laws are enforced and ensure that women have equal, effective access not only to formal status but to the benefits of that status as well. Establishing accessible systems for birth and marriage registration are also a critical support for ensuring non-discrimination in the impact of nationality laws and procedures.

Addressing and eliminating institutional and structural barriers and stereotypical attitudes is a key dimension of achieving substantive equality. Some of the cases in domestic courts noted earlier in this chapter demonstrate that even where the law recognizes formal equality, gender-biased attitudes may colour the responses of the judiciary in interpreting the law, or encourage administrative regulations that undermine formal equality stated in the constitution and/or the nationality law.

III. Intersectional Discrimination

Achieving the universal standard of substantive equality requires addressing the issue of *de facto* and *de jure* discrimination against specific categories of women who suffer multiple discrimination due to poverty, migration status, ethnicity, religion, social or economic status, and other identity factors. Problems of difference in social and economic status can be addressed through a gender impact assessment of laws and policies, and temporary special measures to eliminate negative outcomes that deny equality. The problem is more complex when multiple discrimination occurs because of diversity in ethnicity and religion.

Cultural differences based on patriarchal values in customary or religious law can be challenged on the basis of constitutional norms, CEDAW, and other treaty standards on gender equality, and the State party's right to limit manifestation of culture and religion in the public interest. This is the justification for many States with plural legal systems to regulate nationality according to uniformly applicable State laws. Cases in domestic courts and the Committee's concluding observations indicate that discriminatory nationality laws that are based on local custom or religious practice can be challenged in the courts.[67]

---

para 89; CO Guyana, A/56/38, 25th Session (2001) para 157; CO Vietnam, A/56/38, 25th Session (2001) para 244; CO Pakistan, A/62/38, 38th Session (2007) para 266; CO Maldives, A/62/38, 37th Session (2007) paras 217 and 219.

[66] UN Doc E/C.12/GC/20 (25 May 2009) para 30.

[67] *Unity Dow v Attorney General of Botswana* (n 35 above); *Meera Gurung v Department of Immigration* (n 35 above); *DNF v HMG*, Nepal, Writ 3303/06, 2 May 2005; *Reshma Thapa v HMG*, Nepal, 12 SCB 2004/2005, 24; *D'Souza v Attorney General & Fisher v Controller of Immigration* (n 35 above) 33; P Fournier,

The Committee has requested States parties to reform customary or personal laws so as to harmonize them with the Convention's general norm of substantive equality.[68] This is especially relevant in the area of nationality for women of minority communities who may acquire nationality on an equal basis but be unable to enjoy the full rights of citizenship available to men and some other women. The Committee has addressed the need to ensure that women of an ethnic minority do not lose citizenship rights.[69] It has also referred to the negative impact of administrative requirements on women migrant workers and those trafficked across borders, who risk losing their citizenship, and requested the States parties to take into consideration the impact of the law when introducing reforms. The Committee has not yet addressed the issue of a secular State party denying nationality on the ground of public policy to an applicant from a community that follows a discriminatory practice such as polygamy.

Religious dogma or values which conflict with the norm of substantive equality in the Convention and Article 9 represent a significant challenge. Islamic State parties frequently have cited religious values based on Sharia law to justify discrimination against women in the area of nationality.[70] Yet scholarship supports the view that there are no constraints in Islam on equal rights to nationality, or on transmitting the mother's nationality to the child. Discriminatory legal values generally reflect the post-colonial impact of civil or common law or customary patriarchal traditions that undermine the Islamic law concept of women as members of the Umma or community.[71] The Committee has drawn attention to the need to use comparative interpretation of Islamic jurisprudence to eliminate discrimination against women in the nationality laws of Islamic State parties.[72]

E. States Parties' Obligations

I. Nature of the Obligations

The States parties' obligations under Article 9 are indicated in the mandatory language of the chapeau: the State 'shall grant equal rights' under Article 9(1) and (2). The language of Article 9(1) also mandates that the State party 'shall ensure' the elimination of specific dimensions of a woman's dependent nationality. This suggests an immediate obligation to

---

'The Reception of Muslim Family Law in Western Liberal States' in *Dossier 27: Muslim Minorities (Women Living Under Muslim Law)* (2005) 63, 66; CO Bhutan, A/59/38, 30th Session (2004) paras 127–8.

[68] CO Singapore, A/56/38, 25th Session (2001) para 74; CO India, A/62/38, 37th Session (2007) paras 147–8; CO Malaysia, A/61/38, 35th Session (2006) para 14; CO Sri Lanka, A/57/38, 26th Session (2002) paras 274–5; CO Lebanon, A/63/38, 40th Session (2008) para 177; CO Burundi, A/63/38, 40th Session (2008) para 127.

[69] CO Bhutan, CEDAW/C/BTN/CO/3 (2004) paras 127–8; CO Indonesia, CEDAW/C/IDN/CO/3 (2007) paras 28–9.

[70] CO Malaysia, CEDAW/C/MYS/CO/2 (2006) paras 9 and 13; CO Saudi Arabia, CEDAW/C/SAU/CO/2 (2008) para 4.

[71] Mayer (n 30 above); Sardar Ali, *Conceptualising Islamic Law* (n 30 above); Kasemsup (n 30 above); Yassin (n 30 above). CO Nigeria, A/63/38, 41st Session (2008) para 316; CO Burundi, A/63/38, 40th Session (2008) para 127; CO Lebanon, A/63/38, 40th Session (2008) para 202; CO Morocco, A/63/38, 40th Session (2008) paras 215 and 252; CO Jordan, A/62/38, 39th Session (2007) para 182; CO Pakistan, A/62/38, 38th Session (2007) paras 254, 265, and 266; CO Kenya, CEDAW/C/KEN/CO/6 (2007) para 32; CO Ghana, CEDAW/C/GHA/CO/5 (2006) paras 25–6; CO Malaysia, CEDAW/C/MYS/CO/2 (2006) paras 13–14; CO Japan, CEDAW/C/JPN/CO/6 (2009) para 6.

[72] CO Jordan, A/62/38, 39th Session (2007) para 183–4; CO Malaysia, CEDAW/C/MYS/CO/2 (2006) para 14; CO Maldives, A/62/38, 37th Session (2007) para 242.

respect these rights by instituting formal equality measures such as constitutional amendments, legislation, and administrative regulations. Some States parties have complied and harmonized constitutional provisions or national legislation with the Convention.[73]

II. Implementation

1. *Obligation to Respect and Protect*

The Committee has indicated that a range of enforcement measures is required to ensure remedies for infringement by State actors as part of the duty to respect women's rights. The State party is considered liable for direct action in infringing women's rights through its agents. The Committee also draws attention to the State party's responsibility to protect and its liability for the acts of non-State actors based on inaction. Actions of non-State actors, including those of employers and family in preventing applications for passports, or the action of traditional tribunals in preventing women from exercising their rights under Article 9, also can be challenged in regional and national courts.[74]

Convention standards, particularly those on violence against women, trafficking, and work, have created a new context in which the 'duty to protect' can be interpreted to place an obligation on the State party to enter into bilateral arrangements and cooperation to afford protection to victims of trafficking and domestic violence, and to women migrant workers for violence and abuse in the host country.[75] Regional treaties such as the SAARC Convention attempt to facilitate such measures.

2. *Obligation to Fulfil*

States parties have a positive obligation to create a supportive context for the exercise of the rights contemplated in Article 9—to fulfil the rights. General Recommendation 21 indicates measures that must be taken to bring the law on family relations in harmony with the mandatory standards of Article 9. In addition, the Committee has suggested generally that administrative measures such as appropriate passport procedures and providing

---

[73] CO Bhutan, CEDAW/C/BTN/CO/3 (2004) paras 127–8; CO Nepal, A/59/39, 30th Session (2004) para 198; CO Ghana, A/61/38, 36th Session (2006) paras 236–7; CO Kenya, A/62/38, 39th Session (2007) para 445; CO Maldives, A/56/38, 24th Session (2001) para 118; CO Singapore, CEDAW/C/SGP/CO/3 (2007) para 26 (amended Constitution and reservation withdrawn). On the need to amend legislation: CO Guinea, A/56/38, 25th Session (2001) paras 124–5; CO Egypt, A/56/38, 24th Session (2001) paras 330–1; CO Vietnam, A/56/38, 25th Session (2001) para 235; CO Sri Lanka, A/57/38, 26th Session (2002) para 274 (law amended (2003)); CO Samoa, A/60/38, 32nd Session (2005) para 42 (law amended); CO Algeria, A/60/38, 32nd Session (2005) paras 141, 142, and 144; CO Vanuatu, A/62/38, 38th Session (2007) para 331; CO Pakistan, A/62/38, 38th Session (2007) para 254; CO Jordan, A/62/38, 39th Session (2007) para 182; CO Morocco, A/63/38, 40th Session (2008) paras 252–3 (Nationality Code amended to harmonize with CEDAW); CO Nigeria, A/63/38, 41st Session (2008) para 317 (not amended); CO Lebanon, A/63/38, 40th Session (2008) para 202.

[74] *Abdulaziz, Cabales and Balkandali v United Kingdom* (n 34 above); *Proposed Amendments to the Naturalization Provisions of the Constitution of Costa Rica* (n 34 above); *In re Aumeeruddy–Cziffra v Mauritius* (n 34 above); *Meera Gurung v Department of Immigration* (n 35 above); *Fisher v Controller of Immigration* (n 35 above); *Unity Dow v Attorney General of Botswana* (n 35 above); *Rattigan and Others v Chief Immigration Officer* (n 35 above); *Salem v Chief Immigration Officer* (n 35 above); *Hambly v Chief Immigration Officer* (n 35 above); CO Sri Lanka, A/57/38, 26th Session (2002) paras 274–5; *Velásquez Rodríguez Case (Interpretation of Compensatory Damages)* Inter-American Court of Human Rights Series C No 4 (29 July 1988) 28 ILM 291 (1989).

[75] GR 21 para 10; Convention on the Reduction of Statelessness (1961); UDHR art 15(1); ICCPR art 24(3); CERD art 5(d)(iii).

access to information and legal aid are required to enable women to exercise these rights.[76] Gender sensitization of judges and immigration officials and incorporating nationality issues into courses on public international law and human rights in State and private institutions in place of the common gender-neutral approaches to the topic, are clearly dimensions of realizing the obligation to fulfil these rights. Providing access to birth and marriage registration procedures, education for children on a basis of equality, and access to health services for persons with resident visas and those who have pending naturalization procedures also are important dimensions of realizing the Article 9 standards. These obligations are incorporated in CESCR General Comment 20, particularly paragraph 30. The Committee has referred to the link between access to registration procedures and nationality rights.[77]

The Committee emphasizes the continuing obligation of States parties to achieve progress in addressing matters prioritized in concluding observations. The Committee sometimes refers to prior concluding observations and emphasizes the State party's failure to address them.[78] This approach is a reminder to States parties that reporting is not a single *ad hoc* response at certain periods. This may help to achieve more progress on the implementation of Article 9. Concluding Comments on the need to integrate a gender perspective into achieving the Millennium Development Goals[79] can also be a motivation to eliminate discrimination in citizenship laws, though that aspect is not specifically covered.

III. Reservations

The Committee has constantly referred to the need to review and withdraw reservations to Article 9.[80] Where constitutional provisions are cited as an explanation for failure to withdraw a reservation, the Committee has called for amendments to the constitution

---

[76] CO Ghana, A/61/38, 36th Session (2006) para 226; CO Mauritania, A/62/38, 38th Session (2007) para 266; CO Greece, A/62/38, 37th Session (2007) paras 527–8; CO Maldives, A/62/38, 37th Session (2007) para 223; CO India, A/62/38, 37th Session (2007) paras 155–6; CO Burundi, A/63/38, 40th Session (2008) para 128; CO Bolivia A/63/38, 40th Session (2008) para 85; CO Indonesia, A/62/38, 39th Session (2007) para 284.

[77] CESCR, 'General Comment 20' (25 May 2009) UN Doc E/C.12/GC/20 part IV para 30; CO Peru, CEDAW/C/PER/CO/6 (2007) para 33.

[78] CO Vietnam, A/62/38, 37th Session (2007) paras 445, 447, and 450; CO Peru, A/62/38, 37th Session (2007) para 601; CO India, A/62/38, 37th Session (2007) paras 144–5; CO Pakistan, A/62/38, 38th Session (2007) para 260; CO Azerbaijan, A/62/38, 37th Session (2007) para 107; CO Netherlands, A/62/38, 37th Session (2007) paras 329 and 367; CO Namibia, A/62/38, 37th Session (2007) para 257; CO France, A/63/38, 40th Session (2008) para 313; CO Saudi Arabia, CEDAW/C/SAU/CO/2 (2008) para 8; CO Lebanon, A/63/38, 40th Session (2008) para 177; CO Burundi, A/63/38, 40th Session (2008) para 127; CO Bolivia, A/63/38, 40th Session (2008) para 66; CO Jordan, A/62/38, 39th Session (2007) para 180.

[79] CO India, A/62/38, 37th Session (2007) para 200; CO Azerbaijan, A/62/38, 37th Session (2007) para 134; CO Namibia, A/62/38, 37th Session (2007) para 280; CO Netherlands, A/62/38, 37th Session (2007) para 363; CO Greece, A/62/38, 37th Session (2007) para 551; CO Peru, A/62/38, 37th Session (2007) para 631; CO Bolivia A/63/38, 40th Session (2008) para 110; CO Saudi Arabia, CEDAW/C/SAU/CO/2 (2008) para 42; CO Maldives, A/62/38, 37th Session (2007) para 245.

[80] CO Jamaica, A/56/38, 24th Session (2001) para 209 (withdrawn); CO Singapore, A/62/38, 39th Session (2007) para 99 (withdrawn); CO Egypt, A/56/38, 24th Session (2001) paras 326, 330, and 331; CO Algeria, A/60/38, 32nd Session (2005) paras 141, 142, and 144; CO Malaysia, CEDAW/C/MYS/CO/2 (2006) paras 4, 9, and 10; CO Jordan, A/62/38, 39th Session (2007) para 182; CO Saudi Arabia, CEDAW/C/SAU/CO/2 (2008) para 27; CO Lebanon, A/63/38, 40th Session (2008) paras 202–3; CO Morocco, A/63/38, 40th Session (2008) paras 215 and 225. Thailand, Fiji, and Liechtenstein withdrew reservations to art 9(2).

to harmonize national law with Article 9.[81] The Committee has also pointed out that dual nationality is not an argument for discrimination against women in transmission of nationality to children born abroad, since this situation would also be created in the case of men who transmit nationality to their children.[82]

The Committee has reiterated the importance of withdrawing a reservation or declaration when the law has been harmonized.[83] States parties may only partially withdraw a reservation to Article 9, leaving part of the reservation in place. The Committee has reminded States parties of the need to adopt a holistic approach and withdraw reservations or declarations to both paragraphs.[84]

The Committee has regularly expressed concern about general reservations, frequently based on Sharia law, as undermining the object and purpose—the basic norms—of the Convention. It has also refused to accept assertions that Sharia law is not subject to interpretation that can harmonize religious law and the Convention. Though a majority of States parties that have entered reservations to Article 9 are Muslim States, the Committee has pointed out that there are interpretations of Islamic law which support equality in regard to nationality of men, women, and children. It has adopted an approach that respects the need for religious and ethnic diversity, but also emphasizes the importance of maintaining universality in human rights standards. The Committee has referred to comparative jurisprudence and reform in countries that follow Islamic law, as a basis for harmonizing the Convention norms in domestic jurisprudence. While its concluding observations on nationality have occasionally referred to this strategy specifically, the Committee more frequently offers a general statement on harmonizing Islamic law and the Convention, which is particularly relevant in the area of nationality, and supported by developments in Muslim States that have eliminated discriminatory nationality laws.[85]

With globalization, nationality laws have acquired great significance for large numbers of low-income women, who cross borders as migrant workers or as trafficked persons. Yet nationality did not merit specific recognition in the Beijing Platform for Action. It has not been given priority in international fora, and is not identified specifically in Millennium Development Goal 3 on the Empowerment of Women. The Committee's focus on reform of nationality laws in General Recommendation 21 and concluding observations has helped women's groups lobbying for law reform, and has led to some States' harmonizing domestic law with the Convention. The Committee's work has also been an impetus to a regional focus on nationality law reform. South Asian regional proposals for State action

---

[81] CO Nepal, A/59/39, 30th Session (2004) para 198; CO Nigeria, A/59/39, 30th Session (2004) para 293.

[82] CO Singapore, A/56/38, 25th Session (2001) para 75; CO Guinea, A/56/38, 25th Session (2001) paras 124–5; CO Egypt, A/56/38, 24th Session (2001) para 326.

[83] CO Jordan, A/62/38, 39th Session (2007) para 182; CO Turkey, A/60/38, 32nd Session (2005) para 353; CO Morocco, A/63/38, 40th Session (2008) paras 215 and 225.

[84] CO Malaysia, CEDAW/C/MYS/CO/2 (2006) paras 4 and 9; CO Thailand, CEDAW/C/THA/CO/5 (2006) paras 31–2; CO Singapore, CEDAW/C/SGP/CO/3 (2007) para 26; CO Jordan, A/62/38, 39th Session (2007) paras 182–4; CO Morocco, A/63/38, 40th Session (2008) para 252.

[85] Sardar Ali, *Conceptualising Islamic Law* (n 30 above); Sardar Ali, 'A Comparative Perspective on the Rights of the Child and Principles of Islamic Law' (n 30 above). On broad reservations based on Islam see CO Jordan, A/62/38, 39th Session (2007) paras 183–4; CO Pakistan, A/62/38, 38th Session (2007) paras 254, 265, and 266; CO Malaysia, CEDAW/C/MYS/CO/2 (2006) paras 13–14; CO Saudi Arabia, CEDAW/C/SAU/CO/2 (2008) paras 4, 27, and 28.

on gender equality refer to repeal and amendment of discriminatory national laws.[86] The important connection between discrimination against women in nationality laws and family values is highlighted in the specific provisions on non-discrimination in nationality laws in the Protocol on the Rights of Women in Africa.[87]

Still, universal norms have not yet been met in domestic jurisdictions in this area.[88] Despite international law developments, the efforts of the Committee, and the importance of nationality status, only a few States parties have withdrawn their reservations.[89] Reservations made to Article 15(4), regarding a woman's right to freedom of movement, reinforce discriminatory approaches to nationality that deny women equal rights.[90] Jurisprudence of national courts on challenges to discriminatory nationality laws has sometimes had a positive impact on domestic law reform.[91] However, this jurisprudence has not been used to motivate law reform even within regions and States that share a common legal tradition. A reference to use comparative regional jurisprudence in this area, integrated into concluding observations, could highlight the importance of looking to a common approach to law reform within regions and similar legal traditions leading to review and withdrawal of reservations.

---

[86] Islamabad Declaration: Review and Future Action Celebrating Beijing Plus Ten, Fifth South Asia Ministerial Conference 3–5 May 2005, Islamabad Pakistan, paras 5(c) and 7(a)(3).

[87] Protocol to the African Charter on the Rights of Women in Africa art 6 (marriage).

[88] Knop and Chinkin (n 7 above). For discussions on legal reforms see: *Sri Lanka Shadow Report to the Committee on Elimination of All Forms of Discrimination against Women*, The Women and Media Collective, Colombo, Sri Lanka, July 2010, available online at <http://www2.ohchr.org/english/bodies/cedaw/docs/ngo/WMD_SriLanka48.pdf> accessed 31 December 2010; I Jalal, 'The Campaign for Gender Equality in Family Law' in *Dossier 27: Muslim Minorities (Women Living Under Muslim Law)* (2005) 27; 'Discriminatory Laws in Nepal and their Impact on Women', Forum for Women, Law and Development, Kathmandu, Nepal (2006) xi–xii, para 96.

[89] Thailand, Fiji and Liechtenstein withdrew reservations to art 9(2), Reservations to CEDAW/SP/1982/2.

[90] CO Jordan, A/62/38, 39th Session (2007) paras 182–3 (withdrawal of reservations to arts 9(2) & 15(4)). Reservations have been entered to both articles by Algeria, Jordan, Morocco, Tunisia, Reservations to CEDAW/SP/1982/2 and available online at <http://treaties.un.org> accessed 31 December 2010.

[91] See *In re Aumeeruddy–Cziffra v Mauritius* (n 34 above); *Meera Gurung v Department of Immigration* (n 35 above); *D'Souza v Attorney General & Fisher v Controller of Immigration* (n 35 above); *Unity Dow v Attorney General of Botswana* (n 35 above). See generally, A M Sood, 'Gender Justice through Public Interest Litigation: Case Studies from India' (2008) 41 *Vanderbilt J Transnational L* 833.

Article 10

States Parties shall take all appropriate measures to eliminate discrimination against women in order to ensure to them equal rights with men in the field of education and in particular to ensure, on a basis of equality of men and women:

(a) The same conditions for career and vocational guidance, for access to studies and for the achievement of diplomas in educational establishments of all categories in rural as well as in urban areas; this equality shall be ensured in pre-school, general, technical, professional and higher technical education, as well as in all types of vocational training;

(b) Access to the same curricula, the same examinations, teaching staff with qualifications of the same standard and school premises and equipment of the same quality;

(c) The elimination of any stereotyped concept of the roles of men and women at all levels and in all forms of education by encouraging coeducation and other types of education which will help to achieve this aim and, in particular, by the revision of textbooks and school programmes and the adaptation of teaching methods;

(d) The same opportunities to benefit from scholarships and other study grants;

(e) The same opportunities for access to programmes of continuing education, including adult and functional literacy programmes, particularly those aimed at reducing, at the earliest possible time, any gap in education existing between men and women;

(f) The reduction of female student drop-out rates and the organization of programmes for girls and women who have left school prematurely;

(g) The same opportunities to participate actively in sports and physical education;

(h) Access to specific educational information to help to ensure the health and well-being of families, including information and advice on family planning.

* For this chapter and the chapter on art 14, I would like to thank Elizabeth Asham for invaluable research assistance. I would also like to thank Sara Waldron and Meredith Owen. Special thanks are also due to Frances Raday, Janie Chuang, and Rikki Holtmaat.

A. Introduction

[E]ducation is a key to the advancement of women and the low level of education of girls and women remains among the most serious impediments to their full enjoyment of human rights and the achievement of women's empowerment.[1]

Article 10 is the first of the economic, social, and cultural rights in the Convention and arguably the most important, facilitating the enjoyment of other rights.[2] Article 10 focuses on the negative impact of discrimination on the realization of the right to education for women and girls. Education is broadly defined to include primary school, vocational training, and functional literacy programmes. Article 10 also aims to meet the educational needs of those girls[3] and women who have had to leave education prematurely. Crucially, Article 10 includes the requirement that States parties provide information on family health and welfare and 'information and advice on family planning.'[4] Furthermore, Article 10 also requires that in providing education, the State should not discriminate between the sexes by ensuring that resources (human and material) are of equal quality and quantity. To facilitate the entry and retention of girls in institutions of learning, it is provided that women and girls should be given the same opportunities to access and to

---

[1] CO Sierra Leone, CEDAW/C/SLE/CO/5 (2007) para 30. See also CO Malawi, CEDAW/C/MWI/CO/5 (2006) para 28; CO Turkey, CEDAW/C/TUR/CO/6 (2010) para 32.

[2] N Burrows, 'The 1979 Convention on the Elimination of all Forms of Discrimination against Women' (1985) 32 *Netherlands Intl L Rev* 419, 435. CO Vietnam, CEDAW/C/VNM/CO/6 (2007) para 19; CO Haiti, CEDAW/C/HTI/CO/7 (2009) para 31; CO Guinea-Bissau, CEDAW/C/GNB/CO/6 (2009) para 34.

[3] Article 10 includes the only specific mention of girls, but the Convention is constructed to apply to women and girls, see GR 28 para 21 and see the discussion in the ch on art 1.

[4] Art 10(h).

benefit from scholarships and educational grants. Article 10 further requires States parties to allow women and girls the same opportunities to engage in sport and other leisure activities in education.

Specific references to education and the provision of information can also be found in Articles 5(b) on parental roles, 11(1)(c) on employment, 14(2)(b) and (d) on rural women, and 16(1)(e) on family and marriage relations. The CEDAW Committee has yet to produce a general recommendation focusing specifically on Article 10. However, it has mentioned the importance of education and the provision of information in a number of its other general recommendations.[5] The Committee also asks States parties to provide training to service providers and the public in its concluding observations.[6]

In its recommendations in both the communications and inquiry procedures under the Optional Protocol, the Committee has enjoined States parties to train service providers and personnel including police and judges to tackle the shortcomings identified.[7] The Committee has received one communication directly on Article 10, which will be considered in the interpretive section of this chapter.[8]

I. Education as a Human Right: International and Regional Perspectives

The right to education has been recognized within both international[9] and regional[10] human rights instruments. The UNESCO Convention against Discrimination in Education is particularly important; like the Convention, it is not only about preventing and eradicating discrimination but also about facilitating the substantive realization of education rights for all.[11]

CESCR General Comment 13 on the right to education is particularly useful in analyzing the obligations of States with respect to education because of its typology of the goals in respect to the full realization of the right to education.[12] The four 'As', described as inter-related and essential, require that education be available, accessible, acceptable,

---

[5] GR 5; GR 6 para 2; GR 9; GR 10 paras 1, 2, and 4; GR 14 paras (a)(i), (iii), (iv), (b), (c); GR 15 paras (a)–(c); GR 18; GR 19 paras 11, 24(b), 24(d), 24(f), 24(q) and 24(t)(ii); GR 21 para 22; GR 23 paras 20(a), 32, 45(c), 48(h), and 50(c)-(d); GR 24 paras 13, 18, 28, and 31(b)-(c); GR 25 paras 2, 23, 31, 32, and 37; GR 26 paras 10, 13, 24(b)(i-vi), and 26(g); GR 28 paras 37(d) and (e).

[6] CO Timor-Leste, CEDAW/C/TLS/CO/1 (2009) para 46; CO Russia, CEDAW/C/USR/CO/7 (2010) paras 35 and 53; CO France, CEDAW/C/FRA/CO/6 (2010) para 30; CO Turkey, CEDAW/C/TUR/CO/6 (2010) paras 13 and 21; CO Sierra Leone CEDAW/C/SLE/CO/5 (2007) para 13. See also CEDAW OP art 13.

[7] *AT v Hungary* CEDAW Communication 2/2003 (2005) CEDAW/C/32/D/2003, views adopted at 32nd Session, para (d); Report on Mexico produced by the Committee under CEDAW OP art 8 and the reply of the Government of Mexico, CEDAW/C/2005.OP.8/Mexico para 278.

[8] *AS v Hungary* CEDAW Communication 4/2004 (2006) CEDAW/C/36/D/4/2004.

[9] See M Ssenyonjo, 'Non-State Actors and Economic, Social and Cultural Rights in M Baderin and R McCorquodale, *Economic, Social and Cultural Rights in Action*' (2009) 359–73; UDHR art 26; Convention relating to the Status of Refugees arts 4 and 22; ICESCR arts 13 and 14; ICCPR art 18(4); CRC arts 28 and 29; ILO Convention 169 arts 26–9 and 31; ICMW arts 30, 43, 45(1)(a)–(b), and 45(2)–(4); CRPD arts 4(1) (h), 4(2), 8(1)(a)-(c), 8(2)(b) and 24.

[10] Ssenyonjo (n 9 above) 373–6; Protocol 1 ECHR art 2; ESC arts 7(3) and 17(1); EU Charter art 14; Banjul Charter arts 17 and 25; ACRWC art 11(3); Protocol on the Rights of Women in Africa arts 1(f), 2(2), 4(2)(d)–(f), 5(a), 5(c), 8(c), 10(2)(a), 12, 14(2)(g), 18(2)(b) and (c); Additional Protocol ACHR (Protocol of San Salvador) art 13; Convention of Belém do Para arts 2(b), 6(b), and 8(a), (c), (e), (f) and (i); Arab Charter art 41.

[11] UNESCO Convention against Discrimination in Education arts 5(e), 5(v), and 7.

[12] CESCR, 'General Comment13' (1999) UN Doc E/C.12/1999/10. See also CESCR 'General Comment 11' (1999) UN Doc E/C.12/1999/4.

and adaptable.[13] 'Accessibility requires the State to ensure that there is no discrimination and that education is physically and economically 'accessible to all, especially the most vulnerable groups, in law and fact'. Acceptability is about ensuring minimum standards and good quality in curricula and teaching methods. It also requires that the education be culturally appropriate. Adaptability requires that education should be flexible enough to meet the changing demands of societies and to respond to their needs.

A number of mechanisms within the human rights framework look at the right to education and specifically, education of girls and the attainment of gender equality generally.[14] The UN Special Rapporteur on Education has analyzed how girls' right to education is often impeded.[15] The Beijing Declaration and Platform for Action examines the reasons for the lower levels of participation of girls in education compared to boys and makes recommendations to governments on how to reverse this situation.[16]

The UNESCO Education for All (EFA) goals include a gender-equality goal.[17] These goals led to the inclusion of universal primary education and the promotion of gender equality and empowerment of women in the Millennium Development Goals (MDGs).[18] The MDGs are part of a non-binding global blueprint to reduce extreme poverty and to facilitate the realization of the targets set out in the eight goals by 2015. Reporting on progress made in realizing the MDGs has now been incorporated into the CEDAW process.[19]

B. Travaux Préparatoires

The first draft was proposed by the Philippines and USSR using the Declaration on the Elimination of Discrimination against Women, 1967 (DEDAW) Article 9 as the basis. The Philippines draft also referenced ICESCR Article 13(1) for its vision of the aims of a good education.[20] Sweden added to the DEDAW reference the importance of consulting the UNESCO Convention.[21] DEDAW Article 9 reads as follows:

All appropriate measures shall be taken to ensure to girls and women, married or unmarried, equal rights with men in education at all levels, and in particular:

---

[13] CESCR General Comment 13 para 6. See also CESCR 'General Comment 16' (2005) UN Doc E/C.12/2005/5 para 30; UNCHR, 'Preliminary Report of the Special Rapporteur on the right to Education, Ms Katarina Tomaševski' (1999) UN Doc E/CN.4/1999/49. See also K Tomaševski, *Human Rights Obligations in Education* (2005).

[14] See also UNGA, 'UN Decade for Human Rights Education and Midterm Review of the Office of the High Commissioner for Human Rights' (2000) UN Doc A/55/360.

[15] UNCHR, 'Report submitted by the Special Rapporteur on the Right to Education, Mr M. Villalobos: Girls' Right to Education' (2006) UN Doc E/CN.4/2006/45.

[16] See Beijing Declaration and Platform for Action (1995) Strategic Objectives B ('Education and Training of Women') and L ('The Girl Child').

[17] UNESCO, 'Dakar Framework for Action' (2000); UNESCO, 'Education for All Monitoring Reports', especially UNESCO, 'The Leap to Equality' (2003). See also UNESCO, 'World Declaration on Education for All' (1990). See also <http://www.right-to-education.org/> accessed 31 December 2010.

[18] UN Millennium Development Declaration (2000) Goal 2 ('Achieve Universal Primary Education') has as one of its targets: 'Ensure that, by 2015, children everywhere, girls and boys alike, will be able to complete a full course of primary schooling'.

[19] CO Cambodia, CEDAW/C/KHM/CO/3 (2006) para 26; CO Vietnam, CEDAW/C/VNM/CO/6 (2007) para 21; CO Sweden, CEDAW/C/SWE/CO/7 (2008) para 43; CO The United Kingdom, CEDAW/C/UK/CO/6 (2008) para 298; CO Cameroon, CEDAW/C/CMR/CO/3 (2009) para 53.

[20] LA Rehof, *Guide to the UN Convention on the Elimination of all Forms of Discrimination against Women* (1993) 112.   [21] Ibid.

(*a*) Equal conditions of access to, and study in, educational institutions of all types, including universities and vocational, technical and professional schools;

(*b*) The same choice of curricula, the same examinations, teaching staff with qualifications of the same standard, and school premises and equipment of the same quality, whether the institutions are co-educational or not;

(*c*) Equal opportunities to benefit from scholarships and other study grants;

(*d*) Equal opportunities for access to programmes of continuing education, including adult literacy programmes;

(*e*) Access to educational information to help in ensuring the health and well-being of families.

The final Article 10 reflects much of the above. Three new provisions were added. These include 10(c) on the elimination of stereotyped concepts of roles for men and women; 10(f) on the reduction of female student drop-out rates and authorizing programmes to ensure that those who have left school early re-enter; and 10(g) on the same opportunities to participate in sports and physical education. One stylistic difference is that in the final Article 10 the phrases 'equal rights' and 'on a basis of equality' are only used in the chapeau to the article and in Article 10(a); the rest of the article uses the 'same' whereas in DEDAW 'equal' and the 'same' are used interchangeably throughout the article. There is no difference in meaning; the central objective of the article and, indeed, the whole Convention, is that it requires States parties to eliminate all discrimination against women and to ensure that women are entitled to the same (equal) conditions in accessing all types of education with teachers and materials of equal quality.

There were some changes to DEDAW provisions, notably the deletion, at the suggestion of the United Kingdom (opposed by Indonesia), of the phrase 'married or unmarried' in the chapeau to DEDAW Article 9.

I. Article 10(a)

Article 10(a) of the Convention on accessing 'educational establishments of all categories' was amended to include the explicit requirement that *all* types of education be available 'in rural as well as in urban areas'. Preschool institutions were also added.[22] Belgium added 'career guidance'.[23] The International Labour Organization observer noted that vocational education should not be separated from vocational training provided for in Article 11 on employment and that this phrase should be added to article 10(a), which it was.[24] Rehof observes that the article was accorded 'considerable latitude in its drafting'.[25]

II. Article 10(b)

Japan suggested that Article 10(b) on equal access to the same curricula and examinations be replaced by 'equal access to the same curricula and examinations of the same or *equivalent* standard'. While 'equivalent' is used in Article 2(a) of the UNESCO Convention, the United Kingdom's proposed use of the word 'same' was preferred and accepted.[26] At the suggestion of Morocco and New Zealand the words 'whether the institutions are co-educational or not' were deleted.

A suggestion made by India, that a further paragraph be inserted into paragraph (b), making provision for special educational institutions and scholarships to bridge the gap

---

[22] Ibid 113–14.   [23] Ibid 114–15.   [24] Ibid 114–15. See also the discussion in ch on art 11.
[25] Ibid 112.   [26] Ibid 116.

between boys' and girls' education, was said to be best considered in a discussion under Article 4 on temporary special measures.[27] India raised this issue again in the discussion of lowering of the female drop-out rates by using temporary special measures in paragraph (f), and again it was said to be better suited to Article 4.[28]

III. Article 10(c)

This paragraph was added at the suggestion of Belgium which called for the 'speedy achievement of co-education'. The Commission on the Status of Women (CSW) adopted the paragraph and added a reference to the elimination of gender stereotypes.[29] The debate that followed included Hungary noting that the provision was already reflected in Article 5. There was also some discussion about whether the aim of co-education was to eliminate stereotyping, with the United States, supported by the UNESCO observer, querying whether co-education was the only means of eliminating gender stereotyping.[30] Rehof notes: 'The aim of the article was "the speedy achievement of co-education". The secondary point of the provision ("stereotyped concepts") at this stage became the main point in the final version.'[31] The draft suggested by Iran is closest to the final version.[32]

IV. Article 10(f)

In addition to seeking to reduce drop-out rates, States, led by Senegal, were keen to provide remedial measures to facilitate a return to education for women and girls who had been forced by circumstance to leave prematurely, hence the addition of 'programmes for girls who have left school too early'.[33] The provision is unique in being the only one in the Convention that expressly mentions girls.[34]

V. Article 10(g)

This is a new provision, there being no mention of sport in DEDAW. A suggestion by Belgium that States also provide 'psycho-sexual education' was resisted. States including Argentina, France, and the USSR suggested that to ensure as wide a ratification of the Convention as possible, provisions that were 'overtly explicit' should be avoided. The phrase was duly dropped and the draft submitted by Cuba stating 'the same right to participate actively in sports and physical education' became the final version.[35]

VI. Article 10(h)

Many states and organizations participated in the discussion on this final paragraph.[36] The Philippines noted that no existing international instrument included a reference to education in family planning.[37] The Swedish view was that the Convention should not 'make a specific link between women and family planning education since this should be

---

[27] Ibid.   [28] Ibid 116, 119.
[29] Ibid 116. See also Convention art 5 and the discussion in ch on art 5.
[30] Ibid 117. The debate continued, 118.   [31] Ibid 117.   [32] Ibid 118.
[33] Ibid 119. See also ibid 120.
[34] GR 28 notes that girls are included in the Convention's entire coverage 'since girls are within the larger community of women and are more vulnerable to discrimination in such areas as access to basic education' para 21. cf Protocol on the Rights of Women in Africa art 1(k) explicitly defining women as including girls.
[35] Rehof (n 20 above) 120.   [36] See also the discussion in the ch on art 12.
[37] Rehof (n 20 above) 120.

seen as a shared responsibility' and not solely the responsibility of women.[38] The UNESCO representative participating as an observer, focused on the education content suggesting that it included the provision of education and information on 'family planning, childcare education of pre-school age children and community development'.[39] The observer from the International Planned Parenthood Federation, supported by Denmark, proposed including 'advice and services'.[40] However, after an objection from Colombia noting that the word services applied to the right of couples to decide on the number and spacing of their children, the word 'services' was deleted and replaced by access to 'information and advice', thus changing the language of DEDAW Article 9(e).[41]

Finally, the same seven States that convened a working group on what eventually became Article 14, suggested that the rights of rural women to receive family planning education and services be included. This suggestion is now included in article 14(2)(b).[42]

C. Issues of Interpretation

States Parties shall take all appropriate measures to eliminate discrimination against women in order to ensure to them equal rights with men in the field of education and in particular to ensure, on a basis of equality of men and women:

While the Committee has not adopted a general recommendation on Article 10, State party obligations under this provision can be discerned through an examination of the Committee's General Recommendation 28.[43] Article 10 imposes both negative and positive obligations on the State. States parties are required to eliminate all discrimination against women in accessing education and also to take steps to facilitate the realization of the right to education.[44] Elements of Article 10 focus on access and equal opportunities for girls and women (both negative and positive obligations), and other elements point at the necessity of changing the content of educational materials and curricula so they no longer form an obstacle to equal opportunities for women or continue to reinforce gender stereotypes. The latter elements point to a positive obligation of States parties to bring about fundamental changes in educational materials and curricula.

I. Taking All Appropriate Measures

The Committee has, in its interpretation of 'all appropriate measures', taken a holistic approach. It has given each State party latitude in devising polices that will be appropriate for its particular circumstances and that can eradicate discrimination impeding women's enjoyment of their rights. Each State party must be able to justify 'the appropriateness of the means...chosen' and to demonstrate 'whether it will achieve the intended effect and result.'[45] In its consideration of Article 10, the Committee regularly urges States parties:

To take measures to eliminate traditional attitudes which perpetuate discrimination and non-compliance with the provisions of article 10 of the Convention. It recommends that the State party take measures to ensure equal access for girls and women to all levels of education and to ensure the retention of girls in school, including through temporary special measures in accordance with article 4, paragraph 1, of the Convention and the Committee's general recommenda-

---

[38] Ibid.   [39] Ibid 121.   [40] Ibid.   [41] Ibid.
[42] See also the discussion in ch on art 14.   [43] GR 28 para 6.   [44] Burrows (n 2 above) 437.
[45] GR 28 para 23. See further section E of this ch on State obligations.

tion 25. The Committee calls on the State party to improve the literacy level of girls and women through the adoption of comprehensive programmes of formal and non-formal education, adult education and training, and the allocation of adequate financial resources.[46]

II. Equality

The requirement in Article 10 that education be enjoyed 'on a basis of equality between men and women' reiterates the principle enunciated in the preambles to the UDHR and the convention that men and women are equal in dignity and rights. Article 10 requires the State party to make the 'same' provision for the education of men and women.[47] 'Same' here goes beyond a formal understanding of equality. The 'same' in Article 10 is not about equivalence, or about treating 'likes alike' or indeed only about passing laws, although that is clearly important. Rather, the Convention requires States parties to recognize that only a substantive understanding, and implementation, of equality policies will suffice.[48] By also requiring measures that aim for structural change of the educational system and the content of educational materials to abolish gender stereotyping, the Committee calls for transformative equality as well. The use of the peremptory 'shall take' in Article 10 makes clear that the State party is required to take as comprehensive an approach as possible to the guarantee of discrimination-free access to education.[49]

1. *Article 10(a)*

The Convention adopts a life cycle model of education progressing from preschool to adulthood. Unlike the UDHR, ICESCR, and CRC, which specify that only primary education is compulsory and should be provided free of charge, the Committee does not make this distinction, seeing all levels and aspects of education as equally important. Discrimination against girls in access to education often starts at a very young age. Learning stereotyped gender roles at the preschool stage can impact on the child's educational experiences in later years.

The Committee constructs the States parties' obligation to provide education for all in its widest terms, noting concern, for example, about 'inadequate educational and rehabilitative programmes for women prisoners'.[50] The Committee has also highlighted the impact of wars, including civil conflict, on the ability of children in general and girls in particular to access education.[51] Moreover, the Committee has identified the access

---

[46] CO Burundi, CEDAW/C/BDI/CO/4 (2008) para 32. See also CO Angola, A/59/38, 31st Session (2004) para 159; CO India, CEDAW/C/IND/CO/3 (2007) paras 33, 34, 35, and 49; CO Jordan, CEDAW/C/JOR/CO/4 (2007) para 30; CO Tajikistan, CEDAW/C/TJK/CO/3 (2007) para 28; CO Serbia, CEDAW/C/SCG/CO/1 (2007) para 30; CO Switzerland, CEDAW/C /CHE/CO/3 (2009) para 36; CO Malawi, CEDAW/C/MWI/CO/6 (2010) para 31; CO Mauritania, CEDAW/C/MRT/CO/1/(2007) para 25.

[47] Art 10(a), (b), (d), (e), and (g). See further section D below on Equality.

[48] GR 25 para 8; GR 28 para 24; Montréal Principles on Women's Economic, Social and Cultural Rights (2004) *Human Rights Quarterly* 760 para 9. See also CESCR, 'General Comment 16' (2005) UN Doc E/C.12/2005/4 paras 7, 8, and 14; S Fredman, 'Providing Equality: Substantive Equality and the Positive Duty to Provide' (2005) 21 *South African J on Human Rights* 163, 165–6.

[49] GR 28 para 21.

[50] CO The United Kingdom, CEDAW/C/UK/CO/6 in A/63/38, 41st Session (2008) para 266. See also CO Germany, CEDAW/C/DEU/CO/6 (2009) para 58.

[51] CO Sierra Leone, CEDAW/C/SLE/CO/5 (2007) para 30; CO Colombia, CEDAW/C/COL/CO/6 (2007) para 30; CO Liberia, CEDAW/C/LBR/CO/6 (2009); Special Rapporteur on the Right to Education (n 15 above) paras 114–20.

difficulties encountered by other groups including migrant and other minority women and 'girls living on the streets'.[52]

Apart from Article 14, Article 10(a) is the only provision in the Convention that expressly refers to rural women.[53] The Committee has noted that rural women, who may include indigenous women and women of different castes or ethnic groups, suffer from higher rates of illiteracy. Concluding one State party report, it expressed concern 'that only 0.2 per cent of women farmers have formal vocational training in agriculture and only 0.3 per cent a polytechnic or university degree in this field'.[54]

The same 'access to studies' requires States parties to remove discriminatory policies, legal, physical, socio-economic, or cultural barriers that impede women and girls from accessing education.[55] Furthermore, the Committee has noted that a violation of the right to equal access to education involves the provision of poor quality or inadequate education as well as the denial of education.[56]

While the Committee praises States parties for 'the high enrolment rates of girls and women at all levels of education',[57] it is clear that a substantial discrepancy remains in participation rates between male and female students at the secondary and higher levels as well as in access to vocational training.[58] This has led the Committee to express concern about 'the lower number of female students at the Ph D level, as well as in competitive research institutions'.[59]

---

[52] CO Egypt, CEDAW/C/EGY/CO/7 (2010) para 31. See also CO Lao People's Democratic Republic, CEDAW/C//LAO/CO/1–5 (2005) para 23; CO Cambodia, CEDAW/C/KHM/CO/3 (2006) para 26; CO Serbia, CEDAW/C/SCG/CO/1 (2007) paras 29–30; CO India, CEDAW/C/IND/CO/3 (2007) paras 32–3; CO Germany, CEDAW/C/DEU/CO/6 (2009) para 34; CO Vietnam, CEDAW/C/VNM/CO/6 (2007) para 21; CO Saudi Arabia, CEDAW/C/SAU/CO/2 (2008) paras 29–30; CO Luxembourg, CEDAW/C/LUX/CO/5 (2008) paras 25–6.

[53] See also art 14(2)(d) of the Convention and the discussion in ch on art 14.

[54] CO Portugal, CEDAW/C/PRT/CO/7 (2008) para 48. See also CO Bhutan, A/59/38, 30th Session (2004) paras 117–18; CO Argentina, A/59/38, 31st Session (2004) para 376; CO Nigeria, A/59/38, 30th Session (2004) para 304; CO Nepal, A/59/38, 30th Session (2004) para 204; CO Ireland, A/60/38, 33rd Session (2005) para 392; CO Malawi, CEDAW/C/MWI/CO/5 (2006) para 27; CO Fiji, CEDAW/C/FJI/CO/4 (2010) para 29; CO Albania, CEDAW/C/ALB/CO/3 (2010) paras 30–1.

[55] CO Vanuatu, CEDAW/C/VUT/CO/3 (2007) paras 30–1; CO Malawi, CEDAW/C/MWI/CO/5 (2006) paras 27–8; CO Saudi Arabia, CEDAW/C/SAU/CO/2 (2008) para 29; CO Guinea-Bissau, CEDAW/C/GNB/CO/6 (2009) paras 33–4. The CESCR divides access into three categories: physical, economic, and non-discrimination. CESCR, 'General Comment 13' (1999) UN Doc E/C.12/1999/10 para 6(a).

[56] S Pimentel, 'Education and Legal Literacy' in HB Schöpp-Schilling and C Flinterman (eds), *The Circle of Empowerment*: Twenty Five Years of the UN Committee on the Elimination of Discrimination against Women (2007) 90, 95.

[57] CO Kuwait, CEDAW/C/KWT/CO/2 (2004) para 59. See also CO Algeria, CEDAW/C/DZA/CO/2 (2005) para 14; CO Samoa, CEDAW/C/WSM/CO/1–3 (2005) para 17.

[58] CO The Netherlands, CEDAW/C/NLD/CO/5 (2010) para 34; UN Millennium Development Goal Report (2009) 15–16.

[59] CO Cyprus, CEDAW/C/CYP/CO/5 (2006) para 23. See also CO Armenia, CEDAW/C/ARM/CO/4/Rev.1 (2009) paras 30–1; CO New Zealand, A/58/38, 29th Session (2003) paras 409–10; CO Nepal, A/59/38, 30th Session (2004) para 204; CO Albania, CEDAW/C/ALB/CO/3 (2010) para 30; CO Rwanda, CEDAW/C/RWA/CO/6 (2009) para 31; CO Angola, A/59/38, 31st Session (2004) para 158; CO Gambia, CEDAW/C/GMB/CO/1–3 (2005) para 37; CO Turkey, CEDAW/C/TUR/CO/6 (2010) para 30; CO Kenya, CEDAW/C/KEN/CO/6 (2007) para 33; CO Vanuatu, CEDAW/C/VUT/CO/3 (2007) para 30; CO Zambia, A/57/38, 27th Session (2002) para 247; CO Egypt, CEDAW/C/EGY/CO/7 (2010) para 31. See also UN Millennium Development Goal Report (2009) 16 and 17.

2. *Article 10(b)*

Both the CEDAW Committee and the Special Rapporteur on Education have noted that quality education is a prerequisite of equality.[60] The Committee has expressed concern about the impact of poor educational infrastructure on women and girls:

reflected in the low budgetary allocation; the lack of, or insufficient number of, schools and teachers; and the poor quality of education (resulting in) a high rate of illiteracy among girls and women, their low enrolment rates in primary, secondary, vocational and higher education, in both urban and rural areas, and in their high drop-out rates.[61]

Even where education of girls is separate from that of boys, curricula, facilities, and teachers are to be of the same quality and to be free from discrimination. The Committee engages States parties about curricula content:

The report indicates that curricula for girls and boys are at the point of being standardized between the sexes from kindergarten through secondary school levels. Please provide further information on this standardization, and its content at the different levels of schooling. Please elaborate in particular whether any measures are being taken to eliminate stereotypical attitudes about the roles and responsibilities of women and men in textbooks, curricula and teacher training, to encourage girls to participate in non-traditional educational, vocational, or professional streams, and to open to women and girls all areas of study in the scientific and technical areas.[62]

Similarly, rural children and those who are sometimes placed in separate schools, including disabled children, are not to be disadvantaged by poor or inadequate facilities and education.[63] Moreover, the Committee has said that there should not be discrimination in the provision of equal quality education dependent on other grounds including minority or other status.[64]

Article 10(b) also requires that there be no discrimination against women in entering the teaching profession, because their presence in educational institutions plays an important symbolic and mentoring role in challenging gender stereotypes about women's work and abilities and provides employment.[65] The Committee has expressed concern 'at the low number of women in academia, as professors, senior lecturers and researchers,

[60] CO Nepal, A/59/38, 30th Session (2004) para 362; CO Haiti, CEDAW/C/HTI/CO/7 (2009) para 23; CO Nigeria, A/59/38, 30th Session (2004) para 303; UNCHR, 'Report submitted by the Special Rapporteur on the Right to Education, Mr M. Villalobos: The Right to Education' (2005) UN Doc E/CN.4/2005/50 paras 107–8.

[61] CO Angola, A/59/38, 31st Session (2004) para 158. See also CO Liberia, CEDAW/C/LBR/CO/6 (2009) para 32; CO Tajikistan, CEDAW/C/TJK/CO/3 (2007) para 27.

[62] List of questions Initial and Second Report Saudi Arabia, CEDAW/C/SAU/Q/2/Add.1 (2007) 19–20. See also CO Malaysia, CEDAW/C/MYS/CO/2 (2006) para 15; CO Estonia, CEDAW/C/EST/CO/4 (2007) para 12; CO Haiti, CEDAW/C/HTI/CO/7(2009) paras 20–1. See also CO Jamaica, CEDAW/C/JAM/CO/5 (2006) para 31; CO Moldova, CEDAW/C/MDA/CO/3 (2006) para 19; CO India, CEDAW/C/IND/CO/3 (2007) paras 34–5; CO Jordan, CEDAW/C/JOR/CO/4 (2007) para 19; CO Niger, CEDAW/C/NER/CO/2 (2007) para 30.

[63] CO Vanuatu, CEDAW/C/VUT/CO/3 (2007) para 30; CO Fiji, CEDAW/C/FJI/CO/4 (2010) para 29.

[64] CO Paraguay, A/60/38, 32nd Session (2005) paras 291–2; CO Nepal, A/59/38, 30th Session (2004) para 204; CO Turkey, A/60/38, 32nd Session (2005) paras 371–2; CO Israel, CEDAW/C/ISR/CO/3 (2005) para 35; CO Canada, A/58/38, 28th Session (2003) para 363; CO India, CEDAW/C/IND/CO/3 (2007) para 32.

[65] CO Brazil, A/58/38, 29th Session (2003) paras 122–3; CO Fiji, CEDAW/C/FJI/CO/4 (2010) para 29; CO Jamaica, CEDAW/C/JAM/CO/5 (2006) para 31; CO Mali, CEDAW/C/MLI/CO/5 (2006) para 27; CO Norway, CEDAW/C/NOR/CO/7 (2007) para 17; Pimentel (n 56 above) 93. See also 'Special Rapporteur on the Right to Education' (2005) (n 60 above) paras 107–8.

and at the decision-making levels in the area of education'.[66] It has recommended that 'the image of teachers be improved through further salary increases, the media and other public forums. The Committee also recommends that additional training be provided to teachers to update their knowledge and teaching methods in the current context of gender equality'.[67]

Research undertaken in monitoring the UNESCO EFA goals has identified high teacher attrition rates, especially in rural areas, as one of the reasons for lower participation levels of girls in education.[68] States parties are obliged to address these situational inequalities by providing adequate money, housing, and other infrastructure services to facilitate teacher retention. Moreover, adequate health care is required, including anti-retroviral drugs to address the high AIDS-related death rates of teachers, particularly women educators who are disproportionately impacted.

Discriminatory policies impacting on women's ability to teach have included the expulsion of female teaching students from colleges due to pregnancy. The Convention was cited in a Zimbabwean case challenging the decision of a private Christian teacher training college which expelled a married woman student who had fallen pregnant during her course in breach of the rules. Citing the Convention, her counsel noted, and the court found, that the rule requiring pregnant students to leave impacted solely on women and was a breach of the right to education, and discriminatory on grounds of sex and gender.[69]

Article 10 of the Convention was cited in a case on stereotyping from Hong Kong, *Equal Opportunities Commission v Director of Education*.[70] The case was brought by the Equal Opportunities Commission and challenged the assignment of boys and girls to secondary schools. Although the schools were all public, some were considered to be particularly good and were thus over-subscribed. In making assignments, the authorities decided to try to 'balance out' the sexes by increasing the allocation of spaces for boys. This practice was based on the argument that girls, who did better on the secondary school entrance examination which formed the basis of the assignment, had an inherent advantage because 'girls matured faster than boys,' and the boys should not be prejudiced by their delayed maturity in accessing the better schools. The Equal Opportunities Commission challenged this practice, based on gender stereotyping, as constituting discrimination against girls. The court found for the Commission and cited Convention Articles 2(a)–(d), 4(1), and 10 in this regard.[71] It found that the discrimination was directly imputable to the gender stereotyping that formed the basis of the policy.

3. *Article 10(c)*

This provision builds on and reinforces Article 10(b). The *travaux préparatoires* to Article 10 indicate that the common aim of States was, in the words of the Kenyan

---

[66] CO Armenia, CEDAW/C/ARM/CO/4/Rev.1 (2009) para 30. See also CO The Netherlands, CEDAW/C/NLD/CO/3 (2010) para 35; CO Rwanda, CEDAW/C/RWA/CO/6 (2009) para 31; CO Japan, CEDAW/C/JPN/CO/6 (2009) para 43; CO Jordan, CEDAW/C/JOR/CO/4 (2007) paras 29–30.

[67] CO Tajikistan, CEDAW/C/TJK/CO/3 (2007) para 28; CO Nepal, CEDAW/C/NPL/CO/3 (2004) paras 204–5; CO Norway, CEDAW/C/NOR/CO/7 (2007) para 18.

[68] UNESCO, 'Teacher Attrition Rates in Sub-Saharan Africa' (2010) 11 et seq.

[69] *Mandizvidza v Chaduka NO, Morgenster College and the Minister of Higher Education* 1999 (2) ZLR 375 (HC). See also CO Belize, CEDAW/C/BLZ/CO/4 (2007) para 23.

[70] *Equal Opportunities Commission v Director of Education* HCLA 1555/2000 reported in 2001 2 HKLRD 690.

[71] Ibid paras 88 ff (see especially paras 109–10).

delegation, 'to eliminate any stereotyped concept of masculine and feminine roles at all levels and in all forms of education'.[72] To this end, teaching materials are to be created that are free of gender stereotyping.[73] Similarly, teaching methods are to be adapted to challenge all forms of discrimination including 'forms that are not explicitly mentioned in the Convention or that are emerging'.[74]

The Committee presses States parties about the impact of stereotyped education, including curricula, on women's life chances and choices including in employment.[75] Instruction that promotes gender stereotypes by providing 'female'-focused subjects for girls is not permitted.[76] The Committee has commented on the 'low participation of girls and women in secondary and tertiary education, including in technology and science-related courses', which may also point to gender-based discrimination in 'tracking' girls into certain study areas.[77] The Committee also engages States parties about 'traditional attitudes that constitute obstacles to girls' education'.[78] It has expressed concern at 'the practice of cross-timetabling, or conflicting class schedules that effectively prevent girls from pursuing courses of study traditionally offered to boys'.[79] The Committee urges States parties to take a comprehensive and holistic approach to address gender stereotyping, encouraging them 'to use all forms of education—formal and informal—including the socialization process through parenting and community social interaction, to eradicate negative stereotypes, attitudes and practices'.[80]

---

[72] Rehof (n 28 above) 117. See also art 5; R Holtmaat, *Towards Different Law and Public Policy: the Significance of article 5a CEDAW for the Elimination of Structural Gender Discrimination* (2004); E Sepper, 'Confronting the "Sacred and Unchangeable": The Obligation to Modify Cultural Patterns under the Women's Discrimination Treaty' (2008) 30 *University of Pennsylvania J Intl L* 585, 594.

[73] Special Rapporteur on the Right to Education (n 15 above) para 104 noting how 'Women teachers' and girls' low expectations are reinforced by textbooks, curricula and assessment material, in which no female figures appear'. See also paras 18–31 and especially paras 19, 21, 24, 25 (on the Convention and the Committee) and 28.

[74] GR 28 para 15.

[75] CO Bosnia-Herzegovina, CEDAW/C/BIH/CO/3 (2006) para 10; CO Republic of Korea, CEDAW/C/KOR/CO/6 (2007) para 26; CO Serbia, CEDAW/C/SCG/CO/1 (2007) para 19; CO Maldives, CEDAW/C/MDV/CO/3 (2007) para 18; CO Pakistan, CEDAW/C/PAK/CO/3 (2007) paras 36–7; CO France, CEDAW/C/FRA/CO/6 (2008) paras 18–19; CO Australia, CEDAW/C/AUS/CO/7 (2010) paras 36–7; CO Turkey, CEDAW/C/TUR/CO/6 (2010) paras 30–1; CO Bolivia, CEDAW/C/BOL/CO/4 (2008) para 20.

[76] CO Bahrain, CEDAW/C/BHR/CO/2 (2008) paras 32–3; CO Turkey, CEDAW/C/TUR/CO/6 (2010) para 30; CO France, CEDAW/C/FRA/CO/6 (2008) para 18; CO Azerbaijan, CEDAW/C/AZE/CO/4 (2009) para 29; CO Australia, CEDAW/C/AUS/CO/7 (2010) paras 36–7; CO Brazil, A/58/38, 29th Session (2003) para 122.

[77] CO Bhutan, A/59/38, 30th Session (2004) para 113. See also CO Croatia, CEDAW/C/CRO/CO/2–3 (2005) para 33; CO Israel, CEDAW/C/ISR/CO/3 (2005) paras 35–6; CO St Lucia, CEDAW/C/LCA/CO/6 (2006) para 27; CO Bosnia-Herzegovina, CEDAW/C/BIH/CO/3 (2006) para 31; CO Slovakia, CEDAW/C/SVK/CO/4 (2008) para 18; CO Luxembourg, CEDAW/C/LUX/CO/5 (2008) paras 15 and 25; CO Switzerland, CEDAW/CHE/CO/3 (2009) para 35.

[78] CO Nigeria, CEDAW, A/59/38, 30th Session (2004) para 304; CO Benin, CEDAW/C/BEN/CO/1–3 (2005) para 30; CO St Lucia, CEDAW/C/LCA/CO/6 (2006) para 28; CO Bhutan, CEDAW/C/BTN/CO/7 (2009) para 25; CO Guinea-Bissau, CEDAW/C/GNB/CO/6 (2009) paras 33–4; CO Vanuatu, CEDAW/C/VUT/CO/3 (2007) para 31; CO Liberia, CEDAW CEDAW/C/LBR/CO/6 (2009) para 33; CO Bolivia; CEDAW/C/BOL/CO/4 (2008) para 20; Combined 3rd, 4th and 5th Periodic Report Paraguay, CEDAW/C/PAR/3–4 (2005) 263; CO Botswana, CEDAW/C/BOT/CO/3 (2010) para 31.

[79] CO Jamaica, CEDAW/C/JAM/CO/5 (2006) para 31.

[80] CO Laos, CEDAW/C/LAO/CO/7 (2009) para 22; See also CO Lebanon, CEDAW/C/LBN/CO/3 (2008) para 25; CO Haiti, CEDAW/C/HTI/CO/7 (2009) para 21; CO Jordan, CEDAW/C/JOR/CO/4 (2007) para 20.

a) Encouraging Coeducation

Encouraging coeducation does not require States parties to make it compulsory, for as noted by the United States during the drafting of the Convention 'it is not the only way of eliminating the stereotyped image of masculine and female roles'.[81] Indeed, coeducation may not be appropriate; in some regions separate schools are the norm, and seeking to overturn that norm may lead to girls no longer being allowed to go to school.[82]

If coeducation is not in place, the State party must guarantee equality by ensuring that quality education—access to the same curricula and teachers trained to the same standard—is respected in separate schools.[83] In States parties which run single-sex institutions, equal numbers of qualified female and male teachers becomes imperative.[84] The Committee has also identified *de facto* segregation as problematic, not least because of its 'consequences for women's professional opportunities, and the high rate of illiteracy among elderly women and, in particular, among Roma women and girls'.[85]

4. Article 10(d)

If poverty or a lack of means is one of the chief impediments to the education of girls and women, then providing scholarships and other forms of assistance becomes crucial.[86] The Committee sees the provision of scholarships as essential to the acceleration of women's participation in education and to the realization of equality between men and women. It has praised those States parties that have set up scholarship schemes for girls.[87] It praised one State party for eliminating difficulties for women in its Student Loan Scheme.[88] The Committee has highlighted that rural girls (and their parents) particularly need financial assistance and other incentives to encourage them to remain in school.[89] The Committee has also urged States parties to 'ensure that women have equal access with men to governmental loans and scholarships for pursuing higher education abroad'.[90]

The Special Rapporteur on Education has noted that although the abolition of fees in many States has led to an increase in the number of girls attending school, the quality of education has declined sharply because the necessary additional teaching staff have not been recruited.[91] This calls for the provision of grants and scholarships to facilitate women's access to teacher training colleges.

---

[81] Rehof (n 20 above) 117.

[82] Combined Initial and Second Report Saudi Arabia, CEDAW/C/SAU/2 (2008) 30. See also CESCR GR 13 para 6(c): 'Acceptability' provides that 'the form and substance' of education must be 'relevant, culturally appropriate and of good quality'. (1999) UN Doc E/C.12/1999/10 para 6(c).

[83] CO Mauritius, CEDAW/C/MAR/CO/5 (2006) paras 24–5.   [84] Rehof (n 20 above) 116

[85] CO Bosnia-Herzogovina, CEDAW/C/BIH/CO/3 (2006) para 24. See also CO Egypt, CEDAW/C/EGY/CO/7 (2010) para 32.

[86] CO Fiji, A/57/38, 26th Session (2002) paras 60–1.

[87] CO Cameroon, CEDAW/C/CMR/CO/3 (2009) para 22; CO Turkey, CEDAW/C/TUR/CO/6 (2010) para 30; CO Ethiopia, A/59/38, 30th Session (2004) para 240; CO Zambia, A/57/38, 27th Session (2002) para 229.

[88] CO New Zealand, A/58/38, 29th Session (2003) para 409. See also CO Ethiopia, CEDAW/C/ETH/CO/1 (2004) para 240.

[89] CO Vanuatu, CEDAW/C/VUT/CO/3 (2007) para 31; CO Bhutan, CEDAW/C/BTN/CO/7 (2009) para 26; CO Haiti, CEDAW/C/HTI/CO/7 (2009) para 31. Responses to the list of questions and issues, Saudi Arabia, CEDAW/C/SAU/Q/2/Add (2007) para 20 (p 19); CO Ecuador, CEDAW/C/ECU/CO/7 (2008) para 31.

[90] CO Bhutan, CEDAW, A/59/38, 30th Session (2004) para 114. See also Responses to the list of issues and questions Saudi Arabia, CEDAW/C/SAU/Q/2/Add.1 (2007) para 23

[91] See Special Rapporteur on the Right to Education (2005) (n 60 above) paras 29–30.

The Committee has pressed States parties about the existence of additional charges and expenses such as purchasing school uniforms, bench levies, and other ancillary costs which are likely to impact disproportionately on girls' access to education, especially if the family has limited resources.[92] With this in mind, the Committee commended a State party for the steps taken:

in the area of education with the assistance of the international community, donor organizations and non-governmental organizations, such as school feeding programmes and the provision of microloans to parents who send their girls to schools . . . and the 2006 resolution . . . which established a 50 per cent quota in granting scholarships.[93]

5. Article 10(e)

The *travaux préparatoires* indicate that in including this provision, States were keen to mitigate the difficulties and disadvantages faced by women who may have had to leave school early, or who may not have received any education at all.[94] The word 'functional' was included before 'literacy' at the behest of the UNESCO observer 'in order to cover programmes teaching reading and writing while imparting practical knowledge'.[95]

The Committee has expressed concern about the continuing discrepancies in literacy rates between men and women, such as 'the high rate of illiteracy, which in 2004 stood at 71 per cent for girls and women . . . which clearly demonstrates patterns of discrimination under article 10'.[96] It has also identified the particular problems faced by older rural, indigenous, and minority women.[97] The Committee has highlighted the importance of addressing the problem of illiteracy as a matter of urgency, including by using

---

[92] CO New Zealand, CEDAW/C/NLZ/CO/6 (2007) paras 32–3; CO Albania, CEDAW/C/ALB/CO/3 (2010) para 30; CO Fiji, CEDAW/FJI/CO/4 (2010) para 28. See Decision T-170/03 *Mora v Bogota District Education Secretary and Others* (28 February 2003) Colombian Constitutional Court, where the transport and opportunity costs to a mother on a low income of having to send her child to a school in a zone different from that in which they lived were held to impinge on the right to education, leading the Colombian Constitutional Court to order the authorities to assign her a school closer to her home. See also *Mohini Jain v State of Karnataka* (1992) 3 SCC 666, 1992 AIR 1858, India Supreme Court.

[93] CO Guinea-Bissau, CEDAW/C/GNB/CO/6 (2009) para 33. See also CO Barbados, CEDAW, A/57/38, Exceptional Session (2002) para 222; CO Zambia, A/57/38, 27th Session (2002) para 229; CO Mauritania, CEDAW/C/MRT/CO/1 (2007) para 36.

[94] See Rehof (n 20 above) 118. SIDA, *Lifelong learning in the South-Critical Issues and Opportunities for Adult Education* (2004); Protocol on the Rights of Women in Africa art 12(2)(a) and (c).

[95] Rehof (n 20 above) 118. See also CESCR, 'General Comment 13' (1999) UN Doc E/C.12/1999/10 paras 15–16.

[96] CO Sierra Leone, CEDAW/C/SLE/CO/5 (2007) paras 30–1; CO Benin, CEDAW/C/BEN/CO/1–3 (2005) para 29; CO Mauritania, CEDAW/C/MRT/CO/1 (2007) para 35; CO Morocco, CEDAW/C/MAW/CO/4 (2008) para 26; CO Saudi Arabia, CEDAW/C/SAU/CO/2 (2008) para 29.

[97] GR 27 para 19; CO Malawi, CEDAW/C/MWI/CO/5 (2006) para 27; CO Turkey, CEDAW/C/TUR/CO/6 (2010) para 30; CO Australia, CEDAW/C/AUS/CO/7 (2010) para 41; CO Paraguay, A/60/38, 32nd Session (2005) para 291; CO El Salvador, A/58/38, 28th Session (2003) para 263; CO Equatorial Guinea, A/59/38, 31st Session (2004) para 193; CO Lao People's Democratic Republic, A/60/38, 32nd Session (2005) para 94; CO Morocco, A/58/38, 29th Session (2003) para 171; CO Yemen, A/57/38, Exceptional Session (2002) para 386; CO Peru, A/57/38, Exceptional Session (2002) para 490; CO Gambia, A/60/38, 33rd Session (2005) para 207; CO Zambia, A/57/38, 27th Session (2002) paras 246–7; CO Guatemala, CEDAW/C/GUA/CO/7 (2009) paras 27–8; CO Ecuador, CEDAW/C/ECU/CO/7 (2008) paras 30–1.

temporary special measures.[98] It has commended States parties which have put resources into addressing women's illiteracy.[99]

The Committee has noted that adult and functional literacy programmes may go beyond teaching basic numeracy and reading skills to incorporate gender and legal literacy which can have a transformative effect on women's lives.[100] Committee expert Silvia Pimentel contends:

> Legal literacy is a crucial tool that empowers women to get past all the 'doorkeepers' standing in their way, so that they can finally reach and move through the 'gate' of law. The CEDAW Convention and its Committee provide key concepts and tools for women, in any part of the world, to pass the 'doorkeepers' and go through the 'gate' to enjoy their rights.[101]

For this reason, the Committee has urged States parties to publicize the Committee's decisions on communications under the Optional Protocol.[102]

6. Article 10(f)

Premature departure from school, usually as a result of early marriage or pregnancy, affects girls and women in many States parties.[103] The Committee has, in General Recommendation 24 and in concluding observations, urged States parties to desist from expelling students because they are pregnant.[104] It has also urged States parties to provide opportunities for premature school leavers to complete their education, while commending those which have made provision for completion.[105] In its questioning of one State party, the Committee requested information on:

> measures taken or envisaged to promote an educational setting that eliminate all barriers that could impede the schooling of pregnant adolescents and young mothers, including physically

---

[98] CO Lao People's Democratic Republic, CEDAW/C/LAO/CO/7 (2009) para 33; CO Peru, A/57/38, Exceptional Session (2002) para 491; CO Yemen, CEDAW/C/YEM/CO/6 (2008) para 25; CO Nigeria, A/59/38, 30th Session (2004) para 304; CO Angola, A/59/38, 31st Session (2004) para 159.

[99] CO Samoa, A/60/38, 32nd Session (2005) para 45; CO Bangladesh, A/59/38, 31st Session (2004) para 233; CO Uganda, A/57/38, Exceptional Session (2002) para 128.

[100] CO Bolivia, CEDAW/C/BOL/CO/4 (2008) paras 17 and 32; CO Lebanon, CEDAW/C/LBN/CO/3 (2008) paras 15 and 25.

[101] Pimentel (n 56 above) 97.

[102] *AT v Hungary* CEDAW Communication 2/2003 (2005) CEDAW/C/32/D/2003 para 9(7). See also eg CO Russian Federation, CEDAW/C/USR/CO/7 (2010) para 15.

[103] CO Equatorial Guinea, A/59/38, 31st Session (2004) para 193; CO Liberia CEDAW/C/LBR/CO/6 (2009) para 32; CO Nepal, A/59/38, 30th Session (2004) para 204; CO Suriname, A/57/38, 27th Session (2002) paras 57–8; CO Zambia, A/57/38, 27th Session (2002) para 246; CO Benin, CEDAW/C/BEN/CO/1–3 (2005) para 30; CO Belize, CEDAW/C/BLZ/CO/4 (2007) paras 23, 24, and 27; CO Bhutan, CEDAW/C/BTN/CO/7 (2009) para 26.

[104] GR 24 para 28; CO Togo, CEDAW/C/TGO/CO/3 (2006) paras 24–5; CO Suriname, A/57/38, 27th Session (2002) para 57; CO Zambia, A/57/38, 27th Session (2002) para 246; CO Jamaica, CEDAW/C/JAM/CO/5 (2006) para 32; CO Malawi, CEDAW/C/MWI/CO/6 (2010) para 31; CO Kenya, CEDAW/C/KEN/CO/6 (2007) para 33; CO Cook Islands, CEDAW/C/COK/CO/1 (2007) para 30.

[105] CO Suriname, A/57/38, 27th Session (2002) paras 57–8; CO Congo, A/58/38, 28th Session (2003) para 171; CO Equatorial Guinea, A/59/38, 31st Session (2004) para 194; CO Cape Verde, CEDAW/C/CPV/CO/6 (2006) para 26; CO Rwanda, CEDAW/C/RWA/CO/6 (2009) para 31; CEDAW CO Fiji, CEDAW/C/FJI/CO/4 (2010) para 28; CO Panama, CEDAW/C/PAN/CO/7 (2010) paras 36–7. See also Pimentel (n 56 above) 97; UNICEF, 'State of the World's Children' (2004) 86. Special Rapporteur on the Right to Education (n 60 above) paras 71–9, 94, and 133.

accessible childcare facilities and to encourage those young mothers who are responsible for the care of their children to complete their schooling.[106]

The Committee has also identified early and forced marriage as problems and enjoined States parties to enact minimum ages for marriage and to ensure that they are the same for men and women.[107] The age specified, eighteen, is designed both to ensure physical maturity as a precursor to childbirth and also to try to keep girls in school for as long as possible. Research indicates that the rate of early marriage falls with increased girls' enrolment in secondary school.[108]

The Committee has addressed the issue of sexual harassment as a factor that sometimes leads to girls abandoning school prematurely. It has noted that 'the lack of trained and qualified teachers, especially female teachers, may increase girls' vulnerability to violence and abuse in schools'.[109] It has noted that rural girls are often targeted and sexually harassed on the way to school, thus impacting attendance and retention.[110]

A lack of toilets leads to absenteeism and premature departure from school. It affects girls disproportionately, particularly with the onset of menses.[111] Work, including home chores such as collecting firewood and getting water, may impact upon a girl's ability to access and stay in education.[112] Failure to take note of the implications of these work requirements in the design of education policy can constitute gender-based discrimination. The Committee has identified the high incidence of child labour as a barrier to education. It asked a State party to take steps to ensure that children, 'especially girls, have access to basic education … and the protection of minimum labour standards elaborated by the International Labour Organization'.[113] To offset the opportunity costs of attending school, States parties may be required to consider making monetary payments or grants available to girls and women hampered by survival pressures that often lead them to give

[106] List of Issues and Questions: Kyrgyzstan, CO CEDAW/C/KGZ/Q/3/Add.1 (2008) Pre-Session Working Group, 42nd Session, para 19. See also CO Belize, CEDAW/C/BLZ/CO/4 (2007) para 23; CO Liberia, CEDAW/C/LBR/CO/6 (2009) para 33; CO El Salvador, CEDAW/C/SLV/CO/7 (2008) para 30.

[107] GR 21 paras 36, 38, and 39. CO Cambodia,CEDAW/C/KHM/CO/3 (2006) para 26; CO Jamaica, CEDAW/C/JAM/CO/(2006) para 40; CO Jordan, CEDAW/C/JOR/CO/4 (2007) paras 35 and 36; CO Bolivia, CEDAW/C/BOL/CO/4 (2008) paras 44 and 45; CO Botswana, CEDAW/C/BOT/CO/3 (2010) paras 31 and 32. See also Art 16(2), ACRWC, Art 21(2), Protocol on the Rights of Women in Africa, Art 6(b); CESCR, 'General Comment 14' (2000) UN Doc E/C.12/2000/4 para 22; CCPR, 'General Comment 28' (2000) UN Doc CCPR/C/21/Rev.1/Add.10 para 23; Special Rapporteur on the Right on Education (n 1 above) paras 73–5 and 78.

[108] Millennium Project, *Taking Action: Achieving Gender Equality and Empowering Women*, Taskforce on Education and Gender Equality (2005) 36 ff. See in particular boxes at 40 and 49; K Watkins, *The OXFAM Education Report* (2000) 195–8; Beijing Declaration and Platform for Action (1995) Strategic Objective L4 paras 279–80. See also CO Bolivia, CEDAW/C/BOL/CO/4 (2008) para 44; CO Fiji, A/57/38, 26th Session (2002) paras 60–1.

[109] CO Guinea-Bissau, CEDAW/C/GNB/CO/6 (2009) paras 33–4. See also CO Lao People's Democratic Republic, CEDAW/C/LAO/CO/7 (2009) para 24; CO Haiti, CEDAW/C/HTI/CO/7 (2009) 23; Combined Third, Fourth and Fifth Reports: Paraguay, CEDAW/C/PAR/3–4 (2005) 263; CO Ecuador, CEDAW/C/ECU/CO/7 (2008) para 32; Protocol on the Rights of Women in Africa art 12(1)(c).

[110] Initial report of States Parties, South Africa, CEDAW/C/ZAF/1(1998) para 119; CO Timor-Leste, CEDAW/C/TLS/CO/1 (2009) para 35; CO Liberia, CEDAW/C/LBR/CO/6 (2009) paras 32–3.

[111] CO Yemen, CEDAW/C/YEM/CO/6 (2008) para 25; CESCR, 'Statement on the Right to Sanitation' (2010) UN Doc E/C.12/45/CRP.1 para 5.

[112] CO Mozambique, CEDAW/C/MOZ/CO/2 (2007) para 30; CO Myanmar, CEDAW/C/MMR/CO/3 (2008) para 34; CO Morocco, CEDAW/C/MAW/CO/4 (2008) paras 26–7; UNDP, 'Beyond Scarcity: Power, Poverty and the Global Water Crisis' (2006) 47.

[113] CO Guatemala, A/57/38, Exceptional Session (2002) paras 202–3. See also CO India, CEDAW/C/IND/CO/3 (2007) para 49.

up on formal education.[114] Finally, the Committee has identified a disproportionately high repetition and drop-out rate among rural, minority, and indigenous girls as being of concern.[115]

7. *Article 10(g)*

The Committee has not paid much attention to this provision. It has however, noted the impact of women's and girls' heavy workloads as barriers to their taking part in sport and physical activities. In light of the information provided in a State party report, that 'stereotypes limit substantially the participation of most poor girls in cultural, sport and other leisure activities' because the girls have to assist mothers in income-generating activities, the Committee requested that the State party 'provide detailed information on any strategies the Government may be contemplating to promote participation of girls especially from rural areas in cultural, sport and other leisure activities and on changing sex role stereotypes that limit such participation'.[116] The Committee has also taken an intersectional approach urging one State party to 'ensure that girls in prison are provided with a full programme of educational activities, including physical education'.[117]

8. *Article 10(h)*

This provision speaks to the importance of providing a base from which decisions about family size and other health related issues can be made.[118] General Recommendation 24 provides that there should not be discrimination in the provision of information on sexual health, education, and services for women and girls.[119] While Article 10(h) is drafted in gender-neutral terms, women bear the disproportionate burden of reproduction. This is recognized by the Committee in its General Recommendation 21:

Decisions to have children or not, while preferably made in consultation with spouse or partner, must not nevertheless be limited by spouse, parent, partner or Government. In order to make an informed decision about safe and reliable contraceptive measures, women must have information about contraceptive measures and their use, and guaranteed access to sex education and family planning services, as provided in article 10 (h) of the Convention.[120]

The Committee has read Article 10(h) with Article 10(f) on premature departure from school as a result of pregnancy. It has recommended that a State party 'ensure that sex education programmes are widely promoted and targeted at girls and boys, and include special attention to the prevention of early pregnancies'.[121]

---

[114] CO Albania, CEDAW/C/ALB/CO/3 (2010) para 30.

[115] CEDAW CO Uruguay, CEDAW/C/URY/CO/7; CO Spain, A/59/38, 31st Session (2004) paras 346–7; CO Israel, A/60/38, 33rd Session (2005) para 256.

[116] Pre-sessional working group, Haiti, CEDAW/C/HTI/Q7, 43rd Session (2008) para 26 on art 13. The Special Rapporteur on Education has in his report on the education of girls noted that while boys are given space to practise certain sports, 'girls are not provided with similar space'. Special Rapporteur on the Right to Education (n 60 above) para 104. See also para 150.

[117] CO Germany, CEDAW/C/DEU/CO/6 (2009) para 58.

[118] It must be read with arts 5(b), 12, 14 (2)(b), 16(1)(e), and 16(2). See also the discussion in ch on art 12.

[119] See also UNCHR, 'The Right to Education: Report submitted by the Special Rapporteur, Katarina Tomaševski' (2004) UN Doc E/CN.4/2004/45 para 36 citing art 10 (h); CRC, 'General Comment 3' (2004) UN Doc A/59/41.

[120] GR 21 para 22. See also CO Jamaica, CEDAW/C/JAM/CO/5 (2006) para 35.

[121] CO Timor-Leste, CEDAW/C/TLS/CO/1 (2009) para 38; CO Namibia, CEDAW/C/NAM/CO/3 (2007) para 22. See also Pimentel (n 56 above) 101.

Despite the acknowledged benefits of education in general, the provision of information on family planning, especially to school-aged children, is controversial.[122] Under socio-cultural and religious influences, some States parties are unwilling to include information on sex education or family planning within their educational curricula.[123] The first Special Rapporteur on Education, Katarina Tomasevki, noted that girls have paid the highest price in the political duels which determine the content of school curricula on human sexuality.[124] The Committee is unyielding and unequivocal in its call to States parties to provide information on health and reproductive matters in schools and to the general public.[125] In General Recommendation 24, the Committee notes that States parties have an obligation to ensure that sexual and reproductive health information is provided to both female and male adolescents 'by properly trained personnel in specially designed programmes that respect their rights to privacy and confidentiality'.[126] Furthermore, in General Recommendation 28, the Committee enjoins States parties to pay attention to the 'specific needs of (adolescent) girls by . . . carrying out programmes that are aimed at the prevention of HIV/AIDS, sexual exploitation and teenage pregnancy'.[127]

Article 10(h) has been the subject of a communication brought to the Committee by a Roma woman who had been sterilized without being given information about the nature of the procedure or the consequences. She had not given her consent prior to the operation being carried out.[128] She claimed a breach of Article 10(h).[129] The State party argued that having had three children previously, the author could be said to have the necessary information on reproductive issues. The Committee found in favour of the author noting, in part, that Article 10(h) had been breached by the failure of the health authorities to give proper counselling and information to the applicant before sterilizing her.[130]

D. Equality in Context

The principles of equality and non-discrimination are overarching. States parties are required to eliminate discrimination wherever it occurs and however caused, and to

---

[122] See eg *Gillick v West Norfolk and Wisbech Area Health Authority* (1985) 3 All ER 402. cf Complaint 45/2007 *International Centre for the Legal Protection of Human Rights (INTERIGHTS) v Croatia* (30 March 2009) European Committee of Social Rights paras 47, 52, and 59 setting out the criteria for the provision of sex education and information within the European context.

[123] Special Rapporteur on the Right to Education (n 119 above) paras 37 and 39.

[124] Special Rapporteur on the Right to Education (n 119 above) para 37.

[125] GR 28 para 21; CO Cape Verde, CEDAW/C/CPV/CO/6 (2006) para 26; CO Chile, CEDAW/C/CHI/CO/4 (2006) paras 17–18; CO Namibia, CEDAW/C/NAM/CO/3 (2007) para 23; CO Uruguay, CEDAW/C/URY/CO/7 (2008) para 39.

[126] GR 24 para 18; CRC, 'General Comment 3' (2004) UN Doc A/59/41 paras 6, 7, 9, 11, 15–18, 20, 23, and 38; CRC, 'General Comment 4' (2004) UN Doc A/59/41 paras 10, 16, 25–8, 30, 31, 39(b) and 40; Beijing Declaration and Platform for Action (1995) para 267.

[127] GR 28 para 21. See also GR 15; UNIFEM *Turning the Tide: CEDAW and the Gender Dimensions of the HIV Pandemic* (2001).

[128] *AT v Hungary* CEDAW Communication 4/2004 (2006) CEDAW/C/36/D/4/2004 para 3.3.

[129] Ibid paras 5.5 and 9.6. To support her argument the author invoked GR 21 para 22. The author also alleged breaches of arts 12 and 16(1)(e) read together with GR 19 and 24 as well as General Comment 28 of the Human Rights Committee; see CCPR, 'General Comment 28' (2000) UN Doc CCPR/C/21/Rev.1/Add.10; paras 3.2, 3.4, 3.5, and 3.6.

[130] *AT v Hungary* CEDAW Communication 4/2004 (2006) para CEDAW/C/36/D/4/2004 para 11.2.

take positive measures to ensure the realization of equality between men and women in education.[131]

I. Formal Equality

Read with Article 1, formal equality in Article 10 requires that the State party take the necessary steps to change the laws and policies removing discriminatory provisions or remedying omissions in the law.[132] Concluding its examination of one State party report, the Committee expressed concern that 'despite strong opposition, the Basic Act on Education has been amended and Article 5, which refers to the promotion of gender equality, has been removed'.[133] Considering Article 10(f), the Committee urged one State party to enact laws prohibiting widespread sexual harassment against women and girls including in education.[134]

II. Moving Beyond Formal Equality

The Committee requires States parties to move beyond formal equality based on adopting a supposedly 'neutral stance' treating men and women the same, towards the attainment of substantive equality. It has observed that 'although there is legal provision (Law 29) mandating continuation of education for girls during and after pregnancy, there is no effective mechanism in place in order to ensure compliance'.[135] By also requiring measures that aim for structural change of the educational system and the content of educational materials in order to abolish gender stereotyping, the Committee calls for transformative equality as well.[136]

III. Substantive Equality

In addition to removing discriminatory laws, substantive equality requires the State party to guarantee that women are enabled to enjoy education in practice, put in place policies to facilitate women's equal participation in education, challenge gender ascriptions in society which may impede women's access to and enjoyment of education, remove structural barriers to women's accessing education as both teachers and learners at all levels, recognize and provide for addressing compound discrimination as a result of intersectional discrimination, and make provision for the use of temporary special measures to achieve the goal of equal access to education for all.[137]

---

[131] GR 28; GR 25 paras 6–10.

[132] CO Canada, A/58/38, 28th Session (2003) para 362; CO Canada, CEDAW/C/CAN/CO/7 (2008) para 43.

[133] CO Japan, CEDAW/C/JPN/CO/6 (2009) para 43.

[134] CO Haiti, CEDAW/C/HTI/CO/7 (2009) paras 16, 23, and 24.

[135] CO Panama, CEDAW/C/PAN/CO/7(2010) para 36. See also CO India, CEDAW/C/IND/CO/3 (2007) para 49; CO Belize, CEDAW/C/BLZ/CO/4 (2007) para 24.

[136] GR 28 paras 5 and 9. See also Special Rapporteur on Education (2006) (n 15 above) para 104.

[137] See the discussion in ch on art 1; GR 28; GR 25 paras 6–10; CO France, CEDAW/C/FRA/CO/6 (2008) para 22; CO Fiji, CEDAW/C/CP/FJI/CO/4 (2010) para 29; CO Australia, CEDAW/C/AUS/CO/7 (2010) paras 2, 13, 26, 40, and 41; CO Turkey, CEDAW/C/TUR/CO/6 (2010) para 31; CO Albania, CEDAW/C/ALB/CO/3 (2010) paras 23 and 31; CO Slovenia, CEDAW/C/SLE/CO/5 (2007) para 18; CO Rwanda, CEDAW/C/RWA/CO/6 (2009) para 32; CO Yemen, CEDAW/C/YEM/CO/6 (2008) para 25; CO Guinea-Bissau, CEDAW/C/GNB/CO/6 (2009) para 34.

The Committee calls on the State party to strengthen implementation of its efforts to tackle, through the education system, the structural causes of the persistent discriminatory attitudes against women. It calls on the State party to overcome expeditiously the de facto segregation in the education system, and to actively encourage the diversification of educational and professional choices for women and men and offer incentives for young women to enter traditionally male dominated fields of study. The Committee calls on the State party to set a clear time frame for the introduction of gender-sensitive educational curricula and teaching methods that address the structural and cultural causes of discrimination against women, and to incorporate sensitization training for teachers both pre- and in-service. It also invites the State party to monitor systematically the impact of measures taken in relation to stated goals and to take corrective measures whenever necessary.[138]

IV. Transformative Equality

Transformative equality involves challenging prevailing gender ideology and calls, in the words of General Recommendation 25, for the transfer of power and resources between men and women.[139] Within the context of Article 10, the biggest challenge facing States parties is the engagement with narrow and discriminatory constructs of culture which lead to the denial of the right to education for women and girls. A transformative model of equality demands that States parties confront the culture conundrum and put in place policies to mitigate the negative impact of gender stereotyping on the educational opportunities of girls. The Committee has identified gender-based discrimination as a universal problem affecting women in the richest and poorest States.

Despite the existence of awareness raising programmes, the Committee is concerned at the persistence of traditional stereotypes relating to the roles and responsibilities of women and men within the family, in the education system and in society in general, which reinforce their sense of inferiority and affect their status in all areas of life and throughout their life cycle. The Committee is concerned that the most recent educational reform has not dealt with these subjects in depth.[140]

Article 10(c) on the elimination of gender stereotypes, points to a revolutionary view of education which requires radical restructuring of society using education as the vehicle for such transformation. The Committee has specifically called on a State party to replace gender-neutral educational curricula with materials that 'address the structural and cultural causes of discrimination against women' which may require that 'gender issues and sensitivity training be made an integral and substantive part of all teacher training'.[141]

---

[138] CO Jamaica, CEDAW/C/JAM/CO/5 (2006) para 32. See also CO Belize, CEDAW/C/BEL/CO/6 (2008) para 24; CO Liberia, CEDAW/C/LBR/CO/6 (2009) para 32; CO Egypt, CEDAW/C/EGY/CO/7 (2010) para 32.

[139] GR 25 para 8. See also Special Rapporteur on the Right to Education (n 15 above) paras 16 and 20; RJ Cook and S Cusack, *Gender Stereotyping: Transnational Legal Perspectives* (2010); R Holtmaat and J Naber *Women's Human Rights and Culture: From Deadlock to Dialogue* (2010).

[140] CO Bolivia, CEDAW/C/BOL/CO/4 (2008) para 20. See also CO Norway, CEDAW/C/NOR/CO/7 (2007) paras 17–18; CO Honduras, CEDAW/C/HON/CO/6 (2007) para 26; CO Pakistan, CEDAW/C/PAK/CO/3 (2007) para 37; CO Jordan, CEDAW/C/JOR/CO/4 (2007) para 19; CO Luxembourg, CEDAW/C/LUX/CO/5 (2008) para 15; CO Republic of Moldova, CEDAW/C/MDA/CO/3 (2006) para 19; CO Tanzania, CEDAW/C/TZA/CO/6 (2008) para 35; CO Armenia, CEDAW/C/ARM/CO/4/Rev.1 (2009) para 20; CO Germany, CEDAW/C/DEU/CO/6 (2009) para 33.

[141] CO Finland, CEDAW/C/FIN/CO/6 (2008) para 182.

V. Direct Discrimination

The Committee has identified different treatment of women based on their sex and gender differences as constituting direct discrimination.[142] Considering Article 10(f), the Committee expressed concern that 'in some educational institutions, teenage mothers are not always readmitted to junior secondary schools because of the perception that "the young mothers would have a negative influence on other girls", while teenage fathers are not prevented from attending schools.'[143]

VI. Indirect Discrimination

The prohibition of indirect discrimination addresses laws or policies that, while gender-neutral on their face, may have a detrimental effect upon and impact disproportionately on women. Formal sex neutrality may mask historical disadvantage of women. Moreover, far from being 'neutral' such policies may actually reflect male experiences, thus ignoring women's lived realities.[144] The Committee has noted that the high rate of female illiteracy in many States parties reflects a pattern of both direct and indirect discrimination.[145]

A problematic issue identified by the Committee, especially in Europe, has been legal bans on wearing of religious dress in public. Although neutral on their face, the bans may constitute indirect discrimination against (mainly Muslim) girls and women who are impacted disproportionately in being denied access to educational establishments in breach of Article 10(a).[146] Together with the CRC and the CCPR, the Committee has identified the gendered impact of the religious dress rule on women and girls. It has requested that the situation of girls who were being expelled from school as a result of the legislation should be closely monitored together with the 'educational achievements of migrant and immigrant girls at all levels'.[147] Of one State's ban on veil wearing in schools and universities, the Committee has requested an account of 'measures taken to eliminate any discriminatory consequences of the ban in the next periodic report'.[148]

Requiring the purchase of school uniforms or the levying of administrative and other fees may also constitute indirect discrimination. The Committee has expressed concern

---

[142] GR 28 para 16.   [143] CO Suriname, A/57/38, 27th Session (2002) para 57.

[144] GR 28 para 16. See also CESCR, 'General Comment 13' (1999) UN Doc E/C.12/1999/10 para 13; CESCR, 'General Comment 16' (2005) UN Doc E/C.12/2005/4 para 13.

[145] CO Saudi Arabia, CEDAW/C/SAU/CO/2 (2008) para 29; CO Morocco, CEDAW/C/MAW/CO/4 (2008) para 26; CO Mauritania, CEDAW/C/MRT/CO/1 (2007) para 35.

[146] GR 25 para 1; CESCR, 'General Comment 13' (1999) UN Doc E/C.12/1999/10 para 13; CESCR, 'General Comment 16' (2005) UN Doc E/C.12/2005/4 para 13. See generally D McGoldrick, *Human Rights and Religion: The Islamic Headscarf Debate* (2006); Human Rights Watch, *Discrimination in the name of Neutrality: Headscarf Bans for Teachers and Civil Servants in Germany* (2009); Human Rights Watch, *Beyond the Burqa* (2009).

[147] CO France, CEDAW/C/FRA/CO/6 (2008) paras 20–1; CRC CO France, CRC/C/155/Add.240 (2004) paras 25–6; CCPR CO France, CCPR/C/FRA/CO/4 (2008); CO Turkey, CEDAW/C/TUR/CO/4–5 (2005) paras 33–4; CO Belgium, CEDAW/C/BEL/CO/6/(2008) paras 35 and 38. See also *MEC for Education, KwaZulu-Natal and Others v Pillay* 2008 1 SA 474 (CC) holding that banning a Hindu girl from wearing a nose ring to school constituted violations of the rights to religion and freedom from discrimination impeding her right to education.

[148] CO Turkey, CEDAW/C/TUR/CO/6 (2010) paras 16–17. *Rahime Kayan v Turkey*, CEDAW Communication 8/2005 (2006) CEDAW/C/34/D/8/2005 (inadmissible). See also CO France, CEDAW/C/FRA/CO/6 (2008) paras 20–1.

at the high drop-out rate from secondary education of rural girls and those belonging to linguistic and ethnic minorities due to the 'secondary costs of education'.[149]

VII. Temporary Special Measures (TSMs)

In General Recommendations 25 and 28, the Committee makes clear that TSMs may be crucial to the acceleration and achievement of equality between men and women.[150] The Committee has proposed that States parties use temporary special measures in areas including sports, culture, and recreation: 'Where necessary such measures should be directed at women subjected to multiple discrimination including rural women.'[151] It has focused on increasing the participation of women as both students and teachers in secondary and higher education.[152] In its General Recommendation 18, the Committee has enjoined States parties to provide information on disabled women, including 'special measures to ensure that they have equal access to education and employment, . . . and to ensure that they can participate in all areas of social and cultural life'.[153]

VIII. Intersectional Discrimination

The Committee has challenged States parties to address intersectional discrimination.[154] Intersectionality recognizes that there are groups of women who, in addition to sex and gender discrimination, may experience discrimination on other grounds including age, disability, indigineity, race, and sexual orientation, simultaneously.[155] The Committee has identified the failure to guarantee access to education, especially to women from minority or other communities, as impacting disproportionately on them in that it harms their life chances and opportunities. The Committee has identified regional differentiation in education and the negative impact of that especially on minority women.[156] Moreover, the Committee has highlighted the impact of allocating inadequate budgetary resources to particular geographical regions where minority or indigenous communities reside and refusal to provide appropriate language facilities, as issues of particular concern.[157] It urged one State party to consider introducing multilingual education and suggested the deployment of university students to the rural areas to help teach language classes.[158]

---

[149] CO Albania, CEDAW/C/ALB/CO/3(2010) para 30.   [150] GR 25; GR 28 para 20.

[151] GR 25 para 38; CO Israel, A/60/38, 33rd Session (2005) para 256; CO Lao People's Democratic Republic, CEDAW/C/LAO/CO/7 (2009) para 34.

[152] CO Japan, CEDAW/C/JPN/CO/6 (2009) para 44; CO Turkey, CEDAW/C/TUR/CO/6 (2010) para 31; CO Albania, CEDAW/C/ALB/CO/3 (2010) paras 23 and 31; CO Uruguay, CEDAW/C/URY/CO/7 (2008) para 33; CO Sierra Leone, CEDAW/C/SLE/CO/5 (2007) para 31. CO Russian Federation, CEDAW/C/USR/CO/7 (2010) paras 34–5; CO France, CEDAW/C/FRA/CO/6 (2008) paras 24–5; CO Sweden, CEDAW/C/SWE/CO/7 (2008) para 24.

[153] GR 18.   [154] GR 28 para 18; GR 27 para 19.

[155] K Crenshaw, 'Demarginalizing the Intersection of Race and Sex: A Black Feminist Critique of Antidiscrimination Doctrine, Feminist Theory and Antiracist Politics' (1989) *University of Chicago Legal Forum* 139; CERD, 'General Recommendation 25' (2000) UN Doc A/55/18, Annex V; CESCR, 'General Comment 15' (2002) UN Doc E/C.12/2002/11 para 5; CESCR, 'General Comment 20' (2009) UN Doc E/C.12/GC/20 paras 17–36; Special Rapporteur on the Right to Education (2005) (n 60 above) paras 87 and 97–101.

[156] CO Serbia, CEDAW/C/SCG/CO/1 (2007) para 29; CO Turkey, CEDAW/C/TUR/CO/6 (2010) para 31; CO Albania, CEDAW/C/ALB/CO/3 (2010) para 30.

[157] CO Turkey, CEDAW/C/TUR/CO/6 (2010) para 31. See also Complaint 13/2002 *Autism Europe v France Case* (2002) European Committee of Social Rights.

[158] CO Lao People's Democratic Republic, CEDAW/C/LAO/CO/7 (2009) para 34.

The Committee has called on States parties to use temporary special measures to address the barriers blocking access to education for indigenous and minority women.[159]

E. States Parties' Obligations

I. The Nature of State Obligations

The chapeau to Article 10 provides that the State party is required to take 'all appropriate measures' to eliminate discrimination against women in order to facilitate their enjoyment of the right to education.[160] The Committee has taken a comprehensive approach to what is appropriate.[161] It has recommended that measures may include: changing the law, ensuring education and social policy is gender-sensitive and facilitates equal access to quality education for women and girls, ensuring adequate infrastructural services including transport and sanitation, facilitating training and retention of female teaching staff especially at the higher levels of education, challenging and removing negative cultural and other barriers to women accessing education or which lead to their leaving prematurely, using gender-disaggregated data at all levels of education to measure progress, providing education that takes on board differences in language, that addresses the urban/rural divide and that is gender-sensitive. The Committee has also called on States parties to provide financial assistance to enable girls to receive an education and recommended the use of international aid to assist in the realization of Article 10 objectives while acknowledging the efforts of those that have done so.[162]

II. Implementation

The obligations of States parties to respect, protect, and fulfil rights have been explored by the Committee in General Recommendations 24 and 28 and apply equally to Article 10.[163] The Committee has noted:

States parties have the responsibility to ensure that legislation and executive action and policy comply with these three obligations. They must also put in place a system which ensures effective judicial action. Failure to do so will constitute a violation . . . .[164]

1. Obligation to Respect

The obligation to respect requires the State party to refrain from taking action which will hinder the enjoyment of the right to education.[165] It also places on States parties the

---

[159] CO Romania, CEDAW/C/ROM/CO/6 (2006) para 27; CO Uruguay, CEDAW/C/URY/CO/7 (2008) para 45. See also CO Bolivia, CEDAW/C/BOL/CO/4 paras 15, 17, and 32; CO Israel, A/60/38, 33rd Session (2005) para 256. See also ACRWC art 11(3)(e) calling on States parties to 'take special measures in respect of female, gifted and disadvantaged children'.

[160] Burrows (n 2 above) 437 on the State's dual obligations.   [161] GR 28 para 23.

[162] CO Timor-Leste, CEDAW/C/TLS/CO/1 (2009) para 36; CO Russian Federation, CEDAW/C/USR/CO/7 (2010) para34; CO Fiji, CEDAW/C/FJI/CO/4 (2010) paras 28–9; CO Guinea-Bissau, CEDAW/C/GNB/CO/6 (2009) para33; CO Vanuatu, CEDAW/C/VUT/CO/3 (2007) para31; CO Cyprus, CEDAW/C/CYP/CO/5 (2006) paras 23–4; CO Sierra Leone, CEDAW/C/SLE/CO/5(2007) para 31; CO Albania, CEDAW/C/ALB/CO/3 (2010) para 31; CO The United Kingdom, CEDAW/C/UK/CO/6 (2008) para 263; CO Finland, A/63/38, 41st Session (2008) para 165.

[163] GR 24 paras 13–18; GR 28 paras 9 and 16 ff. See also CESCR, 'General Comment 13' (1999) UN Doc E/C.12/1999/10 paras 46, 47, and 50. The CESCR further notes that the three obligations must be understood in respect of the 4 As (availability, accessibility, acceptability, adaptability).

[164] GR 24 para 13.   [165] GR 28 para 9.

duty to make education free from any kind of discrimination. The Committee has done a great deal to address barriers to access under Article 10(a) calling upon one State party: 'to provide safe transportation to and from schools as well as safe educational environments free from discrimination and violence'.[166] The Committee has expressed concern about the high rate of sexual harassment against girls, including in education, noting 'the lack of adequate training for teachers to address such harassment'.[167]

2. *Obligation to Protect*

The obligation to protect requires positive action by the State party to make provision for the effective enjoyment of the right and to ensure that third parties do not, by their actions, violate the right to education of women and girls including by refusing to allow them to go to school.[168] Where education is provided in private institutions or by religious or other non-State entities, it should still conform to the equality standard ensuring that there is no sex or gender discrimination in the construction of curricula or the delivery of education. Concluding the examination of one State party report, the Committee reiterated:

its concern about the influence of the church on girls' and young women's right to education. In that regard, the Committee repeats its concern that schools remain free to expel girls because of pregnancy, that only a few secondary schools allow girls to continue their education after pregnancy and that schools are allowed to dismiss unwed teachers who become pregnant.[169]

3. *Obligation to Fulfil*

The obligation to fulfil requires that the State party facilitate access to and provide for the realization of women's rights. This may require it to adopt appropriate measures which include legislative, administrative, and judicial action, adequate budgetary allocations, and the adoption of policies which enhance the enjoyment of the right to education.[170] The Committee noted its appreciation of a State party's 'non-discriminatory provisions in the education law, the various proactive measures and programmes aimed at increasing the participation of girls in the school system, the literacy programmes targeting mainly women, as well as the flexible arrangements to allow girls who drop out of school to continue their studies'.[171]

The Committee enjoins States parties to ensure that discriminatory laws are amended and also that the laws are implemented and enforced: while commending one State party for having enacted legislation proscribing sexual harassment, it noted that in practice, there was still a high incidence of sexual violence in schools.[172] The Committee has reminded one State party of its legal obligations to ensure access to economic, social and cultural rights including education for the people living in territory that it occupies.[173] In its consideration of *AS v Hungary*, under Article 10(h) the Committee recommended that the State consider amending those parts of the Public Health Act that gave discretion

---

[166] CO Timor-Leste, CEDAW/C/TLS/CO/1 (2009) para 36.

[167] CO Finland, A/63/38/, 41st Session (2008) para 181.

[168] GR 28 para 9; CO Tajikistan, CEDAW/C/TJK/CO/3 (2007) para 28.

[169] CO Belize, CEDAW/C/BLZ/CO/4 (2007) para 23. See also CO Jordan, CEDAW/C/JOR/CO/4 (2007) para 19; CO Tajikistan, CEDAW/C/TJK/CO/3 (2007) para 28.

[170] GR 28 paras 9 and 20; CESCR 'General Comment 13' (1999) UN Doc E/C.12/1999/10 para 46.

[171] CO El Salvador, CEDAW/C/SLV/CO/7 (2008) para 29.

[172] Ibid para 23. See also CO Austria, CEDAW/C/AUT/CO/6 (2007) para 30.

[173] CO Israel, CEDAW/C/ISR/CO/3 (2005) paras 23–4.

to a physician to sterilize without the provision of information when he or she deemed it necessary.[174]

The Committee has urged States parties to provide training on changes in legislation and implementation measures to police, judges, health personnel, media, community, and religious leaders. It has also recommended targeting awareness raising campaigns for the benefit of affected women and girls.[175] The Committee has highlighted the role that the media can play in realizing Article 10(c) and (h), urging one State:

to encourage public dialogue on the educational choices girls and women make and their subsequent opportunities and chances in the labour market. It recommends that awareness raising campaigns be addressed to both women and men and that the media be encouraged to project positive images of women and of the equal status and responsibilities of women and men in the private and public spheres.[176]

The Committee has been vigilant in calling the attention of States parties to the discriminatory impact of practices and policies on the lives of women and children and has been urging them to close the educational opportunity gap by using temporary special measures.[177]

The Committee has highlighted the importance of monitoring progress including setting clear time frames and benchmarks 'for the introduction of gender-sensitive educational curricula and teaching methods'[178] and also by collecting data, requiring: 'that data on school retention, completion and achievement in literacy and numeracy be disaggregated and cross-tabulated on the basis of sex, ethnicity and geographical location to ensure that the needs of specific groups can be identified and appropriate interventions applied to eliminate sex-based disparities.'[179]

The Committee recognizes the importance of making adequate budgetary provision to facilitate access to education especially for minority and other under-represented women. In this regard, the Committee also recommends the provision of scholarships.[180] Focusing on rural girls and women, the Committee has urged States parties to take steps to mitigate their particular disadvantage and discrimination by providing books, transport fees, and incidental costs to facilitate access.[181] Adequate boarding facilities for girls

---

[174] *AS v Hungary* CEDAW Communication 4/2004 (2006) CEDAW/C/36/D/4/2004 para 11.5(II).

[175] CO The United Kingdom, A/63/38, 41st Session (2008) paras 277 and 279; CO Bolivia, CEDAW/C/BOL/CO/4 (2008) para 20; CO Uruguay, CEDAW/C/URY/CO/7 (2008) para 21.

[176] CO Lebanon, CEDAW/C/LBN/CO/3 (2008) para 25. See also CO Haiti, CEDAW/C/HTI/CO/7 (2009) para 21.

[177] CO Liberia, CEDAW/C/LBR/CO/6 (2009) para 33. See also GR 25 paras 31, 32, and 37; CO Yemen, CEDAW/C/YEM/CO/6 (2008) para 25; CO Guinea-Bissau, CEDAW/C/GNB/CO/6 (2009) para 34; CO Timor-Leste, CEDAW/C/TLS/CO/1 (2008) para 36.

[178] CO Jamaica, CEDAW/C/CO/5 (2006) para 32. See also CO India, CEDAW/C/IND/CO/3 (2007) para 33.

[179] CO Australia, CEDAW/C/AUS/CO/7 (2010) para 37. See also CO Libyan Arab Jamahiriya, CEDAW/C/LBY/CO/5 (2009) para 32.

[180] CO Samoa, A/60/38, 32nd Session (2005) para 43; CO Albania, CEDAW/C/ALB/CO (2010) para 30; CO Myanmar, CEDAW/C/MMR/CO/3 (2008) para 34; CO India, CEDAW/C/IND/CO/3 (2007) paras 32–3.

[181] CO Uruguay, CEDAW/C/URY/Q/7/Add.1 (2008) para 32; CO Lao People's Democratic Republic, CEDAW/C/LAO/CO/7 (2009) para 33; CO Haiti, CEDAW/C/HTI/CO/7 (2009) para 31; CO Malawi, CEDAW/C/MWI/CO/5 (2006) para 27; CO Vanuatu, CEDAW/C/VUT/CO/3 (2007) para 31; CO Guinea-Bissau, CEDAW/C/GNB/CO/6 (2009) para 34; CO Fiji, CEDAW/C/FJI/CO/4 (2010) para 28.

have also been recommended.[182] The Committee has also highlighted the importance of international cooperation by means of aid and other support in the delivery of the right to education.[183]

III. Reservations

There are no reservations to Article 10. However, a number of reservations to other provisions in the Convention may impact on the enjoyment of the right to education free from sex and gender discrimination. These include the many reservations to Article 16 on marriage and family relations on grounds of personal status laws which may specify different ages of marriage for boys and girls. Moreover, reservations to Article 15(4) based on male guardianship may affect the ability of girls and women to study abroad or to live away from home. This has a direct impact on women, violating their freedom of movement, and an indirect impact in denying them educational opportunities.[184] Similarly, reservations to Article 5 on stereotyping have potentially negative effects on women's ability to enjoy Article 10 rights free from discrimination.

---

[182] CO Vanuatu, CEDAW/C/VUT/CO/3 (2007) para 30; CO Maldives, CEDAW/C/MDV/CO/3 (2007) para 27.

[183] CO Sierra Leone, CEDAW/C/SLE/CO/5 (2007) para 31; CO Niger, CEDAW/C/NER/CO/2 (2007) para 30, CO Mauritania, CEDAW/C/MRT/CO/6 (2007) para 36; CO Burundi, CEDW/C/BDI/CO/4 (2008) para 32.

[184] F Banda, *Project on a Mechanism to Address Laws that Discriminate against Women* (2008) 90.

Article 11

1. States Parties shall take all appropriate measures to eliminate discrimination against women in the field of employment in order to ensure, on a basis of equality of men and women, the same rights, in particular:

(a) The right to work as an inalienable right of all human beings;

(b) The right to the same employment opportunities, including the application of the same criteria for selection in matters of employment;

(c) The right to free choice of profession and employment, the right to promotion, job security and all benefits and conditions of service and the right to receive vocational training and retraining, including apprenticeships, advanced vocational training and recurrent training;

(d) The right to equal remuneration, including benefits, and to equal treatment in respect of work of equal value, as well as equality of treatment in the evaluation of the quality of work;

(e) The right to social security, particularly in cases of retirement, unemployment, sickness, invalidity and old age and other incapacity to work, as well as the right to paid leave;

(f) The right to protection of health and to safety in working conditions, including the safeguarding of the function of reproduction.

2. In order to prevent discrimination against women on the grounds of marriage or maternity and to ensure their effective right to work, States Parties shall take appropriate measures:

(a) To prohibit, subject to the imposition of sanctions, dismissal on the grounds of pregnancy or of maternity leave and discrimination in dismissals on the basis of marital status;

(b) To introduce maternity leave with pay or with comparable social benefits without loss of former employment, seniority or social allowances;

(c) To encourage the provision of the necessary supporting social services to enable parents to combine family obligations with work responsibilities and participation in public life, in particular through promoting the establishment and development of a network of child-care facilities;

(d) To provide special protection to women during pregnancy in types of work proved to be harmful to them.

3. Protective legislation relating to matters covered in this article shall be reviewed periodically in the light of scientific and technological knowledge and shall be revised, repealed or extended as necessary.

* I would like to thank my chief research assistant Revital Tordjman and also research assistants Belle Spivak and Julie Asila for their excellent and indispensable research assistance on this chapter and the chapter on art 4.

A. Introduction

Article 11 of the Convention addresses comprehensively the obligation of States parties to eliminate discrimination against women in employment and occupation, which are key to sustainable development and to the human dignity and personality of the individual. The unique contribution of Article 11 is to create holistic standards for women's rights in employment and occupation, based on recognition of the complex realities of women's economic, family, and employment situation. 'The primary assignment of women to work in the private sphere of the family has usually resulted in severe consequences for them with respect to their equality with men in access to opportunities in labour markets: their work in the family remains largely invisible, it is not accounted for in gross national products, and does not give women economic empowerment.'[1]

Article 11 spans the entire range of measures required to ensure women's access to the labour market and to secure their equal opportunity and conditions as employees. It requires States parties to eliminate discrimination against women in the field of employment and occupation and to secure equality in the right to work, employment opportunities, employment conditions, remuneration, social security, and health and safety. It requires them to prevent discrimination against women on the grounds of marriage or maternity and to ensure their effective right to work. The Article provides the framework for formal and substantive equality and for elimination of structural discrimination in employment and occupation.

I. ILO and Other UN Agencies

Article 11 deals with the subject matter of discrimination in employment and occupation and protection of maternity in parallel with ILO and other UN agency regulation. However, Article 11 remains distinct in its non-symmetrical requirement of eliminating discrimination against women in these areas of economic activity, rather than the gender-neutral prohibition of sex discrimination in the other instruments.

The ILO, from its inception in 1919, promulgated standards intended to protect women specifically, regarding matters such as work in mines, night work, and maternity protection. In 1951, it introduced equal pay for work of equal value for men and women workers. In 1958, the ILO adopted Convention No 111[2] to promote equal opportunity and treatment and to eliminate discrimination in employment on grounds of race, colour, sex, religion, political opinion, national extraction, or social origin. In 1981, the ILO adopted the Workers with Family Responsibilities Convention (Convention No 156),[3] which was inspired by CEDAW,[4] and, in 1998, included elimination of discrimination

---

[1] HB Schöpp-Schilling, 'Impediments to Progress: The Formal Labor Market' in HB Schöpp-Schilling and C Flinterman (eds), *The Circle of Empowerment: Twenty-Five Years of The UN Committee on The Elimination of Discrimination Against Women* (2007) 161.

[2] ILO Convention concerning Discrimination in Respect of Employment and Occupation (ILO Convention No 111) (adopted 25 June 1958, entered into force 15 June 1960) 362 UNTS 31.

[3] ILO Workers with Family Responsibilities Convention (ILO Convention No 156) (adopted 23 June 1981, entered into force 11 August 1983) 1331 UNTS 295.

[4] EC Landau and Y Beigbeder, *From ILO Standards to EU Law: The Case of Equality Between Men and Women at Work* (2008) 17.

in respect of employment and occupation as one of the four principles in the Declaration on Fundamental Principles and Rights at Work.[5]

The UDHR employed the formula for prohibition of discrimination including discrimination on ground of sex[6] which has become the basis for subsequent UN human rights treaties. In the UDHR, the rights and freedoms with regard to which there must be no sex discrimination include the rights to work, to free choice of employment, to just and favourable conditions of work and remuneration and to protection against unemployment, to equal pay for equal work, to social protection, to join trade unions and to special care, and assistance for 'motherhood'.[7] In 1966, these principles were re-enacted in the ICESCR, which further detailed and expanded the employment and occupation rights included in the UDHR, for instance, by introducing rights to training programmes, equal opportunity for promotion, and safe and healthy working conditions, while expressly guaranteeing the equal right of men and women to the enjoyment of such rights.[8]

II. Beijing Platform for Action

The Beijing Platform for Action,[9] reaffirming commitment to the equal rights and human dignity of women and men enshrined in international instruments and in, particular, the CEDAW Convention, commits States to ensuring the full implementation of the human rights of women and of the girl child as an inalienable, integral, and indivisible part of all human rights and fundamental freedoms. The Platform for Action includes employment and occupation rights within the wider context of women and the economy. Taking the holistic approach of Convention Article 11 the Platform for Action analyzes obstacles to women's economic autonomy in economic policy decision-making, remunerated and unremunerated work, formal and informal labour markets, non-standard work, discrimination in education, training, hiring, remuneration for work of equal value, promotion, inadequate sharing of family responsibilities and unpaid domestic work, reduction of public services and public service jobs, unemployment, and globalization. It proposes strategic objectives to be pursued by governments and non-governmental organizations to secure women's access and equal participation in all these aspects of economic life.

III. Millennium Development Goals

The Millennium Development Goals, which set the target of eradicating extreme poverty and hunger by 2015, includes indicators for increasing women's share in wage employment in the non-agricultural sector.[10] Since 2005, the Committee has added a standard paragraph in its concluding observations taking note of the linkages between the MDGs and the Convention.

---

[5] Declaration on Fundamental Principles and Rights at Work, International Labour Conference, 86th Session (adopted 19 June 1998).

[6] UDHR art 2.   [7] Ibid arts 23 and 25(2).   [8] ICESCR arts 2(2), 3, 6, 7, 8, 9, and 10(2).

[9] Beijing Declaration and Platform for Action (Beijing Declaration) (adopted 15 September 1995) UN Doc A/CONF.177/20 and A/CONF.177/20/Add.1.

[10] Millennium Development Goals Indicators, 'Share of women in wage employment in the non-agricultural sector' at <http://unstats.un.org/unsd/mdg/SeriesDetail.aspx?srid=722> accessed 31 December 2010.

B. Travaux Préparatoires

I. Differing Perspectives in Western, Socialist, and Developing Economies

At the very outset of the discussion on the Preamble, the USSR emphasized 'the dependence of the general development and prosperity of all countries on women assuming a full part in all spheres of state and local life. They considered that mention should also be made of... the contribution of women "... to the material and spiritual values of society...", the importance of motherhood and woman's role in the family...'[11] Differences of approach were apparent in western, socialist, and developing economies' perspectives.[12] The western countries adopted a liberal model promoting the concept of equal opportunity, while the socialist bloc and developing countries insisted on detailed protective measures for women's health, safety, motherhood, and role in the family.

II. Reproductive Function

In discussion of 'the reproductive function of women', the United States maintained that 'special protective legislation for women in employment in fact operated against women's interests and should be extended to men as well'. The USSR took the view that the Convention was aimed at elimination of discrimination against women and 'references to men, who—so far as [the representative] was aware—were not particularly disadvantaged in the matter of employment, was therefore out of place'. Supported by Byelorussia, it proposed limiting the employment of women in heavy labour and in work which could be physically harmful to them or 'prejudicial to their social function of reproduction'. The United Kingdom, India, and Belgium promoted a compromise solution which resulted in adoption of the text of Article 11(1)(f): 'the right to protection of health and safety in the working environment, including the safeguarding of the function of reproduction' and Article 11(2)(d)'s obligation 'to provide special protection to women during pregnancy in types of work proved to be harmful to them'.

III. Family Responsibilities

As regards protection for family responsibilities, Belgium indicated three categories for protection: marital status, maternity, and motherhood or responsible parenthood. The USSR, Czechoslovakia, and the Philippines were of the opinion that there should be protective measures 'to enable women to combine the fulfilment of family and maternal obligations'. Sweden, Canada, and Finland took the view that men be given the opportunity to assume their share of the responsibility for family and children, and that 'reference should be made to "parents" in general rather than specifically to "mothers"'. The version adopted in Article 11(2) refers to prevention of discrimination against women 'on grounds of marriage or maternity' together with 'enabling parents to combine family obligations with work responsibilities'.

---

[11] LA Rehof, *Guide to the Travaux Préparatoires of the United Nations Convention on the Elimination of All Forms of Discrimination against Women* (1993) 32.

[12] Ibid 122–43.

IV. Costs of Maternity Protections and Social Services

France, Belgium, and the ILO, were of the opinion that the costs of maternity protections should not be borne by the individual employer but by social security and public funds. The United States opposed this view.[13] In the final result, Article 11 mentions 'paid leave' without reference to the cost-bearer and falls short of imposing an obligation on the State to provide 'social services to enable parents to combine family obligations with work responsibilities', only requiring them to support provision of such services.

V. Pensionable Age and Part-time Work

Some of the more far-reaching socialist proposals from the USSR, such as a proposed guarantee that all the rights, benefits, and privileges of full-time work would be given to women in part-time work, did not find their way into the Convention.[14] The USSR, Egypt, and Bulgaria were in favour of a lower pensionable age for women but Canada, France, the UK, and the International Association for Social Progress believed that inclusion of special pension conditions for women would be protectionist, discriminatory, and inappropriate.[15]

C. Issues of Interpretation

I. Concepts

Article 11 divides the elimination of discrimination against women in the employment context into two separate concepts: the first, in Article 11(1), relates to elimination of discrimination against women in order to ensure them the same employment rights, on a basis of equality of men and women, and the second, in Article 11(2), relates to the need to prevent discrimination against women on the grounds of marriage or maternity and to ensure their effective right to work. This conceptualization highlights the duality of discrimination against women and of the measures required to eliminate it.

As regards Article 11(1), the discrimination to be eliminated is against women as such, and measures of formal and substantive equality, prevention of direct and indirect discrimination, and temporary special measures are needed in order to secure equal employment opportunity. As regards Article 11(2), the discrimination against women which is to be eliminated is on grounds of marriage or maternity, as wives or mothers, requiring measures of substantive or *de facto* equality, elimination of structural discrimination, including stereotyping, and conceptual and institutional transformative equality, to ensure women's effective right to work. These various methods to be used in eliminating discrimination in all its forms are required under Article 11, in conjunction with Articles 1–5.

States parties' obligation to eliminate discrimination in the field of employment and occupation applies to both the public and the private sectors, in accordance with Article 2(e), which requires elimination of discrimination by 'any person, organization or enterprise'. There is perhaps no other article in Parts II and III of the Convention on which this provision has greater impact. While policy for political and public life, education, health, family law, and banking and rural development is to a great extent under the direct control of State authorities, private employers play a central part in determining employment policy.

---

[13] Ibid 139.   [14] Ibid 125.   [15] Ibid 136.

II. Article 11(1)

'States Parties shall take all appropriate measures to eliminate discrimination against women in the field of employment in order to ensure, on a basis of equality of men and women, the same rights'.

All appropriate measures are to be taken to ensure women rights on 'a basis of equality of men and women' and not the 'same terms as men', a choice of wording made purposefully according to the *travaux préparatoires*.[16]

The significance of this choice of criterion is that, where women and men are not similarly situated, it requires substantive equality measures to secure equal opportunity. In the context of economic, social, and cultural rights the CESCR in General Comment 20 stated:

Since the adoption of the Covenant, the notion of the prohibited ground 'sex' has evolved considerably to cover not only physiological characteristics but also the social construction of gender stereotypes, prejudices and expected roles, which have created obstacles to the equal fulfilment of economic, social and cultural rights. Thus, the refusal to hire a woman on the ground that she might become pregnant, or the allocation of low-level or part-time jobs to women based on the stereotypical assumption that, for example, they are unwilling to commit as much time to their work as men, constitutes discrimination.[17]

Elimination of indirect as well as direct discrimination against women in employment is necessary, as discussed below,[18] to prevent the use of criteria or practices which will have a disparate and adverse impact on women because they are differently situated from men. An act which discriminates against women should be judged objectively on grounds of its adverse impact on them and there is no need to prove that it was committed with an intention to discriminate. It is of primary importance to obviate any requirement to show discriminatory intent, as the holder of the stereotypical beliefs which fuel discriminatory practices 'may not be conscious of them, and [may] be outraged, devastated or bewildered by any suggestions that he or she is sexist'.[19]

III. Article 11(1)(a)

'The right to work as an inalienable right of all human beings'.

The core right to work in the context of Article 11 requires States parties to protect women against discriminatory exclusion from labour markets.[20] The right to work has been recognized by the CESCR in its General Comment 18 as 'essential for realizing other human rights and forms an inseparable and inherent part of human dignity'. The right to work contributes to the survival of the individual and her family.[21]

1. Inalienability and Cultural Restrictions on Women's Right to Work

In CEDAW, unlike other international and regional human rights instruments which guarantee the right to work, the right to work is defined as inalienable.[22] This places it in the category of those rights which cannot by their nature be taken away, providing an

---

[16] Ibid. [17] CESCR, 'General Comment 20' (2009) UN Doc E/C 12/GC/20 para 20.

[18] See the discussion below in section D. II.: *Direct and Indirect Discrimination*.

[19] R Cook and S Cusack, *Gender Stereotyping: Transnational Legal Perspectives* (2009) 18.

[20] M Risse, 'A Right to Work? A Right to Leisure? Labor Rights as Human Rights' (2009) 3 *J of Law & Ethics of Human Rights* 1, 3.

[21] CESCR, 'General Comment 18' (2005) UN Doc E/C 12/GC/18 para 1. [22] Ibid para 3.

essential guarantee for women's economic freedom. This is of particular importance in the context of traditionalist cultural restrictions which may prohibit women's participation in economic enterprise.[23]

The inalienable right to work has, conversely, given rise to claims by traditionalist women that they are being excluded because of their traditionalism. Thus, a teacher in a public school in Turkey, who was dismissed by the Higher Disciplinary Council, complained to the Committee under the Optional Protocol that her dismissal for wearing a Muslim headscarf, contrary to the dress code, was a violation of Article 11.[24] The Committee did not examine the case on the merits and so did not have to consider whether prohibition of the wearing of the Muslim headscarf by a teacher in a secular school would constitute discrimination based on sex or whether it was justified because the headscarf would transmit a patriarchal worldview obstructive to teaching in a secular environment (as held, regarding university students in Turkey, by the ECtHR in the *Leyla Sahin* case[25]).

Gender stereotyping[26] of women as primarily housewives or as service providers, cultural practices which impose care functions on women, and social attitudes according to which women are not equally eligible for full participation in the labour market all adversely impact women's right to work. These discriminatory practices and views are likely to result in failure by States parties to provide equal employment opportunities for women. They are also a central factor in failure to provide proper social services and facilities for child care and care of other dependant family members, which are a precondition to enable caregivers, who are usually in practice women, to exercise the right to work.

2. Realization of Full Employment

Implementation of the right to work requires States to take measures aimed at the realization of full employment.[27] States parties are obliged to take all appropriate measures to facilitate the economic participation of women and, in particular, to reduce women's higher levels of unemployment.

The Committee has frequently addressed the problem of women's low economic participation[28] and has called on States parties to adopt appropriate measures to ensure women's equal access to paid employment. Additionally, the Committee has noted with concern high rates of unemployment for women who are in the labour force[29] and has urged introduction of temporary special measures in creating employment opportunities for women.[30] The Committee has said that it was particularly concerned that women's high educational

---

[23] CO Kuwait, A/59/38 (Supp), 30th Session (2004) paras 72–3.

[24] *Rahime Kayhan v Turkey*, CEDAW Communication 8/2005 (2006) UN Doc CEDAW/C/34/D/8/2005.

[25] F Raday, 'Traditionalist Religious and Cultural Challengers: International and Constitutional Human Rights Responses' (2008) 41 *Israel L Rev* 596–634; *Şahin v Turkey* Application 44774/98, (2005) 41 EHRR 8.

[26] Cook and Cusack (n 19 above) 18–20.

[27] CESCR, 'General Comment 18' (2005) UN Doc E/C 12/GC/18 para 3.

[28] CO Morocco, A/58/38, 29th Session (2003) paras 174–5; CO Sri Lanka, A/57/38, 26th Session (2002) paras 290–3; CO Tunisia, A/57/38, 27th Session (2002) paras 200–1.

[29] CO France, A/58/38, 29th Session (2003) paras 259–62; CO Russian Federation, A/57/38, 26th Session (2002) paras 383–6; CO Zambia, A/57/38, 27th Session (2002) paras 248–9; CO Uganda, A/57/38, Exceptional Session (2002) para 143.

[30] CO New Zealand, A/58/38, 29th Session (2003) paras 411–12; CO Zambia, A/57/38, 27th Session (2002) paras 248–9; CO Russian Federation, A/57/38, 26th Session (2002) paras 383–6.

levels do not seem to result in job opportunity and the growing unemployment rate of female first-job seekers is alarming.[31]

In contrast, the Committee noted that in some States women's rate of participation has been steadily rising and in one State party women's participation in the labour market is 'at an impressive 75%'.[32] The Millennium Development Goals 2008 Report notes that job opportunities for women are opening up and women have more income-earning possibilities than ever before, occupying overall 40 per cent of non-agricultural jobs in 2006 as compared to 35 per cent in 1990; however, they remain trapped in insecure, low-paid positions.[33]

3. *Availability and Accessibility of Decent Work*

The right to work also entails the accessibility of decent work.[34] The ILO has highlighted the fact that gender-equality concerns are central for the promotion of its decent work agenda which targets four strategic objectives: rights at work, employment protection, social protection, and social dialogue. The inclusion of gender mainstreaming in the ILO policy goals is a welcome emphasis in the development of the decent work agenda. However, the view that equality for men and women can be achieved by ILO policy of protection for all workers regardless of sex is dubious. For women to take a full and equal role in labour markets, structural change is required, with targeted programmes for the advancement of women in the labour force and protection for them in their maternity and parenting roles with equality of responsibilities in the family. It is here that the emphasis of the Convention adds a crucial building block to the solid structure of ILO standards and EU law, reminding us that the utopia of the decent work perspective has not yet replaced the need for a woman's perspective.

Women in many countries have an especially acute problem regarding access to decent work in the formal economy. Under Article 11(1)(a), States parties are required to address the concentration of women in the informal sector of the economy, in unpaid family work, and in export processing zones, where labour standards are not enforced, and ensure the application of general labour standards to women working in these sectors. Most informal workers—workers without a regular contract, casual day labourers without a fixed employer, temporary agency workers, part-time workers, outworkers for formal firms, and employees of informal enterprises—are deprived of secure work, worker's benefits, social protection, and representation or voice and a higher percentage of them are poor as compared with those working in the formal economy.[35] In 2008, the Millennium Development Goals Report records that two-thirds of women in the developing world work in vulnerable jobs as own-account and unpaid family workers and that in South Asia and Africa, this type of work accounts for more than 80 per cent of all jobs for women.[36] The concern

---

[31] CO Slovenia, A/58/38, 29th Session (2003) paras 212–13.

[32] CO Switzerland, A/58/38, 28th Session (2003) para 130; CO Denmark, A/57/38, 27th Session (2002) para 325.

[33] Report of the Secretary General, 'The Millennium Development Goals Report' (2008) 18, at < http://www.un.org/millenniumgoals/2008highlevel/pdf/newsroom/mdg%20reports/MDG_Report_2008_ENGLISH.pdf > accessed 31 December 2010.

[34] CESCR, 'General Comment 18' (2005) UN Doc E/C 12/GC/18 para 12.

[35] ILO, 'Women and Men in the Informal Economy: A Statistical Picture' (2002) 12.

[36] The Millennium Development Goals Report (n 33 above) 18.

for protection of women's rights in the informal economy is included expressly in the Protocol on the Rights of Women in Africa.[37]

In General Recommendation 16, the Committee noted that a high percentage of women work without payment, social security, and social benefits in rural and urban family enterprises, usually owned by a male member of the family, and affirmed that such unpaid work constitutes a form of women's exploitation. The Committee recommended that States parties collect data on women's unpaid work in family enterprises and take the necessary steps to guarantee payment, social security, and social benefits for women working in these enterprises.[38] The Committee has expressed concern[39] at the complete lack of protection for women working in the informal sector, such as domestic service, and the lack of enforcement of laws to protect women workers in export processing zones or *maquila* industry. It called upon States parties to provide adequate protection and ensure enforcement of labour laws for women workers in all areas.[40]

In General Recommendation 17, the Committee drew attention to the unremunerated domestic activities of women and called on States parties to collect sex-disaggregated data on the division of time spent in household activities and in the labour market and to report on incorporation of unremunerated domestic activities in the gross national product.[41]

The ILO includes part-time work within the conceptual framework of informal sector work.[42] The Committee is concerned at the precarious conditions of women working in the informal sector and at part-time work, who have no labour protection, no access to social security, and no due respect for their labour rights.[43] The measures to be applied regarding part-time work are discussed below under Article 11(1)(b).

IV. Article 11(1)(b)

'The right to the same employment opportunities, including the application of the same criteria for selection in matters of employment'.

1. *Employment Opportunities*

The right to the 'same employment opportunities' which constitutes the first part of this section should be read as inclusive of the right to education and training necessary for the same employment opportunities, as well as the right of access to the employment opportunities for which the woman is qualified.

Horizontally-segregated job markets, which invariably involve women's exclusion from certain branches of employment activity, represent a failure to meet the standards of Article 11(1)(b). The Committee has frequently called on States parties to eliminate occupational segregation, in particular, through education and training.[44] Nevertheless, the Committee has noted that, even where women have a high education level, the position of

---

[37] Protocol on the Rights of Women in Africa art 13.   [38] GR 16 para 241.

[39] CO Brazil, A/58/38, 29th Session (2003) paras 124–5; CO Mexico, A/57/38, Exceptional Session (2002) paras 441–2; CO Peru, A/57/38, Exceptional Session (2002) para 478; CO Sri Lanka, A/57/38, 26th Session (2002) paras 290–3.

[40] CO Peru, A/57/38, Exceptional Session (2002) para 479; CO Sri Lanka, A/57/38, 26th Session (2002) para 291.

[41] GR 17 para 242.

[42] ILO, 'Women and Men in the Informal Economy: A Statistical Picture' (2002) 7–8.

[43] CO Germany, A/59/38, 30th Session (2004) paras 388–9.

[44] CO Peru, A/57/38, Exceptional session (2002) paras 478–9; CO Switzerland, A/58/38, 28th Session (2003) paras 130–3; CO Slovenia, A/58/38, 29th Session (2003) paras 212–13; CO Japan, A/58/38, 29th

women in the labour market is characterized by a strong occupational segregation with a concomitant wage differential.[45] The Committee also, on occasions, expressed its concern at the under-representation of women in qualified positions in some areas of professional and public life, such as the judiciary and public affairs.[46] Occupations in prisons, police, and the military have frequently been barred to women and the European Court of Justice has ruled that this violates the principle of equal access for women.[47]

The Committee has linked the existence of a segregated labour market and low pay for women with gender stereotypes, which perpetuate the attitude that women play a secondary role in the workforce and are available as cheap, part-time workers.[48] Physical segregation of men and women at work may result from traditionalist religious edicts, which prohibit the intermingling of men and women: the ILO has addressed the problem of segregation at work under Sharia law and noted that separation of men and women at the workplace or vocational guidance of women towards typically female sectors, whether it be a prohibition of co-mingling at work or the limited training of women, may result in occupational segregation according to sex.[49] It is clear under Articles 11(1)(b) and 5 that States parties must take all appropriate measures to modify these restrictive cultural patterns where they result in the exclusion of women from access to the same employment opportunities as men.

2. Selection for Employment

The right to application of the same criteria for selection in matters of employment—equal treatment in acceptance for employment—is important in conceptual terms as well as legal terms. Employers, public and private, are not free to discriminate against women when taking on new employees, even prior to the existence of a contractual relationship, and hence recruitment policy must conform to the non-discrimination principles of the Convention, as is made clear by the addition of the requirement of 'the same criteria for selection' in Article 11(1)(b).

V. Article 11(1)(c)

'The right to free choice of profession and employment, the right to promotion, job security and all benefits and conditions of service and the right to receive vocational training and retraining, including apprenticeships, advanced vocational training and recurrent training'.

1. Free Choice of Profession and Employment

Article 11(1)(c) continues the theme of the previous sections, addressing access to the labour market and guaranteeing women's right to free choice of profession and occupation. To this end, the Committee has urged efforts in education, training, and retraining,[50]

Session (2003) paras 212–13; CO New Zealand, A/58/38, 29th Session (2003) para 412; CO Kyrgyzstan, A/59/38, 30th Session (2004) paras 155–6.

[45] CO Estonia, A/57/38, 26th session (2002) paras 105–8.   [46] Ibid.

[47] Landau and Beigbeder (n 4 above) 105–9.

[48] CO Iceland, CEDAW/C/ICE/CO/6 (2009) paras 29–30; CO Norway, CEDAW/C/NOR/CO/7 (2007) paras 17, 18, 25, and 26.

[49] ILO, 'Special Survey on Equality in Employment and Occupation' (1996) para 173.

[50] CO Estonia, A/57/38, 26th Session (2002) para 108; CO Czech Republic, A/57/38, Exceptional Session (2002) paras 99–100; CO Mexico, A/57/38, Exceptional Session (2002) para 444; CO Ukraine, A/57/38, 27th Session (2002) paras 293–4.

curricula reform to combat traditional attitudes, and creation of an enabling environment for women's presence in high-level and well-paid positions.[51]

2. Equal Treatment in Employment Conditions

Article 11(1)(c) requires the same rights on a basis of equality of men and women, in promotion, job security, benefits and conditions of service, training, retraining and recurrent training. The Committee's concluding observations on equal treatment in employment conditions have largely addressed the issue of promotion. The Committee has termed women's concentration in low-paid jobs as being a result not only of horizontal job segregation (occupational segregation) but also vertical segregation (segregation in promotion).[52] It expressed particular concern that although women have a higher level of education than men in some States parties, this has not been translated into promotion of women to senior posts in the public and private sectors[53] and that, in others, in spite of their higher level of university education women remain under-represented in Parliament, in academia, and in the economic sector.[54] The Committee has urged adoption of proactive TSMs including quotas to encourage qualified women to apply for high-ranking posts in academia.[55]

3. Sexual Harassment

The Committee has addressed the issue of sexual harassment as a phenomenon which has contributed to widespread discrimination against women.[56]

Sexual harassment has been defined as 'any form of unwanted verbal, non-verbal or physical conduct of a sexual nature ... with the purpose or effect of violating the dignity of a person, in particular when creating an intimidating, hostile, degrading, humiliating or offensive environment'.[57] It is discriminatory in its impact because a worker victimized by sexual harassment will frequently be affected in wages, promotion, or dismissal (*quid pro quo* harassment) or, even in the absence of direct measures of economic blackmail where the harassment creates a hostile environment, she will be unable to fulfil her professional potential in the workplace.[58] Sexual harassment is clearly a result of discriminatory organizational culture in workplaces.[59]

Sexual harassment has been regarded variously, in different international and national contexts, as discrimination in employment conditions, sexual violence in the workplace, and a violation of the employee's human dignity. The Committee has primarily dealt with sexual harassment in the workplace in its General Recommendation 19 on violence against

---

[51] CO Trinidad and Tobago, A/57/38, 26th Session (2002) paras 151–2.
[52] CO Switzerland, A/58/38, 28th Session (2003) para 124; CO Brazil, A/58/38, 29th Session (2003) para 124.
[53] CO Saint Kitts and Nevis, A/57/38, 27th Session (2002) para 99.
[54] CO Greece, A/57/38, Exceptional Session (2002) para 287.
[55] CO Greece, A/57/38, Exceptional Session (2002) para 288.
[56] CO Samoa, A/60/38, 33rd Session (2005) paras 54–5; CO Argentina, A/59/38, 30th Session (2004) paras 121, 122 & 162; CO New Zealand, A/58/38, 28th Session (2003) paras 166–7; CO South Africa, A/53/38/Rev.1, 19th Session (1998) para 104.
[57] Council Directive (EC) 2002/73 on the implementation of the principle of equal treatment for men and women as regards access to employment, vocational training and promotion, and working conditions [2002] OJ L269/15 art 2(2).
[58] ILO, 'General Observation: Concerning Convention No 111' (2002); Council Directive (EC) 2006/54 on the implementation of the principle of equal opportunities and equal treatment of men and women in matters of employment and occupation (recast) [2006] OJ L204/23 para 6.
[59] European Commission 'Sexual harassment in the Workplace in the European Union' (1998) at <http://www.un.org/womenwatch/osagi/pdf/shworkpl.pdf> accessed 31 December 2010.

women, emphasizing that this is not only a phenomenon of discrimination at work but also of sexual violence against women: 'Equality in employment can be seriously impaired when women are subjected to gender-specific violence, such as sexual harassment in the workplace'.[60] The Committee's policy on sexual harassment as violence in the workplace is elaborated below, in the context of health and safety in the workplace.[61]

4. Vocational Training, Retraining, and Recurrent Training

The emphasis on vocational training, retraining, and recurrent training is especially significant in view of the interrupted career or labour market participation pattern of women's work.[62] The Committee has recommended education, training, and retraining as a way to eliminate occupational segregation[63] and has recommended job-training programmes for different groups of unemployed women.[64]

5. Part-time Work

The issue of part-time work brings into question both women's right to free choice of employment and their right to equal treatment in employment conditions.

The Committee has expressed concern at the high concentration of women in part-time employment.[65] This has been criticized as indicating a failure to accept women's family role. However, contextually understood, the Committee is indicating that the high concentration of women in part-time work may be evidence of structural failure to facilitate full employment for women, whether as a result of lack of child care facilities or as a result of failure to eliminate cultural stereotypes which place child care responsibility solely on women and regard their work in the labour market as of secondary importance. States parties must 'improve the conditions for working women so as to enable them to choose full-time, rather than part-time, employment in which they are currently over-represented'.[66] The Committee has played an important role in emphasizing the problem of women being forced into part-time work and in identifying a State obligation to take all appropriate measures to enable them to choose full-time work if they wish. The Committee's approach, focusing as it does on the problem of relegating women to part-time work, is in contrast with the approach reflected in the ILO Convention on Part-Time Work, which justifies part-time work as a means of increasing employment opportunities and requires freedom of choice not to work part-time only for those workers previously employed full-time.[67] The Committee regards it as an obligation on States parties to secure conditions which will allow all women to make their own choice as to whether to work full-time or part-time.

---

[60] GR 19 para 17.

[61] See the discussion below in section C on health and safety in the workplace. See also the discussion in ch on Violence against Women.

[62] Schöpp-Schilling (n 1 above) 174–5.

[63] CO Ukraine, A/57/38/, 27th Session (2002) para 294; CO Peru, A/57/38/, Exceptional Session (2002) para 479.

[64] CO New Zealand, A/58/38/, 29th Session (2003) para 412.

[65] CO New Zealand, A/58/38/, 29th Session (2003) para 411; CO Japan, A/58/38/, 29th Session (2003) para 369.

[66] CO The Netherlands, A/56/38, 25th Session (2001) para 214.

[67] ILO Convention concerning Part-Time Work (ILO Convention No 175) (adopted 24 June 1994, entered into force 28 February 1998) 2010 UNTS 51 arts 9–10.

The need to determine whether disadvantageous treatment of part-time workers constitutes indirect discrimination arose in the *Nguyen* Communication under the Optional Protocol.[68] The right to equal treatment in part-time work had been established in the ILO Convention on Part-Time Work,[69] in the EC Part-Time Work Directive,[70] and in the case law of the ECJ,[71] which has held that disadvantageous treatment of part-time workers constitutes indirect discrimination against women as it adversely affects a much greater number of women than of men. The Communication raised the issue of a non-accumulation clause in the maternity leave benefit for self-employed women, depriving them of the benefit where they, concurrently, receive an equivalent benefit on the basis of salaried employment. The Committee found no violation, with the majority stating that the Convention leaves States parties a margin of discretion to devise a system of maternity leave benefits. Dissenting Committee members were, however, of the opinion that the non-accumulation clause might constitute indirect discrimination against women who work as part-time salaried workers, in addition to working in self-employment as family helpers in their husbands' enterprises, by depriving them of maternity benefits based on the overall number of hours in their combined working situations.

VI. Article 11(1)(d)

'The right to equal remuneration, including benefits, and to equal treatment in respect of work of equal value, as well as equality of treatment in evaluation of the quality of the work'.

In 1989, in General Recommendation 13 on equal remuneration for work of equal value, the Committee encouraged States parties, which had not yet done so, to ratify the 1951 ILO Equal Remuneration Convention (ILO Convention No 100),[72] which is considered a core convention of the ILO.

The word 'remuneration' in Article 11(1)(d) is intended, as agreed in the *travaux préparatoires*, to incorporate the wide definition of pay in ILO Convention No 100.[73] Thus, remuneration includes 'the ordinary, basic or minimum wage or salary and any additional emoluments, whatsoever payable directly or indirectly, whether in cash or in kind, by the employer to the worker and arising out of the worker's employment'.[74] The kind of payments or benefits which are included in a wide definition are: expatriation allowance, contributions to retirement benefits schemes, severance pay, unfair dismissal compensation, free travel facilities for retired employees, and holiday bonuses.[75]

The right to equal pay for work of equal value takes account of the fact that lower wages for women are not only a result of direct discrimination but also, and perhaps chiefly, of the horizontal segregation of jobs and the payment of lower wages in feminized

---

[68] *Ms Dung Thi Thuy Nguyen v The Netherlands* Communication 3/2004 (2006) CEDAW/C/36/D/3/2004.

[69] ILO Convention No 175 arts 1(c)(ii) and 5.

[70] Council Directive (EC) 97/81 concerning the Framework Agreement on part-time work concluded by UNICEF, CEEP, and the ETUC [1997] OJ L14/9; SI 2000/1551 The Part-time Workers (Prevention of Less Favourable Treatment) ('Part-time Work Directive) Regulations 2000 (UK).

[71] Landau and Beigbeder (n 4 above) 183–205.

[72] ILO Convention concerning Equal Remuneration for Men and Women Workers for Work of Equal Value (ILO Convention No 100) (adopted 29 June 1951, entered into force 23 May 1953) 165 UNTS 303.

[73] Rehof (n 11 above) 136.   [74] ILO Convention No 100 art 1(a).

[75] Landau and Beigbeder (n 4 above) 69, 81–8.

occupations or professions.[76] The Committee has frequently brought the causal connection between the wage gap and occupational segregation to the attention of States parties.[77] The Committee has urged States parties to promote job evaluation measures, to accelerate the eradication of pay discrimination[78] or to give wage increases in the female-dominated sectors of public employment to decrease the wage gap.[79]

General Recommendation 13 noted, in 1989, that 'more remains to be done to ensure application of [the] principle' of equal remuneration for work of equal value. It called for the creation of implementation machinery wherever possible. Nearly twenty years later, the ILO Committee of Experts still notes that difficulties in applying ILO Convention No 100 in law and in practice result, in particular, from a lack of understanding of the scope and implications of the concept of work of equal value. Proof of discrimination in work of equal value cases is difficult to establish, and effective implementation of the principle requires shifting the burden of proof to the individual employers to justify the pay gap between their male and female employees by objective factors unconnected to sex.[80]

Article 11(1)(d) regards job evaluation as an inherent part of the process of proving that work performed by women is of equal value to that performed by men in the workplace,[81] in contrast to the ECJ which has held that the right to make a claim should not be conditioned on job evaluation.[82] Job evaluation entails assessment of the tasks and the demands made on workers in carrying them out, such as skill, effort, and responsibility.[83] There is a risk of sex bias in the evaluation process as a result of the pervasive undervaluation of tasks performed predominantly by women. ILO Convention No 100 required that, where there is job evaluation, the appraisal must be 'objective'.[84] Article 11(1)(d) of the Convention expressly requires 'equality of treatment in the evaluation of the quality of work', and the Committee, in General Recommendation 13[85] and in State party reviews,[86] suggested that States parties should consider the study, development, and adoption of job evaluation systems which are based on gender-neutral criteria.

---

[76] ILO, 'Report of the Committee on the Application of Standards' (2007).

[77] CO Estonia, A/57/38, 26th Session (2002) para 107; CO Trinidad and Tobago, A/57/38, 26th Session (2002) para 151; CO Ukraine, A/57/38, 27th Session (2002) para 293; CO Hungary, A/57/38, Exceptional Session (2002) para 327.

[78] CO Denmark, A/57/38, 27th Session (2002) para 326; CO Hungary, A/57/38, Exceptional Session (2002) para 328; CO Luxembourg, A/58/38, 28th Session (2003) para 315; CO Norway, A/58/38, 28th Session (2003) para 430.

[79] CO Estonia, A/57/38, 26th Session (2002) para 108.

[80] CCPR CO Iceland, A/60/40 Vol. I, 83rd Session (2005) para 87(5) (noting that 'the burden of proof rests with the employer, who must demonstrate that any difference in wages paid to men and women for work of equal value is based on factors other than the gender of the employees'); see also Case C-236/98 *Jämställdhetsombudsmannen v Örebro läns landsting* [2000] ECR I-2189.

[81] There were disagreements in the Working Group as to whether this inclusion might be unduly burdensome, especially for developing countries: Rehof (n 11 above) 135.

[82] Case 61/81 *Commission v UK* [1982] ECR 2601.

[83] Case C-127/92 *Dr Pamela Enderby v Sec of State for Health* [1993] ECR I-5535. Examples of national applications of the requirement of equal remuneration for work of equal value are wardens in sheltered accommodation (predominantly women) vis-à-vis security guards in offices (predominantly men), school meal supervisors vis-à-vis garden and park supervisors, speech therapists vis-à-vis pharmacists.

[84] ILO Convention No 100 art 3.   [85] GR 13 para 2.

[86] CO Switzerland, A/58/38, 28th Session (2003) para 131; CO Finland, A/56/38, 24th Session (2001) para 283.

VII. Article 11(1)(e)

'The right to social security, particularly in cases of retirement, unemployment, sickness, invalidity and old age and other incapacity to work, as well as the right to paid leave.'

Social security is an umbrella term for social insurance programmes which provide protection in defined situations of need. In the context of Article 11, the situations of need referred to are those resulting from various kinds of incapacity to work, whether temporary or long-term: 'retirement, unemployment, sickness, invalidity and old age and other incapacity to work'. Social security may be provided through social insurance programmes funded by employer and/or employee contributions to a public or private insurance scheme or may be directly funded by the State.

Women are disproportionately represented amongst those in situations of need. The Committee has noted that the impact of poverty is greater among women and has expressed concern about the feminization of poverty.[87] The Committee has expressed concern as to the high percentage of women living in poverty.[88] It has drawn attention to the barriers in relation to access to education, employment, health care, and other social services faced by vulnerable groups of women.[89] It has addressed the problem of women migrant workers and advised that insurance should cover disabled and jobless women after they are repatriated.[90] It has commented that States parties have not applied the gender perspective in their national activities to combat poverty and urged States parties to assess the gender impact of anti-poverty measures. It has called on them to increase their efforts to combat poverty among women in general and vulnerable groups of women, in particular, and to ensure women's access to production resources, education, and technical training.[91]

1. *Coverage of Social Security Schemes*

Women in precarious work will often not be eligible for social security. The Committee has expressed concern regarding social security eligibility of women in the informal economy[92] and has called on States parties to ensure that women domestic workers (including migrant workers), temporary wage earners, women in the informal sector, and rural and indigenous women have access to social security.[93] In the *Nguyen* Communication, dissenting Committee members drew attention to the need to guarantee full social security benefits for women in part-time work.[94] The CESCR has noted that some social security schemes exclude, among others, women who are homemakers, due to their inability to make sufficient voluntary contributions.[95]

The right to equality in social security precludes denying married women benefits to which married men would be entitled. The Human Rights Committee held that the Netherlands had violated women employees' right to equal protection of the law by

---

[87] CO Belarus, A/59/38, 30th Session (2004) para 353.

[88] CO Canada, A/58/38, 28th Session (2003) para 357; CO Sri Lanka, A/57/38, 26th Session (2002) paras 296–7.

[89] See the discussion below in section D. V.: Intersectional Discrimination.

[90] CO Sri Lanka, A/57/38, 26th Session (2002) para 293.

[91] CO Canada, A/58/38, 28th Session (2003) paras 346, 357, and 358; CO Costa Rica, A/58/38, 29th Session (2003) paras 66–7; CO Costa Rica, A/58/38, 29th Session (2003) para 67.

[92] CO The Philippines, CEDAW/C/PHI/CO/6 (2006) para 25.

[93] CO Costa Rica, A/58/38 (Supp), 26th Session (2003) para 63.

[94] *Ms Dung Thi Thuy Nguyen* (n 68 above) para 10.5 (dissent).

[95] CESCR Report E/2006/22 (2005) UN Doc E/C.12/2005/5 para 207(e).

denying long-term unemployment benefits to a married woman because she was not the family 'breadwinner', while married men could receive unemployment benefits even if their wife was the principal income earner.[96]

2. Retirement

Older women are one of the population's most vulnerable to poverty. Older women who have been employed in the labour force generally receive lower pension payments than men, as a result both of the lower wages paid to women and the fewer number of years they work on average.[97] The Committee has expressed concern regarding the level of women's pension benefits.[98] It has pointed out that older women are disadvantaged by having experienced multiple forms of discrimination throughout their economically active years and recommended that women's unpaid and paid employment patterns be taken into consideration in order to avoid a discriminatory impact.[99] Their income after leaving the labour force is affected by their age of eligibility for a pension. The idea of allowing a lower pensionable age for women was raised but was a subject of contention in the *travaux préparatoires*.[100] The compromise in Article 11 was to leave open the possibility of allowing an option of earlier retirement by providing that the retirement conditions did not need to be on the 'same terms as men' but rather must be 'equally with men'.[101]

It is clear under Article 11(1)(e) that women cannot be forced to retire earlier than men. However, the possibility of allowing an option of early retirement remains open and may be desirable: the Committee has expressed concern about the situation of women over the age of forty in the labour market[102] and eligibility for pension at an earlier age might reduce the risk of poverty for some of the women in this group. The CESCR has noted with concern different retirement ages for men and women, commenting that they in practice result in lower pensions for women and recommending the adoption of the same age of retirement for men and women,[103] but that Committee did not consider the possibility of allowing women an option of earlier retirement which would allow individual women to choose the best course of action for themselves.

3. Paid Leave

The right of women to paid leave on equal terms with men taken at its narrowest means the right to the same 'periodic holidays with pay, as well as remuneration for public holidays' as is guaranteed to all workers under Article 7(b) of the ICESCR. Additionally, ICESCR 7(d) includes the right to 'rest, leisure and reasonable limitation of working hours' and this provision should, by association, draw attention to the wider problem of women's leisure time when compared with men: 'almost everywhere women are now working more outside the home, but there has not been a parallel lightening of their responsibility for unremunerated work in the household and in the community'.[104] Addressing the full scope of Article 7(b) under CEDAW Article 11(1)(e) might provide

---

[96] *FH Zwaan-de Vries v The Netherlands*, CCPR Communication No 182/1984 (1987) UN Doc CCPR/C/29/D/182/1984.

[97] See the discussion below in section D. V.: Intersectional Discrimination.

[98] CO Iceland, A/57/38, 26th Session (2002) para 250.

[99] CO France, A/58/38, 29th Session (2003) paras 263–4.   [100] Rehof (n 11 above) 136.

[101] Ibid.   [102] CO Croatia, A/60/38, 32nd Session (2005) para 194.

[103] CESCR Report E/2003/22 (2003) UN Doc E/2003/22 paras 360 and 382.

[104] Department of Economic and Social Affairs (Statistics Division), 'World's Women 2005 Progress in Statistics' (New York 2005) 47.

a basis for exploring flexible work, job-sharing, and other forms of scheduling which would ensure women rest and leisure on a basis of equality with men.

VIII. Article 11(1)(f)

'The right to protection of health and to safety in working conditions, including the safeguarding of the function of reproduction.'

1. *Safe and Healthy Working Conditions*

Article 11(1)(f) ensures women the same right to safe and healthy working conditions as men and also adds the right to safeguarding of the function of reproduction.[105] This section is particularly important as women's employment in low-paid and precarious work is liable to expose them also to unsafe and unhealthy working conditions. The Committee has expressed concern regarding women's occupational health, citing on one occasion conditions in the tobacco-growing industry and on another that 12 per cent of women were working in conditions which did not meet health and safety standards.[106]

ILO conventions, from the beginning of the twentieth century, imposed prohibitions on women's night work, underground work, and heavy lifting.[107] These prohibitions disadvantaged women in the labour market by stereotyping them and by excluding them from remunerative employment.[108] The key breakthrough in the progressive cancellation of protective measures for women, except for maternity protection, was in the 1975 ILO Resolution and Plan of Action which required ongoing review of protective legislation in the light of scientific knowledge and technological advances.[109] Similarly, Article 11(3) of the Convention requires periodic review of protective measures on the basis of scientific and technological change.

The prohibitions on night work and underground work have been progressively modified in the ILO context[110] and the ECJ has held that any prohibition of night work for women constitutes discrimination.[111] The issue of prohibition of women's work in these areas has not yet been addressed by the Committee.

---

[105] The right to safe and healthy working conditions is guaranteed to all workers under the CESCR and the ILO Occupational Safety Health Convention. CESCR art 7(b); ILO Convention concerning Occupational Safety and Health and the Working Environment (ILO Convention No 155) (adopted 22 June 1981, entered into force 11 August 1983) 1331 UNTS 279.

[106] CO Republic of Moldova, A/55/38, 23rd Session (2000) paras 109–10; CO Russian Federation, A/57/38, 26th Session (2002) para 385.

[107] ILO Convention concerning Night Work (ILO Convention No 171) (adopted 26 June 1990, entered into force 4 January 1995) 1855 UNTS 305; Underground Work Convention (ILO Convention No 45) (adopted 21 June 1935, entered into force 30 May 1937) 40 UNTS 63; ILO Convention concerning the Maximum Permissible Weight to be Carried by One Worker (ILO Convention No 127) (adopted 28 June 1967, entered into force 10 March 1970) 721 UNTS 305. See Landau (n 4 above) (noting that Convention No 127 is under revision) 129.

[108] WB Creighton, *Working Women and the Law* (1979) 26–37; Schöpp-Schilling (n 1 above) 173–4.

[109] Landau and Beigbeder (n 4 above) 116.

[110] ILO Convention No 171; ILO Convention No 45; Safety and Health in Mines Convention (ILO Convention No 176) (adopted 22 June 1995, entered into force 5 June 1998) 2029 UNTS 207.

[111] Case C-345 *Ministere Public v Stoeckel* [1989] ECR I-4047; Case C-197/96 *Commission v France* [1996] ECR I-l 489. The ECJ held that prohibition of night work for women was a violation of the principle of equal treatment and if women are exposed to greater risk of attack at night, appropriate measures can be taken to diminish it.

2. Safeguarding of the Function of Reproduction

Article 11(1)(f) specifically requires States parties to take all appropriate measures to safeguard the function of reproduction in the workplace, under the chapeau of ensuring the same rights on a basis of equality of men and women.

In the case of both men and women, protection of their reproductive function may require prohibition of their exposure to certain industrial processes or chemicals, such as radiation. In the case of pregnant women, an additional reason for protection may be to protect the foetus or to protect the newborn children of mothers who are breast-feeding.[112] The Committee has addressed the need for breast-feeding breaks to be implemented in legislation.[113]

The Article 11(1)(f) obligation to safeguard reproductive health in the workplace is especially important in view of the fact that this is not a view that had been universally adopted.[114] Article 11(1)(f) does not allow for 'equal' removal of protection for the function of reproduction, but indicates, instead, the requiremen t of providing equal protective measures to safeguard the reproductive functions of both men and women.

3. Sexual Violence in the Work Environment

Women are also exposed to gendered health and safety risks in the work environment as a result of sexual violence. The Committee in its General Recommendation 19, analyzing sexual harassment in the workplace, asserted that sexual harassment can be humiliating and may constitute a health and safety problem and recommended measures to prevent it.[115] This approach is well founded in regional research which has concluded: 'Sexual harassment pollutes the working environment and can have a devastating effect upon the health and safety of those affected by it'.[116]

The Indian Supreme Court relied on India's ratification of the Convention to hold, in the case of *Vishaka v State of Rajasthan*, that the gang rape of a social worker was prohibited, although there was no law prohibiting sexual harassment in the workplace. A set of guidelines binding public and private employers was introduced, closely following the standards laid down in General Recommendation 19.[117] In a later case,[118] the Supreme Court of India held that dismissal of an employee, after rejection of her allegation of attempted sexual harassment had been rejected by a court, was wrongful. The Court stated that the message of the Convention and other international agreements was to direct State parties 'to take appropriate measures to prevent discrimination of all forms against women besides taking steps to protect the honour and dignity of women'.

---

[112] As indicated in Council Directive (EC) 92/85 on the introduction of measures to encourage improvements in the safety and health at work of pregnant workers and workers who have recently given birth or are breastfeeding [1992] OJ L348.

[113] CO Democratic People's Republic of Korea, A/60/38, 33rd Session (2005) para 32; CO Estonia, A/57/38, 26th Session (2002) para 83; CO Panama, A/40/45, 4th Session (1985) paras 197–8.

[114] The US Supreme Court took the contrary position that 'fetal protection policy' limits women's equal employment opportunity and constitutes a discriminatory practice: *International Union v Johnson Controls* 499 US 187, 111 SCt 1196 (1991).

[115] GR 19 para 18.

[116] M Rubenstein, *The Dignity of Women at Work: A Report on the Problem of Sexual Harassment in the Member States of the European Communities* (1987) Appendix.

[117] *Vishaka v State of Rajasthan* (1997) AIR 1997 SC 3011 (Supreme Court of India); EOC 92–222 *Aldridge v Booth* (1988) 80 ALR 1.

[118] *Apparel Export Promotion Council v AK Chopra* (1999) 1 SCC 759 (Supreme Court of India).

In extreme situations, women's exposure to sexual violence at work has gone as far as rape and murder. The Committee in its inquiry under the Optional Protocol on the cases of abduction, rape, and murder of hundreds of women in Cuidad Juárez, Mexico, situated the problem in the establishment of the *maquilas* and the creation of jobs mainly for women, while the social change in women's roles had not been accompanied by a change in traditionally patriarchal attitudes and mentalities.[119] The Committee commented: 'Some high-level officials…have gone so far as to publicly blame the victims themselves for their fate, attributing it to their manner of dress, the place in which they worked, their conduct, the fact that they were walking alone, or parental neglect.'[120] This kind of risk has been one of the rationales given in the past for prohibiting night work for women. Under the Convention, the risk of sexual violence must be met by eliminating the violence and turning the workplace into a safe environment for women rather than by restricting women's freedom of choice and right to work.

IX. Article 11(2)

'In order to prevent discrimination against women on the grounds of marriage or maternity and to ensure their effective right to work'.

Article 11(2) requires elimination of discrimination against women on grounds of marriage or maternity. The principle of equality makes it essential to offset the disadvantage faced by women as to conditions for access to and participation in the labour market, which reflect gender stereotypes that women are chiefly responsible for unpaid work related to looking after a family, as wives or mothers, while paid work derived from an economic activity is mainly the responsibility of men.

The Committee has expressed:

concern at the overemphasis on legislative protection of and cultural promotion of motherhood and family roles for women, rather than on women as individuals in their own right. The traditional, stereotyped view of women as mothers is thereby reinforced and negates the participation of fathers in child care. That perception reflects a misunderstanding of such critical concepts as gender roles, indirect discrimination and de facto inequality.[121]

Ensuring women's effective right to work requires not only removal of stereotypes but also protection of women's employment status during pregnancy and maternity leave and provision of supporting social services to enable parents to combine family obligations with work responsibilities. In this context, Article 11(2) requires States parties to take appropriate measures to secure the right to job security and the right to maternity leave with pay, to encourage the provision of child care facilities and to provide special protection regarding harmful work during pregnancy. The principles of maternity protection have been universally embraced and at least some of the basic elements of maternity protection have been adopted into the legislation of virtually every nation in the world.[122]

---

[119] 'Report on Mexico produced by the Committee on the Elimination of Discrimination against Women under article 8 of the Optional Protocol to the Convention, and reply from the Government of Mexico' (2005) CEDAW/C/2005/OP.8/MEXICO para 25.

[120] Ibid para 67.

[121] CO Slovakia, A/53/38, 19th Session (1998) para 74. For similar sentiments, see also CO Greece, A/57/38, Exceptional Session (2002) para 285; CO Czech Republic, A/41/45, 5th Session (1986) para 185.

[122] International Labour Conference, 88th Session, *Concerning Maternity Protection Health and Safety in Agriculture* (Geneva 29 May 2000).

X. Article 11(2)(a)

'States are required to take appropriate measures to prohibit, subject to the imposition of sanctions, dismissal on the grounds of pregnancy or of maternity leave and dismissals on the basis of marital status'.

1. Prohibition of Dismissal

Article 11(2)(a) prohibits dismissal on the grounds of pregnancy, maternity leave, or marital status. The Committee has called on States parties to take measures to prevent the practice of illegal dismissal of women in cases of pregnancy and childbirth.[123]

Article 11(2)(a) was relied upon by the Supreme Court of Belize. A teacher was dismissed from a Catholic school because she was an unmarried mother and had failed to comply with an alleged contractual undertaking to live in accordance with Jesus' teaching on marriage and sex. The Court held, citing Article 11(2)(a) as a primary ground, that the dismissal was discrimination on the basis of pregnancy and of marital status and was in violation of her constitutional rights.[124]

2. Discrimination in Conditions of Employment and in Acceptance to Employment

Read in the context of the chapeau of Article 11(2), which addresses the need to ensure women's 'effective right to work', the focus on dismissal in Article 11(2)(a) should not be taken to have a narrow meaning. The overall problem addressed in Article 11(2) is the effective right to work, which entails prevention of discrimination not only in dismissal but also in conditions of employment, the worsening of which might constitute constructive dismissal. It also entails prevention of discrimination in acceptance to work, which would result in excluding pregnant women or women who are parents of young children from work. In this context, the Committee has expressed concern regarding the persistence of women's exclusion from employment on the grounds of pregnancy and in compulsory pregnancy testing as a condition for employment.[125] Additionally, unfavourable treatment on grounds of pregnancy or maternity might properly be regarded as discrimination against women in employment, under Article 11(1)(b).[126]

XI. Article 11(2)(b)

'To introduce maternity leave with pay or with comparable social benefits without loss of former employment, seniority or social allowances'.

1. Right to Leave

The right to maternity leave provides for integration of women's childbearing role in the workplace, which is essential for implementation of women's effective right to work.[127]

---

[123] CO Japan, CEDAW/C/JPN/CO/6 (2009) paras 45–6; CO Finland, CEDAW/C/FIN/CO/6 (2008) paras 25–6; CO Dominican Republic, A/59/38, 31st Session (2004) para 306.

[124] *Roches v Wade* (30 April 2004) Action No 132 (SCt Belize), extracted in M Shivas and S Coleman (eds), *Without Prejudice: CEDAW and the Determination of Women's Rights in a Legal and Cultural Context* (2010) 149.

[125] CO Mexico, CEDAW/C/MEX/CO/6 (2006) para 30, CO Dominican Republic, A/59/38/, 31st Session (2004) para 306.

[126] See, eg, Council Directive 2006/54 (n 58 above) para 24: 'It is clear from the case law of the Court of Justice that unfavourable treatment of a woman related to pregnancy or maternity constitutes direct discrimination on grounds of sex'.

[127] *Municipal Corporation of Delhi v Female Workers (Muster Roll)* (2000) AIR 2000 SC 1274 (Supreme Court of India). The Supreme Court of India awarding employees who were not 'regular employees' full

No minimum length of maternity leave is established in Article 11. The first international minimum standard for maternity leave was set by the ILO Maternity Protection Convention in 1919 at six weeks, extended in 2000 to fourteen weeks:[128] ILO Maternity Protection Recommendation 2000 sets the desirable standard at eighteen weeks.[129] The need underlying the requirement of mandatory leave for the mother in childbearing is physiological and is, hence, a maternal rather than a parental right.[130] The Committee should consider whether, under Article 11(2)(b), a distinction can be made between mandatory and optional leave periods which would make it possible for women to opt out of the non-mandatory period of maternity leave. It follows that the optional part of the maternity leave should be parental leave, transferable to the father, as discussed below.

2. With Pay or Comparable Social Benefits

The requirement of pay or comparable social benefits during the leave is the essence of Article 11(2)(b). Most working women depend on their wages for income and cannot afford to take maternity leave without pay. ILO Convention No 183 of 2000 sets minimum benefits at a level which ensures that a woman can maintain herself and her child in proper conditions of health and with a suitable standard of living, and where, under national law or practice, benefits are based on previous earnings, they must not be less than two-thirds of the woman's previous earnings.[131]

ILO Convention Nos. 103 and 183 set the principle that in order to protect the situation of women in the labour market, maternity leave benefits must be provided through compulsory social insurance or public funds and that an employer should not be individually liable for the direct cost, without that employer's specific agreement. However, in 2000, the ILO established exceptions to the rule. The shift to allowing the employer to be the cost-bearer increases the likelihood of discrimination in employment of women of childbearing age.[132] Nevertheless, Article 11(2)(b) leaves open both the possibility of the employer directly paying the employee her wages during the leave or of the State providing comparable social benefits.[133] The Committee has said that States parties are required to provide for maternity leave in legislation and to regulate employers' obligation to pay wages or must provide comparable social benefits, funded from national insurance or public funds.[134]

---

statutory rights to maternity leave, said that art 11 of the Convention which governs marriage and maternity must 'be read into the contract of service' between the Corporation and the women employees.

[128] ILO Convention No 100; ILO Convention concerning Maternity Protection (Revised 1952) (ILO Convention No 103) (adopted 28 June 1952, entered into force 7 September 1955) 214 UNTS 321; ILO Convention concerning the Revision of the Maternity Protection Convention (revised) (ILO Convention No 183) (adopted 15 June 2000, entered into force 7 February 2002) 2181 UNTS 253.

[129] ILO Recommendation R191: Maternity Recommendation Concerning the Revision of the Maternity Protection Recommendation (1952), 88th Conference Session, Geneva, 30 May 2000.

[130] *Schachter v The Queen* [1988] Trial Div. T. 2345–86 (Fed Ct of Canada).

[131] ILO Convention No 183 art 6(3).

[132] CO Jordan, A/55/38, 22nd Session (2000) para 185; CO New Zealand, A/53/38/Rev.1, 19th Session (1998) para 269.

[133] Rehof (n 11 above) 139–40.

[134] CO Bangladesh, A/59/38, 31st Session (2004) para 254; CO Dominican Republic, A/59/38, 31st Session (2004) para 303; CO Switzerland, A/58/38, 28th Session (2003) para 133; CO Guyana, A/56/38, 25th Session (2001) para 169.

3. *Protection of Employment Status*

Article 11(2)(b) protects women against loss of employment, seniority, or social allowances as a result of maternity leave. This section goes beyond protection against dismissal and loss of pay discussed above. It seeks to maintain the continuity of women's employment status as it was at the time of commencement of maternity leave.[135]

XII. Article 11(2)(c)

'To encourage the provision of the necessary supporting social services to enable parents to combine family obligations with work responsibilities and participation in public life, in particular through promoting the establishment and development of a network of childcare facilities'.

1. *Affordable and Accessible Child Care Facilities*

Provision of affordable and accessible child care facilities is essential to allow two parents or single parents to participate in the labour market. Since, in the vast majority of families, women are still the primary caretaker, child care facilities are in general essential to women's rather than men's equal employment opportunity. According to UNICEF,[136] a majority of the rising generation in economically advanced societies is spending a significant part of childhood in out-of-home child care.

The Convention was the first international convention to refer expressly to the need for provision of child care facilities to enable parents to combine family obligations with work responsibilities and participation in public life. Shortly after the Convention's adoption, in 1981, the ILO provided that all measures compatible with national conditions and possibilities shall be taken to develop or promote community services, public or private, such as child care and family services and facilities.[137]

The period of leave which is not to meet the physiological needs of the mother is more properly to be regarded as child care leave and as a parental obligation, as is required under Article 5(b) of the Convention, which requires State parties to recognize the common responsibility of men and women in the upbringing and development of their children. The Committee has encouraged the introduction of parental leave and has called for incentives for men to take up parental leave.[138] The Committee has applauded States parties which have encouraged male employees to use their right to paternity leave and to increase their involvement as caretakers.[139]

2. *Encourage or Provide*

The Convention does not impose an obligation on States parties to provide child care services but only an obligation to encourage their provision. It also does not impose any

---

135 CO Timor-Leste, CEDAW/C/TLC/CO/1 (2009) paras 39–40; CO Jordan, A/55/38, 22nd Session (2000) para 185.

136 P Adamson, *'The child care transition: a league table of early childhood education and care in economically advanced countries'* in *Innocenti Research Centre Report Card 8* (UNICEF, 2008).

137 ILO Workers with Family Responsibilities Convention (ILO Convention No 156) (adopted 23 June 1981, entered into force 11 August 1983) 1331 UNTS 295, art 5.

138 CO Germany, CEDAW/C/DEU/CO/6 (2009) para 38; CO Sweden, CEDAW/C/SWE/CO/7 (2008) para 27; CO Czech Republic, CEDAW/C/CZE/CO/3 (2006) para 26; CO Canada, A/58/38, 28th Session (2003) para 381; CO Finland, A/56/38, 24th Session (2001) para 298.

139 CO Canada, CEDAW/C/CAN/CO/7 (2008) para 6; CO Luxembourg, A/58/38, 28th Session (2003) para 298; CO Norway, A/50/38, 14th Session (1995) para 486; CO Finland, A/50/38, 14th Session (1995) para 388.

obligation with regard to state funding of child care. It will be up to the Committee to introduce guidelines which will interpret 'the necessary supporting social services' as services which render child care affordable and accessible. Some indication of the Committee's preparedness to impose an obligation on States to provide such services can be inferred from its recommendation that a 'State party . . . ensure that maternity leave is available in all public and private employment, especially through the enactment of a law on maternity leave, and expand the number of crèches available for working mothers'.[140]

XIII. Article 11(2)(d)

'To provide special protection to women during pregnancy in types of work proved to be harmful to them'.

There is considerable overlap between this provision and that of Article 11(1)(f). The difference is that Article 11(1)(f) refers to both men's and women's reproductive health, while this provision focuses only on the state of pregnancy.

The Committee has expressed concern that a danger of discrimination against pregnant women arises from protective provisions on occupational health, recommending, for example, that a State party review its occupational health and safety legislation and standards, with a view to reducing protective standards, which often have a discriminatory effect on women in general and pregnant women in particular.[141] The intention is not, of course, to reduce standards genuinely required for protection of pregnant women but to eliminate discrimination against women where protection of their reproductive role is used as a pretext.

XIV. Article 11(3)

'Protective legislation relating to matters covered in this article shall be reviewed periodically in the light of scientific and technological knowledge and shall be revised, repealed or extended as necessary.'

Article 11(3) reflects the necessity of reviewing and revising protective legislation in light of changes in scientific and technological knowledge to determine whether it remains necessary. Unnecessary mandatory protection limits women's equality of opportunity in employment by excluding them from specific jobs or tasks and by perpetuating negative stereotypes regarding their need for protection. It has been observed that protective legislation for working mothers in the socialist economies of Central and Eastern Europe 'became major negative influences on women's equal opportunities in the newly emerging private labor markets under neo-liberal or welfare-State oriented governments'.[142] The Committee needs to consider the proper balance between protection of women's capability of integrating maternity and employment as against the desirability of non-intervention in regulation of women's opportunity to compete in neo-liberal labour markets. One possible way of dealing with this dilemma is perhaps by converting mandatory exclusions to optional protections, thus leaving individual women a choice.

---

[140] CO Maldives, CEDAW/C/MDV/CO/3 (2007) para 30; CO Bangladesh, A/59/38, 31st Session (2004) paras 253–4; CO Switzerland, A/58/38, 28th Session (2003) para 133; CO Guyana, A/56/38, 25th Session (2001) para 169.

[141] CO Belarus, A/55/38, 22nd Session (2000) para 374.

[142] Schöpp-Schilling (n 1 above) 174.

D. Equality in Context

I. Formal and Substantive Equality

Article 11 requires both formal and substantive equality in the field of employment. The Committee has urged States parties both to ensure equal opportunity for men and women in the labour market (formal equality) and to accelerate the realization of women's *de facto* equality with men in the areas of public and private employment (substantive equality).[143] Specifically, Article 11(1)(c) requires States parties to ensure the right to vocational training, retraining, and recurrent training; this provision is responsive to women's reality of interrupted career patterns, usually as a result of family responsibilities, and of concentration in low-paid occupational sectors. Elaborating on the measures needed to achieve *de facto* equality, the Beijing Declaration and Platform for Action calls for measures to ensure access to ongoing training, including for unemployed women and women re-entering the labour market after an extended temporary exit from employment owing to family responsibilities; to expand training for women in non-traditional areas; promote employment programmes for women entering and re-entering the labour market; to promote equal participation of women in high-skilled jobs, and encourage them to take up non-traditional jobs, especially in science and technology.[144] The Article 11(1)(d) right to equal pay for work of equal value is an additional measure of *de facto* equality, which takes account of the need to change the negative impact on women's pay which results from occupational segregation. Finally, all the measures to ensure women's effective right to work without being prejudiced by their marital status, pregnancy, or maternity also promote *de facto* equality.

II. Direct and Indirect Discrimination

In all aspects of their employment relationship, including access to jobs, employment conditions, and dismissal, women may be victims of direct or indirect discrimination. Both direct and indirect discrimination are prohibited under Article 11 combined with Article 1.

'Direct discrimination' occurs where the difference of treatment disadvantages women as such. Thus, for instance, barring certain occupations to women where there is no good faith, occupational qualification which requires the employment of men is direct discrimination. Payment of lower wages to women for the same job is direct discrimination. Direct discrimination also includes detrimental acts or omissions on the basis of prohibited grounds where there is no comparable similar situation (eg the case of a woman who is pregnant).[145]

'Indirect discrimination' refers to laws, policies, or practices which appear neutral at face value, but have a disproportionate impact on women. There may be indirect discrimination in a criterion which bars women's access by requiring a qualification which excludes women because of their average physiological characteristics, such as a weight or height requirement for police work, or disadvantages them because of biological difference, such as lower pension payments actuarially calculated on the basis of expected longevity. As

---

[143] CO Dominican Republic, A/59/38, 31st Session (2004) para 303.
[144] Beijing Declaration and Platform for Action (n 9 above) Strategic objective F.5 (e) and (g).
[145] CESCR, 'General Comment No 20' (2009) UN Doc E/C 12/GC/20 para 10(a).

discussed above, disadvantageous conditions for part-time workers have been held by the ECJ to be a form of indirect discrimination against women, as they adversely affect a much greater number of women than men, and a minority individual opinion in a case under the Optional Protocol adopted this approach.[146] Article 11(1)(d)'s requirement of the right to equal pay for work of equal value also addresses a form of indirect discrimination. It is the concentration of women in segregated occupational sectors which is the root cause of gender differentials in pay for work of equal value, and its prevention under Article 11(d) is part and parcel of the requirement to eliminate indirect as well as direct discrimination.

III. Elimination of Structural Discrimination Including Gender Stereotyping

The elimination of gender stereotyping or prejudices based on the inferiority of either of the sexes is required under Article 5(a) of the Convention. Article 11 is in its essence an application of this requirement to all issues of women's participation in the labour market. The most universally prevalent gender stereotype still attached to women in all cultures, religious and secular, is that they are primarily homemakers and that their role in the public sphere in general and in the labour market in particular is subordinate to that of men. Thus, all sections of Article 11 and all Committee concluding observations which address women's right to equal opportunity in acceptance to employment and promotion, their right to equal wages for work of equal value, and the need to eliminate occupational segregation in the labour market are directed to eliminating cultural stereotyping and prejudices based on the perceived inferiority of women as workers.

Article 11(2) expressly addresses this problem, obliging States parties to prevent discrimination against women on grounds of marriage or maternity. The Committee has identified overemphasis on women's role in the family as a gender stereotype which widely affects women's equality of opportunity in the labour market.[147] Measures to facilitate the combination of paid work and care activities that are directed solely at women are rejected by the Committee as being gender stereotypical in themselves.[148] The Committee's call to modify 'existing social, religious and cultural norms that recognize men as the head of the family and breadwinner and confine women to the roles of mother and wife'[149] is not a requirement that they neglect their family role. Rather, the basic human rights theme of the Convention is that stereotypes of women's family role must not be allowed to create barriers to women's enjoyment of their rights to work and to equal employment opportunity or to justify their exploitation as lower paid or unpaid workers.

IV. Transformative Equality

In requiring States parties to prevent discrimination against women on grounds of marriage and maternity and to ensure their effective right to work, Article 11(2) institutes a

---

[146] *Ms Dung Thi Thuy Nguyen v The Netherlands* (n 68 above).
[147] CO Georgia, CEDAW/C/GEO/CO/3 (2006) para 17.
[148] eg CO Egypt, A/56/38, 24th Session (2001) para 332.
[149] CO Yemen, CEDAW/C/YEM/CO/6 (2008) para 15; CO Syrian Arab Republic, CEDAW/C/SYR/CO/1 (2007) para 28; CO Uzbekistan, CEDAW/C/UZB/CO/3 (2006) para 20; CO Indonesia, A/53/38, 18th Session (1998) para 289; CO Croatia, A/53/38, 18th Session (1998) para 103; CO Czech Republic, A/53/38/Rev.1, 18th Session (1998) paras 185 and 196.

regime of transformative equality on both a conceptual and institutional level. It requires elimination of gender stereotyping which has fully or partially excluded women from the labour market because of their role in the family. The Committee has articulated the need for transformative equality and structural change, laying down the requirement that 'legislation and policies create the structural and systemic framework that will lead to women's long-term participation in the labour force on a basis of equality with men'.[150] The Committee has contributed to implementing transformative equality by requiring parental leave for child care.

Institutionally, Article 11(2) requires change in the workplace to prevent discrimination and exclusion of women on account of pregnancy, maternity, or marriage and to require accommodation of women's need for paid maternity leave. It also requires States parties to encourage the provision of social services which will enable parents to combine family obligations with participation in the labour market. The Beijing Declaration and Platform for Action elaborates on the action which must be taken by governments, in coordination with NGOs and the private sector, to provide affordable support services such as high-quality child care which address the needs of working men and women.[151] Effective development of transformative equality under the Convention in this context will require a shift from the mere encouragement of social services for care of children and other dependant family members to a fully-fledged social and economic right to such services.

V. Intersectional Discrimination

The Committee has identified various subgroups of women who are subject to intersectional discrimination in the labour market. These subgroups divide into general categories of discrimination: race, ethnicity, nationality, family status, disability and age; and labour force categories of discrimination such as employment in precarious work. In all these situations, sex discrimination is exacerbated by the layer of discrimination added on the basis of the woman's additional group identity.

As regards these groups of women, the Committee has focused on the need to address their low level of participation in the labour market or the problem of job segregation compounded by race and ethnicity.[152] The Committee has expressed concern as to the high percentage of women living in poverty, in particular, older women living alone, female single parents, aboriginal women, women of colour, immigrant women, and women with disabilities.[153] It has drawn attention to the barriers in relation to access to education and employment faced by vulnerable groups of women, including rural women, older women, Traveller women, women who are single parents, and women with disabilities.[154]

---

[150] CO Ireland, A/54/38, 21st Session (1999) para 182.

[151] Beijing Declaration and Platform for Action (n 9 above) Strategic Objective F.3 (f) and (g).

[152] CO Brazil, A/58/38, 29th Session (2003) para 124; CO New Zealand, A/58/38, 29th Session (2003) paras 421–2.

[153] CO Ethiopia, A/59/38, 30th Session (2004) para 259; CO Canada, A/58/38, 28th Session (2003) para 357.

[154] CO Ireland, A/60/38 (Supp), 33rd Session (2005) paras 392–3.

The Committee has expressed special concern about the difficult situation of older women, which arises in large measure from women's labour market participation patterns:

Older women for a variety of reasons, including their work as unpaid family members in the informal sector, part-time work, interrupted career patterns and concentration in low-paying jobs, are often insufficiently covered by health insurance and pension schemes. The Committee recommends that the issue of the care required for older women be addressed through public policy measures in order to establish societal responsibility for their well-being. Care given to them by family members should be socially and financially recognized and encouraged. Special recognition should be provided to the contribution of women to their families, the national economy and civil society throughout their life span: stereotypes and taboos that restrict or limit older women from continuing to contribute should be eliminated.[155]

Intersectional discrimination can be used to describe not only the dual discrimination encountered by women in general categories of discrimination, but also that encountered by women who belong to an economic class which is subject to discrimination, characterized by poverty, low educational or skill levels, and social exclusion or vulnerability. Labour force categories of intersectional discrimination affect women employed in precarious work, non-standard employment which is poorly paid, insecure, unprotected, and cannot support a household. Precarious work is of a gendered nature, with women over-represented as domestic workers, women working in free trade zones or the *maquila* industry, temporary workers, and women working in the informal sector.[156] The Committee has focused on the special problems of women employed in precarious work, calling on States parties to address lack of social security and other labour benefits, including paid maternity leave, in this kind of work. It has also called on States parties to take steps to ensure the implementation and enforcement of labour legislation to guarantee the protection of women employed in precarious work and the punishment of perpetrators of violence against them.[157]

The dual discrimination suffered by women in the context of the labour force sector in which they are employed is analyzed as regards migrant workers in General Recommendation 26:

Although both men and women migrate, migration is not a gender-neutral phenomenon. The position of female migrants is different from that of male migrants in terms of legal migration channels, the sectors into which they migrate, the forms of abuse they suffer and the consequences thereof. To understand the specific ways in which women are impacted, female migration should be studied from the perspective of gender inequality, traditional female roles, a gendered labour market, the universal prevalence of gender-based violence and the worldwide feminization of poverty and labour migration.[158]

The Committee mandates countries of origin and destination to formulate a comprehensive gender-sensitive and rights-based policy to regulate and administer all aspects and

---

[155] CEDAW, 'Ending discrimination against older women through the Convention', A/57/38 (2002) Part I, Decision 26/III, paras 430–6.

[156] J Fudge and R Owens, *'Precarious Work, Women, and the New Economy: The Challenge to Legal Norms'* (2006) 3–27.

[157] CO Dominican Republic, A/59/38, 31st Session (2004) paras 303 and 306–9; CO Mexico, A/57/38, Exceptional Session (2002) paras 441, 442, 445, and 446.

[158] GR 26 para 5.

stages of migration. In particular, it calls on States parties to facilitate access of women migrant workers to work opportunities abroad and to ensure protection of the rights of women migrant workers.[159] They should seek the active involvement of women migrant workers and relevant non-governmental organizations in policy formulation, implementation, monitoring, and evaluation.[160]

E. States Parties' Obligations

I. Nature of the Prohibition of Discrimination

1. 'All Appropriate Measures', Including the Need for Application of TSMs[161]

Article 11(1) in its chapeau expressly requires States parties to take all appropriate measures to eliminate discrimination against women in the field of employment. Article 11(2) requires States parties to take 'appropriate measures' rather than 'all appropriate measures', perhaps underlining the nature of most of the article as establishing social and economic rights. Nevertheless, the distinction between appropriate and all appropriate measures is somewhat semantic and does not derogate from the immediacy and totality of the States parties' obligations under Article 11(2).

2. Immediate or Gradual Implementation

The negative rights set out in Articles 11(1) and 11(2)(a) are in essence political and civil rights, as well as having social and economic implications, and hence require immediate implementation. They require elimination of discrimination against women, guarantee of the same rights as men in the field of employment, and prohibition of discrimination on grounds of marriage and maternity. 'The right to non-discrimination and to the exercise and enjoyment of economic, social and cultural rights imposes an immediate obligation on States'.[162]

The positive obligations imposed on States parties in Article 11(2)(b), (c), and (d) are to provide social and economic rights and benefits. In contrast with the CESCR, CEDAW does not include a general provision limiting the pace of implementation to the 'maximum of a State's available resources'. Hence, the immediacy of required implementation depends on the language of each section. Accordingly, the obligation to introduce maternity leave with pay and the obligation to provide special protection in harmful work during pregnancy are of immediate application. Only Article 2(c) uses language that suggests the possibility of gradual implementation: States parties need only 'encourage' provision of support services through 'promoting' establishment and 'development' of child care facilities.

II. Implementation

The obligation to respect women's equality rights under the Convention is the direct responsibility of States parties and of all State agencies to abide by the provisions of the Convention and to guarantee that these provisions will be applied and implemented in

---

[159] Ibid para 23(a).   [160] Ibid para 23(b).   [161] See the discussion in ch on art 4.
[162] F Banda, 'Understanding Women's Economic and Social Human Rights' [2006] 12 *East African J of Peace & Human Rights* 233, 239; CESCR, 'General Comment 16' (2005) UN Doc E/C.12/2005/4, part II para 16; CESCR, 'General Comment 20' (2009) UN Doc E/C.12/GC/20, part II.

all activities for which the State party is responsible as legislature, adjudicator, executive, or public employer. Under this head, the Committee has called upon States parties to enact equal employment opportunity legislation for both the public and private sectors of employment.[163] It has also called upon States parties to enact equal pay for work of equal value legislation for both the public and private sectors of employment.[164]

The obligation to protect women against violation of their Article 11 rights is, in large part, an indirect obligation of the State, which must be implemented by exercising due diligence over the activities of private employers and trade unions. Article 2(e), which obliges States parties to take all appropriate measures to eliminate discrimination against women by any person, organization, or enterprise, hence constitutes an essential element in the effectiveness of Article 11. The Committee has called on States parties to enforce women's rights under Article 11 against private as well as public employers.[165] As regards private employers, the States' obligation is due diligence; however, as regards the public employer, there is additionally direct liability for violation and not merely the obligation of due diligence.

The obligation to fulfil requires the States parties to take all appropriate measures to enforce and implement the Convention provisions. Under this obligation, States parties must develop institutions, mechanisms, and strategies which will ensure that the Convention provisions will become living law and practice. The Committee has called on States parties to ensure access to courts and tribunals which can give effective remedies for violation of women's Article 11 rights.[166] However, the Committee has not yet developed detailed policy on the issue of implementation of Article 11. An important point of reference will undoubtedly be the ILO Special Survey of 1996.[167] It indicates that there has been a substantial shift in national policies from standard-setting to economic and social measures.[168] The measures reported include the setting up of specialized institutional machinery, definition of a range of penalties, judicial enforcement of individual rights, shifting the burden of proof in discrimination cases,[169] and implementation of affirmative action programmes.[170] Among the recommendations made by the ILO are that States should ensure that employers may not terminate the employment of discrimination victims and merely pay compensation,[171] should provide free legal assistance for victims who do not have the financial means to bring actions,[172] and should promote the participation of women in trade unions.[173] The Beijing Declaration and Platform for Action requires governments, trade unions, and women's organizations to establish mechanisms

---

[163] CO New Zealand, CEDAW/C/NZL/CO/6 (2007) para 19; CO Dominican Republic, A/59/38, 31st Session (2004) para 303; CO Tunisia, A/57/38, 27th Session (2002) para 201.

[164] CO Samoa, A/60/38, 32nd Session (2005) paras 54–5; CO Lebanon, A/60/38, 33rd Session, (2005) para 110; CO Bangladesh, A/59/38, 31st Session (2004) para 254; CO Russian Federation, A/57/38, 26th Session (2002) para 384; CESCR CO Sweden, UN Doc E/2002/22 (2001) para 737.

[165] CO Dominican Republic, A/59/38, 31st Session (2004) para 303.

[166] CO Bosnia-Herzegovina, CEDAW/C/BIH/CO/3 (2006) para 14; CO Albania, A/58/38 (Supp), 28th Session (2003) para 63; CO Switzerland, A/58/38, 28th Session (2003) para 107.

[167] ILO Special Survey 1996 (n 49 above) para 165.

[168] ILO, 'General Survey on Equality in Employment and Occupation' (1988) 75th Session, Geneva, para 163.

[169] N Rubin (ed), *Code of International Labour Law: Law, Practice and Jurisprudence* (2005) 485. For more on the rights of rural women, see ibid 492; see also the discussion in ch on art 14.

[170] Ibid 488. The ILO reports that a number of States give subsidies to employers who recruit a woman to a traditionally male occupation, ibid 484.

[171] Ibid 493.   [172] Ibid.   [173] Ibid 493–5.

to adjudicate wage discrimination, to encourage job evaluation schemes, and to recognize collective bargaining as a right and as an important mechanism for eliminating wage inequality for women.[174]

Effective implementation of equal employment opportunity includes harmonization of work and family responsibilities for women and men. The Beijing Declaration and Platform for Action requires governments to ensure that full- and part-time work can be freely chosen by men and women, to secure the appropriate protection of labour laws and social security benefits for both, to make provision for job-protected parental leave,[175] and to promote flexible working arrangements and on-site child care.[176]

III. Reservations

There are very few reservations to Article 11. Ireland reserved the right for the time being to maintain provisions of Irish legislation in the area of social security which are more favourable to women than men; such provisions may not actually be contrary to the requirements of Article 11 which requires elimination of discrimination against women in the right to social security. The United Kingdom reserved the right to apply all United Kingdom legislation and the rules of pension schemes affecting retirement pensions, survivors' benefits and other benefits in relation to death or retirement (including retirement on grounds of redundancy); it is not clear which of these statutory provisions are contrary to Article 11. The sole reservation which clearly runs contrary to the requirements of Article 11 is that of Micronesia, which advises that it is not at present in a position to enact comparable worth legislation or to enact maternity leave with pay or with comparable social benefits; Finland objected to the reservation as being incompatible with the object and purpose of the Convention.

---

[174] Beijing Declaration and Platform for Action (n 9 above) Strategic Objective F.4 (h); ILO 'Gender Equality and Decent Work: Good Practices at the Workplace' (2004) 37 and 27–9.

[175] Beijing Declaration and Platform for Action (n 9 above) Strategic Objective F.6.

[176] See ibid; see also 'Gender Equality and Decent Work: Good Practices at the Workplace' (n 174 above) 8, 63, and 64.

Article 12

1. States Parties shall take all appropriate measures to eliminate discrimination against women in the field of health care in order to ensure, on a basis of equality of men and women, access to health care services, including those related to family planning.

2. Notwithstanding the provisions of paragraph 1 of this article, States Parties shall ensure to women appropriate services in connection with pregnancy, confinement and the post-natal period, granting free services where necessary, as well as adequate nutrition during pregnancy and lactation.

* We are grateful to Monica Arango, Luisa Cabal, Oscar Cabrera, Alejandra Cardenas, Simone Cusack, Bernard Dickens, Sandra Dughman, Joanna Erdman, Linda Hutjens, Eszter Kismodi, Adriana Lamackova, Jenny Leon, Charles Ngwena, Mindy Roseman, Iqbal Shah, and Christina Zampas for their comments and help on previous drafts of this chapter, to Global Justice Center for its bank of cases referencing the Convention, and Articulación Feminista for its *Observatorio de Sentencias Judiciales*, which provides Latin American court decisions referencing the Convention.

A. Introduction

Article 12 obliges States parties 'to eliminate discrimination against women in the field of health care'. States parties are required to address such discrimination 'in order to ensure, on a basis of equality of men and women, access to health care services'. Article 12(1) requires ensuring women's access to general health care services equally with men and access to services that predominantly women employ, illustrated by its specification of family planning.

Article 12(2) recognizes that equality includes treatment regarding sex-specific health care needs by requiring appropriate services for women relating to pregnancy, confinement, and the post-natal period, and adequate nutrition during pregnancy and lactation. Article 12(2) is consistent both with the preambular paragraph, which states that 'the role of women in procreation should not be a basis for discrimination', and with Article 4(2), which explains that 'adoption by State Parties of special measures...aimed at protecting maternity shall not be considered discriminatory'. In recognizing the need to accommodate women's sex-specific differences in reproduction, Article 12 underscores the importance of ensuring substantive equality in the field of health care.

General Recommendation 24 is a basic guide to the application of Article 12. A number of other general recommendations are relevant, such as those concerning specific health problems,[1] or health problems that certain subgroups of women face,[2] and those general recommendations concerning overarching obligations, such as on temporary special measures[3] and core obligations.[4] General Recommendation 24 recognizes the interconnection of Article 12 with other Convention articles.[5] For instance, Article 10(h) provides for access to health-related education, 'including information and advice on family planning',[6] and Article 11(2) protects employed women against discrimination related to pregnancy and maternity leave.[7] Article 14(2)(b) requires that women in rural areas 'have access to adequate health care facilities, including information, counselling and services in family planning',[8] and Article 16(1)(e) recognizes rights 'to decide freely and responsibly on the number and spacing of their children, and to have access to the information, education and means to enable them to exercise these rights' to ensure equality in marriage and family relations.[9]

Additional articles are also relevant to health, particularly as they address some of the social determinants of health,[10] such as the unequal distribution of power, money and resources.[11] This inequality can be addressed through Article 7, which requires women's equal participation in government.[12]

Other guides to the application of Article 12 are the Committee's concluding observations on reports of States parties. The Committee's decisions under the Communications[13]

---

[1] GR 14; GR 15; GR 19.   [2] GR 18; GR 26; GR 27.   [3] GR 25.   [4] GR 28.
[5] GR 24 para 28.   [6] See the discussion in ch on art 10.   [7] See the discussion in ch on art 11.
[8] See the discussion in ch on art 14.
[9] GR 21 paras 21–3 and 36; see the discussion in ch on art 16.
[10] WHO, 'Closing the Gap in a Generation: Health Equity through Action on the Social Determinants of Health' (Final Report of the Commission on Social Determinants of Health) (2008) <http://www.who.int/social_determinants/thecommission/finalreport/en/index.html> accessed 31 December 2010.
[11] Ibid part 4, 109–75.   [12] See the discussion in ch on art 7.
[13] *Ms AS v Hungary* CEDAW Communication No 4/2004 (2006), CEDAW/C/36/D/4/2004 (involuntary sterilization of a Romani woman).

and Inquiry[14] procedures of the Optional Protocol have further clarified States parties' obligations regarding equal access to health care services, and decisions that are pending under these respective procedures will give further insight into the nature and the scope of the health obligation.[15] Domestic court decisions applying Article 12 to country-specific health issues also provide illumination. For instance, a court applied Articles 5, 11, and 12 of the Convention to hold that a woman had the right of access to contraceptive sterilization, even though she did not meet legal requirements that restricted sterilization to therapeutic grounds.[16]

Elaboration of the content and meaning of Article 12 has evolved in tandem with the development of understanding of women's health,[17] medico-legal,[18] and programme[19] guidelines; UN conference outcome documents;[20] and the reports of the UN Special Rapporteur on Health.[21] In addition, the application of rights to health by the CESCR,[22] CERD,[23] and CRC,[24] and of health-related rights by the CCPR,[25] will continue to impact the meaning of Article 12. The European Commission of Human Rights,[26] the European

[14] 'Report on Mexico produced by the Committee on the Elimination of Discrimination against Women under article 8 of the Optional Protocol to the Convention, and reply from the Government of Mexico'(2005) CEDAW/C/2005/OP.8/MEXICO (failure to investigate disappearances of women in Ciudad Juárez).

[15] *Alyne da Silva Pimentel v Brazil* (avoidable maternal mortality) (filed 30 November 2007, pending); *LC v Peru* (pregnant girl suicide attempt and subsequent denial of treatment) (filed 18 June 2009, pending); Inquiry request submitted to CEDAW by the Center for Reproductive Rights, International Women's Rights Action Watch-Asia Pacific and a coalition of Philippine NGOs regarding ban on the distribution of hormonal contraception in Manila City public health system, 2010.

[16] Superior Tribunal de Justicia de Corrientes F, ML c/Hospital Vidal de la Ciudad de Corrientes y/o Ministerio de Salud Pública de Corrientes y/o Estado de la Provincia de Corrientes s/Amparo (12/04/06) para VI.

[17] WHO, 'Women and Health: Today's Evidence, Tomorrow's Agenda' (2009) <http://www.who.int/gender/documents/9789241563857/en/index.html> accessed 31 December 2010.

[18] WHO, 'Guidelines for Medico-legal Care for Victims of Sexual Violence' (2003) <http://www.who.int/violence_injury_prevention/publications/violence/med_leg_guidelines/en/index.html> accessed 31 December 2010; WHO 'Safe Abortion: Technical and Policy Guidance for Health Systems' (2003) <http://www.who.int/reproductivehealth/publications/unsafe_abortion/9241590343/en/index.html> accessed 31 December 2010 [revised edition forthcoming, 2011].

[19] WHO, 'Integrating Gender into HIV/AIDS Programmes in the Health Sector' (2009) <http://www.who.int/gender/documents/hiv/9789241597197/en/> accessed 31 December 2010.

[20] GR 24 para 3; Report of the International Conference on Population and Development Cairo; (1994) UN Doc A/CONF.171/13/Rev.1 (ICPD); Beijing Declaration and Platform for Action; UNGA, 'Report of the World Conference against Racism, Racial Discrimination, Xenophobia and Related Intolerance' (2001) UN Doc A/CONF.189/12 (Durban).

[21] UN Special Rapporteur on the Right of Everyone to the Enjoyment of the Highest Attainable Standard of Physical and Mental Health <http://www.ifhhro.org/information-centre/documents-un-special-rapporteur> accessed 31 December 2010.

[22] CESCR, 'General Comment 14' (2000) UN Doc E/C.12/2000/4.

[23] CERD, 'General Recommendation 25' (2000) UN Doc A/55/18, annex V.

[24] CRC, 'General Comment 4' (2000) UN Doc CRC/GC/2003/4; CCPR, 'General Comment 28' (2000) UN Doc CCPR/C/21/Rev.1/Add.10.

[25] *KL v Peru* CCPR Communication No 1153/2003 (2005), CCPR/C/85/D/1153/2003; *LMR v Argentina* CCPR/C/101/D/1608/2007.

[26] *Bruggemann and Scheuten v Federal Republic of Germany* (1981) App 6959/75, 3 EHRR 244 (abortion regulation not always cause of an interference with women's rights); *Paton v United Kingdom* (App 8416/78) (1980) EHRR 408 (spousal authorization impermissible); *RH v Norway* (App 17004/90) (1992) 73 DR 155 (spousal authorization impermissible); *Tavares v France* (App 16593/90) (1991) (claim for wrongful maternal death inadmissible but positive obligations exist to prevent loss of life).

Court of Human Rights,[27] the Inter-American Commission on Human Rights,[28] and the Inter-American Court of Human Rights[29] will continue to bring new dimensions to the meaning of Article 12, as will the African human rights system.[30]

Human rights aspects of women's health have been addressed by UN specialized agencies such as WHO,[31] UNFPA,[32] ILO,[33] and UNAIDS.[34] The Committee collaborates with these agencies pursuant to Convention Article 22.[35]

B. Travaux Préparatoires

The drafting history shows that in all the working documents leading up to the version of the convention drafted by CSW and ECOSOC there was no separate article on the elimination of discrimination against women in the field of health care.[36] The health concerns of women first emerged as a separate topic in the context of Article 11, on employment,

---

[27] *A., B. & C. v Ireland* [GC](App 25579/05) (2010) (clarification of life indication for abortion required); *Boso v Italy* (App 50490/99) (2002) (spousal authorization impermissible); *Evans v United Kingdom* [GC] (App 6339/05) (2007) (denial of a woman's access to her embryo permissible because of sperm donor's refusal); *KH and Others v Slovakia* (App 32881/04) (2009) (denial of medical records impermissible); *Open Door Counselling v Ireland* (App 14234/88) (1993) (upheld rights to information on foreign legal abortions); *Pichon and Sajous v France* (App 49853/99) (2001) (claim of pharmacists to object on grounds of conscience to selling contraceptives held inadmissible, but limitations on conscience permissible when necessary for women's health); *SH and Others v Austria* (App 57813/00) (2001) (Grand Chamber decision pending) (prohibition of particular forms of infertility treatment); *Ternovsky v Hungary* (App 67545/09) (2010) (health professionals' inability to assist in home births) (possible appeal to Grand Chamber); *Tysiac v Poland* (App 5410/03) (2007) (transparency in accessing abortion services); *Vo v France* [GC] (App 53924) (2005) (criminal law not required to remedy the negligent death of a foetus); *Women on Waves and Others v Portugal* (App 31276/05) (2009) (restrictions on freedom of expression regarding abortion impermissible).

[28] *Case 2141 ('Baby Boy')* (United States of America) Resolution No 23/8 (6 March 1981) *Hum Rts L. J.* 2 (1981) 110 (abortion permissible); *Case 12.041 Marina Machaca,* Peru (6 March 2000) Friendly Settlement (rape of a girl and subsequent denial of remedies); *Case 12.191 Maria Mamérita Mestanza Chávez,* Peru (22 October 2003) Friendly Settlement (involuntary sterilization causing death); *Paulina del Carmen Ramírez Jacinto,* México, Report N°21/07, Petition 161–2 (9 March 2007) Friendly Settlement (rape of a girl causing unwanted pregnancy and subsequent denial of abortion).

[29] *De La Cruz Flores v Peru* (2004) Merits. Judgment, Inter-American Court of Human Rights Series C No 115 (criminal prosecution of doctor for confidential provision of care impermissible); *Xákmok Kásek Indigenous Community v Paraguay,* Merits, Reparations and Costs. Judgment of 24 August 2010. Series C No 214 (failure to prevent maternal death of an indigenous woman).

[30] Banjul Charter art 16; Protocol on the Rights of Women in Africa art 14.

[31] WHO, 'Multi-Country Study on Women's Health and Domestic Violence against Women: Initial Results on Prevalence, Health Outcomes and Women's Responses' (2005) <http://www.who.int/gender/violence/who_multicountry_study/en/> accessed 31 December 2010.

[32] UNFPA, 'Publications: Fistula [and Female Genital Mutilation/Cutting]' <http://www.unfpa.org/public/home/publications/pubs_fistula> accessed 31 December 2010.

[33] The United Nations Interagency Task Force on Adolescent Girls, 'Girl Power and Potential: A Joint Programming Framework for Fulfilling the Rights of Marginalized Adolescent Girls' (2007) <http://www.unicef.org/adolescence/files/FINAL-UNJointFramewokrpdf.pdf> accessed 31 December 2010.

[34] Joint United Nations Programme on HIV/AIDS, 'International Guidelines on HIV/AIDS and Human Rights 2006 Consolidated Version' (2006), HR/PUB/06/9 <http://data.unaids.org/Publications/IRC-pub07/jc1252-internguidelines_en.pdf> accessed 31 December 2010; UNAIDS 'UNAIDS Guidance Note on HIV and Sex Work' (2009) <http://data.unaids.org/pub/BaseDocument/2009/jc1696_guidance_note_hiv_and_sexwork_en.pdf> accessed 31 December 2010.

[35] WHO, 'Women's Health and Human Rights: Monitoring the Implementation of CEDAW' (2007) <http://www.who.int/reproductivehealth/publications/gender_rights/9789241595100/en/index.html> accessed 31 December 2010. See discussion in ch on art 22.

[36] LA Rehof, *Guide to the Travaux Préparatoires of the United Nations Convention on the Elimination of All Forms of Discrimination against Women* (1993) 145.

probably due to the ILO's history of protecting the health of women in the workplace.[37] In the course of elaborating the issue, however, and in view of the length and detail of Article 11, it was decided to separate the focus on health into a self-contained article, which became Article 12.

DEDAW contained no specific provision directly concerned with health care for women. It referred only to educational information 'ensuring the health and wellbeing of families', in Article 9(e), and protection of maternity of working women, in Article 10(2) and (3).[38] The lack of provision in DEDAW is curious, given that it was adopted one year after the adoption of the ICESCR, which recognizes in its Article 12 'the right of everyone to the highest attainable standard of physical and mental health' and the means to take steps to realize this right.

This omission of an article on women's health in DEDAW might explain the undeveloped nature of the right to health care services in the text of the Convention. The final version of the Convention consists of the briefest of statements in Article 12(1) to eliminate discrimination in the field of health care, and requires health care to be available on the basis of equality of men and women. The article, as adopted, lacks an introductory chapeau, consistent with its origins under the umbrella of Article 11.

C. Issues of Interpretation

I. Health and its Sex and Gender Dimensions

The Committee interprets the term 'health' consistently with the WHO description of health as a state of 'physical, mental and social well-being and not merely the absence of disease or infirmity'.[39] This is because the WHO description is almost universally used and because States parties to the Convention are also members of WHO. A domestic court has stated that health must be understood according to the WHO description when it applied Article 12 to require appropriate services to be provided to a pregnant girl who had been raped by her father.[40]

General Recommendation 24 explains that distinctive health features and factors that differ for women in comparison to men, or for some subgroups of women,[41] include:

- biological factors such as their reproductive functions;[42]
- socio-economic factors that vary for women in general and some groups of women in particular, such as unequal power relationships negatively affecting women's ability to negotiate safe sexual practices with men, increasing their risk of infection with HIV/AIDS;[43]

---

[37] Ibid 241.

[38] J Tadaakira, 'Article 12: Elimination of Discrimination against Women in Health Care' in Japanese Association of International Women's Rights (ed), *Convention on the Elimination of All Forms of Discrimination against Women: A Commentary* (1995) 241, 242–5.

[39] Constitution of the WHO, Preamble.

[40] Juzgado de Instrucción N°II–San Carlos de Bariloche, Argentina, NRF s/abuso sexual. Incidente de solicitud de interrupción de embarazo formulado por TN (05/04/2010) para XI.

[41] GR 24 para 12.   [42] CO Mauritania, CEDAW/C/MRT/CO/1 (2007) paras 39–40.

[43] CO El Salvador, CEDAW/C/SLV/CO/7 (2008) paras 35–6; CO Kenya, CEDAW/C/KEN/CO/6 (2007) paras 39–40; CO Tanzania, A/63/38, 41st Session (2008) paras 138–9.

- psychosocial factors, such as depression in general and post-partum depression in particular, and other psychological conditions including those that lead to eating disorders, notably anorexia and bulimia;[44] and
- health system factors, such as the establishment of standards to ensure protection of confidentiality in the delivery of health care to women.[45]

The Committee requires States parties to interpret rights relating to health 'from the perspective of women's needs and interests'.[46] Interpreting Article 12, therefore, requires understanding the sex and gender dimensions of health. Sex concerns particular biological needs, for example, regarding women's reproductive health care requirements, and gender concerns social constructions of women,[47] including their social roles and their capacities to make their own decisions about their health care. Social practices of gender subordination exacerbate the multiple risk factors for women's poor health throughout their lives. Risk factors are those conditions that put people at greater hazard of poor health. The Committee persists in asking States parties to address the general and particular risk factors that women face, such as smoking,[48] alcoholism,[49] stress-related conditions,[50] mental instability,[51] unsafe abortion,[52] malnutrition and anaemia,[53] and poverty.[54] States parties are required to ensure women's access to services that address such risk factors, and collect statistics on the conditions and diseases of subgroups.[55]

Understanding the sex and gender dimensions of health helps to make visible human rights violations that otherwise would not be identified. For instance, the Committee has consistently raised maternal mortality as a human rights concern.[56] A maternal death is defined as 'the death of a woman while pregnant or within 42 days of termination of pregnancy, irrespective of the duration and site of the pregnancy, from any cause related to or aggravated by the pregnancy or its management but not from accidental or incidental causes'.[57] It is estimated that maternal deaths now reach around 358,000 annually.[58] Even though the scale of maternal mortality is larger than that of many human rights violations, it is only recently that maternal death has attracted attention of the international human rights community, through the work of the Committee, other treaty bodies,[59] the Office

---

[44] CO Finland, A/63/38, 41st Session (2008) paras 185–6.
[45] GR 24 para 12(d); see also paras 18, 22, and 31(e).   [46] GR 24 para 12.   [47] GR 28 para 5.
[48] CO Luxembourg, CEDAW/C/LUX/CO/5 (2008) paras 27–8.
[49] CO Iceland, A/63/38, 41st Session (2008) paras 234–5.
[50] CO Sweden, CEDAW/C/SWE/CO/7 (2008) paras 34–5.
[51] CO China, CEDAW/C/CHN/CO/6 (2006) para 28.
[52] CO India, CEDAW/C/IND/CO/3 (2007) paras 40–5.
[53] CO Myanmar, CEDAW/C/MMR/CO/3 (2008) paras 38–9.
[54] CO Colombia, CEDAW/C/COL/CO/6 (2007) paras 30–3.
[55] GR 24 paras 9–10; CO The Netherlands, CEDAW/C/NLD/CO/4 (2007) paras 35–6.
[56] CO Cambodia, CEDAW/C/KHM/CO/3 (2006) paras 29–30; CO Sierra Leone, CEDAW/C/SLE/CO/5 (2007) paras 34–5; CO Peru, CEDAW/C/PER/CO/6 (2007) paras 24–5; CO Azerbaijan, CEDAW/C/AZE/CO/3(2007) paras 25–6.
[57] WHO, 'Trends in Maternal Mortality: 1990 to 2008: Estimates developed by WHO, UNICEF, UNFPA and The World Bank' (2010) 4 at <http://whqlibdoc.who.int/publications/2010/9789241500265_eng.pdf> accessed 31 December 2010.
[58] Ibid 17.
[59] CESCR, 'General Comment 14' (2000) UN Doc E/C.12/2000/4 para 21; 'Access to Maternal Health Care from a Human Rights Perspective' OEA/Ser.L/V/II. Doc 69, 7 June 2010, <http://cidh.org/women/SaludMaterna10Eng/MaternalHealth2010.pdf> accessed 31 December 2010.

of the United Nations High Commissioner for Human Rights,[60] the Human Rights Council,[61] and the UN Special Rapporteur on Health.[62]

II. The Field of Health Care

Read as a whole, Article 12 implicates both individual and collective dimensions of rights, since an individual's access to health services is frequently a function not only of individual circumstances, but also of the collective nature of health care systems.

The Committee mandates that States parties place 'a gender perspective at the centre of all policies and programmes affecting women's health and should involve women in planning, implementation and monitoring of such policies and programmes and in the provision of health services to women'.[63] States parties must consider these aspects of health systems from the perspective of women,[64] and of subgroups including rural women.[65] It obliges States parties to design and implement a comprehensive gender-sensitive national strategy to promote women's health throughout their life cycle.[66] The Committee requires States parties to address the underlying determinants that positively affect women's health, such as good public health and sanitation services,[67] and determinants that negatively affect women's health, including violence against women,[68] cultural and traditional practices such as female genital mutilation (FGM),[69] and laws, regulations, and institutional practices.[70] Compliance requires appropriate measures aimed at the early detection and treatment of diseases, such as breast and cervical cancers.[71] Consideration is needed of 'diseases…and conditions hazardous to health that affect women or certain groups of women differently from men, as well as information on possible intervention in this regard'.[72]

III. Access to Health Care Services

Article 12 protects the right to non-discriminatory access to health care services, rather than the right to health as such. The phrase 'health care services' should be interpreted in the context of universal coverage which WHO has defined as 'access to key promotive, preventive, curative and rehabilitative health interventions for all at an affordable cost'.[73] The three dimensions of coverage are: (1) the proportion of the population served'

---

[60] UNCHR, 'Report of the Office of the United Nations High Commissioner for Human Rights on Preventable Maternal Mortality and Morbidity and Human Rights' (16 April 2010) UN Doc A/HRC/14/39, 14th Session.

[61] UN Human Rights Council, Preventable Maternal Mortality and Morbidity and Human Rights, UN Doc A/HRC/11/L.16/Rev. 1 (16 June 2009); UN Human Rights Council, Preventable Maternal Mortality and Morbidity and Human Rights, UN Doc A/HRC/15/L.27 (27 Sept 2010).

[62] UNCHR, 'Report of the Special Rapporteur on the right of everyone to the highest attainable standard of health. Addendum: Mission to India' (15 April 2010) UN Doc A/HRC/14/20/Add.2.

[63] GR 24 para 31(a).   [64] CO Nigeria, A/63/38, 41st Session (2008) paras 334–5.

[65] CO Suriname, CEDAW/C/SUR/CO/3 (2007) paras 31–2.   [66] GR 24 para 2.

[67] CO Cook Islands, CEDAW/C/COK/CO/1 (2007) para 8.

[68] GR 24 paras 15 and 29; GR 19 paras 1–5, 19, 22, and 24(m); see discussion in ch on violence against women; CO Tanzania, A/63/38, 41st Session (2008) para 120.

[69] GR 14; GR 24 para 18; CEDAW CO Yemen, A/63/38, 41st Session (2008) paras 379–80.

[70] GR 24 paras 9, 14, 15, 17, 19, and 31(c).

[71] CO Bahrain, CEDAW/C/BHR/CO/2 (2008) paras 36–7.   [72] GR 24 para 10.

[73] WHO, 'Social health insurance-Report by the Secretariat' UN Doc A/58/20 (7 April 2005) para 2 <http://apps.who.int/gb/ebwha/pdf_files/WHA58/A58_20-en.pdf> accessed 31 December 2010.

(2) the level of services; and (3) the proportion of health costs covered by prepaid pooled funds.[74]

Health care services that should be covered will depend in part on the incidence levels for women of diseases and conditions hazardous to their health in their community, but requires the inclusion of sex-specific services. The application of Article 12 is not limited by the legal or occupational status of health care providers or States parties' determinations of what they will fund. Providers can include, among others: doctors, dentists, clinical psychologists, social workers, nurses, and midwives.[75]

A key criterion of compliance with Article 12 is access, which presupposes the availability of sustainable services, including information about the services. The Committee requires States parties to 'report on measures taken to eliminate barriers that women face in gaining access to health care services and what measures they have taken to ensure women timely and affordable access to such services'.[76] States parties are urged to identify the test by which to assess whether a distinction in a health law, policy, or practice impairs women's access to health care services.[77] Many health laws, policies, and practices make distinctions between women and men. Some distinctions are justified, such as those that serve a legitimate purpose of accommodating women's sex differences in reproductive cancers, including cervical cancer.

Other distinctions are not justified, such as those that do not serve a legitimate objective in that they deny women access to services, such as distinctions that stereotype women as incapable of making medical decisions. The Committee consistently encourages States parties to remove unjustifiable distinctions against women's equal access with men to health care services, such as gendered barriers, legal and regulatory obstacles, barriers resulting from women's lack of information about services, barriers relating to lack of procedures to ensure free and informed consent, and economic barriers.

Gendered barriers to health care services can be understood as the many obstacles that women face on their various pathways to obtaining health services because they are women.[78] Gendered barriers sometimes compound with other barriers such as those based on age[79] and cultural affiliation.[80] The elimination of negative attitudes of health workers is necessary to ensure women's equal access to health services.[81] Another gendered barrier is objection of providers on grounds of conscience to supplying medical care on which women are particularly dependent, coupled with their failure to refer women to willing providers.[82]

Article 12 is read in conjunction with the Convention's Preamble paragraph 2, stating that individuals are 'equal in dignity', to require the protection of women's human dignity in the field of health care throughout their life cycle.[83] States parties are required to take appropriate measures to ensure access. This requires that health services are delivered

---

[74] WHO, 'World Health Report: Health Systems Financing: the Path to Universal Coverage' (2010) xv, 12 at <http://www.who.int/whr/2010/en/index.html> accessed 31 December 2010.

[75] CO Guatemala, CEDAW/C/GUA/CO/7 (2009) paras 35–6.

[76] GR 24 para 21 (emphasis in the original).   [77] GR 24 para 19.

[78] GR 24 para 2; CO Liechtenstein, CEDAW/C/LIE/CO/3 (2007) paras 25–6.

[79] CO Canada, CEDAW/C/CAN/CO/7 (2008) paras 41–2; CO Republic of Korea, CEDAW/C/KOR/CO/6 (2007) para 18; CO Luxembourg, CEDAW/C/LUX/CO/5 (2008) paras 27–8.

[80] CO Ecuador, CEDAW/C/ECU/CO/7 (2008) paras 38–9.

[81] CO Kenya, CEDAW/C/KEN/CO/6 (2007) paras 37–8; CO Tanzania: A/63/38, 41st Session (2008) paras 136–7.

[82] GR 24 para 21.   [83] Ibid.

in a manner that is acceptable to women, including respectful, dignified treatment.[84] Unacceptable and dignity-denying treatment comes in many forms, including failure to obtain free and informed consent,[85] such as through involuntary sterilization on grounds of minority ethnicity,[86] and genital mutilation of girls.[87] The Committee requires States parties to ensure acceptable and dignified access to care through the protection of women's confidentiality,[88] and securing their right to be free from cruel, inhuman, and degrading treatment.[89]

The Committee has identified multiple legal and regulatory barriers to access to health services. Laws criminalizing medical procedures, such as contraception and abortion, act as legal barriers to women's access to effective health care.[90] A domestic court explained that 'CEDAW has emphasized that laws criminalizing medical interventions that specially affect women constitute a barrier to women's access to needed medical care, compromising women's right to gender equality in the area of health'.[91]

Other legal and regulatory barriers include third party authorization requirements, such as by courts, parents, guardians, partners or husbands.[92] A domestic court has built on Article 12 to recommend elimination of the requirement of court authorizations for therapeutic abortions, where they are legal, to save the health of women. The court was concerned that health authorities take steps to clarify the law because its lack of transparency particularly prejudices young women in accessing services.[93] Laws relating to provision of health services should be clear to providers, prospective recipients, and the wider community the law affects.[94] Transparent access requires that information about services and counselling about treatment options for health care are accessible and understandable in order to ensure access for women. Moreover, the information and counselling have to be provided in understandable languages in order to ensure access to women who face language barriers.[95]

Women's practical access to services depends on their possession and comprehension of necessary information, for instance, of care options, their effectiveness, risks and benefits, service locations and hours of operation, and the legal permissibility of services.[96] Information regarding risks and benefits of possible options is central to informed decision-making with respect to health care services.[97] Health ministries must ensure that women possess the knowledge of available services and how to obtain them, and ensure public availability of such information, through, for example, the media.[98]

The Committee obliges States parties to ensure women's physical access to health care, irrespective of their geographic location.[99] In particular, it is concerned that women in

---

[84] Ibid para 22.   [85] CO Korea, CEDAW/C/KOR/CO/6 (2007) paras 29–30.
[86] *AS v Hungary* (n 13 above); CEDAW CO Czech Republic, CEDAW/C/CZE/CO/5 (2010) paras 34–5.
[87] CO Togo, CEDAW/C/TGO/CO/5 (2006) para 15.   [88] GR 24 paras 22 and 31(e).
[89] CO Cameroon, CEDAW/C/CMR/CO/3 (2009) paras 28–9.   [90] GR 24 paras 14, 26, and 31(c).
[91] Corte Constitucional de Colombia, C-355/06 (10 May 2006) s 7.
[92] GR 24 para 14; CO Cook Islands CEDAW/C/COK/CO/1 (2007) paras 34–5; CO Saudi Arabia, CEDAW/C/SAU/CO/2 (2008) para 33; CO Syrian Arab Republic, CEDAW/C/SYR/CO/1 (2007) paras 29–30; CO Benin, CEDAW/C/BEN/CO/1–3 (2005) para 31; CO Saint Lucia, CEDAW/C/LCA/CO/6 (2006) para 32.
[93] Juzgado de Instrucción N°II (n 40 above) paras VIII and X.
[94] GR 24 paras 9, 17, 21, and 23; CO Portugal, CEDAW/C/PRT/CO/7 (2008) paras 42–3.
[95] CO New Zealand, CEDAW/C/NZL/CO/6 (2007) paras 38–9.   [96] GR 24 para 20.
[97] CO Cuba, CEDAW/C/CUB/CO/6 (2006) para 27.
[98] CO Kyrgyzstan, CEDAW/C/KGZ/CO/3 (2008) paras 37–8.
[99] CO Syrian Arab Republic, CEDAW/C/SYR/CO/1 (2007) paras 29–30.

rural areas may lack access to health care services,[100] including therapeutic drugs, such as emergency contraception,[101] and appropriate services for the prevention of suicide.[102] Physical access requires States to ensure that health care services are within reach of geographically remote, disabled or otherwise disadvantaged women.[103]

The Committee is concerned about eliminating economic barriers to health care services so that all women, irrespective of income level, have the same access to affordable services that men have, and have reasonable access to services that are necessary for their specific health needs, such as maternity care.[104] Economic barriers are particularly problematic for women because of their generally low economic status and opportunities and lack of access to family resources. States are required to report on 'requirements or conditions that prejudice women's access such as high fees for health care services...'.[105] Official, user, or 'informal' fees for health care services[106] increase the risk of poor women either forgoing services or settling for substandard services, perhaps from unqualified providers.[107] Drugs essential to women's health, such as contraceptives, need to be registered in national essential drug lists to keep costs low and maximize availability.[108] Article 12(2) explicitly requires States parties to provide 'free services where necessary' for 'pregnancy, confinement and the post-natal period', and the Committee consequently commends States for ensuring free maternity care,[109] and asks all States to report on their affordability.[110]

IV. Reproductive and Sexual Health Services

The Convention is the first human rights treaty explicitly to require States parties to ensure access to family planning.[111] The Committee requires that appropriate measures are taken to ensure women's access to services 'in the areas of family planning, pregnancy, confinement and during the post-natal period,'[112] and to sexual and reproductive health services.[113] States parties' failure to remove barriers to women's effective access to reproductive and sexual health services constitutes discrimination against women.[114]

The Committee interprets sexual and reproductive health consistently[115] with the definitions found in the 1994 UN International Conference on Population and Development Programme of Action[116] and the 1995 UN Fourth World Conference on Women Platform for Action.[117] These documents explain that '[r]eproductive health is a state of complete physical, mental and social well-being and not merely the absence of disease or infirmity, in all matters relating to the reproductive system and to its functions and processes'.[118] The explanation addresses the reproductive processes, functions, and system at all stages

---

[100] CO Mauritania, CEDAW/C/MRT/CO/1 (2007) paras 41–2; CO Saint Lucia, CEDAW/C/LCA/CO/6 (2006) para 32; CO Maldives, CEDAW/C/MDV/CO/3 (2007) paras 31–2; CO China, CEDAW/C/CHN/CO/6 (2006) para 28; CO Bosnia-Herzegovina, CEDAW/C/BIH/CO/3 (2006) para 36.

[101] CO Peru, CEDAW/C/PER/CO/6 (2007) paras 24–5.

[102] CO China, CEDAW/C/CHN/CO/6 (2006) para 28.

[103] GR 24 para 7; CO Lebanon, CEDAW/C/LBN/CO/3 (2008) para 34.

[104] GR 24 paras 7, 12(b), 21, 26–7, 30–1(d); CO Ecuador, CEDAW/C/ECU/CO/7 (2008) paras 38–9.

[105] GR 24 para 21.   [106] Ibid paras 21 and 27.

[107] CO China, CEDAW/C/CHN/CO/6 (2006) paras 27–8.

[108] CO Azerbaijan, CEDAW/C/AZE/CO/3 (2007) paras 25–6.

[109] CO Ecuador, CEDAW/C/ECU/CO/7 (2008) paras 38–9.   [110] GR 24 paras 26–7.

[111] Arts 12(1), 10(h), 14(2)(b), and 16(1)(e).   [112] GR 24 para 2.   [113] Ibid paras 11 and 29.

[114] GR 24 paras 11, 14, and 17.   [115] Ibid para 3.

[116] ICPD (n 20 above) para 7.2.

[117] Beijing Declaration and Platform for Action (n 20 above) para 94.

[118] ICPD (n 20 above) para 7.2; Beijing Declaration and Platform for Action (n 20 above) para 94.

of life, in the context of 'complete physical, mental and social well-being'.[119] In signing these documents, States parties have agreed to fulfil the 'right of men and women to be informed and to have access to safe, effective, affordable and acceptable methods of family planning of their choice, as well as other methods of their choice for regulation of fertility which are not against the law, and the right of access to appropriate health-care services that will enable women to go safely through pregnancy and childbirth and provide couples with the best chance of having a healthy infant'.[120]

These documents state that reproductive health includes sexual health, 'the purpose of which is the enhancement of life and personal relations, and not merely counselling and care related to reproduction and sexually transmitted disease'.[121] The WHO has refined the definition of sexual health as a:

state of physical, emotional, mental and social well-being in relation to sexuality; it is not merely the absence of disease, dysfunction or infirmity. Sexual health requires a positive and respectful approach to sexuality and sexual relationships, as well as the possibility of having pleasurable and safe sexual experiences, free of coercion, discrimination and violence. For sexual health to be attained and maintained, the sexual rights of all persons must be respected, protected and fulfilled.[122]

The Committee underscores the importance of ensuring access to reproductive health services, because neglect of these services disproportionately burdens women. It encourages improved access to a wide range of contraceptive methods,[123] and recommends the repeal of laws banning the display or sale of contraceptives.[124] It requires availability of contraceptives for men, so that women will no longer bear the primary responsibility for family planning,[125] and it will be understood that reproductive and sexual health are the responsibility of both partners.[126]

Moreover, the Committee requires that States parties report on measures they have taken regarding the sex-specific services affecting pregnancy, confinement, and the post-natal period, on how they have reduced maternal mortality and morbidity rates,[127] and whether free services are available for women who cannot pay for them.[128] States must report on maternal mortality rates among vulnerable groups of women, and what they have done to ensure reasonable allocation of resources to maximize safe motherhood, and reduce maternal mortality,[129] including where it arises from unsafe abortions.[130]

The Committee never misses an opportunity to underscore the importance of ensuring adolescent girls' access to sexual and reproductive health services.[131] It expressed concerns

---

[119] Ibid.   [120] Ibid.   [121] Ibid.

[122] WHO, 'Developing Sexual Health Programmes' (2010) 3 at <http://whqlibdoc.who.int/hq/2010/WHO_RHR_HRP_10.22_eng.pdf> accessed 31 December 2010.

[123] CO Kazakhstan, CEDAW/C/KAZ/CO/2 (2007) paras 25–6; CO Chile, CEDAW/C/CHI/CO/4 (2006) para 19; CO Serbia CEDAW/C/SCG/CO/1 (2007) para 33; CO Macedonia CEDAW/C/MKD/CO/3 (2006) para 32; CO Azerbaijan CEDAW/C/AZE/CO/3 (2007) paras 25–6.

[124] CO Suriname, CEDAW/C/SUR/CO/3 (2007) paras 31–2.

[125] CO Portugal, CEDAW/C/PRT/CO/7 (2008) paras 42–3; CO Thailand CEDAW/C/THA/CO/5 (2006) paras 39–40.

[126] CO Democratic People's Republic of Korea, CEDAW/C/PRK/CO/1 (2005) para 46; CO Gambia, CEDAW/C/GMB/CO/1–3 (2005) para 36.

[127] GR 24 para 26; CO Mauritania CEDAW/C/MRT/CO/1 (2007) paras 39–40.

[128] GR 24 para 27.

[129] GR 24 para 18; CO Democratic Republic of Congo, CEDAW/C/COD/CO/5 (2006) para 35.

[130] CO Uruguay, CEDAW/C/URY/CO/7 (2008) paras 38–9.

[131] GR 24 paras 18, 23, and 31(b); GR 28 para 21.

about lack of implementation of a decision on a communication by the CCPR.[132] This CCPR communication found a violation of an adolescent girl's right to be free from cruel, inhuman, and degrading treatment when a public hospital forced her to carry an anencephalic foetus (a non-viable foetus lacking an upper brain) to term and to breast-feed the dying child. The hospital did so knowing that the criminal law allowed for abortion in such cases, and that the newborn infant would die predictably within a few days after birth.[133]

A domestic court relied on Article 12 and General Recommendation 24 to uphold the constitutionality of a law requiring the provision of sexual and reproductive health services to all fertile persons, especially adolescent girls.[134] Another domestic court relied on Article 12 to permit lawful abortion in the case of a 15-year-old girl who was raped, because forcing her to carry a pregnancy to term resulting from rape would deny her the right to be equal in dignity and would treat her as 'a mere instrument'.[135] This court cited General Recommendation 19, requiring States parties to take measures to prevent coercion of women regarding reproduction and to ensure that they do not have to undergo high-risk procedures such as illegal abortions due to the lack of appropriate services for fertility control.[136]

The Committee's overriding concern as to punitive abortion laws is the increased probability of higher maternal mortality and morbidity rates and denial of women's substantive equality, thereby contravening Article 12.[137] It reads Article 12 together with Article 2(g) to require repeal of 'all national penal provisions which constitute discrimination against women'[138] and continually asks States to remove penalties for women undergoing abortion.[139]

The Committee commends States parties when they decriminalize abortion, for example, in cases of risk to life, health, foetal malformation, and rape.[140] It is concerned when States parties lack information on the consequences of unsafe abortion.[141] The Committee raises concerns when States parties attempt to restrict grounds for abortion,[142] such as criminalizing therapeutic abortion.[143] The Committee is concerned when States parties fail to operationalize abortion in cases of rape.[144] It requires implementation of regulations

---

[132] CO Peru, CEDAW/C/PER/CO/6 (2007) paras 24–5.   [133] *KL v Peru* (n 25 above).

[134] Tribunal Superior de Justicia de la Ciudad Autónoma de Buenos Aires, Argentina, Liga de Amas de Casa, Consumidores y Usuarios de la República Argentina y otros c/CGBA s/acción declarativa de inconstitucionalidad, 14/10/2003, Judge Alicia E.C. Ruiz, paras 3–4.

[135] Tribunal Superior de Justicia de Chubut, Argentina, F, AL s/Medida Autosatisfactiva, 08/03/2010, Judge Passuti, para IV, subpara VII.

[136] Ibid, Judge Royer, para VI.3.   [137] GR 24 paras 14, 26, and 31(c).   [138] GR 28 para 31.

[139] CO Andorra, A/56/38, 25th Session (2008) para 48; CO Belize A/54/38, 21st Session (1999) para 57; CO Burkina Faso, A/55/38, 22nd Session (2000) para 276; CO Cameroon, A/55/38, 23rd Session (2000) para 60; CO Chile, CEDAW/C/CHI/CO/4 (2006) paras 19–20; CO Ireland, A/54/38, 21st Session (1999) para 186; CO Jordan, A/55/38, 20th Session (2000) para 181; CO Namibia, A/52/38/Rev.1, 17th Session (1997) para 127; CO Nepal, A/54/38, 21st Session (1999) paras 139 & 148; CO Nicaragua, CEDAW/C/NIC/CO/6 (2007) paras 17–18; CO Pakistan, CEDAW/C/PAK/CO/3 (2007) paras 40–1; CO United Kingdom A/55/38, 21st Session (1999) para 310.

[140] CO Colombia, CEDAW/C/COL/CO/6 (2007) paras 22–3.

[141] CO Guatemala, CEDAW/C/GUA/CO/7 (2009) paras 35–6.

[142] CO Lithuania, A/63/38, 41st Session (2008) paras 80–1.

[143] CO Nicaragua, CEDAW/C/NIC/CO/6 (2007) para 18.

[144] CO Cameroon, CEDAW/C/CMR/CO/3 (2009) paras 40–1.

for the laws allowing legal therapeutic and ethical abortion, so that abortion provisions are clear to the providers and to women.[145]

Domestic courts and parliaments build on Article 12 to ensure women's access to lawful abortion. One court used Article 12 in interpreting its national constitution to hold that the criminal prohibition of abortion in all circumstances is a disproportionate measure because it infringes the rights to health of the pregnant woman.[146] Another domestic court relied on Convention Article 12 to uphold a law permitting abortion on request during the first twelve weeks of pregnancy because the law was necessary to eliminate discrimination in the field of health care.[147] A parliament cited Convention Article 12 in a preamble to a law, explaining that gender equality requires the availability of abortion on request during the first fourteen weeks of pregnancy and on therapeutic and eugenic grounds until twenty-two weeks.[148] This same law requires that contraceptives be covered by the national health system as a way of preventing unwanted pregnancies and abortion.

The Committee continually highlights the need to address the gendered dimensions of the AIDS pandemic. It asks States parties to adopt measures to eliminate discrimination against women and girls infected with HIV/AIDS,[149] and commends them for adopting laws to prevent the spread of HIV/AIDS,[150] particularly plans to address the feminization of HIV/AIDS and other sexually transmitted diseases.[151]

D. Equality in Context

I. Formal Equality

Applying the Article 1 definition of 'discrimination against women' to the field of health care requires determining how various laws, policies, or practices make a 'distinction, exclusion or restriction' that impairs or nullifies women's access to health care services on the basis of equality with men.[152] Different treatment of women and men in analogous health situations, or limiting women's access to health care, without a reasonable justification is discriminatory.[153] The Committee observes that men's authority to veto women's decisions regarding their health is contrary to formal equality. It unjustifiably denies women equal access to health services, entrenches women's inferior status in their marriages, families, and societies, and negatively stereotypes women as incapable of making decisions.[154]

Not every distinction, exclusion, or restriction made on the basis of sex in access to health care services will violate Article 12. For example, as Article 12(2) indicates,

---

[145] CO Bolivia, CEDAW/C/BOL/CO/4 (2008) paras 42–3.

[146] Corte Constitucional de Colombia C-355/06 (n 91 above) s 10.1.

[147] Constitutional Court of the Slovak Republic, *Decision-PL. ÚS 12/01-297* (4 December 2007).

[148] Spanish Law on Sexual and Reproductive Health and the Voluntary Interruption of Pregnancy, Ley Orgánica 2/2010, 3 March 2010 <http://www.boe.es/boe/dias/2010/03/04/pdfs/BOE-A-2010-3514.pdf> accessed 31 December 2010.

[149] CO Jamaica, CEDAW/C/JAM/CO/5 (2006) para 36.

[150] CO Azerbaijan CEDAW/C/AZE/CO/3 (2007) para 5; CO Kenya CEDAW/C/KEN/CO/6 (2007) paras 39–40.

[151] CO Brazil, CEDAW/C/BRA/CO/6 (2007) paras 29–30.   [152] GR 24 para 19.

[153] CO Sweden, CEDAW/C/SWE/CO/7 (2008) paras 34–5.

[154] GR 24 para 14; CO Indonesia, CEDAW/C/IDN/CO/5 (2007) paras 16–17.

distinctions in service delivery to attend to women's sex-specific health care needs are necessary and therefore do not constitute discrimination.

II. Substantive Equality

The elimination of *de facto* discrimination in order to realize substantive equality requires, among other measures, reforming laws, policies, and practices that are sex-neutral on their face, but that in practice negatively affect the health of women or specific groups of women. For example, criminalizing contraception is sex-neutral because it applies to both men and women. However, lack of contraceptives disproportionately affects women's health because only women become pregnant. The Committee is also concerned about sex-neutral laws that force victims of sexual violence to report to police immediately, prior to seeking health care, because such reporting may disproportionately prejudice female victims in accessing health, especially psychological, services.[155]

The Committee states that 'identical or neutral treatment of women and men might constitute discrimination against women if such treatment resulted in or had the effect of women being denied the exercise of a right because there was no recognition of the pre-existing gender-based disadvantage and inequality that women face'.[156] Gender-based disadvantage and inequality in the field of health care often is caused, for example, by the neglect, lack of accommodation, or underfunding of sex-specific health care needs or diseases, health conditions, or risk factors that predominantly affect women. Substantive equality necessitates attending to the risk factors that disproportionately affect women's health.[157]

The Committee consistently requires States parties to accommodate the sex-specific health needs of marginalized women, such as Romani[158] or Muslim[159] women, women in prostitution,[160] single women,[161] and refugee and internally displaced women,[162] by taking appropriate measures to address their marginalization, in order to ensure their access to health services. Substantive equality requires going beyond merely comparing the formal treatment of individuals in similar situations; it requires paying sufficient attention to women who suffer historical or persistent prejudice. Substantive equality necessitates decriminalizing treatment of women with stigmatized conditions, such as HIV/AIDS,[163] or women in stigmatized work, such as sex work,[164] because criminalizing denies such women equal access to health services.

The Committee interprets substantive equality as justifying different treatment of men and women in dissimilar situations when necessary to achieve access to health care services.[165] In such situations, the relevant question is whether men and women are treated appropriately according to their sex- and gender-based health differences.

---

[155] CO Myanmar, CEDAW/C/MMR/CO/3 (2008) paras 22–3.   [156] GR 28 para 5.
[157] GR 24 para 12.   [158] CO Slovenia, CEDAW/C/SVN/CO/4 (2008) paras 35–6.
[159] CO Myanmar, CEDAW/C/MMR/CO/3 (2008) paras 42–3.   [160] GR 24 paras 6 and 18.
[161] CO Maldives, CEDAW/C/MDV/CO/3 (2007) paras 33–4.
[162] CO Azerbaijan, CEDAW/C/AZE/CO/3 (2007) para 31–2.
[163] CO Myanmar, CEDAW/C/MMR/CO/3 (2008) paras 40–1.
[164] UNAIDS, 'UNAIDS Guidance Note on HIV and Sex Work' (2009) 8–14 <http://data.unaids.org/pub/BaseDocument/2009/jc1696_guidance_note_hiv_and_sexwork_en.pdf> accessed 31 December 2010; UNCHR, 'Report of the Special Rapporteur on the right of everyone to the highest attainable standard of health' (27 April 2010) UN Doc A/HRC/14/20, paras 36–45.
[165] CO Cook Islands, CEDAW/C/COK/CO/1 (2007) para 35.

The Committee elaborates that while 'lack of respect for the confidentiality of patients will affect both men and women, it may deter women from seeking advice and treatment and thereby adversely affect their health and well-being' when men would not be deterred.[166]

Where an apparently sex-neutral rule disproportionately prejudices the health of women, and no justification for such rule can be shown, a State party will have to reform the law to ensure substantive equality. The Committee rejects governmental attempts to use cost considerations to justify policies that disproportionately impair women's health.[167] A domestic court, building on its own constitutional provision regarding access to health care which, the court said, had the same content as Article 12, rejected a law that allowed disproportionately higher fees for women's care than men's in the private health system. The court considered that these higher fees burden women's access, thus denying them equal access to services.[168]

III. Transformative Equality

Realizing transformative equality[169] in the field of health care requires understanding how the structures of subordination of women in legal, social, economic, political, or cultural sectors of society impede women's access to health care.[170] States parties should 'allocate adequate budgetary, human and administrative resources to ensure that women's health receives a share of the overall health budget comparable with that for men's health, taking into account their different health needs'.[171] Transformative equality requires reallocation or reorientation of health care resources, including budgets and health personnel, to achieve universal coverage for women on a basis of equality with men. The Committee is concerned about how the restructuring of health services can decrease the number of clinics and health resources available to women.[172] Unfair discrimination also occurs when States parties fail to reasonably accommodate the different health situations of men and women. For health expenditures to be equal, States parties are required to treat men and women by reference to their relative incidence levels of conditions of ill-health or diseases in their populations.[173]

Transformative equality requires States parties to dismantle demeaning stereotypes of women and subgroups of women in the health sector to accelerate the achievement of *de facto* equality.[174] Persistent stereotypes that inhibit women's equal access are those that consider women as incompetent and irrational decision-makers, lacking the capacity for medical and moral agency and self-determination, so they are denied the opportunity to make their own health care decisions.[175] The Committee reads Article 12 in conjunction with Articles 2(f) and 5(a) to require States parties to expose stereotypes detrimental to women in accessing health services, and show how they discriminate against women or otherwise deny them their rights.[176] It is concerned about stereotypes that treat women as

---

[166] GR 24 para 12(d).   [167] CO Kyrgyzstan, CEDAW/C/KGZ/CO/3 (2008) paras 37–8.
[168] Tribunal Constitucional de Chile, Constitucionalidad del artículo 38 ter de la Ley Nº 18.933, Rol Nº 1710-10 Inc. (06/08/2010) paras 103, 155–6.
[169] GR 25 paras 6–7.   [170] CO Haiti, CEDAW/C/HTI/CO/7 (2009) paras 38–9.
[171] GR 24 para 30.   [172] CO Poland, CEDAW/C/POL/CO/6 (2007) para 24.
[173] CO Armenia, CEDAW/C/ARM/CO/4/Rev.1 (2009) paras 36–7.
[174] CO Indonesia, CEDAW/C/IDN/CO/5 (2007) paras 16–17.
[175] *AS v Hungary* (n 13 above); CO Canada, CEDAW/C/CAN/CO/7 (2008) paras 43–4.
[176] CO Maldives, A/56/38, 24th Session (2001) para 142.

vectors of disease, thus blaming them for the spread of diseases, such as HIV/AIDS, and ignoring men's responsibilities in preventing such diseases.[177]

IV. Direct vs Indirect Discrimination

The Committee explains that:

direct discrimination against women constitutes different treatment explicitly based on grounds of sex and gender differences. Indirect discrimination against women occurs when a law, policy, programme or practice appears to be neutral as it relates to men and women, but has a discriminatory effect in practice on women, because pre-existing inequalities are not addressed by the apparently neutral measure. Moreover, indirect discrimination can exacerbate existing inequalities owing to a failure to recognize structural and historical patterns of discrimination and unequal power relationships between women and men.[178]

Indirect discrimination appears when the application of gender-neutral norms or practices results in women being disproportionately and negatively affected by them. Indirect discrimination also occurs where laws, policies, or practices do not recognize and accommodate the ways in which women are different from men or differently situated from men. The Committee explains that 'if a health care system lacks services to prevent, detect and treat illnesses specific to women', it is discriminatory.[179] For example, this occurs when there is no health care for female prisoners, including pregnant women.[180]

Measures that allow for health care providers' conscientious objection to deliver lawful care may be indirectly discriminatory. Such measures appear to be sex-neutral because they are not specifically aimed at women. However, health care providers generally object on grounds of conscience primarily to the provision of sexual and reproductive health care services to women, disproportionately prejudicing their access. The Committee recognizes the importance of accommodating health providers' exercise of their conscience but requires States parties to inform women of all of their options, and to refer women in good time to non-objecting providers, ensuring that referral does not frustrate or prejudice access to lawful care.[181]

V. Intersectional Discrimination

Intersectional discrimination is often evidenced by disparities in health status among particular subgroups of women marginalized by their identities, such as girl children,[182] adolescent women,[183] unmarried women including single mothers,[184] lesbian women,[185] elderly women,[186] women in prostitution,[187] indigenous women,[188] racialized women,[189]

---

[177] CO Guyana, CEDAW/C/GUY/CO/3-6 (2005) para 38.   [178] GR 28 para 16.
[179] GR 24 para 11.   [180] CO Yemen, A/63/38, 41st Session (2008) paras 391–2.
[181] GR 24 para 11; CO Slovakia, CEDAW/C/SVK/CO (2008) para 29; CO Portugal, CEDAW/C/PRT/CO/7 (2008) paras 42–3; CO Poland, CEDAW/C/POL/CO/6 (2007) paras 24–5.
[182] GR 24 para 6.   [183] GR 24 para 18; CO Sweden CEDAW/C/SWE/CO/7 (2008) paras 34–5.
[184] CO Armenia, CEDAW/C/ARM/CO/4/Rev.1 (2009) paras 36–7.   [185] GR 28 paras 18 and 31.
[186] GR 27 paras 11, 12, 14, 21, 32, and 45–6; CO Kazakhstan, CEDAW/C/KAZ/CO/2 (2007) paras 26–7; CO France, CEDAW/C/FRA/CO/6 (2008) paras 38–9.
[187] GR 24 paras 6 and 18.
[188] GR 24 para 6; CO Ecuador, CEDAW/C/ECU/CO/7 (2008) paras 24–5.
[189] CO New Zealand, CEDAW/C/NZL/CO/6 (2007) paras 38–9.

rural women,[190] or women who are migrants, internally displaced, asylum seekers or refugees.[191] The Committee elaborates that 'discrimination on the basis of sex or gender may affect women belonging to such groups to a different degree or in different ways than men'.[192]

Often, discrimination against subgroups of women compounds with discrimination on the basis of health conditions, such as mental health problems,[193] HIV positivity,[194] or disabilities,[195] to deny women with such conditions access to appropriate health care services. A domestic court has relied on the Convention to require the State to provide specialized mental health services to displaced women who are victims of armed conflict.[196] Another domestic court relied on Article 12 to hold that the exclusion of infertility treatment from public health services is a form of discrimination against infertile women.[197]

VI. Temporary Special Measures (TSMs)

States parties might have to adopt temporary special measures to ensure equality for women in the field of health care.[198] The measures should be specifically designed to be temporary and to eliminate the effects of discrimination. The temporary nature might be measured by a time frame, such as the amount of time necessary to introduce a vaccine to accelerate the reduction of cervical cancer among certain groups where prevalence rates have been historically higher than the general population of women. The Committee has suggested the use of TSMs to eliminate discrimination against aboriginal, ethnic, minority,[199] or rural women[200] to accelerate their access to health care until such time as their access is the same as the general population of women.

E. States Parties' Obligations

I. Nature of the obligations

1. 'All Appropriate Measures'

States parties must justify the appropriateness of the particular measures they have chosen to ensure equality[201] in accessing health care services. While they may use discretion in selecting the measures employed to achieve equality in the field of health care, 'ultimately,

---

[190] CO Bolivia, CEDAW/C/BOL/CO/4 (2008) paras 42–3; CO Colombia, CEDAW/C/COL/CO/6 (2007) paras 22–3.

[191] GR 24 paras 6 and 16. CO Austria, CEDAW/C/AUT/CO/6 (2007) paras 29–30.

[192] GR 28 para 18.

[193] CO Guatemala, CEDAW/C/GUA/CO/7 (2009) paras 41–2; CO The United Kingdom, A/63/38, 41st Session (2008) paras 292–4; CO Luxembourg, CEDAW/C/LUX/CO/5 (2008) paras 27–8; CO China, CEDAW/C/CHN/CO/6 (2006) para 28.

[194] CO Myanmar, CEDAW/C/MMR/CO/3 (2008) paras 40–1.

[195] CO Australia, CEDAW/C/AUS/CO/5 (2006) para 27; CO Pakistan, CEDAW/C/PAK/CO/3 (2007) paras 42–3.

[196] Corte Constitucional de Colombia, *T-045/10* (02 February 2010) s 6.4 No 5.

[197] Cámara Segunda de Apelaciones en lo Civil, Sala Primera, Provincia de Entre Ríos, Argentina, Pannuto Martin Javier y Otra c/Instituto de Obra Social de la Provincia de Entre Ríos (I.O.S.P.E.R.) s/Acción de Amparo (02/06/2009) para II.2.

[198] Art 4(1); GR 25 para 7.

[199] CO Canada, CEDAW/C/CAN/CO/7 (2008) paras 43–4; CO Slovakia, A/63/38, 41st Session (2008) paras 36–7; CO Venezuela, CEDAW/C/VEN/CO/6 (2006) para 16.

[200] CO Morocco, CEDAW/C/MAR/CO/4 (2008) paras 32–3.   [201] GR 28 para 23.

it is for the Committee to determine whether a State party has indeed adopted all necessary measures at the national level aimed at achieving the full realization of the rights recognized in the Convention'.[202]

Appropriateness requires States parties to 'demonstrate that health legislation, plans and policies are based on scientific and ethical research and assessment of health status and needs of women'.[203] When laws, policies, or practices regarding women's health are not based on reliable scientific evidence, but on prejudices, pseudo-science, or patriarchal customs, alternate measures that are evidenced-based, transparent, and otherwise appropriate to women's health needs and circumstances are necessary.[204]

A 'policy must be action- and results-oriented in that it should establish indicators, benchmarks and timelines, ensure adequate resourcing for all relevant actors and otherwise enable those actors to play their part in achieving the agreed benchmarks and goals'.[205] Ensuring that measures are appropriate in the field of health care requires the use of health indicators to monitor the provision of services to women, to ensure that they are appropriate and affordable, and to monitor continuously whether gender and diversity perspectives are included in health reporting.[206]

The Committee uses a variety of indicators, including health status indicators, health service indicators, and structural indicators.[207] Health status indicators measure the outcomes of health services, such as maternal mortality ratios (maternal deaths per 100,000 live births).[208] Health service indicators, also known as process indicators, measure the nature and delivery of a service. They include the percentage of women who are attended at birth by skilled health personnel,[209] and benchmarks that show whether health services are affordable.[210]

Structural indicators include health laws, constitutional provisions on rights relating to health, professional ethical codes of medical, nursing and midwifery associations, and the ratification of human rights treaties. These indicators show the degree of compliance with the human rights of women, including the rights to autonomy, privacy, and informed choice.[211] Such indicators determine whether laws and policies have been established to ensure women equal access to health care services.[212] Where equal access has been denied, indicators will show the extent to which there has been effective use of remedial procedures of investigation or appeal.[213]

General appeal procedures, such as through courts, national human rights institutions, public defenders of rights or ombudspersons,[214] might be used to investigate alleged violations within the health system. Specialized investigational and appeal procedures might also be established within a health care system, such as the appointment of female health

---

[202] Ibid.   [203] GR 24 para 9.   [204] Ibid.   [205] GR 28 para 28.

[206] GR 24 paras 29 and 31(d); CO Canada, CEDAW/C/CAN/CO/7 (2008) paras 41–2.

[207] UNCHR, 'Report of the Special Rapporteur on the right of everyone to the highest attainable standard of health' (2008) UN Doc A/HRC/7/11.

[208] GR 24 para 17; WHO (n 57 above).

[209] WHO, 'National-Level Monitoring of the Achievement of Universal Access to Reproductive Health: Conceptual and Practical Considerations and Related Indicators'. Report of a WHO/UNFPA Technical Consultation (2007) <http://www.searo.who.int/LinkFiles/Publications_national_level_monitoring.pdf> accessed 31 December 2010.

[210] GR 24 para 9.   [211] GR 24 para 31(e).

[212] GR 24 para 9; CO Colombia, CEDAW/C/COL/CO/6 (2007) para 6.

[213] GR 24 para 15(c); GR 28 para 34; *Karen Tayag Vertido v The Philippines* CEDAW Communication No 18/2008 para 8.3.

[214] CO Czech Republic, CEDAW/C/CZE/CO/5 (2010) para 17.

ombudspersons to investigate suspected infractions. Health ombudspersons might be more accessible than courts, and might be more effective in ensuring that States parties meet their obligations in the health sector.[215]

Indicators are usually designed in a sex-neutral manner, but more refined gender-sensitive indicators might be needed to ensure measures are appropriate for achieving *de facto* equality, particularly for subgroups of women, such as those at higher risk of poor health outcomes due to socio-economic factors.[216] Such indicators would show the degree to which services are appropriate, affordable, and adequate to meet the needs of all women, and are of a nature that women find acceptable.[217] Acceptability is a qualitative assessment and includes criteria related to privacy of service delivery, and sensitivity to life cycle, gender, and cultural[218] requirements.

The Committee obliges States parties to 'collect relevant sex-disaggregated data, to enable effective monitoring, facilitate continuing evaluation and allow for the revision or supplementation of existing measures and the identification of any new measures that may be appropriate'[219] for women and particular groups of women.[220] Data disaggregated by, for example, age, rural status, and ethnicity, is often required to show the degree to which particular subgroups of women lack equal access to services.[221] When States parties do not produce 'reliable data disaggregated by sex on the incidence and severity of diseases and conditions hazardous to women's health',[222] the Committee asks them to ensure that measures are appropriate to achieve indicators and benchmarks.[223]

2. Immediate vs Gradual Implementation

States parties have immediate obligations of compliance to eliminate discrimination against women in the field of health care to ensure women have equal access to health care services. Immediate obligations include requirements to identify and abolish discriminatory laws, policies, and health care practices that are barriers to women's equal access. This includes requiring States parties to ensure availability of health services that only women need,[224] such as those relating to pregnancy and its complications.

Immediate obligations exist to eliminate discrimination against particular subgroups of women where they have been harmed, such as through governmental failure to ensure sufficient distribution of health services. Obligations are also immediate when conditions of ill-health are preventable, such as preventable causes of maternal mortality and morbidity[225] and tuberculosis.[226] Under Article 12(2), States parties 'shall ensure to women appropriate services in connection with pregnancy, confinement and the post natal period'. The use of the term 'ensure' means that the nature of the obligations under Article 12(2) is immediate.

The obligation may be more gradual where a therapeutic drug has recently been approved as safe and effective, but is initially too expensive for public distribution. Gradually, as a

---

[215] GR 24 paras 29–31.   [216] CO Poland, CEDAW/C/POL/CO/6 (2007) paras 28–9.
[217] GR 24 para 22.   [218] CO Ecuador, CEDAW/C/ECU/CO/7 (2008) paras 38–9.
[219] GR 28 para 28.   [220] GR 24 para 10.
[221] CO Lithuania, A/63/38, 41st Session (2008) paras 84–5; CO Cameroon, CEDAW/C/CMR/CO/3 (2009) paras 40–1.
[222] GR 24 para 9.   [223] GR 28 para 23.
[224] GR 24 para 14; CO Sweden, CEDAW/C/SWE/CO/7 (2008) paras 34–5.   [225] GR 24 para 17.
[226] Ibid.

drug becomes less expensive through the availability of a generic equivalent, States parties will be obliged to distribute it in public health clinics.

3. Specific/Non-specific

Article 12 requires States parties to ensure access to specific services 'related to family planning' and 'appropriate services in connection with pregnancy, confinement and the post-natal period, and adequate nutrition during pregnancy and lactation'. Article 12(2) is also specific as to the obligation to grant 'free services, where necessary'. The Committee specifies that States parties develop a comprehensive gender-sensitive national strategy to promote women's health throughout their life cycle,[227] and to collect statistics disaggregated by sex.[228] Article 12(1) includes non-specific obligations in that States parties may choose the measures they determine to be appropriate to ensure women's equal access to health services in the national context,[229] even though the choice is subject to Committee oversight.[230]

II. Implementation

1. Obligation to Respect

The obligation to respect rights requires States parties:

> **to refrain from obstructing action taken by women in pursuit of their health goals...States parties should not restrict women's access to health services or to the clinics that provide those services on the ground that women do not have the authorization of husbands, partners, parents or health authorities or because they are unmarried or because they are women.[231]**

This obligation also requires States parties to reform laws 'that criminalize procedures only needed by women and that punish women who undergo those procedures'.[232] The Committee recommends the review of laws on abortion with a view to eliminating punitive provisions for women who undergo this procedure.[233]

Ministries of Health are obliged to provide women with effective access to lawful services, to investigate whether women are actually receiving such services through, for example, the collection of official statistics, and to attend to the health burdens of unavailable, inaccessible, or unsafe services.[234] States parties are accountable for the arbitrary exercise of power through health ministries, resulting in women's preventable deaths and disabilities that Article 12 obliges States parties to prevent.[235] Where women do not have effective access to safe services, failure to identify, respond to, and remedy the deficiency aggravates the violation.[236]

---

[227] Ibid para 2; CO Bolivia, CEDAW/C/BOL/CO/4 (2008) paras 42–3.
[228] GR 24 para 9; CO Portugal, CEDAW/C/PRT/CO/7 (2008) paras 42–3.   [229] GR 24 para 9.
[230] GR 28 para 23.   [231] GR 24 para 14.   [232] Ibid.
[233] CO Andorra, A/56/38, 25th Session (2008) para 48; CO Belize A/54/38, 21st Session (1999) para 57; CO Burkina Faso A/55/38, 22nd Session (2000) para 276; CO Cameroon A/55/38, 23rd Session (2000) para 60; CO Chile, CEDAW/C/CHI/CO/4 (2006) paras 19–20; CO Ireland A/54/38, 21st Session (1999) para 186; CO Jordan A/55/38, 20th Session (2000) para 181; CO Namibia, A/52/38/Rev.1, 17th Session (1997) para 127; CO Nepal, A/54/38, 21st Session (1999) paras 139 and 148; CO Nicaragua, CEDAW/C/NIC/CO/6 (2007) paras 17-18; CO Pakistan, CEDAW/C/PAK/CO/3 (2007) paras 40–1; CO The United Kingdom, A/55/38, 21st Session (1999) para 310.
[234] *KL v Peru* (n 25 above).   [235] CO Mongolia, CEDAW/C/MNG/CO/7 (2008) paras 33–4.
[236] CO Cameroon, CEDAW/C/CMR/CO/3 (2009) paras 40–1.

2. Obligation to Protect

The obligation 'to protect rights relating to women's health requires States parties, their agents and officials to take action to prevent and impose sanctions for violations of rights by private persons and organizations'.[237] The positive obligation to prevent and respond to acts of discrimination by non-State actors is subject to the due diligence standard in the health sector.[238] This standard requires the State party to establish effective systems as well as effective measures to prevent and respond to acts of discrimination by particular non-State actors.[239] The Committee reports annually on what States parties have done to implement its recommendations about systemic reforms and remedies for the individual victims in the particular communications.[240]

The establishment of effective systems requires mechanisms for monitoring provision of health care services, and the enactment and effective enforcement of policies regarding, for instance, 'health care protocols, hospital procedures to address violence against women and abuse of girl children'.[241]

The transfer by States parties of health care service delivery to private agencies may adversely impact women's ability to access such services,[242] particularly women and girls from poor rural areas and women with disabilities.[243] Consequently, States parties should carefully monitor the privatization of health care and its impact on the health of women[244] and report on what they have done 'to organize governmental processes and all structures through which public power is exercised to promote and protect women's health'.[245]

The obligation to protect according to the due diligence standard requires ensuring adequate prosecution and punishment of individuals who violate women's rights, such as those who perform female genital mutilation.[246] The obligation also exists when an infringement has been found in a case of domestic violence; the State party is required to ensure that the victim 'receives reparation proportionate to the physical and mental harm undergone and to the gravity of the violation of her rights'.[247]

The obligation to protect requires States parties 'to protect women against discrimination by private actors and take steps directly aimed at eliminating customary and all other practices that prejudice and perpetuate the notion of inferiority or superiority of either of the sexes, and of stereotyped roles for men and women'.[248] This requires at a minimum instituting protocols to ensure respect for women's dignity as they access both the public and private health care systems and implementing programs such as to eliminate FGM.[249]

---

[237] GR 24 para 15.   [238] GR 28 para 13.

[239] *Goekce v Austria* CEDAW Communication No 5/2005 (2007) CEDAW/C/39/D/5/2005 paras 12.1.1, 12.1.2, and 12.1.4; *Yildirim v Austria* CEDAW Communication No 6/2005 (2007) CEDAW/C/39/D/6/2005 paras 12.1.5 and 12.3.

[240] UNGA, 'Report of the CEDAW Committee Forty-fourth and Forty-fifth Sessions' (2010) UN Doc A/65/38, 110–15.

[241] GR 24 para 15(a); CO Korea, CEDAW/C/KOR/CO/6 (2007) para 18; *Ms AS v Hungary* (n 13 above) para 11.5-II.

[242] CO Haiti, CEDAW/C/HTI/CO/7 (2009) paras 34–5; CO India, CEDAW/C/IND/CO/3 (2007) paras 40–1.

[243] CO Lebanon, CEDAW/C/LBN/CO/3 (2008) para 34.

[244] CO Italy, CEDAW/C/ITA/CC/4–5 (2005) para 33.   [245] GR 24 para 17.

[246] CO Mauritania, CEDAW/C/MRT/CO/1 (2007) paras 27–8.

[247] *Ms AT v Hungary* CEDAW Communication No 2/2003 (2005), CEDAW/C/32/D/2003 para 9.6.

[248] GR 28 para 9.   [249] CO Portugal, CEDAW/C/PRT/CO/7 (2008) para 31.

The obligation to protect women's access to health care services requires States parties to prevent marginalization of women with stigmatized diseases, such as sexually transmitted infections including HIV/AIDS,[250] and those with stigmatized conditions, such as obstetric fistula[251] and mental health disorders.[252]

3. *Obligation to Fulfil*

The obligation to fulfil requires States parties 'to facilitate access to and to provide for the full realization of women's rights'.[253] This overarching obligation requires States parties to 'take appropriate legislative, judicial, administrative, budgetary, economic and other measures to the maximum extent of their available resources to ensure that women realize their rights to health care'.[254] It requires instituting a gender-sensitive public health infrastructure that addresses the magnitude of women's ill-health, particularly when it arises from preventable conditions.[255] It obliges States parties to allocate the necessary budgetary resources 'to prevent, detect, and treat illness specific to women.'[256] The Committee has commended States for subsidizing basic medicines such as contraceptives[257] and condoms.[258]

III. Reservations

States parties have entered no reservations to Article 12.

F. Conclusion

Many of the laws, policies, and practices regarding women's equality in access to health care services have emerged in specific areas of women's health that are of pressing contemporary concern. While this chapter elaborates on how Article 12 has been applied to date, it is an interpretive guide to how the article could be applied to discriminatory situations that are not yet visible, as well as to emerging or future health issues of concern to women.

The nature and scope of the specific and general obligations with regard to the elimination of all forms of discrimination against women in the field of health care will evolve as understanding of women's health needs deepens in the medical, public health, and social sciences. The content and meaning of Article 12 will continue to be elaborated through the Committee's work[259] and the practice of States parties, influenced by the work of other human rights bodies, such as through cases pending before

---

[250] CO Tanzania, A/63/38, 41st Session (2008) paras 138–9.
[251] CO Sierra Leone, CEDAW/C/SLE/CO/5 (2007) para 22.
[252] CO Guatemala, CEDAW/C/GUA/CO/7 (2009) paras 35–6.   [253] GR 28 para 20.
[254] GR 24 para 17.   [255] Ibid para 17.   [256] Ibid para 11.
[257] CO Burkina Faso, CEDAW/C/BFA/CO/4–5 (2005) para 35.
[258] CO Ghana, CEDAW/C/GHA/CO/5 (2006) para 32.
[259] *Alyne da Silva Pimentel v Brazil* (n 15 above); *LC v Peru* (n 15 above).

the European Court of Human Rights[260] and the Inter-American Commission on Human Rights.[261]

Addressing discrimination against women in the field of health care also requires engaging with different disciplines and methods that provide evidence of distinction, exclusion, or restriction, and of measures to improve women's access to health services. These disciplines and methods might be drawn, for instance, from analytical processes within the medical sciences, public health sciences, social sciences, health systems,[262] and ethics.[263] Evidence may also come from research on women's health,[264] and on particular barriers affecting particular subgroups of women regarding, for instance, access to new vaccines such as those to prevent cervical cancer.[265] Interpretation of evidence often incorporates interdisciplinary knowledge applied to determining the evolving obligations to ensure women's equality rights in the field of health care, or to assessing related 'human rights and fundamental freedoms in the political, economic, social, cultural, civil or any other field'.[266]

[260] *Červeňáková v Czech Republic* (involuntary sterilization of a Romani woman) (filed May 2009, App 26852/09); *Ferenčíková v Czech Republic* (involuntary sterilization of a Romani woman) (April 2010); *IG, MK and RH v Slovakia* (involuntary sterilization of Romani women) (filed April 2004); *NB v Slovakia* (involuntary sterilization of a Romani woman) (filed May 2010); *RK v Czech Republic* (involuntary sterilization of a Romani woman) (filed January 2008); *S & T v Poland* (restrictive access to legal abortion for adolescents) (filed May 2009); *RR v Poland* (denial of appropriate care to assess genetic condition because of her pregnant status) (filed December 2004); *VC v Slovakia* (involuntary sterilization of a Romani woman) (filed April 2007); *Z v Moldova* (denial of appropriate post abortion care despite continuous bleeding) (filed February 2009); *Z v Poland* (denial of appropriate care to treat ulcerative colitis because of her pregnant status, resulting in death) (filed September 2008).

[261] *AN v Costa Rica* (denial of abortion for a high risk pregnancy of a foetus with severe brain abnormality) (filed October 2008); *FS v Chile* (involuntary sterilization of an HIV-positive woman) (filed February 2009); *IV v Bolivia* (involuntary sterilization of a woman) (admissible July 23, 2008); *Ana Victoria Sanchez Villalobos and Others v Costa Rica* (prohibition of IVF treatment) (filed March 2004).

[262] WHO, 'Everybody's Business: Strengthening Health Systems to Improve Health Outcomes' (2007) 3 at <http://who.int/healthsystems/strategy/everybodys_business.pdf> accessed 31 December 2010.

[263] FIGO Committee for the Study of Ethical Aspects of Human Reproduction and Women's Health, 'Ethical Issues in Obstetrics and Gynecology' (2009) <http://www.figo.org/about/guidelines> accessed 31 December 2010.

[264] G Sen and P Östlin (eds), *Gender Equity in Health: The Shifting Frontiers of Evidence and Action* (New York: Routledge, 2010).

[265] JN Erdman, 'Human Rights in Health Equity: Cervical Cancer and HPV Vaccines' (2009) 35 *Am J of Law & Medicine* 365–87.

[266] See the discussion in ch on art 1.

Article 13

States Parties shall take all appropriate measures to eliminate discrimination against women in other areas of economic and social life in order to ensure, on a basis of equality of men and women, the same rights, in particular:

(a) The right to family benefits;

(b) The right to bank loans, mortgages and other forms of financial credit;

(c) The right to participate in recreational activities, sports and all aspects of cultural life.

* I would like to thank Anna Maria Paulus for superb research assistance.

A. Introduction

Article 13 obliges States parties to ensure women's equality in all areas of economic and social life, including cultural life. It complements both the Convention provisions covering political life and those pertaining to the private sphere. Article 13 thus reaffirms the indivisibility of all human rights and the central Convention premise that women are entitled to participate in all areas of life on a basis of equality.[1] According to UDHR Article 22, economic, social, and cultural rights are indispensable to leading a life of dignity and freedom to develop one's personality. The CEDAW Committee underscores this premise in General Recommendation 28, noting that the principle of equality 'entails the concept that all human beings...are free to develop their personal abilities, pursue their professional careers and make choices without the limitations set by stereotypes, rigid gender roles, and prejudices'.[2] Recognizing that women, like men, are entitled freely to choose economic activity according to their own aspirations, Article 13 guarantees women's right to earn their livelihood and to autonomy in the economic sphere.[3] This independence is essential to realizing other Convention rights: economic independence empowers women to make decisions in their personal lives, in particular, to choose whether and with whom to enter into marriage. Economic independence is also a gateway to women's participation in public life.[4]

Article 13 acknowledges the human need for social interaction and its importance for the free and full development of one's personality.[5] It also acknowledges that social life is where many gender-based stereotypes are lived and perpetuated, which either prevent women from engaging in social interaction beyond the family circle or restrict them to specific social roles. Achieving women's equality in this sphere particularly requires rooting out social customs and norms that perpetuate gender stereotypes (Article 5).

Article 13 sets forth women's right to equality in economic and social life comprehensively, as opposed to the approach of other human rights treaties, which list specific rights in respect of which equality is to be ensured.[6] It obliges States parties to examine the full range of women's economic and social reality so they can take appropriate measures to realize equality. Article 3 takes the same approach. As emphasized by the Beijing Declaration and Platform for Action, economic structures and policies that produce or perpetuate women's inequality including access to resources such as land and credit, must be targeted.[7]

The potential of Article 13 is underdeveloped in the work of the Committee. The practice of other human rights bodies, in particular the CESCR, and of the special procedures of the Human Rights Council, could be used as inspiration for understanding and applying the article.

---

[1] Preamble, paras 2 and 7.   [2] GR 28 para 18.

[3] See also: Montréal Principles on Women's Economic, Social and Cultural Rights, 26 *Human Rights Quarterly* 760 (2002) 762.

[4] Ibid.

[5] See also UDHR art 29(1), which links life in a human community to the development of one's personality.

[6] As examples of this approach see ICERD art 5, ICCPR art 2(1), and ICESCR art 2(2).

[7] Beijing Platform for Action, Strategic Objective F ('Women and the Economy') § 44. See also the Beijing Declaration, Critical Area of Concern No 6, § 35.

B. Travaux Préparatoires

The drafting history of Article 13 reflects development towards a comprehensive understanding of women's equality in the areas of economic, social, and cultural life. The draft adopted by the Working Group of the CSW in 1976 did not contain a specific provision on women's equality in economic and social life.[8] Some elements, such as a right to non-discrimination with respect to family allowances, were contained in provisions concerning only employment; the problem of equal access to financial credit was discussed later and in relation only to women in rural areas.[9] A separate article was proposed when the discussion reached the Third Committee. It consisted of those elements of Article 11 that were not limited to employment.[10] The right to financial credit was added to this proposal,[11] and the provision became comprehensive through the inclusion of an introductory sentence referring to equality in economic and social life in general.[12] Finally, the right to participation in leisure and cultural activities, which had been proposed for the provision on non-discrimination in employment, was moved here and reworded to specify that recreational activities and sports as well as all cultural activities were covered.[13] Thus, the right contained in section (c) advanced from an accessory right of employed women to a right of all women irrespective of the existence of an employment relationship.

C. Issues of Interpretation

The structure of Article 13 mirrors this drafting history. The chapeau lays down women's right of non-discrimination in 'other' areas of economic and social life. Thus, the guarantee is comprehensive and complements the Convention provisions that refer to particular rights, such as education, formal and informal employment and employment-related economic benefits, rural women's rights to social security, and the rights to conclude contracts and to enjoy economic equality in marriage and to choose an occupation. In some respects the article may be seen as subsidiary to other more specific articles, but it also carries its own specificity as to certain matters listed in sections (a–c).

This structure may well explain why the Committee has rarely referred to Article 13 explicitly in its practice and has not yet adopted a general recommendation on it. However, the Committee has implicitly dealt with Article 13 by making recommendations on areas covered by it, often linked with general obligations of States parties under Articles 1, 2, and 3. Examples are the Committee's request that all poverty alleviation programmes fully benefit women;[14] that States parties put into place programmes promoting women's economic

---

[8] L Rehof, *Guide to the Travaux Préparatoires of the United Nations Convention on the Elimination of All Forms of Discrimination against Women* (1993) 148. Art 10 DEDAW contains such a right, but then focuses on women in employment situations.

[9] Proposal by Egypt, India, Indonesia, Iran, Pakistan, Thailand, and the US, UN Docs E/CN.6/L.687 and E/CN.6/L.681/Add.1, 23–5, see Rehof (n 8 above).

[10] UN Doc A/C.3/33/L.47 (Denmark and the Netherlands), see Rehof (n 8 above) 149.

[11] UN Doc A/C.3/33/WG.1/CRP.5/Add.4 (Guyana), see Rehof (n 8 above) 150.

[12] See Rehof (n 10 above).

[13] UN Doc A/C.3/33/WG.1/CRP.5/Add.4, see Rehof (n 8 above) 150. Cuba proposed a different wording, which did not entail any substantive change, UN Doc A/C.3/33.L.47 paras 126–7.

[14] CO Belarus A/59/38, 30th Session (2004) para 354; CO Dominican Republic A/58/38, 31st Session (2004) para 283.

independence;[15] that development cooperation programmes address the socio-economic causes of discrimination against women;[16] and that a gender perspective be incorporated into all social and economic policies, programmes, and projects.[17] The Committee has also emphasized that States parties must make women equal participants and actors in designing social and economic policies and programmes, not merely beneficiaries of these measures.[18]

To the extent that economic policies are determined in international institutions or through inter-State cooperation, the extraterritorial reach of Article 13 is at stake where the effects of a State party's decisions affect women elsewhere.[19] States parties must strive to ensure that economic and social rights are protected by international policies, and they must create favourable conditions for the realization of all economic and social rights.[20]

Article 13 has considerable potential because it applies to overarching economic and social policies as well as to the vast area of social interactions where gender stereotypes are formed, reinforced, and perpetuated.[21] An increased focus on ensuring women's equality in economic life will significantly contribute to empowering women in all other areas of life.

I. Chapeau

1. 'To Eliminate Discrimination'. . . in Order to Ensure. . . the Same Rights'

As in Article 11, the reference to 'the same rights' in the chapeau of Article 13 may give rise to the misunderstanding that the provision aims at formal equality only. However, States parties are obliged 'to eliminate discrimination against women'. Thus, the provision refers to the comprehensive understanding of discrimination as contained in Article 1. It requires States parties to address direct, indirect, and structural discrimination. The purpose of eliminating discrimination is complemented by the aim of ensuring that women can exercise all their rights and have access to all opportunities and benefits available within a State and society.[22] This is expressed by the chapeau through the words 'on a basis of equality of men and women', which specify the obligation to ensure 'the same rights'. The ultimate aim is not the sameness of rights, but their equal enjoyment in fact.

---

[15] CO Gambia A/60/38, 33rd Session (2005) para 198.

[16] CO Angola A/59/38, 31st Session (2004), para 149; CO Burkina Faso A/60/38, 33rd session (2005).

[17] CO Argentina A/59/38, 31st Session (2004) para 373.

[18] CO Argentina, A/59/38, 31st Session (2004) para 372bis.

[19] See the discussion on extraterritorality in ch on art 2.

[20] CO Burkina Faso A/60/38, 33rd session (2005) para 348; CO Democratic Republic of the Congo, CEDAW/C/COD/CO/5, 36th Session (2006) para 16 (on development cooperation). See generally: SI Skogley and M Gibney, 'Transnational Human Rights Obligations' (2002) 24 *Human Rights Quarterly* 781–98, 790–3, with reference to CESCR, 'General Comment No 2: International Technical Assistance Measures (art. 22)' (1990) paras 86–8, and to Vienna Declaration and Programme of Action, Part I, para 13. See generally: M Ssenyonjo, 'Non-State Actors and Economic, Social and Cultural Rights', in M Baderin and R McCorquodale, *Economic, Social and Cultural Rights in Action* (2007) 109 and 120, and M Gondek, *The Reach of Human Rights in a Globalising World. Extraterritorial Application of Human Rights Treaties* (2009) 336.

[21] As discussed at length in ch on art 5.

[22] On the complementary character of the two concepts see A Bayefsky, 'The Principle of Equality or Non-Discrimination in International Law' (1990) 12 *Human Rights L J* 1; OM Arnardóttir, *Equality and Non-Discrimination under the European Convention on Human Rights* (2003) 8–10.

2. 'In Other Areas of Economic and Social Life'

The Chapeau is closely modelled after that of Article 11, which applies to 'the field of employment'. This explains why Article 13 covers 'other' areas of economic and social life. The reference to areas of life instead of rights echoes the scope of the definition of discrimination contained in Article 1 and of the States parties' obligations under Article 3. Both refer to the human rights and fundamental freedoms in, *inter alia*, the economic and social 'field'. Thus, they extend the reach of the Convention in several directions: they include all rights not explicitly mentioned in it, but which are relevant in the economic and social fields. This encompasses civil and political rights to the extent that they are necessary to participate in economic and social life. Finally, the reference to 'areas of life' requires looking beyond rights guaranteed and taking into account the denial of access to resources and opportunities.[23] Thus, Article 13 can be characterized as a convention within the Convention.[24]

a) Economic and Social Rights not Protected by other CEDAW Provisions

As the Committee has emphasized, the Convention is part of a comprehensive international human rights framework that, explicitly or implicitly, aims at ensuring the enjoyment of all rights by all.[25] Therefore, and as in Article 1, the rights relevant in the economic and social field can be found in other international treaties, irrespective of their binding force for a State party to CEDAW, in customary international law, and even in non-binding documents.[26] In addition, Article 13 arguably even surpasses these international sources by referring to 'rights' in these areas in general. Hence, it allows taking into account rights that are granted under national law in these fields and that go farther than international human rights law.

Accordingly, the most relevant sources for identifying such rights are the ICESCR and regional human rights treaties.[27] Their analysis reveals the following social and economic rights, some of which Article 13 lists explicitly:

the right to an adequate standard of living and continuous improvement of living conditions,[28] including

- the right to adequate food and to be free from hunger;[29]
- the right to adequate housing;[30]
- the right to adequate clothing;[31]

---

[23] See the discussion in ch on art 3.

[24] On the incorporation of other rights into the Convention see: A Byrnes, 'The Convention on the Elimination of All Forms of Discrimination against Women' in W Benedek, E Kisaakye, and G Oberleitner (eds), *Human Rights of Women International Instruments and African Experiences* (2002) 119, 124.

[25] GR 28 para 3.   [26] See the discussion in ch on art 1.

[27] The African Charter of Human Rights and Peoples' Rights (esp. arts 14–17), and its Protocol on the Rights of Women in Africa (2003) (esp. art 13), the European Social Charter and the Revised European Social Charter, and the Additional Protocol to the American Convention on Human Rights in the Area of Economic, Social and Cultural Rights (Protocol of San Salvador).

[28] ICESCR art 11(1), CRC art 27(1).   [29] ICESCR art 11(1) and (2).

[30] ICERD art 5(e)(iii), CESCR art 11(1), Revised ESC art 31.   [31] ICESCR art 11(1).

- the right to social services[32] and of access to basic public services.[33] This right is partly covered by Article 11 and partly by Article 13(a);
- right to protection against poverty and social exclusion;[34]
- the right to water;[35]
- the right to sanitation;[36]
- the right to live in a healthy environment,[37] which is covered, in part, by Article 12;
- the right of access to any place or service intended for use by the general public, such as transport, hotels, restaurants, cafes, theatres, and parks;[38]
- the right to equal participation in cultural activities[39] and to participate at all levels in the determination of cultural policies.[40] This is explicitly protected by Article 13(c);
- the right to equal participation in recreational, leisure, and sporting activities,[41] also explicitly protected by Article 13(c); and
- authors' rights[42] (equally contained in Article 13(c)).

Additionally, a State party must take into account social and economic rights guarantees in its national law.

b) Civil and Political Rights Necessary for Participating in Economic and Social Life

Participation in economic and social life entails interactions with other members of society. For this reason, civil and political rights that guarantee these interactions must also be safeguarded for women on the basis of equality. The Committee has recognized this connection, albeit only specifically as to Articles 1 through 5 and 24.[43] Freedom of association, for example, is necessary to set up business associations, professional societies, or social clubs; freedom of opinion is essential to meaningful exchanges with other people on issues of economic and social life, and for publicizing one's economic activities. Moreover, freedom of movement within the territory of the State of residence is indispensable for conducting business as well as for maintaining social contacts.[44] Finally, the right to privacy, which protects communications by mail, telephone, or other technical means, is essential to effectively carrying out economic or social activities.

---

[32] ICERD art 5(e)(iv), ECC art 13 (right to social assistance for all persons without adequate resources) and art 14 (right to benefit from social welfare services), see also Montréal Principles (n 3 above), Point II.1.(c).

[33] Additional Protocol to the American Convention on Human Rights in the Area of Economic, Social and Cultural Rights (Protocol of San Salvador) art 11(1).

[34] Revised ESC art 30.

[35] See CESCR, 'General Comment 15: The right to water (Articles 11 and 12)' (2002) UN Doc E/C.12/2002/12. The right to water also follows from the rights to the highest attainable standard of health. Further sources are the right to life and human dignity (ibid para 3).

[36] See 'Report of the independent expert on the issue of human rights obligations related to access to safe drinking water and sanitation, C de Albuquerque', UN Doc A/HRC/12/24 (2009) paras 60–81.

[37] Additional Protocol to the American Convention on Human Rights in the Area of Economic, Social and Cultural Rights (Protocol of San Salvador) art 11(1); see also: Montréal Principles (n 3 above), II.1.(j).

[38] ICERD art 5(f).

[39] ICERD art 5(e)(vi), ICESCR art 15(1)(a), CRC art 31(1) and (2), CRPD art 30(1).

[40] Protocol to the African Charter on the Rights of Women in Africa art 17(1).

[41] CRC art 31(1); CRPD art 30(5).   [42] CESCR art 15(1)(c).   [43] GR 28 para 7.

[44] CCPR, 'General Comment 27' (1999) UN Doc CCPR/C/21/Rev.1/Add.9 para 1 (liberty of movement as an 'indispensable condition for the free development of a person').

c) Access to Resources and Opportunities in Social and Economic Life

As shown above, a systematic interpretation of Article 13 in light of Article 3 requires also taking into account situations in which women are denied equal access to resources and opportunities in social and economic life. Instead of centring on rights, this approach focuses on obstacles to economic and social activities. Some treaties reflect this approach by underscoring the need for women's equality in particular areas of economic and social life, such as in tax law[45] or through the recognition of the economic value of the work of women in the home.[46] Other documents do so by emphasizing duties of the State to promote opportunities for self-employment, entrepreneurship, the development of cooperatives, and starting one's own business.[47] In order to detect other obstacles, the terms 'economic' and 'social' must be clarified.

Ordinarily, 'economic' refers to the production, development, and management of material resources. Such gains are obtained by producing and selling goods or services either at one's own risk or that of another, ie as a self-employed person or as an employee. For the purposes of Article 13, only self-employed activities fall under 'economic life' because the Committee has consistently considered informal dependent work[48] as falling under Article 11.[49] Moreover, material resources can be increased by financial activities, such as banking or investment in another person's economic activities. Finally, the state or private actors may provide persons with material resources, eg through social security or insurance schemes. Again, they fall under Article 11 if they depend on an employment relationship. 'Economic life' also extends to activities that support gaining material resources. Examples are access to immaterial resources, such as professional networks and knowledge.

'Social' has a double meaning: On the one hand, it denotes matters affecting human welfare, as in 'social politics'; on the other hand, it relates to living together in communities. In its first-mentioned meaning, 'social' overlaps with 'economic'. This overlap is reflected in some theoretical concepts of economic and social rights.[50] For others, social rights are fundamentally about distributive justice; they aim at bringing about social cohesion, solidarity, and inclusion.[51] This approach is closer to an understanding of 'social' as relating to living together in communities. For the purpose of Article 13, it appears more helpful to apply this latter interpretation, as it encompasses all forms of human

---

[45] Protocol to the African Charter on the Rights of Women in Africa art 13(j).

[46] Protocol to the African Charter on the Rights of Women in Africa art 13(i). See also Montréal Principles (n 3 above) para 24.

[47] CRPD art 27(1)(f).

[48] For the Committee's understanding of 'informal' see P Patten, *'Opportunities and Traps—The Informal Labor Market'* in HB Schöpp-Schilling and C Flinterman (eds), *The Circle of Empowerment: Twenty Five Years of the UN Committee on the Elimination of Discrimination against Women* (2007) 179–82.

[49] See the discussion in ch on art. 11.

[50] For a broad understanding of 'economic' as encompassing rights to social security and to an adequate standard of living permitting a life in dignity, see S Hertel, 'Why Bother? Measuring Economic Rights—The Research Agenda' 7 (3) *Intl Studies Perspectives* 215–30 (2006); S Hertel and LP Minkler, 'Introduction' in S Hertel and LP Minkler (eds), *Economic Rights: Conceptual, Measurement, and Policy Issues* (2008) 1–35, 3–4. The definition of economic rights as rights of access to resources indispensable for creating or exchanging goods and services is similarly broad; for this approach see C Gorga, 'Toward the Definition of Economic Rights' (1999) 2 *J of Markets & Morality* 88–101, 89; and M Langford (ed), *Social Rights Jurisprudence* (2008).

[51] K Rittich, 'Social Rights and Social Policy—Transformation of the International Landscape' in D Barak-Erez and AA Gross (eds), *Exploring Social Rights* (2007) 107–34, 109.

interaction for the development of one's personality. It reflects human nature as a 'social animal' and the fundamental right to personal autonomy. 'Social' life extends to interactions within the family to the extent that they are not covered by Article 16, but it does not encompass public and political life which falls under Article 7.

The following section brings together the three components (described at a), b), and c) above) to determine the scope of application of the chapeau of Article 13. Beyond the rights and areas outlined below, States parties must continuously monitor whether there are obstacles to women's participation in economic and social life.

d) Conclusion: Scope of Application of the Chapeau

aa) *Right to Self-employed Economic Activities*

Women's equal right to carry out economic activities as a self-employed person follows from the definition of 'economic life'. The Committee has rarely looked at this issue, and when doing so, it has focused on female entrepreneurs in developing countries.[52] However, women in industrialized countries also are under-represented in independent economic activities.[53] A greater emphasis on women as entrepreneurs would help combat gender-based stereotypes by shifting the perception from women as victims of human rights violations to women in charge of their own fates.

Article 13 prohibits directly and indirectly discriminatory rules on the conditions for exercising a self-employed activity and on social security for the self-employed. Discriminatory laws concerning women's legal capacity are proscribed by Article 15. States are also obliged to prevent and punish discrimination by third parties that occurs in economic life, such as when women are prevented from, or harassed for pursuing an independent economic activity. Substantive equality requires States parties to take into account the social reality of women when making laws and designing policy measures. In particular, it encompasses providing adequate possibilities for child care and care of the elderly to enable women to exercise a profession.[54] In this context, they must pay special attention to situations of intersectional discrimination resulting in the exclusion of women with disabilities from independent economic activities.

Transformative equality calls for eliminating structural obstacles, eg by eradicating stereotypes concerning 'typical feminine professions' (retail, personal service, health), and for State initiatives to provide information, training, support, and public or private funding to self-employed women. Possible temporary special measures are to give preference, in public procurement decisions, to women-owned enterprises or to enterprises carrying out a policy of advancing women within their workforce as well as increasing their representation in decision-making bodies in economic life.[55]

bb) *Right to Food*

Women's equal right to food is under-reported by States and underdeveloped by Committee recommendations.[56] The Committee has dealt with women's equal access to

---

[52] CO Guinea CEDAW/C/GIN/CO/6, 39th Session (2007) para 37; CO Tanzania, CEDAW/C/TZA/CO/6, 41st Session (2008) para 38.

[53] OECD Factbook 2008: Economic, Environmental, and Social Statistics (2008) 138–9; see also comparison of twenty-nine industrialized states at <http://www.nationmaster.com/graph/lab_emp_sel_sel_rat_wom-labor-employment-self-rates-women> accessed 31 December 2010.

[54] CO Samoa, CEDAW/C/WSM/CC/1–3, 32nd Session (2005) para 28.

[55] CO Austria, CEDAW/C/AUT/CO, 37th Session (2009) para 27.

[56] I Rae, *Women and the Right to Food* (2008) 29–30.

food in emergency situations,[57] with rural women's right to food under Article 14,[58] and with adequate nutrition for women during pregnancy and lactation and malnutrition as a risk factor for women's health, under Article 12.[59]

Seventy per cent of the world's hungry are women, and they are disproportionately affected by malnutrition and food insecurity.[60] The right to food encompasses not only the right to be free from hunger (Article 11(2) ICESCR), but also the right to adequate food (Article 11(1) ICESCR). Measures taken to combat hunger and to realize the right to adequate food have to target men and women equally. National strategies for the realization of the right to food must contain gender-sensitive targets, goals, and benchmarks.[61] This requires gathering sex-disaggregated data. In implementing MDG 1, according to which the proportion of people who suffer from hunger is to be halved by the year 2015, the target must be to reach women in proportion to their percentage among those suffering from hunger. In situations of hunger after a (natural or man-made) disaster, gender-based stereotypes of the lesser value of girls and women must be considered in designing assistance strategies.

The right to adequate food is fully realized when every person has physical and economic access to adequate food at all times.[62] Adequacy presupposes availability, accessibility, and acceptability.[63] All three criteria must be met to ensure women *de facto* equality. 'Availability' denotes the quantity and quality sufficient to satisfy individuals' dietary needs, including women's varying needs during their life cycle.[64] 'Accessibility' means physical and economic accessibility; obstacles for women include distance from sources and unsafe travel. Acceptability depends on convictions about the appropriateness of food beyond its nutrient value.

The State must not prevent women from realizing their right to food (duty to respect), eg by hindering their access to, and control over means of food production. It is also obliged to take protective measures against interference with this right by private persons, such as by combating customary practices prohibiting women from eating before men are fed, allowing women only less nutritious food,[65] or food taboos for women.[66] States parties also have a duty to fulfil women's equal right to adequate food, obliging them to promote women's access to methods of, knowledge on, and opportunities for food production and purchase.[67]

---

[57] CO Democratic People's Republic of Korea A/60/38, 33rd Session (2005) para 53; Statement by the CEDAW Committee in regard to the tsunami disaster that occurred in South-East Asia on 26 December 2004, A/60/38, 32nd Session (2005), Annex II para 2.

[58] See the discussion in ch on art 14. Rural women's rights are emphasized in CO Democratic People's Republic of Korea A/60/38, 33rd Session (2005) para 60; see also GR 27 para 24 (older women in rural areas).

[59] CO Myanmar, CEDAW/C/MMR/CO/3 (2008) paras 38–9 (malnutrition). See also the discussion in ch on art 12.

[60] Human Rights Council Advisory Committee, Study on discrimination in the context of the right to food, UN Doc A/HRC/AC/6/CRP.1 (2010) para 38.

[61] CESCR, 'General Comment 12' (1999) UN Doc E/C.12/1999/5 para 29.   [62] Ibid para 6.

[63] For the following ibid para 7–13.   [64] As emphasized by CESCR, GC 12 para. 9.

[65] CESCR, 'General Comment 16: The Equal Right of Men and Women to the Enjoyment of all Economic, Social and Cultural Rights (art 3)' (2005) UN Doc E/C.12/2005/4 para 28.

[66] CO Democratic Republic of the Congo, A/55/38, 22nd Session (2000) para 232.

[67] See the discussion in ch on art 14.

cc) Right to Adequate Housing

Women encounter manifold obstacles in the realization of their right to adequate housing.[68] It encompasses access to, and enjoyment of, land and accommodation.[69] The Committee has taken up women's right to housing with relatively narrow focus, for example, looking at the situation of refugee and internally displaced women,[70] women belonging to minorities,[71] and women in vulnerable situations.[72]

The adequacy of housing depends on various factors, such as legal security of tenure, availability of services (energy, water), facilities and infrastructure, affordability, habitability (including a healthy environment), accessibility, location, and cultural adequacy.[73] Under Article 13, States parties must consider these factors in light of women's factual situations.[74] For example, legal security of tenure also extends to protection of women against traditional practices allowing relatives or in-laws to evict them after the death of their father or husband. Availability of services must take into account that women may face danger when using communal toilets at night or when getting water from distant places. Affordability must be determined in view of women's lower average income.

Women's equal right to adequate housing may be jeopardized by legal norms and culturally motivated actions. Article 15(2) provides for legal protection, ensuring equality with respect to women's legal capacity to conclude contracts, such as sale of land and rent agreements, to administer property, including real estate, and to inherit property. Equal access to marital assets upon divorce or the husband's death is guaranteed by Article 16(1). Article 13 applies to all other legal norms, including customary or religious law recognized by the State, that discriminates against women, such as State or community rules that divest an indigenous woman of her right to live on community land, when she marries a man from outside the group.[75] Abolishing such norms is an aspect of the State party's duty to respect.

Article 13 pertains to discriminatory social and cultural norms that jeopardize women's equal right to housing, such as landlords' rejection of single female tenants or women's hesitance to claim inheritance because of a norm of male control over all property.[76] The

---

[68] See L Farha, 'Women and Housing' in K Askin and D Koenig (eds), *Women and International Human Rights Law, Vol. 1* (1999) 483.

[69] Beijing Platform for Action para 31; Habitat II Agenda, para 40(b). See also: L Farha, 'Is there a Woman in the House? Reconceiving the Human Right to Housing', 14:1 *Canadian J of Women and the L* 118–36 (2002) and generally: B Wilson, 'Le droit à un logement suffisant au sens du Pacte international relatif aux doits économiques, sociaux et culturels des Nations Unies (Pacte I)' 18:5 *Revue Suisse de Droit International et Européen* (2008) 431–56.

[70] CO United Kingdom, CEDAW/C/UK/CO/6, 41st Session (2008) para 295 (women with insecure immigration status); CO Azerbaijan, CEDAW/C/AZE/CO/4, 44th Session (2009) para 37.

[71] CO Spain, A/59/38, 31st session: (2004) para 345 (Roma women); CO Israel A/60/38, 33rd session (2005) para 259 (Bedouin women); CO Slovenia CEDAW/C/SVN/CO/4, 42nd Session (2008) para 35 (Roma women); CO Lithuania, CEDAW/C/LTU/CO/4, 41st Session (2008) para 28 (older women, women with disabilities, migrant women, women belonging to ethnic minorities).

[72] Committee Report on Mexico CEDAW/C/2005/OP.8/Mexico, 32nd Session (2005) para 289 (poverty and extreme poverty); GR 27 para 12 (older women).

[73] CESCR, 'General Comment 4: The Right to Adequate Housing (art 11(1))' (1991) UN Doc E/1992/23 para 8.

[74] For the following analysis see also I Westendorp, *Women and Housing, Gender Makes a Difference* (2008) 242–3.

[75] 'Report by the Special Rapporteur on adequate housing as a component of the right to an adequate standard of living, and on the right to non-discrimination, M Kothari', UN Doc E/CN.4/2006/118 (27 February 2006) 13 para. 44.

[76] Ibid 12–13 paras 41–4.

State party must take protective action against interference by private persons and must combat pertinent gender-based stereotypes.

The equal right to adequate housing is also put at risk by privatization of land and housing. Privatization is particularly hard on women if the reform programmes do not take into account the specific obstacles that women face in obtaining credit. States parties must also ensure that property titles are granted to women on an equal basis—avoiding grants to male proxies (relatives); and granting title to both husband and wife[77] and preventing discrimination in distribution of communal land within indigenous communities, where women may be under-represented in the decision-making body.[78] Forced eviction, whether in the context of privatization or other projects, may also have a greater impact on women than on men.[79] States parties must offer non-discriminatory measures to prevent homelessness and alleviate other consequences such as trauma and loss of livelihood because of relocation.[80] Women belonging to groups in vulnerable situations— older women, women with disabilities, refugee and migrant women, women belonging to ethnic minorities or indigenous groups, or women with HIV/AIDS[81]—suffer multiple discriminations in these circumstances.

The duty to respect obliges the State party to abstain from carrying out evictions that discriminate against women in these ways. The duty to protect requires the State party to enact and enforce laws prohibiting private property owners from evicting persons if no protection is available for the victims. Under its duty to fulfil, the State party must provide for such protection, such as relocation policies that meet women's particular circumstances.

Inadequate housing can render women more vulnerable to violence, especially where the housing does not provide sufficient protection against intrusions, such as in cases of relocation after an eviction or a natural or man-made disaster.[82] Conversely, violence against women can entail a violation of their right to adequate housing when women cannot find safe housing in cases of domestic violence.[83] The Committee has recognized this connection but has not located the issue within the scope of Article 13, dealing with it under Articles 2, 5, and 16.[84]

dd) Right to an Adequate Standard of Living

The right to an adequate standard of living encompasses more than the rights to food, housing, and clothing. It covers all facets of a life in dignity and autonomy. Sufficient financial or other material resources are indispensable to its realization. States parties must meet this need through non-contributory social security for lack of livelihood in circumstances beyond an individual's control and through old-age benefits.[85] Social

---

[77] Ibid 15 para 54 and p 13 para 45. [78] Ibid 15 para. 54 and 13, para. 45.

[79] CESCR, 'General Comment 7' (1997) UN Doc HRI/GEN/1/Rev.7 p 46 para 3.

[80] Ibid para 10.

[81] Ibid; Report of the Special Rapporteur on adequate housing (n 75 above) p 10 para 30 and pp 14–15 paras 47–53.

[82] Statement by the CEDAW Committee in regard to the tsunami disaster that occurred in South-East Asia on 26 December 2004, UN Doc A/60/38, 32nd Session (2005) Annex II para 4.

[83] Report of the Special Rapporteur on adequate housing (n 75 above) para 32. For details, see G Paglione, 'Domestic Violence and Housing Rights' (2006) 28:1 *Human Rights Quarterly* 125.

[84] *AT v Hungary*, CEDAW Communication No 2/2003 (2005), CEDAW/C/32/D/2003 para 9.6, Recommendation I.(b). See also the discussion in ch on violence against women.

[85] For non-contributory social security see: CESCR, 'General Comment 19' (2008) UN Doc E/C.12/GC/19 paras 4(b) and 23, for non-contributory old-age benefits see: CESCR, 'General Comment 6' (1995) UN Doc

security with respect to temporary inability to work (maternity, sickness, work-related injury, unemployment) is covered by Article 11; family benefits fall under Article 13(a). In respect of the remaining rights to social security, women's equality under the chapeau of Article 13 obliges States parties to take into account women's devotion of their time to unpaid work in the home, including care for family members, that does not provide opportunity to contribute to a social security scheme based on their own income.[86] To the extent that social security schemes for the situations described above are based on contributions, they must be devised with a view to the situation of women.[87]

The road and transport infrastructure may have a different impact on women than on men. Where women rely more on public transportation than men do, States parties must provide transportation on schedules that protect women's access to livelihoods and are safe.[88]

As the Convention Preamble emphasizes, women suffer disproportionately more than men in situations of poverty.[89] The Committee has found this to be the case particularly in countries with a persisting gender pay gap or during economic restructuring.[90] Moreover, the Committee has noted a 'feminization' of poverty, especially among vulnerable groups of women, such as those heading households, older women, and rural women.[91] According to ICESCR Article 11, States parties must take measures to eradicate extreme poverty (the lack of means of survival)[92] as well as to combat relative poverty, which often is defined as an income that amounts to 50 per cent or less of the average income in a State.[93] Convention Article 13 requires States parties to examine women's *de facto* situation in designing policies and measures and to target them accordingly.[94] In addition, States parties must analyze the possible effects of their actions on women, and must adapt them if these actions are expected to have a disparate negative impact on them.[95] Conversely, the promotion of gender equality and empowerment of women is an effective way to combat poverty.[96]

E/1996/22 paras 20–1 and 30. See generally: C Krause and M Scheinin, 'The Right Not to be Discriminated against: The Case of Social Security' in TS Olin, A Rosas, and M Scheinin (eds), *The Jurisprudence of Human Rights Law. A Comparative Interpretive Approach* (2000) 253–86; L Lamarche, 'Le Pacte international relatif aux droits économiques, sociaux et culturels, les femmes et le droit à la sécurité sociale : des considérations et des propositions pour un droit «universel» a la sécurité sociale' (2002) 14:1 *Canadian J of Women and the L* 53–97.

[86] CESCR, 'General Comment 19' (2008) UN Doc E/C.12/GC/19 para 32. [87] Ibid.

[88] See Committee Report on Mexico CEDAW/C/2005/OP.8/Mexico, 32nd Session (2005) para 289.

[89] 8th Preamble Paragraph, see the discussion in ch on Preamble.

[90] CO Georgia, CEDAW/C/GEO/CO/3 (2006) paras 84–5.

[91] CO Belarus, A/59/38, 30th session (2004) para 353.

[92] C Apodaca, 'Measuring Women's Economic and Social Advancement' (1998) 20 *Human Rights Quarterly* 139–72, 166.

[93] M Langford, 'Poverty in Developed States: International Human Rights Law and the Right to a Remedy' (2008) 51 *German Ybk of Intl L* 251–89, 252.

[94] CO Belarus, A/59/38, 30th Session (2004) para 354; CO Angola A/59/38, 31st Session (2004) para 149; CO Dominican Republic A/59/38, 31st Session (2004) para 238; CO Guinea CEDAW/C/GIN/CO/6 (2007) para 42.

[95] CO Argentina A/59/38, 31st Session (2004) para 373.

[96] UN Millennium Declaration (UN Doc A/55/2 of 18 September 2000) III.20. See also 'Report of the Independent Expert on the question of human rights and extreme poverty, Ms MM Sepúlveda Carmona, to the General Assembly on the importance of social protection measures in achieving Millennium Development Goals (MDGs)', UN Doc A/65/259 (2010).

ee) Right to Water

The right to water is closely connected to the right to life and to human dignity, as well as to the right to an adequate standard of living and the right to the highest attainable standard of health.[97] The Committee has dealt with women's equal access to water especially in rural areas.[98] However, the right also applies to women living in other areas, such as slums or other unrecognized settlements.[99] The Committee has not spelled out the contents of States parties' obligations as to these situations.

As with the right to food, availability (for personal and domestic uses), quality, physical accessibility, and affordability are the decisive factors for determining the content of the right to water.[100] Under traditional, gender-based division of household chores, women and girls are responsible for obtaining water, frequently from distant locations. They often are in danger of being assaulted on their way. States parties must provide for accessibility in terms of both location and safety.

Water must be affordable; States parties must offer subsidies where necessary, allocated on the basis of women's individual income and responsibilities for dependent family members. Where water is limited, Article 13 requires women's equal participation in decision-making as to its use (personal consumption, irrigation, production of goods).

ff) Right to Sanitation

The right to adequate sanitation is a component of the right to an adequate standard of living and arguably is developing into an independent human right that protects human dignity.[101] The right falls under Article 13, which encompasses all social rights not contained elsewhere in the Convention. The Committee has dealt with women's right to sanitation primarily as to rural areas, under Article 14,[102] but has paid less attention to the right as to women in urban areas, including in slums or other informal housing.[103]

The lack of access to sanitation has a disproportionate impact on women and girls.[104] Where adequate sanitation is not available, they run the risk of assault in dealing with their physical needs and may drop out of school for lack of facilities. As with other rights emanating from the right to an adequate standard of living, the criteria for determining adequacy are availability, quality, accessibility, affordability, and acceptability.[105] Consequently, sanitation facilities must be provided in a number sufficient to prevent

---

[97] UN Docs A/RES/64/292 (2010) para 1; A/HRC/RES/15/9 (2010) para 3.

[98] CO Ethiopia, A/59/38 (Supp), 30th Session (2004) para 260; CO Bangladesh, A/59/38, 31st session: (2004) para 260; CO Benin, A/60/38, 33rd session (2005) para 159; CO Democratic Republic of the Congo, CEDAW/C/COD/CO/5, 36th Session (2006) para 17.

[99] CO Israel, A/60/38, 33rd Session (2005) para 259 (Bedouin women).

[100] CESCR, 'General Comment 15' (2003) UN Doc E/C.12/2002/11 para. 12.

[101] 'Report of the independent expert C de Albuquerque' (n 36 above) paras 14–19 and 59; CESCR Statement on the Right to Sanitation, UN Doc E/C.12/45.CRP.1 (2010) paras 7–8.

[102] CO Gabon, A/60/38 (Supp), 32nd Session (2005) para 247 (on rural women); CO Pakistan, CEDAW/C/PAK/CO/3 (2007) paras 42–3 (on rural women); CO Democratic Republic of the Congo, CEDAW/C/COD/CO/5 (2006) para 17, CO Tanzania, CEDAW/C/TZA/CO/6 (2008) para 44; CO Suriname, CEDAW/C/SUR/CO/3 (2007) para 31 (on rural women); CO Thailand, CEDAW/C/THA/CO/5 (2006) para 288 (on rural and hill tribe women); CO The Philippines, CEDAW/C/PHI/CO/6 (2006) (also on Muslim women in Mindanao). See also the discussion in ch on art 14.

[103] Committee Report on Mexico CEDAW/C/2005/OP.8/Mexico, 32nd Session (2005) para 289; CO Israel, A/60/38, 33rd Session (2005) para 259 (Bedouin women in unrecognized villages).

[104] Report of the independent expert C de Albuquerque (n 36 above) para 51; Statement of CESCR (n 101 above) para 5.

[105] Report of the independent expert C de Albuquerque (n 36 above) paras 70–80.

unreasonably long waiting times, they must be close to households, workplaces, and public institutions, including schools and health institutions, and they must be safe to use. If cultural norms require separate sanitation facilities for women and men, they must be provided, and in appropriate ratios.

gg) Tax Laws

Women's equal participation in economic life pursuant to Article 13 also extends to the impact of tax laws. The Committee has addressed some tax issues, and two States parties entered reservations to Article 13 relating to qualifying the income of a married woman as part of the taxable income of her husband under certain circumstances.[106] Even if such tax laws do not negatively affect women's income and thus do not directly interfere with their equal participation in economic life, the Committee considered that they may be indirectly discriminatory by perpetuating gender-based stereotypes, for example, the expectation that married women give up their careers to take on family responsibilities.[107] Because of the complexity of tax systems, discrimination against women is often indirect,[108] and it can be brought about by the complicated interplay between different taxes. Therefore, Article 13 obliges States parties to monitor the impact of tax rules, and to adapt them so as to ensure substantive equality for women as a prerequisite for equal participation in economic life.

hh) Right to Participate in Social Life

The Committee has rarely dealt with women's equal right to participate in 'social life'. As explained above (at C. I.2.c), this right extends to all activities outside the family and not belonging to political and public life, whether in person or through communication. Women's equal enjoyment of this right entails equal access to any place or service intended for use by the general public, irrespective of whether the service is offered by the State or by a private actor.[109] This follows from the State party's duties to respect and to protect, respectively. A service is intended for use by the general public when it is offered to all irrespective of the recipient's identity.[110] Relevant services are, for example, transport, hotels, restaurants and cafes, shopping centres, as well as parks and other public spaces. Health care services fall under Article 12; educational establishments are included in Article 10, and cultural institutions are covered by Article 13(c).

Equal participation in public life also extends to conditions for personal contact, which relates to freedom of movement. Examples of interference with this right are legal rules or social norms barring women from appearing in public without a male relative or prohibiting them from driving a car.[111] Other examples are State-enforced or State-

---

[106] Reservation by the UK (concerning income and capital gains tax), withdrawn in 1995; Malta (income tax; reservation extant). It was intended to be of a transitional nature 'until those laws are completely superseded'. Thirteen years later and in the absence of exceptional circumstances that prevented the State from amending its law, the Committee expressed strong dissatisfaction, CO Malta, CEDAW/C/MLT/CO/1-3, 31st Session (2004), para 99.

[107] CO Germany, CEDAW/C/DEU/CO/6 (2009) para 30.

[108] For a typology, see K Barnett and C Grown, *Gender Impacts of Government Revenue Collection: The Case of Taxation* (2004) 26–49; D Elson, *Budgeting for Human Rights* (2006) 76–95.

[109] See also: High Court of Zambia, *Longwe v Intercontinental Hotels*, Judgment of 4 November 1992, per Musumali, J. (basing the right of access on arts 1, 2, and 3 CEDAW).

[110] M Fries, *Die Bedeutung von Art. 5(f) der Rassendiskriminierungskonvention im deutschen Recht* (2003) 24–40.

[111] CO Saudi Arabia, CEDAW/C/SAU/CO/2 (2008) paras 15–16.

protected restrictions on clothing for women appearing in public, such as an obligation to wear a burqa outside the house or a prohibition of wearing a burqa in public.[112] Women migrant workers experience violations of their equal right to freedom of movement when employers or recruiters confiscate their passports or when employers lock domestic workers in their houses.[113]

Women's equal participation in social life is often restricted by structural discrimination that is based on culturally supported stereotypes. Rules on the 'correct' conduct of women in public, and thus in social life, often are emanations of gender-based stereotypes.[114] They must be eradicated through education, awareness-raising campaigns, and a critical public discussion about such stereotypes and the underlying cultural norms. Article 13 requires that women equally participate in these debates to shape culture.[115]

ii) Right to Communication in Economic and Social Life

Economic and social interactions also occur through means of communication such as correspondence, telecommunication, and new media.[116] Consequently, women's equal participation in economic and social life requires that they enjoy equal freedom of opinion and have equal access to these means of communication.[117] This presupposes at least primary education (reading and writing) and basic computer skills. Programmes for improving computer literacy must target women specifically, if gender-based stereotypes prevent their using modern technologies. The 'digital divide' between men and women[118] may also result from women's lack of access to computers due to their lower income and lower levels of education. When States adopt online access to services, such as distance education, permits for economic activities, or applications for social services, they must take into account the gendered digital divide and must ensure that their services remain accessible to women.

II. Article 13(a): The Equal Right to Family Benefits

1. Concepts

Article 13(a) guarantees women's equality in a particularly important area of economic life, the provision of material resources by the State party or private actors. 'Family benefits' are payments made, or other financially relevant advantages provided to families to enhance their well-being, through social security systems or other public assistance programmes for families. If such benefits are granted in connection with an employment relationship, they are covered by Article 11.

The expression 'family benefits' has a wide scope of application because during the drafting process, 'family allowance' was revised to read 'family benefits'. Consequently, the term not only covers financial support (direct or through tax concessions), but also

---

[112] For an example of an obligation to wear a burqa see 'Report of the Special Rapporteur on violence against women, its causes and consequences, Y Ertürk, on her mission to Saudi Arabia', UN Doc A/HRC/11/6/Add.3 (2009) para 48.

[113] GR 26 para 26(d).   [114] See the discussion in ch on art 5.   [115] See n 136 below.

[116] As recognized by CESCR, 'General Comment 5' (1994) UN Doc E/1995/22 para 37 (with respect to persons with disabilities).

[117] Also recognized by the World Summit on the Information Society, Tunis Commitments, UN/ITU Doc. WSIS/05/ZUNIS/DOC7-E (2005) para 23.

[118] J Cooper, 'The Digital Divide: The Special Case of Gender' (2006) 22 *J of Computer-Assisted Learning* 320–34.

extends to all other material support given to families, such as priority access to public housing, health insurance coverage for the whole family at reduced rates or without additional contributory payment, and public subsidies for mortgages. Education benefits, such as reduced fees or school uniforms or school books provided free of charge, fall under Article 10 if they discriminate between girls and boys. Non-discrimination in respect of family benefits is an expression of the principle of equality of spouses pursuant to Article 16(1)(c), particularly relating to the material support of their children.

The CEDAW Committee has not defined the term 'family'. Like the CCPR, it considers that, in view of the different concepts worldwide, there is no standard definition.[119] Consequently, the term 'family' is to be defined by national law, but it must respect the principle of equality of women and men, enshrined in Article 16(1)(d). Where national law deems a couple to be a 'family', both spouses are equally entitled to receive family benefits.[120]

Moreover, the domestic definition of 'family' must respect the right to family life guaranteed under ICCPR Article 17. This right encompasses the relations between a biological or adoptive parent and a child as well as persons who provide a home for children in the absence of their parents. Article 13(a) requires States parties to provide family benefits to adults caring for children on a basis of equality between women and men regardless of marital status: to unmarried (heterosexual and same-sex) couples raising children,[121] and to single parents. In the case of couples, women's equality requires the payment of family benefits to both partners when they are legally recognized as parents. Single women who are head of a household must be treated in a way that ensures their substantive equality with single men heading a household.[122]

2. Equality in Context

The obligation to ensure women *de jure* equality with respect to family benefits requires that payments be made in a way that provides men and women equal access to the benefits. Therefore, a State party may not make benefits payable to the husband without the wife's consent, for example, by presuming that he is the head of the household.[123]

The obligation to ensure *de facto* equality requires States parties to safeguard women's effective access to family benefits. They must take into account social norms preventing single or divorced mothers from accessing a bank account independently of their male family members. States parties also may not set up substantive obstacles, such as conditioning family benefits to single mothers upon their having exhausted legal remedies against the father for payment of child support. The elimination of structural discrimination with respect to family benefits includes eradicating legal and social norms

---

[119] GR 21 para 13; CCPR, 'General Comment 19' (1990) UN Doc HRI/GEN/1/Rev.9 (Vol. I) para. 2. See the discussion in ch on art 16.

[120] CO Guinea, CEDAW/C/GIN/CO/6 (2007) paras 40–1 (payment to the husband as the 'head of the household').

[121] CCPR *Joslin v New Zealand*, CCPR/C/75/D/902/1999, annex, individual opinion Rajsoomer Lallah and Martin Scheinin (exclusion of same-sex couples with respect to benefits requires additional justification), confirmed by *Young v Australia*, CCPR/C/78/D/941/2000 para 10.

[122] Particularly emphasized with respect to the right to adequate housing: CESCR, 'General Comment 7' (1997) UN Doc HRI/GEN/1/Rev.7 p. 46 para 6.

[123] See the Committee's critical reaction to such reservation by Malta, CO Malta, CEDAW/C/MLT/CO/1–3 (2004) para 99.

that treat men as heads of the household and of norms that discriminate against unwed mothers.

Moreover, States parties may not introduce social security provisions more favourable to women than to men unless these provisions serve to attain substantive equality for women.[124] If, however, the provisions are based on gender-based stereotypes, they are inconsistent with the Convention as they contravene Article 5.

III. Article 13(b): The Equal Right to Bank Loans, Mortgages, and Other Forms of Financial Credit

1. Concepts

Article 13(b) serves to ensure women's economic autonomy.[125] The obligation extends to the provision of these services by both public and private institutions, following both from the unrestricted wording of Article 13 and from Article 2(d) and (e). The change from 'access' to financial services to the 'equal right to' made during the drafting process underscores that the right not only covers the provision of financial services, but also the conditions under which they are granted.

The term 'bank loan' refers to the provision of money by a bank and the duty to repay that sum. Collateral security may be part of the loan contract, but is not necessary. The provision covers other forms of for-profit banking, such as Islamic banking, and interest-free loans, usually granted by public entities for a specific purpose. 'Mortgages' means the conveyance of an interest in real estate as security for the repayment of money borrowed. 'Financial credit' encompasses any other situation in which money is made available, either through a credit institution other than a bank (micro-credit, credit union, or self-help group) or through other means, such as by postponing the repayment of a financial obligation.

2. Equality in Context

Ensuring women's right to equality with respect to all financial instruments listed in section (b) requires focusing particularly on indirect discrimination. In many States parties, women encounter difficulties in obtaining bank loans and public subsidies and have less access to finance for business purposes. Typical obstacles are conditions that women frequently cannot meet because of past discrimination: the requirement of a certain amount of prior experience, of an uninterrupted employment history, or of individually owned assets. As such requirements commonly are justified by the lender's interest in securing repayment of the debt, States parties should take positive measures to assist women in gaining a place at this bargaining table[126] by adopting policies aimed at closing the gender pay gap, increasing women's home ownership, and providing for equal property rights. Temporary special measures may be warranted, such as public loan programmes for women or State guarantees for loans granted to women by private banks. In addition, practices related to determining qualification for credit should be transparent and non-discriminatory.

---

[124] Such provisions were the object of a reservation to art 13(a) made by Ireland, see Multilateral Treaties Deposited with the Secretary-General, UN Doc/ST/LEG/SER.E/27 (2010) ch IV n28.

[125] See above at A.   [126] Farha (n 68 above) 123–4.

Educational measures and media campaigns may help eliminate structural discrimination. Women often lack financial education and access to relevant information. Primary and secondary education should include basic financial education for all children. In addition, special advisory services for women might be set up outside the education systems.

All these measures must take into account intersectional discrimination. Older women, disabled women, and women belonging to ethnic minorities or other groups that experience discrimination, may be particularly disadvantaged in obtaining loans because of stereotypical assumptions about their personal capabilities that are unrelated to the facts of their financial qualification for credit. Women migrant workers may face difficulties in accessing formal financial institutions for securely sending remittances.[127]

IV. Article 13(c): The Equal Right to Participate in Recreational Activities, Sports, and all Aspects of Cultural Life

Article 13(c) safeguards women's equality in cultural life, which the Convention treats as part of social life. Cultural life is a significant component of human dignity[128] because it relates to the development and expression of an individual's world view and thus to identity.[129] Recreational activities and sports are a part of social and cultural life to be enjoyed on an equal basis with men, and help preserve physical and mental health as a basis for the enjoyment of all other rights.[130]

1. Concepts

Culture is understood as 'the set of distinctive spiritual, material, intellectual and emotional features of society or a social group'.[131] It encompasses arts and literature, rites and ceremonies, sports and games, methods of production of technology, lifestyles, ways of living together, value systems, traditions, and beliefs.[132] Individuals have the right to express, enjoy and shape culture, individually and in community with others; this includes the right to contest dominant norms and values within the communities to which an individual chooses to belong.[133] Freedom of choice as to the culture(s) in which the individual participates is crucial to self-realization.[134] The cultural group may have the ultimate say in deciding on its membership if its survival is at issue,[135] but the principle of non-discrimination under Article 13 establishes a boundary on such decisions. The processes of developing and defining cultural norms must engage women on an equal basis with men.[136] Reflecting this imperative, Article 17(1) of the Protocol to

---

[127] GR 26 para 24 (g).   [128] See the discussion of the concept of dignity in ch on Preamble.

[129] 'Report of the independent expert in the field of cultural rights, Farida Shaheed, UN Doc A/HRC/14/36' (2010) para 3.

[130] See generally: UNGA RES/A/58/5 'Sport as a means to promote education, health, development and peace' (2005); and UN Division for the Advancement of Women, 'Women, gender equality and sport'(2007).

[131] UNESCO Universal Declaration on Cultural Diversity, of 2 November 2001, 5th Preamble Paragraph.

[132] UNESCO Declaration on Cultural Diversity; CESCR, 'General Comment 21' (2009) UN Doc E/C.12/CG21 para 13.

[133] Report of the independent expert in the field of cultural rights, Farida Shaheed (n 129 above) para 10.

[134] E Stamatopoulou, *Cultural Rights in International Law* (2007) 129–32.

[135] CCPR, *Sandra Lovelace v Canada*, Communication No 24/1977, UN Doc A/36/40 (1983) para 16; affirmed in CCPR, *Kitok v Sweden*, Communication No 197/1985, A/43/40, Annex 7 (G) (1988) para 9.8.

[136] Women who participated in the 1993 World Conference on Human Rights emphasized the frequent exclusion of women from these processes. See DJ Sullivan, 'Women's Human Rights and the 1993 World

the African Charter on the Rights of Women in Africa expressly guarantees women the right to live in a positive cultural context and to participate at all levels in the determination of cultural policies. Article 13 emphasizes the dimension of 'cultural rights' as individual rights, including the right to determine whether to participate in a particular culture,[137] and of 'culture' as a dynamic concept, not a fixed state.[138]

Recreational activities cover leisure as well as hobbies, diversions, or other pastime occupation, carried out alone or in groups and providing relaxation and rest. If such activities are offered against payment, they fall under the right to equality with respect to services intended for use by the general public. Sports relates to any physical activity, whether or not in recognized form and/or according to specific rules. A minimum of physical activity is necessary, but intellectual activity may be predominant (as in chess). Sports carried out as an economic activity falls under the chapeau of Article 13. Sport activities may be organized by the State or by private actors.

2. *Equality in Context*

Formal equality requires that women are not excluded from any of these areas by law. If the State party supports culture and sports, it must do so equally for women's and men's activities, and it must ensure respect for women's equality by the public or private organizer.[139]

States parties must also refrain from indirectly discriminating against women. Consequently, a State party that financially supports cultural, recreational, or sports activities that are carried out predominantly by men has to support those of women equally. Furthermore, the duty to protect obliges the State party to prevent private organizers of cultural and sports events from discriminating directly or indirectly against female participants, for example, by excluding women from certain sports because of gender-based stereotypes.

States parties must eliminate culturally supported stereotyping, such as restricting women to 'women's cultural activities' and 'women's sports'[140]. Female artists and athletes should be promoted as role models. States parties must put into place programmes that permit girls and women to participate in sports in school and in the community, and they must ensure women's access to sport facilities to achieve substantive equality.[141] When doing so, States must take into account intersectional discrimination encountered by girls, older women, disabled women, and women belonging to minorities.[142]

Transformative equality is particularly important with respect to women's participation in cultural life. Culture (as defined above) must be shaped by women on an equal basis with men. Hence, women must have equal access to the formal and informal processes

---

Conference on Human Rights' (1994) 88 *Am J of Intl L* 152, 157. See also CESCR, 'General Comment 21' (2009) UN Doc E/C.12/CG21 paras 15(a), 22, 25, 49(a), 52(b).

[137] As underscored also by CESCR, 'General Comment 21' (2009) UN Doc E/C.12/CG21 para 15. For the impact of the individual dimension see also: L Reidel, 'What are Cultural Rights? Protecting Groups with Individual Rights' (2010) 9 *J of Human Rights* 65–80, 75.

[138] CESCR, 'General Comment 21' (2009) UN Doc E/C.12/CG21 para 11; Y Donders, *Towards a Right to Cultural Identity?* (2002) 33–3.

[139] See the discussion on art 2(e) in ch on art 2.

[140] Women, gender equality and sport (n130 above) 20.

[141] Beijing Platform for Action, Critical Area of Concern B, Education and training of women, Strategic Objective B.2, para 83(m), and Critical Area of Concern C, Women and health, Strategic Objective C.2, para 107(f).

[142] GR 27 para 47 (with respect to older women); CESCR, 'General Comment 5' (1994) UN Doc E/1995/22 para. 36 (with respect to persons with disabilities).

that create cultural norms, and their voices must have equal weight in the societal debates. Cultural and sports institutions must establish structures to ensure awareness of gender equality issues, and women and men must be equally represented in these institutions.[143] Here, temporary special measures under Article 4, such as quotas, may be particularly helpful.[144]

D. States Parties' Obligations

I. Nature of the Obligation

States parties must 'take all appropriate measures' to 'ensure' women's equality in economic and social life. These measures may be constitutional and legal reform or other policy measures.[145] The measures must be chosen on the basis of being the best for realization of women's equality. Consequently, States parties are under an immediate obligation to assess discrimination in these fields, to enact or repeal legislation, and to adopt a plan to address the problem.[146] This blueprint for reform must be adapted continuously, requiring States parties to monitor the effect of measures taken under the plan. Discriminatory laws and policies must be abolished immediately and gaps in provisions to prohibit discrimination by third parties and on remedies must be filled without delay.

II. Implementation—Respect, Protect, and Fulfil

Under their obligation to respect, States parties are duty-bound to abolish all discriminatory legal rules as described above and to ensure that State authorities do not discriminate by action or omission. Within the context of Article 13, the obligation to protect is of central importance because discrimination frequently is perpetrated by private persons individually or collectively. States parties must exercise due diligence to prevent and eradicate discrimination by these non-State actors.[147] A key instrument is anti-discrimination statutes that extend to all areas of economic and social life and bind private actors. These laws must provide remedies to alleged victims of discrimination and must ensure them effective access to judicial review. The CEDAW Committee considers as good practice anti-discrimination laws that also permit claims to be made on behalf of a victim, not only by the victim herself.[148] Procedures can be rendered more effective if the claimant's burden of proof is alleviated or even shifted to the defendant.[149] Sanctions for discrimination must be dissuasive and should include compensation for the immaterial damage suffered. States parties must also disseminate pertinent legal information.

One potentially effective method of complying with the States parties' obligation to fulfil—to create an environment conductive to the realization of the right concerned— is establishing an independent anti-discrimination body with investigative and sanction powers.[150] Moreover, in allocating their budgets, States parties must ensure that the benefits granted in the areas of economic, social, and cultural activities (such as subsidies or

---

[143] Beijing Platform for Action, Critical Area of Concern G, Women in power and decision-making.
[144] GR 25 para 38.   [145] See the discussion in ch on art 3.
[146] See the discussion in ch on art 3.   [147] GR 28 para 13.
[148] CO Germany CEDAW/C/DEU/CO/6 (2009) paras 19–20.
[149] CO Germany CEDAW/C/DEU/CO/6 (2009) paras 17–18.
[150] CO Germany CEDAW/C/DEU/CO/6 (2009) paras 19–20.

tax benefits), reach women on an equal footing with men.[151] Legal and policy measures in the field of economics are often viewed as 'gender-neutral', but may be indirectly discriminatory because they either reinforce gender-based stereotypes or because they do not take into account women's different social reality. Therefore, States parties also must carry out gender-impact analyses of their laws, both before and after enactment, in developing strategies in economic, social, and cultural policies.

III. Reservations

In light of the broad scope of Article 13, the dearth of reservations may seem surprising. One reservation to the provision as a whole was entered on the basis of religion; it has been withdrawn.[152] Other reservations concerned tax law,[153] or more advantageous social security benefits for women.[154] However, reservations to other CEDAW provisions, in particular to Article 15 (equality before the law and in civil matters)[155] greatly affect the realization of their economic and social rights.

---

[151] See the discussion in ch on art 3.
[152] Bangladesh: Reservation to art 13(a) (also relating to arts 2 and 16(1)(c) and (f)) 'as they conflict with *Sharia* law based on the Holy Quran and Sunna'. Withdrawn in 1997.
[153] n 106 above.   [154] n 124 above.   [155] See the discussion in ch on art 15.

Article 14

1. States Parties shall take into account the particular problems faced by rural women and the significant roles which rural women play in the economic survival of their families, including their work in the non-monetised sectors of the economy, and shall take all appropriate measures to ensure the application of the provisions of the present Convention to women in rural areas.

2. States Parties shall take all appropriate measures to eliminate discrimination against women in rural areas in order to ensure, on a basis of equality of men and women, that they participate in and benefit from rural development and, in particular, shall ensure to such women the right:

a. to participate in the elaboration and implementation of development planning at all levels;

b. to have access to adequate health care facilities, including information, counselling and services in family planning;

c. to benefit directly from social security programmes;

d. to obtain all types of training and education, formal and non-formal, including that relating to functional literacy, as well as, inter alia, the benefit of all community and extension services, in order to increase their technical proficiency;

e. to organise self-help groups and co-operatives in order to obtain equal access to economic opportunities through employment or self-employment;

f. to participate in all community activities;

g. to have access to agricultural credit and loans, marketing facilities, appropriate technology and equal treatment in land and agrarian reform as well as in land resettlement schemes;

h. to enjoy adequate living conditions, particularly in relation to housing, sanitation, electricity and water supply, transport and communications.

* For this chapter and the chapter on art 10, I would like to thank Elizabeth Asham for invaluable research assistance. I would also like to thank Sara Waldron and Meredith Owen. Special thanks are also due to Rikki Holtmaat, Frances Raday, and Janie Chuang.

A. Introduction

Rural women 'produce on average more than half of all the food that is grown' yet 'they own only two per cent of land,... receive only one percent of all agricultural credit' and 'represent two thirds of all illiterate people'.[1]

The particularity of rural women's experiences is the focus of Article 14.[2] The article requires States parties to take the necessary measures to integrate rural women in their implementation of the Convention and reminds them that the experiences and needs of rural women should not be forgotten or ignored. While recognizing that all the other articles in the Convention apply to rural women, Article 14 highlights issues which impact disproportionately on this group. A primary issue is that of discrimination in accessing land and, by implication, the enjoyment of the right to food. The gender dimensions of the right to water are highlighted. The focus on rural women's right to participate in development planning is also critical, and unique.

While other human rights instruments mention rural people, the CEDAW Convention is the only human rights treaty that includes a provision directly and exclusively addressing rural women.[3] Indeed, it is the only provision in the Convention that targets a

---

[1] Food 2050, 'Women: The Linchpin to Food Security' online blog posted 9 November 2010 (citing statistics from the International Federation of Agricultural Producers) <http://food2050.eu/women-the-linchpin-to-food-securi/ accessed 31 December 2010.

[2] A Gonzalez Martinez, 'Rights of Rural Women: Examples from Latin America' in HB Schöpp-Schilling and C Flinterman (eds), *The Circle of Empowerment: Twenty Five Years of the UN Committee on the Elimination of Discrimination against Women* (2007) 212. LA Rehof, *Guide to the Convention on Discrimination against Women* (1993) 151–61.

[3] Compare CRPD arts 9(1), 25(c), 26(1)(b). The Protocol to the African Chater on Human and People's Rights on the Rights of Women in Africa (2003) includes provisions covering similar issues to those covered

specific group. Article 14 of the Convention is one of the least controversial articles in the Convention and received universal support for its inclusion. Despite its importance, Article 14 has received relatively little attention in legal academic writing.[4] To date, no claims relating to this article or to rural women have been brought to the Committee under the Optional Protocol communication procedure.

I. Who is a Rural Woman?

The Committee constructs 'rural' as related to both geography and exclusion from services and opportunities.[5] It concludes that rural living increases women's socio-economic disadvantages due to lack of access to services including health, education, water, sanitation, and transport. Their vulnerability to poverty is further exacerbated by legal and social policies that exclude them from land ownership and deny their right to voice their opinions in development planning and in local government.[6]

Other factors including disability and age have also been identified as having a disproportionate impact on rural women.[7] Moreover, while indigeneity is not always linked to rural living, in many instances the intersectional discrimination faced by indigenous women is exacerbated by their rural living environment. Concluding the examination of one report, for example, the Committee expressed concern about 'rural minority women, including Tibetan women, who face multiple forms of discrimination based on sex, ethnic or cultural background, and socio-economic status.[8]

While widespread urbanization has led to a global decrease in rural populations, in many non-industrialized regions in the world a very large proportion of women continue to live in rural areas and to contribute to subsistence agricultural labour.[9] They are

in art 14 of CEDAW. These can be found in multiple articles including arts 13–21. See also UN Declaration on the Rights of Indigenous People arts 2, 22, and 23. Declaration of Rights of Peasants: Women and Men, 2009 (non binding), annexed to *Preliminary Study of the Human Rights Council Advisory Committee on discrimination in the context of the right to food* (2010) UN Doc A/HRC/13/32.

[4] See eg CI Nyamu, 'The International Human Rights Regime and Rural Women in Kenya' (2000) *East African J of Peace and Human Rights* 1; CI Nyamu, 'Rural Women in Kenya and the Legitimacy of the Human Rights Discourse and Institutions' in EK Quashigah and OC Okafor (eds), *Legitimate Governance in Africa* (1999) 263; L Pruitt, 'Migration, Development and the Promise of CEDAW for Rural Women' (2009) 30 *Michigan J of Intl L* 710.

[5] CO Morocco, A/58/38, 29th Session (2003) paras 170, 171, and 176; CO Albania, CEDAW/C/ALB/CO/3 (2010) para 36; CO Ireland, CEDAW/C/IRL/CO/4–5 (2005) paras 392–3. See also Report of the Secretary-General, 'Improvement of the Situation of Women in the Rural Areas' (2009) UN Doc A/64/190, 29; World Bank, International Fund for Agriculture and Development (IFAD) and Food and Agriculture Organization (FAO), *Gender and Agriculture Sourcebook* (2009).

[6] CO Albania, A/58/38, 28th Session (2003) para 76; CO Ireland, CEDAW/C/IRL/CO/4–5 (2005) para 392; CO China, CEDAW/C/CHN/CO/6 (2006) para 27; CO Uruguay, CEDAW/C/URY/CO/7 (2008) para 42; CO Sierra Leone, CEDAW/C/SLE/CO/5 (2007) para 36; CO Mongolia, CEDAW/C/MNG/CO/7 (2008) paras 35 and 37.

[7] GR 27 paras 12, 19, 24, 32, 44, and 47; CO Argentina, CEDAW/C/ARG/CO/6 (2010) paras 41–2; Report of the Secretary-General (2009) (n 5 above) paras 56–60, 66–9, and 72(j) and (k).

[8] CO China, CEDAW/C/CHN/CO/6 (2006) para 27. See also CO Israel, CEDAW/C/ISR/CO/3 (2005) para 39; CO The Philippines, CEDAW/C/PHI/CO/6 (2006) paras 29–30; CO Peru, CEDAW/C/PER/CO/6 (2007) para 36; CO Canada, CEDAW/C/CAN/CO/7/Add.1/Corr.1 (2008) para 43; CO Australia, CEDAW/C/AUS/CO/7 (2010) paras 26 and 41. See also 'Gender and Indigenous Peoples' Human Rights' (2010) Permanent Forum on Indigenous Issues, OSAGI, and DAW, Briefing Note No 6.

[9] CO Papua New Guinea, CEDAW/C/PNG/CO/3 (2010) para 45; CO Lao People's Democratic Republic, CEDAW/C/LAO/CO/7 (2009) para 44. UN DAW, *2009 Survey on the Role of Women in Development* (2009) 29. Report of the Secretary-General, 'The Improvement of the Situation of Women in Rural Areas' (1995) UN Doc A/50/257/Rev.1 paras 15–20.

often excluded from more lucrative farming including commercial farming and growing cash crops, thus denying them the economic empowerment opportunities afforded to men.

The challenges faced by rural women are not confined to developing States. One European State party, for example, notes in its 2008 report to the Committee that 'Compared to men, women in rural areas have a lower professional level, fewer permanent appointments, less opportunity for independent entrepreneurship, a bigger chance of working part-time and more frequent participation in non-qualifying education'.[10]

II. Rural Women: From Development to Rights

The concerns of rural women have generally been considered as part of the development agenda.[11] The conceptual approach to rural women's concerns has evolved since the mid-twentieth century, shifting from a focus on women in development (WID),[12] to looking at women and development (WAD), then on to gender and development (GAD),[13] and finally on to the rights-based approach to development (RBAD).[14] These conceptual developments are reflected in UN women's conferences.[15] The CEDAW Committee takes a human rights approach.[16] It engages States parties on progress made in the realization of the Millennium Development Goals (MDGs).[17] The Committee has emphasized that 'the full and effective implementation of the Convention is indispensable for achieving the MDGs'.[18]

---

[10] CO The Netherlands, CEDAW/C/NLD/5 (2008) 93.

[11] I Rae, *Women and the Right to Food* (2008); UNGA Res 3523 (15 December 1975) UN Doc A/RES/3523(XXX); UNGA Res 3524 (15 December 1975) UN Doc A/RES/3524(XXX); UNGA Res 62/136 (18 December 2007) UN Doc A/RES/62/136; 'Rural Women in Kenya and the Legitimacy of the Human Rights Discourse and Institutions' (n 4 above) 266.

[12] WAD highlighted the importance of integrating women into development. E Boserup, *Women's Role in Economic Development* (1970).

[13] WAD highlighted the importance of factoring in the impact of global inequalities in economic relations between States and their impact on women while GAD focused on the importance of recognizing women's reproductive and economic work especially in the non-monetized sector as well as acknowledging the paramount impact of gender on women's lives. EM Rathgeber, 'WID, WAD, GAD: Trends in research and practice' (1990) *J of Developing Areas* 489.

[14] RBAD was based on Sen's capabilities approach and moved the issue from welfare to rights and entitlement. A Sen, *Development as Freedom* (1989); M Nussbaum, *Women and the Human Right to Development: The Capabilities Approach* (2000). UNDP, 'Human Rights and Human Development' (2000).

[15] 'Report of the World Conference of the International Women's Year' (Mexico City 19 June to 2 July 1975) UN Doc E.CONF.66/37 (1976) (hereafter Mexico Conference) paras 8, 9, 14, 16, 18, 22, 145, 147, 163, and 169; 'Report of the World Conference of the UN Decade for Women: Equality, Development and Peace' (Copenhagen 14–30 July 1980) UN Doc A/CONF.94/35 (hereafter Copenhagen conference) paras 3, 4, 8, 10–16, 43–5; 'Report of the World Conference to review and appraise the achievements of the UN Decade for Women, Equality, Development and Peace'(Nairobi 15–26 July 1985) UN Doc A/CONF.116/28/Rev.1 (hereafter Nairobi Conference) paras 17, 18, 25, 26, 123, 134, 174, and 196. Rural women did not make it into the list of twelve critical areas of concern at the 1995 Beijing Conference. They were, however, mentioned including in paras 16, 26, 27, and 36. Report of the Secretary-General (1995) (n 9 above) para 2. See also Beijing+10 Declaration (2005) para 4.

[16] CO Jamaica, CEDAW/C/JAM/CO/5 (2006) para 37.

[17] UNGA Res 55/2, 'UN Millennium Declaration' (18 September 2000) UN Doc A/RES/55/2; See also C Hayes, 'Out of the Margins: The MDGs through a CEDAW lens' (2005) 13 *Gender and Development* 67. See the discussion in the Introduction.

[18] CO Sierra Leone, CEDAW/C/SLE/CO/5 (2007) para 44; see also Sixth Periodic Report Malawi, CEDAW/C/MW/I/6 (2008) paras 71, 80, and 102; CO Malawi, CEDAW/C/MWI/CO/6 (2010) para 47; CO The Netherlands, CEDAW/C/NLD/CO/5 (2010) para 49; CO Panama, CEDAW/C/PAN/CO/7 (2010) para 55; CO Russian Federation, CEDAW/C/USR/CO/7 (2010) para 52.

III. Rural Women within UN Structures

In the first years after the Convention came into force, institutional support for the rights of rural women within the UN system was notably provided by the Food and Agricultural Organization (FAO). It initially took up the Convention Article 22 invitation to specialized agencies to contribute to the work of the Committee by producing reports and offering technical assistance to States parties on writing reports and produced guidelines on reporting under Article 14.[19] The United Nations Development Fund for Women (UNIFEM) has been an important agent urging States to implement the Convention in national development programmes.[20] In 2007, the UN General Assembly voted to establish an International Day of Rural Women in recognition of 'the critical role and contribution of rural women, including indigenous women, in enhancing agricultural and rural development, improving food security and eradicating rural poverty'.[21]

A focus on gender is also included in the mandates of the Special Rapporteurs on Food,[22] Health,[23] Housing,[24] Indigenous People,[25] Poverty,[26] and Water,[27] and they have considered rural women in their work.[28]

B. Travaux Préparatoires

The drafting of Article 14 was uncontroversial.[29] Initially, rural women had only been considered in provisions on employment and education.[30] It was at the 26th session of the Commission on the Status of Women (CSW) in 1976 that a representative of the FAO raised the plight of rural women. She suggested that the existing drafts of the Convention did not take adequate notice of the challenges faced by rural women. The FAO representative reminded delegates about the concerns expressed at the Mexico Conference and beyond.[31] Following the Mexico Conference, States were keen to

---

[19] FAO, *CEDAW: Guidelines for Reporting under Article 14* (2005). See also <http://www.fao.org> accessed 31 December 2010.

[20] UNIFEM, *CEDAW and the Human Rights Based Approach to Programming: A UNIFEM Guide* (2007).

[21] UNGA Res 62/136 (18 December 2007) UN Doc A/RES/62/136 para 8.

[22] HRC, 'Mandate of the Special Rapporteur on Food' (27 September 2007) UN Doc A/HRC/RES/6/2 para 2(c).

[23] UNCHR, 'Special Rapporteur of the Commission on Human Rights on the right of everyone to the enjoyment of the highest attainable standard of physical and mental health' UNCHR. Res 2002/31 (establishing mandate) and UNCHR Res. 2005/24 (extending mandate).

[24] UNCHR, 'Special Rapporteur on adequate housing as a component of the right to an adequate standard of living, and on the right to non discrimination in this context' UNCHR Res 2000/9 (establishing mandate).

[25] UNCHR, 'Special Rapporteur on the situation of human rights and fundamental freedoms of indigenous peoples,' UNCHR Res 2001/57 (establishing mandate) and UNCHR Res 2004/62 (extending mandate).

[26] UNCHR, 'Independent expert on the question of human rights and extreme poverty' UNCHR Res. 1998/25 (establishing mandate) and UNCHR Res.2004/23 (extending mandate).

[27] HRC, 'Human Rights and access to safe drinking water and sanitation' (28 March 2008) UN Doc A/HRC/RES/7/22 para 2(d).

[28] See also 'Report of the Independent Expert in the field of cultural rights, Ms Farida Shaheed' (2010) UN Doc A/HRC/14/36 paras 34, 37, and 61–3.

[29] N Burrows, 'The Convention on the Elimination of all Forms of Discrimination against Women' (1985) *Netherlands Intl L Rev* 419,446; Rehof (n 2 above)153; Nyamu 'Rural Women in Kenya and the Legitimacy of the Human Rights Discourse and Institutions' (n 4 above) 266–7; Pruitt (n 4 above) 731–3.

[30] Rehof (n 2 above). 153.

[31] See eg UNGA Res 3521 (15 December 1975) UN Doc A/RES/3521(XXX); UNGA 3523 (15 December 1975) UN Doc A/RES/3523(XXX).

emphasize the importance of engaging rural women in development, exemplifying the WID analysis.[32]

A small working group comprising Egypt, India, Indonesia, Iran, Pakistan, Thailand, and the United States was convened to consider drafting a provision on rural women. Its draft was presented to the CSW by India, which noted that two-thirds of the world's women lived in rural areas and deserved specific focus.[33] The aim of proposing a separate article was to enable rural women 'to participate, equally with men, in agricultural and rural development and to enjoy all the resulting benefits such as planning, health, training, community activities, credit, agricultural reform, etc.'[34] The first draft provided:

States Parties shall take all measures to eliminate discrimination against women in rural areas in order to guarantee them equality as participants and as beneficiaries of agricultural and rural development and particularly the right to:

(a) **Participate fully in the formulation and implementation of development planning from the local to the national levels;**

(b) **Receive adequate medical and health facilities, including family planning advice and services;**

(c) **Obtain all types of training, formal and non-formal, as well as community and extension services;**

(d) **Participate equally in all community activities including co-operatives;**

(e) **Obtain equal access to credit and loans; marketing facilities; and equal treatment in land and agrarian reform as well as land resettlement schemes.[35]**

The working group draft was warmly welcomed and broadly accepted.[36] Missing in the first draft but added later was a provision on social security sponsored by Byelorussia, Egypt, and the USSR.[37] Also added was a provision, suggested by Kenya, on adequate living conditions including the provision of housing, water, electricity, transport, and sanitation. This became final Article 14(2)(h). France's suggestion that provisions on rural women should be read into all the other substantive parts of the Convention instead of being contained in a separate article was rejected.[38] The reiteration, in Article 14, of some of the issues already covered elsewhere in the Convention, was seen as important in 'stressing the situation of rural women'.[39]

I. Other Issues Discussed and Amendments Made

1. Coverage

Argentina suggested that the introductory paragraph be expanded to encompass rural women and other disadvantaged groups in both rural and urban areas. Hungary thought the rural focus should be maintained.[40] Bangladesh proposed the inclusion of a provision on the important work done by rural women in the survival of their families. This was broadened to include their work in the non-monetized sector.[41] This became final Article 14(1).

---

[32] UNGA 3505 (15 December 1975) UN Doc A/RES/3505(XXX), Mexico Conference (n 15 above).

[33] UN Doc E/CN.6/L.687, Burrows (n 29 above) 446, Rehof (n 2 above) 153. Ibid.

[34] Rehof (n 2 above) 153.   [35] UN Doc E/CN.6/L.687 (1976)   [36] Rehof (n 2 above) 154.

[37] Ibid 159.   [38] Ibid 156; see also UN Doc. E/CN.6/SR.658 (1976) para 3.   [39] Ibid 157.

[40] Ibid 156. The issue of coverage also arose over provisions on health, social security, self-help groups and cooperatives, and living conditions. Rehof (n 2 above) 158–60.

[41] Ibid 157.

2. Equality

The United Kingdom (UK) suggested that the word 'equal' be removed from each sub-paragraph and be placed in the introductory paragraph instead. This was done and 'equality between men and women' is now found only in Article 14(2). The UK also suggested that the qualifying word 'appropriate' be placed before 'measures' to prevent any extreme measures being taken in the elimination of discrimination against women. Again this was accepted.[42]

3. Health and Family Planning

Three issues arose. New Zealand proposed an amendment that would ensure that quality of care was the same between men and women and also that men should have equal access to family planning advice. Greece expressed reservations about the inclusion in paragraph (b) of family planning because it might provoke negative reactions.[43] Bangladesh proposed expanding the scope of coverage to include receiving adequate nutrition during pregnancy and lactation. It was agreed to place this in Article 12.[44]

4. Education

The provision on training in paragraph (c) of the working group draft was broadened, at the suggestion of Cuba, to include the word 'education'.[45] Also added to the provision after 'formal and non-formal' were the words 'including functional literacy'. Finally, the aim of accessing these different types of education and training, 'to increase technical proficiency' was noted.[46]

5. Self-help Groups and Cooperatives

The USSR queried the specificity of the reference to opportunities to organize self-help groups and cooperatives in what is now Article 14(2)(e). It preferred a more general right to 'different economic opportunities'. However, the original draft suggested by Bangladesh was kept.[47]

C. Issues of Interpretation

Both the State party reports and the Committee's concluding observations reflect an inconsistent approach to Article 14. The Committee's attention to rural women is not systematic. Commentary on each of the substantive provisions through Article 12 may include allusion to the situation of rural women. Article 14 may not be specifically addressed, and rural women may be included under the headings 'vulnerable'[48] or 'economic empowerment'[49]—or not at all.[50] Rural women appear to be mainly dealt with in the context of intersectionality—an analysis of discrimination that involves taking into consideration the additional disadvantage experienced by women as a result of

---

[42] Ibid 155.   [43] Ibid 158.   [44] Ibid.   [45] Ibid 159.
[46] Ibid 159–60.   [47] Ibid 160.
[48] eg CO Panama, CEDAW/C/PAN/CO/7 (2010) paras 46 and 49; CO South Africa, A/53/38/Rev.1, 19th Session (1998) paras 135–6.
[49] eg CO Botswana, CEDAW/C/BOT/CO/3 (2010) paras 39–40. However, in addition to considering economic empowerment, the United Arab Emirates merited a separate consideration of rural women. CO United Arab Emirates, CEDAW/C/ARE/CO/1 (2010) paras 41–2.
[50] CO The United Kingdom, CEDAW/C/UK/CO/6 (2008).

an identity factor or situation in addition to their sex. Both the Committee's concluding observations and questions to States parties are replete with reference to the importance of addressing this multiple discrimination.[51]

In addressing Article 14, States parties appear to be selective in the provisions on which they choose to focus.[52] The Committee has expressed concern about 'the lack of comprehensive information and statistical data on the situation of rural women'.[53]

I. Article 14(1)

Article 14 requires States parties to take 'appropriate measures' to ensure that the Convention is applied to rural women. What is 'appropriate' may relate as much to the socio-economic, political, and legal framework of the State party under consideration as to the types of measures that can be taken to address a particular problem. The Committee requires each State party to justify its chosen means for meeting its obligations and also to 'demonstrate whether it will achieve the intended effect and result'.[54] The Committee envisages comprehensive measures which go beyond an exclusively legal focus. States parties cite lack of resources as a major factor hampering their ability to fully implement some provisions, and the Committee has acknowledged these limitations.[55]

1. Significant Roles Which Rural Women Play in the Economic Survival of their Families

General Recommendation 16, the only general recommendation that explicitly mentions rural women in its title, focuses on women's unpaid work in rural and urban family enterprises. The Committee notes that unpaid work constitutes exploitation of women, highlights the silence in State party reports on women's contributions, and requests States parties to provide more data on the legal and social situation of women working in family enterprises.[56]

General Recommendation 16 builds on General Recommendation 9 (on gathering statistical data) and focuses on recognition in national accounts of women's contributions in the non-monetized sector. Similarly, in General Recommendation 17, the Committee enjoins States to quantify women's unpaid domestic work and to include it in the calculation of the gross national product and in national accounts.[57] The general recommendation refers to the Nairobi Declaration, which called on governments to take concrete steps to quantify the contributions of women to 'agriculture, food production, reproductive and

---

[51] CO Panama, CEDAW/C/PAN/CO/7 (2010) para 46; List of Questions Uganda, CEDAW/C/UGA/Q/7 (2010) paras 26–7; CO Egypt, CEDAW/C/EGY/CO/7 (2010) para 43; CO Bolivia, CEDAW/C/BOL/CO/4 (2008) paras 2 and 17; CO Lebanon, CEDAW/C/LBN (2008) paras 36–7; CO Albania, CEDAW/C/ALB/CO/3 (2010) paras 18, 19, 23, and 35–7.

[52] Rae (n 11 above) 28–30. Pruitt (n 4 above) 736, see also Gonzalez Martinez (n 2 above) 222. Compare brief overview approach taken in Combined 5th, 6th, and 7th periodic report Sri Lanka, CEDAW/C/LKA/5-7 (2010) with the more comprehensive approach in 7th periodic report, Ukraine, CEDAW/C/UKR/7 (2008).

[53] CO Bhutan, CEDAW/C/2004/CRP.3/Add.3/Rev.1 (2004) para 112; CO Algeria, A/60/38, 32nd Session (2005) para 159; CO The Netherlands, CEDAW/C/NLD/CO/5 (2010) para 44; CO Turkey, CEDAW/C/TUR/CO/6 (2010) paras 36–7; CO Ukraine, CEDAW/C/UKR/CO/7 (2008) paras 42–3; CO Uzbekistan, CEDAW/C/UZB/CO/3 (2006) para 29; CO Uruguay, CEDAW/C/URY/CO/7 (2008) para 43; CO United Arab Emirates, CEDAW/C/ARE/CO/1 (2010) para 41.

[54] GR 28 para 23.   [55] Gonzalez Martinez (n 2 above) 212–13.

[56] CO Estonia, A/57/38, 26th Session (2002) para 113; CO Turkey, CEDAW/C/TUR/CO/6 (2010) para 36.

[57] GR 17 paras (b) and (c).

household activities'.[58] The link between the undervaluation of women's work and their low status in society is clear. Rural women whose work is not within the waged sector are particularly disadvantaged by this disregard.

II. Article 14(2)

A primary theme of the Convention and the Committee's work is elimination of all discrimination against women, whatever its source or claimed justification.[59] As one State party with a largely rural population describes the situation:

The quality of life in rural areas remains much lower than in urban areas. A large percentage of the rural population are predominantly subsistence farmers and women account for 80 per cent... Rural women are subjected to more discrimination than their urban counterparts. They have been stereotyped as weaker and [sic] subservient beings than men... Some of these attitudes are entrenched by customary laws... Within the domestic setting, power relations remain titled in favour of men. Most rural women face violence or physical assaults. They have no or limited contribution to the number and spacing of children. Any attempt to interfere with the husband's key decisions often results in divorce or physical abuse. Unfortunately, rural women are socially and culturally expected to put up with such abuse and this is reinforced by traditional and religious beliefs and practices.[60]

1. Participation

Participation is a recurring theme in Article 14 and in the Committee's work.[61] Article 14(2) recognizes that women's exclusion from voicing their opinions in development planning has often resulted in planners' failure to take their needs into account.[62] In General Recommendation 23, the Committee notes that an examination of States parties' reports reveals a link between women's full and equal participation in public life and an improvement in Convention implementation.[63] The Committee has noted its concern 'about the possible adverse impact of agricultural trade liberalization on women and women's low level of participation in trade negotiations'.[64] It has also identified the under-representation of, amongst others, 'indigenous women and women from remote or rural communities'

---

[58] Nairobi Conference (n 15 above) para 120.

[59] GR 25 para 5; GR 28 paras 24–9. See the discussion in ch on art 1. See also section D on Equality below.

[60] 6th Periodic Report Malawi, CEDAW/C/MWI/6 (2008) para 267. See also Combined 2nd and 3rd periodic report India, CEDAW/C/IND/2-3 (2005) paras 289 and 317–19; CO Nicaragua, CEDAW/C/NIC/CO/6 (2007) para 29; CO Mongolia, CEDAW/C/MNG/CO/7 (2008) para 35; CO Russian Federation, CEDAW/C/USR/CO/7 (2010) para 42; Combined 2nd, 3rd, and 4th periodic report South Africa, CEDAW/C/ZAF/2–4 (2009) para 14.12.

[61] Art 14(2)(a) and (f). See also GR 23 paras 5, 9, 17, 30, and 31; CO Albania, A/58/38, 28th Session (2003) para 76; CO Argentina, A/59/38, 31st Session (2004) para 377; CO Mongolia, CEDAW/C/MNG/CO/7 (2008) para 35; CO Nigeria, CEDAW/C/NGA/CO/6 (2008) para 339. See also the discussion in chs on arts 7 and 8.

[62] Marking International Day of Rural Women 2009, International Fund for Agricultural Development (IFAD) noted that there was 'a dramatic disproportion between rural women's voice and decision making role and their enormous contribution to agricultural marketing, production and livelihoods', IFAD International Day of Rural Women 2009 at <http://www.ifad.org/media/events/2009/rural_women.htm> accessed 31 December 2010.

[63] GR 23 para 14.   [64] CO Niger, CEDAW/C/NER/CO/2 (2007) para 35.

in leadership and decision-making positions, as well as in their 'equal access to education, employment and health' as significant implementation issues.[65]

2. Article 14(2)(a)

The *travaux préparatoires* show that States were concerned to ensure that women were able to participate at all levels of government, whether local, national, or regional.[66] This provision reinforces the Convention Preamble: 'Convinced that the full and complete development of a country ... requires the participation of women in equal terms with men in all fields'. In General Recommendation 28 and in its dialogues with States parties, the Committee highlights the importance of ensuring that women are able to participate in development planning. For example, the Committee:

urges the State party to make the promotion of gender equality an explicit component of its national development plans and policies, and in particular those aimed at poverty alleviation and sustainable development. It urges the State party to pay special attention to the needs of rural women, ensuring that they participate in decision making processes.[67]

The Committee has also identified the international dimension of development programmes noting the importance of focusing on rural women and urging one State party 'to place emphasis on women's rights in all development cooperation programmes with international organizations and bilateral donors'.[68] The Committee has commended one State party for putting in place regional and sectoral development policies which had led to an improvement in rural women's quality of life.[69]

General Recommendation 23 identifies barriers to women's participation as including the burdens of domestic work, economic dependence on men, long and inflexible hours of work including the 'double burden' of unrecognized homework and paid work outside the home, stereotyping in society, illiteracy, and women's lack of confidence.[70] These barriers certainly have an impact on women's participation in the public endeavour of development planning.

3. Article 14(2)(b)

The health care issues outlined in Article 12[71] are of particular concern to rural women and occur throughout their life cycle.[72] They lack access to acceptable, affordable, appropriate,

---

[65] CO Australia, CEDAW/C/AUS/CO/7 (2010) para 26. See also CO Nicaragua, CEDAW/C/NIC/CO/6 (2007) para 31; CO Vietnam, CEDAW/C/VNM/CO/6 (2007) para 29; CO Peru, CEDAW/C/PER/CO/6 (2007) para 37; GR 27 para 49.

[66] See Rehof (n 2 above) 158; CO United Arab Emirates, CEDAW/C/ARE/CO/1 (2010) para 44.

[67] CO Equatorial Guinea, A/59/38, 31st Session (2004) para 190. See also GR 28 para 27; CO Paraguay, A 60/38, 32nd Session (2005) para 290; CO Gambia, A/60/38, 33rd Session (2005) para 211; Combined 2nd and 3rd periodic report India, CEDAW/C/IND/2-3 (2005) para 292; CO Nigeria, CEDAW/C/NGA/CO/6 (2008) para 36; CO Uzbekistan, CEDAW/C/UZB/CO/4 (2010) para 37; CO Turkey, CEDAW/C/TUR/CO/6 (2010) para 37. See also the discussion in the Preamble ch.

[68] CO Burkina Faso, A/60/38, 33rd Session (2005) para 348. See also CO Equatorial Guinea, A/59/38, 31st Session (2004) para 190; CO Guyana, A/60/38, 33rd Session (2005) para 308; CO Peru, CEDAW/C/PER/CO/6 (2007) para 37; UNGA Res 62/136 (18 December 2007) UN Doc A/RES/62/136 para 7.

[69] CO Tunisia, A/57/38, 27th Session (2002) para 187. See also CO Ethiopia, A/59/38, 30th Session (2004) para 259.

[70] GR 23 paras 8–12 and 20.

[71] See the discussion in ch on art 12. See also Convention art 14(2)(h); GR 24 para 28.

[72] CO Serbia, CEDAW/C/SCG/CO/1 (2007) para 33; CO Panama, CEDAW/C/PAN/CO/7 (2010) para 41; GR 24 paras 2, 7, 8, and 28. See also UNGA Report of the Secretary-General (2009) (n 5 above) paras 40–8.

and adequate health care as envisaged in General Recommendation 24.[73] The urban focus of most health care services means that rural people only have access to basic, often inadequate primary health care facilities.[74]

The problem of 'budgetary discrimination' against rural women, identified during the drafting of the Convention, remains to this day.[75] The Committee has expressed concern that the impact of restructuring of the health sector has led to a 'decrease in the number of clinics and health services available to women, particularly in the rural areas'.[76] It has recommended that a State party offer free access to health services in all rural areas and that it seek to reduce the high suicide rate in rural areas by 'enhancing the availability of affordable quality mental health and counselling services'.[77] Noting high cervical cancer death rates in a State party that cited high medical costs and inaccessible services, the Committee also asked it to 'elaborate on the efforts taken to increase awareness for the need for regular pap smears and to provide cervical cancer screenings for women, including women in rural areas'.[78]

Both the Committee and the UN Secretary-General have noted that the gender discriminatory factors that place women in a subordinate position lead to their being at an increased risk of violence and contracting HIV.[79] The Secretary-General's report notes that 'In many countries, rural women and girls are disproportionately affected.'[80] Rural women's distance from centralized health systems means that they are, therefore, less able to access anti-retroviral drugs and information.[81] The Committee has urged a State party to educate women about the disease and how to protect themselves 'particularly in the rural areas'. It also urged the State party to ensure that women and girls are accorded equal rights and access to HIV/AIDS detection and related health care and social services.[82]

The violence suffered by rural women has been singled out for attention in General Recommendation 19, which requires States parties to 'report on the risks to rural women, the extent and nature of violence and abuse to which they are subject, their need for

---

[73] GR 24 paras 21, 22, and 28. See also GR 27 paras 21 and 45; CESCR, 'General Comment 14' (2000) UN Doc E/2001/22; CO Nicaragua, CEDAW/C/NIC/CO/6 (2007) para 17.

[74] The issue was noted during the drafting, Rehof (n 2 above) 154. CO Guatemala, A/57/38, Exceptional session (2002) para 193; CO Congo, A/58/38, 28th Session (2003) para 174; CO Morocco, A/58/38, 29th Session (2003) paras 172, 173, and 177; CO Argentina, A/59/38, 31st Session (2004) para 376; CO Equatorial Guinea, A/59/38, 31st Session (2004) para 205; CO Lao People's Democratic Republic, A/60/38, 32nd Session (2005) para 96.

[75] Rehof (n 2 above) 158. Gonzalez Martinez (n 2 above) 220; CO Myanmar, CEDAW/C/MMR/CO/3 (2008) paras 38–9.

[76] CO Poland, CEDAW/C/POL/CO/6 (2007) para 24.

[77] CO China, CEDAW/C/CHN/CO/6 (2006) para 28. GR 24 para 25.

[78] List of issues and questions Uganda, CEDAW/C/UGA/Q/7 (2010) para 24.

[79] GR 24 paras 5, 12, and 18; GR 15; Report of the Secretary-General (2009) (n 5 above) para 42; CO Congo, A/38/58, 28th Session (2003) paras 175–6; CO El Salvador, A/58/38, 28th Session (2003) para 260; CO Papua New Guinea, CEDAW/C/PNG/CO/3 (2010) para 43; CO Botswana, CEDAW/C/BOT/CO/5 (2010) paras 37–8.

[80] Report of the Secretary-General (n 5 above) para 42.

[81] GR 24 paras 18 and 31(b). See also CRC, 'General Comment 3' (2003) UN Doc CRC/GC/2003 para 21.

[82] CO Panama, CEDAW/C/PAN/CO/7 (2010) para 45. See also CO Suriname, A/57/38, 27th Session (2002) para 65; CO Papua New Guinea, CEDAW/C/PNG/CO/3 (2010) para 43; CO Nepal, A/59/38, 30th Session (2004) para 213. See also GR 27 para 21. cf Protocol on the Rights of Women in Africa art 14(1)(e).

and access to support and other services and the effectiveness of measures to overcome violence'.[83]

The Committee has highlighted the problem of maternal (and infant) mortality in rural areas and called on States parties to address it.[84] The Committee has also made the link between the denial of abortion and the rise in maternal mortality, expressing concern 'that many women, in particular in rural areas, give birth at home, and that the practice of illegal and unsafe abortions increases the high rate of maternal mortality'.[85]

Also highlighted as an area of concern by the Committee has been the effect of the improper extensive use of fertilizers and pesticides which are harmful to rural women and their dependants.[86]

4. Accessing Information

Because of their workload—sourcing water, food, and fuel—many rural women, and adolescent girls in particular, are unable to attend school.[87] High levels of illiteracy impede their access to information on sexual and reproductive issues.[88] This leads to an increase in unplanned pregnancies.[89] This leads to a higher than average conception and birth rate with poor development outcomes for the children.[90] It also perpetuates inter-generational cycles of poverty.[91] The Committee has urged a State party to strengthen and expand efforts to increase knowledge of and access to affordable contraceptive methods and provide emergency contraception and also recommended that in family planning education programmes the State party 'take due account of traditions and physical barriers of women in rural areas'.[92] Identifying a 3 per cent contraception prevalence, the

[83] GR 19 para 24 (q). See also paras 24 (a) and 21; CO Brazil, A/58/38, 29th Session (2003) para 114; CO Nicaragua, CEDAW/C/NIC/CO/6 (2007) para 20. The 'Report of the Secretary General' (n 5 above) para 50 also identifies rural women as being particularly vulnerable to violence due to the 'inaccessibility of law enforcement and protection services'.

[84] CO Guatemala, A/57/38, Exceptional Session (2002) paras 192–3; CO Uganda, A/57/38, Exceptional Session (2002) para 147; Dominican Republic, A/59/38, 31st Session para 309; CO Myanmar, CEDAW/C/MMR/CO/3 (2008) para 38; CO Yemen,CEDAW/C/YEM/CO/6 (2008) para 28; CO Panama CEDAW/C/PAN/CO/7 (2010) para 42; CO Sierra Leone, CEDAW/C/SLE/CO/5 (2007) para 34; CO Nigeria, CEDAW/C/NGA/6(2008) para 337.

[85] CO Timor-Leste, CEDAW/C/TLS/CO/1 (2009) para 37. See also CO Uganda, A/57/38, Exceptional Session (2002) para 147; CO Botswana, CEDAW/C/BOT/CO/3 (2010) para 35; CO Mali, CEDAW/C/MLI/CO/5 (2006) para 34; CO Benin, A/60/38, 33rd Session (2005) paras 157–8; CO Cape Verde, CEDAW/C/CPV/CO/6 (2006) para 30; CO Sierra Leone, CEDAW/C/SLE/CO/5 (2007) para 35; CO Nigeria, CEDAW/C/NGA/CO/6 (2008) para 337; CO Congo, A/38/58, 28th Session (2003) para 151. See also GR 24 para 31(c).

[86] CO Paraguay, A/60/38, 32nd Session (2005) para 289.

[87] Combined 2nd, 3rd, and 4th periodic report South Africa, CEDAW/C/ZAF/2–4 (2010) para 14.4; CO Sierra Leone, CEDAW/C/SLE/CO/5 (2007) paras 31 and 36; CO Angola, A/59/38, 31st Session (2004) paras 158 and 164. See also Beijing (1995) para 92.

[88] GR 28 para 28; CO Ecuador, A/58/38, 29th Session (2003) paras 317–18; CO El Salvador, A/58/38, 28th Session (2003) para 259.

[89] CO Brazil, A58/38, 29th Session (2003) para 127; CO Benin, A/60/38, 33rd Session (2005) paras 157–8; CO The Philippines, CEDAW/C/PHI/CO/6 (2006) para 27; CO Serbia, CEDAW/C/SCG/CO/1 (2007) para 33; CO Egypt, CEDAW/C/EGY/CO/7 (2010) paras 39–40; CO Turkey, CEDAW/C/TUR/CO/6 (2010) paras 34–5; GR 24 para 21.

[90] CO El Salvador, A/58/38, 28th Session (2003) paras 259–60; Sixth Periodic Report Malawi, CEDAW/C/MWI/8 (2008) para 269.

[91] *Preliminary Study of the Human Rights Council Advisory Committee on discrimination in the context of the right to food* (2010) UN Doc A/HRC/13/32 para 58. See also GR 24 para 7.

[92] CO Lao People's Democratic Republic, CEDAW/C/LAO/CO/7 (2009) para 38. See also CO Peru, CEDAW/C/PER/CO/6 (2007) para 23; CO Yemen, CEDAW/C/YEM/CO/6 (2008) para 29.

Committee recommended the speedy review and repeal of a law prohibiting 'the advertising of contraceptives, thereby limiting women's access to family planning'.[93]

5. Article 14(2)(c)

The Convention's drafting history shows vigorous debate over whether social security should only be payable to those in formal employment or to all citizens including rural women engaging in subsistence agriculture.[94] Few States parties in the developing world make provision for social security.[95] Many States parties that do provide social security require the beneficiary to have contributed to a central scheme in order to collect.[96] Rural women are particularly disadvantaged by not having the means to make contributions, not least because their income frequently is irregular and unrecorded. The Committee has specifically expressed concern 'about the situation of women agricultural workers who are excluded from the protection of the Labour Code and who consequently do not benefit from social security or other benefits'.[97] The Committee, in General Recommendation 16, calls on States parties to 'take the necessary steps to guarantee payment, social security and social benefits for women who work without such benefits in enterprises owned by a family member'.[98]

State party obligations in respect of social security are underscored by other human rights treaties. CESCR General Comment 19, which is cited in General Recommendation 27,[99] identifies States parties' obligation to ensure that social security is available, adequate, accessible (covering everyone without discrimination), and affordable.[100]

Both CEDAW and CESCR emphasize the importance of taking into consideration women's disproportionate caring burdens and unique work patterns, which may also require breaks for childbearing and childrearing.[101] Also of concern is the common practice of States parties mandating lower retirement ages for women than for men, which may result in lower contributions to social security funds and thus lower pensions.[102] Rural women may be further prejudiced by not having the requisite identification documents to prove entitlement to State assistance and also by the location of the State offices in

---

[93] CO Congo, A/38/58/, 28th Session (2003) para 175; cf Combined 5th, 6th, and 7th periodic report Sri Lanka, CEDAW/C/LKA/5-7 (2010) para 136.

[94] Rehof (n 2 above) 153, 159, and 161. Social Security is also provided for in Convention art 11(1)(e) on employment. See the discussion in ch on art 11. See also UDHR arts 22 and 25(1); CESCR art 9; CESCR, 'General Comment 19' (2008) UN Doc E/C.12/GC/19.

[95] CO Zambia, A/57/38, 27th Session (2002) para 248; CO Mauritania, CEDAW/C/MRT/CO/1 (2007) para 41.

[96] GR 27 para 2; CESCR, 'General Comment 19' (2008) UN Doc E/C.12/GC/19 para 7, recommends that States parties put in place non-contributory schemes covering everyone.

[97] CO Lebanon, CEDAW/C/LBN/CO/3 (2008) para 36. On the exclusion of domestic workers see CO Jamaica, A/58/38, 24th Session (2001) para 215; CO Canada, A/58/38, 28th Session (2003) paras 365–6; CO Costa Rica, A/58/38, 29th Session (2003) para 63; CO The Philippines, CEDAW/C/PHI/CO/6 (2006) para 25.

[98] GR 16 para (c). See also Protocol on the Rights of Women in Africa art 13(f); CESCR, 'General Comment 19' (2008) UN Doc E/C.12/GC/19 paras 50–1; CO Turkey, CEDAW/C/TUR/CO/6 (2010) paras 32–3.

[99] CEDAW GR 27 para 20.

[100] CESCR, 'General Comment 19' (2008) UN Doc E/C.12/GC/19 paras 11–28.

[101] CO Canada, CEDAW/C/2003/1/CRP.3/Add.5/Rev.1 (2003) paras 49, 50, 57, and 58; CESCR, 'General Comment 19' (2008) UN Doc E/C.12/GC/19 para 32.

[102] CO Austria, A/58/38, 23rd Session (2000) para 236; GR 27 paras 20, 24, 42, and 44.

urban areas.[103] For example, South Africa noted in a report to the Committee the efforts of the Government to remedy the lack of access to 'social services such as social grants, housing and development opportunities' resulting from the denial, during the apartheid era, of identification cards. The most affected were 'black rural residents with many of these being elderly women, single mothers, women looking after children of relatives and women with disabilities'.[104] The Committee has also highlighted the disproportionate disadvantage in accessing social services and benefits, faced by minorities and indigenous women of not having birth certificates and identity documents.[105]

The Committee also has identified the problem of marital status discrimination affecting widowed, never-married, or divorced women. In General Recommendation 27, the Committee links the poverty experienced by older women and their lack of access to social security to their ability to buy food. It recommends that the States parties provide adequate non-contributory pensions on an equal basis, and where older women have insufficient income security, that they provide allowances. Moreover, given inter-generational care obligations for grandchildren and other relatives, General Recommendation 27 makes clear that older women in general should also be given child care benefits and support.[106]

6. Article 14(2)(d)

This provision focuses on all types of education without hierarchy.[107] Unlike ICESCR and CRC, it does not describe any form of education as compulsory, suggesting that all are equally important.[108] CEDAW Convention Article 14(2)(d) reinforces Convention Article 10(a) on education in rural areas, and the two must be read together.[109] Article 10(a) reads, in part, that States parties undertake to provide 'the same conditions . . . for access to studies and for the achievement of diplomas in educational establishments of all categories in rural as well as in urban areas'.[110] States parties should not seek to limit, or narrowly construct rural women's education rights to those listed in Article 14. It would be inconsistent to provide in Article 10 for equal access to all forms of education for both urban and rural women, while seeking to limit that coverage in another article. To seek to do so would be to create a two-tier educational system and constitute discrimination on grounds of residence or location, in short, to breach the Convention's key objective, the elimination of all discrimination.[111]

---

[103] CO China, CEDAW/C/CHN/CO/6 (2006) para 32; CO Peru, CEDAW/C/PER/CO/6 (2007) paras 32–3; CO Egypt, CEDAW/C/EGY/CO/7 (2010) paras 43–4; CESCR, 'General Comment 19' (2008) UN Doc E/C.12/GC/19 para 27.

[104] Combined 2nd, 3rd, and 4th periodic report South Africa, CEDAW/C/ZAF/2–4 (2010) para 14.32.

[105] CO Bolivia, CEDAW/C/BOL/CO/4 (2008) para 19.

[106] GR 27 paras 24, 43, and 44. See also CO Belarus, A/59/38, 30th Session (2004) para 353; CO China, CEDAW/C/CHN/CO/6 (2006) para 32; List of issues and questions Bangladesh, CEDAW/C/BGD/Q/7 (2010) paras 22 and 27.

[107] CO Nepal, A/59/38, 30th Session (2004) para 205.

[108] CO Sierra Leone, CEDAW/C/SLE/CO/5 (2007) para 31; cf CESCR arts 13 and 14; CRC arts 28 and 29.

[109] See also Gonzalez Martinez (n 2 above) 214. See also the discussion in ch on art 10.

[110] During the drafting of art 10, Finland queried whether it was too ambitious to expect rural areas to receive the same coverage as urban areas. UN Doc E/CN.6/591 (1976) para 115. It preferred to a guarantee that 'women would have access to all educational establishments irrespective of their place of residence'. Rehof (n 2 above) 115.

[111] GR 28. See also CESCR, 'General Comment 20' (2009) UN Doc E/C.12/GC/20 para 34.

The focus of Article 14(2)(d) on providing education beyond the formal, classroom-based model, is particularly important to rural women not least because their difficulties in accessing educational institutions result in lower levels of formal education and an increase in functional illiteracy. They are also more likely to drop out of school than those living in urban areas.[112] During the drafting process it was noted that the aim of both formal and informal education included increase in technical proficiency, which is clearly important to rural women.[113] The Committee asks questions about differences in 'the quality of education between rural and urban areas' and 'the gender gap at the technical/vocational and tertiary education levels'.[114] The Committee has expressed particular concern that 'only 0.2 per cent of women farmers have formal vocational training in agriculture and only 0.3 per cent a polytechnic or university degree in this field'[115] and also about rural women's 'limited participation in agricultural and animal husbandry training programmes' and recommended that the State party ensure that rural women and girls have access to vocational training.[116]

While the Convention highlights the importance of not discriminating against women and girls in the provision of education, in the absence of a general recommendation on the subject, CESCR General Comment 13 (on education) may be consulted as the template for implementing the right to education. According to CESCR, States are obliged to ensure that education is available, accessible, acceptable, and adaptable.[117]

Both States parties' reports and the Committee's concluding observations clearly indicate that rural girls and women are disproportionately disadvantaged in accessing good quality education and information.[118] Where schools are distant from girls' homes, fear of harassment and violence en route to school hinders access.[119] Boarding schools may help to address this problem in some situations.[120] Similarly, the Committee has identified the charging of fees and related costs including for transport, the purchase of uniforms and equipment as constituting barriers to rural women's and girls' access to education.[121]

---

[112] CO Peru, CEDAW/C/PER/CO/6 (2007) para 26. See also CO Albania, A/58/38, 28th Session (2003) para 76; CO Niger, CEDAW/C/NER/CO/2 (2007) para 30; CO Nigeria, CEDAW/C/NGA/CO/6 (2008) paras 35–6. On difficulties experienced by indigenous and minority women see CO Canada, CEDAW/C/CAN/CO/7/Add.1/Corr.1 (2008) para 43; CO Azerbaijan, CEDAW/C/AZE/CO/3 (2007) para 31. See also GR 27 paras 19 and 40.

[113] Rehof (n 2 above) 159. See also CO Sierra Leone, CEDAW/C/SLE/CO/5 (2007) para 31.

[114] List of issues and questions Bangladesh, CEDAW/C/BGD/Q/7 (2010) para 14. See also CO Tuvalu, CEDAW/C/TUV/CO/2 (2007) para 39.

[115] CO Portugal, CEDAW/C/PRT/CO/7 (2008) para 48. See also para 49.

[116] CO Bhutan, A/59/38, 30th Session (2004) paras 117–18. See also Combined 5th and 6th periodic report China, CEDAW/C/CHN/5–6 (2004) paras 33–4.

[117] CESCR, 'General Comment 13' (1999) UN Doc E/C.12/1999/10 para 6. See also the discussion in ch on art 10.

[118] CO Ecuador, A/58/38, 29th Session (2003) para 319; CO Nepal, A/59/38, 30th Session (2004) paras 204–5; CO Tajikistan, CEDAW/C/TJK/CO/3 (2007) para 33; CO Kenya, CEDAW/C/KEN/CO/6 (2007) para 33; CO Uruguay, CEDAW/C/URY/CO/7 (2008) paras 32, 42, and 43; CO Yemen, CEDAW/C/YEM/CO/6 (2008) para 36; CO Turkey, CEDAW/C/TUR/CO/6 (2010) para 30; CO China, CEDAW/C/CHN/CO/6 (2006) para 27; CO Bhutan, CEDAW/C/BTN/CO/7 (2009) para 26; CO Lao People's Democratic Republic, CEDAW/C/LAO/CO/7 (2009) para 33; Combined 2nd, 3rd, and 4th periodic report South Africa, CEDAW/C/ZAF/2–4 (2010) para 14.33.

[119] CO Bhutan, CEDAW/C/BTN/CO/7 (2009) para 26; CO Timor-Leste, CEDAW/C/TLS/CO/1 (2009) paras 35–6.

[120] Combined 2nd and 3rd periodic report India, CEDAW/C/IND/2-3 (2005) para 98; CO Maldives, CEDAW/C/MDV/CO/3 (2007) para 27; CO Vanuatu, CEDAW/C/VUT/CO/3 (2007) para 30.

[121] CO China, CEDAW/C/CHN/CO/6 (2006) para 28; CO Fiji, CEDAW/C/FJI/CO/4 (2010) para 28.

Interventions include the provision of scholarships and other financial assistance. The Committee congratulated a State party for abolishing interest payments on student loans, which, it had previously noted, 'had a potentially unfavourable impact on women'.[122]

Indigenous girls and women are further disadvantaged by language discrimination. The Committee has noted as to one State party, for example, 'that women and girls...whose mother tongue is not the primary national language continue to face educational disadvantages, particularly in the rural areas and...insufficient information, including data, has been provided by the State on the issue'.[123]

The Committee has urged States parties to use special measures to improve the educational opportunities of rural women and girls and to reduce their drop-out rates.[124] The Committee has highlighted that States parties have a duty to ensure that rural women are legally literate so they can vindicate their rights and recommended that 'information on the content of the Convention be disseminated in the educational system, including in the rural (atoll) areas'.[125]

7. Article 14(2)(e)

While it may seem tautologous to have included self-help groups and cooperatives in the same provision, the drafting history indicates the difference: the Chair explained that a self-help group was 'an arrangement of a cooperative kind which is not established as a formal cooperative.'[126] The provision recognizes that due to discrimination, women are not always given opportunities for economic self-empowerment, thus the necessity of having their own organizations to facilitate it.[127] The Committee has specifically noted the importance of these opportunities, asking how many women participate in the management of agricultural cooperatives and whether they have the same access to credit as men,[128] and requesting a State party to provide detailed information about measures taken to enable women to realize equal opportunities in income-generation activities.[129] While commending another State party on its economic empowerment initiatives, the Committee expressed concern about 'widespread poverty among women, particularly rural women and women head of households'. It urged the State party to ensure that rural women had access to 'income-generating projects'.[130]

---

[122] CO New Zealand, CEDAW/C/NZL/CO/6 (2007) para 9; see also CO Albania, CEDAW/C/ALB/CO/3 (2010) para 30; CO Vanuatu, CEDAW/C/VUT/CO/3 (2007) para 31.

[123] CO Turkey, CEDAW/C/TUR/CO/6 (2010) para 30. See also CO Timor-Leste, CEDAW/C/TLS/CO/1 (2009) para 36; CO Panama, CEDAW/C/PAN/CO/7 (2010) para 35; Combined 2nd and 3rd periodic report India, CEDAW/C/IND/2-3 (2005) para 97. See also Protocol on the Rights of Women in Africa art 18(2)(a) calling on States to protect and enable the development of women's indigenous knowledge systems.

[124] CO South Africa, A/53/38/, 19th Session (1998) paras 135–6; CO Peru, A/57/38, Exceptional Session (2002) para 491; CO Former Yugoslav Republic of Macedonia, CEDAW/C/MKD/CO/3 (2006) para 28.

[125] CO Maldives, CEDAW/C/MDV/CO/3 (2007) para 18. See also CO Vietnam, CEDAW/C/VNM/CO/6 (2007) para 29; CO Russian Federation, CEDAW/C/USR/CO/7 (2010) paras 42 and 53.

[126] Rehof (n 2 above) 160.

[127] Ibid. See Initial Report United Arab Emirates, CEDAW/C/ARE/1 (2010) 56.

[128] List of issues and questions Russian Federation, CEDAW/C/USR/Q/7 (2009) para 27. See also List of issues and questions Bangladesh, CEDAW/C/BGD/Q/7 (2010) para 21.

[129] CO Sierra Leone, CEDAW/C/SLE/CO/5 (2007) para 33. See also CO Albania, A/58/38, 28th Session (2003) para 77; CO Estonia, A/57/38, 26th Session (2002) para 114.

[130] CO Nigeria, CEDAW/C/NGA/CO/6 (2008) paras 35–6. See also CO Serbia, CEDAW/C/SCG/CO/1 (2007) para 32; Combined 2nd and 3rd periodic report India, CEDAW/C/IND/2-3 (2005) paras 282 and 294; CO India, CEDAW/C/IND/CO/3 (2007) para 37; CO Mozambique, CEDAW/C/MOZ/CO/2 (2007) para 41.

8. *Article 14(2)(f)*

The focus of Article 14(2)(f) again concerns women's participation. Article 14(2)(f) seeks to address the often socially and culturally based rationales for the exclusion of women and must be read with Articles 5(a) and 7.[131] General Recommendation 23 links women's inequality to their low level of participation in public and political life.[132] Participation in community life is particularly important for rural women, who are often far removed from interaction with formal State institutions and who therefore rely on male family members as well as local authorities and institutions to facilitate their enjoyment of rights.[133] The Committee has remarked:

Considering the fact that 80 per cent of the population lives in rural areas and that the village chiefs and the village councils handle most everyday matters, the Committee is very concerned that less than 1 per cent of the village chiefs are women and only one member of the Women's Union represents women in the village council.[134]

The Committee has emphasized the need for States parties to address women's under-representation in community organizations.[135] It has called on States parties 'to ensure the participation of women in the council of elders'[136] and noted with concern that a 'revision of the Organic Law of the Villagers' Committees does not call for women's equal representation on villagers' committees'.[137] It has called for gender sensitization of community bodies, including village mediation units which also deal with violence.[138]

The Committee also recognizes that participation in communal activities is particularly important to indigenous women and other women who belong to minority groups.[139] While it is important to recognize cultural and other differences between groups, the preservation of cultural norms cannot be invoked to justify discrimination against women.[140] Approving of a State party's recognition of cultural differences, the Committee cautioned, 'while the recognition of community justice by the State party might make it easier for indigenous and rural people to have access to justice, it might operate to perpetuate stereotypes and prejudices that discriminate against women and violate the human rights enshrined in the Convention'.[141]

---

[131] CO Fiji, CEDAW/C/FJI/CO/4 (2010) para 26; CO Sierra Leone, CEDAW/C/SLE/CO/5 (2007) para 21; GR 23 paras 8–10. See also Protocol on the Rights of Women in Africa art 17 on women's right to participate in the elaboration of cultural values.

[132] GR 23 para13; CO Papua New Guinea, CEDAW/C/PNG/CO/3 (2010) para 46.

[133] GR 23 para 12. See also 'Rural Women in Kenya and the Legitimacy of the Human Rights Discourse and Institutions' (n 4 above) 263; 'Report of the Independent Expert in the field of cultural rights' (n 28 above) paras 34, 61–4. See also *Shilubana and Others v Nwamitwa (Commission for Gender Equality as amicus curiae)* 2007 (2) SA 432.

[134] CO Lao People's Democratic Republic, A/60/38, 32nd Session (2005) para 104. See also Combined 5th, 6th, and 7th periodic report Sri Lanka, CEDAW/C/LKA/5-7 (2010) para 144.

[135] GR 27 para 23; CO Mozambique, CEDAW/C/MOZ/CO/2 (2007) para 40; CO Nigeria, CEDAW/C/NGA/CO/6 (2008) para 36. See also Combined 2nd and 3rd periodic report India, CEDAW/C/IND/2-3 (2005) para 286.

[136] CO Russian Federation, CEDAW/C/USR/CO/7 (2010) para 44.

[137] CO China, CEDAW/C/CHN/CO/6 (2006) para 25; CO Lao People's Democratic Republic, CEDAW/C/LAO/CO/7 (2009) para 44.

[138] CO Lao People's Democratic Republic, CEDAW/C/LAO/CO/7 (2009) para 24.

[139] Co Guyana, A/60/38, 33rd Session (2005) paras 307–8; CO Argentina, CEDAW/C/ARG/CO/6 (2010) para 41; CO Peru, CEDAW/C/PER/CO/6 (2007) para 36.

[140] 'Report of the Independent Expert in the field of cultural rights' (n 28 above) para 64.

[141] CO Bolivia, CEDAW/C/BOL/CO/4 (2008) para 22.

9. *Article 14(2)(g)*

The Committee has identified the denial of credit and loans to women as barriers to their participating in economic life as equal citizens in States parties at all income levels.[142] Referring to a key industry in an economically developed State party, the Committee linked women's low rate of participation in the fishery industry to sex- and gender-based discrimination, including in relation to 'access to grants and loans'.[143] As to another State party, the Committee expressed its concern 'that women lack access to credit and banking facilities which is a major constraint to their participation in small business projects'. It went on to urge the State party to ensure that women 'have access to income-generation opportunities, including access to training, markets and credit'.[144] As to a State party that was facilitating the establishment of a Women's Bank, the Committee expressed concern that 'loans are still given to women at high interest and that burdensome conditionalities, which undermine women's development still prevail'.[145]

Women's lack of access to immoveable property and low participation in the formal economy which guarantees a regular income means that they do not have collateral, negatively affecting their ability to secure loans and credit. The Committee has asked a State party to include in its next report data on the situation of rural women 'including the causes of the low percentage of women, as compared with men, who own land and have full access to credit facilities'.[146]

a) Appropriate Technology

Rural women have long been associated with non-mechanized subsistence level food production. This is in no small part a result of their limited access to more advanced means of production because of discrimination as well as the general shortage of technology in rural areas.[147] The Committee has noted that one of the benefits of development for rural women is access to (environmentally sound) technological advances.[148]

b) Equal Treatment in Land

This is arguably the most important provision to rural women, and the Committee gives it a great deal of attention.[149] Lack of rights to land makes women extremely

---

[142] See also the discussion on loans in ch on art 13. See also GR 27 para 47; CO Estonia, A/57/38, 26th Session (2002) para 114; CO Albania, A/58/38, 28th Session (2003) para 76; CO Uruguay, CEDAW/C/URY/CO/7 (2008) para 33; CO Lebanon, CEDAW/C/LBN/CO/3 (2008) paras 36–7; CO Nigeria, CEDAW/C/NGA/CO/6 (2008) para 35.

[143] CO Iceland, CEDAW/C/ICE/CO/6 (2008) para 31. See also CO Morocco, A/58/38, 29th Session (2003) para 174; CO Fiji CEDAW/C/FJI/CO/4 (2010) para 34.

[144] CO Papua New Guinea, CEDAW/C/PNG/CO/3 (2010) paras 45–6; CO Sierra Leone, CEDAW/C/SLE/CO/5 (2007) para 33; List of issues and questions Bangladesh, CEDAW/C/BGD/Q/7 (2010) para 23.

[145] CO Tanzania, CEDAW/C/TZA/CO/6 (2008) para 37. See also CO Azerbaijan, CEDAW/C/AZE/CO/3 (2007) para 23; CO India, CEDAW/C/IND/CO/3(2007) para 36.

[146] CO Uzbekistan, CEDAW/C/UZB/CO/4 (2010) para 37. See also Combined 2nd and 3rd periodic report India, CEDAW/C/IND/2-3 (2005) para 283; CO Nigeria, CEDAW/C/NGA/CO/6 (2008) paras 338–9; List of Questions, Uganda, CEDAW/C/UGA/Q/7 (2010) para 26; 6th periodic report Malawi, CEDAW/C/MW/1/6 (2008) 266; Initial Report United Arab Emirates, CEDAW/C/ARE/1 (2010) 56; CO United Arab Emirates, CEDAW/C/ARE/CO/1 (2010) para 43; CO Papua New Guinea, CEDAW/C/PNG/CO/3 (2010) paras 45–6.

[147] Combined 5th, 6th, and 7th periodic report Sri Lanka, CEDAW/C/LKA/5-7 (2010) para 141.

[148] CO Lao People's Democratic Republic, A/60/38, 33rd Session (2005) para 93; CO Paraguay, A/60/38, 32nd Session (2005) para 290.

[149] International Land Coalition, IFAD and FAO, *Rural Women, Land and CEDAW* (2004); CO Kenya, A/58/38, 28th Session (2003) paras 223–4; CO Uzbekistan, CEDAW/C/UZB/CO/3 (2006) para 29; CO

vulnerable to poverty and eviction and negatively affects their economic options. The ability to access land is also important because of its linkage to food security.[150] Women's access to land is in many places limited by both legally and culturally enshrined discrimination.[151] The co-existence of multiple and varying personal law systems, some of which permit discrimination against women, makes both ownership and land usage conditional upon the dictates of community rules which may not recognize women's rights.[152] This constitutes discrimination against women and contravenes Convention Articles 2(f), 15, and 16, as well as General Recommendation 21, particularly the provisions relating to distribution of property on death and divorce.[153] Even where the constitutional framework guarantees equality before the law for all, gender prejudice may lead to denial of women's access to land.[154] Some constitutions privilege personal status laws over the right to equality to the detriment of women's property rights. Even where constitutions formally offer equal protection, as the Committee notes, 'the precedence of constitutional law over customary law is not always ensured in practice'.[155]

c) Land Reform and Resettlement

The Committee has identified implementation of land laws and policies as a particular problem. The gendered notion of a man as the head of the household means that women without the protection of a man are often left out of land resettlement schemes, heightening poverty especially of vulnerable groups, including indigenous women, widows, and other women who head households. The Committee has noted that women are 'considerably disadvantaged by the process of privatization, as most lands and livestock were registered under the male heads of households leaving women without legal title or control over their assets'.[156] In General Recommendation 21, the Committee calls on States parties undertaking land redistribution programmes among groups of different ethnic origins to guarantee the rights of women, regardless of marital status, to share the redistributed land.[157] The Committee applauded a State party on adopting a Law on Contracting Rural Land providing for land to be allocated to married, divorced, and widowed women,

India, CEDAW/C/IND/CO/3 (2007) para 47; CO Pakistan, CEDAW/C/PAK/CO/3 (2007) para 42; CO Tajikistan, CEDAW/C/TJK/CO/3 (2007) paras 19 and 34; CO Bolivia, CEDAW/C/BOL/CO/4 (2008) para 11; CO Lebanon, CEDAW/C/LBN/CO/3 (2008) para 36; CO Nigeria, CEDAW/C/NGA/CO/6 (2008) paras 35–6; CO Timor-Leste, CEDAW/C/TLS/CO/1 (2009) para 42; CO Papua New Guinea, CEDAW/C/PNG/CO/3 (2010) para 45.

[150] GR 21 para 26; GR 24 para 7; GR 27 para 24; Rae (n 11 above) 12. FAO *Improving Gender Equity in access to land* (2006) 2. See also C Chinkin and S Wright 'The Hunger Trap: Women, Food and Self-Determination' (1993) 4 *Michigan J of Intl L* 262.

[151] GR 27 para 26; CO Papua New Guinea, CEDAW/C/PNG/CO/3 (2010) paras 45 and 46; CO Nigeria, CEDAW/C/NGA/CO/6 (2008) para 338; UNCHR, 'Report of the Special Rapporteur on Adequate Housing, Women's equal ownership of, access to and control over land and the equal rights to own property and to adequate housing' (2002) UN Doc. E/CN.4/2002/53.

[152] Sixth Periodic Report Malawi, CEDAW/C/MWI/6 (2008) para 272; CO Uganda, A/57/38, Exceptional Session (2002) paras 151–3; CO Uganda, CEDAW/C/UGA/CO/7 (2010) paras 41 and 42; CO Kenya, A/58/38, 28th Session (2003) paras 223 and 224.

[153] CEDAW GR 21 paras 26, 34, and 35.

[154] CO Uganda, A/57/38, Exceptional session (2002) paras 151–3; CO Uganda, CEDAW/C/UGA/CO/7 (2010) paras 41 and 42; CO Lebanon, CEDAW/C/LBN/CO/3 (2008) para 37; CO Papua New Guinea, CEDAW/C/PNG/CO/3 (2010) para 45; CO Fiji, CEDAW/C/FJI/CO/4 (2010) para 34. See also B Oomen, *Chiefs in South Africa: Law, Power and Culture in the Post-Apartheid Era* (2005) 158.

[155] CO Botswana, CEDAW/C/BOT/CO/3 (2010) para 13. See also *Magaya v Magaya* (1999) 1 ZLR 100. See also related discussion in chs on arts 15 and 16.

[156] CO Mongolia, CEDAW/C/MNG/CO/7 (2008) para 37.   [157] GR 21 para 27.

also noting that '70 per cent of the rural landless are women'. The Committee suggested remedial action including 'measures and steps to change customs that result in discrimination against women'.[158] The Committee enjoined one State party to 'ensure that surplus land given to displaced rural and tribal women is cultivable'.[159] The Committee has pointedly noted 'the need for rural women's participation in land reform programmes' and recommended that 'the national machinery for women ... work actively on matters of land reform policy and problems of rural women to ensure their active participation in those areas'.[160] In a subsequent report to the Committee, the same State party acknowledged that women were often excluded from speaking in meetings and giving their opinions about development projects and what to do with compensation for land expropriation. It reported that it had begun holding separate meetings for men and women to address women's exclusion from participation.[161]

The Convention has been cited in a number of cases pertaining to challenges brought by women to customary law norms denying them the right to inherit property because of their sex. In *Ephraim v Pastory*,[162] a woman from a rural area in Tanzania contested a Haya customary rule that allowed women to inherit land but not to sell it; their inheritance rights were limited to use during their lifetime (life estate or usufruct). When the woman sought to sell the land, her nephew challenged the sale on the ground that it violated customary norms. Holding for the woman, the court noted that customary law had to cede to international norms of equality and non-discrimination, including those of the Convention. This decision is in keeping with Convention Articles 2(f) and 15(1). The *Ephraim* decision also accords with General Recommendation 21 and has been followed in two Kenyan cases, both of which identified Convention Article 1 as a basis for upholding the principle of non-discrimination and allowing women to inherit on equal terms with men.[163]

10. Article 14(2)(h)

Article 14(2)(g) guarantees women the right to 'adequate living conditions, particularly in relation to housing, sanitation, electricity, and water supply, transport and communications'. The Committee has not focused in detail on issues covered by this provision. Rather, it tends to list them cursorily as issues of concern while urging States parties to take measures to improve upon provision of these resources.[164] The Committee has occasionally

---

[158] CO China, CEDAW/C/CHN/CO/6 (2006) paras 5 and 27. See also CO Mozambique, CEDAW/C/MOZ/CO/2 (2007) para 40; CO Tajikistan, CEDAW/C/TJK/CO/3 (2007) para 34.

[159] CO India, CEDAW/C/IND/CO/3 (2007) para 47.

[160] CO South Africa, A/53/38/Rev.1, 19th Session (1998) paras 135 and 136.

[161] Combined 2nd, 3rd, and 4th periodic report South Africa, CEDAW/C/CO/ZAF/2–4 (2010) para 14.12.

[162] *Ephraim v Pastory* [1990] LRC 757. See also *Dhungana v Nepal* Supreme Court Writ No 3392, 2 August 1995; *Bhe v Magistrate Khayelitsha* [2005] 1BCLR 1.

[163] GR 21 paras 34 and 35. *Rono v Rono &* another [2008] 1KLR 803, 812–13. *In the matter of the estate of Lerionka Ole Ntutu (deceased)* Succession Cause No 1263 of 2000 [2008] KLR 1, 5–6.

[164] CO Mauritania, CEDAW/C/MRT/CO/1 (2007) paras 41–2; CO Pakistan, CEDAW/C/PAK/CO/3 (2007) paras 40 and 42; CO Mozambique, CEDAW/C/MOZ/CO/2 (2007) para 41; CO Canada, CEDAW/C/CAN/CO/7/Add.1/Corr.1 (2008) para 43; CO Yemen, CEDAW/C/YEM/CO/6 (2008) para 36; CO Nigeria, CEDAW/C/NGA/CO/6 (2008) para 36; CO Timor-Leste, CEDAW/C/TLS/CO/1 (2009) para 42; CO Uganda, CEDAW/C/UGA/CO/7 (2010) para 42.

expressed concern over the lack of data in State party reports on these issues.[165] It has also acknowledged resource constraints as the reason for States parties' failure to implement the provision.[166] In several general recommendations, the Committee has identified access to Article 14(2)(h) rights as important.[167]

a) Housing

The First World Conference on Women noted that women spent disproportionately more time in and near the home than men and, therefore, should be consulted about the location and type of housing, and that it should be organized to reduce 'labour as well as travel for vital needs such as water, food, fuel and other necessaries'.[168] Rural women continue to be disadvantaged in accessing adequate housing, particularly because of legal and social factors which deny them the right to purchase or access land and housing.[169] In many States parties, women's rights to housing are mediated through fathers and husbands as head of household; they do not have independent rights to housing.[170] This ignores the high number of households headed by women, including widows.[171] Among other issues, the denial of an independent right to housing has been recognized as placing women at greater risk of violence.[172]

Discriminatory laws on the allocation of property after divorce may also leave women homeless.[173]

The Committee has taken an intersectional approach, identifying certain groups including aboriginal, minority, refugee and displaced women and girls as particularly disadvantaged in their access to and enjoyment of the right to housing. Concluding its examination of one State party report, the Committee expressed concern 'with the situation of Bedouin women who live in unrecognized villages with poor housing conditions and limited or no access to water, electricity and sanitation'.[174] In the follow-up reporting cycle, the Committee again asked about the condition of Bedouin women and requested the State party to indicate 'the measures taken . . . to ensure that the rights of Palestinian

---

[165] CO United Arab Emirates, CEDAW/C/ARE/CO/1 (2010) para 42; CO Uzbekistan, CEDAW/C/CO/4 (2010) para 36.

[166] Gonzalez Martinez (n 2 above) 213.

[167] GR 21 para 26; GR 24 para 28; GR 27 paras 24 and 47–9; GR 28.

[168] Mexico Conference (n 15 above) para 151. See also ibid paras 148–53. CESCR, 'General Comment 4' (1999) UN Doc E/1992/23 para 8 on the core components of a right to adequate housing.

[169] UNHCHR, 'Report of the Special Rapporteur on adequate housing on Women and adequate housing' (2006) UN Doc E/CN.4/2006/118.

[170] GR 21 paras 30–5; GR 27 paras 26–8 and 51–3. See also *Preliminary Study of the Human Rights Council Advisory Committee on discrimination in the context of the right to food* (2010) UN Doc A/HRC/13/32 para 58; cf Protocol on the Rights of Women in Africa art 16, granting women the right to housing irrespective of marital status. cf also Combined 2nd and 3rd periodic report India, CEDAW/C/IND/2-3 (2007) 299, noting a scheme that provides rural women with funding to build houses and also lists the woman as sole or joint owner.

[171] CO Mongolia, CEDAW/C/MNG/CO/7 (2008) para 37; CO Nigeria, CEDAW/C/NGA/CO/6 (2008) para 36; CO Fiji, CEDAW/C/FJI/CO/4 (2010) para 34; CO Botswana, CEDAW/C/BOT/CO/3 (2010) para 41.

[172] UNCHR, 'Report of the Special Rapporteur on Adequate Housing' (n 169 above) para 16. See also the discussion in the ch on Violence against Women.

[173] GR 21 paras 25–33. See also the discussions in the chs on arts 15 and 16.

[174] CO Israel, CEDAW/C/ISR/CO/3 (2005) para 39. See also CO Azerbaijan, CEDAW/C/AZE/CO/3 (2007) para 31; CO Canada, CEDAW/C/CAN/CO/7/Add.1/Corr.1 (2008) para 43.

Arab Bedouin women who have lost their ancestral land due to home demolitions are fully protected'.[175]

The Special Rapporteur on the Right to Adequate Housing has consulted the Committee in his work and notes that the Committee has accepted his recommendation that it prepare and adopt a general recommendation on the right to housing and land.[176] This has yet to occur.

b) Water

The Committee has not focused in any depth on the right to water or explored the gendered dimensions of water usage and access.[177] However, in General Recommendation 24, the Committee noted that the rights contained in Article 14(2)(h) are 'critical for the prevention of disease and the promotion of good health care'.[178] The Committee sometimes briefly refers to the right to water and the provision of sanitation, in a list of matters that the State should consider improving.[179]

CESCR General Comment 15 cites CEDAW Article 14(2)(h) and notes that the lack of access to clean water supply constitutes discrimination against women.[180] It continues: 'States Parties have an obligation to progressively extend safe sanitation services, particularly to rural and deprived urban areas, taking into account the needs of women and children.'[181]

Water is particularly important to rural women because of the gendered division of labour in which water collection and related activities including cooking, cleaning, and washing are 'women's work'.[182] Environmental changes which have led to greater water scarcity have a disproportionate impact on women,[183] increasing the distances they must travel to source water and exposing them to violence in the process. Concluding the examination of one State party where arsenic poisoning of water had been identified, the Committee noted the disproportionate impact on rural women of reproductive age. It urged the State party to seek to encourage those responsible directly or indirectly for the poisoning to compensate the victims and also to:

put in place measures for ensuring that safe drinking water is available to all, and particularly to affected rural women and their families. The Committee calls on the State party to prepare without delay a plan of action containing preventative and remedial measures, and prioritizing technologies favoured by rural women, their families and local communities that are risk-free, cost-effective and provide alternatives to underground water withdrawal.[184]

---

[175] List of issues and Questions Israel, CEDAW/C/ISR/Q5 (2010) para 33. See also ibid paras 34–5.

[176] UNCHR, 'Report of the Special Rapporteur on Adequate Housing' (n 169 above) paras 16 and 81.

[177] See A Hellum, 'Engendering the Right to Water and Sanitation: A Woman Focused and Grounded Approach' in M Langford and A Russell (eds), *The Right to Water: Theory, Practice and Prospects* (forthcoming 2011).

[178] GR 24 para 28.

[179] CO Lao People's Democratic Republic, CEDAW/C/LAO/CO/7 (2008) para 38; CO Yemen, CEDAW/C/YEM/CO/6 (2008) para 36; CO Canada, CEDAW/C/CAN/CO/7/Add.1/Corr.1 (2008) para 43; CO Morocco, CEDAW/C/MAR/CO/4 (2008) para 32; CO Mongolia, CEDAW/C/MNG/CO/7 (2008) para 36.

[180] CESCR, General Comment 15' (2003) UN Doc E/C/12/2002/11 para 4. See also paras 13, 15, 16(a), and 17.

[181] CESCR, 'General Comment 15' (2003) UN Doc E/C/12/2002/11 para 29.

[182] Combined 4th and 5th periodic report Nepal, CEDAW/C/NPL/4–5 (2010) para 251.c; CESCR, 'General Comment 15' (2003) UN Doc E/C/12/2002/11 para 12(a).

[183] CO Mongolia, CEDAW/C/MNG/CO/7(2008) paras 35–6.

[184] CO Bangladesh, A/59/38, 31st Session (2004) paras 259–60.

Lack of adequate sanitation facilities has been linked to denial of the right of education, particularly for girls.[185] In light of growing privatization of water delivery, economic accessibility is particularly important to women, who often do not have the same financial resources as men to purchase water.[186] CESCR notes that State party obligations include intervention to facilitate access to water when individuals are unable to do so on their own[187] and requires States parties to alleviate the disproportionate burden of water collection borne by women. It further emphasizes the importance of ensuring that women are included in decision-making processes concerning water.[188]

c) Electricity, Communication, and Transport

General Recommendation 27 highlights the difficulties faced by older rural women in participating in economic and community activities and in accessing services, due to lack of transport.[189] General Recommendation 24 identifies 'the absence of convenient and affordable public transport' as a barrier to accessing health care.[190] Women's access to transport is hampered by lack of money and, particularly in rural areas, lack of navigable roads. States parties' reports identify the long distances that they have to walk as key to women's inability to access health facilities, to higher infant and maternal mortality rates, and to lack of contraception and family planning advice.[191] The Committee's Mexico Inquiry, where it investigated the disappearance and murder of over 300 women and the lack of due diligence by the State party, highlighted the impact on women of the lack of safe transport as well as the absence of electricity.[192] The Committee has otherwise commented only rarely on the provision of electricity.[193]

Communication comes in many forms. As already noted, the Committee encourages States to ensure that citizens are informed in their own languages about the Convention and States parties' obligations.[194] A UNIFEM programme used an innovative art project to raise awareness about the Convention, bringing together 200 marginalized women, including poor rural women, to identify challenges facing them and to make a quilt with the Convention as the central theme. For rural women, difficulties included 'limited access to agricultural equipment, seeds, fertilizers and transport mean that they cannot make a profit from their agricultural activities'.[195] Many rural women have not ben-

---

[185] CESCR, 'General Comment 15' (2003) UN Doc E/C/12/2002/11 para 16(b), UNDP 'Human Development Report 2006: Water' (2006).

[186] CESCR, 'General Comment 15' (2003) UN Doc E/C/12/2002/11 paras 27 and 44(a).

[187] Ibid para 25.

[188] Ibid para 16(a). See also Combined 2nd and 3rd periodic report India, CEDAW/C/IND/2–3 (2005) paras 300 and 319.

[189] GR 27 paras 24 and 47.   [190] GR 24 para 21.

[191] 6th periodic report Malawi, CEDAW/C/MWI/6 (2008) 268; 6th periodic report Yemen, CEDAW/C/YEM/6 (2007) 66.

[192] Mexico, CEDAW Optional Protocol Article 8 Examination Concerning Gender Discrimination, CEDAW/A59/38 part II (2004) paras 64, 69, 188, and 290. On the impact of lack of safe transportation on rural girls' access to education see, CO Bhutan, CEDAW/C/BTN/CO/7 (2009) para 25; Responses to the list of issues and questions South Africa, CEDAW/C/ZAF/Q4/Add.1 (2010) para 2.9.1.6.2.

[193] CO Nigeria, CEDAW/C/NGA/CO/6 (2008) para 339; CO Yemen, CEDAW/C/YEM/CO/6 (2008) para 36; CO Israel, CEDAW/C/ISR/CO/3 (2005) para 39.

[194] CO Papua New Guinea, CEDAW/C/PNG/CO/3 (2010) paras 15, 17, 18, and 58; CO Uzbekistan, CEDAW/C/UZB/CO/3 (2006) paras 14 and 38.

[195] A Divinskaya, 'CEDAW in Kyrgyzstan: movement towards *justice*' UNIFEM Community Art Project (UNIFEM undated) 2, <http://www.unifem.org/cedaw30/attachments/success_stories/3ADCommunityArtProject_en.pdf> accessed 31 December 2010.

efited from the global technology boom because of their low levels of education, lack of knowledge about the availability of the technology, and, even if aware, lack of financial resources to access it.[196]

D. Equality in Context

The objective of the Convention is the elimination of discrimination in all spheres.[197]

I. Formal Equality

A key State party obligation under the Convention is to ensure that no laws or policies exist that discriminate against women. In societies with plural legal systems, formal equality requires the State party to ensure that all of its laws comply with all the provisions of the Convention and that they are applied. The Committee has noted with concern, for example, that 'continuing discrimination against women' results from application of customary law in village courts despite its being subordinate to the Constitution and statutory laws.[198]

II. Substantive Equality

In General Recommendations 25 and 28, the Committee has noted that changing the law to remove discriminatory provisions is a start, but is, by itself, insufficient.[199]

Substantive equality requires the State party to move beyond formal legal equality to look at women's lived experiences. It requires a consideration of the effect of the law, policies, and practices on the enjoyment, or otherwise, of the rights in question. The Committee asked one State to provide information on the impact of its policies on rural women:

Please provide information regarding the closure regime and related restrictions on movement in the West Bank, and what impact they have on women living in rural areas of the West Bank and their ability to enjoy the rights provided by the Convention, in particular those provided for under article 14. This information is particularly relevant with regard to the access of women to adequate health care, formal and non-formal education, adequate living conditions and empowerment, equality with respect to economic life and also their right to enjoy family life. Please also inform the Committee about measures taken to ensure that women living in rural areas are able to access and cultivate their land in areas behind the wall and around settlements.[200]

Effectiveness is important to the realization of substantive equality. The Committee has noted with concern, for example, that despite adoption of a new law, rural women 'continue to have limited access to land ownership and to credit facilities and extension services, thus perpetuating their poor social and economic conditions'.[201] Substantive equality may also require the State party to address historically embedded discrimination faced by

---

[196] GR 27 para 12.   [197] GR 28 paras 4, 14, and 15.
[198] CO Papua New Guinea, CEDAW/C/PNG/CO/3 (2010) para 17.
[199] GR 25 para 8; GR 28 para 16.
[200] List of issues and questions Israel, CEDAW/C/ISR/Q/5 (2010) para 35.
[201] CO Paraguay, A/60/38, 32nd Session (2005) para 289. See also CO Mongolia, CEDAWC/MNG/CO/7 (2008) para 36.

women in policy and law by making use of temporary special measures to accelerate the realization of equality.[202]

III. Transformative Equality

Transformative equality is concerned with addressing structural discrimination. In its consideration of Article 14, the Committee has noted its concern 'that traditional female stereotypes are most prevalent in the rural communities and that rural women are often relegated to tasks related to farming and raising children and have no opportunity for wage employment'.[203] It has called on States parties to address discrimination that is grounded in social and cultural constructions of the roles of men and women (gender) and stereotyping focusing on 'the impact of negative customs and traditional practices which affect full enjoyment of the right to property by women'.[204]

IV. Direct Discrimination

General Recommendation 28 defines direct discrimination as 'different treatment explicitly based on grounds of sex or gender differences'.[205] In its General Recommendation 24 and consideration of State party reports under Article 14(2)(b), the Committee has identified the denial of services needed only by women such as abortion as constituting direct discrimination.[206] The Committee has also identified discriminatory inheritance and land laws as constituting direct discrimination and as requiring review under Article 14(2)(g).[207]

V. Indirect Discrimination

In General Recommendation 28, the Committee notes that indirect discrimination may include laws and policies that are on their face neutral, but which, in practice, impact disproportionately on women.[208] The Committee has expressed concern, for example, about rural policies and programmes that are 'mostly gender neutral' and that were 'formulated without attention to gender perspectives and to discrimination and inequality faced by women and girls'.[209] Moreover, the Committee has called a State party's attention to 'indirect discrimination against women because they have limited access to credit, owing to their lack of collateral'.[210]

---

[202] CO Algeria, A/60/38, 32nd Session (2005) para 160.

[203] CO Myanmar, CEDAW/C/MMR/CO/3 (2008) para 44.

[204] CO Uganda, CEDAW/C/UGA/CO/7 (2010) para 42. See also CO Sierra Leone, CEDAW/C/SLE/5 (2007) para 20; Combined 2nd and 3rd periodic report India, CEDAW/C/IND/2–3 (2005) paras 307 and 317; CO Botswana,CEDAW/C/BOT/CO/3/(2010) para 23; CO Uganda, A/57/38, 27th Session (2002) para 134; CO Egypt, CEDAW/C/EGY/CO/7 (2010) paras 21–2. See also GR 25 para 38. See generally R Cook and S Cusack, *Gender Stereotyping; Transnational Legal Perspectives* (2009).

[205] GR 28 para 16.

[206] GR 24 paras 11, 14, and 19. CO Nigeria, CEDAW/C/NGA/CO/6 (2008) para 337. See also CO Congo, A/58/38, 28th Session (2003) para 151.

[207] CO Kenya, A/58/38, 28th Session (2003) paras 223–4; CO Sierra Leone, CEDAW/C/SLE/CO/5 (2007) para 37; CO Lebanon, CEDAW/C/LBN/CO/3 (2008) para 37; South Africa: Responses to the list of issues and questions, CEDAW/C/ZAF/Q4/Add.1 (2010) para 2.12.1.2. cf Combined 2nd and 3rd periodic report India, CEDAW/C/IND./2–3 (2005) paras 279 and 319.

[208] GR 27 para 16.

[209] CO Bhutan, CEDAW/C/2004/1/CRP.3/Add3/Rev.1 (2004) para 105.

[210] CO Botswana, CEDAW/C/BOT/CO/3 (2010) para 39.

VI. Intersectionality

The Committee pays particular attention to the impact of intersectional discrimination.[211] Considering Article 14(2)(b), the Committee has expressed concern 'about the situation of rural women, particularly older women and indigenous women, in view of their extreme poverty, marginalization and frequent lack of access to health care'.[212] The Committee asks States parties to provide 'comprehensive information including sex-disaggregated data and trends over time, on the *de facto* holistic position of rural and ethnic minority women and on the impact of measures taken and results achieved in the implementation of policies and programmes for these groups of women and girls'.[213]

VII. Temporary Special Measures (TSMs)

Temporary special measures are a means to accelerate the realization of equality by tackling the unfair discrimination women face as result of historical and structural discriminatory policies and practices.[214] To address barriers to women's participation in development planning, General Recommendations 23 and 25 recommend that States parties use temporary special measures to address women's under-representation.[215] The Committee has specifically noted that temporary special measures, 'especially with regard to access to education, public services, justice, health care and micro-financing', would be appropriate in a State party where the majority of the women are rural.[216]

E. States Parties' Obligations

Article 14(1) and (2) require the State party to take 'all appropriate measures'. In General Recommendation 28, the Committee offers guidance to States parties on the measures that they are required to take.[217] With regard to Article 14, the Committee has recommended that States parties adopt policies that will remove barriers to women's enjoyment of rights. The Committee has engaged States parties about changing laws, providing adequate budgetary support to rural women, making available scholarships to overcome the low levels of participation of rural girls in education, providing gender-disaggregated data including for rural areas, examining the gendered impact of development and agrarian policies before implementation, and also using temporary special measures to accelerate the elimination of discrimination against women and the realization of their rights.[218] The

---

[211] GR 28 para 18.

[212] CO Argentina, CEDAW/C/ARG/CO/6 (2010) para 41. See also CO China, CEDAW/C/CHN/CO/6 (2006) para 28, Combined 2nd and 3rd periodic report India, CEDAW/C/IND/2–3 (2005) para 317.

[213] CO Vietnam, CEDAW/C/VNM/CO/6 (2007) para 29. See also, CO Serbia, CEDAW/C/SCG/CO/1 (2007) paras 37–8; CO Mauritania, CEDAW/C/MRT/CO/1 (2007) para 42.

[214] See Convention art 4 and the discussion in ch on art 4. See also GR 25; CO Australia, CEDAW/C/AUS/CO/7 (2010) para 26.

[215] GR 23 para 15; GR 25 para 32.

[216] CO Yemen, CEDAW/C/YEM/CO/6 (2008) para 37. See also GR 25 para 38.

[217] GR 28 paras 23–42.

[218] CO Egypt, CEDAW/C/EGY/CO/7 (2010) para 43; CO Uzbekistan, CEDAW/C/UZB/CO/4 (2010) paras 16, 34, and 36; CO Ukraine, CEDAW/C/UKR/CO/7 (2010) paras 37 and 43; CO Yemen, CEDAW/C/YEM/CO/6 (2008) para 37; CO Bolivia, CEDAW/C/BOL/CO/4 (2008) para 33; CO Turkey, CEDAW/C/TUR/CO/6 (2010) para 37; CO China, CEDAW/C/CHN/CO/6 (2006) paras 16, 23, 28, 32, 36, and 38.

Committee has noted that States parties undertake to respect, protect, and fulfil their obligations.[219]

I. Obligation to Respect

This requires the State party to refrain from engaging in or supporting any activity or practice that leads to a breach of Convention rights.[220] While noting that there will sometimes be a need for very large development projects, the Committee has expressed concern about the displacement of tribal women and urged a State party 'to study the impact of megaprojects on tribal and rural women and to institute safeguards against their displacement and violation of their human rights'.[221]

II. Obligation to Protect

This obligation requires the State party to take steps to eliminate discrimination resulting from the actions of non-State actors.[222] Focusing on Article 14(2)(b), the Committee has noted the lack of health services including low rates of contraceptive use and recommended an improvement of access to reproductive and family planning services 'without requiring the permission of the husband'.[223] Discussing Article 14(2)(d), the Committee urged a State party 'to take steps to overcome traditional attitudes that in some rural areas may constitute obstacles to the education of women and girls and to keep girls in school'.[224]

III. Obligation to Fulfil

This obligation requires a State party to take positive measures to facilitate the realization and effective enjoyment of Convention rights. In its consideration of State party reports under Article 14, the Committee has made a number of recommendations, including requiring the State party to '[e]stablish a clear legislative framework to protect women's rights to inheritance and ownership of land'.[225] Considering Article 14(2)(a), the Committee has suggested that development projects should be implemented 'only after conducting gender impact assessments involving rural women, and it should conduct awareness raising campaigns on gender equality, with the focus among key State officials responsible for reforming the gender sector on the gender aspects of rural development'.[226] Focusing on Article 14(2)(b), the Committee has highlighted the importance of the State party providing adequate budgetary resources and access to affordable health care in particular 'prenatal and obstetric services' including in emergencies.[227] It has recommended that a State party offer free access to health services in all rural areas and that it seek to reduce the high suicide rate in rural areas by 'enhancing the availability of affordable

---

[219] GR 24 paras 13–18; GR 28 paras 9 and 16 ff.   [220] GR28 paras 35 and 37(a).
[221] CO India, CEDAW/C/IND/CO/3 (2007) para 47.   [222] GR 28 para 9.
[223] CO Benin, A/60/38, 33rd Session (2005) para 158.
[224] CO Egypt, CEDAW/C/EGY/CO/7 (2010) para 32. See also CO Uganda, CEDAW/C/UGA/CO/7 (2010) para 42.
[225] CO Burkina Faso, A/60/38, 33rd Session (2005) para 348; See also CO Lebanon, A/60/38, 33rd Sesson (2005) para 118; CO Lebanon, CEDAW/C/LBN/CO/3 (2008) para 37.
[226] CO Uzbekistan, CEDAW/C/UZB/CO/4 (2010) para 37; See also CO Turkey, CEDAW/C/TUR/CO/6 (2010) para 37; CO China, CEDAW/C/CHN/CO/6 (2006) para 28; CO Nigeria, CEDAW/C/NGA/CO/6 (2008) para 339.
[227] CO Nigeria, CEDAW/C/NGA/CO/6(2008) para 337.

quality mental health and counselling services'.[228] The Committee has also identified international cooperation and the provision of assistance as important to the realization of Article 14. It has encouraged a State party 'to seek assistance from the international community with trying to meet its obligations to provide adequate housing, education and health'.[229] The Committee has also highlighted the importance of States parties' addressing intersectional discrimination and recommended the implementation of special programmes for vulnerable groups of women in rural areas.[230]

Considering Article 14(2)(h), the Committee, in General Recommendation 27, enjoins States parties to provide 'affordable and accessible public transport to meet the needs of older women'.[231] Focusing on Article 14(2)(d), the Committee has urged States parties to use special measures to improve the educational opportunities of rural women and girls.[232] It has also engaged States parties on the importance of educating the rural population about their rights and specifically making them aware of the Convention, including in languages with which they are familiar. It has highlighted that States parties have a duty to ensure that rural women are legally literate to enable them to vindicate their rights.[233]

The Committee is clear that States parties must take targeted, concrete, and measurable steps to realize Article 14 rights.[234] In 2010, the Committee commended a State party for the steps it had taken to develop 'indicators on gender equality including data on indigenous people, people with disabilities and people from lower socio-economic and rural and remote backgrounds'.[235] In its consideration of Article 14(2)(b), the Committee asked one State party to provide gender-disaggregated information on urban/rural figures for infant mortality,[236] while urging another to 'assess the actual causes of maternal mortality and set targets and benchmarks within a time frame for its reduction'.[237] Focusing on Article 14(2)(c), the Committee recommended that one State party whom it had asked to ensure that birth certificates and identity documents be issued to indigenous rural women should 'establish concrete goals and timetables for this process and provide information on the progress achieved in its next report'.[238] Considering Article 14(2)(f), the Committee asked one State party to put in place 'monitoring mechanisms to regularly assess progress made toward the achievement of established goals, with the participation of tribal chiefs and women's organisations'.[239]

---

[228] CO China, CEDAW/C/CHN/CO/6 (2006) para 28; GR 24 para 25.

[229] CO Papua New Guinea, CEDAW/C/PNG/CO/3 para 45. See also GR 28 para 29; CO Democratic People's Republic of Korea, A/60/38, 33rd Session (2005) para 60; CO Guyana, A/60/38, 33rd Session (2005), para 308; CO Sierra Leone, CEDAW/C/SLE/CO/5 (2007) paras 17, 31, and 34, CO Ukraine, CEDAW/C/UKR/CO/7 (2010) para 45.

[230] GR 27 paras 24, 32, and 47.   [231] GR 27 para 24.

[232] CO South Africa, A/53/38/Rev.1, 19th Session (1998) paras 135–6.

[233] CO Guyana, A/60/38, 33rd Session (2005) para 291; CO Panama, CEDAW/C/PAN/CO/7 (2010) para 15; CO Uzbekistan, CEDAW/C/UZB/CO/4 (2010) paras 11–12; List of Issues and Questions Uganda, CEDAW/C/UGA/Q/7 (2010) paras 1, 5, and 26; CO Bolivia, CEDAW/C/BOL/CO/4 (2008) para 17; CO Egypt, CEDAW/C/EGY/CO/7(2010) para 17; CO Russian Federation, CEDAW/C/USR/CO/7 (2010) paras 42 and 53; CO China, CEDAW/C/CHN/C0/6 (2006) para 11; cf African Protocol art 8.

[234] CO Lebanon, CEDAW/C/LBN/CO/3 (2008) para 37; CO Poland, CEDAW/C/POL/CO/6 (2007) para 27.

[235] CO Australia, CEDAW/C/AUS/CO/7 (2010) para 2.

[236] CO Uzbekistan, CEDAW/C/UZB/OC/4 (2010) paras 34–5.

[237] CO Sierra Leone, CEDAW/C/SLE/CO/5 (2007) para 35.

[238] CO Bolivia, CEDAW/C/BOL/CO/4 (2008) para 19.

[239] CO Sierra Leone, CEDAW/C/SLE/CO/5 (2007) para 21.

F. Reservations

One State party, France, has formally entered two reservations to Article 14. The first is arguably a declaration. It relates to Article 14(2)(c) on social security and guarantees 'that women who fulfil the conditions relating to family or employment required by French legislation for personal participation shall acquire their own rights within the framework of social security'. The second, to Article 14(2)(h), provides that the article 'should not be interpreted as implying the actual provision, free of charge, of the services mentioned in that paragraph'.

During the consideration of France's sixth periodic report, Committee member Mr Flinterman raised the issue, noting that 'the reservation to Article 14(2)(h) did not appear to restrict the State Party's obligations under the Convention' and should therefore be withdrawn.[240] The French representative responded by saying that withdrawing the reservation to 14(2)(h) was 'imminent'. With regard to Article 14(2)(c), the representative noted that there had been major changes to the French legal system since ratification and that the government was prepared 'to conduct a fresh round of consultations'.[241] The Committee encouraged the State party to finalize the withdrawal of the Article 14(2)(c) reservation. It further noted that the State party should 'initiate as soon as possible the procedure to withdraw its declaration and reservation to Article 14(2)(h), which in the opinion of the Committee have the character of an interpretive declaration'.[242]

Although not citing Article 14, the reservations of some States to Articles 2(f) on modifying or abolishing discriminatory customs and practices and Article 5(a) can have a negative impact on rural women. In addition, reservations relating to succession to customary and other titles is problematic for rural women, as it means that they cannot succeed to chieftaincy and other hereditary titles that have great symbolic and, in some cases, practical importance. This limits their participation rights.[243]

Moreover, reservations to Articles 15 on equality before the law and freedom of movement and 16 on family life, have a significant impact on rural women's enjoyment of their rights. Specifically, limitations pertaining to equality in women's access to property, including discriminatory inheritance laws, have a particular impact on rural women because frequently their well-being is tied to access to land and related property. Implementation of Article 14(2)(g) is thus affected. The Committee's requests to States parties to withdraw these reservations have gone largely unheeded.[244]

---

[240] CEDAW, 'Summary Record of the 817th Meeting', UN Doc CEDAW/C/SR/.817 (2008) para 14.
[241] Ibid paras 31–2.   [242] CO France, CEDAW/C/FRA/CO/6 (2008) para 11.
[243] See reservations for Cook Islands, Lesotho, Micronesia and Niger available at: <http://treaties.un.org/> 31 December 2010. See also Papua New Guinea, CEDAW/C/PNG/CO/3 (2010) paras 25, 26, and 45.
[244] See GR 21 paras 41, 42, and 44–7; CO Egypt, CEDAW/C/EGY/CO/7 (2010) para 13. F Raday, 'Culture, Religion and Gender' (2003) *International J of Constitutional L* 663; J Connors, 'The Women's Convention in the Muslim World' in JP Gardener (ed), *Human Rights as General Norms and a State's Right to Opt Out* (1997) 85.

Article 15

1. States Parties shall accord to women equality with men before the law.

2. States Parties shall accord to women in civil matters a legal capacity identical to that of men, and the same opportunities to exercise that capacity. In particular they shall give women equal rights to conclude contracts and to administer property and shall treat them equally in all states of procedure in courts and tribunals.

3. States Parties agree that all contracts and all other private instruments of any kind with a legal effect which is directed at restricting the legal capacity of women shall be deemed null and void.

4. States Parties shall accord to men and women the same rights with regard to the law relating to movement of persons and the freedom to choose their residence and domicile.

* I would like to thank Allison Sherrier for her research assistance on the chapters on arts 9 and 15.

A. Introduction

Article 15(1) states in simple and explicit language the norm on equality between men and women before the law that underpins the entire Convention. Article 15(1) is followed by additional provisions which deal with equality in regard to women's legal capacity in specific areas of civil law, and the same right as men to acquire a domicile and by implication to be governed by a legal system of their choice, through freedom of movement and residence. This article must be understood in the context of the evolving meaning of the concept of 'equality before the law'.

Constitutional provisions on equality in domestic jurisdictions and international human rights instruments use the phrase 'equality before the law' and 'equal protection of the law'. 'Equal protection of the law' represents an expansion of the concept of equality that emerged from Enlightenment ideologies in the Western liberal democratic tradition of the eighteenth and nineteenth centuries.[1] 'Equality before the law' means that everyone is subject to the same system of law, with equal access to the same courts and tribunals, and has the same right to non-discriminatory administration of justice. 'Equality before the law' is thus inherently connected to the idea of non-discrimination in law enforcement and in all courts—civil, criminal, and administrative.[2] The concept has expanded to 'equal protection of the law'. This phrase is broader in scope, and includes the idea of equality and non-discrimination in the substantive content of law. Laws and procedures should conform to a standard of equality and non-discrimination and non-arbitrariness, affording equal protection to all through the legal system.

Over time, these two phrases have been combined in defining the legal guarantees of equality. UDHR Article 7 declares that 'all persons are equal before the law and entitled without discrimination to equal protection of the law'. ICCPR Article 26 uses the same language to combine the two concepts. It expands upon this norm by adding that 'the law shall prohibit any discrimination and guarantee to all persons equal and effective protection against discrimination on any grounds' including sex. National constitutions and regional human rights treaties also combine the phrases 'equality before the law' and 'equal protection of the law' as one norm.[3] CEDAW builds on these earlier provisions through its specificity to women.

Courts in domestic jurisdictions with constitutions that refer only to 'equality before the law' have interpreted them as affording equal protection of the law in all areas of governance.[4] The Fourteenth Amendment of the US Constitution, adopted in 1868, refers only to 'equal protection of the law' but has been interpreted to cover the concept of non-arbitrary enforcement of the law by courts and administrative agencies.[5] The Canadian Charter of Rights and Freedoms and the new Constitution of South Africa, both of which

---

[1] M Nowak, 'Civil and Political Rights' in J Symonides (ed), *Human Rights Concepts and Standards* (2000) 69, 98.

[2] PG Polyviou, *The Equal Protection of the Laws* (1980) 1–5; Constitution of West Germany art 3(1); Constitution of Ireland art 40(1); Canadian Bill of Rights 1960 s 1(b).

[3] eg Constitution of India art 14; Constitution of Sri Lanka art 12(1); Constitution of the Republic of South Africa (1996) s 9; Constitution of Colombia art 13; Canadian Charter of Rights and Freedoms (1985) s 15; Banjul Charter s 3; ACHR art 24; ECHR art 14 and Protocol No 12 (TS 177, 2000).

[4] G Hogan and G Whyte, JM Kelly (eds): *The Irish Constitution*, 3rd edn (1994) 712–43. cf PW Hogg, *Constitutional Law of Canada*, 4th edn (1997) 1240–1.

[5] LG Forer, *Unequal Protection: Women, Children, and the Elderly in Court* (1991) 36–44; Polyviou (n 2 above) 4.

were adopted after the CEDAW Convention came into force in 1981, have incorporated definitions of equality that expand even beyond the combined standard of 'the right to equality and equal protection of the law' to include 'equal benefit of the law'.[6]

Article 15 of the Convention only addresses equality before the law. However, Article 2 of the Convention creates the positive requirement for States parties to ensure legal protection of the rights of women and to enforce this protection through the judiciary. Article 15 enables women to effectively use the legal protections guaranteed under Article 2. Together, these articles provide women with the necessary legal support to claim all the other rights of the Convention. With equality before the law and equal protection of the law guaranteed, women become empowered to demand the standards of equality outlined by the Convention.[7]

The Committee has not interpreted the phrase 'equality before the law' with specific reference to Article 15. Articles 15 and 16 are often considered together. One reason is that both provisions are based on DEDAW Article 6, creating the impression that Article 15 strengthens Article 16. Equality before the law does not seem to have been envisaged as it can be interpreted: to reinforce Articles 1 and 2. General Recommendation 21 reflects the same approach. It considers equality in the family and comments on sub-articles in Article 15 that are linked to Article 16. Moreover, when the Committee arrives at Article 15 towards the end of the time-consuming constructive dialogue with States parties, there is a perception that equality issues raised by Article 15 have already been dealt with. Hence, there is a tendency to move on to Article 16. This approach is compounded by the fact that the vast majority of women from developed countries are not affected by issues covered by Article 15, such as civil law standards on matters of legal capacity or contracts.

The Committee's use of the phrase in general recommendations and concluding observations, however, establishes a broad norm of equality which addresses discrimination in impact. This focus on equality in fact is clear from its use of the phrase 'equality before the law' and 'on a basis of equality with men' in general recommendations[8] and its emphasis on incorporating the norm of equality before the law, in conjunction with laws prohibiting discrimination based on sex, in several concluding observations.[9] The recognition of a right to equality is considered a manifestation of respect for human dignity as underlined in DEDAW and the CEDAW Preamble.

B. Travaux Préparatoires

Article 15 of the Convention was based on DEDAW Article 6, which dealt with the areas covered by Articles 15 and 16.[10] The inclusion of these articles as Part IV of the Convention, which was originally entitled Civil and Family Rights,[11] reflects this link. DEDAW Article 6(1) prefaces the provisions on equal rights of women with a reference to 'safeguarding

---

[6] Canadian Charter of Rights and Freedoms s 15(1); Constitution of the Republic of South Africa (1996) s 9.

[7] See the discussion in chs on arts 2 and 3.

[8] GR 21 (on arts 9, 15, and 16) and GR 25 reflect the concept of substantive equality. GR 19 includes 'equal protection under the law' in para 7(e) as an aspect of CEDAW art 1.

[9] CO Jordan, A/55/38, 22nd Session (2000) para 168; CO Barbados, A/57/38, Exceptional Session (2002) para 225; CO Costa Rica, A/58/38, 29th Session (2003) para 52. See discussion below in Section D. II. : Substantive equality.

[10] UN doc E/CN.6/573 (1973) para 71.   [11] UN doc A/C.3/33/L.47/Add.2 (1978).

the unity and harmony of the family, which remains the basic unit of any society', then goes on to address equality in legal capacity and women's right to freedom of movement. DEDAW Article 6(2) deals with the equal status of husband and wife. Article 15 thus reinforces Article 16, linking the legal standards of non-discrimination in family relations and personal and legal status.

The Convention drafting discussions focused on the importance of specifically recognizing women's legal capacity and legal status to 'perform legally binding acts'.[12] The aspect of equal personal and property rights of women using a male comparator emerges in the discussions suggesting that 'equality before the law' was also meant to refer to equality and non-discrimination in the content of the law or 'equal protection of the law'. *Locus standi* ('standing') or status in civil and criminal cases and equal rights in all stages of procedure in courts and tribunals were also raised as important issues that should be covered in Article 15.

I. Article 15(1)

Some interventions in the discussions on Article 15(1) focus on the need to remove obstacles imposed in legal systems that fail 'to accord recognition and dignity to the status of women as adult individuals'.[13] These disabilities are often based on consideration of women as minors in domestic legal systems. This general recognition of equality before the law is similar to the guarantee set forth in ICCPR Article 26 and reinforces the applicability of this guarantee to women as a fundamental human right.[14] In addition, this guarantee has a broad reach as Article 15(1) clearly was meant to include both criminal and civil legal procedures. This is indicated in the text of the Convention itself by the conscious use of the word 'law' with no limiting category in this provision as compared to the reference specifically to 'civil matters' in Article 15(2) and, impliedly, in Article 15(3).

II. Article 15(2)

The discussions on the 'same opportunities to exercise' legal capacity in Article 15(2) were linked to the need for identical ages of majority for women and men.[15] Discussions at the drafting stage also indicate that recognizing women's legal capacity to contract was not meant to eliminate other restrictions on legal capacity such as insanity.[16] These interventions reflect awareness of some legal cultures that classify women, minors, and insane persons together as persons who lacked legal capacity.[17]

Additionally, some State delegations pointed out during the drafting process that ICCPR Article 16 on legal personality was not meant to address legal capacity to act.[18] Therefore, no international conventions existed that specifically guaranteed 'women the right, on the same terms as men, to perform legally binding acts'.[19] The specific recognition in Article 15(2) that women have a 'legal capacity identical to that of men' to conclude

---

[12] LA Rehof, *Guide to the Travaux Préparatoires of the UN Convention on the Elimination of All Forms of Discrimination against Women* (1993) 162 and 167; A Tomoko, 'Article 15: Equality of Men and Women before the Law' in Japanese Association of International Women's Rights (ed) *Convention on the Elimination of All Forms of Discrimination against Women: A Commentary*, Japanese Association of International Women's Rights (1995) 281, 283–6.

[13] UN Doc E/CN.6/591 (1976) para 153. See also Rehof (n 12 above) 164.   [14] ICCPR art 26.

[15] Rehof (n 12 above) 165.   [16] UN Doc A/C.3/33/L.47/Add.2 (1978) para 186.

[17] Rehof (n 12 above) 165.   [18] UN Doc E/CN.6/552 (1972) para 58.

[19] UN Doc E/CN.6/573 (1973) para 94.

legal agreements and contracts addresses this concern. This language reflects both the need to recognize women's legal capacity and the need to avoid conflict with limitations on legal capacity relating to insanity or minority.

III. Article 15(3)

Article 15(3) stands out from the other articles in that it does not begin with the mandate 'State Parties shall'. Rather, Article 15(3) asserts that 'State Parties agree' to make certain contracts and other legal instruments null and void if they fall under this provision. This is the language in the original draft adopted by the CSW.[20] The language 'States agree' may have followed from one of the earliest suggestions in the CSW Working Group that the new convention include a provision stating that States parties 'undertake to remove any restrictions on the capacity and competence of women'.[21] In 1976, the CSW considered and adopted Article 15(3) with the phrase 'States agree' already in place and without any alternative suggestions—indicating that the drafters reached a consensus on the language early on.[22]

The more controversial section of Article 15(3) was the addition of the phrase 'other private instruments with any kind of legal effect'. Some States felt that this phrase would have the effect of nullifying existing private agreements and would, therefore, create a 'disquieting legal vacuum'.[23] This concern was rebutted by the understanding that the purpose of this phrase was to prevent abuse of the right to contract granted in the Convention by not allowing women to waive this right.[24] Additionally, the words 'other private instruments' are meant to allow this provision to apply broadly to include both commercial contracts and civil matters of a private nature.[25]

IV. Article 15(4)

The guarantee of the right to freedom of movement in Article 15(4) comes from DEDAW Article 6(1). The Convention drafters added the right of a woman to choose her own residence or domicile. The discussions on Article 15(4) indicate that the words 'domicile' and 'residence' were both used because domicile meaning 'permanent home' was not synonymous with residence, which can refer to a person's current, but not necessarily permanent, place of habitation. Some drafts of Article 15(4) only included the word 'residence',[26] but Belgium proposed adding 'domicile' because some legal systems make a distinction between the two concepts, and this provision is intended to include the freedom for women to choose both their domicile and their residence.[27]

This provision necessarily applies equally to married and unmarried women because it must be read in conjunction with Article 1, which defines discrimination against women 'irrespective of marital status'. Some States objected to Article 15(4) on the ground that women did not have freedom of movement and choice of residence under Islamic or national law.[28]

---

[20] UN Doc E/CN.6/589 (1974) 41; UN Doc E/CN.6/608 (1976) para 137. See also UN Doc A/C.3/33/L.47/Add.2 (1978) para 181.

[21] UN Doc E/CN.6/AC.1/L.2 (1974) 7.   [22] UN Doc E/CN.6/608 (1976) para 137.

[23] UN Doc A/C.3/33/L.47/Add.2 (1978) para 180.   [24] Ibid para 183.   [25] Ibid para 184.

[26] UN Doc E/CN.6/591/Add.1/Corr.1 (1976) paras 87, 95, and 104.   [27] Ibid 6.

[28] UN Doc E/CN.6/608 (1976) para 134; Rehof (n 12 above).

C. Issues of Interpretation

I. Article 15(1)

All the sub-sections of Article 15 follow the broad statement of equality before the law found in Article 15(1), yet these subsequent sections specifically refer to equality in legal capacity and in civil matters. This could be interpreted to mean that the phrase 'equality before the law' in Article 15 is limited to its narrower meaning of equal access to civil courts and tribunals and non-discriminatory administration of justice. However, the Committee applies this provision to address issues of equal protection of the law as well. Therefore, the right to equality before the law must be interpreted broadly. It encompasses all decision-making bodies, executive or judicial, including civil, criminal, and administrative courts and tribunals. Article 15 also applies to traditional legal systems.

Equal legal capacity is linked to women's achieving equality in status within the family. Several issues of women's civil legal capacity are also covered in Article 16(1)(d), 16(1)(f), and 16(1)(g). Women's right to administer property is covered in specific language in Article 15(2) as well as Article 16(1)(h).

The link between legal capacity and women's status in the family has been recognized and explored in General Recommendation 21, describing the specific interventions required to implement Article 15. Addressing the linkage between Articles 15 and 16 in General Recommendation 21 paragraphs 25 to 29, the Committee highlighted the need to transform family relations in light of the basic equality standard stated in Article 15 and to create the context for responding to the discrimination addressed in Articles 15 and 16.

The Committee rarely notes Article 15 specifically, but many concluding observations of a general nature refer to the need for law reform to conform to Articles 15 and 16.[29] As a general and fundamental statement of women's status in the law, Article 15(1) could be invoked to deal with areas not specifically covered by other articles. For example, Article 15(1) could be used to raise gender equality issues connected with trade unions and responses to conflict and natural disasters.[30] Aspects of substantive law and procedure that deny equal protection under the law to women affected by violence in these situations could also be appropriately considered under Article 15(1). This approach would reinforce the transformative potential of this section.

1. *Equality and Administration of Criminal Justice*

Article 15(2)–(4) clearly contemplate a standard of equality before the law with reference to proceedings connected with civil law. However, as the phrase 'equality before the law' in Article 15(1) in general contemplates equality in the enforcement of the law, it can be read

---

[29] CO Suriname, A/57/38, 27th Session (2002) para 68; CO Mauritania, CEDAW/C/MRT/CO/1 (2007) para 44; CO Kenya, CEDAW/C/KEN/CO/6 (2007) para 44; CO Tanzania, CEDAW/C/TZA/CO/6 (2008) para 51; CO Malawi, CEDAW/C/MWI/CO/6 (2010) para 43; CO Guinea-Bissau, CEDAW/C/GNB/CO/6 (2009) para 42; CO Myanmar, CEDAW/C/MMR/CO/3 (2008) para 47; CO Tuvalu, CEDAW/C/TUV/CO/2 (2009) para 52; CO Vanuatu, CEDAW/C/VUT/CO/3 (2007) para 39; CO Timor-Leste, CEDAW/C/TLS/CO/1 (2009) para 46.

[30] CO Nicaragua, A/56/38, 25th Session (2001) paras 293 and 297; CO Sri Lanka, A/57/38, 26th Session (2002) paras 286, 298, and 299; CO India, CEDAW/C/CIND/CO/3 (2007) para 50; CO Lebanon, A/63/38, 40th Session (2008) paras 200 and 266; CO Morocco, A/63/38, 40th Session (2008) paras 256–7; CO Burundi, A/63/38, 40th Session (2008) para 137; GR 19 paras 7(c) and 16.

to include criminal proceedings.[31] The *travaux préparatoires* also suggest that there was a concern with including criminal proceedings in Article 15.[32] The administration of criminal justice is also included in General Recommendation 19, in the context of violence against women.

Article 15(1) is a response to the gender bias in legal systems, in particular, in relation to criminal law and family law. For example, according to English common law principles, the concept of unity of personality between husband and wife (coverture) meant that adultery was a criminal offence and women were punished more harshly for the offence in both family law and criminal law.[33] In addition, the substantive law on rape, including marital rape, failed to recognize the infringement of a woman's right to bodily integrity,[34] and although a variety of laws existed that might apply to violent attacks (eg assault and battery), the concept of domestic violence was not recognized until the twentieth century. Procedural laws were equally biased; Sir Edward Coke remarked that 'in some cases women are by law wholly excluded to bear testimony'.[35] This exclusion was based on the reasoning that women were considered unreliable witnesses because of their 'frailty'.[36] Women also were not eligible to serve on juries in trials for crimes prosecuted under the common law.[37]

Other legal systems also reflected patriarchal values in the area of criminal justice. Civil law, which was influenced by the Roman law concept of *patria potestas* or the all powerful male head of the family, also had discriminatory provisions relating to sexual crimes and criminal justice.[38] For this reason, it criminalized adultery, did not provide for the criminal prosecution of marital rape, and excluded women from sitting as judges or serving on juries.

Despite Islamic law provision for women's separate legal identity and contractual and property rights, the approach to women in the criminal justice system sometimes reflected inherent gender biases. Procedurally, a woman's evidence was considered half the value of a man's.[39] However, it should be noted that the Quran has been interpreted to treat men and women equally,[40] and gender bias has mainly arisen in different countries through legal codification, jurisprudence, and application.[41]

Legal systems in Asia, Africa, and Latin America that were colonized by the British, French, Spanish, and other European powers absorbed a good deal of the legal values of the colonizers and retained many of them after independence.[42] Examples of such

---

[31] Polyviou (n 2 above) 2.　　[32] Rehof (n 12 above) 164.

[33] See generally W Blackstone, *Commentaries on the Laws of England*, 16th edn (1825) 144 ff. See also, Sir Edward Coke, *Institutes of the Laws of England* (1797) Vol. I cited in Forer, (n 5 above) 96 and 238. See generally, H Barnett, *Introduction to Feminist Jurisprudence* (1998) for an analysis of violence against women based on traditional legal systems and feminist theory.

[34] Blackstone (n 33 above); Hogan and Whyte (n 4 above) 713.　　[35] Cited in Forer (n 5 above) 96.

[36] Ibid.　　[37] Ibid.

[38] eg Mendez, 'A Comparative Study of the Impact of the Convention on the Rights of the Child: Law Reform in Selected Civil Law Countries' in *Protecting the World's Children* (2007) 100. CF Amerasinghe, *Aspects of the Actio Injuriarum in Roman Dutch Law* (1966) 180–1.

[39] S Sardar Ali (ed), *Conceptualising Islamic Law, CEDAW and Women's Human Rights in Plural Legal Settings*, UNIFEM South Asia Regional Office New Delhi (2006) 19–20; Pakistan's Rules of Evidence, art 17 of the Qanun-e-Shahadat Order, 1984.

[40] Sardar Ali (n 39 above).

[41] See EY Krivenko, *Women, Islam and International Law* (2009) 44, 57, and 58.

[42] For more a detailed history, see generally ES Burrill, RL Roberts, and E Thornberry (eds), *Domestic Violence and the Law in Colonial and Postcolonial Africa* (2010).

remnants are the lack of criminal punishment for marital rape and lack of criminal laws prohibiting domestic violence in many States.[43] The British codification of criminal law, evidence, and procedure was introduced in India and absorbed into other colonies in Asia and Africa. This eighteenth- to nineteenth-century colonial law still provides the foundation of criminal law in many former colonial States, which has not (even in the countries of the Indian subcontinent) been changed for centuries. The Committee has commended the revocation or modification of such discriminatory provisions.[44]

Changes in international criminal justice have taken account of feminist concerns about gender bias, for example, the assertion of the jurisdiction of the International Criminal Court with respect to such crimes as rape, sexual slavery, enforced prostitution, enforced sterilization, and other forms of sexual violence.[45] In addition, regional tribunals have developed jurisprudence to recognize rape and domestic violence as infringements of a woman's right to bodily integrity.[46] International and regional jurisprudence on rape and sexual violence provides support for similar developments in States parties' domestic law and, in turn, allow States parties to give effect to the guarantees of Article 15.

National Constitutions and fundamental rights guarantees on freedom from torture and the right to equality and equal protection and the right to life have been used to transform legal approaches to domestic violence, rape, and torture.[47] However, many States parties continue to impose the burden of these discriminatory principles on women in criminal law and procedure, and there has been no holistic or consistent approach to legislative reform based on Convention commitments. Gender bias in criminal investigations, sentencing policies, and award of compensation to victims of sexual crimes, as well as State party inaction in law enforcement, remain significant obstacles to equality.[48] In 2008, the Committee considered gender bias issues in national judicial procedures through the individual complaints process.[49] In *Vertido v The Philippines*, the Committee found a violation of State obligations under Articles 2 and 5 based on

[43] CO Lao People's Democratic Republic, A/60/38, 32nd Session (2005) para 109; CO Gabon, A/60/38, 32nd Session (2005) para 236; CO Guinea, A/56/38, 25th Session (2001) para 96; CO Haiti, CEDAW/C/HTI/CO/7 (2009) para 24. See also, Jessica Neuwirth, 'Inequality Before the Law: Holding States Accountable for Sex Discriminatory Laws under the Convention on the Elimination of all Forms of Discrimination against Women and Through the Beijing Platform for Action' (2005) 18 *Harvard Human Rights J* 19, 24.

[44] eg CO Uruguay, CEDAW/C/URY/CO/7 (2008) paras 24 and 25; CO Chile, CEDAW/C/CHI/CO/4 (2006) para 6; CO Trinidad and Tobago, A/57/38, 26th Session (2002) para 136; CO Cape Verde, CEDAW/C/CPV/CO/6 (2006) para 19.

[45] Barnett (n 33 above) 251–75; Rome Statute of the International Criminal Court (1998) art 7(1)(g), crime against humanity, and art 8(2)(b)(xxii) violation of the laws and customs of war.

[46] *MC v Bulgaria*, Application 39272/98 (ECHR 2003); Prosecutor v Kunarac, Kovac & Vukovic (Judgment) ICTY-96–23/1-T (22 February 2001).

[47] See also, *Discriminatory Laws in Nepal and their Impact on Women*, Forum for Women, Law and Development, Kathmandu, Nepal (2006) for case law and S Goonesekere (ed), *Violence, Law and Women's Rights in South Asia* (2004) 13, 30–32.

[48] CO Vietnam, A/56/38, 25th Session, (2001) para 258; CO Maldives, A/56/38, 24th Session (2001) para 137; CO Egypt, A/56/38, 24th Session (2001) para 344; CO Nicaragua, A/56/38, 25th Session (2001) paras 308–9; CO Sri Lanka, A/57/38, 26th Session (2002) para 284; CO Peru, A/62/38, 37th Session (2007) para 610; CO Pakistan, A/62/38, 38th Session (2007) paras 17–18; CO Singapore, A/62/38, 39th Session (2007) para 27; CO India, CEDAW/C/IND/CO/3 (2007) para 22; CO Bolivia, A/63/38, 40th Session (2008) para 67; CO Lebanon A/63/38, 40th Session (2008) paras 186–7.

[49] *Vertido v The Philippines* CEDAW Communication 18/2008 (2010) CEDAW/C/46/D/18/2008. See also the discussion in ch on the Optional Protocol.

numerous gender-based myths and stereotypes in the country's rape laws and in judicial interpretation and application of the rape laws.[50]

II. Article 15(2)

Article 15(2) and 15(3) are closely connected. Article 15(2) sets out the general norms regulating legal capacity in civil matters. Article 15(3) prohibits contracts that are contrary to the standard of Article 15(2).

The standards stated in Article 15(2) are clearly restricted to non-criminal matters as indicated by the use of the term 'civil'. In common law legal systems, the term distinguishes between the criminal and non-criminal (civil) branches of the law. Similarly, in civil law systems, 'civil' denotes legal relations between private persons as opposed to legal relations between a private person and a holder of state power. The term 'civil' was included in Article 15(2) to denote this distinction. The Committee has not adopted a broader interpretation of 'civil', as, for example, the European Court of Human Rights has in applying the term to encompass all issues concerning economic interests of individuals.[51]

1. Identical Legal Capacity

The use of the term 'identical' in reference to a male comparator as opposed to 'same' or 'equal' emphasizes the response to legal cultures which completely denied women legal capacity. In the English common law and the Roman law-based codes, a married woman was subject to 'coverture' or 'marital power'. This meant that she had no separate legal status or identity. Women were classified with minors and insane persons as lacking all legal capacity. Women in non-marital relationships were also discriminated against in important areas of law such as family support. Cohabitation relationships were not recognized by law to create an obligation of support. Proving the paternity of a non-marital child was difficult because corroboration of women's evidence on paternity was required in order to claim maintenance for the child.[52] These factors inhibited women's legal capacity to claim rights, and similar values are reflected in other legal traditions.[53] According to the text of Manu in Hindu Law, 'the father protects a woman in childhood, her husband protects her in youth, and her sons protect her in old age; a woman is never fit for independence.'[54] Though some schools of Islamic law recognize the property and contractual rights of women, one State party to the Convention has reserved Article 15 asserting that full legal

---

[50] *Vertido v The Philippines* (n 49 above) paras 8.8 and 8.9. cf *AT v Hungary* CEDAW Communication 2/2003 (2005) CEDAW/C/32/D/2003.

[51] eg, *Case of Gorou v Greece (No 2)*, Application 12686/03 (ECtHR 2009) para 26; *Case of Syngelidis v Greece*, Application 24895/07 (ECtHR 2010) para 29. The ECtHR also finds personal rights and a right to education to be civil in nature, see *Ganci v Italy*, Application 41576/98 (ECtHR 2004) para 25 and *Emine Araç v Turkey*, Application 9907/02 (ECtHR 2008) para 25. See also, J Frowein and W Peukert, *Europäische Menschenrechtskonvention: EMRK Kommentar* (2009) art 6, paras 15–18.

[52] Common law: Blackstone (n 33 above); Sir Edward Coke (n 33 above) 96, 238; Barnett (n 33 above) Part II at 83–117, Part III at 121–204; Hogan and Whyte (n 4 above) 713. Civil law: Mendez (n 38 above); HR Hahlo, *The South African Law of Husband and Wife*, 5th edn (1985) 1–13; RW Lee, *An Introduction to Roman-Dutch Law* (5th edn, 1953) 63 and 241. S Goonesekere, 'Family Support and Maintenance: Emerging Issues in Some Developing Countries with Mixed Jurisdictions' (2006) 44 *Family Court Rev* 361, 361–75.

[53] See generally, RJ Cook, 'Reservations to the Convention on the Elimination of all Forms of Discrimination against Women' (1990) 30 *Virginia J Intl L* 643, 699–700.

[54] P Diwan, *Law of Adoption, Minority Guardianship and Custody* (1989) 178.

capacity and contractual freedom for women is incompatible with Sharia law.[55] In some States, the belief that women lack capacity, and are, therefore, always dependent on a man, is reflected in laws requiring a male guardian to be present for a legal act to be valid.[56] Discriminatory laws affecting women's legal capacity pervade all areas of law including property law, access to health care, and employment law.[57]

By focusing on achieving identical legal capacity with a male comparator, the Convention addresses the disempowerment of women because of their sex that is embedded in major legal systems. However, achieving formal equality is not the only standard in the Convention. Article 15(2) states that women must be given the 'same opportunities to exercise' legal capacity. This necessarily means that a supportive context must be created by providing for exercise of the social and economic rights incorporated in the Convention, especially Article 10 on women's education and Articles 3 and 14 which implicitly address women's poverty. Legal literacy schemes that provide information on exercising legal rights are a crucial aspect of the standards set by Article 15(2). Implementation of Articles 5 and 16 are also critical to women's exercising their right as persons with full legal capacity.

2. *Equality in Contractual and Property Transactions*

The importance of equality in contractual and property transactions has been highlighted in General Recommendation 21. Article 13(a) and (b), on equal rights to family benefits, bank loans, mortgages, and credit also underscore the significance of this aspect of Article 15. The relationship between Articles 15 and 13 is yet another example of how the rights in Article 15 are linked with many of the other rights enumerated in the Convention. Under Article 15(2), a woman has the right to own and administer property; Article 13 makes it possible for women to exercise this right to land by giving women equal access to the financial means necessary to procure and manage property. In addition, owning property is often a prerequisite to obtaining loans and building credit.

In English common law the status of married women as legal minors meant that they were under guardianship or wardship, thereby lacking independent contractual capacity and dependent on a male head of household who was perceived as the breadwinner. Coverture meant that the husband acquired ownership of a woman's property on marriage. This disempowered legal status of married women meant that they had no right to enter into contracts or own or manage property.[58] Married women's testamentary capacity or right to alienate or dispose of property was not recognized. Civil law systems recognized the husband's marital power in relation to contract and property, although in some exceptional situations a married woman could acquire separate property rights and enter into contracts. The first legislative reforms to confer equal property and contractual rights in English law, the Married Women's Property Act (1882), equated the status of a married woman to a '*femme sole*'—a single woman (whether never married, widowed, divorced or otherwise) who was not dependent on a man and who could own property. Civil law

---

[55] D Pearl, *A Textbook on Muslim Personal Law*, 2nd edn (1987) 75; Sardar Ali (n 39 above) 20. United Arab Emirates' Reservation to CEDAW art 15(2); see also Krivenko (n 41 above) 126–7. Other Islamic States parties have entered more general reservations to any provisions that conflict with Sharia law.

[56] eg Zimbabwe Family Code, Customary Marriages Act Ord 5/1917; Civil Code of Cameroon art 74 Ord 81-02. See also CO Libyan Arab Jamahiriya, CEDAW/C/LBY/CO/5 (2009) para 38; generally, Krivenko (n 41 above).

[57] Neuwirth (n 43 above) 23–4.

[58] Forer (n 5 above) 33; *Bromley's Family Law*, 10th edn (2007) 106–48.

systems, however, considered unmarried women as lacking the full legal capacity of a male. Hence, they needed a male guardian to perform legal actions. Both systems discriminated against unmarried women who had children or lived with a man as a cohabiting partner.[59]

Islamic law and some customary laws in Asia and Africa confer equal access to property and contract rights for women. In these systems, women are often recognized as economic producers and persons with legal capacity, property and contractual rights, and rights of use or rights to ownership and management of separate economic assets.[60] The number and variations of customary systems, however, militates against accounting for all situations, and many customary systems deny women these rights. Many States parties still retain property and contract laws which do not confer equal rights on women at all stages of their lives.[61] Even where legal reform has been introduced, women may in fact lack management rights and access to property.

Legal restraints on contract and property rights also have the effect of denying women equal opportunities in relation to other matters, such as access to credit, loans, suretyship, and other commercial transactions in their own name. Women can be prevented from obtaining social security benefits and pensions as widows or female heads of household and cohabiting partners or never-married women. They may be unable to act as executors and administrators of family property. These legal limitations have sometimes been challenged in national courts, citing the Convention or constitutional provisions that reflect its norms.[62]

The Committee regularly highlights the lack of consistent effort to reform these laws to provide for women's contractual capacity and property management rights.[63]

---

[59] Hahlo (n 52 above); Barnett (n 33 above) 127 and 133; Lee (n 52 above) 63–71; Bromley (n 58 above).

[60] Sir J Muria, 'Personal Common law Conflicts and Women's Human Rights' in A Byrnes, J Connors, and L Bik (eds), *Advancing the Human Rights of Women: Using International Human Rights in Domestic Litigation* (1997) 138; Sardar Ali (n 39 above) 21; P Kameri-Mbote, 'Gender Dimensions of Law, Colonialism and Inheritance in East Africa: Kenyan Women's Experience,' International Environment Law Research Centre (2002); S Goonesekere, 'Colonial Legislation and Sri Lankan Family Law: The Legacy of History' in KM de Silve et al (eds), *Asian Panorama* (1990) 193; MV Tran, 'The Position of Women in Traditional Vietnam' in KM de Silve et al (eds), *Asian Panorama* (1990) 274–83.

[61] eg CO Kenya, CEDAW/C/KEN/CO/6 (2007) paras 41–2; CO Liberia, CEDAW/C/LBR/CO/6 (2009) paras 40–1; CO Mauritania, CEDAW/C/MRT/CO/1 (2007) paras 43–4. See generally eg Federation of Women Lawyers-Kenya and International Women's Human Rights Clinic, 'Kenyan Laws and Harmful Customs Curtail Women's Equal Enjoyment of ICESCR Rights' (2008) Georgetown University Law Center 12–13.

[62] F Butegwa, 'Using the African Charter on Human and Peoples' Rights to Secure Women's Access to Land in Africa' in RJ Cook (ed), *Human Rights of Women: National and International Perspectives* (1994) 495–9; *Ephraim v Pastory* (n 47 above); *Joli v Joli* and *Noel v Toto* (n 47 above); Case 5 SCC 125 *Kishwar and others v State of Bihar and others* AIR 1996 (1996) India Supreme Court (applying constitutional norms reflecting CEDAW standards); *Daniel Latifi v Union of India*, Civil No 868/1986 (decided 28 September 2001); *Annama v Ibrahim*, CA 419/757 (1982) [Sri Lanka].

[63] Property Rights: CO Nepal, A/59/38, 30th Session (2004) para 217; CO Sri Lanka A/57/38, 26th Session (2002) para 274; CO Vietnam, A/56/38, 25th Session (2001) para 271; CO Bolivia, A/63/38, 49th Session (2008) para 71; CO Morocco, A/63/38, 40th Session (2008) para 251; CO Namibia, A/62/38, 37th Session (2007) paras 255 and 277. Contracts, Commercial transactions and Social Security: CO Bolivia, A/63/38, 40th Session (2008) paras 67 and 78; CO Lebanon, A/63/38, 40th Session (2008) para 192; CO Bangladesh, A/59/38, 31st Session (2004) para 232; CO Morocco, A/58/38, 29th Session (2003) paras 174–5. Family Responsibility: CO Namibia, A/62/38, 37th Session (2007) para 255; CO Sri Lanka, A/57/38, 26th Session (2002) para 297; CO Venezuela, A/61/38, 34th Session (2006) para 312; CO Burundi, A/63/38, 40th Session (2008) para 123.

3. *Equality in Access to Procedures in Civil Courts and Tribunals*

Since Article 15(2) refers to equal treatment in courts and procedures as an aspect of civil legal capacity, it covers the legal issue of *locus standi* as well as *de facto* capacity to participate fully in civil courts and administrative and other tribunals. States parties have the related positive obligation under Article 2 of ensuring that tribunals and other public institutions are accessible to women. The importance of affording access to justice in this manner has been emphasized in General Recommendation 21 and concluding observations.[64]

The concept of coverture and marital power in common law and civil law respectively, meant that a married woman had no *locus standi in judicio* or legal capacity and status in court. She did not have the right to sue and be sued in court in her independent capacity, without the assistance of her husband. Her right to represent children in court was limited. Unmarried women also faced discrimination in civil actions for family support because of their limited rights to claim maintenance. These limitations have been eliminated in many jurisdictions but have been retained in others in the post-colonial period.[65]

III. Article 15(3)

The phrase 'States parties agree' seems to refer to a consensus regarding the need for time-bound targets to ensure that contracts or private instruments that seek to restrict women's legal capacity do not have any legal consequences. This provision seeks to prevent women from signing away their rights under contracts and agreements. States parties must demonstrate to the Committee that in their legal system provisions restricting women's legal capacity in a contract or other instrument are illegal and void, as contrary to public policy.

Article 15(3) refers to 'all other private instruments of any kind' and, therefore, covers non-commercial agreements such as those relating to medical procedures, marriage contracts, and access to pharmaceuticals, as well as commercial agreements. Though Article 15(2) refers only to equal rights to conclude contracts, the general reference to legal capacity in the text and Article 15(3) clarify that women should also have equal rights to conclude private instruments of a non-contractual nature, such as creating a will or trust. As indicated in the section on the *travaux préparatoires*, the purpose of this broad language was to ensure that Article 15 was as inclusive as possible.[66]

Article 15(3) makes discriminatory contracts and private agreements 'null and void'. This creates an expectation that provisions of civil and private legal instruments will be unenforceable if the aim (or result) of the provision is to discriminate against women. This has been interpreted narrowly to nullify the offensive provision and not the entire instrument.[67] For example, Article 15 creates an expectation that States parties will enact

---

[64] CO Tunisia, A/57/38, 27th Session (2002) para 184; CO Romania, CEDAW/C/ROM/CO/6 (2006) para 12; CO Turkmenistan, CEDAW/C/TKM/CO/2 (2007) para 12; CO Colombia, CEDAW/C/COL/CO/6 (2007) para 18; CO Vanuatu, CEDAW/C/VUT/CO/3 (2007) para 39; CO Kenya, CEDAW/C/KEN/CO/6 (2007) para 41; CO Tuvalu, CEDAW/C/TUV/CO/2 (2009) para 18.

[65] Hahlo (n 52 above); Lee (n 52 above) 63–4; Forer (n 5 above); Bromley (n 58 above) 107.

[66] See above, section B: *Travaux Préparatoires*. See also UN Doc A/C.3/33/L.47/Add.2 (1978) para 184.

[67] eg *Uganda v Matovu*, Criminal Session Case No 146 of 2001, High Ct of Uganda at Kampala (21 October 2002). See also, United Kingdom Understanding on art 15(3) ('understands the intention of this provision to be that only those terms or elements of a contract or other private instrument which are discriminatory in the sense described are to be deemed null and void, but not necessarily the contract or instrument as a whole').

and enforce legislation ensuring that women can enter into their own marriage contracts without a guardian. Article 15(3) can also be interpreted to nullify marriage contracts that aim at 'restricting the legal capacity of women', such as the capacity to own property as a married woman. To avoid nullifying marriage contracts and other important private instruments, States parties and national courts applying Article 15(3) may interpret the provision to void only the restricting clause of contracts and private agreements and not the entire contract.

IV. Article 15(4)

This provision addresses specific circumstances in which women's right to freedom of movement is circumscribed. It complements the Convention standards on nationality in Article 9 and elaborates on UDHR Article 13 and ICCPR Article 12. These rights are also recognized in regional human rights instruments such as the American Convention on Human Rights, the African Charter, the European Convention on Human Rights, and national constitutions.[68]

Domicile determines the jurisdiction and the law applicable to personal status.[69] Domicile and residence are connected concepts since domicile is defined as a person's legal home or place of permanent residence.[70] Domicile in common and civil law is acquired at birth, and can be changed by acquiring a new domicile of choice in another State. In the case of married women, the concept of consortium and marital rights and duties imposed a legal obligation to live together as husband and wife. Coverture and the husband's marital power in the common law and civil law respectively, meant that the husband's domicile at the time of marriage determined the domicile of the wife, and this followed any change in his domicile even when she did not reside with him. His domicile was thus considered the domicile of the spouses, and a refusal by the wife to move with him was a ground for divorce in the common law. A woman who wanted matrimonial relief had to file her case in the courts of the jurisdiction in which her husband was domiciled.[71] In States influenced by these legal systems the principle of domicile seriously limited a woman's choice of residence and movement until the dissolution of the marriage and the acquisition of a new domicile of choice. Family support laws that emphasized the concept of male head of household and breadwinner reinforced this principle.

In Islamic law the husband's right to control and guidance has been interpreted as justifying restrictions on the wife's freedom of movement. However, other interpretations of the relevant text suggest that such a right is inconsistent with other principles relating to women's legal capacity and status.[72]

The Convention in Article 15(4) rejects the principle of dependent domicile. General Recommendation 21 and concluding observations have addressed the necessity of States parties eliminating the concept of the wife's dependent domicile and restrictions on

---

[68] ACHR art 22; Banjul Charter art 12; ECHR Protocol 4 art 2 (TS 046, 1963); Canadian Charter of Rights and Freedoms (1985) s 6(1); Constitution of the Republic of South Africa (1996) s 21; Constitution of India art 19(d) and (e).

[69] Hahlo (n 52 above) 128. eg *Bromley's Family Law* (n 58 above) 265–6.

[70] Fawcett, Carruthers, and North (eds), *Cheshire, North, & Fawcett: Private International Law*, 14th edn (2008) 154–71.

[71] Ibid 178 and 966; *Le Mesurier v Le Mesurier* (1895) 1 NCR 160 PC, overruled by Supreme Court of Sri Lanka in *Ashokan v Ashokan* (1994) 1 Sri LR 413.

[72] Sardar Ali (n 39 above) 35.

freedom of movement and choice of residence. The Committee has called upon States parties to end the practice of male guardianship over women, which results in *de facto* restrictions on women's freedom of movement.[73]

D. Equality in Context

I. Formal Equality

Each provision of Article 15 gives priority to achieving formal equality, on the basis of a male comparator, as the fundamental first step. Some States parties still entrench formal inequality with a range of discriminatory laws that impose legal disabilities on women. The Committee consistently recognizes the importance of this first step.[74] The expansive interpretation of Article 15(1) to include the concept of equal protection of the law, as discussed above in the Introduction, requires States parties to take measures to implement substantive equality. General Recommendations 19, 21, and 25 are particularly relevant to such efforts.

II. Substantive Equality

Achieving substantive equality with respect to Article 15 means that legal literacy and legal aid must be accessible to women to claim their rights in civil courts and tribunals. This is especially relevant in States parties where poverty, illiteracy, lack of rights awareness, and access to information and legal literacy programmes, as well as cultural norms relating to women's movements in public, may place relief through the formal legal system, courts and tribunals, out of the reach of a majority of women. Gender insensitivity among the judiciary and law enforcement agencies may contribute to problems of access to justice through these fora.[75] The Committee has called upon States parties to address these problems proactively.[76]

The Committee, in linking Articles 15 and 16 in its concluding observations, has shown that achievement of equality standards set out in Article 16 on family relations will also

---

[73] See the discussion in ch on art 9; GR 21 paras 9–10; CO Saudi Arabia, CEDAW/C/SAU/CO/2 (2008) paras 15–16; CO Myanmar, CEDAW/C/MMR/CO/3 (2008) paras 42–3; CO United Arab Emirates, CEDAW/C/ARE/CO/1 (2010) para 46; CO Libyan Arab Jamahiriya, CEDAW/C/LBY/CO/5 (2009) paras 37–8; CO Yemen, CEDAW/C/YEM/CO/6 (2008) paras 387–8.

[74] CO Serbia, CEDAW/C/SCG/CO/1 (2007) para 8; CO Myanmar, CEDAW/C/MMR/CO/3 (2008) para 47; CO Tuvalu, CEDAW/C/TUV/CO/2 (2009) para 52. See the discussion in ch on art 9. On women's activism for law reform: *Discriminatory Laws in Nepal and their Impact on Women* (n 47 above); I Jalal, 'The Campaign for Gender Equality in Family Law' in *Dossier 27: Muslim Minorities (Women Living Under Muslim Law)* (2005); S Goonesekere (ed), *Violence, Law and Women's Rights in South Asia* (2004) 13, 30; MI Plata, 'Reproductive Rights as Human Rights: The Colombian Case' in RJ Cook (ed), *Human Rights of Women: National and International Perspectives* (1994) 515.

[75] Goonesekere (n 74 above).

[76] CO Guinea, A/56/38, 25th Session (2001) para 135; CO Vietnam, A/56/38, 25th Session (2001) para 257; CO Uzbekistan, A/56/38, 24th Session (2001) para 177; CO Egypt, A/56/38, 24th Session (2001) para 345; CO Sri Lanka, A/57/38, 26th Session (2002) para 285; CO Bhutan, A/59/38, 30th Session (2004) para 18; CO Nigeria, A/59/38, 30th Session (2004) para 298; CO Malaysia, A/61/38, 35th Session (2006) para 12; CO Greece, A/62/38, 37th Session (2007) paras 527–8; CO Peru, A/62/38, 37th Session (2007) paras 614–15; CO Pakistan, A/62/38, 38th Session (2007) para 23; CO Maldives, A/62/38, 37th Session (2007) para 20; CO India, CEDAW/C/IND/CO/3 (2007) paras 18–19; CO Saudi Arabia, A/63/38, 40th Session (2008) paras 27 and 37; CO Bolivia, A/63/38, 40th Session (2008) para 85; CO Burundi, A/63/38, 40th Session (2008) para 129; *Vertido v The Philippines* (n 49 above) para 8.9.

have an impact on achieving the standards of equal access to courts and tribunals, especially in the areas of divorce, child custody, and maintenance.[77]

An important aspect of women's access to civil courts and tribunals is gender sensitivity and gender balance in the judiciary and administrative tribunals. Some administrative tribunals and bodies that engage in alternative dispute resolution, such as mediation tribunals and customary courts, may not have any female representation on the panels or may not allow women to represent petitioners. The Committee has addressed the need for judicial training and a gender balance in all courts and tribunals and the need to bring informal dispute resolution institutions within these norms.[78]

III. Transformative Equality Including Elimination of Structural Obstacles and Gender Stereotyping

Some specific aspects of Article 15 such as the phrase 'same opportunities to exercise [legal] capacity' and equal treatment 'in all stages of procedure in courts and tribunals' highlight the need to achieve a model of transformative equality, eliminating gender stereotypes and institutionalized discrimination in the judicial process, as well as addressing the need for a transformation of attitudes and values in the family and community towards women. States parties must address the aspect of indirect discrimination and distinctions which impact or have the effect of creating disadvantages and denying equality to women. According to the Committee, interventions could include the introduction of temporary special measures according to Article 4(1) and General Recommendation 25, especially in regard to giving women access to legal aid and legal literacy, and providing access to courts and tribunals.[79] General Recommendation 21 states the necessity of achieving substantive equality in regard to property rights, since economic policies and women's lack of awareness of their rights can restrict or deny their access to land ownership, or to effective management and control even when equal rights of ownership and possession are recognized by law.[80]

Women's equal access to justice and full realization of their economic and social rights, thus, are closely linked. This linkage is also emphasized in Article 8 of the Protocol on the Rights of Women in Africa, setting specific regional standards for access to justice, which cover a wide range of socio-economic rights.

---

[77] eg CO Suriname, A/57/38, 27th Session (2002) para 68; CO Mauritania, CEDAW/C/MRT/CO/1 (2007) para 44; CO Kenya, CEDAW/C/KEN/CO/6 (2007) para 44; CO Tanzania, CEDAW/C/TZA/CO/6 (2008) para 51; CO Malawi, CEDAW/C/MWI/CO/6 (2010) para 43; CO Guinea-Bissau, CEDAW/C/GNB/CO/6 (2009) para 42; CO Myanmar, CEDAW/C/MMR/CO/3 (2008) para 47; CO Tuvalu, CEDAW/C/TUV/CO/2 (2009) para 52; CO Vanuatu, CEDAW/C/VUT/CO/3 (2007) para 39; CO Timor-Leste, CEDAW/C/TLS/CO/1 (2009) para 46.

[78] CO Uzbekistan, A/56/38, 24th Session (2001) para 177; CO Pakistan, A/62/38, 38th Session (2007) para 24; CO Bangladesh, A/59/38, 31st Session (2004) para 242; CO Namibia, A/62/38, 37th Session (2007) para 265. Judicial training: CO Togo, CEDAW/C/TGO/5 (2006) para 11; CO Turkmenistan, CEDAW/C/TKM/CO/2 (2006) para 12; CO Ghana, CEDAW/C/GHA/CO/5 (2006) para 13; CO China, CEDAW/C/CHN/CO/6 (2006) para 12; CO Costa Rica, A/58/38, 29th Session (2003) para 53.

[79] CO Guinea, A/56/38, 25th Session (2001) para 132; CO Sweden A/56/38, 25th Session (2001) para 346; CO Kuwait, A/59/38, 30th Session (2004) para 79; CO Pakistan, A/62/38, 38th Session (2007) para 32; CO Maldives, A/62/38, 37th Session (2007) para 25; CO Singapore, A/62/38, 39th Session (2007) paras 19–20; CO Bolivia, A/63/38, 40th Session (2008) paras 90–1; CO India, CEDAW/C/IND/CO/3 (2007) paras 42–3.

[80] GR 21. See also K Rittich, 'The Properties of Gender Equality' in P Alston and M Robinson (eds), *Human Rights and Development Towards Mutual Reinforcement* (2005) 87.

IV. Intersectional Discrimination

General Recommendation 25 specifically addresses the need to ensure that women do not suffer additional discrimination because of the interface of gender and other factors. Women can suffer multiple discriminations as to all the provisions of Article 15, particularly on the basis of ethnicity or religion.

Article 15 provisions on equality, legal capacity, and domicile are challenged in many countries by the State's 'defence' of the need to respect diversity and the cultural rights of minority communities. Similarly, the right to freedom of religion is represented as a 'conflicting' human right which prevents elimination of discriminatory provisions in this area. Concluding observations on the reports of States parties indicate a range of such practices.[81] Customs such as a rapist marrying a victim are justified as a community response that prevents a woman being marginalized in her own community because of an act of sexual violence.

The Committee has consistently adopted a universalist approach to women's human rights, in general recommendations as well as in its concluding observations which refer to these practices. The Committee has emphasized the importance of developing harmonized civil codes in place of diverse personal laws to create common legal rights based on the norms of Articles 15 and 16.[82] It has encouraged reference to comparative jurisprudence and legal developments in similar jurisdictions fertilized by the same legal tradition such as between States with legal systems based on Islamic law, on common law, or on civil law.[83] The transformative potential of the Convention is best captured in the Protocol on Women's Rights in Africa. It is the only regional instrument that has set a broad spectrum of standards that are based on and indeed reinforce the Convention and the Committee's views on the changeable and evolving nature of culture and tradition.

The very application of personal laws to some groups of women has been deeply influenced by the concepts of unity of personality, marital power, and male breadwinner derived from colonial legal systems. Colonial legislation applied these concepts to ensure

---

[81] F Raday, 'Culture, Religion and CEDAW's art 5(a)' in HB Schöpp-Schilling and C Flinterman (eds), *The Circle of Empowerment: 25 Years of the UN Committee on the Elimination of Discrimination against Women* (2007) 68, 76; M Siesling, 'Cultural Defence in Criminal Law,' paper presented at Colloquium: Women's Human Rights v Religion, Culture and Tradition, Ministry of Foreign Affairs Netherlands, 12 May 2009; CO Guinea, A/56/38, 25th Session (2001) paras 122 and 128; CO Nepal, A/59/38, 30th Session (2004) paras 208–9; CO India, CEDAW/C/IND/CO/3 (2007) paras 8 and 28; CO Bolivia, A/63/38, 40th Session (2008) para 67; CO Saudi Arabia, A/63/38, 40th Session (2008) para 232; CO Lebanon, A/63/38, 40th Session (2008) para 187; CO Egypt, A/56/38, 24th Session (2001) para 344; CO Turkey, A/60/38, 32nd Session (2005) paras 363–4; CO Jordan, A/62/38, 39th Session (2007) para 23; CO Pakistan, A/62/38, 38th Session (2007) para 5. Cultural and religious practices of Roma and Muslim women in Europe: CO Greece, A/62/38, 37th Session (2007) paras 529, 530, and 545; CO Sweden, A/63/38, 40th Session (2008) para 378.

[82] GR 14; GR 19 para 11; GR 21 paras 7, 8, 16, 25, and 26; CO Greece, A/62/38, 37th Session (2007) para 545; CO Jordan, A/62/38, 39th Session (2007) para 12; CO India, A/62/38, 37th Session (2007) paras 10–11; CO Sri Lanka, A/57/38, 26th Session (2002) para 275; CO Bangladesh, A/59/38, 31st Session (2004) para 248; CO Burundi, A/63/38, 40th Session (2008) para 127; CO Lebanon, A/63/38, 40th Session (2008) para 178; CO Tanzania, CEDAW/C/TZA/CO/6 (2008) para 51; CO Timor-Leste, CEDAW/C/TLS/CO/1 (2009) para 46; CO Liberia, CEDAW/C/LBR/CO/6 (2009) para 41; CO Cook Islands, CEDAW/C/COK/CO/1 (2007) para 23; CO Papua New Guinea, CEDAW/C/PNG/CO/3 (2010) para 26.

[83] CO Malaysia, A/61/38, 35th Session (2006) para 14; CO Maldives, A/56/38, 24th Session (2001) paras 140–1; CO Maldives, A/62/38, 37th Session (2007) paras 241–2; CO Pakistan, A/62/38, 38th Session (2007) para 29; CO Singapore, A/62/38, 39th Session (2007) para 16; CO Jordan, A/62/38, 39th Session (2007) para 12; CO Sri Lanka, A/57/38, 26th Session (2002) para 275; CO United Arab Emirates, CEDAW/C/ARE/CO/1 (2010) para 46.

that a woman who married a man governed by a system of personal law became subject to his personal law, whereas a woman lost her right to be governed by her own personal law upon marriage to a man not governed by that system. *Lovelace v Canada*, a case before the CCPR, raised this issue on the basis of legislation that prior to amendment in 1983 reflected this approach.[84] In the *Lovelace* case, an ethnic Indian woman lost her right to remain on her Indian reservation upon her marriage to a non-Indian male, and this restriction continued after the marriage was dissolved. The CCPR found this combined discrimination based on the claimant's gender and ethnicity to be a violation of her rights.[85] These male-biased principles, as pointed out in the *Lovelace* case, result in a limitation on a woman's choice of residence. They clearly infringe the standards set by Article 15(1) and 15(4).

Article 15 and the Committee's general recommendations draw attention to the need to focus on multiple discriminations suffered by rural women, women in low income households, and female heads of households, including widows and older women. They may not have independent legal status, or any of the specific property and other rights referred to in Article 15, because of economic factors, customary practices, and laws and policies that focus exclusively on men as heads of households. Restrictions on remarriage of widows, domestic violence, including forced marriage, and denial of access to courts and tribunals can prevent single women, including widows and older women, from having equal opportunities to access legal remedies in civil matters.[86] The Committee has clarified these realities, as well as the importance of eliminating both formal discrimination and disadvantages in impact because of these factors in a number of State party reviews.[87]

Women with mental disabilities have suffered multiple discriminations in the law because their legal incapacity has been institutionalized in legal systems both as women and as 'insane persons'. The latter are sometimes grouped in some systems with minors and suffer the same legal limitations. The concept of 'protection' by a guardian or curator may in fact result in violations of their fundamental human rights, including bodily integrity. The CRPD now deals specifically with this topic, incorporating a definition of discrimination very similar to CEDAW Article 1. The Committee addressed issues concerning mentally disabled women in General Recommendation 15 and in a number of State party reviews.[88]

---

[84] *Lovelace v Canada*, Communication R.6/24 (1981) UNHRC, UN Doc Supp No 40, A/36/40, 166.

[85] Ibid.   [86] GR 27.

[87] GR 21 paras 7, 8, 16, and 28; CO Bangladesh, A/59/38, 31st Session (2004) para 260; CO Malaysia, A/61/38, 35th Session (2006) para 30; CO Thailand, A/61/38, 34th Session (2006) para 274; CO Peru, A/62/38, 37th Session (2007) para 628; CO Nicaragua, A/62/38, 37th Session (2007) paras 585 and 593; CO Bolivia, A/63/38, 40th Session (2008) para 71; CO Andorra, A/56/38, 25th Session (2001) para 47; CO Guinea, A/56/38, 25th Session (2001) para 122; CO Sri Lanka, A/57/38, 26th Session (2002) paras 296–7; CO Burundi, A/63/38, 40th Session (2008) para 125; CO Venezuela, A/61/38, 34th Session (2006) para 312; CO Sri Lanka, A/57/38, 26th Session (2002) para 297; CO Bolivia, A/63/38, 40th Session (2008) para 71; CO France, A/63/38, 40th Session (2008) para 343; CO Ethiopia, A/59/38, 30th Session (2004) para 268.

[88] CO Nicaragua, A/56/38, 25th Session (2001) paras 293 and 297; CO Sri Lanka, A/57/38, 26th Session (2002) paras 286, 298, and 299; CO India, CEDAW/C/IND/CO/3 (2007) para 50; CO Lebanon, A/63/38, 40th Session (2008) paras 200 and 266; CO Morocco, A/63/38, 40th Session (2008) paras 256–7; CO Burundi, A/63/38, 40th Session (2008) para 137; CO Bolivia, A/63/38, 40th Session (2008) para 78; CO Ethiopia, A/59/38, 30th Session (2004) para 268.

E. States Parties' Obligations

I. Nature of the obligation

The obligation of the States parties under Article 15 is indicated in mandatory terms by using the phrase 'shall accord' in Article 15(1), (2), and (4). The Committee has clarified that there is a specific and immediate obligation to promote and implement these standards by law reform that eliminates any limitations on legal capacity in the areas covered by Article 15(2) and 15(4). It has consistently used language that emphasizes the importance of reforming laws and implementing them as quickly as practicable, calling for such law reform to be a 'priority' and for States to 'expedite' or 'accelerate' legal reforms,[89] on occasion explicitly referring to Article 15.[90] The States parties' obligation to respect the broad standard of equality before the law in Article 15, as interpreted by the Committee, requires formal recognition in legal instruments such as constitutions or specific legislation such as gender equality laws.[91] Family law reform, as related closely to the capacity issues addressed in Article 15, often accompanies these formal efforts under Article 15.

Article 15(3), using the phrase 'State Parties agree', establishes a different standard of State obligation. The language suggests an ongoing obligation rather than immediate legal reform to ensure that such contracts and instruments are void, as illegal and contrary to public policy. The obligation under Article 15(3) is negative—a requirement to not enforce restrictive agreements. During the drafting process, one State explained that under this provision 'if a woman voluntarily agreed she would not sign any checks or enter into any contract without her husband's consent, paragraph 3 would make such agreement between husband and wife null and void'.[92] To fulfil this negative obligation, States may have to enact legislation incorporating the norms of Article 15 and provide for judicial review of restrictive agreements.

II. Implementation

International, regional, and domestic constitutional jurisprudence now recognizes that States have a duty to protect individuals from violations of their human rights by both State and non-State actors,[93] which includes violation of one's right to 'equality before the law'. When specific legislation is enacted to guarantee a general norm of equality or to confer equal rights and remove disabilities, private actors are required to conform to these standards. The Committee has emphasized that gender equality norms must not be merely aspirational, but that States parties must make available effective remedies such as

---

[89] CO Mauritania, CEDAW/C/MRT/CO/1 (2007) para 44; CO Malawi, CEDAW/C/MWI/CO/6 (2010) para 43; CO Guinea-Bissau, CEDAW/C/GNB/CO/6 (2009) para 42; CO Timor-Leste, CEDAW/C/TLS/CO/1 (2009) para 46.

[90] CO Kenya, CEDAW/C/KEN/CO/6 (2007) para 44; CO Tanzania, CEDAW/C/TZA/CO/6 (2008) para 51; CO Myanmar, CEDAW/C/MMR/CO/3 (2008) para 47; CO Tuvalu, CEDAW/C/TUV/CO/2 (2009) para 52; CO Vanuatu, CEDAW/C/VUT/CO/3 (2007) para 39.

[91] GR 21 para 49. See, eg, CO Chile, CEDAW/C/CHI/CO/4 (2006) para 9.

[92] UN Doc A/C.3/33/L.47/Add.2 (1978) para 183.

[93] See eg *Vertido v The Philippines* (n 49 above) para 8.9; *AT v Hungary* (n 50 above); cf *Velásquez Rodríguez Case (Interpretation of Compensatory Damages)* Inter-American Court of Human Rights Series C No 4 (29 July 1988), 28 ILM 291 (1989) paras 172–3; *Saheli Women's Resource Centre v Commissioner of Police, Delhi*, AIR 1990 SC 513 (Supreme Ct of India, 1990); *Faiz Mohomed v Attorney General*, 1995 1 Sri LR 372 (Supreme Ct of Sri Lanka).

constitutional litigation and writs for infringement of individual rights by both State and non-State actors.[94]

The 'obligation to protect' requires that women have equal access to remedies for infringement of these rights. This may mean monitoring the impact of conciliation procedures and adopting reasonable requirements of *locus standi*.[95] Human rights groups and activists should be allowed to represent women whose rights are violated, in harmony with the broad concept of *locus standi* incorporated in the Optional Protocol.[96] Public interest litigation is especially relevant in both promoting State accountability to realize social and economic rights regarding access to health, education, and shelter, and ensuring that women have access to the superior courts that hear constitutional cases.[97]

States parties also have a positive obligation to fulfil the social and economic rights enumerated in the Convention—access to health, education, and shelter in particular are essential—to create substantively equal opportunities for women to exercise the rights referred to in Article 15(2), 15(3), and 15(4). While gradual implementation may be justified as a practical matter, the Committee indicates clearly that indefinite postponement of the obligation to fulfil social and economic rights is unacceptable.[98] Monitoring the impact of economic policies, in particular, is essential to realizing women's property and land rights and addressing the reality of gender-based discrimination and disadvantage.[99]

III. Reservations

The Committee has noted that cultural diversity, religion, and domestic law have often been cited by States parties as the basis for entering reservations or declarations to Article 15.[100] The reserving States parties are usually those in which harmonization is a major issue, and they enter reservations or declarations to address the problem of current incompatibility of treaty standards with domestic law. However, some States parties ratify and do not enter reservations or declarations, even though they have not harmonized their domestic law. These States parties are obligated by international treaty law to harmonize their domestic laws immediately but have often done so in an ad hoc manner or have not done so at all.[101]

---

[94] CO Andorra, A/56/38, 25th Session (2001) para 34; CO Singapore, A/56/38, 25th Session (2001) para 89; CO Vietnam, A/56/38, 25th Session (2001) para 244; CO Nicaragua, A/56/38, 25th Session (2001) para 279; CO Pakistan, A/62/38, 38th Session (2007) para 8; CO Colombia, CEDAW/C/COL/CO/6 (2007) para 18; CO Tuvalu, CEDAW/C/TUV/CO/2 (2009) paras 21–2. See also GR 19; Finding and Recommendation in Mexico Inquiry Report CEDAW/C/2005/OP/8 Mexico 27 Jan 2005.

[95] See concluding observations (n 94 above).   [96] See the discussion in ch on the Optional Protocol.

[97] Optional Protocol art 2. See also cases in *Discriminatory Laws in Nepal and their Impact on Women* (n 47 above); Goonesekere (n 74 above) 13, 30. See generally AM Sood, 'Gender Justice through Public Interest Litigation: Case Studies from India' (2008) 41 *Vanderbilt J Transnational L* 833.

[98] CO Chile, CEDAW/C/CHI/CO/4 (2006) para 9; CO Burkina Faso, A/60/38, 33rd Session (2005) paras 335–6; CO Lao People's Democratic Republic, A/60/38, 32nd Session (2005) para 95; CO Nigeria, A/59/38, 30th Session (2004) paras 294 and 304.

[99] GRs 24 and 25, reinforced in CESCR, 'General Comment 20' (25 May 2009) UN Doc E/C.12/GC/20 para 40; Rittich (n 80 above) 87. CO Panama, CEDAW/C/PAN/CO/7 (2010) para 47; CO Ecuador, CEDAW/C/ECU/CO/7 (2008) para 19; CO El Salvador, CEDAW/C/SLV/CO/7 (2008) para 38; CO Jamaica, CEDAW/C/JAM/CO/5 (2006) para 38; CO Egypt, A/56/38, 24th Session (2001) para 351; CO Estonia, A/57/38, 26th Session (2002) para 114; CO Lithuania, A/55/38, 23rd Session (2000) para 161.

[100] Morocco, Tunisia, Algeria, Pakistan, Bahrain, Niger, Oman, Syrian Arab Republic, India, and United Arab Emirates.

[101] CO Nigeria, A/59/38, 30th Session (2004) paras 295–6; CO Nigeria, CEDAW/C/NGA/CO/6 (2008) paras 17–18; CO Yemen, CEDAW/C/YEM/CO/6 (2008) para 46; CO Cameroon, CEDAW/C/CMR/CO/3 (2009) para 13.

Several States parties, particularly Islamic states, have entered reservations to provisions of Article 15, most commonly to Article 15(4). These reservations are usually combined with reservations to Article 9.[102] A few States parties entered general reservations limiting their obligation to introduce initiatives that conflict with Sharia, also covering Article 15. It is in this context that the Committee has consistently, in both general recommendations and concluding observations, adopted an approach of asking States parties to review and withdraw their reservations and declarations, and to set a timetable for doing so. The Committee has been particularly concerned about broad reservations based on cultural diversity and religion, even when a State party has assured that the reservation does not prevent harmonization of its laws with the Convention.[103] In 2008, the Committee specifically referred to reservations to Article 15(4) as contrary to the object and purpose of the Convention.[104]

Some States parties have withdrawn their reservations and have been commended by the Committee for doing so.[105] Others, mainly Islamic states, maintain their reservations to these articles, even when the law has been harmonized.[106] The Committee has encouraged States parties with domestic laws based on Sharia to use comparative jurisprudence in harmonizing domestic law with the Convention norms. Progress has been slow.

The maintenance of these restrictions, and the continuing legal disabilities in domestic law in regard to choice of residence, freedom of movement, and contractual capacity, do not conform to social and economic realities in some of the States parties which have entered reservations and declarations. Low-income women are permitted to enter these countries and live and work overseas as migrant workers. They do so for economic survival. Those engaged in business or professions may also live and work overseas for economic reasons. Women of all classes work as economic producers and traders engaged in contractual transactions. Reservations reflect an insistence on retaining discriminatory norms in domestic law, even when there is an urgent need to bring domestic laws in line with the social and economic realities in women's lives—and with the Convention.

F. Conclusion

At first glance, it appears that there has been relatively little discussion of Article 15 by the Committee in both concluding observations and general recommendations. Considering the fundamental importance of equal legal standing and legal capacity to the realization

---

[102] See the discussion in ch on art 9. Algeria, Morocco, Qatar, Tunisia, Bahrain, Niger, Oman, and Syrian Arab Republic. See Reservations on UN Treaty Database on CEDAW: <http://treaties.un.org/> accessed 31 December 2010.

[103] CO Switzerland, A/58/38, 28th Session (2003) para 100; CO Pakistan, A/62/38, 38th Session (2007) para 13; CO Saudi Arabia, CEDAW/C/SAU/CO/2 (2008) para 10; CO Malaysia, A/61/38, 35th Session (2006) para 9; CO Niger, CEDAW/C/NER/CO/2 (2007) para 10; GR 4, GR 20 and GR 21 paras 41–7.

[104] CO Bahrain, CEDAW/C/BHR/CO/2 (2008) para 16.

[105] CO Brazil, A/58/38, 29th Session (2003) para 91; CO France, CEDAW/C/FRA/CO/6 (2008) para 8; CO Jamaica, A/56/38, 24th Session (2001) para 210; CO Libyan Aran Jamahiriya, CEDAW/C/LBY/CO/5 (2009) para 13; CO Switzerland, CEDAW/C/CHE/CO/3 (2008) para 4; CO Thailand, A/54/38/Rev.1, 20th Session (1999) para 223; CO Turkey, CEDAW/C/TUR/CO/6 (2010) para 4; CO Cook Islands, CEDAW/C/COK/CO/1 (2007) para 5; CO Bangladesh, A/52/38/Rev.1, 17th Session (1997) para 424.

[106] eg CO Morocco, CEDAW/C/MAR/CO/4 (2008) para 14; CO Tunisia A/57/38, 27th Session (2002) para 188. Brazil, France, Ireland, Jordan, Thailand, and Turkey have withdrawn reservations to art 15, see Reservations at <http://treaties.un.org/> accessed 31 December 2010.

of numerous other rights such as health, housing, and economic independence, it would seem that Article 15 should be referred to often by the Committee. A perusal of the Committee's concluding observations, however, indicates that principles embedded in Article 15 are incorporated. For example, concluding observations discussing economic security based on women's ability to own and control land directly relates to Article 15(2), which obligates States parties to ensure that women have capacity equal to that of men to administer property.[107] Other concluding observations refer exclusively to Article 16, or do not refer to any article, when such laws also implicate a woman's legal capacity and freedom to conclude contracts.[108]

The failure of the Committee to rely on Article 15 more regularly is to be regretted in so far as States may not recognize the implicit link in many recommendations. The principles underlying Article 15 are, however, often discussed and should be considered among the most important in the Convention. Legal capacity, property ownership and administration, and equality under the law are necessarily related to other social and economic rights. A specific general recommendation from the Committee giving guidance on each provision of Article 15, rather than one linking it to other provisions, would underscore the importance of this provision.

Article 15 does not specify precise legal reforms since the details of implementation will vary with each legal system. Article 15 does, however, provide a common standard of equality that requires States parties to recognize gender-biased and discriminatory assumptions ingrained in their different legal systems and to address the manner in which these assumptions restrict women's exercise of legal personality.

---

[107] CO Guatemala, CEDAW/C/GUA/CO/7 (2009) para 34; CO China, CEDAW/C/CHN/6 (2006) paras 37–8; CO Chile, CEDAW/C/CHI/CO/4 (2006) paras 9–10; CO Democratic Republic of Congo, A/55/38, 22nd Session (2000) para 230.

[108] CO Libyan Arab Jamahiriya, CEDAW/C/LBY/CO/5 (2009) para 38; CO Saudi Arabia, CEDAW/C/SAU/CO/2 (2008) paras 15–16; CO Yemen, CEDAW/C/YEM/CO/6 (2008) paras 387–8; CO Jordan, A/55/38, 22nd Session (2000) para 172. None of these concluding observations explicitly mentions Article 15(2) in expressing concern over these practices.

Article 16

1. States Parties shall take all appropriate measures to eliminate discrimination against women in all matters relating to marriage and family relations and in particular shall ensure, on a basis of equality of men and women:

(a) The same right to enter into marriage;

(b) The same right freely to choose a spouse and to enter into marriage only with their free and full consent;

(c) The same rights and responsibilities during marriage and at its dissolution;

(d) The same rights and responsibilities as parents, irrespective of their marital status, in matters relating to their children; in all cases the interests of the children shall be paramount;

(e) The same rights to decide freely and responsibly on the number and spacing of their children and to have access to the information, education and means to enable them to exercise these rights;

(f) The same rights and responsibilities with regard to guardianship, wardship, trusteeship and adoption of children, or similar institutions where these concepts exist in national legislation; in all cases the interests of the children shall be paramount;

(g) The same personal rights as husband and wife, including the right to choose a family name, a profession and an occupation;

(h) The same rights for both spouses in respect of the ownership, acquisition, management, administration, enjoyment and disposition of property, whether free of charge or for a valuable consideration.

2. The betrothal and the marriage of a child shall have no legal effect, and all necessary action, including legislation, shall be taken to specify a minimum age for marriage and to make the registration of marriages in an official registry compulsory.

* I greatly appreciate helpful comments on drafts from Prof. Ruth Halperin-Kaddari and Prof. Barthazar Rwezaura as well as research assistance from Taylor Pierce, Lindsey Smith, and Kavinvadee Suppapongtevasadul.

A. Introduction

Article 16 provides for equality between women and men in all aspects of marriage and dissolution of marriage, prohibits child marriage, and provides for States parties to enact a minimum age for marriage and to require marriage registration. The two parts of the article are grounded in and expand on the language of Article 16 of the UDHR and subsequent articulations of the rights stated in that article.

Because 'the family is the natural and fundamental group unit of society',[1] and because marriage remains the norm for the vast majority of women at some point in their lives, the impact on women's lives of inequality between men and women within the construct of marriage is deep and broad. Marriage-based restrictions on women's property rights, mobility, and choice of occupation, and marriage-based imposition of household duties, have major consequences for women's education, economic status, health and ability to avoid or escape violent relationships, and their ability to care for themselves, their children, and others for whom they take responsibility.[2]

The language of the UDHR (and ICCPR Article 23 and ICESCR Article 10(1)) presents a potential tension between traditional concepts of 'protecting' the family unit and the concept that spouses individually have 'equal rights to marriage, during marriage, and at its dissolution'. Pursuing the elimination of discrimination breaks the presumptive privacy barrier that has historically prevented examination of the family equality and power dynamic in the name of 'protecting the family'. Article 16 provides a map for examining that dynamic, indicating that protection of the family requires protection of spouses' individual human rights and promotion of equality between them, rather than maintaining family 'protection' at the expense of its female members.

Customs, traditions, religious law and practice, and gender stereotyping have perhaps a greater impact on implementation of Article 16 than on any other article in the Convention. Family role assignments, and family identity as a whole, are defined through a long history of gender-based stereotypes and patriarchal control of family systems. The gender roles related to the inescapable biology of reproduction place women in a double-edged position of prime nurturer and prime object of control. Legal provisions to promote formal equality may have unintended consequences, such as inadequate post-divorce support awards based on unwarranted assumptions that equal employment laws have an instantaneous impact on women's economic status. Achievement of substantive equality may be particularly challenging, because of deeply held prejudices and accepted cultural traditions and attitudes specifically related to women's reproductive and family roles. Understanding and implementation of Article 5 are central to implementing all parts of Article 16.

Article 16, in conjunction with Articles 2 and 5, requires States parties to prohibit discrimination, to eliminate discrimination in personal status laws, and to address the gender stereotyping and customary and religious law and practice that support persistent inequality within the family. The Committee consistently reviews these three overarching requirements within the framework of Article 2 and General Recommendation 28, commenting on States parties' progress towards their achievement and emphasizing the areas still to be addressed. States parties that formally retain discriminatory laws and

---

[1] UDHR art 16(3).

[2] The literature on discrimination against women in the family is enormous, as is the material on multiple legal systems and on gender issues in specific family law regimes. For overviews see F Banda, *Women, Law and Human Rights: An African Perspective* (2005); A Hellum, J Stewart, SS Ali, and A Tsanga (eds), *Human Rights, Plural Legalities and Gendered Realities: Paths are Made by Walking*, Southern and Eastern African Regional Centre for Women's Law (2007); KM Cuno and M Desai (eds), *Family, Gender, and Law in a Globalizing Middle East and South Asia* (2009); Z Anwar (ed), *Wanted: Equality and Justice in the Muslim Family* (2009); International Council on Human Rights Policy, *When Legal Worlds Overlap: Human Rights, State and Non-State Law* (2009); Organising Committee of the Commission on European Family Law, Series: European Family Law in Action, vols I–IV (2003–2009).

customs are instructed to change them.[3] States parties that have made some effort are commended and are urged to deal with remaining issues.[4] States parties that have taken significant steps to formally abolish discriminatory laws and customs are instructed to focus on implementation and to address attitudes, foster awareness, and promote women's access to legal remedies.[5]

I. Preliminary History

The 1964 Convention on Consent to Marriage, Minimum Age for Marriage and Registration of Marriages (the Marriage Convention)[6] states that abusive marriage 'customs, ancient laws and practices' contravene the UDHR injunction of equality 'as to marriage, during marriage and at its dissolution'. The Marriage Convention was a watershed call for States to firmly commit to eliminating discrimination in marriage customs and practices. However, the Convention fails to specify a minimum age of marriage and allows for marriage by proxy.[7] These limitations resonate to the present, as early and forced marriages remain among the most difficult discriminatory practices to eliminate.

The 1967 Declaration on the Elimination of All Forms of Discrimination against Women (DEDAW) addresses equality in the family somewhat more specifically. DEDAW Article 6(1)(a) provides for equality in the acquisition, management, and inheritance of property, 'including property acquired during marriage', and Article 6(2) refers to equal consent to marriage, equal rights during marriage and at its dissolution, and equal rights with respect to children. Article 6(3) reiterates the prohibition of child marriage and

---

[3] CO Albania, A/58/38, 28th Session (2003) para 61; CO Bangladesh, A/59/38, 31st Session (2004) para 248; CO Burundi, A/56/38, 24th Session (2001) para 56; CO Cameroon, CEDAW/C/CMR/CO/3 (2009) paras 15–17; CO Indonesia, CEDAW/C/IDN/CO/5 (2007) paras 18–19; CO Jordan, CEDAW/C/JOR/CO/4 (2007) para 18; CO Lebanon, CEDAW/C/LBN/CO/3 (2008) para 19 ('urgently'; Committee had recommended the same in 2005, A/60/38, 60th Session (2005) para 100); CO Malawi, CEDAW/C/MWI/CO/5 (2006) para 14; CO Nicaragua, A/56/38, 25th Session (2001) para 313 and CEDAW/C/NIC/CO/6 (2007) para 8 (reiterating recommendation of 2001); CO Rwanda, CEDAW/C/RWA/CO/6 (2009) para 42; CO Samoa, A/60/38, 32nd Session (2005) para 65; CO Singapore, CEDAW/C/SGP/CO/3 (2007) para 16; CO Syrian Arab Republic, CEDAW/C/SYR/CO/1 (2007) para 18.

[4] These Concluding Observations refer to proposed legal (statutory) changes that are not yet enacted or to statutes that address some but not all of the equality obligations under art 16. CO Benin, A/60/38, 33rd Session (2005) para 148; CO Burkina Faso, A/55/38, 22nd Session (2000) para 282; CO Cambodia, CEDAW/C/KHM/CO/3 (2006) para 34; CO Japan, CEDAW/C/JAM/CO/5 (2006) para 18; CO Maldives CEDAW/C/MDV/CO/3 (2007) paras 12 and 36; CO Morocco, CEDAW/C/MAR/CO/4 (2008) paras 35–9; CO Turkey A/60/38, 32nd Session (2005) para 364; CO Tanzania, CEDAW/C/TZA/CO/6 (2009) para 30; CO Uruguay, CEDAW/C/URY/CO/7 (2008) para 47 (citing earlier review as well as CRC recommendation).

[5] CO Switzerland CEDAW/C/CHE/CO/3 (2009) para 38 (tax structure); CO Eritrea, CEDAW/C/ERI/CO/3 (2006) para 29; CO Ethiopia, A/59/38(Supp), 30th Session (2004) para 244; CO Jamaica, CEDAW/C/JAM/CO/5 (2006) para 26; CO Kyrgyzstan, CEDAW/C/KGZ/CO/3 (2008) para 18; CO Mauritius, CEDAW/C/MAR/CO/5 (2006) para 33; CO Mozambique, CEDAW/C/MOZ/CO/2 (2007) paras 23 and 45; CO The Netherlands, CEDAW/C/NLD/CO/4 (2007) para 20; CO Togo, CEDAW/C/TGO/CO/5 (2006) para 13; CO The United Kingdom, CEDAW/C/UK/CO/6 (2009) para 291 (study impact of 1996 family law).

[6] Convention on Consent to Marriage, Minimum Age for Marriage and Registration of Marriages (hereinafter Marriage Convention) (adopted 7 November 1962, entered into force 9 December1964) 521 UNTS 231.

[7] Marriage Convention art 1(2). The Marriage Convention has only fifty-four ratifications and accessions, some undertaken since CEDAW's entry into force. Some States parties reserved art 1(2), thereby rejecting any possibility of marriage by proxy.

the requirement of a minimum age of marriage and prohibits betrothal of 'girls before puberty'. It also confirms the importance of marriage registration.

II. Travaux Préparatoires

Rehof notes that the record of negotiations on the text of the Convention reveals various geopolitical and philosophical tensions, including 'the role of religion in society'.[8] Many of these issues continue to affect Convention implementation.

The issues that gave rise to the most complex discussions during the drafting process relate to the characterization and rights of unmarried women, particularly with respect to child custody and out of wedlock children; guardianship, wardship and adoption; and equal property rights. The Third Committee Working Group of the Whole (Working Group) deliberated on Article 16 in eight meetings in November 1978.

Discussion of the chapeau centred on inclusion of the phrase 'whether married or unmarried'. It was deleted because it was part of the definition of discrimination in Article 1. However, Cuba indicated that it should remain because of the 'special nature of this article'.[9] There was a similar discussion during consideration of Article 16(1)(d) relating to care and custody of children. The draft language adopted by the CSW had indicated that women have the 'same rights and responsibilities, whether married or not'. The United Kingdom proposed amended language: 'irrespective of their marital status'. Egypt 'expressed reservations with respect to this subparagraph'.[10] However, the language 'irrespective of their marital status' was adopted in the final version of Article 16(1)(d).

The text relating to guardianship and adoption that was transmitted by the CSW to the UNGA and referred on to the Third Committee, read: '(e) Recognition of equal rights to be guardians and trustees, and also of an equal right to adopt children'. The discussion of this provision in the Third Committee Working Group centred on inclusion of language deferring to the varying national laws with respect to guardianship, wardship, trusteeship, and adoption. A number of States do not provide for adoption at all as being contrary to religious law. Many provide that fathers are the sole guardians of children. The representative of Bahrain offered an amendment that addressed the issue:

Recognition of equal rights and duties of both men and women in respect of wardship of children in such a way that does not run counter to the interests of the children and conform with the rules and regulations of society derived from the provision of the applicable religious and positive laws prevailing in the society.[11]

Sweden proposed language in accordance with the Declaration on the Rights of the Child[12] ('the interest of the children shall be paramount'), and Morocco proposed deletion of the entire provision. 'After a long discussion on whether the ideas of the subparagraph should be retained or deleted,' the Working Group determined to 'try to find a generally acceptable formulation'.[13] Ultimately, Bahrain proposed somewhat different language that captured the idea of varying forms of protection and control of children: 'or similar social forms when these concepts exist in national legislation'. Additional

---

[8] LA Rehof, *Guide to the Travaux Préparatoires of the United Nations Convention on the Elimination of All Forms of Discrimination against Women* (1993) 2.

[9] UN Doc A/34/60 (1979) paras 192–3, 195–6, 198.   [10] Ibid paras 209, 211–13.

[11] Ibid para 217.

[12] Declaration on the Rights of the Child (20 November 1959) UNGA Res 1386 (XIV).

[13] UN Doc A/34/60 para 223.

discussion ensued, in which the representatives of Algeria, Bangladesh, Pakistan, and Morocco supported this amendment, and the representative of Portugal pointed out that 'the conformity of national legislation comes at a later stage of ratification. If a similar procedure had been applied, it would not have been possible to adopt the International Convention on the Suppression and Punishment of the Crime of Apartheid'.[14]

After further discussion this language was adopted.[15]

The wording of Article 16(1)(h) relating to equal property rights in marriage was also discussed at length. The source of contention was property regimes in a number of States. Morocco proposed an amendment that recognized 'equal rights of both spouses in respect of the ownership, acquisition, management, administration, enjoyment and disposition of property, whether free of charge or for a valuable consideration' but continued with a provision to allow for unequal or no inheritance rights: 'The same shall apply in the case of inheritance of property, whether it be property owned by one spouse or property "acquired" in common, unless the internal law relating to personal status and inheritance provides otherwise'.[16]

The representatives of Bangladesh, Bahrain, and Mauritania supported this amendment. Others supported deleting it. The United Kingdom, noting that the proposed amendment's language would allow a State to change its law to eliminate equality in inheritance, offered a formulation that did not defer to personal status law. After several other amendments were proposed, the Working Group determined to transmit alternative texts to the Third Committee 'as a consensus could not be reached'.[17] In the next Working Group meeting, the United States and Morocco proposed an amendment that omitted any reference to inheritance.[18] This version was adopted, thereby eliminating the reference to equal inheritance rights that had been included in DEDAW Article 6(1)(a). This issue remains problematic for women in many States parties and is addressed in General Recommendation 21.

The Working Group revisited the issue of unmarried women in considering whether to include a third paragraph in Article 16(2), relating to the rights of children born out of wedlock and their mothers. The CSW had adopted a paragraph on this issue. The Third Committee discussion 'repeatedly brought up the argument of whether the convention applied only to women or should incorporate the child born out of wedlock. Opinion was divided, and some delegates considered the subject too sensitive to be treated in an international instrument'.[19] The representative of Spain noted that 'if the Convention was to appropriately reflect existing reality', the issue of discrimination against 'so-called illegitimate children and unmarried mothers' should be included, and the representative of Belgium agreed. The representative of the USSR noted, *inter alia*, that the Commission on Human Rights was at that time working on a draft Convention on the Rights of the Child. The majority agreed to delete the paragraph.[20]

The suggestions and compromises made during the drafting process foreshadowed the challenges to Convention implementation related to culture, tradition, and various State party approaches to personal status law. The Committee adopted General

---

[14] Ibid para 230.   [15] Ibid paras 217–32.   [16] Ibid para 234.   [17] Ibid para 252.
[18] Ibid para 253.
[19] Rehof (n 8 above) 185. Rehof refers specifically to Egypt, Iran, and Pakistan as considering the issue of unmarried mothers 'very sensitive', ibid 186.
[20] UN Doc A/34/60 paras 256–8.

Recommendation 21 to note the contextual obstacles to equality in the family and to provide guidance to States parties in eliminating these obstacles.

III. General Recommendation 21

The Committee adopted General Recommendation 21, on Articles 9, 15, and 16, in 1994. After more than ten years of experience reviewing States parties' reports, the Committee took the opportunity of the International Year of the Family (1994) to examine these 'three articles in the Convention that have special significance for the status of women in the family'.[21] The prefatory paragraphs emphasize that the Convention 'goes further' than the UDHR and earlier treaties relating to the rights of women, 'by recognizing the importance of culture and tradition in shaping the thinking and behaviour of men and women and the significant part they play in restricting the exercise of basic rights by women'.[22] General Recommendation 21 is an unequivocal confirmation of the relationship between culture and tradition, equality in the family, and women's equal enjoyment of all other human rights. It is explicit in remarking the inequality perpetuated by patriarchal traditions and customs, and in recommending their elimination. General Recommendation 21 also broke new ground in specifically stating that polygamy 'contravenes a woman's right to equality with men, and should be discouraged and prohibited'.[23] As of December 2010, the Committee is engaged in adoption of a General Recommendation on the Economic Consequences of Marriage, *de facto* Relationships, and Their Dissolution.[24]

B. Issues of Interpretation

I. Chapeau

The chapeau includes a number of concepts that are not defined within the Convention and which have evolved with global changes in social attitudes and structures. The Committee has not addressed all of these issues directly, but its concluding observations and decisions under the Optional Protocol provide some guidance as to its approach.

1. 'All Appropriate Measures . . . and in Particular'

Most of the chapeau is in language common to those of the other articles, discussed at some length in the chapter on Article 2. Application of Article 16 is illuminated additionally by comments made by several members of the Committee, in dissents to two decisions under the Optional Protocol, on the meaning of 'and in particular'. They suggest that the wording of the chapeau indicates the intent to cover all issues related to equality in the family, including those not enumerated in the specific language of Article 16.[25] The Committee has not commented further on this question. However, its practice in general recommendations and concluding observations, for example, with respect to polygamy

---

[21] GR 21 para 5.   [22] Ibid para 3.   [23] Ibid para 14.

[24] Working title as of 2010. The general approach is outlined in the Concept Note on the General Recommendation on Economic Consequences of Marriage and its Dissolution, CEDAW/C/2009/II/WP.2 (2009).

[25] *Group d'Intérêt pour le Matronyme*, Communication No 12/2007, CEDAW/C/44/D/12/2007 (2009); *SOS Sexisme*, Communication No 13/2007, CEDAW/C/44/D/13/2007 (2009). In both cases the majority did not address the language of the chapeau.

and violence against women, has included elaboration well beyond the specific language of the Convention.

2. The 'Same Rights and Responsibilities'

The subject matter of Article 16 raises a special issue with respect to States parties' obligations to provide the 'same rights and responsibilities' as articulated not in the chapeau but in Article 16(1)(c), (1)(d), and (1)(f). States are obligated to adopt and implement laws providing the same—equal—rights and responsibilities for women and men as spouses, parents, and guardians of children. All such laws and structures, however, operate on a formal, public level. By definition, they cannot reach the operational level within the family, nor can they spell out every detail of potential responsibilities, disputes, and inequality.

Most inequalities within families do not reach the public, formal level of evaluation and decision-making, as those mechanisms usually are invoked only when a family experiences a death or a breakup. The quotidian dynamic of sharing responsibilities within intact families occurs behind the real or virtual walls that surround families in every social and cultural context. The operation of 'same rights and responsibilities' is worked out in negotiations based on unwritten rules that may or may not be subject to discussion. The negotiations are private, between spouses and between them and other family members.

3. 'Marriage and Family Relations'

The chapeau reference to 'marriage and family relations' raises multiple issues. It is somewhat broader than the language of UDHR Article 16, which refers to the right to 'marry and to found a family'. Neither the UDHR nor the Convention defines 'marriage', 'family', or 'family relations'. The UDHR and the Marriage Convention provide for 'equal rights as to marriage, during marriage and at its dissolution' but do not refer specifically to other family forms or personal relationships.

The definition of 'marriage' is embedded in the laws, cultures, and religions of individual States parties and their subdivisions. In obliging States parties to provide for equality of men and women upon entering marriage, during the marriage, and at its dissolution, the Convention implies a structural definition that includes mutual and equal obligations between the parties. The Committee has not addressed same-sex marriage or other relationships with a view to defining them, but it has recognized the reality of same-sex relationships and indicated that States parties must provide for equality between the parties.[26]

Other international instruments are not helpful in elucidating the concept of 'family'. Neither the ICCPR nor the ICESCR are informative as to the definition, although their monitoring bodies address the question to a limited extent. The ICESCR refers to the family as the fundamental unit of society and specifically addresses only consent to marriage.[27] CESCR General Comment 4 (on the right to adequate housing) states that 'the concept of "family" must be understood in a wide sense'.[28] ICCPR Article 23(3) and (4) indicates that equality in undertaking marriage, during marriage, and its dissolution are fundamental civil and political rights but does not refer to other relationships. CCPR in its General Comments 19 and 28 acknowledges the 'various forms of family',

---

[26] CO Lithuania, CEDAW/C/LTU/CO/4 (2008) para 23; CO Sweden, CEDAW/C/SWE/CO/7 (2008) para 9 (commending action plan including violence in same-sex relationships); see the discussion of sexual orientation in ch on art 1.
[27] ICESCR art 10(1).   [28] ICESCR, 'General Comment 4' (1992) UN Doc E/1992/23 para 6.

although it specifically identifies only single-parent families and unmarried parents as among the 'various forms'.

The CMW defines 'family' for purposes of that Convention as:

persons married to migrant workers or having with them a relationship that, according to applicable law, produces effects equivalent to marriage, as well as their dependent children and other dependent persons who are recognized as members of the family by applicable legislation or applicable bilateral or multilateral agreements between the States concerned.[29]

This definition is more restrictive than that suggested in the General Comments to the two Covenants and is somewhat circular, as, with respect to persons other than spouses, it relies on States parties' formal (legislative or other) recognition of dependence rather than evaluating the nature of the relationship to confer family membership.

According to UN SG's 1995 Report on the International Year of the Family, 'families assume diverse forms and functions among and within countries'.[30] The United Nations Programme on the Family, in a collection of papers issued on the tenth anniversary of the Year of the Family, explores the changes in family formation and functions in view of national and global economic and social developments and underscores the diversity and the fluidity of definitions.[31]

As the 'fundamental unit of society,' to be 'protected,'[32] families historically have been the site of fundamental inequality. In the name of protecting the family, States have supported male authority over the actions of wives, daughters, and other family members and over the accumulation and use of property. Divorce has been made extraordinarily difficult for women to initiate, and upon divorce women experience far greater negative financial and social consequences than men. Patriarchal traditions and attitudes inform laws, policies, and customs relating to all aspects of marriage and family life. For purposes of implementing the Convention, as underscored in General Recommendation 21 paragraph 13, the core issue is the elimination of discrimination against women within the family, regardless of its size and membership. States parties are obligated to address the discriminatory aspects of all the various forms of family and family relationships. This is critical not only as to the transactions within the family, but because discrimination within the family is a fundamental factor in discrimination against women outside the family. The Convention requires States parties to address these traditions and attitudes and to open family law and policy to the same scrutiny that is given to the 'public' aspects of individual and community life.

4. De Facto Relationships

General Recommendation 21, paragraph 18 states that the elimination of discrimination against women in *de facto* relationships is included in State party obligations under Article 16(1). The Committee is concerned about the lack of legal frameworks for *de facto* unions and the results of dissolution of such a relationship in which women may not have

---

[29] CMW art 4.

[30] Report of the Secretary-General, 'Observance of the International Year of the Family' (1995) UN Doc A/50/370 para 14.

[31] UN Division for Social Policy and Development, 'International Year of the Family, Major Trends Affecting Families' (2004), <http://social.un.org/index/Family/Publications/MajorTrendsAffectingFamilies. aspx> accessed 31 December 2010.

[32] UDHR art 16(3).

clear legal rights with respect to division of property.[33] The Committee recommends equal property rights for the parties in *de facto* relationships.[34]

However, the nature of a *de facto* relationship that confers rights between the partners is not precisely defined by the Committee or by the other treaty monitoring bodies that have addressed 'family' issues.[35] The CMW Article 4 refers to individuals having 'a relationship that, according to applicable law, produces effects equivalent to marriage'. Since this leaves the defining elements of such relationships to the domestic law of each State it adds little clarity to the position under international human rights law.

The UN Food and Agriculture Organization is clearer. It defines a *de facto* relationship as 'cohabitation of a man and woman with a view to a long-term partnership'.[36] A sampling of States parties' laws relating to *de facto* relationships reveals no uniform or clear definition as well as a pattern of connecting the concept to common law marriage. Australia, for example, defines a *de facto* relationship with legal consequences as 'the relationship of a man and a woman who are living together as husband and wife on a genuine domestic basis, although not married'.[37] In Canada, the legal status of *de facto* partners has been clearly differentiated from those in civil unions, marriage, and common law marriage.[38]

All of these definitions share the practical problem of evidence: to obtain the benefits of any State law or policy, individuals must demonstrate that they are in a recognized relationship. This is generally more complicated than proving the existence of a registered marriage. Because women frequently are at a disadvantage in meeting complex requirements for claiming or retaining rights, they may also be at a disadvantage in negotiating the consequences of a *de facto* relationship.

5. Unregistered Marriages as De Facto Unions

Marriages that are concluded under religious and customary practices that are not recognized by the State party, and therefore cannot be registered, create a particular equality issue.[39] The parties and their communities see themselves as married, but the State party does not. Upon dissolution of the relationship by divorce or death, women in these marriages are subject to discriminatory custom or religious law of their communities, without the protection of rights they could have under civil law—assuming the State party has adopted a civil marriage law—if the marriage were registered.[40] State party recognition and regulation of these arrangements as *de facto* relationships can protect women's property and custody rights. In South Africa, where Muslim marriages cannot be registered and are not recognized by the State, the Constitutional Court has held that the nature of the relationship must be acknowledged such that widows in both monogamous and

---

[33] CO Norway, CEDAW/C/NOR/CO/7 (2007) para 31.   [34] Ibid para 32.

[35] Neither CCPR 'General Comment 19' (1990) UN Doc HRI/GEN/1/Rev.6 para 2 nor GC 28 para 27 suggest standards for recognition of 'couples' for purposes such as dependent social security benefits or property division upon dissolution of the relationship.

[36] UN Food and Agriculture Organization, '"De Facto Unions." The Legal Status of Rural Women in 19 Latin American Countries' (1994) para 2.4 ('de facto unions') <http://www.fao.org/DOCREP/U5615e/u5615e03.htm#P457_72830> accessed 31 December 2010.

[37] Family Law Amendment (Shared Parental Responsibility) Act 2006, part 4, § 25(4)(1).

[38] N Roy, *De Facto Union in Quebec* (2005) <http://www.canada-justice.org/eng/pi/icg-gci/dfu-udf/dfu-udf.pdf> accessed 31 December 2010.

[39] CO Kazakhstan, CEDAW/C/KAZ/CO/2 (2007) para 29; CO Azerbaijan, CEDAW/C/AZE/CO/4 (2009) paras 39–40. See the discussion on art 16(2) see B. III below.

[40] CO Azerbaijan, CEDAW/C/AZE/CO/4 (2009) paras 39–40.

polygynous Muslim marriages have the rights of a surviving 'spouse' under the Succession Act.[41]

Such unrecognized marriages must be distinguished from religious or customary marriages for which the State party does not require registration in order for them to be recognized as valid, eg, customary marriage in some sub-Saharan African States parties and religious marriage in Syrian Arab Republic and Pakistan, and most marriages in India.[42]

The Committee has stated that States parties must 'have consensual unions recognized as a source of rights'.[43] In 1992, it closely questioned a State party on the status of *de facto* (common-law) relationships and the property rights of women in those relationships.[44] It has required States parties to develop a framework for property distribution in relation to *de facto* relationships and to report more fully on 'property distribution upon dissolution of marriage or a *de facto* relationship'.[45] It has queried States parties about the disadvantages faced by women in *de facto* or common-law relationships with respect to rights upon ending the relationship.[46] In 2007, the Committee stated that States parties must 'ensure the same protection of women's rights in marriage and in situations of cohabitation'.[47]

State party obligations to address domestic violence include recognition of *de facto* relationships for the purposes of holding perpetrators accountable. The Committee has indicated that domestic violence legislation and programmes must apply to partners and former partners as well as husbands[48] and other 'intimate relationships'.[49]

6. Polygamy

The Committee has asserted that polygamy (which in practice means polygyny) is fundamentally unequal and must be 'discouraged and prohibited' by law.[50] While the Committee has clearly indicated in General Recommendation 21 and in many of its concluding observations[51] that polygamy is a violation of the Convention and should be abolished, it also

---

[41] *Daniels v Campbell NO and Others* (2004) CCT 40/03; *Hassam v Jacobs NO and Others* (2008) 4 All SA350 C.

[42] eg Botswana, CEDAW/C/BOT/CO/3 (2010) para 41; CO India, CEDAW/C/IND/CO/3 (2007) paras 58-9; CO Namibia, CEDAW/C/NAM/CO/3 (2007) paras 28-9; CO Pakistan, CEDAW/C/PAK/CO/3 (2007) paras 34-5; CO Syrian Arab Republic, CEDAW/C/SYR/CO/1 (2007) para 34.

[43] CO Dominican Republic, A/59/38, 31st Session (2004) para 287.

[44] CO Barbados, A/47/38, 18th session (1992) paras 42–8.

[45] CO Canada, CEDAW/C/CAN/CO/7 (2008) para 48; CO Norway C/NOR/CO/7 (2007) para 31.

[46] CO Antigua and Barbuda, A/52/38/Rev.1, 17th Session (1997) paras 237, 262, and 271.

[47] CO Estonia, CEDAW/C/EST/CO/4 (2007) para 31.

[48] CO Armenia, CEDAW/C/ARM/CO/4/Rev.1 (2009) para 22; CO Barbados, A/47/38, 18th Session (1992) para 421; CO Japan, CEDAW/C/JPN/CO/6 (2009) para 31; CO Slovenia, CEDAW/C/SVN/CO/4 (2008) para 24.

[49] CO Japan, CEDAW/C/JPN/CO/6 (2009) para 31; CO Slovenia, CEDAW/C/SVN/CO/4 (2008) para 24. See the discussion in ch on violence against women.

[50] GR 21 para 14; CO Bhutan, CEDAW/C/BTN/CO/7 (2009) para 34 (reiterating A/59/38, 30th Session (2004) para 116); CO Greece, CEDAW/C/GRC/CO/6 (2007) para 34; CO Uzbekistan, CEDAW/C/UZB/CO/4 (2010) paras 42–3 (reiterating similar observations in CEDAW/C/UZB/CO/3 (2006) para 38 and A/56/38, 24th Session (2001) paras 187–8); CO Vanuatu, CEDAW/C/VUT/CO/3 (2007) para 38; CO Algeria, A/60/38, 32rd Session (2005) para 143; CO Bangladesh, A/59/38, 31st Session (2004) paras 245–6; CO Egypt, CEDAW/C/EGY/CO/7 (2010) paras 47–8 (reiterating A/56/38, 24th Session (2001) paras 354–5); CO Ghana, CEDAW/C/GHA/CO/5 (2006) paras 35–6; CO Indonesia, CEDAW/C/IDN/CO/5 (2007) para 18; CO Israel, A/60/38(Supp) 33rd Session (2005) paras 261–2; CO Lao People's Republic, CEDAW/C/LAO/CO/7 (2009) paras 48–9; CO Madagascar, CEDAW/C/MDG/5 (2008) paras 36–7.

[51] GR 21 para 14; CO South Africa, A/53/38 (1998), para 115; CO Cape Verde, CEDAW/C/CPV/CO/6 (2006) paras 33–4; CO Ghana, CEDAW/C/GHA/CO/5 (2006) paras 35–6; CO Kyrgyzstan, CEDAW/C/KGZ/CO/3 (2008) paras 21–2; CO Tajikistan, CEDAW/C/TJK/CO/3 (2007) paras 35–6.

recognizes the necessity of protecting the well-being of the millions of women who are in polygamous marriages. Some States parties have adopted laws requiring a first wife's consent or judicial permission to take another wife,[52] or requiring property division upon divorce or death of the husband to account for the property rights of all wives. However, the Committee has concluded that such provisions do not adequately address the issue.[53]

7. Equality in the Family and Multiple Legal Systems

Many States parties relegate family law issues, referred to as personal status law,[54] to the law or custom of ethnic and religious communities. State party reports and Committee reviews frequently disclose significant discrimination against women under these laws and customs, in contravention of Convention Articles 1, 2, 5, 15, and 16.

Relegation of personal status law to religious or other communities may be a matter of State policy, reflected in States parties' reservations to the Convention.[55] Some States parties simply apply religious law in matters of personal status. Some such States parties have reserved Article 16 or have entered a general reservation based on conflict with their respective constitutions, which declare a State religion.[56]

A number of States parties' Constitutions specifically provide that personal status laws are exempt from constitutional provisions prohibiting discrimination. This means that constitutional equal protection and non-discrimination provisions are 'ring-fenced' and so do not protect women from the discriminatory effects of marriage under custom, thereby providing to communities constitutional protection that is denied to women. The Committee has recommended that these States parties amend their constitutions to eliminate this exemption.[57]

The Committee seeks evidence that the State party is making progress in changing its laws despite obstacles that it might face. It has noted a number of stagnant situations, such as a State party that adopted a Constitution enshrining equality but which has made no progress in adopting legislation to eliminate the discriminatory aspects of its multiple family law regimes,[58] or States parties that adopted laws that were progressive for their

---

[52] See eg Tanzania Law of Marriage Act 1971, ss 18–22; CO United Republic of Tanzania, CEDAW/C/TZA/CO/6 (2008) paras 21–2.

[53] GR 21 para 14; CO South Africa, A/53/38, 19th Session (1998) para 115; CO Cape Verde, CEDAW/C/CPV/CO/6 (2006) paras 33–4; CO Ghana, CEDAW/C/GHA/CO/5 (2006) paras 35–6; CO Kyrgyzstan, CEDAW/C/KGZ/CO/3 (2008) paras 21–2; CO Tajikistan, CEDAW/C/TJK/CO/3 (2007) paras 35–6.

[54] Personal status law refers to marriage and its dissolution, child custody, adoption, and inheritance.

[55] Singapore, Israel, India. See UN Treaty Database on CEDAW Reservations: <http://treaties.un.org/> accessed 31 December 2010.

[56] eg Constitution of the Arab Republic of Egypt art 2 (Islam the State religion and the 'principal source of legislation'); Constitution of Tunisia art 1 (Islam the State religion); Constitution of Malaysia art 3 (Islam the State religion).

[57] A number of British Commonwealth States adopted constitutions at independence that provide for equality under the law and before the law and/or prohibit discrimination on the basis of sex, but—in the spirit of self-determination—exempt personal status law from this prohibition. This results in preservation of highly sex-discriminatory customary practices with no constitutional recourse. See eg CO Gambia, CEDAW/C/GMB/CO/1-3 (2005) paras 19 and 20; CO Zambia, A/57/38, 27th Session (2002) paras 230–1; CO Botswana, CEDAW/C/BOT/CO/3 (2010) para 11.

[58] CO Uganda, A/57/38, Exceptional Session (2002) paras 129–30; CO South Africa, A/53/38, 19th Session (1998) para 115; CO India, CEDAW/C/IND/CO/3 (2007) paras 10–11.

time in addressing the multiple family law systems but have not revisited them in decades to eliminate remaining discriminatory practices that are now ripe for change.[59]

Some States parties that reserve personal status issues to the law and custom of communities limit individual choice as to the legal system under which they may marry. States parties may not have a civil code under which individuals may marry and divorce, or they may require that members of religious and ethnic communities marry only under their personal law and custom, without providing individuals with a 'right of exit' to a civil law.[60] This limits the legal regulation of family matters to identity-based regimes that preserve inequality and are not accountable externally for violations of human rights. The Committee has declared unequivocally that the preservation of multiple legal systems results in discrimination against women and consistently recommends that States parties 'harmonize' their multiple laws and customary practices with the principles of the Convention.[61]

The Committee has frequently observed that 'culture is dynamic and subject to change'[62] and that culture and religion, frequently cited as the basis for discriminatory family law, are not static and are subject to evolution and interpretation. It has indicated to States parties that change is expected. With respect to Islamic law, it has 'encourage[d]' States parties 'to obtain information on comparative jurisprudence and legislation, where more progressive interpretations of Islamic law have been codified in legislative reforms'.[63]

The existence of a civil marriage and divorce law does not guarantee equality between women and men in marriage and family relationships. Civil family laws may well enshrine stereotypes and gendered expectations of spousal roles and responsibilities. As the Committee frequently notes, and as discussed below, States parties do not consistently meet their obligation to implement the norms of the Convention in civil laws.[64] Reserving personal status law and custom to communities, to be designed and implemented by community authorities or institutions that are not accountable under the Convention or

---

[59] CO United Republic of Tanzania, CEDAW/C/TZA/CO/6 (2008) paras 146–7 (referring to Law of Marriage Act 1971); CO Kenya, CEDAW/C/KEN/CO/6 (2007) paras 41–4 (referring to Law of Succession Act 1979).

[60] CO Singapore, CEDAW/C/SGP/CO/3 (2007) para 16: 'ensure that Muslim women have full, easy and affordable access to civil law in all matters'. In a public consultation on art 16, held in New York, 26 July 2009, several academic experts affirmed the necessity of the 'right of exit'. Notes of the author.

[61] CO Republic of Congo, A/58/38, 28th Session (2003) paras 160–61; CO Lebanon, CEDAW/C/LBN/CO/3 (2008) paras 18–19 (and referring to CEDAW/C/LBN/CO/2 (2005) on the same subject); CO Equatorial Guinea, A/59/38, 31st Session (2004) para 191; CO Malaysia, CEDAW/C/MYS/CO/2 (2006) paras 13–14; CO The Philippines, CEDAW/C/PHI/CO/6 (2006) paras 11–12; CO Kenya, CEDAW/C/KEN/CO/6 (2007) paras 43–4; CO Greece, CEDAW/C/GRC/CO/6 (2007) paras 33–4; CO Niger, CEDAW/C/NER/CO/2 (2007) paras 15–16; CO Canada, CEDAW/C/CAN/CO/7 (2008) paras 17–19 (abolish discriminatory matrimonial property law applied under Indian Act); CO United Republic of Tanzania, CEDAW/C/TZA/CO/6 (2008) paras 146–7; CO Cameroon, CEDAW/C/CMR/CO/3 (2009), para 15; CO Myanmar, CEDAW/C/MMR/CO/3 (2008) para 47; CO Nigeria, CEDAW/C/NGA/CO/6 (2008) para 18.

[62] CO Jordan, CEDAW/C/JOR/CO 4 (2007) para 20; CO Eritrea, CEDAW/C/ERI/CO/3 (2006) para 15; CO Guinea, CEDAW/C/GIN/CO/6 (2007) para 24; CO Kenya, CEDAW/C/KEN/CO/6 (2007) para 22; CO Lao People's Democratic Republic, CEDAW/C/LAO/CO/7 (2009) para 22; CO Liberia, CEDAW/C/LBR/CO/6 (2009) para 19; CO Madagascar, CEDAW/C/MDG/CO/5 (2008) para 17; CO Mali, CEDAW/C/MLI/CO/5 (2006) para 18; CO Mauritania, CO C/MRT/CO/1 (2007) para 22; CO Timor-Leste, CEDAW/C/TLS/CO/1 (2009) para 28; CO Tuvalu, CEDAW/C/TUV/CO/2 (2009) para 28.

[63] CO Malaysia, CEDAW/C/MYS/CO/2 (2006) para 14; CO Jordan, CEDAW/C/JOR/CO/4 (2007) para 12; CO Indonesia, CEDAW/C/IDN/CO/5 (2007) para 13; CO Sri Lanka, A/57/38, 26th Session (2002) para 275; CO Singapore, CEDAW/C/SGP/CO/3 (2007) para 16.

[64] See the discussion in ch on art 2.

under the national constitution and laws relating to sex discrimination and equality, is a clear failure to meet Convention obligations.

II. Article 16(1)

1. *Article 16(1)(a) The Same Right to Enter into Marriage*

The right to enter into marriage may be limited by formal restrictions related to affinity, prior marriage, widowhood, age, and/or required consent of parents or guardians. Under the Convention, women, having the 'same right' to enter into marriage, cannot be subject to restrictions to which men are not subject.

Women's *de facto* enjoyment of their right to enter marriage is limited by religious and customary practices and social attitudes, such as:

- Right of divorced women to remarry. Some states provide for a waiting period of anywhere from ninety days to almost one year before a woman can remarry after a divorce,[65] while similar restrictions are not mandated for men.
- Right of widowed women to remarry. The Committee has expressed concern about discriminatory widowhood rituals[66] or a required waiting period for widows before remarrying.[67] Widows may be forced to undergo 'cleansing' or other degrading widowhood rituals and be required to live apart from their community or in seclusion for a period of time.[68] They may be forced, or heavily pressured, to marry a brother of their late husband (levirate marriage, known also as widow inheritance), on grounds that the widow, her children, and her reproductive capacity belong to the husband's family.[69] Women may also be subject to sororate marriage, the custom requiring families to 'replace' a deceased wife by offering her sister to the widower.[70] Men are not subject to these limitations and pressures.

2. *Article 16(1)(b) The Same Right Freely to Choose a Spouse and to Enter into Marriage only with their Free and Full Consent*

The standard of freedom to choose a spouse and freely consent to marriage is established in the Marriage Convention Article I, which states that:

No marriage shall be legally entered into without the full and free consent of both parties, such consent to be expressed by them in person after due publicity and in the presence of the authority competent to solemnize the marriage and of witnesses, as prescribed by law.

---

[65] CO Japan, CEDAW/C/JPM/CO/6 (2009) paras 17–18; CO Thailand, CEDAW/C/THA/CO/5 (2006) para 19 (310 day waiting period); CO Timor-Leste, CEDAW/C/TLS/CO/1(2009) para 45; CO Turkey, CEDAW/C/TUR/CO/6 (2010) paras 40–1; CO Madagascar, CEDAW/C/MDG/CO/5 (2008) paras 36–7.

[66] CO Togo, CEDAW/C/TGO/CO/5 (2006), para 15; CO Equatorial Guinea, A/59/38, 31st Session (2004) para 196; CO Gabon, A/60/38, 32nd Session (2005) para 239.

[67] CO Luxembourg, CEDAW/C/LUX/CO/5 (2008) para 34 (State party failed to address the matter after two prior reviews noted it).

[68] See eg NKA Busia, Jr, 'Ghana: Competing Visions of Liberal Democracy and Socialism' in AA An-Na'im (ed), *Human Rights under African Constitutions* (2003) 52–96, 89; Banda (n 2 above) 155–7; Protocol on the Rights of Women in Africa (2003) art 20(a).

[69] CO Mali, CEDAW/C/MLI/CO/5 (2005) paras 18, 35, 36; CO Burkina Faso, A/60/38, 33rd Session (2005) para 341; CO Guinea-Bissau, CEDAW/C/GNB/CO/6 (2009) para 41; CO Ethiopia, A/59/38, 30th Session (2004) paras 251–2. The Committee expressed concern over 'widow inheritance' in Uganda, A/57/38, Exceptional Session (2002) para 153.

[70] CO Mali, CEDAW/C/MLI/CO/5 (2005) paras 35–6; CO Guinea, A/56/38, 24th Session (2001) para 122; CO Burkina Faso, A/60/38, 33rd Session (2005) para 341.

General Recommendation 21, paragraph 16 provides that States parties must ensure by law that women have the right to choose whether to marry, whom to marry, and when to marry:

A woman's right to choose a spouse and enter freely into marriage is central to her life and to her dignity and equality as a human being. An examination of States parties' reports discloses that there are countries which, on the basis of custom, religious beliefs or the ethnic origins of particular groups of people, permit forced marriages or remarriages. Other countries allow a woman's marriage to be arranged for payment or preferment and in others women's poverty forces them to marry foreign nationals for financial security. Subject to reasonable restrictions based, for example, on a woman's youth or consanguinity with her partner, a woman's right to choose when, if, and whom she will marry must be protected and enforced at law.

'Free and full consent' to marriage can only be legally given by persons who are recognized by law to have the capacity to consent: adults, defined in General Recommendation 21 as eighteen years of age.

Women's full enjoyment of the right to enter marriage on an equal basis with men requires a seismic shift in individual and community attitudes about women's roles and expectations. Where women are primarily expected to marry, care for children and other family members, and maintain the household, they may be denied or forego education and may have limited or self-limited employment prospects. These limitations, in turn, reinforce the necessity of marriage. States parties are obligated to address the traditional attitudes and gender stereotyping and to eliminate the discrimination in education and employment that limit women's choices as to whether, when, and whom to marry.[71] Breaking the circle of limited expectations and choices as to marriage is critical to achieving substantive equality under Article 16.

a) Arranged Marriage and Forced Marriage

Human rights concepts of free choice of spouse and 'free and full consent' to marriage operate in complex contexts. Marriage negotiations between prospective spouses and their families fall within a continuum of parental and prospective spousal consent. Despite laws protecting parties' free and full consent, their choices may be constrained by cultural expectations of marriage based on class, ethnic, religious, or other identity factors. Where families are traditionally involved in choosing children's spouses, one or both of the prospective spouses may have the right to refuse a match offered by the parents; or children may consider a prospective spouse but must request parents or other designated relatives to negotiate the match and arrange meetings between the intended spouses; or a self-chosen couple may be expected to obtain the approval of parents or other powerful members of the extended family. Marriage in all legal and cultural contexts is also an economic transaction that circulates wealth in the community, involving financial negotiations such as gift exchanges between the betrothed and between their families, gifts to the couple from extended family and friends, dowry, marriage settlements, bridewealth, and payment for substantial wedding celebrations.

The Committee has consistently noted with concern the economic aspects of marriage formation that discriminate against women. General Recommendation 21 paragraph 16 alludes to the arrangement of marriage 'by payment or preferment' as a violation of women's right to freely choose a spouse. The Committee has expressed concern over any

---

[71] See the discussion in ch on art 5.

requirement of bridewealth or bride price (a payment of cattle, goods, or other assets by a prospective husband's family to the family of the prospective wife) or dowry (payment of goods and/or cash by the bride's family to the husband's family) and recommends that both be abolished.[72]

In formal terms, various forms of arranged marriage may not violate the guarantee of equal right to choose a spouse and consent to marriage, as both spouses' rights may be equally limited. In substantive terms, however, women often are not situated equally with men with respect to negotiating marriage. Gendered role expectations create pressure on women to marry (and to marry 'suitably'), to become mothers, and to give priority to the wishes of others.[73] Gendered power relations result in greater familial (frequently fathers') assertion of control over young women's movements and choice of companions than over those of young men. Economic inequality limits women's bargaining power; they may need marriage to survive. They may be seen as a financial drain on their family of origin, or unlikely to add to their family's economic well-being and incapable of supporting parents as they age, and, therefore, must be married off to another family.

Forced marriage, in which parents or other individuals in a position of control determine when and whom a woman will marry without consulting her in any way, is the ultimate denial of women's free and full consent to marriage and as such is condemned.[74] In such situations, the woman frequently is a child by any definition. She may be threatened with force, including death, or exile from the family if she attempts to refuse[75] and may indeed be killed if she does so.[76] The Committee has expressed concern over particular forms of forced marriage, such as widow inheritance (forced marriage to a deceased husband's brother)[77] and bride abduction (where consent of the bride is irrelevant, and which may occur with the complicity of the bride's family).[78]

Some States parties have made efforts to address forced marriage in immigrant communities through awareness-raising[79] or criminal sanctions[80] and through immigration policies placing age restrictions on family reunification (with fiancés and spouses). The

---

[72] CO Uganda, A/57/38, Exceptional Session (2002) paras 153–4. CO India, CEDAW/C/IND/CO/3 (2007) para 26 (same concern expressed in prior reviews). The terms are sometimes used interchangeably, designating a payment to the husband's family as 'dowry'. Regardless of terminology, required payment or exchange of property is the concern.

[73] As noted in ch on art 5.

[74] CO Bhutan, A/59/38, 30th Session (2004) para 126; CO Mali, CEDAW/C/MLI/CO/5 (2006) paras 17, 18, 35, 36; CO Pakistan, CEDAW/C/PAK/CO/3 (2007) paras 45–6; CO Malawi, CEDAW/C/MWI/CO/6 (2010) para 42; CO Mozambique, CEDAW/C/MOZ/CO/2 (2007) para 22; CO Uganda, A/57/38, Exceptional Session (2002) para 153; CO Turkey, A/60/38, 32nd Session (2005) para 367; CO Tuvalu, CEDAW/C/TUV/CO/(2009) para 51; CO Vietnam, A/56/38, 25th Session (2001) para 258.

[75] CO Turkey, A/60/38, 32nd Session (2005) paras 363–7; CO Jordan, A/55/38, 22nd Session (2000) para 179.

[76] eg CO Lebanon, A/60/38, 33rd Session (2005) para 103. See the discussion of this issue in ch on violence against women.

[77] See n 69 above and accompanying text.

[78] CO Kyrgyzstan, A/59/38, 30th Session (2004) paras 169–70. See, noting the persistence of the practice, 'Report of the Special Rapporteur on violence against women, its causes and consequences, Rashida Manjoo: Mission to Kyrgyzstan' (2010) UN Doc A/HRC/14/22/Add.2 para 23.The High Court of Tanzania held a marriage by abduction invalid under the Tanzania Law of Marriage Act and CEDAW art 16(1)(b), *Jonathan v Republic*, Criminal Appeal No 53/2001, High Court of Tanzania at Moshi (2001).

[79] CO Denmark, CEDAW/C/DEN/CO/7 (2009) paras 40–1, following up on prior reviews, A/57/38, 27th Session (2002) paras 345–6 and CEDAW/C/DEN/C/6 (2006) paras 30–1; CO The United Kingdom, CEDAW/C/UK/CO/6 (2009) paras 276–7.

[80] CO Belgium, CEDAW/C/BEL/CO/6 (2008) paras 43–4.

Committee, while acknowledging the efforts, has expressed concern about and recommended examination of the impact of the restrictive immigration policies on families and the development of action plans.[81] It has also expressed concern about the forced marriage of migrant women in receiving countries and recommended sub-regional efforts to combat it.[82]

3. *Article 16(1)(c) The Same Rights and Responsibilities During Marriage and at its Dissolution*

Article 16(1)(c) is a framing statement, indicating that from the beginning to the end of a marital relationship the partners are equal in capacity and rights. General Recommendation 21, paragraph 17, referring to the discrimination that results from States parties' reliance 'on the application of common law principles, religious or customary law, rather than by complying with the principles contained in the Convention', underscores their obligation to provide a comprehensive legal framework for women's equal enjoyment of their human rights within the family structure. The 'same rights in marriage and at its dissolution' also apply to the ownership and management of property, division of property upon dissolution of a marriage or *de facto* relationship, and inheritance of property upon death of one party. These issues are covered under Article 16(1)(g).

a) **During Marriage**

The Committee has noted in a variety of contexts that, as stated in General Recommendation 21, the 'husband being accorded the status of head of household and primary decision maker...contravene[s] the provisions of the Convention'.[83]

b) **Dissolution of Marriage**

General Recommendation 21 is silent on matters relating to the divorce process as opposed to the property aspects. The application of civil, customary, or religious law with respect to divorce grounds and processes frequently results in contravention of the Convention's non-discrimination norm.

aa) *Grounds for Divorce*

The Committee has stated that grounds for all divorces must be the same for women as for men, both in law and as applied. However, its concluding observations and jurisprudence do not illuminate the issues in detail. General Recommendation 21 does not discuss dissolution under Article 16(1)(c) and refers to divorce only in paragraph 28, relating to property.

Where divorce is a formal process under civil or religious law that requires a finding of fault on the part of one of the spouses, men should not be allowed to divorce at will, without stated grounds, or to cite grounds for divorce that women cannot.[84] Women should not be required to state grounds if men are not, nor should they be limited to relatively

---

[81] CO Denmark, CEDAW/C/DEN/CO/7 (2009) paras 40–1; CO Norway, A/58/38, 28th Session (2003) paras 425–6 and CEDAW/C/NOR/CO/7 (2007) para 29.

[82] CO Tajikistan, CEDAW/C/TJK/CO/3 (2007) paras 37–8.

[83] Para 17. See also CO Fiji, A/57/38, 26th Session (2002) paras 54–5; CO Indonesia, CEDAW/C/IDN/CO/5 (2007) para 18; CO Singapore, A/56/38, 25th Session (2001) para 79; CO Burundi, CEDAW/C/BDI/CO/4 (2008) para 12; CO Guinea, CEDAW/C/GIN/CO/6 (2007) para 44; CO Mali, CEDAW/C/MLI/CO/5 (2006) para 11.

[84] CO Thailand, CEDAW/C/THA/CO/5 (2006) para 19 (differing standards for adultery grounds); CO Sierra Leone, CEDAW/C/SLE/CO/5 (2007) para 38.

extreme ones such as abandonment or precluded from citing physical or psychological abuse.

Marriage dissolution under custom involves standards of behaviour and fault that are not formally documented.[85] Marital behaviour and dissolution norms are established by the community, reflecting many aspects of gender stereotyping and inequality in that community. Women might have the nominal capacity to leave their marriage, but they are more likely than men to be economically dependent on remaining in the household and to be subject to family pressure to remain married. As the Committee has noted with concern, physical violence and other forms of maltreatment may be considered according to community norms to be a standard element of marriage[86] and an insufficient reason for dissolution.[87] Where children by applicable law or custom belong to the husband's family, leaving a marriage can mean leaving one's children behind, for many women a reason to remain despite having sufficient grounds for dissolution, including violence.

bb) Process and Procedure

Women have the right to access divorce procedures on a basis of equality with men. In formal terms, this requires States parties' recognition of equal legal capacity and equal standing before any court or tribunal that is empowered to grant dissolution of a marriage.[88] Any requirements as to documentation, witnesses, notice, and recording of the process must be the same for women and men. Women must have the same right as men to initiate and to complete a divorce; the Committee specifically recommends elimination of repudiation.[89] Where procedures are less formal, as in customary systems, women and men must be acknowledged within their community to have the same right to end a marriage.

Differences in the situation of women and men result in substantive inequality in access to and use of marriage dissolution procedures. Women's access to formal courts may be limited by poverty, illiteracy, social expectation concerning public activity or confrontation, and lack of knowledge.[90] Even well-educated and financially comfortable women may be intimidated by the expense, stigma, and complexity of a civil legal process. In many States parties the judiciary remains largely male; the judges on religious courts, which may be the only possible venue for a dissolution procedure, are almost invariably male.[91]

---

[85] A Armstrong et al, 'Uncovering Reality: Excavating Women's Rights in the African Family'(1993) 7 *Intl J of L, Policy and the Family* 314, 350, quoted in Banda (n 2 above) 127. See also Report of States parties: Kenya, CEDAW/C/KEN/7 (2010) para 255.

[86] CO Guinea-Bissau, CEDAW/C/GNB/CO/6 (2009) para 23; CO Liberia, CEDAW/C/LBR/CO/6 (2009) para 18; CO Myanmar, CEDAW/C/MMR/CO/3 (2008) para 20; CO United Republic of Tanzania, CEDAW/C/TZA/CO/6 (2009) para 21. The Committee also notes a 'culture of silence' and women's lack of awareness of their rights relating to violence: CO Bhutan, CEDAW/C/BTN/CO/7 (2009) para 19.

[87] CO Vietnam, A/56/38, 25th Session (2001) para 258. See the discussion in ch on violence against women.

[88] See the discussion in ch on art 15.

[89] Repudiation is the right of a husband to unilaterally divorce a wife, under Islamic law. CO Guinea, A/56/38, 25th Session (2001) para 134; CO Mauritania, CEDAW/C/MRT/CO/1 (2007) para 43; CO Greece, A/57/38, Exceptional Session (2002) para 295; CO Niger, CSEDAWC/NER/CO/2 (200) para 17; CO Togo, CEDAW/C/TGO/CO/5 (2006) para 14; as to equality in initiating divorce in non-Muslim states, CO Chile, A/54/38/Rev.1, 21st Session (1999) para 222; CO The Philippines, CEDAW/C/PHI/CO/6 (2006) para 32.

[90] CO Botswana, CEDAW/C/BOT/CO/3 (2010) paras 13, 17, and 18.

[91] eg reservation of Israel to art 7(b); CO Pakistan, CEDAW/C/PAK/CO/3 (2007) paras 24–5.

Some States parties' procedures include counselling, review, or decision-making by a marriage council or a council of elders or religious authorities.[92] A community-based panel may replicate in its make up unequal power relationships between women and men in that community.[93] The Committee has noted that such tribunals 'might operate to perpetuate stereotypes and prejudices that discriminate against women and violate the human rights enshrined in the Convention'.[94]

4. Article 16(1)(d) The Same Rights and Responsibilities as Parents, Irrespective of their Marital Status, in Matters Relating to their Children; in all Cases the Interests of the Children Shall Be Paramount

The UDHR is silent on the issue of equal parental rights and responsibilities. Article 25(2) provides only that '[m]otherhood and childhood are entitled to special care and assistance. All children, whether born in or out of wedlock, shall enjoy the same social protection'. DEDAW Article 6(2)(c) expands upon the rights and responsibilities of parenthood: 'Parents shall have equal rights and duties in matters relating to their children. In all cases the interest of the children shall be paramount.'

'Equal rights and duties [or responsibilities]' as parents was a revolutionary concept in 1967 and remains so in many quarters. The language echoes across the Convention, appearing as well in Articles 5(b) and 11(2)(c). Both provisions underpin the Committee's statements on the subject, linking the issues of traditional gender roles and stereotypes, the structure of the workplace, and family roles and expectations with respect to caring for children. Preservation of traditional gender roles may result in a father and his family by law or custom having considerably greater authority over children than practical responsibility for their care. States parties are required to encourage attitude change towards equal parental responsibility, using all available means of addressing stereotypes and providing economic support and incentives for both parents to care for their children.

The Committee has not addressed this obligation extensively under Article 16 but has noted with concern laws that designate a husband as head of household.[95] It has commended a State party for adopting a law that 'sets out to apply the concept of co-parenting based on three principles of equality between parents, equality between children, and the child's right to her or his two parents'.[96] It recommended to a State party that a pilot parenting programme for fathers be extended throughout the country.[97] The Committee also repeated in two consecutive reviews its recommendation to a State party that the State party strengthen awareness-raising measures to 'promote and implement the equal sharing of domestic and family responsibilities, including the idea of joint parental responsibility between women and men'.[98]

---

[92] eg Tanzania Law of Marriage Act 1971, ss 102–4, 106(3); B Rwezaura, 'Gender Justice and Children's Rights: A Banner for Family Law Reform in Tanzania' in A Bainham (ed), *International Survey of Family Law 1997*, 413, 421–5 (describing Tanzania's comprehensive attempt to formalize and regulate the role of community marriage tribunals, and proposed changes).

[93] CO Zambia, A/57/38, 27th Session (2002) para 250.

[94] CO Bolivia, CEDAW/C/BOL/CO/4 (2008) para 22; see also CO Malawi, CEDAW/C/MWI/CO/5 (2005) paras 17–18.

[95] See n 83 above.   [96] CO France, A/58/38, 29th Session (2003) para 249.

[97] CO Saint Kitts and Nevis, A/57/38, 27th Session (2002) para 104.

[98] CO Mongolia, CEDAW/C/MNG/CO/7 (2008) para 24, repeating recommendation in CO Mongolia, A/56/38, 24th Session (2001) para 270.

Reference to shared responsibility for children appears most consistently as a comment on parental leave policy or the lack thereof. The Committee encourages States parties to adopt parental leave and child care policies that allow parents to share care of children and to balance work and family.[99] Well into the twenty-first century, however, it appears that sharing responsibilities remains a challenge, as the Committee has encouraged a number of States parties to find incentives for men to take parental leave.[100]

Article 16(1)(d) requires States parties to eliminate laws and customs that grant fathers sole or greater authority over children. To provide for women's *de facto* enjoyment of the right to equal authority over the children, States parties must ensure that State agencies and employees and private enterprises accept the equal authority of mothers in all matters involving their children, such as education, consent to health care, and travel.[101]

a) Child Custody in Divorce: In all Such Cases, the Interest of the Children Shall Be Paramount

Article 16(1)(d) also relates to the determination of child custody upon dissolution of marriage or *de facto* union. Each parent's ability to care for the children should be evaluated without recourse to gender stereotypes relating to parenting capabilities. Such stereotypes underlie rules or presumptions that children of a certain age belong with one or the other parent.[102] Legal and customary rules based on gender stereotypes or lineage discount the individual circumstances, abilities, and relationships that determine parents' fitness to raise the child and 'the best interest of the child' and are inherently discriminatory.

'The interest of the children shall be paramount' is carried over directly from DEDAW. It does not appear in the UDHR. The standard is stated in the CRC as 'the best interest of the child'.[103] Convention Article 5(b) states, 'the interest of the children is the primordial consideration in all cases'. The Committee has not commented specifically on this provision. However, considerable literature exists on the application of the standard under the CRC, including its discriminatory impact on women.[104] Legislatures, courts, or other family tribunals may determine that the 'best interest of the child' is served, for example, by awarding custody to fathers in a patrilineal society, by applying discriminatory religious law, or by awarding custody to the parent who has greater financial resources (generally the father).[105]

---

[99] CO Luxembourg, CEDAW/C/LUX (2008) para 17; CO Hungary, A/57/38, Exceptional Session (2002) para 320; CO Japan, CEDAW/C/JPN/CO/6 (2009) paras 47–8; CO New Zealand, A/58/38, 29th Session (2003) paras 411–12 and CEDAW/C/NZL/CO/6 (2007) paras 36–7; CO Switzerland, CEDAW/C/CHE/CO/3 (2009) paras 37–8.

[100] CO Denmark, CEDAW/C/DEN/CO/7 (2009) paras 11–12, reiterating CEDAW/C/DEN/CO6 (2006) paras 14–15; CO Finland, CEDAW/C/FIN/6 (2008) paras 25–6; CO Germany, CEDAW/C/DEU/CO6 (2009) paras 7, 27, 38, and 39 (also in prior reviews, A/59/38, 30th Session (2004) paras 388–9 and A/55/38, 22nd Session (2000) para 314); CO Lithuania, CEDAW/C/LTU/4 (2008) paras 20–21; CO Sweden, CEDAW/C/SWE/CO/7 (2008) paras 26–7; CO The United Kingdom, CEDAW/C/UK/CO/6 [part of A/63/38] (2008) para 287; CO Japan, CEDAW/C/JPN/CO/6 (2009) paras 47–8. See the discussion in ch on art 11.

[101] CO Libyan Arab Jamahiriya, CEDAW/C/LBY/CO/5 (2009) paras 18–19 (travel).

[102] See eg Rwezaura (n 92 above) outlining the presumptions and stereotypes that are obstacles to application of 'best interest of the child' standard in religious and customary tribunals.

[103] CRC art 3. The only other human rights treaty that refers to the standard is the CRPD art 7.2.

[104] eg M Freeman, *A Commentary on the United Nations Convention on the Rights of the Child: Article 3, The Best Interests of the Child* (2007) 53.

[105] CRC CO Greece, CRC/C/114 (2002) paras 144–5; CO Niger, CRC/C/118 (2002) paras 163–4; CO Islamic Republic of Iran, CRC/C/146 (2005) para 462; CO Togo, CRC/C/146 (2005) para 541; CO Indonesia, CRC/C/137 (2004) paras 53, 54, 65, 66, and 72; CO Pakistan, CRC/C/133 (2003) paras 210–11.

Widows and divorced women may lose custody upon remarriage.[106] The CRC has determined that such practices do not meet the 'best interest' standard, expressing concern where 'children's lives are governed by family customs and religious law rather than by State law'.[107]

b) Children Born Out of Wedlock

Children born of unmarried parents may bear the stigma of 'out of wedlock' (or less elegant language). While Article 16 is not specific as to this issue, the UDHR Article 2 is specific, and General Recommendation 21, paragraph 19 alludes to it: 'the children of such unions do not always enjoy the same status as those born in wedlock'. The Committee has expressed to several States parties its concern over the *de jure* and *de facto* discrimination women experience on the basis of their unwed motherhood.[108]

In some systems, if all the elements of marriage formation are not completed, children are considered to belong only to the mother's lineage, and she and her family are solely responsible for them.[109] Where law or custom provides for fathers' responsibility to financially support children born out of wedlock, as a practical matter, if the father does not voluntarily acknowledge paternity, the mother will have full responsibility to obtain proof of paternity, pursue an order for child support (maintenance), and collect it. Even where single (divorced or unmarried) mothers have adequate access to child support payments, they may have far more daily responsibility for their children's physical and emotional care than the father. States parties have a responsibility to make every effort to eliminate stigma, to support women's pursuit of maintenance for their children, and to promote unwed fathers' involvement with their children.[110]

5. *Article 16(1)(e) The Same Rights to Decide Freely and Responsibly on the Number and Spacing of their Children and to Have Access to the Information, Education, and Means to Enable them to Exercise these Rights*

This provision echoes the language of Articles 10, 12, and 14 in reaffirming the right freely to choose the number and spacing of children and the obligation of States parties to provide education and services to fulfil this right. Article 16 places the right specifically in the context of marriage and, according to the Committee, *de facto* relationships. General Recommendation 21, paragraphs 21–23 offer commentary on the impact of fertility on women's lives and choices and grounds their right to control their fertility in that narrative. It focuses on women's right to independence in making decisions with respect to number and spacing of children, directly linking the right to choice with the norm of equality in the family.

---

[106] Ibid.

[107] Freeman (n 104 above) 53 (quoting CRC CO Bangladesh, CRC/C/15/Add.74 (1997) para 12).

[108] CO Japan, A/58/38, 29th Session (2003) para 371 and CEDAW/C/JPN/CO/6 (2009) para 17 (issue cited in 2003 remains); CO Tunisia, A/57/38, 27th Session (2002) paras 204–05; CO Uruguay, CEDAW/C/URY/CO/7 (2008) paras 48–9.

[109] Banda (n 2 above) 109 (in patrilineal cultures children belong to the father's kin group upon payment of bridewealth, as does paternal responsibility).

[110] CO Tuvalu, CEDAW/C/TUV/CO/2 (2009) paras 51–2; CO Uruguay, CEDAW/C/URY/CO/7 (2008) paras 48–9; CO Kenya, CEDAW/C/KEN/CO/6 (2007) para 44.

General Recommendation 24, on women and health (Article 12), explicates women's right to health throughout their life span, including adolescence and later years.[111] It focuses primarily on the right of access to health care and the legal, cultural, and structural barriers to access,[112] including those that arise in the context of family relationships, primarily issues of consent by husbands or other male relatives[113] and the imbalance of power in the family.[114]

The core meaning of Article 16(1)(e) lies in reading it in conjunction with the other provisions of Article 16.[115] Women can exercise the 'same' right as their partner to decide on the number and spacing of children only if they have equal power to make decisions affecting their individual and their family's well-being. Equality in decision-making is grounded in recognition of women's rights to enter marriage, choose a family name, own and manage property, choose an occupation, share responsibility for children, and end marriage, on an equal basis with men. If women do not have the same rights as men with regard to these matters, the very concept of their making a decision about childbearing is inapplicable.

Decisions on whether and when to have children are among the most intimate decisions individuals make, within a context that is the most intimate of all settings for addressing equality issues. If States parties fail to meet their obligations with respect to equality in the establishment and maintenance of families, they cannot meet the obligation to provide for the same rights to decide on the number and spacing of children.

6. *Article 16(1)(f) The Same Rights and Responsibilities With Regard to Guardianship, Wardship, Trusteeship, and Adoption of Children, or Similar Institutions Where these Concepts Exist in National Legislation; in all Cases the Interests of the Children Shall Be Paramount*

This language can be read to cover all possibilities in which adults are designated to care for children who are not biologically related to the parents, as equal responsibility for 'their children' is dealt with in Article 16(1)(d). However, the *travaux préparatoires* suggest that the primary issue meant to be addressed is equal authority over biological children.[116] General Recommendation 21, paragraph 20 suggests that the 'legal concepts of guardianship, wardship, trusteeship and adoption' are applied to biological children as well. The designation could be established by custom, religious law, or civil law. Preference for either males or females to execute these responsibilities is contrary to the Convention. Despite the considerable amount of contentious discussion during the drafting, the Committee has rarely alluded to this provision. It has not explored to date the meaning of 'same rights and responsibilities' with respect to the roles of persons who are not parents in caring for children and the protection of property for their benefit.

'Guardianship, wardship, [and] trusteeship' could refer to physical custody; responsibility for a child's welfare, including education and medical care decisions, regardless of where the child lives; fiduciary responsibility to manage property and financial affairs of a minor; or any combination of these responsibilities. The Committee has noted with

---

[111] Paras 8 and 18.   [112] See ch on art 12 for full discussion of information and access issues.
[113] GR 24 paras 14 and 21.   [114] GR 24 para 12(b).
[115] The Committee has not commented specifically on art 16(1)(e) but rather subsumes these equality issues in observations relating to art 12.
[116] See the discussion related to nn 13–15 above.

concern that certain customs and religious laws favour a male guardian or trustee for biological children[117] even where mothers have custody,[118] on the stereotypical assumption that women do not have the capacity to deal with financial, educational, and other decisions that affect the welfare of minors.

7. Article 16(1)(g) The Same Personal Rights as Husband and Wife, Including the Right to Choose a Family Name, a Profession, and an Occupation

a) Right to Choose a Family Name

The family name provision was not included in DEDAW. General Recommendation 21, paragraph 24 grounds the right to choose a family name in considerations of individual identity in the community. A woman's choice or retention of a family name different from that of her husband, a husband's decision to take the wife's family name, or a couple's decision to choose a name together, are all related to the balance of power between the spouses. That choice becomes the public face of the marriage, emblematic of the parties' identity in relationship to the community and the State.

Beyond the statement in General Recommendation 21, the Committee has offered little commentary in State party reviews on the individual identity aspect of the family name. In two cases determined under the Optional Protocol,[119] the nature of the right has been contested within the Committee. In both cases, the majority stated that the provision 'aims to enable a married woman or a woman living in a husband-and-wife relationship to keep her maiden name, which is part of her identity, and to transmit it to her children, and as such its beneficiaries are only married women, women living in *de facto* union and mothers'.[120] However, a minority of seven experts supported a broader definition of the right, indicating that (a) the rights enumerated in Article 16(1)(a–g) are not exhaustive,[121] and (b) the State party's refusal to allow the victims to change their respective family names at this point, which would redress the discriminatory ('sexist') law and custom that prevented the victims' mothers from transmitting their family name to their children, is itself discriminatory in violation of the Convention.[122] According to this view, equality as to choice of family name extends to every aspect of that choice, at every point in life where the choice may be made.[123]

The Committee has generally commended statutory changes to provide for equal rights[124] or has urged States parties to do so.[125] Its comments on transmission of the family name to children have indicated that prohibiting women in a marriage or *de facto* relationship from giving the children their family name,[126] providing the father a right

---

[117] CO Sierra Leone, CEDAW/C/SLE/CO/6 (2007) para 38; CO Kuwait, A/59/38, 30th Session (2004) paras 66–7.

[118] eg CO Morocco, CEDAW/C/MAR/CO/4 (2008) paras 38–9.

[119] *Group d'Intérêt pour le Matronyme* (n 25 above); *SOS Sexisme* (n 25 above). In determining the communications to be inadmissible, the Committee extensively discussed the nature of the right.

[120] *Group d'Intérêt pour le Matronyme* (n 25 above) para 11.10; *SOS Sexisme* (n 25 above) para 10.6.

[121] As discussed in text related to n 25 above.

[122] *Group d'Intérêt pour le Matronyme* (n 25 above) paras 12.15 and 12.17; *SOS Sexisme* (n 25 above) paras11.12 and 11.14.

[123] Art 16(1)(g) is cited in *Ünal Tekeli v Turkey* (16 November 2004) ECHR Application no 29865/96, holding that the law prohibiting a married woman from using her family name is discriminatory.

[124] CO Thailand, CEDAW/C/THA/CO/5 (2006) para 6; CO Tunisia, A/57/38, 27th Session (2002) para 184: CO Luxembourg, A/55/38, 22nd Session (2000) para 402.

[125] CO Jordan, A/55/38 (2000) para 175; CO Japan, CEDAW/C/JPN/CO/6 (2009) paras 17–18.

[126] CO Belgium, CEDAW/C/BEL/CO/6 (2008) paras 27–8.

to veto transmission of the mother's family name if they do not agree,[127] and giving the father the final decision if the parents cannot agree on a name[128] are all limitations that constitute sex discrimination.

b) Right to Choose a Profession and an Occupation

The DEDAW provision on this subject is in the article on employment.[129] Its position in the Convention article on equality in the family underscores the substantive issue: the impact of family power dynamic and stereotypes on women's basic economic choices. General Recommendation 21, paragraph 24 refers to employment choice as a matter of promoting family stability by providing for 'equity, justice, and individual fulfilment' of family members. It indicates that laws and customs requiring a husband's permission for a wife to work outside the home, and limiting permission to certain occupations, contravene the Convention. With rare exception, however,[130] the Committee addresses choice of occupation and profession under Article 11. States parties have an obligation to eliminate laws that proscribe certain occupations for women and those that support male authority over their work and career choices. They also are obligated to promote equality in education and the workplace, adopting laws and policies that require employers and educational institutions to eliminate barriers to their entry and their success.[131] Most significantly, they are required to make every effort to change the attitudes that result in these obstacles and that reinforce male authority over women's employment decisions.

8. *Article 16(1)(h) The Same Rights for Both Spouses in Respect of the Ownership, Acquisition, Management, Administration, Enjoyment, and Disposition of Property, Whether Free of Charge or for a Valuable Consideration*

This provision goes to the heart of women's property rights in marriage and *de facto* relationships. Legal capacity as articulated in Article 15 is critical to all the enumerated elements; DEDAW includes legal capacity and property rights in marriage in a single article,[132] which evolved into Convention Articles 15 and 16. Ownership, acquisition, management, administration, enjoyment, and disposition of property can rest only in individuals whose legal capacity is recognized formally and substantively.[133] General Recommendation 21, paragraphs 25 and 26 link the content of Article 15 and property issues. The Committee's concluding observations with respect to property rights are grounded in the premise that the Convention requires legal and *de facto* recognition of women's capacity to own and manage property.[134]

a) Acquisition and Ownership, Management, and Administration During the Marriage

Unless the State party has adopted legislation to modify it, ethnic or indigenous custom may not recognize women's capacity to own and manage property. Women who have married according to custom cannot claim an interest in most of the property accumulated during the marriage, regardless of their contribution. The Committee has

---

[127] CO France, CEDAW/C/FRA/CO/6 (2008) para 34.
[128] CO The Netherlands, CO/C/NLD/CO/4 (2007) paras 33–4.   [129] DEDAW art 10(1)(a).
[130] CO Jordan, A/55/38, 22nd Session (2000) paras 174–5.
[131] See the discussion in chs on arts 10 and 11.   [132] DEDAW art 6.
[133] See the discussion in ch on art 15.   [134] GR 21 paras 25–9.

expressed concern over women's lack of property rights in customary marriage in such States parties.[135]

Limitations on the right to acquire and manage property have a particularly deep impact on rural women, whose livelihood and family welfare depend largely on access to land. Women's or wives' lack of recognized legal capacity to own or inherit land and lack of entitlement to shares under land distribution schemes, either as individuals or as co-owners with their husbands, result in economic vulnerability that undermines equality. The Committee generally discusses this issue under Article 14.[136]

The Committee has expressed concern over inequality in spouses' rights to manage property in a number of States parties.[137] Where a community property regime is the norm, nominally providing that the marital property is equally theirs, women still may not have the right to manage the property. If property accumulated by virtue of women's economic activity is considered to belong to a marital household, managed by the husband, women are rendered continuously dependent.[138]

Some civil and religious legal regimes provide for women and men to maintain separate property throughout the marriage, and in some States parties spouses may choose at the commencement of the marriage whether to establish community or separate property. The Committee has not commented on any management or mutual decision-making issues that may arise under separate property arrangements.

b) Division of Property upon Dissolution of Marriage or *De Facto* Relationship

The core issue with respect to women's economic equality upon dissolution is whether they share equally in property accumulated during the relationship.[139] The specific issues vary considerably from State party to State party and include: whether women have legal capacity to own and manage property; the definition of marital property, or property available for division between the parties; recognition of non-financial contribution to marital property, including loss of economic opportunity and financial or non-financial investment in development of the parties' economic potential; and laws and customs relating to division of marital property.

The definition of marital property for purposes of division upon dissolution is variable. A comprehensive definition includes all property accumulated during the marriage, including real estate; household goods; savings and investments; business enterprises; interest in pensions, retirement accounts or other entitlements that are acquired during the relationship but paid out later in life; and increase in value of non-marital property.[140]

---

[135] CO Uganda, A/57/38, Exceptional Session (2002) paras 153–4; CO Samoa, A/60/38, 32nd Session (2005) paras 60–1; CO Albania, A/58/38, 28th Session (2003) paras 68–9; CO Kenya, CEDAW/C/KEN/CO/6 (2007) paras 41–2.

[136] See the discussion in ch on art 14.

[137] CO Guinea, CEDAW/C/GIN/CO/6 (2007) para 44; CO Cameroon, CEDAW/C/CMR/CO/3 (2009) para 46.

[138] CO Burundi, A/56/38, 24th Session (2001) para 56 and CO Burundi, CEDAW/C/BDI/CO/4 (2008) para 12 (no change); CO Guinea, CEDAW/C/GIN/CO/6 (2007) paras 40–4; CO Indonesia, CEDAW/C/IDN/CO/5 (2007) para 18 (noting discrimination concerns expressed in prior review); CO Mali, CEDAW/C/MLI/CO/5 (2006) para 11; CO Singapore, A/56/38, 25th Session (2001) para 79; CO Fiji, A/57/38, 26th Session (2002) paras 54–5. See also *ME Morales de Sierra*, Inter-American Commission on Human Rights, Report No 4/10 (19 January 2001) paras 28, 37–9, and 41–4.

[139] CO Lebanon, CEDAW/C/LBN/CO/2 (2008) paras 44–5; CO India, CEDAW/C/IND/CO/3 (2007) paras 54–5; CO Turkey, CEDAW/C/TUR/CC/4-5 (2005), paras 25–6.

[140] Generally, non-marital property is that owned individually by a spouse prior to the marriage or acquired as an individual inheritance or gift.

In States parties that recognize women's full legal capacity and require division of marital property upon dissolution, the nature of each party's contribution to the marital estate may be an issue: property may be divided on the basis of title, which as a practical matter usually favours the male; or be based on the relative proportion of financial contribution, also usually favouring the male. Laws providing for 'equitable' division of property frequently do not define 'equitable' and, with property division resting in the discretion of judges or negotiation between spouses, may result in wives receiving less than half the marital estate. The Committee has recommended that unequal results be remedied by recognizing non-financial contributions to marital property.[141]

The Committee also has recommended that States parties recognize the contribution to marital property that consists of a wife's financial and household support of a husband's education, which is her investment in the development of his 'human capital'.[142] This is not measured in cash terms but as an equal contribution to the ultimate growth of the marital estate.

A regime of separate property prevails in some States parties. Each individual keeps property owned at the commencement of the marriage, and any increase in value is attributed to the original owner. While such arrangements appear to be equal on their face, as a practical matter the wife may have less property than the husband upon entry into marriage and because of household duties, lack of education, systemic economic discrimination, and similar factors, is less able to increase her property during the marriage.[143] Where custom or civil or religious law limits post-marital financial support, upon dissolution of these marriages women may well be left with no home, little or no property, and no continuing financial support.

Where women's legal capacity and marital property rights are still entirely or partly unrecognized, they are particularly vulnerable to eviction from the marital home. Women in customary marriages may live on property that belongs to the husband's family or clan, without title residing in any individual. Upon dissolution of the marriage, women traditionally were expected to return to the home of their parents (leaving their children with the father, to whose family they were considered to belong).[144] This expectation has been disrupted by economic and cultural change, including global acknowledgment of the pervasiveness of violence against women and the recognition that women should not be required to remain in violent marriages.[145] However, some States parties, including those that have nominally recognized the realities of domestic violence, have failed to adopt marital property laws that provide for women to obtain a share of the accumulated marital property and to stay in their homes. The Committee has noted with concern the failure of these States parties to protect women's rights upon dissolution of marriage and recommended that they adopt appropriate laws.[146]

---

[141] CO Fiji, A/57/38, 26th Session (2002) paras 54–5; CO Guyana, A/60/38, 33rd Session (2005) paras 289–90.

[142] CO Slovenia, CEDAW/C/SVN/CO/4 (2008) paras 33–4; CO Switzerland, CEDAW/C/CHE/CO/3 (2009) paras 41–2.

[143] 'Freedom to dissipate nothing is no freedom at all': Banda (n 2 above) 132.

[144] This applies to patrilineal custom and patrilocal marriage; matrilineal and matrilocal marriage customs result in a different situation. Banda (n 2 above) 129–32.

[145] See the discussion in ch on violence against women.

[146] CO Kenya, CEDAW/C/KEN/CO/6 (2007) paras 17–18; CO Uganda, A/57/38, Exceptional session (2002) paras 153–4.

The Committee has also noted that even where the formal law provides nominally for equal rights to acquire and manage property, for equal distribution of property upon divorce, and for widows' inheritance rights, poor implementation of these laws may produce an unequal economic result.[147]

c) Inheritance

The Committee has consistently expressed concern over discrimination against women with respect to inheritance despite the lack of specific language in the Convention. It generally recommends that States parties 'introduce legislative reforms to provide women with equal rights in...inheritance'.[148] A number of States parties, including some in which widows do have inheritance rights, do not recognize the right of daughters and other female relatives to inherit or to inherit equally with sons and other male relatives. In addressing the issue in State party reviews the Committee has not clearly differentiated between the inheritance rights of widows and those of daughters.[149] However, in General Recommendation 27 on the rights of older women, the Committee has recognized the inheritance issues specific to widows, including those in polygamous marriages.[150]

Inheritance is also frequently referred to under Article 14, underscoring its particular importance to rural women as the sole source of survival. Concluding observations relating to Article 14 typically recommend or 'urge' States parties to 'take appropriate measures to eliminate all forms of discrimination with respect to ownership and inheritance of land'.[151]

The Committee has noted that 'widow inheritance', the discriminatory custom of requiring a widow to marry her late husband's brother in order to remain on the family property and to be supported by the late husband's family or clan, is inextricably linked to widows' lack of property rights[152] and affects rural women in particular. If a woman does not have any rights to the land and livelihood that had been provided by her deceased husband, such levirate marriage may be her only economic choice.

The Committee also has expressed concern over the practice that is referred to vividly and accurately as 'property grabbing'.[153] While rural families may live on land that belongs to a clan or community rather than to individuals, and no individual would be in a position to inherit this land, in some States parties the concept of clan or community

---

[147] CO Benin, CEDAW/C/BEN/CO/1–3 (2005) paras 19–22; CO Burkina Faso, CEDAW/C/BFA/CO/4–5 (2005) paras 27–8.

[148] CO United Arab Emirates, CEDAW/C/ARE/CO/1 (2010) para 48.

[149] CO Azerbaijan, CEDAW/C/AZE/CO/3 (2007) para 28; CO Bahrain, CEDAW/C/BHR/CO/2 (2008) para 38; CO Bangladesh, A/59/38, 31st Session (2004) paras 247–8; CO Cameroon, CEDAW/C/CMR/CO/3 (2009) para 46 (citing issues in 2000 review, A/55/38); CO Ghana, CEDAW/C/GHA/CO/5 (2006) para 35; CO Greece, CEDAW/C/GRC/CO/6 (2007) para 33 and A/57/38, Exceptional Session (2002), para 295; CO India, A/55/38, 22nd Session (2000) paras 82–3; CO Kyrgyzstan, A/59/38, 30th Session (2004) paras 171–2; CO Libyan Arab Jamahiriya, CEDAW/C/LBY/CO/5 (2009) paras 17–18; CO Myanmar, CEDAW/C/MMR/CO/3 (2008) para 44; CO Timor-Leste, CEDAW/C/TLS/CO/1 (2009) paras 42, 46; CO Singapore, CEDAW/C/SGP/CO/3 (2007) para 15; CO United Republic of Tanzania, CEDAW/C/TZA/CO/6 (2009) paras 18, 19, 44; CO Vanuatu, CEDAW/C/VUT/CO/3 (2007) paras 38–39.

[150] GR 27 paras 26–8 and 51–3.

[151] CO Botswana, CEDAW/C/BOT/CO/3 (2010) para 40 (referring to art 14). See also CO Burkina Faso, A/60/38, 33rd Session (2005) para 348; CO Guinea, CEDWA/C/GIN/CO/6 (2007) para 43; CO India, A/55/38, 22nd Session (2000) para 83; CO Malawi, CEDAW/C/MWI/CO/5 (2006) para 33; CO Switzerland, CEDAW/C/CHE/CO/3 (2009) para 39. See also the discussion in ch on art 14.

[152] CO Ethiopia, A/59/38, 30th Session (2004) paras 251–2.

[153] CO Malawi, CEDAW/C/MWI/CO/6 (2010) paras 42–3.

ownership is extended by custom to exclude widow(s)' inheritance of *any* property. This can result in the late husband's family descending on the widow(s) and claiming all the property accumulated during the marriage, including such items as houses and businesses that are not on clan land, home furnishings, cars, and bank accounts—a fundamental violation of wives' equal right to property upon dissolution of marriage by death.

III. Article 16(2)

Child marriage remains a matter of concern with respect to many States parties. State obligations to institute a minimum age of marriage, right to consent to marriage, and registration of marriage were first enshrined in the Convention of that title, adopted in 1964.[154] Despite decades of discussion and universal condemnation of child marriage in international fora, the practice persists, grounded in tradition and defended on the basis of culture and religious law.[155] While the prohibition of child marriage applies equally to girls and boys, its effect is largely asymmetrical; girls are much more frequently subjected to it.[156] The Committee invariably comments on States parties' failure to protect against early and forced marriage.[157]

1. Definition: 'a Child'

The definition of 'child' in international law is not uniform, nor is its formal demarcation, age of majority. The CRC provides a guideline rather than an absolute definition: 'a child means every human being below the age of eighteen years unless under the law applicable to the child, majority is attained earlier.'[158] The *ICCPR Commentary* concludes that under ICCPR Article 23, States parties must set a minimum age of marriage, which according to the *travaux préparatoires* should be no lower than fifteen.[159] The Convention on the Civil Aspects of International Child Abduction (The Hague Convention) applies only to children below the age of sixteen.[160] The United Nations Programme on Youth sees 'youth' as individuals between the ages of fifteen and twenty-four years.[161] The African Charter on the Rights and Welfare of the Child states that a child is a 'human being less than 18

---

[154] Marriage Convention (n 6 above).

[155] See eg UNICEF, 'Early Marriage: A Harmful Traditional Practice' (2005), <http://www.unicef.org/publications/files/Early_Marriage_12.lo.pdf> accessed 31 December 2010; CO Israel, A/60/38 (2005) paras 261–2 (State party cited 'privacy').

[156] CO Morocco, CEDAW/C/MAR/CO/4 (2008) para 34 ('vast majority' of court-approved child marriage relates to girls); UNICEF addresses it as an issue affecting only girls (n 155 above).

[157] CO Lao People's Democratic Republic, A/60/38, 32nd Session (2005) paras 110–11; CO Paraguay, A/60/38, 32nd Session (2005) paras 281–2; CO Bangladesh, A/59/38, 31st Session (2004) paras 257–8; CO Indonesia, CEDAW/C/IDN/CO/5 (2007) para 18; CO Japan, CEDAW/C/JPN/CO/6 (2009) paras 17–18 (failure to change law after prior review); CO Hungary, A/57/38, Exceptional Session (2002) paras 333–4; CO Bhutan, CEDAW/C/BTN/CO/7 (2009) para 34 (State party did not address 'illegal child marriages' noted in prior review, A/59/38, 30th Session (2004)) paras 125–6; CO Suriname, A/57/38, 27th Session (2002) paras 67–8; CO Tajikistan, CEDAW/C/TJK/C/3 (2007) paras 35–6 (minimum age reduced to 17); CO Chile, CEDAW/C/CHI/CO/4 (2007) paras 21–2; CO Trinidad and Tobago, A/57/38, 26th Session (2002) paras 157–8; CO Nigeria, A/59/38, 30th Session (2004) para 299 and CEDAW/C/NGA/CO/6 (2008) paras 318, 319. Forced marriage is discussed in section II. 2. a) Arranged Marriage and Forced Marriage, above.

[158] CRC art 1.

[159] M Nowak, *UN Covenant on Civil and Political Rights: A Commentary*, 2nd edn (2005) 527–8, 534–5.

[160] Para 4.

[161] The United Nations 'Youth and the United Nations: Frequently Asked Questions [FAQS/Q&A]' <http://social.un.org/index/Youth/FAQ.aspx> accessed 31 December 2010 (citing General Assembly, A/36/215 and resolution 36/28 (1981)).

years of age'. The Committee states unequivocally that a 'child' is a person below the age of eighteen.[162]

2. Betrothal and Marriage of a Child

The preamble to the 1964 Marriage Convention cites the UNGA[163] 'that certain customs, ancient laws and practices relating to marriage and the family [are] inconsistent with the principles set forth in the Charter of the United Nations and in the Universal Declaration of Human Rights', and indicates that States:

should take all appropriate measures with a view to abolishing such customs, ancient laws and practices by ensuring, *inter alia*, complete freedom in the choice of a spouse, eliminating completely child marriages and the betrothal of young girls before the age of puberty, establishing appropriate penalties where necessary and establishing a civil or other register in which all marriages will be recorded.

These rights and State responsibilities were restated in DEDAW Article 6(2)(a), providing for equality in choice of spouse and consent to marriage. DEDAW Article 6(3) states that 'child marriage and the betrothal of young girls before puberty should be prohibited' and requires establishment of a minimum age for marriage and 'compulsory' marriage registration.

The Convention provision underscores States parties' obligations to eliminate child marriage and to protect individuals by requiring a minimum age of marriage and registration of marriage. The Third Committee Working Group discussed whether to refer only to girls and whether the prohibition of betrothal should apply only to girls prior to puberty. Ultimately, it adopted language, alluding to children rather than only to girls and prohibiting 'betrothal and marriage of a child'.[164] The significance of this language is that it protects the rights of all children with respect to being pledged in marriage without their consent or knowledge and eliminates any support for cultural practices that distinguish between girls and boys as to their presumed readiness for marriage at puberty.

3. Shall Have No Legal Effect

Article 16(2) of the Convention emphasizes the offensiveness of child marriage, beyond the prohibition in DEDAW, by stating that such marriages 'shall have no legal effect'. The Committee has not discussed the issue of invalidity as a universal legal remedy for child marriage as suggested by the language of Article 16(2). A marriage may be declared to have 'no legal effect', or be invalidated, through a prescribed legal process to declare it void *ab initio*.[165] This process protects the child parties by restoring their status as single, never-married (rather than divorced) persons and, to the extent possible, voiding any property transactions relating to the marriage and restoring property to the original owners. A State party must provide for a process that places the girl in a position to be properly married as an adult without stigma related to her child marriage.[166]

---

[162] GR 21 para 36.   [163] UNGA Res 843 (IX) (17 December 1954).

[164] Rehof (n 8 above) 184; UN Doc A/34/60, Annex, para 254.

[165] A marriage that is void *ab initio* (from the beginning) places the parties in the position of being never-married.

[166] CO India, CEDAW/C/IND/CO/3 (2007) para 56.

4. *Minimum Age for Marriage*

Article 16(2) (like the earlier Marriage Convention) does not designate a preferred minimum age, and the *travaux préparatoires* do not indicate any discussion of a specific age for marriage.[167] With the adoption of General Recommendation 21, the definition of 'child' for purposes of age for marriage has been clarified as less than eighteen years.[168]

The Committee regularly comments on the persistent laws and practices that permit a lower minimum age of marriage for females than for males and insists that the age of consent to marriage should be the same for both.[169] Many States parties that do provide for a minimum age set it at less than eighteen, and many also allow a lower age of marriage for females than for males. A few States parties do not require a minimum age at all.[170]

As the Committee notes with concern, the exploitive nature of child marriage is visited much more intensely on females than on males. Girls may be given in marriage to pay a debt or as compensation for a wrong committed against the male's family. They may be given to men who are much older. Child brides suffer extreme disadvantage in losing their opportunities for education and personal freedoms as compared to boys of the same age.[171] Frequently their health suffers as well because of very early sexual contact and childbearing.[172]

5. *Marriage Registration*

The Committee notes that registration protects women and girls from men's undertaking multiple unreported marriages, engages the State in ascertaining that individuals are of legal age and are not constrained by consanguinity or other appropriate limitations, and provides proof of marriage for purposes of establishing property rights during marriage and at its dissolution.[173] It also has a bearing on children's legal and social status in many places.[174]

IV. Equality in Context

1. *Formal Equality*

The nature of the family setting renders formal laws particularly inadequate to ensure equality within it. Still, State party commitment, in the form of legal provisions, is essential to implementation of the equality norm in fact. As long as States parties retain inadequate

---

[167] One State noted that the CRC was in drafting process at the same time as CEDAW, but the record does not indicate any discussion of the age issue as related to the CRC. UN Doc A/34/60 para 256.

[168] See discussion of 'child' in section B. III. 1.

[169] CO Burkina Faso, A/60/38, 33rd Session (2005) paras 339–40; CO Samoa, A/60/38, 32nd Session (2005) paras 60–1; CO France, A/58/38, 29th Session (2003), paras 267–8; CO Guatemala, A/57/38, Exceptional Session (2002) paras 196–7; CO Mexico, A/57/38, Exceptional Session (2002), paras 449–50; CO Armenia, C/ARM/CO/4/Rev.1 (2009) para 14; CO Venezuela, CEDAW/C/VEN/CO/6 (2006) para 34.

[170] CO Saudi Arabia, CEDAW/C/SAU/CO/2 (2008) paras 35–6.

[171] CO Guatemala, A/57/38, Exceptional Session (2002) para 197; CO Yemen, CEDAW/C/YEM/CO/6 (2009) para 31; CO Peru, A/57/38, Exceptional Session (2002) para 489; CO Timor-Leste, CEDAW/C/TLS/CO/1 (2009) para 35.

[172] See GR 24 paras 15(d), 28; CO Nigeria, CEDAW//NGA/CO/6 (2008) para 33 (child marriage contributes to extraordinarily high maternal mortality rate).

[173] CO India, A/55/38, 22nd Session (2000) para 62; CO Syria, CEDAW/C/SYR/CO/1 (2007) para 34; CO Yemen, C/YEM/CO/6 (2009) para 31; CO Azerbaijan, CEDAW/C/AZE/CO/4 (2009) paras 39–40.

[174] See the discussion of children born out of wedlock in section B. II.4. b above.

laws or position customary and religious systems as superior to the Convention or to constitutional norms that apply in other areas, equality in the family will remain out of reach.[175]

The Committee has pointedly noted that the fluidity of custom and the possibility of interpretation of religious law offer potential for progress towards equality,[176] which it expects States parties to explore. Ultimately, the achievement of equality in the family requires as a foundation a comprehensive and coherent formal legal structure that meets the standards of Article 16.[177]

2. Substantive and Transformative Equality

In the context of the family, substantive equality—the *de facto* enjoyment of rights provided by law—can only be achieved through efforts to transform the institution itself. The gendered nature of interests and power distribution between family members must be examined, and power must be redistributed on a basis of equality.

States parties are obligated under Article 16 to provide for the conditions that promote and support the equal power of women and men in making decisions within and about families. Meeting the substantive obligations of Articles 5 and 15, in particular, is crucial to meeting the substantive equality obligations of Article 16. Some States parties have attempted to mandate equality in distributing household tasks;[178] others have mandated inequality, frequently in the name of custom or religion.[179] As a practical matter, laws providing for equality in sharing household tasks and care of children are not amenable to enforcement.[180] States cannot monitor whether daily decision-making is based on imbalance of power between the parties and traditional gender roles. They can and must, however, provide for full legal capacity and economic equality and work towards elimination of customs and stereotypes that prevent women from engaging on an equal basis with men in making these decisions. Changing this dynamic transforms the institution.

C. States Parties' Obligations

I. Implementation

1. Obligation to Respect

Article 16(1) requires States parties to refrain from preserving or enacting laws and policies that undermine equality between women and men in the family. This includes eliminating State party recognition of written and unwritten religious law and customary

---

[175] Reservations on this basis are discussed below in Section C. II.

[176] CO Malawi, CEDAW/C/MWI/CO/6 (2010) para 21 ('The Committee urges the State party to view culture as a dynamic dimension of the country's life and social fabric, subject to many influences over time and therefore to change'); CO Tunisia, A/57/38, 27th Session (2002) para 184 (commending the State party's reform of its [Islamic] Personal Status Code); CO United Arab Emirates, CEDAW/C/ARE/CO/1 (2010) para 44.

[177] CO Lebanon, A/60/38, 33rd Session (2005) paras 99–100.

[178] eg the Family Code of Cuba, described in Combined Fifth and Sixth State Party Report, CEDAW/C/CUB/5–6 (2006) paras 53–6, 694–714.

[179] The reservations entered by Egypt and Niger state this quite clearly. See also *Morales de Sierra* (n 138 above) paras 28, 39, 41, and 44.

[180] As the Government of Cuba acknowledged, see Combined Fifth and Sixth State Party Report, CEDAW/C/CUB/5–6 (2006) paras 170–4.

practices that discriminate against women; refraining from preservation or enactment of family codes that enshrine discriminatory community customs and practices; and eliminating or changing statutory codes that permit or encourage any form of discrimination in the family as described in Article 16.

States parties also are obligated to provide for marriage and *de facto* relationships and their dissolution, with all their implications as to property rights, decision-making, and custody of children, according to a non-discriminatory statutory code that all individuals may invoke regardless of ethnic, religious, or other identity.

2. *Obligation to Protect*

States parties are obligated to protect women from discriminatory actions by other individuals and by institutions and 'enterprises'.[181] In the family context, the obligation to protect is not readily distinguishable from the obligation to respect, as enactment of the laws and regulations necessary to protect women from the discriminatory actions of spouses and other family members, also meets the States parties' 'obligation to respect' the right to non-discrimination as described in section C.I.1. These laws and regulations should provide for equality in making decisions relating to marriage, *de facto* relationships, and their dissolution; require an individual's free consent to marriage and specifically prohibit forced marriage and child marriage; and provide for equality between women and men as to all aspects of care and custody of children and of property ownership, control, and inheritance. States parties must ensure that gender stereotypes and role assumptions are not perpetuated in undertaking family law reform and redesign.

States parties are required to prohibit and prevent actions by family members that harm women in the name of family solidarity or honour. This includes effectively addressing 'crimes of honour', marital rape, and other violence,[182] forced marriage, and reproductive choice within relationships.

3. *Obligation to Fulfil*

The obligation to fulfil human rights norms places responsibility on States parties to invest in programmes and infrastructure that ensure that individuals can enjoy their rights. With respect to discrimination in the family, States parties must provide a system of courts or other independent and impartial tribunals, properly trained in matters of attitude as well as in law, in which women can claim their rights. They also must provide women with competent legal assistance to access these decision-makers or bodies. Under Article 16(2), States parties must establish an infrastructure for the registration of marriage.

States parties have an obligation to take measures to eliminate forced marriages and to enforce those measures effectively. They must devote resources to changing social and cultural attitudes to eliminate the stereotypical assumptions that marriage is required to complete women's lives and that women's primary value lies in their reproductive roles. States parties are obligated to expand women's educational and employment opportunities so they can avoid forced marriage and to provide shelter and support for women who flee it.[183]

States must also provide for education on family life issues from an early age, and for other efforts to change attitudes, with a view towards addressing gender stereotypes and

---

[181] CEDAW art 2(e).   [182] See the discussion in ch on violence against women.
[183] Ibid.

power imbalances between male and female that support child marriage and perpetuate inequality in the family. The deep infrastructure of inequality must be addressed under every article of the Convention, beginning and ending with the family.

II. Reservations

Article 16 is the most reserved substantive article in the Convention. As of 31 December 2010, thirty-four States parties have reserved specifically all or part of Article 16. Others, as the Committee has noted, have not reserved but perpetuate 'certain laws' that 'do not actually conform to the provisions of the Convention'.[184]

The reservations are remarkable for their content as well.[185] In General Recommendation 21 the Committee:

> noted with alarm the number of States parties which have entered reservations to the whole or part of article 16, ... claiming that compliance may conflict with a commonly held vision of the family based, *inter alia*, on cultural or religious beliefs or on the country's economic or political status. ... Many of these countries hold a belief in the patriarchal structure of a family which places a father, husband or son in a favourable position. In some countries where fundamentalist or other extremist views or economic hardship have encouraged a return to old values and traditions, women's place in the family has deteriorated sharply.[186]

The Article 16 reservations fall into several categories. Some clearly reject its premises on the basis of conflict with religious law.[187] Three States parties reserved Article 16 on the ground that matters relating to personal status are reserved to their 'communities'—essentially carving out discriminatory family law as an exception to non-discrimination provisions in those States parties' respective constitutions or basic laws.[188] Others have reserved specific provisions, indicating some attention to the particularities of inequality in the family.[189] Several States parties entered a general reservation to the entire Convention, indicating that the State's religious law or its constitution is deemed superior to the norms of the treaty.[190]

General Recommendation 21, paragraph 44 urges States parties to 'resolutely discourage any notions of inequality of women and men which are affirmed by laws, or by religious or private law or by custom, and progress to the stage where reservations, particularly to article 16, will [be] withdrawn'. In 1998, in its statement for the fiftieth anniversary of the UDHR, the Committee stated that it considers Articles 2 and 16 'to be core provisions of the Convention...central to the objects and purpose of the Convention', and that reservations to Article 16 are impermissible.[191] The Treaty-Specific Reporting Guidelines adopted in 2008 requires States parties to 'report on the interpretation and the effect' of reservations to, *inter alia*, Article 16 and on 'any reservations or declarations they may have lodged with regard to similar obligations in other human rights treaties'.[192] Several States parties consistently enter objections to these reservations,

---

[184] GR 21 para 45. [185] See the discussion in ch on Reservations.
[186] GR 21 paras 41–2. [187] eg Egypt. [188] India, Israel, Singapore.
[189] eg Malaysia, Libyan Arab Jamahiriya, Bangladesh. [190] eg Tunisia, Brunei Darussalam.
[191] 'Report of the Committee on the Elimination of Discrimination against Women' (1998) UN Doc A/53/38/Rev.1 19th Session, Annex, 47–50.
[192] 'Report of the Committee on the Elimination of Discrimination against Women' (2008) UN Doc A/63/38(Supp), 41st Session, Annex, 78–83.

sometimes stating specifically that they consider the reservation to be contrary to the object and purpose of the Convention.[193]

1. *Withdrawal of Reservations*

The Committee regularly engages States parties in a discussion of reservations during the constructive dialogue and urges them to withdraw them. Several States parties have modified reservations to Article 16[194] but very few have completely withdrawn them.[195] One State party as of 2010 has failed to submit a formal notice of withdrawal despite announcing to the Committee in 2006 that it would do so.[196]

The characterization of the Article 16 reservations as contrary to the object and purpose of the Convention is more than a legal formality. The Committee has determined that equality in the family is essential to women's full enjoyment of their human rights. It therefore continues to pursue the subject, consistently indicating to all States parties their obligation to promote evolution of religion, culture, and tradition to integrate the Convention norm of equality in the family.

2. *Reservations and the Optional Protocol*

In 2007, the Committee had before it two communications relating to Article 16(1)(g), which had been reserved by the State party at issue. In reviewing the cases, the Committee determined that the petitions were inadmissible and did not address the issue of reservations. A minority of seven experts produced dissenting opinions in both cases. The minority concluded in both opinions, after analyzing the status of the petitioners as 'victims', that the petitioners' claims should be examined 'in light of Articles 2, 5, and 16(1)'.[197] The minority opinions noted the majority's failure to address the reservations issue, stating that since the majority examined the petitions only on the basis of Article 16(1)(g), the reservation should have been addressed. The Committee's approach to petitions based on reserved provisions remains unresolved.

---

[193] See the discussion of objections in ch on Reservations.

[194] Malaysia (partial withdrawal/modification), Libya (modification), France (partial withdrawal).

[195] A detailed description of withdrawal and modification of reservations to art 16 is included in the ch on Reservations.

[196] Morocco, CEDAW/C/MAR/CO/4 (2008) paras 14–15.

[197] *Group d'Intérêt pour le Matronyme* (n 25 above); *SOS Sexisme* (n 25 above).

Violence Against Women

A. Introduction

There is no provision in either the Declaration (DEDAW) or Convention on the Elimination of All Forms of Discrimination against Women (the Convention) that explicitly addresses violence against women. This contrasts with the ICERD Article 4(a) which requires States parties to declare as 'an offence punishable by law...all acts of violence...against any race or group of persons of another colour or ethnic origin'. Instead,

   * I would like to thank Lena Skoglund for her valuable contribution as a research assistant; I would also like to thank Professor Hilary Charlesworth for her helpful comments on the chapter on art 3 and the chapter on Violence against Women and, as always, for her encouragement and support.

States parties' obligations with respect to the elimination of violence against women have been developed by a number of international institutional initiatives in which the Committee has played a key role.[1] By requiring a holistic approach to the different manifestations of violence against women, identifying violence as discrimination against women, and thereby adopting a rights-based approach, General Recommendation 19, on Violence against Women, 1992 was the instrument that brought violence against women unequivocally into the domain of international human rights law.

B. General Recommendation 19

I. Background to General Recommendation 19

The failure to include violence against women within the Convention is explained by the institutional understanding of the issue at the time of its adoption and its late entry onto the international agenda.[2] The World Plan of Action adopted by the Conference of the International Women's Year, Mexico City, 1975, did not refer explicitly to violence against women but called upon women to proclaim their solidarity in support of the elimination of gross violations of human rights 'involving acts against the moral and physical integrity of individuals'.[3] It also referred to the need for education programmes based on the ideals of 'mutual respect' and for resolving family conflict in ways that ensure the dignity, equality, and security of each of its members.[4] The Declaration of Mexico on the Equality of Women and their Contribution to Development and Peace,[5] paragraph 11, stated an aim of social education to be to teach 'respect for physical integrity' and that the 'human body, whether that of woman or man, is inviolable and respect for it is a fundamental element of human dignity'. Paragraph 28 recognized some forms of violence against women, including 'rape, prostitution, physical assault, mental cruelty, child marriage, forced marriage and marriage as a commercial transaction'.

In drafting the Convention Article 6, Belgium proposed including the words 'attacks on the physical integrity of women',[6] echoing the language of the Mexico Declaration. The proposal was not supported. Portugal 'touched upon' the issue again but this was apparently the limit of attempts to include any direct reference to violence against women in the Convention.

The Second World Conference on Women in 1980, adopted a Resolution on '[b]attered women and violence in the family'[7] that identified geographic and social isolation, alcohol

---

[1] Report of the Secretary-General, 'In-depth Study on All Forms of Violence against Women' (2006) UN Doc A/61/122/Add.1, 13 para 31.

[2] On the history of violence against women as a matter of international concern see J Connors, 'Violence against Women', Background Paper, United Nations Fourth World Conference on Women (1995) reprinted in H Barnett, *Sourcebook on Feminist Jurisprudence* (1997) 558; E Evatt, 'Finding a Voice for Women's Rights: The Early Years of CEDAW', 34 *George Washington Intl L R* (2002–2003) 515, 543–51.

[3] 'Report of the World Conference of the International Women's Year', Mexico City (hereafter Mexico Conference) (2 July 1975) UN Doc E/CONF.66/34 para 51.

[4] Ibid paras 124 and 131.

[5] Mexico Conference (n 3 above).

[6] L Rehof, *Guide to the Travaux Préparatoires of the United Nations Convention on the Elimination of All Forms of Discrimination against Women* (1993) 91.

[7] 'Report of the World Conference of the United Nations Decade for Women, Copenhagen', (1980) UN Doc A/CONF.94/35 Resolution 5.

and drug abuse, and low self-esteem as contributing factors to violence. Violence against women was located as a social problem within the ambit of health policies. Among the objectives for health care were the 'development of programmes aimed at eliminating all forms of violence against women and children' and 'the protection of women of all ages from the physical and mental abuse resulting from domestic violence, sexual assault, sexual exploitation and any other form of abuse'.[8]

Following the Copenhagen Conference, various UN bodies began to attend to violence against women, most notably the UN Committee on Crime Prevention and Control. In 1982, the Committee identified violence, including violence against family members, as an important issue of crime prevention and control and put violence against women on the agenda for its Seventh Congress, scheduled to take place in 1985.

Also in 1982, the UNECOSOC, acting on CSW's recommendation, adopted Resolution 1982/22. The resolution noted the persistent concern expressed by the international community at the 'blatant and inhuman' abuses of women and children, including battered women and children, violence in the family, rape, prostitution, and the inevitable serious problems of mental and physical health. The resolution called upon member States to take 'immediate and energetic steps' to combat these social evils.[9]

The special areas of concern identified at the 1985 Third World Conference on Women at Nairobi included abused women and the need to intensify efforts to introduce national legislation and programmes to ascertain the causes of such violence, to prevent and eliminate it. The Forward-Looking Strategies for the Advancement of Women adopted at the Conference (FLS) asserted that 'gender specific violence is increasing'[10] and that violence against women 'exists in various forms in everyday life in all societies'.[11] The introduction of preventive policies, legal measures, national machinery, and comprehensive assistance for women victims of violence were called for. In 1987, the CSW identified violence against women within the family and society as falling within the FLS priority theme of peace.

In 1985, the UNGA adopted its first resolution on domestic violence, in which it recognized that 'abuse and battery in the family are critical problems that have serious physical and psychological effects on individual family members'.[12] Although the resolution 'had regard' to the Convention, it did not identify women as the main victims of such violence and its recommendations were directed towards the UN SG to intensify research on domestic violence from a criminological perspective, rather than towards institutions for the guarantee of women's human rights.

Thus, at the end of the UN Decade for Women, violence against women was entering the international agenda but was perceived primarily as a social matter of crime prevention and criminal justice. The form of violence most commonly considered at the international level was family or domestic violence, although there was some attention to other forms of violence such as sexual assault, prostitution, and coerced marriage. Requests for research into violence and for policy responses were directed towards the institutional bodies for crime control, not those for the guarantee of human rights. Violence was often perceived as a private act, that is, as the deviant behaviour of an individual rather than

---

[8] Ibid para 141(f).   [9] See also ECOSOC Res 1984/14 (24 May 1984) on violence in the family.

[10] 'Report of the World Conference to Review and Appraise the Achievements of the United Nations Decade for Women: Equality, Development and Peace, Nairobi' (1985) para 288; para 76 asserted that 'Legislation should be passed and laws enforced in every country to end the degradation of women through sex-related crimes'.

[11] Ibid para 258.   [12] UNGA Res 40/36 (29 November 1985) UN Doc A/RES/40/36.

as sustained and acquiesced in by the organizational structures of society (for example, prisons, police, courts, religious institutions). Other lenses through which violence was viewed were those of health and social welfare of all family members. 'In addition, with the adoption of the "harmful traditional practices" agenda by the UN in the 1980s, violence against women came to be associated with traditional societies, thus de-linking the problem from structural inequalities inherent in existing gender relations'.[13] A collective mind shift was needed to see the multiple local forms of violence committed against women as constituting a pattern of global behaviour and thus to expose the systemic and structural nature of that violence. Such a mind shift was necessary to bring violence against women within the framework of international human rights law incurring State responsibility for its continuance.

The beginning of that mind shift came through a number of initiatives in the late 1980s. One facet was a global campaign on violence against women, led by activist women's movements and sustained since at least the early 1980s.[14] Another was at the institutional level. In 1986, an Expert Group on Violence in the Family with Special Emphasis on its Effects on Women was organized by the UN. This was followed in 1989 by a special study on violence against women in the family, which highlighted its endemic nature and occurrence across social divides including those of class, culture, and religion.[15] The study showed that such violence may be tolerated, condoned, or acquiesced in by the community or the State. It identified domestic violence as complex and multi-factoral but concluded that 'violence against wives is a function of the belief, fostered in all cultures, that men are superior and that the women they live with are their possessions or chattels that they can treat as they wish and as they consider appropriate.'[16]

UNECOSOC Resolution 1988/2, on Efforts to eradicate violence against women within the family and society, noted the relevant provisions of the ICESCR, but not those of the Convention. It called for consolidated efforts between intergovernmental organizations and NGOs for the eradication of violence against women within the family and society. In a further resolution on domestic violence in 1990, the UNGA commended the efforts that had been made through the UN, including through the Convention, to guarantee the human rights of women and children, but maintained the criminal justice approach. It recognized that domestic violence may cause physical and psychological harm to members of the family and requested the SG to convene a further expert working group to draw up guidelines on domestic violence.[17]

In 1990, Charlotte Bunch argued that 'sexism kills women' before birth, during childhood, and throughout adulthood. This violence is not random but is profoundly political, resulting from structural relationships of power, domination, and privilege. Unlike the UNGA resolutions, her article explored the importance of connecting women's life experiences of violence to human rights and suggested ways of furthering this approach.[18]

[13] *15 Years of the United Nations Special Rapporteur on violence against women* (1994–2009)—A Critical Review, 2008, 15, 33 (hereinafter Special Rapporteur '15 Years').

[14] Report of the Secretary-General (n 1 above) para 23; see also Special Rapporteur ' 15 Years' (n 13 above) 3. Their crucial role has continued; P Antrobus, *The Global Women's Movement: Origins, Issues and Strategies* (2004).

[15] *Violence against Women in the Family*, UN, 1989, UN Sales No E.89.IV.5.   [16] Ibid 33.

[17] UNGA Res 45/114 (14 December 1990) UN Doc A/RES/45/114.

[18] C Bunch, 'Women's Rights as Human Rights: Toward a Re-Vision of Human Rights' (1990) 12 *Human Rights Quarterly* 486.

The Committee first addressed violence against women through General Recommendation 12 in 1989. General Recommendation 12 stated that Articles 2, 5, 11, 12, and 16 impose obligations on States parties to protect women against acts of violence; identified the sites of violence as the family, the workplace, and other areas of social life; and recommended that States report on legislation and other measures to protect women against violence, support services for victims, and statistical data on the incidence of violence. In its General Recommendation 14, the Committee reverted to the more usual analysis by identifying female circumcision as a traditional practice harmful to women's health and recommending measures for its eradication.

II. General Recommendation 19

The 1989 UN Study had recommended that the necessary fundamental change might best be commenced through implementation of the 'ideals and goals' of the Convention, along with those of the FLS.[19] The adoption of General Recommendation 19 in 1992 was a major step towards this as it delivered the 'missing link'[20] in understanding violence against women as a matter of human rights. In anticipation of the 1993 World Conference on Human Rights, in 1991, the Committee decided to allocate part of its 11th session in 1992 to discussing and studying articles of the Convention relating to violence. At the 11th session it adopted General Recommendation 19, which became the basis of the Committee's subsequent work on the issue.

'General Recommendation 19 is a detailed and an in-depth review of the issue of violence against women containing general comments, comments on specific articles of the Convention and specific recommendations'.[21] It locates violence against women within the framework of inequality between women and men, asserting that all forms of such violence constitute a form of sex-based discrimination under Article 1, and that discrimination is a major cause of such violence. It defines gender-based violence against women in a holistic way that encompasses all its diverse forms and sites. This constitutes a significant move away from the more restricted and itemized understanding of violence against women as primarily (but not exclusively) domestic or familial violence. It requires States parties to prevent, investigate, and punish acts of violence against women whether committed by public authorities or private bodies and to provide for reparation. It spells out that 'the full implementation of the Convention require[s] States to take positive measures to eliminate all forms of violence against women'. Detailed recommendations for practical steps to achieve this are provided.

III. Subsequent International Instruments

General Recommendation 19 brought violence against women within the terms of the Convention[22] and thus squarely into the language, institutions and processes of

---

[19] *Violence against Women in the Family* (n 15 above) 105.

[20] H Shin, 'CEDAW and Violence against Women: Providing the "Missing Link"' in HB Schöpp-Schilling and C Flinterman (eds), *The Circle of Empowerment: Twenty-Five Years of The UN Committee on The Elimination of Discrimination against Women* (2007) 223.

[21] T Van Boven, 'Study Concerning the Right to Restitution, Compensation and Rehabilitation for Victims of Gross Violations of Human Rights and Fundamental Freedoms' (1996) UN Doc E/CN.4/SUB.2/1993, reprinted in 59 *Law and Contemporary Problems* 283.

[22] The first Special Rapporteur on violence against women concurred that although '[v]iolence is not expressly mentioned... a proper interpretation of the definition [of discrimination in CEDAW art 1] allows it

international human rights law. In June 1993, the World Conference on Human Rights recognized that '[g]ender-based violence and all forms of sexual harassment and exploitation ... are incompatible with the dignity and worth of the human person, and must be eliminated'.[23]

This was followed by the Declaration on the Elimination of Violence against Women (DEVAW), drafted by CSW and adopted by the UNGA in December 1993.[24] DEVAW affirms the importance of universal application to women of their human rights and recognizes that effective implementation of the Convention 'would contribute to the elimination of violence against women'. It reiterates the rights-based approach, affirming that 'violence against women constitutes a violation of the rights and fundamental freedoms of women and impairs or nullifies their enjoyment of those rights and freedoms'. Significantly, it then locates that violence historically as a consequence of patriarchy is a 'manifestation of historically unequal power relations between men and women, which have led to domination over and discrimination against women by men ... is one of the crucial social mechanisms by which women are forced into a subordinate position compared with men'.

DEVAW defines gender-based violence and sets out States' obligations with respect to its condemnation, echoing General Recommendation 19 in its assertion of the standard of due diligence for the prevention, investigation, and punishment of violence against women, 'whether those acts are perpetrated by the State or by private person'. Importantly, it states that States 'should not invoke any custom, tradition or religious consideration to avoid their obligations with respect to its elimination'. DEVAW sets out a range of measures that should be undertaken by States and by international organizations within their fields of competence.

DEVAW is applicable to all UN member States, not just States parties to the Convention, as is the case with General Recommendation 19.[25] As a UNGA resolution it is not legally binding but as a consensus statement of the global political body it has significant weight. There are differences between General Recommendation 19 and DEVAW. The former follows the articles of the Convention and is directed towards State party reporting, while the latter looks to a broader range of State activity, for example, budgeting and developing national plans of action and the role of UN organs, specialized agencies. General Recommendation 19 incorporates more forms of violence than DEVAW, for example, by explicitly including pornography and incest. The Committee has been guided by both instruments in determining States parties' obligations to combat violence against women.

Another important step taken in 1993 was the adoption by the UNCHR of the mandate for a Special Rapporteur on the causes and consequences of violence against women (SR VAW).[26] The Special Rapporteurs' annual and country visit reports are a source of information for the Committee. In 1995, the Beijing Declaration and Platform for Action included violence against women as an Area of Critical Concern. Five years later, the Beijing + 5 outcome document, *Women 2000: Gender Equality, Development and Peace for*

---

to be included by implication'. Special Rapporteur on violence against women 'Preliminary Report' (1994)UN Doc E/CN.4/1995/42 para 85.

[23] Vienna Declaration and Programme for Action A/CONF.157/23 (1993) 1, 18; II, 38.

[24] UNGA Res 48/104 (20 December 1993), 'Declaration on the Elimination of Violence against Women' UN Doc A/RES/48/104. On the adoption of DEVAW see the discussion in ch on the Optional Protocol.

[25] This was important because while in 2010 there are 186 States parties to the Convention, there were many fewer in 1993.

[26] UNCHR UN Doc E/CN .4/RES/1994/45 (4 March 1994).

the Twenty-first Century declared that '[i]t is widely accepted that violence against women and girls, whether occurring in public or private life, is a human rights issue'.[27]

The UNGA has continued to address violence against women, including in the Millennium Declaration[28] and the Outcome Document of the 2005 World Summit.[29] In 2003, it asked the UN SG to prepare an In-Depth Study on Violence against Women.[30] The Study provides a 'state of the art' overview of the forms and manifestations of violence against women, its consequences, indicators, State obligations, and promising practices in implementation and prevention. Its first recommendation for the national level is to secure gender equality and protect women's human rights.[31] Taking note of the Study, in 2006, the GA requested an annual report on implementation of its recommendations, including follow-up procedures.[32]

At its annual sessions CSW regularly takes up various facets of the topic and has made elimination and prevention of violence against women and girls its priority theme for 2013.[33] Within its mandate for the maintenance of international peace and security, the UNSC has called upon States to protect women and girls from gender-based violence in armed conflict[34] and more forcefully has demanded the complete 'cessation by all parties to armed conflict of all acts of sexual violence'.[35] Other UN bodies continue to engage with the issue within the terms of their own competence; for example, the UN Commission on Crime Prevention and Criminal Justice determined in 2008 that violence against women and girls would be central to its work over the ensuing seven years.

At the regional level, the Convention of Belém do Pará, adopted by the Inter-American system in 1994, was the first treaty on violence against women, and the Assembly of the African Union adopted the Protocol to the African Charter on Human and Peoples' Rights on the Rights of Women in Africa in 2003.[36] The Council of Europe Committee of Ministers has adopted a non-binding recommendation on the protection of women against violence.[37]

Thus, by 2010, multiple global and regional institutions had incorporated issues of violence against women into their work, thereby incurring the possibility that the work of the Committee might become marginalized or overlooked. However, the importance of the Convention as the global, international legally binding instrument prohibiting discrimination, and, thus, gender-based violence, against women, is recognized and

---

[27] UNGA Res S-23/3, rev. 1 (16 November 2000) 'Further actions and initiatives to implement the Beijing Declaration and Platform for Action' UN Doc A/RES/S-23/3 (2000 Outcome Document) para 13.

[28] UNGA Res 55/2 (8 September 2000) UN Doc A/RES/55/2 para 25. The CEDAW Committee routinely refers States to the Millennium Development Goals in its concluding observations.

[29] UNGA Res 60/L.1 (15 September 2005) UN Doc A/RES/60/L.1 para 58(f): 'we resolve to ... eliminate pervasive gender discrimination ... and violence against women and the girl child'.

[30] UNGA Res 58/185 (22 December 2003) UN Doc A/RES/58/185.

[31] Report of the Secretary-General (n 1 above) 104.

[32] UNGA Res 61/143 (19 December 2006). In 2008, the Secretary-General launched a Campaign *UNITE to End Violence against Women*, 2008–2015.

[33] CSW, 'Report on the Fifty-Third Session (2–13 March 2009) ECOSOC OR (2009) Supp N0 7, E/2009/27, UN Doc E/CN.6/2009/15, 19.

[34] UNSC Res 1325 (31 October 2000) On Women, Peace and Security, UN Doc S/RES/1325.

[35] UNSC Res 1820 (19 June 2008) UN Doc S/RES/1820; UNSC Res 1888 (30 September 2009) UN Doc S/RES/1888; UNSC Res 1889 (5 October 2009) UN Doc S/RES/1889; UNSC Res 1960 (16 December 2010) UN Doc S/RES/1960.

[36] Provisions on violence against women in the Protocol include arts 1(j), 3(4), 4(2), 5, 11, 12(d), 13(c), 20, 22(b), 23(b). See F Banda, *Women, Law and Human Rights: an African Perspective* (2005) ch 5.

[37] Recommendation Rec (2002) 5.

affirmed in many of the subsequent instruments and reports.[38] The SR VAW recognizes that 'it is important to keep the work of CEDAW in view when working on her own mandate'[39] and the UN SG's Study affirms that 'adherence to the Convention . . . , its Optional Protocol and other relevant international human rights treaties . . . constitute measures to address violence against women'.[40] The Study draws upon States parties' reports to the Committee[41] and, in turn, the Committee draws States' attention to the UN SG's Report.[42] The regional human rights bodies have drawn upon General Recommendation 19 and the work of the Committee in interpreting and applying their own instruments.[43] The Committee refers to regional instruments, for example, recommending to States in the Inter-American system that they comply with the Convention of Belém do Pará and use indicators approved by the Committee of Experts on Violence of the Inter-American Commission of Women.[44]

C. Violence against Women: Interpretive Issues

General Recommendation 19 requires States parties to report on measures for the prevention, prosecution, and punishment of violence against women, which they have widely done. The Committee invariably includes reference to the issue in its concluding observations. Through these and its jurisprudence under the OP to the Convention, the Committee has elucidated its understanding of gender-based violence against women and States parties' obligations with regard to its prevention and punishment. The Committee has focused upon particular manifestations of violence, highlighted deficiencies in States parties' responses, and made positive recommendations as to appropriate measures that should be adopted in compliance with States parties' obligations. Many recommendations are now more or less standard and are repeated for most countries, for example, that 'priority attention' be given to addressing violence against women.[45]

I. Violence against Women within an Equality Paradigm

The object and purpose of the Convention is the elimination of all forms of discrimination against women. General Recommendation 19 accordingly tackles 'the problem of violence within an equality paradigm'.[46] It asserts that gender-based violence against women is a form of discrimination within Article 1 of the Convention, despite the omission of any explicit article on the subject. It is 'a form of discrimination that seriously inhibits women's ability to enjoy rights and freedoms on a basis of equality with men'

---

[38] eg DEVAW, Preamble; Protocol on the Rights of Women in Africa, Preamble.

[39] Special Rapporteur '15 Years' (n 13 above) 4.

[40] Report of the Secretary-General (n 1 above) para 262. [41] Ibid para 18.

[42] eg CO Cook Islands, CEDAW/C/COK/CO/1 (2007) para 25; CO Serbia, CEDAW/C/SCG/CO/1 (2007) para 22; CO Bahrain, CEDAW/C/BHR/CO/2 (2008) para 25.

[43] eg *Opuz v Turkey* ECHR 33401/02 (9 June 2009) para 185; *González et al ('Cotton Field') v Mexico* (Preliminary Objection, Merits, Reparations, and Costs), Inter-American Court of Human Rights Series C No 205 (16 November 2009) especially paras 394–5.

[44] eg CO Ecuador, CEDAW/C/ECU/CO/7 (2008) para 21.

[45] eg CO Republic of Congo, A/58/38, 28th Session (2003) para 167; CO Slovenia, A/58/38, 29th Session (2003) para 207; CO Benin, CEDAW/C/BEN/CO/1-3 (2005) para 24; CO FYROM (Macedonia), CEDAW/C/MKD/CO/3 (2006) para 24; CO Mozambique, CEDAW/C/MOZ/CO/2 (2007) para 25.

[46] J Fitzpatrick, 'The Use of International Human Rights Norms to Combat Violence against Women' in R J Cook (ed) *Human Rights of Women: National and International Perspectives* (1994) 532, 535.

and, as such, constitutes discrimination in and of itself and signifies lack of respect for women's integrity and dignity. Gender-based violence is thus a violation of women's human rights.

This rights-based approach recognizes that women are entitled to be free from violence and the fear of violence, and that States parties have a legal obligation to ensure this right. This entails a move from seeing women as victims to recognizing that they have rights which have been violated: shifting the language from that of 'natural' or 'inevitable' violence to failure of States parties' obligations. The SR VAW has explained that by applying a human rights perspective to violence a momentum for breaking the silence surrounding it and for connecting the diverse struggles across the globe has been created. 'Today, a life free of violence is increasingly accepted as an entitlement rather than merely a humanitarian concern'.[47] States must not only understand and implement their positive obligations for preventing, prosecuting, and punishing violence against women, but must also promote a rights awareness in victims and potential victims.[48] The Convention provides the international legal framework for application in national institutions that can be used to instill the requisite awareness in both States parties and women who have experienced violence.

Within a human rights framework gender-based violence impedes enjoyment of specific rights listed in General Recommendation 19, paragraph 7: the rights to life; not to be subject to torture or to cruel, inhuman, or degrading treatment or punishment; to equal protection according to humanitarian norms in time of international or internal armed conflict; to liberty and security of person; to equal protection under the law; to equality in the family; to the highest standard attainable of physical and mental health; to just and favourable conditions of work. DEVAW Article 3 lists the same rights, with the addition of the right to be free from all forms of discrimination.

Some of these rights are spelled out in the Convention[49] while others are drawn from a range of human rights instruments and international humanitarian law treaties. The guarantee of 'human rights and fundamental freedoms' in Convention Articles 1 and 3 provides the basis for the linkage between other human rights treaties, the Convention and General Recommendation 19.

The Committee has given weight to women's right to be free from violence as integral to their human right to life and to physical and mental integrity and has indicated that it cannot be superseded by claims to other rights, including rights to property and privacy,[50] freedom of movement, and fair trial.[51] This balance of rights has been expressly adopted by the European Court of Human Rights.[52]

---

[47] Special Rapporteur '15 Years' (n 13 above) 35.

[48] SE Merry, 'Rights Talk and the Experience of Law: Implementing Women's Human Rights to Protection from Violence', 25 *Human Rights Quarterly* (2003) 343–4.

[49] GR 19 para 6 clarifies that '[g]ender-based violence may breach specific provisions of the Convention, regardless of whether those provisions expressly mention violence'.

[50] *Ms AT v Hungary* CEDAW Communication No 2/2003(2005) CEDAW/C/32/D/2003 para 9.4.

[51] *Şahide Goekce v Austria* CEDAW Communication No 5/2005 (2007) CEDAW/C/39/D/5/2005 para 12.1.5; *Fatma Yildirim (deceased) v Austria* CEDAW Communication No 6/2005 (2007) CEDAW/C/39/D/6/2005.

[52] *Opuz v Turkey* (n 43 above) para 147.

II. Definition of Gender-based Violence against Women

General Recommendation 19 provides the first holistic international law definition of gender-based violence against women. Since violence can and does occur to anyone, the definition must distinguish between random violence and violence that is specifically directed at women. A definition is also required to emphasize that gender-based violence has multiple forms in addition to domestic violence, which had previously been the focus of attention within UN bodies. All forms of violence against women are a matter of concern to the Committee.

General Recommendation 19 defines gender-based violence against women as 'violence that is directed against a woman because she is a woman or that affects women disproportionately'. This definition expresses more explicitly than subsequent definitions the relationship between the violence and the sex of the victim.[53] The violence does not just happen to occur to women, but is motivated by 'factors concerned with gender',[54] such as the need to assert male power and control, to enforce assigned gender roles in society, and to punish what is perceived as deviant female behaviour. In its Inquiry into the deaths of women in Ciudad Juárez, the Committee criticized a practice that 'discriminates against women whose conduct may not conform to the accepted "moral code", but who have an equal right to life'.[55] The Committee has distinguished between sex-based and gender-based violence, regarding the latter 'as an infringement of the right to personal security'.[56]

The Committee did not explain 'disproportionately' in General Recommendation 19, but it is apparent that it applies both to forms of violence that are committed against women in greater numbers than against men, and violence that has a disparate impact upon women's lives. There are many examples of the first and the Committee frequently expresses its disquiet about the 'high incidence',[57] 'high'[58] or 'continuing'[59] 'persistence'[60] or 'increase'[61] of violence against women. The Committee has rejected the view that forms of violence such as domestic violence that are committed to a greater extent against women, largely by men, and which have significantly greater potential to disrupt women's lives than is the case for men, can be described in gender-neutral language that conceals the gender-based quality of violence against women and undermines the notion that such violence is a form of discrimination against women.[62]

---

[53] DEVAW does not define 'gender-based violence'; nor does the Beijing Platform for Action, para 113; the Convention of Belém do Pará, art 1 defines violence against women 'as any act or conduct, based on gender'; the Protocol on the Rights of Women in Africa, art 1 states that violence against women 'means all acts perpetrated against women'.

[54] Connors (n 2 above) 558, 562.

[55] Report on Mexico produced by the Committee on the Elimination of Discrimination against Women under article 8 of the Optional Protocol to the Convention, and reply from the Government of Mexico, CEDAW/C/2005/OP8/Mexico (27 January 2005) para 275 (hereinafter Mexico Inquiry).

[56] CO Kyrgyzstan, A/54/38, 20th Session (1999) para 122.

[57] eg CO Republic of Congo, A/58/38, 28th Session (2003) para 166.

[58] eg CO FYROM (Macedonia), CEDAW/C/MKD/CO/3 (2006) para 23; CO Ireland, CEDAW/C/IRL/CO/4-5 (2005) para 28.

[59] eg CO The United Kingdom, CEDAW/C/UK/CO/6 (2008) para 280.

[60] eg CO Canada, A/58/38, 28th Session (2003) para 369; CO Brazil, A/58/38, 29th Session (2003) para 112.

[61] eg CO Romania, A/55/38, 23rd Session (2000) para 306.

[62] eg CO The Netherlands, CEDAW/C/NLD/CO/4 (2007) para 19; repeated CO The Netherlands CEDAW/C/NLD/CO/5 (2010) para 10; CO Finland CEDAW/C/FIN/CO/6 (2008) para 173.

The Committee expressed concern to Algeria about 'the large number of women murdered, raped, abducted, and subjected to serious physical abuse by terrorist groups in recent years'.[63] Undoubtedly, men were also subject to terrorist violence but the 'large numbers' of attacks against women brought them within the Committee's frame of reference. In a perhaps more obvious example of disproportionate incidence of violence against women, the Committee has expressed its serious concern about 'most cruel forms, such as acid throwing, stoning and dowry death',[64] all manifestations of violence that are committed almost exclusively—and thus disproportionately—against women.

'Disproportionately' also applies to the impact of violence. The Committee is concerned that 'women victims of violence are advised to return to their abusive partners by authority figures, including the police and magistrates'.[65] Since men are unlikely to be given the same advice, this is an indication of the disproportionate effect of this form of violence on women. The consequences of rape impact disproportionately upon women, for example, through the possibility of pregnancy, raped women being pressured to forgive or marry the rapist (who is thence pardoned or given a reduced sentence),[66] and social attitudes.

Under General Recommendation 19, violence against women encompasses acts that inflict physical, mental, or sexual harm or suffering, threats of such acts, coercion and other deprivations of liberty.[67] None of these terms is defined, but they are elucidated through the Committee's concluding observations. Economic harm is not included as it is in the Protocol on the Rights of Women in Africa. However, the Committee has taken account of economic harm, for example, by expressing concern where only 'acts leading to physical injury' are criminalized and not verbal, psychological, and economic violence;[68] that widows often become 'vulnerable to violence and economic deprivation as a result of entrenched mindsets';[69] and recommending 'particular attention to the physical, emotional and financial abuse of elderly women'.[70]

D. Gender-Based Violence against Women: Sites and Forms

I. Introduction

General Recommendation 19 follows the structure of the Convention, article by article. In its concluding observations and jurisprudence under the OP, the Committee has

---

[63] CO Algeria, A/54/387, 20th Session (1999) paras 77–8.
[64] eg CO Bangladesh A/52/387, 17th Session (1997) para 436; see also CO FYROM (Macedonia), CEDAW/C/MKD/CO/3 (2006) para 23.
[65] eg CO Belize, CEDAW/C/BLZ/CO/3 (2007) para 19.
[66] eg 'Reparatory marriage', CO Romania, A/55/387, 23rd Session (2000) para 306; Issues and questions Lebanon, CEDAW/PSWG/2005/II/CRP.1/Add.8 (2005) para 9; CO Eritrea, CEDAW/C/ERI/CO/3 (2006) para 77; CO Fiji, A/57/387, 26th Session (2002) para 58 (practice of *bulubulu*, whereby the rapist may marry the victim on receipt of apology and, thus, supposedly inducing reconciliation); CO the Philippines, CEDAW/C/PHI/CO/6 (2006) paras 523–4. On the debate over *bulubulu* see SE Merry, *Human Rights and Gender Violence: Translating International Law into Local Justice* (2006) 113–33.
[67] DEVAW states that violence against women means 'any act of gender-based violence that results in, or is likely to result in, physical, sexual or psychological harm or suffering to women, including threats of such acts, coercion or arbitrary deprivation of liberty, whether occurring in public or in private life'. This definition is cited by the Committee (n 55 above) para 52.
[68] CO Madagascar, CEDAW/C/MDG/CO/5 (2008) para 18.
[69] CO Nepal, CEDAW/C/NPL/CO/3 (2004) para 206.
[70] CO Austria, A/55/38 (Supp) 23rd Session (2000) para 230.

addressed violence against women as a separate topic. The Committee encourages States parties to have regard to General Recommendation 19 in their reports and regularly asks them for details about the forms and extent of violence within the State party and the strategies adopted to combat it. The information received and the Committee's responses provide an expanded analysis of the problems States parties face in tackling the forms of violence against women within their national jurisdictions[71] and potential responses. Categorization is not always easy and there is considerable overlap between forms (or manifestations) and sites of violence. For example, a woman migrant worker is described as vulnerable to various forms of violence, such as sexual abuse, sexual harassment, physical violence, food and sleep deprivation, which may occur in diverse sites, such as within the household where she is employed or in other work environments, such as on farms or in the industrial sector.[72]

The Committee's work on violence maps the methodology of the DEVAW Article 2, which was adopted by the first Special Rapporteur on violence against women[73] and followed in the UN SG's Report, that is violence occurring in the family, violence occurring within the community, and violence perpetrated or condoned by the State.[74]

II. Violence in the Family[75]

Family violence is a form of discrimination[76] that is 'one of the most insidious forms of violence against women ... [that] is prevalent in all societies',[77] whether or not identified as such by the State.[78] The Committee has identified patriarchal attitudes and stereotypes with respect to women's and men's roles and responsibilities in the family as a root cause of violence against women.[79] It has emphasized the physical safety and autonomy of women over 'the sacredness and permanency of the family'[80] and over property and privacy rights.[81]

Although it is concerned that a State should distinguish between family violence and that committed by a stranger,[82] the Committee has not defined the former and has

---

[71] Merry (n 66 above).   [72] GR 26 para 20.

[73] The Special Rapporteur on violence against women, 'Preliminary Report' (1994) UN Doc E/CN.4/1995/42 paras 117–313.

[74] The Special Rapporteur on violence against women suggested 'adding the "transnational arena", which, due to globalisation and increased transnational processes, has emerged as a fourth level where women are encountering new vulnerabilities'. Special Rapporteur '15 Years' (n 13 above) 5.

[75] See Report of the Secretary-General (n 1 above) paras 111–25; The Special Rapporteur on violence against women, 'Report on Violence in the Family' (1996) UN Doc E/CN.4/1996/53; DO Thomas and ME Beasley, 'Domestic Violence as a Human Rights Issue' (1993) 15 *Human Rights Quarterly* 36; K Roth, 'Domestic Violence as an International Human Rights Issue' in RJ Cook (ed) *Human Rights of Women: National and International Perspectives* (1994) 326; B Meyersfeld, *Domestic Violence and International Law* (2010).

[76] In *Opuz v Turkey* the ECtHR noted that '[t]he CEDAW Committee has reiterated that violence against women, including domestic violence is a form of discrimination against women' (n 43 above) para 187. In *S v Baloyi (Minister of Justice and Another Intervening)* 2000 (2) SA 425 the Constitutional Court of South Africa noted the positive obligation imposed by the Convention to eliminate discrimination as relevant in interpreting national legislation with respect to domestic violence.

[77] GR 19 para 23.

[78] CO Democratic People's Republic of Korea, CEDAW/C/PRK/CO/1 (2005) para 37.

[79] GR 19 para 11 ('traditional attitudes by which women are regarded as subordinate to men or as having stereotyped roles perpetuate widespread practices involving violence or coercion'); CO The Philippines CEDAW/C/PHI/CO/6 (2006) para 17.

[80] Merry (n 66 above) 77.   [81] *Ms AT v Hungary* (n 50 above) para 9.4.

[82] eg CO Albania, A/58/38, 28th Session (2003) para 72.

variously referred (without definition) to domestic,[83] intrafamilial[84] or intimate partner[85] violence. It has not explicitly addressed violence within same-sex relationships. General Recommendation 19 brings battering, rape, other forms of sexual assault, mental and other forms of violence within its ambit,[86] while DEVAW adds sexual abuse of female children in the household, dowry-related violence, female genital mutilation, and other traditional practices harmful to women, non-spousal violence, and violence related to exploitation. The Committee has expressly addressed marital rape,[87] crimes committed in the name of honour,[88] forced marriage,[89] bride abduction,[90] early or child marriage,[91] dowry death,[92] lobola,[93] incest,[94] female infanticide and sex selective abortion,[95] and polygamy.[96] A particular form of assault within the home or institutions is corporal punishment,[97] or chastisement,[98] the social acceptance of which legitimates violence. This leads to silence about its occurrence, a culture of impunity and under-reporting for fear of retaliation.[99] It has frequently expressed concern at States parties' failure to adopt holistic or comprehensive measures to address the multiple forms of violence that occur within this site.

The OP has given the Committee new tools to give effect to women's right to be free from violence, and it has used the right of individual communication to articulate States parties' obligations with respect to domestic violence in three cases that have come before

---

[83] UNGA Res 58/147 (19 February 2004) UN Doc A/RES/58/147: domestic violence is 'violence that occurs within the private sphere, generally between individuals who are related through blood or intimacy'. It takes 'many different forms, including physical, psychological and sexual violence'. This conforms with the Committee's understanding of domestic violence.

[84] eg CO Mexico, A/53/38, 18th Session (1998) para 379; this includes violence between 'partners who have not lived together', Issues and Questions, Venezuela CEDAW/C/VEN/Q/4–6 (2006) para 14.

[85] eg CO Norway, CEDAW/C/NOR/CO/7 (2007) para 19.

[86] In GR 21 para 40 the Committee reiterated the importance of GR 19 in 'considering the place of women in the family'.

[87] eg CO Vietnam, A/56/38, 25th Session (2001) para 258; CO Mexico, A/53/38, 18th Session (1998) para 379; CO Romania, A/55/38, 23rd Session (2000) para 306; CO Republic of Congo, A/58/38, 28th Session (2003) para 167; CO Serbia, CEDAW/C/SCG/CO/1 (2007) para 21; CO Singapore, CEDAW/C/SGP/CO/3 (2007) para 27; CO Cook Islands, CEDAW/C/COK/CO/1, (2007) para 24.

[88] eg CO Pakistan, CEDAW/C/PAK/CO/3 (2007) para 23; see J Connors, 'United Nations Approaches to "Crimes of Honour"' in L Welchman and S Hossain (eds) *'Honour' Crimes, Paradigms and Violence against Women* (2005) 22, 29–31.

[89] eg GR 19 para 11 (on arts 2(e) and (f) and 5); CO Algeria, A/54/38, 20th Session (1999) para 91; CO Vietnam, A/56/38, 25th Session (2001) para 258; Issues and Questions, CO Benin, CEDAW/PSWG/2005/II/CRP.1/Add.1 (2005) para 12; Issues and Questions, Pakistan, CEDAW/C/PAK/Q/3 (2005) para 13; CO The United Kingdom, CEDAW/C/UK/CO/6 (2008) para 277.

[90] eg CO Kyrgyzstan, CEDAW/C/KGZ/CO/3 (2008) para 22.

[91] eg CO Israel, CEDAW/C/ISR/CO/3 (2005) para 42; CO Vietnam, A/56/38, 25th Session (2001) para 258; CO Nepal, CEDAW/C/NPL/CO/3 (2004) para 208.

[92] GR 19 para 11; CO India, CEDAW/C/IND/CO/3 (2007) para 26; CO Bangladesh, A/52/38, 17th Session (1997) para 436.

[93] CO Zimbabwe, A/53/38, 18th Session (1998) para 141.

[94] GR 19 para 24 (ensuring support for families where incest has occurred); CO The Philippines, CEDAW/C/PHI/CO/6 (2006) paras 523–4; CO Portugal, A/57/38, 26th Session (2002) para 334.

[95] eg CO China, CEDAW/C/CHN/CO/6 (2006) para 31.

[96] eg CO Zimbabwe, A/53/38, 18th Session (1998) para 141; CO Israel, CEDAW/C/ISR/CO/3 (2005) para 42; CO Indonesia, CEDAW/C/IDN/CO/5 (2007) para 18.

[97] CO The United Kingdom, CEDAW/C/UK/CO/6 (2008) para 280; CO Ecuador, CEDAW/C/ECU/CO/7 (2008) para 21.

[98] eg CO Fiji, A/57/38, 26th Session (2002) para 58.

[99] eg CO Madagascar, CEDAW/C/MDG/CO/5 (2008) para 18.

it.[100] All three have demonstrated a high threshold of such violence involving threats, intimidation, beating, and battering, which in two cases resulted in killing. In *Ms AT v Hungary*,[101] a woman complained that Hungary's failure to provide her with effective protection from her violent former common law husband violated the Convention. The Committee found that the ineffective responses by the authorities to many years of severe domestic violence, often taking place when the husband was drunk, constituted violations of Articles 2(a), (b), and (e) and 5(a), linked with Article 16. It noted that Hungary admitted that there were no remedies available capable of protecting Ms AT and that although legal reforms had been commenced they remained inadequate to benefit the complainant.

Ms Şahide Goekce (deceased) v Austria and *Ms Fatma Yildirim (deceased) v Austria*[102] are 'companion' cases commenced by the same bodies (the Vienna Intervention Centre against Domestic Violence and the Association for Women's Access to Justice). Both cases involved repeated spousal domestic violence resulting in death. The Committee noted Austria's comprehensive system to address violence against women but considered that:

in order for the individual woman victim of domestic violence to enjoy the practical realisation of the principle of equality of men and women and of her human rights and fundamental freedoms, the political will that is expressed in the aforementioned comprehensive system of Austria must be supported by State actors, who adhere to the State party's due diligence obligations.[103]

In none of the above cases did the Committee elucidate its understanding of domestic violence, apparently taking it as evident from the strong facts of each case.

The Committee took a flexible approach to admissibility in these cases indicating that it will not allow formal requirements to prevent its examination of serious cases of domestic violence. For example, in *Ms AT v Hungary*, the Committee considered that pending domestic civil proceedings were unlikely to bring the complainant effective relief and that a delay of over three years in criminal proceedings since the violent incident was an 'unreasonably prolonged delay' in the terms of OP Article 4. Further, although most of the violence had occurred before the OP's entry into force for Hungary (one serious attack took place after that time) it was persuaded that Hungary's inaction covered all the violence that had continued since 1998. This reflects the reality of domestic violence as ongoing and incessant, often over the many years of a relationship.

III. Violence Occurring in the Community

1. Physical Violence in the Community

The Committee has addressed some of the diverse forms of physical and psychological violence that women face within their communities, including rape, gang rape,[104] and sexual assault, much of which is extreme. In concluding observations it has expressed concern where a State's criminal law defines rape in terms of force rather than consent,[105] perceives

---

[100] *Ms NSF v United Kingdom*, Communication No 10/2005 (2007) CEDAW/C/38/D/10/2005, also concerned domestic violence, including allegations of marital rape and death threats. The Communication was found inadmissible because of failure to exhaust domestic remedies.

[101] (n 50 above).   [102] (n 51 above).   [103] Ibid para 12.1.2.

[104] eg CO Kyrgyzstan, A/54/38, 20th Session (1999) para 122.

[105] eg CO Azerbaijan, CEDAW/C/AZE/CO/4 (2009) para 37.

rape as a crime against chastity rather than as a crime against the person,[106] or qualifies sexual abuse as a crime of morality rather than as a violent crime.[107] It has required States parties to 'widen the definition of rape... to reflect the realities of sexual abuse experienced by women'[108] and sought information about the levels of rape within a State party and the steps taken to address it.[109]

Vertido v the Philippines[110] (a case of acquaintance rape) provided the Committee with an opportunity to expand on some of its concerns. It clarified that rape is to be understood as violating a woman's right to 'personal security and bodily integrity'.[111] It recommended a legislative definition of rape that places 'the lack of consent at its centre' and removes requirements that sexual assault be committed by force or violence and that penetration be proved. To minimize secondary victimization of the survivor a definition of sexual assault should either require:

the existence of 'unequivocal and voluntary agreement' and requiring proof by the accused of steps taken to ascertain whether the complainant was consenting; or

...that the act take place in 'coercive circumstances' and includes a broad range of coercive circumstances.[112]

A detailed analysis of violence within the community is provided by the Committee's Inquiry under OP Article 8 into the multiple murders, abductions, and rapes of women that occurred over a period of more than ten years in Ciudad Juárez, Mexico.[113] General Recommendation 19, paragraph 21 highlighted the special risk of violence faced by girls from rural communities who migrate to seek employment in towns. The women who had been murdered and disappeared in Ciudad Juárez were at 'high risk' of violence in the *maquilas* where they worked and lived in poverty or extreme poverty. They were exposed to other forms of community violence: organized crime, drug trafficking, illegal migration, trade in women, prostitution, exploitation of prostitution, and pornography.[114] The Committee found that the repetition of such serious acts of violence over a sustained period of time constituted systemic violence 'founded in a culture of violence and discrimination, based upon women's alleged inferiority' that has developed specific characteristics 'marked by hatred and misogyny' and has given rise to a culture of impunity.[115] The social and cultural environment that constructed women as poor, vulnerable, and insignificant facilitated human rights abuses.[116] The widespread kidnappings, disappearances, rapes, mutilations, and murders have been termed 'femicide'—the 'gender-based murder of a woman'.[117]

---

[106] CO The Philippines, CEDAW/C/PHI/CO/6 (2006) para 523 (welcoming a change in the law in this regard).

[107] eg CO Belgium, CEDAW/C/BEL/CO/6 (2008) para 29.

[108] CO India, CEDAW/C/IND/CO/3 (2007) para 23.

[109] eg Issues and Questions, Ireland, CEDAW/PSWG/2005/II/CRP.1/Add.6 (2005) para 10.

[110] Communication No 18/2008 (2010) CEDAW/C/46/18/2008.   [111] Ibid para 8.7.

[112] Ibid para 8.8(b)(i) and (ii).

[113] See also CO Mexico, A/57/38, Exceptional Session (2002) para 439; CO Mexico, CEDAW/C/MEX/CO/6 (2006) paras 597–8; *González* et al ('*Cotton Field*') *v Mexico* (n 43 above).

[114] Mexico Inquiry (n 55 above) para 289; SE Merry, *Gender Violence: A Cultural Perspective* (2009) 120–5.

[115] Mexico Inquiry (n 55 above) paras 66 and 261.   [116] Ibid para 38.

[117] Report of the Secretary-General (n 1 above) para 127; see also Mexico Inquiry (n 55 above) para 74; CO Mexico, CEDAW/C/MEX/CO/6 (2006) para 596.

2. Exploitation

The Committee has identified multiple other forms of and susceptibilities to violence within the community, in general terms in General Recommendation 19 and contextually in response to States parties' reports. These include commercial exploitation of women as sexual objects,[118] sex tourism,[119] forced prostitution and organized marriages between women from developing countries and foreign nationals. These may not involve violence per se but create situations of vulnerability in which violence may occur. Prostitution, in particular, involves marginalization and inadequate protection from violence. The Committee has expressed concern at lack of economic alternatives to prostitution,[120] and has urged the development of effective strategies and programmes to address the demand for prostitution,[121] but has only obliquely suggested that it constitutes violence of itself.[122]

3. Harmful Practices

Various forms of violence are 'rooted in custom as an infringement of women's human rights',[123] some of which are associated with family relationships,[124] while others are located within both the family and community. For example, *sati* is based in the relationship between the woman and her deceased husband but takes place within a community setting.[125] The Committee has declared some specific practices to be contrary to the Convention, for example, witch hunting ('an extreme form of violence'),[126] *deuki* (dedicating girls to a god and goddess), *jhuma* (second sisters remaining unmarried and spending their lives in monasteries), *kumari pratha* (having a girl child as living goddess) and *badi* (ethnic practice of prostitution among young girls).[127]

The Committee has voiced its concern at the number of women and girls who have undergone, or are at risk of undergoing, female genital mutilation, a practice also located within the community and family. The issue first came before the Committee in its 7th session in 1988 in the context of reports from Senegal and Nigeria and proved to be divisive between members.[128] In General Recommendation 14 (1990) it recommended 'appropriate and effective' steps for its eradication to be undertaken by health, education, religious, social, and cultural bodies, including collection of data and providing support to women's organizations. The Committee has taken up the issue with specific States parties, noting the entrenched cultural underpinnings of the practice,[129] but also describing the practice as injurious to the physical and psychological well-being of girls.[130] It has commended States that have taken steps to eliminate the practice, regretted ineffective legislation,[131] and indicated the desirability of prosecution of perpetrators[132] to combat impunity. Such

---

[118] GR 19 para 12.   [119] Ibid para 14.

[120] eg CO Malawi, CEDAW/C/MWI/CO/5 (2006) para 23.

[121] eg CO Australia, CEDAW/C/AUS/CO/7 (2010) para 33.

[122] The Declaration of Mexico (1975) para 28 included prostitution as a violation of women's human rights. The Committee has requested adequate information on prostitution; eg CO Zimbabwe, A/53/38, 18th Session (1998) para 162.

[123] CO India, CEDAW/C/IND/CO/3 (2007) para 27.   [124] Merry (n 66 above) 127–55.

[125] CO India, CEDAW/C/IND/CO/3 (2007) para 26.   [126] Ibid.

[127] CO Nepal, CEDAW/C/NPL/CO/3 (2004) para 208.   [128] Evatt (n 2 above) 515, 525.

[129] eg CO Eritrea, CEDAW/C/ERI/CO/3 (2006) para 78–9.

[130] GR 19 para 12; eg CO Cameroon, A/55/38, 23rd Session (2000) para 43.

[131] eg CO Benin, CEDAW/C/BEN/CO/1-3 (2005) para 21; CO Cameroon, A/55/38, 23rd Session (2000) para 43; CO Nigeria, CEDAW/C/NGA/CO/5 (2004) para 299.

[132] eg CO The United Kingdom, CEDAW/C/UK/CO/6 (2008) para 279.

concerns are expressed both to countries where the practice is long established[133] and those where it is associated with certain sectors of the population.[134]

Other forms of violence are normalized by social practices, for example, the ready availability of pornography, pornographic and violent video games and cartoons. The Committee has urged their banning.[135]

4. Workplace Violence

General Recommendation 19 identifies the workplace as a site of violence and sexual harassment of women. It does not refer to schools, but the Committee has done so in its concluding observations.[136] Sexual harassment subjects women to humiliation and may constitute a health and safety concern. Its incidence denies women's equality in the workplace and is discriminatory, especially where a woman 'has reasonable grounds to believe that her objection would disadvantage her in connection with her employment, including recruitment or promotion, or when it creates a hostile working environment'.[137] The Committee understands sexual harassment as 'unwelcome sexually determined behaviour as physical contact and advances, sexually coloured remarks, showing pornography and sexual demand, whether by words or actions'.[138] It has expressed concern about the prevalence of such conduct and failure to criminalize it,[139] or to ensure the effectiveness of relevant legislation.[140]

Some forms of work create particular vulnerability to violence and harassment, for example, domestic work,[141] especially for women migrant workers who 'are scarcely ever out of sight of their employers' and may be unable to register with their embassies or file complaints.[142] Migrant workers remain the concern of their State of origin which should have appropriate mechanisms to respond to abuses of its national women working abroad. The Committee reminded Indonesia of this when it noted that the State party's report did not address 'reports of the death as a result of mistreatment and abuses of Indonesian migrant women abroad, as well as cases of trafficking for the purposes of prostitution'.[143]

An especially serious case of sexual violence at work occurred in the case of *Vishakha v State of Rajasthan*.[144] A woman social worker was employed to go to rural areas to educate the population about such issues as dowry and child marriage. She was allegedly gang raped in an incident which 'reveals the hazards to which a working woman may be exposed and the depravity to which sexual harassment can degenerate; and the urgency for safeguards by an alternative mechanism in the absence of legislative measures'.[145] In civil proceedings the Supreme Court of India noted that there was no relevant domestic legislation on sexual harassment at work. Laying down detailed guidelines for

---

[133] eg CO Zimbabwe, A/53/38, 18th Session (1998) para 141.

[134] eg Canada, A/58/38, 28th Session (2003) para 341.

[135] eg CO Japan, CEDAW/C/JPN/CO/6 (2009) paras 35–6.

[136] eg CO Republic of Congo, A/58/38, 28th Session (2003) para 166; CO Ecuador, CEDAW/C/ECU/CO/7 (1998) para 20.

[137] GR 19 para 18.　　　[138] Ibid.

[139] eg CO Romania, A/55/38, 23rd Session (2000) para 306; CO Brazil, A/58/38, 29th Session (2003) para 93.

[140] eg Issues and Questions, Venezuela, CEDAW/C/VEN/Q/4-6 (2006) para 16.

[141] eg CO Morocco, A/58/38, 29th Session (2003) para 68.　　　[142] GR 26 paras 20–1.

[143] CO Indonesia, A/53/38/Rev.1, 18th Session (1998) para 296.　　　[144] (1997) 6 SCC 241.

[145] Ibid.

safeguarding women's rights at work, the Supreme Court asserted the significance of international conventions and norms for the 'purpose of interpretation of the guarantee of gender equality, right to work with human dignity' in accordance with the Indian Constitution. Specifically, Convention Article 11 and General Recommendation 19 were resorted to for guidance 'in construing the nature and ambit of constitutional guarantee of gender equality'. These guidelines were approved in a subsequent case of workplace harassment,[146] in which the Supreme Court described the message of the Convention and the Beijing Declaration as 'loud and clear': 'sexual harassment of a female at the place of work is incompatible with the dignity and honour of a female and needs to be eliminated and that there can be no compromise with such violations, admits of no debate'.

IV. Violence Condoned or Perpetrated by the State

In accordance with the general international law principles on State responsibility for international wrongful acts attributable to the State,[147] the Convention 'applies to violence perpetrated by public authorities'.[148] This requires the State to investigate alleged abuses committed by its agents or within its institutions and to prosecute and punish those found responsible. Failure to do so creates a climate of impunity[149] while complying with the obligation facilitates 'the maximum protection of the law'.[150] The Committee has clarified that this encompasses State agents such as the military,[151] police[152] and security forces,[153] prison officers,[154] diplomatic staff,[155] and State-run institutions such as prisons, police stations, detention centres,[156] schools, and camps for refugees and internally displaced persons.[157] Where State actors commit severe acts of violence, including sexual violence, it may constitute torture.[158] State policies may constitute forms of violence against women, for example, compulsory sterilization or abortion, which 'adversely affects women's physical and mental health'.[159] *Ms AS v Hungary*[160] concerned the forcible sterilization of a Roma woman. The Committee found this to be a violation of Convention Article 10(h) but perhaps surprisingly did not consider the case in terms of gender-based violence.

---

[146] *Apparel Export Promotion Council v AK Chopra*, (1999) 1 SCC 759.

[147] International Law Commission, Articles on Responsibility of States for Internationally Wrongful Acts, UNGA Res 56/83 (12 December 2001) arts 1–4.

[148] GR 19 para 8.   [149] eg CO Myanmar, CEDAW/C/MMR/CO/3 (2008) para 24.

[150] *Ms AT v Hungary* (n 50 above) recommendations, II(b).

[151] eg CO India, CEDAW/C/IND/CO/3 (2007) para 9; CO Myanmar, CEDAW/C/MMR/CO/3 (2008) para 24.

[152] eg Issues and Questions, Pakistan, UN Doc CEDAW/C/PAK/Q/3, 38th Session (2006) para 16; CO Russian Federation, A/57/38, 26th Session (2002) para 391; CO India, CEDAW/C/IND/CO/SP.1 (2010) para 19.

[153] eg CO Sri Lanka, A/57/38, 26th Session (2002) para 286.

[154] eg CO Russian Federation, A/57/38, 26th Session (2002) para 391.

[155] GR 26 para 21 notes sexual abuse and violence committed by diplomats against women migrant domestic workers while enjoying diplomatic immunity.

[156] eg CO China, CEDAW/C/CHN/CO/6 (2006) para 22.

[157] 'Report of the Special Rapporteur on violence against women' (1998) UN Doc E/CN.4/1998/54 provides many examples.

[158] Report of the Secretary-General (n 1 above) para 258.   [159] GR 19 para 22.

[160] CEDAW Communication No 4/2004 (2006) CEDAW/C/36/D/4/2004.

V. Violence in Armed Conflict[161]

The Convention does not specify that it is applicable in armed conflict,[162] but General Recommendation 19, paragraph 16 notes that wars, armed conflict, and occupation often 'lead to increased prostitution, trafficking in women and sexual assault of women'. The World Conference on Human Rights affirmed that 'Violations of the human rights of women in situations of armed conflict are violations of the fundamental principles of international human rights and humanitarian law'.[163] The Beijing Declaration and Platform for Action made Women and Armed Conflict its Critical Area of Concern E.

The Committee has affirmed the continued applicability of the Convention to 'all persons brought under the jurisdiction or effective control of a State party'[164] in conditions of violence, armed conflict, and occupation. This applies to women serving in the military[165] and to civilians. Thus, in 2009, it issued a statement recalling the applicability of international human rights and humanitarian law 'in all circumstances and at all times' and noting 'that the human rights of women and children in Gaza, in particular to peace and security, free movement, livelihood and health, have been seriously violated during this military engagement'.[166] Without spelling out the basis for its remarks, the Committee has referred to the 'comfort women', the women across Asia who were forced into prostitution by Japanese military during the Second World War. These events occurred long before the drafting of the Convention and Japan's ratification (1985). Nevertheless, some members of the Committee suggested that the Japanese Government should pay compensation to victims and create a fund in memory of those who had died. They requested an explanation about the measures the State party was planning to take to assist those women.[167]

The Committee has requested countries involved in the conflicts surrounding the disintegration of the Former Yugoslavia to submit on an exceptional basis reports addressing acts of violence against women and children, including mass rapes and rape used as a weapon of war.[168] It sought to break the silence about sexual abuse and aggression against women, to alleviate the situation of women victims of armed conflict and to prevent further violence. Accordingly, the Committee has asked about the facilities for rape victims, mechanisms for informing women about the Convention, and the consequences of rape, especially forced pregnancies. The Committee has called upon women not to remain

---

[161] The Special Rapporteur on violence against women, 'Violence Against Women Perpetrated and/ or Condoned by the State During Times of Armed Conflict (1997–2000)' UN Doc E/CN.4/2001/73 (23 January 2001); J Gardam and H Charlesworth, 'Protection of Women in Armed Conflict' (2000) 22 *Human Rights Quarterly*; J Gardam and M Jarvis, *Women, Armed Conflict, and International Law* (2001); N Quénivet, *Sexual Offenses in Armed Conflict and International Law* (2005); C Abaka, 'Women in War and its Aftermath: Liberia' in Schöpp-Schilling and Flinterman (eds) (n 20 above) 234; MU Walker, 'Gender and Violence in Focus: A Background for Gender Justice in Reparations' in R Rubio-Marin (ed), *The Gender of Reparations* (2009) 18.

[162] In contrast to the Convention on the Rights of the Child, 1989, art 38(4).

[163] Vienna Declaration and Programme for Action (1993) II, 38.

[164] CO Israel, CEDAW/C/ISR/CO/3 (2005) paras 23–4 (applicability of the Convention in the Occupied Territories).

[165] eg CO Indonesia, A/53/38/Rev.1, 18th Session (1998) para 295.

[166] Decision 43/III, Statement by the Committee on the Elimination of Discrimination against Women on the situation in Gaza, A/64/38 (2009) Annex II.

[167] CO Japan, A/49/38, 13th Session (1994) para 576; CO Japan, CEDAW/C/JPN/CO/6 (2009) para 37.

[168] CO Croatia, A/50/38, 14th Session (1995) paras 585–6; Bosnia-Herzegovina, A/49/38, 13th Session (1994) para 736.

passive but to make themselves visible at governmental and non-governmental levels in order to generate the political will requisite for change.[169]

The Committee has recognized that sexual violence against women continues in the apparent aftermath of armed conflict with long-lasting effects. It is deeply concerned about the continuing occurrence of rapes in the Democratic Republic of the Congo and has urged the State party to end the impunity of perpetrators.[170] Some ten years after the end of the armed conflict in Bosnia-Herzegovina, it remained concerned at the situation of wartime victims of sexual violence, including the disadvantage experienced by female heads of household and internally displaced persons who are often not sufficiently recognized in post-conflict legal frameworks. It urged the State party to protect these women through legislation and allocation of financial resources for adequate social provision, including health insurance and housing, at a level comparable to that applicable to military victims of war.[171]

Violence in armed conflict encompasses political violence that conditions people to tolerate violence in general,[172] including communal and intra-state[173] violence. In this regard, the Committee repeatedly sought information from India about the Gujarat massacre of 2002, requesting details on the number of reported cases of sexual assault and violence against women, victim protection measures and their impact, arrests and punishments for perpetrators (including State officials), gender-specific measures for the rehabilitation and compensation of women victims, and the number of women who have benefited from such measures.[174] In 2009, India belatedly reported on an exceptional basis on the impact of the violence in Gujarat on women.[175] The Committee expressed its regret that the report was overdue, vague, and inadequately addressed the issues and its concern at the Government's lack of due diligence in many aspects of its substantive response to the situation.[176]

The Committee sees women's participation in peace processes as important in seeking to end violence against women in armed conflict, in accordance with UNSC resolutions.[177] It has, thus, encouraged States parties, 'to fully involve all women concerned in all stages of the peace process'.[178] This endorsement has, however, had little impact and women remain largely excluded from peace processes.

---

[169] eg CO Bosnia-Herzegovina, A/49/38, 13th Session (1994) paras 753–7.

[170] CO Democratic Republic of Congo, CEDAW/C/COD/CO/5 (2006) para 338.

[171] CO Bosnia-Herzegovina, CEDAW/C/BIH/CO/3 (2006) paras 37–8; see also Issues and Questions, Mozambique, CEDAW/C/MOZ/Q/2 (2007) para 13; CO Guatemala, A/57/38, Exceptional Session (2002) para 205.

[172] CO Guatemala, A/49/38, 13th Session (1994) para 47.

[173] eg CO Russian Federation, A/57/38, 26th Session (2002) para 391 (rape and sexual violence in the armed conflict in Chechnya); CO Russian Federation CEDAW/C/USR/CO/7 (2010) para 24 (increasing rates of violence there and the Northern Caucasus).

[174] CO India, CEDAW/C/IND/CO/3 (2007) paras 67–8; CO India CEDAW/C/IND/CO/SP.1 (2010) para 2.

[175] UN Doc CEDAW/C/IND/SP.1 (2009).

[176] CO India, CEDAW/C/IND/CO/SP.1 (2010) paras 2–4.

[177] eg CO Myanmar, CEDAW/C/MMR/CO/3 (2008) para 25.

[178] eg CO Israel, CEDAW/C/ISR/CO/3 (2005) para 22; CO Cyprus, CEDAW/C/CYP/CO/5 (2006) para 270; Statement on the situation in Gaza (n 166 above).

E. Violence against Women: Equality in Context

I. Formal, Substantive, and Transformative Equality

Without the understanding that gender-based violence against women constitutes sex- and gender-based discrimination, legal and policy requirements for formal equality will not achieve substantive equality. Substantive equality requires recognition of and appropriate responses to gender-specific harms that will not be addressed by gender-neutral (formal equality) measures.[179] The assertion in General Recommendation 19 that '[g]ender-based violence is a form of discrimination' is thus a critical step in moving from formal to substantive equality. At the same time, the elimination of discrimination against women is a crucial element in the prevention of violence against women, which is 'an outcome of gender discrimination that shapes social, economic, cultural and political structures, rather than being independent of them'.[180] Accordingly, measures to combat gender-based violence against women should be framed in the context of the promotion and practical realization of equality through eliminating sex- and gender-based discrimination, and changing patriarchal structures and attitudes, and gendered stereotypes as required by Article 5. General Recommendation 19, the Committee's concluding observations, and jurisprudence are all directed towards transformative equality and the advancement and empowerment of women.

The Committee understands that patriarchal attitudes,[181] cultural stereotypes (such as those of the 'macho image of men'),[182] and prejudice are structural and systemic (not private[183] or sporadic),[184] subordinate women, and create deep-rooted impediments to the eradication of violence against them.[185] They may also undermine the effectiveness of measures addressing violence against women, including reforming legislation. In *Ms AT v Hungary* the Committee noted that it had 'stated on many occasions that traditional attitudes by which women are regarded as subordinate to men contribute to violence against them'.[186] While concentration on isolated cases may conceal the structural dimensions of violence, in *Ms AT v Hungary*, the Committee recognized 'aspects of the relationships between the sexes and attitudes towards women' in the country as a whole. Similarly, 'focusing solely on the murders and disappearances as isolated cases in [Ciudad Juárez] would not appear to be the answer in terms of resolving the underlying sociocultural problem'.[187] Failure by the State party to eradicate stereotypes that contribute to violence against women entails violation of Article 5(a).

---

[179] eg the reaction of the Committee to the gender-neutral laws adopted by the Netherlands and Finland (n 62 above).

[180] Special Rapporteur '15 Years' (n 13 above) 34 (citing Convention art 1 and GR 19); see also DEVAW, Preamble.

[181] eg CO Benin, CEDAW/C/BEN/CO/1-3 (2005) para 21; CO Pakistan, CEDAW/C/PAK/CO/3 (2007) para 28.

[182] CO Jamaica, CEDAW/C/JAM/CO/5 (2006) para 385.

[183] eg CO Bulgaria, A/53/38, 18th Session (1998) para 255; CO Russian Federation, CEDAW/C/USR/CO/7 (2010) para 25.

[184] Mexico Inquiry (n 55 above) para 159.   [185] GR 19 para 11; see also DEVAW, Preamble.

[186] *Ms AT v Hungary* (n 50 above) para 9.4.

[187] Mexico Inquiry (n 55 above) para 34. MR Tavares da Silva and Y Fener-Gómez, 'The Juárez Murders and the Inquiry Procedure' in Schöpp-Schilling and Flinterman (eds), (n 20 above) 298, 304, describe the 'violent society, with social and familial tensions, within a culture of misogyny and discrimination, where women were easily devalued and discarded'.

The structural nature of gender violence demands societal transformation in changing attitudes and behaviours. The Committee believed that responses in Ciudad Juárez to the murders and disappearances of hundreds of women did not explore the potential for such transformation. Officials could have focused 'on promoting social responsibility, change in social and cultural patterns of conduct of men and women and women's dignity', but instead they had tended to make 'potential victims responsible for their own protection by maintaining traditional cultural stereotypes'.[188] Placing the burden on victims transfers the responsibility from the State and third parties and denies women's entitlement to security. The Committee indicated how States parties might respond differently to fulfil their obligation to achieve the required transformation. Appropriate behaviours include 'specific policies on gender equality . . . and a gender perspective integrated into all public policies',[189] education, public information programmes and awareness campaigns,[190] the use of media, popular music, theatre, and working with civil society, including women's organizations. Overall, what is sought is 'a global and integrated response, a strategy aimed at transforming existing sociocultural patterns, especially with regard to eradicating the notion that gender violence is inevitable'.[191] This approach, emphasizing women's empowerment, is endorsed by the SR VAW:

> Empowerment discourse—through interventions ranging from education, skills training, legal literacy, access to productive resources, among others—aims to enhance women's self-awareness, self-esteem, self-confidence and self-reliance. This enables women to understand that subordination and violence are not fate; to resist internalising oppression; to develop their capabilities as autonomous beings; and constantly negotiate the terms of their existence in public and private spheres.[192]

II. Intersectional Discrimination

While all women are potentially targets of gender-based violence, some women are especially at risk. The Committee has built up a considerable catalogue of women who are susceptible to intersectional discrimination that increases the likelihood of violence and heightens its adverse consequences when it occurs. Vulnerability to violence may stem from the position of particular women in specific States parties or more generally, and is enhanced by impunity. Vulnerability is exacerbated by legal marginalization (for example, criminalization of prostitution, undocumented migrants,[193] imprisonment,[194] detention or being under investigation,[195] seeking asylum);[196] from social isolation (for example, rural women and girls,[197] refugees,[198] internal migration and displacement, women of lower castes,[199] women in prostitution);[200] from being identified as belonging

---

[188] Mexico Inquiry (n 55 above) para 57.   [189] Ibid para 34.
[190] GR 19 para 24(f), (t)(ii); CO Bulgaria, A/53/38, 18th Session (1998) para 255.
[191] Mexico Inquiry (n 55 above) paras 159 and 287.
[192] Special Rapporteur '15 Years' (n 13 above) 35.   [193] GR 26.
[194] eg CO UK, CEDAW/C/UK/CO/6 (2008) para 267; CO Bangladesh, A/52/38, 17th Session (1997) paras 443 and 452.
[195] CO Russian Federation, A/57/38, 26th Session (2002) para 392.
[196] eg CO Austria, A/55/38 23rd Session (2000) para 221.
[197] GR 19 para 24(o) and (q); CO Nicaragua, A/56/38, 25th Session (2001) para 298.
[198] eg CO Nepal, CEDAW/C/NPL/CO/3 (2004) paras 218–19.
[199] eg CO India, CEDAW/C/IND/CO/3 (2007) para 28 (Dalits).
[200] eg GR 19 para 15 (on art 6); CO Kyrgyzstan, CEDAW/C/KGZ/CO/3 (2008) para 43.

to a certain group such as a religious, ethnic,[201] racial, sexual, or other minority, or an indigenous community;[202] from age (young[203] or elderly);[204] from disability;[205] and from low social status (widowhood).[206] Social constructions of women as inferior, as poor, as lacking agency all contribute to vulnerability, including to harassment by State officials with whom they come into contact. Other isolating factors may be linguistic, women's lack of knowledge of their rights and entitlements, and lack of mobility.[207] These may well be intertwined and the Committee may address multiple forms of disadvantage together, without identifying differences between them. For example, it expressed its concern to Ireland 'about violence suffered by women from marginalised and vulnerable groups, including Traveller women, migrant women, asylum-seeking and refugee women and women with disabilities'.[208]

The Committee has linked vulnerability to violence with inadequate guarantee of economic, social, and cultural rights and has urged their implementation, including through temporary special measures, for example, for indigenous women.[209] It has also urged reconciliation between different ethnic groups where violence has erupted, calling for 'appropriate measures to ensure long-term integration of the affected communities into the previous communities'.[210]

F. States Parties' Obligations

I. Nature of States Parties' Obligations

1. Appropriate and Effective Measures

The Committee has clarified the nature of States parties' obligations with respect to the elimination of violence against women. General Recommendation 19, paragraph 24(a) requires States parties to take 'appropriate and effective measures to overcome all forms of gender-based violence, whether by public or private act'.[211] Although this does not indicate the timeline within which States parties should act, in line with DEVAW Article 4 ('should pursue . . . without delay a policy of eliminating violence against women'), the Committee has urged States parties to act immediately,[212] without delay,[213] expeditiously,[214] or to

---

[201] eg CO Sri Lanka, A/57/38, 26th Session para 286 (Tamil women); CO Myanmar, CEDAW/C/MMR/CO/3 (2008) para 24 (rural ethnic women).

[202] eg CO Brazil, A/58/38, 29th Session (2003) para 114; CO Australia, CEDAW/C/AUS/CO/7 (2010) paras 40–1.

[203] eg CO Canada, A/58/38, 28th Session (2003) para 369; CO Brazil, A/58/38, 29th Session (2003) para 112. Girls are especially susceptible to certain forms of violence: early marriage, female genital mutilation, child sexual exploitation, and prostitution, GR 19 para 15.

[204] eg CO Austria, A/55/38 23rd Session (2000) para 230.   [205] eg ibid para 221.

[206] eg CO Nepal, CEDAW/C/NPL/CO/3 (2004) para 206.

[207] eg GR 26 para 21 (migrant workers may be confined to their work or living sites, prohibited from using telephones, or banned from joining groups or cultural associations).

[208] CO Ireland, CEDAW/C/IRL/CO/4-5 (2005) paras 28–9.

[209] eg CO Australia, CEDAW/C/AUS/CO/7 (2010) para 41.

[210] CO India, CEDAW/C/IND/CO/SP.1 (2010) para 37(c).

[211] See also DEVAW art 1; Convention of Belém do Pará art 1; Protocol on the Rights of Women in Africa art 1(j).

[212] eg CO Slovenia, A/58/38, 29th Session (2003) para 207.

[213] eg CO Cook Islands, CEDAW/C/COK/CO/1, (2007) para 25; Mexico, CEDAW/C/MEX/CO/6 (2006) para 596.

[214] eg CO Morocco, A/58/38, 29th Session (2003) para 169.

give high priority[215] to adopting and implementing measures to combat violence against women. In *Ms AT v Hungary*, the Committee recommended that Hungary take 'immediate and effective measures to guarantee the physical and mental integrity of AT and her family'. This followed the Committee's earlier recommendation for interim measures of protection under the Convention OP Article 5(1). The Committee had sent a *note verbale* to Hungary requesting that it adopt 'immediate, appropriate and concrete preventive interim measures of protection . . . in order to avoid irreparable damage'.[216] It also moved beyond the specific position of the complainant to the State party's general obligations with respect to violence against women and girls by requiring Hungary to 'implement expeditiously and without delay' its concluding observations to Hungary's combined fourth and fifth periodic reports, delivered some three years earlier.

2. Duty of Due Diligence

General Recommendation 19, paragraph 24 requires that States parties exercise due diligence[217] in combating gender-based violence. It spells out that 'under general international law and specific human rights covenants, States may also be responsible for private acts if they fail to act with due diligence to prevent violations of rights or to investigate and punish acts of violence, and for providing compensation'.[218] The duty of due diligence with respect to the acts of private actors arises when there is a situation of extreme danger of violence of which the State authorities 'knew or should have known'.[219] This approach has been continued in subsequent instruments,[220] throughout the work of the SR VAW[221] (who has noted the Committee's important contribution in this regard)[222] and is endorsed in the Secretary-General's Study.[223]

3. The Standard of Due Diligence

The standard of due diligence is high. The Committee observed that Austria had a 'comprehensive model to address domestic violence that includes legislation, criminal and civil-law remedies, awareness raising, education and training, shelters, counselling for victims of violence and work with perpetrators'.[224] In both *Fatma Yildirim* and *Şahide Goekce*, the authorities had prosecuted the perpetrators 'to the full extent of the law' but, nevertheless, there was a failure to exercise due diligence and, thus, violation of the Convention. Having a system in place to address the problem is insufficient; it must be put into effect by State actors who understand and adhere to the obligation of due

---

[215] eg CO Slovenia, A/58/38, 29th Session (2003) para 207; CO Benin, CEDAW/C/BEN/CO/1-3 (2005) para 23; CO DPR Korea, CEDAW/C/PRK/CO/1 (2005) para 38; CO FYROM (Macedonia), CEDAW/C/MKD/CO/3 (2006) para 24.

[216] *Ms AT v Hungary* (n 50 above) para 4.2.

[217] C Benninger-Budel (ed), *Due Diligence and Its Application to Protect Women from Violence* (2008).

[218] This principle is reasserted in *Ms AT v Hungary* (n 50 above) para 9.2; *Şahide Goekce v Austria* (n 51 above) para 12.1.1; *Fatma Yildirim v Austria* (n 51 above) para 12.1.1.

[219] *Şahide Goekce v Austria* (n 51 above) para 12.1.4; *Fatma Yildirim v Austria* (n 51 above) para 12.1.4.

[220] DEVAW art 4(c); Convention of Belém do Pará art 7(b).

[221] 'Report of the Special Rapporteur on violence against women 'Standard of Due Diligence'' (2006) UN Doc E/CN.4/2006/6.

[222] Preliminary Report (1994) UN Doc E/CN.4/1995/42 para 106; Special Rapporteur '15 Years' (n 13 above) 9.

[223] Report of the Secretary-General (n 1 above) paras 254–60.

[224] *Fatma Yildirim v Austria* (n 51 above) para 12.1.2; *Şahide Goekce v Austria* (n 51 above) para 12.1.2.

diligence.[225] Determining whether the authorities 'knew or should have known' of the danger of violence is context-specific, as especially illustrated by the facts in *Fatma Yildirim*. Although there was an interim injunction prohibiting him from returning to the couple's apartment, the immediate surroundings, and her workplace, Fatma Yildirim's husband had continuously contacted and threatened to kill her. There had been regular police interventions. Another factor that increased the danger was that the husband stood to lose his residence permit in Austria if the marriage was terminated.[226] The failure of the authorities to detain him breached the due diligence obligation to protect Fatma Yildirim; they did not take the decisive steps when the facts showed that they knew, or should have known, of the extreme danger.

In Ciudad Juárez there was no serious investigation into each murder and disappearance and impunity had prevailed for a decade. This constituted a failure of due diligence by the authorities.[227] Particular deficiencies were obtaining false confessions through torture, cases being closed without any arrests or punishments of perpetrators, irregularities in forensic examinations, failure to identify victims, and inadequate records and files.[228]

The Committee has suggested that due diligence requires zero-tolerance, for example, in urging States to 'launch a zero-tolerance campaign on violence against women'[229] with the objective of raising awareness of the problem and to make it 'socially and morally unacceptable'.[230]

II. Implementation of States Parties' Obligations

To comply with the obligation of due diligence States parties should adopt, implement, and monitor[231] legislation and policies with respect to violence against women applicable to their own agents and to non-State actors in all relevant fields, including employment, health, social services, education, business, and trade.

In order to clarify States parties' obligations under the Convention, the Committee has expressly adopted the 'respect, protect, promote and fulfil' typology.[232] However, although the Committee has provided many examples of what it regards as 'immediate and effective measures' in compliance with States parties' obligations, it does not expressly categorize them in this way. The following section provides examples of legal, social, rehabilitative, and educative measures the Committee has recommended, some of which may come under more than one of the levels of obligation. Lawyers must work alongside experts in other disciplines such as sociology, social policy, social work, public health, and economics, and legal initiatives must operate in conjunction with social,

---

[225] Ibid.

[226] *Fatma Yildirim v Austria* (n 51 above) para 12.1.4.

[227] Mexico Inquiry (n 55 above) paras 273–6; see also *González* et al *('Cotton Field') v Mexico* (n 43 above) especially paras 283, 284, 293, 300, and 388.

[228] The Committee found the investigation into the violence against women in Gujarat to be 'flawed from the outset': CO India, CEDAW/C/IND/CO/SP.1 (2010) paras 13–14.

[229] eg CO Iraq, A/55/38, 23rd Session (2000) para 190; CO Republic of Congo, A/58/38, 28th Session (2003) para 166; CO Cameroon, A/55/38, 23rd Session (2000) para 50; CO Romania, A/55/38, (Supp) 23rd Session (2000) para 307; CO Benin, CEDAW/C/BEN/CO/1-3 (2005) para 24.

[230] CO Romania, A/55/38, 23rd Session (2000) para 307.

[231] eg CO Nicaragua, A/56/38 (Supp) 25th Session (2001) para 309; CO Brazil, A/58/38, 29th Session (2003) para 113.

[232] *Ms AT v Hungary* (n 50 above) Recommendations, II(a).

economic, and political reforms. The Committee has not directly adopted the terminology of the CESCR that practices adopted to combat violence against women should be available, accessible, affordable, and appropriate.[233] However, this language pervades the Committee's concluding observations and recommendations.

1. *Obligation to Respect*

A State party's obligation to respect women's human rights is owed both to its immediate society and to the international community.[234] It requires States parties 'to refrain from discriminatory actions that directly or indirectly result in the denial of the equal right of men and women to their enjoyment of [human] rights'.[235] The obligation to respect women's right to be free from violence includes the duty to ensure that criminal, civil, administrative, and labour laws are not discriminatory and that they provide an effective legal framework for combating violence against women.

The Committee has frequently expressed concern at the lack, or inadequacy, of an appropriate legislative framework to combat forms of violence against women and routinely recommends its adoption or strengthening.[236] It urges States parties to adopt 'a specific law on domestic violence against women which provides for effective protection of victims, including restraining orders, and their access to legal aid'.[237] States parties must criminalize violence against women and girls.[238] The Committee consistently calls upon States parties to adopt penal law provisions, repealing those that define rape and sexual violence inappropriately, or which undermine the value of women's testimony.[239] It has also called for reform of laws or judicial practices that allow for defences of honour,[240] or for the perpetrator to escape punishment, for example, by allowing a victim (or the victim's heir) to decide whether to exact retribution or payment of compensation, or to pardon the accused.[241] Where women are killed in 'crimes of honour' perpetrators should be prosecuted in the same way as for other homicides.[242]

Where apposite legislation is in place the Committee may recommend strengthening its implementation and monitoring.[243] Adequate and allocated funding is essential for the proper operation of national strategies,[244] functioning of legal processes, and provision of social and medical care, including crisis service and shelters.[245] While women themselves must not be made responsible for ensuring freedom from violence,[246] self-help

---

[233] eg CESCR, 'General Comment 12' (1999) UN Doc E/C.12/1999/5.

[234] eg Mexico Inquiry (n 55 above) para 272.

[235] CESCR, 'General Comment 16' (2005) UN Doc E/C.12/2005/4 para 18.

[236] eg CO Hungary, CEDAW/C/HUN/CO/6 (2007), repeated in *Ms AT v Hungary* (n 50 above) para 9.3; CO Mexico, A/53/38, 18th Session (1998) para 411; CO Bulgaria, A/53/38, 18th Session (1998) para 255; CO Benin, CEDAW/C/BEN/CO/1-3 (2005) para 23.

[237] eg CO Hungary, CEDAW/C/HUN/CO/6 (2007) para 18.

[238] eg CO Tajikistan, CEDAW/C/TJK/CO/3 (2007) para 22.

[239] eg CO Pakistan, CEDAW/C/PAK/CO/3 (2007) para 16.

[240] GR 19 para 24(r)(ii); CO Lebanon, CEDAW/C/LBN/CO/2 (2005) para 28, reiterated CEDAW/C/LBN/CO/3 (2008) para 27; CO Brazil, A/58/38, 29th Session (2003) para 106.

[241] eg CO Pakistan, CEDAW/C/PAK/CO/3 (2007) paras 22–3.

[242] eg CO Iraq, A/55/38, 23rd Session (2000) para 194.

[243] *Şahide Goekce v Austria* (n 51 above) para 12.3(a); *Fatma Yildirim v Austria* (n 51 above) para 12.3(a); CO Nicaragua, A/56/38, 25th Session (2001) para 309.

[244] eg CO Belgium, CEDAW/C/BEL/CO/6 (2008) para 32.

[245] eg CO Canada, A/58/38, 28th Session (2003) para 369.

[246] Mexico Inquiry (n 55 above) para 57.

efforts should be respected and may be material in determining whether the State party has exercised due diligence.[247] States should assist women in this regard.[248]

The Committee has sought to make States parties comply with their positive duty to ensure that all State officials and public authorities respect their obligations. It has repeatedly said that officials, 'especially law enforcement personnel, the judiciary, health-care providers and social workers' must be 'fully familiar with applicable legal provisions and...sensitized to all forms of violence against women and respond adequately to them'.[249] Not only must officials not themselves commit acts of gender-based violence, they must also respond effectively and promptly to allegations of such violence. Inappropriate behaviour and attitudes, or giving effect to prejudices and gender stereotypes by State officials (for example, in rape trials)[250] lessens women's understanding of themselves as rights-holders and condones the violence, potentially discouraging women from reporting violence,[251] dropping charges, or otherwise withdrawing from the legal process.[252] This contributes to revictimization of women in a climate of impunity.[253]

2. Obligation to Protect

The obligation to protect—or to ensure respect[254]—is the positive obligation upon States parties to exercise due diligence to protect women from violence committed by non-State actors, for instance, individual family members, people within the community, or paramilitaries. The obligation to protect includes combating a climate of impunity and silence whereby violence is socially legitimated and women suffer extreme violence without criminal accountability for perpetrators.[255] Such impunity feeds further spirals of violence. Combating impunity requires prompt, thorough, impartial, and serious investigation of allegations of violence against women. The Mexico Inquiry illustrates inadequate investigation. The Committee found that 'no case of homicide linked to sexual violence was investigated in depth, the scene of the crime was not preserved, evidence was destroyed, accusations were ignored, defendants were framed, evidence was lost, pages were removed from files, and some of them have only a few pages, indicating that years had gone by without any investigation whatsoever'.[256] Inefficiency, complicity, and negligence in public authorities charged with investigating allegations of violence should be investigated and adequately sanctioned.[257]

---

[247] The Committee noted the 'positive and determined efforts' Fatma Yildirim made to save her own life; moving out of the apartment with her daughter, establishing ongoing contact with the police, seeking an injunction, and authorizing her husband's prosecution. *Fatma Yildirim v Austria* (n 51 above) para 12.1.3.

[248] GR 14, Preamble recognizes that 'important action that is being taken by women and by all interested groups [to combat practices prejudicial to the health and well-being of women] needs to be supported and encouraged by Governments'.

[249] eg CO Hungary, CEDAW/C/HUN/CO/6 (2007) para 19.

[250] *Vertido v The Philippines* CEDAW Communication No 18/2008 (2010) CEDAW/C/46/D/18/2008 paras 8.4, 8.5, and 8.6.

[251] eg CO Jordan, CEDAW/C/JOR/CO/4 (2007) para 22.   [252] Merry (n 48 above) 347.

[253] DEVAW art 4(f).

[254] The Committee recommended that the Mexican authorities '[u]rgently implement or strengthen effective measures for the protection of persons or institutions working to clear up the facts and ensure respect for human rights in Ciudad Juárez and Chihuahua state', Mexico Inquiry (n 55 above) para 282.

[255] eg CO Mozambique, CEDAW/C/MOZ/CO/2 (2007) para 24.

[256] Mexico Inquiry (n 55 above) para 88.

[257] Ibid para 274; CO India, CEDAW/C/IND/CO/SP.1 (2010) para 15.

Following investigations, the State party must ensure that accused perpetrators are vigilantly prosecuted in a timely fashion. This may have a symbolic effect in conveying 'to offenders and the public that society condemns cases where the perpetrator in a domestic violence situation poses a dangerous threat to the victim'.[258] Prosecution may be effectuated in the absence of a complaint by the victim.[259] Where convicted, offenders must be sentenced appropriately.[260] Rehabilitation[261] or therapeutic[262] programmes for offenders may also be considered. The Committee has expressed caution about informal forms of dispute resolution[263] and mediatory procedures that favour reconciliation in situations of violence, for example, within the family, and has recommended that States scrutinize such processes closely.[264]

Criminal law must be used alongside other high quality and effective protective measures, such as twenty-four-hour hotlines, restraining or other civil law orders,[265] and early warning and emergency search mechanisms for cases involving missing women and girls.[266] Protection orders must be available after normal working hours for all victims of violence.[267]

Women must be able to access justice. Accordingly, the State party should ensure the elimination of 'obstacles that may be encountered by women victims of violence in obtaining precautionary measures against perpetrators of violence and to ensure that such measures remain easily accessible to them'.[268] Protective measures for witnesses, victims, and victims' families need to be ensured.[269] Hungary was advised to provide 'victims of domestic violence with safe and prompt access to justice, including free legal aid where necessary, in order to ensure them available, effective and sufficient remedies and rehabilitation'.[270] Women may find their interactions with the legal system alienating, especially where their assertion of rights is met with hostility from the perpetrator and his family.[271] Specialized bodies such as victim-friendly[272] or family violence courts,[273] domestic violence and sex crimes units within law enforcement agencies,[274] or increasing the number of women in judicial and law enforcement roles,[275] are practical measures that the Committee has suggested or commended.

Victims of violence do not only need provision for legal assistance and access to justice. Medical, psychological, and other social and economic support services are also

---

[258] *Şahide Goekce v Austria* (n 51 above) para 12.3(b); *Fatma Yildirim v Austria* (n 51 above) para 12.3(b).

[259] eg CO Bulgaria, A/53/38, 18th Session (1998) para 255.   [260] GR19 para 24(g) and (t)(i).

[261] *Ms AT v Hungary* (n 50 above) para 9.6 II(h) (recommending that offenders be provided with rehabilitation programmes and programmes on non-violent conflict resolution methods).

[262] eg CO Austria, A/55/38 23rd Session (2000) para 230.

[263] CO Pakistan, CEDAW/C/PAK/CO/3 (2007) paras 24–5.

[264] eg CO Vietnam, A/56/38, 25th Session (2001) para 259; CO DPR Korea, CEDAW/C/PRK/CO/1 (2005) paras 39–40; CO Finland, CEDAW/C/FIN/CO/6 (2008) para 173.

[265] *Ms AT v Hungary* (n 50 above) para 9.4.   [266] Mexico Inquiry (n 55 above) para 276.

[267] eg CO Cook Islands, CEDAW/C/COK/CO/1 (2007) para 24.

[268] CO Venezuela, CEDAW/C/VEN/CO/6 (2006) para 26.

[269] CO Democratic Republic of Congo, CEDAW/C/COD/CO/5 (2006) paras 338–9.

[270] *Ms AT v Hungary* (n 50 above) para 9.6. II(g). On legal aid see also, eg, CO The Netherlands, CEDAW/C/NLD/CO/4 (2007) repeated CO The Netherlands, CEDAW/C/NLD/CO/5 (2010) para 26.

[271] Merry (n 48 above) 343.   [272] eg CO Zimbabwe, A/53/38, 18th Session (1998) para 137.

[273] eg CO Canada, A/58/38, 28th Session (2003) para 345; CO The Philippines, CEDAW/C/PHI/CO/6 (2006) para 523.

[274] eg CO Ecuador, CEDAW/C/ECU/CO/7 (2008) para 20.

[275] eg CO Belize, CEDAW/C/BLZ/CO/3 (2007) para 20.

necessary.[276] The Committee has requested information on the provision of support services such as refuges[277] (including safe accommodation for dependant children),[278] rape crisis centres, counselling, and other protective services.[279] Where these are inadequate or insufficient it urges States parties to take steps to improve the situation.

The obligation to protect includes the provision of adequate and effective remedies and reparation for victims of violence.[280] In *Ms AT v Hungary*, the Committee recommended reparation 'proportionate to the physical and mental harm undergone and to the gravity of the violations'[281] but did not suggest amounts,[282] or even whether reparation should be financial.[283] In response to the Gujarat massacre the Committee recommended 'effective and gender-specific measures to rehabilitate and compensate women victims of violence'.[284] Remedies should also be provided to the relatives of those who have suffered violence. For example, the Committee recommended that Mexico:

consider the need to facilitate adoption procedures for the grandmothers who have taken the children of the murdered and abducted women into their care and keeping so that they can receive the benefits to which they are entitled and have access to the social security benefits and social assistance which they would be entitled to receive through their mothers.[285]

The obligation to protect women from gender-based violence requires addressing cultural stereotypes, prejudices, and women's subordination in order to challenge the culture of impunity around violence against women. In *Ms AT v Hungary*, the Committee linked the unavailability of appropriate shelters and civil protection orders under Hungarian law with traditional attitudes that regard women as subordinate to men. The media are one instrument of changing attitudes. 'States should introduce education and public information programmes to help eliminate prejudices that hinder women's equality'.[286] General Recommendation 19 reaffirms in this context General Recommendation 3, which urges the adoption of education and public information programmes, to help eliminate prejudices and current practices that hinder women's enjoyment of social equality. The Committee has recommended awareness campaigns, in conjunction with civil society and the media, and capacity building for public officials.[287]

3. *Obligation to Promote and Fulfil*

The obligation to promote requires States parties to be forward-looking and to adopt short-, medium-, and long-term policies to combat violence against women in all its forms and manifestations, aiming at eventually fulfilling the goal of its elimination. Strategies and policies must vary according to the nature of violence, its incidence, and

---

[276] eg CO Bulgaria, A/53/38, 18th Session (1998) para 255.

[277] GR 19 para 24(t)(iii).

[278] *Ms AT v Hungary* (n 50 above) Recommendation I(b).

[279] GR 19 para 24(k); 24(r)(iii).

[280] GR 19 para 24(i). DEVAW art 4(d).

[281] *Ms AT v Hungary* (n 50 above) Recommendation I(b). It made no such recommendation in *Şahide Goekce v Austria* (n 51 above) or *Fatma Yildirim v Austria* (n 51 above).

[282] The Committee noted that compensation 'though inadequate' had been paid to the families of those who had died in the Gujarat massacre, widows, and injured women; CO India, CEDAW/C/IND/CO/SP.1 (2010) para 11.

[283] R Rubio-Marin (ed), *The Gender of Reparations* (2009); Special Rapporteur on violence against women 'Reparations for Women Subjected to Violence' (2010) UN Doc A/HRC/14/22 paras 12–86.

[284] eg CO India, CEDAW/C/IND/CO/SP.1 (2010) para 35(a).

[285] Mexico Inquiry (n 55 above) para 292.

[286] GR 19 para 24(d); CO Bulgaria, A/53/38, 18th Session (1998) para 255.

[287] Mexico Inquiry (n 55 above) para 288.

the social and economic context. Accordingly, there must be multiple strategies involving a range of agencies, NGOs, and other civil society institutions. The Committee has indicated some approaches to societal transformation through the eradication of violence against women.

The Committee regularly commends the adoption of a national plan or strategy for addressing violence against women,[288] and the institution of appropriate national machinery, such as a Taskforce for Action, especially one that brings together stakeholders from government, law enforcement agencies, and civil society.[289] A national strategy should be comprehensive, concerted, long-term, multidisciplinary, and coordinated and include legal, educational, financial, and social components.[290] It must also be implemented, regularly monitored, and evaluated.[291] Sufficient resources must be allocated for its implementation and should not be allowed to be depleted, including for NGO services.[292] A close relationship with civil society involving dialogue and information sharing in the development and implementation of national policies is recommended.[293] The Committee questions States parties about the efficacy of their plans, identifies weaknesses in analysis and research,[294] and recommends their strengthening.[295]

The Committee's proposals for long-term fulfilment of States parties' obligations encompass social, educational, and technical measures, including coordination between different branches of government and between law enforcement and judicial officers in addressing gender-based violence; regular gender training to, and sensitization of, all public officials, in particular, judges, lawyers, law enforcement officials, parliamentarians, teachers, and social workers;[296] public awareness campaigns on all forms of violence against women and girls[297] that address men and boys as well as women and girls;[298] the Convention and General Recommendation 19 to be made known and adhered to by health professionals; rehabilitation programmes; programmes in non-violent conflict resolution for perpetrators; ensuring autonomy and independence of forensic departments and experts in their investigation of crimes of violence against women.

The Committee is aware that information and data on gender-based violence remain inadequate, has noted the scarcity of disaggregated statistical data on many occasions,[299] and has appreciated appropriate research.[300] General Recommendation 19, paragraph 24(c) encourages the 'compilation of statistics and research on the extent,

---

[288] eg CO Morocco, A/58/38, 29th Session (2003) para 169.

[289] eg CO New Zealand, CEDAW/C/NZL/CO/6 (2007) para 8.

[290] eg CO Belgium, CEDAW/C/BEL/CO/6 (2008) para 31.

[291] *Ms AT v Hungary* (n 50 above) Recommendation II(c).

[292] eg CO The United Kingdom, CEDAW/C/UK/CO/6 (2008) para 280.

[293] eg Mexico Inquiry (n 55 above) para 270; CO Bahrain, CEDAW/C/BHR/CO/2 (2008) para 25.

[294] eg CO New Zealand, CEDAW/C/NZL/CO/6 (2007) para 24.

[295] eg CO Nicaragua, A/56/38, 25th Session (2001) para 292.

[296] This is an often repeated recommendation; eg CO Vietnam, A/56/38, 25th Session (2001) para 259; CO Republic of Congo, A/58/38, 28th Session (2003) para 167; CO Brazil, A/58/38, 29th Session (2003) para 107; CO Slovenia, A/58/38, 29th Session (2003) para 207; CO Ireland, CEDAW/C/IRL/CO/4-5 (2005) para 28; CO Belize, CEDAW/C/BLZ/CO/3 (2007) para 20; CO Australia, CEDAW/C/AUS/CO/5 (2006) para 19; *Vertido v the Philippines* (n 250 above) para 8.8(b)(iii) and (iv).

[297] eg CO Vietnam, A/56/38, 25th Session (2001) para 259; CO Slovenia, A/58/38, 29th Session (2003) para 207; CO Ireland, CEDAW/C/IRL/CO/4-5 (2005) para 29.

[298] CO The Philippines, CEDAW/C/PHI/CO/6 (2006) para 526.

[299] eg CO Libya, A/49/38 13th Session (1994) para 133; CO Japan, A/49/38, 13th Session (1994) para 577; CO Bangladesh, A/52/38 17th Session (1997) para 442.

[300] eg CO The Netherlands, A/49/38 (Supp) 13th Session (1994) para 310.

causes and effects of violence, and on the effectiveness of measures to prevent and deal with violence'. The Committee has been forceful in urging States parties to devise and improve structures for systematic data collection. It has called upon them to study data on incidences of different types of violence disaggregated by sex, age, ethnicity, urban/rural setting, and the relationship of the perpetrator with the victim, as well as quantitative research to make findings in order to address violence against women.[301] The Committee has also encouraged States parties to collect data on criminal proceedings related to such violence.[302]

G. Conclusions

General Recommendation 19 has been the basis of the Committee's work on violence against women. Since 1992, the Committee's work has been supplemented by that of other UN and regional bodies. Many of the issues raised by the Committee have been more comprehensively analyzed elsewhere, perhaps most notably by the Special Rapporteurs on Violence against Women. They have used their mandate to provide fuller accounts of the causes and consequences of the multiple forms and sites of violence, as well as exploring in greater detail the complexities of such issues as the relationship between violence and culture,[303] violence against women in armed conflict, and the transformative potential of the concept of due diligence,[304] which were all flagged in General Recommendation 19. The structure and limitations of State party reporting constrain the Committee from exploring issues in depth. Its function is to engage in constructive dialogue and to encourage States parties to change their laws and practices in conformity with their obligations under the Convention. While the SR VAW can devote her country missions to examination of violence, States parties' reports and the Committee's concluding observations must give attention to all Convention articles. However, when able to do so, as in the Mexico Inquiry, the Committee has explored more fully the linkages between exploitive labour, women's migration for work, poverty, patriarchy, social constructions of women and gender relations, official apathy and complicity in creating an environment hostile to women's security and well-being.

The Committee has not always gone as far as some of the reports of the SR VAW and academics have sought. For example, it has not designated even extreme forms of domestic violence resulting in death as in the cases of Şahide Goekce and Fatma Yildirim as torture,[305] but has rather focused on making feasible recommendations directed at the authorities for the prevention, protection, and punishment of violence against women. It has, nevertheless, not been inhibited from making strong statements, for example, placing women's right to be free from violence high in the hierarchy of rights and emphasizing the

---

[301] eg CO Slovenia, A/58/38, 29th Session (2003) para 207; CO France, CEDAW/C/FRA/CO/6 (2008) para 29; CO Norway, CEDAW/C/NOR/CO/7 (2007) para 19.

[302] eg CO Austria, A/55/38 23rd Session (2000) para 239.

[303] The Special Rapporteur on violence against women 'Intersections Between Culture and Violence Against Women' (2007) UN Doc A/HRC/4/34.

[304] Report of the Special Rapporteur (n 221 above).

[305] As suggested in the Special Rapporteur on violence against women 'Violence in the Family' (1996) UN Doc E/CN.4/1996/53; R Copelon, 'Intimate Terror: Understanding Domestic Violence as Terror' in Cook (ed) (n 46 above) 116; CA MacKinnon, 'On Torture: A Feminist Perspective on Human Rights' in KE Mahoney and P Mahoney (eds), *Human Rights in the 21st Century: A Global Perspective* (1993) 21.

duty to criminalize all forms of violence against women, alongside measures for protection, support, and rehabilitation.

In line with the UN policy of gender mainstreaming, women's human rights, including the right to be free from violence, have been addressed by other treaty bodies and mandate holders. The CCPR[306] and the CESCR[307] have adopted general comments on gender equality within the context of the two Covenants, which address forms of gender-based violence, but without reference to General Recommendation 19 or to the Committee's work on the subject. The Special Rapporteur on Torture has examined how to develop a gender-sensitive interpretation of torture.[308]

In 2010, the 15 Year Review of the Beijing Declaration and Platform for Action was carried out in the CSW. The Secretary-General's Report included a review of the twelve Critical Areas of Concern addressed in Beijing. It states that since 1995, combating violence against women has become a priority in many parts of the world and that there have been positive results, notably: strengthened and more comprehensive legal, policy, and institutional frameworks; increased availability and quality of services for victims/survivors of violence; engagement of multiple stakeholders to prevent violence against women; and improvements in data collection and analysis.[309] Continuing gaps and concerns are also identified.

These are all issues that the Committee has raised with States parties. However, the language of the rights-based approach to violence against women—that violence against women, including in situations of armed conflict, has become recognized as violation of women's human rights—is not widely incorporated in the Review Document beyond acknowledging that 'States are continuing to eliminate discriminatory provisions in such laws and incorporate new provisions to ensure the protection of women's human rights throughout the criminal justice system'.[310] CEDAW, the Beijing Declaration and Platform for Action, and Outcome document are all reaffirmed in the Declaration adopted by CSW on 2 March 2010,[311] but there is no explicit mention of violence against women, nor any overarching resolution on the topic. The language is rather that of gender equality, empowerment, and affirmation of the MDGs.

Perhaps the rights-based approach to gender-based violence is now so widely accepted that it does not need to be spelled out again. If this is the case, the constant questioning by the Committee of States parties about implementation of their obligations under the Convention and exhortations to adopt national strategies, legislation, and practices to reduce its incidence and to provide a legal framework for accountability have contributed significantly to this achievement. The Committee ensures that the language of rights is not forgotten.

[306] CCPR, 'General Comment 28' (2000) UN Doc CCPR/C/21/Rev.1/Add.10.
[307] CESCR, 'General Comment 16' (2005) UN Doc E/C.12/2005/4 uses the CEDAW art 1 definition of discrimination; see also CESCR 'General Comment 20' (2009) UN Doc E/C.12/GC/20.
[308] 'Report of the Special Rapporteur on torture and other cruel, inhuman or degrading treatment or punishment' (2008) UN Doc A/HRC/7/3.
[309] Report of the Secretary-General, 'Review of the Implementation of the Beijing Declaration and Platform for Action, the Outcomes of the Twenty-Third Special Session of the General Assembly and its Contribution to Shaping a Gender Perspective Towards the Full Realization of the Millennium Development Goals' (2010) UN Doc E/2010/4*–E/CN.6/2010/2* (Review Document) para 121.
[310] Ibid para 291.   [311] UN Doc E/CN.6/2010/L.1.

Article 17

1. For the purpose of considering the progress made in the implementation of the present Convention, there shall be established a Committee on the Elimination of Discrimination against Women (hereinafter referred to as the Committee) consisting, at the time of entry into force of the Convention, of eighteen and, after ratification of or accession to the Convention by the thirty-fifth State Party, of twenty-three experts of high moral standing and competence in the field covered by the Convention. The experts shall be elected by States Parties from among their nationals and shall serve in their personal capacity, consideration being given to equitable geographical distribution and to the representation of the different forms of civilization as well as the principal legal systems.

2. The members of the Committee shall be elected by secret ballot from a list of persons nominated by States Parties. Each State Party may nominate one person from among its own nationals.

3. The initial election shall be held six months after the date of the entry into force of the present Convention. At least three months before the date of each election the Secretary-General of the United Nations shall address a letter to the States Parties inviting them to submit their nominations within two months. The Secretary-General shall prepare a list in alphabetical order of all persons thus nominated, indicating the States Parties which have nominated them, and shall submit it to the States Parties.

4. Elections of the members of the Committee shall be held at a meeting of States Parties convened by the Secretary-General at United Nations Headquarters. At that meeting, for which two thirds of the States Parties shall constitute a quorum, the persons elected to the Committee shall be those nominees who obtain the largest number of votes and an absolute majority of the votes of the representatives of States Parties present and voting.

5. The members of the Committee shall be elected for a term of four years. However, the terms of nine of the members elected at the first election shall expire at the end of two years; immediately after the first election the names of these nine members shall be chosen by lot by the Chairman of the Committee.

6. The election of the five additional members of the Committee shall be held in accordance with the provisions of paragraphs 2, 3 and 4 of this article, following the thirty-fifth ratification or accession. The terms of two of the additional members elected on this occasion shall expire at the end of two years, the names of these two members having been chosen by lot by the Chairman of the Committee.

7. For the filling of casual vacancies, the State Party whose expert has ceased to function as a member of the Committee shall appoint another expert from among its nationals, subject to the approval of the Committee.

8. The members of the Committee shall, with the approval of the General Assembly, receive emoluments from United Nations resources on such terms and conditions as the Assembly may decide, having regard to the importance of the Committee's responsibilities.

9. The Secretary-General of the United Nations shall provide the necessary staff and facilities for the effective performance of the functions of the Committee under the present Convention.

---

* I would like to thank Marie Elske Gispen for her assistance on the chapters on arts 17, 18, 19, 20, 21, and 22 of the Commentary.

A. Introduction

Article 17 of the Convention provides for the establishment of the Committee on the Elimination of Discrimination against Women.[1] Article 17 resembles the provisions establishing the other United Nations human rights treaty monitoring bodies, with a noteworthy difference in the envisaged enlargement of the Committee from eighteen to twenty-three members after the thirty-fifth ratification. The primary function of the Committee envisaged in the Convention is to consider progress in the implementation of the Convention by means of the reporting procedure (Article 18), which was later supplemented by the individual communications procedure and inquiry procedure of the Optional Protocol. Articles 18–22 provide further details about the reporting procedure (Article 18), the adoption of the Committee's Rules of Procedure (Article 19), its meetings (Article 20), its reports (Article 21), and the role of the specialized agencies (Article 22). The provisions are not detailed, leaving room for the Committee to develop its methods of work over the years. Since 1987, the Committee has participated in the meetings of Chairpersons of the Human Rights Treaty Bodies (hereafter 'Chairpersons'), a forum in which problems that the treaty bodies have in common are discussed, and where working methods are streamlined. These meetings have had an impact on the work of the Committee, and vice versa.

The Convention entered into force on 3 September 1981. The first Meeting of States Parties took place on 16 April 1982, electing the first Committee members. The Committee held its first session from 18–22 October 1982. As the number of ratifications had already reached thirty five in March 1982, the Committee was composed of twenty-three members from the outset.

---

[1] See further A Byrnes, 'The Committee on the Elimination of Discrimination Against Women' in P Alston and F Mégret (eds), *The United Nations and Human Rights. A Critical Appraisal*, 2nd edn (forthcoming); HB Schöpp-Schilling, 'The nature and mandate of the Committee' in HB Schöpp-Schilling and C Flinterman (eds), *The Circle of Empowerment: Twenty-Five Years of the UN Committee on the Elimination of Discrimination Against Women* (2007) 248–61.

B. Travaux Préparatoires

Both the Commission on the Status of Women (CSW) and the Third Committee of the General Assembly intensely discussed the question of Convention implementation, in particular, as to whether the CSW should be entrusted with consideration of the status of the Convention, or whether a new body should be established for that purpose.

The Working Group's draft text submitted to the 25th session of the CSW contained alternative texts for various articles, including those dealing with the consideration of the status of the Convention. The first option entrusted 'consideration of the question of the status of the implementation of the Convention' to the CSW,[2] and the second provided for the establishment of a Committee.[3]

Some CSW members expressed the fear that 'the creation of a committee would deprive the Commission of competence with respect to the application of the convention and this might be used as an excuse to do away with the Commission',[4] and noted that the review of States parties' progress in implementation could be successfully fulfilled by the CSW, and that granting that power to the CSW would be the 'simplest, most logical and effective process'.[5] Arguments in favour of a Committee included the already heavy workload of the CSW and the preference for the supervision to be entrusted to a body of independent experts rather than government representatives.[6]

At its 26th session, the CSW was still 'sharply divided' over what constituted the most suitable mechanism.[7] New amendments were introduced, most of which proposed the establishment of a working group by the CSW, of either ten or ten to fifteen members.[8] Another draft proposed the establishment of a special committee of fifteen members elected by the CSW, but serving in their personal capacity.[9] The text adopted (then Article 19) referred to an ad hoc group of ten to fifteen members elected by the CSW from among States parties to the Convention, serving in their personal capacity.[10]

Discussions continued until the final stages of the drafting process in the Third Committee of the General Assembly. The Third Committee had before it three proposals, including the version submitted by the CSW, a proposal providing for the establishment of an ad hoc group of twenty-three States parties and members of the Economic and Social Council, and a proposal providing for the establishment of a Committee.[11] This last proposal was adopted, with an amendment to the effect that the United Nations would be responsible for the expenses of the Committee, rather than the States parties.[12]

During the discussion in the Third Committee Working Group, some States favoured the establishment of a body of twenty-three members, 'even if this added to the costs, as this number would be more consonant with the expanded membership of the United Nations and would permit a more adequate representation of the smaller countries

---

[2] UN Doc E/CN.6/574 (1974) 17.
[3] UN Doc E/CN.6/574 (1974) 18, along the lines proposed by Egypt, Nigeria, and Zaire.
[4] UN Doc E/CN.6/589 (1974) para 81.   [5] UN Doc E/CN.6/591 (1976) para 183.
[6] UN Doc E/CN.6/591 (1976) para 182.   [7] UN Doc E/CN.6/608 (1976) para 178.
[8] Amendments proposed by India, Iran, and Egypt reproduced in UN Doc E/CN.6/608 (1976) paras 185, 189, and 190, respectively.
[9] Amendment proposed by Denmark UN Doc E/CN.6/608 (1976) para 191.
[10] UN Doc E/CN.6/608 (1976) paras 185–205.
[11] UN Doc A/C.3/34/14, Annex I (1979) 10–15 for Swedish proposal.
[12] UN Doc A/C.3/34/SR.72 (1979) paras 52–65, proposal on expenses by Bangladesh.

within the requirements of equitable geographic distribution'.[13] Those in favour of a committee of eighteen members pointed to the excellent work of the CERD, and the fact that a body of twenty-three members was in conflict with the requirement of twenty States parties for the Convention to enter into force. It was then suggested to enlarge membership at a later stage, pursuant to which the proposal was amended to the effect that membership would be enlarged to twenty-three pursuant to the fortieth ratification. A subsequent amendment changed 'fortieth' to 'thirty-fifth'.[14]

The final text provides that Committee members must be experts of high moral standing. It was suggested to include a requirement that individuals nominated shall have been involved in the advancement of equality of rights of men and women, and that not less than half of the members should be women. Both suggestions were rejected.[15] Consequently, the Convention does not contain specific requirements regarding qualifications of members other than the general 'competence' requirement, nor does it lay down incompatibilities for membership.

C. Internal Organization and Engagement with Other Entities

I. Subsidiary Bodies

The Convention does not deal with the establishment of subsidiary bodies of the Committee; this is dealt with in the Committee's Rules of Procedure.[16] Under Rule 41, it may set up ad hoc subsidiary bodies and define their composition and mandates. The Committee's Rules of Procedure provide for a number of working groups to assist it with its main functions. At its 6th session, the Committee established two working groups. Working Group I would consider and suggest ways and means of expediting the work of the Committee, and Working Group II would deal with ways and means of implementing Article 21.[17] Following a recommendation of Working Group I, the Committee decided at its 8th session to establish a pre-session working group that assists it in preparing the consideration of States' reports.[18] At the 26th session, the Committee decided to take up issues on implementation of Article 21 and on ways and means of expediting the work of the Committee, through a Working Group of the Whole.[19]

The Committee may establish working groups and designate rapporteurs to assist it in any manner on which it may decide,[20] thus allowing flexibility in dealing with communications under the Optional Protocol. It can also establish a working group to assist it in carrying out its duties under the Optional Protocol inquiry procedure.[21] General recommendations under Article 21 are drafted in working groups established for that purpose. When the Committee has undertaken the drafting of several general recommendations simultaneously, it can establish more than one working group under this rule. Throughout the years, the Committee has established various ad hoc working groups, such as a working

---

[13] UN Doc A/C.3/34/SR.72 (1979) para 11, proposal by Libya.
[14] UN Doc A/C.3/34/SR.72 (1979) para 11. France proposed the two stages, Sweden amended its own proposal.
[15] Amendments proposed by the United States, reproduced in UN Doc E/CN.6/608 (1976) para 197.
[16] See the discussion in ch on art 19.
[17] UN Doc A/42/38 (1987) paras 26 and 28; Rules of Procedure 54. See the discussion in ch on art 21.
[18] UN Doc A/44/38 (1989) paras 19 and 22; Rules of Procedure 4.
[19] UN Doc A/57/38 (2002) para 19.   [20] Rules of Procedure 62(1).
[21] Rules of Procedure 8(3). See the discussion in ch on Optional Protocol.

group to review its guidelines for reporting subsequent to the Chairpersons' adoption of the revised harmonized reporting guidelines. In addition, the Committee has created the function of country rapporteur and has established country task forces to prepare for the consideration of reports.[22]

II. Interaction with Other Entities in the UN System

Over the years, the Committee's interaction with the other treaty monitoring bodies has increased significantly. At its 15th session, it decided to designate members to act as focal points on each of the other human rights treaty bodies and to inform the Committee on relevant activities.[23] Focal points for interaction with the specialized agencies also were appointed in 1998.[24] In light of the enhanced interaction with various entities, the Committee at its 37th session decided to discontinue the focal points.[25]

The Committee Chairperson participates in the Meetings of the Chairpersons of the Human Rights Treaty Bodies and, with a member of the bureau, in the Inter-Committee Meetings. In addition, the Secretariat informs the Committee about relevant developments in the human rights regime in its note on the 'Ways and means of expediting the work of the Committee on the Elimination of Discrimination against Women' prepared for each session.

Over the years, the Committee has held discussions with relevant Special Procedures of the Commission on Human Rights (since 2006, the Human Rights Council) and the former Sub-Commission on Human Rights. By the end of 2010, however, there was no institutionalized relationship between the treaty bodies and the Human Rights Council. The Committee has indicated that it looks forward to developing one.[26] The Chairpersons agree that the treaty system and the Universal Periodic Review are 'complementary and mutually reinforcing'.[27] The Committee has not designated an observer to follow the Universal Periodic Review process.

III. The Committee and Treaty Body Reform

The Committee has actively contributed to the long-term discussion on treaty body reform.[28] In 2006, it issued a statement in which it formulated a number of concerns about the HCHR's proposal on a unified standing treaty body.[29] While acknowledging the challenges faced by the treaty bodies, the Committee did not consider that the establishment of a unified treaty body would respond to such challenges. It held that the plan implied 'a serious risk of undermining the differentiation and specificity of human rights as enshrined in the seven major international human rights treaties'.[30] The Committee

---

[22] See the discussion in ch on art 18. [23] UN Doc A/51/38 (2006) para 337.

[24] UN Doc A/53/38/Rev.1 (1998) paras 431–3. [25] UN Doc A/62/38 (2007) para 659.

[26] CEDAW, 'Ways and means of expediting the work of the Committee on the Elimination of Discrimination against Women' (2006) CEDAW/C/2009/II/4 para 39.

[27] UNGA, 'Report of the chairpersons of the human rights treaty bodies on their twentieth meeting' (2008) UN Doc A/63/280, Annex, para 24(d).

[28] See Schöpp-Schilling and Flinterman (n 1 above).

[29] 'Plan of action submitted by the United Nations High Commissioner for Human Rights' in Report of the Secretary-General, 'In larger freedom: Towards development, security and human rights for all' (2005) UN Doc A/59/2005/Add.3, Annex, para 147; further elaborated in Report by the Secretariat, 'Concept paper on the High Commissioner's proposal for a unified standing treaty body' (2006) HRI/MC/2006/2.

[30] CEDAW Statement, 'Towards a harmonized and integrated human rights treaty body system' (2006) UN Doc A/61/38, 35th Session, Annex I, para 4.

favoured an approach in which the treaty bodies work as much as possible as a harmonized and integrated system so as to enhance their visibility, accessibility, and effectiveness. While advocating further harmonization, coordination, and integration of the various aspects of their mandates, the Committee stressed that this should not lead to losing the specificities of their different roles.[31] Its concern was based on the experience in its own work and of other bodies dealing specifically with gender issues.

D. Committee Practice

I. Article 17(1)

... experts of high moral standing and competence in the field covered by the Convention.

The Committee is the only treaty body in which women are a large majority; indeed, very few men have been members during its existence.[32] Gender balance has by far not been achieved in any of the treaty bodies, despite the recommendation by the Chairpersons that States parties should give due consideration to, among others, balanced gender representation.[33]

The biographical data show a wide diversity of expertise among past and present members.[34] Almost all members have significant expertise in and commitment to gender issues, either as academics, policy advisers, in legal practice or the judiciary. They have backgrounds in fields such as social or political sciences, media, law, education, human rights and equal treatment, and medicine. Most members have previous experience in regional or international bodies, either in expert bodies dealing with gender issues or in political organs such as the CSW.

As is the case for all treaty bodies, the Convention does not pose specific professional requirements for membership. Neither is there a provision comparable to ICCPR Article 28(2) or CAT Article 17(1) that States parties shall bear in mind the participation of some persons having legal experience. This can be explained by the original lack of an individual complaints procedure. Diverse knowledge and expertise as well as practice in international relations are important for the performance of the Committee's functions, in particular in the consideration of reports. In light of the Committee's function under the Optional Protocol, it has become necessary to have a number of members with legal expertise.

The experts ... shall serve in their personal capacity.

The independence of members is essential. Members may not be subject to direction or influence of any kind, or to pressure from a State party or its agencies in regard to the performance of their duties. As the CCPR stated in guidelines for the exercise of

---

[31] CEDAW Statement (n 30 above) paras 5–7.

[32] Johan Nordenfelt (Sweden) 1982–1984; 2001–2004; Göran Melander (Sweden) 2001–2004; Cees Flinterman (The Netherlands) 2003–2010; Niklas Bruun (Finland) since 2009. See A Byrnes, 'The "Other" Human Rights Treaty Body: The work of the Committee on the Elimination of Discrimination Against Women' (1989) 14 *Yale J of Intl L* 1, 8–9.

[33] UNGA, 'Report of the chairpersons of the human rights treaty bodies on their twenty-first meeting' (2009) UN Doc A/64/280 para 18(d), referring to UNGA Res 63/167 (2008) UN Doc A/RES/63/167 para 4.

[34] Available in reports of the Meetings of States Parties online at <http://www.un.org/Depts/los/meeting_states_parties/meeting_states_parties.htm> accessed 31 December 2010.

their functions by Committee members: 'they are not accountable to their State, but are accountable only to the Committee and their own conscience.'[35] The Convention does not formulate incompatibilities for membership. Consequently, government officials, including ambassadors, are not excluded from membership. This may raise questions as to whether they serve, or can be perceived to serve, 'in their personal capacity'. The importance of members' independence is reiterated in the solemn declaration members make upon assuming their duties, both upon election and re-election:

I solemnly declare that I shall perform my duties and exercise powers as a member of the Committee on the Elimination of Discrimination against Women honourably, faithfully, impartially and conscientiously.[36]

Members' positions as independent experts is reflected in Rule 60 of the Rules of Procedure, providing that members may not take part in the examination of a communication if the member is a national of the State party concerned.[37] Similar rules do not exist for the Committee's activities under the reporting procedure and the inquiry procedure, but the established practice that members do not engage in the constructive dialogue with the State party of which they are a national, nor in the adoption of the concluding observations, was reaffirmed in a decision.[38] The same practice will be applied with regard to the inquiry procedure. This practice is in accordance with the statement adopted by the Chairpersons about the independence of experts, which reads 'The chairpersons recommended that members of treaty bodies refrain from participating in any aspect of the consideration of the reports of the States parties of which they were nationals, or communications or inquiries concerning those States parties, in order to maintain the highest standards of impartiality, both in substance and in appearance.'[39] The Committee could formalize this practice by incorporating it in its Rules of Procedure.

Members play an important role in enhancing Convention implementation at the national and global level more generally. They participate in technical assistance activities at the request of States parties, organized by the DAW, OHCHR, and other United Nations entities.[40] At its 44th session, the Committee adopted a decision that 'experts from individual States parties may advise their Governments during the reporting process, including the preparation of the report under Article 18 of the Convention, but should not lead or write the report'.[41]

The Chairpersons have called on States parties to refrain from nominating or electing persons 'performing political functions or occupying positions which were not readily reconcilable with the obligations of independent experts under the given treaty'.[42]

---

[35] CCPR, 'Guidelines for the exercise of their functions by members of the Human Rights Committee' (1998) UN Doc A/53/40, Vol. I, Annex III, para 1. CEDAW has not adopted similar guidelines.

[36] Rules of Procedure 15.   [37] Rules of Procedure 60(1)(c).

[38] CEDAW, 'Consideration of reports' (1998) UN Doc A/53/38/Rev.1, Decision 18/III.

[39] UNGA, 'Report of the eighth meeting of persons chairing the human rights treaty bodies' (1997) UN Doc A/52/507 para 67.

[40] CEDAW, 'Ways and means of expediting the work of the Committee on the Elimination of Discrimination against Women' (2009) UN Doc CEDAW/C/2009/II/4 para 41.

[41] CEDAW, 'Scope of Committee members acting in their personal capacities'(2009) UN Doc A/65/38, 47th Session, Decision 44/I, para 1.

[42] 'Report of the eighth meeting of persons chairing the human rights treaty bodies' (n 39 above) para 68, reiterated by the 21st meeting, 'Report of the chairpersons of the human rights treaty bodies on their twenty-first meeting' (n 33 above) Annex I, para 17(a), endorsing the points of agreement of the inter-

Nevertheless, States parties have continued to nominate and elect persons who hold or have held high political positions.

…consideration being given to equitable geographical distribution and to the representation of the different forms of civilization as well as the principal legal systems.

The 'equitable geographical distribution' clause refers to the fundamental principle of the United Nations to reflect the entire membership in UN-related bodies. The Convention does not allocate seats to regional groups. The Rules of Procedure of the Meeting of States Parties, the body responsible for the election of Committee members, do not further specify how equitable geographic distribution is to be achieved. Nor do the Rules specify measures that could be taken if elections result in an imbalanced composition, as has occurred.[43] The Committee has five officers: a Chairperson, three Vice-Chairpersons, and a Rapporteur, who are elected from among its members 'with due regard to equitable geographical representation'.[44] Members of Working Groups are generally selected with a view to regional balance. Further, a 'fair geographical balance of experts' is taken into account when the Committee works in parallel chambers to consider States parties' reports.[45]

The General Assembly has called on States parties to ensure equitable geographical distribution in the membership of the human rights treaty bodies. It has encouraged States parties to 'consider and adopt concrete actions, *inter alia*, the possible establishment of quota distribution systems by geographical region' for the election of the members of the treaty bodies.[46] It suggested a quota of seats for each regional group in proportion to regional representation among the States parties.

II. Article 17(2)

…Each State Party may nominate one person from among its own nationals.

This clause is comparable to ICERD Article 8(1) and differs from ICCPR Article 29 which provides that States parties may nominate not more than two persons. Although not explicitly stated, candidates may be renominated after election, and if they have not been elected. The Committee's Rules of Procedure underline the personal nature of the candidacy and membership, stating that members may not be represented by alternates.[47]

III. Practice and Developments relating to Article 17(3) and (4)

…a meeting of States Parties…

The Meeting of States Parties is held biannually, generally for one day. Its main agenda item is the election of members of the Committee. The nominations submitted by States parties are distributed by the Secretary-General. The documents containing the nominations, biographical data, and CVs have always been public and are now published on

committee meeting, as submitted in UNGA 'Report of the ninth inter-committee meeting of human rights treaty bodies' (2009) UN Doc A/64/276, Annex II, para 46(j).

[43] See generally UNGA, 'Report of the United Nations High Commissioner for Human Rights on the equitable geographical distribution in the membership of the human rights treaty bodies' (2009) UN Doc A/64/212, table 1.

[44] Rules of Procedure 16. See the discussion in ch on art 19.

[45] CEDAW Report (2006) UN Doc A/61/38, 34th Session para 366.

[46] UNGA Res 64/173 (18 December 2009) UN Doc A/RES/64/173 para 1.

[47] Rules of Procedure 11.

the OHCHR Website.[48] Rule 13 of the Meeting of States parties' Rules of Procedure largely restates the treaty provisions on the election of members, and Rule 14 adds that the elections shall be held by secret ballot.[49] Some NGOs have taken initiatives to lobby for the nomination and election of candidates, but States parties are not required to consult NGOs, nor do they play any formal role in this procedure.

The Meeting is informed on the status of declarations, reservations, objections, and notifications of withdrawal of reservations made by States parties,[50] and while a role for the States parties might seem obvious, in practice the Meeting is not used as a forum for formal discussion of reservations.

IV. Article 17(5)

The clause providing for a term of two years only for nine members elected at the inception of the Committee is common in human rights treaties establishing a treaty monitoring body. It must be read in conjunction with Article 17(6), which provides for the expansion of the Committee from eighteen to twenty-three members following the 35th ratification. As that number had been achieved before the establishment of the Committee, it has been composed of twenty-three members from the outset. Consequently, every two years the term of eleven or twelve members expires. The clause ensures continuity in membership: every two years no more than twelve vacancies exist. In practice, a significant number of members serve more than one term.

The Convention does not impose a limit on the number of terms a member may serve, so they can be re-elected indefinitely. In practice, some members have served on the Committee for a very long time. The longest continuously serving member was Hanna Beate Schöpp-Schilling, who was a member from 1989–2008.[51] Members' terms of office begin on 1 January of the year following their election by the meeting of States parties and ends on 31 December four years later.[52]

V. Article 17(6) and 17(7)

Article 17(7) is based on ICERD Article 8(5). Most other United Nations human rights treaties provide for the State that had nominated the candidate who cannot complete the term to appoint a new member. The exception is the ICCPR, which provides that all States parties may nominate a new member. CAT provides that the States parties must approve of the appointment of the new member, and other treaties require approval by the Committee (ICERD, CEDAW, CRC, ICMW), whereas the CRPD simply states that the State concerned may appoint a new member, and requires approval neither by the Committee nor by the States parties. The Committee's role in this respect is relevant, as it could, for example, block the appointment of members who do not meet the requirements.

---

[48] This information is available at <http://www2.ohchr.org/english/bodies/cedaw/> under 'Meeting of States parties' accessed 20 December 2010.

[49] 'Draft Rules of Procedure of the Meeting of States parties to the Convention on the Elimination of All Forms of Discrimination against Women' (1982) UN Doc CEDAW/SP/2/Rev.1, rule 14.

[50] Meeting of States Parties to CEDAW, 'Declarations, reservations, objections and notifications of withdrawal of reservations relating to the Convention on the Elimination of All Forms of Discrimination against Women' (2010) UN Doc CEDAW/SP/2010/2.

[51] An overview of the Committee's membership 1982–2007 can be found on <http://www2.ohchr.org/english/bodies/cedaw/docs/CEDAWListMembersNew.pdf> accessed 31 December 2010.

[52] Rules of Procedure 12.

The Committee's Rules of Procedure elaborate that a 'casual' vacancy may occur through death, inability of a member to perform her or his function as a member of the Committee, or resignation of a member.[53] Several members have died during their term and were succeeded by a new member. In addition, a number of members have resigned upon taking up other prominent functions, such as a position as judge in the International Criminal Court or a Minister in the national government.[54] When a State party does not nominate a new candidate, the vacancy remains unfilled.[55]

VI. Article 17(8)

The lack of an honorarium for members remains an issue of concern. Until 2002, members received an honorarium, which was reduced to one US dollar per year by the General Assembly in 2002.[56] Membership requires a considerable time commitment, especially since the number of sessions has increased to three. Taking into account the time needed for adequate preparation of consideration of State reports and participation in Working Groups, members spend some three months annually on their work for the Committee. This time commitment may constitute an obstacle for qualified candidates who might have to take unpaid leave from employment or who have very demanding positions.

VII. Article 17(9)

The Secretary-General of the United Nations shall provide...

The specific tasks of the Secretary-General are not elaborated in the Convention, but are dealt with in Rules 21–23 of the Rules of Procedure: the Secretary-General shall provide the secretariat of the Committee and its subsidiary bodies and shall be present at the meetings of the Committee and may make oral or written statements. In practice, at the opening of its sessions the Committee is welcomed by the HCHR or her representative.

From the first CEDAW session in 1982 through its 39th session in 2007, the Division for the Advancement of Women (DAW) was responsible for providing the necessary services to the Committee.[57] DAW was established in 1946 as the Section on the Status of Women, Human Rights Division, Department of Social Affairs. In 1972, the section was upgraded as the Branch for the Promotion of Equality for Men and Women under the newly created Centre for Social Development and Humanitarian Affairs of the United Nations Office

---

[53] Rules of Procedure 13.

[54] Akua Kuenyehia was elected as a judge the ICC as of 11 March 2003; Fumiko Saiga was elected on 30 November 2007. Their resignation was not required by CEDAW, but by art 40 of the ICC Statute. Asha Rose Mtengeti-Migiro of Tanzania was elected to Parliament and appointed Minister for Community Development, Women Affairs and Children during the year she joined the CEDAW Committee. She attended the eleventh session in August 2000 before resigning from the Committee.

[55] Hazel Gumede Shelton of South Africa was elected in June 2006 and resigned in 2007. The State party did not nominate a successor and the seat remained vacant through 2010. UN Doc A/65/38, 44th Session (2009) para 11 (South Africa had not yet nominated a candidate).

[56] UNGA Res 56/272 (2002) UN Doc A/RES/56/272. See UNGA, 'Report of the Chairpersons of the human rights treaty bodies on their fifteenth meeting' (1993) UN Doc A/58/350 para 57. The General Assembly (Res 2489 (XXIII) of 21 December 1968, reaffirmed several times) generally prohibits remuneration other than subsistence allowance for members of UN bodies unless specifically approved by the GA; the CEDAW honorarium had been one of the exceptions.

[57] Details on this history are available online at <http://www.un.org/womenwatch/daw/daw/history.html> accessed 31 December 2010.

in Vienna. In 1978, it was renamed as the Branch for the Advancement of Women. In August 1993, the unit was moved to New York as the Division for the Advancement of Women, where it formed part of the Department of Policy Coordination and Sustainable Development (DPCSD). As a result of restructuring, the Division became part of the Department of Economic and Social Affairs (DESA) in 1996.

For a long time, the Committee was the only treaty body that was not serviced by the OHCHR and the only treaty body that did not meet in Geneva. From the 40th session in 2008, the Committee has been serviced by the OHCHR in Geneva and now meets in Geneva and New York.[58]

The move to OHCHR Geneva was discussed repeatedly for years before it occurred. The question of location and the need for cooperation with the other human rights treaty bodies appeared regularly on the Committee's agenda. In 1996, the Secretary-General decided, contrary to the Committee's own wishes,[59] that it would continue to be serviced by the DAW to provide for a strong and unified programme for the advancement of women within the United Nations.[60] The Chairpersons supported the Committee's position.[61] After 1996, emphasis shifted towards seeking ways to ensure cooperation between the Committee and the other human rights treaty bodies and their secretariats, rather than to continue to seek relocation.[62]

The discussion was renewed when the HCHR proposed relocation to Geneva in the context of her proposals on treaty body reform.[63] The Committee did not wish to rush decision-making, but urged to await further elaboration of the HCHR's plans, and to allow for its own input.[64] The Committee was informed in October 2006 of the Secretary-General's decision to transfer servicing of the Committee to the OHCHR. It was initially somewhat reluctant because it did not want to lose the quality of servicing it received from DAW. Further, it wished to be informed about other relevant developments that had an impact on the duties of the OHCHR such as the establishment of the Human Rights Council in 2006.[65] Following discussions with the HCHR, the Committee asked for implementation of the decision as of 2008.[66]

The Secretariat prepares for each CEDAW session a Note on the meetings and substantive activities of the other treaty bodies and relevant political organs such as CSW and the Human Rights Council.[67]

---

[58] See the discussion in ch on art 20(2).   [59] UN Doc A/50/38, 14th Session (1995) Decision 14/II.

[60] Letter of the Secretary-General to the Chairperson of the Committee, 8 February 1996, quoted in Report by the Secretariat, 'Ways and means of expediting the work of the Committee' (1997) UN Doc CEDAW/C/1997/5 para 3.

[61] UNGA, 'Report of the seventh meeting of persons chairing the human rights treaty bodies' (1996) UN Doc A/51/482 para 46.

[62] See eg UNCHR and UNCSW, 'Joint work plan of the Division for the Advancement of Women and the Office of the United Nations High Commissioner for Human Rights, Report of the Secretary-General' (2004) UN Docs E/CN.4/2004/65–E/CN.6/2004/7.

[63] Plan of Action UN HCHR (n 29 above) paras 100 and 148.

[64] UN Doc A/61/38, 34th Session (2006) Decision 34/I'.

[65] 65 Schöpp-Schilling and Flinterman (n 1 above) 219.

[66] 'Ways and means of expediting the work of the Committee on the Elimination of Discrimination against Women' (2007) CEDAW/C/2007/II/4 para 15.

[67] See 'Ways and means of expediting the work of the Committee on the Elimination of Discrimination against Women' (2008) UN Doc A/63/38, 40th Session paras 402–9. For sessions serviced by DAW see <http://www.un.org/womenwatch/daw/cedaw/sessions.htm> accessed 31 December 2010.

...the necessary staff and facilities for the effective performance of the functions of the
Committee...

The Committee's official languages are Arabic, Chinese, English, French, Russian, and
Spanish,[68] and statements made in one official language shall be translated into the other
official languages. While the Rules of Procedure adopted at the first session did not include
Arabic as a working language, the relevant rule was amended quickly.[69] All official languages are also working languages of the Committee.[70] All official documents and all
formal decisions shall be in all official languages. The Secretary-General is responsible for
providing the Committee with summary records of its meetings.[71]

As a consequence of the financial crisis of the United Nations, the General Assembly
decided in 1986 that the Committee would be entitled to summary records in English
and French only and suggested that summary records be provided only on substantive
matters such as the consideration of States parties' reports, and that the length of its report
be limited.[72] The Committee had to accept the decision, but disapproved and emphasized
that it would accept it only for that session. It pointed out that its budget had been underestimated from the beginning, and further cutbacks could affect its work negatively.[73]
Publication of summary records was again on the agenda in the 29th session, and the 31st
session, where the Committee expressed a preference for digital sound recordings of the
proceedings made available in all six official languages on the website. It also expressed
its concern that no summary records had been issued for various years.[74] At the 34th session, the Committee expressed its appreciation for publication of summary records of the
previous three sessions on the DAW website. On the occasion of the Committee's 25th
anniversary, DAW published a compilation of documents on a CD.[75]

Article 17(9) refers explicitly to the Committee's functions under the Convention, thus
necessitating a decision on additional resources required for the new functions bestowed
on it under the Optional Protocol.[76] The General Assembly requested the Committee to
hold meetings to exercise its functions under the Optional Protocol after its entry into
force, in addition to its meetings held under Article 20. It provided that the duration
of such meetings would be determined and, if necessary, reviewed by a meeting of the
States parties to the Optional Protocol, subject to the approval of the General Assembly.
It further requested the Secretary-General to provide the staff and facilities necessary for
the effective performance of the functions of the Committee under the Optional Protocol
after its entry into force.[77]

With regard to the term 'necessary', it must be noted that the lack of human and financial resources is a constant concern of the Committee, as well as of the other treaty bodies.
The Chairpersons have suggested that the allocation of significant human, financial, and

---

[68] Rules of Procedure 24.   [69] UN Doc A/39/45, 2nd Session (1983) para 18.
[70] Originally, Arabic was not a working language, see UN Doc A/38/45, 1st Session (1982), Annex III,
rule 19.
[71] Rules of Procedure 27.
[72] UN Doc A/42/38, 6th Session (1987) para 5; UNGA Decision 41/466 (11 December 1986).
[73] UN Doc A/42/38, 6th Session (1987) paras 38–9.
[74] UN Doc A/59/38, 31st Session (2004) paras 443–4.
[75] For further information, see <http://www.un.org/womenwatch/daw/cedaw/cdrom_cedaw/EN/files/
cedaw25years/start.html> accessed 31 December 2010.
[76] See the discussion in ch on Optional Protocol.
[77] UNGA Res 54/4, 'Optional Protocol to the Convention on the Elimination of All Forms of Discrimination
against Women' (1999) UN Doc A/RES/54/4, paras 5–6.

technical resources to the Universal Periodic Review performed by the Human Rights Council might affect the effective functioning of the treaty bodies.[78] The Chairpersons' meetings and the Inter-Committee Meeting consistently stress the need for the OHCHR to allocate adequate human and financial resources to the Human Rights Treaties Branch to ensure effective and continuous support for the work of the treaty bodies.[79]

The Committee's decision to request an extension of its meeting time[80] obviously had budgetary implications.[81] It requested authorization to hold three annual sessions of three weeks as a permanent measure from 2008 onwards, to hold as a temporary measure part of one annual session in parallel chambers, and to hold three annual meetings of the Working Group on Communications. It explained in detail the financial implications of this request, and the additional activities it would be able to perform.[82] This illustrates the position of the Committee as a treaty organ. While it is independent in the sense that it is not subject to instructions by any United Nations organ or by any State, its functioning depends on OHCHR decisions on resource allocation and the General Assembly's determination of the budget. In its request, the Committee elaborates on the necessity of extended meeting time that requires additional funding, to deal with the backlog of State party reports and with its duties under the Optional Protocol.

The General Assembly authorized the convening of three annual sessions of three weeks from January 2010 rather than from 2008. It requested the Secretary-General to provide the resources, including staff and facilities, necessary for the effective functioning of the Committee within its full mandate, taking into account in particular the entry into force of the Optional Protocol.[83]

---

[78] 'Report of the chairpersons of the human rights treaty bodies on their twenty-first meeting' (n 33 above) Annex I, para 7.
[79] 'Report of the chairpersons of the human rights treaty bodies on their twenty-first meeting' (n 33 above) Annex I, paras 24 and 49(d).
[80] See the discussion in ch on art 20.
[81] UN Doc A/62/38, 39th Session (2007) Decision 39/I, 226–7.
[82] CEDAW, 'Request for extension of the meeting time of the Committee on the Elimination of Discrimination against Women' (2007) UN Doc A/62/38, 39th Session, Annex X.
[83] UNGA Res 62/218 (2007) UN Doc A/RES/62/218 para 21.

Article 18

1. States Parties undertake to submit to the Secretary-General of the United Nations, for consideration by the Committee, a report on the legislative, judicial, administrative or other measures which they have adopted to give effect to the provisions of the present Convention and on the progress made in this respect:

(a) Within one year after the entry into force for the State concerned;

(b) Thereafter at least every four years and further whenever the Committee so requests.

2. Reports may indicate factors and difficulties affecting the degree of fulfilment of obligations under the present Convention.

A. Introduction

Article 18 deals with States parties' reports, the main procedure for reviewing their implementation of Convention obligations. Until the adoption of the Optional Protocol, this constituted the only procedure. The reporting procedure is comprehensive, covering all substantive articles of the Convention, and it is periodic, thus allowing the Committee

* I would like to thank Marie Elske Gispen for her assistance on the chapters on arts 17, 18, 19, 20, 21, and 22 of the Commentary.

to identify trends within States parties and at the international level. Article 18 provides no details as to how the Committee should undertake this task, merely stating that it shall 'consider' reports. This left much room for the Committee to apply the provision in a way that best contributes to its general mandate under Article 17, 'considering the progress made in the implementation of the present Convention'. The absence of details also allowed for developing its work methods over the years, to make the reporting procedure more effective. The ever increasing workload and the failure of many States parties to submit their reports on time, or to submit a report at all, necessitated regular discussions of the Committee's methods of work. Other treaty bodies face the same problems, as has been discussed in the Meetings of Chairpersons of the Human Rights Treaty Bodies and the Inter-Committee Meetings. Decisions adopted in these meetings have led to a number of changes in the Committee's guidelines for reporting and in its working methods.

The Committee has held a number of informal meetings, financially supported by the respective States parties, to discuss its working methods.[1] An informal meeting in Geneva in October 2007 provided for discussion of revising reporting guidelines, follow-up to concluding observations, and issues concerning the Committee's relocation to Geneva.[2]

The most important procedure changes that have occurred since the Committee's inception include the adoption of concluding observations upon the consideration of States parties' reports and the follow-up procedure developed subsequently, the streamlining of States parties' report submissions and of the reviews, and the use of information from national human rights institutions, non-governmental organizations, and the specialized agencies.

B. Travaux Préparatoires

In the early drafting stages, there was discussion on the consideration of Convention implementation in relation to procedures under other treaties relating to women's rights. The need to avoid duplication and overlap was pointed out.[3] This must be seen in light of an ECOSOC resolution requesting the General Assembly to integrate existing reporting requirements on implementation of DEDAW and treaties relevant to the protection of women's rights, such as the Convention on the Political Rights of Women, and the various conventions relating to the abolition of slavery and traffic in persons.[4]

The discussion on the reporting procedure was intertwined with intense discussion on the question of the most suitable organ for considering implementation.[5] The need for periodic review of the progress made in implementing the Convention was 'fully endorsed'.[6] Both in the CSW and the Third Committee, the discussion on international implementation measures focused mainly on the periodicity of reporting and on the information to be contained in the reports. The version adopted by the CSW in 1976

---

[1] Lund, Sweden, April 2002; May 2004 in Utrecht, the Netherlands; May 2006 in Berlin. Other State-supported informal meetings: April 1995, Madrid (preparation of comments for the Fourth World Conference on Women); May 2010, Paris (discussion of discriminatory laws and the role of national parliaments).

[2] CEDAW, 'Ways and means of expediting the work of the Committee on the Elimination of Discrimination against Women' (2008) UN Doc CEDAW/C/2008/I/4, Annex III.

[3] CSW, 'Working paper by the Secretary-General' (1973) UN Doc E/CN.6/573 paras 100–11.

[4] ECOSOC Res 1978/28, ECOSOC Official Records (Supp No 1) (1978) UN Doc E/1978/78, 30; UNGA Res 33/186 (29 January 1979) UN Doc A/RES/33/186.

[5] See the discussion in ch on art 17.   [6] UN Doc E/CN.6/591 (1976) para 181.

required States parties to submit a report every two years after the Convention's entry into force.[7]

In the Third Committee, it was argued that a four-year reporting cycle would permit planning and implementation of national measures, whereas a two-year cycle would place more pressure on States parties to implement the Convention. Another suggestion was not to include reporting periodicity, as was also the case in ICCPR Article 40.[8] It was agreed to establish a duty to report at least every four years 'and further whenever the [body] so requests',[9] which included the possibility for the Committee to 'request further information from States Parties'.[10]

With respect to the contents of the report, there was some discussion in the CSW. Iran suggested requesting information on 'legislative, administrative and practical measures'. Egypt suggested 'legislative, judicial, administrative or other measures' and Denmark suggested 'legislative, judicial, administrative and other measures' and that reports 'may indicate factors and difficulties affecting the degree of fulfilment of obligations'. These States then submitted a joint proposal, requesting information on legislative, judicial, administrative, or other measures and the reference to the factors and difficulties.[11] This language remained unchanged in the Third Committee.[12]

C. Committee Practice

I. The Obligation to Submit Country Reports
States Parties undertake to submit...

1. *Encouraging the Submission of Reports—Avoiding Duplication in Reporting*
States parties' delays and failures to submit reports have been a long-term concern of the Committee. Many States parties submit their reports late, or have failed to submit any report since ratification.[13] The Committee was expressing its concern about delays in the submission of reports as early as at its 4th session.[14]

All human rights treaty monitoring bodies face this problem. Various reasons for non-submission have been identified, including the burden of reporting under human rights treaties, difficulties faced by small States, the delay between submission and the scheduling of the consideration and a lack of commitment from governments.[15] The Meetings of Chairpersons have discussed the issue repeatedly, resulting in various measures. The first

---

[7] CSW, 'Report on the twenty-sixth and resumed twenty-sixth sessions' (1976) UN Doc E/CN.6/608 paras 172–205.
[8] UNGA, 'Report of the Working Group of the Whole on the drafting of the Convention on the Elimination of All Forms of Discrimination against Women' (1979) UN Doc A/C.3/34/14, 9.
[9] Report of Working Group of the Whole (n 8 above) 10 (brackets in original).
[10] Report of Working Group of the Whole (n 8 above) 10.
[11] CSW, 'Report on the twenty-sixth session' (n 7 above) paras 189–92.
[12] Report of Working Group of the Whole (n 8 above) 10.
[13] For an overview see UN Doc A/65/38, 44th Session (2010), Annex IX. See also documentation prepared by the Secretariat, 'Status of submission of reports by States parties under article 18 of the Convention' in CEDAW, 'Ways and means of expediting the work of the Committee on the Elimination of Discrimination against Women' (2010) UN Doc CEDAW/C/2010/45/2.
[14] UN Doc A/40/45, 4th Session (1985) para 22.
[15] A Byrnes, 'The Committee on the Elimination of Discrimination Against Women' in P Alston and F Mégret (eds), *The United Nations and Human Rights. A Critical Appraisal*, 2nd edn (forthcoming).

was the adoption of consolidated guidelines in 1991, requesting States parties to submit a core document under the various human rights instruments containing general information required by each treaty body.[16] Further developments include the adoption in 2006 of harmonized guidelines for reporting, including guidelines for a common core document and treaty-specific documents,[17] which led to amendment of the Committee's own guidelines in 2008.[18]

A far-reaching proposal, suggesting that each State party submit a single report for all treaty bodies, was accepted neither by the Inter-Committee Meeting nor the Meeting of Chairpersons. This position was endorsed by the Committee, since it 'would not adequately meet the overriding concerns and objectives of strengthening the implementation of human rights obligations at the national level'. Allowing States parties to submit an expanded core document was acceptable.[19]

2. *Allowing Combined Reports*

In 1986, the General Assembly encouraged the Committee to examine ways and means to deal with the problem of the backlog of reports awaiting consideration, 'including possible adjustment of the reporting system'.[20] In response, the Committee agreed that the Convention did not permit it to make adjustments in required periodicity.[21] Gradually, however, the Committee has accepted combined reports, as a way for States parties to catch up when they are far behind in meeting their reporting obligations. In 1991, the Committee decided that States parties whose reports were overdue by the conclusion of the 10th session could submit a combined report to the Committee. If this included an initial report, the combined report should be comprehensive, covering all aspects of the Convention and the Committee's general recommendations, and should describe the current situation of women and indicate the changes which had been made since the entry into force of the Convention and the obstacles encountered in its implementation.[22] Subsequently, at the 16th session, the Committee decided, on an exceptional basis and as a temporary measure, to invite States parties to combine a maximum of two of the reports required under Article 18.[23] Then, at the 23rd session, it extended this approach by inviting States parties with overdue reports to combine all their outstanding reports in a single document.[24] At the 40th session, it decided to request States parties reporting

---

[16] 'Consolidated guidelines for the initial part of the reports of States parties' (1991) HRI/1991/1, published as annex to HRI/CORE/1.

[17] Inter-Committee Meeting of the human rights treaty bodies Meeting of chairpersons, 'Harmonized guidelines on reporting under the international human rights treaties, including guidelines on a common core document and treaty-specific documents. Report of the Inter-Committee Technical Working Group' (2006) HRI/MC/2006/3.

[18] CEDAW, 'Convention-specific reporting guidelines of the Committee on the Elimination of Discrimination against Women' (2008) UN Doc A/63/38, 40th Session Annex I.

[19] UN Doc A/58/38, 29th Session (2003) para 450; see discussion below, section C. II. 1. on the form and content of reports.

[20] UNGA Res 41/108 (4 December 1986) UN Doc A/RES/41/108 para 8.

[21] UN Doc A/42/38, 6th Session (1987) para 41.

[22] UN Doc A/46/38, 10th Session (1991) para 370.

[23] UN Doc A/52/38, 16th Session (1997) para 375 and Decision 16/III.

[24] UN Doc A/55/38, 23rd Session (2000) Decision 23/II. It took into account the practice of other treaty bodies, as described in CEDAW 'Ways and means of expediting the work of the Committee' (2000) UN Doc CEDAW/C/2000/II/4 paras 4–15.

at that session to present their subsequent two reports as combined reports,[25] including States parties whose reports were not overdue.

3. *Persuading States Parties to Submit Reports*

Other methods to encourage States parties to submit reports on time include systematically sending reminders, drawing attention to the possibility of combining reports and receiving technical assistance for the preparation of reports; intensifying high-level secretariat encouragement of reporting through bilateral and multilateral contacts; informal contacts of Committee members, bureau members, or Chairpersons with non-reporting States parties; and convening meetings with States parties concerned.[26] The Committee formalized its 'incremental approach to encourage reporting' at the 29th session. It formulated a procedure for sending reminders and their contents. It also decided to include a list of States parties that have not responded to reminders in its annual report.[27]

At the 28th session, the Committee decided to convene a meeting during its 29th session with States parties whose reports had been due for over five years.[28] This resulted in the submission of initial reports by a number of States parties, while others informed the Committee of the status of report preparation. Further action in that regard would also be influenced by the Committee's ability to consider reports received within a reasonable period of time.[29] In 2008, it held another meeting with the States parties to update them on its working methods, including its efforts to encourage States parties to submit long-overdue initial reports.[30]

While hesitant at first,[31] the Committee decided at its 31st session that it would, like some of the other treaty bodies, consider Convention implementation by a State party in the absence of a report, but only as a measure of last resort and in the presence of a government delegation. The question of whether the treaty bodies have the power to take these steps has been raised, but there are 'persuasive legal arguments that such measures fall within the implied powers of the committees.'[32] The Meeting of Chairpersons also accepts this approach, provided it is used a measure of last resort.[33] The Committee takes such decisions on a case-by-case basis, in particular, in instances where a State party has not submitted an initial report many years after ratification and in light of the Committee's assessment of possible reasons for non-reporting. This step is preceded by other efforts, including notification to the State party of the Committee's intention to take up implementation of the Convention at a designated future session, inviting the State party to submit the requested report before the designated session. Designation of

---

[25] UN Doc A/63/38, 40th Session (2008) Decision 40/IV.

[26] UN Doc A/57/38, 27th Session (2002) para 368.

[27] UN Doc A/58/38, 29th Session (2003) para 456 and Decision 29/I.

[28] UN Doc A/58/38, 28th Session (2003) Decision 28/II.

[29] UN Doc A/59/38, 30th Session (2004) para 422.

[30] UN Doc A/63/38, 41st Session (2008) para 420.

[31] No agreement could be reached at the Lund seminar, 'Decisions made during the seminar on working methods of the Committee on the Elimination of Discrimination against Women Reporting by States parties' in 'Ways and means of expediting the work of the Committee' (2002) UN Doc CEDAW/C/2002/II/4, Annex I.

[32] Byrnes (n 15 above).

[33] UNGA, 'Report of the chairpersons of the human rights treaty bodies on their twenty-first meeting' (2009) UN Doc A/64/276, Annex I, para 17(a), as submitted in UNGA, 'Report of the ninth inter-committee meeting of human rights treaty bodies'(2009) UN Doc A/64/276, Annex II, para 49(f).

a future session is made allowing the State party sufficient time to prepare and submit its report.[34] At its 32nd session, the Committee for the first time notified two States parties, Cape Verde and Saint Lucia, whose initial reports were more than ten years overdue, of its intention to take up their implementation of the Convention at the 35th session. It invited both States parties to submit all their overdue reports as combined reports by June 2005. The Committee further stated that it would consider their implementation of the Convention in the absence of a report if the reports were not submitted by the designated time.[35]

The experience with Cape Verde and Saint Lucia was considered positive; each submitted its six long-overdue reports in one report. The extension of the Committee's meeting time and work in parallel chambers significantly reduced the backlog in considering reports. Consequently, the Committee could request States parties to submit long-overdue reports, knowing that it could schedule these for consideration within a reasonable time.[36] It has since then invited a large number of States parties whose reports were very long overdue. Four States parties that were more than twenty years overdue in submitting their initial report under Article 18 were requested to submit all their overdue reports as combined reports. With respect to these States parties, the Committee further decided that, as a measure of last resort, if the reports were not submitted it would consider the implementation of the Convention in the absence of a report.[37]

Despite these measures, the number of outstanding reports remains high. Of the twelve States parties that were notified at the 37th session in 2007, five submitted a report. By the end of 2010, the situation in one State party was considered in the absence of a report, in the presence of a delegation, and for one State party a list of issues has been prepared in the absence of a report. The remaining reports are outstanding and no consideration has been scheduled.[38] As of the 46th session, which took place in 2010, nineteen States parties' reports were five years or more overdue.[39]

II. Reporting Requirements

...a report on the legislative, judicial, administrative or other measures which they have adopted to give effect to the provisions of the present Convention and on the progress made in this respect...

Reports may indicate factors and difficulties affecting the degree of fulfilment of obligations under the present Convention.

---

[34] UN Doc A/59/38, 31st Session (2004) Decision 31/III, para 439.

[35] UN Doc A/60/38, 32nd Session (2005) para 408.

[36] CEDAW, 'Ways and means of expediting the work of the Committee on the Elimination of Discrimination Against Women' (2007) UN Doc CEDAW/C/2007/I/4 para 39.

[37] Dominica, Guinea-Bissau, Haiti, and Liberia. UN Doc A/62/38, 37th Session (2007) para 653. The situation in Dominica was considered in the absence of a report (CEDAW/C/DMA/CO/AR). Guinea-Bissau, Haiti, and Liberia submitted combined reports (CEDAW/C/GNB/6, CEDAW/C/HTI/7 and CEDAW/C/LBR/6, respectively).

[38] Ways and Means report (2010) (n 13 above).

[39] CEDAW, 'Status of submission of reports by States parties under article 18 of the Convention: Report of the Secretary-General' (2010) UN Doc CEDAW/C/2010/46/2, Annex II. Furthermore, the Committee did not consider reports from any of these nineteen States parties at its 47th Session (2010) CEDAW/C/2010/47/1 para 4.

1. *Form and Contents of Reports*

Article 18 does not provide details as to the content of States parties' reports, other than that they should contain information on legislative, judicial, administrative, or other measures. The Committee adopted guidelines for initial reports at its 2nd session.[40] These were amended in 1995, to incorporate the recommendations of the Meeting of Chairpersons concerning the first part of States parties' reports that should be submitted in accordance with the consolidated guidelines for the initial part of reports of States parties (core document). Other amendments incorporated various suggestions that had been made over the years, such as requests for data on maternal mortality, fertility rates, and female-headed households. The amended rules reflected the technical and financial capacity of the Secretariat as regards distribution of documentation submitted by States parties and the Committee's practice under Article 18 with respect to subsequent reports. Further, the amended rules included a request for detailed information about reservations in periodic reports.[41]

Guidelines for the preparation of second and subsequent reports were adopted in 1988. As a general rule, these reports should focus on the period between the consideration of the prior report and the preparation of the current one. States should take into account the Committee's proceedings regarding the previous report. Reports should include legal and other measures adopted since the previous report; actual progress made to promote and ensure the elimination of discrimination against women; any significant changes in the status and equality of women; any remaining obstacles to the participation of women on an equal basis with men in the political, social, economic, and cultural life of their country; and matters raised by the Committee which could not be dealt with when the previous report was considered.[42]

In light of the Beijing Declaration and Platform for Action, the guidelines for both initial and periodic reports were revised to include 'information on measures taken to implement the Platform for Action in order to facilitate the work of the Committee on the Elimination of Discrimination Against Women in monitoring effectively women's ability to enjoy the rights guaranteed by the Convention'. States were invited, in particular, to address the twelve Critical Areas of Concern identified in the Platform for Action. The Committee stressed that these were compatible with the articles of the Convention and therefore within its mandate.[43]

During the 2002 seminar in Lund, the Committee decided to revise the reporting guidelines, primarily to include requirements to report on the implementation of outcome documents of various world conferences and the special session of the General Assembly (Beijing + 5, 2000),[44] and in the case of periodic reports, the Committee's concluding observations on the most recent State party review. The guidelines were also to indicate that States parties should provide concise reports and provide guidance as to the format

---

[40] UN Doc A/39/45, 2nd Session (1984) ch III.

[41] UN Doc A/50/38, 14th Session (1995) para 652; CEDAW, 'Ways and means of expediting the work of the Committee' (1995) UN Doc CEDAW/C/1995/6 paras 17–22 and Annex II.

[42] CEDAW, 'Guidelines for the preparation of second and subsequent periodic reports'(1988) UN Doc A/43/38, 7th Session, Annex IV.

[43] UN Doc A/51/38, 15th Session (1996) para 355.

[44] A standard paragraph requesting such information was formulated, see UN Doc A/57/38, 27th Session (2002) para 375.

of reports, including length.[45] Accordingly, the Committee adopted revised reporting guidelines, to be followed for initial as well as periodic reports at its 27th session.[46]

At the 35th session, the Committee endorsed the adoption by the Inter-Committee Meeting of the harmonized guidelines, including guidelines on a common core document.[47] Subsequent to the adoption of the harmonized guidelines, the Committee revised its own guidelines and adopted the 'Convention-specific reporting guidelines of the Committee on the Elimination of Discrimination against Women' at its 40th session,[48] which must be applied in conjunction with the harmonized reporting guidelines for the common core document. These revised guidelines replace all earlier guidelines.

This reporting structure requires States parties to submit a common core document, containing information of a general and factual nature, that constitutes the first part of all State parties' reports and need not be repeated in the Convention-specific document submitted to the Committee. If a State party has not submitted a common core document, or if the information therein has not been updated, relevant information must be included in the Convention-specific document. The Committee stressed the importance of referring to the sex and gender dimensions of information included in the common core document. The common core document should provide information about the general framework for the protection and promotion of human rights disaggregated according to sex and should include information on non-discrimination and equality and effective remedies. The Convention-specific report should provide information of a more analytical nature on 'the impact of laws, the interaction of plural legal systems, policies, and programmes on women'. The report should contain analytical information on the progress made in ensuring enjoyment of rights under the Convention by all groups of women throughout their life cycle within the territory or jurisdiction of the State party. The guidelines set out in detail which information should be included in States parties' reports, distinguishing between initial and periodic reports.

At its 6th session, the Committee had discussed whether it could reject a short report that failed to comply with the requirements. Since the delegation of the State party concerned was present and had not been informed in advance that the report would not be considered, it was agreed that the report would be considered.[49] In its concluding observations, the Committee addressed in general terms the quality of reports and the extent of compliance with the reporting guidelines, expressing its regret, for example, at the lack of sex-disaggregated statistics and references to previous concluding observations or general recommendations, and the overdue status of reports. It reminded States parties of the need to comply with reporting obligations in a timely manner, 'as delays in reporting may have a negative impact on the implementation of the Convention', and encouraged them to seek technical assistance for the preparation of reports.[50]

---

[45] 'Decisions of the Lund seminar' (n 31 above).

[46] CEDAW, 'Revised reporting guidelines' (2002) UN Doc A/57/38, 27th Session, Annex.

[47] UN Doc A/61/38, 35th Session (2006) para 384. For the text of the harmonized guidelines see HRI/MC/2006/3 (n 17 above).

[48] CEDAW, 'Convention-specific reporting guidelines of the Committee on the Elimination of Discrimination against Women' (2008) UN Doc A/63/38, 40th Session, Annex I, Decision 40/I. The guidelines are also available on the OHCHR website: <http://www2.ohchr.org/english/bodies/cedaw/docs/AnnexI.pdf> accessed on 31 December 2010.

[49] UN Doc A/42/38, 6th Session (1987) para 187, initial report of Sri Lanka.

[50] CO Libyan Arab Jamahiriya, CEDAW/C/LYB/CO/5 (2009) para 2.

2. *NGOs and their Involvement in the Preparation of States Parties' Reports*

The reporting obligation belongs to the State party. Nevertheless, the Committee sees an important role for NGOs in the preparation of reports and recommends that States parties consult NGOs when they prepare their report, without implying that NGOs take over the actual writing of the report or that it should result in a joint State-NGO report. It emphasizes that at all times the report has to be that of the State party, and that the NGO involvement should not exclude the possibility of submitting their own report.[51]

III. The Committee's Role

...for consideration by the Committee...

The consideration of reports takes up most of the Committee's meeting time. At its 5th session, it noted that it could only examine eight reports per ten-day session in order to discharge its duties responsibly.[52] At that session, the Committee already faced a backlog of thirty reports.[53] As of 2010, with three annual sessions of three weeks,[54] the Committee schedules up to twenty-eight reports for consideration each year. The Committee has expressed confidence that three annual sessions, at least one of which is held in two chambers, is adequate and ensures that the Committee can discharge all its responsibilities under the Convention as well as the Optional Protocol in a timely manner.[55]

1. *Preparing for the Dialogue with States Parties*

The Committee's increasing workload has necessitated greater efficiency in the consideration of reports. At its 6th session, it set up two Working Groups, one of which would deal with ways and means of expediting the work of the Committee. This Working Group recommended the establishment of two standing working groups.[56] At the 7th session, the Working Group's recommendations to coordinate the questions to be put to representatives by following the order of the Convention[57] were accepted with some reservations by some members, who feared that the related proposal to develop a list of issues and questions by groups of Committee members would be too bureaucratic[58] and might hinder the Committee from having a genuine dialogue. However, the Committee's first experiences with this method of work, which also involved an analysis of information prepared by the Secretariat, was fruitful and saved time.[59] The procedure was continued at the next session, with the Working Group preparing the lists of issues, which were transmitted to the representatives of the State party to prepare replies for presentation at the same session.[60] In 1989, in light of the increase in the number of periodic reports the Committee agreed to hold a pre-session working group of five members to prepare

---

[51] 'Statement by the Committee on the Elimination of Discrimination against Women on its relationship with non-governmental organizations' (2010) UN Doc A/65/38, 45th Session, Annex V, Decision 45/VI, para 8.

[52] UN Doc A/41/45, 5th Session (1986) para 21.　　[53] UN Doc A/41/45, 5th Session (1986) para 15.

[54] On the extension of the meeting time, see the discussion in ch on art 20.

[55] UN Doc A/62/38, 37th Session (2007) para 649.

[56] UN Doc A/42/38, 6th Session (1987) paras 26 & 37.

[57] UN Doc A/42/38, 6th Session (1987) para 40.

[58] UN Doc A/42/38, 6th Session (1987) para 51.

[59] UN Doc A/43/38, 7th Session (1988) paras 43–4.

[60] UN Doc A/44/38, 8th Session (1989), para 21.

the lists of issues and questions relating to reports to be considered at that session.[61] The report of the pre-session working group was to indicate matters which members had asked to be included in the periodic reports during the consideration of the initial report; important progress or significant change; and remaining obstacles and matters on which further information was needed.[62]

From the 11th session, the pre-session working group began grouping questions under each of the articles.[63] At its 16th session, the Committee decided to change its methods of work. The pre-session working group would formulate a list of questions concentrating on the major areas of concern as to Convention implementation. These written questions would be submitted to the State party to be answered in writing prior to the session for which the review is scheduled.[64] Further, the pre-session working group would convene at least one session prior to the one at which the report would be considered,[65] which was subsequently changed to at least two sessions in advance.[66] From the 20th session, each pre-session working group has convened in the week after the full working session ends.[67]

At its 19th session, the Committee introduced the function of country rapporteur, tasked with seeking additional information on the situation of women in the country under review and a role in the preparation of concluding observations.[68] The informal meeting in Utrecht in 2004 led to the establishment, on an experimental basis, of a country task force for one of the States parties that would report at the 31st session.[69] The Committee subsequently established task forces for a limited number of reports but has not used this mechanism frequently.[70] At the 35th session, acting on the agreement reached in the informal meeting in Berlin, the Committee agreed to further strengthen and enhance the role of the country rapporteur in the various stages of the consideration of States parties' reports: preparation of a list of issues and questions, identification of issues and priorities to be raised during the constructive dialogue, and drafting of the concluding comments. The country rapporteur is responsible for facilitating inputs from all Committee experts to this process. At the 35th session, the Committee adopted guidelines on the role and functions for the country rapporteur.[71] The experience gained with country task forces was used to coordinate among experts to ensure that all critical issues would be covered adequately in the constructive dialogue. Country rapporteurs take a lead role in coordinating this effort.[72]

During the 2002 Lund meeting, the Committee decided to cluster questions according to the four substantive parts of the Convention.[73] At the 2004 Utrecht meeting, the Committee decided to further structure consideration of reports. Since then initial reports have been considered on an article-by-article basis, with the exception of Articles 1 and 2,

---

[61] UN Doc A/44/38, 8th Session (1989) para 24, decision approved by UNGA Res 44/73 (8 December 1989) UN Doc A/RES/44/73 para 10.
[62] UN Doc A/45/38, 9th Session (1990) paras 29–30.
[63] UN Doc A/47/38, 11th Session (1992) para 14.
[64] UN Doc A/54/38/Rev.1, 20th Session (1999) para 412.
[65] UN Doc A/52/38, 16th Session (1997) para 369 and Suggestion 16/2.
[66] UN Doc A/54/38/Rev.1, 20th Session (1999) para 412.
[67] UN Doc A/53/38/Rev.1, 18th Session (1998) paras 436–8 and Suggestion 18/1.
[68] UN Doc A/53/38/Rev.1, 19th Session (1998) paras 395–7 and Decision 19/II.
[69] UN Doc A/59/38, 31st Session (2004) para 420.
[70] eg UN Doc A/64/38 42nd Session (2008) to lead to the consideration of reports at the 43rd Session.
[71] UN Doc A/61/38, 35th Session (2006) paras 388–96.
[72] UN Doc A/61/38, 35th Session (2006) paras 370–5.
[73] Decisions at the Lund seminar (n 31 above).

7 and 8, and 15 and 16, which are considered in clusters. The Chair organizes the dialogue by inviting the State party to respond after a series of questions is asked. Periodic reports are considered in accordance with the four substantive parts of the Convention.[74]

The main trend that can be discerned from these changes is that a large amount of the work is now undertaken prior to the session, resulting in better preparation of the Committee members and the States parties. This leads to a more focused and more in-depth dialogue during the session, and consequently enhances the quality of the concluding observations.

In 2005, the General Assembly authorized the Committee to meet in parallel chambers,[75] and at the 2006 Berlin meeting, the Committee discussed its working methods for the consideration of periodic reports when meeting in parallel chambers. At the 35th session, it decided on the working methods and established criteria for determining membership of the two chambers: fair geographical balance; length of experts' service on the Committee; assignment of experts who are nationals of reporting States parties to the chamber that is not considering those reports; assignment of Committee bureau members to each chamber; and to the extent possible, geographical balance of State party reviews assigned to each chamber.[76]

2. The Constructive Dialogue

From the beginning, the term 'consideration' was interpreted as involving a constructive dialogue at a public meeting with representatives of the State party. Especially during dialogues on periodic reports, State party representatives should be prepared to engage in 'an open and in-depth dialogue'.[77] States parties may introduce their reports in oral presentations with strict time limits, shortened over the years to thirty minutes.[78] Committee members' interventions are also subject to limitations of three minutes each, and each expert may make no more than two interventions per State party.[79] When the Committee meets in parallel chambers, members' interventions continue to be limited to two per State, and for not more than five minutes each.[80]

The Committee attaches great value to the presence of State party representatives: the consideration is rescheduled if they are absent, even though this disturbs the programme of work. In its Convention-specific reporting guidelines, the Committee recommends that States parties' delegations should include persons who, 'through their knowledge and competence and their position of authority or accountability, are able to explain all aspects of women's human rights in the reporting State and are able to respond to the Committee's questions and comments concerning the implementation of the Convention'.[81]

Committee members often raise critical questions and point to what they consider shortcomings in implementation. Nevertheless, the Committee does not act as a court

[74] UN Doc A/59/38, 31st Session (2004) paras 422–3.
[75] For more on the process leading to the authorization to work in parallel chambers, see the discussion in ch on art 20.
[76] UN Doc A/61/38, 35th Session (2006) para 366.
[77] UN Doc A/54/38/Rev.1, 20th Session (1999) para 408.
[78] UN Doc A/59/38, 31st Session (2004) para 418.
[79] UN Doc A/59/38, 31st Session (2004) para 419. In 2002, it was set at three to five minutes, Decisions at the Lund seminar (n 31 above).
[80] UN Doc A/61/38, 35th Session (2006) para 376.
[81] CEDAW, 'Convention-specific reporting guidelines of the Committee on the Elimination of Discrimination against Women' (2008) UN Doc A/63/38, 40th Session, Annex I, Decision 40/I, para 33.

and does not pass judgement, using the ' "carrot" rather than the "stick." '[82] The consideration of reports is to be seen as a form of assistance to States parties in implementing their Convention obligations. The Committee provides 'specific guidance' for each State party, recommending the adoption of measures to advance implementation, which may include a recommendation to seek technical assistance from the Office of the High Commissioner for Human Rights (OHCHR) or specialized agencies.[83]

IV. Periodic Reporting Requirements and Committee Review

(a) Within one year after the entry into force for the State concerned;
(b) Thereafter at least every four years and further whenever the Committee so requests.

At its 21st session, the Committee decided that it may sometimes be necessary to request exceptional reports from States parties under Article 18(1)(b) to examine information on an actual or potential violation of women's human rights, where there is special cause for concern about such a violation. It adopted the following standards and guidelines:

(a) There should be reliable and adequate information indicating grave or systematic violations of women's human rights, in whatever situation;
(b) Such violations are those that are gender-based or directed at women because of their sex;
(c) Reports should focus on a particular issue or issues identified by the Committee;
(d) States parties shall submit their reports for consideration at such session as the Committee determines.[84]

NGOs are encouraged to submit information on situations warranting such exceptional reports.[85]

The Committee has requested and received five reports on an exceptional basis: from the Federal Republic of Yugoslavia (Serbia and Montenegro, oral report), Bosnia and Herzegovina (oral report), Croatia (written report), Rwanda (oral report), and the Democratic Republic of the Congo (oral report).[86] The Committee has also taken the less emphatic measure of making a special request for a report that is already due. Subsequent to the events in Gujarat, the Committee decided at its 29th session to request the Government of India to indicate the anticipated date of submission of its combined second and third periodic reports, including information on the events in Gujarat and their impact on women.[87] When India failed to comply with this request, the Committee reiterated it at its 30th session and further decided that the Chairperson would request a meeting with the Representative of India to the United Nations while attending the 48th session of the

---

[82] E Evatt, 'Finding a voice for women's rights: The early days of CEDAW' (2002) 34 *George Washington Intl L Rev* 515, 530.

[83] HB Schöpp-Schilling, 'The Nature and Mandate of the Committee' in HB Schöpp-Schilling and C Flinterman (eds), *The Circle of Empowerment: Twenty-Five Years of the UN Committee on the Elimination of Discrimination Against Women* (2007) 248, 253.

[84] As amended, UN Doc A/59/38, 31st Session (2004) para 438; original version, UN Doc A/54/38/Rev.1, 20th Session (1999) Decision 21/I. The only amendment is that the original version did not contain the words 'in whatever situation'.

[85] Statement on relationship with NGOs (n 51 above) para 12.

[86] UN Doc A/59/38, 31st Session (2004) Annex VI.

[87] UN Doc A/58/38, 29th Session (2003) para 459. India was asked to do so by 15 December 2003; its combined second and third periodic reports were due on 8 August 1998 and 8 August 2002, respectively.

CSW (March 2004) to seek clarification from the Government on the status of the preparation of the report.[88] The report was submitted in October 2005 but did not comply with the Committee's specific request for information on the Gujarat violence. Discussing it at the 37th session, the Committee expressed its dissatisfaction with this lack of information and noted that the additional information provided during the constructive dialogue was not sufficient. Consequently, referring to Article 18(1)(b), it requested the State party to submit a follow-up report in January 2008 for consideration by the Committee later in 2008. It did not use the term 'exceptional report', but stressed that this follow-up report would not replace the submission of a combined fourth and fifth periodic report. It indicated in detail what information should be included in the follow-up report.[89] This report was indeed submitted in December 2009, which, remarkably, was entitled 'Report on an exceptional basis'.[90] The Committee eventually considered the report at the 47th session, and while it appreciated the submission of the report, it was critical of the contents.[91]

1. Concluding Observations

After some discussions on its mandate, the Committee decided in 1994 to adopt concluding comments upon the conclusion of the consideration of reports.[92] Since then, the procedure for adoption has undergone changes, as have the structure and content. At its 40th session, the Committee decided to change the title to 'concluding observations', in line with efforts to harmonize the working methods of the human rights treaty bodies.[93]

2. Format of the Concluding Observations

The Committee determined that the concluding observations should cover the most important points raised during the constructive dialogue, emphasizing both positive aspects of the reports and matters on which the Committee had expressed concern, and should clearly indicate what the Committee wished the State party to include in its next report. For second and subsequent reports, the concluding observations should take into account the findings of the pre-session working group as well as the constructive dialogue.[94] At the 31st session, the Committee introduced the term 'focused concluding comments'. It agreed to prioritize 'a limited number of focused critical concerns of an emerging or persistent nature' in the concluding observations on periodic reports.[95] At its 32nd session, the Committee decided to include a new standard paragraph as the first in the section on 'principal areas of concern and recommendations'. This paragraph refers to the State party's obligation to implement the Convention in its entirety and points out that the concerns and recommendations identified in the concluding observations require the State party's priority attention.[96]

The concluding observations initially followed a standard pattern that had been elaborated at the 15th session in 1996. The original standard format had five headings; an introduction, factors and difficulties affecting the implementation of the Convention,

---

[88] UN Doc A/59/38, 30th Session (2004) para 425.

[89] CO India, CEDAW/C/IND/CO/3 (2007) paras 67–8. For the report see CEDAW/C/IND/2–3 covering 1997–2005.

[90] State Party Report: India, CEDAW/C/IND/SP.1.   [91] CO India, CEDAW/C/IND/CO/SP.1 (2010).

[92] See the discussion in ch on art 21.   [93] UN Doc A/63/38, 40th Session (2008) Decision 40/III.

[94] See the discussion in ch on art 22. For the decision to adopt concluding observations, see UN Doc A/49/38, 13th Session (1994) paras 812–17.

[95] UN Doc A/59/38, 31st Session (2004) para 429.

[96] UN Doc A/60/38, 32nd Session (2005) para 405.

positive aspects, principal areas of concern, and suggestions and recommendations.[97] At the 19th session, the Committee decided to combine the sections relating to principal areas of concern and recommendations and suggestions into one section 'principal areas of concern and recommendations',[98] reducing the format to four headings. At the outset, the concluding observations were preceded by a summary of the State party's presentation prepared by the Secretariat.[99] At the 34th session, the Committee decided to dispense with this practice for budgetary reasons.[100] This decision was implemented immediately. Statements by States parties' representatives are now made available on the website of the OHCHR.

The introduction to the concluding observations reflected on compliance of the report with the Committee's guidelines and on issues such as the inclusion of statistical data disaggregated by sex, the nature and quality of the oral report; and comments on the existence and status of reservations.[101] In the first years of this practice, the Committee used a heading entitled 'factors and difficulties affecting the implementation of the Convention', describing the major areas of the Convention that have not been implemented by the State party. It covered aspects such as the status of the Convention in domestic law, legislation to implement the Convention, and the presence of overarching social factors such as tradition and cultural and behavioural patterns. This section also addressed the State party's reservations and other legal impediments to implementation. In 2002, the Committee decided to reserve this section only for the most exceptional circumstances, and no longer to refer to factors such as the persistence of stereotypical attitudes relating to the roles of men and women.[102] An example of such an exceptional circumstance is the devastating effect of a hurricane.[103]

The section on principal areas of concern and recommendations identifies problems and suggests approaches to compliance with the Convention. The concluding observations may include specific suggestions to seek technical assistance from the OHCHR or other parts of the United Nations system.[104] Since January 2005, this section has begun with a paragraph assessing the general framework for Convention implementation in the State party. This paragraph further reflects on the action taken with respect to issues of concern identified in previous concluding observations.[105]

The section on positive aspects is organized in the order of the Convention's articles, while the section on principal areas of concern is organized in the order of importance of the particular issue in the State party. Further, the concluding observations include a reference to commitments the State party made at the Fourth World Conference on Women and closes with a recommendation relating to dissemination of the Convention, the reports, and the concluding comments.[106] At the 41st session, the Committee decided

---

[97] UN Doc A/52/38, 16th Session (1997) paras 354–61 and Decision 16/I.
[98] UN Doc A/53/38/Rev.1, 19th Session (1998) para 395.
[99] UN Doc A/53/38/Rev.1, 19th Session (1998) para 397.
[100] UN Doc A/61/38, 34th Session (2006) para 365.
[101] UN Doc A/53/38/Rev.1, 19th Session (1998) para 397.
[102] UN Doc A/57/38, 27th Session (2002) para 374.
[103] CO Saint Kitts and Nevis, A/57/38, 27th Session (2002) para 92.
[104] UN Doc A/53/38/Rev.1, 19th Session (1998) para 397.
[105] UN Doc A/59/38, 31st Session (2004) para 429.
[106] UN Doc A/52/38, 16th Session (1997) paras 354–61 and Decision 16/I.

to include subject headings in the concluding observations,[107] which makes them more informative.

3. *Procedure for Adopting Concluding Observations*

The Committee decided in 1994 that two Committee members would draft the concluding observations to be considered for adoption. To the extent possible, at least one of these rapporteurs should be from the region of the reporting State party. As to periodic reports, these members consulted with the members of the pre-session working group. The draft concluding observations are considered in closed meetings and are included as adopted in the Committee's annual report.[108]

Significant changes to the procedure were introduced at the 16th session.[109] It was decided that a large part of the preparatory work would be done prior to the constructive dialogue. The procedure was further developed at the 19th session.[110] The country rapporteur would seek additional information on the report under review, and present her findings as an introduction to the report at a closed meeting, before the State party's presentation. The concluding observations drafted thereafter reflected the views expressed at the meetings during which the report was presented rather than the views of the individual rapporteur.[111]

The Committee agreed at its 35th session that, following the constructive dialogue either in chambers or in plenary, a closed meeting would be held to consider the main issues to be reflected in the concluding observations. Only issues and concerns raised during the constructive dialogue may be included in the concluding observations. Concluding observations, therefore, reflect the issues retained as significant by the Committee, and do not reflect the views of the individual country rapporteur. The country rapporteur prepares the first draft of the concluding observations with the support of the Secretariat and coordinates further comments and inputs by Committee experts before finalizing the draft.[112]

After an assessment of working methods at the 37th session, the responsibility of the country rapporteurs in preparing and conducting the constructive dialogue was further enhanced to help ensure that all members can contribute to the dialogue in a timely and meaningful manner. The country rapporteur circulates succinct country briefing notes seven to ten days prior to the beginning of a session. These notes should include all critical issues to be covered in the constructive dialogue. The country rapporteur takes a lead role in ensuring that all pending critical issues are brought up in follow-up questions. The country rapporteur also introduces the draft concluding comments in plenary, prior to their consideration and adoption. All concluding observations are adopted by the Committee in closed plenary meetings.[113]

---

[107] UN Doc A/63/38, 41st Session (2008) Decision 41/II and Annex X, Subject headings (titles) to be used in concluding observations.

[108] UN Doc A/49/38, 13th Session (1994) paras 812–17.

[109] UN Doc A/52/38, 16th Session (1997) paras 354–61 and Decision 16/I.

[110] UN Doc A/53/38/Rev.1, 19th Session (1998) paras 395–7. Upheld at the Lund seminar, see Decisions of the Lund seminar (n 31 above).

[111] UN Doc A/52/38, 16th Session (1997) paras 354–61 and Decision 16/I.

[112] UN Doc A/61/38, 35th Session (2006) paras 397–8.

[113] UN Doc A/62/38, 37th Session (2007) paras 650–1.

At the conclusion of the constructive dialogue, the Committee holds a closed meeting to reflect on the main issues and tendencies to be discussed in the concluding observations.[114] As from the 42nd session in 2008, the concluding observations are no longer included in the Committee's annual reports to the General Assembly. The report refers to the Official Document System of the UN and to the relevant document symbols.

4. Follow-up to Concluding Observations

As a rule, the Committee requests States parties to disseminate the concluding observations widely, in all appropriate languages, with a view to providing for public discussion to promote implementation.[115] The OHCHR publishes all concluding observations on its website. To facilitate follow-up by States parties—and for the purposes of monitoring implementation—concluding observations should be sufficiently precise and give details as to what is expected from States parties. The Committee strives to formulate concluding observations with 'concrete, achievable, but non-prescriptive recommendations'.[116] An adequate follow-up mechanism is crucial to the effectiveness of the reporting procedure, in which NGOs and NHRIs play an important role.

The Committee did not immediately focus on establishing a procedure for the follow-up of concluding observations when the subject was first discussed at the 2004 Inter-Committee Meeting, because of its already heavy workload.[117] However, it did adopt the procedure at its 41st session, deciding to include a request to each State party in its concluding observations that information on steps taken to implement specific recommendations be provided to the Committee within two years.[118]

The methodology for the procedure was further refined in the 45th session. States parties are requested to submit information within one or two years on action taken to implement the recommendations selected under the follow-up procedure.[119] Usually two recommendations are selected for the procedure. A list of States parties that have submitted follow-up information is made available in the annual report and can be retrieved through the OHCHR website.[120] The Committee's rapporteur on follow-up of concluding observations can respond and, when appropriate, request further clarifications.[121]

An effective follow-up mechanism provides additional force to the reporting procedure, which continues to be the primary process for monitoring Convention implementation. The Inter-Committee Meetings have taken up follow-up as a key element of treaty implementation, and the 10th Inter-Committee Meeting (December 2009) agreed on a number of procedural aspects.[122] Suggestions for further reinforcing follow-up include convening workshops and meetings and, on the invitation of the State party concerned,

---

[114] UN Doc A/52/38, 16th Session (1997) paras 354–61 and Decision 16/I.

[115] CEDAW, 'Convention-specific reporting guidelines of the Committee on the Elimination of Discrimination against Women' (2008) UN Doc A/63/38, 40th Session, Annex I, Decision 40/I, para 34.

[116] UN Doc A/63/38, 41st Session (2008) para 418.

[117] UNGA, 'Report of the chairpersons of the human rights treaty bodies on their sixteenth meeting' (2004) UN Doc A/59/254, Annex, para 16.

[118] UN Doc A/63/38, 41st Session (2008) Decision 41/III. The procedure will be assessed in 2011.

[119] UN Doc A/65/38, 45th Session (2010) para 25.

[120] <http://www2.ohchr.org/english/bodies/cedaw/followup.htm> accessed 31 December 2010.

[121] The letters in which the rapporteur responds are also available on the website.

[122] UNGA, 'Report of the chairs of the human rights treaty bodies on their twenty-second meeting, Annex I, Report of the tenth inter-committee meeting of the human rights treaty bodies' (2010) UN Doc A/65/190 para 40(e)–(g).

country visits.[123] The Chairpersons at their 22nd meeting established a Working Group on Follow-up, to meet in the period between Chairpersons Meetings.[124] NGOs and NHRIs play an important role in the follow-up procedure, in disseminating the concluding observations and by monitoring closely States parties' activities in the period between the submission of reports and encouraging them to take necessary action.

V. The Role of Other Entities

1. Information from National Human Rights Institutions

At the 32nd session, the Committee expressed its interest in establishing interaction with national human rights institutions and decided to discuss the modalities for such interaction at the next session. Representatives of national human rights institutions were invited to present information.[125] At that session, the Committee had before it a report of the Irish Human Rights Commission. In the absence of an agreed procedure for dealing with such reports, it allocated a separate segment during the informal meeting with NGOs. The Committee agreed that modalities for interaction with national human rights institutions should be developed in coordination with other human rights treaty bodies.[126] Subsequently, at its 40th session, it adopted a statement on its relations with national human rights institutions, stressing the need for close cooperation in the light of the common goals of protecting, promoting, and fulfilling the human rights of women and girls.

The Committee identified an important role for national human rights institutions in the promotion of Convention implementation at the national level, in the protection of women's human rights as well as the enhancement of public awareness. It noted that national human rights institutions could physically attend and provide information orally in the meetings allocated to them in the pre-session working groups and sessions of the Committee.[127]

The Committee has suggested that NHRIs provide comments and suggestions on States parties's reports, and information in relation to the mandate of the Committee under the Optional Protocol to conduct an inquiry. It invited NHRIs to submit country-specific information on States parties' reports that are before the pre-session working group or the Committee and to make presentations at a time specifically allocated to them in the pre-session working groups and Committee sessions.[128]

2. Information from Non-Governmental Organizations

Additional information is indispensable to the Committee in the performance of its tasks. State party reports are often incomplete, in that they are too brief, provide information only on laws and not on practice, and may offer an unrealistically positive picture of Convention implementation. The process of regular NGO submissions was established

---

[123] Report of the 21st meeting of Chairpersons (2009) (n 33 above) para 49(h).

[124] UNGA, 'Report of the chairpersons of the human rights treaty bodies on their twenty-second meeting' (2010) UN Doc A/65/190 para 35(b).

[125] UN Doc A/60/38, 32nd Session (2005) para 414.

[126] UN Doc A/60/38, 33rd Session (2005) para 426.

[127] 'Statement by the Committee on the Elimination of Discrimination against Women on its relationship with national human rights institutions' (2008) UN Doc A/63/38, 40th Session, Annex II, Decision 40/II.

[128] Ibid.

by an international NGO, upon invitation by the Committee,[129] and many domestic, regional, and international NGOs and coalitions now regularly submit information. The OHCHR website for CEDAW (and all other treaty bodies) contains a section for 'Information provided to the Committee', linking to the reports submitted by NGOs for each session.

The relevance of NGO contributions was first discussed extensively at the Committee's 10th session. The Committee considered means of involving NGOs from developing countries, given the resource constraints, and noted the facilitating role of international NGOs such as the International Women's Rights Action Watch to encourage the development of national NGOs.[130] The contribution of NGOs was acknowledged in general terms in the Working Group's report in the 11th session.[131]

At its 16th session, the Committee decided to further open to NGOs and recommended that the Secretariat facilitate an informal meeting with NGOs, if possible with interpretation, during the first two days of the session. The initial hesitancy of some Committee members to make use of such information is reflected in the report. It was explicitly stated that such information 'did not compromise the independence of the members, who had been selected on the basis of expertise and integrity', and that 'the input of non-governmental organizations should not be perceived as clandestine material given to Committee members'. The Committee decided to recommend to States parties that they consult NGOs in the preparation of their reports. It recommended that international non-governmental organizations and United Nations agencies, funds, and programmes be encouraged to facilitate attendance of NGO representatives at Committee sessions. Further, it saw a role for UN offices in the field working with NGOs to disseminate information on the Convention and on the work of the Committee.[132]

The important role of NGOs in the reporting procedure was acknowledged in the Committee's 2010 statement on NGOs. It noted that it was necessary that the constructive dialogue be based on information received from not only States parties, UN entities, and National Human Rights Institutions, but also from NGOs to ensure a constructive dialogue. The Committee encouraged NGOs to provide reports, which could relate either to the implementation of provisions of the Convention or to specific themes focusing on gaps in implementation or the Committee's concluding observations. The Committee also welcomed comments and suggestions on the State party's reports.[133]

NGO reports are most useful when received in a timely manner for consideration by the Committee's pre-session working group. NGOs are invited to participate at the meeting of the working group and to make oral presentations and provide clarifications related to the preparation of the list of issues and questions. During the full session, NGO reports, oral presentations to the Committee, and presence during the examination of the State party by the Committee are welcomed. The Committee holds a public meeting with

---

[129] See generally, M Freeman, 'The Committee on the Elimination of Discrimination against Women and the Role of Civil Society in Implementing International Women's Human Rights Norms' (2010) 16 *New England J of Intl and Comparative L* 25.

[130] UN Doc A/46/38, 10th Session (1991) para 389.

[131] UN Doc A/47/38, 11th Session (1992) para 14.

[132] UN Doc A/52/38, 16th Session (1997) para 362 and Decision 16/II. The Committee's decision was taken on the basis of an extensive overview of the practice of other treaty bodies, see CEDAW, 'Ways and means of expediting the work of the Committee' (1997) UN Doc CEDAW/C/1997/5 paras 28–48.

[133] Statement on relationship with NGOs (n 51 above) paras 1–6.

NGOs on the first day of the first and second week of each session. During these meetings, NGOs make oral presentations of their written reports and respond to additional questions by Committee members. In addition, NGOs can provide further information to the Committee during informal lunch hour briefings (side events), usually held the day before the consideration of the State party's report.[134] Obviously, for many NGOs, physically attending the Committee's sessions in Geneva or New York is not possible due to resource constraints. The input can also be provided with 'the use of new technology, such as videoconference links and webcasting'.[135]

While acknowledging the important role of NGO input in general terms, the Committee does not cite NGO reports when considering States parties' reports.

3. Role of the Secretariat

The large number of reports to be dealt with, and the changes in the working methods have resulted in increased demands on the Secretariat.[136] For consideration of States parties' reports the Secretariat provides analysis based on the reports and supplementary statistical data from other United Nations sources, reports prepared by other treaty bodies, and information provided by specialized agencies. The Secretariat provides information on the status of submission of reports and about the activities and working methods of other treaty bodies. This enables the Committee to better focus its questions and to pay closer attention to achievements, remaining obstacles, and matters on which further information was required.[137]

---

[134] Ibid paras 9–10.   [135] Ibid paras 15.
[136] See the discussion in ch on art 17 for more on the functions of the Secretariat.
[137] UN Doc A/49/38, 13th Session (1994) para 18.

Article 19

1. The Committee shall adopt its own rules of procedure.

2. The Committee shall elect its officers for a term of two years.

A. Introduction

All the human rights treaty bodies may adopt—and amend—their own rules of procedure. Some treaties prescribe certain procedural requirements. For example, ICCPR Article 39(2) prescribes the number of members that constitute a quorum, and that decisions shall be made by a majority vote of the members present. CEDAW Article 19 is identical to ICERD Article 10(1) and (2). All of the human rights treaties leave to the respective treaty bodies the determination of number and type of officers. The CEDAW Committee has determined that it shall have five officers: one Chairperson, three Vice-Chairpersons, and a Rapporteur.

B. Travaux Préparatoires

The provision on the rules of procedure found its origin in the proposal to establish a committee to consider the status of Convention implementation.[1]

C. Committee Practice

I. Article 19(1)

The Committee shall adopt its own rules of procedure.

The Committee adopted rules of procedure at its first session in 1982.[2] At its 12th session, it changed its working methods with respect to the consideration of States parties reports,

---

* I would like to thank Marie Elske Gispen for her assistance on the chapters on arts 17, 18, 19, 20, 21, and 22 of the Commentary.

[1] UNGA Third Committee, 'Report of the Working Group of the Whole on the drafting of the Convention on the Elimination of All Forms of Discrimination against Women' (1979) UN Doc A/C.3/34/14, Annex I, 10–15 for Swedish proposal.

[2] UN Doc A/38/45, 1st Session (1982) Annex III.

which required it to change its Rules of Procedure.[3] At the 13th session, the Secretariat was asked to prepare draft revised rules reflecting the Committee's practice as it had developed over the years.[4] The rules were to reflect, among other matters, the Committee's decision to include Arabic as a working language.[5] Other amendments concerned the duration of sessions, the responsibilities of the Chairperson with regard to representing the Committee at United Nations meetings in which the Committee is officially invited to participate, the consideration of reports submitted by States parties, the formulation of suggestions and recommendations, and the participation of the specialized agencies and non-governmental organizations. Finalizing the revised rules took several years, delayed by other matters on the Committee's agenda (including the Fourth World Conference on Women), as well as developments relating to the Optional Protocol. Adoption of the Optional Protocol resulted in a major addition: Part Three, the Rules of Procedure for the Optional Protocol to the Convention on the Elimination of All Forms of Discrimination against Women. The Rules relating to the Optional Protocol were finalized at an expert meeting in Berlin in 2000.[6] The draft was adopted by the Committee at its 23rd session and, after editing by the Secretariat, was formally adopted at the 24th session in 2001.[7]

Since this major revision, the Rules have undergone further changes in light of experience in working with the Optional Protocol. In 2006, the Committee's Working Group on Communications requested the Secretariat to prepare a compilation of those Rules of Procedure which may require amendments in the light of practice and experience gained so far.[8] This resulted in amendments to a number of rules concerning the complaints procedure.[9]

The Rules are divided into three parts. The first part contains the general rules, dealing with issues such as convening sessions, officers of the Committee, duties of the Secretariat, and the conduct of business during meetings. Part Two deals with the reporting procedure and general discussions. Part Three deals with the two procedures under the Optional Protocol.

The procedures concerning the conduct of business at meetings and voting procedures are found in Rules 28–40. Rule 29 states that twelve members of the Committee shall constitute a quorum. The Committee aims to take all decisions by consensus and resorts to voting only when all efforts to reach consensus have been exhausted. Decisions are then taken by a simple majority of members present and voting (Rule 31), which means

---

[3] UN Doc A/48/38, 12th Session (1993) paras 627–33. At its 12th Session, the Committee considered the reports of two working groups: the Working Group to consider ways and means of expediting the work of the Committee (WG I) and the Working Group on ways and means of implementing Article 21 (WG II). The decision to change its working methods was based on the report of WG I. See also the discussion on these Working Groups in ch on art 21 in Section C.I.1.

[4] UN Doc A/49/38, 13th Session (1994) para 811. The Secretariat's proposals are included in CEDAW, 'Draft amendment to the rules of procedure of the Committee on the Elimination of Discrimination against Women' (1995) UN Doc CEDAW/C/1995/6, Annex I.

[5] UN Doc A/39/45, 2nd Session (1984) para 18. See the discussion in ch on art 30.

[6] UN Doc A/56/38, 24th Session (2001) para 24.

[7] 'Rules of procedure of the Committee on the Elimination of Discrimination against Women' (2001) UN Doc A/56/38, 24th Session, Decision 24/I and Annex I.

[8] 'Report of the Working Group on Communications under the Optional Protocol to the Convention on its seventh session' (2006) UN Doc A/61/38, 35th Session, Annex IX, para 8(b).

[9] 'Amendments to rules of procedure' (2007) UN Doc A/62/38, 39th Session paras 655–61 and Appendix. The adoption of the amendments has not resulted in the publication of a fully revised document containing the Rules of Procedure.

members casting an affirmative or negative vote. Members who abstain from voting are considered not to be voting (Rule 32(2)). The Committee shall normally vote by show of hands, but a member may request a roll call (Rule 34). Voting in elections is by secret ballot (Rule 39). In practice, however, election of officers takes place by acclamation (with the exception of the election of the first Chairperson at the first session) after confidential consultations among Committee members. This practice, common among all treaty bodies, has been criticized by commentators, since the actual decision-making takes place outside the context of formal meetings and the principle of election by secret ballot is not applied in practice.

Concluding observations on States parties' reports are adopted by consensus. The Committee also seeks to adopt decisions and views under the Optional Protocol by consensus, but Committee members may append individual opinions to inadmissibility decisions and views (Rules 70(3) and 72(6) respectively).[10]

Meetings shall be public unless the Committee decides otherwise (Rule 28(1)); however, meetings at which concluding observations on States parties' reports are discussed as well as meetings of pre-session and other working groups shall be closed unless the Committee decides otherwise (Rule 28(2)). Further, the examination of communications takes place in closed meetings (Rule 74(1)), and meetings related to the consideration of inquiries under Article 8 of the Optional Protocol are closed as well (Rule 81(1)).

The Committee's official documents are for general distribution, unless the Committee decides otherwise (Rule 43). This implies that the Committee's reports, formal decisions, pre-session documents, and all other official documents of the Committee and its subsidiary bodies are public. The same holds true for reports and additional information submitted by States parties under Article 18 of the Convention. The term 'public' has acquired an entire new meaning since the launch of websites by the various UN bodies. A wealth of information is available through the website of the Office of the High Commissioner for Human Rights (OHCHR).[11] Most States parties' reports are available from the 13th session and concluding observations from the 15th session onwards. For sessions held since the Committee's move to Geneva in 2008, the website also includes the Committee's Lists of Issues and written replies from States parties, and reports from non-governmental organizations. Information for the first twelve sessions is not available on the OHCHR or DAW websites, but some annual reports are available through other UN websites. Other official documents available online include the Committee's agenda, reports from specialized agencies, documents concerning the Committee's methods of work (the 'ways and means' reports), and general recommendations.

Another important issue dealt with in the Rules of Procedure is the establishment of subsidiary bodies. Rule 41 provides that the Committee may set up ad hoc subsidiary bodies and will define their composition and mandates. Such bodies shall elect their own officers and will apply the Rules of Procedure. The Committee has established various working groups, such as for the preparation of the consideration of reports, the consideration of individual communications, and to examine ways and means to expedite the functions of the Committee.[12]

---

[10] See the discussion in ch on the Optional Protocol.
[11] Home page for the Committee <http://www2.ohchr.org/english/bodies/cedaw/index.htm> and for treaty bodies' documents <http://tb.ohchr.org/default.aspx> accessed 31 December 2010.
[12] See the discussion in ch on art 17.

The Rules of Procedure may be amended by a decision taken by a two-thirds majority of the members present and voting.[13]

II. Article 19(2)

The Committee shall elect its officers for a term of two years.

This provision is reaffirmed in Rule 17, which adds that the officers are eligible for re-election provided that the principle of rotation is upheld. If an officer ceases to be a member of the Committee, she or he may not continue to hold office. From among its members, the Committee elects as officers a Chairperson, three Vice-Chairpersons, and a Rapporteur, with due regard to equitable geographical representation. Applying the principle of equitable geographical distribution, the five officers are generally from the five regions.[14] In addition, it is customary for the Chairperson to be limited to serving one term.[15]

The functions of the Chairperson include representing the Committee at UN meetings in which the Committee is officially invited to participate, chairing sessions of the Committee and maintaining order at the meetings.[16] If the Chairperson is unavailable, she may designate another officer of the Committee, or another member (Rule 18(3)). The Chairperson reports to the Committee on her activities between sessions. Until 2005, these activities were summarized in detail in the annual reports; since then reference is made only to the meeting at which the Chairperson reported, though the Chairperson's statements are available on the OHCHR website. Meetings and events at which the Committee is generally officially represented include meetings of the CSW, the Human Rights Council, the General Assembly, World Conferences, Chairpersons meetings, and the Inter-Committee Meetings. The Chairpersons have established short-term working groups on common procedural issues such as the development of harmonized reporting guidelines and reservations. Various Committee members have represented the Committee in such working groups where specific expertise has played a role in distributing tasks. Other activities include participation in technical cooperation missions to States parties on the implementation of the Convention.

The decision to work in parallel chambers led to a discussion on the question of whether it was necessary to have a Rapporteur in each of the chambers. The Committee agreed that there was no need to have the function of Rapporteur in each of the chambers and that all its office holders could contribute to chairing the sessions of the two chambers.[17]

---

[13] Rules of Procedure 93.
[14] Rules of Procedure 16.
[15] An exception to this custom was made when Ivanka Corti served two terms, for the sake of continuity during the Committee's involvement with the Fourth World Conference on Women.
[16] Rules of Procedure 30.
[17] UN Doc A/61/38, 35th session (2006) paras 368–9.

Article 20

1. The Committee shall normally meet for a period of not more than two weeks annually in order to consider the reports submitted in accordance with article 18 of the present Convention.

2. The meetings of the Committee shall normally be held at United Nations Headquarters or at any other convenient place as determined by the Committee.

A. Introduction

Article 20 sets the frequency and location of the Committee's sessions. It limits the Committee's meeting time to one session of a maximum of two weeks. This is unique in the UN human rights treaty system; none of the other treaties prescribes the monitoring body's meeting time. As the number of States parties increased, one annual two-week meeting turned out to be clearly inadequate for consideration of all the reports and the Committee's other work. This became even more problematic after the Optional Protocol entered into force.

Extending the Committee's meeting time requires an amendment of the clause 'not more than two weeks annually'. While such an amendment has been proposed,[1] as of 2010, it has not received the required number of ratifications by States parties. Nevertheless, additional meeting time has been granted to the Committee on the basis of General Assembly resolutions. Further, Article 20 is somewhat different from comparable treaty provisions, which provide in general terms that the monitoring body shall perform the functions described in the treaty, rather than referring exclusively to the consideration of reports. However, this limitation has not been an obstacle to the Committee's expanding agenda and programme of work.

---

* I would like to thank Marie Elske Gispen for her assistance on the chapters on arts 17, 18, 19, 20, 21, and 22 of the Commentary.

[1] 'Report of the States Parties' (1995) UN Doc CEDAW/SP/1995/2 paras 4–8.

B. Travaux Préparatoires

The nature of the body that would monitor the Convention was the subject of intense discussion. The question of whether it should be entrusted to the CSW or to a special treaty body was not resolved until the very last stage. The various proposals concerned the establishment of the body as well as a number of logistical issues such as the meeting time, which in the final version was included in a separate article. The clause restricting the meeting time to 'not more than two weeks' was introduced by Iran at the 26th session of the CSW, in a proposal based on Article IX of the International Convention on the Suppression and Punishment of the Crime of Apartheid. Under the Apartheid Convention a group of three members of the Commission on Human Rights considers State reports during a period of not more than five days. Under this model, experts would have been chosen from the CSW and there would not have been a separate CEDAW Committee[2]—The limited membership and time was ultimately not sustainable with the large number of States parties and, therefore, States party reports associated with the CEDAW Convention. The text the CSW submitted to the Third Committee, however, included this limitation of the meeting time.[3] The alternative proposal offered by Sweden, providing for the establishment of a committee of independent experts,[4] was largely modelled on ICERD Article 9, and the two-week limit was included in that proposal as well.

The Third Committee was under considerable pressure to complete the Convention before the end of 1979 so it could be opened for signature at the Second World Conference on Women in Copenhagen in 1980.[5] This resulted in voting without in-depth discussions of the various proposals, which may have contributed to the adoption of a provision containing some elements that appear illogical. The limited two-week meeting time might have been appropriate for a working group that would meet prior to the annual CSW session, but not for a human rights treaty body comparable to CERD and the HRC. The *travaux préparatoires* do not reveal why the reference to two weeks of meeting time was included in the alternative proposal establishing a committee.

C. Committee Practice

I. 'The Committee shall normally meet for a period of not more than two weeks annually...'

As the number of States parties and reports increased, the Committee needed much more time than one annual two-week session to perform its tasks. Various modest ad hoc measures were taken starting in 1987, when the Convention had ninety-two States parties. At its 6th session, the Committee considering that 'an extension of a session, in exceptional cases, was not in contradiction of Article 20 of the Convention',[6] decided to request

---

[2] UN Doc E/CN.6/591 para 186.   [3] UN Doc E/CN.6/608 (1976) paras 189–92.
[4] UNGA, 'Report of the Working Group of the Whole on the drafting of the Convention on the Elimination of All Forms of Discrimination against Women' (1979) UN Doc A/C.3/34/14 Annex I.
[5] See also ME Galey, 'International enforcement of women's rights' (1984) 6 *Human Rights Quarterly* 463, 481.
[6] UN Doc A/42/38, 6th Session (1987) paras 52, 580, and Decision 1.

an extended session. The General Assembly granted the request,[7] so the 7th session was indeed extended by four days (eight meetings). At its 8th session, the Committee decided to establish a pre-session working group to prepare the consideration of reports.[8] At its 10th session, the Committee again requested four days of additional meeting time and suggested that States parties should consider the problem with a view to searching for a long-term solution, including amending Article 20.[9] The General Assembly allowed the Committee to hold three-week sessions in 1993 and 1994[10] but did not respond to the suggestion concerning the amendment of Article 20(1).

One argument raised by Committee members was that the Committee had to consider many more periodic reports than other treaty bodies.[11] In 1994, the Committee noted that the temporary extension was not sufficient to cope with the backlog of reports to be considered, and reiterated its recommendation for a structural solution in the form of an amendment of Article 20. It further recommended that the General Assembly, pending the completion of an amendment process, authorize the Committee to meet exceptionally for two sessions of three weeks' duration each, preceded by a pre-session working group, starting in 1995 and in the biennium 1996–1997.[12] The General Assembly responded by recommending that the States parties to the Convention consider the possibility of amending Article 20 to allow for sufficient meeting time for the Committee.[13] The request for two sessions in 1995 and 1996 was, however, not granted.

At its 14th session, the Committee adopted General Recommendation 22, in which it:

1. Recommends that the States parties favourably consider amending Article 20 of the Convention in respect of the meeting time of the Committee, so as to allow it to meet annually for such duration as is necessary for the effective performance of its functions under the Convention, with no specific restriction except for that which the General Assembly shall decide;
2. Recommends also that the General Assembly, pending the completion of an amendment process, authorize the Committee to meet exceptionally in 1996 for two sessions, each of three weeks' duration and each being preceded by pre-session working groups;
3. Recommends further that the meeting of States parties receive an oral report from the Chairperson of the Committee on the difficulties faced by the Committee in performing its functions[.][14]

A statement as referred to in the above-cited paragraph was delivered to the Meeting of States parties by the Chairperson of the Committee, Ivanka Corti. Finland, supported by a large number of other States parties, introduced a draft resolution to amend Article 20(1). The amendment as adopted by the Meeting of States parties reads as follows:

The Committee shall normally meet annually in order to consider the reports submitted in accordance with article 18 of the present Convention. The duration of the meetings of the

---

[7] UNGA Res 42/60 (30 November 1987) UN Doc A/RES/42/60 para 13, in which the Committee was allowed to hold, 'on an exceptional basis, no more than eight additional meetings to its eighth session in 1988 to advance consideration of reports already submitted to it'.

[8] UN Doc A/44/38, 8th Session (1989) para 22.

[9] UN Doc A/46/38, 10th Session (1991) paras 377–8.

[10] UNGA Res 47/94 (16 December 1992) UN Doc A/RES/47/94 para 13.

[11] UN Doc A/49/38, 13th Session (1994) para 796.

[12] UN Doc A/49/38, 13th Session (1994) paras 13–14.

[13] UNGA Res 49/164 (23 December 1994) UN Doc A/Res/49/164 para 8.

[14] UN Doc A/50/38, 14th Session (1995) 1–2.

Committee shall be determined by a meeting of the States parties to the present Convention, subject to the approval of the General Assembly.[15]

This call for the amendment was supported by the Fourth World Conference on Women,[16] and the proposal to amend the Convention was formally endorsed by the General Assembly, which urged States parties to the Convention to take appropriate measures so that acceptance by a two-thirds majority of States parties could be reached as soon as possible in order for the amendment to enter into force.[17] However, despite broad support in the political organs, fifteen years later only 60 out of 186 States parties, less than one-third, have accepted the amendment.[18] As a consequence, the Committee depends on authorization by the General Assembly for its additional meeting time. Over the years, the Committee has received authorization to extend its meeting time on a more or less structural basis, allowing the Committee to actually meet twice annually from 1997–2005 (and thrice in 2002) and increasing this to three meetings per year in 2006.[19]

The first step towards meeting three times annually was taken in 2002. Following a request by the Committee,[20] the General Assembly authorized it to hold a three weeks' exceptional session 'to be used entirely for the consideration of the reports of the States parties in order to reduce the backlog of reports'.[21] This backlog was seen as constituting a 'disincentive' for States parties to report in a timely manner.[22] Subsequently, in 2005, the Committee made a request for three annual three-week sessions, effective from January 2006, and for authorization to hold part of its sessions in parallel working groups for the consideration of reports.[23] The General Assembly authorized three three-week sessions as a temporary measure, and granted the request to meet in parallel working groups for up to seven days on an exceptional and temporary basis. It urged the Committee to assess the situation with regard to the meeting time after two years.[24] The Committee did so at its 37th session, assessing its workload on the basis of the remaining backlog of reports awaiting consideration, the projected future availability of reports, and its other responsibilities under the Convention and the Optional Protocol. It concluded that the Committee should be provided with the opportunity to hold three sessions per annum, of which at least one would meet in parallel chambers.[25] In response, the General Assembly authorized the Committee to meet on an exceptional and temporary basis in a total of five sessions in 2008–09, of which three would occur in parallel chambers. More importantly, the General Assembly authorized the Committee to hold three annual sessions of three weeks

---

[15] 'Report of the States Parties' (1995) UN Doc CEDAW/SP/1995/2, Annex.

[16] 'Report of the Fourth World Conference on Women, Beijing 4–15 September 1995' (17 October 1995) UN Doc A/CONF.177/20 and Add.1, ch I, resolution 1, Annex II, para 230(j).

[17] UNGA Res 50/202 (22 December 1995) UN Doc A/RES/50/202 para 6. Article 26 of the Convention provides that the General Assembly shall decide how a request for a revision shall be dealt with; the requirement of a two-thirds majority is not stated in the Convention.

[18] The full list of State party ratifications of the amendment to art 20(1) is available online at <http://treaties.un.org> accessed 31 December 2010. The General Assembly continues to urge acceptance of the amendment, eg UNGA Res 64/138 (18 December 2009) UN Doc A/RES/64/138 paras 9–10.

[19] Meeting reports are available online at <http://treatybodyreport.org/cedaw-ars.html> accessed 31 December 2010.

[20] UN Doc A/56/38, 25th Session (2001) Decision 25/I.

[21] UNGA Res 56/229 (24 December 2001) UN Doc A/RES/56/229 para 13.

[22] UN Doc A/59/38, 30th Session (2004) para 420.

[23] UN Doc A/60/38, 33rd Session (2005) Decision 33/I.

[24] UNGA Res 60/230 (23 December 2005) UN Doc A/RES/60/230 paras 14–17.

[25] UN Doc A/62/38, 37th Session (2007) Decision 37/I.

each, for an interim period effective from January 2010, pending the entry into force of the amendment to Article 20(1). Each session may be preceded by a one-week pre-session working group. Further, the Working Group on Communications under the Optional Protocol may also hold three annual sessions.[26] This situation appears to be a structural resolution—although the General Assembly theoretically could reverse it.

II. '...in order to consider the reports submitted in accordance with article 18 of the present Convention.'

While Article 17 states that 'there shall be a Committee for the purpose of considering the progress made in the implementation of the Convention', Article 20(1) seems to limit the purpose of sessions to the consideration of reports. The Convention provides for additional functions of the Committee in Article 21, including drawing up a report to be submitted to the General Assembly and making suggestions and recommendations based on the examination of reports. The entry into force of the Optional Protocol also has had significant consequences for the Committee's agenda. The Committee's agenda and annual reports indicate that it spends quite some time on issues that would fall under the more general heading of considering progress in the implementation of the Convention, rather than just the consideration of reports. Examples include the exchange of information on activities, discussions on the methods of work, adoption of general recommendations, and the adoption of statements on topical issues.

The General Assembly resolutions relating to extended meeting time refer to the 'purpose of considering reports of States parties' and not to what the Committee calls its 'other responsibilities' under the Convention.[27] Clearly, the Committee uses the meeting time also for the adoption of general recommendations and statements.

III. 'The meetings of the Committee shall normally be held at United Nations Headquarters or at any other convenient place as determined by the Committee.'

Logistical matters were an obstacle to organizing the Committee's first session in New York, and as ECOSOC had expressed the wish that the Committee begin its work as soon as possible, it held its first session in Vienna. The first session was organized by the Branch for the Advancement of Women, at the Vienna International Centre.[28] From the 4th session, the Committee held meetings in Vienna and New York alternately; New York sessions were scheduled in the years when meetings of the States parties to the Convention were held.[29] The Assistant Secretary-General suggested that the Committee reconsider this decision in light of the support of the Vienna-based Centre for Social Development and Humanitarian Affairs for the Committee's work. The Committee turned down this request, as meeting exclusively in Vienna would require amending the Rules of Procedure; moreover, members pointed to the available facilities and publicity for its meetings at UN Headquarters and to the fact that most States parties had permanent missions in New York.[30] The request was made again at the Committee's

---

[26] UNGA Res 62/218 (22 December 2007) UN Doc A/RES/62/218 paras 14–15.
[27] UN Doc A/62/38, 37th Session (2007) Decision 37/I.
[28] UN Doc A/38/45, 1st Session (1982) para 7.   [29] UN Doc A/39/45, 2nd Session (1983) para 6.
[30] UN Doc A/40/45, 4th Session (1985) paras 19–21.

7th session; for budgetary reasons the General Assembly invited the Committee and the States parties to hold future sessions in Vienna.[31] The Director of the Branch for the Advancement of Women explained that the cost of servicing the Committee could be reduced if it met at the established headquarters of its substantive unit, which was Vienna.[32] The Committee observed that the difference in cost (amounting to US$900) was negligible, and reiterated its preference for holding sessions in New York, rather than exclusively in Vienna. It further noted that it could be useful to hold some sessions in Geneva, in order to establish a closer relationship with other treaty bodies and to have access to legal advice and assistance.[33]

The secretariat moved from Vienna to New York in 1993, and all Committee sessions between 1994 and 2007 were held in New York. With the relocation of the secretariat to Geneva in 2008,[34] the Committee's sessions are organized there, with one of the three annual sessions held in New York. The Committee has indicated that this facilitates and encourages cooperation between the Committee and the United Nations gender equality bodies.[35]

---

[31] UNGA Res 42/60 (30 November 1987) UN Doc A/RES/42/60 para 14.
[32] UN Doc A/43/38, 7th Session (1988) para 4.
[33] UN Doc A/43/38, 7th Session (1988) para 57. See also GR 7 para 2.
[34] See the discussion in ch on art 17.   [35] UN Doc A/62/38, 39th Session (2007) Decision 39/I.

Article 21

1. The Committee shall, through the Economic and Social Council, report annually to the General Assembly of the United Nations on its activities and may make suggestions and general recommendations based on the examination of reports and information received from the States Parties. Such suggestions and general recommendations shall be included in the report of the Committee together with comments, if any, from States Parties.

2. The Secretary-General of the United Nations shall transmit the reports of the Committee to the Commission on the Status of Women for its information.

A. Introduction

Article 21 combines two distinct topics. First, the Committee must report annually on its activities to the General Assembly. This clause can be found in all human rights treaties, though not all treaties include a role for ECOSOC. The Convention is the only treaty that provides also that CSW shall receive the Committee's annual reports, though only 'for its information'. The second topic is the reference to 'suggestions and general recommendations' based on the examination of States parties' reports. In the early years of the Committee, members debated the scope of this provision, especially the question of whether the Committee had the mandate to evaluate or assess an individual State party's performance in implementing the Convention. While it first held the view that it could only adopt general recommendations addressed to all States parties, from 1994 onwards it has adopted concluding observations (for many years called 'concluding comments') containing suggestions and recommendations addressed to individual States parties.

* I would like to thank Marie Elske Gispen for her assistance on the chapters on arts 17, 18, 19, 20, 21, and 22 of the Commentary.

B. Travaux Préparatoires

The subject of reporting on Convention implementation was closely associated with the discussions on the nature of the monitoring body.[1] Proposals suggesting that the CSW was the most appropriate body provided for the submission of a report on the status of Convention implementation to the CSW's parent body, ECOSOC, every four years.[2] The alternative proposal, providing for the establishment of a committee of independent experts, referred annual reports of the Committee to the General Assembly, through the Secretary-General. The latter proposal included the possibility of issuing suggestions and general recommendations and States parties' comments, but it did not refer to a role for the CSW.[3] During the discussion, the Federal Republic of Germany observed that close cooperation between the Committee and the CSW should be ensured.[4]

The draft Convention adopted by the CSW provided that the ad hoc group to be established by the CSW would submit to the CSW a report of its activities with general recommendations based on the examination of States parties' reports. The CSW was then to transmit that report, together with its own comments, to ECOSOC. In turn, ECOSOC would periodically submit to the General Assembly reports with recommendations of a general nature and a summary of the information received from the States parties and the specialized agencies.[5] The Third Committee of the General Assembly had various drafts before it. Following the decision to establish a committee of independent experts,[6] it was decided that an annual report should be submitted to the General Assembly, through the ECOSOC, and to the CSW for information.

There was no discussion on the motivation for the submission of a report to the General Assembly. Discussions during the drafting of the ICCPR reveal that the purpose of the annual reporting requirement was to solidify the relationship between the treaty body and the United Nations.[7]

C. Committee Practice

I. Article 21(1)

The Committee shall, through the Economic and Social Council, report annually to the General Assembly of the United Nations....

The Committee elects a Rapporteur for a period of two years, with due regard to equitable geographical representation.[8] The Committee adopts a report at the end of each session.[9] The Secretary-General submits a note on the results of the Committee's sessions to ECOSOC, announcing that the report of the sessions will be transmitted to the

---

[1] See the discussion in ch on art 17.   [2] UN Doc E/CN.6/574 (1974) 17.
[3] UN Doc E/CN.6/574 (1974) 19.   [4] UN Doc E/CN.6/591 (1976) para 182.
[5] UN Doc E/CN.6/608 (1976) paras 192 and 202.
[6] UNGA, 'Report of the Working Group of the Whole on the drafting of the Convention on the Elimination of All Forms of Discrimination against Women' UN Doc A/C.3/34/14 (1979) Annex I, 10–15.
[7] M Nowak, *UN Covenant on Civil and Political Rights: CCPR commentary*, 2nd edn (2005) 793.
[8] Rules of Procedure 16 and 17.
[9] At the 2nd Session, the Committee failed to adopt a complete report, see UN Doc A/39/45, Vol. 2, 3rd Session (1984) paras 7–12.

General Assembly.[10] This refers to a report on the results of the most recent sessions of the Committee which is available online as well as to the Committee's annual report to be submitted to the General Assembly.[11] ECOSOC does not discuss the Committee's report under a separate agenda item, but relevant issues come up when the Council considers the CSW report on the follow-up to the Fourth World Conference on Women and to the 23rd special session of the General Assembly, in which the CSW played a leading and coordinating role.[12] ECOSOC has stressed that the follow-up to the outcome documents of these political meetings and the fulfilment of the obligations under the Convention 'are mutually reinforcing in achieving gender equality and the empowerment of women'.[13]

The General Assembly deals with the Committee's reports biannually in the Third Committee, under the agenda item 'Advancement of women', rather than 'Promotion of human rights', where the reports of the other treaty bodies are dealt with. This agenda item covers various other issues such as the implementation of the Beijing Declaration and Platform for Action, the report of the Special Rapporteur on Violence against Women, and the report of UNIFEM. The Third Committee has before it the Committee's annual report and a report of the Secretary-General on Convention ratifications and reservations.[14] The Secretary-General's report also provides information on the Committee's progress in the consideration of States parties' reports and their compliance with their reporting obligations. In its resolutions, the General Assembly typically encourages States that have not ratified the Convention to do so and urges States parties to comply with their obligations and to take into consideration the Committee's concluding observations and general recommendations. States parties are further called upon to make every possible effort to submit their reports on time, without, however, a reminder that this too constitutes an obligation under the Convention.[15]

...on its activities...

The Convention does not specify the contents of the Committee's report to the General Assembly, other than that it must concern the Committee's activities.[16] The annual reports are a valuable source of information about all aspects of the Committee's work. They provide details on the Committee's working methods and contain its decisions, statements, and general recommendations. As from the 42nd session, the concluding observations are no longer published in the reports but are available on the OHCHR

---

[10] UN Doc E/2010/74 (2010).

[11] eg UN Doc E/2010/74 (2010) referring to UN Doc E/CN.6/2010/CRP.2. The first five annual reports were published as Supplement No 45; since then they have been published as Supplement No 38 to the General Assembly's Official Records.

[12] UN Doc E/CN.6/2010/11 (2010) 54–87. See also Five-year Review of the Implementation of the Beijing Declaration and Platform for Action, 5–9 June 2000, for more on the issues raised at the 23rd special session of the General Assembly.

[13] ECOSOC Res 2009/15 (28 July 2009) preamble.

[14] Report of the Secretary-General, 'Status of the Convention on the Elimination of All Forms of Discrimination against Women' (2009) UN Doc A/64/342.

[15] UNGA Res 64/138 (18 December 2009) UN Doc A/RES/64/138.

[16] See the discussion in ch on the Optional Protocol, on the requirement to include a summary of the Committee's activities under the Optional Protocol in its annual report.

website.[17] The reports contain an overview of the status of ratification, the submissions and consideration of States parties' reports, and organizational matters such as the Committee's membership and the composition of subsidiary bodies.

The Committee (...) may make suggestions and general recommendations based on the examination of reports and information received from the States Parties. (...)

1. Assessing States Parties' Reports

In the early stages of its work, there was no consensus among Committee members on its mandate under Article 21. The Committee, therefore, requested advice from the United Nations Office of Legal Affairs. At the 5th session, a representative of the Office explained the terms 'suggestions and recommendations'. In the absence of guidance in the *travaux préparatoires*, he referred to the background of the adoption of similar terminology in ICERD, by which the Committee could be guided. That would imply that it could be flexible in making suggestions on the basis of States parties' reports without qualification as to whether they should be addressed to general situations or specific situations and to make recommendations of a general nature addressed to all States parties. He also pointed out that Rule 46 of the Committee's Rules of Procedure was more limited in scope than Article 21 of the Convention.[18] Following discussions in a working group, the Committee agreed that a general recommendation could be made as a result of examination of reports by States parties and could be addressed to all States parties.[19]

The Committee extensively discussed at its 6th session the question of whether it could include in its report a paragraph of general appraisal and assessment of States parties' reports. The Working Group to consider ways and means of expediting the work of the Committee (WG I) proposed to adopt a paragraph of general appraisal at the end of the question period. While some members held the view that such a paragraph could encourage States parties to take action and would be helpful in drafting subsequent reports, others believed that a general paragraph might give an inaccurate picture of the Committee's view on a report. The latter group doubted whether the Committee could reach a unanimous position. After some discussion, the Committee decided to make a general comment on a States party's report after its consideration, when appropriate. If the Committee could not reach consensus, it would state no more than that the report had been received and considered, and that it felt that not all questions had been dealt with. Discouraging comments would be avoided.[20]

At the same session, the Working Group on ways and means of implementing Article 21 (WG II) agreed that general recommendations and suggestions could be addressed to all States parties, but it was divided as to whether the Committee was authorized to address a suggestion to one State party.[21] It was pointed out that this differed from the general paragraph at the end of a discussion. Ultimately, the Committee agreed that it could, in an appropriate case, make suggestions and general recommendations based on the examination of a report and information received from a State party. This decision, however, was

---

[17] Contra, Rules of Procedure 42 (stating that the annual report shall contain the concluding comments of the Committee relating to each State party's report).

[18] UN Doc A/41/45, 5th Session (1986) para 359.

[19] UN Doc A/41/45, 5th Session (1986) para 362, considering the suggestions put forth by an open-ended working group created to recommend methods of improving efficiency.

[20] UN Doc A/42/38, 6th Session (1987) paras 42, 44, and 45.

[21] UN Doc A/42/38, 6th Session (1987) para 56.

not reached by consensus, and the dissenting members insisted that their objections be reflected in the annual report.[22]

As a consequence, at the same session, the Committee for the first time discussed general paragraphs that had been drafted for inclusion in the annual report as comments on reports of States parties. Agreeing that the annual report of the 6th session accurately reflected those proposals, all drafts were withdrawn, except the one on Greece, which had already been adopted.[23] The reports from this session all conclude with a similar structure in which 'the Committee' or 'members of the Committee' express a number of compliments and make a specific request concerning the provision of information in subsequent reports.[24]

A renewed discussion took place at the 10th session, which did not result in a clear conclusion.[25] Three years later, the Committee formally decided to follow the other human rights treaty bodies and to adopt concluding observations on the reviews of States parties' reports, and it established the procedure for preparing these comments.[26] This was a major step forward. The adoption of conclusions by the Committee as a whole strengthened the reporting procedure as a tool for advancing Convention implementation. The concluding observations make the scope of the obligations more concrete and provide a basis for preparation of subsequent reports. Further, the concluding observations constitute a tool for the Committee to measure progress and to discern trends. They can be used by NGOs and NHRIs to play their own role at the domestic level. Finally, the concluding observations are the basic component of the Committee's jurisprudence, providing guidance to all States parties on the content of Convention obligations.

2. *General Recommendations*

Having decided that it could formulate general recommendations, the Committee at its 5th session adopted its first general recommendation, on Article 18.[27] It also adopted a suggestion to the effect that States parties might consider the establishment of public institutions to ensure elimination of discrimination against women.[28] Furthermore, it adopted 'general observations' reflecting the opinion of 'many members of the Committee' on rural women.[29] At the 6th session, it decided to establish a standing working group on ways and means of implementing Article 21.[30]

During the Committee's 9th session, the Working Group on Article 21 had considered six draft general recommendations, two of which were submitted for approval by the Committee: on female circumcision and on avoiding discrimination against women

---

[22] UN Doc A/42/38, 6th Session (1987) paras 57–60. See also A Byrnes, 'The "Other" Human Rights Treaty Body: The Work of the Committee on the Elimination of Discrimination Against Women' (1989) 14 *Yale J Intl L* 1, 43–4; E Evatt, 'Finding a voice for women's rights: The early days of CEDAW' (2002) 34 *George Washington Intl L Rev* 515, 532–3.

[23] UN Doc A/42/38, 6th Session (1987) para 54.

[24] See generally UN Doc A/42/38, 6th Session (1987).

[25] UN Doc A/46/38, 10th Session (1991) para 392.

[26] UN Doc A/49/38, 13th Session (1994) para 812, although one Committee member continued to object, see CEDAW/C/SR.255. For more on the procedure for the adoption of concluding observations, see the discussion in ch on art 18.

[27] UN Doc A/41/45, 5th Session (1986) para 362.

[28] UN Doc A/41/45, 5th Session (1986) para 363.

[29] UN Doc A/41/45, 5th Session (1986) para 365.

[30] UN Doc A/42/38, 6th Session paras (1987) paras 28 and 37.

in national strategies for the prevention and control of AIDS.[31] At the 10th session, it adopted General Recommendation 16 on unpaid women workers in rural and urban family enterprises; General Recommendation 17 on the measurement and quantification of the unremunerated domestic activities of women and their recognition in the gross national product; and General Recommendation 18 on disabled women.[32] These general recommendations are brief, point to a specific issue, explain it in the context of the Convention, often request States parties to collect statistical data, and contain a generally formulated recommendation to improve women's situations.

At its 10th session, the Committee decided to prepare comments on articles of the Convention, as preparatory work for the adoption of general recommendations. The Secretariat was asked to prepare background documents on the basis of reports from States parties, reports of the Committee, the Nairobi Forward Looking Strategies, other UN documents, and reports from the specialized agencies and non-governmental organizations.[33] This practice resulted in the adoption of more detailed and comprehensive general recommendations. This new format was first implemented in General Recommendation 19 on violence against women.

In 1997, the Committee decided to work in three stages when formulating general recommendations. The first stage consists of an open dialogue between the Committee, NGOs, and others on the topic of the general recommendation. A Committee member then drafts the general recommendation, which is discussed by the Committee (in closed plenary session). At a subsequent session, the revised draft is adopted by the Committee.[34] In its 2010 statement on NGOs, the Committee reiterated that NGOs are encouraged to provide inputs on general recommendations under elaboration and to make use of the Committee's general recommendations in their own work.[35] The process of drafting and adopting a general recommendation can take several years to complete.

In the final stage of drafting the general recommendation on migrant women, the Committee collaborated with the Committee on Migrant Workers and organized a joint meeting.[36] The Inter-Committee Meetings and Chairpersons Meetings have acknowledged that exploring the possibilities of adopting joint general recommendations on common thematic issues would be useful.[37]

3. Statements

In addition to general recommendations, the Committee has adopted a number of statements in which it clarifies 'its position on major international developments and

---

[31] UN Doc A/45/38, 9th Session (1990) paras 42–8; texts adopted in Annex IV of the report.

[32] UN Doc A/46/38, 10th Session (1991) paras 1–3.

[33] UN Doc A/46/38, 10th Session (1991) paras 380–1.

[34] CEDAW, 'Overview of the working methods of the Committee on the Elimination of Discrimination against Women in relation to the reporting process' (2009) UN Doc CEDAW/C/2009/II/4, Annex III, paras 33–5.

[35] 'Statement by the Committee on the Elimination of Discrimination against Women on its relationship with non-governmental organizations' UN Doc A/65/38, 45th session (2010) Annex V, Decision 45/VI, para 13.

[36] UN Doc A/63/38, 40th Session (2008) para 411. The contribution of the Committee on the Protection of the Rights of All Migrant Workers and Members of Their Families to the preparation of GR 26 was acknowledged in the final text, see UN Doc A/64/38, 42nd Session (2008) Annex I, Decision I.

[37] UNGA, 'Report of the chairpersons of the human rights treaty bodies on their twentieth meeting' (2008) UN Doc A/63/280, Annex, para 42(s).

issues that bear upon the implementation of the Convention'.[38] Statements may address thematic issues or a situation in a State party. For example, the Committee adopted a statement on the situation of women in Iraq, dealing specifically with unequal status of women in legislation;[39] on Haiti after the earthquake in January 2010;[40] and on the inclusion of Afghan women in the process of peace building, security, and reconstruction in Afghanistan.[41] The subjects of thematic statements have included reservations,[42] treaty body reform,[43] and gender and climate change.[44]

II. Article 21(2)

The Convention provides for only a limited role for the CSW, to the effect that it receives the Committee's reports 'for its information'. The CSW does not address the Convention specifically but refers to it under the agenda item relating to the Fourth World Conference and its follow-up. For example, at its 53rd session, the CSW dealt with the equal sharing of responsibilities between women and men, including care giving in the context of HIV/AIDS. The background report prepared by the Secretariat recalled the relevant provisions of the Convention, among other documents, and recommended in general terms its full implementation.[45] The CSW's agreed conclusions reiterate that the Convention provides a legal framework and a comprehensive set of measures for the promotion of equal sharing of responsibilities between women and men, and urges the ratification of the Convention, the limitation of the extent of reservations and the withdrawal of reservations that are incompatible with the object and purpose of the Convention, and the full implementation of the Convention, putting in place effective national legislation, policies, and action plans.[46]

The Committee can provide input to the CSW on specific agenda items. For the CSW session on Beijing +15 in 2010, the Committee adopted a statement, recalling the commitments States made in the Beijing Declaration and Platform for Action, and reiterating the strong links between the outcome documents and the Convention. It emphasized the need for States to do more to guarantee women's access to justice, including by ensuring that judicial systems and law enforcement facilitate women's capacity to claim their rights,

---

[38] CEDAW, 'Overview of the current working methods of the Committee on the Elimination of Discrimination against Women' UN Doc A/59/38, 31st Session (2004) Annex X, para 34.

[39] UN Doc A/59/38, 31st Session (2004) Annex II.

[40] 'Statement of the Committee on the Elimination of Discrimination against Women on the Situation on Haiti' UN Doc A/65/38, 45th Session (2010) Annex II, Decision 45/III.

[41] 'Statement of the Committee on the Elimination of Discrimination against Women on the inclusion of Afghan women in the process of peacebuilding, security and reconstruction in Afghanistan' UN Doc A/65/38, 45th Session (2010) Annex III, Decision 45/IV.

[42] 'Statements on reservations to the Convention on the Elimination of All Forms of Discrimination against Women adopted by the Committee on the Elimination of Discrimination against Women' UN Doc A/53/38, 19th Session (1998) paras 47–50.

[43] 'Statement by the Committee on the Elimination of Discrimination against Women, towards a harmonized and integrated human rights treaty body system' UN Doc A/61/38, 35th Session (2006) Annex I, para 4.

[44] 'Statement of the Committee on the Elimination of Discrimination against Women on gender and climate change' UN Doc A/65/38, 44th session (2009) Annex II, Decision 44/II.

[45] Report of the Secretary-General, 'The equal sharing of responsibilities between women and men, including care giving in the context of HIV/AIDS' (2008) UN Doc E/CN.6/2009/2.

[46] CSW, 'Agreed conclusions on the equal sharing of responsibilities between women and men, including care giving in the context of HIV/AIDS' (2009) UN Doc E/CN.6/2009/15 (2009) paras 3 and 15(b).

and to ensure that all discriminatory laws are repealed and that they exercise due diligence in pursuing violations perpetrated by private actors.[47]

The Committee has discussed its relationship with the CSW on a number of occasions. At the 24th session, the Committee decided to develop closer links with the CSW. In that regard, it drew attention to the willingness of Committee members to serve in expert group meetings convened to prepare for Commission sessions and as panellists during the sessions.[48] The CSW can, of course, seek the Committee's views on issues on its agenda. Having before it a report of the Secretary-General on the advisability of the appointment of a Special Rapporteur on laws that discriminate against women, the Commission invited the Committee to forward its views on ways and means that could best complement the work of the existing mechanisms and enhance the Commission's capacity with respect to discriminatory laws.[49] The Committee responded positively and suggested that it would contribute an analysis of its consideration of the theme concerned, drawing mainly from the concluding comments of the Committee in that regard. It also observed that Committee experts could participate in any panel discussion organized in conjunction with the consideration of the theme in the CSW.[50]

---

[47] 'Statement of the Committee on the Elimination of Discrimination against Women on the 15-year review of the implementation of the Beijing Declaration and Platform for Action' UN Doc A/65/38, 45th Session (2010) Decision 45/V, para 6.

[48] CEDAW 'Links with the Commission on the Status of Women' UN Doc A/56/38, 24th Session (2001) Decision 24/III.

[49] UN Doc E/CN.6/2006/15 (2006) 20–1; Report of the Secretary-General 'Advisability of the appointment of a special rapporteur on laws that discriminate against women' (2006) UN Doc E/CN.6/2006/8.

[50] UN Doc A/61/38, 36th Session (2006) paras 641–2.

Article 22

The specialized agencies shall be entitled to be represented at the consideration of the implementation of such provisions of the present Convention as fall within the scope of their activities. The Committee may invite the specialized agencies to submit reports on the implementation of the Convention in areas falling within the scope of their activities.

A. Introduction

The Committee's practice under Article 22 has developed significantly over the years. The text refers exclusively to specialized agencies, although in its current practice the Committee invites other UN entities to submit reports. In the early years, the Committee did not ask the specialized agencies to submit country-specific information to be used in the consideration of States parties' reports, as some members believed this was beyond the Committee's mandate. Gradually, it allowed a larger role for these agencies in the reporting procedure, and it welcomes country-specific information as well as input at the pre-session working group. Further, it considers the specialized agencies to be valuable partners in assisting States parties in implementing the Convention at the domestic level.

B. Trauvaux Préparatoires

The main points of discussion in the Working Group of the Third Committee concerned, in the first place, the role of the reports to be submitted by the specialized agencies; some States held the view that such reports would be submitted to the monitoring body for its information only.[1] Second, the Working Group noted that information from the specialized agencies should focus on the Convention and not on treaties adopted by the agencies. Third, the question arose of whether specialized agencies should be obliged to submit reports. The Working Group adopted the text of Article 22, leaving open which body would receive the reports.[2] The final text thus leaves the initiative for requesting

---

* I would like to thank Marie Elske Gispen for her assistance on the chapters on arts 17, 18, 19, 20, 21, and 22 of the Commentary.

[1] At this stage, it had not yet been decided what organ would consider Convention implementation.

[2] UNGA Third Committee, 'Report of the Working Group of the Whole on the drafting of the Convention on the Elimination of All Forms of Discrimination against Women' (1979) UN Doc A/C.3/34/14, 34th Session, para 15.

reports with the Committee and does not formulate it as a right or obligation of the specialized agencies. The reference in earlier drafts to specialized agencies' involvement in Convention implementation at the national level, and the possibility of their providing technical assistance, were not included.[3]

C. Committee Practice

In the early stages of the Committee's work, Article 22 was the subject of controversy concerning the submission of country-specific information which could be used in the consideration of States parties' reports. Some members believed this would be outside the Committee's mandate. At the 2nd session, the Committee decided by consensus to invite specialized agencies whose activities were relevant, to prepare reports on programmes that might promote Convention implementation as well as additional information.[4] The decision does not specify which specialized agencies fall within the scope of Article 22, nor does it indicate what the Committee intends to do with the information.

From the late 1980s, the Committee further developed the role of the specialized agencies. It invited them to report on their programmes and activities which might promote the implementation of the Convention. It further invited them to provide additional information submitted to the specialized agencies by States parties concerning the relevant articles of the Convention and within the framework of the Committee's agenda.[5] It did not go so far as to request the specialized agencies to submit their own information on the situation in States parties, but information they have received from States parties could be forwarded. A next step was to invite the specialized agencies to undertake activities to ensure broader implementation within their spheres of competence.[6] At this stage, the relationship was said to be 'extremely disappointing'. The few reports submitted to the Committee did not specifically address the Convention and were of limited use in the State party reviews. At the same time, the Committee has only made limited use of the specialized agencies reports, typically using the reports for background information.[7]

In the early 1990s, the Committee decided to provide opportunities in plenary for representatives of the specialized agencies and other UN bodies to present information related to specific articles of the Convention or to issues considered for general recommendations and suggestions. These individuals could be invited to participate as resource persons for the Working Groups.[8] As noted by the 1994 Chairpersons Meeting, the desire to increase the effectiveness of cooperation with the specialized agencies changed the atmosphere.[9] For the Committee, the Beijing Declaration and Platform for Action constituted a new impetus for further involvement of the specialized agencies. The Committee made its invitation to submit reports more specific by indicating how the specialized agencies could best contribute to its work in following up on the recommendations of the Beijing

---

[3] See text of original draft in Third Committee Report of the WG (1979) (n 2 above), Annex I, para 15.

[4] UN Doc A/39/45/Vol. 1, 2nd Session (1983) para 25.

[5] UN Doc A/42/38, 6th Session (1987) para 580, Decision 2.

[6] UN Doc A/43/38, 7th Session (1988) para 48.

[7] A Byrnes, 'The "Other" Human Rights Treaty Body: the Work of the Committee on the Elimination of Discrimination Against Women' (1989) 14 *Yale J Intl L* 1, 38–9.

[8] UN Doc A/46/38, 10th Session (1991) para 373.

[9] UNGA, 'Report of the fifth meeting of persons chairing the human rights treaty bodies' (1994) UN Doc A/49/537 paras 23 and 37–40.

Platform for Action. The Committee established a list of areas of engagement with the various agencies, corresponding to the Beijing Platform's Critical Areas of Concern.

In 1997, the Committee took an important decision, requesting the specialized agencies to submit their information in a more structured manner, and that it be country-specific and include information from country or regional studies about the State party, new statistics collected by the agencies, and a description of the agencies' country-level programmes. At the same time, it underlined the relevance of its own work for the specialized agencies. It stressed that particularly those with field offices should keep in mind the principles and recommendations of the Committee in defining their work programmes.[10]

In 1998, the Committee decided that specialized agencies should be invited to submit their information to the pre-session working group and to address the Committee as a whole in a closed meeting on States parties under initial review.[11] The Committee further decided to nominate individual members to act as focal points for each agency or organization and to request the organization to nominate a member to serve as a focal point for the Committee.[12] The World Bank and the International Monetary Fund were added to the invitation list, 'to present an analysis of the impact of their policies on women's enjoyment of their rights'.[13]

At its 25th session, the Committee adopted guidelines for the reports submitted by UN bodies and specialized agencies, stressing again the relevance of such information. It suggested that country-specific information be complemented with additional information on the agency's programmes in the country or region. Further, it observed that it was most beneficial to have written reports to be presented by the representative of the UN body or specialized agency during the closed meeting.[14]

The Committee was not satisfied with the information provided to it. At the 29th session, it observed that only a limited number of agencies and entities took advantage of the opportunity to provide the Committee with country information in a closed meeting at the beginning of the session and during the pre-session working group. Some Committee members also noted that the system of focal points for liaising with certain UN entities did not seem to function very well. The Committee decided again to encourage the relevant entities to designate their own focal points for liaising with the relevant Committee member and to establish contact to discuss ways and means of interaction with the Committee.[15] The concern was reiterated at the 33rd session, and the Committee pointed to the 'apparent indifference of some entities', particularly the United Nations Development Programme, in relation to the Committee's work. It pointed out that the central offices did not provide information available from the field. It decided to revise its guidelines for reports of UN bodies and specialized agencies to make them clearer and more specific. Members remained dissatisfied with the functioning of the focal points, and it was decided to discuss this matter in the Inter-Committee Meeting.[16] New guidelines specifically requesting extensive information were adopted at the 34th session.[17]

---

[10] UN Doc A/52/38, 16th Session (1997) para 365.
[11] UN Doc A/53/38/Rev.1, 18th Session (1998) Decisions 18/I and 18/II.   [12] Ibid paras 431–3.
[13] Ibid para 438.   [14] UN Doc A/56/38, 25th Session (2001) paras 392–5.
[15] UN Doc A/58/38, 29th Session (2003) paras 462–3.
[16] UN Doc A/60/38, 33rd Session (2005) paras 437–41.
[17] CEDAW, 'Guidelines for submission of reports by United Nations specialized agencies and other bodies' (2006) UN Doc A/61/38, 34th Session, Annex II para 6.

The Committee further indicated that it preferred succinct, country-specific written reports, made available to the pre-session working group. Representatives are invited to update this information and present it to the Committee during the closed meetings which the Committee convenes at each session with representatives of the UN system.[18] The Committee's practice was stated in the relevant rules of procedure.[19] In light of the enhanced interaction with various entities, the Committee discontinued its practice of focal points.[20]

As the process has developed, the ILO, FAO, and UNESCO regularly submit informa-tion, which is made available on the OHCHR website. Representatives of agencies and entities whose work is relevant for the Committee (and for whom the Committee's work is relevant), appear regularly at the Committee's sessions. The concluding observations do not make explicit reference to the information submitted by the specialized agencies, as is the Committee's practice with respect to all sources of information other than States par-ties' reports. Where appropriate, the Committee encourages States parties to seek techni-cal assistance from specialized agencies and programmes of the UN system.[21]

Finally, the Committee 'warmly welcomes' the information it receives from United Nations country teams. It considers that the country teams can play a role not only in submitting information on States parties under review, but in addition 'to undertake fol-low-up activities on the basis of the Committee's concluding comments and to support States parties in their implementation of the concluding comments at the country level, and to submit further information at the time the respective State party reports the next time'.[22]

---

[18] Ibid paras 7–8.   [19] Rules of Procedure 44–5.
[20] UN Doc A/62/38, 37th Session (2007) para 659.
[21] eg CO Uganda, CEDAW/C/UGA/CO/7 (2010) para 56.
[22] UN Doc A/61/38, 36th Session (2006) para 634; UN Doc A/62/38, 39th Session (2007) para 677.

Article 23

Nothing in the present Convention shall affect any provisions that are more conducive to the achievement of equality between men and women which may be contained:

(a) In the legislation of a State Party; or

(b) In any other international convention, treaty or agreement in force for that State.

A. Introduction

Article 23 is a savings clause,[1] the purpose of which is to clarify the relationship between the provisions of the Convention and those contained in other treaties or national law. It is intended to ensure that the highest standard for the protection of women's human rights is observed by a State party, whether the source of that obligation is the Convention, another treaty, or national law.

Where a national law provides better protection for women's equality than the Convention does, Article 23(a) provides that the national provision should prevail. In this respect Article 23(a) states explicitly what the position would have been in any event, as the treaty does not restrict a State party from providing for a higher level of protection.

The adoption of any new treaty often gives rise to the question of how the obligations of States parties under that treaty relate to their obligations under other conventions, and which standard is to prevail if obligations under two treaties conflict.[2] The matter is

* I would like to thank Professor Dianne Otto for her comments on the chapters on arts 1 and 2; Luke Beck, Renée Chartres, Maria Herminía Graterol, and Eleanor Bath for their research assistance, and the University of New South Wales for Goldstar and Faculty of Law funding to support research for this chapter and the chapters on arts 1, 2, and 24.

[1] See generally N Matz-Lück, 'Treaties, Conflict Clauses' in R Wolfrum (ed), *The Max Planck Encyclopedia of Public International Law* (2008) online edition <http://www.mpepil.com> accessed 31 December 2010.

[2] See generally, A Sadat-Akhavi, *Methods of Resolving Conflicts Between Treaties* (2003); Matz-Lück (n 1 above); *Conclusions of the Work of the Study Group on the Fragmentation of International Law: Difficulties Arising from the Diversification and Expansion of International Law*, Report of the International Law Commission at

further complicated if the States parties to the earlier treaty are not the same as the States parties to the later treaty.[3] Article 23(b) addresses this issue.

B. Travaux Préparatoires[4]

The Convention was drafted against the background of existing international and regional human rights treaties, including those that addressed the situation of women, and of a range of national laws that prohibited discrimination against women. One of the concerns of the drafters was to ensure that gains already made at the domestic level that were greater than those required by any international treaty would not be undermined by its adoption. A further concern was clarifying the potential impact of the new convention on existing international and regional treaties which regulated specific aspects of the human rights of women in greater detail than the new convention was likely to do.

Some existing treaties were consistent with the Convention, or may even have provided a higher level of human rights protection, but others arguably were not. For example, various forms of protective legislation, such as restrictions on night work by women or on women's employment in certain industries designated in ILO conventions, were of particular concern. Indeed, the ILO sought to avoid any conflicts by suggesting a clause safeguarding ILO conventions from any adverse impact of the Convention.[5]

The initial CSW draft contained a savings clause only with respect to national measures that provided more extensive protection of women's human rights than would be provided for by the Convention: 'None of the provisions of this Convention may be regarded as diminishing the significance of the existing domestic legislation of countries if that legislation provides for more extensive rights for women'.[6]

That provision was amended to clarify its meaning, and the text adopted by the CSW and forwarded to ECOSOC at the end of 1976 read: 'Nothing in the present Convention shall affect the provisions of domestic legislation in force in a State party if they are more favourable to women'.[7]

An additional clause was proposed to cover existing international treaties. The effect of the initial proposal would have been that the Convention would not have affected the operation of existing treaties in any way.[8] However, the language that was forwarded by the CSW to ECOSOC in 1976 made it clear that existing conventions were protected only if they contained provisions more favourable to women: 'Similarly, nothing in the present Convention shall affect existing conventions adopted under the auspices of the United

---

its 58th session, UN Doc A/61/10 (2006) para 251; and T Meron, *Human Rights Law-Making in the United Nations: A Critique of Instruments and Process* (1986) especially ch IV.

   [3] See United Nations, *Final Clauses of Multilateral Treaties Handbook* (2003) 84–8.

   [4] See generally Sadat-Akhavi (n 2 above) 220–2.

   [5] The clause proposed by the ILO read: 'Nothing in this Convention shall prejudice, or be so applied as to prejudice, the provisions of International Labour Conventions which deal in greater detail with the matters covered by Articles 12 [11 in the final text] and 13 [11] of this Convention.' LA Rehof, *Guide to the Travaux Préparatoires of the United Nations Convention on the Elimination of All Forms of Discrimination Against Women* (1993) 218.

   [6] UN Doc E/CN.6/589 (1974) 42.   [7] UN Doc E/CN.6/608 (1976) 9.

   [8] Proposed by Hungary: UN Doc E/CN.6/589 (1974) para 90.

Nations or the specialized agencies and having as their object the regulation of various aspects of the status of women if they provide for more extensive rights for women.'[9]

The ILO considered that this draft rendered uncertain the extent of States parties' obligations under earlier treaties, and preferred the version of the paragraph without the last clause.[10] As a result of further discussions and amendments in the Working Group of the Third Committee,[11] the final content and wording was agreed,[12] making it clear that the Convention did not intend to undermine in any way either national provisions or other international provisions that were 'more conducive to the achievement of equality between men and women'. Thus, the standard adopted was not whether provisions were more favourable to women, but whether they promoted equality of women and men.

C. Issues of Interpretation

I. Nothing in the Present Convention Shall Affect Any Provisions that Are More Conducive to the Achievement of Equality Between Men and Women Which May Be Contained:

It is difficult to imagine a domestic or international measure promoting equality for women that would go beyond what is permissible under the Convention. Among other provisions, Articles 3 and 24 oblige States parties to 'take all appropriate measures...to ensure the full development and advancement of women' and to 'take all necessary measures...aimed at the full realization of the rights recognized in the...Convention'. Article 23 reflects a concern that the Convention might be restrictively interpreted or used to preserve measures, such as some forms of protective legislation, which, although described as more 'favourable' to women, were in fact based on stereotypes about women's roles.

1. (a) In the Legislation of a State Party; or

This phrase covers national legislation that is more conducive to the attainment of women's equality than the provisions of the Convention. In contrast to other treaties, there is no reference to more favourable 'practice' in a State party.[13]

Article 23(a) does not directly address the relationship between the Convention and a national law that is inconsistent with an obligation imposed by it, for example, a constitutional provision that prohibits temporary special measures that may be required by the Convention. As a matter of international law, the Convention would prevail over

---

[9] Draft art 16(2), UN Doc E/CN.6/608 (1976) 9.

[10] See Communication dated 15 March 1977 addressed to the Secretary-General of the United Nations by the Director-General of the International Labour Office, 'Draft Convention on the Elimination of Discrimination against Women (Article 16, paragraph 2)', Memorandum by the Director-General of the International Labour Office, E/5938 (24 March 1977). See also International Labour Office, 'Note on the Question of Compatibility between the UN Convention on the Elimination of All Forms of Discrimination against Women and Certain ILO Conventions on the Protection of Women', *ILO Official Bulletin*, vol LXVIII, Ser. A, 1985, 40–2.

[11] T Saeki, 'Article 23: Preferential Application of National and International Legislation of Higher Levels of Protection than the Present Convention' in Japanese Association of International Women's Rights (ed), *Convention on the Elimination of All Forms of Discrimination against Women: A Commentary* (1995) 366, 367–8; Rehof (n 5 above) 216–22.

[12] Based on a compromise text almost identical to the final version proposed by the United Kingdom: Rehof (n 5 above) 221.

[13] eg CMW art 81(1).

an inconsistent national law,[14] and the State party's obligation would be to amend the inconsistent national law.

2. (b) In Any Other International Convention, Treaty or Agreement in Force for that State

This phrase covers both universal and regional treaties, and includes both multilateral and bilateral treaties. Article 23(b) provides guidance only as to cases in which the provisions of the Convention and another treaty (whether prior or subsequent) overlap but are consistent with each other, with the other treaty providing for a higher standard—it ensures that the higher standard is applied.

For example, if an earlier treaty required States parties to provide unpaid maternity leave, while a later one required the provision of paid maternity leave, a State party could comply with both obligations by providing paid maternity leave. Or, assume that another human rights treaty required States parties to guarantee not only the right of women to transmit their surnames to their children (required by Convention Article 16(1)(g)), but also the independent right of children to use their mothers' surnames (a right not clearly covered by the Convention[15]). The State party would plainly be obliged to ensure the children's right to assert a separate right to use such names, by virtue of the other treaty. To the extent that this other obligation is intended to remedy the effects of sex discriminatory legislation which allows fathers but not mothers to transmit their surnames as a matter of course, it would be 'conducive to the achievement of equality between men and women', and more so than the Convention. But the situation would be the same in the absence of Article 23(b), whether these provisions appeared in a treaty that preceded the Convention or in a subsequent treaty.

Article 23 does not provide any guidance in relation to cases in which an actual or potential conflict exists between obligations under the Convention and under another treaty, although the early drafts of the article sought to do so by providing for the continuation of existing treaty obligations in relation to women if they conflicted with the new convention. For example, if a treaty adopted prior to the Convention obliged States parties to prohibit women from undertaking night work or underground work, and the Convention required a State party not to discriminate in employment on the ground of sex, the apparent inconsistency in obligation would need to be resolved.[16] The resolution could be reached either by interpretation to harmonize the obligations or by preferring one obligation over another, based on some principle such as *lex specialis* prevailing, or the clear intention of the Convention to override earlier inconsistent treaties.[17] Another example might be a conflict that might arise between a State party's obligations under the Convention to ensure the equality of women and its obligations under the ICCPR to ensure the free exercise of religious beliefs where those beliefs or practices are inconsistent with the Convention's standard of equality.[18]

A further example might be a conflict between the scope of temporary special measures permitted or required by the Convention and the more limited use of special

[14] VCLT art 27.
[15] *Duvauferrier and Frey v France* CEDAW Communication No 12/2007 (2009) para 11.10 (though six Committee members held otherwise in a dissenting opinion).
[16] See Meron (n 2 above) 208–9.
[17] See M Nowak, *UN Covenant on Civil and Political Rights*, 2nd rev edn (2005) 111–12, 117–19.
[18] See Meron (n 2 above) 153–60.

measures permitted under another international or regional treaty. In one case in which this type of issue was raised,[19] a regional court rejected a State party's argument that its use of fixed quotas for certain academic positions in areas where women were grossly under-represented were special measures that did not constitute discrimination (and were therefore not caught by the prohibition on sex discrimination in employment in Directive 76/207/EEC) and that in any case the relevant EC law on the subject should be read in light of its Convention obligations. The Court argued that the Convention's provisions relating to special measures were 'permissive rather than mandatory'[20] and applied the more narrow case law of the ECJ on special measures permitted by Article 2(4) of the Directive, finding the measures to be discriminatory under that Directive.[21] Given that the Convention entered into force for the State party after the adoption of the relevant Directive and that the Committee has taken the view that in some cases special measures may be obligatory to redress persistent inequality, this finding is open to question. However, it is not surprising that a regional court would prefer to prioritize its own regionally based law over a more broadly based international regime, a view apparently shared by the State party.[22]

The general law of treaties provides some guidance for avoiding or resolving conflicts between treaties, although it does not provide completely satisfactory answers where the parties to earlier and later treaties are not the same, and where the treaties overlap but do not completely cover the same subject matter, particularly as regards human rights treaties.[23]

II. Other International Law

In contrast to the savings clauses of CRC Article 41 and CRPD Article 4(4),[24] Article 23 makes no reference to '(other) international law in force' for a State—in effect customary international law. A State's entry into a treaty that covers an area that is also the subject of similar obligations under customary international law does not necessarily displace the customary international law obligation, as this can coexist with the treaty obligation.[25]

The extent to which the non-discrimination norm of the Convention has become part of customary international law is contested. However, it is clear that the norm can be argued in a number of respects to constitute customary international law. If a State party entered a reservation to a Convention provision that was shown to reflect a norm of customary

---

[19] Case E-1/02, *EFTA Surveillance Authority v Norway*, Court of the European Free Trade Association (24 January 2003).

[20] Para 58.   [21] Para 59.

[22] The Norwegian Government representative informed the Committee that the EEA Agreement which incorporated the EC Directive 'had precedence over the Convention because it was a "horizontal" instrument that regulated all aspects of her country's relationship with the European Union (EU)'. UN Doc CEDAW/C/SR.804 (B), 39th Session (2007) paras 48, 49, and 51.

[23] Matz-Lück (n 1 above); Meron (n 2 above).

[24] See, in relation to CRC art 41, United Nations, *Legislative History of the Convention on the Rights of the Child* (2007) vol II, 805–11; S Detrick, 'Article 41' in S Detrick, *A Commentary on the United Nations Convention on the Rights of the Child* (1999) 712–22; and in relation to the right to education in KD Beiter, *The Protection of Right to Education by International Law Including a Systematic Analysis of Article 13 of the International Covenant on Economic, Social and Cultural Rights* (2005) 122–3.

[25] International Court of Justice, *Military and Paramilitary Activities in and against Nicaragua (Nicaragua v United States of America)*, Judgment of 27 June 1986 [1986] ICJ Rep 14 paras 175–8.

international law, then the State would still be bound by the corresponding customary international law rule.[26] Furthermore, if a State party were bound by a customary law norm, the performance of that obligation might be subject to monitoring or adjudication in some other forum, even if its performance did not formally fall within the jurisdiction of the Committee under the reporting or communications procedures.[27]

Nor does Article 23 provide any guidance for the resolution of a conflict between a State party's obligation under the Convention and its obligations under customary international law. What would the relationship be, for example, between a State party's obligation under the Convention to provide a remedy for sexual harassment in employment that takes place within its territory, if the alleged harasser is entitled to claim diplomatic immunity under treaties or customary international law, or the claim is also brought against the foreign State as employer? Would Article 23(b) require the State party to give priority to its obligation under Article 2(b) of the Convention and override any claim to immunity based on treaty or customary international law? Or is the sending State, if a party to the Convention, obliged to waive its immunity to give effect to its own Convention obligations?

The answer to both questions is probably no, whether the source of the obligation to afford immunity is a prior treaty, such as the Vienna Convention on Diplomatic Relations, or a subsequent treaty such as the United Nations Convention on the Jurisdictional Immunities of States and Their Property 2004, or customary international law. The rationale for this conclusion is likely to be couched in terms of the maxim *lex specialis derogat lege generali* (specific provisions prevail over general provisions) or as following from the requirement that in the interpretation of a treaty States must take into account 'any relevant rules of international law applicable in the relations between the parties'[28] (here State or diplomatic immunity, which can generally only be lifted by express words or necessary intendment[29]); or that this is a reasonable limitation on the right of the person, particularly if in theory options exist to bring a case against the person in the other State.[30]

D. Interpretation by the Committee—General Approach

The Committee has made few explicit references to Article 23. However, it has occasionally commented on the effect of Article 23 in cases where the State party has entered reservations to the Convention that seek to preserve national laws that are more favourable to women or that the State party considers may not be fully in compliance with the Convention, in some cases as the result of an abundance of caution on the State's part. For example, in one case where the Committee considered that a State party was unduly cautious in considering that its legislation was not consistent with the Convention, it urged the State party 'to study carefully the nature and thrust of the remaining reservations within the context of article 23 of the Convention . . . and the Vienna Convention

---

[26] Ibid.   [27] Ibid.   [28] VCLT art 31(3)(c).

[29] cf *Al-Adsani v United Kingdom*, Application No 35763/07, European Court of Human Rights, judgment of the Grand Chamber (21 November 2001); *Fogarty v United Kingdom*, Application No 37112/97, European Court of Human Rights, judgment of the Grand Chamber (10 October 2001).

[30] cf *Cudak v Lithuania*, Application No 15869/02, European Court of Human Rights, judgment of the Grand Chamber (23 March 2010).

on the Law of Treaties, with the aim of withdrawing them as soon as possible'.[31] The Committee has also called on one State party to withdraw reservations to the Convention where it 'ha[d] not entered reservations to other human rights treaties, which all contain the principle of equality between women and men and the prohibition of discrimination on the basis of sex',[32] and noted that another State party, despite entering reservations to the Convention 'did not enter any reservations to the International Covenant on Civil and Political Rights, which also requires equality between women and men' in relation to inheritance and marriage and divorce.[33] This underlines that, notwithstanding their reservations to the Convention, these States parties would still be internationally obligated under those other treaties not to discriminate in this manner, and there would appear to be little point in maintaining reservations to the Convention since the more extensive obligation under the other treaty would prevail.[34]

E. Reservations, Declarations, and Understandings

A number of States parties have made declarations or entered 'reservations' that attempt to preserve national measures that are 'more favourable' to women than to men. For example, France 'declare[d] that no provision of the Convention must be interpreted as prevailing over provisions of French legislation which are more favourable to women than to men'. Similar declarations were made by Monaco, Ireland, and the United Kingdom.

The point of such 'reservations' is that because the Convention obliges States parties to address discrimination against women, and these measures—if discriminatory at all—could only involve discrimination against men, they would not be inconsistent with the Convention (though they might be covered by the obligation in other treaties not to discriminate on the ground of sex). Of course, some of these measures might be intended to achieve substantive equality or temporary special measures. If so, they would be consistent with the Convention[35] and would not violate other treaty obligations to ensure gender equality.

However, not all provisions that are 'more favourable to women' are thereby free of discrimination against women. Some protective legislation is based on stereotypes that ultimately disadvantage women and would therefore be inconsistent with the Convention, unless covered by provisions such as Article 11(3). In such cases, the declarations would constitute genuine reservations to the Convention, and the question of their compatibility with the object and purpose of the treaty would arise.

---

[31] See CO Ireland, A/60/38, 33rd Session (2005) para 399 and discussion at CEDAW/C/SR.693 para 56 (2005) (Ms Schöpp-Schilling).

[32] CO Niger, CEDAW/C/NER/CO/2 (2007) para 9 and CEDAW/C/SR.789 (2007) para 7 (Ms Schöpp-Schilling).

[33] CO Libya, CEDAW/C/LBY/CO/5 (2009) para 13. See also CO Tunisia, CEDAW/C/TUN/CO/6 (2010) para 12 and CEDAW/C/SR.949 (2010) para 11 (Mr Flinterman).

[34] See also L Lijnzaad, *Reservations to UN-Human Rights Treaties: Ratify and Ruin?* (1995) 370.

[35] CO Ireland, A/60/38, 33rd Session (2005) para 399 and discussion at CEDAW/C/SR.693 (2005) para 56 (Ms Schöpp-Schilling).

Article 24

States Parties undertake to adopt all necessary measures at the national level aimed at achieving the full realization of the rights recognized in the present Convention.

A. Introduction

Article 24 at first sight seems to state an obvious principle of international law: that States parties must take measures at the domestic level to give effect to the obligations they accept under the treaty. It also appears to repeat, and to be largely subsumed by, other general obligations set out earlier in the Convention, in particular Articles 2, 3, 4, and 5. The placement of the article—which imposes substantive obligations—in a part of the Convention which otherwise deals with formal matters and establishes the machinery for the international monitoring of the Convention, is awkward.

As noted above,[1] Articles 2, 3, and 24 are closely linked and overlapping articles, and it is difficult to suggest that the omission of Article 24 from the Convention would have any significant impact on the broad obligations of the State party to take all necessary measures to achieve the realization of its Convention obligations at the national level. Indeed, some commentators have suggested that Article 24 may be 'redundant'.[2] None the

---

* I would like to thank Professor Dianne Otto for her comments on the chapters on arts 1 and 2; Luke Beck, Renée Chartres, Maria Herminía Graterol, and Eleanor Bath for their research assistance, and the University of New South Wales for Goldstar and Faculty of Law funding to support research for this chapter and the chapters on arts 1, 2, and 23.

[1] See the discussion in chapter on art 2.

[2] N Burrows, 'The 1979 Convention on the Elimination of All Forms of Discrimination Against Women' (1985) 32 *Netherlands Intl L Rev* 419, 427. Takeshi Yamashita makes a similar comment: 'Article 24: The Full Realization of the Rights Recognized in the Convention' in Japanese Association of International Women's Rights (ed), *Convention on the Elimination of All Forms of Discrimination against Women: A Commentary* (1995) 373, 376.

less, the drafters included Article 24 in the Convention as a separate article; accordingly, it is appropriate to consider its history and potential additional role, as well as to analyze the reference States parties and the Committee have made to Article 24 in their practice under the Convention.[3]

B. Travaux Préparatoires

What was to become Article 24 started life as part of proposals related to the monitoring and implementation machinery for the Convention put forward at the 1976 session of the CSW. Separate proposals put forward by Egypt and Denmark[4] were combined into a draft (then draft Article 19[5]) which provided that 'the States Parties undertake to adopt measures at the national level, including the establishment of machinery and procedures aimed at achieving the full realization of the rights recognized in the present Convention'.

The draft article also provided that States parties would submit reports on their implementation of the Convention to the Secretary-General of the United Nations, for consideration by a working group of the CSW which would report to the Commission. The drafts provided that States parties 'shall make use of national machinery established to promote the advancement of women', as well as of NGOs.[6] Some minor changes were made to the draft when it reached the Working Group of the Third Committee of the General Assembly. These included the omission of the references to 'machinery' (some States supported this amendment because it would make the article 'more comprehensive') and to 'the establishment of procedures', while the words 'all' and 'necessary' were added before 'measures'.[7] The language adopted by the Working Group and the Third Committee as draft Article 20(1) thus contained the wording that now appears in Article 24, though it was still part of an article which included international monitoring procedures. Draft Article 20(1) was removed from the monitoring provisions in draft Article 20 (now Articles 17 and 18) and included as a separate Article 24.

C. Issues of Interpretation

The inclusion of Article 24 as an independent article in the Convention and the drafting history indicates that the drafters intended it to have some substantive content. The article can be viewed as affirming that the Convention is an instrument which imposes obligations to take positive measures at the national level to ensure the realization of equality between women and men in addition to the emphasis in Article 2 on eliminating discrimination, and that these measures should be comprehensive and should also include national level machinery to give effect to the Convention. The emphasis is on 'full realization' of the rights guaranteed. One commentator suggests that this article might be seen as a response to any perception that the Convention was merely a

---

[3] See Yamashita (n 2 above) 376.
[4] UN Doc E/CN.6/508 paras 190–1. Egypt's draft provided: '1. Each State Party undertakes to promote the establishment at the national level of procedures aimed at achieving progressively the full realization of the rights recognized in the present Convention.' (UN Doc E/CN.6.L.708).
[5] UN Doc E/CN.6/L.715 in E/CN.6/508 para 192.   [6] Draft art 19(b).
[7] UN Doc A/C.3/34/14, 9.

programmatic or policy instrument that did not impose legally binding obligations on States parties.[8]

I. Undertake to Adopt

The word 'undertake' indicates the acceptance of a legal obligation—here to 'adopt' the measures referred to in the article. The question arises whether this is an obligation of immediate applicability or one which indicates some form of progressive realization of the specified goals.[9] As the word 'progressively' was eliminated from the early draft of the article, and an obligation to 'promote' was replaced by an obligation 'to adopt',[10] the obligation became immediate and action-oriented.

This obligation is to 'adopt' measures formulated with the purpose of achieving the full realization of rights and tailored to their achievement; it does not necessarily suggest an obligation of immediate realization of the goals set out.

II. All Necessary Measures

The phrase '[all] necessary measures' appears only here in the Convention—other references are to 'appropriate measures'. The language connotes a broad commitment. The word 'all' underlines that States parties' commitments are not to be half-hearted or partial; the phrase has 'a fairly strong connotation'.[11] The word 'necessary' is not limiting but rather underlines the need for States parties to take decisive action, to do everything that is necessary to achieve the full realization of the rights. The inclusion of the word 'all' and the removal of the reference to machinery and procedures during the drafting underline the comprehensive scope of the required measures. They should involve a comprehensive strategy and programme to achieve the goals of the Convention, as reinforced by the phrase 'aimed at achieving the full realization' of the rights. The use of the phrase 'necessary measures' implies that a range of legislative, policy, programmatic, educational, and similar measures may need to be used, and the phrase would also include positive action or temporary special measures referred to in Article 4.[12]

III. At the National Level

This reference reflects the article's origin as part of a provision that included both international and national level measures. These include measures to be taken by the executive, the legislature, and the judiciary, and include the translation of the rights under the Convention into the domestic legal system, though this would not necessarily require direct incorporation of the treaty into domestic law.[13] Educational measures, including dissemination of material about the Convention and the Committee, are also included.

---

[8] See Yamashita (n 2 above) 376, referring to McKean's assertion that 'this Convention is promotional and programmatic; it does not impose immediately binding legal obligations but requires parties to take "all appropriate measures"' (WA McKean, *Equality and Discrimination under International Law* (1983) 193).

[9] See Yamashita (n 2 above) 379. LA Rehof, *Guide to the Travaux Préparatoires of the United Nations Convention on the Elimination of All Forms of Discrimination Against Women* (1993) 224–5.

[10] Yamashita (n 2 above) 379.   [11] Ibid 378.   [12] See GR 25 para 24.

[13] Though Yamashita (n 2 above) 382–4 suggests this.

IV. Aimed at Achieving the Full Realization

The phrase 'full realization' makes it clear that the obligation is a comprehensive one, to cover all areas of life, and also that it would extend not just to *de jure* but also to *de facto* enjoyment of rights.

V. Of the Rights Recognized in the Present Convention

The Convention contains few provisions which are actually statements of rights guarantees (Articles 9 and 15 are two such statements). However, the language of this phrase is not 'the rights set forth in the Convention', as it is in Article 2 of the Optional Protocol, but the 'rights recognized in the...Convention'. This phrase has a parallel in ICCPR Article 2(1) ('rights recognised in the present Covenant').

This language raises a question as to the scope of the Article 24 obligation: is it limited to those provisions of the Convention that can be viewed as setting out guarantees of rights; does it extend to all the substantive areas mentioned in the Convention (the State party's obligation to eliminate discrimination can be read as implying a corresponding right not to be subject to discrimination in those areas); or does it include all human rights and fundamental freedoms referred to in the definition of 'discrimination against women' in Article 1?

One commentator has suggested that the scope of Article 24 is limited to the areas covered in the Convention's substantive articles, and that the article's distinctive contribution is a focus on the positive aspects of ensuring the enjoyment of equality in those areas, as opposed to the Article 2 focus on eliminating discrimination.[14] However, this seems an unduly narrow interpretation of a provision intended by the drafters to be comprehensive in scope, in a human rights convention which should normally be construed generously. Furthermore, the Preamble to the Convention states:

> Noting that the Universal Declaration of Human Rights affirms the principle of the inadmissibility of discrimination and proclaims that all human beings are born free and equal in dignity and rights and that everyone is entitled to all the rights and freedoms set forth therein, without distinction of any kind, including distinction based on sex,

> Noting that the States Parties to the International Covenants on Human Rights have the obligation to ensure the equal right of men and women to enjoy all economic, social, cultural, civil and political rights...

This appears to be a clear recognition in the Convention of a comprehensive set of human rights and fundamental freedoms, and the better interpretation of Article 24 would be that it extends, as does Article 1, to eliminating discrimination against women and promoting equality in the enjoyment of all fundamental human rights and freedoms.

D. Interpretation by the Committee—General Approach

The Committee's practice gives little guidance as to whether Article 24 has independent content. The Committee frequently refers to States parties' obligations under 'Articles 2, 3, and 24' together, but rarely refers to Article 24 alone.

---

[14] Ibid 377.

For example, General Recommendation 12 (equality in family life) states:

43. Consistent with articles 2, 3 and 24 in particular, the Committee requires that all States parties gradually progress to a stage where, by its resolute discouragement of notions of the inequality of women in the home, each country will withdraw its reservation, in particular to articles 9, 15 and 16 of the Convention...

50. Assisted by the comments in the present general recommendation, and as required by articles 2, 3 and 24, States parties should introduce measures directed at encouraging full compliance with the principles of the Convention, particularly where religious or private law or custom conflict with those principles.[15]

The Committee's reference to Article 24 in concluding observations has been inconsistent, reflecting, in part, its method of examining reports and the structure of its concluding comments, which generally proceed sequentially through the substantive articles of the Convention. Article 24, which appears in the procedural implementation section, therefore receives little or no focused attention. Nevertheless, on some occasions the Committee has referred to it, making specific suggestions at the end of its concluding observations and referring to the article. On other occasions, however, it makes similar recommendations without any reference to Article 24.

In its concluding observations on the report of one State party, the Committee stated:

In line with article 24 of the Convention and article 13 of its Optional Protocol, the Committee calls upon the State party to take concrete measures to make the Convention and its Optional Protocol widely known. In this respect, the Committee requests the State party to undertake public awareness and training programmes on the Convention and its Optional Protocol, as well as on the Committee's general recommendations.[16]

Similarly, in its concluding observations on another State party, the Committee called on the State party:

to take additional measures to ensure that the Convention is sufficiently known and applied by all branches of Government as a framework for all laws, court verdicts and policies on gender equality and the advancement of women, including the adoption of a new classification system of court cases. The Committee also calls upon the State party to take, in line with its obligations under article 24 of the Convention and article 13 of its Optional Protocol, concrete measures to make the two treaties, as well as the Committee's general recommendations, widely known.[17]

Similar recommendations made to other States parties in the same time frame made no reference to Article 24.[18]

In 2008, the Committee adopted a structure of headings to be used in its concluding observations,[19] which includes, towards the end of the list of topics to be addressed, national human rights institutions, national parliaments, collection of sex-disaggregated data and statistics, and dissemination of information about the Convention. This suggests that the Committee sees these as falling within Article 24, as they relate to implementation

---

[15] See GR 12 and GR 28.   [16] CO The United Kingdom, A/63/38, 41st Session (2008) para 263.
[17] CO Lithuania, CEDAW/C/LTU/CO/4(2008) para 67.
[18] CO The Netherlands, CEDAW/C/NLD/CO/5(2010) para 51. See also CO Egypt, CEDAW/C/EGY/CO/7 (2010) para 57.
[19] UN Doc A/63/38 part II (2008) Annex X, 261.

measures 'at the national level' as mandated by the article.[20] But equally, the Committee has referred to these matters in the context of other articles, including Articles 2 and 3. The following section discusses two national mechanisms to which the Committee has devoted significant attention in its practice and concluding observations.

I. Parliaments/Legislatures

The Committee has long stressed the important role that parliaments play in Convention implementation. In its 2010 statement on the issue, the Committee drew on its experience to set out the various contributions that parliaments can make.[21] It noted that 'Parliaments and their members have a vital role to play in ensuring respect for the principles enunciated in the Convention and they have a wide range of tools at their disposal to do so'.[22] It sees parliaments as playing both a substantive and a procedural role in the implementation by holding the executive government accountable and taking 'active measures to ensure that laws, policies, actions, programmes and budgets reflect the principles and obligations in the Convention'.[23]

The Committee has also noted that parliaments can play an important and beneficial role in the reporting process, in particular, by following up the concluding observations of the Committee as well as through their overall monitoring role. The Committee now includes in its concluding observations a standard paragraph on the role of legislatures, generally along the following lines:

> While reaffirming that the Government has the primary responsibility, and is accountable in particular, for the full implementation of the State party's obligations under the Convention, the Committee, stressing that the Convention is binding on all branches of Government, invites the State party to encourage its national Parliament, in line with its procedures, where appropriate, to take the necessary steps with regard to the implementation of the present concluding observations and the Government's next reporting process under the Convention.[24]

II. National Human Rights Institutions

The Committee has placed increasing emphasis on the role that independent national human rights institutions can play in the implementation of the Convention. In its 2008 statement on its relationship with NHRIs, it noted that NHRIs play an 'important role in the promotion of the implementation of the Convention . . . at the national level, the protection of women's human rights as well as the enhancement of public awareness of such rights'.[25] It has urged NHRIs to ensure that their activities reflect the principles of formal and substantive equality embodied in the Convention, that women have ready access to NHRIs for the protection of their rights, and that NHRIs have a gender-balanced membership and staff.[26] The Committee has also called on NHRIs to disseminate the

---

[20] Though the Committee's statements on NHRIs or on national parliaments makes specific reference to art 24. See nn 24 and 28 below.

[21] *National Parliaments and the Convention on the Elimination of All Forms of Discrimination against Women: Statement by the Committee on the Elimination of Discrimination against Women on its Relationship with Parliamentarians*, Decision 45/VII, A/65/38 (Supp) part II, 45th Session (2009) Annex VI, 84.

[22] Ibid para 4.   [23] Para 4.   [24] CO Botswana, CEDAW/C/BOT/CO/3 (2010) para 8.

[25] *Statement by the Committee on the Elimination of Discrimination against Women on its Relationship with National Human Rights Institutions*, Decision 40/II, A/63/38 (Supp) part I, 40th Session (2008) Annex II, 142 para 3.

[26] Ibid para 4.

Convention and the OP, and its concluding observations, general recommendations, and views, as well as to monitor implementation of the Convention.[27]

The Committee has noted the significant role that NHRIs may play in the reporting procedure by providing independent information to it and addressing it, as well as by supporting alleged victims in bringing cases to the Committee.[28] The Committee regularly receives information from, and is addressed by NHRIs.

The Committee urges States parties that have not yet established independent NHRIs which comply with the Paris Principles[29] to do so, and to ensure that the institutions have an appropriate mandate to monitor the effective implementation of the Convention and promote women's equality.[30]

E. Reservations, Declarations, and Understandings

There are no reservations or declarations relating specifically to Article 24, though general reservations to the Convention would apply to it. Where a State party has entered a broad reservation to Article 2, but no similar reservation to Article 24, the question arises of whether the State party is bound by Article 24 if it covers similar obligations to those in the provisions to which reservations have been made.

---

[27] Ibid para 5.   [28] Ibid paras 6–7.
[29] *Principles Relating to the Status of National Institutions*, GA resolution 48/134, Annex (1993).
[30] See eg CO Lao PDR, CEDAW/C/LAO/CO/7 (2010) paras 13–14; CO Papua New Guinea, CEDAW/C/PNG/CO/3 (2010) paras 19–20; CO Turkey, CEDAW/C/TUR/CO/6 (2010) paras 42–3; CO Botswana, CEDAW/C/BOT/CO/3 (2010) paras 17–18; CO Iceland, A/63/38 part II, 41st Session (2008) para 239; CO Japan, A/58/38 part II, 29th Session (2003) para 374.

Article 25

(1) The present Convention shall be open for signature by all States.

(2) The Secretary-General of the United Nations is designated as the depositary of the present Convention.

(3) The present Convention is subject to ratification. Instruments of ratification shall be deposited with the Secretary-General of the United Nations.

(4) The present Convention shall be open to accession by all States. Accession shall be effected by the deposit of an instrument of accession with the Secretary-General of the United Nations.

A. Introduction

Article 25 stipulates the procedures required to become a party to the Convention through signature and ratification; it declares the UN Secretary-General (UN SG) as the depositary; and it allows for accession which, in practice, includes succession.[1] The Convention is open to all States in the world.

* I would like to thank Sahrah Al-Nasrawe-Sözeri, Benjamin Feyen, Ines Franke, Anna-Maria Paulus, Allison Sherrier, and Eric Veillerobe for their assistance on this chapter and on the chapters on arts 26, 27, 29, and 30.

[1] See section D. IV. below.

B. Travaux Préparatoires

The content of this article only came up at the final deliberations on the Convention. The USSR proposed a draft article whereby States were able to sign or accede to the Convention.[2] The United Kingdom and UNESCO argued for more specificity insofar as signature is followed by ratification.[3] The ILO issued a statement which aimed at governments having to ensure, *inter alia,* that obligations under the Convention would not conflict with obligations already incurred under existing international instruments.[4] At the 26th session of the CSW, the text was divided into three paragraphs with a separate paragraph dedicated to ratification. During the meetings of the Working Group of the Third Committee of the UNGA, a further paragraph was added at the initiative of the United Kingdom, the USSR, and the Byelorussian SSR stipulating the UN SG as depositary of the Convention. The phrase 'by any State' was revised to 'by all States' to emphasize the goal of universality.

C. Practice of States Parties

The Convention was adopted by the UNGA in resolution 34/180 on 18 December 1979, and was open for signature at the Copenhagen Conference on 17 July 1980, where sixty-four States signed it. As of 31 December 2010, 186 States[5] have become parties to the Convention, 96 by means of signature and ratification, 82 States by accession, and 8 States by way of succession.[6] By signing the Convention, the State party is obliged to refrain from acts which would defeat the object and purpose of a treaty.[7]

D. Issues of Interpretation

The Convention's final provisions, Articles 25, 26, 27, 29, and 30, have not been a major subject of interpretation by the Committee. Thus, unlike other chapters in the Commentary, the chapters on these Articles make little mention of the Committee approach. Final provisions are dealt with in general terms in the VCLT and the specific provisions supplement it. The UN Treaty Handbook also provides information on UN practice.

I. Article 25(1)

Article 25(1) opens the Convention for signature by all States, both UN member States and non-member States, in accordance with the drafters' intent that it would be an instrument of universal scope. The Convention remains open for signature indefinitely as is the case with most multilateral human rights treaties for which universal participation is a paramount goal. Signing a treaty is, apart from its function of authentication

---

[2] UN Doc E/CN.6/AC.1/L.2 (1974) 10; LA Rehof, *Guide to the Travaux Préparatoires of the United Nations Convention on the Elimination of All Forms of Discrimination against Women* (1993) 226–7.

[3] Rehof (n 2 above) 227.   [4] Ibid.

[5] Number of States parties to other international human rights treaties: 147 (CAT), 141 (Genocide Convention), 137 (CERD), 193 (CRC), 88 (CRPD), 166 (ICCPR), 160 (ICESCR).

[6] See <http://treaties.un.org/Pages/ViewDetails.aspx?src=TREATY&mtdsg_no=IV-8&chapter=4&lang=en> accessed 31 December 2010.

[7] See the discussion in the Introduction (history) and ch on art 27.

of the text, one of the most common first steps in the process of becoming party to that treaty. The Convention must be signed by someone with full powers under the VCLT,[8] typically one of the three authorities specified in the UN Treaty Handbook: the Head of State, Head of Government, or Minister for Foreign Affairs.[9] Signature implies the State's intention to take measures to express its will to be bound by the treaty at a later date[10] and entitles it to proceed to ratification, as well as to receive depositary notifications and communications relating to the Convention.[11] According to VCLT Article 18(a), signature also incurs the obligation to refrain in good faith from acts which would defeat the object and purpose of the treaty.

In contrast to the earlier UN human rights treaties, which provide for signature by UN member States only,[12] the Convention takes a comprehensive approach by opening it to non-member States of the UN, such as Switzerland, which ratified the Convention in 1987 but joined the UN in 2002, and also to States other than the negotiating ones. The Convention changed the practice in this regard since the later UN human rights treaties almost all allow for 'all States'.[13] However, the phrase 'all States' implies that only independent States which fulfil all the elements of statehood under international law are entitled to sign, ratify, or accede to the Convention.[14] This raises the question whether territories or entities, whose status as sovereign States is unclear or contested, are able to do so. The UN SG is not competent to determine whether a certain territory or entity falls within this wording.[15]

Since the Convention does not contain a specific territorial application clause,[16] it is—in accordance with the basic principle of VCLT Article 29—binding upon a State in respect to its entire territory. Difficulties as to the duty to report can arise when parts of a State's territory become autonomous but remain within the binding effect of the Convention. Such a situation may arise in the case of non-State entities such as crown dependencies, overseas territories, former colonies, *de facto* regimes, or non-State subjects of international law and municipalities. The following sections illustrate the issues which can arise.

1. Crown Dependencies and Overseas Territories; Former Colonies

a) United Kingdom

The United Kingdom crown dependencies and overseas territories are not part of the UK, but the UK is responsible for their external affairs. UK legislation does not extend to them. The UK's 1986 instrument of ratification specified ratification in respect of the United Kingdom of Great Britain and Northern Ireland, the Isle of Man, British Virgin Islands, Falkland Islands (Malvinas), South Georgia and the South Sandwich

---

[8] VCLT art 7.   [9] UN, *Treaty Handbook* (2006) 10.   [10] VCLT art 14.

[11] VCLT art 77(1)(e).

[12] ICESCR art 26; ICCPR art 48. ICERD art 17 is somewhat broader, allowing for ratification by UN Member States, members of the specialized agencies, parties to the Statute of the ICJ, and States invited by the UNGA to ratify.

[13] CAT art 25; CRC art 46; CMW art 86 and CRPD art 42; except CED art 38 ('all Member States of the United Nations').

[14] I Brownlie, *Principles of Public International Law*, 7th edn (2008) 69–70.

[15] Compare section D. II. below on UNGA guidance to UN SG on this issue.

[16] A treaty provision whereupon a State party can declare that the treaty shall extend to all or specific of the territories for whose international relations it is responsible; eg ECHR art 63.

Islands, and Turks and Caicos Islands.[17] The UK reports for its crown dependencies and overseas territories and is currently working towards extending the UK's ratification of the Convention to all populated overseas territories.

b) The Netherlands

The Netherlands ratified the Convention in 1991 for the Kingdom in Europe, the Netherlands Antilles and Aruba.[18] The Antilles and Aruba submit separate reports (although the Netherlands should provide one consolidated report).[19] As of 10 October 2010, the Antilles was dissolved as a unified political entity.[20] This may imply that the two new territories Curaçao and Sint Maarten will submit their own reports, as has been the case for Aruba.[21]

c) New Zealand

New Zealand's 1985 instrument of ratification indicated that the Convention should extend to the Cook Islands and Nuie. Formerly administered by New Zealand, the Cook Islands and Niue currently have the status of self-governing States in free association with New Zealand. The responsibility of the Cook Islands and Niue to conduct their own international relations and particularly to conclude treaties has evolved substantially over the years. As a result of these developments, the UN SG, as Convention depositary, recognized the full treaty-making capacity of the Cook Islands in 1992 and of Niue in 1994. The Cook Islands acceded to the Convention on 11 August 2006 whereas Niue has not done so. Arguably, the Convention is applicable to Niue through automatic succession.[22]

d) Hong Kong

The Convention has applied to Hong Kong since 14 October 1996, when the UK Government extended the Convention to the then dependent territory which had been a British colony for 156 years. Under the Sino-British Joint Declaration,[23] the People's Republic of China (the PRC) resumed sovereignty over Hong Kong on 1 July 1997. From that date, the Convention, which the PRC had ratified on 4 November 1980, has continued to apply to the Hong Kong Special Administrative Region pursuant to the assumption by the Central People's Government of the PRC of obligations under the Convention in relation to Hong Kong. The PRC made the same declarations and reservations *mutatis mutandis* which were made by the UK in connection with the extension of the Convention to Hong Kong.[24] Although it remains doubtful whether such a declaration is of declaratory or constitutive nature, the possibility of its producing a binding effect cannot be dismissed. The only reservation the PRC had made upon its

---

[17] See <http://treaties.un.org/Pages/ViewDetails.aspx?src=TREATY&mtdsg_no=IV-8&chapter=4&lang=en#63> accessed 31 December 2010.

[18] See <http://treaties.un.org/Pages/ViewDetails.aspx?src=TREATY&mtdsg_no=IV-8&chapter=4&lang=en#43> accessed 31 December 2010.

[19] CO The Netherlands, CEDAW/C/NLD/CO/5 (2010) paras 14–15.

[20] Bonaire, Saba, and Sint Eustatius became Dutch special municipalities.

[21] CO The Netherlands, CEDAW/C/NLD/CO/4 (2007) para 2; CO The Netherlands, CEDAW/C/NLD/CO/5 (2010) para 2.

[22] See section D. IV. below.

[23] Joint Declaration of the Government of the United Kingdom of Great Britain and Northern Ireland and the Government of the People's Republic of China on the Question of Hong Kong 1984, 1339 UNTS 36.

[24] <http://treaties.un.org/Pages/ViewDetails.aspx?src=TREATY&mtdsg_no=IV-8&chapter=4&lang=en#14> accessed 31 December 2010.

ratification was that it does not consider itself bound by Article 29(1).[25] In view of the so-called 'moving treaty boundaries' principle,[26] as codified in Article 15 of the Vienna Convention on Succession of States in Respect of Treaties and recently applied to Hong Kong,[27] the Convention including the reservations made by the PRC extends *ipso facto* to Hong Kong.

2. De Facto Regimes, Non-State Subjects of International Law, and Municipalities

a) *De Facto* Regimes, Including Taiwan

De facto regimes are entities claiming to be States or governments, which control more or less clearly defined territories without being recognized—at least by many States—as States or governments.[28] *De facto* regimes such as Taiwan (Republic of China) cannot become bound to human rights treaties directly, because Article 25(1) permits signature only by States. *De facto* regimes can become bound to treaties by means of special agreements with another State or an international organization.[29] They do not become States parties to the Convention, and are bound under international law only in relation to the other party to the special agreement. Such special agreements refer to the substantive but not the procedural obligations of the treaty. Since Taiwan has not concluded any special agreements it is not bound to the Convention. In 2007, Taiwan's legislative Yuan incorporated the stipulations of the Convention into its domestic legislation, but in accordance with the UNGA resolution on the restoration of the lawful rights of the People's Republic of China in the United Nations[30] the UN SG did not consider this act as ratification.[31] Therefore, Taiwan is not bound to the Convention under international law, but internally.

b) Holy See

The Holy See, whose international legal personality is best defined *sui generis*,[32] is legally competent to ratify multilateral treaties.[33] It has not signed or ratified the Convention. The Holy See Mission to the UN, as a permanent observer at the UN, has stated that there are parts of the Convention (Articles 12, 14, and 16 as regards the rights of women to access family planning services) which make it impossible for the Holy See to accept obligations under the Convention.[34]

---

[25] See the discussion in ch on art 29(1).

[26] The 'moving treaty boundaries' principle means that when an existing State acquires territory, it does not succeed to the predecessor State's treaties; but its own treaty ratifications normally become applicable to that territory.

[27] A Zimmermann, 'State Succession in Treaties' in R Wolfrum (ed), *The Max Planck Encyclopedia of Public International Law* (2008) para 8, online edition <www.mpepil.com> accessed 31 December 2010.

[28] JA Frowein, 'De facto regimes' in R Wolfrum (ed), *The Max Planck Encyclopedia of Public International Law* (2008) para 1, online edition <www.mpepil.com> accessed 31 December 2010.

[29] The most frequent examples are human rights agreements within the framework of restoring peace or of humanitarian assistance; M Schoiswohl, *Status and (Human Rights Obligations) of Non-Recognized De Facto Regimes in International Law: The Case of Somaliland* (2004) 221.

[30] UNGA Res 2758 (XXVI) (25 October 1997).

[31] Government Information Office, Republic of China (Taiwan) 'Taiwan Aims to Sign Up Against Discrimination' (2006).

[32] G Westdickenberg, 'Holy See' in R Wolfrum (ed), *The Max Planck Encyclopedia of Public International Law* (2008) para 3, online edition <www.mpepil.com> accessed 31 December 2010.

[33] The Holy See has ratified ICERD, CRC, and CAT.

[34] <http://www.wf-f.org/CEDAW-ActionAlert.html> accessed 31 December 2010.

c) São Paulo State, Brazil

In 1992, the State of São Paulo and many São Paulo municipalities adopted the 'Paulista Convention on the Elimination of All Forms of Discrimination against Women'[35] following negotiations between women's NGOs and local government authorities. Since municipalities do not have international legal personality, no obligations under international law flow from this act. However, actions such as this can make the CEDAW Convention part of public administration. The Paulista Convention contains detailed responsibilities for State and local governments to advance women's human rights in the areas of public administration, day care, education, health care, employment, and the prevention of violence against women.[36]

d) San Francisco, California, USA

In 1998, San Francisco adopted the Convention as a city ordinance.[37] The underlying principles of the Convention take effect as a matter of local government policy.[38] The city of Los Angeles, California did the same in 2003. Since the United States is one of the few States which have not ratified the Convention, this local ordinance reflecting the Convention's principles can be considered as moral leverage to promote US ratification, as well as to promote realization of its principles on a municipal level.

II. Article 25(2)

Article 25(2) designates the UN SG as the depositary of the Convention. The provision refers to the deposit of the text of the Convention and everything which is not mentioned in Article 25(3) and (4) (instruments of ratification and accession, including reservations and interpretive declarations attached thereto)[39] or Article 30 (text in all six authentic languages).[40]

All treaties concluded under UN auspices should be worded to confer depositary functions only on the UN SG.[41] The role and function of the UN SG are determined by the relevant provisions of the Convention and VCLT Articles 76 and 77. As depositary, the UN SG is responsible for ensuring the proper execution of all treaty actions. Among the duties of the depositary is that of informing all interested parties, by way of depositary notifications, of any action relating to the treaties deposited with the UN SG. Other communications concerning agreements which the UN SG may find necessary to circulate for the information of UN member States, are circulated by him as Chief Administrative Officer of the UN and not as treaty depositary. The depositary's duties are

---

[35] Paulista Convention on the Elimination of All Forms of Discrimination against Women (*Convencão Paulista Sobre a Eliminação de Todas as Formas de Discriminação contra a Mulher*), International Women's Rights Action Watch translation of the Portuguese original.

[36] I Landsberg-Lewis (ed), *Bringing Equality Home: Implementing the Convention on the Elimination of All Forms of Discrimination Against Women* (1999), see <http://www.unifem.undp.org/cedaw/indexen.htm> accessed 31 December 2010.

[37] CEDAW Ordinance, City and County of San Francisco Municipal Code Administrative Code §12K.1 (2000). The original City and County of San Francisco Ordinance 128–98 was approved on 13 April 1998. It was renumbered and amended by Ordinance 325-00, File No. 001920, approved on 31 December 2000, see <http://www.sfgov3.org/index.aspx?page=130> accessed 31 December 2010.

[38] The local ordinance established a CEDAW Committee which works with the Commission and city departments to identify discrimination against women and girls, and to implement human rights principles throughout the city.

[39] See section D. III. and IV. below.   [40] See the discussion in ch on art 30.

[41] UN, *Summary of Practice of the Secretary-General as Depositary* (1994) (ST/LEG/7/Rev.1) 7.

international in character and must be performed impartially.[42] In practice, the UN SG has assigned depositary functions to the Treaty Section of the UN Office of Legal Affairs of the Secretariat because of the paramount concern that these functions be performed in a legally correct and absolutely consistent manner and that all information on UN treaties be available in and published by one office.[43] For example, after the deposit of a binding instrument with the UN SG, the Office of Legal Affairs must make sure that the instrument submitted is correct as to form and content.[44]

As the principal depositary, the UN SG is frequently consulted on treaty questions, such as with respect to final clauses and amendment procedures. Upon request, the UN SG, as depositary, provides up-to-date information on the status of the treaties[45] (in addition to the circulation of the publication Multilateral Treaties Deposited with the UN SG[46]). The Office of Legal Affairs provides on his behalf, for example, updated information for inclusion in the UN SG's report to the Meeting of States Parties to the Convention on the Elimination of All Forms of Discrimination against Women.[47] The UNGA has determined that the UN SG is not competent as depositary to determine whether a territory or another entity would fall within the 'all States' formula.[48] It issued a general understanding[49] in 1973 stating that 'the Secretary-General, in discharging his functions as a depositary of a convention with an "all States" clause, will follow the practice of the Assembly in implementing such a clause and, whenever advisable, will request the opinion of the Assembly before receiving a signature or an instrument of ratification or accession.'[50] Since this statement, the UNGA has occasionally given guidance on whether it considered a certain territory or entity to be a State,[51] which the UN SG follows.

III. Article 25(3)

Article 25(3) provides that the Convention requires ratification as the final procedural step for its entry into force for signatory States. Most multilateral treaties provide for signature subject to ratification;[52] the Convention provides for ratification with or without preceding signature. The Convention provides no time limit for ratification after signature. Ratification is a formal declaration by the organ of a State with the authority under internal law to conclude treaties, by which that State expresses its consent to be bound by the treaty.[53] Through that concrete act, the State demonstrates its acceptance of the formal and substantive rights and obligations contained in the Convention. Providing for signature subject to ratification allows States time to seek approval for the Convention at the domestic level and to enact any legislation necessary to implement it domestically, prior to undertaking the legal obligations of the treaty at the international level.[54] Domestic law may require the approval of the legislature before ratification.

---

[42] VCLT art 76(2).   [43] Ibid.   [44] UN (n 41 above) 36.

[45] Since there has not been a female Secretary-General so far, the male term is used.

[46] ST/LEG/SER.E/-   [47] 1249 UNTS 13.

[48] UNGA Res 1993 (XVIII) (17 December 1963) UN Doc A/RES/1993 (XVIII).

[49] UNGA Supplement No.30 (12 December 1973) UN Doc A/9030.

[50] UN Juridical Yearbook (1973) 79, n 9 and UN Juridical Yearbook (1974) 157.

[51] eg in relation to Guinea-Bissau and Democratic Republic of Vietnam UNGA Res 3067 (XXVIII) (16 November 1973) UN Doc A/RES/3067 (XXVIII).

[52] Or acceptance or approval.   [53] VCLT arts 11 and 14.

[54] UN, *Final Clauses of Multilateral Treaties: Handbook* (2003) 36.

Upon ratification at the international level, a State is obliged to implement the treaty domestically. Under international law a State party's domestic law cannot be invoked as a justification for failure to perform treaty obligations.[55] Upon ratification, the State becomes legally bound under the Convention in accordance with the terms of Article 27(1) and (2).[56]

At the time of ratification, a State can enter reservations—as a number of States have. Article 28 expressly provides for reservations.[57]

In accordance with the usual policy for multilateral treaties, the second sentence of Article 25(3) requires the deposit of instruments of ratification with the UN SG at UN Headquarters in New York. They are effective only from the date of deposit, generally recorded as that on which the instrument is received at Headquarters. States are asked to deliver their instrument of ratification directly to the UN Treaty Section to ensure the action is promptly processed. The UN recommends that States provide courtesy translations in English and/or French of instruments in other languages submitted for deposit with the UN SG, to facilitate prompt processing.[58]

IV. Article 25(4)

'Accession' is the means by which a State that did not sign a treaty already subscribed to by other States, formally accepts its provisions and expresses its consent to be bound by it. Any State can accede to the Convention by depositing an instrument of accession with the UN SG without first signing or ratifying the Convention and without seeking approval of the other States parties.[59] A newly emergent State may accede to a treaty to which it did not wish to become bound through succession, which is generally considered to be effective from the date that the new State becomes responsible for its international affairs.[60] Accession has the same legal effect as ratification. Article 25(4) provides that the Convention shall be open to accession by all States, without any further qualification. Hence, any State that might gain independence in the future is entitled to become a party to the Convention at any time. This Article also illustrates the drafters' intention to make the Convention as universally applicable as possible. The UN SG is also the depositary for instruments of accession.[61]

State succession[62] is not explicitly mentioned as a means of becoming party to the Convention. However, succession was the preferred instrument of the successor States of the former Yugoslavia and the former Czechoslovakia, and eight such States have become parties to the Convention through this means.[63] After 1992, the situation of the Federal Republic of Yugoslavia posed difficulties with respect to its participation in the UN and in

---

[55] VCLT art 27; International Law Commission Articles on Responsibility of States for Internationally Wrongful Acts 2001 art 32.

[56] See the discussion in ch on art 27(1) and (2).   [57] See the discussion in ch on art 28.

[58] UN (n 9 above) 11.

[59] T Kitajima 'Article 25': Signature, Ratification, Accession and Deposit in Japanese Association of Women's Rights (ed), *Convention on the Elimination of All Forms of Discrimination against Women: A Commentary* (1995) 385–92, 391.

[60] UN (n 54 above) 38.   [61] VCLT art 16(b).

[62] See Vienna Convention on Succession of States in Respect of Treaties, 1978, art 2(1)(b).

[63] Slovenia (6 July 1992), Croatia (9 September 1992), Czech Republic (22 February 1993), Slovakia (28 May 1993), Bosnia-Herzegovina (1 September 1993), the former Yugoslav Republic of Macedonia (18 January 1994), Serbia (12 March 2001), Montenegro (23 October 2006).

multilateral treaties.[64] The former Yugoslavia had signed the Convention on 17 July 1980 and ratified it on 26 February 1982. While the 1992 annual report lists the State party as Yugoslavia,[65] the Committee decided at its 12th session in 1993 that it should request the States of the territory of the former Yugoslavia to submit reports on an exceptional basis.[66] Thereupon, Bosnia-Herzegovina and the Federal Republic of Yugoslavia (Serbia and Montenegro) submitted reports to the Committee for consideration at its 13th session.[67] Croatia's report was considered at the 14th session.[68] Slovenia's initial report was discussed at the Committee's 16th session.[69]

The initial report of Serbia[70] submitted in May 2006 included Montenegro and Kosovo. The partially recognized Republic of Kosovo[71] is not a party to the Convention. But under the Special Representative of the UN SG in UNMIK, Section 3.2 of the Constitutional Framework for Provisional Self-Government states that:

the Provisional Institutions of Self-Government shall observe and ensure internationally recognized human rights and fundamental freedoms, including those rights and freedoms set forth in: . . . (e) The Convention on the Elimination of All Forms of Discrimination Against Women;

which in effect makes the Convention directly applicable in courts in Kosovo under UNMIK.[72] UNMIK also submits reports for Kosovo to the CCPR.[73] Since all treaty obligations undertaken by Serbia and Montenegro would continue to apply with respect to the Republic of Serbia (effective from the date of Montenegro's independence, 3 June 2006), consideration of the combined report was allowed. Montenegro's independent report is overdue. The combined initial, second, and third periodic report of the former Yugoslav Republic of Macedonia was considered at the 34th session.[74]

Since the Russian Federation is considered as the only successor State of the former USSR, it deposited neither an instrument of accession nor of succession after the dissolution of the Soviet Union. The other former Soviet Republics acceded to the Convention with the exception of Belarus and Ukraine. These States had been considered as separate subjects of international law during the Soviet era, albeit formally part of the USSR,[75] and had separately ratified the Convention in 1981.

The complex law on State succession of treaties remains contentious, and international practice is not uniform. However, human rights treaties are generally considered to be

---

[64] For the discussions by the ICJ in the various stages of the case 'Application of the Convention on the Prevention and Punishment of the Crime of Genocide' brought by Bosnia and Herzegovina against Serbia and Montenegro see <http://www.icj-cij.org/docket/index.php?p1=3&k=f4&p3=4&case=91> accessed 31 December 2010.

[65] CEDAW UN Doc A/46/38(Supp) (1993).   [66] UN Doc A/49/38 (1994) para 730.
[67] Ibid (1994) paras 732–57, 758–76.   [68] UN Doc A/50/38 (1995) paras 556–91.
[69] CEDAW/C/SVN/1 (1997).   [70] CEDAW/C/SCG/1 (2006).

[71] Upon request of Serbia, the UNGA adopted a resolution on 8 October 2008 asking the ICJ for an advisory opinion on the issue of Kosovo's declaration of independence. On 22 July 2010, the ICJ ruled that Kosovo's declaration of independence did not violate international law, see 'Accordance with International Law of the Unilateral Declaration of Independence in Respect of Kosovo (Advisory Opinion)' <http://www.icj-cij.org/docket/index.php?p1=3&p2=4&k=21&case=141&code=kos&p3=4> accessed 31 December 2010.

[72] Constitutional Framework for Provisional Self-Government UNMIK/REG/2001/9 (15 May 2001).

[73] CCPR, 'Report submitted by the United Nations Interim Administration Mission in Kosovo to the Human Rights Committee on the Human Rights Situation in Kosovo since June 1999' (2006) UN Doc CCPR/C/UNK/1.

[74] CEDAW/C/MKD/CO/3 (2006).

[75] Along with the USSR, the Ukrainian Soviet Socialist Republic and the Belorussian Soviet Socialist Republic were founding members of the UN in 1945.

governed by the rule of automatic succession. The CCPR has asserted that once the rights of individuals have been recognized by treaty, they cannot simply be denied due to the succession of a State.[76] In effect, the Committee acted in accordance with this view in asking for exceptional reports from the successor States of the former Yugoslavia even though no instruments of accession were deposited. Human rights treaties do not generally contain termination clauses, underlining the irreversible character of human rights obligations. Thus, the general rule of automatic succession remains applicable.[77]

V. Absence of a Withdrawal Clause

The question of succession is closely related to the question of denunciation or withdrawal because in both cases treaty obligations may come to an end. A withdrawal clause had been included in the draft Convention prepared by the Working Group of the 25th session of the CSW.[78] The decision to abandon this clause can probably be explained by the drafters' intent to discourage States parties from relinquishing their incurred obligations. It should not be possible to denounce the Convention and then ratify it again with new reservations. In accordance with VCLT Article 56, if a treaty is silent as to denunciation or withdrawal, a State party may only withdraw from it if it is established that the parties intended to admit the possibility of withdrawal, or if the right of denunciation or withdrawal may be implied by the nature of the treaty. Thus, consistent with this conclusion and VCLT Article 54, withdrawal from the Convention would not be possible unless all States parties so agreed. In this respect, the Convention is stronger than CAT, CRC, ICMW, and CRPD, which do have denunciation clauses.

---

[76] CCPR, 'General Comment 26' (1997) UN Doc CCPR/C/21/Rev.1/Add.8/Rev.1 para 4.
[77] ILA Committee on State Succession, Resolution 3/2008 'Aspects of the Law on State Succession' 73rd Conference of the International Law Association (Rio de Janeiro, Brazil, 17–21 August 2008) para 11.
[78] Kitajima (n 59 above) 391.

Article 26

(1) A request for the revision of the present Convention may be made at any time by any State Party by means of a notification in writing addressed to the Secretary-General of the United Nations.

(2) The General Assembly of the United Nations shall decide upon the steps, if any, to be taken in respect of such a request.

A. Introduction

As a 'revision clause', Article 26 of the Convention seeks to provide both stability of the text and the necessary flexibility for change. Other human rights treaties also provide for revision, although the procedures may differ. Article 26 provides that a revision may be requested by notification from a State party in written form addressed to the UN SG and empowers the UNGA to establish the procedure for possible amendment.[1]

B. Travaux Préparatoires

The USSR draft for the present Article 26 contained a provision on withdrawing from the Convention, in case of extraordinary events coercing the State to do so, but it was later deleted.[2] Finland, Singapore, and the United Kingdom were concerned that such a provision weakened the Convention, since it was difficult to determine those extraordinary events. This could open the door for circumventing domestic implementation problems.[3]

---

* I would like to thank Sahrah Al-Nasrawe-Sözeri, Benjamin Feyen, Ines Franke, Anna-Maria Paulus, Allison Sherrier, and Eric Veillerobe for their assistance on this chapter and on the chapters on arts 25, 27, 29, and 30.

[1] Same procedure is stipulated in art 45 of the Convention Relating to the Status of Refugees, art 16 of the Convention on the Prevention and Punishment of the Crime of Genocide, and ICERD art 23. In contrast, ICESCR art 29, ICCPR art 51, CRC art 50, ICMW art 90, and CRPD art 47 stipulate a more complex procedure to determine whether the proposed amendment is accepted for ratification. CAT art 29 is based on the Covenants but does not require the approval of the UNGA.

[2] UN Doc E/CN.6/AC.1/L.2 (1974); LA Rehof, *Guide to the Travaux Préparatoires of the United Nations Convention on the Elimination of All Forms of Discrimination against Women* (1993) 228–30, 229.

[3] Rehof (n 2 above) 229.

C. Practice of States Parties

One amendment has been put forward since the Convention entered into force in 1981. As the Convention gained wider acceptance, the limitation of the Committee's meeting time in Article 20(1) became increasingly problematic.[4] In 1995, the Committee noted that it was the only UN human rights treaty body whose meeting time was limited by its treaty, and recommended an amendment.[5] The amendment was proposed by Denmark, Iceland, Finland, Norway, and Sweden. At their 8th meeting in May 1995—in a procedure that does not meet the terms of Article 26(1)—the States parties amended Article 20(1) by providing that the Committee meet annually, but that the duration of its meeting would be determined by a meeting of States parties, subject to the approval of the UNGA.[6] The amendment, which was noted with approval by the UNGA, will enter into force after it has been accepted by a two-thirds majority of the States parties to the Convention.[7] As of 31 December 2010, only 57 of the 186 States parties to the Convention had accepted the amendment. As the amendment is not yet in force, the Committee remains dependent on the repeated authorization from the UNGA for its additional meeting time.[8]

D. Issues of Interpretation

The text of a treaty may be amended in accordance with VCLT Articles 39–41 unless the treaty provides for its amendment process, which supersedes the VCLT provisions. The Vienna Convention uses the terms 'amendment' and 'modification' and not 'revision'. Revision of a treaty means amendment of a comprehensive nature,[9] but also encompasses amendments to a specific provision. VCLT Article 40, which stipulates the amendment procedure for multilateral treaties, may be superseded by the relevant provisions of a treaty. Thus, the text of the Convention may be altered in accordance with its amendment rules in Article 26. Where Article 26 is silent on particular issues, the subsidiary rules of Article 40 of the VCLT may be applied.

I. Article 26(1)

According to Article 26(1), only States parties to the Convention may initiate the amendment procedure, and they may do so at any time. This means that neither non-party States nor any body such as the Committee is competent to do so. States parties must provide their request for revision in writing addressed to the UN SG. Notifications are simply statements providing the required information. VCLT Article 40(2) stipulates that all contracting States must be notified of all proposals for amendment of a multilateral treaty. The UN SG, as treaty depositary, circulates amendment proposals. The treaty secretariat is in the best position to determine the validity of the proposed amendment

---

[4] See the discussion in ch on art 20(1).
[5] 'Report of the Eighth Meeting of the States Parties to the Convention on the Elimination of All Forms of Discrimination against Women' (1995) CEDAW/SP/1995/2 para 2.
[6] Ibid para 5.
[7] UNGA Res 50/202 (23 February 1996) UN Doc A/RES/50/202.
[8] See the discussion in chs on 17–22, especially ch 20 on Committee meetings.
[9] UN, *Final Clauses of Multilateral Treaties Handbook* (2003) 106.

and to carry out any necessary consultations.[10] It is not within the UN SG's discretion to decide upon what steps are to be taken.

II. Article 26(2)

Paragraph 2 stipulates the UNGA as the organ empowered to determine the steps for amendment of the Convention, as opposed to the amendment power allocated to the States parties under VCLT Article 40(2).[11] Thus, it is up to the discretion of the UNGA to decide on the measures to be taken to enact the amendment, including delegating the amendment process to another body. One possible explanation for not placing the right to amend with the States parties is that the Convention seeks to create a universal regime, under which amendment should be at arm's length rather than in the hands of the States parties, which are directly affected by any changes to the Convention. This was particularly relevant at the time the Convention was adopted, as the small number of States parties might have been considered to offer a less global vision than the full UNGA.[12]

Once the UNGA is notified of the request, there are two options for action. If the UNGA determines that a specific measure is necessary, it is authorized to decide upon the action to be taken. Alternatively, the UNGA may decide against further steps, essentially denying the request for an amendment. The UN SG, upon being informed of the decision, duly communicates it to all States parties and circulates the relevant information for publication.[13]

VCLT Article 40(4) provides that an amendment, upon its entry into force, binds only those States which have formally accepted it; Convention Article 26 does not speak to this issue. This creates different regimes under the same treaty, with negative implications,[14] and indeed may not even be feasible. For example, with regard to the amendment to Convention Article 20, the Committee can only have one set of sessions that affects all the States parties. As a practical matter, the technique developed by the International Telecommunication Union could be applied, whereby the amendment, once it enters into force, replaces the earlier provision in its entirety.[15] Since the Convention does not provide for a withdrawal clause, States parties that have not voted for it must, nevertheless, accept the amendment.

The amendment process under Article 26 has proven to be cumbersome, and it appears particularly so in view of the only amendment proposed thus far, pertaining to a procedural matter that would seem to be relatively uncontroversial. However, given the effort that was expended in drafting the Convention and its far-reaching content, the high procedural bar may be reasonable protection from frivolous or politicized amendments.

---

[10] UN, *Treaty Handbook* (2006) 22–3.

[11] VCLT art 40(2) states that each one of the contracting States shall have the right to take part in: (a) the decision as to the action to be taken in regard to such proposal; and (b) the negotiation and conclusion of any agreement for the amendment of the treaty.

[12] This has of course changed dramatically, as ratification has become near-universal.

[13] UN, *Summary of Practice of the Secretary-General as Depositary* (1999) (ST/LEG/7/Rev.1) 75–6.

[14] UN (n 9 above) 98–9.

[15] J Klabbers, 'Treaties, Amendment and Revision' in R Wolfrum (ed), *The Max Planck Encyclopedia of Public International Law* (2008) para 10, online edition <www.mpepil.com> accessed 31 December 2010.

Article 27

(1) The present Convention shall enter into force on the thirtieth day after the date of deposit with the Secretary-General of the United Nations of the twentieth instrument of ratification or accession.

(2) For each State ratifying the present Convention or acceding to it after the deposit of the twentieth instrument of ratification or accession, the Convention shall enter into force on the thirtieth day after the date of the deposit of its own instrument of ratification or accession.

A. Introduction

In accordance with Article 27(1), the Convention entered into force on 3 September 1981, the thirtieth day after the deposit of the twentieth instrument of accession by St Vincent and the Grenadines.

B. Travaux Préparatoires

The USSR proposed a draft article with the wording of the final Article 27(1) but left open the necessary number of instruments of ratification or accession.[1] The United Kingdom suggested at least twenty-seven, following the precedent of ICERD Article 19, or even thirty-five, following the International Covenants on Human Rights.[2] The United States suggested that the number of ratifications or accessions should be at least one-third of the UN member States, while Hungary and the USSR suggested that the number should be as low as possible so the Convention could enter into force at the earliest possible date.[3]

* I would like to thank Sahrah Al-Nasrawe-Sözeri, Benjamin Feyen, Ines Franke, Anna-Maria Paulus, Allison Sherrier, and Eric Veillerobe for their assistance on this chapter and on the chapters on arts 25, 26, 29, and 30.

[1] LA Rehof, *Guide to the Travaux Préparatoires of the United Nations Convention on the Elimination of All Forms of Discrimination against Women* (1993) 232.

[2] ICCPR art 49; ICESCR art 27.   [3] Rehof (n 1 above) 232.

Ultimately, this provision was adopted without a vote at this meeting since the CSW agreed on the majority preference for twenty instruments.[4]

The Working Group of the UNGA adopted the finalized text of the present Article 27 without further changes.[5]

C. Practice of States Parties

The first twenty States to sign and ratify or accede to the Convention were Sweden, German Democratic Republic, Poland, Portugal, Cuba, Guyana, Dominica, Barbados, China, Cape Verde, Hungary, USSR, Belarus, Rwanda, Ukraine, Mexico, Norway, Haiti, Mongolia, and St Vincent and the Grenadines.[6] The Convention entered into force less than twenty-one months after its adoption, which was at that time more quickly than any human rights treaty.[7]

Article 17(1) provides that the Committee to be established should at the time of the Convention's entry into force consist of eighteen experts, to be increased to twenty-three after the thirty-fifth ratification or accession. When the first Committee members were elected during the first meeting of the States parties on 16 April 1982, the number of the instruments of ratification or accession had already reached thirty-five. Hence, the Committee consisted of twenty-three members from its first session in October 1982.[8]

D. Issues of Interpretation

Since both paragraphs of Article 27 refer to ratification and accession, it is apparent that accession can take place prior to as well as after the Convention's entry into force. Similarly, since the Convention does not provide any deadline for signature, States may still sign and ratify the Convention after its entry into force.

I. Article 27(1)

Article 27(1) defines the 'manner' and 'date' for the Convention to enter into force, as is provided for by VCLT Article 24(1).[9] Paragraph 1 repeats that the UN SG acts as depositary.[10] The depositary provides the information that establishes when the treaty enters into force.[11] Article 27(1) stipulates that thirty days must elapse between the date on which the required number of instruments is deposited and the date of entry into force. This period is required to ensure that preconditions are met and gives the depositary time to notify contracting States of the pending entry into force.[12]

---

[4] M Honda, 'Article 27': Entry into Force in Japanese Association of Women's Rights (ed), *Convention on the Elimination of All Forms of Discrimination against Women: A Commentary* (1995) 397–401, 398.

[5] Rehof (n 1 above) 233.   [6] See the discussion in ch on art 25.

[7] Subsequently, the CRC entered into force more quickly, less than ten months after its adoption.

[8] See the discussion in ch on art 17(1).

[9] VCLT art 24(1) (stating that 'a treaty enters into force in such manner and upon such date as it may provide or as the negotiating States may agree').

[10] See the discussion in ch on art 25(2) and (3).

[11] VCLT art 77(1)(f) stipulates the task to 'inform the States entitled to become parties to the treaty when the number of signatures or of instruments of ratification, acceptance, approval or accession required for the entry into force of the treaty has been received or deposited'.

[12] UN, *Final Clauses of Multilateral Treaties: Handbook* (2003) 59.

The drafters' compromise of twenty instruments of ratification or accession as condition for the Convention's entry into force became a model for subsequent UN human rights treaties.[13]

II. Article 27(2)

The domestic effect of the Convention's coming into force depends upon the relationship between domestic and international law in the State party's legal system.[14] In States parties in which international law is directly applicable (monist systems), the Convention's application depends only on paragraph 2. In States in which the Convention must be translated into domestic law (dualist systems), the Convention's application additionally depends on the State party's constitutional requirements. However, regardless of the domestic system, once a State party has committed to the Convention's entry into force for itself, it is obliged under international law—at least—with respect to other States parties and has exposed itself to monitoring by other States parties, UN Charter bodies and the Committee with regard to the rights of women within its jurisdiction.[15]

Article 28 of the VCLT states the general principle that a treaty shall not be applied retroactively 'unless a different intention appears from the treaty or is otherwise established'. In the absence of a contrary intention, a treaty cannot apply to acts or facts which took place, or situations which ceased to exist, before the date of its entry into force. Although no Convention provision suggests any intent of retroactive application, the Committee has referred to issues concerning the sexual exploitation of Asian women (the 'comfort women') by the Japanese military during the Second World War. This forced prostitution took place long before the drafting of the Convention and its coming into force for Japan in 1985.[16] Without providing a basis for this retroactive application, the Committee has made recommendations on lasting solutions.[17] However, analogous to the *Ms AT v Hungary* case,[18] it can be argued that the Committee is competent on the premise of continuing harm. Ms A.T. experienced further domestic violence after the Convention came into force for Hungary; while this was not the case for the Asian women, the harm suffered by them can be considered as continuing because of the Japanese government's failure to provide compensation or find any enduring solutions. These women continue to experience discrimination, disadvantage, and humiliation which constitute independent continuous violations.[19]

---

[13] cf CAT art 27; CRC art 49; CMW art 87; CRPD art 45; CED art 39. In contrast, the (earlier) two International Covenants required thirty-five and ICERD twenty-seven instruments.

[14] See discussion of the Convention in monist and dualist systems in ch on art 2.

[15] See the discussion in the Introduction and chs on arts 1 and 2 respectively.

[16] See the discussion in ch on Violence against Women.

[17] CO Japan, CEDAW/C/JPN/CO/6 (2009) paras 37–8.

[18] *Ms AT v Hungary* CEDAW Communication No 2/2003 (2005) para 8.5.

[19] The Committee is also concerned about the deletion of references to this issue in school textbooks, CO Japan, CEDAW/C/JPN/CO/6 (2009) para 37.

Article 28

1. The Secretary-General of the United Nations shall receive and circulate to all States the text of reservations made by States at the time of ratification or accession.

2. A reservation incompatible with the object and the purpose of the present Convention shall not be permitted.

3. Reservations may be withdrawn at any time by notification to this effect addressed to the Secretary-General of the United Nations, who shall then inform all States thereof. Such notification shall take effect on the date on which it is received.

A. Introduction[1]

Article 28 of the Convention on the Elimination of All Forms of Discrimination against Women (the Convention) explicitly envisages that States ratifying or acceding to the Convention may do so with reservations, indicating that these shall be received by the Secretary-General and circulated to all States. Article 28(3) indicates that reservations may be withdrawn at any time through notification to the Secretary-General, with the withdrawal taking effect on the date on which that notification is received. Article 28(2) mirrors Article 19(c) of the 1969 Vienna Convention of the Law of Treaties (VCLT), prohibiting reservations that are incompatible with the Convention's object and purpose.

* I would like to thank Stephanie Jensen-Cormier, Heather Northcott, Nathalie Stadelmann, and Mercedes Morales (OHCHR) for their assistance on this chapter and on the chapter on the Optional Protocol.

[1] The views expressed in this chapter are those of the author and do not necessarily reflect the views of the United Nations.

There are no provisions in the Convention described as non-derogable, nor is there any provision which identifies articles which may not be subject to reservations.

B. Travaux Préparatoires

During the negotiation of the Convention, one State suggested that no reservations should be permitted,[2] but others were of the view that States should be able to enter a limited number of reservations to some provisions for a limited time during which changes in legislation and/or educative measures could clear the way to their removal. One State referred to Article 19 of the VCLT and considered that it was essential that reservations which were not incompatible with the treaty's object and purpose should be permissible.[3] The draft text of the Convention presented by Belgium referenced to 'denunciations' in draft Article 24.[4]

During the resumed 26th session of the CSW, Denmark proposed a separate article on reservations[5] which included most of the elements of Article 28 as it appears in the Convention, but also indicated that any State party which objected to a reservation had ninety days in which to notify the Secretary-General that it did not accept it. In addition to providing that a reservation incompatible with the Convention's object and purpose was impermissible, the draft article stated that 'a reservation the effect of which would inhibit operation of the Committee established by the Convention' would not be allowed. Importantly, this draft article also included a formula for the identification of invalid reservations, based on Article 20 of ICERD,[6] providing that a reservation shall be considered 'incompatible or inhibitive' if it attracted objections from at least two-thirds of the Convention's States parties.

Following minor modifications, the draft article was adopted, as orally revised, without a vote in the CSW, although there was discussion on whether there was a need to include an article on reservations in the Convention or if the provisions of the VCLT or the ICERD should be used as the basis for such an article.[7] The draft Convention as a whole, including this article, was adopted by the CSW in its resolution 1 (XXVI) and submitted to the Economic and Social Council. Comments submitted on the draft to the General Assembly called for a clearer and simpler provision, based on the VCLT. One State considered that it was unclear whether a reservation would be considered incompatible only if there were objections from two-thirds or more of the States parties, or whether reservations could be considered incompatible in the event that the threshold was not reached. It was also suggested that the implications of an incompatible reservation for the reserving State party were unclear.[8] Other States had similar concerns, with some considering the provision to be unnecessary given that the VCLT sets out the rules relating to reservations,

---

[2] UN Doc E/CN.6/573 (1973) para 113.   [3] UN Doc E/CN.6/591 (1976) para 166.

[4] UN Doc E/CN.6/591/Add.1 (1976); LA Rehof, *Guide to the Travaux Préparatoires of the United Nations Convention on the Elimination of All Forms of Discrimination against Women* (1993) 234–7.

[5] UN Doc E/CN.6/L.701.

[6] B Clark, 'The Vienna Convention Reservations Regime and the Convention on Discrimination against Women' (1991) 85 *Am J of Intl L* 281, 283 (suggesting that this provision has been an effective restraint on reservations to the ICERD).

[7] UN Doc E/CN.6/608 (1976) paras 214–16.

[8] Report of the Secretary-General, 'Draft Convention on the Elimination of Discrimination against Women' (1977) UN Doc A/32/218 para 158.

while others called for the retention of a formula to identify incompatible reservations.[9] Discussion of the draft article continued in the Working Group of the General Assembly which considered the Convention's final provisions at the beginning of the Assembly's 34th session in 1979, during which the formula to identify incompatible reservations was deleted.[10] The provision as it appears in the treaty text was adopted by the Third Committee and the Plenary of the General Assembly.[11]

C. Reservations to the Convention

At 31 December 2010, 59 of the then 186 States parties to the Convention maintained reservations or declarations[12] entered on ratification or accession, many to more than one article. Forty of these have reservations to Article 29(1), which invests the ICJ with jurisdiction for the settlement of disputes relating to implementation of the Convention.[13] Reservations to Article 29(1) are permitted by Article 29(2).

Several reservations, including those concerning relations with Israel, may be described as 'political'.[14] A significant number are, however, substantive, with one commentator suggesting that they go 'to the heart of both values of universality and integrity'[15] in international human rights law generally, and that relating to women in particular. The background of many stems from different cultural and religious approaches to the role of women, frequently reflected in domestic laws on nationality, property rights, including in relation to women's inheritance, economic opportunities, freedom of movement, and

---

[9] UNGA, 'Addendum 2 to the Report of the Secretary-General' (1977) UN Doc A/32/218/Add 2 para 24.

[10] UNGA, 'Report of the Working Group of the Whole on the Drafting of the Convention on the Elimination of Discrimination against Women' (1979) UN Doc A/C.3/34/14, 16–18.

[11] UN Doc A/34/830 (1979) Annex para 18 and UNGA Res 34/180 (18 December 1979) UN Doc A/RES/34/180 Annex.

[12] VCLT art 2 defining a reservation as a 'unilateral statement, however phrased or named, made by a State, when signing, ratifying, accepting, approving or acceding to a treaty whereby it purports to exclude or to modify the legal effects of certain provisions of the treaty in their application to that State'. The Netherlands entered an interpretive declaration to Preamble paragraph 10 which is unlikely to meet this definition. France, Germany, and the Netherlands entered a similar interpretative declaration to Preamble paragraph 11. See L Lijnzaad, *Reservations to UN-Human Rights Treaties: Ratify and Ruin?* (1995) 304–5. These preambular paragraphs were adopted after a recorded vote with 108 votes in favour, none against and 26 abstentions. UNGA Verbatim Record (18 December 1979) UN Doc A/34/PV.107. Reservations, objections, and withdrawals of reservations can be found at Status of Treaties <http:/treaties.un.org> accessed 31 December 2010.

[13] Algeria, Argentina, Bahamas, Bahrain, Brazil, Brunei Darussalam, China, Cuba, Democratic People's Republic of Korea, Egypt, El Salvador, Ethiopia, France, India, Indonesia, Iraq, Israel, Jamaica, Kuwait, Lebanon, Mauritius, Micronesia (Federated States of), Monaco, Morocco, Myanmar, Niger, Oman, Pakistan, Qatar, Saudi Arabia, Singapore, the Syrian Arab Republic, Thailand, Trinidad and Tobago, Tunisia, Turkey, United Arab Emirates, Venezuela, Vietnam, and Yemen have reserved this provision. The Byleorussian Soviet Socialist Republic (Belarus), Bulgaria, Czechoslovakia, Hungary, Mongolia, Poland, Romania, the Ukrainian Soviet Socialist Republic (Ukraine), and the Union of Soviet Socialist Republics (Russian Federation) have withdrawn their reservations to this provision.

[14] Iraq and the Syrian Arab Republic indicated that approval of the Convention in no way implies recognition of or entry into any relations with Israel. Israel, which was not at that time a State party to the Convention, indicated to the Secretary-General on 12 December 1986 that it considered the Iraq declaration as explicitly of a political character and incompatible with the purposes and objectives of the Convention and that it could not in any way affect whatever obligations are binding upon Iraq under general international law or under particular conventions. Israel also noted that it would adopt an attitude of complete reciprocity to Iraq.

[15] RJ Cook, 'Reservations to the Convention on the Elimination of All Forms of Discrimination against Women' (1990) 30 *Virginia J of Intl L* 643, 644.

choice of residence. Many, including some which have been withdrawn, were foreshadowed in the debates during the negotiations of the Convention, the report of the Third Committee transmitting the Convention to the General Assembly,[16] and the Official Records of the final adoption.[17]

Reservations to human rights treaties generally,[18] and the Convention in particular, have been discussed by many commentators,[19] and this chapter does not repeat their analysis. Rather, it surveys the existing pattern of reservations, activity by States parties and the Committee to address them, and their removal and modification.

I. General reservations

The majority of reservations to the Convention is directed at individual articles of the treaty, but a minority is general. These include those of Brunei Darussalam, Liechtenstein, Malaysia, Mauritania, Oman, Pakistan, Saudi Arabia, and Tunisia. Brunei Darussalam maintains reservations regarding provisions that may be contrary to its Constitution and the beliefs and principles of Islam, its official religion. Liechtenstein reserves the right, in light of Article 1, to apply with respect to all the Convention obligations, Article 3 of its Constitution, providing that determination of succession to the throne, and related issues concerning Liechtenstein's Princely House, are governed by the laws of that House. Malaysia's reservation indicates that its accession is subject to the understanding that the provisions of the Convention do not conflict with the provisions of the Islamic Sharia and its Constitution. Mauritania indicates that it approves each and every part of the Convention which is not contrary to the Sharia and is in accordance with its Constitution. Oman indicates that it subjects all provisions of the Convention not in accordance with the Sharia and legislation in force in Oman to reservations. Pakistan's reservation makes clear that its accession is subject to its Constitution, while Tunisia's 'general declaration' indicates that it shall not take any organizational or legislative decision in conformity with the requirements of the Convention where such would conflict with the

---

[16] UN Doc A/34/830 (1979).

[17] UNGA, 'Official Records of the 107th Plenary Meeting of the Thirty-Fourth Session of the General Assembly' (1979) UN Doc A/34/PV.107 paras 1–88.

[18] CJ Redgwell, 'Reservations to Treaties and Human Rights Committee General Comment No 24 (52)' (1997) 46 *Intl Comparative L Quarterly* 390; R Baratta, 'Should Invalid Reservations to Human Rights Treaties be Disregarded?' (2000) 11/2 *Eur J of Intl L* 413; B Simma, 'Reservations to Human Rights Treaties: Some Recent Developments' in G Hafner et al (eds), *Liber Amicorum: Professor Ignaz Seidl-Hohenveldern—in Honour of his 80th Birthday* (1998) 659; R Goodman, 'Human Rights Treaties, Invalid Reservations, and State Consent' (2002) 96/531 *Am J of Intl L* 531; I Boerefijn, 'Impact on the Law on Treaty Reservations' in MT Kamminga and M Scheinin (eds), *Impact of Human Rights Law on General International Law* (2009) 63.

[19] Cook (n 15 above); Clark (n 6 above); A Jenefsky, 'Permissibility of Egypt's Reservations to the Convention on the Elimination of All Forms of Discrimination against Women' (1991) 15/2 *Maryland J Intl . & Trade* 199; HB Schöpp-Schilling, 'Reservations to the Convention on the Elimination of All Forms of Discrimination against Women: An Unresolved Issue or (No) New Developments?' in I Ziemele (ed), *Reservations to Human Rights Treaties and the Vienna Convention Regime: Conflict, Harmony or Reconciliation* (2004) 3; J Riddle, 'Making CEDAW Universal: A Critique of CEDAW's Reservation Regime under Article 28 and the Effectiveness of the Reporting Process' (2002) 34 *George Washington L Rev* 605; C Chinkin, 'Reservations and Objections to the Convention on the Elimination of All Forms of Discrimination against Women' in JP Gardner (ed), *Human Rights as General Norms and a State's Right to Opt Out: Reservations and Objections to Human Rights Conventions* (1997) 64; J Connors, 'The Women's Convention in the Muslim World' in JP Gardner (ed), ibid 85; Amnesty International, *Reservations to the Convention on the Elimination of All Forms of Discrimination against Women: Weakening the Protection of Women from Violence in the Middle East and North Africa Region* (2004).

provisions of Chapter I of its Constitution, the first Article of which declares Islam to be the official religion of the State. Similarly, Saudi Arabia's reservation states that in case of contradiction between the Convention and norms of Islamic law, Saudi Arabia is not under any obligation to observe the contradictory terms of the Convention.

II. Articles 1 to 5

The significance of the Convention's first five articles to the fulfilment of its objectives has been repeatedly stressed by the Committee and others, but a large number of reservations and declarations have been made to these articles. Several States parties have formulated differently phrased reservations indicating that the Convention is not binding for them insofar as its provisions may conflict with the Islamic Sharia. Others indicate that the State concerned is prepared to comply with the Convention, provided that such compliance does not contradict the Sharia. As is the case with general reservations, these reservations are viewed by many commentators as imprecise and indeterminate, and render unclear the content of the legal obligation that the State party accepts through ratification or accession. This is particularly so where the reservation does not explain its legal and practical scope. Where these reservations are explained on the basis of the Sharia, uncertainty is even more acute as there are different views among Islamic scholars as to the precise requirements of the Sharia, and whether it is subject to evolving interpretation and practice. States parties which explain their reservations as being based on the Sharia do not refer to the same provisions of the Convention in their reservations. In addition, not all States parties with large Muslim populations have entered reservations, suggesting that there is no firm view among countries as to whether the Sharia precludes implementation of any of the provisions of the Convention.

Reservations to Article 2 justified on religious grounds include those of Bahrain which encompass the entirety of Article 2, in order to ensure its implementation within the bounds of the provisions of the Islamic Sharia, and those of Bangladesh and Egypt. Although not explicitly indicated, Syria's reservation to Article 2 appears to be motivated by that article's perceived incompatibility with the Sharia, as does Iraq's reservation to Article 2(f) and (g). Libya indicates that Article 2 shall be implemented with due regard for the peremptory norms of the Islamic Sharia relating to inheritance. Morocco's reservation expresses the State party's readiness to apply Article 2 provided that its provisions do not conflict with the provisions of the Islamic Sharia. It explains that certain of the provisions contained in the Moroccan Code of Personal Status according women rights that differ from the rights conferred on men may not be infringed upon or abrogated because they derive primarily from the Islamic Sharia, which strives to strike a balance between the spouses in order to preserve the coherence of family life. In view of its multiracial and multi-religious society, and the need to respect the freedom of minorities to practise their religious and personal laws, Singapore reserves the right not to apply the provisions of Article 2 where such application would be contrary to those religious and personal laws. The United Arab Emirates' reservation to Article 2(f) is also based on its view that this paragraph violates Islamic rules on inheritance.

Many reservations to Article 5 are also explained on the basis of custom or religion. India declares that it shall abide by Article 5(a), requiring States parties to take all appropriate measures to modify the social, cultural and patterns of conduct of men and women in order to achieve the elimination of prejudices and customary and all other practices based on the idea of the inferiority or superiority of either of the sexes, or stereotyped roles for men and women, in conformity with its policy of non-interference in the personal affairs of any community without its initiative or consent. The reservation of the Federated States of Micronesia to Article 5 is explained in light of its capacity as trustee of the heritage of diversity within its States in respect of succession to traditional titles and marital customs. Niger, a predominantly Muslim State, also expresses reservations to Article 5(a), not on the basis of the Sharia, but because Article 5(a) and (b), relating to the inclusion of a proper understanding of maternity as a social function, and the common responsibility of men and women in their children's upbringing and in family education cannot be applied immediately, as they contravene existing customs and practices that evolved over time. In what it describes as a declaration, Qatar indicates that modification of 'patterns' in Article 5(a) must not be understood as encouraging women to abandon their roles as mothers and their role in child-rearing, thereby undermining the structure of the family. Both France and Niger declare that 'family education' in Article 5(b) should be interpreted as education in the family, which is subject to the guarantee of privacy set out in Article 17 of the ICCPR.

Reservations and declarations to Articles 1 to 5 are not all based on religion and custom. The United Kingdom, also on behalf of its dependent territories, expresses its understanding that the main purpose of the Convention, in light of the definition of discrimination against women in Article 1, is the reduction of discrimination against women, and indicates that it therefore does not regard the Convention as imposing any requirement to repeal or modify any existing laws, regulations, customs, or practices by which women are treated more favourably than men. The United Kingdom extends this understanding to the construction of Article 4(1) on temporary special measures aimed at accelerating *de facto* equality between women and men. The United Kingdom's ratification is also expressed to be subject to the understanding that none of its obligations under the Convention shall be treated as extending to the succession to, or possession and enjoyment of, the throne, the peerage, titles of honour, social precedence, or armorial bearings, or the affairs of religious denominations or orders or any act to ensure the combat effectiveness of the armed forces. Similarly, Monaco subsumes its ratification to the constitutional provisions governing succession to the throne, as do Morocco and Spain. Qatar declares that it accepts Article 1 provided that, in accordance with the provisions of Islamic law and Qatari legislation, the phrase 'irrespective of their marital status' is not intended to encourage family relationships outside legitimate marriage.

Algeria's reservation to Article 2 indicates that it is prepared to apply its provisions on condition that they do not conflict with the provisions of the Algerian Family Code. Qatar's reservation to Article 2(a), in connection with the rules on hereditary transmission of authority, is based on its consideration that the paragraph is inconsistent with Article 8 of its Constitution. The Bahamas' reservation states, without explanation, that it does not consider itself bound by Article 2(a) which requires a State party to embody, where this has not already occurred, the principle of the equality of men and women in its national constitution or other legislation and to ensure, through law or other appropriate means, the practical realization of this principle. The reservation of the Democratic People's Republic of Korea states that it does not consider itself bound by Article 2(f) which requires States parties to take all appropriate measures, including legislation, to modify or abolish existing laws, regulations, customs and practices which constitute discrimination against women. Lesotho's reservation indicates that it does not consider itself bound by

Article 2 to the extent that it conflicts with Lesotho's constitutional stipulations relative to succession to the throne and the law relating to succession to chieftainship. Similarly, the Federated States of Micronesia reserves the right not to apply Article 2(f) in respect of succession to certain well-established traditional titles, and to marital customs that divide tasks or decision-making in purely voluntary or consensual private conduct, a reservation it extends to Articles 5 and 16. Niger also expresses reservations in relation to Article 2(d) and (f), 'concerning the taking of all appropriate measures to abolish all customs and practices which constitute discrimination against women, particularly in respect of succession'. These, it indicates, cannot be applied immediately as they are contrary to existing customs and practices which, by their nature, can be modified only with the passage of time and the evolution of society and not by an act of authority.

III. Articles 7–9

Article 7 has attracted reservations from several States parties, on various grounds, although a number of these have been withdrawn. Expressing the view that women take a prominent part in all aspects of public life in the State party, Israel maintains a reservation to Article 7(b), preserving the right of the laws of any of the religious communities in Israel to discriminate against women in the appointment of women to religious courts. Monaco reserves the right not to apply Article 7(b) in respect of recruitment to the police force.

A number of States parties which originally entered reservations to Article 9, obliging States parties to grant women equal rights with men in relation to their nationality and that of their children, have withdrawn them. Those reservations that remain are generally to paragraph 2 relating to nationality of children. Unexplained reservations to Article 9(1) and (2) are maintained by Iraq, Monaco, and the United Arab Emirates, with Monaco describing the provisions of Article 9 as incompatible with its nationality laws, and the United Arab Emirates expressing the view that the acquisition of nationality is an internal matter to be governed by national legislation. Article 9(2) is subjected to unexplained reservations by the Bahamas, Bahrain, Brunei Darussalam, the Democratic People's Republic of Korea, Jordan, Lebanon, Malaysia,[20] Oman, Saudi Arabia, and Syria. Morocco's reservation to Article 9(2) explains that the Law of Moroccan Nationality permits a child to bear the nationality of his or her mother only where the child is born in Morocco to an unknown or stateless father as a means of guaranteeing each child's right to nationality. The reservation is also explained on the basis that a child born in Morocco to a Moroccan mother and a foreign father may acquire Moroccan nationality by declaring within two years of reaching the age of majority, her or his desire to acquire such citizenship, in circumstances where she or he resides in Morocco. Kuwait's reservation to this provision indicates that it is inconsistent with the Kuwaiti Nationality Act which stipulates that a child's nationality shall be determined by that of her or his father. Similarly, Qatar and Tunisia maintain reservations on the basis that Article 9(2) is inconsistent with their nationality legislation. The United Kingdom's reservation to Article 9 is explained

---

[20] On 6 February 1998, Malaysia sought to modify its reservation to Article 9(2) to declare that its reservation will be reviewed if the Government amends the relevant law. This modification failed as a result of an objection by France on 20 July 1998. The Netherlands submitted a similar objection on 21 July 1998, one day after the 90-day deadline. On the practice of modifying reservations, see P Kohona, 'Some Notable Developments in the Practice of the UN Secretary-General as Depositary of Multilateral Treaties: Reservations and Declarations' (2005) 99/2 *Am J of Intl L* 433.

as aimed at preserving temporary and transitional provisions relating to the January 1983 entry into force of the 1981 British Nationality Act, which might be discriminatory.

IV. Articles 11–14

A small number of States parties maintain reservations to specific parts of Articles 11 to 14. Many of those relating to Article 11, concerning equality in employment, entered on ratification or accession have been withdrawn, and those that remain are narrow. Most of these reservations are based on stereotypical assumptions of the roles of women and men. Australia, in a modification of a wider reservation, does not accept the application of the Convention insofar as it would require alteration of Defence Force policy which excludes women from combat duties. Austria reserves the right to apply Article 11 as far as night work of women and special protection of working women is concerned, within the limits established by national legislation. Malta and Singapore interpret Article 11(1) in light of Article 4(2), which defines special measures, including those in the Convention aimed at protecting maternity as non-discriminatory, as not precluding prohibitions, restrictions, or conditions on the employment of women in certain areas, or the work done by them where this is considered necessary or desirable to protect the health and safety of women or the human foetus. Malta notes that obligations imposed on it by other international treaties, including various ILO treaties aimed at the protection of women workers, are also incorporated into its reservation. A number of States parties to the Convention have withdrawn from these ILO treaties on the ground that while protective, they limit women's right to work. Several reservations to Article 11 relate to a State party's obligation to introduce maternity leave with pay or comparable social benefits throughout the State party. Australia indicates that it is not at present in a position to comply with this obligation, although many women in Australia are provided with such benefits. A similar reservation is maintained by the Federated States of Micronesia. The United Kingdom maintains reservations relating to pension schemes and retirement benefits, and qualifying periods of employment or insurance in relation to maternity benefits, while Ireland reserves the right to regard its legislation relating to employment opportunities and pay as sufficient implementation of Article 11. Malaysia indicates that it interprets the provisions of Article 11 as relating to discrimination between women and men only, while Singapore indicates that it considers legislation to implement Article 11 unnecessary for the minority of women who do not fall within the ambit of its employment legislation.

The few reservations to Article 13, which requires elimination of discrimination in economic and social life, include that of Ireland directed to maintaining social security legislation more favourable to women than men; and of Malta, which reserves the right to continue to apply taxation legislation which deems the income of a married woman to be the income of her husband, and, until such time as the relevant legislation is reformed, discriminatory aspects of family property law. Monaco also reserves the right to continue to implement its social security laws which envisage payment of benefits to the head of household, who is presumed to be the husband. Narrow reservations are maintained by France in relation to Article 14(2)(c) and (h) concerning rural women, with the former indicating that women who fulfil the conditions relating to family or employment required by French legislation for personal participation shall acquire their own rights within the framework of social security, and the latter indicating that paragraph 2(h) should not be interpreted to imply the actual provision, free of charge, of housing, sanitation, electricity, water supply, transport, and communications.

V. Articles 15–16

Article 15 requires States parties to accord women equality with men before the law, equal legal capacity, including with respect to contracts, the administration of property, and in court proceedings, as well as equality in relation to personal movement, and right to choose their residence and domicile. Qatar entered a reservation to Article 15(1) in relation to matters of inheritance and testimony, on the basis of its inconsistency with Islamic law. It also entered a reservation to Article 15(4) on the basis of it being inconsistent with the provisions of family law and established practice. The United Arab Emirates explains that Article 15(2) relating to equal legal capacity conflicts with the precepts of the Sharia regarding this issue, testimony, and the right to conclude contracts, and, therefore, does not consider itself bound by its terms. Switzerland indicates that it will apply this provision subject to several interim provisions relating to matrimonial law. The United Kingdom explains that it understands that only those elements of a contract which restrict the legal capacity of women shall be deemed null and void by virtue of Article 15(3), rather than the contract as a whole.

Reservations to Article 15(4) on choice of residence and domicile could be predicted from the drafting discussions in the CSW, during which the representative of Egypt, supported by the representatives of Indonesia and the Islamic Republic of Iran, indicated that according to the Holy Quran, the husband must choose the site of the matrimonial home and the wife has the same domicile as her husband.[21] The reservations of Algeria, Morocco, and Tunisia subsume the right of women to choose their residence and domicile to domestic personal laws. Bahrain, Oman, and Syria also entered reservations to this provision, but with no explanation. Niger declares that these freedoms can only apply to unmarried women. Malta's reservation expresses its commitment to remove discriminatory family property law, but that it will continue to apply that legislation until that time.

Reservations to all or part of Article 16, which guarantees equality between women and men in marriage and family life, are maintained by a large number of States parties. As is the case of reservations to Article 15, these reservations could be predicted from the process of drafting Article 16, which was difficult. Attempts were also made by some States, even in the discussions in the Third Committee of the General Assembly, to amend the draft Convention to conform with their domestic law.[22] The Committee has been particularly critical of these reservations, suggesting that they manifest rejection of the applicability of human rights protection in the private sphere, and entrench an inferior role for women in domestic life.

Several of the reservations which apply to Article 16 in its entirety, provide a detailed explanation, generally based on the Islamic Sharia. These include those of Egypt which explains that the Sharia accords women rights equivalent to those of their spouses so as to ensure a just balance between them, with an equivalency of rights and duties ensuring 'complementarity which guarantees true equality between the spouses,

---

[21] Rehof (n 4 above) 166–7.

[22] Ibid 168–86. For example, the representative of Morocco argued that the roles of men and women were not 'traditional,' but had arisen in the deep consciousness of the human race and that to provide for equality for men and women would affect the 'psychic and moral balance of children', UNGA Summary Record of the Third Committee of the General Assembly Meetings No 70–71 (6–7 December 1979) UN Doc A/C.3/34/SR.70–71.

not a quasi-equality that renders the marriage a burden on the wife'. The reservation explains that the Sharia allows women to enjoy certain advantages through marriage, which are balanced against advantages that men possess. Accordingly, it states that the Sharia provides that the husband must pay bridal money to the wife, maintain her fully, and provide a payment on divorce, while the wife retains full rights to her property, and is not obliged to spend anything on her keep. In light of this, the Sharia restricts the wife's rights to divorce by making this contingent on a judge's ruling, a restriction which does not apply to the husband. Morocco's reservation to this provision is similar, indicating that the equality envisaged in the Article is incompatible with the Sharia which guarantees to each of the spouses rights and responsibilities within a framework of equilibrium and complementarity. Iraq's reservation to Article 16 describes the Sharia as according women rights equivalent to those of their spouses to ensure a just balance between them, while that of the United Arab Emirates explains that the financial obligations and rights of spouses under the Sharia makes a woman's right to divorce conditional on a judicial decision. General reservations, also based on the Sharia, but not including an explanation, were entered by Bahrain and Maldives. Algeria and Israel subsume the application of Article 16 to their domestic legislation on personal status, while India declares that it will apply Article 16(1) in conformity with its policy of non-interference in the personal affairs of any community without its initiative and consent.

Other reservations to Article 16 are directed at particular parts of the provision. Some of these, such as those of Bangladesh to paragraph 1(c) requiring equality in marriage and on its dissolution; Kuwait to paragraph 1(f) on equality of rights in relation to children; Malaysia to paragraph 1(a), enshrining the equal right of women to enter into marriage, and (c), (f), and (g), requiring equal rights to choose a family name, a profession, and an occupation; and Oman and Qatar, to paragraph 1(a), (c), and (f), are explained as based on the Sharia. Niger's reservations to paragraph 1(c), (e), and (g) are justified on the basis that these obligations cannot be applied immediately as they are contrary to existing customs and practices which can only be modified with the passage of time and the evolution of society. Tunisia indicates that implementation of paragraphs 1(g) and (h) must not conflict with its domestic legislation on family names and inheritance.

Some reservations to Article 16 are unexplained. These include those of the Bahamas, to paragraph 1(h) relating to equal property rights; Jordan, to paragraph 1(c), (d), and (g); Lebanon to paragraph 1(c), (d), (f), and (g); and Tunisia to paragraph 1(c), (d), and (f). Some States parties have entered very precise reservations to particular elements of Article 16. Ireland's reservations to Article 16(1)(d) and (f) constitute a statement of its view that the attainment of the objectives of the Convention does not require extension to men of the same rights as women in respect of children born out of marriage. The United Kingdom maintains a similar reservation to paragraph 1(f) indicating that decisions in relation to adoption give principal consideration of promotion of the child's welfare, rather than placing her or his interests paramount. France, Monaco, the Republic of Korea, and Switzerland maintain reservations to paragraph 1(g) on the right to choose a family name. Malta's reservation asserts its right to apply discriminatory legislation relating to family property pending its reform, while Switzerland subjects the application of paragraph 1(h) on equal property rights to interim provisions in its matrimonial legislation. Malta and Monaco entered reservations to paragraph 1(e) requiring equality between women and men in respect of the number and spacing of children insofar as that provision might be interpreted as imposing an obligation to legalize abortion, with Monaco extending this to legalization of sterilization.

India entered a specific reservation to Article 16(2), which provides that the betrothal and marriage of a child shall have no legal effect, and that all necessary action, including legislation shall be taken to specify a minimum age for marriage and make registration of marriages in an official registry compulsory. The State party indicated that while it fully supports the principle of compulsory registration of marriages, this was not practical in a vast country such as India with its variety of customs, religions, and levels of literacy.

D. Activity to Address Reservations to the Convention

I. Objections by States Parties

Article 20 of the VCLT provides that States parties to a treaty may object to reservations made by other States parties within twelve months from the date of the depositary notification of the reservation or that on which the reserving State expressed its consent to be bound by the treaty, whichever is later. Several commentators have noted States parties' general unwillingness to object to incompatible reservations, owing to diplomatic sensitivities, as well as the practical difficulties and resource constraints they face in monitoring and formulating their positions on doubtful reservations, particularly taking into account the short time frame for objection.[23] The limited practical effect of objections is a factor which may be likely to discourage States parties from submitting objections, with one commentator suggesting that their main function is to 'preclude a particular interpretation of the treaty from gaining influence'.[24] Some suggest that the lack of objection by many States parties to the numerous reservations which may be contrary to the object and purpose of the Convention creates an impression that it is not as binding an international commitment as other human rights treaties, and that the religious and cultural sensitivities that its full implementation might generate lead States parties to be tolerant of these reservations.[25] Others argue that a large number of objections might have discouraged ratification and led States parties to withdraw from the Convention. However, some very significant reservations which attracted objections have been withdrawn, and it is likely these objections were one factor leading to that result.

Austria, Belgium, Canada, the Czech Republic, Denmark, Estonia, Finland, France, Germany, Greece, Hungary, Ireland, Italy, Latvia, Mexico, the Netherlands, Norway, Poland, Portugal, Romania, Slovakia, Spain, Sweden, and the United Kingdom have exercised their right to object to reservations to the Convention. Some of these States parties have submitted repeated objections, testifying to their vigilance with regard to the Convention.[26] Argentina, Israel, and the former Union of Soviet Socialist Republics

---

[23] Chinkin (n 19 above) 76–7; Kohona (n 20 above) 442.   [24] Lijnzaad (n 12 above) 54.

[25] Chinkin (n 19 above) 77.

[26] It should be noted that the Ad Hoc Committee of Legal Advisers on Public International Law of the Council of Europe (CAHDI) acts as a European observatory of reservations to international treaties and discusses this issue at regular meetings. On 18 May 1999, the Council of Europe Committee of Ministers to Member States adopted Recommendation No R(99)13 on Responses to Inadmissible Reservations to International Treaties and attached model response clauses. On 5 May 2000, the Committee of Ministers' Deputies of the Council of Europe adopted Decision (2000)708 on Practical Issues Regarding Reservations to International Treaties.

submitted what can be described as political objections.[27] Some States parties have also submitted objections after the twelve-month period provided for in Article 20 has elapsed, with some indicating their view that despite the provisions of the VCLT, there is no time limit for objections.[28] These are usually circulated by the Secretary-General as communications but are not submitted for registration, nor published in the United Nations Treaty Series.

Objections by States parties vary from an unexplained statement of objection[29] to indications that the objecting State considers that the reservation is subject to the general principle of treaty interpretation according to which a party may not invoke the provisions of its internal law as justification for failure to perform a treaty.[30]. Others, particularly more recent objections, provide explanations for the objecting State's view that the reservations are incompatible with the object and purpose of the Convention.[31] Several indicate that the reservations, if implemented, would inevitably result in discrimination against women on the basis of sex, which is contrary to the object and purpose of the Convention[32] or all the articles of the Convention and the principles of equal rights of women and men and non-discrimination on the basis of sex set forth in the UN Charter, the UDHR, or other international instruments signed or ratified by the reserving State.[33] Some indicate that incompatible reservations are not acceptable because they would render a basic international obligation of a contractual nature meaningless, and that such reservations, particularly when framed generally, not only cast doubt on the commitment of the reserving State to the object and purpose of the Convention, but contribute to the undermining of international contractual or treaty law, or international law generally.[34] Several objections

[27] On 15 April 1986, the former Soviet Union objected to the declaration made by Germany extending its application to West Berlin, which it considered unlawful and not legally valid; on 4 April 1989, Argentina objected to the extension of the United Kingdom's ratification to the Falkland Islands (Malvinas), South Georgia, and the South Sandwich Islands, as communicated on 27 November 1989. Israel objected to Iraq's declaration relating to recognition of the former (n 14 above).

[28] See eg the communication received from Denmark in relation to Kuwait's reservation received on 12 February 1997, more than two years after Kuwait's accession, and the communication from Sweden on 13 August 1997 in relation to Singapore's reservation received almost two years after Singapore's accession.

[29] The United Kingdom to the reservation of Micronesia (Federated States of) to art 11(1)(d) on enactment of comparable worth legislation.

[30] Denmark to the reservation made on accession by Libya; Finland to Maldives; Norway to Algeria, Kuwait, Lesotho, Malaysia, Maldives, Pakistan, and Singapore.

[31] Austria to Maldives; Canada to Maldives; Finland to Libya; Germany to Algeria, Bangladesh, Brazil, Egypt, Iraq, Jamaica, the Republic of Korea, Libya, Malawi, Maldives, Malaysia, Mauritius, Pakistan, Thailand, Tunisia, and Turkey; The Netherlands to Bangladesh, Brazil, Egypt, Kuwait, Iraq, India, Jamaica, Lebanon, Libya, Malawi, Maldives, Mauritius, Morocco, Republic of Korea, Thailand, Tunisia, and Turkey; Poland to the United Arab Emirates; Portugal to Maldives; Sweden to Bangladesh, Brazil, Thailand, and Tunisia; The United Kingdom to Micronesia (Federated States of).

[32] Czech Republic, Denmark, Estonia, Germany, Latvia, Romania, and Sweden to Oman; Czech Republic, Denmark, Estonia, Germany, Hungary, Italy, Latvia, and Romania to Brunei Darussalam; Estonia to Syrian Arab Republic; Sweden to Kuwait; Austria, Belgium, Czech Republic, Hungary, Italy, Poland, Romania, Slovak Republic, and Sweden to Qatar.

[33] Mexico to Bangladesh, Cyprus, Egypt, Iraq, Libya, Mauritius, New Zealand (in relation to the Cook Islands), Thailand, and Turkey; Sweden to Bangladesh, Brazil, Brunei Darussalam, Egypt, Iraq, Jordan, Libya, Maldives, Malawi, Mauritius, Micronesia (Federated States of), New Zealand (in relation to the Cook Islands), Republic of Korea, Thailand, Tunisia, and United Arab Emirates.

[34] Sweden to Bangladesh, Brazil, Egypt, Iraq, Kuwait, Libya, Malawi, Mauritius, New Zealand (in relation to the Cook Islands), Oman, Republic of Korea, Thailand, and Tunisia; The Netherlands to Algeria, Bahrain, Fiji, Lesotho, Malaysia, Mauritania, Pakistan, Saudi Arabia, Singapore, and Syrian Arab Republic; Norway to Kuwait, Libya and Maldives; Norway to Algeria, Brunei Darussalam, Libya, Malaysia and Singapore;

indicate that it is in the common interest of States that treaties to which they have chosen to become parties are respected, as to their object and purpose, by other parties.[35]

A number of States parties' objections to reservations subsuming implementation of the Convention to the Islamic Sharia, the reserving State's Constitution, or national legislation is based on the view that such reservations, without further clarification, raise doubts as to the degree of commitment assumed by the State party in becoming party to the Convention,[36] are of an unlimited or undefined character,[37] or subject to interpretation, modification, and selective application in different States parties.[38] Explanations of this nature often appear in objections to general reservations, usually based on Islamic law, which fail to specify the provisions of the Convention to which they apply or the extent of the derogation.[39] Some objecting States indicate that such reservations limit or exclude the application of the Convention on a vaguely defined basis,[40] fail to clarify for other States parties the provisions which might be affected or might be affected in the future, thus leaving them unclear as to the obligations accepted by the reserving State or its commitment to the object and purpose of the treaty.[41] Others indicate that general and indeterminate reservations, such as those ruling out the application of the Convention or subordinating it to the Sharia or national laws, deprive the Convention of any effect.[42] Similarly, objections to broad reservations to particular articles, such as Articles 2, 15, and 16, which often are based on Islamic law, and do not clearly specify how far the reserving State accepts the provision, explain that the reservations are of unlimited scope and undefined or general character,[43] or consist of a general reference to a system of law without specifying its content,[44] making it impossible for other States parties to determine how far

Poland to United Arab Emirates; Portugal to Oman, Brunei Darussalam, Micronesia (Federated States of), and United Arab Emirates; Ireland to Brunei Darussalam and Oman.

[35] Sweden to Bangladesh, Brazil, Democratic People's Republic of Korea, Egypt, Iraq, Republic of Korea, Libya, Malawi, Mauritania, Mauritius, Micronesia (Federated States of), New Zealand, Saudi Arabia, Thailand, and Tunisia; The Netherlands to Algeria, Bahrain, the Democratic People's Republic of Korea, Fiji, Lesotho, Malaysia, Mauritania, Pakistan, Saudi Arabia, and Syrian Arab Republic; The Netherlands and Norway to Singapore; Norway to Libya, Maldives, and Lesotho; Austria, Norway, Portugal, and Sweden to United Arab Emirates; Austria, Czech Republic, The Netherlands, and Portugal to Brunei Darussalam; Austria, Czech Republic, The Netherlands, and Portugal to Oman; Austria, Belgium, Czech Republic, and Sweden to Qatar.

[36] Germany, The Netherlands, and Norway to Algeria; Austria, Germany, The Netherlands, and Sweden to Mauritania; The Netherlands to Fiji, Lesotho, Libya, Malaysia, Pakistan, Singapore; Germany, The Netherlands, Spain, and Sweden to Saudi Arabia; Finland, The Netherlands to Maldives; Estonia and Finland to Qatar; Austria, Ireland, The Netherlands, Portugal, Romania to Brunei Darussalam; Austria, Ireland, The Netherlands, Portugal, Romania to Oman; Portugal to United Arab Emirates.

[37] Denmark to Mauritania and Saudi Arabia; Denmark, Greece, Poland, and Slovakia to Oman; Denmark, Greece, and Poland to Brunei Darussalam.

[38] Norway to Kuwait, Libya and Maldives; Canada and Czech Republic to Oman.

[39] Austria to Lebanon; Finland and Germany to Malaysia; Finland to Maldives; Austria and Germany to Pakistan; Finland, Norway, and Portugal to Mauritania; Austria, Finland, Ireland, Norway, and Portugal to Saudi Arabia; Finland and Slovakia to Brunei Darussalam; Slovakia to Oman.

[40] Portugal to Mauritania and Saudi Arabia.

[41] France and The United Kingdom to Saudi Arabia; Belgium, Canada, Czech Republic, Estonia, France, Italy, Spain, Sweden, and The United Kingdom to Brunei Darussalam; Germany, Hungary, Italy, Spain, United Kingdom to Oman; Belgium, Latvia, and The Netherlands to Qatar; The United Kingdom to Mauritania.

[42] France to Oman and Brunei Darussalam.

[43] Denmark and Greece to Bahrain; France and Greece to Syrian Arab Republic; Greece to Oman and United Arab Emirates.

[44] The United Kingdom to United Arab Emirates.

the reserving State has undertaken the obligations of the Convention,[45] or creating doubts as to the degree of commitment assumed.[46]

A significant number of objections relate to reservations to Article 2 or any of its paragraphs, containing the obligation of States parties to condemn discrimination against women in all its forms, and to pursue by all appropriate means and without delay, a policy of elimination of discrimination against women, including through various steps identified by other articles in the Convention including Articles 5(a), 9, 15, and 16 on equality in marriage and family life. A number of these objections are explained on the grounds that reservations to these provisions are directed at provisions which the objecting State party considers to be basic or fundamental or go to the very essence of the objective of the elimination of discrimination against women.[47] Finland explained its objection to Kuwait's reservation to Article 7 on elimination of discrimination against women in political and public life,[48] which has been withdrawn, on the basis that this provision is fundamental, with its implementation being essential to the fulfilment of the Convention's object and purpose.

Article 20 of the VCLT provides that an objection to a reservation does not preclude the entry into force of the treaty between the reserving State and the objecting State unless the latter definitely expresses a contrary intention. Only one objection—that of Sweden with regard to the reservations of Maldives on accession—expressly states that the objecting State party considers that the reservations constitute an obstacle to the entry into force of the Convention between the two States. Most specify that they do not affect the entry into force of the treaty between the parties, allowing the Convention to remain in force between the reserving State and the objector. Some indicate that the reservation cannot alter or modify in any respect the obligations arising from the Convention for any State party.[49] Others suggest that the reservation should be considered invalid,[50] while some indicate that the Convention remains in force without the reserving State benefiting from the reservation.[51] Several suggest that the reserving State reconsider its

---

[45] France and The United Kingdom to Bahrain; Norway, Estonia, and The United Kingdom to Syrian Arab Republic; Germany, Latvia, Netherlands, Spain, and The United Kingdom to United Arab Emirates; Poland to Qatar.

[46] Austria, Finland, Germany, The Netherlands, Sweden to Bahrain; Austria, Estonia, Finland, Germany, Italy, The Netherlands, Spain, Sweden to Syrian Arab Republic; Finland, Norway, Portugal, Sweden to United Arab Emirates; Estonia and Finland to Oman; Sweden to Qatar; Portugal to Micronesia (Federated States of).

[47] Greece to the Syrian Arab Republic's reservation to art 2; Austria, Denmark, Finland, Germany, The Netherlands, Norway, Portugal, Spain, and the United Kingdom to the Democratic People's Republic of Korea's reservation to art 2(f); Italy to Qatar's reservations to arts 2 and 16; Finland to Malaysia's reservations to arts 2(f) and 5(a); Austria, Denmark, Finland, Germany, Norway, Portugal, and Spain to the Democratic People's Republic of Korea's reservation to art 9(2); Denmark, Finland and Norway to Niger's reservations to arts 2(d) and (f), 5(a), 15(4), and 16(1)(c), (e), and (g); Denmark, Finland, Ireland, Portugal, Norway, and Spain to Saudi Arabia's reservation to art 9(2); Finland to Brunei Darussalam's and Qatar's reservations to art 9(2); Portugal to reservations of United Arab Emirates and Oman in respect of parts of arts 2, 9, 15, and 16; Portugal, Slovakia, and Spain to the reservation of Brunei Darussalam to art 9(2); Finland and The Netherlands to Qatar's reservations to arts 15(1) and (4) and 16(1)(a), (c), and (f); Norway and Spain to Qatar's reservations to arts 2(a), 9, 15(1) and (4), and 16; Latvia to Qatar's reservation to art 2(a).

[48] Finland to Kuwait.   [49] Portugal to Maldives.   [50] Mexico to Mauritius.

[51] Jan Klabbers describes the origin of this approach, in particular with respect to human rights treaties, drawing attention to the model responses to reservations annexed to the Council of Europe's Committee of Ministers Recommendation R(99)13 on Responses to Inadmissible Reservations to International Treaties. J Klabbers, 'Accepting the Unacceptable? A New Nordic Approach to Reservations to Multilateral Treaties' (2000) 69 *Nordic J of Intl L* 179.

reservations,[52] while others implicitly do so by drawing attention to the unlimited scope and undefined character of the reservation, thereby encouraging the reserving State to define its reservation more narrowly.

II. Meeting of States Parties

The Committee has expressed concerns about reservations to the Convention from its inception. In response, Canada, which had not submitted objections, included the subject of reservations in the agenda of the third meeting of States parties to the Convention, held in New York on 25 March 1986. After a short general exchange of views, during which the Committee's views on reservations were noted and concern expressed at some reservations that could be considered incompatible with the Convention, the meeting requested the Secretary-General to seek the views of States parties on the question of reservations to the Convention and report on those views to the General Assembly at its 41st session. The meeting also decided to place reservations on the agenda of the next meeting of States parties, which would be held in 1988.[53]

Sponsors of the resolution on the status of the Convention at the regular session of the Economic and Social Council in May 1986 sought to include the decision of the meeting of States parties in the resolution's text.[54] This was controversial, because at that time, Bangladesh and Egypt had entered the broadest reservations, based on perceived conflict of the Convention with the Sharia, and some delegations suggested that the draft resolution was anti-Islamic.[55] On 30 May 1986, pursuant to the decision of the meeting of States parties, the Secretary-General invited Member States to submit their views on the question of reservations that could be considered incompatible with the object and purpose of the Convention and, therefore, within the scope of Article 28(2). Only seventeen States parties, or less than 20 per cent of the Convention's then eighty-seven parties, responded.[56] Most of these responses were cursory, with one commentator concluding that their small number and poor quality reflected a view that the Convention was somehow separate and distinct from other multilateral treaties, of lesser status than those treaties because of its culturally sensitive content, and perceived as a statement of intent or rhetoric, rather than a codification of internationally-binding obligations.

In a full analysis of the report compiling the responses, a scholar points out that less than half addressed the questions of compatibility and admissibility of reservations.[57] Some substantive responses made proposals on strategies to address them. Canada proposed a multi-faceted approach including discussions among States and consideration at meetings of States parties and meetings of the Committee, and suggested that guidelines on the nature and scope of the substantive articles of the Convention, particularly Articles 9, 11, 15, and 16, were essential to assist States to understand the objectives of the Convention and the nature of the obligations it involved. Canada also suggested that consideration

---

[52] Denmark to Brunei Darussalam, Oman, Mauritania, Saudi Arabia, Niger, United Arab Emirates; Estonia to Syrian Arab Republic.

[53] 'Report of the Third Meeting of the States parties to CEDAW' (1986) UN Doc CEDAW/SP/10.

[54] ECOSOC Res 1986/4 (21 May 1986).   [55] Clark (n 6 above) 284.

[56] Canada, China, Cuba, Czechoslovakia, Denmark, France, Gabon, Federal Republic of Germany, Ireland, Japan, Mexico, Portugal, Saint Lucia, Spain, Sweden, Turkey, and the Union of Soviet Socialist Republics. Compiled in the Report of the Secretary-General, 'Status of the Convention on the Elimination of All Forms of Discrimination Against Women' (1986) UN Docs A/41/608 and A/41/608/Add.1.

[57] Clark (n 6 above) 283–4.

be given to the appointment in 1987, of a Special Rapporteur to the Committee, or a three-person working group, to prepare the guidelines for the Committee's consideration at its 7th session and States parties' discussion during their 4th meeting in 1988. Sweden proposed revision of Article 28, through an amendment to the Convention pursuant to Article 26(1), which would define articles against which no reservation would be allowed or establish a procedure along the lines of ICERD Article 20(2) providing that a proportion of States parties could determine the permissibility of reservations.

The Third Committee's consideration of the Secretary-General's report compiling these views during the General Assembly's 41st session in 1986 proved difficult, with some States alleging cultural insensitivity on the part of others, and interference with their sovereign right to enter reservations. The resolution on the Convention recalled the decision of the 3rd meeting of States parties to request States parties' views on the matter, but merely took note of the Secretary-General's report. Beyond emphasizing the importance of the strictest compliance by States parties with their obligations under the Convention, it did not directly address reservations,[58] and did not take up the suggestions of Canada and Sweden for the creation of a mechanism to address them.

The topic of reservations was included in the agenda of the 4th meeting of States parties in March 1988, although Egypt reserved its position on the inclusion of this item. No substantive discussion took place, with the meeting adopting a decision recalling that of the 3rd meeting of States parties, noting the report to the General Assembly and the various views expressed at meetings of the General Assembly, ECOSOC, and States parties in 1986 and 1988.[59]

The biennial meetings of States parties to the Convention continue to receive a report on declarations, reservations, objections, and withdrawal of reservations to the Convention,[60] but there has been no discussion of this report or of the general issue during these meetings since 1986. However, several United Nations World Conferences and their follow-up reviews have addressed reservations to the Convention. These have included the 1993 Vienna Declaration and Programme of Action, the Beijing Declaration and Platform for Action,[61] and the Beijing + 5 review by the 23rd Special Session of the General Assembly.[62] Operative paragraphs in General Assembly, ECOSOC, and CSW resolutions on the Convention routinely include language noting that some States parties have modified their reservations, and expressing satisfaction at the fact that some reservations have been withdrawn. These resolutions also urge States parties to limit the extent of any reservations they lodge, formulate them as precisely and narrowly as possible to ensure that no reservations are incompatible with the object and purpose of the Convention, review them regularly with a view to their withdrawal, and withdraw reservations that are contrary to the

[58] UNGA Res 41/108 (4 December 1986) UN Doc A/RES/41/108.

[59] 'Report of the Fourth Meeting of the States parties to CEDAW' (1988) UN Doc CEDAW/SP/11, 2.

[60] eg 'Declarations, reservations, objections and notifications of withdrawal of reservations relating to the Convention on the Elimination of All Forms of Discrimination against Women' (2010) UN Doc CEDAW/SP/2010/2.

[61] UNGA, 'Report of the Fourth World Conference on Women' (1995) UN Docs A/CONF.177/20 and A/CONF.177/20/Add.1 paras 230(c)–(d).

[62] UNGA Res S-23/3 (16 November 2000) UN Doc A/RES/S-23/3 para 68(c).

Convention's object and purpose.[63] In Resolution 6/30 on integrating the human rights of women throughout the United Nations system, the Human Rights Council urged all States parties to withdraw reservations to treaties which are incompatible with their object and purpose. The reservations of States parties to the Convention have also been raised in dialogue in the Council's Universal Periodic Review working group, and actions in relation to reservations have been included amongst the relevant State's commitments or the recommendations of the working group.[64]

III. The Work of the Committee

Since its establishment, the Committee has routinely raised reservations with individual States parties during constructive dialogue, urging their removal and commending those which have objected to the reservations of other States parties. Two of the Committee's general recommendations directly concern reservations, and other general recommendations also address the question in the context of their subject matter. The Committee's Suggestion 4 also deals with reservations, while its contribution to the fiftieth anniversary of the adoption of the UDHR and the five-year review of the Vienna Declaration and Programme of Action is a statement on reservations. Successive reporting guidelines adopted by the Committee have also required that States parties provide information on any reservations they may maintain, their effect, and the plans for their removal.

The Committee first took up reservations during its 3rd session in 1984, during the consideration of the initial report of Egypt,[65] when experts discussed the State party's reservations, suggesting that their wording gave no guidance on the extent to which they limited the applicability of the Convention in Egypt. Experts also requested information on how the requirements of the Convention and Islamic law were reconciled.[66] At that session, the Committee also asked for legal advice on its functions in respect of reservations. The Treaty Section of the UN Office of Legal Affairs provided an opinion[67] which indicated that the Secretary-General as depository had no power to interpret the Convention, but was bound to circulate reservations as received. The opinion concluded that the functions of the Committee 'did not appear to include a determination of the incompatibility of reservations, although reservations undoubtedly affect the application of the Convention and that the Committee might have to comment thereon in its reports in this context'. The opinion also indicated that in the absence of a specific regime such as that in the ICERD 'a question of interpretation of the Convention is involved here' and suggested that formal dispute mechanisms, such as arbitration or referral to the International Court of Justice (ICJ), would become applicable in the event of a dispute as to the permissibility of a reservation.

During its 3rd session, the Committee decided to annex reservations and objections to its reports on States parties concerned.[68] At its 5th session in 1986, several experts proposed that the Committee adopt a general recommendation on reservations, although a

---

[63] eg UNGA Res 64/138 (16 February 2010) UN Doc A/RES/64/138 para 6.

[64] See the reports of the Human Rights Council's Working Group on the Universal Periodic Review on Algeria (A/HRC/WG.6/1/DZA/4), Bahrain (A/HRC/WG.6/1/BHR/4), India (A/HRC/WG.6/IND/4), Morocco (A/HRC/WG.6/1/MAR/4), and Tunisia (A/HRC/WG.6/TUN/4).

[65] Initial report of Egypt, CEDAW/C/5/Add.10 and Amend.1 (1983).

[66] UNGA, 'Report of the CEDAW Committee—Third Session' (1984) UN Doc A/39/45 paras 190–3.

[67] Ibid Annex III.   [68] Ibid paras 349 and 357–9.

number of other experts were strongly of the view that the formulation of general recommendations on this or any other subject interpreting the Convention did not fall within the Committee's mandate.[69]

Amongst the reports considered by the Committee at its 6th session were those of Bangladesh,[70] which had reservations to Article 2, Article 13(a), and Article 16(1)(c) and (f); France,[71] which had reservations to parts of Articles 15 and 16; the Republic of Korea,[72] which had reservations to parts of Articles 9 and 16; and Spain,[73] which had a reservation to Article 7 relating to succession to the throne. In addition to commenting in its report on Convention implementation by each State party in light of these reservations,[74] the Committee adopted General Recommendation 4 in which it expressed concern at 'the significant number of reservations that appeared to be incompatible with the object and purpose of the Convention,' welcomed the decision of the States parties to consider the issue of reservations at their meeting in 1988, and suggested that States parties 'reconsider these reservations with a view to withdrawing them'.[75] The Committee did not identify any existing reservation as being incompatible or otherwise, perhaps in an effort to comply with the opinion of the Office of Legal Affairs.[76]

More controversially, and linked to the consideration of the report of Bangladesh during which experts had expressed concern about the effects of Islamic law on the rights of women,[77] the Committee requested that Bangladesh's next report include a special section on family law and the Islamic Sharia, and recommended that research should be carried out on the rights of women under Islamic law.[78] The Committee also requested the United Nations system as a whole, the specialized agencies, and the CSW 'to promote or undertake studies on the status of women under Islamic law and customs and, in particular, on the status and equality of women in the family on issues such as marriage, divorce, custody and property rights and their participation in public life of the society, taking into consideration the principle of *El Ijtihad* in Islam'.[79]

The Committee's request for studies on the status of women in Islam proved controversial. Bangladesh, in ECOSOC, urged 'the greatest caution in using the Convention as a pretext for doctrinaire attacks on Islam'.[80] During the ECOSOC session, suggestions by the delegations of Bangladesh and Egypt that the Committee was indulging in cultural imperialism and religious intolerance appeared to attract support, as ECOSOC resolution 1987/3 to the General Assembly recommended that no further action be taken on the Committee's request for studies on women and Islam. This recommendation was accepted by the General Assembly, which in its resolution 42/60 took note of the views on the Committee's report expressed by delegations in the ECOSOC and decided to take no

---

[69] UNGA, 'Report of the CEDAW Committee—Fifth Session' (1986) UN Doc A/41/45 para 364. See also E Evatt, 'Finding a Voice for Women's Rights: The Early Years of CEDAW' (2002) 34 *George Washington Intl L Rev* 535–9 (discussing the disagreement within the Committee as to the meaning of Article 21 empowering the Committee to make suggestions and general recommendations).

[70] Initial report of Bangladesh, CEDAW/C/5/Add.34 (1986).

[71] Initial report of France, CEDAW/C/5/Add.33 and Amend.1 (1986).

[72] Initial report of the Republic of Korea, CEDAW/C/5/Add.35 (1986).

[73] Initial report of Spain, CEDAW/C/5/Add.30 and Amend.1 (1985).

[74] UNGA, 'Report of the CEDAW Committee—Sixth Session' (1987) UN Doc A/42/38 paras 134 and 157 (Republic of Korea); 260 (Spain); 394 and 419 (France); 512 and 543 (Bangladesh).

[75] Ibid para 579.   [76] Schöpp-Schilling (n 19 above) 14.

[77] UN Doc A/42/38 (n 74 above) paras 513, 517, and 540.   [78] Ibid para 570.

[79] Ibid Decision 4 para 583.   [80] ECOSOC Summary Record (1987) UN Doc E/1987/SR.11, 13.

action on the Committee's request. The General Assembly also called on the Committee to review its request, in light of the views of delegations expressed in the ECOSOC and the 3rd Committee of the General Assembly,[81] and made no mention of reservations in the resolution.

Despite the views of the ECOSOC and the General Assembly, at its 7th session in 1988, the Committee reiterated its position that given the direct or indirect references by States parties to Islamic religion, traditions, and customs as a source of, or influence on, laws relating to the status of women, studies on the subject would assist it in carrying out its mandate. The Committee also made clear that it had not intended to criticize any religion, but that its request had arisen as a result of the consideration of the reports of more than one State party, and it was deeply concerned at the misunderstanding that its request had generated in the political bodies.[82]

The study requested by the Committee has never been prepared. However, the impact of reservations on implementation of the Convention in individual States parties has remained high on its agenda. A strict interpretation of the VCLT reservations regime, which leaves the determination of the permissibility of reservations to States parties, with no authority being given to any monitoring or supervisory body, might suggest that questioning States parties on areas subject to reservations is outside its mandate, but the Committee has continued to engage States parties on the issue during consideration of reports, as well as through its lists of issues and questions submitted in advance of such consideration. To date, no State party has objected to this line of questioning, and many have provided detailed information on the practical effect of reservations on implementation of the Convention in the respective State party, and plans for their removal.

The Committee adopted a second general recommendation on reservations at its 11th session in 1992, in the run-up to the World Conference on Human Rights (WCHR). As in the case of General Recommendation 4, General Recommendation 20 does not analyze the compatibility of reservations to the Convention, but suggests that States parties should raise the question of the validity and the legal effect of reservations to the Convention in the context of reservations to other human rights treaties; reconsider such reservations with a view to strengthening the implementation of all human rights treaties; and consider introducing a procedure on reservations to the Convention comparable with that of other human rights treaties. Also at the 11th session, the Committee tasked its Chairperson to place the 'global issue of reservations to human rights conventions' on the agenda during her participation on the preparatory committee for the WCHR.[83]

At its 12th session in early 1993, the year of the WCHR, the Committee adopted Suggestion 4, reiterating its concern at the large number and scope of reservations, and, in a phrase going beyond the general recommendations, expressing its opinion that some of these appeared to be of questionable compatibility with the object and purpose of the Convention. It recommended that States parties review the compatibility of these reservations with those to other human rights conventions, and the need for and desirability of withdrawing them. It also recommended that States parties keep the number and scope of

---

[81] UNGA Res 42/60 (30 November 1987) UN Doc A/RES/42/60 paras 8–9.
[82] UNGA, 'Report of the CEDAW Committee—Seventh Session' (1988) UN Doc A/43/38 paras 64–71.
[83] UNGA, 'Report of the CEDAW Committee—Eleventh Session' (1992) UN Doc A/47/38 para 469. The Sub-Commission adopted a resolution on CEDAW in 1991. See ECOSOC, 'Report of the Sub-Commission on Prevention of Discrimination and Protection of Minorities—Forty-Third Session' (1991) UN Doc E/CN.4/Sub.2/1991/65 (E/CN.4.1992/2).

reservations to a minimum, make them as specific as possible, and give full consideration to lodging objections to reservations entered by other States parties whenever such action is appropriate.[84] At the same session, the Committee decided that it would support steps recommended by the Sub-Commission on Prevention of Discrimination and Protection of Minorities in its resolution 1992/93, if taken in common with other human rights treaty bodies, to seek an advisory opinion from the ICJ that would clarify the issue of reservations to human rights treaties and thereby assist States parties in their ratification and implementation.[85]

An advisory opinion was not sought. However, the WCHR adopted paragraph 39 of the Vienna Declaration and Programme of Action,[86] supporting the Committee's approach, which encouraged finding ways and means of addressing the particularly large number of reservations to the Convention, called on the Committee to continue its review of reservations, and urged States parties to withdraw reservations that are contrary to the object and purpose of the Convention or which are otherwise incompatible with international treaty law.

The Committee built on the outcome of the WCHR with respect to reservations at its 13th session in 1994. First, it adopted General Recommendation 21 on non-discrimination and equality in marriage and family relations, which, *inter alia*, expressed alarm at the number of reservations to the Convention; the combined effect of reservations to Articles 2 and 16 based on cultural and religious beliefs and customs, which seemed to nullify any hope for change; the persistence and re-emergence of patriarchal family structures; and old values and traditions due to fundamentalist or other extremist views or economic hardships. The general recommendation pointed out that Articles 2, 3 and 24 required all States parties to progress gradually to a stage where reservations, particularly to Articles 9, 15, and 16, could be withdrawn. It also requested reserving States parties to report on whether their laws complied with Articles 9, 15, and 16 and if not, explain their religious and private laws or customs which impeded the realization of the Convention, and progress in respect of removal of reservations to these provisions, including the introduction of measures 'directed at full compliance.'[87]

Second, the Committee amended its guidelines for the preparation of initial and periodic reports required by Article 18, to request States parties which had entered substantive reservations to report specifically with regard to their reservations, why they considered them to be necessary, their precise effect on national law and policy, and whether they had entered similar reservations to other human rights treaties which guarantee similar rights. Reserving States parties were also required to indicate plans they might have to limit the effect of the reservations or withdraw them and, where possible, specify a timetable for withdrawing them. The Committee made particular reference to those States parties which had entered general reservations, or to Articles 2 or 3, stating for the first time that it considered such reservations to be incompatible with the Convention's object and purpose, and requiring a special effort from these States parties, which were directed to report on the effect and interpretation of their reservations.[88] Successive reporting guide-

---

[84] UNGA, 'Report of the CEDAW Committee—Twelfth Session' (1993) UN Doc A/48/38, 1–4.
[85] Ibid section I para 5.
[86] Vienna Declaration and Programme of Action (25 June 1993) UN Doc A/CONF.157/23.
[87] UNGA, 'Report of the CEDAW Committee—Thirteenth Session' (1994) UN Doc A/49/38.
[88] Consolidated guidelines were issued by the Committee at its Fourteenth Session. See, UNGA, 'Report of the CEDAW Committee—Fourteenth Session' (1995) UN Doc A/50/38 para 652.

lines issued by the Committee take this approach, with the current guidelines requiring reporting on reservations in the common core document to be submitted to all treaty bodies, with specific information being required in the Convention-specific report.[89]

Third, the Committee decided that a section reflecting its views on reservations would be included in its concluding observations on States parties' reports. It also requested that a special letter be sent by the Secretary-General to those States parties that had entered substantive reservations to the Convention, drawing attention to the Committee's concern. It was noted that this concern should be brought to the attention of the 7th meeting of States parties, the Commission on Human Rights, and the CSW and other human rights treaty bodies. It also recommended that the programme of advisory services of the Centre for Human Rights and the DAW be made available to provide advice to States parties on the withdrawal of reservations, and requested that the Secretariat provide information on reservations to other human rights treaties in its analysis of States parties' reports which it provides to the Committee.[90] Finally, noting that some States parties objected to reservations they consider to be contrary to the object and purpose of the Convention, the Committee encouraged objecting States parties to enter into a bilateral dialogue with reserving States parties, with a view to finding a solution.

During its 15th session in 1996, the Committee's attention was drawn to the Human Rights Committee's General Comment 24 on reservations,[91] which, *inter alia*, asserted that Committee's view that its role included the determination of the compatibility of reservations with the object and purpose of the ICCPR and described the consequences of its determination that a reservation was incompatible particularly in the context of individual communications. The Committee requested information from the Secretariat on responses to reservations to human rights treaties,[92] including by human rights treaty bodies, which it received at its 16th session in 1997.[93] On the basis of this report, the Committee decided on the placement of the issue of reservations in its concluding observations,[94] information that should be provided in the Secretariat's analyses of States parties' reports,[95] and the need for international and regional seminars on reservations.[96] The Committee's General Recommendation 23 on women in public life, also adopted at

---

[89] Paragraph 40(b) of the guidelines for the common core document calls for reporting on reservations, while paragraph C.3 of the CEDAW-specific reporting guidelines requires explanation of existing reservations and their continued maintenance clarified. States parties which have general reservations or those to Article 2 and/or 7, 9, and 16 should report on the interpretation and effect of those reservations. Report of the Secretary-General, 'Compilation of guidelines on the form and content of reports to be submitted by States parties to the International Human Rights Treaties' (2009) UN Doc HRI/GEN/2/Rev.6, Chapter I para 40(b) and CEDAW, 'Reporting Guidelines' (2008) UN Doc A/63/38, Annex I para C.3.

[90] UNGA, 'Report of the CEDAW Committee—Thirteenth Session' (1994) UN Doc A/49/38 paras C.1 (4)–(11).

[91] CCPR, 'General Comment 24' (1994) UN Doc CCPR/C/21/Rev.1/Add 6 reprinted in UN Doc HRI/GEN/1/Rev.9 (2008).

[92] UNGA, 'Report of the CEDAW Committee—Fifteenth Session' (1996) UN Doc A/51/38 para 346.

[93] Report by the Secretariat, 'Reservations to the Convention on the Elimination of All Forms of Discrimination against Women' (1996) UN Doc CEDAW/C/1997/4. Further information was provided to the Committee on the same topic in 2001. Report by the Secretariat, 'Ways and Means of Expediting the Work of the Committee' (2000) UN Doc CEDAW/C/2001/II/4 paras 20–56.

[94] UNGA, 'Report of the CEDAW Committee—Sixteenth Session' (1997) UN Doc A/52/38/Rev.1, Part I para 357.

[95] Ibid para 368.

[96] Ibid para 374.

that session,[97] called on States parties to explain the reason for and effect of any reservations to Articles 7 or 8, keep these under close review, and include a timetable for their removal in their reports. If the reservations reflected traditional, customary, or stereotyped attitudes towards women's roles in society, States parties should report on steps being taken to change these attitudes.[98]

At its 17th session, the Committee decided that its contribution to the 1998 fiftieth anniversary of the adoption of the UDHR and the five-year review of the Vienna Declaration and Programme of Action would be a statement on reservations, 'particularly in the context of Article 2 of the Convention,' and designated one of its members to submit a draft for discussion at its 18th session in 1998.[99]

Adopted at its 19th session later in 1998, this statement is the most comprehensive formulation of the Committee's approach to reservations.[100] It highlights the Committee's extensive experience with the impact of reservations on women's achievement of full and substantive equality with men gained through its examination of States parties' reports and the increasing concern expressed by other human rights treaty bodies, United Nations World Conferences, States, and the International Law Commission (ILC) and notes that the Committee has observed that some States parties with reservations to the Convention have not entered reservations to analogous provisions in other treaties. It also notes that a number of States parties seek to justify reservations to particular articles on the ground that national law, tradition, religion, or culture are not congruent with Convention principles. Recognizing that the Convention does not prohibit reservations which are compatible with its object and purpose, the statement indicates that the Committee considers Articles 2 and 16 to be core provisions of the Convention, with Article 2 being central to its object and purpose and reservations to Article 16 being incompatible with the Convention and therefore impermissible.

The statement describes reservations as preventing the Committee from assessing progress in Convention implementation, limiting its mandate and potentially affecting the entire human rights regime. Reservations to the Convention are also described as expressing a State party's unwillingness to comply with an accepted human rights norm, ensuring that women's inequality with men is entrenched at the national level. This, the Committee considers, not only affects women's ability to exercise and enjoy their rights, but guarantees that they will remain inferior to men and have less access to the full range of civil, political, economic, social, and cultural rights enjoyed by men, leading women to compete with men on an unequal footing for such rights as equality in income, access to education, housing, and health care, and equality of rights and responsibilities within the family. In the Committee's view, reservations to Articles 2 and 16 'perpetuate the myth of women's inferiority and reinforce the inequalities in the lives of millions of women throughout the world', thereby ensuring that they continue to be treated in both public and private life as inferior to men, and to suffer greater violations of their rights in every sphere of their lives. The statement reiterates the view of Mr Alain Pellet, the ILC's Special Rapporteur on reservations, that a reserving State has the option of maintaining

---

[97] Ibid para 387. The edited GR can be found in UNGA, 'Report of the CEDAW Committee—Seventeenth Session' (1997) UN Doc A/52/38/Rev.1, Part II, I, A.

[98] Ibid para 44.   [99] Ibid para 483.

[100] UNGA, 'Report of the CEDAW Committee—Nineteenth Session' (1998) UN Doc A/53/38/Rev.1, Part II, A.

reservations after a good faith examination, withdrawing or replacing impermissible reservations with permissible reservations, or renouncing being a party to the treaty.[101] It also indicates that the Committee recognizes and appreciates the positive impact objections by other States parties can have in encouraging reserving States to withdraw or modify reservations, and the empowering effect these objections have for women in the State party. The statement also makes clear that objections not only exert pressure on reserving States, but serve as a guide to the Committee in its assessment of the permissibility of reservations.

The statement asserts that the Committee has an important role to play, discharged through its consideration of reports and formulation of concluding observations which routinely express concern about reservations to Articles 2 and 16 and the failure of States parties to withdraw or modify them. It recognizes the Special Rapporteur's view that control of the permissibility of reservations is the primary responsibility of States parties, but expresses its grave concern at the number and extent of impermissible reservations, and at the reluctance of States parties to remove or modify them, even where other States parties object. No reference is made to the Human Rights Committee's General Comment 24, and unlike in the case of that General Comment, the statement does not indicate clearly whether the Committee is of the view that its role includes the determination of the impermissibility of reservations. However, it very clearly identifies Article 2 as central to the Convention's object and purpose, and reservations to Article 16 as incompatible with the Convention and therefore impermissible, and in asserting a role, albeit unclear, for the Committee in relation to reservations, moves beyond the views held by the Special Rapporteur at the time of the statement's adoption, that only States parties had a role in respect of reservations.

Beyond calling for revision of substantive reservations to the Convention with the aim of their possible withdrawal in its contribution to the WCHR,[102] and in its statement on the 10-year review and appraisal of the Beijing Declaration and Platform for Action,[103] the Committee has made one further formal statement on reservations in its General Recommendation 28 on the core obligations of States parties under Article 2 of the Convention, adopted at its 47th session in 2010. This reiterates its view that Article 2 is the very essence of States parties' obligations under the Convention and that any reservations to it, or any of its paragraphs, are, in principle, incompatible with the Convention's object and purpose and therefore impermissible under Article 28(2). General Recommendation 28 also makes clear that reservations to Article 2 do not relieve the State party of the need to comply with its other obligations under other human rights treaties to which it is party and with customary international law relating to the elimination of discrimination against women.

---

[101] UNGA, 'Report of the International Law Commission on the Work of its Forty-Ninth Session (1997) UN Doc A/53/10 para 86; the initial work of the Special Rapporteur on reservations and human rights treaties is contained in his second report, ILC 'Second report on reservations to treaties' UN Doc A/CN.4/477 (1996) paras 52–82.

[102] UNGA, 'Report of the CEDAW Committee—Twenty-Fourth Session' (2001) UN Doc A/56/38/Rev.1, Part I paras 384–5.

[103] 'Statement of the Committee on the Elimination of Discrimination against Women on the Occasion of the 10-year Review and Appraisal of the Beijing Declaration and Platform for Action' (2005) UN Doc A/60/38, Part I, Annex I para 3.

The Committee has also provided information to the ILC's Special Rapporteur on reservations, who has produced some sixteen reports since 1995,[104] meeting with him during its 37th session on 1 February 2007.[105] It was also represented at a meeting with representatives of human rights treaty bodies convened during the ILC's 59th session during May of that year.[106] The Committee provided similar input to the expert of the Sub-Commission on Prevention of Discrimination and Protection of Minorities who was tasked with the preparation of a study on the subject.[107]

In 2000, the Committee requested an analysis of the practices of human rights treaty bodies relating to reservations, in the context of both the reporting and petitions process.[108] The Committee, possibly because of lack of time, has never discussed this analysis, which highlights the Human Rights Committee's General Recommendation 24 and that Committee's decision to sever what it determined to be an invalid reservation and consider a case submitted under the First Optional Protocol to the ICCPR which concerned a provision in that treaty to which the State party concerned had entered a reservation.[109] The Special Rapporteur of the ILC, however, refers to this analysis as 'important,' indicating that human rights treaty bodies, including the Committee, are anxious to engage in a dialogue with reserving States, encouraging them to withdraw their reservations rather than rule on their impermissibility.[110]

Consistent with the Special Rapporteur's view, the Committee has continued to address reservations constructively. Its dialogues with reserving States parties are similar, and while the statements in its concluding observations vary, it is possible to discern some general trends.[111] It usually commends States parties when considering their initial reports for their ratification or accession without reservations, and all States parties for withdrawing reservations, committing themselves to do so, considering such a step, or objecting to the reservations of other States parties which are incompatible with the object and purpose of the Convention. If States parties have reservations, the committee sometimes makes what could be described as neutral remarks, expressing concern or disappointment, or calling on States parties to make efforts to withdraw reservations and to provide a timeline for withdrawal,[112] particularly when States parties maintain reservations over successive reporting rounds and there have been legislative reforms.[113] In such

---

[104] Available at <http://untreaty.un.org/ilc/guide/1_8.htm> accessed 31 December 2010.

[105] UNGA, 'Report of the CEDAW Committee—Thirty-Seventh Session' (2007) UN Doc A/62/38, Part I para 662.

[106] ILC, 'Report of the Special Rapporteur on Reservations to Treaties: Meeting with Human Rights Bodies' (2007) UN Doc ILC(LIX)/RT/CRP.1.

[107] UNGA, 'Report of the CEDAW Committee—Twentieth Session' (1999) UN Doc A/54/38/Rev.1 para 421.

[108] Report by the Secretariat, 'Ways and Means of Expediting the Work of the Committee' (2000) UN Doc CEDAW/C/2001/II/4 paras 20–56.

[109] *Rawle Kennedy v Trinidad and Tobago* CCPR Communication No 845/1999 UN Doc CCPR/C/67/D/845/1999. See also Schöpp-Schilling (n 19 above) 29.

[110] ILC, 'Seventh Report of the Special Rapporteur on Reservations to Treaties' (2002) UN Doc A/CN.4/525 paras 49–51; see also ILC, 'Eighth Report of the Special Rapporteur on Reservations to Treaties' (2003) UN Doc A/CN.4/535 paras 21–2.

[111] See Schöpp-Schilling (n 19 above) 35, expressing the view that what she describes as 'inconsistencies' may be based on a 'conscientious evaluation of the factual legal situation in the respective countries, on political considerations of the Committee or on mere oversight'.

[112] CO Switzerland, CEDAW/C/CHE/CO/3 (2010) paras 11–12.

[113] CO Malta, CEDAW/C/MLT/CO/4 (2010) paras 12–13; CO Australia, CEDAW/C/AUS/CO/7 (2010) paras 14–16; CO Bangladesh, CEDAW/C/BGD/CO/7 (2011) paras 12–13; CO Israel, CEDAW/C/ISR/CO/5 (2011) paras 8–9; CO Liechtenstein CEDAW/C/LIE/CO/4 (2011) paras 12–13.

cases the Committee makes very critical remarks, frequently suggesting that reservations impede, seriously hinder, or are obstacles or impediments to full implementation of the Convention.[114] It also draws attention to the effect of these reservations on *de facto* implementation of the Convention, and sometimes suggests that this is in contradistinction to the State party's legislation.[115]

The Committee has implicitly identified reservations as contrary to the object and purpose of the Convention in many instances. For example, in its concluding observations on Egypt and Iraq the Committee referred to its view expressed in its statement on reservations, that Articles 2 and 16 are central to the object and purpose of the Convention and that in accordance with Article 28(2), reservations to these articles should be withdrawn.[116] Recent concluding observations are more explicit and declare that certain reservations are contrary to the Convention's object and purpose. Thus, in its concluding observations on the initial reports of Mauritania[117] and Saudi Arabia,[118] the Committee expressed concern that the reservations of these States parties were drawn so widely that they were contrary to the object and purpose of the Convention. Similarly, its concluding observations on the initial reports of Bahrain[119] and the Democratic People's Republic of Korea[120] describe reservations to parts of Articles 2 and 9 as contrary to the object and purpose of the Convention, while those on Lebanon[121] express concern at its reservations to Articles 9 and 16 which the Committee considers as contrary to the object and purpose of the Convention, with a similar statement being made in the concluding observations on Syria.[122] The concluding observations on the combined first and second report of Morocco, express the Committee's deep concern at the number and importance of its reservations, particularly to Article 2, indicating that it 'considers any reservation to that article to be contrary to the object and purpose of the Convention and incompatible with international law',[123] a view it reiterates in its concluding observations on Morocco's combined third and fourth periodic reports in 2008 in relation to both Articles 2 and 16.[124] A similar view is expressed in its concluding observations on Algeria[125] and the third periodic report of Singapore,[126] while those on the initial report of the United Arab Emirates express the opinion that Articles 2, 9, 15, and 16 are central to the object and purpose of the Convention and reservations should be withdrawn.[127] Although welcoming Egypt's progress in withdrawing reservations, the Committee's 2010 concluding observations on its combined sixth and seventh report urge it to review and withdraw its reservations to

---

[114] See the reports on reservations submitted to the annual Meetings of Chairpersons of the Human Rights Treaty Bodies and the Inter-Committee Meetings of the Human Rights Treaty Bodies between 2005 and 2008: HRI/MC/2005/5, 52–69; HRI/MC/2006/5/Rev.1; HRI/MC/2007/5, 14–16 and HRI/MC/2007/5/Add.1, 4–7; HRI/MC/2008/5, 6–11.

[115] CC Jordan, A/62/38, part III, 39th Session (2007) paras 182–3.

[116] CC Egypt, A/56/38, part I, 24th Session (2001) para 327; CC Iraq, A/55/38, part II, 23rd Session (2000) para 186.

[117] CC Mauritania, A/62/38, part II, 38th Session (2007) para 24.

[118] CO Saudi Arabia, A/63/38, part I, 40th Session (2008) para 24.

[119] CO Bahrain, CEDAW/C/BHR/CO/2 (2008) para 16.

[120] CC Republic of Korea, A/60/38, part II, 33rd Session (2005) paras 33–4.

[121] CC Lebanon, A/60/38, part II, 33rd Session (2005) paras 93–4.

[122] CC Syrian Arab Republic, A/62/38, part II, 38th Session (2007) para 122.

[123] CC Morocco, A/52/38/Rev.1, 16th Session (1997) para 59.

[124] CO Morocco, A/63/38, part I, 40th Session (2008) para 226.

[125] CC Algeria, A/60/38, part I, 32nd Session (2005) para 141.

[126] CC Singapore, A/62/38, part III, 39th Session (2007) para 105.

[127] CO United Arab Emirates, CEDAW/C/ARE/CO/1 (2010) paras 16–17.

Articles 2 and 16, which the Committee indicates are incompatible with the Convention's object and purpose.[128] The concluding observations on Israel,[129] Libya,[130] Malaysia,[131] Maldives,[132] Malta,[133] Morocco,[134] Niger,[135] Singapore,[136] and Thailand[137] similarly define reservations to Article 16 as contrary to the Convention's object and purpose. Those on Israel,[138] Kuwait,[139] and Maldives[140] also express the Committee's view that reservations to any part of Article 7 are incompatible with the Convention's object and purpose.

A number of concluding observations also make clear that the Committee has maintained its early interest in the compatibility of Islamic law with the requirements of the Convention, but their careful wording also indicates that the Committee is alert to the controversy that surrounds this issue. Accordingly, based on the State party's explanation that its reservations to Article 16 of the Convention cannot be removed for religious reasons, its concluding observations on Jordan invite it to revise its Personal Status Act in the light of comparative jurisprudence where more progressive interpretations of Islamic law have been codified in legislative reforms to give women equal rights in marriage, divorce, and custody of children and to withdraw its reservations.[141] Similarly, the concluding observations on Morocco express the Committee's concern that the combination of reservations to Articles 2 and 15 leave no room for evolving concepts of Islamic law,[142] while those on Malaysia express the Committee's particular concern at the position expressed by the State party that laws based on Sharia interpretation cannot be reformed.[143]

The concluding observations on the initial and first reports of Singapore note that some reforms have already been introduced in Muslim personal law, and urge the State party to continue this process in consultation with members of different ethnic and religious groups, including women. The Committee also recommends that Singapore study reforms in other countries with similar legal traditions with a view to reviewing and reforming personal laws so they conform to the Convention and result in withdrawal of the State's reservations.[144] The concluding observations on the initial report of Saudi Arabia urge it to consider the withdrawal of its general reservation, particularly in light of the delegation's assurance that there is no contradiction in substance between the Convention and the Sharia.[145]

To date, the Committee has not addressed reservations in its consideration of individual communications or in relation to its inquiry competence, although reservations

[128] CO Egypt, CEDAW/C/EGY/CO/7 (2010) paras 13–14.
[129] CC Israel, A/60/38, part II, 33rd Session (2005) para 246.
[130] CO Libya, CEDAW/C/LBY/CO/5 (2009) para 13.
[131] CC Malaysia, A/61/38, part II, 35th Session (2007) para 27.
[132] CC Maldives, A/62/38, part I, 37th Session (2007) para 217.
[133] CO Malta, CEDAW/C/MLT/CO/4 (2010) para 13.
[134] CO Morocco, A/63/38, part I, 40th Session (2008) para 226.
[135] CC Niger, A/62/38, part II, 38th Session (2007) para 215.
[136] CC Singapore, A/62/38, part III, 39th Session (2007) para 105.
[137] CC Thailand, A/61/38, part I, 34th Session (2006) para 266.
[138] CC Israel, A/60/38, part II, 33rd Session (2005) para 246.
[139] CC Kuwait, A/59/38, part I, 38th Session (2004) para 61.
[140] CC Maldives, A/62/38, part I, 37th Session (2007) para 217.
[141] CC Jordan, CEDAW/C/JOR/CO/4 (2000) para 12.
[142] CC Morocco, A/52/38/Rev.1, 16th Session (1997) para 59.
[143] CC Malaysia, A/61/38, part II, 35th Session (2007) para 26.
[144] CC Singapore, A/62/38, part III, 39th Session (2007) para 105.
[145] CO Saudi Arabia, A/63/38, part I, 40th Session (2008) para 10.

have been raised by the relevant States parties to claim inadmissibility of three communications. In *Salgado v United Kingdom*, on discrimination against women in relation to their right to pass their nationality to their children, the United Kingdom contested the case's admissibility in light of its reservation to Article 9 which privileged discriminatory, but temporary and transitional provisions, noting that neither the Committee nor States parties had objected to the reservation.[146] In *Groupe d'Intérêt pour le Matronyme v France*[147] and *SOS Sexisme v France*,[148] concerning equality in choice of family name, the State party contested admissibility on the basis of its reservation to Article 16(1)(g). In all three cases, the Committee chose to declare the cases admissible on other grounds. However, the Committee has adopted a formal decision stating that the determination of the permissibility of a reservation falls within its functions in the examination of individual complaints.[149] The Committee will be unable to avoid discussion of reservations in the context of communications and inquiries, and should carefully analyze the content of its concluding observations in relation to reservations to ensure a consistent approach, at least in terms of which of the articles of the Convention it considers to constitute its object and purpose, with a view to developing a comprehensive general comment on the issue. As the next section of this chapter indicates, moreover, it is likely that ultimately reservations may be maintained only by those States parties whose legal systems include elements of the Islamic Sharia.

E. Removal and Modification of Reservations

Limited attention has been paid to the fact that a significant number of reservations entered by States parties at the time of accession or ratification have been modified or removed entirely. Indeed, more reservations to the Convention have been modified or removed than those to any other human rights treaty. These actions have affected general reservations, as well as reservations to particular provisions of the Convention, including Article 29(1) relating to dispute settlement.[150] Accordingly, the Committee's statement on the 15-year review of the implementation of the Beijing Declaration and Platform for Action notes the steady progress that has been made in this context and encourages other States parties to follow suit, including by drawing on the experience of States that have withdrawn reservations.[151]

Withdrawal or modification of reservations has usually occurred because changes in the State party's legislation or policy have rendered the reservations unnecessary. In some cases, the language of the reservations had indicated that the State party would work towards full compliance with the Convention and their removal. Some States parties modified or withdrew reservations after the presentation of their reports to the Committee,

---

[146] *Salgado v United Kingdom* CEDAW Communication No 11/2006 (2007) CEDAW/C/37/D/11/2006 paras 4.18 and 6.4.

[147] *Groupe d'Intérêt pour le Matronyme v France* CEDAW Communication No 12/2007 (2009) CEDAW/C/44/D/12/2007 paras 4.1, 4.2, 6.1, 6.2, 10.1, and 10.2.

[148] *SOS Sexisme v France* CEDAW Communication No 13/2007 (2009) CEDAW/C/44/D/13/2007 paras 4.1, 4.2, 6.1, 6.4, 9.2, and 9.3.

[149] CEDAW Decision 41/I (2008) UN Doc A/63/38, Part II, Chapter 1.

[150] The Byleorussian Soviet Socialist Republic (Belarus), Bulgaria, Czechoslovakia, Hungary, Mongolia, Poland, Romania, the Ukrainian Soviet Socialist Republic (Ukraine), and the Union of Soviet Socialist Republics (Russian Federation) have withdrawn their reservations to this provision.

[151] CEDAW Decision 45/V (2010) UN Doc A/65/38, Annex IV para 2.

during which the impact of reservations and their retention had been discussed. Some States parties have withdrawn reservations in the lead-up to or after their considera-tion under the Universal Periodic Review procedure of the Human Rights Council. The actions of these States parties may have been directly affected by the constructive dialogue with the Committee or the Universal Periodic Review. Civil society may have used these procedures in their advocacy for change at the national level.

As for general reservations, on 24 October 1991, Malawi withdrew its far-reach-ing reservation which had indicated that '[o]wing to the deep-rooted nature of some traditional customs and practices of Malawians, the Government of the Republic of Malawi shall not, for the time being, consider itself bound by such of the provisions of the Convention as require immediate eradication of such traditional customs and practices'. On 25 August 2004, Lesotho modified a similar declaration indicating that the Government would not take any legislative measures under the Convention that would be incompatible with the Lesotho Constitution. On 5 July 1995, the Libyan Arab Jamahiriya replaced its general reservation which subsumed its accession to the Convention to the laws on personal status derived from the Islamic Sharia, with a more specific reservation indicating that Article 2 would be implemented in light of the 'per-emptory norms' of the Islamic Sharia relating to inheritance and that the implementation of Article 16(1)(c) and (d) would be without prejudice to any of the rights guaranteed to women by the Islamic Sharia. This modification was submitted after Libya had pre-sented its report to the Committee, on which occasion the Committee and the delega-tion discussed its far-reaching reservation in detail, exploring ways in which it could be drawn more precisely. In early 1999, the Maldives also modified its reservation made on accession, which had stated that the State party would 'comply with the provisions of the Convention, except those which the Government may consider contradictory to the principles of the Islamic Sharia upon which the laws and traditions of the Maldives is founded', and that the 'Maldives does not see itself bound by any provisions of the Convention which obliges to change its Constitution or laws in any manner', replacing it with more specific reservations concerning Articles 7(a) and 16.[152]

Two States parties have withdrawn reservations which sought to preserve customs relat-ing to inheritance of chiefly titles from the reach of the Convention (Cook Islands, 30 July 2007; Fiji, 24 January 2000). One reservation relating to succession to the throne or noble titles has also been removed (Luxembourg, 9 January 2008). Malaysia withdrew its reservation to Article 5(a) which had subjected its application to the Sharia law on divi-sion of inherited property on 19 July 2010.[153] On 22 December 2003, France withdrew its reservation to Article 5(b) which had indicated that it was not to be interpreted as imply-ing joint exercise of parental authority in situations where French legislation envisaged exercise of this authority by only one parent.

---

[152] Germany objected that this modification did not constitute a withdrawal or partial withdrawal of the reservation, but rather new reservations after the ninety-day time limit then set by the depositary, and thus the objection did not affect the modification. In 2000, the time limit for objecting to late and modified reservations was extended to twelve months from the date of the depositary notification. Palitha Kohona indicates that this case led to the extension of the time limit for objecting to late and modified objections to twelve months as set out in the United Nations Legal Counsel, Note Verbale 'Modification of Reservations' (4 April 2000) LA 41 TR/221 (23–1), Kohona (n 20 above) 437–8. Maldives' reservation to Article 7(a) has been withdrawn.

[153] Malaysia's attempt to modify its reservations to Articles 5(a), 7(b), 9(2), and 16(1)(a) on 6 February 1998 failed because of an objection by France (n 20 above).

Reservations relating to Article 7, concerning equality in public life participation, have been withdrawn by a number of States parties. Belgium withdrew its reservation reserving the exercise of royal powers to men, as well as the function of ex officio senators to male members of the royal family, on 14 September 1998; France, its reservation subsuming Article 7 to its electoral code, on 26 March 1984; Kuwait its reservation to Article 7(a), restricting the right to vote and be eligible for election to males on 9 December 2005; Maldives its reservation to Article 7(a), which had subsumed the application of the provision to its Constitution; and Thailand, its reservation restricting the application of Articles 7 and 10, on equality between women and men in education in light of national security, maintenance of public order, and service or employment in the military or paramilitary, on 1 August 1996. Malaysia withdrew its reservation to Article 7(b) on 19 July 2010.

Reservations relating to equality of women with men in citizenship, and the capacity to devolve citizenship on their children have also been withdrawn: Algeria, to Article 9(2), 15 July 2009; Cyprus, to Article 9(2), 28 June 2000; Egypt, to Article 9(2), 4 January 2008; Fiji, to Article 9, 24 January 2000; Ireland, to Article 9(1), 19 December 1996; Jamaica, to Article 9(2), 8 September 1995; Liechtenstein, to Article 9(2), 3 October 1996; Malaysia, Article 9(1), 6 February 1998; Republic of Korea, Article 9, 24 August 1999; Thailand, to Article 9(2), 26 October 1992; and Turkey, its declaration relating to Article 9(1), 29 January 2008.

On 24 July 2007, Singapore withdrew a general reservation relating to employment and citizenship which had stated that as 'Singapore is geographically one of the smallest independent countries in the world and one of the most densely populated, the Republic of Singapore accordingly reserves the right to apply such laws and conditions governing the entry into, stay in, employment in and departure from its territory of those who do not have the right under the laws of Singapore to enter and remain indefinitely in Singapore, and to the conferment, acquisitions and loss of citizenship of women who have acquired such citizenship by marriage and of children born outside Singapore'.

The United Kingdom withdrew reservations preserving the freedom of parental choice with regard to education of children, its right not to interfere with the liberty of individuals and bodies to establish and direct educational institutions, and in relation to teaching curriculum, provision of text books and teaching methods, as well as coeducation on 22 March 1996. Several States parties have withdrawn or modified reservations excluding women from particular forms of employment, such as night work (Austria, 14 September 2000), underground work in mines (New Zealand, 13 January 1989; The United Kingdom, 4 January 1995), in the military (Austria, 14 September 2000; Australia, 30 August 2000; Cook Islands, 30 July 2007; Germany, 10 December 2001; New Zealand, 5 July 2007; Switzerland, 29 April 2004), and law enforcement (Cook Islands, 30 July 2007; New Zealand, 5 July 2007). Canada withdrew its declaration relating to Article 11(1)(d) on 28 May 1992 and Ireland those reservations to Article 11(1) which had expressed its right to consider its domestic legislation as sufficient implementation of this provision on 9 December 1996. A general declaration with a similar objective was withdrawn by the United Kingdom on 22 March 1996. Mauritius withdrew its unexplained reservations to Article 11(1)(b) and (d) on 5 May 1998, and Thailand withdrew its reservations insofar as they applied to Article 11(1)(b) on 25 January 1991. New Zealand withdrew the reservation relating to Article 11(2)(b) requiring the introduction of maternity leave with pay on 5 September 2003, but did not extend this to Tokelau.

Bangladesh withdrew its reservation to Article 13(a) relating to the right to family benefits, which had been explained as conflicting with the Sharia, on 23 July 1997. Ireland withdrew its reservation to the same article which had been explained as based on its desire to apply more favourable social security conditions for women than men pending the entry into force of envisaged legislation, on 19 December 1996; Ireland withdrew similarly worded reservations to Article 13(b) and (c) concerning access to credit and other financial services, and recreational activities provided by private persons, organizations, or enterprises, on 11 June 2004, while the United Kingdom withdrew reservations to this article based on the impact of taxation legislation on married women on 4 January 1995, and in regard to certain social security benefits on 22 March 1996.

Some States parties have withdrawn or modified reservations to Article 15 guaranteeing equality before the law. Belgium withdrew its reservation to Article 15(2) and (3), which was directed to providing a transitional rule that couples could maintain their prior (and discriminatory) marriage contracts, on 8 July 2002. France withdrew reservations to the same provisions on 21 July 1986 following the amendment of discriminatory legislation. Ireland withdrew its reservation to Article 15(3) which had stated that it would not supplement existing provisions in Irish law which accorded women identical capacity to men in this context on 24 March 2000, while Thailand withdrew its unexplained reservation to Article 15(3) on 25 January 1991. Reservations to Article 15(4) requiring States parties to accord to women and men the same rights relating to movement and choice of residence and domicile have been withdrawn by Brazil on 20 December 1994 and Ireland on 19 December 1986, following amendment of domestic legislation. The United Kingdom also withdrew its reservation to this paragraph which had subsumed its application to its immigration legislation on 24 July 2007, and Jordan did so on 5 May 2009.

Very few States parties have withdrawn their reservations to Article 16 on equality in marriage and family life. On 22 March 1996, the United Kingdom withdrew a reservation explaining that its acceptance of Article 16(1) shall not be treated as limiting personal freedom to dispose of property or giving a person a right to property the subject of such a limitation. Brazil withdrew unexplained reservations to Article 16(1)(a), (c), (g), and (h) providing for equal rights to enter into marriage, the same rights and responsibilities during marriage, the same personal rights as husband and wife, including the right to choose a family name, a profession, and occupation and with regard to property, on 20 December 1994. The Republic of Korea withdrew unexplained reservations relating to Article 16(1)(c), (d), and (f) on 15 March 1991. France withdrew its reservations to Article 16(1)(c), (d), and (h) on 21 July 1986, in light of the repeal of discriminatory legislation relating to family property. On 23 July 1997, Bangladesh withdrew its reservation relating to Article 16(1)(f) providing that States parties shall ensure women and men the same rights and responsibilities with regard to guardianship, trusteeship, and adoption of children, which had been explained as conflicting with Sharia law. Mauritius withdrew its reservations to Article 16(1)(g), on the personal rights of husband and wife, including the right to choose a family name, a profession, and an occupation, on 5 May 1998. Malaysia withdrew its reservations to Article 16(1)(b), (d), (e), and (h) which had been subjected to the application of the Islamic Sharia and the Federal Constitution, on 6 February 1998. Luxembourg withdrew its reservation to Article 16(1)(g) on the right to choose a family name on 9 January 2008. Malaysia's reservation to Article 16(2) was removed on 19 July 2010.

F. Conclusion

The current situation in relation to reservations to the Convention is a significant improvement on that of its early years, when many States parties had expressed a limited commitment to its principles by entering far-reaching reservations on accession or ratification. However, while reservations have been gradually removed, those that remain are noteworthy. Few which are explained on the basis of culture and religion have been withdrawn, and it is likely that in the near future reservations which meet the definition of incompatibility in Article 28 will be maintained by those States parties whose legal systems include elements of the Islamic Sharia. Other States parties should continue to object to any new reservations, and the Committee will need to approach this area with sensitivity, while maintaining its constructive approach. It may also wish to reiterate its early requests for studies on the compatibility of the Convention with the Sharia, particularly taking account of the growing number of Islamic scholars who have produced studies in this area.[154] The Committee may also wish to consider developing other tools, such as a procedure to follow up statements by delegations during constructive dialogue that reservations are in the process of being reconsidered and withdrawn. In 2008, Beate Schöpp-Schilling suggested that such statements should be tracked by the Committee, and should be followed up by a letter if the promised action did not occur within a year of the relevant reporting round.

---

[154] See, for example, the sources at www.musawah.org, including Musawah 'CEDAW and Muslim Family Laws: In Search of Common Ground' (Sisters in Islam, 2011). N Abaid, 'Sharia, Muslim States and International Treaty Obligations: A Comparative Study' (British Institute of International and Comparative Law, 2008) 59–99.

Article 29

(1) Any dispute between two or more States Parties concerning the interpretation or application of the present Convention which is not settled by negotiation shall, at the request of one of them, be submitted to arbitration. If within six months from the date of the request for arbitration the parties are unable to agree on the organization of the arbitration, any one of those parties may refer the dispute to the International Court of Justice by request in conformity with the Statute of the Court.

(2) Each State Party may at the time of signature or ratification of the present Convention or accession thereto declare that it does not consider itself bound by paragraph 1 of this article. The other States Parties shall not be bound by that paragraph with respect to any State Party which has made such a reservation.

(3) Any State Party which has made a reservation in accordance with paragraph 2 of this article may at any time withdraw that reservation by notification to the Secretary-General of the United Nations.

A. Introduction

In contrast to other UN human rights treaties,[1] the Convention does not provide for a special inter-State complaints mechanism. Hence, the Article 29 'settlement of disputes clause' is an important tool for maintaining the integrity of the text and monitoring the implementation of the Convention. The only other monitoring regime provided for within the Convention itself is the Committee review of State party reports. The Democratic Republic of the Congo invoked Article 29, as well as similar provisions of other human rights treaties, in an unsuccessful attempt to establish the jurisdiction of the ICJ in its dispute with Rwanda in the Case concerning Armed Activities on the Territory of the Congo.[2]

* I would like to thank Sahrah Al-Nasrawe-Sözeri, Benjamin Feyen, Ines Franke, Anna-Maria Paulus, Allison Sherrier, and Eric Veillerobe for their assistance on this chapter and on the chapters on arts 25, 26, 27, and 30.
[1] eg ICCPR art 41; ICERD art 22; CAT art 21.
[2] *Armed Activities on the Territory of the Congo (New Application) (Democratic Republic of the Congo v Rwanda)* [2006] ICJ Rep 6 paras 80–93. In its request for provisional measures the DRC unsuccessfully

B. Travaux Préparatoires

No article corresponding to the present Article 29 was discussed until the final deliberations on the Convention in the Working Group of the Third Committee of the UNGA.
Some delegates raised the need to have a process for inter-State complaints regarding the
Convention's implementation and for complaints by individuals and/or by national and
international NGOs regarding violations of the Convention.[3] No such processes were
included in the final text.[4]

An article on the settlement of disputes was first introduced by the United States[5] with a
text based on the similar provision of ICERD Article 22.[6] The prototype for ICERD Article
22 (as well as dispute settlement clauses in other human rights treaties) was Article IX
of the Convention on the Prevention and Punishment of the Crime of Genocide.[7] The
United States' proposal was opposed on the ground that the inclusion of this Article would
be outside the scope of the Convention by dealing with domestic rather than international
affairs, as well as on the ground that it conflicted with the Statute of the ICJ, without
specifying the objection. Some representatives were concerned about any mention of the
ICJ. Supporters of the article argued that its absence could be understood as a decision by
the international community not to seriously uphold women's rights.[8] Moreover, provision for the settlement of disputes about human rights cannot be considered as an internal
affair. France demurred that the United States' proposal was not sufficiently explicit in
terms of negotiations prior to the request to the ICJ. Its proposed compromise text was
identical to Article 16 of the International Convention against the Taking of Hostages.[9]
The United States orally proposed to add two sentences to paragraph 2, which provided
for settlement of disputes by conciliation. After discussions on the preference for either the
original text proposed by the United States or the compromise text proposed by France,
the latter version was adopted unamended by the Working Group.[10] No further problems
were noted during the discussion in the Third Committee, and the Article was adopted as
Article 29 of the draft Convention.[11]

---

sought to establish prima facie jurisdiction on the basis of dispute settlement clauses in other human rights
conventions including ICERD art 22; the Convention on the Prevention and Punishment of Genocide
art IX.

[3] UN Doc E/CN.6/573 paras 101, 104, and 105; see LA Rehof, *Guide to the Travaux Préparatoires of the
United Nations Convention on the Elimination of All Forms of Discrimination against Women* (1993) 238–9.

[4] See the discussion in ch on the Optional Protocol.   [5] Rehof (n 3 above) 239.

[6] ICERD art 22 provides for any dispute between States parties with respect to the interpretation or
application of the Convention, which is not settled by negotiation 'or by the procedures expressly provided
for in this Convention' to be referred to the ICJ at the request of either party to the dispute. A procedure expressly provided for is the mandatory inter-State communication procedure stipulated in ICERD
arts 11–13.

[7] This provision stipulates that any dispute between States parties 'relating to the interpretation, application or fulfilment', of the Convention shall be submitted to the ICJ at the request of any State party to the
dispute.

[8] K Abe, 'Article 29': Settlement of Disputes in Japanese Association of Women's Rights (ed), *Convention
on the Elimination of All Forms of Discrimination against Women: A Commentary* (1995) 414, 415.

[9] Ibid; see also UN Doc A/C.3/34/WG.1/CRP.2/Add.3 (1979).   [10] Rehof (n 3 above) 239.

[11] Abe (n 8 above) 416.

C. Practice of States Parties

Article 29(1) is the only Convention article for which reservation is expressly allowed. It is unsurprisingly the most reserved article. Thirty-nine States parties entered reservations upon signature, ratification, or succession in conformity with Article 29(2), excluding themselves from the dispute settlement procedures provided for in paragraph 1. Nine States parties have withdrawn their original reservations, according to Article 29(3).

D. Issues of Interpretation

A dispute settlement clause contributes to the effective implementation of a treaty. Therefore, all States parties are authorized to rely on the clause. Any State party can intervene if it considers that another State party impedes the aim of the Convention, by characterizing the issue as a matter of interpretation and application of the Convention. Article 29 favours the dispute resolution processes listed in the UN Charter Article 33—negotiation, ad hoc arbitration and adjudication—rather than a more specific inter-State complaint procedure. Article 29 also establishes the compulsory jurisdiction of the ICJ in accordance with Article 36(1) of its Statute, if the pre-conditions of Article 29 are met. Although it is placed with the procedural clauses, the dispute settlement clause remains a substantive provision of the Convention.[12]

I. Article 29(1)

Article 29(1) provides for negotiation, arbitration, and the ICJ as possible mechanisms to resolve a dispute. It provides for recourse to the ICJ regarding any dispute between two or more States parties concerning the interpretation or application of the Convention, on the preconditions that it has not been possible to settle the dispute by negotiation; that following this failure, the dispute has, at the request of one of the States parties, been submitted to arbitration; and if the parties have been unable to agree on the organization of the arbitration, a period of six months has elapsed from the date of the request for arbitration. The ICJ has determined in its decision *Democratic Republic of Congo (DRC) v Rwanda* from the wording of Article 29(1) that these conditions are cumulative.[13] In this case, the ICJ found in 2006 that it had no jurisdiction in the case of the *Armed Activities on the Territory of the Congo (New Application: 2002)*. The DRC had instituted proceedings against Rwanda in respect of a dispute concerning 'massive, serious and flagrant violations of human rights and of international humanitarian law' allegedly committed by Rwanda on the territory of the DRC.[14] The Court examined eleven bases of jurisdiction (such as, *inter alia,* Convention Article 29(1)) put forward by the DRC and concluded that none of the bases could be accepted to establish its jurisdiction in this case. The court based its judgment on the arguments that the DRC had failed to prove it had attempted to settle the dispute amicably or seek arbitration which is a precondition to any application; and that Rwanda had rejected the court's jurisdiction. Following this decision, Article 29(1) requires a dispute about the Convention and negotiations

---

[12] S Rosenne, 'Final Clauses' in R Wolfrum (ed), *The Max Planck Encyclopedia of Public International Law* (2008) para 16 online edition <www.mpepil.com> accessed 31 December 2010.
[13] *Armed Activities on the Territory of the Congo* (n 2 above) para 87.   [14] Ibid para 1.

about this dispute. Negotiations must take place and be relevant in that they refer to the interpretation or application of the Convention. Article 29(1) requires that any dispute be subject to negotiation prior to arbitration, and then there must be a positive attempt at arbitration;[15] it is not sufficient to presume it will be a failure. A separate opinion is held by judge Al-Khasawneh who argues that there are no special requirements that negotiations should be itemized.[16]

Interpretation of a treaty (the giving of meaning to a text) is generally sought in connection with application of the treaty to a given situation, which will be crucial in defining the issues for interpretation and may affect the process of interpretation.[17] Interpretation and application of a treaty also encompass the consequences of a violation of individual rights under the treaty.[18] Since it is not possible to apply a treaty except on the basis of some interpretation, there is little practical distinction between the two elements of the formula.[19] In the application of dispute settlement clauses they tend to converge.[20]

If negotiations fail, arbitration proceedings are to be initiated. Lack of agreement between the parties on the organization of arbitration cannot be presumed since the condition is formally set out in Article 29.[21] If the States parties cannot agree on organization of the arbitration within the determined time period, the dispute may be referred to the ICJ by one or all States parties in conformity with Article 36(1) of the Statute of the ICJ. Application of Article 29 goes to establishment of the Court's jurisdiction, not to the admissibility of the case.[22] The possibility for all States parties to the dispute to invoke the ICJ emphasizes the universal and objective rather than reciprocal character[23] of the Convention.[24]

Since this procedure has not yet been successfully applied, the Committee's general recommendations are all the more important as to the interpretation and application of the Convention.[25]

II. Article 29(2)

By its terms, reservations to Article 29 are not contrary to the object and purpose of the Convention.[26] This paragraph is a (practical) means to allow States that do not accept the jurisdiction of the ICJ to become parties to the Convention.[27] The second sentence of

---

[15] Ibid para 83.

[16] Separate opinion of Judge Khasawneh para 13 <http://www.icj-cij.org/docket/files/126/10445.pdf> accessed 31 December 2010.

[17] VCLT arts 31–3.

[18] *LaGrand (Germany v United States of America)* [2001] ICJ Reps 466–517 para 42. The dispute related, *inter alia*, to whether there had been violation of Vienna Convention on Consular Relations Arts 36(1)(a) and (c) in consequence of the breach of 36(1)(b) and whether the dispute came within the Optional Protocol art 1 whereby 'disputes arising out of the interpretation or application of the Convention shall lie within the compulsory jurisdiction of the International Court of Justice...'. See also *Oil Platforms (Islamic Republic of Iran v United States of America)* [1996] ICJ Reps 803–21 paras 16–20.

[19] *Applicability of the Obligation to Arbitrate under Section 21 of the United Nations Headquarters Agreement of 26 June 1947 (Advisory Opinion)* [1988] ICJ Rep 57 para 59 (separate opinion Judge Shahabuddeen).

[20] C McLachlan, 'The Principle of Systemic Integration and Article 31(3)(c) of the Vienna Convention' (2005) 54 *Intl and Comparative L Quarterly* 279, 286.

[21] *Armed Activities on the Territory of the Congo* (n 2 above) para 92.   [22] Ibid para 88.

[23] *Reservations to the Convention on the Prevention and Punishment of the Crime of Genocide (Advisory Opinion)* [1951] ICJ 15 Rep 12.

[24] Recourse to the ICJ has the added benefit to the parties of being funded by member contributions to the UN budget; UN, *Final Clauses of Multilateral Treaties: Handbook* (2003) 89.

[25] See the discussion in the ch on art 21.   [26] Abe (n 8 above) 419.   [27] Ibid 417.

the paragraph means that the consequence of a reservation of Article 29(1) is that other States parties are not bound by paragraph 1 with respect to any State party which has made such a reservation. This accords with the ICJ history that compulsory jurisdiction has never been accepted.[28] If one party to a dispute has opted out, no other State party may invoke the procedure against the opting-out State party. Nor is the reserving State party allowed to bring a claim under Article 29 against any other State party.

A reservation under Article 29(2) can be made at the time of signature and ratification or accession, but not upon succession.[29]

III. Article 29(3)

Reservations under paragraph 2 may be withdrawn any time through notification to the UN SG.[30] Such a withdrawal is irreversible. After a reservation has been withdrawn, no new reservation under Article 29(2) would be possible because the time for entering such a reservation has expired.[31]

---

[28] Social States in particular did not accept the compulsory jurisdiction.
[29] Compare VCLT art 19.   [30] See the discussion in ch on art 25(2).
[31] See section D.II. above.

Article 30

The present Convention, the Arabic, Chinese, English, French, Russian and Spanish texts of which are equally authentic, shall be deposited with the Secretary-General of the United Nations.

IN WITNESS WHEREOF the undersigned, duly authorized, have signed the present Convention.

A. Introduction

It is current practice that treaties concluded under the auspices of the UN provide in their final clauses that the texts are equally authentic in all the official languages of the UN and officially recognized at the date the treaty was adopted.[1] The official languages are Arabic, Chinese, English, French, Russian, and Spanish.[2] These are the languages in which the meaning of the Convention's provisions is to be determined and only the wording of one of the six authentic languages is binding.

B. Travaux Préparatoires

The first version of the final provisions in the draft Convention proposed by the USSR did not include Arabic as one of the authentic languages and provided that the Convention should be deposited in the UN archives and that 'duly certified copies of this Convention shall be transmitted to the governments of the signatory and acceding States'.[3] Neither suggestion was adopted in the final text. Syria orally proposed to add Arabic.[4] According to Benin's proposal, the languages were listed alphabetically.[5] The United Kingdom suggested including a second paragraph stipulating that 'the Secretary-General of the United Nations shall transmit to the Governments of the signatory and acceding States, duly

---

* I would like to thank Sahrah Al-Nasrawe-Sözeri, Benjamin Feyen, Ines Franke, Anna-Maria Paulus, Allison Sherrier, and Eric Veillerobe for their assistance on this chapter and on the chapters on arts 25, 26, 27, and 29.

[1] cf eg ICERD art 25; ICCPR art 53; ICCPR OP I art 14; ICCPR OP II art 11; ICESCR art 31; CAT art 33; OPCAT art 37; CRC art 54; CMW art 93; CEDAW OP art 21; CPRD art 50.

[2] Arabic was first recognized in 1973 as the sixth official UN language; UNGA Res 3190 (XXVIII) (18 December 1973).

[3] UN Doc E/CN.6/AC.1/L.2 (1974) art 23; LA Rehof, *Guide to the Travaux Préparatoires of the United Nations Convention on the Elimination of All Forms of Discrimination against Women* (1993) 295.

[4] Rehof (n 3 above) 241.   [5] Ibid.

certified copies of the present Convention'[6] which was later withdrawn.[7] The final text of the final article was adopted along with the rest of the draft Convention.[8]

C. Practice of the Secretary-General

Under Article 77(1)(b) of the VCLT, the UN SG as depositary circulates certified true copies (accurate duplication) of the Convention to all States and entities which may become parties to the Convention. The UN SG no longer sends hard copies of the Convention to States parties since it is available in all languages online[9] and on the UN Official Document System. The treaty section of the UN Office of Legal Affairs sends a depositary notification to States via e-mail.[10]

D. Issues of Interpretation

According to VCLT Article 33(3), the terms of a treaty, which has been authenticated in multiple languages are presumed to have the same meaning in each authentic text. However, it might be possible that the comparison of the authentic texts reveals a difference in meaning. In that case, the true meaning is to be identified by applying the rules of interpretation from VCLT Articles 31, 32, and 33(4) whereby the object and purpose of the Convention are the pivotal factors. The goal is not to find the meaning which can best be reconciled with the object and purpose, but to balance the differences and find a common tenor among the different versions. It is not acceptable to use one text and ignore the others to avoid ambiguities.[11]

The Committee supports popularization of the Convention and welcomes its translation into local languages.[12] Domestic application of the Convention is likely to use a translation into the local language, if available. This version might be an official translation authorized by the government. Translation mistakes might occur, but they do not affect the substance of the Convention and VCLT Article 79 does not apply.[13] Such translation merely reflects the interpretation by the individual State party. Any act of public authorities (including of the courts) based on domestic translation is legally assailable under international law and may need to be reversed.

Although neither the Convention nor the Committee[14] require that the text be made available in accessible format for persons with disabilities, the Convention should be

---

[6] Similar wording is an integral part of comparable provisions such as CERD art 25; CCPR art 53; CCPR OP I art 14; CCPR OP II art 11; CESCR art 31; CAT art 33; OPCAT art 37; CRC art 54; CMW art 93; CEDAW OP art 21.

[7] Rehof (n 3 above) 241.

[8] K Abe 'Article 30: Authentic Text' in Japanese Association of Women's Rights (ed), *Convention on the Elimination of All Forms of Discrimination against Women: A Commentary* (1992) 420, 421.

[9] <http://www2.ohchr.org/english/bodies/cedaw/convention.htm> accessed 31 December 2010.

[10] M Nowak and E McArthur, *The United Nations Conventions Against Torture: A Commentary* (2008) art 33 para 4.

[11] Abe (n 8 above) 422.

[12] GR 28 para 1. cf eg, CO Eritrea, CEDAW/C/ERI/CO/3 (2006) para 8; CO Timor-Leste, CEDAW/C/TLS/CO/1 (2009) para 20.

[13] VCLT art 79 deals with the correction of errors in texts or in certified copies of treaties.

[14] The Committee invites States parties at least to expand its online infrastructure and promote the use of media and information and communication technologies to facilitate access to the Convention, see eg CO Turkmenistan, CEDAW/C/TKM/CO/2 (2006) para 13.

construed in light of subsequent treaties such as CRPD Article 49. States parties have started distributing the Convention or State party reports in Braille and in electronic formats and audio tape, as well as in all official languages,[15] although the Convention and the Committee do not call for this explicitly.

The repetition of the UN SG's function as depositary in connection with the authenticity of languages must be seen in light of his task to add to the text of the Convention a 'multilingual' title page and 'signature page', on which the names of the States parties concerned appear in all official UN languages.[16] The article also indicates that all authentic versions are to be deposited in the same way. The depositary is charged with ensuring that the final version of the text is a faithful reproduction of that which was agreed upon by the contracting parties and with correcting any errors, as well as with verifying the authenticity of the translated material. Although errors in the treaty text, often caused by translation difficulties, do not affect the validity of a treaty, the UN SG is responsible for correcting them and is encouraged to find a remedy to correct drafting oversights.[17]

---

[15] South Africa, Combined Second, Third and Fourth Periodic Report of States Parties, CEDAW/C/ZAF/2–4 (2010) 22.

[16] UN, *Summary of Practice of the Secretary-General as Depositary* (1999) UN Doc ST/LEG/7/Rev.1 12.

[17] R Caddell, 'Depositary' in R Wolfrum (ed), *The Max Planck Encyclopedia of Public International Law* (2008) paras 1, 9, and 10, online edition <http://www.mpepil.com> accessed 31 December 2010.

Optional Protocol

* I would like to thank Stephanie Jensen-Cormier, Heather Northcott, Nathalie Stadelmann, and Mercedes Morales (OHCHR) for their assistance on this chapter and on the chapter on art 28.

A. Introduction[1]

The Optional Protocol (OP) to the Convention on the Elimination of All Forms of Discrimination against Women was adopted by consensus by the UNGA on 6 October 1999.[2] It was opened for signature, ratification, and accession for all States parties to the Convention on 10 December 1999 and entered into force on 22 December 2000. At 31 December 2010, 100 States from all regions of the world were party to the Protocol. Accordingly, individuals or groups of individuals claiming to be victims of those States' violations of Convention rights have the opportunity to complain of those alleged violations to the Committee on the Elimination of Discrimination against Women. The OP also invests the Committee with competence to conduct an inquiry into reliable allegations of grave or systematic violations of the rights in the Convention in individual States parties. Three States parties have opted out of this procedure.[3]

This section surveys the background to the OP. It is followed by a commentary on each provision which compares the OP with provisions in other human rights treaties, highlights its drafting history, and describes its interpretation by the Committee.

B. Background

I. Negotiations of the Convention

During the negotiations of the Convention in the Commission on the Status of Women (CSW) from 1972 to 1976 and the Third Committee of the UNGA from 1977 to 1979, the inclusion of a petitions procedure as a means of overseeing Convention implementation was proposed by several Member States. In the early stages of the drafting process, Canada suggested 'that careful thought be given to setting up a ... reporting procedure within the Commission on the Status of Women and a method for handling complaints by States and individuals regarding violations of the new convention'. Sweden suggested considering a procedure for international supervision similar to that in ICERD and the ICCPR OPI. It stressed 'that it is essential that such supervision provisions should also provide for the right of private persons to lodge complaints concerning a State party's implementation of the Convention'.[4] The drafts considered by CSW, however, did not contain a concrete proposal for an individual complaints procedure.

During the 1976 CSW session, Belgium submitted a draft article providing that as soon as the Convention entered into force, States parties would undertake to examine in the CSW the possibility of establishing procedures for the implementation of the Convention with a view to enabling States parties and their nationals to address themselves to the ad hoc group which was being proposed as the monitoring body for the Convention. Belgium considered that the suggested reporting procedure was a 'minimalist' solution, and that the precedents of the ICCPR's First OP and the ICERD provision for individual complaints after domestic remedies had been exhausted, should be the point of departure, as the Convention should not lag behind those precedents.[5]

---

[1] The views expressed in this chapter are those of the author and do not necessarily reflect the views of the United Nations.

[2] UNGA Res 54/4 (6 October 1999) UN Doc A/RES/54/4.   [3] Bangladesh, Belize, and Colombia.

[4] UN Doc E/CN.6/573 (1973) paras 104–7.

[5] ECOSOC, 'CSW Summary Record' (1976) UN Doc E/CN.6/SR.673 paras 93–4.

Although there was some support for the proposal, it was rejected by eleven votes to eight, with three abstentions.[6] Some queried whether it was appropriate to refer such a matter to the CSW, with several delegations suggesting that a complaints procedure was not appropriate for the Convention, distinguishing between conventions on 'serious international crimes', such as apartheid and racial discrimination and those dealing with areas such as discrimination against women where States had already begun to cooperate and where it would be inappropriate to establish a body which would act as a 'court of judgement.'[7] Some viewed the proposal as legally controversial as States would only be able to modify the Convention in accordance with its amendment provisions. Others considered the CSW reporting procedure to be adequate, with concerns being raised that inclusion of the article might discourage ratification and accession and jeopardize the reporting provision.[8]

The inclusion of an individual complaints procedure was raised again after the CSW forwarded the completed draft Convention to the 32nd session of the UNGA in 1977, when the Netherlands suggested that the Convention should contain a provision for inter-State complaints. It also suggested that 'serious consideration be given to including in the draft Convention the right of individual petition, providing persons under the jurisdiction of the States parties with the opportunity to submit complaints to the supervisory body'.[9] No draft proposal was submitted, and thus the Convention confers on the Committee one monitoring procedure: the consideration of States parties' reports.

II. The Campaign for Further Monitoring Procedures

The CEDAW Committee started work in 1982, focusing first on the development of working methods and establishing the reporting procedure as an effective mechanism to encourage implementation of the Convention at the national level.

Early commentators on the Committee noted that its monitoring procedures were limited in comparison with those of other UN human rights treaty bodies, and that the tools available to it to encourage implementation were also comparatively weak.[10] Individual Committee members raised the possibility of strengthening the Convention and the Committee through an optional protocol which would include a petitions procedure, and at its 10th session in 1991, it was suggested that the Committee should propose this possibility as part of its contribution to the forthcoming Second World Conference on Human Rights to be held in Vienna in 1993.[11]

Strengthening available international mechanisms for monitoring women's human rights and the possible creation of new mechanisms were raised in 1991 in a UN SG report

---

[6] ECOSOC, 'Report of the CSW—Twenty-Sixth and Resumed Twenty-Sixth Sessions' (1977) UN Doc E/CN.6/608 para 208.

[7] ECOSOC, 'CSW Summary Record' (1976) UN Doc E/CN.6/SR.674 paras 4 and 14.

[8] 'Report of the CSW—Twenty-Sixth and Resumed Twenty-Sixth Sessions' (n 6 above) paras 207–8.

[9] Report of the Secretary-General, 'Draft Convention on the Elimination of Discrimination against Women' (1977) UN Doc A/32/218 para 151.

[10] A Byrnes and J Connors, 'Enforcing the Human Rights of Women: A Complaints Procedure for the Convention on the Elimination of All Forms of Discrimination against Women?' (1996) 21/3 *Brooklyn J of Intl L* 679, 689 n 20; see also T Meron, 'Enhancing the Effectiveness of the Prohibition of Discrimination against Women' (1990) 84 *Am J Intl L* 213, 216.

[11] A Byrnes, *CEDAW #10: Building on a Decade of Achievement: A Report on the Tenth Session of the Committee on the Elimination of Discrimination against Women* (1991) 22–3.

to the CSW which examined its communications procedure.[12] This report concluded that the CSW procedure was weak compared with other UN human rights procedures, and that little attention was given to the human rights concerns of women by those procedures. The procedure does not provide individuals with an opportunity to seek redress, nor does it provide an opportunity to undertake a detailed study on any particular situation.[13] The report made several proposals to strengthen procedures for women, including the addition of an optional protocol to the Convention which would give the Committee competence to receive and consider individual communications alleging violations of the Convention by a State party that had accepted this competence. The report noted that the HRC, CERD, and CAT had this capacity.[14] The CSW took no action on these proposals.

Proposals were also made during this period for an instrument giving the Committee competence to consider petitions to strengthen the international framework to confront violence against women. In November 1991, the UN convened an expert group meeting to consider options in this context. These included a substantive protocol to the Convention which would address violence against women; a protocol to the Convention which would include substantive elements on violence against women as well as a complaints mechanism relating to such violence; a protocol which would provide the Committee with competence to consider complaints relating to all the rights in the Convention; and the elaboration and adoption of a new declaration or convention on violence against women.[15] The expert group recommended the elaboration and adoption of a declaration on violence against women, a recommendation endorsed by the CSW and the UNGA. This led to the negotiation of the Declaration on the Elimination of Violence against Women, adopted in 1993.[16]

Strengthening the international human rights framework for women and girls was amongst the demands made by the highly organized international women's movement which mobilized before the Vienna World Conference on Human Rights. Throughout the preparations for the Conference, NGOs and other actors demanded that greater attention be paid to women's human rights in all UN activities, and the strengthening of existing UN institutions whose main focus was the advancement of women and women's human rights.[17] They also called for the addition of an optional protocol to the Convention which

---

[12] Report of the Secretary-General 'Monitoring the Implementation of the Nairobi Forward-Looking Strategies for the Advancement of Women: Examining Existing Mechanisms for Communications on the Status of Women' (1991) UN Doc E/CN.6/1991/10.

[13] Report of the Secretary-General, 'Advisability of the appointment of a special rapporteur on laws that discriminate against women' (2006) UN Doc E/CN.6/2006/8 paras 33–4.

[14] Report of Secretary-General (n 12 above) paras 155–6.

[15] 'Report of the Expert Group Meeting on Violence against Women' (1991) UN Doc EGM/VAW/1991/1 paras 34–7; Report of the Secretary-General 'Violence against women in all its forms' (1991) UN Doc E/CN.6/1992/4; Working Paper presented by the Government of Canada, *Issues in the Development of an International Instrument on Violence against Women* (1991) UN Doc EGM/VAW/WP.1; A Byrnes, *Observations on the Background Paper Prepared by the Government of Canada on Issues in the Development of an International Instrument on Violence against Women* (1991).

[16] UNGA Res 48/104 (20 December 1993) UN Doc A/RES/48/104.

[17] DJ Sullivan, 'Women's Human Rights and the 1993 Word Conference on Human Rights' (1994) 88 *Am J Intl L* 152; J Connors, 'Non-Governmental Organizations and the Human Rights of Women' in P Willets (ed), *The Conscience of the World: The Influence of Non-Governmental Organizations in the United Nations System* (1996) 147; S Marks, 'Nightmare and Noble Dream: the 1993 World Conference on Human Rights' (1994) 53 *Cambridge LJ* 54, 58–60; Report submitted by UNIFEM to the World Conference on Human Rights (1993) UN Doc A/CONF.157/PC/61/Add.17 paras 19–20.

would include the right of individual petition.[18] This advocacy was well repaid, with the final document of the Conference calling on the CSW and the Committee to 'quickly examine the possibility of introducing the right of petition through the preparation of an optional protocol to the Convention'.[19]

In January 1994, the CEDAW Committee suggested that the CSW request that an expert group meeting be convened in 1994 to prepare a draft optional protocol providing a complaints procedure. It indicated that the expert group should be composed of five to ten independent experts, including a member of the Committee designated by the Chairperson, with knowledge of the different forms of civilization, the principal legal systems and international law, and the experience of the other human rights treaty bodies in the preparation and operation of optional protocols. The report of the expert group would then be presented to the Committee for comments, and thereafter to the CSW for action.[20]

When the CSW met in March 1994, it considered the Vienna Conference outcome, but did not endorse the Committee's proposal for the Secretary-General to convene an expert group meeting. Rather, the Commission, through ECOSOC, agreed to examine the feasibility of introducing the right to petition under the Convention at its 39th session in 1995, 'taking into account the results of any governmental expert group meeting that may be convened prior to that session'.[21] No meeting was convened, but, during 1994, an independent expert group meeting was organized by the Women in Law Project of the International Human Rights Law Group, with the Maastricht Centre for Human Rights at the University of Limburg in the Netherlands.[22] Participants came from all regions, and included three members of CEDAW, members of other treaty bodies, and international human rights and women's human rights experts. The outcome of the meeting was a draft optional protocol ('the Maastricht draft') which provided the Committee with competence to receive and consider individual complaints alleging violations of the Convention and inquire into allegations of serious or systematic violations of its terms.[23] The Maastricht draft built on existing human rights procedures but also contained innovative elements which sought to make its procedures more accessible to women.

The Maastricht draft was presented to the Committee by one of its members in a paper that outlined the content of the draft, raised a number of questions, and recommended that the Committee endorse the draft and recommend its adoption by the UNGA.[24]

---

[18] NGO Forum Final Report, 'All Human Rights for All: Recommendations adopted by the Forum of Non-Governmental Organizations at the World Conference for Human Rights: The New Consensus, June 1993' in M Nowak (ed), *World Conference on Human Rights, Vienna, June 1993: The Contributions of NGOs Reports and Documents* (1994) 230, 231 para 6 and 235 para 4.

[19] Vienna Declaration and Programme of Action (25 June 1993) UN Doc A/CONF.157/23 (Part II), ch 111, sec II, para 40.

[20] CEDAW *Suggestion No 5* on the feasibility of preparing an optional protocol to the Convention in UNGA, 'Report of the CEDAW Committee—Thirteenth Session' (1994) UN Doc A/49/38.

[21] ECOSOC Res 1994/7 (21 July 1994) UN Doc E/RES/1994/7.

[22] The then-Director of the Women in Law Project of the Law Group, Ms Donna Sullivan was the driving force behind the initiative.

[23] The Maastricht draft is appended to Byrnes and Connors (n 10 above), which also provides information on the background to its formulation.

[24] SR Cartwright, 'An Optional Protocol to the Convention on the Elimination of All Forms of Discrimination against Women' presented to the Fourteenth Session of the Committee on the Elimination of Discrimination against Women (1995) UN Doc CEDAW/C/1995/WG.1/WP.1. The Committee also had before it a paper prepared by Philip Alston, then-Chairperson of CESCR, on a draft optional protocol to the ICESCR, submitted to the Committee at its Fourteenth Session in 1995. P Alston, 'Draft Optional Protocol Providing for the Consideration of Communications' (1994) UN Doc E/C.12/1994/12.

After discussion by a working group, the Committee adopted *Suggestion No 7* almost unanimously,[25] outlining elements it considered should be included in an optional protocol.[26] The Committee decided not to present a draft protocol, as it believed that the proposal would have greater success in intergovernmental processes if a draft instrument emanated from an intergovernmental body, such as ICRMW.

Suggestion No 7 largely corresponds to the Maastricht draft, and envisages two procedures: a communications and an inquiry procedure. As in the case of the Maastricht draft, *Suggestion No 7* did not include a provision for complaints between States relating to a State party's fulfilment of its obligations under the Convention.[27] The Committee's elements reflect existing human rights instruments which establish complaints and inquiry procedures and developed practice. They included interim measures to avoid irreparable harm,[28] follow-up, and remedial measures.[29] There were several innovations. One was a wide approach to standing, allowing communications to be submitted by an individual, group, or organization suffering detriment from a violation of rights in the Convention, or claiming to be directly affected by the failure of a State party to comply with its obligations under the Convention, or by a person or group having sufficient interest in the matter.[30] *Suggestion No 7* also envisaged that the Committee might, with the consent of the State party concerned, visit its territory while examining a communication.[31] Emphasis was placed on mediation and settlement, and the importance of publicity for the Convention and the new protocol, as well as resources for its operation.

Based on its recommendation, which had been approved by ECOSOC,[32] the CSW took up the question of preparing a petition procedure for the Convention at its 39th session in March 1995, this time with the benefit of the Committee's *Suggestion*.[33] The CSW was preoccupied during this session with preparations for the forthcoming Fourth World Conference on Women and did not discuss the *Suggestion*. Rather, it recommended that the Secretary-General seek the views of governments, intergovernmental organizations, and NGOs on an optional protocol to the Convention, taking into account *Suggestion No 7*, which would be presented in a report of the Secretary-General to its 40th session in 1996. The CSW also recommended that an open-ended in-session working group be established

[25] CEDAW Summary Record (1995) UN Doc CEDAW/C/SR.282 paras 13–19.

[26] CEDAW *Suggestion No 7* on Elements for an optional protocol to the Convention in UNGA, 'Report of the CEDAW Committee—Fourteenth Session' (1995) UN Doc A/50/38.

[27] The Maastricht meeting agreed not to include an inter-State complaints procedure because such procedures, included in the ICCPR OPI, the ICERD, and the CAT had never been used. Byrnes and Connors (n 10 above) 704–8. Such a procedure is included in ICRMW art 76; CPED art 32; and ICESCR OP art 10. In written comments on *Suggestion No 7*, NGOs called for the inclusion of an inter-State procedure: Report of the Secretary-General, 'Views submitted by Governments, intergovernmental and non-governmental organizations on the elaboration of a draft optional protocol to the Convention on the Elimination of All Forms of Discrimination against Women' (1996) UN Doc E/CN.6/1996/10 para 124 and Report of the Secretary-General, 'Additional views of Governments, intergovernmental and non-governmental organizations on an optional protocol to the Convention' (1997) UN Doc E/CN.6/1997/5 para 299. One commentator suggests that the omission of an inter-State communications procedure from the Optional Protocol reinforces the different and unequal treatment of women's rights compared with other rights and that the threat of the activation of inter-State procedures has been used as a diplomatic bargaining chip (A Edwards, *Violence against Women under International Human Rights Law* (2011) 117–18).

[28] 'CEDAW *Suggestion No 7*' (1995) UN Doc A/50/38 (n 26 above) para 10.   [29] Ibid paras 13–14.

[30] Ibid para 7.   [31] Ibid para 12.

[32] ECOSOC Res 1994/7 (21 July 1994) UN Doc E/RES/1994/7.

[33] ECOSOC, 'Results of the Fourteenth Session of the Committee on the Elimination of Discrimination against Women' (1995) UN Doc E/CN.6/1995/CRP.1.

to meet in parallel to its 40th session to consider the views received 'with a view to elaborating a draft optional protocol'. These proposals were approved by ECOSOC.[34] The Beijing Platform for Action expressed support for the process initiated by the Commission to elaborate a draft optional protocol that could enter into force as soon as possible.[35]

III. The Drafting Process in the CSW

The intergovernmental process relating to the OP began with the first session of the Working Group which met in parallel to the 40th session of the CSW in March 1996. A compilation of views submitted by eighteen States and nineteen NGOs on the feasibility of an optional protocol, taking account of the Committee's *Suggestion No 7* was before it. The majority expressed support for development of an optional protocol, and identified *Suggestion No 7* as an important basis for work. These views also identified issues requiring further clarification and obstacles. Several of these became recurring themes in discussions in the Commission over the next four years. They included whether a protocol, on the lines suggested by *Suggestion No 7*, would overlap with existing human rights procedures, leading to duplication of work and waste of human and financial resources. Whether the Convention obligations, some of which were considered to be framed in general terms, were appropriate for an enforceable system of individual rights that could be measured by a quasi-judicial body—in other words 'justiciable'—was also questioned. Specific concerns relating to elements of *Suggestion No 7* included whether the protocol should provide for both a petition and inquiry procedure; whether the proposed broadened standing should be accepted; and the explicit provision of interim measures and follow-up procedures.[36]

Discussions during the first session of the Working Group began slowly. None the less, views were exchanged on the feasibility of a protocol, and a number of key issues, as well as the elements of *Suggestion No 7*. Extensive consideration was given to the question of the justiciability of the Convention,[37] and the Committee's suitability to consider communications or to embark on investigations as envisaged in *Suggestion No 7*.[38] A paragraph-by-paragraph discussion of *Suggestion No 7* focused on its innovative elements, in particular its suggestion of broad standing,[39] explicit inclusion of interim measures,[40] identification of remedial measures,[41] and an explicit power of follow-up.[42] The need for an inquiry procedure, given that the model for the procedure, CAT Article 20, had been used infrequently, was discussed, as was the threshold required for the initiation of any such inquiry. The Working Group also addressed the impact of reservations to the Convention

---

[34] ECOSOC Res 1995/29 (24 July 1995) UN Doc E/RES/1995/29.

[35] UNGA, 'Report of the Fourth World Conference on Women' (1995) UN Doc A/CONF.177/20/Rev.1 para 230(k).

[36] Report of the Secretary-General 'Views submitted by Governments, intergovernmental and non-governmental organizations on the elaboration of a draft optional protocol to the Convention on the Elimination of All Forms of Discrimination against Women' (1996) UN Doc E/CN.6/1996/10 and Corr.1, Add.1 and Add.2.

[37] The Chairperson's summary of exchange of views on elements contained in *Suggestion No 7* held in the open-ended working group in 1996 is outlined in the 'Report of the Open-ended Working Group on the Elaboration of a Draft Optional Protocol to CEDAW' contained in ECOSOC, 'Report of the CSW—Fortieth Session' (1996) UN Doc E/1996/26, Annex III. The summary of discussions on justiciability appears in paras 104–11.

[38] Ibid para 111.   [39] Ibid paras 29–38.   [40] Ibid paras 10–57.   [41] Ibid paras 71–7.

[42] Ibid paras 78–80.

on the operation of the protocol and the capacity of the Committee to pronounce on such reservations.[43] Support was expressed for the Committee's Element 28, precluding reservations to the optional protocol, although some expressed concern that such a provision might discourage ratification, and the view that ratifying States should be able to opt out of either the petition and inquiry procedure, or the inquiry procedure.[44]

ECOSOC renewed the Working Group's mandate to meet in parallel to the 41st session of the Commission in 1997 and authorized the participation of a representative of the Committee in its meetings as a resource person.[45] The Working Group's requests that further views of governments and other actors on an optional protocol be canvassed and compiled for its next session and the Secretary-General provide a comparative summary of existing treaty- and Charter-based communications and inquiry procedures to that session, were also approved.[46]

The Working Group's 1997 session considered a draft optional protocol[47] prepared by the Chairperson on the basis of *Suggestion No 7*, views expressed by governments and others in written submissions[48] and proposals made during the Working Group's first session. The draft included an individual complaints procedure and an inquiry procedure. Although influenced by the Maastricht draft, the Chairperson's draft did not include many of its more innovative features. It did, however, retain the notion of widened standing, a conciliatory function for the Committee, provided that its decisions would be legally binding, and that no reservations to the protocol would be permitted. A brief general debate was followed by a first reading of the Chairperson's text.

On the basis of the Chairperson's draft Working Group, participants focused on formulating a text acceptable to all.[49] Some advocated a protocol which built on existing procedures and their practice which responded to the disadvantages women face in accessing international procedures. Others proposed a narrow protocol which replicated the text of existing instruments. Issues flagged as controversial during the 1st session—standing, the status of the Committee's 'views', the proposed inquiry procedure and reservations—were again the subject of hot debate. The Working Group requested renewal of its mandate so it could meet twice more, in parallel to the Commission's 42nd and 43rd sessions in 1998 and 1999, again with the assistance of a resource person

[43] Ibid paras 22 and 103.   [44] Ibid para 103.

[45] ECOSOC Decision 1996/240 'Renewal of the Mandate of the Open-ended Working Group on the Elaboration of a Draft Optional Protocol to CEDAW' (22 July 1996) UN Doc E/DEC/1996/240. The General Assembly authorized convening of the working group on 20 November 2006.

[46] CSW Resolution 40/8, ECOSOC, 'Report of the CSW—Fortieth Session' (1996) UN Doc E/1996/26.

[47] Text submitted by the Chairperson of the Open-Ended Working Group of the CSW on the Elaboration of a Draft Optional Protocol to CEDAW in 1997. ECOSOC, 'Annex: Draft Optional Protocol to CEDAW' (1997) UN Doc E/CN.6/1997/WG/L.1 in United Nations, *The Optional Protocol: Text and Materials* (2000) UN Sales No E.00.IV.2, 30–3.

[48] Additional views from twenty-one States, twelve NGOs, one representing forty-nine NGOs, and one IGO had been submitted in response to the Secretary-General's request for further views. Report of the Secretary-General, 'Additional views of Governments, intergovernmental and non-governmental organizations on an optional protocol to the Convention' (1997) UN Doc E/CN.6/1997/5.

[49] Chairperson's summary of views and comments made by delegations during the negotiations on a draft protocol to CEDAW in 1997, ECOSOC, 'Report of the CSW—Forty-First Session' (1997) UN Doc E/1997/27, Annex II, Appendix II.

from the Committee.[50] It also requested that the Secretariat submit to it a document comparing the Chairperson's draft and amendments proposed by the Working Group with the provisions of existing human rights instruments.[51]

As the third session of the Working Group convened in March 1998, a number of delegations and NGOs were determined to celebrate the fiftieth anniversary of the adoption by the UNGA in 1948 of the UDHR with the adoption of a protocol providing women with the right to petition the CEDAW Committee. The UNHCHR underlined the importance of finalization and rapid entry into force of the Protocol. The Chairperson had engaged in intersessional informal discussions and delegations had agreed on a cleaner text for negotiation.[52] However, as agreement on parts of the text emerged, areas of difficulty became clearer. These included the question of standing,[53] the appropriateness of the inquiry procedure, and the prohibition of reservations. Accordingly, the Working Group was unable to complete its task during the anniversary year.

Participants in the general debate on the first day of the Working Group's 4th session, in March 1999, urged completion of negotiations and the adoption of a consensus text at that session, particularly in light of the twentieth anniversary of the adoption of the Convention which would fall on 18 December 1999. A second revised text, taking account of proposals made at the third session of the Working Group, was submitted by the Chairperson.[54] On 11 March 1999, at its second and third meetings, the Working Group adopted the draft OP to the Convention and an enabling resolution through which it would be submitted to the CSW, ECOSOC, and the UNGA.

A number of issues which had been proposed for inclusion in the Protocol appear in the resolution which transmitted the Protocol. These include paragraph 3, which stresses that States parties to the Protocol should undertake to respect the rights and procedures provided by the Protocol and cooperate with the Committee at all stages of its proceedings; paragraph 4, stressing that in the fulfilment of its mandate the Committee should continue to be guided by the principles of non-selectivity, impartiality, and objectivity; and paragraphs 5 and 6 relating to meeting time and staff and facilities so that the Committee could effectively fulfil its functions under the Protocol.[55]

Twenty-five interpretative statements, which the Working Group agreed would be compiled and form part of its report, were made after the Protocol's adoption by the

---

[50] CSW Resolution 41/3, ECOSOC 'Report of the CSW—Forty-First Session' (1997) UN Doc E/1997/27; ECOSOC Decision 1997/227, 'Renewal of the Mandate of the Open-ended Working Group on the Elaboration of a Draft Optional Protocol to CEDAW' (21 July 1997) UN Doc E/DEC/1997/227.

[51] Report of the Secretary-General, 'Annotated comparison of the draft optional protocol and the amendments proposed thereto with the provisions of existing human rights instruments' (1998) UN Doc E/CN.6/1998/7.

[52] Revised draft optional protocol submitted by the Chairperson on the basis of the compilation text contained in document E/CN.6/1997/WG/L.1 and proposals made at the forty-first session of the CSW, ECOSOC, 'Report of the CSW—Forty-First Session (1997) UN Doc E/1997/27, Annex III, Appendix I.

[53] Chairperson's summary of views and comments made by delegations during the negotiations on a draft optional protocol to CEDAW in 1998, ECOSOC, 'Report of the CSW—Forty-Second Session' (1998) UN Doc E/1998/27, Annex II, Appendix II, paras 2–8.

[54] Revised draft optional protocol submitted by the Chairperson on the basis of the compilation text contained in document E/CN.6/1997/WG/L.1 and proposals made at the 42nd session of the CSW, ECOSOC, 'Report of the CSW—Forty-Second Session' (1998) UN Doc E/1998/27, Annex II, Appendix I.

[55] Ibid draft art 7(1), the alternative to draft art 16 and the resources paragraph.

Working Group.[56] These statements express the views of States on the Protocol in general, and also address a number of its provisions. China, Costa Rica, also on behalf of Argentina, Bolivia, Chile, Colombia, Dominican Republic, Ecuador, El Salvador, Panama, Peru, and Venezuela, Egypt, Italy, The Netherlands, the Philippines and the United Kingdom, also speaking on behalf of Sweden, and Germany on behalf of all the member States of the European Union, the Central and Eastern European countries associated with the European Union, and other associated countries expressed the view that the Optional Protocol provided strong procedures for the enforcement of the human rights of women. Costa Rica and the Philippines indicated that they had been motivated by the plight of women throughout the negotiations, with the Philippines dedicating the outcome to the most marginalized, vulnerable, oppressed, and silenced women. The Philippines and Italy also highlighted the role of women's groups and NGOs as the driving force behind the Protocol, and thanked them for their contributions to the negotiations. Other interpretative statements were more cautious. Australia made clear that it would carefully consider and consult on the text at the domestic level, noting that its domestic treaty-making procedures required a high level of consultation at the national level, including the involvement of parliamentarians, State, and Territory Governments within its federal system and the wider community. Morocco stressed that the interpretation of the provisions of the Protocol would be subordinated to absolute respect for its sovereignty and moral and spiritual values and to the compatibility of those provisions with its Constitution. Tunisia, while stressing the importance of the Protocol in promoting the rights of women and ensuring respect for such rights in practice in order to bring parity and equality of opportunity, considered that the Protocol could only be ratified within the framework of respect for constitutional legality in each country and each country's national sovereignty. Interpretative statements relating to specific provisions of the text are addressed below in the commentary on those provisions.

The CSW,[57] the ECOSOC,[58] and the UNGA[59] all adopted the OP by consensus. A special signing ceremony was convened at UN Headquarters on 10 December 1999, with twenty-three States[60] becoming signatory to the instrument. During a panel event later that day, Kofi Annan, the then-Secretary-General, made clear that he could think 'of no better way to celebrate this last Human Rights Day of a century which has seen great advances in women's rights, than by adding this important instrument to our tool-kit for ensuring that women really do enjoy those rights'.[61]

---

[56] Interpretative statements on the draft optional protocol to CEDAW, ECOSOC, 'Report of the CSW—Forty-Third Session' (1999) UN Doc E/1999/27, Annex II.

[57] ECOSOC, 'Report of the CSW—Forty-Third Session (1999) UN Doc E/1997/27, Chapter I, A; DPI Press Release *Draft Optional Protocol to Women's Anti-discrimination Convention approved by Commission on the Status of Women* UN Doc WOM/1117 (12 March 1999).

[58] ECOSOC Resolution 1999/13 (28 July 1999) UN Doc E/RES/1999/13.

[59] UNGA Res 54/4 (6 October 1999) UN Doc A/RES/54/4.

[60] Austria, Belgium, Bolivia, Chile, Colombia, Costa Rica, Czech Republic, Denmark, Ecuador, Finland, France, Germany, Greece, Iceland, Italy, Liechtenstein, Luxembourg, Mexico, The Netherlands, Norway, Senegal, Slovenia, Sweden.

[61] IPS Daily Journal vol. 7, No 238 (13 December 1999).

IV. The Work of the Committee under the Optional Protocol

Between the adoption of the OP by the UNGA and its entry into force, the Committee prepared itself for the new competencies it conferred. Ms Silvia Cartwright was tasked to prepare a working paper on the new procedures,[62] which the Committee discussed at its 23rd session. The working paper proposed the establishment of a five-member standing working group to discharge identified functions in relation to the Protocol, devolution of decisions of prima facie admissibility of communications to the Secretariat and elements to be contained in the Committee's Rules of Procedure relating to the Protocol. Ms Cartwright then prepared draft Rules of Procedure relating to the Committee's functions under the Protocol which were discussed by members at an informal meeting held in Berlin, Germany in December 2000. These were adopted by the Committee at its 24th session in January 2001.[63] The rules, *inter alia*, regulate transmission of communications to the Committee[64] and the maintenance of a register of communications[65] and indicate that the Secretary-General may request clarification or additional information from authors of communications.[66] They also regulate how communications will be considered,[67] including by providing that a Committee member will not join in the examination of a communication if she or he has a personal interest in the case, has participated in any decision on the case other than under the OP, or is a national of the State party concerned.[68]

In 2001, as envisaged by Rule 62 of its Rules of Procedure, the Committee established a five-member standing Working Group on the OP whose members would be elected every two years. The Working Group was renamed the Working Group on Communications under the Optional Protocol at the Committee's 28th session in January 2003,[69] in order to make clear that its mandate is confined to communications under the Protocol, while the Article 8 inquiry procedure is administered by the Committee as a whole. The Working Group prepares initial drafts for the Committee on the admissibility and merits of communications. It has developed a model communications form to assist petitioners,[70] and a Fact Sheet on submitting individual complaints. It also has developed administrative procedures to provide for efficient and timely processing of communications and ensured that the Secretariat has provided background papers on procedural and substantive issues relating to the Protocol.

Women's advocates worldwide were delighted with the negotiation of the Protocol and its rapid entry into force. They expected that many would take advantage of its procedures. They have been disappointed, however; few petitions have been submitted, from a limited number of States. The Committee has not had the opportunity to develop a comprehensive

---

[62] CEDAW, 'Working paper on proposed procedures for the administration of the Optional Protocol to CEDAW: Note prepared by SR Cartwright' (2000) UN Doc CEDAW/C/2000/II/WP.2.

[63] CEDAW Rules of Procedure, UNGA, 'Report of the CEDAW Committee—Twenty-Fourth Session' (2001) UN Doc A/56/38, Annex I, Parts XVI and XVII. Amendments to the rules were adopted at the Committee's thirty-ninth session, UNGA, 'Report of the CEDAW Committee—Thirty-Ninth Session' (2007) UN Doc A/62/38, Chap V, paras 653–5 and Appendix.

[64] Rules of Procedure 56.   [65] Rules of Procedure 57.   [66] Rules of Procedure 58.

[67] Rules of Procedure 64–9.   [68] Rules of Procedure 60.

[69] UNGA, 'Report of the CEDAW Committee—Twenty-Eighth Session' (2003) UN Doc A/58/38, Part I, ch V para 435.

[70] Ibid para 406. The revised communications form and the Fact Sheet are available at <http://www2.ohchr.org/english/law/cedaw-one.htm > accessed 31 December 2010.

jurisprudence, although it has made significant contributions in some areas, in particular violence against women and women's right to reproductive health.

As of 31 December 2010, twenty-seven cases had been registered under the Protocol. Fourteen cases had been decided, with eight being held inadmissible, and views being pronounced on six. Three cases had been discontinued and ten were pending. The decided cases concern nine States, all but one members of the Council of Europe and thus subject to a regional human rights régime. All but one of the petitioners lived in a Council of Europe State. The Committee has conducted only one inquiry.

Under-usage of the Protocol's procedures may be explained by the weaknesses that affect these procedures generally. They are not well-known and can be difficult to access and use, especially for those without legal assistance. Both the communications and inquiry procedures are slow, with the former requiring the exhaustion of domestic remedies before the merits of the case may be considered. Although the 'views' or decisions adopted by the Committee on petitions are authoritative, they are not binding, and there is no enforcement procedure. Would-be petitioners may also have a choice of avenues for complaint, including those at the regional level which have binding outcomes. The fact that the Convention's provisions are formulated in terms of obligations rather than rights may be a challenge for those seeking to elaborate claims. Fewer women than men use the human rights communications and inquiry procedures,[71] with one commentator suggesting that these 'litigation-style' processes do not serve them as well as men because of the systematic power imbalance and disadvantage women experience and their lack of resources, literacy, and access to legal aid.[72] The requirement that domestic remedies be exhausted before the Committee will consider a communication also poses a particular challenge for women in jurisdictions where their access to courts is limited. That these procedures relate to alleged violations by a State party poses a further difficulty where the facts of the case relate to non-State action, such as domestic violence, or transnational violations, such as trafficking.

Despite their small number, the Committee's views on communications and the results of the single inquiry have been influential in the creation of a women's human rights jurisprudence, including in relation to the State's obligation to exercise due diligence to prevent or prosecute human rights violations, which has been relied on by the European Court of Human Rights[73] and the Inter-American Court of Human Rights.[74]

C. Commentary

I. The Preamble

The States parties to the present Protocol,

Noting that the Charter of the United Nations reaffirms faith in fundamental human rights, in the dignity and worth of the human person and the equal rights of men and women,

---

[71] Edwards (n 27 above) 123–36.   [72] Ibid 125–9.

[73] *Opuz v Turkey* [2009] ECHR 33401/02 (9 June 2009). See also the discussion in the Introduction and ch on Violence against Women.

[74] *Claudia González y Otras v Mexico* ('*Campo Algodonero*' or '*Cotton Field*' case) Inter-American Court of Human Rights Series C No 205 (16 November 2009).

Also noting that the Universal Declaration of Human Rights proclaims that all human beings are born free and equal in dignity and rights and that everyone is entitled to all the rights and freedoms set forth therein, without distinction of any kind, including distinction based on sex,

Recalling that the International Covenants on Human Rights and other international human rights instruments prohibit discrimination on the basis of sex,

Also recalling the Convention on the Elimination of All Forms of Discrimination against Women ('the Convention'), in which the States Parties thereto condemn discrimination against women in all its forms and agree to pursue by all appropriate means and without delay a policy of eliminating discrimination against women,

Reaffirming their determination to ensure the full and equal enjoyment by women of all human rights and fundamental freedoms and to take effective action to prevent violations of these rights and freedoms,

Have agreed as follows:

The short preamble, in contrast to the lengthy preamble to the CEDAW, elements of which have raised objections from some States parties, builds on the two-paragraph preamble included in the draft optional protocol submitted by the Chairperson to the CSW Working Group.[75]

During negotiations many delegations expressed a preference for a short, succinct preamble.[76] Some had suggested reference to the Vienna Declaration and Programme of Action and the Beijing Platform for Action,[77] but it was agreed that these references would be included in the resolution adopting the OP.[78]

The preamble recalls the UN Charter; Articles 1 and 2 of the UDHR; ICESCR Article 2(2); ICCPR Article 2(1) and the chapeau to CEDAW Article 2.

Article 31(1) of the VCLT provides that a treaty is to be interpreted in good faith in accordance with the ordinary meaning to be given to the terms of the treaty in their context and in light of its object and purpose, with the context comprising, *inter alia*, its text, including its preamble and annexes (Article 31(2)). The Committee has not explicitly addressed the preamble in its work under the OP, but has implicitly pursued the objective of ensuring women's full and equal enjoyment of all human rights and fundamental freedoms and taking effective action to prevent violations of those rights set out in its final paragraph.

II. Article 1

A State Party to the present Protocol ('State Party') recognizes the competence of the Committee on the Elimination of Discrimination against Women ('the Committee') to receive and consider communications submitted in accordance with article 2.

Article 1 establishes the Committee's competence in relation to communications, providing that a State party to the Protocol recognizes its competence to receive and consider communications in accordance with Article 2.

---

[75] 'Text submitted by the Chairperson of the Open-Ended Working Group of the CSW' (1997) UN Doc E/CN.6/1997/WG/L.1 (n 47 above) Preamble. See also the discussion in ch on art 28.

[76] 'Chairperson's summary of views and comments' (1997) UN Doc E/1997/27, Annex II, Appendix II (n 49 above) para 5; 'Chairperson's summary of views and comments' (1998) UN Doc E/1998/27, Annex II, Appendix II (n 53 above) para 1.

[77] 'Chairperson's summary of views and comments' (1998) UN Doc E/1998/27, Annex II, Appendix II (n 53 above) para 1.

[78] UNGA Res 54/4 (6 October 1999) UN Doc A/RES/54/4, Preamble.

Article 1 recalls the first part of ICCPR OPI Article 1, the first part of CRPD OP Articles 1 and 1(1), and ICESCR OP Article 1(1). In these cases, the communications procedure is contained in a separate procedural protocol while in the ICERD, the CAT, the CMW and the CED the communications procedure is part of the treaty, and States parties are required to recognize the competence of the relevant treaty body to receive and consider communications through a declaration, rather than through ratification or accession.

Unlike the ICCPR OPI, CAT, and CMW, ICESCR OP, and ICRMW, the CEDAW OP Article 1 does not explicitly state that only States parties to the Convention may become States parties to the OP. Instead, it refers to States parties to the present Protocol, as does the CRPD OP. The procedure for becoming a State party is covered in OP Article 15. The phrase 'in accordance with article 2,' relating to submission of communications, recalls the first clause of the ICCPR OPI Article 2, which provides that the right to submit communications is subject to the provisions of its Article 1.

Element 5 of the Committee's *Suggestion No 7* envisaged that States parties to the Convention should have the opportunity to ratify or accede to the OP.[79] Governments, intergovernmental organizations, and NGOs generally supported this, but several recommended inclusion of language reflecting the procedure for signing, ratifying, and acceding to the OP,[80] or the inclusion of a provision identical to ICCPR OPI Article 1. Some NGOs suggested that no State could be required to ratify the protocol, and that no additional obligations would be imposed on States parties to the Convention which chose not to ratify it.[81] At the 1st session of the Working Group in 1996, most considered Element 5 to be generally acceptable. However, questions relating to the status and impact of reservations on the admissibility of communications under the OP and the justiciability of the provisions of the Convention were raised.[82]

Article 1 of the draft optional protocol submitted by the Chairperson to the 2nd session of the Working Group in 1997 consisted of two sub-paragraphs, the first providing that a State party to the Convention that becomes a party to the present Protocol recognizes the competence of the CEDAW Committee to receive and examine communications, and the second that no communication shall be received by the Committee if it concerns a State party to the Convention which is not a party to this Protocol.[83]

During the 2nd session of the Working Group, delegations expressed a preference for a concise Article 1, limited to the question of the Committee's competence to receive and consider complaints, as proposed in the Chairperson's draft, and accordingly, agreed *ad referendum* to the proposal. Some considered that the article should also address the question of standing and that communications would be submitted in accordance with the provisions of the Protocol. Although there was some support for maintaining a separate subparagraph explicitly providing that no communications would be received in respect of a State party which was not party to the Protocol, most considered this to be redundant

---

[79] 'CEDAW *Suggestion No 7*' (1995) UN Doc A/50/38 (n 26 above).

[80] Ukraine in 'Views submitted by Governments, IGOs and NGOs' (1996) UN Doc E/CN.6/1996/10 and Corr.1, Add.1 and Add.2 (n 36 above) para 61.

[81] Ibid para 62.

[82] 'Report of the Open-ended Working Group on the Elaboration of a Draft Optional Protocol to CEDAW' (1996) UN Doc E/1996/26, Annex III (n 37 above) paras 21–5.

[83] 'Text submitted by the Chairperson of the Open-Ended Working Group of the CSW' (1997) UN Doc E/CN.6/1997/WG.L.1 (n 47 above) art 1.

so the sub-paragraph was deleted.[84] Based on these discussions, Article 1 of the revised draft optional protocols submitted by the Chairperson to the Working Group's 1997 and 1998 sessions provided that a State party to the Protocol recognizes the competence of the Committee to receive and consider communications, and maintained 'submitted in accordance with article 2' in brackets.[85] The provision in its final form was agreed during the Working Group's 1999 session.

III. Article 2

Communications may be submitted by or on behalf of individuals or groups of individuals, under the jurisdiction of a State party, claiming to be victims of a violation of any of the rights set forth in the Convention by that State Party. Where a communication is submitted on behalf of individuals or groups of individuals, this shall be with their consent unless the author can justify acting on their behalf without such consent.

Optional Protocol Articles 2, 3, and 4 contain criteria which must be fulfilled to enable the Committee to receive and consider a communication. If any of these criteria is not met, the communication will be declared inadmissible and will not be considered on its merits. The mandatory nature of these criteria is underlined by the Committee's Rules of Procedure: Rule 67 provides that the Committee, a working group, or a rapporteur shall apply the criteria in OP Articles 2, 3, and 4 to decide on the admissibility of a communication, and Rule 72(4) clarifies that the Committee shall not decide on the merits of a communication without having first considered all of the grounds for admissibility. The Committee usually refers explicitly to these rules in the first paragraph of its decisions on admissibility.[86]

Rule 64 provides that admissibility decisions are made by a simple majority. A working group may also declare a communication admissible, provided that all members eligible to participate so decide. Rule 66 provides that the Committee may decide the question of admissibility and the merits of a communication separately.

The Committee's procedures with respect to communications received, including time limits, are set out in Rule 69. This rule provides that as soon as possible after the

---

[84] 'Chairperson's summary of views and comments' (1997) UN Doc E/1997/27, Annex II, Appendix II (n 49 above) paras 6–7.

[85] 'Revised draft optional protocol' (1997) UN Doc E/1997/27, Annex III, Appendix I (n 52 above); 'Revised draft optional protocol' (1998) UN Doc E/1998/27, Annex II, Appendix I (n 54 above).

[86] *B.-J. v Germany* CEDAW Communication No 1/2003 (2004) UN Doc CEDAW/C/36/D/1/2003 paras 8.1–8.2; *AT v Hungary* CEDAW Communication No 2/2003 (2005) UN Doc CEDAW/C/36/D/2/2003 para 8.1; *Dung Thi Thuy Nguyen v The Netherlands* CEDAW Communication No 3/2004 (2006) UN Doc CEDAW/C/36/D/3/2004 para 9.1; *AS v Hungary* CEDAW Communication No 4/2004 (2006) UN Doc CEDAW/C/36//D/4/2004 para 10.1; *Şahide Goekce v Austria* CEDAW Communication No 5/2005 (2007) UN Doc CEDAW/C/39/D/5/2005 para 7.1; *Fatma Yildirim v Austria* CEDAW Communication No 6/2005 (2007) UN Doc CEDAW/C/39/D/6/2005 para 7.1; *Cristina Muñoz-Vargas y Sainz de Vicuña* CEDAW Communication No 7/2005 (2007) UN Doc CEDAW/C/39/D/7/2005 paras 11.1–11.2; *Rahime Kayhan v Turkey* CEDAW Communication No 8/2005 (2006) UN Doc CEDAW/C/34/D/8/2005 paras 7.1–7.2; *N.S.F v United Kingdom* CEDAW Communication No 10/2005 (2007) UN Doc CEDAW/C/38/D/10/2005 paras 7.1–7.2; *Salgado v United Kingdom* CEDAW Communication No 11/2006 (2007) UN Doc CEDAW/C/37/D/11/2006 paras 8.1–8.2; *Zhen Zhen Zheng v The Netherlands* CEDAW Communication No 15 (2009) UN Doc CEDAW/C/42/D/15/2007 para 7.1; *Groupe d'Intérêt pour le Matronyme v France* CEDAW Communication No 12 (2009) UN Doc CEDAW/C/44/D/12/2007 paras 11.1–11.2; *SOS Sexisme v France* CEDAW Communication No 13/2007 (2009) UN Doc CEDAW/C/44/D/13/2007 paras 10.1–10.2; *Karen Tayag Vertido v The Philippines* CEDAW Communication No 18 (2010) UN Doc CEDAW/C/46/D/18/2008 para 6.1.

communication has been received, and provided that the complainant(s) consent to the disclosure of their identity to the State party concerned, the Committee, working group, or rapporteur shall bring the communication confidentially to the State party's attention and request that it submit a written reply. The request must state that it does not imply that any decision has been reached on the admissibility of the communication. The State party is required to submit written statements to the Committee on the admissibility or merits of any such communication within six months of receiving it. The State party may also request in writing that the communication be rejected as inadmissible, setting out the grounds for admissibility, within two months of the Committee's request.[87] The Committee is entitled to request written explanations or statements that relate only to the admissibility of a communication, but where it does so the State party may respond with respect to both the admissibility and the merits of the communication, provided that these are submitted within six months of the Committee's request.[88] Rule 70 mandates the Committee to communicate any decision of inadmissibility, together with its reasons, to the author of the communication and the State party as soon as possible. Any inadmissibility decision may be reviewed by the Committee upon receipt of a written request by or on behalf of the author(s) of the communication containing information indicating that the reasons for inadmissibility no longer apply. Where the issue of admissibility is decided before the State party's written explanations or statements on the merits of a communication are received, that decision and all other relevant information is to be submitted through the Secretary-General to the State party. The author of the communication shall also be informed.[89] The Committee may revoke its decision that a communication is admissible in the light of any explanation submitted by the State party.

Article 2 sets out who may submit a communication, or standing. First, it confines standing to individuals, or groups of named individuals. Second, it requires that the individual or groups of individuals claim to be victims of a violation of any Convention rights. Third, the individual or groups of individuals must be under the jurisdiction of the State party against whom the communication is submitted. Fourth, it allows petitions to be submitted on behalf of victims, provided they consent to the petition being submitted on their behalf, unless the author can justify acting without consent.

1. Individuals or Groups of Individuals

All international human rights communications procedures provide that communications may be submitted by individuals. ICERD extends this to 'groups of individuals' and CAT, CMW, and CPED provide that communications may also be submitted on 'behalf of individuals'. The CEDAW OP goes further, providing the Committee with competence to receive and consider communications from or on behalf of individuals or groups of individuals, as do the CRPD OP and the ICESCR OP. These instruments and the CEDAW OP require the consent of those individuals or groups of individuals, unless the author can justify acting on their behalf without such consent.

The rules of procedure and practice of the HRC, CAT, and CERD committees allow alleged victims to be represented by duly designated representatives. These treaty bodies have also accepted communications on behalf of victims where it appears that they are

---

[87] Rules of Procedure 69(5).   [88] Rules of Procedure 69(4).
[89] Rules of Procedure 71(1).

unable to submit a communication or designate a representative, but they require those submitting the communication to justify acting on behalf of the victim.

Prior to, and throughout, the negotiations of the CEDAW OP, proposals were made to broaden standing beyond that enjoyed by other treaty bodies to allow CEDAW to receive and consider communications from individuals, groups, or organizations with sufficient interest in the matter, but who were not victims per se. Such proposals, which were contained in the Maastricht draft[90] were justified on the basis of the disadvantages women face in accessing legal remedies generally, and international legal remedies in particular.

Element 7 of the Committee's *Suggestion No 7*[91] took up these ideas, providing that communications could be submitted by an individual, group, or organization suffering detriment from a violation of rights in the Convention, or claiming to be directly affected by the failure of a State party to comply with its obligations under the Convention, or by a person or group having a sufficient interest in the matter. Governments described the idea of broadened standing as 'innovative', with some welcoming the proposal in light of the structural discrimination women experience. Others considered that standing should be limited to individual victims or groups of victims.[92] In contrast, NGOs expressed strong support for broadened standing, pointing out that because of the resource constraints women often face, individuals, groups, and NGOs should be able to submit petitions, to protect victims and to address group violations.[93] These views were reiterated during the first session of the Working Group. The question of who would be entitled to complain was also linked by some to the issue of justiciability and whether all Convention provisions would be subject to petition under the OP.[94]

Article 2 of the Chairperson's draft maintained the idea of broadened standing, providing that communications could be submitted by an individual, group or organization claiming to have suffered a violation of any of the rights in the Convention or claiming to be directly affected by the failure of a State party to comply with its obligations under the Convention. It also provided that individuals, groups, or organizations claiming that a State party had violated any Convention rights or was failing to comply with its Convention obligations would be able to submit communications if in the opinion of the Committee they had sufficient interest in the matter.[95] Some support was expressed for this formulation during the 2nd session of the Working Group as it was seen as a means to overcome the obstacles women face in accessing international redress procedures, but opinions differed on those who should have standing to complain ranging from individuals only; individuals and groups of individuals; to individuals, groups of individuals, groups, and organizations with sufficient interest in the matter. Those who supported investing organizations with sufficient interest in the matter with the right to complain

[90] Art 1(b) of Maastricht draft. See Appendix of Byrnes and Connors (n 10 above).

[91] 'CEDAW *Suggestion No 7*' (1995) UN Doc A/50/38 (n 26 above) para 7.

[92] 'Views submitted by Governments, IGOs and NGOs' (1996) UN Doc E/CN.6/1996/10 and Corr.1 (n 36 above) paras 64–70; Add.1, para 10; 'Additional views by Governments, IGOs and NGOs' (1997) UN Doc E/CN.6/1997/5 (n 48 above) paras 74–97.

[93] 'Views submitted by Governments, IGOs and NGOs' (1996) UN Doc E/CN.6/1996/10 (n 36 above) paras 71–3; 'Additional views by Governments, IGOs and NGOs' (1997) UN Doc E/CN.6/1997/5 (n 48 above) para 98.

[94] 'Report of the Open-ended Working Group on the Elaboration of a Draft Optional Protocol to CEDAW' (1996) UN Doc E/1996/26, Annex III (n 37 above) paras 29–35.

[95] 'Text submitted by the Chairperson of the Open-Ended Working Group of the CSW' (1997) UN Doc E/CN.6/1997/WG/L.1 (n 47 above) art 2.

argued that this would address situations of systematic and widespread violations of women's rights or where groups of women had suffered violations. Others considered that these situations were better addressed through an inquiry procedure, as the main purpose of a communications procedure is to deal with the violations of individual rights.[96] Some supported standing for representatives of alleged victims, with proposals being made to provide for the submission of communications 'on behalf of' victims, with consideration being given to whether representative communications could be lodged in the absence of the victim's consent.[97]

The revised draft submitted by the Chairperson to the 3rd session of the Working Group encapsulated all the ideas relating to standing which had been put forward.[98] During that session, all delegations agreed that the OP should entitle individuals and groups of individuals to submit communications. Some considered that groups should also be entitled to do so, with several being of the view that organizations should also have standing as they could be victims of human rights violations. In light of existing instruments and the practice of the CCPR, there was support for language indicating that communications could be submitted on behalf of complainants, although several suggested that this should be limited to representatives designated by victims.[99]

The Chairperson's 2nd revised draft presented alternative, simplified versions of Article 2, envisaging that communications could be submitted by individuals or groups of individuals or groups, or on their behalf by organizations or designated representatives. The 4th session of the Working Group agreed on Article 2 as it appears in the Protocol. This allows for communications to be submitted by individuals or groups of individuals, but not groups per se or organizations. Communications may be submitted on behalf of individuals or groups of individuals, but this must be with their consent unless the author can justify acting on their behalf without such consent.

A number of States expressed disappointment with Article 2 on the adoption of the Protocol by the Working Group.[100] Ghana (also on behalf of other African States) considered that the adopted draft fell far below the threshold they would have preferred for a mechanism that dealt with matters as peculiar and far-reaching as providing legal remedies for violations of women's rights. They thought that the realities in their countries and the high rate of legal illiteracy meant that the majority of women are unaware of their rights within their own national jurisdictions, let alone those in international human rights instruments, and that Article 2 made accessibility to this Protocol for these women even more difficult.

Others stated that they interpreted the provision narrowly. China indicated that Article 2 should ensure that victims will be able to submit communications to the Committee, but at the same time prevent totally irrelevant persons from taking advantage of the special situation of victims for their own purposes by acting in their name.

---

[96] 'Chairperson's summary of views and comments' (1997) UN Doc E/1997/27, Annex II, Appendix II (n 49 above) paras 8–15.

[97] Ibid para 13.

[98] 'Revised draft optional protocol' (1997) UN Doc E/1997/27, Annex III, Appendix I (n 52 above) draft art 2.

[99] 'Chairperson's summary of views and comments' (1998) UN Doc E/1998/27, Annex II, Appendix II (n 53 above) paras 2–6.

[100] 'Interpretative statements on the draft optional protocol to CEDAW' (1999) UN Doc E/1999/27, Annex II (n 56 above).

China also considered that any representative should be from the same country as the victim. Egypt stressed that the provision on submission of communications on behalf of victims in Article 2 was conditional on exceptional and compelling circumstances making it impossible to obtain the victim's consent. It also thought that the term 'groups of individuals' required each individual in the group to be identified separately, a point also made by Japan. Israel interpreted the requirement of consent of a group of individuals on whose behalf a complaint has been filed to refer to the consent of each individual in the group.

Other interpretative statements signalled a broad interpretation of Article 2, a view which has been supported by an academic commentator on the provision.[101] Canada considered that the article gave the Committee authority to determine the question of consent according to the particular circumstances of each case and that it should be interpreted no less favourably than the existing practices and procedures of other human rights treaty bodies. Costa Rica's understanding of the phrase 'on behalf of individuals or groups of individuals' was that a broad-based approach would be taken in determining who would be entitled to submit communications in order to ensure effective access to justice.

As to the consent of victims, Costa Rica assumed that the personal, social, and cultural conditions of women who have suffered the alleged violation would be taken into account. Denmark, also speaking on behalf of Finland, Iceland, and Norway, expressed disappointment that it was not possible for delegations to agree on NGOs bringing communications to the Committee in their own right, but took comfort in the reference to 'groups of individuals', which it took to mean that NGOs alleging they were victims of a violation could submit a communication. Italy expressed confidence that the Committee's approach would develop in light of the practice of other human rights treaty bodies and of the Convention, which provides for a wider scope of social and cultural rights than other instruments. It expected the Committee to adopt a broad interpretation of the provision, enabling NGOs and others acting on behalf of victims to do so without their consent where it was impossible or very difficult for victims to act personally or to give their consent. Italy also indicated that it understood the formulation 'groups of individuals' to include NGOs acting on behalf of individuals and in their own capacity. Germany, also on behalf of the European Union and associated countries, Japan and New Zealand indicated that 'on behalf of' was to be interpreted in light of practices under other human rights instruments. Ghana indicated its understanding that the Committee would take account of the peculiarities of the Convention when developing its Rules of Procedure. India recognized the need for broad 'standing' to provide for cases where women are not able to bring complaints themselves for various reasons, but considered that those acting on behalf of an alleged victim should be able to demonstrate sufficient interest to justify so acting, and a standing association with the individual concerned. India also interpreted 'consent' as not acting contrary to the wishes of the victim and without violating her right to privacy. Indonesia noted that victims must be able to choose for themselves whether to pursue redress through the OP and recognized that there were situations in which the victims' consent could not be obtained, but that these should be approached in line with

---

[101] K Tang, 'Internationalizing Women's Struggle against Discrimination: The UN Women's Convention and the Optional Protocol' (2004) 34 *British Journal of Social Work* 1173, 1181. Tang indicates that this 'gives NGOs or community advocates the opportunity to launch their complaints to the monitoring body on behalf of individuals'.

the interpretation of the existing human rights treaty bodies. The Philippines understood Article 2 in light of the practices of existing treaty bodies, and considered that the justification of an author to act on behalf of others must take into consideration the political, social, and cultural constraints and obstacles in women's public and private lives. The Philippines made clear that these structural constraints place women in situations where they may not be able to exercise their rights fully, or give their consent in crises and emergencies. It broadly interpreted the circumstances justifying an author acting on behalf of a victim to include where women are at risk because they are illiterate or have no legal capacity to represent themselves, where they are in detention or at risk of ill-treatment, intimidation, or reprisals. It also indicated that complaints on behalf of individuals or groups of individuals could be made by NGOs.

The Committee's Rules of Procedure take a broad approach to the question of who may submit communications. Rule 68 provides that communications may be submitted by individuals or groups of individuals who claim to be victims of violations of the rights set forth in the Convention, or by their designated representatives, or by others on behalf of an alleged victim where the alleged victim consents, thus assuming consent of the victim or victims where the communication is submitted by their designated representatives.[102] In cases where a communication is submitted on behalf of a victim or victims in the absence of consent, the author must provide written reasons justifying such action.

The Committee has not been required to address the issue of representation in the communications it has decided. A number have been submitted by legal counsel,[103] independent researchers, and NGOs[104] on behalf of alleged victims with their consent. Two were submitted on behalf of deceased victims by NGOs with the written consent of the victims' survivors or their guardians. They also justified their action by the fact that the deceased were their clients with whom they had a special relationship and because they were organizations for women victims of domestic violence.[105]

2. *Victims of a Violation*

Article 2 provides that a communication will be admissible only if it claims that the author is a victim of a State party's violation of any of the rights set forth in the Convention. This prerequisite is common to all international communications procedures,[106] with the ICESCR OP adding that the CESCR may decide not to consider a communication if it does not reveal that the author has suffered a clear disadvantage, unless the Committee considers that it raises a serious issue of general importance.[107] The requirement means that the communication must show clearly that the law, policy or practice, act or omission of the State party directly affects the petitioner or group of petitioners or it will be inadmissible. In other words, it is insufficient to claim that the action or omission of the State party is discriminatory or a violation of the Convention generally.

---

[102] Rules of Procedure 68.

[103] *Dung Thi Thuy Nguyen v The Netherlands* (n 86 above); *Cristina Muñoz-Vargas y Sainz de Vicuña v Spain* (n 86 above); *Zhen Zhen Zheng v The Netherlands* (n 86 above); *Karen Tayag Vertido v The Philippines* (n 86 above).

[104] *AS v Hungary* (n 86 above); *Groupe d'Intérêt pour le Matronyme v France* (n 86 above); *SOS Sexisme v France* (n 86 above).

[105] *Şahide Goekce v Austria* (n 86 above) para 3.13; *Fatma Yildirim v Austria* (n 86 above) para 3.13.

[106] ICCPR OPI art 1; ICERD art 14(1); CAT art 22(1); CRPD OP art 1(1); ICESCR OP art 2; CED art 31(1).

[107] ICESCR OP art 4.

Element 7 of *Suggestion No 7* envisaged this requirement in relation to communications from individuals, groups, or organizations suffering detriment from a violation of Convention rights or claiming to be directly affected by the failure of a State party to comply with its Convention obligations, but not in relation to claims from those with sufficient interest in the matter. The Netherlands welcomed the avoidance of the word 'victim' in the Committee's formulation.[108] Most States, however, considered that admissible communications should be limited to those where petitioners claimed to have suffered an injury or were directly affected by a State party's lack of compliance with the Convention.[109]

Article 2 of the Chairperson's text submitted to the 2nd session of the Working Group did not explicitly require that petitioners claim to be victims, but required that they claim to have 'suffered' from a violation of any Convention right or to be 'directly affected' by the failure of a State party to comply with its Convention obligations. The word 'victim' did not appear in any of the alternative formulations of Article 2 submitted to the third session of the Working Group. During the third session, however, the Chairperson submitted a new draft Article 2 to the Working Group more closely reflecting language in existing instruments.[110] Alternative proposals for Article 2 in the revised draft submitted to the 4th session included the requirement that communications claim that the individual or individuals who are the subject of the communications are victims.[111]

A number of the communications considered by the Committee have raised the issue of whether the Article 2 requirement that the petitioner(s) claim to be victims of a violation of Convention rights by the State party concerned has been satisfied. In *B.-J. v Germany*,[112] the petitioner alleged that she suffered gender-based discrimination under the statutory regulations on the legal consequences of divorce. The State party argued that the author had not satisfied the victim requirement as her claim amounted to a request for a general and fundamental review of German law on the legal consequences of divorce, rather than an allegation that she had been directly and adversely affected by the application of the law.[113] The Committee held the communication inadmissible on other grounds and did not address the victim requirement.

In *Salgado v United Kingdom*,[114] the petitioner claimed to be a victim of violations of the Convention in that as a British woman married to a foreigner she was prevented from transmitting her British nationality to her son, born in 1954, while a British man married to a foreigner would have been able to do so. The State party argued that the communication was inadmissible because the author had ceased to be a victim of the State party's denial of its citizenship to her son when he reached majority.[115] While not addressing the issue directly, the Committee concluded that the alleged discrimination against the author stopped on the date of her son's majority, after which he had the primary right in respect of his nationality.[116]

---

[108] 'Views submitted by Governments, IGOs and NGOs' (1996) UN Doc E/CN.6/1996/10 (n 36 above) para 66.

[109] Ibid paras 68–70 and Corr.1 para 10; 'Additional views by Governments, IGOs and NGOs' (1997) UN Doc E/CN.6/1997/5 (n 48 above) paras 84, 92 and 95.

[110] 'Chairperson's summary of views and comments' (1998) UN Doc E/1998/27, Annex II, Appendix II (n 53 above) para 2.

[111] 'Revised draft optional protocol' (1998) UN Doc E/1998/27, Annex II, Appendix I (n 54 above).

[112] *B.-J. v Germany* (n 86 above).   [113] Ibid para 4.4.

[114] *Salgado v United Kingdom* (n 86 above).   [115] Ibid para 4.11.   [116] Ibid para 8.4.

In two communications alleging violations of the Convention by nine named petitioners as a result of legislation on family names which prevented them taking their mothers' family names, or transmitting their family names to their children, France[117] argued that the petitioners were not victims under Article 2. Eight of the authors were unmarried without children or married with adult children, and, as such, France argued they could not be victims of violations of Convention Article 16(1)(g) 2, 5, or 16(1) generally.[118] It maintained there was no discrimination against the unmarried authors because the family name was not dependent on their sex, because girls and boys were equally affected by the legislation. However, their mothers could have been victims of a violation as they were unable to transmit their family names to their children.[119] Relying on *Salgado v United Kingdom*,[120] France argued that any discrimination against mothers of the adult children ended when their children reached majority, when the issue of their family name would be in the adult children's hands.[121]

A majority of the Committee agreed that although they might be indirectly affected by a violation of their parents' rights, unmarried and childless complainants did not meet the victim requirement for the purposes of Article 2, as Convention Article 16(1)(g) benefited married women, women living in *de facto* unions or mothers. In addition, they had not suffered any sex-based discrimination in bearing their fathers' family name, as all children, be they girls or boys, were affected by the legislation.[122] A majority also considered that although the authors with adult children might have met the definition of 'victim' of discrimination against women, the discrimination against them ended on their children's majority, at which time the children became the primary rights holders in relation to their names.[123] A minority of the Committee took a different view, concluding that those authors who wished to take their mothers' names were victims as they satisfied the applicable test which was whether they had directly and personally suffered the violations alleged. The minority concluded that these authors had acquired a family name under a rule which amounted to sex-based discrimination against women under Articles 2, 5, and 16 of the Convention, as it only applied to women's family names.[124]

3. *Under the Jurisdiction of the State Party*

All international human rights communications procedures provide that communications must emanate from petitioners 'within' (ICERD Article 14(1)), 'subject to' (ICCPR OPI, ICESCR OP, CAT Article 22(1), ICRMW Article 77(1)) or 'under' the jurisdiction of the State party concerned. However, no jurisdictional requirement was included in *Suggestion*

---

[117] *Groupe d'Intérêt pour le Matronyme v France* (n 86 above) and *SOS Sexisme v France* (n 86 above).

[118] Group d'Intérêt pour le Matronyme based its case on art 16(1)(d), while SOS Sexisme claimed that the authors were victims of violation of the Convention generally. The Committee invited the authors to provide observations in relation to arts 2, 5, and 16(1) in an interim decision taken at its forty-second session. *SOS Sexisme v France* (n 86 above) para 7; *Groupe d'Intérêt pour le Matronyme v France* (n 86 above) para 8. See also the discussion in ch on art 16.

[119] *Groupe d'Intérêt pour le Matronyme v France* (n 86 above) paras 4.3–4.4; *SOS Sexisme v France* (n 86 above) paras 4.3, 4.4, and 4.7.

[120] *Salgado v United Kingdom* (n 86 above).   [121] *SOS Sexisme v France* (n 86 above) para 4.8.

[122] *Groupe d'Intérêt pour le Matronyme v France* (n 86 above) paras 11.9–11.13; *SOS Sexisme v France* (n 86 above) paras 10.6–10.8.

[123] *SOS Sexisme v France* (n 86 above) para 10.9.

[124] *Groupe d'Intérêt pour le Matronyme v France* (n 86 above) paras 12.5–12.7 and 12.17; *SOS Sexisme v France* (n 86 above) paras 11.11–11.14 and 11.16–11.17.

No 7. Several States indicated in written comments that the person or persons must be under the jurisdiction of the State against which the communication was brought,[125] but this was not included in the draft submitted to the Working Group by the Chairperson. When the draft was discussed, some delegations indicated that only victims subject to the jurisdiction of the State party should be entitled to submit a communication, but emphasized that this would include women refugees and migrant women.[126] The Chairperson's revised drafts included this concept.[127]

In its interpretative statement, China asserted that not only the alleged victims, but those who submit communications on behalf of victims should be from the same country to prevent irrelevant persons from taking advantage of them. This interpretation would preclude non-national and international organizations raising complaints on behalf of alleged victims under the jurisdiction of that State party. The issue has not arisen before the Committee as victims and their representatives have all been under the jurisdiction of the State party concerned. One commentator considers that a strength of the OP is that the jurisdiction requirement applies to the victim, but not her representative or those acting on her behalf.[128]

4. The Rights Set Forth in the Convention

All international instruments require communications to fall within the scope of the relevant human rights treaty.[129]

In order to address the fact that many of the provisions of the Convention do not set out 'rights' per se, but identify appropriate measures to be taken by States parties to eliminate discrimination against women on the basis of sex in respect of particular rights,[130] in line with the Maastricht draft,[131] Element 7 of *Suggestion No 7* provided that authors could claim to be suffering detriment from a violation of rights in the Convention or claim to be directly affected by the failure of a State party to comply with its obligations under the Convention. This formulation was taken up in Article 2 of the Chairperson's draft protocol,[132] although some written comments[133] on *Suggestion No 7* suggested a preference for the language contained in existing instruments.

---

[125] 'Views submitted by Governments, IGOs and NGOs' (1996) UN Doc E/CN.6/1996/10 (n 36 above) paras 68–9; 'Additional views by Governments, IGOs and NGOs' (1997) UN Doc E/CN.6/1997/5 (n 48 above) paras 84 and 88.

[126] 'Chairperson's summary of views and comments' (1997) UN Doc E/1997/27, Annex III, Appendix II (n 49 above) para 19.

[127] 'Revised draft optional protocol' (1997) UN Doc E/1997/27, Annex III, Appendix I (n 52 above) and 'Revised draft optional protocol' (1998) UN Doc E/1998/27, Annex II, Appendix I (n 54 above).

[128] MGE Bijnsdorp, 'The Strength of the Optional Protocol to the United Nations Women's Convention' (2000) 18/3 *Netherlands Quarterly of Human Rights* 329, 336.

[129] ICCPR OPI art 1; ICERD art 14(1); CAT art 22(1); CRPD OP art 1(1); CED art 31(1); ICESCR OP art 2.

[130] Byrnes and Connors discuss the types of obligations contained in the Convention (n 10 above) 717–34.

[131] Ibid art 2 of the Maastricht draft.

[132] 'CEDAW *Suggestion No 7*' (1995) UN Doc A/50/38 (n 26 above); and art 2 of the Chairperson's draft, see 'Text submitted by the Chairperson of the Open-Ended Working Group of the CSW' (1997) UN Doc E/CN.6/1997/WG/L.1 (n 47 above).

[133] Mexico, Colombia, and Japan in 'Views submitted by Governments, IGOs and NGOs' (1996) UN Doc E/CN.6/1996/10 (n 36 above) paras 68–70. Australia indicated that further elaboration on the formula was required, ibid para 65; China, Mexico, Morocco, Panama, and Venezuela in 'Additional views by Governments, IGOs and NGOs' (1997) UN Doc E/CN.6/1997/5 (n 48 above) paras 80, 84, 86, and 95–6.

During the negotiations, some States sought to restrict the scope of the Protocol to only some of the Convention rights. During the Working Group's second session, many delegations expressed the view that communications would need to allege a violation of Convention rights, arguing that failure to comply with Convention obligations was a violation of rights and, thus, explicit inclusion of this phrase was unnecessary. Others wished to see reference to failure to comply with Convention obligations as a basis for a communications, as this would emphasize the comprehensive framework of the Convention which covered a broad range of rights. Some also pointed out that the Convention's scope is more than clearly identifiable rights, and that inclusion of the notion of failure to comply would make it clear that the Committee was empowered to deal with direct violations and the failure of States parties to take measures to implement the Convention.[134]

The revised draft submitted to the Chairperson to the 3rd session of the Working Group contained alternative formulations of this element in Article 2.[135] Many delegations expressed the view that it was important to make clear in the Protocol that violations of Convention rights would address acts of States parties, as well as their failure to act. Several were of the view that the term 'violations of the Convention' encompassed both these concepts and that this formulation was sufficient.[136] Article 2 of the Chairperson's second revised draft reflected these positions,[137] with the 3rd session of the Working Group agreeing on the succinct formulation in the Protocol.

Several interpretative statements address the meaning of 'violation of any of the rights set forth in the Convention', emphasizing that as the Convention requires States parties not only to refrain from conduct that infringes directly on the rights it contains, but also to take positive measures to ensure that the rights can be effectively enjoyed, the Committee would be able to accept communications concerning each and every substantive provision of the Convention, and would examine whether the State party has taken all the necessary steps to fulfil the Convention's obligations.[138]

Article 2 makes clear, however, that to be admissible a communication must relate to Convention rights, or concern discrimination against women. Decisions of the Committee under the Protocol address issues which are explicitly addressed in the Convention and those which are not explicitly addressed but which meet the definition of discrimination against women on the basis of sex. Thus, the Committee has taken up cases of domestic violence, which is not addressed in the Convention, but is the subject of General Recommendation 19. It has also indicated that the situation in which women who have fled their country because of fear of domestic violence often find themselves to be the subject of a communication.[139]

---

[134] 'Chairperson's summary of views and comments' (1997) UN Doc E/1997/27, Annex II, Appendix II (n 49 above) paras 16–18.

[135] Proposals for art 2 in 'Revised draft optional protocol' (1997) UN Doc E/1997/27, Annex II, Appendix I (n 52 above).

[136] 'Chairperson's summary of views and comments' (1998) UN Doc E/1998/27, Annex II, Appendix II (n 53 above) para 7.

[137] 'Revised draft optional protocol' (1998) UN Doc E/1998/27, Annex II, Appendix I (n 54 above).

[138] Austria, Canada, Costa Rica, Denmark, Germany, Ghana, Italy in 'Interpretative statements on the draft optional protocol to CEDAW' (1999) UN Doc E/1999/27, Annex II (n 56 above).

[139] *N.S.F v United Kingdom* (n 86 above).

IV. Article 3

Communications shall be in writing and shall not be anonymous. No communication shall be received by the Committee if it concerns a State Party to the Convention that is not a party to the present Protocol.

Article 3 elaborates the basic threshold criteria for admissibility of communications common to all UN communications procedures. These require that communications be in writing[140] and not be anonymous.[141] Article 3 also highlights the optional nature of the procedure, indicating that communications may not be received if they concern a State party to the Convention which is not a party to the Protocol.[142] OP Article 15(2) and (3) make clear that ratification of, or accession to, the Convention is required prior to ratification or accession of the Protocol.

Element 8 of *Suggestion No 7* provided that communications would be in writing, while Element 9(a) indicated that the communication would be inadmissible if the State party concerned had not ratified or acceded to the OP. Paragraph (b) of the same Element precluded anonymous communications.

One State indicated that it was important to ensure that the communications procedure did not indirectly discriminate against or disenfranchize individuals or groups. A requirement of written submission, while easier for States and the Committee, could discriminate against women with low levels of print literacy and consideration should be given to alternative means of communication.[143] The possibility of video submission or oral presentations in exceptional cases when the Committee deemed that there was no other reasonable way to lodge a communication was also addressed,[144] although practical difficulties and financial implications were raised.[145]

Article 3 of the draft optional protocol submitted by the Chairperson to the second session of the Working Group provided that communications shall be in writing and shall not be anonymous, with Article 1(2) providing that no communication shall be received by the Committee if it concerns a State party to the Convention which is not a party to this Protocol.[146] The Chairperson's draft Article 3 was adopted *ad referendum* during the Working Group's second session,[147] with the additional element drawn from draft Article 1 being included and agreed by referendum during its 3rd session.[148]

---

[140] The requirement for communications to be in writing is contained in ICCPR OPI art 2 and ICESCR OP art 3(2)(g).

[141] ICCPR OPI art 3; ICERD art 14(6)(a); CAT art 22(2); CMW art 77(2); CRPD OP art 2(a); ICESCR OP art 3(2)(g); CED art 31(2)(a).

[142] ICCPR OPI art 1; CRPD OP art 1(2); ICESCR OP art 1(2). A declaration accepting the Committee's competence to receive and consider communications is required in respect of other communications procedures: ICERD art 14(1); CAT art 22(1); ICRMW art 77(1)i and CPED art 31(1).

[143] Australia in 'Views submitted by Governments, IGOs and NGOs' (1996) UN Doc E/CN.6/1996/10 (n 36 above) para 75.

[144] 'Report of the Open-ended Working Group on the Elaboration of a Draft Optional Protocol to CEDAW' (1996) UN Doc E/1996/26, Annex III (n 37 above) para 39.

[145] 'Additional views by Governments, IGOs and NGOs' (1997) UN Doc E/CN.6/1997/5 (n 48 above) paras 99–100.

[146] 'Text submitted by the Chairperson of the Open-Ended Working Group of the CSW' (1997) UN Doc E/CN.6/1997/WG/L.1 (n 47 above).

[147] 'Chairperson's summary of views and comments' (1997) UN Doc E/1997/27, Annex II, Appendix II (n 49 above) para 21.

[148] 'Chairperson's summary of views and comments' (1998) UN Doc E/1998/27, Annex II, Appendix II (n 53 above) para 9.

Accordingly, the 1998 revised draft optional protocol contains Article 3 as it appears in the adopted text.[149]

Rule 56(3) of the Committee's Rules of Procedure provides that no communication shall be received by the Committee if it concerns a State that is not a party to the Protocol, is not in writing, or is anonymous. Communications with these flaws which are received by the Committee's secretariat are brought to the attention of the Chairperson of the Working Group on Communications, but not to the State party concerned and are not registered. Information on the number of such communications received is provided to the Working Group at each of its sessions.

V. Article 4

1. The Committee shall not consider a communication unless it has ascertained that all available domestic remedies have been exhausted unless the application of such remedies is unreasonably prolonged or unlikely to bring effective relief.
2. The Committee shall declare a communication inadmissible where:
   (a) The same matter has already been examined by the Committee or has been or is being examined under another procedure of international investigation or settlement;
   (b) It is incompatible with the provisions of the Convention;
   (c) It is manifestly ill-founded or not sufficiently substantiated;
   (d) It is an abuse of the right to submit a communication;
   (e) The facts that are the subject of the communication occurred prior to the entry into force of the present Protocol for the State party concerned unless those facts continued after that date.

Article 4 sets out a number of admissibility criteria, some of which render communications prima facie inadmissible, while others require consideration and decision by the Committee.

Some of these criteria are drawn from existing communications procedures, and were included in *Suggestion No 7*.[150] *Suggestion No 7* proposed two additional admissibility criteria which do not appear in the OP: that a communication should disclose an alleged violation of rights or an alleged failure of a State party to give effect to obligations under the Convention and that the author should within a reasonable period provide adequate substantiating information.[151] Written comments on *Suggestion No 7* dealt with each criterion proposed, with one State indicating that each communication must describe the facts, indicate the object of the petition, and the rights allegedly violated.[152] Several suggested additional criteria. These included a time limit for submission of communications ranging from three to twelve months,[153] that the object of the communication must not be incompatible with the principles of the UN Charter,[154] that it should comply with the

---

[149] 'Revised draft optional protocol' (1998) UN Doc E/1998/27, Annex III, Appendix I (n 54 above).

[150] 'CEDAW *Suggestion No 7*' (1995) UN Doc A/50/38 (n 26 above) para 9(d), (e) and (g).

[151] Ibid para 9(c) and (g).

[152] Cuba in 'Additional views by Governments, IGOs and NGOs' (1997) UN Doc E/CN.6/1997/5 (n 48 above) para 110.

[153] 'Additional views by Governments, IGOs and NGOs' ibid paras 132–3, 134(f), and 137. ICESCR OP art 3(2)(a) provides that a communication shall be considered inadmissible if it is not submitted 'within one year after the exhaustion of domestic remedies, except in cases where the author can demonstrate that it had not been possible to submit the communication within that time limit'.

[154] Cuba in 'Additional views by Governments, IGOs and NGOs' ibid para 134(a).

principles of objectivity, justice, and impartiality,[155] and that it should include information on legal remedies or reparations, if any, undertaken by the State party.[156] It was also suggested that no communication with openly political motives, or references which the State in question found insulting, or from the mass media should be accepted, while each should emanate from a reliable and well-founded source.[157] During the 1st session of the Working Group, support was expressed for a time limit for the lodging of communications and for a requirement that they comply with the principles of objectivity and justice and include legal remedies or reparations, if any, undertaken by the State party.[158]

The Chairperson's draft provided that the Committee shall declare a communication inadmissible where it considered it to be an abuse of the right of submission or incompatible with the Convention. It also provided that the Committee shall not declare a communication admissible unless it had ascertained that all available domestic remedies had been exhausted, unless it considered this requirement unreasonable; and that the same matter is not being examined under another procedure of international investigation or settlement, unless that procedure is unreasonably prolonged. Additional requirements that the communication comply with the principles of objectivity and impartiality and include information of legal remedies or reparation undertaken by the respective State party were also included in the draft.[159]

The inclusion of a number of these elements in the Protocol was agreed in principle during the Working Group's second session, although many delegations preferred to place the Protocol on an equal footing with similar international procedures, on the basis that a higher admissibility threshold would discriminate against women,[160] and did not support the inclusion of admissibility criteria relating to principles of objectivity and impartiality.[161]

The Chairperson's revised text included the concepts which had attracted the broad support of the Working Group in the various alternatives to Article 4, but put the criterion of compliance with objectivity and impartiality in brackets.[162] During the 3rd session of the Working Group, some delegations insisted that these principles should be maintained in the consideration of communications, and suggested that instead of these being included as part of the admissibility criteria, they could appear in another part of the Protocol. Others disagreed with the inclusion of the principles.[163] The revised draft protocol submitted to the 4th session did not contain the principles in the admissibility criteria, but included a paragraph in brackets in draft Article 7 stating that while exercising its function under the Protocol, the Committee should act in compliance with the

---

[155] Cuba, China, and Panama in 'Additional views by Governments, IGOs and NGOs' ibid paras 134 (d), 135, and 138.

[156] China in 'Additional views by Governments, IGOs and NGOs' ibid para 135.

[157] Cuba in 'Additional views by Governments, IGOs and NGOs' ibid para 134.

[158] 'Report of the Open-ended Working Group on the Elaboration of a Draft Optional Protocol to CEDAW' (1996) UN Doc E/1996/26, Annex III (n 37 above) paras 50–1.

[159] 'Text submitted by the Chairperson of the Open-Ended Working Group of the CSW' (1997) UN Doc E/CN.6/1997/WG/L.1 (n 47 above) art 4.

[160] 'Chairperson's summary of views and comments' (1997) UN Doc E/1997/27, Annex II, Appendix II (n 49 above) para 22.

[161] Ibid para 31.

[162] 'Revised draft optional protocol' (1997) UN Doc E/1997/27/, Annex III, Appendix I (n above 52) art 4.

[163] 'Chairperson's summary of views and comments' (1997) UN Doc E/1997/27, Annex II, Appendix II (n 49 above) para 13.

principles of objectivity and impartiality.[164] The principles are not included in the OP, but paragraph 3 of its enabling UNGA resolution stresses that the Committee should continue to be guided by the principles of non-selectivity, impartiality, and objectivity.[165] Several interpretative declarations made in the CSW addressed Article 4. China indicated that it was general practice that politically motivated communications are inadmissible. It considered that the phrase 'an abuse of the right to submit a communication' applied to communications submitted for political purposes. India called on the Committee, when interpreting the admissibility criteria, to guard against insufficiently substantiated and politically motivated complaints, particularly where such motivation has an international character intended to exploit the procedure for ends unrelated to the protection of the rights of women.[166]

1. All Available Domestic Remedies Have Been Exhausted Unless the Application of Such Remedies is Unreasonably Prolonged or Unlikely to Bring Effective Relief

UN communications procedures provide that a communication shall not be considered by the relevant committee unless it has ascertained that all available domestic remedies have been exhausted.[167] Exceptions to this general rule are made if the application of such remedies is unreasonably prolonged[168] or unlikely to bring effective relief.[169]

Element 9(f) of *Suggestion No 7* indicated that a communication would be declared inadmissible by the Committee if all domestic remedies had not been exhausted, unless the Committee considered that requirement unreasonable. This Element was welcomed by NGOs, which suggested that the requirement should not obstruct the filing of claims, but enable States parties with effective domestic remedies to address a complaint before it reached the international level, thereby advancing the principle of accountability at the domestic level.[170] The Element was also supported by most States,[171] although some called for further discussion and analysis of the proposed criteria to be used to determine whether the exhaustion of domestic remedies was not reasonable and how that determination would be made.[172] Several suggested a clearer formulation, for example, that communications would be inadmissible if available domestic remedies had not been exhausted, except where it had been shown convincingly that such remedies were inefficient or that they were

---

[164] 'Revised draft optional protocol' (1998) UN Doc E/1998/27, Annex II, Appendix I (n 54 above) para 4.

[165] UNGA Res 54/4 (6 October 1999) UN Doc A/RES/54/4.

[166] 'Interpretative statements on the draft optional protocol to CEDAW' (1999) UN Doc E/1999/27 Annex II (n 56 above).

[167] ICCPR OPI arts 2 and 5(2)(b); ICERD art 14(7)(a); CAT art 22(5)(b); CMW art 77(3)(b); CRPD OP art 2(d); ICESCR OP art 3(1)i and CPED art 31(2)(d).

[168] ICCPR OPI art 5(2)(b); ICERD art 14(7)(a); ICESCR OP art 3(1); CPED art 31(2)(d). CMW art 77(3)(b) provides for this exception if 'in the view of the Committee' the application of the remedies is unreasonably prolonged.

[169] CAT art 22(5)(b); ICRMW art 77(3)(b); CRPD OP art 2(d).

[170] 'Views submitted by Governments, IGOs and NGOs' (1996) UN Doc E/CN.6/1996/10 (n 36 above) paras 85–6.

[171] 'Additional views by Governments, IGOs and NGOs' (1997) UN Doc E/CN.6/1997/5 (n 48 above) paras 115–23. Cuba did not consider there should be an exception where the remedy was unreasonably prolonged. Ibid para 121.

[172] Mexico in 'Views submitted by Governments, IGOs and NGOs' (1996) UN Doc E/CN.6/1996/10 (n 36 above) para 83; China, Luxembourg, Mexico, Morocco, Venezuela in 'Additional views by Governments, IGOs and NGOs' (1997) UN Doc E/CN.6/1997/5 (n 48 above) paras 118, 120 and 122.

unjustifiably prolonged.[173] During the 1st session of the Working Group, there was support for the Committee's Element, although delegations preferred that the formulation of the provision correspond with that in existing instruments, in particular, the Convention against Torture and the International Convention on the Rights of All Migrant Workers and Members of Their Families, which incorporated the practice of the Human Rights Committee which interpreted the ICCPR provision to include the absence of effective remedies, their lack of effectiveness or denial of a remedy. It was also suggested that more general wording might be needed to include situations where the victim was unaware of domestic remedies or their availability. The inclusion of 'available' before 'domestic remedies' in line with other instruments was also proposed.[174]

Article 4(2)(a) of the Chairperson's draft provided that the Committee shall not declare a communication admissible unless it has ascertained that all available domestic remedies have been exhausted, unless it considers this requirement unreasonable. The 2nd session of the Working Group agreed that this criterion should be included, although some suggested adding a qualification, such as exhaustion should be determined in accordance with generally recognized rules of international law.[175] The Chairperson's revised text reflected these ideas in alternative formulations.[176] The 3rd session of the Working Group agreed that admissibility criteria would be contained in two separate paragraphs, the first dealing with exhaustion of domestic remedies and the second the remaining criteria. Some delegations also considered that it should be up to the author to demonstrate that the application of domestic remedies is unreasonably prolonged or unlikely to bring effective relief, while others considered that the criterion should be determined in accordance with generally recognized rules of international law.[177] The Chairperson reflected these ideas in the revised draft, with the 4th session of the Working Group agreeing on a stream-lined subparagraph.

Two interpretative statements were made on Article 4(1) in the CSW. India indicated that 'unreasonably prolonged' should be interpreted in the light of the normal speed of justice in the State party, and that it should generally be possible to establish that delay itself is discriminatory. Costa Rica made clear that the exhaustion rule was to be understood as being of benefit to States and accordingly may be waived.[178]

The petitioner's failure to exhaust domestic remedies has been raised by all but one State party in the Committee's fourteen concluded communications. In the remaining case, *AT v Hungary*,[179] the State chose not to raise any preliminary objections on admissibility, although it indicated that the author had not made effective use of the domestic remedies available to her, which it admitted were not capable of providing her with immediate

---

[173] Colombia in 'Views submitted by Governments, IGOs and NGOs' (1996) UN Doc E/CN.6/1996/10 (n 36 above) paras 83–4.

[174] 'Report of the Open-ended Working Group on the Elaboration of a Draft Optional Protocol to CEDAW' (1996) UN Doc E/1996/26, Annex III (n 37 above) para 48.

[175] 'Chairperson's summary of views and comments' (1997) UN Doc E/1997/27, Annex II, Appendix II (n 49 above) para 25.

[176] 'Revised draft optional protocol' (1997) UN Doc E/1997/27, Annex III, Appendix I (n 52 above) draft art 4(1) and alternative draft art 4(iv).

[177] 'Chairperson's summary of views and comments' (1998) UN Doc E/1998/27, Annex II, Appendix II (n 53 above) paras 10–1.

[178] 'Interpretative statements on the draft optional protocol to CEDAW' (1999) UN Doc E/1999/27, Annex II (n 56 above).

[179] *AT v Hungary* (n 86 above).

protection from her violent partner.[180] The Committee also considered that any further domestic remedies would not bring effective relief or were unreasonably prolonged.[181]

The Committee has relied on the extensive jurisprudence which has been developed by other human rights treaty bodies, and particularly the Human Rights Committee.[182] The CEDAW Committee has taken the view that OP Articles 2, 3, and 4 and its Rules of Procedure require it to apply the admissibility criteria actively.[183] Thus, it raises the issue of exhaustion of domestic remedies even where the State party does not do so, or explicitly or implicitly waives its right to do so.[184] Authors are required to provide details of the steps they have taken to exhaust domestic remedies, or that the requirement is not applicable because they would be ineffective or unreasonably prolonged. Rule 69(6) of the Committee's Rules of Procedure, however, shifts the burden of showing that there are specific applicable and available remedies that have not been exhausted to the State party where the State party disputes the claim that all available domestic remedies have been exhausted.[185]

The question of exhaustion of domestic remedies is determined by the Committee as of the time it considers a communication, rather than at the time of its submission, on the basis that rejecting a communication as inadmissible when domestic remedies had been exhausted by the time of its consideration would be pointless as the author could submit a new communication relating to the same alleged violation. Thus, in *Yildirim v Austria*,[186] the Committee did not review its decision that the communication was admissible, as the civil liability proceedings pursued by the victim's daughter, still in process when the submission was made, were finalized before the Committee's consideration. Rule 70 of its Rules of Procedure also allows the Committee to review inadmissibility decisions when the reasons for inadmissibility no longer apply.

The Committee also considers that authors are required to raise the substance of the alleged violation in domestic courts explicitly to enable the State party to remedy the violation before it can be raised before the Committee,[187] emphasizing that the underlying rationale of the exhaustion requirement is to give States parties an opportunity to remedy a violation of any of the rights set forth in the Convention through their legal systems before the Committee addresses the same issues.[188] It requires authors to comply properly with domestic procedural requirements, including formal requirements for filing and time limits. Accordingly, in *B.-J. v Germany*;[189] the Committee held the petition inadmissible because some aspects of the case were pending in the domestic courts, and other aspects had not been properly made the subject of appeal or correctly brought to the Federal Constitutional Court. The author had not filed her complaint in accordance with the formal requirements for constitutional claims, had missed deadlines, and had

---

[180] Ibid para 5.6.   [181] Ibid para 8.4.

[182] For an overview of this see DJ Sullivan, *Overview of the rule requiring exhaustion of domestic remedies under the Optional Protocol to CEDAW* OP-CEDAW Technical Papers 1 (2008).

[183] Rules of Procedure 67 and 72(4).

[184] *AT v Hungary* (n 86 above).

[185] CEDAW rules of procedure, UNGA, 'Report of the CEDAW Committee—Twenty-Fourth Session' (2001) UN Doc A/56/38, Annex I, Parts XVI and XVII. Amendments to the rules were adopted at the Committee's thirty-ninth session, UNGA, 'Report of the CEDAW Committee—Thirty-Ninth Session' (2007) UN Doc A/62/38, Chap V, paras 653–5 and Appendix.

[186] *Fatma Yildirim v Austria* (n 86 above) para 11.3.

[187] *Salgado v United Kingdom* (n 86 above) para 8.5.

[188] *Şahide Goekce v Austria* (n 86 above) para 7.2.   [189] *B.-J. v Germany* (n 86 above).

not exhausted her claims in the lower courts. Also the Committee was not convinced that the proceedings were unreasonably prolonged or unlikely to bring effective relief.[190] Similarly, in *Salgado v the United Kingdom*,[191] the Committee concluded that the petitioner had never applied to register her son as a British citizen, nor challenged the refusal of the United Kingdom authorities to grant her son nationality in the High Court.[192] In *Kayhan v Turkey*,[193] where the petitioner claimed violations of her right to work, equal employment opportunities, and equal treatment under Article 11 of the Convention, the communication was held inadmissible because although she had raised discrimination, the petitioner had not explicitly raised discrimination on the basis of sex in proceedings against her and in her appeal in Turkey. As such, the Committee considered that the Turkish administrative and judicial bodies had not had the opportunity to consider the case from the perspective of domestic remedies, or the substance of the case presented to the Committee, and, thus, domestic remedies had not been exhausted.[194] A similar approach was taken in *N.S.F v United Kingdom*,[195] where the petitioner, an asylum seeker with two young children, claimed that she feared for her life because of the violence of her former husband in Pakistan and the future and education of her two sons if she were deported. The Committee held the communication inadmissible because discrimination against women on the basis of sex had not been raised explicitly in any of the relevant asylum proceedings in the United Kingdom, nor in her application to the European Court of Human Rights.[196] In *Zhen Zhen Zheng v The Netherlands*,[197] the Committee held the petitioner's claim to be a victim of a violation of Convention Article 6 inadmissible for non-exhaustion because Article 6 had not been raised in domestic proceedings.[198] The petitioner had failed to access an available avenue of appeal, and the Committee concluded that she had not provided convincing arguments that the remedy would be unreasonably prolonged or unlikely to give effective relief. Non-exhaustion of domestic remedies also rendered inadmissible the communication submitted by Ms Delange, one of the nine petitioners who claimed to be victims of a violation by France of the Convention, because she was unable to transmit her family name to her minor child on a basis of equality with her father, because she had made no effort to bring any domestic proceedings.[199]

The Committee's decisions indicate that the authors of communications are required to exhaust any judicial, administrative, and extraordinary remedy which is available in practice, provides relief for the harm suffered, and is effective for the objective sought by the author in the particular circumstances of the case. Most decisions have concerned ordinary judicial remedies. The Committee concluded that Ms Salgado did not satisfy this admissibility criterion by pursuing administrative and legislative procedures, when there were available judicial procedures.[200]

In *AS v Hungary*,[201] the Committee was faced with the question of whether the victim was required to exhaust an extraordinary constitutional remedy of revision of judgment applicable in cases where a review is needed because the issue concerns a point of law of general importance. Although the question of whether extraordinary remedies must be exhausted was not addressed by the Committee, it concluded that the author was not

---

[190] Ibid paras 8.5–8.6.   [191] *Salgado v United Kingdom* (n 86 above) para 8.5.
[192] Ibid para 8.5.   [193] *Rahime Kayhan v Turkey* (n 86 above).
[194] Ibid paras 7.5–7.7.   [195] *N.S.F v United Kingdom* (n 86 above).   [196] Ibid para 7.3.
[197] *Zhen Zhen Zheng v The Netherlands* (n 86 above).   [198] Ibid para 7.3.
[199] *SOS Sexisme v France* (n 86 above) para 10.12.
[200] *Salgado v United Kingdom* (n 86 above) para 8.5.   [201] *AS v Hungary* (n 86 above).

required to avail herself of revision of judgment because it was ineffective and unavailable to her.[202] It remains to be seen whether the Committee will take the approach of other human rights treaty bodies which require exhaustion of extraordinary remedies that offer an effective and sufficient means of redress and are based on legal principles, rather than the discretion of the decision-maker.[203]

The Committee has also made clear that the exhaustion requirement only applies to remedies which are available to the author. Thus, in *Şahide Goecke v Austria*,[204] the Committee concluded that the deceased victim was not required to avail herself of an action of 'associated prosecution' in respect of her violent husband after the Public Prosecutor had decided to drop the charges against him. The Committee considered that this remedy was *de facto* unavailable to the victim as it was subject to stringent legal rules, German was not Ms Goecke's mother tongue, and, most importantly, because she was in a situation of protracted domestic violence and threats of violence. The fact that the State party raised this remedy late in the proceedings also led the Committee to conclude that the remedy was 'rather obscure'.[205] Similarly, in *Vertido v The Philippines*,[206] the Committee concluded that the special remedy of *certiorari* was not available to the victim as it was available only to the 'People of the Philippines' represented by the Solicitor General, and in any event only addressed errors of jurisdiction, and not the error of judgment comprising sex-based discrimination underlying the acquittal of a man who had been prosecuted for Ms Vertido's rape, which was the basis of her communication.[207]

The Committee has applied the exceptions to the exhaustion requirement in a number of cases. In *AT v Hungary*,[208] it concluded that a delay of over three years from the dates of the incidents that were the subject of criminal proceedings for assault and battery amounted to an unreasonably prolonged delay within the meaning of Article 4(1), particularly as the author had been at risk of irreparable harm and threats to her life during that period. The Committee noted that the author had no possibility of obtaining temporary protection while criminal proceedings were ongoing, the defendant had at no time been detained, and the State party itself had admitted that the remedies pursued by the author were not capable of providing immediate protection.[209] This contrasts with the Committee's approach in *B.-J. v Germany*, where the majority concluded that the author had not demonstrated that the remedies were unreasonably prolonged. Two Committee members, however, considered that domestic remedies had been unreasonably prolonged in relation to some parts of the claim, on the basis that the matter required the determination and granting of financial or material resources essential for the survival of the author, and that this should have been finalized with the speed and efficiency of the parties' divorce.[210]

Several communications have raised the issue of whether a remedy, although available, is unlikely to bring effective relief. Spain argued that domestic remedies had not been exhausted by Ms Muñoz-Vargas y Sainz de Vecuña because her *amparo* appeal was pending, and entry into force of new legislation providing for equality between women and men in succession to titles of nobility would apply retroactively to her case. This issue and

---

[202] Ibid para 10.3.   [203] Sullivan (n 182 above) 6–7.
[204] *Şahide Goekce v Austria* (n 86 above).
[205] Ibid para 11.3.   [206] *Karen Tayag Vertido v The Philippines* (n 86 above).
[207] Ibid para 6.2.   [208] *AT v Hungary* (n 86 above).   [209] Ibid para 8.4.
[210] *B.-J. v Germany* (n 86 above) Appendix, individual opinion of Committee members Krisztina Morvai and Meriem Belmihoub-Serdani (dissenting).

counter arguments put forward by the author were not addressed by the Committee, which held the communication inadmissible *ratione temporis*.[211] In *AT v Hungary*, the author argued that her pending appeal to the Supreme Court was unlikely to be successful in light of settled case law and, therefore, that exhaustion of this remedy should not be required. Although the Committee indicated that the eventual outcome of the appeal was not likely to bring effective relief in light of her life-threatening situation, it preferred to conclude that the communication was admissible as the available remedies were unduly prolonged, rather than on the basis that Supreme Court jurisprudence indicated that the remedies were unlikely to bring relief.[212] The life-threatening and dangerous situation of the victim in *Yildirim v Austria* was also a factor leading the Committee to conclude that a complaint under legislation designed to determine the lawfulness of official actions of a public prosecutor was unlikely to bring her effective relief.[213] In *Nguyen v The Netherlands*, the Committee was faced with the question of whether an earlier decision in proceedings brought by the author excused her from bringing proceedings in relation to a second alleged violation based on facts identical to those in the first proceedings. The author argued that she had exhausted all domestic remedies because she had appealed the outcome of a decision concerning benefits available to her during her maternity leave to the highest administrative court. She had appealed the decision concerning benefits relating to a second maternity leave, but withdrew this appeal after losing the final appeal in respect of the first maternity leave. The Committee concluded that in the absence of information on this issue from the State party and the author and in light of the unambiguous wording of the decision of the highest administrative court, proceedings relating to the second maternity leave benefits were unlikely to bring relief.[214] In *Groupe d'Intérêt pour le Matronyme v France*, although holding the communication inadmissible because the petitioners were not victims within Article 2, the Committee considered that the procedure for change of name set out in the French Civil Code was unlikely to bring effective relief to a group of petitioners seeking to take their mothers' family names, and was also unreasonably prolonged.[215] Additionally, based on *Sahide Goekce v Austria*, the Committee is likely to consider it doubtful that remedies of an abstract nature will bring effective relief. Accordingly, Ms Goekce's heirs were not required to initiate a constitutional procedure aimed at bringing about an amendment of legal provisions which had barred her from appealing against the decisions of the public prosecutor not to detain her husband who ultimately killed her.[216]

It has been suggested that, except in cases where the subject of the communication is violence, the Committee's approach to exhaustion of domestic remedies has been conservative and it has not approached the criterion flexibly in the spirit of the Convention's object and purpose. Here, comparisons have been drawn between the approach to the exhaustion criterion in *B.-J. v Germany* and the more flexible approach in *AT v Hungary*. It should be noted, however, that inadmissibility decisions have not all been unanimous, and dissenters have approached the criterion of exhaustion from a gender perspective. In *Zhen Zhen Zheng v The Netherlands*, the individual opinion of the three dissenters

---

[211] *Cristina Muñoz-Vargas y Sainz de Vicuña* (n 86 above).   [212] *AT v Hungary* (n 86 above) para 8.4.
[213] *Fatma Yildirim v Austria* CEDAW Communication No 6/2005 (2007) UN Doc CEDAW/C/39/D/6/2005 para 11.4.
[214] *Dung Thi Thuy Nguyen v The Netherlands* (n 86 above) para 9.3.
[215] *Groupe d'Intérêt pour le Matronyme v France* CEDAW Communication No 12 (2009) UN Doc CEDAW/C/44/D/12/2007 paras 11.7–11.8.
[216] *Sahide Goekce v Austria* (n 86 above) para 11.2.

concludes that Article 4(1) was irrelevant as the substance of the complaint concerned the State party's obligations under Article 6, particularly in light of the nature of trafficking and the difficulty victims face in reporting this crime.[217]

2. *The Same Matter*

This provision, designed to ensure that there is no duplication in consideration of communications at the international level, requires the Committee to declare a communication inadmissible where it has already examined the same matter, or if the same matter has already been examined, or is being examined by another international procedure of investigation or settlement. Similar provisions are contained in CAT, ICRMW, CRPD OP, and ICESCR OP.[218] The ICCPR OPI and CPED exclude only those cases that are being examined by such a procedure simultaneously.[219]

Element 9(f) of *Suggestion No 7* envisaged that if the same matter were being examined under another international procedure, the Committee would declare the communication inadmissible unless it considered that procedure unreasonably prolonged. States welcomed the first part of this element considering that it would streamline processes and reduce duplication of efforts.[220] The proposal that the Committee could consider communications being examined by other international procedures if they were unreasonably prolonged was not supported, however, as this would involve the Committee judging the working of other bodies.[221] Several comments called for the Protocol explicitly to exclude any communication from the Committee's consideration that had already been examined under another international procedure. The Council of Europe drew attention to reservations entered by Council of Europe Member States to the ICCPR OPI Article 5(2) which excluded matters already considered, or simultaneously being considered, by the European Court of Human Rights from the Human Rights Committee's petitions competence.[222] Support was expressed for language, mirroring that of CAT or ICRMW, which would limit the Committee's competence to matters which had not been and were not being examined by another treaty body.[223]

The Chairperson's draft protocol provided, in Article 4(2)(b), that the Committee shall not declare a communication admissible unless it has ascertained that the same matter is not being examined under another procedure of international investigation or settlement, unless that procedure is unreasonably prolonged.[224] During the Working

---

[217] *Zhen Zhen Zheng v The Netherlands* CEDAW Communication No 15 (2009) UN Doc CEDAW/C/42/D/15/2007, individual opinion of Committee members Mary Shanti Dairiam, Violeta Neubauer and Silvia Pimentel (dissenting).

[218] CAT art 22(5)(a); ICRMW art 77(3)(a); CRPD OP art 2(c) CPED and ICESCR OP art 3(2)(c).

[219] ICCPR OPI art 5(2)(a); CED art 31(2)(c). See also CERD rule 84(1)(g). C Phuong, 'The Relationship Between the European Court of Human Rights and the Human Rights Committee: Has the "Same Matter" Already Been Examined?' (2007) 7/2 *Human Rights L Rev* 385.

[220] 'Views submitted by Governments, IGOs and NGOs' (1996) UN Doc E/CN.6/1996/10 (n 36 above) paras 82–3; 'Additional views by Governments, IGOs and NGOs' (1997) UN Doc E/CN.6/1997/5 (n 48 above) paras 124, 126, 127 and 129.

[221] 'Additional views by Governments, IGOs and NGOs' (1997) UN Doc E/CN.6/1997/5 (n 48 above) paras 125–7.

[222] Ibid paras 126 and 130.

[223] 'Report of the Open-ended Working Group on the Elaboration of a Draft Optional Protocol to CEDAW' (1996) UN Doc E/1996/26, Annex III (n 37 above) para 49.

[224] 'Text submitted by the Chairperson of the Open-Ended Working Group of the CSW' (1997) UN Doc E/CN.6/1997/WG/L.1 (n 47 above).

Group's 2nd session, all agreed that an inadmissibility criterion relating to duplication of procedures should be included, but differed as to whether only simultaneous consideration should be precluded or also matters already considered by another procedure, or by the Committee itself. There was also agreement that it would be inappropriate for the Committee to consider whether another procedure was unreasonably prolonged.[225] The Chairperson's revised text included these ideas in alternative formulations,[226] and with the exception of the chapeau, the revised text submitted to the 4th session of the Working Group is that in the Protocol.[227]

The Committee has followed the jurisprudence of other treaty bodies, in particular, the Human Rights Committee, which has reduced the effects of the limitation by holding that 'same matter' refers to communications which involve the same set of facts, the same individuals, the same violations,[228] and the same substantive rights.[229] Thus, in *Rahime Kayhan v Turkey*,[230] where the State party sought to have the case held inadmissible on the basis that a similar case had been held inadmissible by the European Court of Human Rights,[231] the Committee concluded that Article 4(2)(a) was not applicable, as it concerned a different individual.[232]

The jurisprudence of other human rights treaty bodies also indicates that communications procedures of the CSW and the special procedures of the former Commission on Human Rights, and now the Human Rights Council, are not an 'international procedure of investigation or settlement'.[233] As the 1503 procedure of the former Commission on Human Rights did not fall within this definition,[234] it is assumed that its successor, the complaints procedure of the Human Rights Council,[235] also does not constitute an international procedure of investigation or settlement so as to render inadmissible a communication considered or being considered under these processes.

3. Incompatible

UN communications procedures provide that communications which are considered to be incompatible with the provisions of the relevant treaty shall be considered inadmissible.[236] This criterion was not included in *Suggestion No 7*, but appeared in the Chairperson's draft text.[237] The criterion was agreed to *ad referendum* during the 2nd

---

[225] 'Chairperson's summary of views and comments' (1997) UN Doc E/1997/27, Annex II, Appendix II (n 49 above) paras 28–30.

[226] 'Revised draft optional protocol' (1997) UN Doc E/1997/27, Annex III, Appendix I (n 52 above).

[227] 'Revised draft optional protocol' (1998) UN Doc E/1998/27, Annex II, Appendix I (n 54 above).

[228] *Fanali v Italy* CCPR Communication No 075/1980 (1983) UN Doc CCPR/C/18/D/75/1980 para 7.2.

[229] *Petersen v Germany* CCPR Communication No 1115/2002 (2004) UN Doc CCPR/C/80/D/1115/2002 para 6.3.

[230] *Rahime Kayhan v Turkey* (n 86 above).

[231] *Leyla Şahin v Turkey* [2009] ECHR 44774/98 (29 June 2004).

[232] The Committee did not address claims of inadmissibility under art 42(a) raised by States parties in *Cristina Muñoz-Vargas y Sainz de Vicuña v Spain* (n 86 above); *N.S.F v United Kingdom* (n 86 above); and *SOS Sexisme v France* (n 86 above).

[233] See UNGA 'Report of the Human Rights Committee—Forty-Ninth, Fiftieth and Fifty-First Sessions' (1994) UN Doc A/49/40, Vol. I para 402.

[234] Ibid. [235] HRC Res 5/1 (18 June 2007) UN Doc A/HRC/RES/5/1.

[236] ICCPR OPI art 3; CAT art 22(2); ICRMW art 77(2); CRPD OP art 2(a); CPED art 31(2)(b); ICESCR OP art (3)(d).

[237] 'Text submitted by the Chairperson of the Open-Ended Working Group of the CSW' (1997) UN Doc E/CN.6/1997/WG/L.1 (n 47 above) art 4(1).

session of the Working Group,[238] and was included in the revised draft texts submitted by the Chairperson to the Working Group.[239]

Turkey argued that Ms Kayhan's communication, alleging a violation of Convention Article 11 through her dismissal as a civil servant because she wore a headscarf was inadmissible, *inter alia,* because it violated the spirit of the Convention as her claim did not concern the definition of discrimination against women in Article 1. The regulations governing civil servants' attire applied to women and men equally, as did the disciplinary and legal consequences.[240] Turkey rejected the claim that Ms Kayhan would not have been dismissed had she been a man or had failed to comply with other civil service dress code requirements. It indicated that she was dismissed because she had continued to wear the headscarf despite warnings and penalties because of her political and ideological opinions and the same sanction would have been applied to a man who breached the dress code regulations. The Committee did not discuss the incompatibility criterion, finding Ms Kayhan's communication to be inadmissible on other grounds.

A minority of the Committee addressed the incompatibility criterion in *Muñoz-Varas y Sainz de Vicuna v Spain*, where the author claimed to be the victim of a violation of Convention Article 2(c) and (f) as a result of rules of succession to titles of nobility which gave her younger brother precedence.[241] The minority considered that the Convention protects women's rights to be free from all forms of discrimination, commits States parties to ensuring practical realization of the principle of equality of women and men, and sets out the normative standards of such equality and non-discrimination in all fields, and to that end Article 1 provides a comprehensive definition of discrimination against women. It considered that it was undisputed that the title under consideration was purely symbolic and honorific, devoid of legal or material effect. Hence, the committee deemed a claim of succession was not compatible with the Convention, which is aimed at protecting women from discrimination which has the effect or purpose of impairing or nullifying the recognition, enjoyment, or exercise by women on a basis of equality of men and women, of human rights and fundamental freedoms in all fields.[242]

In contrast, one member of the Committee acknowledged that the right to titles of nobility is not a fundamental right and may have little material consequence, but, nevertheless, considered that male precedence in this context was a violation, in principle, of women's right to equality, as it subverted progress towards the elimination of discrimination against women, reinforced male superiority and maintained the status quo. This member also emphasizes that the inalienable right to non-discrimination on the basis of sex is a stand-alone right which must be recognized regardless of its material consequences, and that the intent and spirit of the Convention should be taken into account in the determination of the compatibility of communications with the provisions of the Convention.[243]

---

[238] 'Chairperson's summary of views and comments' (1997) UN Doc E/1997/27, Annex II, Appendix II (n 49 above) para 25.

[239] 'Revised draft optional protocol' (1997) UN Doc E/1997/27, Annex III, Appendix I (n 52 above) art 4(2)(i); and 'Revised draft optional protocol' (1998) UN Doc E/1998/27, Annex II, Appendix I (n 54 above) art 4(2)(ii).

[240] *Rahime Kayhan v Turkey* (n 86 above) paras 4.4 and 6.3.

[241] *Cristina Muñoz-Vargas y Sainz de Vicuña* (n 86 above).   [242] Ibid para 12.2.

[243] Ibid paras 13.5, 13.7–13.9.

4. *Manifestly Ill-founded or Not Sufficiently Substantiated*

UN communications procedures which pre-date the OP do not contain these inadmissibility criteria, although the Human Rights Committee's rules of procedure provide that a communication must be submitted in a manner sufficiently substantiated.[244] *Suggestion No 7* indicated that a communication would be inadmissible if the author within a reasonable period failed to provide adequate substantiating information,[245] but did not refer to 'manifestly ill-founded' petitions.

These criteria were proposed during the Working Group's 1st session,[246] but were not included in the Chairperson's draft. Some delegations reiterated their proposal for the inclusion of the criteria during the 2nd session of the Working Group, while others argued that they were not in any comparable international procedure, although they were in regional instruments.[247] The criteria were included in brackets in the alternative versions of Article 4 in the Chairperson's revised draft. The sub-paragraph relating to manifestly ill-founded petitions also provided for inadmissibility on the basis that the communication was obviously politically motivated.[248] It was agreed during the 3rd session of the Working Group,[249] that the criteria of manifest ill-foundedness and lack of substantiation would be combined in one sub-paragraph and the Chairperson's revised text submitted to the 4th session reflected this in bracketed text.[250]

Several delegations remained uncomfortable with these criteria. Thus, in its interpretative declaration in the CSW, the Netherlands indicated its view, drawn from the practice of other international human rights treaty bodies, that the inadmissibility criteria of excluding manifestly ill-founded or not sufficiently substantiated complaints were concrete illustrations of the general admissibility criterion which provides that a communication should be compatible with the provisions of the Convention.

Although States have sought to have communications held inadmissible as ill-founded[251] or because of lack of substantiation,[252] the Committee has not addressed these criteria. It may do so in the future, as other communications procedures adopted since the OP contain a provision indicating that a communication shall be considered inadmissible if it is manifestly ill-founded or not sufficiently substantiated.[253] ICESCR OP Article 3(2)(e) also provides that the CESCR shall declare a communication inadmissible when it is exclusively based on reports disseminated by mass media.[254]

---

[244] CCPR, rule 90.

[245] 'CEDAW *Suggestion No 7*' (1995) UN Doc A/50/38 (n 26 above) Element 9(g).

[246] 'Report of the Open-ended Working Group on the Elaboration of a Draft Optional Protocol to CEDAW' (1996) UN Doc E/1996/26, Annex III (n 37 above) para 50.

[247] 'Chairperson's summary of views and comments' (1997) UN Doc E/1997/27, Annex II, Appendix II (n 49 above) para 26.

[248] 'Revised draft optional protocol' (1997) UN Doc E/1997/27, Annex III, Appendix I (n 52 above) alternative 1 draft art 4(2)(iii), alternative para 2(iii) and para 2(iii *bis*) and alternative para 2 (iii *bis*).

[249] 'Chairperson's summary of views and comments' (1998) UN Doc E/1998/27, Annex II, Appendix II (n 53 above) para 12.

[250] 'Revised draft optional protocol' (1998) UN Doc E/1998/27, Annex II, Appendix I (n 54 above) draft art 4(2)(iii).

[251] *N.S.F v United Kingdom* (n 86 above); *Salgado v United Kingdom* (n 86 above).

[252] *B.-J. v Germany* (n 86 above); *N.S.F v United Kingdom* (n 86 above); *Zhen Zhen Zheng v the Netherlands* (n 86 above); *SOS Sexisme v France* (n 86 above).

[253] CRPD OP art 2(e); ICESCR OP art 3(2)(e).

[254] Cuba proposed that the CEDAW OP should provide that communications from the mass media should not be accepted. See 'Additional views by Governments, IGOs and NGOs' (1997) UN Doc E/CN.6/1997/5 (n 48 above) para 134(e).

5. *Abuse of the Right to Submit a Communication*

With the exception of ICERD, each communication procedure expressly provides for inadmissibility of a communication if the Committee considers it to be an abuse of the right to submit a communication.[255]

Element 9(e) of *Suggestion No 7* included this concept. Several States suggested adding related prerequisites, such as that the communication should not contain offensive or insulting language directed at the State party against which the communication is lodged,[256] or that the communications procedure should not be applied so as to authorize anyone to make unfounded accusations against a State party or make use of distorted facts.[257] During the first session of the Working Group, this element garnered broad support, and draft Article 4 of the Chairperson's text provided that the Committee shall declare a communication inadmissible which it considers to be an abuse of the right of submission. The 2nd session of the Working Group agreed *ad referendum* to the inclusion of this criterion in the Protocol. Some delegations sought to add explicit reference to obvious political motivation, but others argued that this was included in the concept of an abuse of the right to submit a communication.[258] During the 3rd session of the Working Group, some proposed that a further criterion of inadmissibility, that the communication was 'vexatious,' be added.[259]

These additional admissibility criteria are not included in the Protocol, although in its interpretative declaration China stated that the phrase 'abuse of the right to submit a communication' applied to communications submitted for political purposes.[260] The Committee has not addressed Article 4(2)(d) in any of the communications it has considered.

6. *The Facts… Occurred Prior to the Entry into Force of the Protocol for the State Party Concerned, Unless those Facts Continued after that Date*

Article 4(2)(e) renders communications which rely on facts occurring prior to the OP's entry into force for the State party concerned inadmissible unless those facts continued after that date. Communications procedures adopted prior to the CEDAW OP do not expressly address the timing of the relevant facts (*ratione temporis*), and the relevant human rights treaty bodies have not taken the issue up in their rules of procedure. In practice, the Human Rights Committee declares such communications inadmissible unless the facts have had continuing effects since the entry into force of the ICCPR OPI, which themselves

---

[255] ICRMW OPI art 3; CAT art 22(2); ICRMW art 77(2); CRPD art 2(b); CPED art 31(2)(b); ICESCR art 3(2)(e).

[256] 'Views submitted by Governments, IGOs and NGOs' (1996) UN Doc E/CN.6/1996/10 (n 36 above) para 80; Cuba in 'Additional views by Governments, IGOs and NGOs' UN Doc E/CN.6/1997/5 (n 48 above) para 134(c).

[257] 'Additional views by Governments, IGOs and NGOs' (1997) UN Doc E/CN.6/1997/5 (n 48 above) paras 114 and 134(c).

[258] 'Chairperson's summary of views and comments' (1997) UN Doc E/1997/27, Annex II, Appendix II (n 49 above) para 26.

[259] 'Chairperson's summary of views and comments' (1998) UN Doc E/1998/27, Annex II, Appendix II (n 53 above) para 12.

[260] 'Interpretative statements on the draft optional protocol to CEDAW' (1999) UN Doc E/1999/27, Annex II (n 56 above).

constitute violations of the Covenant.[261] Communications procedures adopted since the CEDAW OP was adopted address the temporal dimension of admissibility.[262]

Suggestion No 7's Element 9(d) provided that the admissibility of a communication depended on its relating to acts or omissions that occurred after the State party ratified or acceded to the Convention, unless the violation or failure to give effect to those obligations or the impact continued after the protocol took effect for that State party. Several States pointed to a lack of clarity, with one considering that the right of petition should be based on the date on which the Protocol entered into force for the State party, which changed nothing with regard to its substantive obligations.[263] Others emphasized that communications must concern acts or omissions taking place after the entry into force of the Protocol for the State concerned in order to comply with the general legal principle of non-retroactivity of norms.[264] China suggested the deletion of admissibility where the facts had continuing effects after the entry into force of the Protocol.[265] During the 1st session of the Working Group, it was noted that this criterion was not included in comparable procedures, with some considering that an optional protocol should apply to acts that had occurred after the entry into force of the Protocol for the State party and others that the date of entry into force of the Convention for the State party was the relevant time.[266]

The criterion was not included in the Chairperson's draft.[267] Some delegations called for its inclusion during the 2nd meeting of the Working Group, while others argued that it was unnecessary as international treaties were non-retroactive by definition.[268] The Chairperson's revised draft included a bracketed subparagraph providing that the Committee shall declare inadmissible a communication that relates to facts that occurred before the entry into force of the Protocol for the State party concerned, unless those facts continued after its entry into force, with this latter phrase further bracketed.[269] The revised text submitted to the 3rd session of the Working Group contained the criterion as it appears in the Protocol.

States parties have frequently invoked Article 4(2)(e). Unsurprisingly for a body commencing a new mandate, the Committee held a number of early cases inadmissible on

---

[261] eg *Lovelace v Canada* CCPR Communication No 24/1977 (1981) UN Doc CCPR/C/13/D/24/1977 para 7.3; *Gueye v France* CCPR Communication No 196/1985 (1989) UN Doc CCPR/C/35/D/196/1985 para 5.3; *Armand Anton v Algeria* CCPR Communication No 1424/2005 (2006) UN Doc CCPR/C/88/D/1424/2005 (declared inadmissible) para 3.6; CCPR, 'General Comment 33' CCPR/C/GC/33 (2008) UN Doc CCPR/C/GC/33 para 9. For CAT, see *AA v Azerbaijan* CAT Communication No 247/2004 (2005) UN Doc CAT/C/35/D/247/2004 (declared inadmissible) para 6.4.

[262] CRPD OP art 2(f); ICESCR OP art 3(b). CED art 35(2) limits the Committee's competence to enforced disappearances occurring after the entry into force of the Convention for the State party concerned.

[263] The Netherlands in 'Views submitted by Governments, IGOs and NGOs' (1996) UN Doc E/CN.6/1996/10 (n 36 above) para 78.

[264] 'Views submitted by Governments, IGOs and NGOs' (1996) UN Doc E/CN.6/1996/10 (n 36 above) para 78; Cuba, Denmark, Luxembourg, Mexico, Morocco, Panama, Spain in 'Additional views by Governments, IGOs and NGOs' (1997) UN Doc E/CN.6/1997/5 (n 48 above) paras 112–13.

[265] 'Additional views by Governments, IGOs and NGOs' (1997) UN Doc E/CN.6/1997/5 (n 48 above) para 111.

[266] 'Report of the Open-ended Working Group on the Elaboration of a Draft Optional Protocol to CEDAW' (1996) UN Doc E/1996/26, Annex III (n 37 above) para 47.

[267] 'Text submitted by the Chairperson of the Open-Ended Working Group of the CSW' (1997) UN Doc E/CN.6/1997/WG/L.1 (n 47 above).

[268] 'Chairperson's summary of views and comments' (1997) UN Doc E/1997/27, Annex II, Appendix II (n 49 above) para 27.

[269] 'Revised draft optional protocol' (1997) UN Doc E/1997/27, Annex III, Appendix I (n 52 above) art 4(2) alternative 1(iv); art 4(2), alternative 2(v).

this basis. In *B.-J. v Germany*,[270] the Committee concluded that the facts of the petitioner's claim had occurred prior to the entry into force of the Protocol for Germany on 15 April 2002, as the divorce became final on 28 July 2000. The majority of the Committee was unconvinced that the facts continued after the date of the divorce. The Committee held the communication in *Salgado v United Kingdom*[271] inadmissible on this ground. The petitioner's son was born in 1954, and any right to his nationality was vested in him alone when he came of age in 1972, both events occurring many years before the elaboration of the Convention and the OP and their entry into force for the United Kingdom. A similar approach was taken in *SOS Sexisme v France*.[272] The Committee concluded that the facts, including the period of time during which the authors could have initiated proceedings to change their children's family names, had occurred prior to the OP's entry into force for France.[273] A majority of the Committee held the claim in *Cristina Muñoz-Vargas y Sainz de Vicuna v Spain*[274] inadmissible *ratione temporis* because the facts underpinning the communication, the issuance of the royal decree of succession to the petitioner's younger brother, occurred prior to the entry into force of the Convention and the OP for Spain and were not considered to be of a continuous nature. The Committee also rejected the petitioner's argument that the alleged violation continued because all court actions relating to her claim had not concluded by the time the OP entered into force for Spain.

Two of the Committee's decisions holding communications inadmissible from a temporal perspective have not been unanimous, with the dissenters being more flexible. In *B.-J. v Germany*,[275] the dissentients considered the proceedings relating to accrued gains and maintenance to be ongoing as they had not been resolved five years after the petitioner's divorce. The dissenter in *Cristina Muñoz-Vargas y Sainz de Vicuna v Spain*[276] held that the petition was not temporally barred because the violation continued beyond the issuance of the royal decree of succession as each of the court judgments dismissing her claim, which had been rendered after entry into force of the OP for Spain, constituted an act affirming the earlier violation of the State party.[277]

The Committee has also rejected States parties' claims of inadmissibility on the basis of this criterion. Although it ultimately concluded that there was no violation on the merits, in *Dung Thi Thuy Nguyen v The Netherlands*,[278] the Committee took the view that part of the communication alleging a violation of Convention Article 11 was admissible *ratione temporis*, as the author's maternity leave lasted four days beyond the entry into force of the OP for The Netherlands. The Committee thought that the central issue to be resolved was when the Dutch legislation had been applied to the alleged detriment of the author.[279]

The Committee has also held the temporal admissibility criterion to be satisfied on the basis of facts with continuing effects. In *AT v Hungary*,[280] although the State party did not raise this issue, the Committee concluded it was competent *ratione temporis* to consider a communication relating to severe domestic violence beginning prior to the entry into force of the OP for Hungary because the facts covered a series of severe incidents and threats of further violence that had uninterruptedly continued since 1998.[281] In *AS v Hungary*,[282] the Committee concluded that although the involuntary sterilization of the author had

[270] *B.-J. v Germany* (n 86 above). [271] *Salgado v United Kingdom* (n 86 above).
[272] *SOS Sexisme v France* (n 86 above). [273] Ibid paras 10.10 and 11.21.
[274] *Cristina Muñoz-Vargas y Sainz de Vicuña* (n 86 above). [275] *B.-J. v Germany* (n 86 above).
[276] *Cristina Muñoz-Vargas y Sainz de Vicuña* (n 86 above). [277] Ibid para 13.10.
[278] *Dung Thi Thuy Nguyen v The Netherlands* (n 86 above). [279] Ibid paras 9.4–9.5.
[280] *AT v Hungary* (n 86 above). [281] Ibid para 8.5. [282] *AS v Hungary* (n 86 above).

occurred a little over three months prior to the entry into force of the OP for Hungary, it had continuing effects, given the low success rate of surgery to reverse the procedure and the risk factors involved.[283] In *Kayhan v Turkey*,[284] the Committee decided that the facts had continuing effects, because although the author had been dismissed over two years before the entry into force of the OP for Turkey, her loss of status as a civil servant, her means of subsistence, her pension entitlements, interest on her salary and income, education grant, and health insurance all continued after its entry into force.[285]

As in the case of the Committee's approach to exhaustion of domestic remedies, there has been criticism of the Committee's approach to *ratione temporis*, suggesting that its jurisprudence is internally inconsistent, and inconsistent with other human rights treaty bodies and international procedures.[286] The Committee's conservative approach to this criterion in *B.-J. v Germany, Salgado v United Kingdom* and *Muñoz-Varas y Sainz de Vicuna v Spain* has been compared to its more flexible approach in *AT v Hungary, AS v Hungary* and *Kayhan v Turkey*. Critics have suggested that the Committee has not analyzed the concept of continuing as opposed to completed violations sufficiently and has failed in this context to adopt a gender perspective. In particular, the majority's approach to Ms B-J's communication has been highlighted as rigid, especially its pithy conclusion that 'the author has not made any convincing arguments that would indicate that the facts, insofar as they relate to the equalization of pensions, continued'.[287] Perhaps this can be explained by the fact that the communication was also held inadmissible on other grounds and because this was the Committee's first communication. It should be noted that the criterion has been applied more flexibly in *Kayhan v Turkey*[288] and *Dung Thi Thuy Nguyen v The Netherlands*,[289] which like Ms B.-J.'s communication allege violations resulting in financial disadvantage. Accordingly, the suggestions of those critics that the Committee is less sympathetic to such claims than those raising physical danger and invasion appear unfounded.

VI. Article 5

1. At any time after the receipt of a communication and before a determination on the merits has been reached, the Committee may transmit to the State Party concerned for its urgent consideration a request that the State Party take such interim measures as may be necessary to avoid possible irreparable damage to the victim or victims of the alleged violation.

2. Where the Committee exercises its discretion under paragraph 1 of the present article, this does not imply a determination on admissibility or on the merits of the communication.

An important innovation in the Protocol is an explicit power of the Committee to transmit to a State party a request that it take such interim measures as may be necessary to avoid possible irreparable damage to the victim(s) of the alleged violation. The power to request interim measures is reflected in the rules of procedure of CERD,[290] CCPR,[291] CAT,[292] and explicitly included in the CRPD OP, CED, and ICESCR, although the

---

[283] Ibid para 10.4.   [284] *Rahime Kayhan v Turkey* (n 86 above).   [285] Ibid para 7.4.
[286] A Byrnes and E Bath, 'Violence against Women, the Obligation of Due Diligence and the Optional Protocol to the Convention on the Elimination of All Forms of Discrimination against Women—Recent Developments' (2008) 8/3 *Human Rights L Rev* 517, 531–2.
[287] *B.-J. v Germany* (n 86 above) para 8.4.   [288] *Rahime Kayhan v Turkey* (n 86 above).
[289] *Dung Thi Thuy Nguyen v The Netherlands* (n 86 above).   [290] CERD rule 94(3).
[291] HRC rule 92.   [292] CAT rule 108.

formulation in the latter two instruments differs from that of the CEDAW OP.[293] Interim measures in relation to the CEDAW OP may be requested at any time after the receipt of a communication by the Committee and before a determination on the merits, and do not imply any determination of the admissibility or merits of the case.

The power to request interim measures had been envisaged by the Committee in Element 10 of *Suggestion No 7*, which provided that pending examination of a communication, the Committee should have the right to request that the status quo be preserved, and a State party should give an undertaking to that effect in order to avoid irreparable harm. *Suggestion No 7* also indicated that such a request should be accompanied by information confirming that no inference could be drawn that the Committee had determined the merits of the communication. Written comments on Element 10 noted its innovative character, with some States supporting its inclusion, others suggesting that a power of this nature should be included in the Committee's Rules of Procedure, others suggesting clarification of its scope, and others suggesting that it be deleted.[294] Similar sentiments were expressed during the 1st session of the Working Group.[295]

The draft submitted by the Chairperson to the Working Group's 2nd session provided that the Committee may request the State party concerned to take interim measures as may be necessary to preserve the status quo or to avoid irreparable harm at any time after the receipt of the communication and before a determination on the merits, and the State party shall comply with such request. Many delegations supported the provision as it accorded with the practice of similar international procedures and would constitute a progressive codification of international law and enhance the transparency of the procedure. Many called for language to enable the Committee to 'recommend' such measures, while others indicated that this would deviate from the practice of similar bodies. Many considered that the term 'preservation of the status quo' was unclear, with others maintaining this was a well-known concept. Some noted that the term 'damage' rather than 'harm' was used in the rules of procedure of other treaty bodies. Some objected on the ground that a request for interim measures might suggest prejudgement of the outcome of the communication, and suggested that a paragraph be added indicating that such a request in no way implies a determination of the admissibility or merits of a communication. Others questioned the need for an explicit requirement that the State party act in accordance with the request, and many called for the deletion of the provision, rather than its reformulation.[296]

The Chairperson's revised draft retained Article 5, although bracketed. The article included a draft sub-paragraph 2 *bis* providing that where the Committee exercised its power under paragraph 1, this did not imply a determination on the merits or admissibility of the communication.[297] During the 3rd session of the Working Group, delegations agreed on a formulation whereby the Committee may transmit to a State party a request

---

[293] CRPD OP art 4 and CRPD rule 64; CED art 31(4); ICESCR OP art 5(1).

[294] 'Views submitted by Governments, IGOs and NGOs' (1996) UN Doc E/CN.6/1996/10 (n 36 above) paras 87–8; 'Additional views by Governments, IGOs and NGOs' (1997) UN Doc E/CN.6/1997/5 (n 48 above) paras 139–48.

[295] 'Report of the Open-ended Working Group on the Elaboration of a Draft Optional Protocol to CEDAW' (1996) UN Doc E/1996/26, Annex III (n 37 above) paras 53–7.

[296] 'Chairperson's summary of views and comments' (1997) UN Doc E/1997/27, Annex II, Appendix II (n 49 above) paras 32–6.

[297] 'Revised draft optional protocol' (1997) UN Doc E/1997/27, Annex III, Appendix I (n 52 above).

for interim measures, as this was congruent with the established practice of other human rights treaty bodies and consistent with Article 7 of the draft Protocol. Delegations considered that a State party was under a general bona fide obligation to consider the Committee's request, and agreed to shorten the article to remove specific reference to this obligation. With the exception of whether the State's 'urgent' consideration was required on transmission of the request, agreement was reached on the article, with the inclusion of a sub-paragraph indicating that the use of interim measures did not imply a determination of the admissibility and the merits of the case. The Chairperson's further revised text reflected this understanding.[298]

The Committee's Rules of Procedure empower the Committee and a working group to decide on such requests,[299] but it has authorized the Chairperson of the Working Group on Communications to decide on these matters intersessionally.[300] Communications in which interim measures were requested include *AT v Hungary*, where the author urgently requested effective interim measures 'in order to save her life, which she believed was threatened by her violent former partner.'[301] Ten days later, the Committee requested the State party 'to provide immediate, appropriate and concrete preventive interim measures of protection . . . to avoid irreparable harm to her'.[302] In response, the State party informed the Committee that it had contacted the author, retained a lawyer experienced in domestic violence cases for her, and had established contact with the competent family and child welfare services, requesting a case-conference to work out further measures to protect her and her children effectively.[303] The Working Group on Communications requested follow-up information five months later, regretting that little information had been provided on the interim measures and requesting that A.T. and her children immediately be offered a safe place to live and adequate financial assistance.[304] In its response, Hungary repeated the information already supplied, leading the Committee to note in its views on the merits that 'the lack of effective and other measures prevented the State party from dealing in a satisfactory manner with the Committee's request for interim measures'.[305]

Interim measures were also requested in *N.S.F v United Kingdom*, with the Committee requesting the State party not to deport the author and her two children pending the Committee's decision on admissibility and merits.[306] The State party appears to have complied with the request, although the communication was ultimately held inadmissible. The Committee has not been required to address a refusal to accede to a request for interim measures.[307]

[298] 'Chairperson's summary of views and comments' (1998) UN Doc E/1998/27, Annex II, Appendix II (n 53 above) paras 15–18; 'Revised draft optional protocol' (1998) UN Doc E/1998/27, Annex II, Appendix I (n 54 above).

[299] Rules of Procedure 63(1) and (2). Under rule 63(3), the working group is required to inform the Committee members of the nature of the request and the communication to which the request relates. Rule 63(4) provides that the request for interim measures shall state that it does not imply a determination of the merits of the communication.

[300] Report of the Second Session of the Working Group on Communications in UNGA, 'Report of the CEDAW Committee—Twenty-Ninth Session' (2003) UN Doc A/58/38, Part II, Annex IX, para 8(c).

[301] *AT v Hungary* (n 86 above) para 4.1.

[302] Ibid para 4.2. A corrigendum to this request was sent approximately three weeks later.

[303] Ibid paras 4.4–6.   [304] *AT v Hungary* (n 86 above) para 4.7.   [305] Ibid para 9.5.

[306] *N.S.F v United Kingdom* (n 86 above) para 1.3.

[307] The Human Rights Committee considers that a refusal to accede to a request for interim measures amounts to a violation of the ICCPR OPI. See *Piandiong et al v The Phillippines* CCPR Communication No 869/1999 (2000) UN Doc CCPR/C/70/D/869/1999.

VII. Article 6

1. Unless the Committee considers a communication inadmissible without reference to the State Party concerned, and provided that the individual or individuals consent to the disclosure of their identity to that State Party, the Committee shall bring any communication submitted to it under the present Protocol confidentially to the attention of the State Party concerned.
2. Within six months, the receiving State party shall submit to the Committee written explanations or statements clarifying the matter and the remedy, if any, that may have been provided by that State Party.

Five of the UN human rights communications procedures establish that before the relevant Committee declares a communication admissible, it must be brought to the attention of the State party concerned.[308] In contrast, CEDAW OP Article 6(1) provides that the Committee may decide that a communication is inadmissible without reference to the State party. This approach is also taken in ICESCR OP Article 6(1) while CPED Article 31(3) indicates that the Committee will transmit the communication to the State party if it considers that the communication meets the admissibility requirements set out in the Convention.

The requirement in Article 6(1) that any communication be brought 'confidentially' to the attention of the State party is also found in ICERD, CRPD OP, and ICESCR OP,[309] and the rules of procedure of CAT.[310] Article 6 provides further protection to complainants by requiring their consent to the disclosure of their identity before the communication is transmitted, a provision which is reiterated in the Committee's Rules of Procedure,[311] and is also found in ICERD and the rules of procedure of the CRPD.[312]

Suggestion No 7 Element 11 envisaged that while the State party would be informed confidentially of the nature of the communication, the author's identity would not be revealed without that person's consent. States considered that communications should be brought to the attention of the State party, confidentially and with necessary security safeguards, but that the author's identity would have to be known so the State could respond appropriately. Some States thought that disclosure of the author's identity should not be required in exceptional cases or where this would endanger her health or life. One State suggested that a representative of the State should be present at this stage.[313] Similar views were presented during the 1st session of the open-ended Working Group with delegations indicating that the author's identity would have to be revealed to the State party to enable it to investigate the allegations, remedy the situation, and provide full information to the Committee so that it could decide on admissibility.[314]

The text submitted by the Chairperson of the Working Group to its 2nd session provided in draft Article 6(1) that unless the Committee considers a communication inadmissible without reference to the State party, it would bring any communication submitted to it confidentially to the attention of the State party, but that the author's identity would

---

[308] ICCPR OPI arts 4(1) and 5(4); ICERD art 14(6)(a); CAT art 22(3); ICRMW art 77(4); CRPD OP art 3. See also CERD rule 92(3); and CAT rule 109(8).

[309] ICERD art 14(6)(a); CRPD OP art 3; ICESCR OP art 6(1).   [310] CAT rule 99(5).

[311] CEDAW rules 58(5), 68(1); and 69(1).   [312] ICERD art 14(6)(a); CRPD rule 70(1).

[313] 'Views submitted by Governments, IGOs and NGOs' (1996) UN Doc E/CN.6/1996/10 and Corr.1, Add.1 and Add.2 (n 36 above) paras 90–1; 'Additional views by Governments, IGOs and NGOs' (1997) UN Doc E/CN.6/1997/5 (n 48 above) paras 149–54.

[314] 'Report of the Open-ended Working Group on the Elaboration of a Draft Optional Protocol to CEDAW' (1996) UN Doc E/1996/26, Annex III (n 37 above) paras 58–60.

not be revealed without the latter's express consent.[315] During the Working Group, the Committee's resource person drew attention to the vulnerability of complainants and the particular risks women face. Some delegations expressed support for the Chairperson's formulation. Others saw the need for the State party to be aware of the victim's identity so it could provide explanations and a remedy. Some delegations considered that the victim should be required expressly to consent or object to the revelation of her identity to ensure her safety and protect her from reprisals, while others considered that the protection concerns would be addressed by withholding her identity temporarily during any period of interim measures.[316]

The revised draft optional protocol submitted by the Chairperson to the 3rd session of the Working Group included three formulations of Article 6(1). The 1st provided that the Committee shall bring any communication submitted to it confidentially to the attention of the State party and that it may in exceptional cases involving a threat to the life or physical integrity of authors withhold their identity throughout or during consideration of interim measures; the 2nd that the State party should be informed confidentially of the communication and the identity of the individual should also be revealed unless the individual objects; and the 3rd that the Committee may bring any communication it admitted confidentially to the attention of the State party concerned, but shall not reveal the identity of the author unless prior consent is given.[317] Delegations expressed the view that practical considerations required that the State party be informed of the identity of those submitting communications, but some suggested that claimants should be able to decide whether their identities should be revealed to the State party. Several also drew attention to the changing practice of the CCPR in respect to confidentiality, although others thought that while a communication was pending only the State party, the complainant, and the Committee should be apprised of the proceedings and their content.[318]

Article 6(1) of the revised draft protocol submitted to the 4th session of the Working Group provided that unless the Committee considered a communication inadmissible without reference to the State party and provided that the individual(s) consent to the disclosure of their identity to that State party, the Committee shall bring any communication to the attention of that State party. No prior agreement had been reached that communications should be brought 'confidentially' to the State party's attention, so this word remained bracketed in the text.[319] Delegations agreed to include this element during the Working Group's 4th session. Following adoption in the Commission, the United Kingdom, also on behalf of Sweden, stated its understanding that in cases where the individual(s) refused to consent to the disclosure of their identity, the Committee may not continue to consider their communication, although information received in this context could be considered if relevant to the Committee's other functions.[320]

[315] 'Text submitted by the Chairperson of the Open-ended Working Group of the CSW' (1997) UN Doc E/CN.6/1997/WG/L.1 (n 47 above).

[316] 'Chairperson's summary of views and comments' (1997) UN Doc E/1997/27, Annex II, Appendix II (n 49 above) paras 37–9.

[317] 'Revised draft optional protocol' (1997) UN Doc E/1997/27, Annex III, Appendix I (n 52 above).

[318] 'Chairperson's summary of views and comments' (1998) UN Doc E/1998/27, Annex II, Appendix II (n 53 above) paras 19–20.

[319] 'Revised draft optional protocol' (1998) UN Doc E/1998/27, Annex II, Appendix I (n 54 above).

[320] 'Interpretative statements on the draft optional protocol to CEDAW' (1999) UN Doc E/1999/27, Annex II (n 56 above).

Suggestion No 7 Element 11 had also envisaged that the State party would reply or provide information about any remedy within a specified period. To underline the Committee's view of the cooperative nature of the procedure, it had also indicated that while the process of examination continued, the Committee would work in cooperation with the parties to facilitate a settlement, which, if reached, would be contained in a confidential report of the Committee.

Most written views supported an explicit deadline for receipt of States' responses, ranging from three to six months.[321] These alternative deadlines were included in the drafts submitted by the Chairperson to the 2nd and 3rd sessions of the Working Group.[322] All agreed on a six-month period during the 3rd session.[323]

The text submitted by the Chairperson to the 2nd session of the Working Group retained the Committee's settlement concept in draft Article 6(3). It provided for the Committee to place itself at the disposal of the parties during its examination of a communication with a view to facilitating a settlement on the basis of respect for Convention rights and obligations. A few States welcomed the mediation element.[324] One State indicated the need to publicize the outcome of any settlement with the agreement of the parties, and another that the Committee's working with the parties to facilitate a settlement would suggest acceptance that a violation had occurred. NGOs considered that any provision relating to friendly settlement must be on the basis of respect for Convention rights and obligations, to guard against coercion or intimidation of complainants to agree a settlement.[325] Similar views were voiced in the Working Group, with some delegations welcoming the idea, but stressing that the terms of any settlement would need to be in accordance with the State party's obligation under the Convention, acceptable to both parties and arrived at without pressure on the complainant. Some underlined the importance of a transparent procedure, which would encourage other States to take action and build up the Committee's case law, suggesting that the report of the settlement could be made public if the author and the State party agreed, although the author's name could be withheld.[326] Some delegations suggested that the Committee's potential role as mediator might prevent it from playing its proper role under a communications procedure,[327] and others that the provision was inappropriate in a human rights instrument as it suggested that the Committee had an arbitral role in relation to individual complaints.[328]

[321] 'Additional views by Governments, IGOs and NGOs' (1997) UN Doc E/CN.6/1997/5 (n 48 above) para 155; 'Report of the Open-ended Working Group on the Elaboration of a Draft Optional Protocol to CEDAW' (1996) UN Doc E/1996/26, Annex III (n 37 above) para 60.

[322] 'Text submitted by the Chairperson of the Open-ended Working Group of the CSW' (1997) UN Doc E/CN.6/1997/WG/L.1 (n 47 above) and 'Revised draft optional protocol' (1997) UN Doc E/1997/27, Annex III, Appendix I (n 52 above).

[323] 'Chairperson's summary of views and comments' (1998) UN Doc E/1998/27, Annex II, Appendix II (n 53 above) paras 21 and 23.

[324] 'Additional views by Governments, IGOs and NGOs' (1997) UN Doc E/CN.6/1997/5 (n 48 above) para 156.

[325] 'Views submitted by Governments, IGOs and NGOs' (1996) UN Doc E/CN.6/1996/10 (n 36 above) paras 89–92.

[326] 'Report of the Open-ended Working Group on the Elaboration of a Draft Optional Protocol to CEDAW' (1996) UN Doc E/1996/26, Annex III (n 37 above) paras 61–2.

[327] 'Chairperson's summary of views and comments' (1997) UN Doc E/1997/27, Annex II, Appendix II (n 49 above) para 42.

[328] 'Chairperson's summary of views and comments' (1998) UN Doc E/1998/27, Annex II, Appendix II (n 53 above) para 22.

The revised drafts submitted to the 3rd and 4th sessions of the Working Group both allowed for settlement of a communication at any time before the Committee reached a decision on its merits. Both drafts included bracketed text stating that in the event of agreement between the parties, the Committee shall adopt findings taking note of the settlement.[329] During the 4th session of the Working Group, draft Article 6(3) was deleted.[330]

VIII. Article 7

1. The Committee shall consider the communications received under the present Protocol in the light of all information made available to it by or on behalf of individuals or groups of individuals and by the State party concerned, provided that this information is transmitted to the parties concerned.
2. The Committee shall hold closed meetings when examining communications under the present Protocol.
3. After examining a communication, the Committee shall transmit its views on the communication, together with its recommendations, if any, to the parties concerned.
4. The State Party shall give due consideration to the views of the Committee, together with its recommendations, if any, and shall submit to the Committee, within six months, a written response, including information on any action taken in light of the views and recommendations of the Committee.
5. The Committee may invite the State Party to submit further information about any measures the State party has taken in response to its views or recommendations, if any, including as deemed appropriate by the Committee, in the State Party's subsequent reports under article 18 of the Convention.

Comparable communications procedures set out similar formulations to those contained in CEDAW OP Article 7(1)–(3) which addresses the consideration of communications and their outcome.[331] The OP was the first instrument to provide, in Article 7(4) and (5), an explicit follow-up procedure to communications. ICESCR OP Article 9 follows this model, while CERD, CCPR, and CAT have developed follow-up procedures which are included in their rules of procedure.[332] These Committees monitor compliance through special rapporteurs who evaluate the State party's compliance with views.

1. Consideration of Communications and its Outcome

Element 12 of the Committee's *Suggestion No 7* envisaged that the Committee would examine communications in the light of all information provided by the State party and by the author or received from other relevant sources. These would be transmitted to the

---

[329] 'Chairperson's summary of views and comments' (1997) UN Doc E/1997/27, Annex II, Appendix II (n 49 above) para 42; 'Chairperson's summary of views and comments' (1998) UN Doc E/1998/27, Annex II, Appendix II (n 53 above) para 22.

[330] ICESCR OP art 7 provides that the Committee shall make available its good offices to the parties concerned with a view to reaching a friendly settlement on the basis of the respect for the obligations set forth in the Covenant.

[331] ICCPR OPI art 5; CAT art 22; ICERD art 14; ICRMW art 77; CRPD OP art 5; CED art 31(5); ICESCR OP arts 8(1–2) and (9).

[332] The Human Rights Committee has described the absence of a follow-up power in the OPI as 'a major shortcoming in the machinery established by the Covenant'. Follow-up on views adopted under the Optional Protocol to the International Covenant on Civil and Political Rights' (1993) UN Doc A/CONF.157/TBB/3 reprinted in UNGA, 'Report of the Human Rights Committee—Forty-Eighth Session' (1993) UN Doc A/48/40, Vol. I, Annex X, 222, para 2.

parties for comment, and the Committee would determine its procedures, hold closed meetings when examining communications, and, as a whole Committee, adopt and transmit views and any recommendations to the parties. Visits to a State party with its agreement were also envisaged as part of the process.

Several States were opposed to the Committee considering information other than that provided by the author and the State party[333] but others supported the idea.[334] NGOs were keen to expand the information base available to the Committee by allowing it to receive oral or written evidence and conduct on-site visits.[335] While a few States supported on-site visits with the agreement or on the invitation of the State concerned, most were opposed to this suggestion.[336] These views were restated in discussions in the 1st session of the Working Group. There was some support for the Committee receiving relevant sources of information in cases where women were disempowered or unable to provide information, which could include material from UN mechanisms, and would be made available to both parties. A few delegations also supported on-site visits in exceptional cases if the State party agreed, pointing to their use in regional human rights systems. Some delegations suggested that the Committee should have the power to conduct oral hearings, but most emphasized the written nature of the procedure.[337]

Article 7 of the Chairperson's draft protocol provided that the Committee would consider communications in the light of all information made available to it by or on behalf of the author and the State party concerned, but also allowed the Committee to take into account information obtained from other sources, provided that this information was transmitted to the author and the State party for comment. It provided for the Committee to hold closed meetings when examining communications and to adopt and transmit its views and any recommendations to the State party and the author.

The Working Group's 2nd session agreed *ad referendum* on Article 7(2) providing that the Committee's meetings would be closed when considering communications. Opinion was divided on whether the Committee should be able to resort to sources of information other than that provided by the author and the State party. Some States suggested leaving this to the Committee's Rules of Procedure. Some delegations considered that the State party should be able to appear in the Committee's proceedings, but most emphasized the written nature of similar processes, indicating that were such a provision to be included, the petitioner should be given the same right to appear in person. A number of delegations argued that no reference should be made to the adoption by the Committee of its views or recommendations, with others indicating that this reflected the sequence of events and the established practice of other treaty bodies, and that the paragraph concerned dealt with

[333] 'Views submitted by Governments, IGOs and NGOs' (1996) UN Doc E/CN.6/1996/10 (n 36 above) para 94.
[334] 'Additional views by Governments, IGOs and NGOs' (1997) UN Doc E/CN.6/1997/5 (n 48 above) paras 158–63.
[335] 'Views submitted by Governments, IGOs and NGOs' (1996) UN Doc E/CN.6/1996/10 (n 36 above) para 95.
[336] 'Additional views by Governments, IGOs and NGOs' (1997) UN Doc E/CN.6/1997/5 (n 48 above) paras 164–6.
[337] 'Report of the Open-ended Working Group on the Elaboration of a Draft Optional Protocol to CEDAW' (1996) UN Doc E/1996/26, Annex III (n 37 above) paras 66–9.

the conclusion of the Committee's examination after the State party had been given the opportunity to submit information and comments.[338]

During the 3rd session of the Working Group, Article 7 paragraph 3 was adopted *ad referendum*. Discussion focused on whether the Committee should only use written information, particularly in light of the constraints women in developing countries might face in that regard. The revised draft protocol submitted to the Working Group in 1998 and 1999 maintained, in brackets, capacity for the Committee to take into account information obtained from other sources, provided that this information was submitted to the author and State party for comment, and entitling the State party to make oral and written submissions. The revised draft protocol submitted to the Working Group in 1999, also included a bracketed proposal requiring the Committee to comply with the principles of objectivity and impartiality.[339]

During discussions in the Working Group, some delegations noted the need to verify other sources of information, that participation of the State and complainants in communications proceedings was not the practice of other treaty bodies, and the resource implications of introducing such a practice.[340] The adopted text does not require the information considered by the Committee to be written and allows it to be made available by or on behalf of the author and the State party concerned, with the caveat that it must be transmitted to the parties. Rule 72(1) and (2) of the Committee's Rules of Procedure provide that the Committee shall consider and formulate its views on communications in light of all written information made available to it by its author(s) and the State party, provided that this information has been transmitted to the other party concerned. The rules also provide that at any time in the course of the examination, the Committee may obtain any documentation from the UN or from other bodies that might assist it. Each party must be given an opportunity to comment on this information or documentation. Additional material, including amicus briefs, may not be submitted by third parties, but may be submitted by the parties to the communication. An amicus brief, prepared by the Center for Reproductive Rights Inc, was submitted by the author in *AS v Hungary* in her supplementary submissions to the Committee, and was considered by the Committee.[341] The OP does not provide for the participation of the State or the author in the proceedings other than by written submissions. The proposal relating to the Committee's compliance with the principles of objectivity and impartiality is not included in the OP as these ideas are included in paragraph 4 of the resolution through which it was adopted.

In line with OP Article 7(2), the Committee adopts views and recommendations after it has considered communications. Views identify the provisions of the Convention that the Committee considers the State party has violated, drawing (where appropriate) on its general recommendations to interpret the Convention.[342]

---

[338] 'Chairperson's summary of views and comments' (1997) UN Doc E/1997/27, Annex II, Appendix II (n 49 above) paras 43–7.

[339] 'Revised draft optional protocol' (1998) UN Doc E/1998/27, Annex II, Appendix I (n 54 above).

[340] 'Chairperson's summary of views and comments' (1998) UN Doc E/1998/27, Annex II, Appendix II (n 53 above) paras 24–6.

[341] *AS v Hungary* (n 86 above) paras 9.4–9.11.

[342] *Fatma Yildirim v Austria* (n 86 above) paras 12.1–12.2; *Şahide Goekce v Austria* (n 86 above) paras 12.1–12.2; *AT v Hungary* (n 86 above) paras 9.1–9.6; *AS v Hungary* (n 86 above) paras 11.2–11.4; Open Society Justice Initiative (2010) *From Judgment to Justice: Implementing International and Regional Human Rights Decisions* 127–32 highlighting the specificity of the recommendations in CEDAW's views.

Recommendations for action to remedy violations are specific, but allow the State party latitude to determine its means of compliance. They are also more detailed than those of other human rights treaty bodies, and include recommendations specific to the individual victim and more general recommendations. For example, recommendations made for the author's specific relief in domestic violence cases have included that the State party take immediate and effective measures to guarantee the victim's and her family's physical and mental integrity, and that she be given a safe home in which to live with her children and receive reparation proportionate to the physical and mental harm undergone and the gravity of the violation of her rights, as well as compensation.[343] Appropriate compensation commensurate with the gravity of the violations of the victim's rights was also requested in a case where the Committee concluded that a violation of the victim's Convention rights resulted from the duration of trial proceedings and the application of stereotypes and myths leading to the acquittal of the man who had raped her.[344]

The Committee also addresses the systemic and structural causes of individual cases, making recommendations which potentially benefit women in the State party concerned, as well as to prevent future violations.[345] For example, in the two petitions relating to fatal domestic violence brought on behalf of the descendants of the victims, no compensation was ordered, but the Committee called on the State party to act with due diligence to prevent and respond to violence against women by strengthening implementation and monitoring existing legislation.[346] Specific recommendations relating to the conduct of trials of sexual offences, the review of relevant legislation, and training for judges, lawyers, law enforcement officers, and medical personnel to avoid the revictimization of sexual assault victims and to ensure that personal perceptions do not affect decision-making have also been called for.[347] In relation to violations of reproductive rights, the Committee has called on the State party to provide appropriate compensation and take measures to ensure that the provisions of the Convention and relevant general recommendations in relation to women's reproductive health and rights are known and adhered to by all relevant personnel in public and private health centres, including hospitals and clinics. It has also called on the State party to review domestic legislation in respect of informed consent so that fully informed consent is provided by the patient before any sterilization is carried out.[348]

In its views, the Committee routinely requires the State party to give due consideration to its views and recommendations and to submit a written response, within six months on any action taken pursuant to them. The Committee also requests the State party to publish its views and recommendations, translate them in its language(s), and distribute them widely.

2. Follow-up Procedure

Elements 13 and 14 of the Committee's *Suggestion No 7* constitute the genesis of the follow-up procedure for communications contained in OP Article 7(4)–(5). *Suggestion No 7* proposed that when the whole Committee had considered that a communication was

---

[343] *AT v Hungary* (n 86 above) para 9.6.
[344] *Karen Tayag Vertido v The Philippines* (n 86 above) para 8.9.
[345] *AT v Hungary* (n 86 above) paras 9.6–9.7.
[346] *Fatma Yildirim v Austria* (n 86 above) paras 12.3–12.4; *Şahide Goekce v Austria* (n 86 above) paras 12.3–12.4.
[347] *Karen Tayag Vertido v The Philippines* (n 86 above) para 8.9.
[348] *AS v Hungary* (n 86 above) para 11.5.

justified, it might recommend remedial measures, or measures designed to give effect to Convention obligations. It provided for the State party to remedy violations, implement recommendations, and ensure an appropriate remedy (which might include adequate reparation). Details of such remedial measures would be provided to the Committee within a set period. Element 14 envisaged the Committee's power to initiate and continue discussions concerning these measures and remedies, including by inviting the State party to include such information in its reports to the Committee under Convention Article 18.

States raised the concern that a petition procedure might infringe on the independence of their judicial systems and noted that the Committee's views and recommendations (which should be general) should not be legally binding. Others called for clarification, in particular, of the State party's responsibility to redress violations and provide reparations. Some NGOs noted that remedial measures might include reform or repeal of national legislation, payment of damages, other forms of reparation, or steps to prevent future violations, such as reform of administrative procedures.[349] They also supported explicit inclusion of the Committee's follow-up role,[350] as did some States. One State did not consider a follow-up role to be appropriate, and another that it should be limited to an invitation to a State party to provide information on any follow-up in its next periodic report under Article 18.[351] During the first session of the Working Group, these diverse views were again put forward. Some welcomed the reference to remedies, including reparations. Others noted the lack of precedent in other human rights treaties, that it was up to the State party to determine the appropriateness of remedial measures, and that they doubted whether the Committee should have the power to order specific remedial measures.[352]

Article 8 of the Chairperson's draft protocol provided that the Committee may request from the State party concerned specific measures to remedy any violation or failure to give effect to its Convention obligations, that the State party take all steps necessary to comply, and that an appropriate remedy be ensured including, if need be, adequate reparation is provided. Written statements clarifying the matter and the remedy that had been taken by the State party were required to be submitted to the Committee within three or six months. Article 9 of the Chairperson's draft provided that the Committee may invite a State party to discuss with it the measures that it had taken to give effect to the Committee's views, suggestions, or recommendations and that the Committee might invite the State party to include in its periodic report details of any measures taken in response to the Committee's views.

During the 1997 session of the Working Group, some support was expressed for draft Article 8, with several delegations considering that this would be a positive contribution by the Working Group to the progressive development of international law on the right to reparation for human rights violations. However, a number of delegations considered that the inclusion of the provision would be a major step which would need careful

---

[349] 'Views submitted by Governments, IGOs and NGOs' (1996) UN Doc E/CN.6/1996/10 (n 36 above) paras 96–100 and Add.1 para 13; 'Additional views by Governments, IGOs and NGOs' (1997) UN Doc E/CN.6/1997/5 (n 48 above) paras 167–74.

[350] 'Views submitted by Governments, IGOs and NGOs' (1996) UN Doc E/CN.6/1996/10 (n 36 above) para 100.

[351] 'Additional views by Governments, IGOs and NGOs' (1997) UN Doc E/CN.6/1997/5 (n 48 above) paras 175–9.

[352] 'Report of the Open-ended Working Group on the Elaboration of a Draft Optional Protocol to CEDAW' (1996) UN Doc E/1996/26, Annex III (n 37 above) paras 71–80.

consideration, with others considering it to be redundant as States were under an obligation to remedy violations, and that these elements could be included in the Committee's
Rules of Procedure and left to its practice.

There was broad support for draft Article 8(3) which was seen as building on existing procedures of treaty bodies and encouraging a continuing dialogue between the
Committee and the State party after the finding of a violation. Some delegations
thought, however, that this might create a parallel procedure to the Article 18 reporting
procedure. Some also considered that the State party should be given an opportunity
to comment on the Committee's views on a concluded communication, so that any
potential disagreement could be reflected in the Committee's annual report. Others
suggested that the State party should be requested to provide its comments and information at each stage of the process. Some delegations suggested that any follow-up
information, including measures taken by the State party should be included in its
periodic report, while others made clear that the communications and reporting procedures were distinct and follow-up to both should also be distinct. In any event, the
time lag between periodic reports would make follow-up to communications through
the reporting process less meaningful.[353] Broad support was expressed for the long-term
follow-up procedure envisaged in draft Article 9, with several delegations underlining
the fact that absence of such a mechanism was considered a weakness in existing procedures. Streamlining of both draft articles was proposed to make the follow-up process
clear, simple, and effective.[354]

Articles 8 and 9 of the revised draft protocol submitted by the Chairperson to the
1998 session of the Working Group retained these ideas, in alternative formulations. It
was agreed to merge short- and long-term follow-up into a single article, with States parties being required to provide a first follow-up response within six months of receiving
the Committee's views. The Committee's long-term role in follow-up, including through
information provided in States parties' reports under Article 18 of the Convention, was
agreed and the provision adopted *ad referendum*.[355] These elements were merged in the
revised draft optional protocol submitted to the Working Group by the Chairperson
in 1999.

On adoption of the Protocol in the CSW, only India made an interpretative declaration
on Article 7, expressing its view that in applying Article 7(4) the Committee should take
account of the logistical difficulties some, particularly developing, countries can face in
obtaining information.

The Committee has been active in implementing its follow-up competence. On the
advice of the Working Group, it has not established a permanent follow-up mechanism,
but approaches each case in which a violation has been found ad hoc, appointing two Rapporteurs on follow-up to views. These ideally include the case Rapporteur.[356]

[353] 'Chairperson's summary of views and comments' (1997) UN Doc E/1997/27, Annex II, Appendix II
(n 49 above) paras 48–53.
[354] Ibid.
[355] 'Chairperson's summary of views and comments' (1998) UN Doc E/1998/27, Annex II, Appendix II
(n 53 above).
[356] 'Report of the CEDAW Working Group on Communications on its eighth session in UNGA', 'Report
of the CEDAW Committee—Thirty-Sixth Session' (2006) UN Doc A/61/38, Part III, Annex X para 9(c).

Two Committee experts were appointed as Rapporteurs on follow-up to the views of the Committee in *AT v Hungary*.[357] The State party provided additional information, and the Committee decided that any further follow-up information would be requested, in accordance with OP Article 7(5), in the context of the reporting procedure under Article 18.[358] Two experts were also appointed as Rapporteurs on follow-up to the views of the Committee in *AS v Hungary*.[359] They updated the Committee on further information received from the State party, as well as on meetings held with its Permanent Mission in New York.[360] A similar approach was taken with regard to the two cases relating to Austria. Since 2009, information on the Committee's follow-up activities is included in its annual report. The Committee also adopts follow-up decisions based on an analysis of information provided by the State party and/or the complainant, and the Committee will close the case when it considers the follow-up action to be satisfactory.

IX. Article 8

1. If the Committee receives reliable information indicating grave or systematic violations by a State Party of the rights set forth in the Convention, the Committee shall invite that State Party to cooperate in the examination of the information and to this end to submit observations with regard to the information concerned.
2. Taking account of any observations that may have been submitted by the State party concerned as well as any other reliable information available to it, the Committee may designate one or more of its members to conduct an inquiry and report urgently to the Committee. Where warranted and with the consent of the State Party, the inquiry may include a visit to its territory.
3. After examining the findings of such an inquiry, the Committee shall transmit these findings to the State Party concerned together with any comments and recommendations.
4. The State Party concerned shall, within six months of receiving the findings, comments and recommendations transmitted by the Committee submit its observations to the Committee.
5. Such an inquiry shall be conducted confidentially and the cooperation of the State Party shall be sought at all stages of the proceedings.

CEDAW OP Article 8 establishes an inquiry procedure, modelled on CAT Article 20. A similar competence is provided for by CRPD OP Article 6, CED Article 23, and ICESCR OP Article 11.

Article 8 was envisaged in Elements 17 to 22 of the Committee's *Suggestion No 7*. These elements proposed that if the Committee received reliable information indicating a State party's serious or systematic violation of rights under the Convention or a failure to give effect to its Convention obligations, the Committee should have the right to invite that State party to cooperate in examining the information and in submitting observations on it. It also proposed that after the Committee had considered those observations and any

---

[357] UNGA, 'Report of the CEDAW Committee—Thirty-Fourth Session' (2006) UN Doc A/61/38, Part I para 348. See also, C Flinterman, 'Strengthening Women's Human Rights Through Individual Complaints' in HB Schöpp-Schilling and C Flinterman (eds), *The Circle of Empowerment: Twenty-Five Years of the UN Committee on the Elimination of Discrimination against Women* (2007) 286, 295.

[358] UNGA, 'Report of the CEDAW Committee—Thirty-Sixth Session' (2006) UN Doc A/61/38, Part III para 627.

[359] UNGA, 'Report of the CEDAW Committee—Thirty-Eighth Session' (2007) UN Doc A/62/38, Part II para 397; *From Judgment to Justice* (n 342 above) notes that CEDAW's follow-up procedure has had an impressive record of responsiveness and implementation because of the rigorous and systematic approach of its rapporteurs.

[360] UNGA, 'Report of the CEDAW Committee—Thirty-Ninth Session' (2007) UN Doc A/62/38, Part III paras 660–1.

other relevant information, it should have the power to designate one or more of its members to conduct an inquiry and report urgently to the Committee. This inquiry would be conducted with the cooperation of the State party and might, with its agreement, include a visit to its territory. Following an examination of the findings, which would be transmitted to the State party, it would have a set period in which to respond. At all times, the inquiry would be conducted confidentially and with the cooperation of the State party. The Committee would encourage the State party to discuss the steps taken by it as a consequence of the inquiry, after which the Committee would be empowered to publish a report.[361]

In their written comments, several States indicated disagreement with the establishment of an inquiry procedure, including on the ground that it would undermine State sovereignty.[362] Others considered that the appropriateness of an inquiry procedure needed further study, as did the criteria for such a procedure.[363] Other States supported inclusion of an inquiry procedure in the Protocol, although one was of the view that an inquiry should be initiated exclusively on the basis of a communication, and follow the same requirements and procedures as the complaints procedure. It also considered that the financial implications of introducing such a procedure should be examined thoroughly.[364] Although it supported investing the Committee with competence to undertake inquiries, as that would allow it to address a broader range of issues than was possible through individual complaints, and to recommend measures for combating structural causes of violation, one State considered that the inquiry procedure should be provided for in another protocol as it might delay the decision on the complaints protocol.[365] Some States also raised the question of the threshold which would generate an inquiry, suggesting that the procedure should be reserved for serious, systematic, or widespread violations of women's human rights.[366] NGOs expressed strong support for an inquiry procedure as it would facilitate the examination of widespread violations, including those that crossed national borders and implicated several governments. They also considered that inquiries could have an educational effect in bringing to light violations and/or neglect by States of 'particular' practices.[367]

During the 1st session of the Working Group, delegations were divided on whether an inquiry procedure should be included in the OP. It was noted that the CAT inquiry procedure had been used only once, and that the Committee's existing mandate allowed it to develop such a competence, through, for example, the creation of an early warning mechanism or a time-bound follow-up procedure to its concluding observations. Some were concerned that an inquiry procedure might overlap with or duplicate existing procedures, such as the CSW and Commission on Human Rights 1503 communications procedures. Others drew a distinction between these intergovernmental procedures and the expert character of the proposed inquiry procedure. The threshold of violation required to

---

[361] 'CEDAW *Suggestion No 7*' (1995) UN Doc A/50/38 (n 26 above).

[362] China, Cuba, and Morocco in 'Additional views by Governments, IGOs and NGOs' (1997) UN Doc E/CN.6/1997/5 (n 48 above) paras 191–4.

[363] 'Views submitted by Governments, IGOs and NGOs' (1996) UN Doc E/CN.6/1996/10 and Corr.1, Add.1 and Add.2 (n 36 above) para 109.

[364] Ibid paras 106–9; 'Additional views by Governments, IGOs and NGOs' (1997) UN Doc E/CN.6/1997/5 (n 48 above) paras 194–202.

[365] 'Additional views by Governments, IGOs and NGOs' ibid paras 197–8.   [366] Ibid paras 194–6.

[367] 'Views submitted by Governments, IGOs and NGOs' (1996) UN Doc E/CN.6/1996/10 and Corr.1, Add.1 and 2 (n 36 above) para 110.

trigger the procedure was also discussed, with several delegations suggesting that it should be high, constituting serious and systematic violations of the Convention.[368]

Articles 10 and 11 of the Chairperson's draft protocol submitted to the 2nd session of the Working Group closely followed Elements 17 to 22 of *Suggestion No 7*, providing that if the Committee received reliable information indicating a State party's serious or systematic violation of Convention rights or a failure to give effect to Convention obligations, the Committee shall invite that State party to cooperate in the examination of the information and to submit observations. After taking into account the State party's observations (if any), as well as any other reliable information available, the Committee could designate one or more of its members to conduct an inquiry and report to it urgently. After examining the findings of the inquiry, the Committee would transmit them, and any comments and recommendations to the State. The State party would then have three or six months in which to submit its observations to the Committee. Any inquiry would be conducted confidentially and the cooperation of the State would be sought at all stages. Article 11 established a follow-up stage, whereby the Committee would be empowered to invite the State party to discuss with it the measures it had taken in response to an inquiry. It could also invite the State party to include in its report details of any measures taken in response to the inquiry.

During the 2nd session of the Working Group, delegations were divided between those that supported the provisions and those that did not. The former considered that the inquiry procedure would allow the Committee to focus on the root causes of discrimination and would be of value in cases where individual women who had suffered over and above other women could not be identified. The latter considered that the procedure would be confrontational, would require significant human and financial resources, and was only appropriate in cases of torture. More clarification was required about the sources of information that would trigger an inquiry and how the veracity of the information would be assessed. The threshold for violation was also discussed, with a number of delegations considering that the violation should be both serious and systematic. A provision which would allow a State party to the Protocol to opt out of the procedure was also suggested.[369]

The revised Protocol submitted by the Chairperson to the 3rd session of the Working Group retained Articles 10 and 11 in brackets.[370] Views expressed during the 3rd session indicated that a sharp division of opinion remained on whether such a procedure should be included. Seeking consensus, the Chairperson introduced a provision allowing States parties to opt out of the procedure on signature, ratification, or accession, by declaring that they did not recognize the competence of the Committee under the articles which established the procedure. Although some indicated that they would have preferred an opt-in provision, the Chairperson's new draft article provided the basis for further discussions. Some delegations indicated that they could only consider an opt-out provision in this context if there was a provision precluding reservations to the Protocol.[371]

---

[368] 'Report of the Open-ended Working Group on the Elaboration of a Draft Optional Protocol to CEDAW' (1996) UN Doc E/1996/26, Annex III (n 37 above) paras 87–97.

[369] 'Chairperson's summary of views and comments' (1997) UN Doc E/1997/27, Annex II, Appendix II (n 49 above) paras 58–61.

[370] 'Revised draft optional protocol' UN Doc E/1997/27, Annex III, Appendix I (n 52 above).

[371] 'Chairperson's summary of views and comments' (1998) UN Doc E/1998/27, Annex II, Appendix II (n 53 above) paras 30–4.

The revised draft Protocol submitted by the Chairperson to the fourth session of the Working Group included the inquiry procedure, again in brackets, in Articles 10, 11, and 11 *bis*.[372] Further issues were flagged by internal brackets. These included whether the threshold to trigger an inquiry was serious or systematic violations, a cumulation of serious and systematic violations, whether an inquiry could include a visit to the State party's territory, whether the State party's response to the Committee's findings should be submitted in three or six months, and whether States would be required to opt in or able to opt out of the procedure. During the 4th session of the Working Group, it was agreed that the threshold required to trigger an inquiry was grave or systematic violations; an inquiry might include a visit to the State party's territory where this was warranted and the State party consented. The State party would have six months in which to react to the Committee's findings following an inquiry.

Notwithstanding these agreements, a number of States explained their understanding of the provision relating to the inquiry procedure in interpretative statements on the adoption of the Protocol by the Working Group. Costa Rica, and those on whose behalf it spoke, emphasized the importance of incorporating this procedure in the OP and noted that such a procedure in the Inter-American system was proving its worth as a form of collaboration with States in the fulfilment of their international obligations.

Several States addressed the threshold requirement of 'a grave or systematic violation' of Convention rights. China suggested that in view of the substantial amount of human and financial resources required to carry out an inquiry, the procedure should apply only where women's rights are seriously violated and on a massive scale, and that a single event could not constitute 'grave or systematic' violations. Egypt considered that repeated occurrence of such violations was required. Israel considered that the phrase excluded inquiries into singular, isolated incidents, a view echoed by Japan, which indicated that an inquiry should not be conducted into individual or accidental cases. Statements made by Germany and Canada on behalf of European Union and associated countries made clear that 'grave or systematic' violations could also occur as a result of the State party failing to act. Ghana suggested that the phrase 'grave or systematic' should be construed broadly, so as not to impede the effective functioning of the Committee. The Philippines expressed its understanding that the term 'grave' was distinct from systemic and imposed no higher standard than the term 'serious'. Several statements also underlined that, as in the case of the communications procedure, the inquiry procedure applied to all provisions and obligations in the Convention, and that violations extended to acts, as well as failures to act by States parties.

The Committee's Rules of Procedure provide that an inquiry may be instigated on the basis of information from any source, and that information that appears to be submitted in order to initiate an inquiry must be forwarded by the Secretariat to the Committee and maintained in a permanent register.[373] The Committee may seek to ascertain the reliability of the information and/or its sources through the Secretary-General and may seek further corroborating information.[374] After the Committee has examined the information and ascertained that it is reliable, it must then invite the State party concerned to comment within an identified time limit. The Committee then considers any observations from the State party, and any other reliable information, including from representatives of the State party,

---

[372] 'Revised draft optional protocol' UN Doc E/1998/27, Annex II, Appendix I (n 54 above).
[373] Rules of Procedure 77 and 78.   [374] Rules of Procedure 82.

governmental and non-governmental organizations, individuals, as well as relevant UN documentation.[375] On the basis of this information, the Committee may decide to designate one or more of its members to conduct an inquiry and to report urgently to the Committee. The Committee determines the modalities of the inquiry,[376] but where warranted and with the State party's consent an inquiry may include a visit to its territory. With the exception of the information included in the summary of the Committee's activities in its annual report, as required by Article 12 of the Protocol, all stages of the inquiry are confidential,[377] and the State party's cooperation is sought at all stages of the proceedings.[378]

As of 31 December 2010, the Committee had conducted one inquiry, which included a visit by two members of the Committee. The inquiry was triggered by written and other information provided by international and national NGOs—Equality Now, Casa Amiga, and the Mexican Committee for the Defense and Promotion of Human Rights—received on 2 October 2002 containing allegations of the abduction, rape, and murder of women in and around Ciudad Juárez, Mexico. In particular, it alleged that since 1993 more than 230 young women and girls, most of them *maquiladora* workers, had been killed in or near Ciudad Juárez. It requested the Committee to undertake an inquiry. That this information was required to trigger the inquiry is notable, as a little over one month earlier the Committee itself had raised questions with Mexico on the reports it had received of sexual torture, murder, mutilation, abduction, and disappearance of hundreds of women in Ciudad Juárez and Chihuaha dating from the early 1990s during its discussion of its 5th periodic report. Indeed, the Committee had expressed 'its great concern at the incidents' and 'at the apparent lack of results of the investigations into the causes of the numerous murders of women and the failure to identify and bring to justice the perpetrators of such crimes with a view to protecting women against this type of violence'.[379]

At its 28th session in January 2003, the Committee considered the request presented by the NGOs, and appointed two of its members, Ms Regina Tavares da Silva and Ms Yolanda Ferrer-Gomez, to undertake a detailed evaluation of the information provided, together with data from other sources. The information considered included the reports of the UN Commission on Human Rights Special Rapporteurs on extrajudicial, summary, or arbitrary executions[380] and on the independence of judges and lawyers,[381] and of the Inter-American Commission on Human Rights' Special Rapporteur on the Rights of Women.[382] Based on the information, and the assessment provided by the two Committee

---

[375] CEDAW art 8(2) and Rules of Procedure 82.   [376] Rules of Procedure 87.

[377] Rules of Procedure 80 also indicates that all documents and proceedings of the Committee relating to the conduct of the inquiry shall be confidential and that it may consult with the State party concerned with respect to the summary for the annual report.

[378] Rules of Procedure 85 indicates that the Committee may request the State party concerned to nominate a representative to meet with the member or members designated by the Committee and that it may request the State party to provide the member or members with any information that they or the State party may consider relates to the inquiry.

[379] UNGA, 'Report of the CEDAW Committee—Exceptional Session' (2002) UN Doc A/57/38, Part III para 439.

[380] ECOSOC, 'Report of the Special Rapporteur on extrajudicial, summary or arbitrary executions, Ms Asma Jahangir: Visit to Mexico' (1999) UN Doc E/CN.4/2000/3/Add.3 para 89.

[381] ECOSOC, 'Report of the Special Rapporteur on the independence of judges and lawyers, Dato'Param Cumaraswamy: Mission to Mexico' (2002) UN Doc E/CN.4/2002/72/Add.1.

[382] Report of the IACHR Special Rapporteur on the Rights of Women 'The Situation of the Rights of Women in Ciudad Juárez, Mexico: The Right to be Free from Violence and Discrimination' (2003) OAS Doc OEA/Ser.L/V/II.117, Doc 44.

members, the Committee decided the information was reliable and 'contained substantiated indications of grave and systematic violations of rights' under the Convention that had not been addressed and were ongoing, and decided to invite the Government of Mexico to cooperate and submit its observations in accordance with CEDAW OP Article 8.

At its 29th session in July 2003, the Committee analyzed the information provided by the Government, which showed recognition of the gravity of the situation and a willingness to cooperate, as well as providing details of measures being taken to address the problem. Additional information was also provided by the NGOs which had initiated the inquiry and the Mexican Commission for the Defense and Promotion of Human Rights, suggesting that the murders continued and that there was no solution in sight. On the basis of its review of the information, the Committee decided to initiate a confidential inquiry under OP Article 8(2) to be conducted by Ms Tavares da Silva and Ms Ferrer-Gomez. They visited Mexico in October 2003 for discussions with authorities in institutions at the federal level in Mexico City, in the city of Chihuaha, and in Ciudad Juárez. They interviewed individual members of NGOs, including those that had led a campaign to denounce the crimes, human rights defenders, and victims' families. They also visited sites where bodies had been found, sites of the *maquiladoras*, and the poorest areas of Ciudad Juárez.[383]

In January 2004, during its 30th session, the Committee discussed the findings of the inquiry and adopted its report and recommendations, transmitting these confidentially to the Government of Mexico and requesting, in accordance with OP Article 8(4), that it submit information on measures taken in response to the recommendations within six months. On 21 July 2004, during its 31st session, the State party submitted its observations to the Committee, which also received supplementary information from Equality Now. Ms Ferrer-Gomez and Ms Tavares da Silva were asked to examine the information and report to the Committee. In accordance with OP Article 9(2), the Committee invited the State party to submit by 1 December 2004, a detailed report on steps taken, measures implemented, and results achieved in relation to the Committee's findings. The State party provided preliminary information on 13 December 2004, and additional information on 17 January 2005.[384]

The Committee's report concluded that the facts 'constitute[d] grave and systematic violations of the Convention (in particular, Articles 1, 2, 3, 5, 6, and 15) as well as its General Recommendation 19 on violence against women and the UN Declaration on Violence against Women.'[385] It did not consider the murders to be sporadic incidents, but to involve 'systematic violations of women's rights, founded in a culture of violence and discrimination that is based on women's alleged inferiority: a situation that has resulted in impunity'. The fact that the disappearances and murders in Ciudad Juárez had not been eradicated, effectively punished, and remedied over a decade, indicated to the Committee that there was a systematic pattern to the violations, leading it to conclude that 'overall, despite the new level of awareness and efforts made at various levels, the situation in Ciudad

---

[383] UNGA, 'Report of the CEDAW Committee—Thirty-First Session' (2004) UN Doc A/59/38, Part II paras 399–402.

[384] UNGA, 'Report of the CEDAW Committee—Thirty-Second Session' (2005) UN Doc A/60/38, Part I para 396.

[385] CEDAW, 'Report on Mexico produced by the CEDAW Committee under article 8 of the Optional Protocol to the Convention, and reply from the Government of Mexico' (hereinafter CEDAW 'Report on Mexico') (2005) UN Doc CEDAW/C/2005/OP.8/MEXICO para 259.

Juárez remains highly complex, tragic, prolonged, and full of unacceptable uncertainties, suspicions, and horrors'.[386]

The Committee adopted sixteen recommendations which focused on investigation and punishment of the crimes. Four general recommendations, classified by Ms Tavares da Silva and Ms Ferrer-Gomez in an article on the inquiry as 'overriding dimensions constituting the essential framework of all responses to the situation, whether criminal, social, cultural or any other',[387] address the need for Mexico to comply with its Convention obligations; the full responsibility of all the authorities at all levels of power to prevent violations against women and protect their human rights; the need to incorporate a gender perspective into various social policies, particularly those relating to gender-based violence; and the need to adopt an effective dialogue and close relationship with NGOs and civil society. Eight recommendations address the investigation of the crimes themselves, including the punishment of the perpetrators and support to the victims' families. Recommendations were also made regarding measures to guarantee the respectful and compassionate treatment of mothers and the relatives of the victims and to ensure the protection of families and human rights defenders who had suffered threats and harassment. One recommendation raised the possibility of creating an agreement with the United States, in light of the border elements of the crimes, aimed at systematic cooperation on prevention and solving the crimes. Four recommendations addressed the prevention of violence, guaranteeing security, and the promotion and protection of the human rights of women. They also called for measures to intensify policies and programmes to guarantee security and restore the social fabric, including through the provision of legal support to all victims of violence and their families in their search for justice and of medical and psychological treatment, and economic assistance, where needed. The provision of necessary resources, both human and financial, to combat violence in Ciudad Juárez, and the establishment of a Special Commissioner were also recommended.

Mexico's response emphasized its commitment to the Convention, acknowledged that the murders were a grave attack on the human rights of women, and indicated that it was committed to all efforts to resolve them and eradicate their causes. It set out the various steps it had taken to address the problem generally and in relation to each of the Committee's recommendations. At the same time, Mexico suggested that the murders constituted a breach of women's human rights, the origin of which lay in entrenched cultural patterns of discrimination exacerbated by the authorities' lack of human and financial resources,[388] and there was no question that a deliberate policy of discrimination was being pursued that would make it responsible for the crimes.[389] It also indicated that while it had studied the Committee's recommendations 'it wishes to point out that in order to facilitate its task of implementation, it would have preferred greater analytical rigour on the part of the experts and more information about the reasons on which their recommendations were based'.[390] During its 32nd session on 27 January 2005, at a press conference held at UN Headquarters in New York, the Committee released the report of

---

[386] Ibid para 45.

[387] R Tavares da Silva and Y Ferrer-Gomez, 'The Juárez murders and the Inquiry Procedure' in HB Schöpp-Schilling and C Flinterman (eds) (n 357 above) 298, 304.

[388] CEDAW, 'Report on Mexico' (n 385 above) 93.   [389] Ibid 93.   [390] Ibid 92.

the inquiry, accompanied by observations which had been submitted by the Government of Mexico.[391]

Perhaps because this has been the Committee's only inquiry, it has not had an opportunity to provide a full analysis of Article 8, including the criteria applied to determine if the triggering information is reliable and the threshold required to meet the definition of grave or systematic violations. In their article on the inquiry,[392] Ms Tavares da Silva and Ms Ferrer-Gomez indicate that the reliability of the information required to generate an inquiry is evaluated by the Committee on the basis of its consistency, corroborating evidence, the credibility of its sources, and information from other sources, national or international, official or non-official.[393] They suggest that the information must be as complete and illustrative as possible, including a clear description of the alleged violations, their gravity or systematic nature, their impact and consequences, and the specific provisions of CEDAW alleged to be violated. Information should also be provided on the alleged perpetrators, on complaints filed, on investigations undertaken, on the involvement of the police and other authorities, on support of civil society organizations, women's NGOs, human rights NGOs, and measures taken, or not taken, within the jurisdiction of the State party to respond to the situation. Their view is that this information may be supplied by a person, an organization, who may be, but need not be a national of the State party; it can be in writing, on videotape, provided by other electronic means, or oral, and it can present different types of evidence, according to each specific situation. As to the threshold required, Ms Tavares da Silva and Ms Ferrer-Gomez conclude that the violations can be either grave or systematic, not necessarily both. In their view, a grave violation means that a severe abuse of fundamental rights under the Convention has taken or is taking place; a systematic violation means that the violation is not an isolated case, but rather a prevalent pattern in a specific situation; one that has occurred again and again, either deliberately, with intent, or as the result of customs and traditions, or even as the result of discriminatory laws or policies, with or without such purpose.

X. Article 9

1. The Committee may invite the State Party concerned to include in its report under article 18 of the Convention details of any measures taken in response to an inquiry conducted under article 8 of the present Protocol.
2. The Committee may, if necessary, after the end of the period of six months referred to in article 8.4, invite the State party concerned to inform it of the measures taken in response to such an inquiry.

Article 9, which is replicated in CRPD Article 12 and ICESCR OP Article 12, establishes procedures to follow up implementation of the Committee's recommendations made after an inquiry. These are reflected in Rules 89 and 90 of the Committee's Rules of Procedure. The Committee is thus empowered to invite the State party to include in its report under CEDAW Article 18, details of any measures taken in response to an inquiry. In addition, the Committee may, after six months during which the State party should have provided

---

[391] CEDAW, 'Report on Mexico' (n 385 above). A procedural summary of the inquiry is included in UNGA, 'Report of the CEDAW Committee—Thirty-First Session' (2004) UN Doc A/59/38, Part II paras 393–408.

[392] Tavares da Silva and Ferrer-Gomez (n 387 above) 299–300.   [393] Ibid.

its observations to the Committee, invite the State party to inform it of the measures it has taken in response to an inquiry.

In Element 21 of its *Suggestion No 7*, the Committee had indicated that it would encourage the State party to discuss the steps taken by it following the inquiry and that the discussions might continue until a satisfactory outcome was achieved. The Committee might also ask the State party to report on its response to the inquiry in its report under Article 18.[394] This Element had won favour with some States and NGOs.[395] One State considered it to be inappropriate as the procedure might be never-ending if the Committee found the State's response unsatisfactory.[396] Some delegations suggested that the term 'satisfactory outcome' was unclear, and wondered what the Committee's attitude might be if the State party would not provide the information requested.[397]

Article 11 of the text submitted by the Chairperson to the Working Group's 2nd session allowed for follow-up to an inquiry,[398] and a similar provision was included in the two revised drafts.[399] Negotiations focused on the inquiry as a whole, rather than on this article in particular, and it appears substantively unchanged in Article 9. Several interpretive statements made on adoption of the OP by the CSW concern this article. Ghana indicated that Article 9 should not preclude dialogue between the Committee and a concerned State in the context of an inquiry. Denmark, and those on behalf of which it spoke, took the same approach, expressing the view that the term 'inform' in Article 9(2) should be understood as part of a process of interaction between the States parties and the Committee under the inquiry procedure.[400]

The Committee invoked Article 9(2) at its 32nd session in January 2005, requesting the Government of Mexico to provide additional information, by 1 May 2005, on its follow-up to the Committee's recommendations made upon the Ciudad Juárez inquiry. The Committee also asked the NGOs and the national human rights institution that had provided the information which initiated the inquiry to provide their views on the situation in Ciudad Juárez, as well as their evaluation of the State party's actions in response to the Committee's recommendations.[401]

The Committee considered the information submitted by the Government and the NGOs at its 33rd session. The Committee also requested that Mexico include information on further measures that it had taken in response to the inquiry in its 6th periodic report.[402] The report included new information on actions taken, with analysis of suc-

---

[394] 'CEDAW *Suggestion No 7*' (1995) UN Doc A/50/38 (n 26 above).

[395] 'Views submitted by Governments, IGOs and NGOs' (1996) UN Doc E/CN.6/1996/10 and Corr.1, Add.1 and Add.2 (n 36 above) para 113; and 'Additional views by Governments, IGOs and NGOs' (1997) UN Doc E/CN.6/1997/5 (n 48 above) paras 210–11.

[396] 'Additional views by Governments, IGOs and NGOs' (1997) UN Doc E/CN.6/1997/5 (n 48 above) para 209.

[397] 'Report of the Open-ended Working Group on the Elaboration of a Draft Optional Protocol to CEDAW' (1996) UN Doc E/1996/26, Annex III (n 37 above) para 96.

[398] 'Text submitted by the Chairperson of the Open-ended Working Group of the CSW' (1997) UN Doc E/CN.6/1997/WG/L.1 (n 47 above).

[399] 'Revised draft optional protocol' UN Doc E/1997/27, Annex III, Appendix I (n 52 above); 'Revised draft optional protocol' UN Doc E/1998/27, Annex II, Appendix I (n 54 above).

[400] 'Interpretative statements on the draft optional protocol to CEDAW' UN Doc E/1999/27, Annex II (n 56 above).

[401] UNGA, 'Report of the CEDAW Committee—Thirty-Second Session' (2005) UN Doc A/60/38, Part I para 396.

[402] UNGA, 'Report of the CEDAW Committee—Thirty-Third Session' (2005) UN Doc A/60/38, Part II paras 412–13.

cesses and remaining challenges, which was considered by the Committee at its session in August 2006. Two Government officials involved in the inquiry formed part of the delegation presenting the report. In its concluding observations, the Committee reiterated its recommendations contained in the inquiry report and urged Mexico to establish concrete monitoring mechanisms, as the crimes have continued.[403] Perhaps because it has completed only one inquiry, the Committee has not to date developed a methodology for assessing the quality of the State party's follow-up action.

XI. Article 10

1. Each State Party may, at the time of signature or ratification of the present Protocol or accession thereto, declare that it does not recognize the competence of the Committee provided for in articles 8 and 9.
2. Any State Party having made a declaration in accordance with paragraph 1 of the present article may, at any time, withdraw this declaration by notification to the Secretary-General.

CEDAW OP Article 10 empowers States parties to declare that they do not recognize the Committee's competence provided for in Articles 8 and 9. By 31 December 2010, only three of the 100 States parties to the OP had chosen to make that declaration,[404] despite concerns expressed during negotiations that the opt-out would render this procedure ineffective. Such a declaration may be withdrawn at any time. CAT Article 28 is an equivalent to Article 10, allowing States parties, at the time of signature, ratification, or accession to the Convention, to declare that it does not recognize the inquiry competence of the Committee. CRPD Article 8 does likewise. ICESCR OP Article 11 requires States parties to declare that they recognize the inquiry competence of the Committee before they are bound by it.

Article 10 had not been envisaged by the Committee in *Suggestion No 7* and had not been included in the draft protocol submitted by the Chairperson to the Working Group in 1997 and 1999. During the 1998 session of the Working Group, in response to the divided opinion over an inquiry procedure, the Chairperson introduced Article 11 *bis* which would allow States parties to opt out of the procedure on signature, ratification or accession. Some delegations indicated that they would have preferred an opt-in clause, and others neither an opt-out nor opt-in so as to ensure the integrity of the Protocol.[405] The provision was ultimately adopted. In its interpretative declaration, India made clear that it had accepted Article 10 in a spirit of compromise. India expressed the view that the complaints and inquiry mechanisms should have been in two separate protocols, or that the latter procedure could have been in an additional protocol. In any event, it would have preferred an opt-in provision, which it considered would have captured better the 'additionality' of the inquiry mechanism.[406]

---

[403] UNGA, 'Report of the CEDAW Committee—Thirty-Sixth Session' (2006) UN Doc A/61/38, Part III paras 595–6; and CO Mexico, CEDAW/C/MEX/CO/6 (2006) para 16.

[404] Bangladesh, Belize, and Colombia made an opt-out declaration on ratification or accession to the OP, while Cuba did so on signature of the Protocol.

[405] 'Chairperson's summary of views and comments' (1998) UN Doc E/1998/27, Annex II, Appendix II (n 53 above) paras 33–4.

[406] 'Interpretative statements on the draft optional protocol to CEDAW' (1999) UN Doc E/1999/27, Annex II (n 56 above) para 25.

XII. Article 11

A State Party shall take all appropriate steps to ensure that individuals under its jurisdiction are not subjected to ill-treatment or intimidation as a consequence of communicating with the Committee pursuant to the present Protocol.

In Element 23 of *Suggestion No 7*, the Committee proposed that when ratifying or acceding to the OP, a State party would undertake to assist the Committee in its inquiries and to prevent any obstacles to, or victimization of, any person providing the Committee with information or assisting it in its inquiries.[407] New Zealand commended this innovative proposal. A number of NGOs stated that it would broaden the duty of cooperation which appeared in other human rights instruments by including a duty to protect against victimization by both the State itself and private individuals. They specifically pointed to situations of violence against women, where only the State was in a position to prevent victimization.[408] Panama noted that once a State had ratified the OP it assumed the obligation to cooperate with the Committee,[409] a view reiterated during the 1st session of the Working Group in 1996.[410]

Article 12 of the Chairperson's draft protocol submitted to the Working Group's 2nd session provided that States parties would undertake not to hinder in any way effective exercise of the right to submit communications; to take all necessary steps to prevent any individual, group, or organization from interfering with the exercise of the right of communication or victimizing any individual for exercising this right, or providing information to or assisting the Committee in its inquiries; and to assist the Committee in its proceedings.[411] In negotiations during the 1997 session of the Working Group, some delegations suggested that the provision was unnecessary as ratification of or accession to the Protocol would oblige States parties to ensure that its procedures could be accessed by all persons under its jurisdiction. However, a majority supported the inclusion of an article capturing the spirit of the proposal, but suggested that the formulation should be positive so as to promote the relationship between the Committee and States parties.[412] Several alternative proposals were put forward by the Chairperson in the revised draft submitted to the 1998 session of the Working Group.[413] Noting that existing instruments did not include such a provision, some delegations again suggested that draft Article 12 was unnecessary as ratification or accession would incorporate an obligation to ensure that the Protocol's procedures were accessible and an obligation of cooperation with the Committee. Many, however, supported the provision but thought it should be formulated positively, with some delegations suggesting that the Protocol should explicitly provide

---

[407] 'CEDAW *Suggestion No 7*' (1995) UN Doc A/50/38 (n 26 above). The provision reflects arts 2(1) and 13 of the Maastricht draft.

[408] 'Views submitted by Governments, IGOs and NGOs' (1996) UN Doc E/CN.6/1996/10 and Corr.1, Add.1 and Add.2 (n 36 above) paras 115–16.

[409] 'Additional views by Governments, IGOs and NGOs' UN Doc E/CN.6/1997/5 (n 48 above) para 214.

[410] 'Report of the Open-ended Working Group on the Elaboration of a Draft Optional Protocol to CEDAW' UN Doc E/1996/26, Annex III (n 37 above) para 98.

[411] 'Text submitted by the Chairperson of the Open-Ended Working Group of the CSW' UN Doc E/CN.6/1997/WG/L.1 (n 47 above).

[412] 'Chairperson's summary of views and comments' (1997) UN Doc E/1997/27, Annex II, Appendix II (n 49 above) para 62.

[413] 'Revised draft optional protocol' UN Doc E/1997/27, Annex III, Appendix I (n 52 above).

that States parties would undertake appropriate steps to protect those using the Protocol from interference and reprisals.[414]

Draft Article 12 in the revised text submitted by the Chairperson to the 1999 session of the Working Group, proposed that States parties to the Protocol would undertake to respect the right or procedure it established to submit communications or information to the Committee, to cooperate with the Committee, and take all appropriate steps to protect all persons using the procedures from interference or reprisal.[415] The first two elements of the draft article did not gain consensus, but the provision as adopted establishes a novel duty of States parties, now repeated in the ICESCR OP Article 13 to ensure that individuals under their jurisdiction are not subjected to ill-treatment or intimidation resulting from their use of the Protocol's procedures.[416]

Several States submitted interpretative statements relating to this provision when CSW adopted the Protocol in 1999. China considered that States parties should implement this provision in the framework of their national law and that it should not prevent States parties from taking legal action against those who have committed crimes or otherwise breached the law in the process of communicating with the Committee. Egypt stressed that the duty imposed on States parties by this article should be within the limits of national legislation. Israel stated that the provision applied strictly within the State in question. Japan indicated that any State accepting the Protocol, but making the Article 10 opt-out declaration, would not have obligations in relation to individuals communicating with the Committee under that procedure. Indonesia noted that Article 11 was in line with its proactive policy for the promotion and protection of the human rights of women, and its commitment to the protection of victims who come forward, and provided examples of concrete steps, including legislation and programmes it had taken in this area.[417]

XIII. Article 12

The Committee shall include in its annual report under article 21 of the Convention a summary of its activities under the present Protocol.

The draft protocol submitted to the 1997 CSW Working Group by the Chairperson included this provision in draft Article 13, as did her revised texts submitted to the 1998 and 1999 sessions of the Working Group. Equivalent provisions are found in comparable instruments.[418] A separate chapter containing a summary of the Committee's activities under the OP has been included in the report of each of its sessions submitted to the UNGA starting with the report of the 25th session in July 2001.[419]

---

[414] 'Chairperson's summary of views and comments' (1998) UN Doc E/1998/27, Annex II, Appendix II (n 53 above) paras 35–8.

[415] 'Revised draft optional protocol' UN Doc E/1998/27, Annex II, Appendix I (n 54 above).

[416] UNGA Res 53/144 (9 December 1998) UN Doc A/RES/53/144, Annex art 9(4).

[417] 'Interpretative statements on the draft optional protocol to CEDAW' UN Doc E/1999/27, Annex II (n 56 above).

[418] ICCPR OPI art 6; ICESCR OP art 15 which replicates CEDAW OP art 12. See also CRPD art 39; CAT art 24.

[419] UNGA, 'Report of the CEDAW Committee—Twenty-Fifth Session' (2001) UN Doc A/56/38 paras 361–6.

XIV. Article 13

Each State Party undertakes to make widely known and to give publicity to the Convention and the present Protocol and to facilitate access to information about the views and recommendations of the Committee, in particular on matters involving that State Party.

Element 24 of the Committee's *Suggestion No 7* proposed that the OP include a provision requiring States parties to publicize the Protocol and its procedures and the Committee's views and any recommendations concerning a communication received or inquiry conducted.[420] In the Working Group's 1996 session, delegations emphasized the need to publicize the OP widely, and proposed appropriate formulations, although some considered that this should be addressed by resolution.[421] Similar views were submitted by States and others to the UN Secretary-General.[422]

The draft submitted by the Chairperson to the 1997 meetings of the Working Group included draft Article 14 whereby States parties undertook to publicize the contents of the Protocol, the procedures established under it and the Committee's views, comments, suggestions, and recommendations. Some delegations suggested that the provision was unnecessary, but the majority agreed with the spirit of the provision, but suggested that it be formulated more simply. Some considered that the views of the Committee should be made known to the public by the State party only, while others suggested that it might be burdensome for the State party to be required to publicize the Committee's views on communications and petitions.[423]

The revised draft submitted by the Chairperson to the 1998 meetings of the Working Group contained three alternative formulations relating to dissemination, each containing further alternatives. By the first, States parties undertook to publicize and to make widely known the contents of the Protocol and the procedures established under it or, by appropriate or active means, the provisions of the Protocol. One formulation of this alternative would limit the State party's responsibilities to dissemination in its own country. By the second alternative, States parties undertook to publicize and make as widely known as possible the contents of the Protocol and the procedures established under it and the Committee's views, comments, suggestions, and recommendations concerning communications and inquiries, or their outcome. By the 3rd alternative, States parties undertook to publicize the annual report of the Committee, particularly as it concerns a communication or an inquiry initiated by the Committee involving a particular State party.[424] During negotiations, many delegations continued to stress the importance of wide knowledge of and publicity for the Protocol, its procedures, and the Committee's conclusions and jurisprudence. Several delegations cautioned against involving States parties in onerous obligations, including of a financial nature, with many calling for a simplified provision. Several delegations considered that this provision was unnecessary

---

[420] 'CEDAW *Suggestion No 7*' (1995) UN Doc A/50/38 (n 26 above) para 24.

[421] 'Report of the Open-ended Working Group on the Elaboration of a Draft Optional Protocol to CEDAW' (1996) UN Doc E/1996/26, Annex III (n 37 above) para 99.

[422] 'Additional views by Governments, IGOs and NGOs' (1997) UN Doc E/CN.6/1997/5 (n 48 above) paras 215–16. China and Spain considered the provision should be contained in a resolution, while Panama was of the view that it should be in the text of the Protocol.

[423] 'Chairperson's summary of views and comments' (1997) UN Doc E/1997/27, Annex II, Appendix II (n 49 above) para 64.

[424] 'Revised draft optional protocol' (1997) UN Doc E/1997/27, Annex III, Appendix I (n 52 above) art 14.

and inappropriate and that States parties that had not been subject to the Protocol's procedures should not have obligations to publicize its proceedings.[425]

The draft protocol submitted by the Chairperson to the 1999 Working Group meetings contained a simplified draft Article 14, whereby each State party to the Protocol undertook to make widely known, or known and to give publicity, or due publicity to the Convention and its OP and to facilitate access to information about the views and recommendations of the Committee, in particular, in matters involving that State party.[426] Article 13 of the adopted text reflects this draft. In its interpretative statement, China recalled views expressed during negotiations that the improvement of women's status involved efforts in various fields, including publicizing the Convention and OP, and accordingly developing countries had the right to allocate resources in the best interest of the women in their countries according to their countries' specific situations.[427]

CEDAW OP Article 14 is replicated in ICESCR OP Article 16, which also calls for dissemination in accessible formats for persons with disabilities. Similarly, under CRC Article 42, States parties undertake to make the principles and provisions of the Convention widely known, by appropriate and active means to adults and children alike.

The Committee requests States parties found in communications to be in violation of the Convention to publish its views and recommendations, have them translated into the local language(s), and to ensure their wide distribution to reach all relevant sectors of society.[428] The Committee also investigates the steps States parties have taken to make the Convention, the OP, and the Committee's output widely known during consideration of their reports and routinely expresses concern in its concluding observations about their lack of visibility.[429] It encourages States parties to promote knowledge and understanding of the Convention and the OP in order to increase women's knowledge of their Convention rights and the procedures under the OP so as to enhance their capacity to claim their rights.[430] Compliance by States parties with Article 13 and the implementation of broad-based awareness-raising campaigns by the UN and civil society are particularly important in light of the very small number of petitions against only a limited number of States which have been submitted to the Committee, as well as the rare attempts to generate an Article 8 inquiry.

XV. Article 14

The Committee shall develop its own rules of procedure to be followed when exercising the functions conferred on it by the present Protocol.

---

[425] 'Chairperson's summary of views and comments' (1998) UN Doc E/1998/27, Annex II, Appendix II (n 53 above) paras 40–2.

[426] 'Revised draft optional protocol' (1998) UN Doc E/1998/27, Annex II, Appendix I (n 54 above) art 14.

[427] 'Interpretative statements on the draft optional protocol to CEDAW' (1999) UN Doc E/1999/27 Annex II (n 56 above).

[428] *AT v Hungary* (n 86 above) para 9.6; *Fatma Yildirim v Austria* (n 86 above) para 12.4; *Şahide Goekce v Austria* (n 86 above) para 12.4; *AS v Hungary* (n 86 above) para 11.6.

[429] See eg CO Argentina, CEDAW/C/ARG/CO/6 (2010) paras 13–14; CO Australia, CEDAW/C/AUS/CO/7 (2010) paras 22–3; CO Burkina Faso, CEDAW/C/BFA/CO/6 (2010) paras 11–12; CO Czech Republic, CEDAW/C/CZE/CO/5 (2010) paras 12–13; CO Turkey, CEDAW/C/TUR/CO/6 (2010) paras 12–13.

[430] See eg CO Armenia, CEDAW/C/ARM/CO/4/Rev.1 (2009).

Although CEDAW Article 19(1) provides that the Committee shall adopt its own rules of procedure, Element 25 of *Suggestion No 7* proposed that the Committee develop rules of procedures relating to the OP that would enable it to conduct its work fairly, efficiently, and, as necessary, urgently. Panama submitted the only comment on this element in response to the Secretary-General's 2nd request for views on *Suggestion No 7*. It noted that the OP should state explicitly that the Committee could establish its own rules of procedure, taking into account matters not settled in the Protocol.[431] The Chairperson's drafts submitted to the Working Group sessions in 1997 and 1998 included this provision in Article 15. Although several delegations suggested that the provision was redundant in light of CEDAW Article 19(1), it was adopted *ad referendum* by the Working Group during its 1998 meetings.[432]

ICERD, ICCPR, CAT, ICRMW, CRPD, and CPED[433] include provisions empowering their respective treaty bodies to establish their own rules of procedure, but there is no equivalent to Article 14 in the ICCPR OPI, the CRPD OP, or the ICESCR OP.

The Committee has actively used this power. Rules of procedure relating to the OP were adopted at its 24th session in January 2001.[434] Amendments to these rules were adopted at the 39th session in January 2007.[435]

XVI. Article 15

1. The present Protocol shall be open for signature by any State that has signed, ratified or acceded to the Convention.
2. The present Protocol shall be subject to ratification by any State that has ratified or acceded to the Convention. Instruments of ratification shall be deposited with the Secretary-General of the United Nations.
3. The present Protocol shall be open to accession by any State that has ratified or acceded to the Convention.
4. Accession shall be effected by the deposit of an instrument of accession with the Secretary-General of the United Nations.

Element 27 of *Suggestion No 7* envisaged that procedures for signing, ratification, and accession should be prescribed in the Protocol, and text to that effect, broadly based on CEDAW Article 25 and ICCPR OPI Article 8 was included in Article 17 of the Chairperson's drafts submitted to the 1997 and 1998 sessions of the Working Group.[436] Delegations expressed satisfaction with the article during the Working Group's 1997

---

[431] 'Additional views by Governments, IGOs and NGOs' (1997) UN Doc E/CN.6/1997/5 (n 48 above) para 217.

[432] 'Chairperson's summary of views and comments' (1998) UN Doc E/1998/27, Annex II, Appendix II (n 53 above) para 43.

[433] ICCPR art 39(2); CAT art 18(2); ICERD art 10(1); ICRMW art 75(1); CRPD art 34(10); CED art 26(6).

[434] CEDAW rules of procedure, UNGA, 'Report of the CEDAW Committee—Twenty-Fourth Session' (2001) UN Doc A/56/38, Annex I, Parts XVI and XVII. Amendments to the rules were adopted at the Committee's thirty-ninth session, UNGA 'Report of the CEDAW Committee—Thirty-Ninth Session' (2007) UN Doc A/62/38, Chap V, paras 653–5 and Appendix.

[435] UNGA, 'Report of the CEDAW Committee—Thirty-Ninth Session' (2007) UN Doc A/62/38, Chapter V, paras 653–5 and Appendix.

[436] 'Text submitted by the Chairperson of the Open-ended Working Group of the CSW' (1997) UN Doc E/CN.6/1997/WG/L.1 (n 47 above); and 'Revised draft optional protocol' (1997) UN Doc E/1997/27, Annex III, Appendix I (n 52 above).

session, although they suggested several technical amendments and agreed that these issues should be resolved in the light of legal opinion.[437] The article specifies no time limit during which States may submit signature, ratification, or accession. It was adopted *ad referendum* during the 1998 Working Group session.

XVII. Article 16

1. The present Protocol shall enter into force three months after the date of deposit with the Secretary-General of the United Nations of the tenth instrument of ratification or accession.
2. For each State ratifying the present Protocol or acceding to it after its entry into force, the present Protocol shall enter into force three months after the date of the deposit of its own instrument of ratification or accession.

This article, which stipulates the requirements for entry into force of the Protocol and its entry into force for each State party was envisaged in Element 27 of *Suggestion No 7*. Spain suggested that the Protocol's entry into force should not be tied to an excessively high number of ratifications, while Cuba considered that the highest number of ratifications should be required.[438]

The draft submitted by the Chairperson to the Working Group's 1997 session provided for entry into force three months after the deposit of either the 5th or 10th instrument of ratification or accession.[439] During this session, proposals were made that the OP should enter into force after the 5th instrument of ratification or accession was lodged with the Secretary-General. Others suggested it was important to have wide acceptance of the OP before it entered into force, and that the threshold should be ten States parties, with some being of the view that twenty should be required.[440] These options were reflected in the revised draft submitted by the Chairperson to the 1998 session of the Working Group,[441] during which those delegations which had favoured a threshold of five ratifications or accessions for entry into force joined those that favoured ten. However, several delegations maintained the view that twenty should be required, on the basis of consistency with the Convention's Article 27.[442] Accordingly, the revised draft optional protocol submitted to the 1999 session maintained these three options.[443] As in the case of the ICCPR OPI, the Protocol set a threshold of ten ratifications or accessions,[444] with entry into force occurring three months after the deposit of the tenth instrument with the Secretary-General. The OP entered into force on 22 December 2000, three months after

---

[437] 'Chairperson's summary of views and comments' (1997) UN Doc E/1997/27, Annex II, Appendix II (n 49 above) para 67; 'Chairperson's summary of views and comments' (1998) UN Doc E/1998/27, Annex II, Appendix II (n 53 above) para 47.

[438] 'Additional views by Governments, IGOs and NGOs' (1997) UN Doc E/CN.6/1997/5 (n 48 above) paras 226–7.

[439] 'Text submitted by the Chairperson of the Open-ended Working Group of the CSW' (1997) UN Doc E/CN.6/1997/WG/L.1 (n 47 above) art 18(1).

[440] 'Chairperson's summary of views and comments' (1997) UN Doc E/1997/27, Annex II, Appendix II (n 49 above) para 68.

[441] 'Revised draft optional protocol' (1997) UN Doc E/1997/27, Annex III, Appendix I (n 52 above).

[442] 'Chairperson's summary of views and comments' (1998) UN Doc E/1998/27, Annex II, Appendix II (n 53 above) para 18.

[443] 'Revised draft optional protocol' (1998) UN Doc E/1998/27, Annex II, Appendix I (n 54 above).

[444] A threshold of ten ratifications or accessions is provided for in art 13 of the CRPD OP and art 18 of the ICESCR OP. Similarly, ten declarations under arts 14 of ICERD and 77 of ICRMW are required to bring their optional communications procedure into force, while five declarations were required in the case of CAT's art 22.

the deposit by Italy of its instrument of ratification on 22 September 2000. Entry into force for individual States occurs three months after the deposit of their instrument of ratification or accession.

XVIII. Article 17

No reservations to the present Protocol shall be permitted.

CEDAW OP Article 17 has no equivalent in comparable instruments. The ICCPR OPI and the ICESCR OP are silent on the question of reservations. The CRPD OP provides in Article 14 that reservations incompatible with the Protocol's object and purpose shall not be permitted. None of the other instruments addresses reservations in the context of communications procedures.

The provision is based on Element 28 of the Committee's *Suggestion No 7*,[445] and was the subject of heated debate during the elaboration of the Protocol. Some States supported the prohibition of reservations to the Protocol.[446] There was some concern, however, that a general prohibition on reservations could discourage ratification, and, thus, several States proposed that the approach of the ICCPR OPI, which is silent on reservations, should be followed, particularly as the practice under multilateral treaties is to admit reservations that are compatible with the object and purpose of the treaty concerned.[447] Views supporting inclusion of a general prohibition on reservations, as well as suggesting that it might be necessary to allow States parties to accept the OP with reservations compatible with the VCLT to achieve a large number of ratifications to the instrument, were also put forward in the 1st session of the Working Group.[448]

Article 20 of the draft Optional Protocol submitted by the Working Group's Chairperson to its 2nd session provided that no reservations to the Protocol shall be permitted.[449] The revised drafts submitted to the 3rd and 4th sessions also included this article.[450] Delegations were divided throughout the negotiations, with some considering it to be consistent with existing international practice and appropriate for a modern instrument designed for the twenty-first century, and others that compatible reservations should be permissible.[451] Those who supported inclusion of the provision pointed out that the Protocol was optional and procedural and that its effective functioning would be undermined were reservations to any of its provisions permitted. Some expressed concern about the long-term implications of a complete prohibition of reservations in a human

---

[445] 'CEDAW *Suggestion No 7*' (1995) UN Doc A/50/38 (n 26 above).

[446] 'Views submitted by Governments, IGOs and NGOs' (1996) UN Doc E/CN.6/1996/10 and Corr.1, Add.1 and Add.2 (n 36 above) para 123; 'Additional views by Governments, IGOs and NGOs' (1997) UN Doc E/CN.6/1997/5 (n 48 above) paras 62–70, 228, and 230.

[447] 'Additional views by Governments, IGOs and NGOs' (1997) UN Doc E/CN.6/1997/5 (n 48 above) paras 65 and 68.

[448] 'Report of the Open-ended Working Group on the Elaboration of a Draft Optional Protocol to CEDAW' (1996) UN Doc E/1996/26, Annex III (n 37 above) para 103.

[449] 'Text submitted by the Chairperson of the Open-ended Working Group of the CSW' (1997) UN Doc E/CN.6/1997/WG/L.1 (n 47 above).

[450] 'Revised draft optional protocol' UN Doc E/1997/27, Annex III, Appendix I (n 52 above); 'Revised draft optional protocol' (1998) UN Doc E/1998/27, Annex II, Appendix I (n 54 above).

[451] 'Chairperson's summary of views and comments' (1997) UN Doc E/1997/27, Annex II, Appendix II (n 49 above) para 70.

rights instrument, but indicated that they were willing to discuss options which fell short of an absolute ban that would discourage ratifications.[452]

Throughout negotiations, strong views were expressed that the subject matter of the Convention made inclusion of this provision necessary, and that this protocol was an exceptional case justifying complete prohibition of reservations which could otherwise defeat its purpose.[453] These views prevailed and the provision remains as Article 17. A significant number of interpretative statements on the OP refer to this Article. Algeria, Cameroon, China, Egypt, India, Israel, Jordan, the Russian Federation, and the United States of America indicated that they had accepted the provision in light of the optional and procedural nature of the Protocol and in order to preserve consensus. They emphasized that it should not set a precedent in relation to the 1969 VCLT, and the practice accepted in respect of becoming party to a treaty. Several also expressed concern that inclusion of the article might discourage States from acceding to or ratifying the Protocol.[454]

Notwithstanding Article 17, some countries have made declarations on ratification beyond that provided for in Article 10 relating to the inquiry procedure. Colombia declared on ratification, indicating that it understood Article 5 of the Protocol to mean that interim measures not only preclude 'a determination on admissibility or on the merits of a communication', as established in OP Article 5(2), but also that any measures involving the enjoyment of economic, social, and cultural rights shall be applied in keeping with the progressive nature of these rights. It also declared that no provision of the Protocol and no recommendation of the Committee may be interpreted as requiring Colombia to decriminalize offences against life or personal integrity.

Several declarations have also been made concerning the territorial application of the Protocol. On its accession on 17 December 2004, the United Kingdom indicated that the Protocol applied to the Falkland Islands (Malvinas) and the Isle of Man. On 18 January 2005, the Government of Argentina submitted a communication to the Secretary-General rejecting this declaration which it reiterated on its ratification on 20 March 2007. New Zealand's ratification is subject to a declaration that the ratification does not extend to Tokelau unless and until a declaration to that effect is lodged with the depositary on the basis of appropriate consultation with Tokelau.

XIX. Article 18

1. **Any State Party may propose an amendment to the present Protocol and file it with the Secretary-General of the United Nations. The Secretary-General shall thereupon communicate any proposed amendments to the States Parties with a request that they notify her or him whether they favour a conference of States Parties for the purpose of considering and voting on the proposal. In the event that at least one-third of the States Parties favour such a conference, the Secretary-General shall convene the conference under the auspices of the United Nations. Any amendment adopted by a majority of the States Parties present and voting at the conference shall be submitted to the General Assembly of the United Nations for approval.**

---

[452] 'Chairperson's summary of views and comments' (1998) UN Doc E/1998/27, Annex II, Appendix II (n 53 above) paras 50–6.

[453] Ibid paras 54–6.

[454] 'Interpretative statements on the draft optional protocol to CEDAW' (1999) UN Doc E/1999/27 Annex II (n 56 above) para 25.

2. Amendments shall come into force when they have been approved by the General Assembly of the United Nations and accepted by a two-thirds majority of the States Parties to the present Protocol in accordance with their respective constitutional processes.

3. When amendments come into force, they shall be binding on those States parties that have accepted them, other States Parties still being bound by the provisions of the present Protocol and any earlier amendments that they have accepted.

Element 29 of *Suggestion No 7* indicated that procedures for amendment should be included in any Protocol to the Convention, and a provision to this effect, based on those in existing instruments,[455] was included in the draft protocol submitted by the Chairperson to the Working Group's 1997 session.[456] This provision provides that any State party wishing to amend the Protocol should propose an amendment to the Secretary-General who will then transmit the proposed amendment to the States parties with a request that they notify her or him whether they favour a conference of States parties to consider and vote on the proposal. If one-third or more of the States parties favour such a conference, it shall be convened by the Secretary-General. Any amendment adopted by a majority of the States parties present and voting shall be submitted to the UNGA for approval. Amendments come into force when they have been approved by the Assembly and accepted by two-thirds or more of the States parties to the Protocol.

Delegations agreed with the article *ad referendum* at that session, although suggestions were made that further consideration be given to paragraph 3, providing that amendments that enter into force shall be binding on States parties that have accepted them, with other States parties being bound by the provisions of the Protocol and any earlier amendments that they had accepted.[457] It is likely that these suggestions were made because strict application of the provision to procedural amendments could lead to absurd results.[458] No changes were made to the draft as proposed.

As of 31 December 2010, no State party to the OP has sought to invoke the amendment provision.

XX. Article 19

1. Any State Party may denounce the present Protocol at any time by written notification addressed to the Secretary-General of the United Nations. Denunciation shall take effect six months after the date of receipt of the notification by the Secretary-General.

2. Denunciation shall be without prejudice to the continued application of the provisions of the present Protocol to any communication submitted under article 2 or any inquiry initiated under article 8 before the effective date of the denunciation.

---

[455] ICCPR art 51; ICCPR OPI art 11; CAT art 29.

[456] 'Text submitted by the Chairperson of the Open-ended Working Group of the CSW' (1997) UN Doc E/CN.6/1997/WG/L.1 (n 47 above) art 21.

[457] 'Chairperson's summary of views and comments' (1997) UN Doc E/1997/27, Annex II, Appendix II (n 49 above) para 71.

[458] Manfred Nowak discusses this in the context of ICCPR, art 51(3) in M Nowak, 'UN Covenant on Civil and Political Rights: CCPR Commentary' (2nd rev ed) (2005) 813–14.

No provision allowing for denunciation or withdrawal[459] is contained in the Convention, and, thus, any purported denunciation is subject to the rules of international law and the VCLT.[460]

However, ICCPR OPI Article 12 provides for the denunciation of the Optional Protocol at any time within three months after written notification of denunciation is submitted to the Secretary-General. Element 29 of *Suggestion No 7* indicated that procedures for denunciation should be prescribed in the Protocol, and the Chairperson's draft presented to the 1997 session of the Working Group contained such a provision indicating that denunciation would take effect either three or six months after the Secretary-General had received notification.[461] During its 1997 session, the Working Group agreed with the text, suggesting that its language be revised to follow the ICCPR OPI Article 12, but that denunciation should take effect six months after receipt of the notification by the Secretary-General,[462] rather than three months as in Article 12. The article, as revised, was adopted *ad referendum* during the 1998 session of the Working Group.[463]

As in the case of ICCPR OPI Article 12(2), Article 19(2) provides that denunciation shall be without prejudice to the continued application of the provisions of Protocol to any communication submitted, and in the case of the CEDAW OP, any inquiry initiated, before the effective date of denunciation. No State party has denounced the CEDAW OP, but in accordance with the practice of the Human Rights Committee communications that reach the OHCHR prior to entry into force of any denunciation are to be accepted and considered by the Committee. Thereafter, such communications are to be declared inadmissible, irrespective of whether the alleged violation of the Convention occurred at a date when the Protocol was in force for the State concerned.[464] It is likely that the CEDAW Committee would take the same approach, and with respect to inquiries as well.

Article 20(c) requires the Secretary-General to notify all States, not only States parties to the OP, of any denunciation under Article 19.

XXI. Article 20

The Secretary-General of the United Nations shall inform all States of:

(a) Signatures, ratifications and accessions under the present Protocol;
(b) The date of entry into force of the present Protocol and any amendment under article 18.
(c) Any denunciation under article 19.

The Committee's *Suggestion No 7* did not expressly provide for this provision, which is based on ICCPR OPI Article 8. The Chairperson included such a provision in the first

---

[459] A proposed clause on withdrawal was deleted from the draft Convention by the CSW at its 26th session.

[460] Vienna Convention on the Law of Treaties (VCLT) (23 May 1969) 1155 UNTS 331 arts 54–72. There is no denunciation provision in the Covenants, but such provisions are contained in ICERD art 21; CAT art 31; CRC art 52; CRPD art 48; CRPD OP art 16; and ICESCR OP art 20.

[461] 'Text submitted by the Chairperson of the Open-ended Working Group of the CSW' UN Doc E/CN.6/1997/WG/L.1 (n 47 above) art 22.

[462] 'Chairperson's summary of views and comments' (1997) UN Doc E/1997/27, Annex II, Appendix II (n 49 above) para 72.

[463] 'Chairperson's summary of views and comments' (1998) UN Doc E/1998/27, Annex II, Appendix II (n 53 above) para 57.

[464] *Damian Thomas v Jamaica* CCPR Communication No 800/1998 (1999) UN Doc CCPR/C/65/D/800/1998. See also M Nowak (n 458 above) 906–7.

draft and in the revisions presented to the Working Group in 1997, 1998, and 1999.[465] The article was adopted *ad referendum* during the 1997 and 1998 sessions of the Working Group,[466] although the text of the provision was reformulated in order to provide greater clarity.

XXII. Article 21

1. The present Protocol, of which the Arabic, Chinese, English, French, Russian and Spanish texts are equally authentic, shall be deposited in the archives of the United Nations.
2. The Secretary-General of the United Nations shall transmit certified copies of the present Protocol to all States referred to in article 25 of the Convention.

This article, envisaged in Element 27 of *Suggestion No 7*, and included in the Working Group's Chairperson's draft Protocol, recalls CEDAW Article 30 and corresponds to ICCPR OPI Article 14, which replicates Article 53 of the Covenant. The article was agreed to *ad referendum* by the 1st session of the Working Group,[467] and adopted by referendum by the 2nd session.[468]

Article 21(1) makes equally valid the Protocol text as adopted in each UN language for interpretation purposes. The terms used are assumed to have the same meaning in each language. If a difference in meaning is discerned, the true meaning is to be determined applying the rules of treaty interpretation in Articles 31, 32, and especially 33(4) of the VCLT.

CEDAW Article 25 provides that the Convention is open to signature and accession by all States, as well as being subject to ratification. In accordance with Article 21 of the Protocol, therefore, certified copies are to be transmitted to all States by the Secretary-General, who is designated as the depositary of the Convention in its Article 25(2).

---

[465] 'Text submitted by the Chairperson of the Open-ended Working Group of the CSW' UN Doc E/CN.6/1997/WG/L.1 (n 47 above) art 23; 'Revised draft optional protocol' UN Doc E/1997/27, Annex III, Appendix I (n 52 above) art 23; 'Revised draft optional protocol' (1998) UN Doc E/1998/27, Annex II, Appendix I (n 54 above) art 23.

[466] 'Chairperson's summary of views and comments' (1997) UN Doc E/1997/27, Annex II, Appendix II (n 49 above) para 73; 'Chairperson's summary of views and comments' (1998) UN Doc E/1998/27, Annex II, Appendix II (n 53 above) para 57.

[467] 'Chairperson's summary of views and comments' (1997) UN Doc E/1997/27, Annex II, Appendix II (n 49 above) para 73.

[468] Ibid para 57.

Annexe 1: Table of General Recommendations

General Recommendations*

General Recommendation No 1, 5th Session (1986) on reporting guidelines

General Recommendation No 2, 6th Session (1987) on reporting guidelines

General Recommendation No 3, 6th Session (1987) on education and public information programmes

General Recommendation No 4, 6th Session (1987) on reservations

General Recommendation No 5, 7th Session (1988) on temporary special measures

General Recommendation No 6, 7th Session (1988) on effective national machinery and publicity

General Recommendation No 7, 7th Session (1988) on resources

General Recommendation No 8, 7th Session (1988) on article 8

General Recommendation No 9, 8th Session (1989) statistical data

General Recommendation No 10, 8th Session (1989) on tenth anniversary of the adoption of CEDAW

General Recommendation No 11, 8th Session (1989) on technical advisory services for reporting

General Recommendation No 12, 8th Session (1989) on violence against women

General Recommendation No 13, 8th Session (1989) on equal remuneration for work of equal value

General Recommendation No 14, 9th Session (1990) on female circumcision

General Recommendation No 15, 9th Session (1990) on women and AIDS

General Recommendation No 16, 10th Session (1991) on unpaid women workers in rural and urban family enterprises

General Recommendation No 17, 10th Session (1991) measurement and quantification of the unremunerated domestic activities of women and their recognition in the GNP

General Recommendation No 18, 10th Session (1991) on disabled women

General Recommendation No 19, 11th Session (1992) on violence against women

General Recommendation No 20, 11th Session (1992) on reservations

General Recommendation No 21, 13th Session (1994) on equality in marriage and family relations

General Recommendation No 22, 14th Session (1995) on article 20 of the Convention

General Recommendation No 23, 16th Session (1997) on women in political and public life

General Recommendation No 24, 20th Session (1999) on article 12—women and health

General Recommendation No 25, 30th Session (2004) on article 4 paragraph 1—temporary special measures

General Recommendation No 26, 42nd Session (2008) Women Migrant Workers, UN Doc CEDAW/C/2009/WP.1/R

General Recommendation No 27, 47th Session (2010) Older women and protection of their human rights, UN Doc CEDAW/C/GC/27

General Recommendation No 28, 47th Session (2010) The Core Obligations of States Parties under Article 2 of the Convention on the Elimination of All Forms of Discrimination against Women, UN Doc CEDAW/C/GC/28

---

* General Recommendations 1–25 can be found reprinted at UN Doc HRI/GEN/1/Rev.9 (Vol. II)

Annexe 2: Table of Treaties

Treaty Title	Treaty Abbreviation
1933 Convention for the Suppression of the Traffic in Women of Full Age (adopted 11 October 1933, entered into force 24 August 1934) 150 LNTS 431	
1992 Paulista Convention on the Elimination of All Forms of Discrimination Against Women	
Additional Protocol to the American Convention on Human Rights in the Field of Economic, Social and Cultural Rights (Protocol of San Salvador) (adopted 17 November 1988, entered into force 16 November 1999) OAS TS 69	Protocol of San Salvador
African Charter on Human and Peoples' Rights (Banjul Charter) (adopted 27 June 1981, entered into force 21 October 1986) 21 ILM 58; 1520 UNTS 217	Banjul Charter
African Charter on the Rights and Welfare of the Child (ACRWC) (entered into force 29 November 1999) OAU Doc. CAB/LEG/24.9/49 (1990)	ACRWC
American Convention on Human Rights (ACHR) (adopted 22 November 1969, entered into force 18 July 1978) OAS TS 36; 1144 UNTS 123	ACHR
Arab Charter on Human Rights 2004 (originally adopted 15 September 1994; revised version adopted 22 May 2004; entered into force 15 March 2008)	Arab Charter on Human Rights
Charter of Fundamental Rights of the European Union (EU Charter) (signed 7 December 2000) OJ C364/8	EU Charter
Charter of the United Nations (signed on 26 June 1945, entered into force 24 October 1945) 59 Stat. 1031, T.S. 993, 3 Bevans 1153	
Constitution of the World Health Organization (WHO Constitution) (adopted 22 July 1946, entered into force 7 April 1948) 14 UNTS 185	WHO Constitution
Convention against Torture and Other Cruel, Inhuman or Degrading Treatment or Punishment (CAT) (adopted 10 December 1984, entered into force 26 June 1987) 1465 UNTS 85	CAT
Convention Against Transnational Organized Crime (Organized Crime Convention) (adopted 15 November 2000, entered into force 29 September 2003) 2225 UNTS 209	Organized Crime Convention
Convention concerning the Employment of Women before and after Childbirth (ILO Convention No 3) (adopted 28 November 1919, entered into force 13 June 1921) 38 UNTS 53	ILO Convention No 3
Convention for the Protection of Human Rights and Fundamental Freedoms (European Convention on Human Rights) (Rome, 4 November 1950; TS 71 (1953))	European Convention on Human Rights or ECHR

Treaty Title	Treaty Abbreviation
Convention for the Suppression of the Traffic in Persons and of the Exploitation of the Prostitution of Others (Trafficking Convention) (opened for signature 21 March 1950, entered into force 15 July 1951) 96 UNTS 271	Trafficking Convention
Convention on Consent to Marriage, Minimum Age for Marriage and Registration of Marriages (Marriage Convention) (adopted 7 November 1962, entered into force 9 December, 1964) 521 UNTS 231	Marriage Convention
Convention on Preventing and Combating Trafficking in Women and Children for Prostitution by the South Asian Association for Regional Cooperation (SAARC Convention) (adopted 5 January 2002, not in force)	SAARC Convention
The Convention on the Civil Aspects of International Child Abduction (The Hague Convention) (concluded 25 October 1980, entered into force 1 December 1983) 1343 UNTS 97	The Hague Convention
Convention on the Elimination of All Forms of Discrimination against Women (CEDAW) (adopted 18 December 1979, entered into force 3 September 1981) 1249 UNTS 13	CEDAW
Convention on the Jurisdictional Immunities of States and Their Property 2004 (adopted 2 December 2004, not in force) UN Doc A/59/508	
Convention on the Nationality of Married Women (adopted 29 January 1957, entered into force 11 August 1958) 309 UNTS 65	Convention on the Nationality of Married Women
Convention on the Political Rights of Women (adopted 20 December 1952, entered into force 7 July 1954) 193 UNTS 135	Convention on Political Rights of Women
Convention on the Prevention and Punishment of the Crime of Genocide (Genocide Convention) (adopted 9 December 1948, entered into force 12 January 1951) 78 UNTS 277.	Genocide Convention
Convention on the Reduction of Statelessness (entered into force 13 December 1975) 989 UNTS 175	
Convention on the Rights and Duties of States adopted by the Seventh International Conference of American States (Montevideo Convention) (adopted 26 December 1933, entered into force 26 December 1934) 165 LNTS 19	Montevideo Convention
Convention on the Rights of Persons with Disabilities (CRPD) (adopted 13 December 2006, entered into force 3 May 2008) UN Doc A/61/106	CRPD
Convention on the Rights of the Child (CRC) (adopted 20 November 1989; entered into force 2 September 1990) 1577 UNTS 3	CRC
Convention Relating to the Status of Refugees (adopted 30 August 1961, entered into force 22 April 1954) 189 UNTS 150	
Convention to Suppress the Slave Trade and Slavery (Slavery Convention) (adopted 25 September 1926; entered into force 9 March 1927) 60 LNTS 253	Slavery Convention
Copenhagen Declaration on Social Development (adopted 14 March 1995) UN Doc A/CONF.166/9	Copenhagen Declaration on Social Development
Council of Europe Convention on Action against Trafficking in Human Beings (Council of Europe Trafficking Convention) (opened for signature 16 May 2005, entered into force 1 February 2008) CETS 197	Council of Europe Trafficking Convention

Treaty Title	Treaty Abbreviation
European Convention on Nationality (opened for signature 6 November 1997, entered into force 1 March 2000) ETS 166	
Geneva Convention for the amelioration of the condition of the wounded and sick in armed forces in the field (First Geneva Convention) (concluded 12 August 1949, entered into force 21 October 1950) 75 UNTS 31	First Geneva Convention
Geneva Convention for the amelioration of the condition of the wounded, sick and shipwrecked members of the armed forces at sea (Second Geneva Convention) (concluded 12 August 1949, entered into force 21 October 1950) 75 UNTS 85	Second Geneva Convention
Geneva Convention relative to the protection of civilian persons in time of war (Fourth Geneva Convention) (concluded 12 August 1949, entered into force 21 October 1950) 75 UNTS 287	Fourth Geneva Convention
Geneva Convention relative to the treatment of prisoners of war (Third Geneva Convention) (concluded 12 August 1949, entered into force 21 October 1950) 75 UNTS 135	Third Geneva Convention
ILO Convention concerning Discrimination in Respect of Employment and Occupation (ILO Convention No 111) (adopted 25 June 1958, entered into force 15 June 1960) 362 UNTS 31	ILO Convention No 111
ILO Convention concerning Equal Remuneration for Men and Women Workers for Work of Equal Value (ILO Convention No 100) (adopted 29 June 1951, entered into force 23 May 1953) 165 UNTS 303	ILO Convention No 100
ILO Convention concerning Forced or Compulsory Labour (ILO Convention No 29) (adopted 28 June 1930, entered into force 1 May 1932) 39 UNTS 55	ILO Convention No 29
ILO Convention concerning Maternity Protection (Revised 1952) (ILO Convention No 103) (adopted 28 June 1952, entered into force 7 September 1955) 214 UNTS 321	ILO Convention No 103
ILO Convention concerning Night Work (ILO Convention No 171) (adopted 26 June 1990, entered into force 4 January 1995) 1855 UNTS 305	ILO Convention No 171
ILO Convention concerning Occupational Safety and Health and the Working Environment (ILO Convention No 155) (adopted 22 June 1981, entered into force 11 August 1983) 1331 UNTS 279	ILO Convention No 155
ILO Convention concerning Part-Time Work (ILO Convention No 175) (adopted 24 June 1994, entered into force 28 February 1998) 2010 UNTS 51	ILO Convention No 175
ILO Convention concerning the Abolition of Forced Labour (ILO Convention No 105) (adopted 25 June 1957, entered into force 17 January 1959) 320 UNTS 291	ILO Convention No 105
ILO Convention concerning the Maximum Permissible Weight to be Carried by One Worker (ILO Convention No 127) (adopted 28 June 1967, entered into force 10 March 1970) 721 UNTS 305	ILO Convention No 127
ILO Convention concerning the Prohibition and Immediate Action for the Elimination of the Worst Forms of Child Labor (ILO Convention No 182) (adopted 17 June 1999, entered into force 19 November 2000) 2133 UNTS 161	ILO Convention No 182

Treaty Title	Treaty Abbreviation
ILO Convention concerning the Revision of the Maternity Protection Convention (revised) (ILO Convention No 183) (adopted 15 June 2000, entered into force 7 February 2002) 2181 UNTS 253	ILO Convention No 183
ILO Protocol of 1990 to the Convention concerning Night Work of Women Employed in Industry (Revised 1948) (adopted 26 June 1990) 1846 UNTS 418	ILO Convention No 89 Protocol
ILO Workers with Family Responsibilities Convention (ILO Convention No 156) (adopted 23 June 1981, entered into force 11 August 1983) 1331 UNTS 295	ILO Convention No 156
Inter-American Convention on the Prevention, Punishment and Eradication of Violence against Women (Convention of Belém do Para) (adopted 9 June 1994, entered into force 5 March 1995) 33 ILM 1534	Convention of Belém do Para
International Convention against the Taking of Hostages (adopted 17 December 1979, entered into force 3 June 1983) 1316 UNTS 205	
International Convention for the Protection of All Persons from Enforced Disappearance (CED) (adopted 20 December 2006, entered into force 23 December 2010) UN Doc A/61/488	CED
International Convention for the Suppression of the Traffic in Women and Children, concluded at Geneva on 30 September 1921, as amended by the Protocol signed at Lake Success, New York, on 12 November 1947 (entered into force as amended 24 April 1950) 53 UNTS 39	
International Convention on the Elimination of All Forms of Racial Discrimination (CERD) (adopted 21 December 1965, entered into force 4 January 1969) 660 UNTS 195	CERD
International Convention on the Protection of the Rights of All Migrant Workers and Members of their Families (CMW) (adopted 18 December 1990, entered into force 1 July 2003) 2220 UNTS 3	CMW
International Convention on the Suppression and Punishment of the Crime of Apartheid (Apartheid Convention) (adopted 30 November 1973, entered into force 18 July 1976) 1015 UNTS 243	Apartheid Convention
International Covenant on Civil and Political Rights (ICCPR) (adopted 16 December 1966, entered into force 23 March 1976) 999 UNTS 171	ICCPR
International Covenant on Economic, Social and Cultural Rights (ICESCR) (adopted 16 December 1966, entered into force 3 January 1976) 993 UNTS 3	ICESCR
Islamabad Declaration: Review and Future Action Celebrating Beijing Plus Ten (adopted 3–5 May 2005, Islamabad Pakistan)	
Optional Protocol to the Convention against Torture and Other Cruel, Inhuman or Degrading Treatment or Punishment (OP CAT) (adopted 18 December 2002, entered into force 22 June 2006) 2375 UNTS 237	OP CAT
Optional Protocol to the Convention on the Elimination of All Forms of Discrimination against Women (OP) or (CEDAW OP) (adopted 6 October 1999, entered into force 22 December 2000) 2131 UNTS 83	OP or CEDAW OP
Optional Protocol to the International Covenant on Civil and Political Rights (ICCPR OPI) (adopted 16 December 1966, entered into force 23 March 1976) 999 UNTS 171	ICCPR OPI

Treaty Title	Treaty Abbreviation
Protocol Additional to the Geneva Conventions of 12 August 1949 and relating to the protection of victims of international armed conflicts (Protocol I to the Geneva Conventions) (concluded 8 June 1977, entered into force 7 December 1978) 1125 UNTS 3	Protocol I to the Geneva Conventions
Protocol Additional to the Geneva Conventions of 12 August 1949 and relating to the protection of victims of non-international armed conflicts (Protocol II to the Geneva Conventions) (concluded 8 June 1977, entered into force 7 December 1978) 1125 UNTS 609	Protocol II to the Geneva Conventions
Protocol Against the Smuggling of Migrants by Land, Sea and Air, supplementing the UN Convention against Transnational Organized Crime (adopted 8 January 2001, entered into force 28 January 2004) 2241 UNTS 507	Protocol Against the Smuggling of Migrants by Land, Sea and Air
Protocol to Prevent, Suppress and Punish Trafficking in Persons, Especially Women and Children, supplementing the United Nations Convention against Transnational Organized Crime (Trafficking Protocol) (adopted 15 November 2000, entered into force 25 December 2003) 2237 UNTS 319	Trafficking Protocol
Protocol to the African Charter on Human and Peoples' Rights on the Rights of Women in Africa (Protocol on the Rights of Women in Africa) (adopted 11 July 2003, entered into force 25 November 2005) OAU AHG/Res.240	Protocol on the Rights of Women in Africa
Protocol to the Convention for the Protection of Human Rights and Fundamental Freedoms (Protocol 12 to the European Convention on Human Rights) (adopted 4 November 2000, entered into force 1 April 2005) CETS 177	Protocol 12 to the European Convention on Human Rights
Protocol to the Convention for the Protection of Human Rights and Fundamental Freedoms as amended by Protocol No 11 (Protocol 1 to the European Convention on Human Rights) (Paris, 1952) (Protocol 11 (ETS 155) entered into force as amended 1 November 1998) ETS 009	Protocol 1 to the European Convention on Human Rights
Rome Statute of the International Criminal Court (The Rome Statute) (adopted 17 July 1998, entered into force 1 July 2002) 2187 UNTS 90	The Rome Statute
ILO Convention concerning Safety and Health in Mines (ILO Convention No 176) (adopted 22 June 1995, entered into force 5 June 1998) 2029 UNTS 207	ILO Convention No 176
Second Optional Protocol to the International Covenant on Civil and Political Rights (ICCPR OP II) (adopted 15 December 1989, entered into force 11 July 1991) 1642 UNTS 414	ICCPR OP II
Supplementary Convention on the Elaboration of Slavery, the Slave Trade and Institutions and Practices Similar to Slavery (Supplementary Slavery Convention) (adopted 7 September 1956, entered into force 30 April 1957) 226 UNTS 3	Supplementary Slavery Convention
Treaty on the Non-Proliferation of Nuclear Weapons (Non-Proliferation Treaty) (concluded 1 July 1968, entered into force 5 March 1970) 729 UNTS 168	Non-Proliferation Treaty
ILO Convention concerning Underground Work (ILO Convention No 45) (adopted 21 June 1935, entered into force 30 May 1937) 40 UNTS 63	ILO Convention No 45
UNESCO Convention against Discrimination in Education (CADE) (adopted 14 December 1962, entered into force 22 May 1962) 429 UNTS 93	CADE

Treaty Title	Treaty Abbreviation
UNESCO Convention on the Protection and Promotion of the Diversity of Cultural Expressions (adopted 20 October 2005, entered into force 18 March 2007) 2440 UNTS 151	
Vienna Convention on Diplomatic Relations (1961) (VCDR) (adopted on 18 April 1961, entered into force on 24 April 1964) 400 UNTS 95	VCDR
Vienna Convention on Succession of States in Respect of Treaties (adopted 23 August 1978, entered into force 6 November 1996) 1946 UNTS 3	
Vienna Convention on the Law of Treaties (VCLT) (adopted 23 May 1969, entered into force 27 January 1980) 1155 UNTS 331	VCLT

Annexe 3: Bibliography

Abaid, Nisrine, 'Sharia, Muslim States and International Treaty Obligations: A Comparative Study' (London: British Institute of International and Comparative Law, 2008).

Abaka, Charlotte, 'Women in War and its Aftermath: Liberia' in Hanna B. Schöpp-Schilling and Cees Flinterman (eds), *The Circle of Empowerment: Twenty-Five Years of The UN Committee on The Elimination of Discrimination against Women* (New York: Feminist Press, 2007) 234–45.

Abe, Kohki, 'Article 29: Settlement of Disputes' in Japanese Association of International Women's Rights (ed), *Convention on the Elimination of All Forms of Discrimination against Women: A Commentary* (Bunkyo: Japanese Association of International Women's Rights, 1995) 414–19.

Abe, Kohki, 'Article 30: Authentic Text' in Japanese Association of International Women's Rights (ed), *Convention on the Elimination of All Forms of Discrimination against Women: A Commentary* (Bunkyo: Japanese Association of International Women's Rights, 1995) 420–4.

Adamson, Peter, *The Child Care Transition: A League Table of Early Childhood Education and Care in Economically Advanced Countries* (Florence: UNICEF, Innocenti Research Centre, 2008).

Alston, Philip, 'Ships Passing in the Night: The Current State of the Human Rights and Development Debate seen through the Lens of the Millennium Development Goals' (2005) 27 *Human Rights Quarterly* 755–829.

Alston, Philip and Robinson, Mary, *Human Rights and Development Towards Mutual Reinforcement* (Oxford: Oxford University Press, 2005).

Amerasinghe, Chtitharanjan Felix, *Aspects of the Actio Injuriarum in Roman Dutch Law* (Colombo: Lake House, 1966).

Amnesty International, *'Reservations to the Convention on the Elimination of All Forms of Discrimination against Women: Weakening the Protection of Women from Violence in the Middle East and North Africa Region'* AI Index: IOR 51/009/2004 (London: Amnesty International, 2004).

Antrobus, Peggy, *The Global Women's Movement: Origins, Issues and Strategies* (London: Zed Books, 2004).

Anwar, Zainah (ed), *Wanted: Equality and Justice in the Muslim Family* (Kuala Lumpur: Musawah, 2009).

Apodaca, Claire, 'Measuring Women's Economic and Social Advancement' (1998) 20 *Human Rights Quarterly* 139–72.

Appiah, Kwame Anthony, 'Stereotypes and the Shaping of Identity' (2000) 88 *Californian Law Review* 41–54.

Armstrong, Alice, Beyani, Chaloka, Himonga, Chuma, Kabeberbi-Macharia, Janet, Molokomme, Athaliah, Ncube, Welshman, Nhlapo, Thandabantu, Rwezaura, Bart and Stewart, Julie, 'Uncovering Reality: Excavating Women's Rights in the African Family' (1993) 7 *International Journal of Law, Policy and the Family* 314–69.

Arnardóttir, Oddný M., *Equality and Non-Discrimination Under the European Convention on Human Rights* (Leiden: Martinus Nijhoff Publishers, 2003).

Arneson, Richard, 'Equality of Opportunity' (October 2002) in Edward N. Zalta (ed), *Stanford Encyclopedia of Philosophy* <http://plato.stanford.edu/entries/equal-opportunity/> accessed 5 May 2009.

Aust, Anthony, *Modern Treaty Law and Practice* (2nd edn, Cambridge: Cambridge University Press, 2007).

Bacchi, Carol, 'The Practice of Affirmative Action Policies: Explaining Resistances and How These Affect Results' in Ineke Boerefijn, Fons Coomans, Jenny Goldschmidt, Rikki Holtmaat and Ria Wolleswinkel (eds), *Temporary Special Measures: Accelerating de facto Equality of Women under Article 4(1) UN Convention on the Elimination of All Forms of Discrimination against Women* (New York: Transnational Publishers, 2003) 75–96.

Baer, Susanne, 'Dignity, Liberty, Equality: A Fundamental Rights Triangle of Constitutionalism' (2009) 59(4) *University of Toronto Law Journal* 417–68.

Ballington, Julie and Matland, Richard E., 'Political Parties and Special Measures: Enhancing Women's Participation in Electoral Processes' EGM/ELEC/2004/EP.8 (16 January 2004) <http://www.un.org/womenwatch/osagi/meetings/2004.EGMelectoral/EP8-Ballington/Matland.PDF> accessed 31 December 2010.

Banda, Fareda, *Women, Law and Human Rights: An African Perspective* (Oxford: Hart Publishing, 2005).

Banda, Fareda, 'Understanding Women's Economic and Social Human Rights' (2006) 12 *East African Journal of Peace and Human Rights* 232–53.

Banda, Fareda, *Project on a Mechanism to Address Laws that Discriminate Against Women* (Geneva: OHCHR, 2008).

Barak-Erez, Daphne, 'Social Rights as Women's Rights' in Daphne Barak-Erez and Aeyal M. Gross (eds), *Exploring Social Rights Between Theory and Practice* (Oxford: Hart Publishing, 2007) 397–408.

Baratta, Roberto, 'Should Invalid Reservations to Human Rights Treaties be Disregarded?' (2000) 11/2 *European Journal of International Law* 413.

Baretto, Manuela and Ellemers, Naomi, 'The Burden of Benevolent Sexism: How it Contributes to the Maintenance of Gender Inequalities' (2005) 35 *European Journal of Social Psychology* 633–42.

Barnett, Hilaire, *Introduction to Feminist Jurisprudence* (London: Cavendish Publishing Ltd, 1998).

Barnett, Kathleen and Grown, Caren, *Gender Impacts of Government Revenue Collection: The Case of Taxation* (London: Commonwealth Secretariat, 2004) 26–49.

Barnidge Jr, Robert P., 'The Due Diligence Principle Under International Law' (2006) 8 *International Community Law Review* 81–121.

Bayefsky, Anne F., 'The Principle of Equality or Non-Discrimination in International Law' (1990) 12 *Human Rights Law Journal* 1–34.

Bayefsky, Anne F., *The UN Human Rights Treaty System: Universality at the Crossroads* (The Hague: Kluwer International Law, 2001).

Beauvoir, Simone de, *The Second Sex* (1949): Howard M. Parshley Translation (1st edn, New York: Alfred A. Knopf, 1989).

Beckwith, Karen and Cowell-Meyers, Kimberly, 'Sheer Numbers: Critical Representation Thresholds and Women's Political Representation' (2007) 5:3 *Perspectives on Politics* 553–65.

Beigbeder, Yves, 'International Civil Service' in Rüdiger Wolfrum (ed), *Max Planck Encyclopedia of International Law* (2008) online edition <http://www.mpepil.com> accessed 31 December 2010.

Beiter, Klaus Dieter, *The Protection of Right to Education by International Law Including a Systematic Analysis of Article 13 of the International Covenant on Economic, Social and Cultural Rights* (Leiden/Boston: Martinus Nijhoff Publishers, 2005).

Benninger-Budel, Carin (ed), *Due Diligence and its Application to Protect Women from Violence* (Leiden/Boston: Martinus Nijhoff Publishers, 2008).

Bijnsdorp, Mireille G.E., 'The Strength of the Optional Protocol to the United Nations Women's Convention' (2000) 18(3) *Netherlands Quarterly of Human Rights* 329–55.

Blackstone, William, *Commentaries on the Laws of England* (16th edn, London: A Straha, 1825).

Boerefijn, Ineke, 'De blinddoek opzij: een mensenrechtenbenadering van geweld tegen vrouwen' (2006) <http://arno.unimaas.nl/show.cgi?did=16239> accessed 31 December 2010, cited in Carin Benninger-Budel (ed), *Due Diligence and its Application to Protect Women from Violence* (Leiden/Boston: Martinus Nijhoff Publishers, 2008).

Boerefijn, Ineke, 'Impact on the Law on Treaty Reservations' in Menno T. Kamminga and Martin Scheinin (eds), *Impact of Human Rights Law on General International Law* (Oxford: Oxford University Press, 2009) 63.

Boerefijn, Ineke, 'The Right to Political Participation: the Case of the SGP' in Rikki Holtmaat and Ineke Boerefijn (eds), *Women's Human Rights and Culture/Religion/ Tradition: International Standards as Guidelines for Discussion?* (Colloquium at the Peace Palace, The Hague 12 May 2009, 2010) SIM Special No 32.

Boerefijn, Ineke, 'The Right to Political Participation: The Case of the SGP' in Rikki Holtmaat and Ineke Boerefijn (eds) *Women's Human Rights and Culture/Religion/ Tradition: International Standards as Guidelines for the Discussion?* (Utrecht: Universiteit Utrecht, 2010).

Bond, Johanna E., 'International Intersectionality: A Theoretical and Pragmatic Exploration of Women's International Human Rights' (2003) 52 *Emory Law Journal* 71–186.

Boserup, Ester, *Women's Role in Economic Development* (London: Earthscan, 1970).

Bourke-Martignoni, Joanna, 'The History and Development of the Due Diligence Standard in International Law and Its Role in the Protection of Women against Violence' in Carin Benninger-Budel (ed), *Due Diligence and its Application to Protect Women from Violence* (Leiden/Boston: Martinus Nijhoff Publishers, 2008).

van Boven, Theo, 'Study Concerning the Right to Restitution, Compensation and Rehabilitation for Victims of Gross Violations of Human Rights and Fundamental Freedoms', UN Doc E/CN.4/SUB.2/1993, reprinted in (1996) 59 *Law and Contemporary Problems* 283.

van den Brink, Marjolein, *Moeders in de Mainstream: een genderanalyse van het werk van het VN-kindercomité*, dissertation Utrecht University with a summary in English: *Mothers in the Mainstream: a Gender Analysis of the Work of the UN Committee on the Rights of the Child* (Nijmegen: Wolf Legal Publishers, 2006).

van den Brink, Marjolein, 'Gendered sovereignty? In Search of Gender Bias in the International Law Concept of State Sovereignty' in Ineke Boerefijn, and Jenny Goldschmidt, (eds), *Changing Perceptions of Sovereignty and Human Rights. Essays in Honour of Cees Flinterman*, (Antwerp: Intersentia, 2008) 65–83.

Boyd, Susan B. (ed), *Challenging the Public/Private Divide: Feminism, Law and Public Policy* (Toronto: University of Toronto Press, 1997).

Boyle, Christine, 'Home Rule for Women: Power Sharing between Men and Women' (1983) 7 *Dalhousie Law Journal* 790–809.

Bridgeman, Jo and Millns, Susan, *Feminist Perspectives on Law: Law's Engagement with the Female Body* (London: Sweet & Maxwell, 1998).

Brownlie, Ian, *Principles of Public International Law* (7th edn, Oxford University Press: 2008).

Bunch, Charlotte, 'Women's Rights as Human Rights: Toward a Re-Vision of Human Rights' (1990) 12 *Human Rights Quarterly* 486–98.

Burrill, Emily S, Roberts, Richard L. and Thornberry, Elizabeth (eds), *Domestic Violence and the Law in Colonial and Postcolonial Africa* (Athens, OH: Ohio University Press, 2010).

Burrows, Noreen, 'The 1979 Convention on the Elimination of All Forms of Discrimination against Women' (1985) 32 *Netherlands International Law Review* 419–60.

Busia Jr, Nana K. A., 'Ghana: Competing Visions of Liberal Democracy and Socialism', in Abdullahi Ahmed An-Na'im (ed), *Human Rights under African Constitutions* (Philadelphia: University of Pennsylvania Press, 2003) 52–96.

Bustelo, Mara R., 'The Committee on the Elimination of Discrimination against Women at the Crossroads' in Philip Alston and James Crawford (eds), *The Future of UN Human Rights Treaty Monitoring* (Cambridge: Cambridge University Press, 2000).

Butegwa, Florence, 'Using the African Charter on Human and Peoples' Rights to Secure Women's Access to Land in Africa' in Rebecca J. Cook (ed), *Human Rights of Women: National and International Perspectives* (Philadephia: University of Pennsylvania Press, 1994).

Butler, Judith, *Gender Trouble: Feminism and the Subversion of Identity*, (London/New York: Routledge, 1990).

Byrnes, Andrew, 'The "Other" Human Rights Treaty Body: The Work of the Committee on the Elimination of Discrimination against Women' (1989) 14 *Yale Journal of International Law* 1, 1–67.

Byrnes, Andrew, *CEDAW #10: Building on a Decade of Achievement: A Report on the Tenth Session of the Committee on the Elimination of Discrimination against Women* (Minneapolis: University of Minnesota, 1991).

Byrnes, Andrew, *Observations on the Background Paper Prepared by the Government of Canada on Issues in the Development of an International Instrument on Violence against Women* (unpublished, 1991).

Byrnes, Andrew, 'The Convention on the Elimination of All Forms of Discrimination against Women' in Wolfgang Benedek, Esther Kisaakye and Gerd Oberleitner (eds), *Human Rights of Women International Instruments and African Experiences* (London: Zed Books, 2002) 119–72.

Byrnes, Andrew, 'The Committee on the Elimination of Discrimination against Women' in Philip Alston and Frédéric Mégret (eds), *The United Nations and Human Rights. A Critical Appraisal* (2nd edn, forthcoming).

Byrnes, Andrew and Connors, Jane, 'Enforcing the Human Rights of Women: A Complaints Procedure for the Women's Convention? Draft Optional Protocol to the Convention on the Elimination of All Forms of Discrimination against Women' (1996) 21 *Brooklyn Journal of International Law* 679–797.

Byrnes, Andrew and Bath, Eleanor, 'Violence against Women, the Obligation of Due Diligence and the Optional Protocol to the Convention on the Elimination of All Forms of Discrimination against Women—Recent Developments' (2008) 8(3) *Human Rights Law Review* 517.

Byrnes, Andrew and Renshaw, Catherine, 'Within the State' in Daniel Moeckli, Sangeeta Shah, Sandesh Sivakumaran and David Harris (eds), *International Human Rights Law* (Oxford: Oxford University Press, 2010).

Caddell, Richard, 'Depositary' in Rüdiger Wolfrum (ed), *The Max Planck Encyclopedia of Public International Law* (2008) online edition <www.mpepil.com> accessed 31 December 2010.

Cartwright, Silvia, 'Interpreting the Convention' in Hanna B. Schöpp-Schilling and Cees Flinterman (eds), *The Circle of Empowerment: Twenty-Five Years of the UN Committee on The Elimination of Discrimination against Women* (New York: Feminist Press, 2007) 30–35.

Charlesworth, Hilary, 'Feminist Methods in International Law' (1999) 93 *American Journal of International Law* 379–94.

Charlesworth, Hilary, 'Concepts of Equality in International Law' in Grant Huscroft and Paul Rishworth (eds), *Litigating Rights: Perspectives from Domestic and International Law* (Oxford: Hart, 2002) 137–47.

Charlesworth, Hilary, 'Not Waving but Drowning: Gender Mainstreaming and Human Rights in the United Nations' (2005) 18 *Harvard Human Rights Journal* 1–18.

Charlesworth, Hilary, 'Human Rights as Men's Rights' in Julie S. Peters and Andrea Wolper (eds), *Women's Rights, Human Rights. International Feminist Perspectives* (New York: Routledge, 1995) 103–13.

Charlesworth, Hilary, Chinkin, Christine and Wright, Shelley, 'Feminist Approaches to International Law' (1991) 85 *The American Journal of International Law* 613–45.

Charlesworth, Hilary and Chinkin, Christine, *The Boundaries of International Law A Feminist Analysis* (Manchester: Manchester University Press, 2000).

Childs, Sarah and Krook, Mona L., 'Critical Mass Theory and Women's Political Representation' (2008) 56 *Political Studies* 725–36.

Childs, Sarah and Krook, Mona L., 'Theorizing Women's Political Representation: Debates and Innovations in Empirical Research' (2008) 17:2 *Femina Politica* 20–30.

Chinkin, Christine, 'Reservations and Objections to the Convention on the Elimination of All Forms of Discrimination against Women' in J.P. Gardner (ed), *Human Rights as General Norms and a State's Right to Opt Out: Reservations and Objections to Human Rights Conventions* (London: British Institute of International and Comparative Law, 1997) 64–84.

Chinkin, Christine and Wright, Shelley, 'The Hunger Trap: Women, Food and Self-Determination' (1993) 4 *Michigan Journal of International Law* 262–321.

Chodorow, Nancy J., *Feminism and Psychoanalytic Theory* (New Haven: Yale University Press, 1989).

Clapham, Andrew, *Human Rights Obligations of Non-State Actors* (Oxford: Oxford University Press, 2006).

Clark, Belinda, 'The Vienna Convention Reservations Regime and the Convention on Discrimination against Women' (1991) 85 *American Journal of International Law* 281, 283.

Sir Coke, Edward, 'Institutes of the Laws of England' (1797) Vol I cited in Lois G. Forer, *Unequal Protection Women, Children, and the Elderly in Court* (New York: WW Norton & Co, 1991).

Combacau, Jean and Sur, Serge, *Droit international public* (6th edn, Paris: Montchrestien, 2004).

Conaway, Camille Pampell and Shoemaker, Jolynn, 'Women in United Nations Peace Operations: Increasing the Leadership Opportunities' (Washington, DC: Georgetown University, *Women in International Security*, 2008).

Connors, Jane, 'Non-Governmental Organizations and the Human Rights of Women' in Peter Willets (ed), *The Conscience of the World: The Influence of Non-Governmental Organizations in the United Nations System* (1996).

Connors, Jane, 'Violence against Women', Background Paper, United Nations Fourth World Conference on Women, 1995, reprinted in Hilaire Barnett, *Sourcebook on Feminist Jurisprudence* (London, Sydney: Cavendish Publishing, 1997) 558–75.

Connors, Jane, 'The Women's Convention in the Muslim World' in J.P. Gardener (ed), *Human Rights as General Norms and a State's Right to Opt Out* (London: B.I.I.C.L., 1997) 85–103.

Connors, Jane, 'United Nations Approaches to "Crimes of Honour"' in Lynn Welchman and Sara Hossain (eds), *'Honour' Crimes, Paradigms and Violence against Women* (London: Zed Books, 2005) 22–41.

Cook, Rebecca J., 'Reservations to the Convention on the Elimination of all Forms of Discrimination against Women' (1990) 30 *Virginia Journal of International Law* 643.

Cook, Rebecca J., 'State Accountability under the Convention on the Elimination of All Forms of Discrimination against Women' in Rebecca J. Cook (ed), *Human Rights of Women: National and International Perspectives* (Philadelphia: University of Pennsylvania Press, 1994) 228–56.

Cook, Rebecca J., 'Obligations to Adopt Temporary Special Measures under the Convention on the Elimination of All Forms of Discrimination against Women' in Ineke Boerefijn, Fons Coomans, Jenny Goldschmidt, Rikki Holtmaat and Ria Wolleswinkel (eds), *Temporary Special Measures: Accelerating de facto Equality of Women under Article 4(1) UN Convention on the Elimination of All Forms of Discrimination against Women* (New York: Transnational Publishers, 2003) 119–42.

Cook, Rebecca J. and Cusack, Simone, *Gender Stereotyping: Transnational Legal Perspectives* (Philadelphia: University of Pennsylvania Press, 2009).

Coomans, Fons and Kamminga, Menno T., *Extraterritorial Application of Human Rights Treaties* (Antwerp: Intersentia, 2004).

Cooper, Joel, 'The Digital Divide: The Special Case of Gender' (2006) 22 *Journal of Computer-Assisted Learning* 320–3.

Copelon, Rhonda, 'Intimate Terror: Understanding Domestic Violence as Terror' in Rebecca J. Cook (ed), *Human Rights of Women: National and International Perspectives* (Philadelphia: University of Pennsylvania Press, 1994) 116–52.

Cowell-Meyers, Kimberly, 'Gender, Power, and Peace: A Preliminary Look at Women in the Northern Ireland Assembly' 23 *Women & Politics* (2001) 55–88.

Craven, Matthew, *The International Covenant on Economic, Social and Cultural Rights: A Perspective on its Development* (Oxford: Oxford University Press, 1995).

Creighton, William B., *Working Woman and the Law* (London: Mansell, 1979).

Crenshaw, Kimberlé, 'Demarginalizing the Intersection of Race and Sex, a Black Feminist Critique of Antidiscrimination Doctrine, Feminist Theory, and Antiracist Politics' in *University of Chicago Legal Forum* (1989) 139–67 (Special Issue: Feminism in the Law: Theory, Practice and Criticism); Reprinted in: Katharine T. Bartlett and Rosanne Kennedy (eds), *Feminist Legal Theory* (Boulder/San Francisco/Oxford: Westview Press, 1991) 57–80.

Cuno, Kenneth M. and Desai, Manisha (eds), *Family, Gender, and Law in a Globalizing Middle East and South Asia* (New York: Syracuse University Press, 2009).

Cusack, Simone and Cook, Rebecca J., 'Combating Discrimination Based on Sex and Gender' in Catarina Krause and Martin Scheinin (eds), *International Protection of Human Rights: A Textbook* (Turku: Åbo Akademi University Institute for Human Rights, 2009) 205–26.

Dahlerup, Drude, 'Conclusion' in Drude Dahlerup (ed), *Women, Quotas and Politics* (New York: Routledge, 2006) 293–307.

De Feyter, Koen and Gómez Isa, Felipe, 'Privatisation and Human Rights' in Id. (eds), *Privatisation and Human Rights in the Age of Globalisation* (Maastricht: Intersentia, 2005)

DeGroot, Gerard J., 'A Few Good Women: Gender Stereotypes, the Military and Peacekeeping' in Louise Olsson and Torunn L. Tryggestad, *Women and International Peacekeeping* (London: Frank Cass Publishers, 2001) 23–38.

Detrick, Sharon, 'Article 41' in Sharon Detrick (ed), *A Commentary on the United Nations Convention on the Rights of the Child* (The Hague/London: Martinus Nijhoff Publishers, 1999) 712–18.

Diwan, Paras, *Law of Adoption, Minority Guardianship and Custody* (Allahabad: Wadhwa & Co, 1989).

Doehring, Karl, *Völkerrecht* (2nd edn, Heidelberg: C.F. Müller, 2005).

Donders, Yvonne, *Towards a Right to Cultural Identity?* (Antwerp: Intersentia, 2002).

Dowell-Jones, Mary, *Contextualising the International Covenant on Economic, Social and Cultural Rights: Assessing the Economic Deficit* (Leiden/Boston: Martinus Nijhoff Publishers, 2004).

Düsing, Sandra, *Traditional Leadership and Democratisation in Southern Africa. A Comparative Study of Botswana, Namibia and South Africa* (2002).

Edwards, Alice, *Violence against Women under International Human Rights Law* (Cambridge: Cambridge University Press, 2011).

Eide, Asbjørn, *Right to Adequate Food as a Human Right*, U.N. Sales No. E.89.XIV.2, (United Nations: New York, 1989).

Eide, Asbjørn, 'Economic, Social and Cultural Rights as Human Rights' in Asbjørn Eide et al (eds), *Economic, Social and Cultural Rights: A Textbook* (1st and 2nd edn, Dordrecht: Martin Nijhoff Publishers, 1995 and 2001) 9–28.

Elson, Diane, *Budgeting for Human Rights* (New York: UNIFEM 2006).

Erdman, Joanna N, 'Human Rights in Health Equity: Cervical Cancer and HPV Vaccines' (2009) 35 *American Journal of Lifestyle Medicine* 365–87.

Evatt, Elizabeth, 'Finding a Voice for Women's Rights: The Early Days of CEDAW' (2002–03) 34 *George Washington International Law Review* 515–53.

Evatt, Elizabeth, 'Private Global Enterprises, International Trade and Finance' in Hanna B. Schöpp-Schilling and Cees Flinterman (eds), *The Circle of Empowerment: Twenty-Five Years of The UN Committee on The Elimination of Discrimination against Women* (New York: Feminist Press, 2007) 106–23.

Facio, Alda and Morgan, Martha, 'Equity or Equality for Women? Understanding CEDAW's Equality Principles', *IWRAW Asia Pacific Occasional Papers Series*, No 14, Kuala Lumpur (2009).

Facio, Alda and Morgan, Martha, 'Equity or Equality for Women? Understanding CEDAW's Equality Principles' (2009) 60 *Alabama Law Review* 1133, 1160–5.

Farha, Leilani, 'Women and Housing' in: Askin Kelly Dawn and Dorean M. Koenig (eds), *Women and International Human Rights Law*, vol. 1 (Ardsley, NY: Transnational Publishers, 1999) 483.

Farha, Leilani, 'Is there a woman in the house? Reconceiving the human right to housing' (2002) 14 *Canadian Journal of Women and the Law* 118–41.

Farha, Leilani, 'Women Claiming Economic, Social and Cultural Rights—The CEDAW Potential', in Malcolm Langford (ed), *Social Rights Jurisprudence Emerging Trends in International and Comparative Law* (Cambridge: Cambridge University Press, 2008) 553–68.

Fawcett, James, Carruthers, Janeen and North, Peter (eds), *Cheshire, North, & Fawcett: Private International Law* (14th edn, Oxford: Oxford University Press, 2008).

Fiske, Susan T., Bersoff, Donald N., Borgida, Eugene, Deaux, Kay and Heilman, Madeline, 'Social Science Research on Trial: Use of Sex Stereotyping Research in *Price Waterhouse v. Hopkins*' (1991) 46 *American Psychologist* 1049–60.

Fitzpatrick, Joan, 'The Use of International Human Rights Norms to Combat Violence against Women' in Rebecca J. Cook (ed): *Human Rights of Women National and International Perspectives* (Philadelphia: University of Pennsylvania Press, 1994) 532–72.

Flinterman, Cees, 'Strengthening Women's Human Rights Through Individual Complaints' in Hanna B. Schöpp-Schilling and Cees Flinterman (eds), *The Circle of Empowerment: Twenty-Five Years of the UN Committee on the Elimination of Discrimination against Women* (New York: Feminist Press, 2007) 286–97.

Fogiel-Bijaoui, Sylvie, 'Familism, Post-Modernity and the State: The Case of Israel' in Jaipaul L. Roopnarine and Uwe P. Gielen (eds), *Families in Global Perspective* (Boston: Allyn and Bacon, 2005) 38–62.

Forer, Lois G., *Unequal Protection: Women, Children, and the Elderly in Court* (New York: WW Norton & Co, 1991).

Fournier, Pascale, 'The Reception of Muslim Family Law in Western Liberal States' (2005) *Dossier 27: Muslim Minorities (Women Living Under Muslim Laws)*.

Fraser, Arvonne S., 'The Convention on the Elimination of All Forms of Discrimination against Women (The Women's Convention)' in Anne Winslow (ed), *Women, Politics and the United Nations* (Westport: Greenwood Press, 1995) 77–94.

Fraser, Arvonne S., 'Becoming Human: The Origins and Development of Women's Human Rights', (1999) 21 *Human Rights Quarterly* 853.

Fredman, Sandra, *Discrimination Law* (Oxford: Oxford University Press, 2002).

Fredman, Sandra, 'Beyond the Dichotomy of Formal and Substantive Equality: Towards a New Definition of Equal Rights' in Ineke Boerefijn, Fons Coomans, Jenny Goldschmidt, Rikki Holtmaat and Ria Wolleswinkel (eds), *Temporary Special Measures: Accelerating de facto Equality of Women under Article 4(1) UN Convention on the Elimination of All Forms of Discrimination against Women* (Antwerp/Oxford/New York: Intersentia, 2003) 111–18.

Fredman, Sandra, 'Providing Equality: Substantive Equality and the Positive Duty to Provide' (2005) 21 *South African Journal on Human Rights* 163–90.

Freeman, Marsha, 'The Committee on the Elimination of all forms of Discrimination against Women and the Role of Civil Society in Implementing International Women's Human Rights Norms' (2010) 16 *New England Journal of International and Comparative Law* 25.

Freeman, Michael, *A Commentary on the United Nations Convention on the Rights of the Child: Article 3, The Best Interests of the Child* (Leiden: Martinus Nijhoff Publishers, 2007).

Fries, Michaela, *Die Bedeutung von Art. 5(f) der Rassendiskriminierungskonvention im deutschen Recht* (Berlin/Heidelberg: Springer, 2003).

Frowein, Jochen, 'The UN Anti-Terrorism Administration and the Rule of Law' in Pierre M. Dupuy, Bardo Fassbender, Malcolm N. Shaw and Karl P Sommermann (eds), *Völkerrecht als Wertordnung/Common Values in International Law: Festschrift für/Essays in Honour of Christian Tomuschat* (Kehl am Rhein: N.P. Engel, 2006) 785–95.

Frowein, Jochen, 'De Facto Regimes' in Rüdiger Wolfrum (ed), *The Max Planck Encyclopedia of International Law* (2008) Para 1 online edition <http:www.mpepil.com> accessed 31 December 2010.

Frowein, Jochen and Peukert, Wolfgang, *Europäische Menschenrechtskonvention: EMRK Kommentar* (Kehl am Rhein: Engel, 2009).

Fudge, Judy and Owens, Rosemary, '*Precarious Work, Women, and the New Economy: The Challenge to Legal Norms*' in Judy Fudge and Rosemary Owens (eds), (Oxford: Hart, 2006).

Galey, Margaret E., 'International enforcement of women's rights' (1984) 6 *Human Rights Quarterly* 463–90.

Galey, Margaret E., 'Promoting Non-Discrimination against Women: The UN Commission on the Status of Women' (1979) 23 *International Studies Quarterly* 273.

Gallagher, Anne, 'Human Rights and the New UN Protocols on Trafficking and Migrant Smuggling: A Preliminary Analysis' (2001) 23 *Human Rights Quarterly* 975–1004.

Gallagher Anne, 'Recent Legal Developments in the Field of Human Trafficking: A Critical Review of the 2005 European Convention and Related Instruments' (2006) 8 *European Journal of Migration and Law* 163–89.

Gallagher, Anne, *The International Law of Human Trafficking* (Cambridge: Cambridge University Press, 2010).

Gallagher, Anne and Pearson, Elaine, 'Detention of Trafficked Persons in Shelters: A Legal and Policy Analysis' (2008) Asia Regional Trafficking in Persons Project (ARTIP).

Gallagher, Anne and Pearson, Elaine, 'The High Cost of Freedom: A Legal and Policy Analysis of Shelter Detention for Victims of Trafficking' (2010) 74 *Human Rights Quarterly* 73–114.

Gardam, Judith and Charlesworth, Hilary, 'Protection of Women in Armed Conflict' (2000) 22 *Human Rights Quarterly* 148–66.

Gardam, Judith and Jarvis, Michelle, *Women, Armed Conflict, and International Law* (The Hague: Kluwer Law International, 2001).

Gardiner, Richard K., Treaty Interpretation (Oxford: Oxford University Press, 2008).

Gaspard, Francoise, 'Unfinishd Battles: Political and Public Life' in Hanna Beate Schöpp-Schilling and Cees Flinterman (eds), *The Circle of Empowerment: Twenty-Five Years of the UN Committee on the Elimination of Discrimination against Women* (New York: Feminist Press, 2007) 145–58.

Gherardi, Silvia, 'The Gender We Think, the Gender We Do in our Everyday Organizational Lives' (1994) 6 *Human Relations* 591–610.

Gierycz, Dorota, 'Human Rights of Women at the Fiftieth Anniversary of the United Nations' in Wolfgang Benedek, Esther M. Kisaakye and Gerd Oberleitner (eds), *Human Rights of Women International Instruments and African Experiences* (London: Zed Books, 2002) 30–49.

Glendon, Mary Ann, *A World Made New: Eleanor Roosevelt and the Universal Declaration of Human Rights* (New York: Random House, 2001).

Goldman, Alan H., 'Affirmative Action' in Marshall Cohen, Thomas Nagel and Thomas Scanlon (eds), *Equality and Preferential Treatment* (Princeton, N.J.: Princeton University Press, 1977) 192–209.

Gondek, Michał, *The Reach of Human Rights in a Globalising World: Extraterritorial Application of Human Rights Treaties* (Antwerp: Intersentia, 2009).

Gonzalez Martinez, Aída, 'Rights of Rural Women: Examples from Latin America' in Hanna B. Schöpp-Schilling and Cees Flinterman (eds), *The Circle of Empowerment: Twenty-Five Years of The UN Committee on The Elimination of Discrimination against Women* (New York: Feminist Press, 2007) 212–22.

Goodman, Ryan, 'Human Rights Treaties, Invalid Reservations, and State Consent' (2002) 96/531 *American Journal of International Law* 531.

Goonesekere, Savitri, 'Colonial Legislation and Sri Lankan Family Law: The Legacy of History' in K.M. de Silva et al (eds), *Asian Panorama* (New Delhi: Vikas Publishing House, 1990).

Goonesekere, Savitri, 'The Conceptual and Legal Dimensions of a Rights-Based Approach, and its Gender Dimensions' in *A Rights-Based Approach to Women's Empowerment and Advancement and Gender Equality*, Workshop Report, UN Division for the Advancement of Women, (October 1998), 52–67.

Goonesekere, Savitri (ed), *Violence, Law and Women's Rights in South Asia* (New Delhi: Sage, 2004).

Goonesekere, Savitri, 'Family Support and Maintenance: Emerging Issues in Some Developing Countries with Mixed Jurisdictions' (2006) 44 *Family Court Review* 361.

Goonesekere, Savitri, 'Universalizing Women's Human Rights through CEDAW' in Hanna B. Schöpp-Schilling and Cees Flinterman (eds), *The Circle of Empowerment: Twenty-Five Years of The UN Committee on The Elimination of Discrimination against Women* (New York: Feminist Press, 2007) 52–67.

Gorga, Camine, 'Toward the Definition of Economic Rights' (1999) 2 *Journal of Markets & Morality* 88–101.

Gosepath, Stefan, 'Equality' (March 2001, revised June 2007), in Edward N. Zalta (ed), *Stanford Encyclopedia of Philosophy* <http://plato.stanford.edu/archives/spr2009/entries/equality/> accessed 31 December 2010.

Grey, Sarah, 'Does Size Matter? Critical Mass Theory and New Zealand's Women MPs' (2002) 55 *Parliamentary Affairs* 19–29.

Groenman, Louise, van Vleuten, Tineke, Holtmaat, Rikki, van Dijk, Ite and de Wildt, Jeroen, *Het Vrouwenverdrag in Nederland anno 1997,* (The Hague: Ministerie van

SZW, 1997). (First Dutch Independent Expert Report on the basis of Article 3 of the Act According the Ratification of CEDAW).

Gross, Aeyal M., 'Sex, Love, and Marriage: Questioning Gender and Sexuality Rights in International Law' (2008) 21 *Leiden Journal of International Law* 235–53.

Hahlo, Herman R. and Kahn, Ellison, *The South African Law of Husband and Wife* (5th edn, Cape Town: Juta & Co, 1985).

Hammouya, Messaoud, *Statistics on Public Sector Employment. Methodology, Structures and Trends* (Geneva: International Labour Office, 1999).

Harris, David J., O'Boyle, Michael, Bates, Ed P. and Buckley, Carla M., *Law of the European Convention on Human Rights* (2nd edn, Oxford: Oxford University Press, 2009).

Hayes, Ceri, 'Out of the Margins: The MDGs though a CEDAW Lens', 13 *Gender and Development* (Oxford: Oxfam, 2005) 67.

Hellum, Anne, 'Engendering the Right to Water and Sanitation: A Woman Focused and Grounded Approach' in Malcolm Langford and Anna Russell (eds), *The Right to Water: Theory, Practice and Prospects* (Cambridge, forthcoming 2011).

Hellum, Anne, Stewart, Julie, Ali, S. Sardar and Tsanga, Amy (eds), *Human Rights, Plural Legalities and Gendered Realities: Paths are Made by Walking*, Southern and Eastern African Regional Centre for Women's Law (Harare: Weaver Press, 2007).

Hepple, Bob, Coussey, Mary and Choudhury, Tufyal, *Equality: A New Framework: Report of the Independent Review of the Enforcement of UK Anti-discrimination Legislation* (Oregon: Hart Publishing, 2000).

Hertel, Shareen, 'Why Bother? Measuring Economic Rights—The Research Agenda' (2006) 7(3) *International Studies Perspectives* 215–30.

Hertel, Shareen and Minkler, Lanse P., 'Introduction' in Shareen Hertel and Lanse P. Minkler (eds), *Economic Rights: Conceptual, Measurement, and Policy Issues* (Cambridge: Cambridge University Press, 2008) 1–35.

Hevener Kaufman, Natalie, 'International Law and the Status of Women: An Analysis of International Legal Instruments Related to the Treatment of Women' (1978) 1 *Harvard Women's Law Journal* 131.

Hevener Kaufman, Natalie, and Lindquist, Stefanie A. 'Critiquing, Gender-Neutral Treaty Language: The Convention on the Elimination of All Forms of Discrimination against Women' in Julie Peters and Andrea Wolper (eds), *Women's Rights, Human Rights* (New York: Routledge, 1995) 114–25.

Hirose, Kasuko, 'Article 1: Definition of Discrimination against Women' in Japanese Association of International Women's Rights (ed), *Convention on the Elimination of All Forms of Discrimination against Women: A Commentary* (Bunkyo: Japanese Association of International Women's Rights, 1995) 39–58.

Hofbauer, Helena, 'Gender-Sensitive Budget Analysis: A Tool to Promote Women's Rights' (2002) 14 *Canadian Journal of Women and the Law* 98–117.

Hogan, Gerard, Whyte, Gerry and Kelly, J.M. (eds), *The Irish Constitution* (3rd edn, Dublin: Butterworths Ltd, 1994).

Hogg, Peter W., *Constitutional Law of Canada* (4th edn, Scarborough: Carswell, 1997).

Holtmaat, Rikki, 'The Power of Legal Concepts: the Development of a Feminist Theory of Law' (1989) 5 *International Journal of the Sociology of Law* 481–502.

Holtmaat, Rikki, 'Towards Different Law and Public Policy: The Significance of Article 5a CEDAW for the Elimination of Structural Gender Discrimination' Ministerie van Sociale Zaken en Werkgelegenheid (Doetinchem: Reed Business Information, 2004).

Holtmaat, Rikki and Naber, Jonneke, *Women's Human Rights and Culture: From Deadlock to Dialogue*, (Antwerp/Oxford/New York: Intersentia, 2010).

Honda, Makoto, 'Article 27: Entry into Force' in Japanese Association of Women's Rights (ed), *Convention on the Elimination of All Forms of Discrimination against Women: A Commentary* (Bunkyo: Japanese Association of International Women's Rights, 1995) 397–401.

hui, tan beng., 'Exploring the Potential of the UN Treaty Body System in Addressing Sexuality Rights' (2007) International Women's Rights Action Watch Asia Pacific Occasional Paper Series, No 11.

Hunter, Rosemary, *Indirect Discrimination in the Workplace* (Sydney: Federation Press, 1992).

Ilic, Zagorka and Corti, Ivanka, *UNITAR Manual on Human Rights Reporting* (New York: United Nations, 1991).

International Law Association, Committee on Feminism and International Law, 'Final Reports on Women's Equality and Nationality in International Law' in *Report of the Sixty Ninth Conference*, (London: International Law Association, 2000).

Iwasawa, Yuji, *International Law, Human Rights, and Japanese Law: The Impact of International Law on Japanese Law* (Oxford: Oxford University Press, 1998) 61–3.

Jalal, Imrana, 'The Campaign for Gender Equality in Family Law' (2005) in *Dossier 27: Muslim Minorities (Women Living Under Muslim Laws)* (Nottingham: The Russell Press, 2005).

Japanese Association of International Women's Rights (ed), *Convention on the Elimination of All Forms of Discrimination against Women: A Commentary* (Bunkyo: Japanese Association of International Women's Rights, 1995).

Jenefsky, Anna, 'Permissibility of Egypt's Reservations to the Convention on the Elimination of All Forms of Discrimination against Women' (1991) 15/2 *Maryland Journal of International Law and Trade* 199.

Jolls, Christine, '*Antidiscrimination Law's Effects on Implicit Bias*', Yale Law School, Public Working Paper No. 148, <http://ssrn.com/abstract=959228> accessed 31 December 2010.

Junko, Torii, 'Article 9: Equality with Respect to Nationality' in Japanese Association of International Women's Rights (ed), *Convention on the Elimination of All Forms of Discrimination against Women: A Commentary* (Bunkyo: Japanese Association of International Women's Rights, 1995) 163–74.

Kadelbach, Stefan, 'The Transformation of Treaties into Domestic Law' (1999) 42 *German Yearbook of International Law* 66–83.

Kägi-Diener, Regula, 'Die Bedeutung internationaler Diskriminierungsverbote, insbesondere von CEDAW, für die schweizerische Rechtsprechung', *Frauenfragen* 1.2009, 42.

Kaiser, Karen, 'Treaties, Direct Applicability' in Rüdiger Wolfrum (ed), *The Max Planck Encyclopedia of Public International Law* (2008) online edition <www.mpepil.com> accessed 31 December 2010.

Kameri-Mbote, Patricia, 'Gender Dimensions of Law, Colonialism and Inheritance in East Africa: Kenyan Women's Experience,' International Environment Law Research Centre (Geneva, 2002).

Kamir, Orit, 'Honor and Dignity Cultures: The Case of *Kavod* and *Kvod Ha-Adam* in Israeli Society and Law' in David Kretzmer and Eckart Klein (eds), *The Concept of Human Dignity in Human Rights Law* (Amsterdam: Kluwer Press, 2002) 231–62.

Kasemsup, Preedee, 'Reception of law in Thailand–a Buddhist society' in Masaji Chiba (ed), *Asian Indigenous Law in Interaction with Received Law* (New York and London: KPI, 1986).

Kawamata, Kazuko, 'Article 7: Equality in Political and Public Life' in Japanese Association of Women's Rights (ed), *Convention on the Elimination of All Forms of Discrimination against Women: A Commentary* (Bunkyo: Japanese Association of International Women's Rights, 1995) 139–50.

Keller, Helen, 'Special Representative' in Rüdiger Wolfrum (ed), *The Max Planck Encyclopedia of International Law* (2008) online edition <http://www.mpepil.com> accessed 31 December 2010.

Khadiagala, Lynn S., 'The failure of popular justice in Uganda: Local councils and women's property rights' (2001) 32 *Development and Change* 55–76.

King, Richard and Sweetman, Caroline, *Gender Perspectives on the Economic Crisis* (Oxford: Oxfam, 2010).

Kitajima, Takae, 'Article 26: Revision' in Japanese Association of Women's Rights (ed), *Convention on the Elimination of All Forms of Discrimination against Women: A Commentary* (Bunkyo: Japanese Association of International Women's Rights, 1995) 393–6.

Klabbers, Jan, 'Accepting the Unacceptable? A New Nordic Approach to Reservations to Multilateral Treaties' (2000) 69 *Nordic Journal of International Law* 179–93.

Klabbers, Jan, 'Treaties, Amendment and Revision' in Rüdiger Wolfrum (ed), *The Max Planck Encyclopedia of Public International Law* (2008) para 10, online edition <http: www.mpepil.com> accessed 31 December 2010.

Klot, Jennifer F., 'Women and Peace Processes—an Impossible Match?' in Louise Olsson (ed), *Gender and Peace Processes—an Impossible Match?* (Uppsala: Collegium of Development Studies, 2003) 17–25.

Knop, K. and Chinkin, C., 'Remembering Chrystal Macmillan: Women's Equality and Nationality in International Law' (2001) 22 *Michigan Journal of International Law* 523–85.

Kohona, Palitha, 'Some Notable Developments in the Practice of the UN Secretary-General as Depositary of Multilateral Treaties: Reservations and Declarations' (2005) 99/2 *American Journal of International Law* 433.

Koukoulis-Spiliotopoulos, Sophia, 'The Limits of Cultural Traditions' (2008) *Annuaire International des Droits de l'Homme III* 411–33.

Kouvo, Sari, 'The United Nations and Gender Mainstreaming: Limits and Possibilities' in Doris Buss and Ambreena Manji (eds), *International Law: Modern Feminist Approaches* (Oxford: Hart, 2005) 237–52.

Krause, Catarina and Scheinin, Martin, 'The Right Not to be Discriminated against: The Case of Social Security' in Theodore S. Olin, Allan Rosas and Martin Scheinin (eds), *The Jurisprudence of Human Rights Law. A Comparative Interpretive Approach* (Turku: Institute for Human Rights, 2000) 253–86.

Krivenko, Ekaterina Yahyaoui, *Women, Islam and International Law* (Leiden/Boston: Martin Nijhoff Publishers, 2009).

Lamarche, Lucie, 'Le Pacte international relatif aux droits économiques, sociaux et culturels, les femmes et le droit à la sécurité sociale: des considérations et des propositions pour un droit « universel » a la sécurité sociale' (2002) 14:1 *Canadian Journal of Women and the Law* 53–97.

Landau, Eve C. and Beigbeder, Yves, *From ILO Standards to EU Law: The Case of Equality Between Men and Women at Work* (Boston: Martinus Nijhoff Publishers, 2008).

Landsberg-Lewis, Ilana (ed), *Bringing Equality Home: Implementing the Convention on the Elimination of All Forms of Discrimination against Women* (New York: UNIFEM, 1999). <http://www.unifem.undp.org/cedaw/indexen.htm> accessed 31 December 2010.

Langford, Malcolm (ed), *Social Rights Jurisprudence* (Cambridge: Cambridge University Press, 2008).

Langford, Malcolm, 'Poverty in Developed States: International Human Rights Law and the Right to a Remedy' (2008) 51 *German Yearbook of International Law* 251–89.

Larserud, Stina and Taphorn, Rita, *'Designing for Equality: Best-fit, Medium-fit and Non-favourable Combinations of Electoral Systems and Gender Quotas'* (Stockholm: International IDEA, 2007).

Lauterpacht, Hersch, 'Foreward to the First Edition' in Paul Weis (ed), *Nationality and Statelessness in International Law* (2nd edn, Alphen aan den Rijn: Sijthoff & Noordhoff, 1979) 11.

Lawson, Rick, 'Life After *Banković*: On the Extraterritorial Application of the European Convention on Human Rights' in Alphonsus Coomans and Menno Kamminga (eds), *Extraterritorial Application of Human Rights Treaties* (Maastricht: Maastricht Centre for Human Rights, Intersentia, 2004) 83–123.

Lee, Robert Warden, *An Introduction to Roman-Dutch Law* (5th edn, Oxford: Oxford Clarendon Press, 1953).

Lijnzaad, Lisbeth, 'Over rollenpatronen en de rol van het Verdrag' in Aalt Willem Heringa, Joyce Hes and Liesbeth Lijnzaad (eds), *Het Vrouwenverdrag. Een beeld van een verdrag* (Antwerp/Apeldoorn: MakluPublishers, 1994) 43–57.

Lijnzaad, Liesbeth, *Reservations to UN-Human Rights Treaties: Ratify and Ruin?* (Dordrecht: Martinus Nijhoff Publishers, 1995).

Lindblom, Anna-Karin, *'The Legal Status of Non-Governmental Organisations in International Law'* (Cambridge: Cambridge University Press, 2001).

Lippincott, Amy, 'Is Uganda's "No Party" System Discriminatory of Women and a Violation of International Law?' (2002) 3 *Brooklyn Journal of International Law* 1137–66.

Mackie, Gerry and LeJeune, John, *'Social Dynamics of Abandonment of Harmful Practices'*, UNICEF Innocenti Working Papers Series, IWP-2009-06 (New York: UNICEF, 2009).

MacKinnon, Catherine A., 'On Torture: A Feminist Perspective on Human Rights' in Kathleen E. Mahoney and Paul Mahoney (eds) *Human Rights in the 21st Century: A Global Perspective* (1993) 21–32.

MacKinnon, Catherine A., *Feminism Unmodified* (Cambridge: Harvard University Press, 1987).

Mansbridge, Jane, 'The Descriptive Political Representation of Gender: An Anti-Essentialist Argument' in Jytte Klausen and Charles S. Maier (eds), *Has Liberalism Failed Women?* (New York: Palgrave, 2001) 19–38.

Marks, Susan, 'Nightmare and Noble Dream: The 1993 World Conference on Human Rights' (1994) 53 *Cambridge Law Journal* 54–62.

Matland, Richard E., 'Enhancing Women's Political Participation: Legislative Recruitment and Electoral Systems' in Julie Ballington and Azza Karam (eds), *Women in Parliament: Beyond Numbers* (Stockholm: International IDEA, 2005) 93–111.

Matz-Lück, Nele, 'Treaties, Conflict Clauses' in Rüdiger Wolfrum (ed), *The Max Planck Encyclopedia of Public International Law* (2008) online edition <www.mpepil.com> accessed 31 December 2010.

Mayer, Ann E, 'Reform of Personal Status Laws in North Africa: A Problem of Islamic or Mediterranean Laws?' (1995) 49 *Middle East Journal* 432–46.

McCrudden, Christopher, 'Human Dignity and Judicial Interpretation of Human Rights' (2008) 19 *European Journal of International Law* 655–724.

McGoldrick, Dominic, '*Human Rights and Religion: The Islamic Headscarf Debate*' (Oxford: Hart Publishing, 2006).

McKean, Warwick A., *Equality and Discrimination under International Law* (Oxford: Clarendon Press, 1983).

McLachlan, Campell, 'The Principle of Systemic Integration and Article 31(3)(c) of the Vienna Convention' (2005) 54 *International and Comparative Law Quarterly* 279–319.

Mégret, Frédéric and Hoffmann, Florian, 'The UN as a Human Rights Violator? Some Reflections on the United Nations Changing Human Rights Responsibilities' (2003) 25 *Human Rights Quarterly* 314–42.

Mendez, Emilio García, 'A Comparative Study of the Impact of the Convention on the Rights of the Child: Law Reform in Selected Civil Law Countries' in *Protecting the World's Children* (Cambridge: Cambridge University Press UNICEF, 2007).

Meron, Theodor, *Human Rights Law-Making in the United Nations: A Critique of Instruments and Process* (Oxford: Clarendon Press, 1986).

Meron, Theodor, 'Enhancing the Effectiveness of the Prohibition of Discrimination against Women' (1990) 84 *American Journal of International Law* 213–17.

Merry, Sally E., 'Rights Talk and the Experience of Law: Implementing Women's Human Rights to Protection from Violence' 25 *Human Rights Quarterly* (2003) 343–81.

Merry, Sally E., *Human Rights and Gender Violence: Translating International Law into Local Justice* (Chicago/London: University of Chicago Press, 2006).

Merry, Sally E., *Gender Violence: A Cultural Perspective* (London: Wiley-Blackwell, 2009).

Meyer, Birgit, 'Much Ado About Nothing? Political Representation Policies and the Influence of Women Parliamentarians in Germany' (2003) 20 *Review of Policy Research* 401–21.

Meyersfeld, Bonita, *Domestic Violence and International Law* (Oxford: Hart Publishing, 2010).

Minow, Martha, *Making All the Difference: Inclusion, Exclusion and American Law* (New York: Cornell University Press, 1999).

Moore, Catherine, 'Women and Domestic Violence: The Public/Private Dichotomy in International Law' (2003) 7 *International Journal of Human Rights* 93–128.

Morsink, Johannes, *Universal Declaration of Human Rights* (Philadelphia: University of Pennsylvania Press, 1999).

Morsink, Johannes, 'Women's Rights in the Universal Declaration' (1991) 13 *Human Rights Quarterly* 229–56.

Morvai, Krisztina, 'Personal Reflection: Rethinking Prostitution and Trafficking,' in Hanna B. Schöpp-Schilling and Cees Flinterman (eds), *The Circle of Empowerment:*

Twenty-Five Years of The UN Committee on The Elimination of Discrimination against Women (New York: Feminist Press, 2007).

Motiejunaite, Jurate, *Women's Rights: the Public/Private Dichotomy* (New York: International Debate, 2005).

Mowbray, Alastair, 'The Consideration of Gender in the Process of Appointing Judges to the European Court of Human Rights' (2008) 8 *Human Rights Law Review* 549–59.

Muria, Sir John, 'Personal Common Law Conflicts and Women's Human Rights' in Andrew Byrnes, Jane Connors and Lum Bik (eds), *Advancing the Human Rights of Women: Using International Human Rights in Domestic Litigation* (Commonwealth Secretariat, 1997).

Neuwirth, Jessica, 'Women and Peace and Security: The Implementation of UN Security Council Resolution 1325' (2002) 9 *Duke Journal of Gender Law and Policy* 253–60.

Nijman, Janne E. and Nollkaemper, André, *New Perspectives on the Divide between National and International Law* (Oxford: Oxford University Press, 2007).

Nose, Kumiko, 'Article 8: Participation in International Activities' in Japanese Association of International Women's Rights (ed), *Convention on the Elimination of All Forms of Discrimination against Women: A Commentary* (Bunkyo: Japanese Association of International Women's Rights, 1995) 151–62.

Novikova, Elvira, 'Poverty, Prostitution, and Trafficking' in Hanna B. Schöpp-Schilling and Cees Flinterman (eds), *The Circle of Empowerment: Twenty-Five Years of The UN Committee on The Elimination of Discrimination against Women* (New York: Feminist Press, 2007) 124–44.

Nowak, Manfred, 'Civil and Political Rights' in Janusz Symonides (ed), *Human Rights Concepts and Standards* (Paris: UNESCO, 2000).

Nowak, Manfred, *UN Covenant on Civil and Political Rights: CCPR Commentary* (2nd revised edn, Kehl am Rhein: N.P. Engel, 2005).

Nowak, Manfred and McArthur, Elizabeth, *The United Nations Conventions Against Torture: A Commentary* (New York: Oxford University Press, 2008).

Nussbaum, Martha, *Sex and Social Justice* (New York: Oxford University Press, 1999).

Nussbaum, Martha, *Women and the Human Right to Development: The Capabilities Approach* (New York: Cambridge University Press, 2000).

Nyamu, Celestine I., 'Rural Women in Kenya and the Legitimacy of the Human Rights Discourse and Institutions' in Edward K. Quashigah and Obiora C. Okafor (eds), *Legitimate Governance in Africa* (The Hague: Kluwer Law International, 1999) 263–308.

Nyamu, Celestine I., 'The International Human Rights Regime and Rural Women in Kenya' (2000) 6 *East African Journal of Peace and Human Rights* 1–33.

Nyamu, Celestine I., 'How should Human Rights and Development Respond to Cultural Legitimization of Gender Hierarchy in Developing Countries?' (2000) 41 *Harvard International Law Journal* 381–418.

Nyamu-Musembi, Celestine, 'Are local Norms and Practices Fences or Pathways? The Example of Property Rights' in An-Na'im, Abdullahi A. (ed), *Cultural Transformation and Human Rights in Africa* (London: Zed Books Ltd, 2002) 126–50.

OHCHR, *UNRPG: Commentary* (2009).

O'Connell Davidson, Julia and Andersen, Bridget, 'Is Trafficking in Human Beings Demand Driven? A Multi-Country Pilot Study' [2003] International Organization for Migration (IOM) Migration Research Series, No 15.

Okin, Susan Moller, 'Is Multiculturalism Bad for Women?' (1997) 22/5 *Boston Review* 25–28.

Oomen, Barbara, *Chiefs in South Africa: Law, Power and Culture in the Post-Apartheid Era* (Oxford: James Currey, 2005).

Otto, Dianne, 'Rethinking the "Universality" of Human Rights Law' (1997–1998) 29 *Columbia Human Rights Law Review* 1–46.

Overy, Clare and White, Robin C. A., *Jacobs & White: The European Convention on Human Rights* (4th edn, Oxford: Oxford University Press, 2006).

Packer, Corinne, *Using Human Rights to Change Tradition* (Antwerp/Oxford/New York: Intersentia, 2002).

Paglione, Giulia, 'Domestic Violence and Housing Rights' (2006) 28:1 *Human Rights Quarterly* 120–47.

Patten, Pramila, *Opportunities and Traps—The Informal Labor Market*, in Hanna B. Schöpp-Schilling and Cees Flinterman (eds), *The Circle of Empowerment: Twenty-Five Years of The UN Committee on The Elimination of Discrimination against Women* (Feminist Press: New York, 2007) 179–82.

Pearl, David, *A Textbook on Muslim Personal Law* (2nd edn, London: Croomhelm, 1987).

Peters, Anne, *Women, Quotas, and Constitutions: A Comparative Study of Affirmative Action for Women under American, German, EC, and International Law* (Boston: Kluwer Law International, 1999).

Petersen, Niels, 'Human Dignity' in Rüdiger Wolfrum (ed), *The Max Planck Encyclopedia of Public International Law* (2008), online edition <www.mpepil.com> accessed 31 December 2010.

Phillips, Anne, 'Defending equality of outcome', (2004) 12 *Journal of Political Philosophy* 1–19 <http://eprints.lse.ac.uk/533/1/equality_of_outcome.pdf> accessed 5 May 2009.

Phillips, Anne, *Multiculturalism Without Culture* (Princeton: Princeton University Press, 2007).

Phillips, Anne, 'Religion: ally, threat or just religion' in Jose Casanova and Anne Phillips, *A Debate on the Public Role of Religion and its Social and Gender Implication, Programme on Gender and Development,* Paper No 5 (Geneva: UNRISD, 2009).

Phuong, Catherine, 'The Relationship Between the European Court of Human Rights and the Human Rights Committee: Has the 'Same Matter' Already Been Examined?' (2007) 7(2) *Human Rights Law Review* 385–95.

Pietilä, Hilkka, *The Unfinished Story of Women and the United Nations* (Geneva: UN Non-Governmental Liaison Service, 2007).

Pimentel, Silvia, 'Education and Legal Literacy' in Hanna B. Schöpp-Schilling and Cees Flinterman (eds), *The Circle of Empowerment: Twenty-Five Years of The UN Committee on The Elimination of Discrimination against Women* (New York: Feminist Press, 2007) 90–103.

Pisillo-Mazzeschi, Ricardo, 'The Due Diligence Rule and the Nature of the International Responsibility of States' (1992) 35 *German Yearbook of International Law* 9–51.

Plata, María Isabel, 'Reproductive Rights as Human Rights: The Colombian Case' in Rebecca J. Cook (ed), *Human Rights of Women: National and International Perspectives* (Philadelphia: University of Pennsylvania Press, 1994).

Polyviou, Polyvios G., *The Equal Protection of the Laws* (London: Duckworth & Co Ltd, 1980).

Pruitt, Lisa R., 'Migration, Development and the Promise of CEDAW for Rural Women' (2009) 30 *Michigan Journal of International Law* 707–61.

Quénivet, Noëlle, *Sexual Offenses in Armed Conflict and International Law* (Ardsley, New York: Transnational Publishers, 2005).

Raday, Frances, 'Culture, Religion, and Gender' (2003) 1 *International Journal of Constitutional Law* 663–715.

Raday, Frances, 'Systematizing the Application of Different Types of Temporary Special Measures under Article 4 of CEDAW' in Ineke Boerefijn, Fons Coomans, Jenny Goldschmidt, Rikki Holtmaat and Ria Wolleswinkel (eds), *Temporary Special Measure: Accelerating de facto Equality of Women under Article 4(1) UN Convention on the Elimination of All Forms of Discrimination against Women* (New York: Transnational Publishers, 2003) 35–44.

Raday, Frances, 'Culture, Religion, and CEDAW's Article 5(a)' in Hanna B. Schöpp-Schilling and Cees Flinterman (eds), *The Circle of Empowerment: Twenty-Five Years of The UN Committee on The Elimination of Discrimination against Women* (New York: Feminist Press, 2007) 68–85.

Raday, Frances, 'Traditionalist Religious and Cultural Challengers: International and Constitutional Human Rights Responses' (2008) 41 *Israel Law Review* 596–634.

Rae, Isabella, *Women and the Right to Food* (Rome: FAO, 2008).

Rathberger, Eva M., 'WID, WAD, GAD: Trends in Research and Practice', *Journal of Computer-Assisted Learning* 320–3.

Rees, Teresa, *Mainstreaming Equality in the European Union: Education, Training and Labour Market Policies* (New York: Routledge, 1998).

Redgwell, Catherine J., 'Reservations to Treaties and Human Rights Committee General Comment No. 24 (52)' (1997) 46 *International Comparative Law Quarterly* 390–412.

Rehof, Lars A., *Guide to the Travaux Préparatoires of the United Nations Convention on the Elimination of All Forms of Discrimination against Women* (Dordrecht/Boston/London: Martinus Nijhoff Publishers, 1993).

Reidel, Laura, 'What are Cultural Rights? Protecting Groups with Individual Rights' (2010) 9 *Journal of Human Rights* 65–80.

Riddle, Jennifer, 'Making CEDAW Universal: A Critique of CEDAW's Reservation Regime under Article 28 and the Effectiveness of the Reporting Process' (2002) 34 *George Washington Law Review* 605–38.

Risse, Mathias, 'A Right to Work? A Right to Leisure? Labor Rights as Human Rights' (2009) 3 *Journal of Law and Ethics of Human Rights* 1–39.

Rittich, Kerry, 'The Properties of Gender Equality' in Philip Alston and Mary Robinson (eds), *Human Rights and Development Towards Mutual Reinforcement* (Oxford: Oxford University Press, 2005)

Rittich, Kerry, 'Social Rights and Social Policy—Transformation of the International Landscape' in Daphne Barak-Erez and Aeyal A. Gross (eds), *Exploring Social Rights* (Oxford and Portland: Hart, 2007).

Romany, Celina, 'State Responsibility goes Private: the Feminist Critique of the Public/Private Distinction in International Human Rights Law' in Rebecca J. Cook (ed), *Human Rights of Women: National and International Perspectives* (Philadelphia: University of Pennsylvania Press, 1994) 85–115.

Rosenne, Shabtai, 'Final Clauses' in Rüdiger Wolfrum (ed), *The Max Planck Encyclopedia of Public International Law* (2008) online edition <www.mpepil.com> accessed 31 December 2010.

Roth, Kenneth, 'Domestic Violence as an International Human Rights Issue' in Rebecca J. Cook (ed), *Human Rights of Women: National and International Perspectives* (Philadelphia: University of Pennsylvania Press, 1994) 326–39.

Roy, Nicole, *De Facto Union in Quebec* (2005) <http://www.canada-justice.org/eng/pi/icg-gci/dfu-udf/dfu-udf.pdf> accessed 31 December 2010.

Rubenstein, Michael, '*The Dignity of Women at Work: A Report on the Problem of Sexual Harassment in the Member States of the European Communities*' (Luxembourg: Office for Official Publications of the European Communities, 1987).

Rubio-Marin, Ruth (ed), *The Gender of Reparations* (New York: Cambridge University Press, 2009).

Rubin, Neville (ed), '*Code of International Labour Law: Law, Practice and Jurisprudence, Volume I* (New York: Cambridge University Press, 2005).

Rudolf, Beate, '*European Union: Compulsory Military Service*' (2005) 3 *International Journal of Constitutional Law* 673–9.

Russell, Ruth B., *A History of the United Nations Charter: The Role of the United States 1940–1945* (Washington, DC: Brookings Institution, 1958).

Rwezaura, Bart, 'Gender Justice and Children's Rights: A Banner for Family Law Reform in Tanzania' in Andrew Bainham (ed), *International Survey of Family Law* (The Hague: XX Publishers 1997) 413–43.

Sacchet, Teresa, 'Political Parties: When do They Work for Women?' EGM/EPWD/2005/E10 (12 December 2005), <http://www.un.org/womenwatch/daw/egm/eql-men/docs/EP.10_rev.pdf> accessed 31 December 2010.

Sadat-Akhavi, Ali, *Methods of resolving conflicts between treaties* (New York: Kluwer Law International, 2003).

Saeki, Tomiki, 'Article 23: Preferential Application of National and International Legislation of Higher Levels of Protection than the Present Convention' in Japanese Association of International Women's Rights (ed), *Convention on the Elimination of All Forms of Discrimination against Women: A Commentary* (Bunkyo: Japanese Association of International Women's Rights, 1995) 366–72.

Sardar Ali, Shaheen (ed), *Conceptualising Islamic Law, CEDAW and Women's Human Rights in Plural Legal Settings* (New Delhi: UNIFEM South Asia Regional Office, 2006).

Sardar Ali, Shaheen, 'A Comparative Perspective of the Convention on the Rights of the Child and the Principles of Islamic Law' in *Protecting the World's Children* (Cambridge University Press and UNICEF, 2007).

Schoiswohl, Michael, *Status and (Human Rights) Obligations of Non-Recognized De Facto Regimes in International Law: The Case of Somaliland* (Leiden/Boston: Martinus Nijhoff Publishers, 2004).

Schöpp-Schilling, Hanna Beate, 'Reflections on a General Recommendation on Article 4 (1) of the Convention on the Elimination of All Forms of Discrimination against Women' in Ineke Boerefijn et al (eds), *Temporary Special Measures. Accelerating the de-facto Equality of Women under Article 4(1) UN Convention on the Elimination of All Forms of Discrimination against Women* (2003) 15.

Schöpp-Schilling, Hanna Beate, 'Reservations to the Convention on the Elimination of All Forms of Discrimination against Women: An Unresolved Issue or (No) New Developments?' in Ineta Ziemele (ed), *Reservations to Human Rights Treaties and the Vienna Convention Regime: Conflict, Harmony or Reconciliation* (Leiden/Boston: Martinus Nijhoff Publishers, 2004) 3–40.

Schöpp-Schilling, Hanna Beate, 'The Nature and Mandate of the Committee' in Hanna Beate Schöpp-Schilling and Cees Flinterman (eds), *The Circle of Empowerment: Twenty-Five Years of The UN Committee on The Elimination of Discrimination against Women* (New York: Feminist Press, 2007) 248–361.

Schöpp-Schilling, Hanna Beate, 'The Nature and Scope of the Convention' in Hanna Beate Schöpp-Schilling and Cees Flinterman (eds), *The Circle of Empowerment: Twenty-Five Years of The UN Committee on The Elimination of Discrimination against Women* (New York: Feminist Press, 2007) 10–29.

Schöpp-Schilling, Hanna Beate, 'Impediments to Progress: The Formal Labour Market' in Hanna Beate Schöpp-Schilling and Cees Flinterman (eds), *The Circle of Empowerment*: Twenty-Five Years of the UN Committee on the Elimination of Discrimination against Women (New York: Feminist Press, 2007).

von Schorlemer, Sabine, 'Article 8' in Bruno Simma (ed), *The Charter of United Nations: A Commentary* (Oxford: Oxford University Press, 2002) 230–46.

Schwelb, Egon, 'The International Convention on the Elimination of All Forms of Racial Discrimination' (1966) 15 *International and Comparative Law Quarterly* 996–1068.

Sen, Amartya, *'Development as Freedom'* (Oxford: Oxford University Press, 1989).

Sen, Gita and Östlin, Piroska (eds), *Gender Equity in Health: The Shifting Frontiers of Evidence and Action* (New York: Routledge, 2010).

Sepper, Elizabeth, 'Confronting the "Sacred and Unchangeable": The Obligation to Modify Cultural Patterns under the Women's Discrimination Treaty' (2008) 30 *University of Pennsylvania Journal of International Law* 585–639.

Sepúlveda, Magdalena, *The Nature of the Obligations under the International Covenant on Economic, Social, and Cultural Rights: Assessing the Economic Deficit* (Utrecht: Intersentia, 2003).

Shachar, Ayelet, 'The Worth of Citizenship in an Unequal World' (2007) 8 *Theoretical Inquiries in Law* 367–88.

Shin, Heisoo, 'CEDAW and Violence against Women: Providing the "Missing Link" ' in Hanna B. Schöpp-Schilling and Cees Flinterman (eds), *The Circle of Empowerment: Twenty-Five Years of The UN Committee on The Elimination of Discrimination against Women* (New York: Feminist Press, 2007) 223–33.

Shivdas, Meena and Coleman, Sarah (eds), *Without Prejudice: CEDAW and the Determination of Women's Rights in a Legal and Cultural Context* (London: Commonwealth Secretariat, 2010).

Simma, Bruno, 'Reservations to Human Rights Treaties: Some Recent Developments' in G Hafner et al (eds), *Liber Amicorum: Professor Ignaz Seidl-Hohenveldern—in Honour of his 80th Birthday* (The Hague: Kluwer, 1998) 659–82.

Simma, Bruno, Khan, Daniel-Erasmus, Zöeckler, Markus and Geiger, Rudolf, 'The role of German courts in the Enforcement of International Human Rights' in Benedetto Conforti and Francesco Francioni (eds), *Enforcing International Human Rights in Domestic Courts* (Leiden: Martinus Nijhoff Publishers, 1997) 71–109.

Skogley, Sigrun I. and Gibney, Mark, 'Transnational Human Rights Obligations' (2002) 24 *Human Rights Quarterly* 781–98.

Smart, Carol, 'The Women in Legal Discourse', (1992) 1 *Social and Legal Studies* 29–44.

Sood, Avani Mehta, 'Gender Justice through Public Interest Litigation: Case Studies from India' (2008) 41 *Vanderbilt Journal of Transnational Law* 833.

Spiro, Erwin, *Law of Parent and Child* (4th edn, Cape Town: Juta & Co, 1985).

Ssenyonjo, Manisuli, 'Non-State Actors and Economic, Social and Cultural Rights' in Mashood Baderin and Robert McCorquodale, *Economic, Social and Cultural Rights in Action* (Oxford: Oxford University Press, 2007) 109–35.

Stamatopoulou, Elsa, *Cultural Rights in International Law* (Leiden/Boston: Martinus Nijhoff Publishers, 2007).

Steiner, Henry J., 'Social Rights and Economic Development: Converging Discourses' (1998) 4 *Buffalo Human Rights Law Review* 25–42.

Steiner, Henry J., Alston, Philip, Goodman, Ryan, *International Human Rights in Context: Law, Politics, Morals* (3rd edn, Oxford: Oxford University Press).

Subedi, Nutan Chandra, 'Elimination of Gender Discriminatory Legal Provision by the Supreme Court of Nepal with Reference to Women's Rights to Property' (2009) 26(1) *Tribhuvan University Journal* 37, 37–54.

Sullivan, Donna J., 'Women's Human Rights and the 1993 World Conference on Human Rights' (1994) 88 *American Journal of International Law* 152.

Sullivan, Donna J., 'The Public/Private Distinction in International Human Rights Law' in Julie S. Peters and Andrea Wolper (eds), *Women's Rights, Human Rights. International Feminist Perspectives* (New York: Routledge, 1995) 126–33.

Sullivan, Donna J., '*Overview of the rule requiring exhaustion of domestic remedies under the Optional Protocol to CEDAW OP*', CEDAW Technical Papers 1 (2008).

Sunder, Madhavi, 'Piercing the Veil' (2002–2003) 112 *Yale Law Journal* 1399–472.

Sweeney, Shawna E., 'Government Respect for Women's Economic Rights' in Shareen Hertel and Lanse Minkler (eds), *Economic Rights Conceptual, Measurement and Policy Issues* (Cambridge: Cambridge University Press, 2007) 233–66.

Swiebel, Joke, 'What Could the European Union Learn From the CEDAW Convention?' in Ineke Boerefijn, Fons Coomans, Jenny Goldschmidt, Rikki Holtmaat and Ria Wolleswinkel (eds), *Temporary Special Measures: Accelerating de facto Equality of Women under Article 4(1) UN Convention on the Elimination of All Forms of Discrimination against Women* (New York: Transnational Publishers, 2003) 51–61.

Tadaakira, Jo, 'Article 12: Elimination of Discrimination against Women in Health Care' in Japanese Association of International Women's Rights (ed), *Convention on the Elimination of All Forms of Discrimination against Women: A Commentary* (Bunkyo: Japanese Association of International Women's Rights, 1995) 241–53.

Tang, Kwong-leung, 'Internationalizing Women's Struggle against Discrimination: The UN Women's Convention and the Optional Protocol' (2004) 34 *British Journal of Social Work* 1173–88.

Tavares da Silva, Maria R. and Ferrer-Gómez, Yolanda, 'The Juárez Murders and the Inquiry Procedure' in Hanna Beate Schöpp-Schilling and Cees Flinterman (eds), *The Circle of Empowerment: Twenty-Five Years of The UN Committee on The Elimination of Discrimination against Women* (New York: Feminist Press, 2007) 298–308.

Thomas, Dorothy O. and Beasley, Michele E., 'Domestic Violence as a Human Rights Issue' (1993) 15 *Human Rights Quarterly* 36–62.

Thomas, Sue, 'The Impact of Women on State Legislative Policies' (1991) 53 *Journal of Politics* 958–76.

Tomasevski, Katarina, *'Human Rights Obligations in Education'* (Nijmegen: Wolf Legal Publishers, 2005).

Tomoko, Arisawa, 'Article 15: Equality of Men and Women before the Law' in Japanese Association of International Women's Rights (ed), *Convention on the Elimination of All Forms of Discrimination against Women: A Commentary* (Bunkyo: Japanese Association of International Women's Rights, 1995) 281–91.

Tran, My Van, 'The Position of Women in Traditional Vietnam' in K.M. de Silve et al (eds), *Asian Panorama* (New Delhi: Vikas Publishing House, 1990).

UN Food and Agriculture Organization, '"De Facto Unions": The legal status of rural women in 19 Latin American countries' (Rome: FAO 1994) <http://www.fao.org/DOCREP/U5615e/u5615e03.htm#P457_72830> accessed 17 December 2010.

United Nations, *Summary of Practice of the Secretary-General as Depositary of Multilateral Treaties* (1999), ST/LEG/7/Rev.1. <http://untreaty.un.org/English/summary.asps> accessed 31 December 2010.

United Nations, *The Optional Protocol: Text and Materials* (New York: Division for the Advancement of Women, 2000).

United Nations, *Final Clauses of Multilateral Treaties: Handbook* (New York: United Nations Publications, 2003).

United Nations, *Treaty Handbook* (New York: United Nations Publications, 2006).

United Nations, *Legislative History of the Convention on the Rights of the Child* (New York and Geneva: Office of the High Commissioner for Human Rights, 2007).

United Nations, *UN 1999 World Survey on the Role of Women in Development* (New York: United Nations Publications, 1999).

Urban Walker, Margaret, 'Gender and Violence in Focus: A Background for Gender Justice in Reparations' in Ruth Rubio-Marin (ed), *The Gender of Reparations* (New York: Cambridge University Press, 2009) 18–62.

Villiger, Mark E., *Commentary on the 1969 Vienna Convention on the Law of Treaties* (Leiden/Boston: Martinus Nijhoff Publishers, 2009).

Vogel-Polsky, Eliane, Positive Action and the Constitutional and legislative Hindrances to its Implementation in the Member States of the Council of Europe (1989) [note: this is a monograph published by the Council of Europe].

Volpp, Leti, 'Blaming Culture for Bad Behaviour', (2000) 12 *Yale Journal of the Humanities* 89–115.

Volpp, Leti, 'Feminism versus Multiculturalism' (2001) 101 *Columbia Law Review* 1181–218.

Wadstein, Margareta, 'Implementation of the UN Convention on the Elimination of all forms of Discrimination against Women' (1988) 10 *Human Rights Quarterly* 5–21.

Westdickenberg, Gerd, 'Holy See' in Rüdiger Wolfrum (ed), *The Max Planck Encyclopedia of Public International Law* (2008) online edition <http://www.mpepil.com> accessed 31 December 2010.

Westendorp, Ingrid, *Women and Housing, Gender Makes a Difference* (Antwerp, Oxford: Intersentia, 2008).

Wilson, Barbara, 'Le droit à un logement suffisant au sens du Pacte international relatif aux doits économiques, sociaux et culturels des Nations Unis (Pacte I)' (2008) 18:5 *Revue Suisse de Droit International et Européen* 431–56.

Wyttenbach, Judith, 'Violence against Women, Culture/Religious Traditions and the International Standard of Due Dilligence' in Carin Benninger-Budel (ed), *Due Diligence and its Application to Protect Women from Violence* (Boston: Martinus Nijhoff Publishers, 2008) 225–39.

Yamashita, Takeshi, 'Article 24: The Full Realization of the Rights Recognized in the Convention' in Japanese Association of International Women's Rights (ed), *Convention on the Elimination of All Forms of Discrimination against Women: A Commentary* (Bunkyo: Japanese Association of International Women's Rights, 1995) 373–84.

Yamashita, Yasuko, 'Article 2: Obligations of States Parties to Eliminate Discrimination against Women' in Japanese Association of International Women's Rights (ed), *Convention on the Elimination of All Forms of Discrimination against Women: A Commentary* (Bunkyo: Japanese Association of International Women's Rights, 1995) 59–82.

Yassin, El Sayed, 'Development of plural structures of law in Egypt' in Masaji Chiba (ed), *Asian Indigenous Law in Interaction with Received Law* (New York and London: KPI, 1986).

Zimmermann, Andreas, 'State Succession in Treaties' in Wolfrum, Rüdiger (ed), *The Max Planck Encyclopedia of Public International Law* (2008) online edition <http://www.mpepil.com> accessed 27 December 2010.

Index